DATE DUE

			PRINTED IN U.S.A.

Literature Criticism from 1400 to 1800

Guide to Gale Literary Criticism Series

When you need to review criticism of literary works, these are the Gale series to use:

If the author's death date is:	You should turn to:
After Dec. 31, 1959 (or author is still living)	***Contemporary Literary Criticism*** for example: Jorge Luis Borges, Anthony Burgess, William Faulkner, Mary Gordon, Ernest Hemingway, Iris Murdoch
1900 through 1959	***Twentieth-Century Literary Criticism*** for example: Willa Cather, F. Scott Fitzgerald, Henry James, Mark Twain, Virginia Woolf
1800 through 1899	***Nineteenth-Century Literature Criticism*** for example: Fedor Dostoevski, Nathaniel Hawthorne, George Sand, William Wordsworth
1400 through 1799	***Literature Criticism From 1400 to 1800*** (excluding Shakespeare) for example: Anne Bradstreet, Daniel Defoe, Alexander Pope, François Rabelais, Jonathan Swift, Phillis Wheatley
	Shakespearean Criticism Shakespeare's plays and poetry
Antiquity through 1399	***Classical and Medieval Literature Criticism*** for example: Dante, Homer, Plato, Sophocles, Vergil, the Beowulf Poet

Gale also publishes related criticism series:

Children's Literature Review

This series covers authors of all eras who have written for the preschool through high school audience.

Short Story Criticism

This series covers the major short fiction writers of all nationalities and periods of literary history.

Poetry Criticism

This series covers poets of all nationalities and periods of literary history.

Drama Criticism

This series covers dramatists of all nationalities and periods of literary history.

ISSN 0740-2880

Volume 18

Literature Criticism from 1400 to 1800

Excerpts from Criticism of the Works
of Fifteenth-, Sixteenth-, Seventeenth-, and
Eighteenth-Century Novelists, Poets, Playwrights,
Philosophers, and Other Creative Writers,
from the First Published Critical Appraisals
to Current Evaluations

James E. Person, Jr.
Editor

Tina N. Grant
Thomas Ligotti
Zoran Minderović
Joann Prosyniuk
Associate Editors

 **Gale Research Inc.** · DETROIT · LONDON

STAFF

James E. Person, Jr., *Editor*

Jelena O. Krstović, Thomas Ligotti, Zoran Minderovic,
Joann Prosyniuk, Joseph C. Tardiff, *Associate Editors*

David J. Engelman, Grace Jeromski, Michael W. Jones,
Christopher K. King, Susan M. Peters, Linda M. Ross, Mark Swartz,
Debra A. Wells, Allyson J. Wylie, *Assistant Editors*

Jeanne A. Gough, *Permissions and Production Manager*

Linda M. Pugliese, *Production Supervisor*
Paul Lewon, Lorna Mabunda, Maureen A. Puhl, Camille Robinson,
Jennifer VanSickle, *Editorial Associates*
Donna Craft, Brandy C. Johnson, Sheila Walencewicz,
Editorial Assistants

Maureen Richards, *Research Supervisor*
Mary Beth McElmeel, *Editorial Associate*
Daniel J. Jankowski, Julie K. Karmazin, Tamara C. Nott,
Julie A. Synkonis, *Editorial Assistants*

Sandra C. Davis, *Text Permissions Supervisor*
Maria L. Franklin, Josephine M. Keene, Denise Singleton,
Kimberly F. Smilay,
Permissions Associates
Rebecca A. Hartford, Michele M. Lonoconus, Shelly Rakoczy,
Shalice Shah, *Permissions Assistants*

Margaret A. Chamberlain, *Permissions Supervisor (Pictures)*
Pamela A. Hayes, *Permissions Associate*
Amy Lynn Emrich, Karla A. Kulkis, Nancy M. Rattenbury, Keith Reed,
Permissions Assistants

Mary Beth Trimper, *Production Manager*
Mary Winterhalter, *External Production Assistant*

Arthur Chartow, *Art Director*
C. J. Jonik, *Keyliner*

Contents

Preface   vii

Acknowledgments   xi

Preface

Literature Criticism from 1400 to 1800 (LC) presents criticism of world authors of the fifteenth through eighteenth centuries. The literature of this period reflects a turbulent time of radical change that saw the rise of drama equal in stature to that of classical Greece, the birth of the novel and personal essay forms, the emergence of newspapers and periodicals, and major achievements in poetry and philosophy. Much of modern literature reflects the influence of these centuries. Thus the literature treated in *LC* provides insight into the universal nature of human experience, as well as into the life and thought of the past.

Scope of the Series

LC is designed to serve as an introduction to authors of the fifteenth through eighteenth centuries and to the most significant interpretations of these authors' works. The great poets, dramatists, novelists, essayists, and philosophers of this period are considered classics in every secondary school and college or university curriculum. Because criticism of this literature spans nearly six hundred years, an overwhelming amount of critical material confronts the student. *LC* therefore organizes and reprints the most noteworthy published criticism of authors of these centuries. Readers should note that there is a separate Gale reference series devoted to Shakespearean studies. For though belonging properly to the period covered in *LC,* William Shakespeare has inspired such a tremendous and ever-growing corpus of secondary material that the editors have deemed it best to give his works extensive coverage in a separate series, *Shakespearean Criticism.*

Each author entry in *LC* attempts to present a historical survey of critical response to the author's works. Early criticism is offered to indicate initial responses, later selections document any rise or decline in literary reputations, and retrospective analyses provide students with modern views. The size of each author entry is intended to reflect the author's critical reception in English or foreign criticism in translation. Articles and books that have not been translated into English are therefore excluded. Every attempt has been made to identify and include the seminal essays on each author's work and to include recent commentary providing modern perspectives.

The need for *LC* among students and teachers of literature was suggested by the proven usefulness of Gale's *Contemporary Literary Criticism (CLC), Twentieth-Century Literary Criticism (TCLC),* and *Nineteenth-Century Literature Criticism (NCLC),* which excerpt criticism of works by nineteenth- and twentieth-century authors. Because of the different time periods covered, there is no duplication of authors or critical material in any of these literary criticism series. An author may appear more than once in the series because of the great quantity of critical material available and because of the aesthetic demands of the series's *thematic organization.*

Thematic Approach

Beginning with Volume 12, roughly half the authors in each volume of *LC* are organized in a thematic scheme. Such themes include literary movements, literary reaction to political and historical events, significant eras in literary history, and the literature of cultures often overlooked by English-speaking readers. The present volume, for example, focuses upon the rise of the English essay. Future volumes of *LC* will devote substantial space to the English Metaphysical poets and authors of the Spanish Golden Age, among many others. The rest of each volume will be devoted to criticism of the works of authors not aligned with the selected thematic authors and chosen from a variety of nationalities.

Organization of the Book

Each entry consists of the following elements: author or thematic heading, introduction, list of principal works (in author entries only), annotated works of criticism (each followed by a bibliographical citation), and a bibliography of further reading. Also, most author entries contain author portraits and other illustrations.

- The **author heading** consists of the author's full name, followed by birth and death dates. If an author wrote consistently under a pseudonym, the pseudonym is used in the author heading, with the real name given in parentheses on the first line of the biographical and critical introduction. Also located here are any name variations under which an author wrote, including transliterated forms for authors whose native languages use nonroman alphabets. Uncertain birth or death dates are indicated by question marks. The **thematic heading** simply states the subject of the entry.

- The **biographical and critical introduction** contains background information designed to introduce the reader to an author and to critical discussion of his or her work. Parenthetical material following many of the introductions provides references to biographical and critical reference series published by Gale in which additional material about the author may be found. The **thematic introduction** briefly defines the subject of the entry and provides social and historical background important to understanding the criticism.

- Most *LC* author entries include **portraits** of the author. Many entries also contain illustrations of materials pertinent to an author's career, including author holographs, title pages, letters, or representations of important people, places, and events in an author's life.

- The **list of principal works** is chronological by date of first book publication and identifies the genre of each work. In the case of foreign authors whose works have been translated into English, the title and date of the first English-language edition are given in brackets beneath the foreign-language listing. Unless otherwise indicated, dramas are dated by first performance, not first publication.

- **Criticism** is arranged chronologically in each author entry to provide a useful perspective on changes in critical evaluation over the years. For the purpose of easy identification, the critic's name and the composition or publication date of the critical work are given at the beginning of each piece of criticism. Unsigned criticism is preceded by the title of the source in which it appeared. All titles by the author featured in the critical entry are printed in boldface type. Publication information (such as publisher names and book prices) and parenthetical numerical references (such as footnotes or page and line references to specific editions of works) have been deleted at the editors' discretion to provide smoother reading of the text.

- Critical essays are prefaced by **annotations** as an additional aid to students using *LC*. These explanatory notes may provide several types of useful information, including: the reputation of a critic, the importance of a work of criticism, the commentator's individual approach to literary criticism, the intent of the criticism, and the growth of critical controversy or changes in critical trends regarding an author's work. In some cases, these notes cross-reference the work of critics within the entry who agree or disagree with each other.

- A complete **bibliographical citation** of the original essay or book follows each piece of criticism.

- An annotated bibliography of **further reading** appears at the end of each entry and suggests resources for additional study of authors and themes. It also includes essays for which the editors could not obtain reprint rights.

Cumulative Indexes

Each volume of *LC* includes a cumulative **author index** listing all the authors that have appeared in *Contemporary Literary Criticism, Twentieth-Century Literary Criticism, Nineteenth-Century Literature Criticism, Literature Criticism from 1400 to 1800,* and *Classical and Medieval Literature Criticism,* along with cross-references to the Gale series *Short Story Criticism, Poetry Criticism, Children's Literature Review, Authors in the News, Contemporary Authors, Contemporary Authors Autobiography Series, Contemporary Authors Bibliographical Series, Dictionary of Literary Biography, Concise Dictionary of Literary Biography, Something about the Author, Something about the Author Autobiography Series,* and *Yesterday's Authors of Books for Children.* Readers will welcome this cumulative author index as a useful tool for locating an author within the various series. The index, which includes authors' birth and death dates, is particularly valuable for those authors who are identified with a certain period but whose death dates cause them to be placed in another, or for those authors whose careers span two periods. For example, F. Scott Fitzgerald is found in *TCLC,* yet a writer often associated with him, Ernest Hemingway, is found in *CLC.*

Beginning with Volume 12, *LC* includes a cumulative **topic index** that lists all literary themes and topics treated in *LC, NCLC* Topics volumes, *TCLC* Topics volumes, and the *CLC* Yearbook. Each volume of *LC* also includes a cumulative **nationality index** in which authors' names are arranged alphabetically under their respective nationalities and followed by the numbers of the volumes in which they appear.

Each volume of *LC* also includes a cumulative **title index,** an alphabetical listing of the literary works discussed in the series since its inception. Each title listing includes the corresponding volume and page numbers where criticism may be located. Foreign-language titles that have been translated are followed by the titles of the translations—for example, *El ingenioso hidalgo Don Quixote de la Mancha (Don Quixote)*. Page numbers following these translated titles refer to all pages on which any form of the titles, either foreign-language or translated, appear. Titles of novels, dramas, nonfiction books, and poetry, short story, or essay collections are printed in italics, while individual poems, short stories, and essays are printed in roman type within quotation marks.

A Note to the Reader

When writing papers, students who quote directly from any volume in the Literary Criticism Series may use the following general forms to footnote reprinted criticism. The first example pertains to material drawn from periodicals, the second to material reprinted from books.

T. S. Eliot, "John Donne," *The Nation and the Athenaeum,* 33 (9 June 1923), 321-32; excerpted and reprinted in *Literature Criticism from 1400 to 1800,* Vol. 10, ed. James E. Person, Jr. (Detroit: Gale Research, 1989), pp. 28-9.

Clara G. Stillman, *Samuel Butler: A Mid-Victorian Modern* (Viking Press, 1932); excerpted and reprinted in *Twentieth-Century Literary Criticism,* Vol. 33, ed. Paula Kepos (Detroit: Gale Research, 1989), pp. 43-5.

Suggestions Are Welcome

In response to various suggestions, several features have been added to *LC* since the series began, including a nationality index, a Literary Criticism Series topic index, thematic entries, a descriptive table of contents, and more extensive illustrations.

Readers who wish to suggest new features, themes, or authors to appear in future volumes, or who have other suggestions, are cordially invited to write to the editor.

Acknowledgments

The editor wishes to thank the copyright holders of the excerpted criticism included in this volume, the permissions managers of many book and magazine publishing companies for assisting us in securing reprint rights, and Anthony Bogucki for assistance with copyright research. We are also grateful to the staffs of the Detroit Public Library, Wayne State University Purdy/Kresge Library Complex, and the University of Michigan Libraries for making their resources available to us. Following is a list of the copyright holders who have granted us permission to reprint material in this volume of *LC*. Every effort has been made to trace copyright, but if omissions have been made, please let us know.

COPYRIGHTED EXCERPTS IN *LC*, VOLUME 18, WERE REPRINTED FROM THE FOLLOWING PERIODICALS:

Encounter, v. XXIX, December, 1967 for "The Spectator as Actor: Addison in Perspective" by Peter Gay. © 1967 by Encounter Ltd. Reprinted by permission of the author.—*Hispania,* v. 63, September, 1980 for "Santa Teresa and the Problem of Desire" by Gari Laguardia. © 1980 The American Association of Teachers of Spanish and Portuguese, Inc. Reprinted by permission of the publisher and the author.—*International Journal of Middle East Studies,* v. 22, February, 1990 for "Steppe Humanism: The Autobiographical Writings of Zahir Al-Din Muhammad Babur, 1483-1530" by Stephen Frederic Dale. Copyright © 1990 Cambridge University Press. All rights reserved. Reprinted by permission of the publisher and the author.—*Journal of Hispanic Philology,* v. III, Winter, 1979. Copyright © 1979 The Journal of Hispanic Philology, Inc. Reprinted by permission of the publisher. Footnotes and page references have been deleted.—*The Monist,* v. 59, October, 1976. Copyright © 1976, The Hegeler Institute, LaSalle, IL 61301. Reprinted by permission of the publisher.—*The New York Times Book Review,* July 24, 1966. Copyright © 1966 by The New York Times Company. Reprinted by permission of the publisher.—*Renascence,* v. XXXIII, Autumn, 1980. © copyright, 1980, Marquette University Press. Reprinted by permission of the publisher.—*The Sewanee Review,* v. XCVI, Fall, 1988. © 1988 by The University of the South. Reprinted by permission of the editor of *The Sewanee Review.*—*Studies in English Literature, 1500-1900,* v. XIX, Summer, 1979 for "The Significance of Addison's Criticism" by Leopold Damrosch, Jr. © 1979 William Marsh Rice University. Reprinted by permission of the publisher and the author.—*Studies in the Literary Imagination,* v. X, Fall, 1977. Copyright 1977 Department of English, Georgia State University. Reprinted by permission of the publisher.—*THOUGHT,* v. LVIII, December, 1983. Copyright © 1983 by Fordham University Press. Reprinted by permission of Fordham University Press, New York.

COPYRIGHTED EXCERPTS IN *LC*, VOLUME 18, WERE REPRINTED FROM THE FOLLOWING BOOKS:

Anderson, Fulton H. From *Francis Bacon: His Career and His Thought.* University of Southern California Press, 1962. Copyright © 1962 by University of Southern California Press. All rights reserved. Reprinted by permission of the publisher.—Bateson, F. W. From "Addison, Steele and the Periodical Essay," in *Dryden to Johnson.* Edited by Roger Lonsdale. Revised edition. Sphere Reference, 1986. © Sphere Books 1971, 1986. Reprinted by permission of the publisher.—Connely, Willard. From *Sir Richard Steele.* Charles Scribner's Sons, 1934. Copyright by Charles Scribner's Sons. Copyright renewed 1962 by Willard Connely. Reprinted with the permission of Charles Scribner's Sons, an imprint of Macmillan Publishing Company.—Emerson, Ralph Waldo. From *The Early Lectures of Ralph Waldo Emerson: 1833-1836, Vol. I.* Edited by Stephen E. Whicher and Robert E. Spiller. Cambridge, Mass.: Harvard University Press, 1959. Copyright © 1959 by the President and Fellows of Harvard College. Renewed 1987 by Elizabeth T. Whicher. Excerpted by permission of the publishers.—Forster, E. M. From *Abinger Harvest.* Harcourt Brace Jovanovich, 1936, Edward Arnold, 1936. Copyright 1936, 1964 by Edward Morgan Forster. Reprinted by permission of Harcourt Brace Jovanovich, Inc. In Canada reprinted by permission of King's College, Cambridge and the Society of Authors as the literary representatives of the E. M. Forster Estate.—Gilson, Etienne and Thomas Langan. From *Modern Philosophy: Descartes to Kant.* Random House, 1963. © copyright, 1963, by Random House, Inc. All rights reserved. Reprinted by permission of the publisher.—Guillén, Jorge. From *Language and Poetry: Some Poets of Spain.* Translated by Stephen Gilman and Ruth Whittredge. Cambridge, Mass.: Harvard University Press, 1961. Copyright © 1961 by the President and Fellows of Harvard College. Renewed 1989 by Mrs. Jorge Guillén. All rights reserved. Excerpted by permission of the publishers.—Hagstrum, Jean H. From *Sex and Sensibility: Ideal and Erotic Love from Milton to Mozart.* The University of Chicago Press, 1980. © 1980 by The University of Chicago. All rights reserved. Reprinted by permission of the publisher.—Hall, Michael L. From "The Emergence of the Essay and the Idea of Discovery," in *Essays on the Essay: Redefining the Genre.*

Joseph Addison

1672-1719

English essayist, critic, dramatist, poet, translator, and librettist.

Addison is considered a masterful essayist whose contributions to the periodicals the *Spectator* and the *Tatler* are highly regarded for their lucid prose style as well as their rational viewpoint on a wide range of subjects including politics, literature, and daily life in eighteenth-century London. Through such fictional personae as Mr. Spectator and Sir Roger de Coverley, Addison created a form of gentle, urbane satire that greatly influenced the course of journalism and, many scholars believe, helped shape the early development of the English novel.

Addison's father, the Reverend Lancelot Addison, was a minister and a scholar who served in Tangier, Morocco and later became dean of Lichfield; Addison was born shortly after his father's return to England from North Africa. When he entered Queens College, Oxford, at age fifteen, it was intended that he would follow his father into the clergy. An interest in Virgil and other Latin poets, however, led to a position at Magdalen College, Oxford, where he resided from 1689 to 1699. After leaving Oxford, Addison spent the next four years traveling extensively in France, Germany, and Italy, preparing for a career as a public servant. Upon his return to London, he joined an informal organization of Whigs called the Kit-Cat Club. The Whigs were Britain's liberal political party, in incessant conflict with their conservative adversaries, the Tories. Since the Tories were in power at the time, Addison had difficulty finding employment. Nevertheless, he was commissioned in 1704 to write a poem celebrating the Duke of Marlborough's victory over French forces at the Battle of Blenheim. *The Campaign* received praise for its skillful poetic style, and Addison's use of a simile comparing Marlborough to an angel established him as a major writer. The poem's success also resulted in the publication of his *Remarks on Several Parts of Italy,* written during his earlier travels, as well as in his appointment to the position of under-secretary of state. He maintained a civil career alongside his literary one, eventually serving as lord commissioner of trade and secretary of state. Addison regularly socialized with other literary figures, becoming a well-known figure in Button's coffeehouse, where he frequently dined with such prominent writers as Jonathan Swift, Lady Mary Wortley Montagu, and Alexander Pope.

In 1709, Richard Steele, a childhood friend of Addison's and a staunch Whig, formed the *Tatler,* a paper distributed three times weekly and written under the collective pseudonym "Isaac Bickerstaff." At Steele's invitation, Addison soon began contributing articles on morality and manners as well as humorous sketches of fictional characters. The *Tatler* continued publishing through 1711, with Addison writing between fifty and sixty pieces. During this time, he independently produced five numbers of the

Whig Examiner, a more expressly political journal. In 1711 Steele began publishing the *Spectator,* a daily paper, and Addison took a more active role in its production, composing almost half of its articles until it folded at the end of 1712. The most popular *Spectator* essays featured Mr. Spectator, a sarcastic Whig, and Sir Roger de Coverley, an aging Tory, in witty discussions of such everyday matters as women's apparel and the use of snuff, but Addison also included more sophisticated material in the form of literary criticism and essays on aesthetics. He stated his intention in *Spectator* 10: "It was said of *Socrates,* that he brought Philosophy down from Heaven, to inhabit among Men; and I shall be ambitious to have it said of me, that I have brought Philosophy out of Closets and Libraries, Schools and Colleges, to dwell in Clubs and Assemblies, at Tea-Tables and in Coffee-Houses." In 1713 Steele started ed a third periodical, the *Guardian,* which Addison joined once he had completed revisions of his tragedy, *Cato.* Addison's last journalistic efforts appeared in the *Freeholder* and the *Old Whig.* He used the latter primarily as a forum for attacking the politics of Steele, with whom his friendship had soured. In 1716 Addison married the countess of Warwick, though his health was failing. He was already suffering from chronic asthma, and when he developed dropsy in 1719 it proved fatal. His dying words to his step-son, "See in what peace a Christian can die," achieved for him a posthumous reputation as a paragon of virtue.

Addison's poetry is largely imitative of the Latin verse he studied and translated during his years at Oxford. Like *The Campaign,* his other poetic works, including "To Sir Godfrey Kneller" and "To Her Royal Highness," exhibit a nationalistic sentiment modelled after that of Virgil, Horace, and Ovid. Addison was valued by the Whig party for the eloquence of his style and the lofty tone of his pane-gyrics to prominent figures, but his favorable reputation as a poet did not last long; as early as 1759, Edward Young dismissed *The Campaign* as a "gazette in rhyme." As a dramatist, Addison completed one work each in the genres of opera, comedy, and tragedy. *Rosamond* features a libretto by Addison recounting Henry II's romance with Rosamond Clifford. The music by Thomas Clayton was reportedly ill-suited to the words, and the opera ran for only three nights in 1707. Similarly, *The Drummer; or, The Haunted House,* a romantic comedy, met with little success due to what many saw as flat characterizations. *Cato,* celebrating the heroism of Marcus Portius Cato the Younger's struggle against an imperious Caesar, is mod-elled on Senecan tragedy, a form that stresses ideas over dramatic action. Addison initially intended it as a play to be read rather than performed, but at Steele's insistence it was brought to the stage. Audiences perceived *Cato* as a compelling political drama relevant to the clash between the Whigs and the Tories, and while some interpreted the play as an allegorical defense of the Whigs, members of both parties praised it highly. Pope, a Tory, wrote a pref-ace to *Cato* as well as a venomous attack on John Dennis, a critic who had published a negative review of the play. The production ran for an unprecedented thirty nights in 1713 and subsequently achieved international acclaim as a powerful statement against tyranny; for this reason, it was staged many years later at Valley Forge before Gener-al George Washington.

Although he achieved renown as a poet and a dramatist, much of Addison's fame was due to his strengths as an es-sayist. Fusing the breezy style of popular newspapers with the essay form devised by Michel de Montaigne in late six-teenth-century France and anglicized by Francis Bacon, Addison and Steele invented an extremely versatile popu-lar literary form. While Steele is credited with creating the framework for bringing informal prose to a cultivated readership, scholars generally acknowledge that Addi-son's contributions most fully explore the possibilities of the familiar essay. As Addison practiced it, the genre em-bodied the neoclassical dictum that a work of art must both instruct and entertain. More than two centuries after his journals ceased publication, Virginia Woolf recognized the durability of "the medium which makes it possible for people of ordinary intelligence to communicate their ideas to the world"; the form persists to the present day in such magazines as the *New Yorker.* Moreover, the fictional pieces in the *Tatler* and the *Spectator* are often viewed as crucial steps leading to the development of the novel. In his essays for the *Tatler,* Addison generally adhered to Steele's conception of Isaac Bickerstaff and his bemused perspective on Londoners and their habits, but he also

began experimenting with enhancing the sketches of the periodical's cast of fictional characters, providing them with family backgrounds and personal lives, and relying on narrative to convey a moral rather than stating it ex-plicitly. Scholars have noted that in some numbers, the re-sult is closer to a short story than an essay. In the *Specta-tor,* Addison continued to contribute fictional sketches, often straying far from the intended lesson in order to re-late a sense of character. Steele had invented the members of "The Spectator Club"—Mr. Spectator, Sir Andrew Freeport, Captain Sentry, the Templar, Will Honeycomb, the Clergyman, and Sir Roger de Coverley—to represent various political or social types, and Addison later added touches to make them seem more like living individuals. Sir Roger, an honest but backward country gentleman and a firm believer in Tory rhetoric, was given the most devel-opment of all, in thirty-three numbers. He is shown visit-ing various locations around England, commenting on topics including the Church, English history, and his own romantic misadventures. Beside lampooning outdated Tory beliefs, the Sir Roger de Coverley papers constitute, perhaps unintentionally, a kind of serial novel. Referring to this aspect of Addison's style, Thomas Babington Ma-caulay, his stalwart advocate from the Victorian period, called him "the forerunner of the great English novelists."

Addison also contributed significantly to the history of lit-erary criticism, and his assessments in the *Spectator* reflect the influence of John Dryden in their rigorous application of classical standards to literature. But, instead of aiming to influence other writers as Dryden did, Addison directed his papers to the educated reader. Furthermore, while Dryden sought to explain the merit of works of established importance, Addison defended lesser-known works in order to bolster their reputations. In his elaborate treat-ment of John Milton's *Paradise Lost* (1667), Addison de-voted one paper to each book of the poem, calling atten-tion to its originality as well as its adherence to epic form. His efforts have been cited as key factors in establishing Milton's critical status as the foremost poet of the English Renaissance. The essays on the English medieval ballad "Chevy Chase" contradicted the prevailing tendency of denigrating the ballad genre, for he contended that the work contains many of the virtues the Neoclassicists had professed to cherish, including heroic action and mimetic descriptions. Although his specific critical pronounce-ments have been surpassed, his critical practice is still re-garded as exemplary. According to C. S. Lewis, "What Addison really shows by his appreciation of the Ballad is his open-mindedness, his readiness to recognize excellence wherever he finds it." In the field of aesthetics, Addison's papers on "the pleasures of the imagination" restated the doctrines of John Locke's *Essay Concerning Human Un-derstanding* (1690) in a way that made it possible for the general audience to understand them. Based on Locke's theory of ideas, Addison's essays stressed personal taste and individual imagination—qualities which many schol-ars believe foreshadow Romantic views on art and artists.

Addison exerted a powerful influence over eighteenth-century letters and the literature of succeeding centuries. Even his political adversaries, Pope and Swift among them, admired the depth of his learning and the force of his opinions. The *Spectator,* the *Tatler,* and *Cato* were among the most popular literature of the period. After his death in 1719, Addison's elevated reputation persisted throughout much of the eighteenth century. In his *Lives of the English Poets* (1781), Samuel Johnson admitted that some of the praise for Addison during his lifetime might have been excessive, especially in regard to his poetry. Still, he affirmed, "Whoever wishes to attain an English style, familiar but not coarse, and elegant but not ostentatious, must give his days and nights to the volumes of Addison." Following the example of Macaulay, a highly influential educator and essayist, English writers of the nineteenth century looked upon Addison as the quintessential man of letters. In 1843 Macaulay wrote a lengthy review of Lucy Aikin's biography of Addison—the review itself was later published as a book—that unreservedly glorified his work as an essayist and poet, stating, "His humanity is without a parallel in literary history." Other Victorian literary figures, including William Makepeace Thackeray, expressed admiration for Addison's gifts as a satirist. At the beginning of the twentieth century, scholars tended to react strongly against what they viewed as the smugness and superficiality of the Victorian age. Writing in 1925, Bonamy Dobrée—recognizing that the Victorians held Addison in such high regard because, in part, they concurred with him on many issues—condescendingly titled his biographical sketch of Addison "The First Victorian." In 1943, C. S. Lewis pronounced, "Addison is, above all else, comfortable," exemplifying the twentieth-century perception that Addison belonged to an age that was at once simpler and more formal, and suggesting that his literary efforts had finally become outmoded. More recent critical assessments of Addison have followed the example of Lee Andrew Elioseff, who in his *Cultural Milieu of Addison's Literary Criticism* (1963) defined Addison as a revolutionary thinker, given the conservatism of his contemporaries. Similarly, the historian Peter Gay has sought to rediscover the cultural context of the *Spectator* essays in order to justify their temperateness, a quality which makes them distasteful to some modern readers. Asserting that Addison's essays are really quite pointed when viewed against the backdrop of eighteenth-century London, a particularly "coarse" place, Gay has argued that "Addison's moderation—his deliberate avoidance of wounding personal allusions, his lighthearted mockery—was itself didactic, designed to teach civility by example." Scholars continue to view Addison as a pivotal writer who epitomized his era and anticipated many later intellectual and literary trends.

(See also *Dictionary of Literary Biography,* Vol. 101.)

PRINCIPAL WORKS

The Campaign (poem) 1705
Remarks on Several Parts of Italy (prose) 1705
"The Present State of the War" (pamphlet) 1707
Rosamond (libretto) 1707
**The Tatler.* 6 vols. [with Richard Steele and others] (essays) 1709-11
†*The Spectator.* 5 vols. [with Richard Steele and others] (essays) 1711-12

Cato (drama) 1713
‡*The Guardian.* 2 vols. [with Richard Steele and others] (essays) 1713
The Drummer; or, The Haunted House (drama) 1716
§*The Works of the Right Honourable Joseph Addison.* 4 vols. (essays, poems, and dramas) 1721
The Works of the Right Honourable Joseph Addison. 6 vols. (essays, poems, and dramas) 1811
The Letters of Joseph Addison (letters) 1941

*Originally published as individual numbers from 12 April 1709 to 2 January 1711.

†Originally published as individual numbers from 1 March 1711 to 6 December 1712.

‡Originally published as individual numbers from 12 March to 1 October 1713.

§Includes essays from the *Whig Examiner,* which was published from 14 September to 12 October 1710, and the *Freeholder,* which was published from 23 December 1715 to 29 June 1716.

Joseph Addison (essay date 1711)

[*In the following essay from the* Spectator, *originally published March 12, 1711, Addison defines the objectives of the periodical and envisions the benefits it will bring to its readers.*]

It is with much Satisfaction that I hear this great City inquiring Day by Day after these my Papers, and receiving my Morning Lectures with a becoming Seriousness and Attention. My Publisher tells me, that there are already Three thousand of them distributed every Day: So that if I allow Twenty Readers to every Paper, which I look upon as a modest Computation, I may reckon about Threescore thousand Disciples in *London* and *Westminster,* who I hope will take care to distinguish themselves from the thoughtless Herd of their ignorant and unattentive Brethren. Since I have raised to myself so great an Audience, I shall spare no Pains to make their Instruction agreeable, and their Diversion useful. For which Reasons I shall endeavour to enliven Morality with Wit, and to temper Wit with Morality, that my Readers may, if possible, both Ways find their Account in the Speculation of the Day. And to the End that their Virtue and Discretion may not be short transient intermittent Starts of Thought, I have resolved to refresh their Memories from Day to Day, till I have recovered them out of that desperate State of Vice and Folly into which the Age is fallen. The Mind that lies fallow but a single Day, sprouts up in Follies that are only to be killed by a constant and assiduous Culture. It was said of *Socrates,* that he brought Philosophy down from Heaven, to inhabit among Men; and I shall be ambitious to have it said of me, that I have brought Philosophy out of Closets and Libraries, Schools and Colleges, to dwell in Clubs and Assemblies, at Tea-Tables and in Coffee-Houses.

I would therefore in a very particular Manner recommend these my Speculations to all well regulated Families, that set apart an Hour in every Morning for Tea and Bread and Butter; and would earnestly advise them for their Good to order [the *Spectator*] to be punctually served up, and to be looked upon as a Part of the Tea Equipage.

Sir *Francis Bacon* observes, that a well-written Book, compared with its Rivals and Antagonists, is like *Moses's* Serpent, that immediately swallow'd up and devoured those of the *Aegyptians*. I shall not be so vain as to think, that where the **SPECTATOR** appears, the other publick Prints will vanish; but shall leave it to my Reader's Consideration, whether, Is it not much better to be let into the Knowledge of one's self, than to hear what passes in *Muscovy* or *Poland;* and to amuse our selves with such Writings as tend to the wearing out of Ignorance, Passion, and Prejudice, than such as naturally conduce to inflame Hatreds, and make Enmities irreconcileable?

In the next Place, I would recommend this Paper to the daily Perusal of those Gentlemen whom I cannot but consider as my good Brothers and Allies, I mean the Fraternity of Spectators who live in the World without having any thing to do in it; and either by the Affluence of their Fortunes, or Laziness of their Dispositions, have no other Business with the rest of Mankind, but to look upon them. Under this Class of Men are comprehended all contemplative Tradesmen, titular Physicians, Fellows of the Royal Society, Templers that are not given to be contentious, and Statesmen that are out of Business; in short, every one that considers the World as a Theatre, and desires to form a right Judgment of those who are the Actors on it.

There is another Set of Men that I must likewise lay a Claim to, whom I have lately called the Blanks of Society, as being altogether unfurnish'd with Ideas, till the Business and Conversation of the Day has supplied them. I have often consider'd these poor Souls with an Eye of great Commiseration, when I have heard them asking the first Man they have met with, whether there was any News stirring? and by that Means gathering together Materials for thinking. These needy Persons do not know what to talk of, 'till about twelve a Clock in the Morning; for by that Time they are pretty good Judges of the Weather, know which Way the Wind sits, and whether the *Dutch* Mail be come in. As they lie at the Mercy of the first Man they meet, and are grave or impertinent all the Day long, according to the Notions which they have imbibed in the Morning, I would earnestly entreat them not to stir out of their Chambers 'till they have read this Paper, and do promise them that I will daily instil into them such sound and wholesom Sentiments, as shall have a good Effect on their Conversation for the ensuing twelve Hours.

But there are none to whom this Paper will be more useful, than to the Female World. I have often thought there has not been sufficient Pains taken in finding out proper Employments and Diversions for the Fair ones. Their Amusements seem contrived for them rather as they are Women, than as they are reasonable Creatures; and are more adapted to the Sex than to the Species. The Toilet is their great Scene of Business, and the right adjusting of their Hair the principal Employment of their Lives. The sorting of a Suit of Ribbons is reckon'd a very good Morning's Work; and if they make an Excursion to a Mercer's or a

Toy-shop, so great a Fatigue makes them unfit for any thing else all the Day after. Their more serious Occupations are Sowing and Embroidery, and their greatest Drudgery the Preparation of Jellies and Sweet-meats. This, I say, is the State of ordinary Women; tho' I know there are Multitudes of those of a more elevated Life and Conversation, that move in an exalted Sphere of Knowledge and Virtue, that join all the Beauties of the Mind to the Ornaments of Dress, and inspire a kind of Awe and Respect, as well as Love, into their Male-Beholders. I hope to encrease the Number of these by Publishing this daily Paper, which I shall always endeavour to make an innocent if not an improving Entertainment, and by that Means at least divert the Minds of my Female Readers from greater Trifles. At the same Time, as I would fain give some finishing Touches to those which are already the most beautiful Pieces in human Nature, I shall endeavour to point out all those Imperfections that are the Blemishes, as well as those Virtues which are the Embellishments, of the Sex. In the mean while I hope these my gentle Readers, who have so much Time on their Hands, will not grudge throwing away a Quarter of an Hour in a Day on this Paper, since they may do it without any Hindrance to Business.

I know several of my Friends and Well-wishers are in great Pain for me, lest I should not be able to keep up the Spirit of a Paper which I oblige my self to furnish every Day: But to make them easie in this Particular, I will promise them faithfully to give it over as soon as I grow dull. This I know will be Matter of great Raillery to the small Wits; who will frequently put me in mind of my Promise, desire me to keep my Word, assure me that it is high Time to give over, with many other little Pleasantries of the like Nature, which Men of a little smart Genius cannot forbear throwing out against their best Friends, when they have such a Handle given them of being witty. But let them remember that I do hereby enter my Caveat against this Piece of Raillery. (pp. 31-4)

> *Joseph Addison, in an excerpt in* Addison &
> Steele and Others: The Spectator, Vol. I, *edited by Gregory Smith, Everyman's Library,*
> *1956, pp. 31-4.*

John Dennis (essay date 1713)

[*Dennis was a minor eighteenth-century English man of letters who is generally esteemed for his astute, wide-ranging literary criticism. However, his several unusually abusive attacks on the character and writings of Alexander Pope have largely diminished his posthumous status in the field. In the following excerpt from a work originally published in 1713, Dennis ridicules Addison's* Cato *for violating Aristotle's rules for tragedy.*]

Probability ought certainly to reign in every tragical action; but though it ought everywhere to predominate, it ought not to exclude the wonderful, as the wonderful which ought everywhere to predominate in epic poetry ought not to exclude the probable. We shall then treat of the improbabilities of this tragedy [*Cato*] when we come to speak of the absurdities with which it throughout abounds from the indiscreet and injudicious observance of some of the Rules of Aristotle. We are at present showing what beauties are wanting to it from the not observing others of those Rules. Here then are none of those beautiful surprises which are to be found in some of the Grecian tragedies and in some of our own, and consequently here is nothing wonderful, nothing terrible or deplorable, which all three are caused by surprise. Now as tragedy is the imitation of an action which excites compassion and terror, and as that alone can be justly accounted a very fine tragical scene which excites one of those two passions, or both, in a very great degree, and as it is impossible either of 'em can be excited in a very great degree without a very great surprise, and there is in this tragedy no very great surprise, we find there is not in this tragedy no not so much as one very fine tragical scene, no not so much as one scene with which we are extremely moved. I sit with indolence from the opening of the play to the very catastrophe; and when at length the catastrophe comes, instead of vehemently shaking with terror or dissolving with melting pity, I rather burn with indignation and I shudder with horror.

> *John Dennis, "Remarks upon Addison's 'Cato, a Tragedy',"* in *Dramatic Essays of the Neoclassic Age, edited by Henry Hitch Adams and Baxter Hathaway, Columbia University Press, 1950, p. 208.*

Richard Steele   (essay date 1716)

[*An Irish-born English politician, dramatist, and essayist, Steele is best known for his journalistic enterprises. Among the many periodicals he founded and edited during the eighteenth century, the two most notable are the* Tatler *and the* Spectator, *the latter a highly popular and influential daily created in collaboration with Addison. Steele was always conscious of the moral intent and effect of his essays, and though they are often diverting and amusing, their ultimate aim is the ethical improvement of the reader. As a dramatist, too, Steele was primarily a moralist; plays such as* The Tender Husband *(1705) and* The Conscious Lovers *(1722) were instrumental in effecting the transition from the decadent, cynical comedies of the Restoration to didactic sentimental comedy. In the following preface to* The Drummer *(1716), Steele praises the humor of the play.*]

Having recommended this Play to the town, and delivered the copy of it to the bookseller, I think myself obliged to give some account of it.

It had been some years in the hands of the author, and falling under my perusal, I thought so well of it, that I persuaded him to make some additions and alterations to it, and let it appear upon the stage. I own I was very highly pleased with it, and liked it the better, for the want of those studied similies and repartees, which we, who have writ before him, have thrown into our Plays, to indulge and gain upon a false taste that has prevailed for many years in the British Theatre. I believe the Author would have condescended to fall into this way a little more than he has, had he, before the writing of it, been often present at theatrical representations. I was confirmed in my thoughts of the Play, by the opinion of better judges, to whom it was communicated, who observed, that the scenes were drawn after Molière's manner, and that an easy and natural vein of humour ran through the whole.

I do not question but the reader will discover this, and see many beauties that escaped the audience; the touches being too delicate for every taste in a popular assembly. My brother sharers were of opinion, at the first reading of it, that it was like a picture in which the strokes were not strong enough to appear at a distance. As it is not in the common way of writing, the approbation was at first doubtful, but has risen every time it has been acted, and has given an opportunity, in several of its parts, for as just and good action as ever I saw on the stage.

The reader will consider that I speak here, not as the author, but as the patentee; which is, perhaps, the reason why I am not diffuse in the praises of the Play, lest I should seem like a man who cries up his own wares, only to draw in customers.

> *Richard Steele, in a preface to* The Drummer (or) The Haunted House: A Comedy *by Joseph Addison, John Bell, 1792, p. Aij.*

Thomas Tickell   (essay date 1721)

[*Tickell was a minor poet and translator and a friend of Addison. His translation of the first book of* The Iliad *(1715) appeared at the same time as that of Alexander Pope. The following is an excerpt from Tickell's preface to a collection of Addison's works, published two years after Addison's death. The preface closes with an elegy.*]

[Addison] first distinguished himself by his Latin compositions, published in the *Musæ Anglicanæ,* and was admired as one of the best authors since the Augustan age, in the two Universities, and the greatest part of Europe, before he was talked of as a poet in town. There is not, perhaps, any harder task than to tame the natural wildness of wit, and to civilize the fancy. The generality of our old English poets abound in forced conceits, and affected phrases, and even those who are said to come the nearest to exactness, are but too often fond of unnatural beauties, and aim at something better than perfection. If Mr. Addison's example and precepts be the occasion, that there now begins to be a great demand for correctness, we may justly attribute it to his being first fashioned by the ancient models, and familiarised to propriety of thought and chastity of style. Our country owes it to him, that the famous Monsieur Boileau first conceived an opinion of the English genius for poetry, by perusing the present he made him of the *Musæ Anglicanæ.* It has been currently reported, that this famous French poet, among the civilities he showed Mr. Addison on that occasion, affirmed, that he would not have written against Perrault, had he before seen such excellent pieces by a modern hand. Such a saying would have been impertinent and unworthy Boileau, whose dispute with Perrault turned chiefly upon some passages in the ancients, which he rescued from the misinterpretations of his adversary. The true and natural compliment made by him was, that those books had given him a very new idea of English politeness; and that he did not question but there were excellent compositions in the native language of a country that possessed the Roman genius in so eminent a degree.

The first English performance made public by him, is a short copy of verses to Mr. Dryden, with a view particularly to his translations. This was soon followed by a version of the fourth Georgic of Virgil, of which Mr. Dryden makes very honourable mention in the postscript to his own translation of all Virgil's Works; wherein I have often wondered that he did not, at the same time, acknowledge his obligation to Mr. Addison, for giving him the Essay upon the Georgics, prefixed to Mr. Dryden's translation. (pp. viii-ix)

Of some other copies of verses printed in the miscellanies while he was young, the largest is *An Account of the Greatest English Poets;* in the close of which he insinuates a design he then had of going into holy orders, to which he was strongly importuned by his father. His remarkable seriousness and modesty, which might have been urged as powerful reasons for his choosing that life, proved the chief obstacles to it. These qualities, by which the priesthood is so much adorned, represented the duties of it as too weighty for him; and rendered him still the more worthy of that honour, which they made him decline. It is happy that this very circumstance has since turned so much to the advantage of virtue and religion, in the cause of which he has bestowed his labours the more successfully, as they were his voluntary, not his necessary employment. The world became insensibly reconciled to wisdom and goodness, when they saw them recommended by him with at least as much spirit and elegance, as they had been ridiculed for half a century.

He was in his twenty-eighth year, when his inclination to see France and Italy was encouraged by the great Lord Chancellor Somers, one of that kind of patriots, who think it no waste of the public treasure to purchase politeness to their country. The poem upon one of King William's campaigns, addressed to his Lordship, was received with great humanity, and occasioned a message from him to the author to desire his acquaintance. He soon after obtained, by his interest, a yearly pension of three hundred pounds from the Crown, to support him in his travels. If the uncommonness of a favour, and the distinction of a person who confers it, enhance its value, nothing could be more honourable to a young man of learning, than such a bounty from so eminent a patron.

How well Mr. Addison answered the expectations of my Lord Somers, cannot appear better, than from the book of Travels he dedicated to his Lordship at his return. It is not hard to conceive why that performance was at first but indifferently relished by the bulk of readers, who expected an account, in a common way, of the customs and policies of the several governments in Italy, reflections upon the genius of the people, a map of their provinces, or a measure of their buildings. How were they disappointed, when, instead of such particulars, they were presented with a journal only of poetical travels, with remarks on the present picture of the country, compared with the landscapes drawn by classic authors, and others the like unconcerning parts of knowledge! One may easily imagine a reader of plain sense, but without a fine taste,

turning over these parts of the volume, which make more than half of it, and wondering how an author, who seems to have so solid an understanding, when he treats of more weighty subjects in the other pages, should dwell upon such trifles, and give up so much room to matters of mere amusement. There are, indeed, but few men so fond of the ancients, as to be transported with every little accident, which introduces to their intimate acquaintance. Persons of that cast may here have the satisfaction of seeing annotations, upon an old Roman poem, gathered from the hills and vallies where it was written. The Tyber and the Po serve to explain the verses that were made upon their banks; and the Alps and Appennines are made commentators on those authors to whom they were subjects so many centuries ago. Next to personal conversation with the writers themselves, this is the surest way of coming at their sense: a compendious and engaging kind of criticism, which convinces at first sight, and shows the vanity of conjectures made by antiquaries at a distance. If the knowledge of polite literature has its use, there is certainly a merit in illustrating the perfect models of it; and the learned world will think some years of a man's life not mis-spent in so elegant an employment. I shall conclude what I had to say on this performance, by observing, that the fame of it increased from year to year; and the demand for copies was so urgent, that their price rose to four or five times the original value before it came out in a second edition.

The Letter from Italy to my Lord Halifax may be considered as the text upon which the book of Travels is a large comment, and has been esteemed by those who have a relish for antiquity, as the most exquisite of his poetical performances. A translation of it by Signior Salvini, professor of the Greek tongue at Florence, is inserted in this edition; not only on the account of its merit, but because it is the language of the country which is the subject of this poem.

The materials for the *Dialogues upon Medals,* now first printed from a manuscript of the author, were collected in the native country of those coins. The book itself was begun to be cast into form at Vienna, as appears from a letter to Mr. Stepney, then minister at that court, dated in November, 1702.

Some time before the date of this letter, Mr. Addison had a design to return to England, when he received advice from his friends, that he was pitched upon to attend the army under Prince Eugene, who had just begun the war in Italy, as secretary from his Majesty. But an account of the death of King William, which he met with at Geneva, put an end to that thought; and as his hopes of advancement in his own country were fallen with the credit of his friends, who were out of power at the beginning of her late Majesty's reign, he had leisure to make the tour of Germany in his way home.

He remained for some time, after his return to England, without any public employment, which he did not obtain till the year 1704, when the Duke of Marlborough arrived at the highest pitch of glory, by delivering all Europe from slavery, and furnished Mr. Addison with a subject worthy of that genius which appears in his Poem called *The Campaign.*—The Lord Treasurer Godolphin, who was a fine judge of poetry, had a sight of this work, when it was only carried on as far as the applauding simile of the Angel; and approved the poem, by bestowing on the author, in a few days after, the place of Commissioner of Appeals, vacant by the removal of the famous Mr. Locke to the council of trade.

His next advancement was to the place of Under Secretary, which he held under Sir Charles Hedges, and the present Earl of Sunderland. The Opera of **Rosamond** was written while he possessed that employment. What doubts soever have been raised about the merit of the music, which, as the Italian taste at that time began wholly to prevail, was thought sufficiently inexcusable, because it was the composition of an Englishman. The poetry of this piece has given as much pleasure in the closet, as others have afforded from the stage, with all the assistance of voices and instruments.

The Comedy called *The Tender Husband* appeared much about the same time, to which Mr. Addison wrote the Prologue. Sir Richard Steele surprised him with a very handsome dedication of this play, and has since acquainted the public, that he owed some of the most taking scenes of it to Mr. Addison.

His next step in his fortune, was to the post of Secretary under the late Marquis of Wharton, who was appointed Lord Lieutenant of Ireland in the year 1709. As I have proposed to touch but very lightly on those parts of his life which do not regard him as an author, I shall not enlarge upon the great reputation he acquired by his turn to business, and his unblemished integrity, in this and other employments. It must not be omitted here, that the salary of Keeper of the Records in Ireland was considerably raised, and that post bestowed upon him, at this time, as a mark of the Queen's favour. He was in that kingdom when he first discovered Sir Richard Steele to be author of **The Tattler,** by an observation upon Virgil, which had been by him communicated to his friend. The assistance he occasionally gave him afterwards in the course of the paper, did not a little contribute to advance its reputation; and upon the change of the ministry, he found leisure to engage more constantly in that work, which, however, was dropped at last, as it had been taken up, without his participation.

In the last paper, which closed those celebrated performances . . . , Sir Richard Steele has given to Mr. Addison the honour of the most applauded pieces in that collection. But as that acknowledgment was delivered only in general terms, without directing the public to the several papers, Mr. Addison, who was content with the praise arising from his own works, and too delicate to take any part of that which belonged to others, afterwards thought fit to distinguish his writings in the **Spectator**s and **Guardian**s, by such marks as might remove the least possibility of mistake in the most undiscerning readers. It was necessary that his share in the **Tatler**s should be adjusted in a complete collection of his works; for which reason Sir Richard Steele, in compliance with the request of his deceased friend, delivered to him by the editor, was pleased to mark with his own hand those **Tatler**s which

are inserted in this edition, and even to point out several, in the writing of which they both were concerned.

The plan of the **Spectator,** as far as it regards the feigned person of the author, and of the several characters that compose his club, was projected in concert with Sir Richard Steele. . . . As for the distinct papers, they were seldom or never shown to each other by their respective authors, who fully answered the promise they had made, and far out-went the expectation they had raised, of pursuing their labour in the same spirit and strength with which it was begun. It would have been impossible for Mr. Addison, who made little or no use of letters sent in by the numerous correspondents of the **Spectator,** to have executed his large share of this task in so exquisite a manner, if he had not ingrafted into it many pieces that had lain by him in little hints and minutes, which he from time to time collected, and ranged in order, and moulded into the form in which they now appear. Such are the **Essays upon Wit, The Pleasures of Imagination, The Critique upon Milton,** and some others. . . . (pp. ix-xv)

The **Tragedy of Cato** appeared in public in the year 1713, when the greatest part of the last act was added by the author to the foregoing, which he had kept by him for many years. He took up a design of writing a play upon this subject, when he was very young at the University, and even attempted something in it there, though not a line as it now stands. The work was performed by him in his travels, and retouched in England, without any formed resolution of bringing it upon the stage, until his friends of the first quality and distinction, prevailed with him to put the last finishing to it, at a time when they thought the doctrine of liberty very seasonable. It is in every body's memory, with what applause it was received by the public; that the first run of it lasted for a month; and then stopped, only because one of the performers became incapable of acting a principal part. The author received a message, that the Queen would be pleased to have it dedicated to her; but as he had designed that compliment elsewhere, he found himself obliged by his duty, on the one side, and his honour on the other, to send it into the world without any dedication. The fame of this Tragedy soon spread through Europe; and it has not only been translated, but acted, in most of the languages of Christendom. The translation of it into Italian, by Signior Salvini, is very well known; but I have not been able to learn, whether that of Signior Valetta, a young Neopolitan nobleman, has ever been made public.

If he had found time for the writing of another tragedy, the death of Socrates would have been the story. And, however unpromising that subject may appear, it would be presumptuous to censure his choice, who was so famous for raising the noblest plants from the most barren soil. It serves to show, that he thought the whole labour of such a performance unworthy to be thrown away upon those intrigues and adventures, to which the romantic taste has confined modern tragedy; and, after the example of his predecessors in Greece, would have employed the drama "to wear out of our minds everything that is mean, or little; to cherish and cultivate that humanity which is the ornament of our nature; to soften insolence, to soothe

Addison's wife, Charlotte Myddelton of Chirk, painted by Van der Mijn.

affliction, and to subdue our minds to the dispensations of Providence" [*Spectator* 39].

Upon the death of the late Queen, the Lords Justices, in whom the administration was lodged, appointed him their Secretary. Soon after His Majesty's arrival in Great-Britain, the Earl of Sunderland being constituted Lord Lieutenant of Ireland, Mr. Addison became a second time Secretary for the affairs of that kingdom; and was made one of the Lords Commissioners of Trade, a little after his Lordship resigned the post of Lord Lieutenant.

The paper called the *Freeholder,* was undertaken at the time when the rebellion broke out in Scotland.

The only works he left behind him for the public, are the *Dialogues upon Medals,* and the *Treatise upon the Christian Religion.* (pp. xv-xvii)

The scheme for the *Treatise upon the Christian Religion* was formed by the author about the end of the late Queen's reign; at which time he carefully perused the ancient writings which furnish the materials for it. His continual employment in business prevented him from executing it till he resigned his office of Secretary of State; and his death put a period to it, when he had imperfectly performed only one half of the design; he having proposed, as appears from the introduction, to add the Jewish to the Heathen testimonies, for the truth of the Christian history. He was more assiduous than his health would well allow in the pursuit of this work; and had long determined to

dedicate his poetry also, for the future, wholly to religious subjects.

Soon after he was, from being one of the Lords Commissioners of Trade, advanced to the post of Secretary of State, he found his health impaired by the return of that asthmatic indisposition which continued often to afflict him during his exercise of that employment, and at last obliged him to beg His Majesty's leave to resign. His freedom from the anxiety of business so far re-established his health, that his friends began to hope he might last for many years; but (whether it were from a life too sedentary, or from his natural constitution, in which was one circumstance very remarkable, that, from his cradle, he never had a regular pulse) a long and painful relapse into an asthma and dropsy, deprived the world of this great man, on the 17th of June, 1719. He left behind him only one daughter, by the Countess of Warwick, to whom he was married in the year 1716.

Not many days before his death, he gave me directions to collect his writings; and at the same time committed to my care the Letter addressed to Mr. Craggs (his successor as Secretary of State) wherein he bequeaths them to him as a token of friendship.—Such a testimony, from the first man of our age, in such a point of time, will be, perhaps, as great and lasting an honour to that gentleman, as any even he could acquire to himself; and yet is no more than was due from an affection, that justly increased towards him through the intimacy of several years. I cannot, without the utmost tenderness, reflect on the kind concern with which Mr. Addison left Me as a sort of incumbrance upon this valuable legacy. Nor must I deny myself the honour to acknowledge, that the goodness of that great man to me, like many other of his amiable qualities, seemed not so much to be renewed, as continued, in his successor; who made me an example, that nothing could be indifferent to him which came recommended by Mr. Addison.

Could any circumstance be more severe to me, while I was executing these last commands of the author, than to see the person, to whom his works were presented, cut off in the flower of his age, and carried from the high office wherein he had succeeded Mr. Addison, to be laid next him in the same grave. I might dwell upon such thoughts as naturally rise from these minute resemblances in the fortune of two persons, whose names probably will be seldom mentioned asunder, while either our language or story subsist, were I not afraid of making this Preface too tedious; especially since I shall want all the patience of the reader, for having enlarged it with the following verses. (pp. xvii-xix)

To The
Right Honourable
The
EARL OF WARWICK, &c.

If, dumb too long, the drooping Muse hath
    stay'd,
And left her debt to Addison unpaid:
Blame not her silence, Warwick, but bemoan,
And judge, oh, judge, my bosom by your own.
What mourner ever felt poetic fires!

Slow comes the verse that real wo inspires:
Grief unaffected suits but ill with art,
Or flowing numbers with a bleeding heart.

Can I forget the dismal night, that gave
My soul's best part for ever to the grave!
How silent did his old companions tread,
By midnight lamps, the mansions of the dead,
Through breathing statues, then unheeded
   things,
Through rows of warriors, and through walks of
   kings!
What awe did the slow solemn knell inspire;
The pealing organ, and the pausing choir;
The duties by the lawn-rob'd prelate pay'd;
And the last words, that dust to dust convey'd!
While speechless o'er thy closing grave we bend,
Accept these tears, thou dear departed friend!
Oh, gone for ever, take this long adieu;
And sleep in peace, next thy lov'd Montagu!

To strew fresh laurels, let the task be mine;
A frequent pilgrim at thy sacred shrine;
Mine with true sighs thy absence to bemoan,
And grave with faithful epitaphs thy stone.
If e'er from me thy lov'd memorial part,
May shame afflict this alienated heart;
Of thee forgetful if I form a song,
My lyre be broken, and untun'd my tongue,
My griefs be doubled, from thy image free,
And mirth a torment, unchastis'd by thee.

Oft let me range the gloomy iles alone,
(Sad luxury! to vulgar minds unknown)
Along the walls where speaking marbles show
What worthies form the hallow'd mould below:
Proud names, who once the reins of empire held;
In arms who triumph'd, or in arts excell'd;
Chiefs, grac'd with scars, and prodigal of blood;
Stern patriots, who for sacred freedom stood;
Just men, by whom impartial laws were given;
And saints, who taught, and led the way to heav-
   en.
Ne'er to these chambers, where the mighty rest,
Since their foundation, came a nobler guest;
Nor e'er was to the bowers of bliss convey'd
A fairer spirit, or more welcome shade.

In what new region, to the just assign'd,
What new employments please th' unbody'd
   mind?
A winged Virtue, through th' ethereal sky,
From world to world, unweary'd does he fly;
Or curious trace the long laborious maze
Of heaven's decrees, where wond'ring angels
   gaze?
Does he delight to hear bold seraphs tell
How Michael battled, and the Dragon fell?
Or, mixt with milder Cherubim, to glow
In hymns of love, not ill essay'd below?
Or dost thou warn poor mortals left behind,
A task well suited to thy gentle mind?
Oh, if sometimes thy spotless form descend,
To me thy aid, thou guardian Genius, lend!
When rage misguides me, or when fear alarms,
When pain distresses, or when pleasure charms,
In silent whisp'rings purer thoughts impart,
And turn from ill a frail and feeble heart;
Lead through the paths thy virtue trod before,
Till bliss shall join, nor death can part us more.

That awful form (which, so ye heavens decree,
Must still be lov'd, and still deplor'd by me)
In nightly visions seldom fails to rise,
Or, rous'd by fancy, meets my waking eyes.
If business calls, or crouded courts invite,
Th' unblemish'd statesman seems to strike my
   sight;
If in the stage I seek to sooth my care,
I meet his soul, which breathes in Cato there:
If pensive to the rural shades I rove,
His shape o'ertakes me in the lonely grove:
'Twas there of Just and Good he reason'd
   strong,
Clear'd some great truth, or rais'd some serious
   song;
There patient show'd us the wise course to steer,
A candid censor, and a friend severe;
There taught us how to live; and (oh! too high
The price for knowledge) taught us how to die.

Thou hill, whose brow the antique struc-
   tures grace,
Rear'd by bold chiefs of Warwick's noble race,
Why, once so lov'd, whene'er thy bower appears,
O'er my dim eye-balls glance the sudden tears?
How sweet were once thy prospects, fresh and
   fair,
Thy sloping walks, and unpolluted air!
How sweet the glooms beneath thy aged trees,
Thy noon-tide shadow, and thy evening breeze!
His image thy forsaken bowers restore;
Thy walks and airy prospects charm no more;
No more the summer in thy gloom's allay'd,
Thy evening breezes, and thy noon-day shade.

From other ills, however Fortune frown'd,
Some refuge in the Muse's art I found:
Reluctant now I touch the trembling string;
Bereft of him who taught me how to sing;
And these sad accents, murmur'd o'er his urn,
Betray that absence they attempt to mourn.
Oh! must I then (now fresh my bosom bleeds,
And Craggs in death to Addison succeeds)
The verse, begun to one lost friend, prolong,
And weep a second in th' unfinish'd song!

These works divine, which, on his death-bed
   laid,
To thee, O, Craggs, th' expiring Sage convey'd;
Great, but ill-omen'd, monument of fame;
Nor he surviv'd to give, nor thou to claim.
Swift after him thy social spirit flies,
And close to his, how soon! thy coffin lies.
Blest pair! whose union future bards shall tell
In future tongues: each other's boast! farewell.
Farewell! whom join'd in fame, in friendship
   try'd,
No chance could sever, nor the grave divide.

(pp. xxi-xxiv)

Thomas Tickell, in a preface to The Works of
the Right Honorable Joseph Addison, Vol. I,
*edited by Thomas Tickell, Jacob Tonson,
1721, pp. vii-xxiv.*

Alexander Pope   (essay date 1734)

[*Pope has been called the greatest English poet of his
time and one of the most important in the history of*

world literature. As a critic and satirical commentator on eighteenth-century England, he was the author of work that represents the epitome of Neoclassicist thought. His famous remark, "The Proper study of mankind is man," perfectly illustrates the temperament of his age, a time when influential thinkers severely narrowed the limits of human speculation. All of Pope's work demonstrates his love of restraint, clarity, order, and that often overused classical term "decorum." His greatness lies in his cultivation of style and wit, rather than sublimity and pathos, and this inclination shaped his criticism of other writers. The following excerpt from Pope's "Epistle to Dr. Arbuthnot," written in 1734, contains his well-known description of "Atticus," mocking Addison's literary influence.]

[Were] there One whose fires
True Genius kindles, and fair Fame inspires;
Blest with each talent and each art to please,
And born to write, converse, and live with ease:
Should such a man, too fond to rule alone,
Bear, like the Turk, no brother near the throne,
View him with scornful, yet with jealous eyes,
And hate for arts that caus'd himself to rise;
Damn with faint praise, assent with civil leer,
And without sneering, teach the rest to sneer;
Willing to wound, and yet afraid to strike,
Just hint a fault, and hesitate dislike;
Alike reserv'd to blame, or to commend,
A tim'rous foe, and a suspicious friend;
Dreading ev'n fools, by Flatterers besieg'd,
And so obliging, that he ne'er oblig'd;
Like Cato, give his little Senate laws,
And sit attentive to his own applause;
While Wits and Templars ev'ry sentence raise,
And wonder with a foolish face of praise—
Who but must laugh, if such a man there be?
Who would not weep, if ATTICUS were he!

(pp. 333-34)

Alexander Pope, in his Pope: Poetical Works, *edited by Herbert Davis, Oxford University Press, London, 1966, 754 p.*

Oliver Goldsmith   (essay date 1759)

[Goldsmith is one of the most important writers of the Augustan age. He distinguished himself during his lifetime as an expressive narrative poet, but has since been acclaimed for two major literary works: The Vicar of Wakefield *(1766), and* She Stoops to Conquer *(1773). Below, he comments briefly on Addison's style.]*

Mr. Addison, for a happy and natural stile, will be always an honour to British literature. His diction indeed wants strength, but it is equal to all the subjects he undertakes to handle, as he never (at least in his finished works) attempts any thing either in the argumentative or demonstrative way. (p. 243)

Oliver Goldsmith, in an originally unsigned essay titled "An Account of the Augustan Age of England," in The Bee: Being Essays on the Most Interesting Subjects, *No. VIII, November 24, 1759, pp. 235-47.*

Edward Young   (essay date 1759)

[Young is best known as the author of The Complaint; or, Night Thoughts on Life, Death, and Immortality *(1742-45), a long blank verse meditation. His* Conjectures on Original Composition in a Letter to the Author of Sir Charles Grandison, *an open letter to Samuel Richardson, was published in pamphlet form. In the following excerpt from that work, Young offers a favorable judgment of* Cato *as a "closet" play and celebrates Addison's character, particularly as exemplified by his dying words.]*

Among the brightest of the moderns, Mr. Addison must take his place. Who does not approach his character with great respect? They who refuse to close with the public in his praise, refuse at their peril. But, if men will be fond of their own opinions, some hazard must be run. He had, what Dryden and Jonson wanted, a warm and feeling heart; but, being of a grave and bashful nature, through a philosophic reserve and a sort of moral prudery, he concealed it where he should have let loose all his fire, and have showed the most tender sensibilities of heart. At his celebrated *Cato* few tears are shed but Cato's own; which, indeed, are truly great, but unaffecting, except to the noble few who love their country better than themselves. The bulk of mankind want virtue enough to be touched by them. His strength of genius has reared up one glorious image, more lofty and truly golden than that in the plains of Dura, for cool admiration to gaze at, and warm patriotism (how rare!) to worship; while those two throbbing pulses of the drama, by which alone it is shown to live, terror and pity, neglected through the whole, leave our unmolested hearts at perfect peace. Thus the poet, like his hero, through mistaken excellence, and virtue overstrained, becomes a sort of suicide; and that which is most dramatic in the drama, dies. All his charms of poetry are but as funeral flowers, which adorn; all his noble sentiments but as rich spices, which embalm, the tragedy deceased.

Of tragedy, pathos is not only the life and soul, but the soul inextinguishable: it charms us through a thousand faults. Decorations, which in this author abound, though they might immortalize other poesy, are the *splendida peccata* which damn the drama; while, on the contrary, the murder of all other beauties is a venial sin, nor plucks the laurel from the tragedian's brow. Was it otherwise, Shakespeare himself would run some hazard of losing his crown.

Socrates frequented the plays of Euripides; and what living Socrates would decline the theatre at the representation of *Cato*? Tully's assassins found him in his litter reading the *Medea* of the Grecian poet to prepare himself for death. Part of *Cato* might be read to the same end. In the weight and dignity of moral reflection, Addison resembles that poet who was called "the dramatic philosopher"; and is himself, as he says of *Cato*, "ambitiously sententious." But as to the singular talent, so remarkable in Euripides, at melting down hearts into the tender streams of grief and pity, there the resemblance fails. His beauties sparkle, but do not warm; they sparkle as stars in a frosty night. There is, indeed, a constellation in his play; there is the philosopher, patriot, orator, and poet; but where is the tragedian? And, if that is wanting,

> Cur in theatrum, Cato severe, venisti? Mart.

And, when I recollect what passed between him and Dryden in relation to this drama, I must add the next line,—

> An ideo tantum veneras, ut exires?

For, when Addison was a student at Oxford, he sent up his play to his friend Dryden, as a proper person to recommend it to the theatre, if it deserved it; who returned it with very great commendation, but with his opinion, that, on the stage, it could not meet with its deserved success. But though the performance was denied the theatre, it brought its author on the public stage of life. For persons in power inquiring soon after of the head of his college for a youth of parts, Addison was recommended, and readily received, by means of the great reputation which Dryden had just then spread of him above.

There is this similitude between the poet and the play: as this is more fit for the closet than the stage, so that shone brighter in private conversation than on the public scene. They both had a sort of local excellency, as the heathen gods a local divinity; beyond such a bound they unadmired, and these unadored. This puts me in mind of Plato, who denied Homer to the public; that Homer which, when in his closet, was rarely out of his hand. Thus, though *Cato* is not calculated to signalize himself in the warm emotions of the theatre, yet we find him a most amiable companion in our calmer delights of recess.

Notwithstanding what has been offered, this, in many views, is an exquisite piece. But there is so much more of art than nature in it, that I can scarce forbear calling it an exquisite piece of statuary,

> "Where the smooth chisel all its skill has shown,
> To soften into flesh the rugged stone."—
> Addison.

That is, where art has taken great pains to labor undramatic matter into dramatic life; which is impossible. However, as it is, like Pygmalion, we cannot but fall in love with it, and wish it was alive. How would a Shakespeare or an Otway have answered our wishes? They would have outdone Prometheus, and, with their heavenly fire, have given him not only life, but immortality. At their dramas (such is the force of nature) the poet is out of sight, quite hid behind his Venus, never thought of till the curtain falls. Art brings our Author forward, he stands before his piece; splendidly, indeed, but unfortunately; for the writer must be forgotten by his audience during the representation, if for ages he would be remembered by posterity. In the theatre, as in life, delusion is the charm; and we are undelighted the first moment we are undeceived. Such demonstration have we that the theatre is not yet opened in which solid happiness can be found by man; because none are more than comparatively good; and folly has a corner in the heart of the wise.

A genius fond of ornament should not be wedded to the tragic muse, which is in mourning: we want not to be diverted at an entertainment where our greatest pleasure arises from the depth of our concern. But whence (by the way) this odd generation of pleasure from pain? The movement of our melancholy passions is pleasant when we ourselves are safe; we love to be at once miserable and unhurt: so are we made; and so made, perhaps, to show us the Divine goodness; to show that none of our passions were designed to give us pain, except when being pained is for our advantage on the whole; which is evident from this instance, in which we see that passions the most painful administer greatly, sometimes, to our delight. Since great names have accounted otherwise for this particular, I wish this solution, though to me probable, may not prove a mistake.

To close our thoughts on *Cato:* he who sees not much beauty in it, has no taste for poetry; he who sees nothing else, has no taste for the stage. While it justifies censure, it extorts applause. It is much to be admired, but little to be felt. Had it not been a tragedy, it had been immortal; as it is a tragedy, its uncommon fate somewhat resembles his who, for conquering gloriously, was condemned to die. Both shone, but shone fatally; because in breach of their respective laws, the laws of the drama, and the laws of arms. But how rich in reputation must that author be who can spare a *Cato* without feeling the loss!

That loss by our author would scarce be felt; it would be but dropping a single feather from a wing that mounts him above his contemporaries. He has a more refined, decent, judicious, and extensive genius than Pope or Swift. To distinguish this triumvirate from each other, and, like Newton, to discover the different colors in these genuine and meridian rays of literary light, Swift is a singular wit, Pope a correct poet, Addison a great author. Swift looked on wit as the *jus divinum* to dominion and sway in the world, and considered as usurpation all power that was lodged in persons of less sparkling understandings. This inclined him to tyranny in wit. Pope was somewhat of his opinion, but was for softening tyranny into lawful monarchy; yet were there some acts of severity in his reign. Addison's crown was elective: he reigned by the public voice:

> —Volentes
> Per populos dat jura viamque affectat Olympo.
> Virg.

But as good books are the medicine of the mind, if we should dethrone these authors and consider them not in their royal, but their medicinal capacity, might it not then be said—that Addison prescribed a wholesome and pleasant regimen which was universally relished and did much good;—that Pope preferred a purgative of satire which, though wholesome, was too painful in its operation—and that Swift insisted on a large dose of ipecacuanha, which, though readily swallowed from the fame of the physician, yet, if the patient had any delicacy of taste, he threw up the remedy instead of the disease?

Addison wrote little in verse, much in sweet, elegant, Virgilian prose; so let me call it, since Longinus calls Herodotus most Homeric, and Thucydides is said to have formed his style on Pindar. Addison's compositions are built with the finest materials, in the taste of the ancients, and (to speak his own language) on truly classic ground; and though they are the delight of the present age, yet am I persuaded that they will receive more justice from posterity. I never read him but I am struck with such a disheartening idea of perfection, that I drop my pen. And, indeed, far superior writers should forget his compositions, if they would be greatly pleased with their own. And yet, (perhaps you have not observed it,) what is the common language of the world, and even of his admirers, concerning him? They call him an elegant writer. That elegance which shines on the surface of his compositions, seems to dazzle their understanding, and render it a little blind to the depth of sentiment which lies beneath. Thus (hard fate!) he loses reputation with them by doubling his title to it. On subjects the most interesting and important, no author of his age has written with greater, I had almost said, with equal, weight. And they who commend him for his elegance, pay him a sort of compliment, by their abstemious praise, as they would pay to Lucretia, if they should commend her only for her beauty.

But you say that you know his value already.—You know, indeed, the value of his writings, and close with the world in thinking them immortal; but I believe, you know not that his name would have deserved immortality though he had never written; and that by a better title than pen can give. You know, too, that his life was amiable; but, perhaps, you are still to learn that his death was triumphant. That is a glory granted to very few; and the paternal hand of Providence, which sometimes snatches home its beloved children in a moment, must convince us that it is a glory of no great consequence to the dying individual; that, when it is granted, it is granted chiefly for the sake of the surviving world, which may profit by his pious example, to whom is indulged the strength and opportunity to make his virtue shine out brightest at the point of death. And here permit me to take notice that the world will probably profit more by a pious example of lay-extraction, than by one born of the church; the latter being usually taxed with an abatement of influence by the bulk of mankind: therefore, to smother a bright example of this superior good influence, may be reputed a sort of murder injurious to the living and unjust to the dead.

Such an example have we in Addison; which, though hitherto suppressed, yet, when once known, is insuppressible, of a nature too rare, too striking to be forgotten. For, after a long and manly, but vain, struggle with his distemper, he dismissed his physicians, and with them all hopes of life. But with his hopes of life he dismissed not his concern for the living, but sent for a youth nearly related and finely accomplished, yet not above being the better for good impressions from a dying friend. He came; but, life now glimmering in the socket, the dying friend was silent. After a decent and proper pause, the youth said, "Dear sir, you sent for me: I believe and I hope that you have some commands; I shall hold them most sacred." May distant ages not only hear, but feel, the reply! Forcibly grasping the youth's hand, he softly said, "See in what peace a Christian can die!" He spoke with difficulty and soon expired. Through grace Divine, how great is man! Through Divine mercy, how stingless death! Who would not thus expire?

What an inestimable legacy were those few dying words to the youth beloved! What a glorious supplement to his own valuable fragment on the truth of Christianity! What

a full demonstration, that his fancy could not feign beyond what his virtue could reach! For when he would strike us most strongly with the grandeur of the Roman magnanimity, his dying hero is ennobled with this sublime sentiment:—

> While yet I live, let me not live in vain. Cato.

But how much more sublime is that sentiment when realized in life; when dispelling the languors, and appeasing the pains of a last hour, and brightening with illustrious action the dark avenue and all-awful confines of an eternity! When his soul scarce animated his body, strong faith and ardent charity animated his soul into divine ambition of saving more than his own. It is for our honor and our advantage to hold him high in our esteem; for the better men are, the more they will admire him; and the more they admire him, the better will they be.

By undrawing the long-closed curtain of his death-bed, have I not showed you a stranger in him whom you knew so well? Is not this of your favorite author,

> —Notâ major imago?— Virg.

His compositions are but a noble preface, the grand work is his death: that is a work which is read in heaven. How has it joined the final approbation of angels to the previous applause of men! How gloriously has he opened a splendid path, through fame immortal, into eternal peace! How has he given religion to triumph amidst the ruins of his nature; and, stronger than death, risen higher in virtue when breathing his last!

If all our men of genius had so breathed their last,—if all our men of genius, like him, had been men of genius for eternals,—then had we never been pained by the report of a latter end—O, how unlike to this! But a little to balance our pain, let us consider that such reports as make us at once adore and tremble, are of use, when too many there are who must tremble before they will adore; and who convince us, to our shame, that the surest refuge of our endangered virtue is in the fears and terrors of the disingenuous human heart.

"But reports," you say, "may be false," and you farther ask me, "If all reports were true, how came an anecdote of so much honor to human nature as mine to lie so long unknown? What inauspicious planet interposed to lay its lustre under so lasting and so surprising an eclipse?"

The fact is indisputably true; nor are you to rely on me for the truth of it. My report is but a second edition; it was published before, though obscurely, and with a cloud before it. As clouds before the sun are often beautiful, so this of which I speak. How finely pathetic are those two lines which this so solemn and affecting scene inspired!—

> "He taught us how to live; and, O, too high
> A price for knowledge, taught us how to die."
> Tickell.

With truth wrapped in darkness, so sung our oracle to the public, but explained himself to me. He was present at his patron's death; and that account of it here given, he gave to me before his eyes were dry. By what means Addison taught us how to die, the poet left to be known by a late and less able hand; but one more zealous for his patron's glory: zealous and impotent, as the poor Egyptian who gathered a few splinters of a broken boat as a funeral-pile for the great Pompey, studious of doing honor to so renowned a name. Yet had not this poor plank (permit me here so to call this imperfect page) been thrown out, the chief article of his patron's glory would probably have been sunk forever, and late ages have received but a fragment of his fame: a fragment glorious indeed, for his genius how bright! But to commend him for composition, though immortal, is distraction now, if there our encomium ends; let us look farther to that concluding scene, which spoke human nature not unrelated to the Divine. To that let us pay the long and large arrear of our greatly posthumous applause.

This you will think a long digression; and justly: if that may be called a digression, which was my chief inducement for writing at all. I had long wished to deliver up to the public this sacred deposit, which by Providence was lodged in my hands; and I entered on the present undertaking partly as an introduction to that which is more worthy to see the light; of which I gave an intimation in the beginning of my letter: for this is the monumental marble there mentioned, to which I promised to conduct you; this is the sepulchral lamp, the long hidden lustre of our accomplished countryman, who now rises, as from his tomb, to receive the regard so greatly due to the dignity of his death: a death to be distinguished by tears of joy; a death which angels beheld with delight.

And shall that which would have shone conspicuous amid the resplendent lights of Christianity's glorious morn, by these dark days be dropped into oblivion? Dropped it is; and dropped by our sacred, august, and ample register of renown, which has entered in its marble memoirs the dim splendor of far inferior worth. Though so lavish of praise, and so talkative of the dead, yet is it silent on a subject which (if any) might have taught its unlettered stones to speak. If powers were not wanting, a monument more durable than those of marble should proudly rise in this ambitious page, to the new and far nobler Addison than that which you and the public have so long and so much admired. Nor this nation only; for it is Europe's Addison, as well as ours; though Europe knows not half his title to her esteem; being as yet unconscious that the dying Addison far outshines her Addison immortal. Would we resemble him? Let us not limit our ambition to the least illustrious part of his character; heads, indeed, are crowned on earth; but hearts only are crowded in heaven; a truth which, in such an age of authors, should not be forgotten.

It is piously to be hoped that this narrative may have some effect, since all listen when a death-bed speaks; and regard the person departing as an actor of a part which the great Master of the drama has appointed us to perform tomorrow. This was a Roscius on the stage of life; his exit how great! Ye lovers of virtue, *plaudite;* and let us, my friend, ever "remember his end, as well as our own, that we may never do amiss." (pp. 66-73)

Edward Young, "Conjectures on Original Composition in a Letter to the Author of Sir Charles Grandison," in his Edward Young's "Conjectures on Original Composition" in England and Germany, *edited by Martin William Steinke, 1759. Reprinted by G. E. Stechert & Co., 1917, pp. 43-73.*

Samuel Johnson   (essay date 1781)

[*Johnson was the major literary figure of the second half of the eighteenth century; his monumental* A Dictionary of the English Language *(1755) standardized for the first time English spelling and pronunciation while his moralistic criticism strongly influenced contemporary tastes. Perhaps the foremost principle in Johnson's critical theory was that a work be evaluated chiefly on its ability to both entertain and instruct the reader. In the following excerpt from his* Lives of the English Poets, *Johnson considers Addison's work in several genres, emphasizing his elegance and consistency as an essayist and dramatist, and his occasional clumsiness as a poet.*]

Before the **Tatler** and **Spectator,** if the writers for the theatre are excepted, England had no masters of common life. No writers had yet undertaken to reform either the savageness of neglect, or the impertinence of civility; to shew when to speak, or to be silent; how to refuse, or how to comply. We had many books to teach us our more important duties, and to settle opinions in philosophy or politicks; but an *Arbiter elegantiarum,* a judge of propriety, was yet wanting, who should survey the track of daily conversation, and free it from thorns and prickles, which teaze the passer, though they do not wound him.

For this purpose nothing is so proper as the frequent publication of short papers, which we read not as study but amusement. If the subject be slight, the treatise is likewise short. The busy may find time, and the idle may find patience.

This mode of conveying cheap and easy knowledge began among us in the Civil War, when it was much the interest of either party to raise and fix the prejudices of the people. At that time appeared *Mercurius Aulicus, Mercurius Rusticus,* and *Mercurius Civicus.* It is said, that when any title grew popular, it was stolen by the antagonist, who by this stratagem conveyed his notions to those who would not have received him had he not worn the appearance of a friend. The tumult of those unhappy days left scarcely any man leisure to treasure up occasional compositions; and so much were they neglected, that a complete collection is nowhere to be found.

These Mercuries were succeeded by L'Estrange's *Observator,* and that by Lesley's *Rehearsal,* and perhaps by others; but hitherto nothing had been conveyed to the people, in this commodious manner, but controversy relating to the Church or State; of which they taught many to talk, whom they could not teach to judge.

It has been suggested that the Royal Society was instituted soon after the Restoration, to divert the attention of the people from publick discontent. The **Tatler** and **Spectator** had the same tendency: they were published at a time when two parties, loud, restless, and violent, each with plausible declarations, and each perhaps without any distinct termination of its views, were agitating the nation; to minds heated with political contest, they supplied cooler and more inoffensive reflections; and it is said by Addison, in a subsequent work, that they had a perceptible influence upon the conversation of that time, and taught the frolick and the gay to unite merriment with decency; an effect which they can never wholly lose, while they continue to be among the first books by which both sexes are initiated in the elegances of knowledge.

The *Tatler* and *Spectator* adjusted, like Casa, the unsettled practice of daily intercourse by propriety and politeness; and, like La Bruyère, exhibited the *Characters and Manners of the Age.* The personages introduced in these papers were not merely ideal; they were then known, and conspicuous in various stations. Of the *Tatler* this is told by Steele in his last paper, and of the *Spectator* by Budgell in the Preface to *Theophrastus;* a book which Addison has recommended, and which he was suspected to have revised, if he did not write it. Of those portraits, which may be supposed to be sometimes embellished, and sometimes aggravated, the originals are now partly known, and partly forgotten.

But to say that they united the plans of two or three eminent writers, is to give them but a small part of their due praise; they superadded literature and criticism, and sometimes towered far above their predecessors; and taught, with great justness of argument and dignity of language, the most important duties and sublime truths.

All these topicks were happily varied with elegant fictions and refined allegories, and illuminated with different changes of style and felicities of invention.

It is recorded by Budgell, that of the characters feigned or exhibited in the *Spectator,* the favourite of Addison was Sir Roger de Coverley, of whom he had formed a very delicate and discriminated idea, which he would not suffer to be violated; and therefore, when Steele had shewn him innocently picking up a girl in the Temple, and taking her to a tavern, he drew upon himself so much of his friend's indignation, that he was forced to appease him by a promise of forbearing Sir Roger for the time to come.

The reason which induced Cervantes to bring his hero to the grave, *para mí solo nació Don Quijote, y yo para él,* made Addison declare, with an undue vehemence of expression, that he would kill Sir Roger; being of opinion that they were born for one another, and that any other hand would do him wrong.

It may be doubted whether Addison ever filled up his original delineation. He describes his Knight as having his imagination somewhat warped; but of this perversion he has made very little use. The irregularities in Sir Roger's conduct seem not so much the effects of a mind deviating from the beaten track of life, by the perpetual pressure of some overwhelming idea, as of habitual rusticity, and that negligence which solitary grandeur naturally generates.

The variable weather of the mind, the flying vapours of incipient madness, which from time to time cloud reason, without eclipsing it, it requires so much nicety to exhibit,

that Addison seems to have been deterred from prosecuting his own design.

To Sir Roger, who, as a country gentleman, appears to be a Tory, or, as it is gently expressed, an adherent to the landed interest, is opposed Sir Andrew Freeport, a new man, a wealthy merchant, zealous for the moneyed interest, and a Whig. Of this contrariety of opinions, it is probable more consequences were at first intended, than could be produced when the resolution was taken to exclude party from the paper. Sir Andrew does but little, and that little seems not to have pleased Addison, who, when he dismissed him from the club, changed his opinions. Steele had made him, in the true spirit of unfeeling commerce, declare that he *would not build an hospital for idle people;* but at last he buys land, settles in the country, and builds not a manufactory, but an hospital for twelve old husbandmen, for men with whom a merchant has little acquaintance, and whom he commonly considers with little kindness.

Of essays thus elegant, thus instructive, and thus commodiously distributed, it is natural to suppose the approbation general and the sale numerous. I once heard it observed, that the sale may be calculated by the product of the tax, related in the last number to produce more than twenty pounds a week, and therefore stated at one and twenty pounds, or three pounds ten shillings a day: this, at a halfpenny a paper, will give sixteen hundred and eighty for the daily number.

This sale is not great; yet this, if Swift be credited, was likely to grow less; for he declares that the *Spectator,* whom he ridicules for his endless mention of the *fair sex,* had before his recess wearied his readers.

The next year (1713), in which *Cato* came upon the stage, was the grand climacterick of Addison's reputation. Upon the death of Cato, he had, as is said, planned a tragedy in the time of his travels, and had for several years the four first acts finished, which were shewn to such as were likely to spread their admiration. They were seen by Pope, and by Cibber; who relates that Steele, when he took back the copy, told him, in the despicable cant of literary modesty, that, whatever spirit his friend had shewn in the composition, he doubted whether he would have courage sufficient to expose it to the censure of a British audience.

The time, however, was now come, when those who affected to think liberty in danger, affected likewise to think that a stage-play might preserve it: and Addison was importuned, in the name of the tutelary deities of Britain, to shew his courage and his zeal by finishing his design.

To resume his work he seemed perversely and unaccountably unwilling; and by a request, which perhaps he wished to be denied, desired Mr. Hughes to add a fifth act. Hughes supposed him serious; and, undertaking the supplement, brought in a few days some scenes for his examination; but he had in the meantime gone to work himself, and produced half an act, which he afterwards completed, but with brevity irregularly disproportionate to the foregoing parts; like a task performed with reluctance, and hurried to its conclusion.

It may yet be doubted whether *Cato* was made publick by any change of the author's purpose; for Dennis charged him with raising prejudices in his own favour by false positions of preparatory criticism, and with *poisoning the town* by contradicting in the *Spectator* the established rule of poetical justice, because his own hero, with all his virtues, was to fall before a tyrant. The fact is certain; the motives we must guess.

Addison was, I believe, sufficiently disposed to bar all avenues against all danger. When Pope brought him the prologue, which is properly accommodated to the play, there were these words, *Britons, arise, be worth like this approved;* meaning nothing more than, Britons, erect and exalt yourselves to the approbation of public virtue. Addison was frighted lest he should be thought a promoter of insurrection, and the line was liquidated to *Britons, attend.*

Now, *heavily in clouds came on the day, the great, the important day,* when Addison was to stand the hazard of the theatre. That there might, however, be left as little to hazard as was possible, on the first night, Steele, as himself relates, undertook to pack an audience. This, says Pope, had been tried for the first time in favour of the *Distrest Mother;* and was now, with more efficacy, practised for *Cato.*

The danger was soon over. The whole nation was at this time on fire with faction. The Whigs applauded every line in which Liberty was mentioned, as a satire on the Tories; and the Tories echoed every clap, to shew that the satire was unfelt. The story of Bolingbroke is well known. He called Booth to his box, and gave him fifty guineas for defending the cause of Liberty so well against a perpetual dictator. The Whigs, says Pope, design a second present, when they can accompany it with as good a sentence.

The play, supported thus by the emulation of factious praise, was acted night after night for a longer time than, I believe, the publick had allowed to any drama before; and the author, as Mrs. Porter long afterwards related, wandered through the whole exhibition behind the scenes with restless and unappeasable solicitude.

When it was printed, notice was given that the Queen would be pleased if it was dedicated to her; *but as he had designed that compliment elsewhere, he found himself obliged,* says Tickell, *by his duty on the one hand, and his honour on the other, to send it into the world without any dedication.*

Human happiness has always its abatements; the brightest sunshine of success is not without a cloud. No sooner was *Cato* offered to the reader, than it was attacked by the acute malignity of Dennis, with all the violence of angry criticism. Dennis, though equally zealous, and probably by his temper more furious than Addison, for what they called liberty, and though a flatterer of the Whig ministry, could not sit quiet at a successful play; but was eager to tell friends and enemies, that they had misplaced their admirations. The world was too stubborn for instruction; with the fate of the censurer of Corneille's *Cid,* his animadversions shewed his anger without effect, and *Cato* continued to be praised.

Pope had now an opportunity of courting the friendship of Addison, by vilifying his old enemy, and could give resentment its full play without appearing to revenge himself. He therefore published *A Narrative of the madness of John Dennis;* a performance which left the objections to the play in their full force, and therefore discovered more desire of vexing the critick than of defending the poet.

Addison, who was no stranger to the world, probably saw the selfishness of Pope's friendship; and, resolving that he should have the consequences of his officiousness to himself, informed Dennis by Steele, that he was sorry for the insult; and that whenever he should think fit to answer his remarks, he would do it in a manner to which nothing could be objected.

The greatest weakness of the play is in the scenes of love, which are said by Pope to have been added to the original plan upon a subsequent review, in compliance with the popular practice of the stage. Such an authority it is hard to reject; yet the love is so intimately mingled with the whole action, that it cannot easily be thought extrinsick and adventitious; for if it were taken away, what would be left? or how were the four acts filled in the first draught?

At the publication the Wits seemed proud to pay their attendance with encomiastick verses. The best are from an unknown hand, which will perhaps lose somewhat of their praise when the author is known to be Jeffreys.

Cato had yet other honours. It was censured as a party-play by a *Scholar of Oxford,* and defended in a favourable examination by Dr. Sewel. It was translated by Salvini into Italian, and acted at Florence; and by the Jesuits of St. Omer's into Latin, and played by their pupils. Of this version a copy was sent to Mr. Addison: it is to be wished that it could be found, for the sake of comparing their version of the soliloquy with that of Bland.

A tragedy was written on the same subject by Des Champs, a French poet, which was translated, with a criticism on the English play. But the translator and the critick are now forgotten.

Dennis lived on unanswered, and therefore little read. Addison knew the policy of literature too well to make his enemy important, by drawing the attention of the publick upon a criticism, which, though sometimes intemperate, was often irrefragable. (pp. 407-14)

Addison, in his life, and for some time afterwards, was considered by the greater part of readers as supremely excelling both in poetry and criticism. Part of his reputation may be probably ascribed to the advancement of his fortune: when, as Swift observes, he became a statesman, and saw poets waiting at his levee, it was no wonder that praise was accumulated upon him. Much likewise may be more honourably ascribed to his personal character: he who, if he had claimed it, might have obtained the diadem, was not likely to be denied the laurel.

But time quickly puts an end to artificial and accidental fame; and Addison is to pass through futurity protected only by his genius. Every name which kindness or interest once raised too high, is in danger, lest the next age should, by the vengeance of criticism, sink it in the same proportion. A great writer has lately styled him *an indifferent poet, and a worse critick.*

His poetry is first to be considered; of which it must be confessed that it has not often those felicities of diction which give lustre to sentiments, or that vigour of sentiment that animates diction: there is little of ardour, vehemence, or transport; there is very rarely the awfulness of grandeur, and not very often the splendour of elegance. He thinks justly, but he thinks faintly. This is his general character; to which, doubtless, many single passages will furnish exceptions.

Yet, if he seldom reaches supreme excellence, he rarely sinks into dulness, and is still more rarely entangled in absurdity. He did not trust his powers enough to be negligent. There is in most of his compositions a calmness and equability, deliberate and cautious, sometimes with little that delights, but seldom with anything that offends.

Of this kind seem to be his poems to Dryden, to Somers, and to the King. His **"Ode on St. Cecilia"** has been imitated by Pope, and has something in it of Dryden's vigour. Of his **"Account of the English Poets,"** he used to speak as *a poor thing;* but it is not worse than his usual strain. He has said, not very judiciously, in his character of Waller:

> Thy verse could shew ev'n Cromwell's inno-
> cence,
> And compliment the storms that bore him
> hence.
> O! had thy Muse not come an age too soon,
> But seen great Nassau on the British throne,
> How had his triumph glitter'd in thy page!—

What is this but to say that he who could compliment Cromwell had been the proper poet for king William? Addison however never printed the piece.

The Letter from Italy has been always praised, but has never been praised beyond its merit. It is more correct, with less appearance of labour, and more elegant, with less ambition of ornament, than any other of his poems. There is, however, one broken metaphor, of which notice may properly be taken:

> Fir'd with that name—
> I bridle in my struggling Muse with pain,
> That longs to launch into a nobler strain.

To *bridle* a *goddess* is no very delicate idea; but why must she be *bridled?* because she *longs to launch;* an act which was never hindered by a *bridle:* and whither will she *launch?* into a *nobler strain.* She is in the first line a *horse,* in the second a *boat;* and the care of the poet is to keep his *horse* or his *boat* from *singing.*

The next composition is the far-famed **Campaign,** which Dr. Warton has termed a *Gazette in Rhyme,* with harshness not often used by the good-nature of his criticism. Before a censure so severe is admitted, let us consider that War is a frequent subject of Poetry, and then enquire who has described it with more justness and force. Many of our own writers tried their powers upon this year of victory, yet Addison's is confessedly the best performance; his poem is the work of a man not blinded by the dust of learn-

ing: his images are not borrowed merely from books. The superiority which he confers upon his hero is not personal prowess, and *mighty bone,* but deliberate intrepidity, a calm command of his passions, and the power of consulting his own mind in the midst of danger. The rejection and contempt of fiction is rational and manly.

It may be observed that the last line is imitated by Pope:

> Marlb'rough's exploits appear divinely bright—
> Rais'd of themselves, their genuine charms they
> boast,
> And those that paint them truest, praise them
> most.

This Pope had in his thoughts; but, not knowing how to use what was not his own, he spoiled the thought when he had borrowed it:

> The well-sung woes shall soothe my ghost;
> He best can paint them who shall feel them
> most.

Martial exploits may be *painted;* perhaps *woes* may be *painted;* but they are surely not *painted* by being *well-sung:* it is not easy to paint in song, or to sing in colours.

No passage in the **Campaign** has been more often mentioned than the simile of the Angel, which is said in the **Tatler** to be *one of the noblest thoughts that ever entered into the heart of man,* and is therefore worthy of attentive consideration. Let it be first enquired whether it be a simile. A poetical simile is the discovery of likeness between two actions, in their general nature dissimilar, or of causes terminating by different operations in some resemblance of effect. But the mention of another like consequence from a like cause, or of a like performance by a like agency, is not a simile, but an exemplification. It is not a simile to say that the Thames waters fields, as the Po waters fields; or that as Hecla vomits flames in Iceland, so Aetna vomits flames in Sicily. When Horace says of Pindar, that he pours his violence and rapidity of verse, as a river swoln with rain rushes from the mountain; or of himself, that his genius wanders in quest of poetical decorations, as the bee wanders to collect honey; he, in either case, produces a simile; the mind is impressed with the resemblance of things generally unlike, as unlike as intellect and body. But if Pindar had been described as writing with the copiousness and grandeur of Homer, or Horace had told that he reviewed and finished his own poetry with the same care as Isocrates polished his orations, instead of similitude he would have exhibited almost identity; he would have given the same portraits with different names. In the poem now examined, when the English are represented as gaining a fortified pass, by repetition of attack and perseverance of resolution; their obstinacy of courage, and vigour of onset, is well illustrated by the sea that breaks, with incessant battery, the dikes of Holland. This is a simile: but when Addison, having celebrated the beauty of Marlborough's person, tells us that *Achilles thus was formed with every grace,* here is no simile, but a mere exemplification. A simile may be compared to lines converging at a point, and is more excellent as the lines approach from greater distance: an exemplification may be considered as two parallel lines which run on together without approximation, never far separated, and never joined.

Marlborough is so like the angel in the poem, that the action of both is almost the same, and performed by both in the same manner. Marlborough *teaches the battle to rage;* the angel *directs the storm:* Marlborough is *unmoved in peaceful thought;* the angel is *calm and serene:* Marlborough stands *unmoved amidst the shock of hosts;* the angel rides *calm in the whirlwind.* The lines on Marlborough are just and noble; but the simile gives almost the same images a second time.

But perhaps this thought, though hardly a simile, was remote from vulgar conceptions, and required great labour of research, or dexterity of application. Of this, Dr. Madden, a name which Ireland ought to honour, once gave me his opinion. *If I had set,* said he, *ten schoolboys to write on the battle of Blenheim, and eight had brought me the Angel, I should not have been surprised.*

The opera of **Rosamond,** though it is seldom mentioned, is one of the first of Addison's compositions. The subject is well chosen, the fiction is pleasing, and the praise of Marlborough, for which the scene gives an opportunity, is, what perhaps every human excellence must be, the product of good-luck improved by genius. The thoughts are sometimes great, and sometimes tender; the versification is easy and gay. There is doubtless some advantage in the shortness of the lines, which there is little temptation to load with expletive epithets. The dialogue seems commonly better than the songs. The two comick characters of Sir Trusty and Grideline, though of no great value, are yet such as the poet intended. Sir Trusty's account of the death of Rosamond is, I think, too grossly absurd. The whole drama is airy and elegant; engaging in its process, and pleasing in its conclusion. If Addison had cultivated the lighter parts of poetry, he would probably have excelled.

The tragedy of **Cato,** which, contrary to the rule observed in selecting the works of other poets, has by the weight of its character forced its way into the late collection, is unquestionably the noblest production of Addison's genius. Of a work so much read, it is difficult to say any thing new. About things on which the public thinks long, it commonly attains to think right; and of **Cato** it has been not unjustly determined, that it is rather a poem in dialogue than a drama, rather a succession of just sentiments in elegant language, than a representation of natural affections, or of any state probable or possible in human life. Nothing here *excites or assuages emotion;* here is *no magical power of raising phantastick terror or wild anxiety.* The events are expected without solicitude, and are remembered without joy or sorrow. Of the agents we have no care: we consider not what they are doing, or what they are suffering; we wish only to know what they have to say. Cato is a being above our solicitude; a man of whom the gods take care, and whom we leave to their care with heedless confidence. To the rest, neither gods nor men can have much attention; for there is not one amongst them that strongly attracts either affection or esteem. But they are made the vehicles of such sentiments and such expression, that there is scarcely a scene in the play which the reader does not wish to impress upon his memory.

When **Cato** was shewn to Pope, he advised the author to print it, without any theatrical exhibition; supposing that it would be read more favourably than heard. Addison declared himself of the same opinion; but urged the importunity of his friends for its appearance on the stage. The emulation of parties made it successful beyond expectation, and its success has introduced or confirmed among us the use of dialogue too declamatory, of unaffecting elegance, and chill philosophy. (pp. 428-33)

Of Addison's smaller poems, no particular mention is necessary; they have little that can employ or require a critick. The parallel of the Princes and Gods, in his verses to Kneller, is often happy, but is too well known to be quoted.

His translations, so far as I have compared them, want the exactness of a scholar. That he understood his authors cannot be doubted; but his versions will not teach others to understand them, being too licentiously paraphrastical. They are, however, for the most part, smooth and easy; and what is the first excellence of a translator, such as may be read with pleasure by those who do not know the originals.

His poetry is polished and pure; the product of a mind too judicious to commit faults, but not sufficiently vigorous to attain excellence. He has sometimes a striking line, or a shining paragraph; but in the whole he is warm rather than fervid, and shews more dexterity than strength. He was, however, one of our earliest examples of correctness.

The versification which he had learned from Dryden, he debased rather than refined. His rhymes are often dissonant; in his *Georgick* he admits broken lines. He uses both triplets and alexandrines, but triplets more frequently in his translations than his other works. The mere structure of verses seems never to have engaged much of his care. But his lines are very smooth in **Rosamond,** and too smooth in **Cato**.

Addison is now to be considered as a critick; a name which the present generation is scarcely willing to allow him. His criticism is condemned as tentative or experimental, rather than scientifick, and he is considered as deciding by taste rather than by principles.

It is not uncommon for those who have grown wise by the labour of others, to add a little of their own, and overlook their masters. Addison is now despised by some who perhaps would never have seen his defects, but by the lights which he afforded them. That he always wrote as he would think it necessary to write now, cannot be affirmed; his instructions were such as the characters of his readers made proper. That general knowledge which now circulates in common talk, was in his time rarely to be found. Men not professing learning were not ashamed of ignorance; and in the female world, any acquaintance with books was distinguished only to be censured. His purpose was to infuse literary curiosity, by gentle and unsuspected conveyance, into the gay, the idle, and the wealthy; he therefore presented knowledge in the most alluring form, not lofty and austere, but accessible and familiar. When he shewed them their defects, he shewed them likewise that they might be easily supplied. His attempt succeeded; enquiry was awakened, and comprehension expanded. An emulation of intellectual elegance was excited, and from his time to our own, life has been gradually exalted, and conversation purified and enlarged.

Dryden had, not many years before, scattered criticism over his Prefaces with very little parsimony; but, though he sometimes condescended to be somewhat familiar, his manner was in general too scholastick for those who had yet their rudiments to learn, and found it not easy to understand their master. His observations were framed rather for those that were learning to write, than for those that read only to talk.

An instructor like Addison was not wanting, whose remarks being superficial, might be easily understood, and being just, might prepare the mind for more attainments. Had he presented *Paradise Lost* to the publick with all the pomp of system and severity of science, the criticism would perhaps have been admired, and the poem still have been neglected; but by the blandishments of gentleness and facility, he has made Milton an universal favourite, with whom readers of every class think it necessary to be pleased.

He descended now and then to lower disquisitions; and by a serious display of the beauties of *Chevy Chase,* exposed himself to the ridicule of Wagstaff, who bestowed a like pompous character on *Tom Thumb;* and to the contempt of Dennis, who, considering the fundamental position of his criticism, that *Chevy Chase* pleases, and ought to please, because it is natural, observes, 'that there is a way of deviating from nature, by bombast or tumour, which soars above nature, and enlarges images beyond their real bulk; by affectation, which forsakes nature in quest of something unsuitable; and by imbecility, which degrades nature by faintness and diminution, by obscuring its appearances, and weakening its effects.' In *Chevy Chase* there is not much of either bombast or affectation; but there is chill and lifeless imbecility. The story cannot possibly be told in a manner that shall make less impression on the mind.

Before the profound observers of the present race repose too securely on the consciousness of their superiority to Addison, let them consider his **"Remarks on Ovid,"** in which may be found specimens of criticism sufficiently subtle and refined; let them peruse likewise his essays on **"Wit,"** and on the **"Pleasures of Imagination,"** in which he founds art on the base of nature, and draws the principles of invention from dispositions inherent in the mind of man, with skill and elegance, such as his contemners will not easily attain.

As a describer of life and manners, he must be allowed to stand perhaps the first of the first rank. His humour, which, as Steele observes, is peculiar to himself, is so happily diffused as to give the grace of novelty to domestick scenes and daily occurrences. He never *outsteps the modesty of nature,* nor raises merriment or wonder by the violation of truth. His figures neither divert by distortion, nor amaze by aggravation. He copies life with so much fideli-

ty, that he can be hardly said to invent; yet his exhibitions have an air so much original, that it is difficult to suppose them not merely the product of imagination.

As a teacher of wisdom, he may be confidently followed. His religion has nothing in it enthusiastick or superstitious: he appears neither weakly credulous nor wantonly sceptical; his morality is neither dangerously lax, nor impracticably rigid. All the enchantment of fancy, and all the cogency of argument, are employed to recommend to the reader his real interest, the care of pleasing the Author of his being. Truth is shewn sometimes as the phantom of a vision, sometimes appears half-veiled in an allegory; sometimes attracts regard in the robes of fancy, and sometimes steps forth in the confidence of reason. She wears a thousand dresses, and in all is pleasing

Mille habet ornatus, mille decenter habet.

His prose is the model of the middle style; on grave subjects not formal, on light occasions not groveling; pure without scrupulosity, and exact without apparent elaboration; always equable, and always easy, without glowing words or pointed sentences. Addison never deviates from his track to snatch a grace; he seeks no ambitious ornaments, and tries no hazardous innovations. His page is always luminous, but never blazes in unexpected splendour.

It was apparently his principal endeavour to avoid all harshness and severity of diction; he is therefore sometimes verbose in his transitions and connexions, and sometimes descends too much to the language of conversation; yet if his language had been less idiomatical, it might have lost somewhat of its genuine Anglicism. What he attempted, he performed; he is never feeble, and he did not wish to be energetick; he is never rapid, and he never stagnates. His sentences have neither studied amplitude, nor affected brevity: his periods, though not diligently rounded, are voluble and easy. Whoever wishes to attain an English style, familiar but not coarse, and elegant but not ostentatious, must give his days and nights to the volumes of Addison. (pp. 445-49)

Samuel Johnson, "Addison," in his The Lives of the English Poets, Vol. I, 1779-81. Reprint by Oxford University Press, 1964, pp. 399-449.

Joseph Warton (essay date 1782)

[*Warton was an accomplished literary critic who is best remembered for* An Essay on the Genius and Writings of Pope. *In the following excerpt from that work, Warton discusses the style and political content of* Cato, *and comments on Addison's writings in other genres.*]

The tragedy of *Cato* . . . is a glaring instance of the force of party [Warton adds in a footnote:" When Addison spake of the secretary of state at that time, he always called him, in the language of Shakespeare, *"That canker'd Bolingbroke."* Notwithstanding this, Addison assured POPE, he did not bring his tragedy on the stage with any party views; nay, desired POPE to carry the poem to the Lords Oxford and Bolinbroke, for their perusal. The play, however, was always considered as a warning to the people, that liberty was in danger during that tory ministry. To obviate the strong impressions, that so popular a performance might make on the minds of the audience, Lord Bolingbroke, in the midst of their violent applauses, sent for Booth, who played Cato, one night, into his box, between the acts, and presented him with fifty guineas; in acknowledgement, as he expressed it with great address, for defending the cause of liberty so well against a perpetual dictator."]; so sententious and declamatory a drama would never have met with such rapid and amazing success, if every line and sentiment had not been particularly tortured, and applied to recent events, and the reigning disputes of the times. The purity and energy of the diction, and the loftiness of the sentiments, copied in a great measure from Lucan, Tacitus, and Seneca the philosopher, merit approbation. But I have always thought, that those pompous Roman sentiments are not so difficult to be produced, as is vulgarly imagined; and which, indeed, dazzle only the vulgar. A stroke of nature is, in my opinion, worth a hundred such thoughts, as,

> When vice prevails, and impious men bear sway,
> The post of honour is a private station.

CATO is a fine dialogue on liberty, and the love of one's country; but considered as a dramatic performance, may as a model of a just tragedy, as some have affectedly represented it, it must be owned to want, ACTION and PATHOS; the two hinges, I presume, on which a just tragedy ought necessarily to turn, and without which it cannot subsist. It wants also CHARACTER, although that be not so essentially necessary to a tragedy as ACTION. Syphax, indeed, in his interview with Juba, bears some marks of a rough African: the speeches of the rest may be transferred to any of the personages concerned. The simile drawn from mount Atlas, and the description of the Numidian traveller smothered in the desert, are indeed in character, but sufficiently obvious. How Addison could fall into the false and unnatural custom of ending his three first acts with similies, is amazing in so chaste and correct a writer. The loves of Juba and Marcia, of Portius and Lucia, are vicious and insipid episodes, debase the dignity, and destroy the unity, of the fable. (pp. 270-72)

It is pity that the tragedy of *Cato,* in which all the rules of the drama, as far as the mechanism of writing reaches, are observed, is not exact with respect to the unity of time. There was no occasion to extend the time of the fable longer than the mere representation takes up; all might have passed in the compass of three hours from the morning, with a description of which the play opens; if the poet, in the fourth scene of the fifth act, had not talked of the *setting* sun playing on the armour of the soldiers.

Having been imperceptibly led into this little criticism on the tragedy of *Cato,* I beg leave to speak a few words on some other of Addison's pieces. The first of his poems, addressed to Dryden, Sir John Somers, and king William, are languid, prosaic, and void of any poetical imagery or spirit. The ***Letter from Italy,*** is by no means equal to a subject fruitful of genuine poetry, and which might have warmed the most cold and correct imagination. One would have expected, a young traveller in the height of his genius and judgment, would have broke out into some strokes of enthusiasm. With what flatness and unfeeling-

ness has he spoken of statuary and painting! Raphäel never received a more flegmatic eulogy. The slavery and superstition of the present Romans, are well touched upon towards the conclusion; but I will venture to name a little piece on a parallel subject, that excels this celebrated Letter; and in which is much lively and original imagery, strong painting, and manly sentiments of freedom. It is a copy of verses written at Virgil's Tomb, and printed in Dodsley's *Miscellanies*.

That there are many well-wrought descriptions, and even pathetic strokes, in the Campaign, it would be stupidity and malignity to deny. But surely the regular march which the poet has observed from one town to another, as if he had been a commissary of the army, cannot well be excused. There is a passage in Boileau, so remarkably applicable to this fault of Addison, that one would almost be tempted to think he had the ***Campaign*** in his eye, when he wrote it, if the time would admit it.

> Loin ces rimeurs craintifs, dont l'esprit phleg-
> matique
> Garde dans ses fureurs un ordre didactique;
> Qui chantant d'un heros les progrés éclatans,
> MAIGRES HISTORIENS, SUIVRONT L'ORDRE DES
> TEMPS;
> Ils n'osent un moment prendre un sujet de vüe,
> Pour prendre Dole, il faut que Lille soit rendüe;
> Et que leur vers exact, ainsi que Mezerai,
> Ait fait déja tomber—les remparts de Coutrai.

The most spirited verses Addison has written, are, an Imitation of the third ode of the third book of Horace, which is indeed performed with energy and vigour; and his compliment to Kneller, on the picture of king George the first. The occasion of this last poem is peculiarly happy; for among the works of Phidias which he enumerates, he selects such statutes as exactly mark, and characterise, the last six British kings and queens.

> Great Pan who wont to chase the fair,
> And lov'd the spreading OAK, was there;
> Old Saturn too, with upcast eyes,
> Beheld his ABDICATED skies;
> And mighty Mars for war renown'd,
> In adamantine armour frown'd:
> By him the childless goddess rose,
> Minerva, studious to compose
> Her twisted threads; the web she strung,
> And o'er a loom of marble hung;
> Thetis the troubled ocean's queen,
> Match'd with a MORTAL, next was seen,
> Reclining on a funeral urn,
> Her short-liv'd darling son to mourn.
> The last was HE, whose thunder flew
> The Titan race, a rebel crew,
> That from a HUNDRED HILLS ally'd,
> In impious league their king defy'd.

There is scarcely, I believe, any instance, where mythology has been applied with more delicacy and dexterity, and has been contrived to answer in its application, so minutely, exactly, in so many corresponding circumstances.— There are various passages in the opera of ***Rosamond,*** that deserve to be mentioned as beautiful, and the versification of this piece is particularly musical.

Whatever censures we have here, too boldly, perhaps, ventured to deliver on the *professed* poetry of Addison, yet must we candidly own, that in various parts of his prose-essays, are to be found many strokes of genuine and sublime poetry; many marks of a vigorous and exuberant imagination. Particularly, in the noble allegory of Pain and Pleasure, the Vision of Mirza, the story of Maraton and Yaratilda, of Constantia and Theodosius, and the beautiful eastern tale of Abdallah and Balsora; and many others: together with several strokes in the Essay on the pleasures of imagination. It has been the lot of many great names, not to have been able to express themselves with beauty and propriety in the fetters of verse, in their respective languages; who have yet manifested the force, fertility, and creative power of a most poetic genius, in prose. This was the case of Plato, of Lucian, of Fenelon, of Sir Philip Sidney, and Dr. T. Burnet, who in his Theory of the Earth, has displayed an imagination, very nearly equal to that of Milton.

> ———————— Mænia mundi
> Discedunt! totum video per Inane geri res!

After all, the chief and characteristical excellency of Addison, was his HUMOUR; for in humour no mortal has excelled him except Moliere. Witness the character of Sir Roger de Coverley, so original, so natural, and so inviolably preserved; particularly, in the month, which the Spectator spends at his hall in the country. Witness also *The Drummer,* that excellent and neglected comedy, that just picture of life and real manners, where the poet never speaks in his own person, or totally drops or forgets a character, for the sake of introducing a brilliant simile, or acute remark: where no train is laid for wit; no JEREMYS, or BENS, are suffer'd to appear. (pp. 275-82)

. . . . .

> See the wild waste of all-devouring years,
> How Rome her own sad sepulchre appears.

This is the opening of [Pope's] epistle to Mr. *Addison,* upon his treatise on medals, written in that pleasing form of composition so unsuccessfully attempted by many modern authors, DIALOGUE. In no one species of writing have the ancients so indisputable a superiority over us. The dialogues of Plato and Cicero, especially the former, are perfect dramas; where the characters are supported with consistency and nature, and the reasoning suited to the characters.

"There are in English *Three* dialogues, and but three" (says a learned and ingenious author, who has himself practised this way of writing with success) "that deserve commendation; namely, the *Moralists* of LORD SHAFTESBURY; Mr. ADDISON'S 'Treatise on Medals'; and the 'Minute Philosopher of Bishop BERKLEY'," ALCIPHRON did, indeed, well deserve to be mentioned on this occasion; notwithstanding it has been treated with contempt by writers much inferior to BERKLEY in genius, learning, and taste. Omitting those passages in the fourth dialogue, where he has introduced his fanciful and whimsical opinions about *vision,* an attentive reader will find that there is scarce a single argument that can be urged in defence of Revelation, but what is here placed in the clearest light,

and in the most beautiful diction: in this work there is a happy union of reasoning and imagination. The two different characters of the two different sorts of free-thinkers, the sensual and the refined, are strongly contrasted with each other, and with the plainness and simplicity of *Euphranor.*

These Dialogues of Addison are written with that *sweetness* and *purity* of style, which constitute him one of the first of our prose-writers. **"The Pleasures of Imagination,"** the **"Essay on the Georgics,"** and his last papers in the **Spectator** and **Guardian,** are models of language. And some late writers, who seem to have mistaken *stiffness* for *strength,* and are grown popular by a pompous rotundity of phrase, make one with that the rising generation may abandon this unnatural, false, inflated, and florid style, and form themselves on the *chaster* model of Addison. The chief imperfection of his treatise on medals, is, that the persons introduced as speakers, in direct contradiction to the practice of the ancients, are *fictitious,* not *real:* for CYNTHIO, PHILANDER, PALAEMON, EUGENIO, and THEOCLES, cannot equally excite and engage the attention of the reader with SOCRATES and ALCIBIADES, ATTICUS and BRUTUS, COWLEY and SPRATT, MAYNARD and SOMERS. It is somewhat singular, that so many modern dialogue-writers should have failed in this particular, when so many of the most celebrated wits of modern Italy had given them eminent examples of the contrary proceeding, and, closely following the steps of the ancients, constantly introduced living and real persons in their numerous compositions of this sort; in which they were so fond of delivering their sentiments both on moral and critical subjects; witness the *Il Cortegiano* of B. CASTIGLIONE, the *Asolani* of P. BEMBO, *Dialoghi* del S. SPERONE, the *Naŭgerius* of FRACASTORIUS, and *Lil.* GYRALDUS *de Poetis,* and many others. In all which pieces, the famous and living geniuses of Italy are introduced discussing the several different topics before them. (pp. 203-07)

> *Joseph Warton, in his* An Essay on the Genius and Writings of Pope, Vols. I & II, *fourth edition, 1782. Reprint by Gregg International Publishers Limited, 1969, 415 p., 423 p.*

The Western Monthly Magazine   (essay date 1835)

[*In the following excerpt, the critic denigrates Addison's thinking as shallow and the style of his essays as artificial. Considering them representative of all Augustan literature, he then broadens his condemnation to include the literary output of the entire Augustan period.*]

The reign of queen Anne has been called the Augustan age of English literature. If, by this expression, is understood no more than that the intellectual manifestations of that reign resemble the finished efforts of those who flourished under the patronage of Mæcenas, there is nothing in it very objectionable. But if it be intended to convey the idea, that the writings of that period are distinguished by any extraordinary excellence, we are disposed to pause, and well to consider, before we assent to the propriety of its application. Our present impression is, that the literary efforts of Anne's time are not only far inferior to those which have given glory to the era of Elizabeth and of James, but are not to be compared with the intellectual achievements of the present century. We apprehend, that a close and serious investigation of the literary character of these widely distinguished epochs, would tend to deepen, rather than to remove this impression. Our present object is, to ascertain, as precisely as we can, how far the *periodical* writings of Anne's reign contribute to sustain the literary preeminence which has been claimed for it. (p. 232)

One of the criteria, by which I propose to determine the character of this literature, is *its value as an agent of improvement to the present age.* If the lawyer, the theologian, the statesman, the literary gentleman,—in short, if the Intellectualist of this century were to imagine himself elevated to some lofty central eminence, wherefrom he might survey all of the past and all of the present, and behold therein one mighty treasure-house of means and aids for self-improvement, and the benefit of the millions around him; what might we reasonably presume to be his first intellectual movement! We answer, to classify these means and aids; to arrange all moral, and mental, and physical agents under their proper heads; to distinguish those influences which God has created, from those which have sprung from the intellect of man, and to assign to each of these influences, and to each class of influences, its proper place in the scale of importance. It is not necessary, nor have we space, to exhibit here our classification of these agents. We will merely state, that of the thousand classes of influences which, at this day, may be brought to bear upon the mind and heart of an individual, or upon the mind and heart of society, polite literature is only *one;* and that in the scale whereby is graduated the value of all the various departments of polite literature, the place, to which the periodical writings of Anne's time are entitled, is, in our judgment, extremely low.

We will present a few of our reasons for this opinion. And first, we ask, what are the *features* by which these writings are characterized? They are said to contain a picture of the taste, the feelings, the opinions, and the manners of the time. We doubt not that sir Roger De Coverley and sir Andrew Freeport, most faithfully and most agreeably represent certain classes of society whereof they were members. We doubt not that many of the essays do most distinctly mirror some of the affectations, and foibles, and vices of that time. Nor are we disposed to doubt, that they are, in general, very correct exponents of the style of feeling and thinking which then pervaded certain portions of the community. Our remark upon this topic is simply this, that conceding all which for this feature has been claimed, we do not deem it of much importance. Whatever has been thought, and felt, and acted by mankind from the birth of time to the present moment, constitutes only *one* branch of human knowledge; and why an Intellectualist of the present day should be in any degree solicitous to know, not what was thought, and felt, and acted in Anne's reign, but merely that small portion thereof which is embodied in the papers of the **Spectator,** and **Tatler,** and **Guardian,** we cannot well conceive. Whenever the taste, feelings, opinions, and manners of the human race are about to be made subjects of attention, only those should be regarded,

which are developed by man in the extraordinary epochs of his earthly progress; those only which give us a clearer and deeper insight into the essential and abiding features of his character. While to us are accessible the Elizabethan era, and the times of the civil wars of England; while we can contemplate the wonderful manifestations of mind and heart furnished by the last seventy years of European and American history, we are not disposed to dwell upon the insipid reign of Queen Anne, nor to care much for its artificial modes of existence, which have been caught up and perpetuated by the genius of its periodical writers. We conclude this topic by observing, that had there been no other reason for remembering Addison and Steele, than the one just considered, we think that long ere this, they should have gone down to that oblivion whereunto they are so rapidly hastening.

Another characteristic feature of the periodical literature of Anne's time, is, *its morality;* by which term I understand, its views of man's domestic, social, and civil relations, and its exhortations to an observance of them. We candidly confess, that we have no spare admiration to bestow upon this morality. We are not so unjust as to charge upon it any positively demoralizing tendency. It does not tend to degrade, neither does it tend to elevate. Its characteristic is, an honest imbecility. It is full of elegantly feeble efforts to charm and whisper men into rectitude. We think that it is pitched upon a very low key—that it is tainted with a paltry worldism. It addresses the servile motives in the human heart. But it was suited to the times, and the times were formed by sensual standards. Where are those lofty strains of piety and devotion, that quicken within the soul a livelier sense of its immortal destinies! Listen to the voice of Addison. Do its tones make the heart throb more quickly? Do they send the blood more swiftly through its channels? Are they remembered in the bright or dreary passages of life? Do we seem to hear them in the still solitude of our chamber? Do they come pealing in upon our hours of gay and worldly festivity? Do they steal into the heart in its moments of sorrow, sustaining and encouraging? We think that they do not. Mr. Addison, the moralist, accomplished none of these ends, and these we reckon among the most legitimate ends of all moral teachings. But not only are they deficient in the traits just designated. They are intolerably dull. Except as opiates, we cannot conceive how the Intellectualist of the present day can, for a moment, endure them. The moral teachings of this literature want life. They want energy. They want the fire and the outbreak of a strong devotional spirit. Truths and appeals are not condensed and compacted into vigorous words. They are diluted by their author's grace and gentleness, and conveyed to the heart only in holiday and lady terms. Some one has said, 'Spread out the thunder into single tones, and it becomes a lullaby for children, pour it forth together in one quick peal, and the royal sound shall move the heavens.' Addison's moral thunder is all spread out into single tones. We desire not to be misunderstood. We do not expect that every sentence of a moral essay shall embody a whole volume of meaning. We do not wish to be startled at every step, by a '*Let there be light!*' or a '*Thou art the man!*' But we do desire, and expect, that when an educated thinker presumes to employ his pen for the purpose of impelling or persuading the heart of man to thoughts and deeds of virtue, he shall do something more than timidly suggest the propriety of being a good husband, a good citizen, or a good patriot—something more than gently to insinuate that the virtues are very beautiful, and that to violate the highest moral obligations, is exceedingly naughty. We are strongly inclined to suspect, that when Mr. Addison addressed himself to moral composition, he was less intent upon the life, and soundness, and worth of thought, than upon the choiceness of phrase, and the sweet falling of clauses. We strongly suspect, that instead of inquiring what changes of moral conduct, what states of moral feeling will be produced by these appeals of mine, he was engaged in asking of a sentence whether it would prefer being terminated by a word of one, or of two syllables; that instead of enlivening his mind with hopes of a wide and lasting improvement of his fellow-beings, he was vexing it with narrow conjectures of the opinion, which the fashionable and artificial circles of the London world would entertain of his speculations. Mr. Addison was too coldly correct, too critically dull to be an impressive and successful moral teacher. He wrote upon moral subjects just as we should expect a man to write, who had been removed from the office of secretary of state, for spending that time and those talents in punctiliously dotting his *i*'s and crossing his *t*'s, which should have been bestowed upon weightier matters. We close our observations on this topic by humbly suggesting, that the Intellectualist of this age would not do wisely, who, in appreciating the various means of nursing into vigor and maturity the moral germs within him, should assign more than an extremely small importance to the moral portion of the periodical literature of Anne's time.

Another characteristic feature of this literature is in *its intellectual department;* embracing the critical and philosophical essays, with the taste and reasoning powers therein manifested. Since a serious conviction of his deficiencies, withheld our applause from Mr. Addison as a moralist, it is probably not anticipated that we shall shower down much eulogy upon his critical and philosophical genius. If we were sometimes sad while reflecting upon the nerveless and worldly character of his morality, we are disposed to smile at his efforts in criticism, while we can hardly refrain from laughing outright at his philosophical reasonings. It is much to be regretted, that we have not sufficient time and space for the introduction of the data whereupon our conclusions are based. We fear we may be charged with want of candor, or, what with some might be deemed less pardonable, with a partial induction of facts. We perhaps may despair of being approved by any who have not become thoroughly acquainted with the length and breadth, and height and depth of these periodical writings; and who have not also been long familiarized with nobler, wider, and mightier standards of intellectual power.

As indications of taste, and as specimens of critical acumen, take the twelve much applauded essays on *Paradise Lost.* We are constrained to say, that the genius of Mr. Addison had not fit wings to bear it onward with the muse of Milton in her majestic flights; for while the imagination of the poet is far away in heavenly realms, among the sphered spirits, and in the presence of the embattled seraphim, that of the critic never seems to range beyond the walls of No. 5, Soho Square. Amidst Milton's gorgeous creations of the upper and the nether worlds, Mr. Addison is as trim, and neat, and finical, as when speaking of affectation, or vanity. We confess, that when reading these papers, we were almost out of patience with their author's want of enthusiastic sympathy with the thoughts that breathe and words that burn in every part of that immortal work—that when we saw his servility to the rules, by which Aristotle imagined all epics must be manufactured, we were almost compelled to throw down his essays with a feeling we do not wish to express. When testing the poetical merit of Milton, he does not ask whether such a character, or such a plot, or such a scene, or such an image, is adapted to the end for which, by the poet, it was designed. Far otherwise. He opens the copy of Aristotle before him, and hunting up the rule, he decides upon the poetry by its conformity or disagreement therewith. To illustrate. Aristotle says there should be no digression in an epic. Hereupon does Mr. Addison most heartily and most candidly condemn, among other things, Milton's beautiful panegyric of marriage, and all those touching and noble lines upon his blindness that follow the invocation 'Hail, holy light.' Mr. Addison seemed to think they had no business there. We think they *had* business there. Our reason is this: John Milton placed them there. With Mr. Addison the example of Homer and the precept of Aristotle, are the *To Kalon* and the *To Prepon* of all epical merit. We shall not so much forget ourself as to presume here to designate *the standards* in the various departments of poetical composition. We will merely recall to mind the truth, that the rules which have been framed for the regulation and advancement of intellectual action, whether in architecture, or painting, or sculpture, or in poetry, are, or should be, derived from a close and philosophical examination of the highest achievements of the highest order of human intellect, in the various spheres just named. As the formation of grammar must be subsequent to the creation of language, so in the fine arts, the formation of rules must be subsequent to the creation of those arts. Would any one, with the exception, perhaps, of Mr. Addison, dream of graduating the merit of the Apollo, or the Medicean Venus, by their conformity with certain rules which a certain soi-disant virtuoso may have oracled from his closet! Certainly not. These rarest monuments of the sculptor's art are themselves the fountain of principles to guide the chisel of the artist. We think Mr. Addison would have been far better employed in testing the rules of Aristotle by the composition of Milton, than in performing the *vice versa* process. If Milton be poetically in the wrong, let all hereafter poets make *the wrong* their beau ideal. They had better err with Milton than be right with Aristotle. Mr. Addison and the class of critics to which he belongs, exhort all genius to obey certain rules, though literary death be the consequence thereof. They resemble the physician of Moliere, who, while destroying his patient with the arbitrary prescriptions of Hippocrates, informed him that, to be sure, he would die, but he would, at least, have the satisfaction of knowing that he died according to the most approved medical rules. We conclude this topic by observing, that to the Intellectualist of this day, we think little or no profit can be derived from a study of Mr. Addison, the critic.

We have but a few remarks to make upon the philosophical essays, which constitute a portion of this literature. If our opinion were to be determined by an examination of those which are most celebrated—the eleven essays on the Pleasures of the Imagination—we fear it would be none of the highest. The two characteristics of these essays, which, we apprehend, cannot but be manifest to the most superficial reader, are, a prim, starched, formal narrowness of conception, and a most unpardonable slovenliness of reasoning. Mr. Addison's philosophical genius seems to be hooped, and corseted, and tricked up in the stiff and artificial finery of the times. There is a want of freedom, of emancipation from the Frenchified and cramped modes of thinking which then prevailed. There is a want of energy, of comprehensive power to impress into his service the ablebodied truths in the wide universe of thought around him. He had not a large intellectual reach. His mental glances did not shoot to and fro, athwart the darkness of the moral world, and reveal its mysteries. His reasonings are full of *non sequiturs.* His propositions are not bound together by strong, invincible chains of ratiocination. His premises are stated, then oftentimes you see a wide chasm, and then comes the lame and impotent conclusion. Mr. Addison's 'for' and 'because' are very much like the 'argal' of the grave digger in *Hamlet.* Instead of dovetailing consecutive thoughts, he shingles them over and over. We might adduce numerous instances to sustain these assertions—we give one of the least exceptionable. Mr. Addison says, 'as the great and only end of these my speculations is, to banish vice and ignorance out of the territory of Great Britain, I shall endeavor, as much as possible, to establish among us a taste of polite literature.' We pause not to cavil at such an expression as, 'taste of polite literature.' We ask the reader to mark the inconsequential character of the reasoning. A taste for polite literature, as that phrase was understood in Queen Anne's time, no more tends to banish vice and ignorance out of a kingdom, than a relish for macaroni and ice-cream tends to banish bad humors out of man's physical constitution. Not only a priori reasoning, but all the past is full of refutations of this unsound conclusion. History and biography have established no truth more firmly than this, that a taste for such literature may coexist with the practice of the most debasing vices, and with the most unpardonable ignorance of all things, save and except the narrow topic of the aforesaid literature. The imbecility of the means, no less than their want of adaptation to the end proposed, must be apparent to every thinker. The instance, just given, is only one of the hundreds, that compel us to the conclusion, that while such thinkers and reasoners as Chillingworth, and Butler, and Edwards, and Burke, and Stewart, are accessible to the Intellectualist of this day, he would run the risk of subjecting himself to laughter, and indeed, to something worse than laughter, did he waste many of his hours in the contemplation of Mr. Addison, the philosopher.

And now, methinks, I hear it whispered—surely while this writer is dealing in such wholesale denunciations of this literature, and its noblest representatives, surely, surely, he has forgotten the clear and classic *taste* therein embodied. Upon this quality of taste, for which this literature has been much admired, we will observe, in the first place, that the relation in which taste stands to the other intellectual powers, is that of a servant to its masters; or, perhaps more properly, of a guide to its superiors. It is the hand which points the other mental powers the course that they should go. It is the compass that guides them in their untracked and starless pathway through the intellectual deep. To be available, it presupposes the existence and activity of these powers. In our judgment, and we hope not to be charged with speaking too confidently, Mr. Addison and his fellow-workers were not gifted with strong mental powers, they wanted vigorous and adventurous talents, and consequently, under the guidance of the most infallible taste, they could have achieved nothing to challenge more than the faintest voice of admiration. But, as we do not feel, so are we not disposed to express, any approbation of their taste. We think it cannot be more truly characterized than as classically and delicately bad. It was tainted with the universal spirit of that time; a spirit which rejoiced in the artificial—which abhorred the simple and the natural; which preferred tripping daintily in buckram, through gardens cut into triangles, and parallelograms, and among groves trimmed into the figures of elephants and pyramids—to wandering in liberty through the beautiful gardens of nature, listening to her thousand simple harmonies, and renewing the freshness of early youth among her hills and her fountains. We think that evidence of this false taste may be perceived throughout all their compositions. We certainly cannot recommend them to the Intellectualist of this day, as models whereupon he might safely endeavor to mould his taste.

Before passing to our concluding topic, we wish to indulge in a few general reflections. One of the qualities inherent in *all* the literature of which we have been speaking is, moral and intellectual barrenness. The compositions of Addison and of Steele are the least *suggestive* of any with which we are acquainted. They do not quicken and create trains of reflection in the minds and hearts of the reader. In the words of Bacon, they do not 'generate still, and cast their seeds in the minds of others, provoking and causing infinite actions and opinions in succeeding ages.' Whatever delight and instruction may be derived from reading them, is derived from *reading* them alone, and not from any awakened recollections and associated ideas, which, as we have already observed, they have not power to arouse. It is doubtless owing to this fact, that to them has been assigned the epithet *classical.* It is this which has so widely contradistinguished them from those intellectual creations which have been denominated *romantic.* The characteristic property of the classical is, to impress, by its own intrinsic beauty and majesty; while the distinguishing character of the romantic is, to move by associated thoughts and images. The Parthenon is classical. It would charm the beholder, if seen upon the centre of a western prairie, and seen by one who never knew that Greece had been crowned with power and with glory, and had at last gone down forever to the sepulchre of dead nations. A gothic castle, which beetles from a precipice, which has laughed to scorn the rage of a thousand tempests, and which tradition tells us was the theatre of some dread exploit, is romantic. An Italian opera, if to us it be any thing, is classical. The epithet romantic may, with propriety, be applied to the melody of 'Auld lang syne,' 'Home, sweet home,' and of other similar songs, whose chief power to move consists in this, that they awaken the slumbering memories of childhood, or recall the image of a friend now no more, or seem to inspire with a momentary life emotions and affections that for years had been lying dead in the still chambers of the heart. Now, Mr. Addison and his coadjutors have been ranked among the classical minds. Surely they are not romantic in the sense which we have endeavored to show belongs to that term. And among the classical writers, we think their place to be very subordinate. Their works want the beautiful proportions, the faultless forms, and the enchanting tones which, so to speak, have embalmed the classic masterpieces of antiquity, and consecrated them to the admiration of all time.

And now we desire to notice another trait which appertains to *all* this literature. We mean its narrowness and particularity as contradistinguished from a wide universality. Its authors did not address the world, nor even Great Britain, nor even London, but they narrowed down their lucubrations to a still narrower set in that metropolis. With a slight modification, what was said of Swift might be applied to them. They wrote 'not satires, but lampoons; not wit for all mankind, but jokes for a particular circle.' Those who are familiar with the essays of Bacon, will understand, that while these are for men in all the successive ages of time, the essays of the **Spectator,** the **Tatler,** and the **Guardian,** though on the same and similar topics, are but for a very small portion of the eighteenth century. We doubt not they touched many of the chords of thinking and of feeling, tuned by the artificial spirit of that brief time. But they have not power to reach those moral harp strings, which have been placed in the human soul by its Creator, and which are enduring as the soul itself. We do not dwell upon this trait as being objectionable. We name it only as *one* of the means for ascertaining what niche in our admiration the periodical literature of Anne's time should occupy. If it be averred that it answered its end; very well. We only say its end was narrow. We only say that the intellectual spirit of its authors did not strike off the chains of the present passion, the present opinion, the present taste, and ascending untrammeled above the nation and the age, did not select topics interesting to all mankind, and exhibit and illustrate them in a manner which to all might be impressive. Their compositions are said to have accomplished their end—that end was temporary. To us they seem marvellously to resemble certain water craft, which having performed its single trip down the western rivers, is ever after consigned to uselessness and decay; while the creations of those minds, to which Mr. Addison and his coadjutors are, in this respect, opposed, may be likened to richly freighted ships that sail forever through the wide seas of time.

As the periodical literature of Anne's reign was only intended to meet and gratify the fashionable spirit of the time, so it is bowing to the fate of all things merely fashionable. The *vivat* of public opinion in one age, has been supplanted by the *pereat* of public opinion in the succeeding. Surely, its admirers cannot anticipate that it shall live and flourish forever in the clear sky of fame. The patience of mankind is not immortal. The gentle sway of the Addisonian dynasty is ceasing. The sceptre, which it has held so long over the hearts and imaginations of men, has, by

their rightful lords, been wrenched away. Its throne has fallen. A spirit, stronger, sterner, and may we not say, lovelier, has come up. It is the spirit of the Elizabethan and the Miltonic age. The applauses, created by the great intellectual achievements of that era, have, after near two centuries, converged into their echoing focus. We rejoice to see a reviving taste for what we have always deemed a fresher, richer, and a nobler literature. We rejoice to see the spirit of the older English writers at length bursting up, like the Arcadian stream after its long subterranean course, to fertilize and beautify the moral landscape of the present century. We beheld, with a melancholy regret, the decline of that spirit, after the exhausting, political, and religious agitations of the sixteenth and seventeenth centuries. It reached its lowest point, during, and immediately after, the reign of Anne. It has now begun to rise. If we may so speak, the pendulum has begun to oscillate upon the other side. We hope that it may continue its upward curve. We hope that the literary power of the nineteenth century may be improved by models of thinking and feeling, created, not in the classical, but in the rich, suggestive, romantic ages of English literature. We can hardly think the world will willingly permit the master-spirits of those ages to be again forgotten. We trust that, leagued with time, they will pass triumphantly down the tide of men's memories, and that, ages hence, their voice will be loud and clear, when the voices of those who, for a brief time, usurped their place, shall be buried in silence.

Our reflections have almost diverted us from our concluding topic, which is, *the style* of this periodical literature. We do not mean style of thinking, but style in the popular acceptation of the term, embracing *language and its construction into sentences.* Much has been said of the classical beauty of Addison's style. His works, like those of Spencer, have been metaphored into 'wells of undefiled English.' Even Dr. Johnson has dictated an oracle upon this subject [*Lives of the Poets,* 1781]. Those who are wont to clap their hands at the sesquipedalianism, and to bow down their intellects before the shrine of this literary autocrat, may have been beguiled into the error, that 'whoever would write English with correctness and elegance, must give his days and nights to the study of Addison.' Samuel Johnson's approbation of a style, is, in our judgment, somewhat equivocal testimony in its favor. If a friend were to inform us that he was charmed and delighted with the style of Mr. Addison, we should prophecy that he would *fail,* did he attempt to move the heart, and mould the opinion of the present age. The style of Addison is no more for the Intellectualist of the present day, than the tactics of Marlborough and Turenne are for its military leaders. And the reasons are obvious. Addison seems to have had but a faint conception of the strength, and compass, and flexibility of the English tongue. His best thoughts are imprisoned in pedantic Gallicisms, and in the Latin and Greek portions of the English language. The Saxon, the melodious, the pliant, the fresh, and maidenly Saxon; the language of Bunyan, of Jeremy Taylor, of Shakespeare, of the Bible,—this language was beginning to be frowned down in the time of Anne. Then was commenced the degradation, consummated under the inglorious dynasty of Johnson. In Addison, we see neat and elegant words, culled and arranged with all the precise formality of a bouquet. The grace, and rosy freshness, and perfume of natural flowers, are not there. We have noted with surprise, how widely different is the influence of the same truths in the style of Addison, from their impressiveness when conveyed in the style of minds belonging to a later day. When uttered by the former, their effect is feeble, and it soon passes away. Enunciated by Robert Hall, or Macaulay, or Dugald Stewart, they impress deeply, and are long remembered. In the former instance, you hear, as it were, a tune delicately executed on a guitar; in the latter, you listen to the same piece of music, embodied in the deep and thrilling tones of a cathedral organ.

But of all writers who have been long in the eye of public favor, perhaps not one can be found, who has been guilty of so many purely grammatical blunders as Mr. Addison. We only suggest a reperusal of Dr. Blair's criticisms of some of his most thoroughly elaborated papers. We declare that we were astonished at the manifold proofs of the abovenamed deficiency, which are candidly revealed by the admiring critic. Words most inappropriate, pronouns without antecedents, adverbs located any where but in their right place, and other similar blunders, of which the merest Sophomore would be ashamed, are continually stumbled upon in going over any of his compositions. And these errors are committed by the correct, the chaste, the finished Mr. Addison! We think that he has completely failed in that very subordinate sphere, in which he was most anxious to succeed, and for which he has been most extravagantly applauded. We take the liberty of here reiterating the truth, which is now beginning to be appreciated, and which we last heard from the lips of Mr. Grimké, that of all English writers who have ever been held up as models of style, the most grammatically incorrect is Mr. Addison.

It cannot be expected that we shall recommend for imitation the *style* of the periodical literature of Anne's time, since we have manifested so much disesteem for that of its purest representative. (pp. 233-44)

> *J. J. J., "Remarks on the Writings of Addison and Steele," in* The Western Monthly Magazine, *Vol. III, No. IV, April, 1835, pp. 232-44.*

Thomas Carlyle   (lecture date 1838)

[*A noted nineteenth-century essayist, historian, critic, and social commentator, Carlyle was a central figure of the Victorian age in England. In his writings, Carlyle advocated a Christian work ethic and stressed the importance of order, piety, and spiritual fulfillment. In the following excerpt from a lecture delivered in 1838, he comments on Addison's place in history.*]

In Queen Anne's time, after that most disgraceful class of people—King Charles' people—had passed away, there appeared the milder kind of unbelief. Complete formalism is the characteristic of Queen Anne's reign. But, amid all this, it is strange how many beautiful indications there are of better things, how many truths were said. Addison was a mere lay preacher, completely bound up in formalism, but he did get to say many a true thing in his generation; an instance of one formal man doing great things. Steele

had infinitely more *naïveté,* but he was only a fellow-soldier of Addison, to whom he subordinated himself more than was necessary. It is a cold vote in Addison's favor that one gives. (pp. 176-77)

> *Thomas Carlyle, "Eighteenth Century in England—Whitfield—Swift—Sterne—Johnson—Hume," in his* Lectures on the History of Literature, *edited by J. Reay Greene, Charles Scribner's Sons, 1892, pp. 169-85.*

Thomas Babington Macaulay   (essay date 1843)

[*Macaulay was a distinguished historian, essayist, and politician of mid-nineteenth-century England. For many years he was a major contributor of erudite, highly opinionated articles to the* Edinburgh Review. *Besides these* Critical and Historical Essays *(1843), his most enduring work is his five-volume* History of England from the Accession of James II *(1849-61), which, despite criticism of its strong bias toward the Whig political party, is revered for its consummate rhetorical and narrative prose. According to Richard Tobias, Macaulay was a writer who "feared sentiment and preferred distance, objectivity, dispassionate vision. Yet withal, he was a brilliant writer who . . . is still capable of moving a reader by sheer verbal excitement." In the following excerpt from his highly influential study of Addison—first published in the* Edinburgh Review *in 1843 as a review of Lucy Aikin's* Life of Joseph Addison *and reprinted in 1896 as* The Life and Writings of Joseph Addison—*Macaulay favorably compares Addison's wit to that of Jonathan Swift and Voltaire and views Addison as a forerunner to the English novelists.*]

To Addison . . . we are bound by a sentiment as much like affection as any sentiment can be which is inspired by one who has been sleeping a hundred and twenty years in Westminster Abbey. We trust, however, that this feeling will not betray us into that abject idolatry which we have often had occasion to reprehend in others, and which seldom fails to make both the idolater and the idol ridiculous. A man of genius and virtue is but a man. All his powers cannot be equally developed, nor can we expect from him perfect self-knowledge. We need not, therefore, hesitate to admit that Addison has left us some compositions which do not rise above mediocrity, some heroic poems hardly equal to [Thomas] Parnell's some criticism as superficial as Dr. [Hugh] Blair's, and a tragedy not very much better than Dr. Johnson's. It is praise enough to say of a writer that, in a high department of literature in which many eminent writers have distinguished themselves, he has had no equal; and this may with strict justice be said of Addison.

As a man he may not have deserved the adoration which he received from those who, bewitched by his fascinating society, and indebted for all the comforts of life to his generous and delicate friendship, worshiped him nightly in his favorite temple at Button's. But, after full inquiry and impartial reflection, we have long been convinced that he deserved as much love and esteem as can be justly claimed by any of our infirm and erring race. Some blemishes may undoubtedly be detected in his character; but the more carefully it is examined, the more will it appear, to use the phrase of the old anatomists, sound in the noble parts, free from all taint of perfidy, of cowardice, of cruelty, of ingratitude, of envy. Men may easily be named in whom some particular good disposition has been more conspicuous than in Addison. But the just harmony of qualities, the exact temper between the stern and the humane virtues, the habitual observance of every law, not only of moral rectitude, but of moral grace and dignity, distinguish him from all men who have been tried by equally strong temptations, and about whose conduct we possess equally full information. (pp. 93-5)

It is probable that Addison, when he sent across St. George's Channel his first contributions to **The Tatler,** had no notion of the extent and variety of his own powers. He was the possessor of a vast mine, rich with a hundred ores; but he had been acquainted only with the least precious part of his treasures, and had hitherto contented himself with producing sometimes copper and sometimes lead, intermingled with a little silver. All at once, and by mere accident, he had lighted on an inexhaustible vein of the finest gold.

The mere choice and arrangement of his words would have sufficed to make his essays classical; for never—not even by Dryden, not even by [Sir William] Temple—had the English language been written with such sweetness, grace, and facility. But this was the smallest part of Addison's praise. Had he clothed his thoughts in the half French style of Horace Walpole, or in the half Latin style of Dr. Johnson, or in the half German jargon of the present day, his genius would have triumphed over all faults of manner. As a moral satirist he stands unrivaled. If ever the best *Tatlers* and *Spectators* were equaled in their own kind, we should be inclined to guess that it must have been by the lost comedies of Menander.

In wit, properly so called, Addison was not inferior to [Abraham] Cowley or [Samuel] Butler. No single ode of Cowley contains so many happy analogies as are crowded into the lines to Sir Godfrey Kneller; and we would undertake to collect from the *Spectators* as great a number of ingenious illustrations as can be found in *Hudibras.* The still higher faculty of invention Addison possessed in still larger measure. The numerous fictions, generally original, often wild and grotesque, but always singularly graceful and happy, which are found in his essays, fully entitle him to the rank of a great poet,—a rank to which his metrical compositions give him no claim. As an observer of life, of manners, of all the shades of human character, he stands in the first class; and what he observed he had the art of communicating in two widely different ways. He could describe virtues, vices, habits, whims, as well as Clarendon. But he could do something better: he could call human beings into existence, and make them exhibit themselves. If wish to find anything more vivid than Addison's best portraits, we must go either to Shakespeare or to Cervantes.

But what shall we say of Addison's humor, of his sense of the ludicrous, of his power of awakening that sense in others, and of drawing mirth from incidents which occur every day, and from little peculiarities of temper and manner such as may be found in every man? We feel the

charm; we give ourselves up to it: but we strive in vain to analyze it.

Perhaps the best way of describing Addison's peculiar pleasantry is to compare it with the pleasantry of some other great satirists. The three most eminent masters of the art of ridicule during the eighteenth century were, we conceive, Addison, Swift, and Voltaire. Which of the three had the greatest power of moving laughter may be questioned; but each of them, within his own domain, was supreme.

Voltaire is the prince of buffoons. His merriment is without disguise or restraint. He gambols; he grins; he shakes the sides; he points the finger; he turns up the nose; he shoots out the tongue. The manner of Swift is the very opposite to this. He moves laughter, but never joins in it. He appears in his works such as he appeared in society. All the company are convulsed with merriment; while the Dean, the author of all the mirth, preserves an invincible gravity and even sourness of aspect, and gives utterance to the most eccentric and ludicrous fancies with the air of a man reading the commination service.

The manner of Addison is as remote from that of Swift as from that of Voltaire. He neither laughs out like the French wit, nor, like the Irish wit, throws a double portion of severity into his countenance while laughing inwardly, but preserves a look peculiarly his own,—a look of demure serenity, disturbed only by an arch sparkle of the eye, an almost imperceptible elevation of the brow, an almost imperceptible curl of the lip. His tone is never that either of a Jack Pudding or of a Cynic. It is that of a gentleman in whom the quickest sense of the ridiculous is constantly tempered by good-nature and good-breeding.

We own that the humor of Addison is, in our opinion, of more delicious flavor than the humor of either Swift or Voltaire. Thus much, at least, is certain, that both Swift and Voltaire have been successfully mimicked, and that no man has yet been able to mimic Addison. The letter of the Abbé Coyer to Pansophe is Voltaire all over, and imposed, during a long time, on the Academicians of Paris. There are passages in [Dr. John] Arbuthnot's satirical works which we, at least, cannot distinguish from Swift's best writing. But of the many eminent men who have made Addison their model, though several have copied his mere diction with happy effect, none has been able to catch the tone of his pleasantry. In *The World,* in *The Connoisseur,* in *The Mirror,* in *The Lounger,* there are numerous papers written in obvious imitation of his *Tatlers* and *Spectators.* Most of those papers have some merit; many are very lively and amusing; but there is not a single one which could be passed off as Addison's on a critic of the smallest perspicacity.

But that which chiefly distinguishes Addison from Swift, from Voltaire, from almost all the other great masters of ridicule, is the grace, the nobleness, the moral purity, which we find even in his merriment. Severity, gradually hardening and darkening into misanthropy, characterizes the works of Swift. The nature of Voltaire was, indeed, not inhuman; but he venerated nothing. Neither in the masterpieces of art nor in the purest examples of virtue, neither in the Great First Cause nor in the awful enigma of the grave, could he see anything but subjects for drollery. The more solemn and august the theme, the more monkey-like was his grimacing and chattering. The mirth of Swift is the mirth of Mephistopheles; the mirth of Voltaire is the mirth of Puck. If, as Soame Jenyns oddly imagined, a portion of the happiness of seraphim and just men made perfect be derived from an exquisite perception of the ludicrous, their mirth must surely be none other than the mirth of Addison,—a mirth consistent with tender compassion for all that is frail, and with profound reverence for all that is sublime. Nothing great, nothing amiable, no moral duty, no doctrine of natural or revealed religion, has ever been associated by Addison with any degrading idea. His humanity is without a parallel in literary history. The highest proof of virtue is to possess boundless power without abusing it. No kind of power is more formidable than the power of making men ridiculous, and that power Addison possessed in boundless measure. How grossly that power was abused by Swift and by Voltaire is well known. But of Addison it may be confidently affirmed that he has blackened no man's character; nay, that it would be difficult, if not impossible, to find in all the volumes which he has left us a single taunt which can be called ungenerous or unkind. Yet he had detractors, whose malignity might have seemed to justify as terrible a revenge as that which men not superior to him in genius wreaked on Bettesworth and on Franc de Pompignan. He was a politician; he was the best writer of his party; he lived in times of fierce excitement,—in times when persons of high character and station stooped to scurrility such as is now practiced only by the basest of mankind: yet no provocation and no example could induce him to return railing for railing.

Of the service which his essays rendered to morality it is difficult to speak too highly. It is true that, when *The Tatler* appeared, that age of outrageous profaneness and licentiousness which followed the Restoration had passed away. Jeremy Collier had shamed the theatres into something which, compared with the excesses of [Sir George] Etherege and [William] Wycherley, might be called decency; yet there still lingered in the public mind a pernicious notion that there was some connection between genius and profligacy, between the domestic virtues and the sullen formality of the Puritans. That error it is the glory of Addison to have dispelled. He taught the nation that the faith and the morality of [Sir Matthew] Hale and Tillotson might be found in company with wit more sparkling than the wit of Congreve, and with humor richer than the humor of Vanbrugh. So effectually, indeed, did he retort on vice the mockery which had recently been directed against virtue, that since his time the open violation of decency has always been considered among us as the mark of a fool. And this revolution, the greatest and most salutary ever effected by any satirist, he accomplished, be it remembered, without writing one personal lampoon.

In the early contributions of Addison to *The Tatler* his peculiar powers were not fully exhibited, yet from the first his superiority to all his coadjutors was evident. Some of his later *Tatler*s are fully equal to anything that he ever wrote. Among the portraits, we most admire Tom Folio, Ned Softly, and the Political Upholsterer. The proceed-

ings of the **"Court of Honor,"** the **"Thermometer of Zeal,"** the story of the **"Frozen Words,"** the **"Memoirs of the Shilling,"** are excellent specimens of that ingenious and lively species of fiction in which Addison excelled all men. (pp. 160-67)

The Spectator himself was conceived and drawn by Addison, and it is not easy to doubt that the portrait was meant to be in some features a likeness of the painter. The Spectator is a gentleman who, after passing a studious youth at the university, has traveled on classic ground, and has bestowed much attention on curious points of antiquity. He has, on his return, fixed his residence in London, and has observed all the forms of life which are to be found in that great city; has daily listened to the wits of Will's, has smoked with the philosophers of the Grecian, and has mingled with the parsons at Child's and with the politicians at the St. James's. In the morning he often listens to the hum of the Exchange; in the evening his face is constantly to be seen in the pit of Drury Lane Theatre. But an insurmountable bashfulness prevents him from opening his mouth, except in a small circle of intimate friends.

These friends were first sketched by Steele. Four of the club—the templar, the clergyman, the soldier, and the merchant—were uninteresting figures, fit only for a background; but the other two,—an old country baronet and an old town rake,—though not delineated with a very delicate pencil, had some good strokes. Addison took the rude outlines into his own hands, retouched them, colored them, and is in truth the creator of the Sir Roger de Coverley and the Will Honeycomb with whom we are all familiar.

The plan of *The Spectator* must be allowed to be both original and eminently happy. Every valuable essay in the series may be read with pleasure separately; yet the five or six hundred essays form a whole, and a whole which has the interest of a novel. It must be remembered, too, that at that time no novel giving a lively and powerful picture of the common life and manners of England had appeared. Richardson was working as a compositor. Fielding was robbing birds'-nests. [Tobias] Smollett was not yet born. The narrative, therefore, which connects together the Spectator's essays gave to our ancestors their first taste of an exquisite and untried pleasure. That narrative was indeed constructed with no art or labor. The events were such events as occur every day. Sir Roger comes up to town to see Eugenio, as the worthy baronet always calls Prince Eugene, goes with the Spectator on the water to Spring Gardens, walks among the tombs in the Abbey, and is frightened by the Mohawks [defined in a footnote as "A set of wild young men who assaulted wayfarers at night, and were suppressed with difficulty"] but conquers his apprehension so far as to go to the theatre when *The Distressed Mother* is acted. The Spectator pays a visit in the summer to Coverley Hall; is charmed with the old house, the old butler, and the old chaplain; eats a jack caught by Will Wimble; rides to the assizes, and hears a point of law discussed by Tom Touchy. At last a letter from the honest butler brings to the club the news that Sir Roger is dead. Will Honeycomb marries and reforms at sixty. The club breaks up, and the Spectator resigns his functions. Such events can hardly be said to form a plot; yet they are related with such truth, such grace, such wit, such humor, such pathos, such knowledge of the human heart, such knowledge of the ways of the world, that they charm us on the hundredth perusal. We have not the least doubt that, if Addison had written a novel on an extensive plan, it would have been superior to any that we possess. As it is, he is entitled to be considered not only as the greatest of the English essayists, but as the forerunner of the great English novelists.

We say this of Addison alone, for Addison is the Spectator. About three sevenths of the work are his, and it is no exaggeration to say that his worst essay is as good as the best essay of any of his coadjutors. His best essays approach near to absolute perfection; nor is their excellence more wonderful than their variety. His invention never seems to flag; nor is he ever under the necessity of repeating himself, or of wearing out a subject. There are no dregs in his wine. He regales us after the fashion of that prodigal nabob who held that there was only one good glass in a bottle. As soon as we have tasted the first sparkling foam of a jest, it is withdrawn, and a fresh draught of nectar is at our lips. On the Monday we have an allegory as lively and ingenious as Lucian's "Auction of Lives;" on the Tuesday, an Eastern apologue as richly colored as the tales of Scheherezade; on the Wednesday, a character described with the skill of La Bruyère; on the Thursday, a scene from common life equal to the best chapters in *The Vicar of Wakefield;* on the Friday, some sly Horatian pleasantry on fashionable follies, on hoops, patches, or puppet shows; and on the Saturday, a religious meditation which will bear a comparison with the finest passages in [Jean Baptiste] Massillon.

It is dangerous to select where there is so much that deserves the highest praise. We will venture, however, to say that any person who wishes to form a just notion of the extent and variety of Addison's powers will do well to read at one sitting the following papers,—the two **"Visits to the Abbey,"** the **"Visit to the Exchange,"** the **"Journal of the Retired Citizen,"** the **"Vision of Mirza,"** the **"Transmigrations of Pug the Monkey,"** and the **"Death of Sir Roger de Coverley."**

The least valuable of Addison's contributions to *The Spectator* are, in the judgment of our age, his critical papers; yet his critical papers are always luminous, and often ingenious. The very worst of them must be regarded as creditable to him, when the character of the school in which he had been trained is fairly considered. The best of them were much too good for his readers. In truth, he was not so far behind our generation as he was before his own. No essays in *The Spectator* were more censured and derided than those in which he raised his voice against the contempt with which our fine old ballads were regarded, and showed the scoffers that the same gold which, burnished and polished, gives lustre to the *Æneid* and the Odes of Horace is mingled with the rude dross of "Chevy Chase."

It is not strange that the success of *The Spectator* should have been such as no similar work has ever obtained. The number of copies daily distributed was at first three thousand. It subsequently increased, and had risen to near four thousand when the stamp tax was imposed. That tax was fatal to a crowd of journals. *The Spectator,* however, stood its ground, doubled its price, and, though its circulation fell off, still yielded a large revenue both to the state and to the authors. For particular papers the demand was immense; of some, it is said, twenty thousand copies were required. But this was not all. To have *The Spectator* served up every morning with the bohea and rolls was a luxury for the few. The majority were content to wait till essays enough had appeared to form a volume. Ten thousand copies of each volume were immediately taken off, and new editions were called for. It must be remembered that the population of England was then hardly a third of what it now is. The number of Englishmen who were in the habit of reading was probably not a sixth of what it now is. A shopkeeper or a farmer who found any pleasure in literature was a rarity. Nay, there was doubtless more than one knight of the shire whose country-seat did not contain ten books, receipt books and books on farriery included. In these circumstances, the sale of *The Spectator* must be considered as indicating a popularity quite as great as that of the most successful works of Sir Walter Scott and Mr. Dickens in our own time. (pp. 173-78)

> *Thomas Babington Macaulay, in his* Life and Writings of Addison, *edited by William P. Trent, Houghton, Mifflin and Company, 1896, 223 p.*

William Makepeace Thackeray   (essay date 1853)

[*Thackeray is one of the most important English novelists of the nineteenth century. During his lifetime he was best known for satiric sketches and stories in which he presented a panoramic view of Victorian society similar to that of Charles Dickens—but of the upper and middle rather than the lower classes. His most famous novel,* Vanity Fair: A Novel without a Hero (1848), *satirizes the corruption of the upper classes and contains, in Becky Sharp, one of the most memorable antiheroines in nineteenth-century fiction. Although intended to serve as the antithesis of the traditionally virtuous and demure female fictional character, the self-serving Sharp engages more reader sympathy and interest than any other character in the novel. Thackeray's criticism—collected in* The English Humourists of the Eighteenth Century (1853) *from lectures he delivered in Europe and the United States—is of mixed quality, but shows interesting aspects of Thackeray's character and the literary taste of his time. In the following excerpt from that work, Thackeray lauds Addison's achievements as a satirist.*]

We have seen in Swift a humorous philosopher, whose truth frightens one, and whose laughter makes one melancholy. We have had in Congreve a humorous observer of another school, to whom the world seems to have no moral at all, and whose ghastly doctrine seems to be that we should eat, drink, and be merry when we can, and go to the deuce (if there be a deuce) when the time comes. We come now to a humor that flows from quite a different heart and spirit—a wit that makes us laugh, and leaves us good and happy; to one of the kindest benefactors that society has ever had; and I believe you have divined already that I am about to mention Addison's honored name.

From reading over his writings, and the biographies which we have of him, amongst which the famous article in the *Edinburgh Review* [July, 1843. Thomas Babington Macaulay's review of *The Life of Joseph Addison*, by Lucy Aikin] may be cited as a magnificent statue of the great writer and moralist of the last age, raised by the love and the marvellous skill and genius of one of the most illustrious artists of our own; looking at that calm, fair face, and clear countenance—those chiselled features pure and cold, I can't but fancy that this great man—in this respect, like [William Congreve]—was also one of the lonely ones of the world. Such men have very few equals, and they don't herd with those. It is in the nature of such lords of intellect to be solitary—they are in the world but not of it; and our minor struggles, brawls, successes, pass under them.

Kind, just, serene, impartial, his fortitude not tried beyond easy endurance, his affections not much used, for his books were his family, and his society was in public; admirably wiser, wittier, calmer, and more instructed than almost every man with whom he met, how could Addison suffer, desire, admire, feel much? I may expect a child to admire me for being taller or writing more cleverly than she; but how can I ask my superior to say that I am a wonder when he knows better than I? In Addison's days you could scarcely show him a literary performance, a sermon or a poem, or a piece of literary criticism, but he felt he could do better. His justice must have made him indifferent. He didn't praise, because he measured his compeers by a higher standard than common people have. How was he who was so tall to look up to any but the loftiest genius? He must have stooped to put himself on a level with most men. By that profusion of graciousness and smiles with which Goethe or Scott, for instance, greeted almost every literary beginner, every small literary adventurer who came to his court and went away charmed from the great king's audience, and cuddling to his heart the compliment which his literary majesty had paid him—each of the two good-natured potentates of letters brought their star and ribbon into discredit. Everybody had his majesty's orders. Everybody had his majesty's cheap portrait, on a box surrounded with diamonds worth twopence apiece. A very great and just and wise man ought not to praise indiscriminately, but give his idea of the truth. Addison praises the ingenious Mr. Pinkethman: Addison praises the ingenious Mr. Doggett, the actor, whose benefit is coming off that night: Addison praises Don Saltero: Addison praises Milton with all his heart, bends his knee and frankly pays homage to that imperial genius. But between those degrees of his men his praise is very scanty. I don't think the great Mr. Addison liked young Mr. Pope, the Papist, much; I don't think he abused him. But when Mr. Addison's men abused Mr. Pope, I don't think Addison took his pipe out of his mouth to contradict them.

Addison's father was a clergyman of good repute in Wiltshire, and rose in the church. His famous son never lost his clerical training and scholastic gravity, and was called "a parson in a tye-wig" in London afterwards at a time

Drawing by William Makepeace Thackeray, "Addison at 'Child's' ".

when tye-wigs were only worn by the laity, and the fathers of theology did not think it decent to appear except in a full bottom. Having been at school at Salisbury, and the Charterhouse, in 1687, when he was fifteen years old, he went to Queen's College, Oxford, where he speedily began to distinguish himself by the making of Latin verses. The beautiful and fanciful poem of **"The Pigmies and the Cranes,"** is still read by lovers of that sort of exercise; and verses are extant in honor of King William, by which it appears that it was the loyal youth's custom to toast that sovereign in bumpers of purple Lyæus: many more works are in the Collection, including one on the Peace of Ryswick, in 1697, which was so good that Montague got him a pension of £300 a-year, on which Addison set out on his travels.

During his ten years at Oxford, Addison had deeply imbued himself with the Latin poetical literature, and had these poets at his fingers' ends when he travelled in Italy. His patron went out of office, and his pension was unpaid: and hearing that this great scholar, now eminent and known to the *literati* of Europe (the great Boileau, upon perusal of Mr. Addison's elegant hexameters, was first made aware that England was not altogether a barbarous nation)—hearing that the celebrated Mr. Addison, of Oxford, proposed to travel as governor to a young gentleman on the grand tour, the great Duke of Somerset proposed to Mr. Addison to accompany his son, Lord Hartford.

Mr. Addison was delighted to be of use to his Grace, and his lordship his Grace's son, and expressed himself ready to set forth.

His Grace the Duke of Somerset now announced to one of the most famous scholars of Oxford and Europe that it was his gracious intention to allow my Lord Hartford's tutor one hundred guineas per annum. Mr. Addison wrote back that his services were his Grace's, but he by no means found his account in the recompense for them. The negotiation was broken off. They parted with a profusion of *congées* on one side and the other.

Addison remained abroad for some time, living in the best society of Europe. How could he do otherwise? He must have been one of the finest gentlemen the world ever saw: at all moments of life serene and courteous, cheerful and calm. He could scarcely ever have had a degrading thought. He might have omitted a virtue or two, or many, but could not have had many faults committed for which he need blush or turn pale. When warmed into confidence, his conversation appears to have been so delightful that the greatest wits sat rapt and charmed to listen to him. No man bore poverty and narrow fortune with a more lofty cheerfulness. His letters to his friends at this period of his life, when he had lost his Government pension and given up his college chances, are full of courage and a gay confidence and philosophy: and they are none the worse in my eyes, and I hope not in those of his last and greatest biographer (though Mr. Macaulay is bound to own and lament a certain weakness for wine, which the great and good Joseph Addison notoriously possessed, in common with countless gentlemen of his time), because some of the letters are written when his honest hand was shaking a little in the morning after libations to purple Lyæus overnight. He was fond of drinking the healths of his friends: he writes to Wyche, of Hamburg, gratefully remembering Wyche's "hoc." "I have been drinking your health to-day with Sir Richard Shirley," he writes to Bathurst. "I have lately had the honor to meet my Lord Effingham at Amsterdam, where we have drunk Mr. Wood's health a hundred times in excellent champagne," he writes again. Swift describes him over his cups, when Joseph yielded to a temptation which Jonathan resisted. Joseph was of a cold nature, and needed perhaps the fire of wine to warm his blood. If he was a parson, he wore a tye-wig, recollect. A better and more Christian man scarcely ever breathed than Joseph Addison. If he had not that little weakness for wine—why, we could scarcely have found a fault with him, and could not have liked him as we do.

At thirty-three years of age, this most distinguished wit, scholar, and gentleman was without a profession and an income. His book of *Travels* had failed: his *Dialogues on Medals* had no particular success: his Latin verses, even though reported the best since Virgil, or Statius at any rate, had not brought him a Government place, and Addison was living up three shabby pair of stairs in the Haymarket (in a poverty over which old Samuel Johnson [in his *Lives of the Poets*, 1781] rather chuckles), when in these shabby rooms an emissary from Government and

Fortune came and found him. A poem was wanted about the Duke of Marlborough's victory of Blenheim. Would Mr. Addison write one? Mr. Boyle, afterwards Lord Carleton, took back the reply to the Lord Treasurer Godolphin, that Mr. Addison would. When the poem had reached a certain stage, it was carried to Godolphin; and the last lines which he read were these:—

> "But, O my Muse! what numbers wilt thou find
> To sing the furious troops in battle join'd?
> Methinks I hear the drum's tumultuous sound
> The victor's shouts and dying groans confound;
> The dreadful burst of cannon rend the skies,
> And all the thunder of the battle rise.
> 'T was then great Marlborough's mighty soul
>   was proved,
> That, in the shock of charging hosts unmoved,
> Amidst confusion, horror, and despair,
> Examined all the dreadful scenes of war:
> In peaceful thought the field of death surveyed,
> To fainting squadrons sent the timely aid,
> Inspired repulsed battalions to engage,
> And taught the doubtful battle where to rage.
> So when an angel, by divine command,
> With rising tempests shakes a guilty land
> (Such as of late o'er pale Britannia passed),
> Calm and serene he drives the furious blast;
> And pleased the Almighty's orders to perform,
> Rides in the whirlwind and directs the storm.

Addison left off at a good moment. That simile was pronounced to be of the greatest ever produced in poetry. That angel, that good angel, flew off with Mr. Addison, and landed him in the place of Commissioner of Appeals—*vice* Mr. Locke providentially promoted. In the following year Mr. Addison went to Hanover with Lord Halifax, and the year after was made Under Secretary of State. O angel visits! you come "few and far between" to literary gentlemen's lodgings! Your wings seldom quiver at second floor windows now!

You laugh? You think it is in the power of few writers now-a-days to call up such an angel? Well, perhaps not; but permit us to comfort ourselves by pointing out that there are in the poem of the *Campaign* some as bad lines as heart can desire: and to hint that Mr. Addison did very wisely in not going further with my Lord Godolphin than that angelical simile. Do allow me, just for a little harmless mischief, to read you some of the lines which follow. Here is the interview between the Duke and the King of the Romans after the battle:—

> Austria's young monarch, whose imperial sway
> Sceptres and thrones are destined to obey,
> Whose boasted ancestry so high extends
> That in the Pagan Gods his lineage ends,
> Comes from afar, in gratitude to own
> The great supporter of his father's throne.
> What tides of glory to his bosom ran
> Clasped in th' embraces of the godlike man!
> How were his eyes with pleasing wonder fixt,
> To see such fire with so much sweetness mixt!
> Such easy greatness, such a graceful port,
> So turned and finished for the camp or court!

How many fourth-form boys at Mr. Addison's school of Charterhouse could write as well as that now? The *Cam-*

paign has blunders, triumphant as it was; and weak points like all campaigns.

In the year 1713 *Cato* came out. Swift has left a description of the first night of the performance. All the laurels of Europe were scarcely sufficient for the author of this prodigious poem. Laudations of Whig and Tory chiefs, popular ovations, complimentary garlands from literary men, translation in all languages, delight and homage from all—save from John Dennis in a minority of one. Mr. Addison was called the "great Mr. Addison" after this. The Coffee-house Senate saluted him Divus: it was heresy to question that decree.

Meanwhile he was writing political papers and advancing in the political profession. He went Secretary to Ireland. He was appointed Secretary of State in 1717. And letters of his are extant, bearing date some year or two before, and written to young Lord Warwick, in which he addresses him as "my dearest lord," and asks affectionately about his studies, and writes very prettily about nightingales and birds'-nests, which he has found at Fulham for his lordship. Those nightingales were intended to warble in the ear of Lord Warwick's mamma. Addison married her ladyship in 1716; and died at Holland House three years after that splendid but dismal union.

But it is not for his reputation as the great author of *Cato* and the *Campaign,* or for his merits as Secretary of State, or for his rank and high distinction as my Lady Warwick's husband, or for his eminence as an Examiner of political questions on the Whig side, or a Guardian of British liberties, that we admire Joseph Addison. It is as a Tatler of small talk and a Spectator of mankind, that we cherish and love him, and owe as much pleasure to him as to any human being that ever wrote. He came in that artificial age, and began to speak with his noble, natural voice. He came, the gentle satirist, who hit no unfair blow; the kind judge who castigated only in smiling. While Swift went about, hanging and ruthless—a literary Jeffreys—in Addison's kind court only minor cases were tried: only peccadilloes and small sins against society: only a dangerous libertinism in tuckers and hoops; or a nuisance in the abuse of beaux' canes and snuff-boxes. It may be a lady is tried for breaking the peace of our sovereign lady Queen Anne, and ogling too dangerously from the side-box; or a Templar for beating the watch, or breaking Priscian's head: or a citizen's wife for caring too much for the puppet-show, and too little for her husband and children: every one of the little sinners brought before him is amusing, and he dismisses each with the pleasantest penalties and the most charming words of admonition.

Addison wrote his papers as gayly as if he was going out for a holiday. When Steele's *Tatler* first began his prattle, Addison, then in Ireland, caught at his friend's notion, poured in paper after paper, and contributed the stores of his mind, the sweet fruits of his reading, the delightful gleanings of his daily observation, with a wonderful profusion, and as it seemed an almost endless fecundity. He was six-and-thirty years old: full and ripe. He had not worked crop after crop from his brain, manuring hastily, subsoiling indifferently, cutting and sowing and cutting again, like other luckless cultivators of letters. He had not done

much as yet; a few Latin poems—graceful prolusions, a polite book of travels; a dissertation on medals, not very deep; four acts of a tragedy, a great classical exercise; and the *Campaign,* a large prize poem that won an enormous prize. But with his friend's discovery of the *Tatler,* Addison's calling was found, and the most delightful talker in the world began to speak. He does not go very deep: let gentlemen of a profound genius, critics accustomed to the plunge of the bathos, console themselves by thinking that he *couldn't* go very deep. There are no traces of suffering in his writing. He was so good, so honest, so healthy, so cheerfully selfish, if I must use the word. There is no deep sentiment. I doubt, until after his marriage, perhaps, whether he ever lost his night's rest or his day's tranquillity about any woman in his life; whereas poor Dick Steele had capacity enough to melt, and to languish, and to sigh, and to cry his honest old eyes out, for a dozen. His writings do not show insight into or reverence for the love of women, which I take to be, one the consequence of the other. He walks about the world watching their pretty humors, fashions, follies, flirtations, rivalries; and noting them with the most charming archness. He sees them in public, in the theatre, or the assembly, or the puppet-show; or at the toyshop higgling for gloves and lace; or at the auction, battling together over a blue porcelain dragon, or a darling monster in japan; or at church, eying the width of their rivals' hoops, or the breadth of their laces, as they sweep down the aisles. Or he looks out of his window at the "Garter" in St. James's Street, at Ardelia's coach, as she blazes to the drawing-room with her coronet and six footmen; and remembering that her father was a Turkey merchant in the city, calculates how many sponges went to purchase her ear-ring, and how many drums of figs to build her coach-box; or he demurely watches behind a tree in Spring Garden 25 Saccharissa (whom he knows under her mask) trips out of her chair to the alley where Sir Fopling is waiting. He sees only the public life of women. Addison was one of the most resolute club-men of his day. He passed many hours daily in those haunts. Besides drinking—which, alas! is past praying for—you must know it, he owned, too, ladies, that he indulged in that odious practice of smoking. Poor fellow! He was a man's man, remember. The only woman he *did* know, he didn't write about. I take it there would not have been much humor in that story.

He likes to go and sit in the smoking-room at the "Grecian," or the "Devil;" to pace 'Change and the Mall—to mingle in that great club of the world—sitting alone in it somehow: having good-will and kindness for every single man and woman in it—having need of some habit and custom binding him to some few; never doing any man a wrong (unless it be a wrong to hint a little doubt about a man's parts, and to damn him with faint praise); and so he looks on the world and plays with the ceaseless humors of all of us—laughs the kindest laugh—points our neighbor's foible or eccentricity out to us with the most good-natured, smiling confidence; and then, turning over his shoulder, whispers *our* foibles to our neighbor. What would Sir Roger de Coverley be without his follies and his charming little braincracks? If the good knight did not call out to the people sleeping in church, and say "Amen" with such a delightful pomposity: if he did not make a speech in the assize-court *àpropos de bottes,* and merely to show his dignity to Mr. Spectator: if he did not mistake Madam Doll Tearsheet for a lady of quality in Temple Garden: if he were wiser than he is: if he had not his humor to salt his life, and were but a mere English gentleman and game-preserver—of what worth were he to us? We love him for his vanities as much as his virtues. What is ridiculous is delightful in him; we are so fond of him because we laugh at him so. And out of that laughter, and out of that sweet weakness, and out of those harmless eccentricities and follies, and out of that touched brain, and out of that honest manhood and simplicity—we get a result of happiness, goodness, tenderness, pity, piety; such as, if my audience will think their reading and hearing over, doctors and divines but seldom have the fortune to inspire. And why not? Is the glory of Heaven to be sung only by gentlemen in black coats? Must the truth be only expounded in gown and surplice, and out of those two vestments can nobody preach it? Commend me to this dear preacher without orders—this parson in the tye-wig. When this man looks from the world, whose weaknesses he describes so benevolently, up to the heaven which shines over us all, I can hardly fancy a human face lighted up with a more serene rapture: a human intellect thrilling with a purer love and adoration than Joseph Addison's. Listen to him: from your childhood you have known the verses; but who can hear their sacred music without love and awe?—

> Soon as the evening shades prevail,
> The moon takes up the wondrous tale,
> And nightly to the listening earth
> Repeats the story of her birth;
> Whilst all the stars that round her burn,
> And all the planets in their turn,
> Confirm the tidings as they roll,
> And spread the truth from pole to pole.
> What though, in solemn silence, all
> Move round the dark terrestrial ball;
> What though no real voice nor sound
> Amid their radiant orbs be found;
> In reason's ear they all rejoice,
> And utter forth a glorious voice,
> For ever singing as they shine,
> The hand that made us is divine.

It seems to me those verses shine like the stars. They shine out of a great deep calm. When he turns to Heaven a Sabbath comes over that man's mind: and his face lights up from it with a glory of thanks and prayer. His sense of religion stirs through his whole being. In the fields, in the town: looking at the birds in the trees: at the children in the streets: in the morning or in the moonlight: over his books in his own room: in a happy party at a country merry-making or a town assembly, good-will and peace to God's creatures, and love and awe of Him who made them, fill his pure heart and shine from his kind face. If Swift's life was the most wretched, I think Addison's was one of the most enviable. A life prosperous and beautiful—a calm death—an immense fame and affection afterwards for his happy and spotless name. (pp. 70-92)

William Makepeace Thackeray, "Congreve and Addison," in his The English Humorists of the Eighteenth Century: Critical Reviews,

the Second Funeral of Napoleon, *Estes & Lauriat, 1891, pp. 48-92.*

W. J. Courthope   (essay date 1884)

[*In the following excerpt from his critical biography of Addison, Courthope details Addison's political opinions, his attitude toward women, and his legacy as a prose stylist.*]

[Addison's history], scanty as it is, goes far towards justifying the glowing panegyric bestowed by Macaulay on "the unsullied statesman, the accomplished scholar, the consummate painter of life and manners, the great satirist who alone knew how to use ridicule without abusing it; who, without inflicting a wound, effected a great social reform; and who reconciled wit and virtue after a long and painful separation, during which wit had been led astray by profligacy and virtue by fanaticism" [*Edinburgh Review,* 1843]. It is wanting, no doubt, in romantic incident and personal interest, but the same may be said of the life of Scott; and what do we know of the personality of Homer and Shakespeare? The real life of these writers is to be found in their work; and there too, though on a different level and in a different shape, are we to look for the character of the creator of Sir Roger de Coverley. But, while it seems possible to divine the personal tastes and feelings of Shakespeare and Scott under a hundred different ideal forms of their own invention, it is not in these that the genius of Addison most characteristically embodies itself. Did his reputation rest on ***Rosamond*** or ***Cato*** or ***The Campaign,*** his name would be little better known to us than any among that crowd of mediocrities who have been immortalised in Johnson's *Lives of the Poets.* The work of Addison consisted in building up a public opinion which, in spite of its durable solidity, seems, like the great Gothic cathedrals, to absorb into itself the individuality of the architect. A vigorous effort of thought is required to perceive how strong this individuality must have been. We have to reflect on the ease with which, even in these days when the foundations of all authority are called in question, we form judgments on questions of morals, breeding, and taste, and then to dwell in imagination on the state of conflict in all matters religious, moral, and artistic, which prevailed in the period between the Restoration and the succession of the House of Hanover. To whom do we owe the comparative harmony we enjoy? Undoubtedly to the authors of the ***Spectator,*** and first among these by universal consent to Addison.

Addison's own disposition seems to have been of that rare and admirable sort which Hamlet praised in Horatio:

> Thou hast been
> As one in suffering all that suffers nothing:
> A man that Fortune's buffets and rewards
> Has ta'en with equal thanks; and blessed are those
> Whose blood and judgment are so well commingled
> That they are not a pipe for Fortune's finger
> To sound what stop she please.

These lines fittingly describe the patient serenity and dignified independence with which Addison worked his way amid great hardships and difficulties to the highest position in the State; but they have a yet more honourable application to the task he performed of reconciling the social dissensions of his countrymen. "The blood and judgment well commingled" are visible in the standard of conduct which he held up for Englishmen in his writings, as well as in his use of the weapon of ridicule against all aberrations from good breeding and common sense. Those only will estimate him at his true worth who will give, what Johnson says is his due, "their days and nights" to the study of the *Spectator.* (pp. 161-63)

[After] the final subversion by the Civil War of the old-fashioned Catholic and Feudal standards of social life, two opposing ideals of conduct remained harshly confronting each other in the respective moral codes of the Court and the Puritans. The victorious Puritans, averse to all the pleasures of sense, and intolerant of the most harmless of natural instincts, had oppressed the nation with a religious despotism. The nation, groaning under the yoke, brought back its banished monarch, but was soon shocked to find sensual Pleasure exalted into a worship and Impiety into a creed. Though civil war had ceased, the two parties maintained a truceless conflict of opinion: the Puritan proscribing all amusement because it was patronised by the godless malignants; the courtiers holding that no gentleman could be religious or strict in his morals without becoming tainted with the cant of the Roundheads. This harsh antagonism of sentiment is humorously illustrated by the excellent Sir Roger, who is made to moralise on the stupidity of party violence by recalling an incident of his own boyhood:—

> The worthy knight, being but a stripling, had occasion to inquire which was the way to St. Anne's Lane, upon which the person whom he spoke to, instead of answering his question, called him a young Popish cur, and asked him who made Anne a saint. The boy, being in some confusion, inquired of the next he met which was the way to Anne's Lane; but was called a prick-eared cur for his pains, and instead of being shown the way, was told that she had been a saint before he was born, and would be one after he was hanged. 'Upon this,' says Sir Roger, 'I did not think it fit to repeat the former question, but going into every lane of the neighbourhood, asked what they called the name of that lane' [*Spectator* 125].

It was Addison's aim to prove to the contending parties what a large extent of ground they might occupy in common. He showed the courtiers in a form of light literature which pleased their imagination, and with a grace and charm of manner that they were well qualified to appreciate, that true religion was not opposed to good breeding. To this class in particular he addressed his papers on Devotion, on Prayer, on Faith, on Temporal and Eternal Happiness. On the other hand, he brought his raillery to bear on the super-solemnity of the trading and professional classes, in whom the spirit of Puritanism was most prevalent. "About an age ago," says he, "it was the fashion in England for every one that would be thought religious to throw as much sanctity as possible into his face, and, in particular, to abstain from all appearances of mirth and

pleasantry, which were looked upon as the marks of a carnal mind. The saint was of a sorrowful countenance, and generally eaten up with spleen and melancholy" [*Spectator* 494].

It was doubtless for the benefit of this class that he wrote his three Essays on Cheerfulness, in which the gloom of the Puritan creed is corrected by arguments founded on Natural Religion.

"The cheerfulness of heart," he observes in a charming passage,

> which springs up in us from the survey of Nature's works is an admirable preparation for gratitude. The mind has gone a great way towards praise and thanksgiving that is filled with such secret gladness. A grateful reflection on the Supreme Cause who produces it, sanctifies it in the soul, and gives it its proper value. Such an habitual disposition of mind consecrates every field and wood, turns an ordinary walk into a morning or evening sacrifice, and will improve those transient gleams of joy, which naturally brighten up and refresh the soul on such occasions, into an inviolable and perpetual state of bliss and happiness.

The same qualities appear in his dramatic criticisms. The corruption of the stage was to the Puritan, or the Puritanic moralist, not so much the effect as the cause of the corruption of society. To Jeremy Collier and his imitators the theatre in all its manifestations is equally abominable; they see no difference between Shakespeare and Wycherley. Dryden, who bowed before Collier's rebuke with a penitent dignity that does him high honour, yet rallies him with humour on this point:

> Perhaps the Parson stretched a point too far
> When with our Theatres he waged a war;
> He tells you that this very Moral Age
> Received the first infection from the Stage;
> But sure a banisht Court with Lewdness fraught
> The seeds of open Vice returning brought;
> Thus lodged (as vice by great example thrives)
> It first debauched the daughters and the wives.

Dryden was quite right. The Court after the Restoration was for the moment the sole school of manners; and the dramatists only reflected on the stage the inverted ideas which were accepted in society as the standard of good breeding. All sentiments founded on reverence for religion, or the family, or honourable industry, were banished from the drama because they were unacceptable at Court. The idea of virtue in a married woman would have seemed prodigious to Shadwell or Wycherley; Vanbrugh had no scruples in presenting to an audience a drunken parson in Sir John Brute; the merchant or tradesman seemed, like Congreve's Alderman Fondlewife, to exist solely that their wives might be seduced by men of fashion. Addison and his disciples saw that these unnatural creations of the theatre were the product of the corruption of society, and that it was men, not institutions, that needed reform. Steele, always the first to feel a generous impulse, took the lead in raising the tone of stage morality in a paper which, characteristically enough, was suggested by some reflections on a passage in one of his own plays. He followed up his attack by an admirable criticism . . . on Etherege's *The Man of Mode,* the hero of which, Sir Fopling Flutter, who had long been the model of young men of wit and fashion, he shows to be "a direct knave in his designs and a clown in his language."

As usual, Addison improves the opportunity which Steele affords him, and with his grave irony exposes the ridiculous principle of the fashionable comedy by a simple statement of fact.

"Cuckoldom," says he,

> is the basis of most of our modern plays. If an alderman appears upon the stage you may be sure it is in order to be cuckolded. An husband that is a little grave or elderly generally meets with the same fate. Knights and baronets, country squires, and justices of the quorum, come up to town for no other purpose. I have seen poor Dogget cuckolded in all these capacities. In short, our English writers are as frequently severe upon this innocent unhappy creature, commonly known by the name of a cuckold, as the ancient comic writers were upon an eating parasite or a vain-glorious soldier.

> . . . I have sometimes thought of compiling a system of ethics out of the writings of these corrupt poets under the title of Stage Morality. But I have been diverted from this thought by a project which has been executed by an ingenious gentleman of my acquaintance. He has composed, it seems, the history of a young fellow who has taken all his notions of the world from the stage, and who has directed himself in every circumstance of his life and conversation by the maxims and examples of the fine gentleman in English comedies. If I can prevail upon him to give me a copy of this new-fashioned novel, I will bestow on it a place in my works, and question not but it may have as good an effect upon the drama as Don Quixote had upon romance [*Spectator* 446].

Nothing could be more skilful than this. Collier's invective no doubt produced a momentary flutter among the dramatists, who, however, soon found they had little to fear from arguments which appealed only to that serious portion of society which did not frequent the theatre. But Addison's penetrating wit, founded as it was on truth and reason, was appreciated by the fashionable world. Dorimant and Sir Fopling Flutter felt ashamed of themselves. The cuckold disappeared from the stage. In society itself marriage no longer appeared ridiculous.

"It is my custom," says the *Spectator* in one of his late papers,

> to take frequent opportunities of inquiring from time to time what success my speculations meet with in the town. I am glad to find, in particular, that my discourses on marriage have been well received. A friend of mine gives me to understand, from Doctor's Commons, that more licenses have been taken out there of late than usual. I am likewise informed of several pretty fellows who have resolved to commence heads of families by the first favourable opportunity.

> One of them writes me word that he is ready to enter into the bonds of matrimony provided I will give it him under my hand (as I now do) that a man may show his face in good company after he is married, and that he need not be ashamed to treat a woman with kindness who puts herself into his power for life. [*Spectator* 525].

So, too, in politics, it was not to be expected that Addison's moderation should exercise a restraining influence on the violence of Parliamentary parties. But in helping to form a reasonable public opinion in the more reflective part of the nation at large, his efforts could not have been unavailing. He was a steady and consistent supporter of the Whig party, and Bolingbroke found that, in spite of his mildness, his principles were proof against all the seductions of interest. He was, in fact, a Whig in the sense in which all the best political writers in our literature, to whichever party they may have nominally belonged—Bolingbroke, Swift, and Canning as much as Somers and Burke—would have avowed themselves Whigs, as one, that is to say, who desired above all things to maintain the constitution of his country. He attached himself to the Whigs of his period because he saw in them, as the associated defenders of the liberties of the Parliament, the best counterpoise to the still preponderant power of the Crown. But he would have repudiated as vigorously as Burke the democratic principles to which Fox, under the stimulus of party spirit, committed the Whig connection at the outbreak of the French Revolution; and for that stupid and ferocious spirit, generated by party, which would deny to opponents even the appearance of virtue and intelligence, no man had a more wholesome contempt. Page after page of the *Spectator* shows that Addison perceived as clearly as Swift the theoretical absurdity of the party system, and tolerated it only as an evil inseparable from the imperfection of human nature and free institutions. He regarded it as the parent of hypocrisy and self-deception.

> Intemperate zeal, bigotry, and persecution for any party or opinion, how praiseworthy soever they may appear to weak men of our own principles, produce infinite calamities among mankind and are highly criminal in their own nature; and yet how many persons eminent for piety suffer such monstrous and absurd principles of action to take root in their minds under the colour of virtues! For my own part I must own I never yet knew any party so just and reasonable that a man could follow it in its height and violence and at the same time be innocent [*Spectator* 399].

As to party-writing, he considered it identical with lying.

"A man," says he,

> is looked upon as bereft of common sense that gives credit to the relations of party-writers; nay, his own friends shake their heads at him and consider him in no other light than as an officious tool or a well-meaning idiot. When it was formerly the fashion to husband a lie and trump it up in some extraordinary emergency it generally did execution, and was not a little useful to the faction that made use of it; but at present every man is upon his guard: the artifice has

been too often repeated to take effect [*Spectator* 507].

Sir Roger de Coverley "often closes his narrative with reflections on the mischief that parties do in the country."

"There cannot," says the *Spectator* himself

> a greater judgment befall a country than such a dreadful spirit of division as rends a government into two distinct people and makes them greater strangers and more averse to one another than if they were actually two different nations. The effects of such a division are pernicious to the last degree, not only with regard to those advantages which they give the common enemy, but to those private evils which they produce in the heart of almost every particular person. This influence is very fatal both to men's morals and to their understandings; it sinks the virtue of a nation, and not only so, but destroys even common sense [*Spectator* 125].

Nothing in the work of Addison is more suggestive of the just and well-balanced character of his genius than his papers on Women. It has been already said that the seventeenth century exhibits the decay of the Feudal Ideal. The passionate adoration with which women were regarded in the age of chivalry degenerated after the Restoration into a habit of insipid gallantry or of brutal license. Men of fashion found no mean for their affections between a Sacharissa and a Duchess of Cleveland, while the domestic standard of the time reduced the remainder of the sex to the position of virtuous but uninteresting household drudges. Of woman as the companion and the helpmate of man, the source of all the grace and refinements of social intercourse, no trace is to be found in the literature of the Restoration except in the Eve of Milton's still unstudied poem; it is not too much to say that she was the creation of the *Spectator.*

The feminine ideal, at which the essayists of the period aimed, is very well described by Steele in a style which he imitated from Addison:—

"The other day," he writes, in the character of a fictitious female correspondent,

> we were several of us at a tea-table, and, according to custom and your own advice, had the *Spectator* read among us. It was that paper wherein you are pleased to treat with great freedom that character which you call a woman's man. We gave up all the kinds you have mentioned except those who, you say, are our constant visitants. I was upon the occasion commissioned by the company to write to you and tell you 'that we shall not part with the men we have at present until the men of sense think fit to relieve them and give us their company in their stead.' You cannot imagine but we love to hear reason and good sense better than the ribaldry we are at present entertained with, but we must have company, and among us very inconsiderable is better than none at all. We are made for the cements of society, and come into the world to create relations amongst mankind, and solitude is an unnatural being to us [*Spectator* 158].

In contrast with the character of the writer of this letter—a type which is always recurring in the *Spectator*—modest and unaffected, but at the same time shrewd, witty, and refined, are introduced very eccentric specimens of womanhood, all tending to illustrate the derangement of the social order, the masculine woman, the learned woman, the female politician, besides those that more properly belong to the nature of the sex, the prude and the coquette. A very graceful example of Addison's peculiar humour is found in his satire on that false ambition in women which prompts them to imitate the manners of men:—

"The girls of quality," he writes, describing the customs of the Republic of Women,

> from six to twelve years old were put to public schools, where they learned to box and play at cudgels, with several other accomplishments of the same nature, so that nothing was more usual than to see a little miss returning home at night with a broken pate or two or three teeth knocked out of her head. They were afterwards taught to ride the great horse, to shoot, dart, or sling, and listed themselves into several companies in order to perfect themselves in military exercises. No woman was to be married till she had killed her man. The ladies of fashion used to play with young lions instead of lap-dogs; and when they had made any parties of diversion, instead of entertaining themselves at ombre and piquet, they would wrestle and pitch the bar for a whole afternoon together. There was never any such thing as a blush seen or a sigh heard in the whole commonwealth" [*Spectator* 434].

The amazon was a type of womanhood peculiarly distasteful to Addison, whose humour delighted itself with all the curiosities and refinements of feminine caprice—the fan, the powder-box, and the petticoat. Nothing can more characteristically suggest the exquisiteness of his fancy than a comparison of Swift's verses on a *Lady's Dressing-Room* with the following, which evidently gave Pope a hint for one of the happiest passages in *The Rape of the Lock:*—

> The single dress of a woman of quality is often the product of a hundred climates. The muff and the fan come together from the different ends of the earth. The scarf is sent from the torrid zone, and the tippet from beneath the Pole. The brocade petticoat rises out of the mines of Peru, and the diamond necklace out of the bowels of Indostan [*Spectator* 69].

To turn to Addison's artistic genius the crowning evidence of his powers is the design and the execution of the *Spectator.* Many writers, and among them Macaulay, have credited Steele with the invention of the *Spectator* as well as of the *Tatler;* but I think that a close examination of the opening papers in the former will not only prove, almost to demonstration, that on this occasion Steele was acting as the lieutenant of his friend, but will also show the admirable artfulness of the means by which Addison executed his intention. The purpose of the *Spectator* is described in the tenth number, which is by Addison [*Spectator*, 1711]:—

"I shall endeavour," said he,

> to enliven morality with wit, and to temper wit
> with morality, that my readers may, if possible,
> both ways find their account in the speculation
> of the day. And to the end that their virtue and
> discretion may not be short, transient, intermit-
> ting starts of thought, I have resolved to refresh
> their memories from day to day till I have recov-
> ered them out of that desperate state of vice and
> folly into which the age has fallen.

That is to say, his design was "to hold as 'twere the mirror
up to nature," so that the conscience of society might recognise in a dramatic form the character of its lapses from
virtue and reason. The indispensable instrument for the
execution of this design was the *Spectator* himself, the silent embodiment of right reason and good taste, who is obviously the conception of Addison.

> I live in the world rather as a spectator of man-
> kind than as one of the species by which means
> I have made myself a speculative statesman, sol-
> dier, merchant, and artizan, without ever med-
> dling with any practical part in life. I am very
> well versed in the theory of a husband, or a fa-
> ther, and can discern the errors in the economy,
> business, and diversion of others better than
> those who are engaged in them; as standers-by
> discover blots which are apt to escape those who
> are in the game. I never espoused any party with
> violence, and am resolved to observe an exact
> neutrality between the Whigs and Tories unless
> I shall be forced to declare myself by the hostili-
> ties of either side. In short, I have acted in all the
> parts of my life as a looker-on, which is the char-
> acter I intend to preserve in this paper.

In order, however, to give this somewhat inanimate figure
life and action, he is represented as the principal member
of a club, his associates consisting of various representatives of the chief "interests" of society. We can scarcely
doubt that the club was part of the original and central
conception of the work, and if this be so, a new light is
thrown on some of the features in the characters of the
Spectator which have hitherto rather perplexed the critics.

"The *Spectator*'s friends," says Macaulay,

> were first sketched by Steele. Four of the club—
> the templar, the clergyman, the soldier, and the
> merchant—were uninteresting figures, fit only
> for a background. But the other two—an old
> country baronet and an old town rake—though
> not delineated with a very delicate pencil, had
> some good strokes. Addison took the rude out-
> lines into his own hands, retouched them, col-
> oured them, and is in truth the creator of the Sir
> Roger de Coverley and the Will Honeycomb
> with whom we are all familiar.

This is a very misleading account of the matter. It implies
that the characters in the *Spectator* were mere casual conceptions of Steele's; that Addison knew nothing about
them till he saw Steele's rough draft; and that he, and he
alone, is the creator of the finished character of Sir Roger
de Coverley. But, as a matter of fact, the character of Sir
Roger is full of contradictions and inconsistencies; and the

want of unity which it presents is easily explained by the
fact that it is the work of four different hands. Sixteen papers on the subject were contributed by Addison, seven by
Steele, three by Budgell, and one by Tickell. Had Sir
Roger been, as Macaulay seems to suggest, merely the
stray phantom of Steele's imagination, it is very unlikely
that so many different painters should have busied themselves with his portrait. But he was from the first intended
to be a *type* of a country gentleman, just as much as Don
Quixote was an imaginative representation of many Spanish gentlemen whose brains had been turned by the reading of romances. In both cases the type of character was
so common and so truly conceived as to lend itself easily
to the treatment of writers who approached it with various
conceptions and very unequal degrees of skill. Any critic,
therefore, who regards Sir Roger de Coverley as the abstract conception of a single mind is certain to misconceive
the character. (pp. 163-75)

Addison may be said to have almost created and wholly
perfected English prose as an instrument for the expression of *social* thought. Prose had of course been written
in many different manners before his time. Bacon, Cowley,
and Temple had composed essays; Hooker, Sir Thomas
Browne, Hobbes, and Locke philosophical treatises; Milton controversial pamphlets; Dryden critical prefaces; Raleigh and Clarendon histories; Taylor, Barrow, South, and
Tillotson sermons. But it cannot be said that any of these
had founded a prose style which, besides being a reflection
of the mind of the writer, could be taken as representing
the genius and character of the nation. They write as if
they were thinking apart from their audience, or as if they
were speaking to it either from an inferior or superior position. The essayists had taken as their model Montaigne,
and their style is therefore stamped, so to speak, with the
character of soliloquy; the preachers, who perhaps did
more than any writers to guide the genius of the language,
naturally addressed their hearers with the authority of
their office; Milton, even in controversy, rises from the
natural sublimity of his mind to heights of eloquence to
which the ordinary idioms of society could not have borne
him; while Dryden, using the language with a raciness and
rhythm probably unequalled in our literature, nevertheless exhibits in his prefaces an air of deference towards the
various patrons he addresses. Moreover, many of the earlier prose writers had aimed at standards of diction which
were inconsistent with the genius of the English tongue.
Bacon, for instance, disfigures his style with the witty an-
titheses which found favour with the Elizabethan and
early Stuart writers; Hooker, Milton, and Browne construct their sentences on a Latin model, which, though it
often gives a certain dignity of manner, prevents anything
like ease, simplicity, and lucidity of expression. Thus
Hooker delights in inversions; both he and Milton pro-
tract their periods by the insertion of many subordinate
clauses; and Browne "projicit ampullas et sesquipedalia
verba" till the Saxon element seems almost eliminated
from his style.

Addison took features of his style from almost all his predecessors: he assumes the characters of essayist, moralist,
philosopher, and critic, but he blends them all together in
his new capacity of journalist. He had accepted the public

as his judges; and he writes as if some critical representative of the public were at his elbow putting to the test of reason every sentiment and every expression. Warton tells us in his *Essay on Pope* [1782] that Addison was so fastidious in composition that he would often stop the press to alter a preposition or conjunction. And this evidence is corroborated in a very curious and interesting manner by the MS. of some of Addison's essays, discovered by Mr. Dykes Campbell in 1858. A sentence in one of the papers on the **Pleasures of the Imagination** shows, by the various stages through which it passed before its form seemed satisfactory to the writer, what nice attention he gave to the balance, rhythm, and lucidity of his periods. In its original shape the sentence was written thus:—

> For this reason we find the poets always crying up a Country Life; where Nature is left to herself, and appears to ye best advantage.

This is rather bald, and the MS. is accordingly corrected as follows:—

> For this reason we find all Fanciful men, and yᵉ poets in particular, still in love with a Country Life; where Nature is left to herself, and furnishes out all yᵉ variety of Scenes yᵗ are most delightful to yᵉ Imagination.

The text as it stands is this:—

> For this reason we always find the poet in love with a country life, where nature appears in the greatest perfection, and furnishes out all those scenes that are most apt to delight the imagination [*Spectator* 414].

This is certainly the best both in point of sense and sound. Addison perceived that there was a certain contradiction in the idea of Nature being "left to herself," and at the same time *furnishing* scenes for the pleasure of the imagination: he therefore imparted the notion of design by striking out the former phrase and substituting "seen in perfection;" and he emphasised the idea by afterwards changing "delightful" into the stronger phrase "apt to delight." The improvement of the rhythm of the sentence in its final form is obvious.

With so much elaboration of style it is natural that there should be in Addison's essays a disappearance of that egotism which is a characteristic—and a charming one—of Montaigne; his moralising is natural, for the age required it, but is free from the censoriousness of the preacher; his critical and philosophical papers all assume an intelligence in his reader equal to his own.

This perfection of breeding in writing is an art which vanishes with the **Tatler** and **Spectator.** Other critics, other humourists have made their mark in English literature, but no second Addison has appeared. Johnson took him for his model so far as to convey lessons of morality to the public by means of periodical essays. But he confesses that he addressed his audience in tones of "dictatorial instruction;" and any one who compares the ponderous sententiousness and the elaborate antithesis of the *Rambler* with the light and rhythmical periods of the **Spectator** will perceive that the spirit of preaching is gaining ground on the genius of conversation. Charles Lamb, again, has passages

which, for mere delicacy of humour, are equal to anything in Addison's writings. But the superiority of Addison consists in this, that he expresses the humour of the life about him, while Lamb is driven to look at its oddities from outside. He is not, like Addison, a moralist or a satirist; the latter indeed performed his task so thoroughly that the turbulent license of Mohocks, Tityre Tus, and such like brotherhoods, gradually disappeared before the advance of a tame and orderly public opinion. To Lamb, looking back on the primitive stages of society from a safe distance, vice itself seemed pardonable because picturesque, much in the same way as travellers began to admire the loneliness and the grandeur of nature when they were relieved from apprehensions for the safety of their purses and their necks. His humour is that of a sentimentalist; it dwells on odd nooks and corners, and describes quaint survivals in men and things. For our own age, when all that is picturesque in society is being levelled by a dull utilitarianism, this vein of eccentric imagination has a special charm, but the taste is likely to be a transient one. Mrs. Battle will amuse so long as this generation remembers the ways of its grandmothers; two generations hence the point of its humour will probably be lost. But the figure of Sir Roger de Coverley, though it belongs to a bygone stage of society, is as durable as human nature itself, and while the language lasts the exquisite beauty of the colours in which it is preserved will excite the same kind of pleasure. Scarcely below the portrait of the good knight will be ranked the character of his friend and biographer, the silent Spectator of men. A grateful posterity, remembering what it owes to him, will continue to assign him the reputation he coveted: "It was said of Socrates that he brought philosophy down from heaven to inhabit among men; and I shall be ambitious to have it said of me that I have brought philosophy out of closets and libraries, schools and colleges, to dwell at clubs and assemblies, at tea-tables and in coffee-houses." (pp. 188-92)

> *W. J. Courthope, in his* Addison, *1884. Reprint by Macmillan and Co., Limited, 1911, 197 p.*

M. O. W. Oliphant   (essay date 1894)

[*Oliphant was a prolific nineteenth-century Scottish novelist, biographer, critic, and historian who contributed regularly to* Blackwood's Edinburgh Magazine. *In the following excerpt, she extols Addison's character and vision.*]

There is not a name in the entire range of English literature to which so full and universal an appreciation has been given by posterity as to that of Addison. He had his critics in his day: he had, indeed, more than critics, and from one quarter at least has received in his breast the fiercest and sharpest sting which a friend estranged could put into poetic vengeance. But the burden even of contemporary voices was always overwhelmingly in his favor, and nowadays there is no one in the world, we believe, who has other than gentle words for the gentle writer—the finest critic, the finest gentleman, the most tender humorist, of his age. It is not only admiration, but a sort of personal affection with which we look back, detecting in all the bustling companies of that witty and depraved period his genial figure, with a delightful simplicity in the midst of all the formalism, and whole-heartedness among the conceits and pretensions, of the fops and the wits, the intriguing statesmen and busy conspirators, of an age in which public faith can scarcely be said to have existed at all. Addison is the very embodiment of that delightful gift of humor on which we pride ourselves so much as a specially English quality. That in its way his style is the perfection of English style is less dear and delightful to us than that what it conveys is the perfection of feeling. His art is the antipodes of that satirical art which allows human excellence only to gird at it, and insinuate motives which diminish or destroy. Addison, on the other hand, allows imperfections which his interpretation turns into something sweeter than virtue, and throws a delightful gleam of love and laughter upon the eccentricities and characteristic follies of individual nature. That he sees everything is one of the conditions of his genial forgiveness of all that is not mean, or base, or cruel. With these he makes no terms. (p. 703)

> M. O. W. Oliphant, "Addison: The Humorist," in The Century, Vol. XLVIII, No. 5, September, 1894, pp. 702-09.

George Saintsbury (essay date 1902)

[*Saintsbury has been called the most influential English literary historian and critic of the late nineteenth and early twentieth centuries. His studies of French literature, particularly* A History of the French Novel *(1917-19), have established him as a leading authority on such writers as Guy de Maupassant and Honoré de Balzac. René Wellek has praised Saintsbury's critical qualities: his "enormous reading, the almost universal scope of his subject matter, the zest and zeal of his exposition," and "the audacity with which he handles the most ambitious and unattempted arguments." In the following excerpt, he assesses Addison's accomplishments as a literary critic, contending that while some assessments of his significance in the evolution of critical and aesthetic theory are exaggerated, many of Addison's writings are still valuable for their sensible judgments on literature.*]

During the latter part of his rather short lifetime Addison, it is hardly necessary to say, enjoyed a sort of mild dictatorship in Criticism as in other departments of literature; and his right to it was scarcely disputed till near the close of the century, though Johnson knew that he was not deep, and tells us that, in his own last days, it was almost a fashion to look down on Addisonian criticism. If, like others, he was displaced by the Romantic revival, he received more lenient treatment than some, in virtue partly of his own general moderation, partly of his championship of Milton. Yet while his original literary gifts recovered high place during the nineteenth century, his criticism has often been considered to possess scarcely more than historic interest, and has sometimes been rather roughly handled—for instance, by Mr Matthew Arnold. But a recent writer [W. Basil Worsfold in his *Principles of Criticism*, 1897], by arguing that Addison's treatment of the Imagination, as a separate faculty, introduced a new principle

into criticism, has at any rate claimed for him a position which, if it could be granted, would seat him among the very greatest masters of the art, with Aristotle and Longinus among his own forerunners. As usual let us, before discussing these various estimates, see what Addison actually did as a critic.

His *début* as such was not fortunate. He was, it is true, only three-and-twenty when at "dearest Harry's" request (that is to say Mr Harry Sacheverell's) he undertook an ***Account of the Greatest English Poets.*** In 1694 nobody, except Dryden, could be expected to write very good verse, so that the poetical qualities of this verse-essay need not be hardly dwelt upon, or indeed considered at all. We may take it, as if it were prose, for the matter only. And thus considered, it must surely be thought one of the worst examples of the pert and tasteless ignorance of its school. Before Cowley nobody but Chaucer and Spenser is mentioned at all, and the mentions of these are simply grotesque. The lines convict Addison, almost beyond appeal, of being at the time utterly ignorant of English literary history up to 1600, and of having read Chaucer and Spenser themselves, if he had read them at all, with his eyes shut. The Chaucer section reads as if it were describing *A C. Merry Tales* or the *Jests of George Peele*. Where Dryden, if he did not understand Chaucer's versification, and missed some of his poetry, could see much even of that, and almost all the humour, the grace, the sweetness, the "God's plenty" of life and character that Chaucer has, Addison sees nothing but a merry-andrew of the day before yesterday. So, too, the consummate art of Spenser, his exquisite versification, his great ethical purpose, and yet his voluptuous beauty, are quite hidden from Addison. He sees nothing but a tedious allegory of improbable adventures, and objects to the "dull moral" which "lies too plain below," much as Temple had done before him. Cowley, Milton, and Waller are mentioned next, in at least asserted chronological order. Cowley is "a mighty genius" full of beauties and faults,

> Who more had pleased us had he pleased us less,

but who is a perfect "milky way" of brilliancy, and has made Pindar himself "take a nobler flight." Milton alternately strikes Addison with awe, rapture, and shock at his politics. He

> Betrays a bottom odious to the sight.

So we turn to Waller, who is not only "courtly" but "moves our passion," (what a pity that he died too soon to "rehearse Maria's charms"!) to Roscommon, who "makes even Rules a noble poetry," and Denham, whose Cooper's Hill "we must," of course, not "forget." "Great Dryden" is then, not unhappily, though not quite adequately, celebrated, and the line on his Muse—

> She wears all dresses, and she charms in all,

is not only neat, but very largely true. When Dryden shall decay, luckily there is harmonious Congreve: and, if Addison were not tired with rhyming, he would praise (he does so at some length) noble Montague, who directs his artful muse to Dorset,

> In numbers such as Dorset's self might use,

as to which all that can be said is that, if so, either the verses of Montague or the verses of Dorset referred to are not those that have come down to us under the names of the respective authors.

To dwell at all severely on this luckless production of a young University wit would be not only unkind but uncritical. It shows that at this time Addison knew next to nothing about the English literature not of his own day, and judged very badly of what he pretended to know.

The prose works of his middle period, the **Discourse on Medals** and the **Remarks on Italy,** are very fully illustrated from the Latin poets—the division of literature that Addison knew best—but indulge hardly at all in literary criticism. It was not till the launching of the **Tatler,** by Steele and Swift, provided him with his natural medium of utterance, that Addison became critical. This periodical itself, and the less known ones that followed the **Spectator,** all contain exercises in this character: but it is to the **Spectator** that men look, and look rightly, for Addison's credentials in the character of a critic. The **Tatler** Essays, such as the rather well known papers on Tom Folio and Ned Softly, those in the *Guardian,* the good-natured puff of Tom D'Urfey, &c., are not so much serious and deliberate literary criticisms, as applications, to subjects more or less literary, of the peculiar method of gently malicious censorship, of laughing castigation in manners and morals, which Addison carried to such perfection in all the middle relations of life. Not only are the **Spectator** articles far more numerous and far more weighty, but we have his own authority for regarding them as, in some measure at least, written on a deliberate system, and divisible into three groups. The first of these groups consists of the early papers on True and False Wit, and of essays on the stage. The second contains the famous and elaborate criticism of Milton with other things; and the third, the still later, still more serious, and still more ambitious, series on the Pleasures of the Imagination. Addison is looking back from the beginning of this last when he gives the general description, and it is quite possible that the complete trilogy was not in his mind when he began the first group. But there is regular development in it, and whether we agree or not with Mr Worsfold's extremely high estimate of the third division, it is quite certain that the whole collection—of some thirty or forty essays—does clearly exhibit that increasing sense of what criticism means, which is to be observed in almost all good critics. For criticism is, on the one hand, an art in which there are so few manuals or trustworthy short summaries—it is one which depends so much more on reading and knowledge than any creative art—and, above all, it is necessary to make so many mistakes in it before one comes right, that, probably, not one single example can be found of a critic of importance who was not a much better critic when he left off than when he began.

In Group One [**Spectator** 58-63] Addison is still animated by the slightly desultory spirit of moral satire, which has been referred to above; and, though fifteen or sixteen years have passed since the *Account,* he does not seem to be so entirely free as we might wish from the crude sciolism, if not the sheer ignorance, of the earliest period. He is often

admirable: his own humour, his taste, almost perfect within its own narrow limits, and his good sense, made that certain beforehand. But he has somewhat overloaded it with unduly artificial allegory, the ethical temper rather overpowers the literary, and there is not a little of that arbitrary "blackmarking" of certain literary things which is one of the worst faults of neo-classic criticism. The Temple of Dulness is built (of course) "after the Gothic manner," and the image of the god is dressed "after the habit of a monk." Among the idolatrous rites and implements are not merely rebuses, anagrams, verses arranged in artificial forms, and other things a little childish, though perfectly harmless, but acrostics—trifles, perhaps, yet trifles which can be made exquisitely graceful, and satisfying that desire for mixing passion with playfulness which is not the worst affection of the human heart.

He had led up to this batch, a few weeks earlier, by some cursory remarks on Comedy, which form the tail of a more elaborate examination of Tragedy, filling four or five numbers [**Spectator** 39, 40, 42, 44, 45]. Readers who have already mastered the general drift of the criticism of the time before him, will scarcely need any long *précis* of his views, which, moreover, are in everybody's reach, and could not possibly be put more readably. Modern tragedies, he thinks, excel those of Greece and Rome in the intricacy and disposition of the fable, but fall short in the moral. He objects to rhyme (except an end-couplet or two), and, though he thinks the style of our tragedies superior to the sentiment, finds the former, especially in Shakespeare, defaced by "sounding phrases, hard metaphors, and forced expressions." This is still more the case in Lee. Otway is very "tender": but it is a sad thing that the characters in *Venice Preserved* should be traitors and rebels. Poetic justice (this was what shocked Dennis), as generally understood, is rather absurd, and quite unnecessary. And the tragi-comedy, which is the product of the English theatre, is "one of the most monstrous inventions that ever entered into a poet's thought." You "might as well weave the adventures of Æneas and Hudibras into one poem" [and, indeed, one might find some relief in this, as far as the adventures of Æneas are concerned]. Tragedies are not even to have a double plot. Rants, and especially impious rants, are bad. Darkened stages, elaborate scenery and dresses, troops of supers, &c., are as bad: bells, ghosts, thunder, and lightning still worse. "Of all our methods of moving pity and terror, there is none so absurd and barbarous as the dreadful butchering of one another," though all deaths on the stage are not to be forbidden.

Now, it is not difficult to characterise the criticism which appears in this first group, strengthened, if anybody cares, by a few isolated examples. It contains a great deal of common sense and good ordinary taste; many of the things that it reprehends are really wrong, and most of what it praises is good in a way. But the critic has as yet no guiding theory, except what he thinks he has gathered from Aristotle, and has certainly gathered from Horace, *plus* Common Sense itself, with, as is the case with all English critics of this age, a good deal from his French predecessors, especially Le Bossu and Bouhours. Which borrowing, while it leads him into numerous minor errors, leads him into two great ones—his denunciations of tragi-comedy, and of the double plot. He is, moreover, essentially arbitrary: his criticism will seldom stand the application of the "Why?" the "*Après?*" and a harsh judge might, in some places, say that it is not more arbitrary than ignorant.

The Second Group [In a footnote, the critic adds, "These began in *Sp.* 267, and were the regular Saturday feature of the paper for many weeks."], or Miltonic batch, with which may be taken its "moon," the partly playful but more largely serious *examen* of *Chevy Chase,* is much the best known, and has been generally ranked as the most important exhibition of Addison's critical powers. It is not, however, out of paradox or desire to be singular that it will be somewhat briefly discussed here. By the student of Addison it cannot be too carefully studied; for the historian of criticism it has indeed high importance, but importance which can be very briefly summed up, and which requires no extensive analysis of the eighteen distinct essays that compose the Miltonic group, or the two on *Chevy Chase.* The critic here takes for granted—and knows or assumes that his readers will grant—two general positions:—

1. The Aristotelian-Horatian view of poetry, with a few of the more commonplace utterances of Longinus, supplies the orthodox theory of Poetics.

2. The ancients, especially Homer and Virgil, supply the most perfect examples of the orthodox practice of poetry.

These things posed, he proceeds to examine *Chevy Chase* at some, *Paradise Lost* at great, length by their aid; and discovers in the ballad not a few, and in the epic very great and very numerous, excellences. As Homer does this, so Milton does that: such a passage in Virgil is a more or less exact analogue to such another in *Paradise Lost.* Aristotle says this, Horace that, Longinus the third thing; and you will find the dicta capitally exemplified in such and such a place of Milton's works. To men who accepted the principle—as most, if not all, men did—the demonstration was no doubt both interesting and satisfactory; and though it certainly did not start general admiration of Milton, it stamped that admiration with a comfortable seal of official orthodoxy. But it is actually more antiquated than Dryden, in assuming that the question whether Milton wrote according to Aristotle is coextensive with the question whether he wrote good poetry.

The next batch is far more important.

What *are* the Pleasures of the Imagination? It is of the first moment to observe Addison's exact definition [in *Spectator* 411]. Sight is the "sense which furnishes the imagination with its ideas; so that by the 'Pleasures of the Imagination' or Fancy, which I shall use promiscuously, I here mean such as arise from visible objects, either when we have them actually in our view, or when we call up their ideas into our minds by paintings, statues, descriptions, or any the like occasion." We can have no images not thus furnished, though they may be altered and compounded by imagination itself. To make this quite sure, he repeats that he means *only* such pleasures as thus arise. He then proceeds, at some length, to argue for the innocence and refinement of such pleasures, their usefulness, and so on; and further, to discuss the causes or origins of pleasure in

sight, which he finds to be three—greatness, uncommonness, and beauty. The pleasantness of these is assigned to such and such wise and good purposes of the Creator, with a reference to the great modern discoveries of Mr Locke's *Essay.*

Addison then goes on to consider the sources of entertainment to the imagination, and decides that, for the purpose, art is very inferior to nature, though both rise in value as each borrows from the other. He adduces, in illustration, an odd rococo mixture of scene-painting and reflection of actual objects which he once saw. Italian and French gardens are next praised, in opposition to the old formal English style, and naturally trained trees to the productions of the *ars topiaria;* while a very long digression is made to greatness in Architecture, illustrated by this remark, "Let any one reflect on the disposition of mind in which he finds himself at his first entrance into the Pantheon at Rome, . . . and consider how little in proportion he is affected with the inside of a Gothic cathedral, though it be five times larger than the other," the reason being "the greatness of the manner in the one, and the meanness in the other."

So the "secondary" pleasures of the imagination—*i.e.,* those compounded and manufactured by memory—are illustrated by the arts of sculpture and painting, with a good passage on description generally, whence he turns to the Cartesian doctrine of the association of ideas, and shows very ingeniously how the poet may avail himself of this. Next comes a curious and often just analysis of the reasons of pleasure in description—how, for instance, he likes Milton's Paradise better than his Hell, because brimstone and sulphur are not so refreshing to the imagination as beds of flowers and wildernesses of sweets. Or we may like things because they "raise a secret ferment in the mind," either directly, or so as to arouse a feeling of relief by comparison, as when we read of tortures, wounds, and deaths. Moreover, the poet may improve Nature. Let oranges grow wild, and roses, woodbines, and jessamines flower at the same time. As for "the fairy way of writing"—that is to say, the supernatural—it requires a very odd turn of mind. We do it better than most other nations, because of our gloominess and melancholy of temper. Shakespeare excels everybody else in touching "this weak superstitious part" of his reader's imagination. The glorifying of the imagination, however, is by no means confined to the poet. In good historians we "see" everything. None more gratify the imagination than the authors of the new philosophy, astronomers, microscopists. This (No. 420) is one of Addison's most ambitious passages of writing, and the whole ends (421) with a peroration excellently hit off.

It is upon these papers mainly that Mr Worsfold bases his high eulogium of Addison as "the first genuine critic," the first "who added something to the last word of Hellenism," the bringer of criticism "into line with modern thought," the establisher of "a new principle of poetic appeal." Let us, as uncontroversially as possible, and without laying any undue stress on the fact that Mr Worsfold practically omits Longinus altogether, stick, in our humdrum way, to the facts.

In the first place, supposing for the moment that Addison

uses "imagination" in our full modern sense, and supposing, secondly, for the moment also, that he assigns the appeal to the imagination as the special engine of the poet, is this an original discovery of his? By no means: there are many *loci* of former writers to negative this—there is one that is fatal. And this is no more recondite a thing than the famous Shakespearian description of

> The lunatic, the lover, and the poet,

as

> Of *imagination* all compact,

with what follows. But this is a mere question of property, plagiarism, suggestion; and such questions are at best the exercises of literary holiday-makers, at the worst the business of pedants and of fools.

A more important as well as a more dangerous question is this. *Does* Addison make "the appeal to the imagination" the test of poetry? It can only be answered that, by his own explicit words, he does nothing of the kind. If he advances anything, it is that the appeal to the imagination is the appeal of art generally—of prose (even of scientific) literary art as well as of poetry, of painting, sculpture, architecture, as well as of literature. In doing this he does a good thing: he does something notable in the history of general æthetics; but in so far as literature, and especially poetry, is concerned, he scarcely goes as far as Longinus in the well-known passage, though he works out his doctrine at much greater length, and with assistance from Descartes and Locke.

But the most important and the most damaging question of all is this, "Are not Addison and his panegyrist using words in equivocal senses? *Does* Imagination in Addison's mouth bear the meaning which we, chiefly since Coleridge's day, attach to the word? Does it even mean what it meant to Longinus, much more what it meant to Shakespeare?

I have no hesitation in answering the two latter questions with an absolute and unhesitating "No!"

It seems indeed extraordinary that, in face of Addison's most careful and explicit limitations, any one should delude himself into thinking that even the Shakespearian and Addisonian Imaginations are identical—much more that Addison's Imagination is the supreme faculty, creative, transcending Fancy, superior to fact, not merely compounding and refining upon, but altogether superseding and almost scorning, ideas of sensation, which we mean by the word, and which Philostratus or Apollonius partly glimpsed. Addison tells us—tells us over and over again—that *all* the ideas and pleasures of the imagination are pleasures of sense, and, what is more, that they are all pleasures of one sense—Sight. Why he should have limited himself in this singular manner it is hard to say; except that he was evidently full of Locke when he wrote, and, indeed, almost entirely under the influence of the *Essay*. That he had a contempt for music is elsewhere pretty evident; and this probably explains his otherwise inexplicable omission of the supplies and assistance given to Imagination by Hearing. His morality, as well as old convention, excluded Touch, Taste, and Smell as low and gross,

though no candid philosophy could help acknowledging the immense influence exercised upon Imagination by at least the first and the last—Taste, because the most definite, being perhaps the least imaginative of all. But the fact that he does exclude even these senses, and still more rigidly excludes everything but Sense, is insuperable, irremovable, ruthless. Addison may have been the first modern critic to work out the appeal of art to the pleasures and ideas furnished by the sense of sight. He is certainly nothing more.

But is he therefore to be ignored, or treated lightly, because of this strange overvaluation of him? Certainly not. Though by no means a very great critic, he is a useful, an interesting, and a representative one. He represents the classical attitude tempered, not merely by good sense almost in quintessence, but by a large share of tolerance and positive good taste, by freedom from the more utterly ridiculous pseudo-Aristotelianisms, and by a wish to extend a *concordat* to everything good even if it be not "faultless." In his **Account** he is evidently too crude to be very censurable: in his first group of essays much of his censure is just. The elaborate vindication of Milton, though now and for a long time past merely a curiosity, is again full of good sense, displays (if not altogether according to knowledge) a real liking for real poetic goodness, and had an inestimable effect in keeping at least one poet of the better time privileged and popular with readers throughout the Eighteenth Century. As for the essay on the Pleasures of the Imagination, the fact that it has been wrongly praised need not in the least interfere with a cordial estimate of its real merits. It is not an epoch-making contribution to literary criticism; it is rather one-sided, and strangely limited in range. But it is about the first attempt at a general theory of æthetics in English; it is a most interesting, and a very early, example of that application of common-sense philosophy to abstract subjects which Locke taught to the English eighteenth century; and many of its remarks are valuable and correct. Moreover, it did actually serve, for those who could not, or who did not, read Longinus, as a corrective to pure form-criticism, to Bysshe with his rigid ten syllables, to bare good sense and conventional rule. Its Imagination was still only that which supplies Images, and was strangely cramped besides; but it was better than mere correctness, mere decency, mere stop-watch. (pp. 437-48)

George Saintsbury, "Eighteenth-Century Orthodoxy: From Addison to Johnson," in his A History of Criticism and Literary Taste in Europe: From the Renaissance to the Decline of Eighteenth Century Orthodoxy, Vol. II, *William Blackwood & Sons Ltd., 1902, pp. 426-500.*

Edward Everett Hale, Jr.   (essay date 1904)

[*Hale was an American literary critic and biographer of his famous father: the social reformer and man of letters best known for his novel* The Man Without a Country *(1865). In the following excerpt from his preface to* The Sir Roger De Coverley Papers, *he discusses the context, style, and ideas of Addison's writings.*]

The *Spectator,* beside being of interest in itself, has a very important place in the history of literature. It gave rise to a whole series of periodicals more or less like itself, gave a definite model to the essay as a literary form, and was of some influence in the development of the novel. We who are surrounded with magazines and novels and essays can hardly imagine a literature when such things were not. Leonora read novels, it is true, but *Cassandra, Cleopatra, Astræa,* the *Grand Cyrus* were books very different from any novel that we ever read. They lacked entirely the presentation of story, character, manners that is so familiar to us. Magazines, Leonora knew nothing of at all, nor of essays.

The *Spectator* and the *Tatler* showed that there could be light and easy writing about matters of great or little importance, that should be amusing and not without character. Prose literature ceased to be a matter of treatises only, of philosophy, of theology, of history. Poetry ceased to be the only form of belles lettres. A different tone began in literature: it ceased to be something for scholars only, and became something for men and women.

There had undoubtedly been Essays in English literature before Addison. Those of Cowley are very charming examples in a limited sphere of much the kind of writing of which Addison was such a master. The Essays of Bacon are brilliant examples of a kind of writing rather different. But whatever essays may have been written, there was not anything till the *Tatler* and the *Spectator* which showed the possibilities of the essay, how it could be light or serious, satirical or humorous, how it could sketch a character, or express a theory, how it could serve as a means of expression for a brilliant mind, continually observing and reflecting on the affairs of the world. Lamb, Hazlitt and Thackeray, Irving, Emerson and Lowell have shown us what may be done with it. The essay is the easy talk of a literary man. It is true that we give the name essay to those famous pieces by Macaulay and Matthew Arnold, that present careful and finished thought on matters of importance. But the characteristic essay is a Roundabout Paper as Thackeray called his, it is Table Talk like Hazlitt's, it is by My Study Window, or Among My Books like Lowell's. And it is this sort of writing in which Addison and Steele excelled. We Americans of the present day sometimes find an essay hard to appreciate, for it does not seem to us to be practical. We ask what it is about, what it tries to say? The true essayist sometimes has something very definite to say, but often enough he is content to suggest an idea or a point of view, as in most of those essays [among Sir Roger de Coverley's] which are not definitely narrative or descriptive.

Those papers that are narrative or descriptive introduce us to another matter. They give us characters and manners, people that we might know living a life which we know of. If there were any story, any plot, the Spectator's visit to Sir Roger would practically be a novel. Yet the first real English novel was not published for thirty years.

Fiction there had been. Sir Thomas More had put his ideas on society in the form of the account given by Raphael Hythloday of the strange country Utopia. Sir Philip Sidney's *Arcadia* was a pastoral poem in prose. In *Euphues*

John Lily had put his ideal of education and gentle life. In the *Pilgrim's Progress* Bunyan had given allegorical figures the likeness and interest of real people. But these are not novels. Even *Robinson Crusoe,* by Defoe, shortly after the *Spectator,* is not a novel according to our present ideas, any more than is *Jack Wilton,* which Thomas Nash wrote long before. No one of these books tried to give a picture of the characters and manners of the life with which we are familiar. But this was one of the chief aims of Addison and Steele. The characters they introduced, the sketches of life that they gave, were perfectly familiar to their readers. If they had written stories, they would have been novelists, and even as it is they have created this one character, Sir Roger de Coverley, the true country gentleman, who is a more definite figure in the mind of the world than many a character of later novelists.

The *Spectator* in its larger aspects, then, is of interest to us because it is so characteristic of the literature of its time, and because it was such an influence upon the literature that followed. Its writers are striking examples of the man of letters and of public affairs so noticeable a figure in the reign of Queen Anne: its pages are full of the most suggestive hints and descriptions that open to us much of the life of that reign. And the *Spectator* was the forerunner of many periodicals and many essays, not in England only and here in America, but on the Continent of Europe. And, further, we may see in the mass of fiction, novel and short story, much that has its forerunner in the *Spectator* account of the old Knight of Coverley Hall.

Let us, however, now fix our attention more particularly upon the *Spectator* itself. Indeed, perhaps, this was the first thing to do: at any rate, this may be done without the other, whereas knowledge about the *Spectator* and its time, without knowledge of the *Spectator* itself, is hardly worth while, save as any historical knowledge is worth while.

And first something must be said of the language, more particularly of the meaning of words. We must remember that language changes in form and in meaning as well. Addison is nearer Shakespeare in point of time than he is to us, and in Shakespeare there are many words which we use in senses very different from those of the plays. It is true that this element in the *Spectator* is not large. Still it is the part of the careful scholar to take account of it. It is better to know a modest number of words and to know them thoroughly, than it is to have an enormous vocabulary and to use it loosely. It is only by having a particular feeling for the meanings of words that we shall follow rightly the full thought of the writer. One word that Addison uses often is *wit:* it was a typical word of the age of Queen Anne. But it was often used in senses not usual to-day: read Pope's *Essay on Criticism* for examples. Addison sometimes means by *wit* what we do, that bright sparkle and brilliancy of speech or thought that gives such a zest to conversation or literature. But he more often means by the word a more general mental power, as in No. 6, where he writes, "wit and sense"; "men of wit"; "wit and learning"; "excellent faculties and abundance of wit"; "wit and angelic faculties"; and in the next paper, "ladies . . . not those of the most wit." Here the word has more the general sense of intellectuality, and if we think of the word in its present sense we gain a false notion. So with the other word that we often contrast with *wit, humor* and the word less common now formed from it, *humorist.* We meet both words frequently in these papers, but rarely with exactly our modern sense: humor means some fanciful or out-of-the-way notion or manner of thought, not necessarily funny or ludicrous, but rather extravagant or fantastic; a humorist is an eccentric. So it is with not a few words: sometimes they have gone out of use; sometimes the meaning has changed. Thus Sir Roger speaks of "men of fine *parts,*" and the Spectator himself, as a boy, is said to have solid *parts.* In like manner England is said to be a *polite* nation, the Lacedæmonians are more virtuous than *polite,* but the meaning is not merely that they were of good manners. The word *conversation* will be found to have a sense somewhat different from that to which we are accustomed. The word *speculation* is used with a particular meaning not common to-day. There are a number of other examples, as "a handsome elocution," "people of quality"; Sir Roger is "a good husband," though not married, and Leonora, in her garden, keeps turtles in cages. One must not think it pedantic to pay attention to these matters. It is certainly pedantic to think that they are of the greatest importance, to spend time upon them that should be given to getting at the ideas. But something of the sort one must do or lose much of the delicacy of the style. A general understanding of what is said anyone may gain at a first reading, but it is the part of the scholar to get the best enjoyment, and that certainly must be based upon a knowledge of what our author had in mind when he wrote. That is the thing we want to get at, and only as it helps us to just that are these written words of value to us.

Having a correct idea of the meanings of his words we shall want to have some notion and appreciation of Addison's style in general, for it is a very famous style. That his manner of writing is marked by ease and elegance will probably be perceived by all, though possibly less attention will be given to these qualities than they deserve, because so many people can write with ease and elegance nowadays, since Addison has shown how it may be done. It will, perhaps, be more readily noted by the close student that this ease and elegance is sometimes attained by a sacrifice of correctness. It is not worth while to cite examples, but almost every paper will offer an instance of some construction which is grammatically careless. Not merely are there constructions once common but now out of use, but there are constructions in which the simplest conventions of syntax are disregarded. The same thing is true to a greater degree with Shakespeare. Our time is more particular about grammatical nicety than was Addison's or Shakespeare's: our thoughts do not seem to be much improved thereby. It does not seem worth while to spend time on these passages. When Addison writes "there is no rank . . . who have not their representatives," we have an example of grammatical carelessness common in Addison's time. Our time is more particular and exact; but it is better to search Addison for points in which he is superior to us than to look for places where he does not come up to our ideas. The main thing about Addison's writing is no particularity about sentences or figures of speech, but the fact that he could write easily and pleasantly about a

very large range of subjects, could make all sorts of things the subject for his thought and the object of our interest. No matter what he writes about—and these papers give at least some idea of his range—he puts his ideas simply and easily and with delicacy and humor, so that, whether he be telling a story or pointing a moral or offering a bit of satire, he is never heavy, nor long-winded, nor pompous, nor wearisome. It will generally be found that he is simpler and clearer in the expression of his ideas than we could be ourselves. Franklin used to try to re-write the essays in the *Spectator* as an exercise in the art of writing, and learned much by comparing his work with the original. Some teachers and students like to do the same thing to-day, and the experiment is pretty sure to show that it is not at all easy to attain the clearness and simplicity of the original, let alone its humor and good sense.

To pass on from the matter of language or style to the matter of these essays, we shall first remark that the . . . papers were not originally written as a single piece.

The *Sir Roger de Coverley Papers* were originally written at one time or another for the *Spectator* by Addison or Steele, whichever happened to feel in the humor. Extracted now and put together, it is clear that they cannot possess that unity of subject or of treatment that we naturally expect in a common piece of writing. The only obvious unity that they have is that all in some way or other mention Sir Roger de Coverley, and in some cases the mention is very slight indeed. But this very lack of unity which in another piece might be annoying, can here be turned to account, for it serves to give us an idea of the general content of the whole work from which these essays are taken. As we see from the essay describing the Club, it was the plan of the *Spectator* that its different ideas should be put forward by different characters, and No. 34 shows us what very different views were possible by this device. So, naturally, several of the papers contain "speculations," as Addison would have said, which are attributed to Sir Roger, only as a mode of presentation. It will be useful to run over all the papers and note of each what its subject is, that we may understand correctly just what we have in these extracts.

First let us note those papers which seem to have for their object merely the presentation of the character of Sir Roger, like No. 2, or that part of it which is given to him. Such papers are 113 in which the Knight gives us an idea of himself in early life, 118 where we have some of his reflections and meditations on the Widow, No. 517 in which we have an account of his death. Other papers, certainly, give us something of his character, but these seem devoted especially to that purpose.

Next come those papers which form the bulk of the collection, in which the Spectator describes his visit to Coverley Hall (Nos. 106, 107, 108, 109, 110, 112, 116, 117, 118, 122, 130), his journey back to London (Nos. 131, 132), and the Knight's return visit to the City (Nos. 269, 329, 335, 383). These make up a sort of story, they require but a little more in the way of plot to be as much of a story as, for instance, *The Legend of Sleepy Hollow.* Their interest is narrative as well as descriptive of manners.

These are the papers distinctly dedicated to Sir Roger de Coverley, but there are a number of others in which he has his part.

Thus Nos. 1, 2, 34, 108, 174, 359, are either character sketches or serve to enforce characters already drawn. No. 34 has its point aside from its personalities, but its interest is largely from the view it gives us of the gentlemen to whom we are introduced in the first account of the Club. No. 108, the account of Will Wimble, has its part in the description of life at Coverley Hall, but it has independent interest, too, as describing a character which we may take as a representative type, fairly presented or not, of an element in society in the time.

The other papers have a general rather than a personal interest, and in this respect are more representative of the *Spectator* than those of which we have been speaking. Some contain chiefly the satire for which Addison is famous, as No. 37, where he presents to us the advanced woman of his day, the club-woman she would be now, or No. 331, where, under the guise of a fantasy on Beards, we have a bit of the satire on fashions of the day of which there is much in the *Spectator.* Rather more of the remaining papers have remarks upon what may be called general topics, as Nos. 125, 126, which contain a discussion of the good and the bad in party spirit, or No. 119, which considers the difference between the manners of the town and the country, or No. 115, which presents the value of exercise. These papers might have been written without any reference to Sir Roger: but it was the plan of the Spectator to give his speculations an intimate, a personal character, or to have them arise naturally out of circumstances in which the reader had an interest. There remain to be noted the two papers on Instinct, which are rather scientific than social in character, but may be included under this head.

Such is the general analysis of the papers in this book, which may be put in a formal way as follows:

I.   Papers pertaining especially to Sir Roger:
   1. His Character: 2, 113, 118, 517.
   2. The Spectator's Visit to him: 106, 107, 108, 109, 110, 112, 116, 117, 118, 122, 130, 131, 132.
   3. His Visit to London: 269, 329, 335, 383.

II. More general Papers:
   1. Presenting Character: 1, 2, 34, 108, 174, 359.
   2. Presenting Satire: 37, 331.
   3. Presenting Observation and Reflection on Life and Society: 6, 114, 115, 119, 120, 121, 123, 125, 126.

It is not enough however to know what a book is about. It is true that by such knowledge we appreciate its ideas better. Still the real object of reading is to get the ideas themselves that they may be to us as much as possible. We want not only to know that some of the Roger de Coverley papers give us the character of the good Knight and country gentleman, but we want to appreciate that character to the full. We want not only to know that other papers describe eighteenth-century life in country and in town, but we want to know what that life was, we want to know it and get the good out of it. And we want not only to know that other papers give us Addison's observations and reflections upon life and society, but we want to know what those observations and reflections were, and further, whether they were sound and good, and whether they were merely temporary, or of some value to us nowadays as we consider the life and society of our own world. In other words we want not only to know what our subject matter is, but we want to know its value.

Of the first two of these matters very little need be said in the way of explanation and commentary, for it is one of the best known parts of literary study to determine them. The characters of Sir Roger, of the Spectator and the others of the Club, of Will Wimble, and even of Tom Touchy, these are particularly presented to us in the Papers, and it would be impertinent to try and summarize here, or to say over, what Addison and Steele say so well later on. It is besides one of the best of exercises for the student to form his own ideas on these things, and to express them either by a talk in class, or by writing a sketch of one character or another, or some adaptation of the circumstances or characters to life with which we are more familiar. It is worth noting that we must not expect the most absolute consistency in these studies of character. They were written at different times by different persons. It seems probable that Addison who elaborated the character thought of him as rather older than did Steele who first sketched it. Thus Steele says particularly that Sir Roger was fifty-six years. Addison always speaks of him as an old man, indeed says that he had courted the widow forty years before, which we otherwise learn was when he was twenty-three or more. Some other slight inconsistencies may be noted, and the fact warns us that it is not in a minor way that we are to draw the character of the country gentleman, but in its general lines. We may perhaps inquire, if Budgell had a correct idea of the old sportsman when he tells that he imported foxes from another country to gain credit by hunting them. But in general we shall find that Addison and Steele had very nearly the same ideas.

In the same way we may form some conception of the life of the time, at least in its more superficial aspects. These little matters alluded to so lightly, the theatre, the puppet-show, the coffeehouse, the club in the town, the hunt, the assizes, the country mansion in the country, these should be hints or suggestions by which we can go farther and form some idea of social life of the day. But such study demands a little more than can be given in a short introduction. . . . Thus the paper on Leonora compared with Will Honeycomb's remarks in No. 34 may make us want to know something about the fine lady of the period, and the account of the clergyman at Coverley Hall may lead us to ask about the religion of the day. The papers on party politics illustrate the history of the time, the paper on manners gives us something of the social life. Everything shows us a life a little different from our own. But, recognizing this difference, we shall generally observe, too, that everything at bottom is not unlike our own life, and that makes it all interesting, to see the mind of man, always much the same, devising all sorts of new forms for himself.

As to the third matter of importance, our authors' observations and reflections, or, in shorter words, their ideas, we are often inclined with such books as the *Spectator* not to consider the value of these matters in themselves. Let us, however, for a moment consider their opinions and see whether they have anything of value for us. For their own day there can be little doubt that they had value: Addison and Steele meant not only to amuse their readers but to help them along, and certainly there is much in the essays of one sort or another which they might readily have taken to heart.

Let us look for a moment at the ideas. In No. 6 we have a discussion which, though put in the mouth chiefly of Sir Roger, was undoubtedly of interest in itself. It is a good exercise to try to sum up in a sentence of, say thirty or forty words, the idea that Steele had it in mind to present. We will not try to do that here, but we will present merely one statement in the paper, namely this: "There is hardly that person to be found who is not more concerned for the reputation of wit and sense, than honesty and virtue." Is this true to-day? and if so what are we to think of it? Can we get anything of value out of Steele's discussion of it that will help us to make up our own minds about it and to follow our own course in the matter?

Or take another idea that may seem a little more to the point. There is the charming Leonora of No. 37. Doubtless there were Leonoras among Addison's readers and many more who saw the point of the humorist's satire. Who was Leonora? She was a lady who had been unfortunately relieved of the duties of a wife and a mother, and who, as the next best thing, turned to self-culture as an object in life. She certainly became a cultivated woman—we shall see that if we read of her indoor amusements and her outdoor employments, and substitute, for what was in fashion two centuries ago, the things that are in fashion to-day. Who can draw a picture of the Leonora of to-day? What is to take the place of the *Grand Cyrus* and the Locke on the Understanding in her library, and of the walks and grottos of her country seat? And if we can form in our own mind a picture of the Leonora of to-day, what shall we say of the Spectator's comment, "I look upon her with a mixture of admiration and pity?" Is there ground for the same satire to-day upon our college women and club women that Addison offered upon the blue stockings of two centuries ago?

What are the ideas worth? That should always be a question with us. We are, some of us, too much in the habit of thinking that if we get at the ideas of the author, know what they are and that they are his, we have done the main thing. But of what use is it to us as reasonable creatures to know that Addison or Steele had such and such thoughts if we do not understand the value of the thoughts and their application to ourselves? Undoubtedly some of the ideas will not have much application: No. 117 is on Witchcraft, and there is little real interest in that subject to-day save as history, nor can we gather much from the paper if we take it as a comment upon superstition in general. But usually the ideas have application. No. 174 gives us an argument which presents the views of the two great elements in English life, the money interest and the landed interest. Undoubtedly we cannot say that those interests exist to-day and in our own country in just the same rela-

tion that they held in the days when Sir Roger and Sir Andrew disputed over them. But there is a money interest in this country and there is what is practically a land interest. Steele's sympathy seems to have been chiefly with the moneyed men, as was not unnatural from his political connections. How would it be with one of us to-day? What sort of discussion could we write if we tried to put No. 174 into modern form?

Let us then think over the ideas and see what we can get out of them. We want to state for ourselves the general idea of any paper and consider it for what it is worth, as, for instance, the idea in Nos. 125, 126, that furious party spirit is likely to result in civil war and bloodshed. Or we want to give fair consideration to particular thoughts as we go along, as to Sir Andrew's remark that "it would be worth while to consider, whether so many artificers at work ten days together by my appointment, or so many peasants made merry on Sir Roger's charge, are the men more obliged." When we have really considered what Addison says, looked at it from different sides, compared it with our own experience, got the reason for it and valued it, then we shall have a far better opinion of Addison's value as a writer than if we knew all that could be said of the qualities of his style. (pp. xi-xxiv)

> *Edward Everett Hale, Jr., in an introduction to* The Sir Roger De Coverley Papers, from the Spectator, *University Publishing Company, 1904, pp. v-xxvi.*

Virginia Woolf (essay date 1919)

[*An English novelist, essayist, and critic, Woolf is one of the most prominent figures of twentieth-century literature. Like her contemporary James Joyce, with whom she is often compared, Woolf employed the stream-of-consciousness technique in her novels. Concerned primarily with depicting the life of the mind, she rebelled against traditional narrative techniques and developed a highly individualized style. Her critical essays, which cover almost the entire range of English literature, contain some of her finest prose and are praised for their insight. In the following essay written in 1919, Woolf emphasizes the enduring worth and the continued relevance of Addison's writings.*]

In July, 1843 [in the *Edinburgh Review*], Lord Macaulay pronounced the opinion that Joseph Addison had enriched our literature with compositions 'that will live as long as the English language'. But when Lord Macaulay pronounced an opinion it was not merely an opinion. Even now, at a distance of seventy-six years, the words seem to issue from the mouth of the chosen representative of the people. There is an authority about them, a sonority, a sense of responsibility, which put us in mind of a Prime Minister making a proclamation on behalf of a great empire rather than of a journalist writing about a deceased man of letters for a magazine. The article upon Addison is, indeed, one of the most vigorous of the famous essays. Florid, and at the same time extremely solid, the phrases seem to build up a monument, at once square and lavishly festooned with ornament, which should serve Addison for shelter so long as one stone of Westminster Abbey stands upon another. Yet, though we may have read and admired this particular essay times out of number (as we say when we have read anything three times over), it has never occurred to us, strangely enough, to believe that it is true. That is apt to happen to the admiring reader of Macaulay's essays. While delighting in their richness, force, and variety, and finding every judgement, however emphatic, proper in its place, it seldom occurs to us to connect these sweeping assertions and undeniable convictions with anything so minute as a human being. So it is with Addison. 'If we wish', Macaulay writes, 'to find anything more vivid than Addison's best portraits, we must go either to Shakespeare or to Cervantes.' 'We have not the least doubt that if Addison had written a novel on an extensive plan it would have been superior to any that we possess.' His essays, again, 'fully entitle him to the rank of a great poet'; and, to complete the edifice, we have Voltaire proclaimed 'the prince of buffoons', and together with Swift forced to stoop so low that Addison takes rank above them both as a humorist.

Examined separately, such flourishes of ornament look grotesque enough, but in their place—such is the persuasive power of design—they are part of the decoration; they complete the monument. Whether Addison or another is interred within, it is a very fine tomb. But now that two centuries have passed since the real body of Addison was laid by night under the Abbey floor, we are, through no merit of our own, partially qualified to test the first of the flourishes on that fictitious tombstone to which, though it may be empty, we have done homage, in a formal kind of way, these sixty-seven years. The compositions of Addison

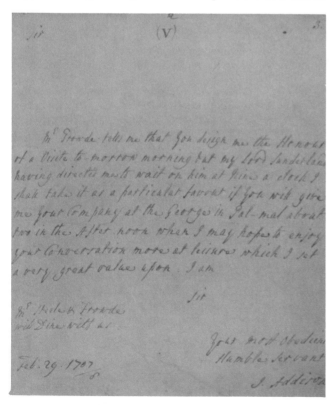

A letter from Addison to Jonathan Swift.

will live as long as the English language. Since every moment brings proof that our mother tongue is more lusty and lively than sorts with complete sedateness or chastity, we need only concern ourselves with the vitality of Addison. Neither lusty nor lively is the adjective we should apply to the present condition of the *Tatler* and the *Spectator.* To take a rough test, it is possible to discover how many people in the course of a year borrow Addison's works from the public library, and a particular instance affords us the not very encouraging information that during nine years two people yearly take out the first volume of the *Spectator.* The second volume is less in request than the first. The inquiry is not a cheerful one. From certain marginal comments and pencil marks it seems that these rare devotees seek out only the famous passages and, as their habit is, score what we are bold enough to consider the least admirable phrases. No; if Addison lives at all, it is not in the public libraries. It is in libraries that are markedly private, secluded, shaded by lilac trees and brown with folios, that he still draws his faint, regular breath. If any man or woman is going to solace himself with a page of Addison before the June sun is out of the sky today, it is in some such pleasant retreat as this.

Yet all over England at intervals, perhaps wide ones, we may be sure that there are people engaged in reading Addison, whatever the year or season. For Addison is very well worth reading. The temptation to read Pope on Addison, Macaulay on Addison, Thackeray on Addison, Johnson on Addison rather than Addison himself is to be resisted, for you will find, if you study the *Tatler* and the *Spectator,* glance at *Cato,* and run through the remainder of the six moderate-sized volumes, that Addison is neither Pope's Addison nor anybody else's Addison, but a separate, independent individual still capable of casting a clear-cut shape of himself upon the consciousness, turbulent and distracted as it is, of nineteen hundred and nineteen. It is true that the fate of the lesser shades is always a little precarious. They are so easily obscured or distorted. It seems so often scarcely worth while to go through the cherishing and humanizing process which is necessary to get into touch with a writer of the second class who may, after all, have little to give us. The earth is crusted over them; their features are obliterated, and perhaps it is not a head of the best period that we rub clean in the end, but only the chip of an old pot. The chief difficulty with the lesser writers, however, is not only the effort. It is that our standards have changed. The things that they like are not the things that we like; and as the charm of their writing depends much more upon taste than upon conviction, a change of manners is often quite enough to put us out of touch altogether. That is one of the most troublesome barriers between ourselves and Addison. He attached great importance to certain qualities. He had a very precise notion of what we are used to call 'niceness' in man or woman. He was extremely fond of saying that men ought not to be atheists, and that women ought not to wear large petticoats. This directly inspires in us not so much a sense of distaste as a sense of difference. Dutifully, if at all, we strain our imaginations to conceive the kind of audience to whom these precepts were addressed. The *Tatler* was published in 1709; the *Spectator* a year or two later. What was the state of England at that particular moment? Why was Addison so anxious to insist upon the necessity of a decent and cheerful religious belief? Why did he so constantly, and in the main kindly, lay stress upon the foibles of women and their reform? Why was he so deeply impressed with the evils of party government? Any historian will explain; but it is always a misfortune to have to call in the services of any historian. A writer should give us direct certainty; explanations are so much water poured into the wine. As it is, we can only feel that these counsels are addressed to ladies in hoops and gentlemen in wigs—a vanished audience which has learnt its lesson and gone its way and the preacher with it. We can only smile and marvel and perhaps admire the clothes.

And that is not the way to read. To be thinking that dead people deserved these censures and admired this morality, judged the eloquence, which we find so frigid, sublime, the philosophy to us so superficial, profound, to take a collector's joy in such signs of antiquity, is to treat literature as if it were a broken jar of undeniable age but doubtful beauty, to be stood in a cabinet behind glass doors. The charm which still makes *Cato* very readable is much of this nature. When Syphax exclaims,

> So, where our wide Numidian wastes extend,
> Sudden, th'impetuous hurricanes descend,
> Wheel through the air, in circling eddies play,
> Tear up the sands, and sweep whole plains away,
> The helpless traveller, with wild surprise,
> Sees the dry desert all around him rise,
> And smother'd in the dusty whirlwind dies,

we cannot help imagining the thrill in the crowded theatre, the feathers nodding emphatically on the ladies' heads, the gentlemen leaning forward to tap their canes, and everyone exclaiming to his neighbour how vastly fine it is and crying 'Bravo!' But how can *we* be excited? And so with Bishop Hurd and his notes—his 'finely observed', his 'wonderfully exact, both in the sentiment and expression', his serene confidence that when 'the present humour of idolizing Shakespeare is over', the time will come when *Cato* is 'supremely admired by all candid and judicious critics'. This is all very amusing and productive of pleasant fancies, both as to the faded frippery of our ancestors' minds and the bold opulence of our own. But it is not the intercourse of equals, let alone that other kind of intercourse, which as it makes us contemporary with the author, persuades us that his object is our own. Occasionally in *Cato* one may pick up a few lines that are not obsolete; but for the most part the tragedy which Dr. Johnson thought 'unquestionably the noblest production of Addison's genius' has become collector's literature.

Perhaps most readers approach the essays also with some suspicion as to the need of condescension in their minds. The question to be asked is whether Addison, attached as he was to certain standards of gentility, morality, and taste, has not become one of those people of exemplary character and charming urbanity who must never be talked to about anything more exciting than the weather. We have some slight suspicion that the *Spectator* and the *Tatler* are nothing but talk, couched in perfect English, about the number of fine days this year compared with the number of wet the year before. The difficulty of getting on to equal terms with him is shown by the little fable which

he introduces into one of the early numbers of the *Tatler,* of 'a young gentleman, of moderate understanding, but great vivacity, who . . . had got a little smattering of knowledge, just enough to make an atheist or a freethinker, but not a philosopher, or a man of sense'. This young gentleman visits his father in the country, and proceeds 'to enlarge the narrowness of the country notions; in which he succeeded so well, that he had seduced the butler by his tabletalk, and staggered his eldest sister. . . . 'Till one day, talking of his setting dog . . . said "he did not question but Tray was as immortal as any one of the family"; and in the heat of the argument told his father, that for his own part, "he expected to die like a dog". Upon which, the old man, starting up in a very great passion, cried out, "Then, sirrah, you shall live like one"; and taking his cane in his hand, cudgelled him out of his system. This had so good an effect upon him, that he took up from that day, fell to reading good books, and is now a bencher in the Middle-Temple.' There is a good deal of Addison in that story: his dislike of 'dark and uncomfortable prospects'; his respect for 'principles which are the support, happiness, and glory of all public societies, as well as private persons'; his solicitude for the butler; and his conviction that to read good books and become a bencher in the Middle-Temple is the proper end for a very vivacious young gentleman. This Mr. Addison married a countess, 'gave his little senate laws', and, sending for young Lord Warwick, made that famous remark about seeing how a Christian can die which has fallen upon such evil days that our sympathies are with the foolish, and perhaps fuddled, young peer rather than with the frigid gentleman, not too far gone for a last spasm of self-complacency, upon the bed.

Let us rub off such incrustations, so far as they are due to the corrosion of Pope's wit or the deposit of mid-Victorian lachrymosity, and see what, for us in our time, remains. In the first place, there remains the not despicable virtue, after two centuries of existence, of being readable. Addison can fairly lay claim to that; and then, slipped in on the tide of the smooth, well-turned prose, are little eddies, diminutive waterfalls, agreeably diversifying the polished surface. We begin to take note of whims, fancies, peculiarities on the part of the essayist which light up the prim, impeccable countenance of the moralist and convince us that, however tightly he may have pursed his lips, his eyes are very bright and not so shallow after all. He is alert to his finger-tips. Little muffs, silver garters, fringed gloves draw his attention; he observes with a keen, quick glance, not unkindly, and full rather of amusement than of censure. To be sure, the age was rich in follies. Here were coffee-houses packed with politicians talking of Kings and Emperors and letting their own small affairs go to ruin. Crowds applauded the Italian opera every night without understanding a word of it. Critics discoursed of the unities. Men gave a thousand pounds for a handful of tulip roots. As for women—or 'the fair sex', as Addison liked to call them—their follies were past counting. He did his best to count them, with a loving particularity which roused the ill-humour of Swift. But he did it very charmingly, with a natural relish for the task, as the following passage shows:

I consider woman as a beautiful romantic animal, that may be adorned with furs and feathers,
pearls and diamonds, ores and silks. The lynx
shall cast its skin at her feet to make her a tippet;
the peacock, parrot, and swan, shall pay contributions to her muff; the sea shall be searched for
shells, and the rocks for gems; and every part of
nature furnish out its share towards the embellishment of a creature that is the most consummate work of it. All this I shall indulge them in;
but as for the petticoat I have been speaking of,
I neither can nor will allow it.

In all these matters Addison was on the side of sense and
taste and civilization. Of that little fraternity, often so obscure and yet so indispensable, who in every age keep
themselves alive to the importance of art and letters and
music, watching, discriminating, denouncing and delighting, Addison was one—distinguished and strangely contemporary with ourselves. It would have been, so one
imagines, a great pleasure to take him a manuscript; a
great enlightenment, as well as a great honour, to have his
opinion. In spite of Pope, one fancies that his would have
been criticism of the best order, open-minded and generous to novelty, and yet, in the final resort, unfaltering in
its standards. The boldness which is a proof of vigour is
shown by his defence of *Chevy Chase*. He had so clear a
notion of what he meant by the 'very spirit and soul of fine
writing' as to track it down in an old barbarous ballad or
rediscover it in 'that divine work' *Paradise Lost*. Moreover, far from being a connoisseur only of the still, settled
beauties of the dead, he was aware of the present; a severe
critic of its 'Gothic taste', vigilant in protecting the rights
and honours of the language, and all in favour of simplicity and quiet. Here we have the Addison of Will's and Button's, who, sitting late into the night and drinking more
than was good for him, gradually overcame his taciturnity
and began to talk. Then he 'chained the attention of every
one to him'. 'Addison's conversation', said Pope, 'had
something in it more charming than I have found in any
other man.' One can well believe it, for his essays at their
best preserve the very cadence of easy yet exquisitely modulated conversation—the smile checked before it has
broadened into laughter, the thought lightly turned from
frivolity or abstraction, the ideas springing, bright, new,
various, with the utmost spontaneity. He seems to speak
what comes into his head, and is never at the trouble of
raising his voice. But he has described himself in the character of the lute better than any one can do it for him.

The lute is a character directly opposite to the
drum, that sounds very finely by itself, or in a
very small concert. Its notes are exquisitely
sweet, and very low, easily drowned in a multitude of instruments, and even lost among a few,
unless you give a particular attention to it. A lute
is seldom heard in a company of more than five,
whereas a drum will show itself to advantage in
an assembly of 500. The lutanists, therefore, are
men of a fine genius, uncommon reflection, great
affability, and esteemed chiefly by persons of a
good taste, who are the only proper judges of so
delightful and soft a melody.

Addison was a lutanist. No praise, indeed, could be less
appropriate than Lord Macaulay's. To call Addison on

the strength of his essays a great poet, or to prophesy that
if he had written a novel on an extensive plan it would
have been 'superior to any that we possess', is to confuse
him with the drums and trumpets; it is not merely to overpraise his merits, but to overlook them. Dr. Johnson superbly, and, as his manner is, once and for all has summed
up the quality of Addison's poetic genius:

His poetry is first to be considered; of which it
must be confessed that it has not often those felicities of diction which give lustre to sentiments,
or that vigour of sentiment that animates diction; there is little of ardour, vehemence, or
transport; there is very rarely the awfulness of
grandeur, and not very often the splendour of elegance. He thinks justly; but he thinks faintly.

The Sir Roger de Coverley papers are those which have
the most resemblance, on the surface, to a novel. But their
merit consists in the fact that they do not adumbrate, or
initiate, or anticipate anything; they exist, perfect, complete, entire in themselves. To read them as if they were
a first hesitating experiment containing the seed of greatness to come is to miss the peculiar point of them. They
are studies done from the outside by a quiet spectator.
When read together they compose a portrait of the Squire
and his circle all in characteristic positions—one with his
rod, another with his hounds—but each can be detached
from the rest without damage to the design or harm to
himself. In a novel, where each chapter gains from the one
before it or adds to the one that follows it, such separations
would be intolerable. The speed, the intricacy, the design,
would be mutilated. These particular qualities are perhaps
lacking, but nevertheless Addison's method has great advantages. Each of these essays is very highly finished. The
characters are defined by a succession of extremely neat,
clean strokes. Inevitably, where the sphere is so narrow—
an essay is only three or four pages in length—there is not
room for great depth or intricate subtlety. Here, from the
Spectator, is a good example of the witty and decisive
manner in which Addison strikes out a portrait to fill the
little frame:

Sombrius is one of these sons of sorrow. He
thinks himself obliged in duty to be sad and disconsolate. He looks on a sudden fit of laughter
as a breach of his baptismal vow. An innocent
jest startles him like blasphemy. Tell him of one
who is advanced to a title of honour, he lifts up
his hands and eyes; describe a public ceremony,
he shakes his head; shew him a gay equipage, he
blesses himself. All the little ornaments of life
are pomps and vanities. Mirth is wanton, and
wit profane. He is scandalized at youth for being
lively, and at childhood for being playful. He sits
at a christening, or at a marriage-feast, as at a funeral; sighs at the conclusion of a merry story,
and grows devout when the rest of the company
grow pleasant. After all Sombrius is a religious
man, and would have behaved himself very
properly, had he lived when Christianity was
under a general persecution.

The novel is not a development from that model, for the
good reason that no development along these lines is possible. Of its kind such a portrait is perfect; and when we

find, scattered up and down the *Spectator* and the *Tatler,* numbers of such little masterpieces with fancies and anecdotes in the same style, some doubt as to the narrowness of such a sphere becomes inevitable. The form of the essay admits of its own particular perfection; and if anything is perfect the exact dimensions of its perfection become immaterial. One can scarcely settle whether, on the whole, one prefers a raindrop to the River Thames. When we have said all that we can say against them—that many are dull, others superficial, the allegories faded, the piety conventional, the morality trite—there still remains the fact that the essays of Addison are perfect essays. Always at the highest point of any art there comes a moment when everything seems in a conspiracy to help the artist, and his achievement becomes a natural felicity on his part of which he seems, to a later age, half-unconscious. So Addison, writing day after day, essay after essay, knew instinctively and exactly how to do it. Whether it was a high thing, or whether it was a low thing, whether an epic is more profound or a lyric more passionate, undoubtedly it is due to Addison that prose is now prosaic—the medium which makes it possible for people of ordinary intelligence to communicate their ideas to the world. Addison is the respectable ancestor of an innumerable progeny. Pick up the first weekly journal and the article upon the 'Delights of Summer' or the 'Approach of Age' will show his influence. But it will also show, unless the name of Mr. Max Beerbohm, our solitary essayist, is attached to it, that we have lost the art of writing essays. What with our views and our virtues, our passions and profundities, the shapely silver drop, that held the sky in it and so many bright little visions of human life, is now nothing but a hold-all knobbed with luggage packed in a hurry. Even so, the essayist will make an effort, perhaps without knowing it, to write like Addison.

In his temperate and reasonable way Addison more than once amused himself with speculations as to the fate of his writings. He had a just idea of their nature and value. 'I have new-pointed all the batteries of ridicule', he wrote. Yet, because so many of his darts had been directed against ephemeral follies, 'absurd fashions, ridiculous customs, and affected forms of speech', the time would come, in a hundred years, perhaps, when his essays, he thought, would be 'like so many pieces of old plate, where the weight will be regarded, but the fashion lost'. Two hundred years have passed; the plate is worn smooth; the pattern almost rubbed out; but the metal is pure silver. (pp. 85-94)

Virginia Woolf, "Addison," in her Collected Essays, Vol. 1, *The Hogarth Press, 1966, pp. 85-94.*

Sir James George Frazer   (essay date 1927)

[*Frazer was a Scottish anthropologist and classical scholar who is best known as the author of* The Golden Bough, *(1890), a vast compendium of anthropological information that is generally credited with generating the enormous interest in anthropology, folklore, myth, and ritual that arose in the late nineteenth and early twentieth centuries. Frazer, who spent a lifetime examining and attempting to explain the primitive bases for human social behavior, was one of the first and most thorough of social anthropologists, and although many of the purely scientific applications of his work have been superceded by subsequent scholarship, his work is seen as central to the shaping of the modern consciousness. In the following excerpt, Frazer provides insight into Addison's experiences and opinions by portraying some aspects of literary society in eighteenth-century London.*]

Joseph Addison was born on the 1st of May 1672, and died on the 17th of June 1719. Thus he lived through the last thirteen years of Charles the Second, the whole of the reigns of James the Second, William the Third, and Anne, and the first five years of George the First. But his memory is chiefly associated with the age of Queen Anne, because that period coincided with the maturity of his genius and witnessed the production of the writings on which his fame securely rests. These writings comprise above all the essays contributed by him to the *Tatler* and the *Spectator,* which ran successively, with breaks of about twenty months, from the 12th of April 1709 to the 20th of December 1714. Thus the time with which we shall be mainly concerned in the following pages includes, roughly speaking, the last six years of the reign of Queen Anne.

As my readers are doubtless aware, the *Spectator* of Queen Anne's time, which published the masterpieces of Addison and many fine papers by his friend Sir Richard Steele, was not a newspaper in the ordinary sense of the word; for it did not attempt to report the current events of the day, and all political discussions, whether of home or foreign affairs, were rigorously excluded. The aim of the writers was to improve the taste and reform the manners and morals of their readers, and they believed that they could better attain their purpose by maintaining a strict neutrality in politics than by plunging into the troubled and angry sea of partisan controversy. But in the essays on social, moral, and literary topics, which formed the whole of the *Spectator* and the chief part of the *Tatler,* the essayists could not wholly abstain from alluding, often in a playful vein, to the public topics which engaged so much of the attention of their contemporaries; and we their successors should but imperfectly understand the life of London in those days if we forgot entirely the great events which were then occurring and the momentous issues which were then being decided in Europe.

While the whole of the *Tatler* and the greater part of the *Spectator* were appearing, the long war with France was still dragging out its weary length to a somewhat indecisive and inglorious close, and Addison makes frequent references to it. He says that news of the war were cried through London with the same precipitation as a fire; that a bloody battle alarmed the town from one end to another in an instant; and that every motion of the French was published in so great a hurry that you might think the enemy were at the gates. News of a great victory were proclaimed to the whole city by the roar of guns from the Tower. In one of his papers Addison professes to have been appropriately awakened from a dream of Fame by the noise of the cannon fired for the taking of Mons. As the ports of France were necessarily closed to English traffic during the war, news of military operations in Flanders and Germany reached England only by the mail from Holland; hence the conspicuous place which the Dutch mail takes in the periodical literature of that age. And as the packet-boat came from the east, and it was long before the invention of steamers, the mail could not arrive so long as the wind sat in the west; accordingly we read that a westerly wind kept the whole town in suspense and put a stop to conversation. Many empty-pated people, says Addison, "do not know what to talk of till about twelve o'clock in the morning; for by that time they are pretty good judges of the weather, know which way the wind sits, and whether the Dutch mail be come in". He tells us of a very grave person, an upholsterer, who ran about the town after the news to the neglect of his family and the ruin of his shop; he always "looked extremely thin in a dearth of news, and never enjoyed himself in a westerly wind".

But the supply of war news fluctuated, not only with the state of the wind, but also with the time of year. For in that easy-going age armies regularly retired in the autumn into winter quarters, from which they came forth, refreshed and invigorated, to resume the business of mutual slaughter in spring. Accordingly a writer who earned his bread by glutting the appetite of the public for sanguinary intelligence was sore put to it to make ends meet during the close season, when little or no blood was flowing. Addison tells of an author who from the beginning of November to the opening of the campaign made shift to live by writing pamphlets and letters to members of parliament or friends in the country; but sometimes he would entertain his ordinary readers with a murder, or pay his weekly bills with the help of strange and lamentable accidents. A little before the armies took the field, his way was to rouse the attention of the public by the report of a prodigy, and if it was tolerably written, it would bring him in two guineas at the lowest price. This prepared his readers for great and bloody news from Flanders in June and July. He always looked well after a battle, and seemed fatter in a fighting year. Happily for himself poor Tom, for that was his name, died before the conclusion of peace, for the cessation of carnage would have taken the bread out of his mouth.

Of the newspapers which reported the course of the campaigns Addison mentions particularly the *Daily Courant,* the *English Post,* the *Post-boy,* the *Postman,* and the *Supplement;* and he says that the political upholsterer spent much time in attempting to reconcile their conflicting reports, when he had much better have been attending to his shop. While the *Spectator* was in course of publication, the Government imposed a tax on paper. This was a heavy blow to the newspapers of the day. The Act of Parliament which imposed the tax was known as the Stamp Act. It was to come into force on the 1st of August 1712; and on the 31st of July, the last day of untaxed newspapers, Addison wrote in the *Spectator* as follows:

> This is the day on which many eminent authors will probably publish their last words. I am afraid that few of our weekly historians, who are men that above all others delight in war, will be able to subsist under the weight of a stamp and an approaching peace. A sheet of blank paper that must have this new imprimatur clapt upon it, before it is qualified to communicate anything to the public, will make its way in the world but very heavily. In short, the necessity of carrying a stamp, and the improbability of notifying a bloody battle, will, I am afraid, both concur to the sinking of those thin folios, which have every other day retailed to us the history of Europe for several years last past. A facetious friend of mine, who loves a pun, calls this present mortality among authors, 'the fall of the leaf' [*Spectator* 445].

These melancholy anticipations were fulfilled. Writing to Stella only five days later Swift says: "Do you know that all Grub Street is dead and gone last week? No more ghosts or murders now for love or money. . . . Every single half sheet pays a halfpenny to the Queen. The *Observator* is fallen; the *Medleys* are jumbled together with the *Flying Post;* the *Examiner* is deadly sick; the *Spectator* keeps on and doubles its price: I know not how long it will last." In consequence of the tax the price of the *Spectator* was raised from one penny to twopence; and the increased cost brought the editors a flood of letters of complaint. One gentleman informed them that he was now deprived of the best part of his breakfast, for since the imposition of the second penny he had been forced every morning to drink his dish of coffee by itself, without the addition of the *Spectator* that used to be better than lace to it. One letter came from a soap-boiler, whose business appears to have suffered from the tax. He wrote in very affectionate terms to the *Spectator* condoling with him on the necessity they both lay under of setting a higher price on their wares and begging the editor, when he next touched on the painful subject, to speak a word or two upon the present duties on Castile soap. Letters from the female world also came in shoals. A large family of daughters drew up a very handsome remonstrance, in which they mentioned, that their father having refused to take in the *Spectator,* since the additional price was set on it, they offered him unanimously to bate him the article of bread and butter in the tea-table account, provided the *Spectator* might be served up to them every morning as usual. To his credit their father, moved by their desire to improve themselves, granted them the continuance both of the *Spectator* and of their bread and butter, giving particular orders that the tea-table should be set forth every morning with its customary bill of fare, and without any manner of defalcation.

In an early number of the *Spectator* Addison congratulates himself and his colleagues on the success of the paper. He says that three thousand copies were distributed every day; so that allowing twenty readers to every copy he reckoned on about sixty thousand daily disciples in the cities of London and Westminster, and he hoped that they would distinguish themselves from the thoughtless herd of their ignorant and unattentive brethren. As Socrates was said to have brought philosophy down from heaven to dwell among men, so, Addison tells us [*Spectator* 10, 1711], it was his ambition to bring philosophy out of closets and libraries, schools and colleges, to dwell in clubs and assemblies, at tea-tables and in coffee-houses. (pp. 148-54)

The principal theatres of London in Addison's time were

the Haymarket and Drury Lane. Of the two, Drury Lane was the older. A theatre stood in Drury Lane in Shakespeare's time; it went by the name of the Phoenix or the Cockpit. After being destroyed by a Puritan mob in 1617, it was rebuilt and existed to 1663, when it was replaced by the first Drury Lane theatre. The new theatre was itself burned down in 1671 or 1672, but was rebuilt by Sir Christopher Wren and opened in 1674 with a prologue by Dryden. This was the Drury Lane theatre frequented by Addison and his contemporaries.

The Haymarket theatre was designed and opened by Vanbrugh in 1706; but at first it was almost a complete failure, partly, it would seem, because it was too distant from the city for the ordinary playgoers, but still more because the convenience of the building for the representation of plays was sacrificed to the magnificence of the architecture. The huge columns, gilded cornices, and immoderately high roof struck the spectators with surprise and wonder, but the voices of the actors were so lost in the void overhead that scarcely one word in ten could be distinctly heard, while the rest was drowned in a sort of confused murmur, like the hum of voices rolling and reverberating among the vaults and along the aisles of a cathedral. But if the stately building was ill-fitted for speech, it was much better adapted for music: the swelling blast of a trumpet and the high notes of a singer lingered lovingly in the hollows of that lofty roof and struck home to the hearts of the rapt listeners with a power and a sweetness they could hardly have attained in a less ample structure. Hence when the Italian opera was introduced into England in the reign of Queen Anne it found its natural home in the Haymarket; and the foreign songs and foreign music saved the theatre from the utter ruin with which it had been threatened by the continuous failure of the English pieces.

It was at the Haymarket that Handel, then a stranger lately arrived in England, produced his opera of *Rinaldo* in February 1711. Though he is said to have devoted only a fortnight to its composition, the opera was highly successful. Addison bore unwilling witness to its popularity. He himself apparently could see nothing in it to admire but much to ridicule. The only design of an opera, he tells us, "is to gratify the senses, and keep up an indolent attention in the audience" [*Spectator* 5]. To do the critic justice, he seems to have conformed his own behaviour very closely to the design of the performance, as he conceived it. For any reference he makes to the music, he might have been deaf; while the rest of the audience sat entranced by the melting airs of *Cara sposa* and *Lascia ch' io pianga,* Addison was calmly sneering at the costumes and the scenery, and was thinking, as he says, how the wits of King Charles's time, those exquisite judges of scenic propriety, would have laughed to see Nicolini exposed to a tempest in robes of ermine and sailing in an open boat upon a sea of pasteboard! what a field for raillery they would have found in painted dragons spitting wildfire, enchanted chariots drawn by Flanders mares, and real cascades in artificial landscapes! In one of the scenes the singer Nicolini engaged in a single combat with a lion on the stage, and this encounter furnished Addison with the material for a whole paper of banter in the **Spectator,** where he gave his readers in an amusing form the pretended result of his in-

quiries into the private history of the lions, or rather of the men in the lion's skin, who fought with Signor Nicolini on the stage to the huge delight of the audience. The first lion, he says, was a candle-snuffer, who, being of a testy choleric temper, outdid his part and would not suffer himself to be killed so easily as the exigencies of the opera required: he was even heard to observe in private life that he had not fought his best, and that he would wrestle Mr. Nicolini for what he pleased, out of the lion's skin. As it was feared that, if he appeared again in the lion's skin, he might carry out his threat by laying the operatic singer on his back on the stage, he was dismissed and the part given to a tailor, a man of a mild and peaceable temper, who conducted himself more like a lamb than a lion on the stage, and only put out his claws to rip up the flesh-coloured doublet of his adversary for the purpose, as was generally supposed, of making work for himself in his private capacity as a tailor. The next lion was a country gentleman, who played the part for his own diversion, but kept his name secret lest his friends should speak of him as "the ass in the lion's skin". His temper was so happily conformed to the character he had to sustain that he surpassed both his predecessors and drew together greater audiences than had been known in the memory of man. As for the report that the lion and Signor Nicolini had been seen smoking a pipe together behind the scenes, it was altogether groundless; for if there was any element of truth in it, this friendly intercourse had not taken place till after the combat was over, when the lion was to be looked upon as dead, according to the received rules of the drama.

From all this agreeable raillery we may infer that the melodies of the great musician spoke to Addison with the accents of a language which he did not understand: he heard with his ears the sounds of the violins and the voices, but the soul of the music escaped him.

In his references to the dramatic as well as the operatic performances of his day Addison paid much attention to the mere outward show and trappings of the pageant. He was particularly sarcastic on stage thunder. He says in one place that last winter he had been at the first rehearsal of the new thunder, which was much more deep and sonorous than any that had been heard before. The lightning flashed more briskly than heretofore, and the clouds were better furbelowed and more voluminous. He was told that the theatre was provided with above a dozen showers of snow consisting of the plays of many unsuccessful poets cut and shredded for the purpose. These were to fall on the head of King Lear at his next appearance on the stage. As for the noise of drums, trumpets, and huzzas, he says it was so loud that when a battle was raging in the Haymarket theatre the sound of it might be heard as far as Charing Cross.

But while he ridiculed the ordinary devices for lending dignity to tragedy, such as the sweeping trains of stage queens and the towering plumes of stage heroes, he was not insensible to the effect of some artifices in moving the awe or pity of the spectators. He tells us that in the parting scene between Jaffeir and Belvidera in Otway's tragedy of *Venice Preserved* the sound of the passing bell, tolling for the execution of Jaffeir's friend Pierre, then about to be broken on the wheel, caused the hearts of the whole audience to quake and made a stronger impression on the mind than mere words could convey. He also speaks with true appreciation and insight of the appearance of the ghost in *Hamlet,* which he calls a masterpiece in its kind, wrought up with every circumstance that could excite the attention of the spectator and chill his blood with horror. He explains, therefore, that he does not find fault with stage artifices when they are skillfully introduced; he would not even banish the handkerchief, which, applied to the eyes of heroines on the stage, drew sympathetic tears from tender-hearted spectators in the audience. He knew that tragedy could not subsist without handkerchiefs; he would only confine the use of that instrument of sorrow within reasonable limits. Similarly he admitted that a disconsolate mother with a child in her hand was a legitimate object of compassion, but he protested that a widow in her weeds, with half-a-dozen fatherless children clinging to her skirts, was more than the most compassionate audience could put up with. (pp. 167-72)

In the pages of Addison we get many glimpses of the audience as well as of the actors in the London theatres of his time. Thus he mentions that of late years there had been a certain person in the upper gallery of the play-house who, when he was pleased with anything that was acted on the stage, expressed his approbation by a loud knock on the benches or wainscot, which might be heard over the whole theatre. Hence this unknown critic in the upper gallery came to be commonly known as the "Trunkmaker in the upper gallery", whether it was that the thwacks which he gave to the boards sounded like the knocking of a carpenter, or whether he was a real trunk-maker who unbent his mind after the labours of the day by laying about him with his hammer. All that was known for certain about him was that he was a large black man who generally leaned forward on a huge oaken plank, paying close attention to everything that passed on the stage. He was never seen to smile, but on hearing anything that pleased him he would take up his staff and apply it to the next piece of timber; after which he composed himself in his former posture till such time as something new set him again at work. It was observed that his blow was so well timed, that the most judicious critic could never except against it. No sooner was a shining thought expressed by the poet or an uncommon grace exhibited by an actor than down came the oaken staff with a resounding thwack on the bench or wainscot. If the audience did not agree with him, he smote a second time; and if they still remained dumb, he looked round him with great wrath and repeated the blow a third time, which never failed to produce a clap. He did not confine his criticisms to a single play-house. Sometimes he plied at the opera, where on Nicolini's first appearance he was said to have demolished three benches in the fury of his applause. He might break as many as half-a-dozen oaken planks in expressing his approval of a popular actor; and he seldom went away from a tragedy of Shakespeare without leaving the wainscot extremely shattered. So useful was he to the theatre by stimulating and directing the applause, that the players cheerfully repaired at their own cost all the damage he made. And once, when he was kept away from the theatre by sickness, the manager paid a man to officiate for him in his absence; but though the substitute laid about him with incredible violence, he did it in such wrong places that the audience soon found out it was not their old friend the trunk-maker.

If the trunk-maker expressed only approval by the well-timed blows of his staff, the audience possessed another implement which they used to show their disapprobation of bad plays and bad players. This was the cat-call. It was a simple musical instrument designed to imitate those melodious sounds with which, in neighbourhoods frequented by cats, the silence of night is often so agreeably broken, and which are commonly known as caterwauling. Played in concert by a number of performers dispersed throughout the theatre, the instrument exerted a powerful effect upon the actors: it struck a damp into generals, and frighted heroes off the stage: at the first sound of it a crowned head has been seen to tremble, and a princess to fall into fits. The notes of it very much improved the sound of nonsense and went along with the voice of the actor who pronounced it as the violin or harpsichord accompanies the Italian recitativo. When the *Humourous Lieutenant* of Beaumont and Fletcher was revived on the stage in Addison's time, it was received with such a chorus of caterwauls as effectually stopped the mirthful sallies of the lieutenant.

At the opera a cluster of ladies in gay hoods sometimes presented as pleasing a spectacle as any on the stage, and diverted the eyes of the audience from the performers. One evening Addison, seated in the back of a box, noticed such a bevy, and compared it to a bed of tulips, the hoods varying in colour from blue to yellow and philomot and pink and pale green. By the unspeakable satisfaction which appeared on the faces of the wearers it was easy to see that their thoughts were more taken up with their pretty hoods than with the singers on the stage. Another time, sitting at an opera in the Haymarket theatre, he observed two parties of very fine women, who had placed themselves in opposite boxes and seemed drawn up in a kind of battle-array one against another. Those on the right were Whigs and those on the left were Tories, and as the badges of their respective parties they had disposed the fashionable black patches of the day on different parts of their faces. The intermediate boxes were occupied by ladies whose principles and patches were midway between these extremes, and who seemed to sit there, singularly enough, for no other purpose but to see the opera. In order to ascertain the state of political opinion among the ladies, Addison had the curiosity to count the patches on both sides, and he found that the Tories had it by about twenty; but the balance of opinion was turned next morning at the puppet-show, where all the ladies were spotted in the Whig manner. Some cynical observers maintained that the ladies spotted their faces black, not so much to display their principles, as to catch husbands, the patches being arranged in the Whig or Tory style according to the political party of the man at whom they had set their cap. But Addison assures us, and we may readily believe him, that whatever might be the motives of a few fantastical coquettes, who patched for their private advantage rather than the public good, there were several women of honour who patched out of principle and with a single eye to the interest of their country.

For women seem to have taken as deep and intelligent an interest in politics in the days of Queen Anne as in our own. Addison describes an encounter between two female politicians across a tea-table, in which the hand of one of the disputants shook so with the earnestness of her feelings, that in the very height of the debate she spilt a dish of tea on her petticoat and scalded her fingers, which naturally broke off the argument, otherwise no one knows how it would have ended. Against such excesses of political zeal Addison earnestly warned his female readers, pointing out to them with great truth that nothing is so bad for the complexion as party spirit, since it flushes the face worse than brandy, besides giving an ill-natured cast to the eye and a disagreeable sourness to the look. On these grounds he advised all young and pretty ladies to abstain from meddling in politics; but as for the old and ugly, if indeed there be any such, he would freely let them be as violent partisans as they pleased, since there was not the least danger of their spoiling their faces or of their convincing anybody.

And as in our own days so in the age of Queen Anne, the passion for learning sometimes burned as warmly in female bosoms as the passion for politics. Addison has described a visit which he paid to a learned lady and has given a catalogue of the books which he found in her library. Some of the volumes, indeed, when he attempted to peruse them, he discovered to be made of wood with no lettering at all except on the back; but others were real books, with paper pages and real printing on them. Among them he lighted upon Ogleby's *Virgil* and Dryden's *Juvenal;* Sir Isaac Newton's *Works; The Grand Cyrus,* with a pin stuck in one of the middle leaves; Locke's *Essay on the Human Understanding,* with a paper of patches in it; a spelling-book; a dictionary for the explanation of hard words; Sherlock, *Upon Death; The Fifteen Comforts of Matrimony;* all the Classic Authors, in wood; a set of Elzevirs, by the same hand; *Clelia,* which opened of itself in the place that describes two lovers in a bower; a *Prayer-Book,* with a bottle of Hungary water beside it; Taylor's *Holy Living and Dying;* and La Ferte's *Instructions for Country Dances.*

But in Queen Anne's time the passion of women for books was equalled and perhaps surpassed by their passion for china. Addison has left on record that there were no inclinations in women which more surprised him than their passions for chalk and china. The taste for chalk wore out in time, but the taste for china lasted for life. An old lady of fourscore might be seen as busy in cleaning what he calls an Indian mandarin as her grand-daughter in dressing a doll. He remembered when there were few china vessels to be seen that held more than a dish of coffee; but in his lifetime they had grown to such a size that many of them could hold half a hogshead. The fashion of the tea-cup, too, within his memory had greatly altered and had run through a wonderful variety of colour, shape, and size. He was informed by his lady friends that the common way of procuring china was by exchanging old suits of clothes for the brittle ware; he himself had known an old petticoat thus metamorphosed into a punch-bowl, and a pair of breeches into a teapot. Against the extravagance into which the taste for china sometimes hurried its votaries,

Addison urged his female readers to remember the vast amount of wrath and sorrow which the breaking of china daily stirred up in the hearts of his dear countrywomen, and he implored them seriously to consider, first, that all china is of a weak and transitory nature; secondly, that the fashion of it is changeable; and thirdly, that it is of no use. He suggested that if women took delight in heaping up piles of earthen platters, brown jugs, and the like useful products of British potteries, there would be some sense in it; for these might be ranged in as fine figures and disposed of in as beautiful pieces of furniture. But on second thoughts he perceived that there was an insuperable objection to the proposal, namely, that the British ware might be of some use, since the dishes might be taken down from the shelf and even eaten and drunk out of; besides which they were intolerably cheap and most shamefully durable and lasting. Under these circumstances it was vain to think of English ware competing with china in the favour of the ladies.

The taste for snuff-taking would seem to have been equally diffused among both sexes in the age of Queen Anne. Men and women alike carried snuffboxes adorned with pictures on the lids. At the time when the infamous impostor and perjured scoundrel, Titus Oates, was in all his glory, posing as an idol of fashionable ladies, a saviour of the State, and a pillar of the Protestant faith, an acquaintance of Will Honeycomb's exhibited a portrait of the so-called doctor on the lid of her snuff-box. And as a singular proof of the extent to which the habit of snuff-taking was carried in the other sex, it may be mentioned that when the head of a beau was dissected after death, the cavities of the skull, which in ordinary people are filled with brains, were discovered to be stuffed with Spanish snuff. Yet in outward shape and appearance the beau in his lifetime had not differed perceptibly from other men; he ate and drank like other people, dressed well, talked loud, laughed frequently, and on several occasions acquitted himself tolerably at a ball; some ladies even took him for a wit. He was cut off in the flower of his age by the blow of a paring-shovel, having been surprised by an eminent citizen as he was tendering some civilities to his wife.

Besides their snuff-boxes, in these days ladies carried fans, and appear to have made great use of them as weapons of offence in their attacks on the male sex. A paper in the **Spectator** contains an account of an academy instituted for the training and discipline of young women in the exercise of the fan. The head of the academy, who contributed the paper, assured his readers that the course of training was not nearly so severe and exacting as might naturally be supposed: a woman of a tolerable genius, who applied her mind to it diligently for only six months, might be able to handle her fan as gracefully as another who had devoted years to the study. Even with regard to the masterpiece of the art, which consisted in fluttering the fan, he said that if a lady did not misspend her time she might make herself mistress of it in three months; while as to the comparatively simple accomplishment of grounding a fan, which only consisted in tossing a fan with an air on a table, he positively affirmed that it might be learned in two days' time as well as in a twelvemonth.

To recur for a moment to the gentleman who perished prematurely by the blow of a paring-shovel, it seems probable that this unfortunate accident prevented him from having the pleasure, or at all events the satisfaction, of meeting the lady's husband in the fields at the back of Montague House, to which gentlemen frequently retired for the settlement of any differences which might have arisen between them, the rural seclusion of the spot being eminently favourable to the calm consideration of the points in dispute. Even on their way to the fields some of the disputants thought better of it and came to an amicable arrangement to be both of them arrested by the police, which saved a needless expenditure of gunpowder and a possible effusion of blood. But it was not always so, nor did the meetings always take place in the fields behind Montague House. On the morning of November 15, 1712, while the *Spectator* was being read at many breakfast tables in London, Lord Mohun fought the Duke of Hamilton in Hyde Park. Lord Mohun was killed on the spot, and the duke mortally wounded. They tried to help him to the cake-house by the ring, in the park, but he died on the grass before he could reach the house.

To abate the frequency of duelling Addison had proposed in the *Tatler* to institute a Court of Honour for the peaceable settlement of disputes which otherwise might have been put to the arbitrament of the sword or the pistol. Indeed, if we may trust the reports of its proceedings which appeared in the *Tatler,* the Court was actually established with Isaac Bickerstaff for its president; and it did adjudicate on not a few nice points of honour. One or two extracts from the journals of the Court may serve to illustrate the nature of the questions which were submitted to its jurisdiction. The jury was composed of twelve gentlemen of the Horse Guards, who unanimously chose Mr. Alexander Truncheon, their right-hand man in the troop, to be their foreman. On being impanelled, the jury drew their swords like one man and saluted the bench with great respect. The first case that came up for trial was an indictment brought by the Honourable Mr. Thomas Gules, of Gule Hall, in the county of Salop, against Peter Plumb, of London, Merchant. The indictment showed forth that, in a conversation between the two in the public street, Plumb had put on his hat two seconds before the Honourable Mr. Thomas Gules, so that for that space of time the Honourable Mr. Thomas Gules had stood bareheaded, while Plumb was covered. The evidence being very full and clear, the jury, without going out of court, declared their opinion unanimously by the voice of their foreman, that the prosecutor was bound in honour to make the sun shine through the criminal, or, as they afterwards explained themselves, to whip him through the lungs. The president, however, judged that the proposed penalty was excessive, and requested the jury to reconsider their verdict. They therefore retired and after an hour's consultation gave as their opinion that in consideration that this was Plumb's first offence he might be allowed to escape with his life and to suffer nothing worse than the slitting of his nose and the cutting off of both his ears. Even in this mitigated form the verdict appeared to the president too severe, and he sentenced the criminal to lose his hat, the instrument of his crime, and ever thereafter to ride in a coach in the streets, leaving the footway open and undisturbed for his betters.

The next case that came up was a difference between a Welshman and a peddling Jew named Dathan. They were indicted by the keeper of an alehouse in Westminster for breaking the peace and two earthen mugs in a dispute about the antiquity of their respective families, to the great detriment of the house and the disturbance of the whole neighbourhood. Dathan said for himself that he was provoked to it by the Welshman, who pretended that the Welsh were an ancienter people than the Jews, "Whereas", said he, "I can show by this genealogy in my hand that I am the son of Mesheck, that was the son of Naboth, that was the son of Shalem, that was the son of—." But before he could climb up his genealogical tree half-way to Adam he was interrupted by the Welshman, who told him that "he could produce shennalogy as well as himself; for that he was John ap Rice, ap Shenkin, ap Shones". The jury did not waste very much of their valuable time over this petty dispute, but gave it as their verdict, that as neither of the disputants wore a sword, they had no right to quarrel on a point of honour; and that both of them should be tossed in the same blanket, and there settle the antiquity of their respective families between themselves as best they could. The president confirmed the verdict. (pp. 174-84)

Sir James George Frazer, "London Life in the Time of Addison," in his The Gorgon's Head and Other Literary Pieces, *Macmillan and Co., Limited, 1927, pp. 148-99.*

C. S. Lewis (essay date 1945)

[*Lewis is considered one of the foremost Christian and mythopoeic authors of the twentieth century. Indebted principally to George MacDonald, G. K. Chesterton, Charles Williams, and the writers of ancient Norse myths, he is regarded as a formidable logician and Christian polemicist, a perceptive literary critic, and—most highly—as a writer of fantasy literature. Lewis also held instructoral posts at Oxford and Cambridge, where he was an acknowledged authority on medieval and Renaissance literature. A traditionalist in his approach to life and art, he opposed the modern movement in literary criticism toward biographical and psychological interpretation. In place of this, Lewis practiced and propounded a theory of criticism that stresses the importance of the author's intent, rather than the reader's presuppositions and prejudices. In the following excerpt from a work originally published in 1945, he evaluates Addison's moral stance as compared with that of the Tory writers of the eighteenth century and credits him with being the originator of numerous "mental habits" that persisted through the Victorian era.*]

'I have always', said Addison, 'preferred Chearfulness to Mirth. The latter I consider as an Act, the former as an Habit of the Mind' [*Spectator* 381]; or again, 'Though I am always serious, I do not know what it is to be melancholy' [*Spectator* 26]. These sentences pretty well give us the measure, if not of the man, yet of the work; just as the limpidity of their style, conveying a distinction of almost a scholastic precision in such manner that even a 'tea-table' could not fail to understand it, gives us the measure of his talent. They serve also to mark the most profound difference between the Whig essayist and his two great Tory contemporaries.

Swift and Pope were by no means always serious and they knew very well what it was to be melancholy. One would have found more mirth in their conversation than in Addison's: not only epigram and repartee, but frolic and extravaganza—even buffoonery. It is true that they regarded satire as a 'sacred weapon', but we must not so concentrate on that idea as to forget the sheer *vis comica* which brightens so much of their work. Swift's 'favourite maxim was *vive la bagatelle*'. *Gulliver* and the *Dunciad* and the whole myth of Scriblerus have missed their point if they do not sometimes make us 'laugh and shake in Rabelais' easy chair'. Even their love of filth is, in my opinion, much better understood by schoolboys than by psychoanalysts: if there is something sinister in it, there is also an element of high-spirited rowdiness. Addison has a sense of humour; the Tories have, in addition, a sense of fun. But they have no 'habit' of cheerfulness. Rage, exasperation, and something like despair are never far away. It is to this that they owe their sublimity—for Pope, no less than Swift, can be sublime. We suspect that the picture he paints of himself is historically false—

> Yes, I am proud; I must be proud to see
> Men not afraid of God, afraid of me.

But it is a sublime poetical image. The picture of surly, contemptuous virtue had often been attempted before—in Chapman's Bussy and Clermont, in Dryden's Almanzor, in Wycherley's Manly, even in the Christ of *Paradise Regained;* but I would give Pope the palm, for in Milton the discrepancy between the known historical character of his Hero and the 'Senecal man' he has painted is more shocking than that between the real and the imagined Pope. There is nothing of so high a reach in Addison. The grandeur of 'cynical asperity' is a flower that grows only in a tropical climate, and in passing to Addison's world we pass to a world where such things are impossible. Surly virtue is not cheerful nor equable: in the long run it is not, perhaps, perfectly consistent with good sense.

This contrast between Addison and the Tories comes out with special clarity in their treatment of enemies. For the Tories, every enemy—whether it be the Duchess of Marlborough or only a Shakespearian editor found guilty of some real English scholarship—becomes a grotesque. All who have, in whatever fashion, incurred their ill will are knaves, scarecrows, whores, bugs, toads, bedlamites, yahoos; Addison himself a smooth Mephistopheles. It is good fun, but it is certainly not good sense; we laugh, and disbelieve. Now mark Addison's procedure. The strength of the Tory party is the smaller country gentry with their Jacobite leanings and their opposition to the moneyed interest. All the material for savage satire is there. Addison might have anticipated Squire Western (as he did later in the *Freeholder*) and painted merely the block-headed, fox-hunting sot, the tyrant of his family and his village. Instead, with the help of Steele he invents Sir Roger de Coverley. The measure of his success is that we can now

think of Sir Roger for a long time without remembering his Toryism; when we do remember it, it is only as a lovable whimsy.

> In all our Journey from *London* to his House we did not so much as bait at a Whig Inn . . . This often betrayed us into hard Beds and bad Cheer; for we were not so inquisitive about the Inn as the Inn-keeper; and provided our Landlord's Principles were sound, did not take any Notice of the Staleness of his Provisions [*Spectator* 126].

As a natural consequence, Mr Spectator soon 'dreaded entering into an House of any one that Sir Roger had applauded for an honest Man'. It is so beautifully done that we do not notice it. The enemy, far from being vilified, is being turned into a dear old man. The thought that he could ever be dangerous has been erased from our minds; but so also the thought that anything he said could ever be taken seriously. We all love Sir Roger; but of course we do not really attend to him as we do—well, to Sir Andrew Freeport. All through the century which Addison ushered in, England was going to attend more and more seriously to the Freeports, and the de Coverleys were to be more and more effectually silenced. The figure of the dear old squire dominates—possibly, on some views, corrupts—the national imagination to the present day. This is indeed to 'make a man die sweetly'. That element in English society which stood against all that Addison's party was bringing in is henceforth seen through a mist of smiling tenderness—as an archaism, a lovely absurdity. What we might have been urged to attack as a fortress we are tricked into admiring as a ruin.

When I say 'tricked' I am not implying that Steele and Addison calculated the whole effect of their creation just as I have set it down. The actual upshot of their work is obvious; their conscious intentions are another matter. I am inclined to think that Addison really loved Sir Roger—with that 'superior love' which, in England, the victorious party so easily accords to the remnants of a vanishing order. Addison is not a simple man; he is, in the older sense of the word, 'sly'. I do not believe for one moment that he was the fiendlike Atticus; but one sees how inevitably he must have appeared so to the losers. He is so cool, so infuriatingly sensible, and yet he effects more than they. A satiric portrait by Pope or Swift is like a thunderclap; the Addisonian method is more like the slow operations of ordinary nature, loosening stones, blunting outlines, modifying a whole landscape with 'silent overgrowings' so that the change can never quite be reversed again. Whatever his intentions, his reasonableness and amiability (both cheerful 'habits' of the mind) are stronger in the end than the Tory spleen. To rail is the sad privilege of the loser.

I have used the word 'amiability'. Should we go further and say 'charity'? I feel that this Christian word, with its doctrinal implications, would be a little out of place when we are speaking of Addison's essays. About the man, as distinct from the work, I will not speculate. Let us hope that he practised this theological virtue. The story that he summoned Lord Warwick to his deathbed *to see how a Christian can die* is ambiguous; it can be taken either as evidence of his Christianity or as a very brimstone proof of the reverse. I give no vote: my concern is with books. And the essays do not invite criticism in terms of any very definite theology. They are everywhere 'pious'. Rational Piety, together with Polite Letters and Simplicity, is one of the hall-marks of the age which Addison was partly interpreting but partly also bringing into existence. And Rational Piety is by its very nature not very doctrinal. This is one of the many ways in which Addison is historically momentous. He ushers in that period—it is just now drawing to a close—in which it is possible to talk of 'piety' or (later) 'religion' almost in the abstract; in which the contrast is no longer between Christian and Pagan, the elect and the world, orthodox and heretic, but between 'religious' and 'irreligious'. The transition cannot be quite defined: absence of doctrine would have to become itself doctrinal for that to be possible. It is a change of atmosphere, which every reader of sensibility will feel if he passes suddenly from the literature of any earlier period to that of the eighteenth century. Hard rocks of Calvinism show up amidst the seemingly innocuous surface of an *Arcadia* or a *Faerie Queene;* Shakespearian comedy reckons on an audience who will at once see the point of jokes about the controversy on Works and Faith. Here also, no doubt, it is difficult to bring Addison to a point. Perhaps the most illuminating passage is the essay on **"Sir Roger at Church",** and specially the quotation from Pythagoras prefixed to it—'Honour first the immortal gods according to the established mode.' That is the very note of Rational Piety. A sensible man goes with his society, according to local and ancestral usage. And he does so with complete sincerity. Clean clothes and the sound of bells on Sunday morning do really throw him into a mood of sober benevolence, not 'clouded by enthusiasm' but inviting his thoughts to approach the mystery of things. (pp. 154-58)

[Addison's] famous defence of 'Chevy Chase' is sometimes taken to show a 'romantic' side in him, but that, I think, is not the best way of considering it. The word 'romantic' is always ambiguous. The paper on 'Chevy Chase' is to be taken in its context. [Lewis's editor adds in a footnote: ' "Chevy Chase" is discussed in *Spectator* 70 and 74.'] It follows a discussion on False Wit. False Wit is taken up by poets who lack the 'Strength of Genius' which gives 'majestick Simplicity to Nature' and who are therefore forced 'to hunt after foreign Ornaments' [*Spectator* 62]. These writers are to poetry what the Goths were to architecture. Ovid is the type of such 'Gothick' poets, and 'the Taste of most of our *English* Poets, as well as Readers, is extremely *Gothick* '. One mark of true poetry is that it 'pleases all Kinds of Palates', whereas the Gothic manner pleases 'only such as have formed to themselves a wrong artificial Taste upon little fanciful Authors' [*Spectator* 70]. It is, therefore, to be expected that common songs or ballads which are 'the Delight of the common People' should be 'Paintings of Nature'. It is after this preamble that Addison proceeds to examine 'Chevy Chase'—according to the rules of Le Bossu—and pronounces in its favour.

No more classical piece of criticism exists. In it Addison touches hands with Scaliger on the one side and Matthew Arnold on the other. What complicates it is, of course, his

peculiar use of the word 'Gothick'. Addison must have known perfectly well that the ballad is just the sort of thing to which his contemporaries would spontaneously have applied that word, and that Ovid and Cowley are not. Very well, then; he will prove that it is the ballad which really follows Nature and that the true Goths are the authors whom the Town in fact prefers. In other words he is calling the neo-classical bluff. It is as if he said, 'You all profess to like a great subject, a good moral, unity of action, and truth to Nature. Well, here they all are in the ballad which you despise; and yonder, in the Cowley which you really enjoy, they are not.' One cannot be certain here, as one could not be certain about the invention of Sir Roger, whether Addison is being 'sly' or really innocent. One sees again what is behind the image of Atticus. The man who writes thus will certainly appear 'sly' to his opponents. But is he consciously setting a trap, or is he merely following the truth as he sees it in all simplicity? Perhaps it does not much matter, for the trap is inherent in the facts, and works whether Addison meant to set it or no; in the sense that if the *nominal* standards of Augustan criticism are ever taken seriously they must work out in favour of the ballads (and much medieval literature) and against most of the poetry the Augustans themselves produced. In other words, if we insist on calling an appreciation of ballads 'romantic', then we must say that Addison becomes a romantic precisely because he is a *real* classic, and that every real classic must infallibly do the same. It is inconceivable that Aristotle and Horace, had they known them, should not have put the *Chanson de Roland* above the *Davideis.* Antiquity and the Middle Ages are not divided from each other by any such chasm as divides both from the Renaissance.

But it is better not to use the word 'romantic' in this context at all. What Addison really shows by his appreciation of the Ballad is his open-mindedness, his readiness to recognize excellence wherever he finds it, whether in those periods which Renaissance Humanism had elected to call 'classical' or in those far longer extents of time which it ignored. The obscurantism of the Humanists is still not fully recognised. Learning to them meant the knowledge and imitation of a few rather arbitrarily selected Latin authors and some even fewer Greek authors. They despised metaphysics and natural science; and they despised all the past outside the favoured periods. They were dominated by a narrowly ethical purpose. *Referenda ad mores omnia,* said Vives; and he thought it fortunate that the Attic dialect contained nearly all the Greek worth reading—*reliquis utuntur auctores carminum quos non tanti est intelligi.* Their philistine attitude to metaphysics is prettily carried off in modern histories by phrases about 'brushing away scholastic cobwebs', but the Humanist attack is really on metaphysics itself. In Erasmus, in Rabelais, in the *Utopia* one recognizes the very accent of the angry *belle-lettrist* railing, as he rails in all ages, at 'jargon' and 'straw-splitting'. On this side Pope and Swift are true inheritors of the Humanist tradition. It is easy, of course, to say that Laputa is an attack not on science but on the aberrations of science. I am not convinced. The learning of the Brobdingnagians and the Horses is ruthlessly limited. Nothing that cannot plead the clearest immediate utility—nothing that cannot make two blades of grass grow where one grew before—wins any approval from Swift. Bentley is not forgiven for knowing more Greek than Temple, nor Theobald for knowing more English than Pope. Most of the history of Europe is a mere wilderness, not worth visiting, in which 'the *Monks* finish'd what the *Goths* begun'. The terror expressed at the end of the *Dunciad* is not wholly terror at the approach of ignorance: it is also terror lest the compact little fortress of Humanism should be destroyed, and new knowledge is one of the enemies. Whatever is not immediately intelligible to a man versed in the Latin and French classics appears to them to be charlatanism or barbarity. The number of things they do not want to hear about is enormous.

But Addison wants to hear about everything. He is quite as good a classical scholar as the Tories but he does not live in the Humanist prison. He notes with satisfaction 'that curiosity is one of the strongest and most lasting Appetites implanted in us, and that Admiration is one of our most pleasing Passions' [*Spectator* 237]. He delights to introduce his readers to the new philosophy of Mr Locke and to explain by it, with aid from Malebranche, 'a famous Passage in the *Alcoran*' [*Spectator* 94]. He remembers with pleasure how 'Mr. *Boyle,* speaking of a certain Mineral, tells us, That a Man may consume his whole Life in the Study of it, without arriving at the Knowledge of all its Qualities'. He gazes on the sea ('the Heavings of this prodigious Bulk of Waters') with 'a very pleasing Astonishment' [*Spectator* 489]. Astronomy, revealing the immensities of space, entertains him with sublime meditations, and his reading, he tells us, 'has very much lain among Books of natural History' [*Spectator* 120]. Mysteries attract him. He loves to lose himself in an *o altitudo* whether on the marvels of animal instinct or on those of the powers enjoyed by the soul in dreams—on which he quotes Browne himself. He lives habitually in a world of horizons and possibilities which Pope touched, I think, only in the *Essay on Man,* and Swift hardly touches at all. It is a cool, quiet world after that of the Tories—say, a water-colour world, but there is more room in it. On those things which it illuminates at all, the wit of Swift and Pope casts a sharper and (in a sense) more beautiful light; but what huge regions of reality appear to them, as Addison says that life itself appears to ignorance and folly, a 'Prospect of naked Hills and Plains which produce nothing either profitable or ornamental'! [*Spectator* 94].

This open-mindedness is not particularly 'romantic', though without it we should have had no Wartons, no Ritson, no Percy, and perhaps no Scott; for the medievalism of the eighteenth century, whatever else it may be, is a mighty defeat of sheer ignorance. But Addison is much more closely connected with the Romantic Movement in quite a different way. He stands at the very turning-point in the history of a certain mode of feeling.

I think that perhaps the best piece of criticism Raleigh ever wrote is in the fourth chapter of his *Wordsworth,* where he sets Claudio's shuddering speech ('To be imprisoned in the viewless winds') beside Wordsworth's longing to retain a body 'endued with all the nice regards of flesh and blood' and yet surrender it to the elements 'As if it were a spirit'. He points out, quite justly, that what is Hell to Claudio is almost Heaven to Wordsworth. Between the two passages a profound change in human sentiment has taken place. Briefly put—for the story has often been told before—it is the change from an age when men frankly hated and feared all those things in Nature which are neither sensuously pleasing, useful, safe, symmetrical, or gaily coloured, to an age when men love and actually seek out mountains, waste places, dark forests, cataracts, and storm-beaten coasts. What was once the ugly has become a department (even the major department) of the beautiful. The first conflict between the old and the new taste received striking expression when Addison was already nine years old, in Thomas Burnet's *Telluris Theoria Sacra.* Burnet cannot quite conceal a certain joy in the awfulness of the Alps, but his very argument depends on the conception that they are deformities—*longaeva illa, tristia et squalentia corpora.* Not that they are the only offence. In the face of this Earth as a whole we find *multa sunt superflua, multa inelegantia:* such beauty *(ornamentum)* as it possesses comes chiefly *cultu et habitatione hominum.*

The position of Addison in this story is very interesting. He divides the sources of imaginative pleasure into three classes—the Great, the Uncommon, and the Beautiful. As specimens of the Great he mentions 'an open Champian Country, a vast uncultivated Desart, of huge Heaps of Mountains, high Rocks and Precipices, or a wide Expanse of Waters'—all of which produce 'a delightful Stilness and Amazement in the Soul'. To a later writer many of these things would have seemed beautiful; to an earlier one they would have seemed simply unpleasant. Addison does not find beauty in them, but he includes them among the sources of pleasure. His category of the Great, clearly distinguished from the Beautiful, exists precisely to make room for them. A similar distinction was, of course, the basis of Burke's treatise on 'The Sublime and Beautiful', and dominated the aesthetic thought of the century. Whether it was not much more sensible than the modern practice of bundling Alps and roses together into the single category of Beauty, I do not here inquire. The interesting thing is that Addison stands exactly at the turn of the tide.

Equally important for the historian of taste is *Spectator,* No. 160, where he contrasts the original 'genius' (which tends to be 'nobly wild and extravagant') and the *Bel Esprit* 'refined by Conversation, Reflection, and the Reading of the most polite Authors'. The taste for 'noble extravagance' is not itself a novelty, for audacities in art and graces that overleap the rules are praised by Dryden, Boileau, and Pope. What is interesting is Addison's belief that even the greatest genius is 'broken' by the rules and in becoming learned 'falls unavoidably into Imitation'. This pessimistic view of culture as something naturally opposed to genius received, no doubt, its extreme expression in Macaulay's essay on Milton; but I think it had also a great deal to do with that crop of forgeries which the eighteenth century produced. If sublime genius lies all in the past, before civilization began, we naturally look for it in the past. We long to recover the work of those sublime prehistoric bards and druids who *must* have existed. But their work is not to be found; and the surviving medieval literature conspicuously lacks the sublimity and mysteriousness we desire. In the end one begins *inventing* what the 'bards', 'druids', and 'minstrels' ought to have written. Ossian, Rowley, and *Otranto* are wish-fulfilments. It is always to be remembered that Macpherson had written original epics about prehistoric Scotland before he invented Ossian. By a tragic chance he and Chatterton discovered that their work was marketable, and so make-believe turned into fraud. But there was a sincere impulse behind it: they were seeking in the past that great romantic poetry which really lay in the future, and from intense imagination of what it must be like if only they could find it they slipped into making it themselves.

So far I have been trying to obey Arnold's precept—to get myself out of the way and let humanity decide. I have not attempted to assess the value of Addison's work, having wished rather to bring out its immense potency. He appears to be (as far as any individual can be) the source of a quite astonishing number of mental habits which were still prevalent when men now living were born. Almost everything which my own generation ignorantly called Victorian seems to have been expressed by Addison. It is all there in the *Spectator*—the vague religious sensibility, the insistence on what came later to be called Good Form, the playful condescension towards women, the untroubled belief in the beneficence of commerce, the comfortable sense of security which, far from excluding, perhaps renders possible the romantic relish for wildness and solitude. If he is not at present the most hated of our writers, that can only be because he is so little read. Everything the moderns detest, all that they call *smugness, complacency,* and *bourgeois ideology,* is brought together in his work and given its most perfect expression.

And certainly, if it were at all times true that the Good is the enemy of the Best, it would be hard to defend Addison. His Rational Piety, his smiling indulgence to 'the fair sex', his small idealisms about trade, certainly fall short of actual Christianity, and plain justice to women, and true political wisdom. They may even be obstacles to them; palliatives and anodynes that prolong the disease. In some moods I cannot help seeing Addison as one who, at every point, 'sings charms to ills that ask the knife'. I believe he could defend himself. He is not attempting to write sermons or philosophy, only essays; and he certainly could not foresee what the search for markets would finally make of international trade. These hostile criticisms, made on the basis of our modern experience when all issues have become sharper, cannot really be maintained. All we can justly say is that his essays are rather small beer; there is no iron in them as in Johnson; they do not stir the depths.

And yet, if I were to live in a man's house for a whole twelve-month, I think I should be more curious about the quality of his small beer than about that of his wine; more curious about his bread and butter and beef than about either. Writers like Addison who stand on the common ground of daily life and deal only with middle things are unduly depreciated today. Pascal says somewhere that the cardinal error of Stoicism was to suppose that we can do always what we do sometimes. No one lives always on the stretch. Hence one of the most pertinent questions to be asked about any man is what he falls back on. The important thing about Malory's world, for example, is that when you fall back from the quest of the Grail you fall back into the middle world of Arthur's court: not plumb down into the level of King Mark. The important thing about many fierce idealists in our own day is that when the political meeting or the literary movement can be endured no longer they fall plumb down to the cinema and the dance band. I fully admit that when Pope and Swift are on the heights they have a strength and splendour which makes everything in Addison look pale; but what an abyss of hatred and bigotry and even silliness receives them when they slip from the heights! The Addisonian world is not one to live in at all times, but it is a good one to fall back into when the day's work is over and a man's feet on the fender and his pipe in his mouth. Good sense is no substitute for Reason; but as a rest from Reason it has distinct advantages over Jargon. I do not think Addison's popularity is likely to return; but something to fill the same place in life will always be needed—some tranquil middle ground of quiet sentiments and pleasing melancholies and gentle humour to come in between our restless idealisms and our equally restless dissipations. Do we not after all detect in the charge of *smugness* and *complacency* the note of envy? Addison is, above all else, comfortable. He is not on that account to be condemned. He is an admirable cure for the fidgets. (pp. 161-68)

C. S. Lewis, "Addison," in his Selected Literary Essays, *edited by Walter Hooper, Cambridge at the University Press, 1969, pp. 154-68.*

Clarence D. Thorpe   (essay date 1951)

[*In the following excerpt, Thorpe describes Addison's legacy as a literary critic, noting that his emphasis on individual taste rather than established principles presages the aesthetics of the Romantic period.*]

One of the favorite clichés of literary historians is that Addison was peculiarly representative of his age. But like most clichés this one may be misleading. For though Addison did belong to his age, he did not belong to it, at least as a critic, in the way that Pope did. Pope's *Essay on Criticism* belongs to the age and to the past; Addison's **"Essay on the Imagination"** belongs to the age and to the future. Pope is performing the office in his essay of a near-perfect synthesizer, giving us in precept and example an epitome of English neo-classicism. But the Augustan age was not a static age; it was a period not only of neat summation and integration, but also of transition and forward movement; it helped to initiate and to transform and transmit the new as well as to take on to itself and make use of the old. Unlike Pope, Addison's peculiar service to aesthetics and criticism was not to utilize the old—though he did some of that, too—but to accept and adapt and transmit the new, and in such a way and to such a degree that he became thereby one of the chief constructive forces in the literary theory of the century that followed. There was a new as well as an old criticism in the Augustan period, just as there is a new and an old criticism today—and of the new critics Addison was the outstanding and distinctive figure.

By the "new criticism" I have in mind that movement in English aesthetic theory, extending roughly from Hobbes to Alison and preparing the way for Wordsworth and Coleridge, which sought means of explaining and evaluating literature on psychological and pragmatic rather than on traditional, formalistic grounds. The key terms of this criticism were Imagination, Taste, Original Genius, Beauty, Sublimity, Novelty, Association of Ideas, Nature. The questions that most concerned it, especially after about 1730, were not those having to do with conformity to the theory and practice of the ancients, with adherence to certain formal patterns or particular stylistic modes, or with evidence of learning and judgment; they were more likely to be, "Does this work please?" "If so, why and how does it please?" "What are the special sources, what are the particular qualities of the pleasure it gives?" "Is it the work of a man of native genius and imagination?"

Most of the new critics still believed in rules or principles; but the principles in which they were interested were those rooted in natural law—the great law of nature. And by nature they came to mean more and more not universal cosmic nature and universal human nature formed in the image of "natural law"—that is, idealized human nature reflecting the inner order and harmony of the universal frame of things—but common human nature as it manifests itself in the passions, motives, and actions of individual men and women. They, therefore, put their main trust not in reason and learning but in natural response, in instinct, emotion, imagination, and original genius.

The theoretical critics of the period were, almost to a man, devotees of the new sensational psychology. The laws they had in mind were psychological laws; and their methods of ascertaining these laws were the empirical ones of appeal to common experience and of observation of the ways of the mind, especially as related to imaginative creation and to response to nature and art. Introspection became increasingly the chief instrument of aesthetic speculation of the time.

Corollary to intensified interest in the ways of the mind was a shift in emphasis in practical criticism from action to character. Likewise, corollary was a shift of attention from mechanical structure to design and to the successive events of a narrative as evidence of the skill with which the author had introduced event and speech to lead to climactic moments and to produce desired effects upon the mind of the observer. Convincing portrayal of individualized characters moved by dominant passions became more important than adherence to decorum in the creation of rigid types. Appeal to the imagination by way of the softer emotions of beauty and novelty and of the great and stirring passion of sublimity, the satisfaction of taste rather than of the reason, rapidly gained ground as the primary aim of the creative artist—though the satisfaction of a "rational" taste was usually considered most desirable.

Addison's role in getting the new criticism going has been described in enthusiastic terms. J. G. Robertson, for example, sees Addison as an originator, who "laid the foundation of the whole romantic aesthetics in England," and who became a significant factor in the "building up of a new aesthetic doctrine in both France and Germany" [*The Genesis of the Romantic Theory in England,* 1923]. W. Basil Worsfold [In his *Principles of Criticism,* 1923] makes similar claims. Professor E. F. Carritt regards Addison as a primary influence on Kant, whose aesthetic theory, he asserts, was little more than a redaction of "distinctions and oppositions current in English for the preceding eighty years." Of Kant's ideas of sublimity and related theories Carritt goes so far as to say, "All is Addison's except the style" ["Effects in England of Kant's Philosophy," *The Monist,* XXXV (1925)]. Through his followers and Kant, Carritt also argues, Addison not only foreshadowed Wordsworth and Coleridge in their most distinctive theories—those of imagination and sublimity—but did much to prepare the way for their practice. Carritt is himself so convinced of the validity of these conclusions and of the general importance of Addison as a critic that he is ready to lay down the proposition that "Addison may justly be thought the father of modern critical theory." Addison, he asserts, owed little to his English predecessors, "but to him the succeeding critics of his century owed almost everything" ["Addison, Kant and Coleridge," *Essays and Studies of the English Association,* XXII (1936)].

Other scholars have recognized Addison's importance in more limited departments. Samuel Monk has shown how large a part he played in giving impetus to the idea of sublimity in the eighteenth century; Edward Niles Hooker has described his role in the development of taste; and Martin Kallich, in his thesis and articles, has accorded him the honor of writing the first systematic treatise on aesthetics in England and of doing much to relate the association of ideas to the imagination.

There is truth in these evaluations, and yet some of them stand in need of qualification. Accuracy requires that we think of the "new criticism" not as having sprung full-blown from the head of one man but rather as having evolved over a long period of time and through the efforts of many important thinkers. In considering this evolution we must not forget such predecessors of Addison as Hobbes, with his seminal speculations on the fancy (imagination), on aesthetic effects, and on the association of ideas, or Dryden, who contributed so much in the way of lively, forward-looking discussion of basic critical problems that it might be argued to some purpose that there was little in Addison's theory that had not been at least intimated in his great essays. We cannot then accept without question Carritt's view that Addison owed little or nothing to his predecessors or the implications of Robertson and Worsfold to the effect that he was the one begetter of a new aesthetics in England.

Nor can Carritt's assertion that succeeding critics of the century owed "almost everything" to Addison quite be taken without reservation. Eighteenth-century criticism is a "mingled skein." Addison contributed much to the final dominant pattern, but others contributed, too, and in ways that went beyond, though rarely if ever entirely outside of Addison's formulation. It will not do, therefore, to minimize the work of the long line of English writers who, after Addison, made notable additions to the new psychological aesthetics: of Burke, who materially broadened and modified concepts of sublimity and taste; of Hume, who developed, most importantly, the principle of association of ideas in relation to the imagination; of Akenside, Young, Tucker, and Duff, of Gerard, Kames, and Blair, Hartley, Beattie, and Alison, who supplied, if not always new ideas, at least ever new variations on the themes of taste, original genius, beauty, sublimity, novelty, association of ideas, and imagination. All of these, neither neoclassic nor yet Romantic critics, but new critics of the transition between the two, were clearing the ground, though sometimes indirectly, for Coleridge and Wordsworth, and were moving, in one way or another, in their general direction.

Addison's place in this evolutionary development need not be overrated to give him ample credit. For, though he was not the sole originator of the new criticism, since most of the separate ingredients of idea and method had already been known and employed by others, it was he who put them together in the first effective atomiclike bombshell of systematic formulation. Faced with a situation where, in constant attempts to find ways to square a native relish of the great English poets with a formalistic aesthetic which had no place for them, compromise had become the rule in English critical practice, Addison cut the Gordian knot by boldly proposing a theory based on psychological rather than on formalistic, rhetorical principle, of such nature and scope as to account for Shakespeare and Spenser as well as for Homer and Sophocles—to account in a general way, indeed, for all great art.

The characteristic fact about Addison as a critic was his zeal for excellence. This was the motivating force in his main critical ventures from the early comment on the *Georgics* to the end. He was interested in what was fine. He thought that the duty of the critic was to discover and explain the specific "distinguishing perfections" of a writer. When he found excellence he was courageous enough to say so and fair enough to offer his reasons. His defense of the old ballads and his championship of true versus false wit are illustrative; also, most importantly, are his papers on *Paradise Lost.* The last twelve of these papers represent a deliberate attempt to isolate for inspection and admiration the "beauties of the several books of this great poem." And Addison clearly shows in his fifth and sixth essays that in doing this he was consciously defying the current fashion of satiric and fault-finding criticism. Addison's quest was for excellence; all that fault-finding could do was to obscure excellence. So his last twelve papers stood as a superb example of the positive method in criticism, for any to follow who would; and as the century went on there were many who chose to follow.

The papers on the imagination likewise represent a quest for excellence, this time especially for its causes and effects. Interestingly enough, the last paragraph of *Spectator* 409, which is, in effect, a prospectus of the theory that is to follow—laying down the issues at stake, announcing the principle of Taste as intrinsic in judgments of literary value, and stating with fair precision Addison's intentions in the forthcoming essay—would suggest that this is to be a part of a long-range, carefully considered campaign, perhaps the final climactic move in this campaign, to give England a better aesthetic and criticism. As a corrective to the English taste for artificial style, Addison tells us, he has written an **"Essay on Wit"** pointing out those false kinds which have been too much admired and showing "wherein the Nature of true Wit consists." Later he has given, in his criticism of the ballads, "an Instance of the great Force which lyes in a natural Simplicity of Thought to affect the Mind of the Reader"; and he has also "examined the Works of the greatest Poet which our Nation or perhaps any other has produced and particularized most of those rational and manly Beauties which give a Value to that Divine Work." Now he is about to enter "upon an Essay *on the Pleasures of the Imagination,* which . . . will perhaps suggest to the Reader what it is that gives a Beauty to many passages of the finest Writers both in Prose and Verse."

Whether they were in fact a part of such a long-range plan as Addison's words imply, it is certain that the papers on the Imagination were not written on the spur of the moment. In their original form they were not written as papers at all, but as a continuous essay, some scholars believe as early as Addison's Oxford days. In *The Spectator* this essay is to appear in much revised, greatly enlarged form, as a professedly deliberate attempt to formulate a new and improved method of dealing with the basic literary problem of excellence versus nonexcellence.

The Sheldonian Latin Oration of 1693 reveals not only that Addison had the right temper of mind but that he was, as early as his college days, in possession of essential equipment for revised thought on aesthetic questions: namely, a spirit receptive to change and a knowledge of and belief in the basic modes and principles of the psychological philosophy of Descartes, Hobbes, and Locke.

This oration exalts the new philosophy at the expense of ancient and scholastic thought. Descartes is played up and Aristotle is played down. The moderns have brought on the stage a new method of philosophizing through which the whole mass of the universe has been so clearly traced "as to leave no occult matter untouched." The net result is emancipation from outworn shibboleths and the gift of improved modes of discovering truth:

> We no longer pay a blind veneration to that barbarous Peripatetic jingle, those obscure scholastic terms of art, once held as oracles; but consult the dictates of our own senses, and by late invented engines force Nature herself to discover plainly her most hidden recesses.

This, of course, smacks of sophomoric bravado, but it suggests, none the less, the extent to which Cartesian and Lockian ideas had fired a youthful receptive mind. The mature writings of Addison show continued interest in the new philosophy. He is intrigued with the wonders of minute life as revealed by the microscope and with the marvels of the heavens disclosed by the telescope. He reflects on the habits of the shellfish, on the multiplicity of living animals, on the remarkably designed chain of being with no gaps below man, with probably no gaps between man and

God; on the phenomenon of pleasure and pain, on pride and ambition, on the ways of the mind in general; on the goodness of Providence in having added to the drab "real qualities" of matter those "imaginary qualities" of colors, sounds, tastes, and smells which brighten the world and cheer the soul of man. Some of these speculations carry a flavor of pseudo science, others suggestions of seventeenth-century divinity, but most of them bear strongly the marks of the new philosophy.

It is not strange, therefore, that when, partly under the cogent influence of Longinus, partly through his own insights and dissatisfactions, Addison had come to feel the inadequacies of the old criticism and the urgent need for some new system which would enable critics to "enter into the very spirit and Soul of fine Writing, and shew us the several sources of that Pleasure which rises in the Mind upon the Perusal of a Noble Work" he turned to the new philosophy for his model. In spirit, method, and substance, the **"Papers on the Imagination"** reveal the fountainhead of Addison's inspiration. Mindful of the fact that in other departments of knowledge new light had come from consulting the "dictates of our own senses," he begins in his search for a fuller understanding of his special subject where Descartes, Hobbes, and Locke had begun: with the ways of human nature and the relation of the external world of sense to the perceiving responsive self. And throughout the essay he follows more or less closely the lead of the new philosophy, with its groundwork of sensational psychology, its reliance on experience, its powerful instrument of empirical inductive investigation.

Isolate the main ideas of this essay for a moment and we may see something of their distinctive character. Instead of the rules, taste is to be the final arbiter of excellence; in decisions of taste the appeal is to the imagination, not to the reason or judgment; to know the ways of the imagination we must know the ways of the mind, especially in its relation to external nature; observation proves that there are three main sources and types of aesthetic appeal—the beautiful, the novel, and the sublime; beauty, novelty, and sublimity are really things of the mind—products of a sort of creative act in a pleasurable response to objects in nature or to literature and art; one factor in the explanation of aesthetic pleasure is the principle of the association of ideas, another is the Lockian theory of the primary and secondary qualities of matter; the power of imagery on the mind is such that even historians, scientists, and philosophers would do well to embellish their writings with allusion and metaphor; aesthetic pleasures are divorced from practical interests, but they have unique values in that they "open a Man's thoughts," raise and "enlarge his Imagination," and in general exert a stimulating, healthful influence on both mind and body.

All these have to do with imaginative response. The list for imaginative creation is shorter—Addison was not too productive on the creative problem. The mind of the poet has the power of selection and combination in representing that which is better and more pleasing than nature (Bacon's version of ideal imitation); the poet may also create worlds and persons that have no existence except in his fancy (Dryden's "Fairy Way of Writing"); success

in this way of writing can be achieved only by a writer endowed with great original genius, such as Shakespeare; the poet should be born with a vigorous faculty of imagination, but he should also educate this faculty with as much pains as a philosopher takes in forming his understanding.

The importance of Addison's theory lies not so much in its overt enunciation of ideas as in its method and spirit, its primary assumptions, the fabrics from which it was created. And it lies less in its actual worth as a completed synthesis than in its implications and its potentialities. Viewed as a systematic presentation of final theory, the essay is as imperfect as can be and is susceptible to all manner of captious or strictly logical criticism. But viewed as a set of tentative pronouncements charged with dynamic suggestion and exemplifying a method of almost illimitable possibilities of development, it is worthy to be classed as one of the great critical documents of all time.

Whatever its imperfections, Addison's treatise carried weight, enough apparently to furnish decisive impetus to a movement that was completely to discredit the merely formalistic parts of neoclassicism and was to eventuate in a new aesthetic for England and to aid in establishing a similar one for Germany and France as well. It is no small thing surely that looking back now we are able to see that virtually all of the outstanding characteristics of the new empirical pragmatic criticism as it evolved in the eighteenth century were in one way or another anticipated by Addison.

Wherever we go in eighteenth-century criticism, whatever the specific subject of speculation, we almost invariably find that Addison had been there. If it is Hutcheson on beauty and aesthetic response, we find parallels to or echoes of Addison's **"Pleasures of the Imagination"**; if it is Burke on taste and sublimity and beauty, Young and Tucker on original genius, Hume and Gerard, and Kames, Blair, and Alison on taste, imagination, sublimity and novelty, the association of ideas, and original genius, we are again in the presence of theory partially developed or at least adumbrated in the *Spectator* papers.

The influence of Addison on subsequent literary thought is nowhere more impressively exemplified than in utterances of such more conservative critics as Hugh Blair and Samuel Johnson. Blair, though rather tightly bound even in his judgments of Shakespeare by the conventions of the older criticism, pays due attention to genius, taste, imagination, and sublimity and gives Addison credit for priority in exploring these fields. It was Addison, he says, who first attempted a regular inquiry into the principles of taste, "and he has the merit of having opened a track, which was before unbeaten." Johnson, rebuking those who feel superior to Addison, invites them to consider Addison's remarks on Ovid as an example of refined criticism. "Let them peruse likewise," he continues, "his essays on wit, and on the pleasure of the imagination in which he founds art on the base of nature, and draws the principles of invention from dispositions inherent in the mind of man, with skill and elegance, such as his contemners will not easily attain."

In practical criticism, too, over and over in the eighteenth century, we see Addison at work. The anonymous essay on *Hamlet* (1736) illustrates the double-barreled effects of his theory and example. Anonymous not only extols Addison but, candidly taking the papers on *Paradise Lost* as his model, proposes to examine a great tragedy "according to the Rules of Reason and Nature, without having any regard to those Rules established by arbitrary Dogmatizing Critics . . . " More specifically, he proposes to show the why of our pleasure in this tragedy: "And as to those things which charm by a certain secret Force and strike us we know not how or why; I believe it will not be disagreeable if I shew to everyone the Reason why they are pleas'd." The spirit and method of Anonymous in fulfilling his promise, his general appeal to common human nature, his analysis of character, his emphasis on psychological preparation, on illusion, on the principle of design, his attention to detailed beauties in a scene-by-scene study of the play, in general disregard of the traditional rules: these are all, often separately it is true, to be repeated again and again in subsequent Shakespearian criticism, in the writings of Kames, Morgann, Richardson, Walter Whiter, even of Warton and Johnson—and they are all Addisonian.

Commenting, in *The Life of Reason,* on the broader influence of Locke, D. G. James has recently said that of early eighteenth-century men, "it was Addison and Butler who had most of Locke's temper and fairness of mind"; and in another passage he remarks that in contrast to Swift and Bolingbroke, Addison had a mind "eminently fair and open to intellectual inquiry." In assessing Addison's contribution to English criticism such a judgment has special pertinence, for it may be truthfully said of Addison that he introduced into aesthetic discussion, more effectively than anyone before him, a spirit of full and free investigation.

Whatever else in the way of specific detail in theory and practice he gave us may be traced for its origin and development to this spirit. One may almost say that Addison was most himself where he questioned the accepted and worked toward something off the main path of current theory and practice. He faced problems squarely and set an example of reaching solutions through the empirical mode of testing fact and experience. Through his adaptation of the new psychology to aesthetic speculation he gave to the theory of judging by taste something of the philosophical foundation that any aesthetic must have before it can gain acceptance by men of thought, and he established a pattern that, broadly speaking, became the norm for his century. It is one thing to assert that "I like what I like, rules or no rules" or to talk about a "I know not what" that gives a work its grace and charm. It is quite another to argue for the integrity of taste on the grounds of "dispositions inherent in the mind of man"—to borrow Johnson's words descriptive of the **"Essay on the Imagination."** Therein, no doubt, is an explanation of why Addison's methods and ideas took hold.

Later critics were to attempt to solve more definitely than Addison what these dispositions were and what laws might be deduced from their operation. But Addison probably did more than any other one man to start his cen-

tury afresh down the long road of exploration of the mysteries of artistic creation and aesthetic response.

Addison's approach to aesthetic problems was basically sensational, but he was not, therefore, a materialist. Though he follows the method of the new philosophy, he holds to the God and the Soul of the Scholastics, and like the Scholastics he sees the soul and body getting on in harmonious relationship. Here as elsewhere Addison's views were essentially moderate. Descartes had set the soul off on its own little island of the pineal gland, restricting the imagination to the sensory and physical, with an essentially mechanical function of supplying the rational soul with materials but otherwise having small traffic with it. Hume, Hartley, and other associationists promoted a tendency to regard the imagination as largely an instrument of mechanical process in a mechanical mind. Their mode was empirical and their chief subject of study the human mind, so that in method and subject they were in the tradition of the new criticism; but in their theory the law of the rules was merely supplanted by the even more mechanical law of association. Addison avoided these extremes. His imagination was an intermediate power lying between the senses and the understanding, owing something to both, and in a rather specific way serving the needs of the whole soul, which in turn had close relations with God. Altogether Addison's ideas were such as to render them more readily assimilable in Romantic theory than were those of the more mechanically minded theorists among his predecessors and successors, with which in the end Coleridge, especially, would have no traffic whatever.

There are, it is true, wide gaps between Addison and the Romantics, differences that may be roughly indicated under four heads: (1) incompatibilities in specific philosophical outlook; (2) inequalities in intellectual last; (3) such divergencies as ordinarily prevail between the incipient and the more fully developed, Addison's best ideas often standing as partial conceptions or hints, sometimes naïvely expressed, which in the Romantic period are to emerge in relatively full-bodied theory; (4) the appearance of concepts in Romantic aesthetics virtually foreign to Addison's view: as, for example, Coleridge's idea of organic form and his theory of the secondary imagination as an esemplastic power operating on the materials of experience subsequent to reflective and subconscious processes. Addison's idea of the function of the creative imagination was the relatively elementary one of enlarging, compounding, and varying materials of experiences or of inventing new forms beyond the realm of experience.

Such differences are, however, relatively unimportant in consideration of the numerous points at which Addison's thought touches that of the Romantics. Basically, the larger concerns of Wordsworth and Coleridge were much the same as Addison's: the aesthetic experience and the imagination as the central facts in matters of art, the ways of the imagination in creation and in aesthetic response, beauty and sublimity, and to a less extent novelty, the problem of excellence in art, the nature of the mind and its relations to its universe, final causes. Their approach, too, was, like Addison's, psychological, and their chief method, also like his, was reasoning from the data of introspection.

Among more particular issues is Addison's idea of the creative perceptive quality of imaginative response, which neighbors closely, it seems to me, the Romantic theory of a modifying, creative imaginative perception. Another is Addison's belief in immediate spontaneous response: "It is but the opening of the Eye and the Scene enters . . . We are struck we know not how, with the symmetry of any thing we see, and immediately assent to the Beauty of an Object . . . " Anticipatory of Wordsworth certainly, as Carritt has pointed out, is Addison's discovery that objects at first sight pleasant "appear more so upon Reflection . . . Memory heightens the Delightfulness of the Original." Addison is once more near Wordsworth, and Keats, too, when he urges that the poet should cultivate his natural imagination and designates as the first step in his education a close acquaintance with and a due relish of "the Works of Nature." A further instance of anticipation occurs in Addison's suggestion, quite in contrast to prevailing neoclassic views, that the aesthetic experience is nonutilitarian and disinterested, which in turn relates closely to his emphasis on pleasure as the primary function of poetry and his belief in the ameliorating effects of the imaginative activity on both soul and body—a good born of and inseparable from pleasure as it were. Addison and Wordsworth would, in fact, have got along very agreeably on the subject of the general beneficent effects of external nature and of good poetry, just as Addison and Shelley would have understood each other quite clearly, up to a point, on the ways in which the imagination can be a blessing to the spirit of man—though, no doubt, Addison would have been a little puzzled by Shelley's more mystical utterances and Shelley would have balked at some of Addison's physiological implications.

These similarities do not necessarily imply influence, either direct or indirect by way of Kant or others. It is perhaps more accurate to describe them in terms of inheritance, a process which in a way is of more honor to the progenitor as an indication of deeply engrained viable qualities than is influence, which may be only a temporary and surface affair. Coleridge and Wordsworth brought into the integration which was their main achievement many and diverse ingredients. The Platonic element was there, accommodated to and supplemented by current transcendental thought; so also were some of the best parts of the psychological modes and discoveries of the past hundred fifty years, as, stripped of their mechanical intentions, they were related to the perceptive and creative functions of mind. But the most fundamental components of this integration bear marks of unmistakable relationship to the ideas of Addison. Modified by a century of intervening Addison-like aesthetic speculation and transformed as they were by the capacious minds of Coleridge and Wordsworth, they still show the certain signs of their ancestry. So that though we may be reluctant to name Addison as father of Romantic criticism, we can safely speak of him as one of its most important grandfathers, through whom were transmitted some of its characteristic dominant traits. (pp. 316-29)

Clarence D. Thorpe, "Addison's Contribution to Criticism," in The Seventeenth Century: Studies in the History of English Thought and Literature from Bacon to Pope *by Richard Foster Jones and others, Stanford University Press, 1951, pp. 316-29.*

Frank Kermode   (essay date 1959)

[*Kermode is an English critic whose career combines modern critical methods with expert traditional scholarship, particularly in his work on Shakespeare. In his discussions of modern literature, Kermode has embraced many of the conceptions of structuralism and phenomenology. In the following review of an edition of collected essays from the* Spectator, *Kermode celebrates Addison's essays as instructive and entertaining.*]

There was no dearth of painless reading matter when the first *Spectator* appeared; yet it did not attempt to conceal from its readers that its object was to civilise them. Clearly there was a general desire for improvement, so long as it was sometimes amusing and always elegant. The *Spectator* arrived six days a week with the morning tea, indefatigably ransacking the moral world for instructive amusement, much as merchants traversed the physical world for the china, the tea and the sugar. But although the ladies might always expect to be entertained by the advertisements, they had no guarantee that the day's essay might not be one of Addison's lay sermons, those expositions of modish philosophy, which might open like this: 'The soul, considered abstractedly from its Passions, is of a remiss and sedentary Nature, slow in its Resolves, and languishing in its executions. The Use therefore of the Passions, &c.' This came out on a Saturday, but Addison continued it on Monday and Tuesday. Once he devoted the papers of a whole week to an essay on Wit; later, Imagination occupied a fortnight without relief. From January 5 to May 3, 1712, the Saturday issues, sometimes double numbers, were given over entirely to Milton; yet the demand for them was so great that Addison had 'no Reason to repent' this journalistic enterprise.

The *Spectator* was not all Roger de Coverley, Will Honeycomb and Steele 'fairsexing it,' as Swift sourly said. Yet its circulation rose from a satisfactory 3,000 to more than 10,000, with a possible peak of 14,000 in No. 384, an unusual political scoop. In the twenty-one months of its life, before Addison removed first Sir Roger and the others, and then himself, from the scene, the success of the paper was such as to establish it as an event of major significance. Throughout seven of the eight familiar volumes (the last one hardly counts, being the record of an artificial revival of the paper in 1714) the authors maintained, and frequently also proclaimed, an admirable balance between good humour and seriousness of purpose. They must have kept in very close touch with their readers, who appeared to enjoy Addison's lectures on such topics as Exercise and Temperance as well as Steele's serial report on prostitution and the little naughtinesses that crept in here and there; these enabled a later generation to congratulate itself on being even more refined than Addison's. The paper justifiably claimed that from day to day it contributed 'something to the polishing of Men's Minds'—and Women's, too. Even Johnson said that these Whig dogs excited 'an emulation of intellectual elegance'; they contrived 'to enliven morality with wit, and to temper wit with morality.' For more than a century the *Spectator* was the Castiglione of the English gentleman.

There have been excessive tributes, Macaulay's for instance [*Edinburgh Review,* 1843]; and Courthope in 1884 represented Addison as virtually the saviour of his country, the man who calmed our social and political turbulence and established 'the comparative harmony we now enjoy.' Having given up the harmony and the Whigs, we may now find less time for Addison; he is probably not much read now, even by schoolboys. As it grows dense with a-numinous objects, we derive less and less comfort from the spacious firmament on high; the market studied by Mr. Davenport has not the simplicity of Sir Andrew Freeport's; and if you think of the two squires, Sir Roger and Strix, certain differences present themselves as obvious. The current *Spectator* has never devoted even one issue to Milton or the Pleasures of the Imagination.

> *Frank Kermode, "Adult Education," in* The Spectator, *Vol. 202, No. 6812, January 16, 1959, p. 83.*

Basil Willey   (essay date 1964)

[*Willey is an English educator and literary scholar. In the following essay, he assesses the intent and the influence of Addison's* Spectator *and* Tatler *essays, noting that Addison was essentially a populariser whose contribution to literature was to voice and address the concerns of the middle class.*]

The Spectator is important not, of course, for any original contribution to ethical theory or speculation, but for its influence in defining the social standards, the norms of approved behaviour, which on the whole were to prevail both then and for a long time to come. If we are to believe J. R. Green, its influence was very great; 'for a whole century', he says, '**The Spectator** had greater weight on moral and religious opinions than all the charges of the bishops'. What strikes us most now, perhaps, is the new 'tone' of **The Spectator;** it represents a new kind of relationship between author and reader—a relationship made possible by the advent of a new and more numerous reading-public. With **The Spectator** the voice of the *bourgeois* is first heard in polite letters, and makes its first decisive contribution to the English moral tradition. Addison is linked by many a thread with the rational divines and the elegant and enlightened philosophers. But though he often echoes the Cambridge Platonists, Halifax, Locke or Shaftesbury, there is usually in what he says a subtle transposition into a bourgeois key: an added touch of complacency, or sentiment, or that sense of security which seems to me his most characteristic note. In him the passion of the seventeenth century has become reverie, its intensity has sunk into contentment, and its speculative attack has subsided into a sober demonstration of the wonderful perfections of the universe, and of the English constitution since 1688.

The eighteenth century in England may not have been a very moral age, but it was certainly an age of moralists. Poets, essayists and novelists preached incessantly; and even the pulpit poured forth exhortations in which the morality was as little touched by emotion as orthodoxy would permit. The age was not left without guidance in any of the departments of conduct, from the management of the passions to the care of the teeth or the cut of a petticoat. Why did morality receive so large a share of attention from the wits and divines and philosophers of the eighteenth century? This sort of question will always be asked, even though no verifiable answer is possible; but Leslie Stephen had a reply to this one. The eighteenth century was moral (in the sense indicated) because theology was then in process of decay. The problem confronting the century is summed up by him thus: 'How could order be preserved when the old sanctions were decaying? Can a society of atheists be maintained? How, to put it bluntly, should morality survive theology?' 'When a creed is dying,' he observes again in another place, 'the importance of preserving the moral law naturally becomes a pressing consideration with all strong natures.' Whether the creed was really as moribund in the eighteenth century as it appeared to the Victorian agnostic and lapsed parson, may perhaps be disputed; certainly the greater number of the English moralists of the eighteenth century would have warmly denied it. Leslie Stephen in this respect, and indeed throughout his *English Thought in the Eighteenth Century,* treated that century as an adumbration of the nineteenth. He is really engaged, throughout, in discussing his own predicament and his own problems, but he does it obliquely, by analysing the thought of his forerunners, the freethinkers of the previous century. What may, I think, be truly said is that in the eighteenth century the pictorial imagery of the traditional faith (the three-decker universe and all its appurtenances) was becoming less and less a part of the mental furniture of educated men, and that this change involved a re-focusing of the moral ideas which had been associated with the older attitude. If a moral law ceases to be thought of, or felt, as the command of a divine Person, ethical speculation will certainly look for other reasons why we should go on being moral.

And other reasons . . . the eighteenth century did find. It discovered the natural moral sense; and it discovered that self-love and social were the same—or, in other words, that the enlightened pursuit of self-interest contributes automatically to the greatest happiness of the greatest number. In a word, it discovered (*a*) the intuitive and (*b*) the utilitarian bases of morality. We must be moral, either because we recognize the beauty of virtue, or because experience proves that what is good for ourselves is good for all—or for both these reasons.

However sceptical one may be about the effectiveness of most moralizing, one is bound to admit that Addison, at least, exerted an influence which lasted well into the nineteenth century. Indeed the Victorians felt a natural affinity with him, and more than one modern critic has detected in him the first accents of the Victorian age. J. R. Green . . . (Introduction to the 'Golden Treasury' volume of *Selections*), called him 'the ancestor of Howard and Wilberforce, the ancestor of Mr Matthew Arnold'. Many years ago, when lecturing to a W. E. A. Class about

The Spectator, I pointed out what seemed to me to be affinities between the *Spectator* programme and the accepted standards of the mid-nineteenth century, and I was consequently both interested and slightly piqued when Mr Bonamy Dobrée, two years later, published his biographical study of Addison under the title 'The First Victorian' [in *Essays in Biography: 1680-1726,* 1925]. As I later discovered, Virginia Woolf, who as the daughter of Leslie Stephen had a vested interest in the eighteenth century, had already, in an essay written in 1919 [in *The Common Reader*], drawn attention to Macaulay's rhetorical overpraise of Addison [in *The Edinburgh Review,* July 1843], and had enquired what remained of him, for us, when 'the deposit of mid-Victorian lachrymosity' had been removed from his reputation.

It is undoubtedly significant that the mid-Victorians, through their spokesman Macaulay, should have fixed upon Addison as their literary Christian hero. For Addison was the first lay preacher to reach the ear of the middle-classes, and to give dignified expression to their ideals and sentiments. The Victorian reading-public agreed with the repentant Pope, that after all 'no whiter page than Addison's remains'. Addison was the safest, the nicest, great writer English literature had produced until the Victorian age itself. He had inculcated a commonsense religion, neither superstitious nor fanatical; he had deplored the vices of the worldly, and cleaned up the Augean stable of the Restoration stage; he had insisted upon the sanctities of the home and of marriage; he had allayed the spirit of faction, chastised the libertine and educated the philistine; he had shown how much joy could be derived from the Pleasures of the Imagination, from the Beauties of Nature, and from that supplement to Holy Scripture, *Paradise Lost.* He had done much more good with his sympathetic humour than Swift with his *saeva indignatio;* indeed he was, in Macaulay's resounding phrases:

> the great satirist who alone knew how to use ridicule without abusing it, who without inflicting a wound effected a great social reform, and who reconciled wit and virtue after a long and disastrous separation, during which wit had been led astray by profligacy, and virtue by fanaticism.

This brings us to the actual aims of the *Tatler* and *Spectator* as conceived by Steele and Addison themselves. We are left in no doubt about this: 'the great aim of these my speculations', says Addison (*Spectator,* 58), 'is to banish vice and ignorance out of the territories of Great Britain'—a sufficiently comprehensive and ambitious programme. They wished to be both censors of manners and arbiters of taste; apostles of a new gospel which was to bring culture, sweetness and light to a generation of Barbarians and Philistines. . . . [The] English nation appears to need the same sort of sermons over and over again throughout the centuries. For indeed, when (to adapt a phrase of Mr Eliot's) [Matthew] Arnold set forth under the banner of criticism to clean up the whole country, he found many of Addison's tasks still waiting to be done, or needing to be done again. In Addison's day the 'Populace' of *Culture and Anarchy* had not lifted its ominous head, but the 'Barbarians' and the 'Philistines', *mutatis mutandis,* were already recognizable as the two main sections of society. And to Addison, as later to Arnold, it seemed that sweet reasonableness, taste, rational religion, and literature, were the best medicines for all cultural ailments. Both aimed at producing, in a nation of shopkeepers, religious sects and political factions, a spirit of calm disinterestedness in which the best ideas could live and grow. Whereas Arnold was compelled to preach to his age the truths they least wanted to hear, Addison believed, with many of his contemporaries, that a polite, learned and rational era was just beginning, perhaps even that the threads left hanging at the overthrow of the ancient world had at last been taken up, ancients and moderns now happily joining hands across the barbarous hiatus of the ages of superstition.

In Addison's time the Barbarian-Philistine classes corresponded fairly closely with the old Cavalier-Roundhead division. On the one hand there were the 'men of wit and pleasure about town', the representatives of the moribund traditions of chivalry, whose manners were those of the Restoration Court and whose social code was that of Restoration Comedy. Their creed consisted of a few simple tenets such as that all religion is hypocrisy; that wit and address are preferable to virtue; that marriage is the grave of love; that every personable woman is fair game for a gallant; that, as between men and women, gallantry is the only possible relation; and, between gentlemen, gambling, conviviality or duelling. To which one might add, that City men, though sometimes the husbands or fathers of the fair, are all snuffling puritans and skinflints.

On the other hand there was the middle class of London, the traditional stronghold of Puritans, and the backbone of the Parliamentary cause in the late troubles. This class lacked the polish and refinement of the other, but was sober and god-fearing, thrifty, home-loving and strict. These were the ancestors of Arnold's Philistines; and they were often illiberal and provincial enough. It must be remembered in justice to them, however, that some of their defects were due to the Clarendon Code, which had excluded Dissenters from the full rights of citizenship and so cut them off from the mainstream of the national life.

In this state of affairs, when wit and refinement were associated with irreligion and libertinism, and religion and morality appeared inseparable from a sour, puritanical or hypocritical temper, there was a need and an opportunity for someone to work out a new intermediate culture, less cynical than that of the gentlemen and less austere than that of the puritans. This was the idea which Steele conceived, and with Addison's help went far to realize. These men were not deep or daring thinkers, in spite of their free use of the words 'speculation' and 'philosophy'; they were just good journalists, with the skill of their trade in feeling the pulse of the times. And they succeeded in making a new compound out of established standards, insisting that virtue and gaiety, polish and moral sentiment, must go together to form a 'humanized puritanism' (as it has been called). It could equally be called a puritanized humanism, less pagan, less courtly, more bourgeois and more sentimental than that of the Renaissance. It was the beginning of the long ascendancy of bourgeois ideals in our literature. In the oft-quoted words of *Spectator* 10:

I shall endeavour to enliven Morality with Wit, and to temper Wit with Morality, that my readers may, if possible, both ways find their account in the Speculation of the Day.

And in No. 179:

I may cast my Readers under two general Divisions, the *Mercurial* and the *Saturnine.* The first are the gay part of my Disciples, who require Speculations of Wit and Humour; the others are those of a more solemn and sober Turn, who find no Pleasure but in Papers of Morality and sound Sense; the former call everything that is Serious, Stupid; the latter look upon everything as Impertinent that is Ludicrous. Were I always Grave, one half of my Readers would fall away from me: were I always Merry, I should lose the other. I make it therefore my endeavour to find out Entertainments of both kinds. . . . I would not willingly Laugh, but in order to Instruct, or if I sometimes fail in this Point, when my Mirth ceases to be Instructive, it shall never cease to be Innocent.

This dual aim, the chastening of the Barbarians and the civilizing of the Philistines, is never lost sight of. First one, then the other, receive their share of attention. As an example of satire on Restoration manners, take No. 158 (Steele), which contains an alleged letter from a gallant of those days:

I am now between 50 and 60, and had the Honour to be well with the first Men of Taste and Gallantry in the joyous Reign of Charles II. We had then, I presume, as good Understandings among us as any now can pretend to. As for yourself, Mr Spectator, you seem with the utmost Arrogance to undermine the very Fundamentals upon which we conducted ourselves. It is monstrous to set up for a Man of Wit and yet deny that Honour in a Woman is anything else but Peevishness, that Inclination is the best Rule of Life, or Virtue and Vice anything else but Health and Disease. We had no more to do but put a Lady in good Humour, and all we could wish followed of course. Then again, your Tully and your Discourses of another Life, are the very Bane of Mirth and good Humour. Prithee don't value thyself on thy Reason at that exorbitant Rate, and the Dignity of humane Nature; take my Word for it, a setting-Dog has as good Reason as any Man in England. . . . I have a great deal more to say to you, but I shall sum it all up in this one Remark, In short, Sir, you do not write like a Gentleman.

Other examples of the overthrow of Restoration values are abundant. In No. 23 Addison shows that it is 'infinitely more honourable to be a Good-natured Man than a Wit'; and in many a paper the state of marriage is extolled, and domestic happiness exalted above worldly pleasures. 'Nothing is a greater Mark of a degenerate and vicious Age, than the common Ridicule which passes on this State of Life' (261). Steele deploys all his considerable reserves of 'sensibility' in depicting tender or affecting family scenes; and his views about the beauty and innocence of childhood, and the brutality of schoolmasters, are in the

tradition running from Montaigne to Rousseau and onwards:

No one who has gone through what they call a great School . . . but must have seen an ingenuous Creature expiring with Shame, with pale Looks, beseeching Sorrow, and silent Tears, throw up its honest Eyes, and kneel on its tender Knees to an inexorable Blockhead to be forgiven the false Quantity of a word in making a Latin Verse (157).

A condemnation of the Restoration dramatists and their followers is only what we should expect from these moralists of the post-Collier period. These authors, says Steele, in a review of *The Scornful Lady,* write as if they thought

there was not one Man of Honour or Woman of Chastity in the House, and come off with Applause: For an Insult upon all the Ten Commandments, with the little Criticks, is not so bad as the Breach of an Unity of Time or Place (270).

The Spectator also attacked the mouldering fabric of 'Barbarism' on its more specious side: the side represented by Quixotism and the chivalric code of honour. If duellists, for example, were to be made to stand in the pillory, 'it would quickly lessen the Number of these imaginary Men of Honour, and put an end to so absurd a Practice' (99).

In No. 6, all the corruptions of the day are traced to the fashionable exaltation of wit at the expense of honest goodness; the men of intelligence have 'lost the taste of Good-will, of Friendship, of Innocence'. Sir Roger de Coverley is here made to say that he is 'so whimsical in a corrupt Age as to act according to Nature and Reason'; his function in *The Spectator* being to represent guileless goodness in contrast to the cynical sophistication of the contemporary Wits. 'Nature and Reason' are of course close yoke-fellows in *The Spectator;* so are 'Reason, Religion and Good Breeding'.

There must have been rich soil lying ready for all this good seed. Steele and Addison, like all good journalists, were sensitive to the movements of public sentiment; the hour was ripe for a rehabilitation of the virtues, and they were the very men for the task. As early as No. 10 Addison complacently announced that already the daily circulation was 3000,

so that if I allow Twenty Readers to every Paper, which I look upon as a modest Computation, I may reckon about Three-score thousand Disciples in London and Westminster, who I hope will take care to distinguish themselves from the thoughtless Herd of their ignorant and unattentive Brethren.

And in a later number (262) he records his gratification on finding that when he 'broke loose from that great Body of Writers who have employed their Wit and Parts in propagating Vice and Irreligion' he was not merely set down as an 'odd kind of Fellow' with a taste for singularity, but has gained a large following.

On the other hand the Philistines are not neglected. 'It is owing,' says Steele, in a paper which contains in brief the substance of his *Christian Hero,* to the forbidding and unlovely Constraint with which men of low Conceptions act when they think they conform themselves to Religion, as well as to the more odious Conduct of Hypocrites, that the word Christian does not carry with it at first view all that is Great, Worthy, Friendly, Generous, and Heroick.

This is in the direct line of descent from the rational theology of the later seventeenth century; and from such a lay-sermon as Halifax's *Advice to a Daughter* (a true literary forerunner of **The Spectator**), in which Halifax says that since nothing else is the better for being sour, why should religion, which is the best of things? It seemed obvious to the moralists in this tradition that the outward and visible sign of inward righteousness should be an open and cheerful demeanour. Was not God himself the best-natured Being in the world? A wise epicure would be religious for the sake of pleasure. Such obvious truths, however, needed stating because of the strange perversity of the kill-joy enthusiasts.

I doubt, however, whether it was entirely the fault of the Puritans that the word 'Christian' did not immediately call to mind either the Aristotelian or the Renaissance ideal of Magnanimity: the Great, Worthy, Friendly, Generous and Heroic man. After all, these are not the virtues that rank highest in Christian ethics. Shaftesbury had recently made ironic use of this in defending his favourite thesis of the *disinterestedness* of true virtue:

> I cou'd be almost tempted to think, that the true Reason why some of the most heroick Virtues have so little notice taken of 'em in our holy Religion, is, because there wou'd have been no room left for *Disinterestedness,* had they been entitled to a share of that infinite Reward, which Providence has by Revelation assigned to other Dutys. *Private Friendship,* and *Zeal for the Publick,* and our *Country,* are Virtues purely voluntary in a Christian (*Sensus Communis,* Part II, Sect. 3).

I [have suggested] that one of the sources of confusion in the moral tradition of Christendom had always lain in the conflict between the Christian ideal which it nominally professed, and the paganism which it really admired and practised. In *Erewhon* they believed in Ydgrun while ostensibly worshipping the gods, and others besides Samuel Butler have held (openly or secretly) that 'the example of a true gentleman is the best of all gospels'. Innumerable as the efforts have been to show that the popular ideal of the Gentleman is really identical with, or at least not incompatible with, the Christian ideal in its purity and rigour, there remains a deep-seated sense that this is not quite the true state of affairs; and a faint tinge of absurdity still clings, in consequence, to the title of Steele's ill-starred treatise, *The Christian Hero.*

An example of Addison's method of handling the enthusiasts may be found in No. 494:

> About an Age ago it was the Fashion in England for every one that would be thought religious, to throw as much Sanctity as possible into his Face, and in particular to abstain from all Appearances of Mirth and Pleasantry, which were

looked upon as the Marks of a Carnal Mind. The Saint was of a sorrowful Countenance, and generally eaten up with Spleen and Melancholy.

And so forth—with a most engaging profusion of capital letters, and with that 'demure serenity, disturbed only by an arch sparkle of the eye and an almost imperceptible elevation of the brow' which Macaulay noted. The ensuing 'character' of Sombrius is one of Addison's best in that kind:

> Sombrius is one of these Sons of Sorrow. He thinks himself obliged in Duty to be sad and disconsolate. He looks on a sudden Fit of Laughter as a Breach of his Baptismal Vow. An innocent Jest startles him like Blasphemy. . . . He sits at a Christening, or a Marriage-Feast, as at a Funeral; sighs at the conclusion of a Merry Story, and grows devout when the rest of the Company grow pleasant. After all, Sombrius is a religious Man, and would have behaved himself very properly, had he lived when Christianity was under a general Persecution.

The rest of this charming and characteristic paper is devoted to a favourite theme of Addison's: the connexion between Religion and Cheerfulness. As if, he exclaims,

> Mirth was made for Reprobates, and Chearfulness of Heart denied those who are the only Persons that have a proper Title to it. . . . The Contemplation of the Divine Being, and the Exercise of Virtue, are in their own Nature so far from excluding all Gladness of Heart, that they are perpetual Sources of it.

Addison returns frequently to this theme—and no wonder, for it is his main message to his age. 'Chearfulness keeps up a kind of Day-Light in the Mind, and fills it with a steady and perpetual Serenity' (381). Unlike 'wanton Mirth', it does not 'throw the Mind into a Condition improper for the present State of Humanity'. Sometimes Addison links it with enjoyment of natural beauty, in a style vastly preferable to Shaftesbury's:

> The Creation is a perpetual Feast to the Mind of a good Man; everything that he sees chears and delights him. Providence has imprinted so many Smiles on Nature, that it is impossible for a Mind which is not sunk in more gross and sensual Delights to take a Survey of them without several secret Sensations of Pleasure. . . . Natural Philosophy quickens this Taste of the Creation, and renders it not only pleasing to the Imagination but to the Understanding. It does not rest in the Murmur of Brooks and the Melody of Birds, in the Shade of Groves and Woods or in the Embroidery of Fields and Meadows, but considers the several Ends of Providence which are served by them, and the Wonders of Divine Wisdom which appear in them. . . . Such an habitual Disposition of Mind consecrates every Field and Wood, turns an ordinary Walk into a morning or evening Sacrifice, and will improve those transient Gleams of Joy, which naturally brighten and refresh the Soul on such Occasions, into an inviolable and perpetual State of Bliss and Happiness (393).

Thus far had the cult of Nature proceeded a hundred years before *The Excursion*! So solicitous has Providence been to maintain this Chearfulness in the mind of man, that it has made it

> capable of conceiving Delight from several Objects which seem to have very little Use in them, as from the Wildness of Rocks and Desarts, and the like grotesque Parts of Nature (387).

But that is not all. Addison, safely becalmed in the long concordat between 'natural philosophy' and religion, goes on to adduce 'one of the finest speculations in that science'—viz. Locke's theory of primary and secondary qualities—in support of his argument:

> if Matter had appeared to us endow'd only with those real Qualities which it actually possesses [i.e. the primary qualities], it would have made but a very joyless and uncomfortable Figure; and why has Providence given it a Power of producing in us such imaginary Qualities [i.e. the secondary] as Tastes and Colours, Sounds and Smells, Heat and Cold, but that Man, while he is conversant in the lower Stations of Nature, might have his Mind cheared and delighted with agreeable Sensations? In short, the whole Universe is a kind of Theatre filled with Objects that either raise in us Pleasure, Amusement or Admiration (*ibid.*).

The authority of Locke appears very strikingly in a naïve concluding paragraph, wherein Addison admits that 'there are many Evils which naturally spring up amidst the Entertainments that are provided for us'. His readers, however, need not worry, for Mr Locke has very satisfactorily explained all this. Evils and dissatisfactions exist here on earth, so that we may be led to seek satisfaction only 'in the Enjoyment of him, with whom there is Fulness of Joy, and at whose Right Hand are Pleasures for evermore'.

Just as he indicates the true mean between the gloom of fanaticism and the mocking laughter of irreligion, so Addison, constant always to the paths of safety and moderation, steers a middle course between those other and still more familiar opposites: Superstition and Enthusiasm. Nowhere is he more entirely at one with the sentiment of his contemporaries. Christendom had laboured for centuries under the one or the other. The dark and monkish Middle Ages had, of course, been utterly given over to superstition; then, at the Reformation, had come an outburst of Zeal of which the best that could be said was that it had indirectly produced the Church of England, but which had unfortunately gone on much further and degenerated into every kind of enthusiastic frenzy. The seventeenth century had witnessed a dire struggle between superstition and zeal, but now in the wholesome daylight of the eighteenth we might at last aspire to a respite from both, and a final union between religion and reason.

Like Swift, but with less intensity, Addison felt that the Church of England did really embody the mean between the two extremes. If Catholics were all superstitious, as of course they were, and dissenters all enthusiasts, as was equally obvious, what reasonable man would be other than an Anglican? The distaste of the eighteenth century for all violent forms of religious emotion was profound and lasting. The lesson of the seventeenth had burnt deep into its soul. 'There is not,' says Addison, 'a more melancholy Object than a Man who has his Head turned with Religious Enthusiasm' (201), and the sentiment was heartily echoed by the poets and novelists as well. 'Most of the Sects that fall short of the Church of England have in them strong Tinctures of Enthusiasm, as the Roman Catholick Religion is one huge overgrown Body of childish and idle Superstitions.' Of Atheism Addison disposes by the argument most commonly used at that time, that to believe it requires more faith than orthodoxy itself. Addison's own faith contained an infusion of the deistic sentiment of the age, but this co-existed in him with an unquestioning acceptance of the tenets of Revealed Religion. On his deathbed he sent for his dissolute stepson to come and see 'how a Christian can die.'

No sketch of *The Spectator* would be complete without some allusion to Addison's campaign on behalf of the Fair Sex; more of the papers were composed for their improvement than for any other single purpose. Indeed this characteristic preoccupation with feminine concerns aroused the scorn of Swift: 'I will not meddle with the Spectator,' he wrote, 'let him fair-sex it to the world's end.' Certainly the predicament of women at this time called for the attention of any *censor morum* and popular educator, and at the very outset Addison announced that there were 'none to whom this Paper will be more useful, than to the Female World':

> I have often thought there has not been sufficient Pains taken in finding out proper Employments and Diversions for the Fair ones. Their Amusements seem to have contrived for them rather as they are Women, than as they are reasonable Creatures; and are more adapted to the Sex, than to the Species . . . etc.

Anyone who wishes to know what the Restoration had done for English upper-class womanhood should read Halifax's *Advice to a Daughter* (the same who became the mother of Lord Chesterfield). A woman's career, we discover, was full of pitfalls. Before marriage, the strictest reserve was imperative, since every woman must consider herself a fortress and every man a potential besieger. The most careful watch must be kept upon the eyes, for the slightest glint of intelligence or friendship there might be interpreted as 'complaisance'; and then, even if the worst were avoided, the tongue of scandal would wag—and this was almost as bad. After marriage, endurance of every kind of marital misery must be cultivated, for fear of ridicule; at best, a degree of influence over a weak husband might be attained by the strategic use of feminine wiles. Such was the lot of womankind in the 'Utopia of gallantry'. It need hardly be said that the corollary of this sort of gallantry is hearty contempt, and few of the writers of the earlier eighteenth century take much trouble to conceal their contempt for all women—except for the exalted few who, as Addison says, 'join all the Beauties of the Mind to the ornaments of Dress, and inspire a kind of Awe and Respect, as well as Love, in their Male Beholders' (10). Virginia Woolf's Orlando knew in her heart, as she poured out tea for Mr Pope, what he really thought of her, even though he sent her copies of verses, solicited her criticism and praised her judgments. Lord Chesterfield tells his son that though women's society must be cultivated for the sake of the Graces, and because of their social influence, they are 'but children of a larger growth. . . . A man of sense only trifles with them, plays with them, humours and flatters them'.

Of this basic contempt subsisting under the mask of gallantry Addison had much less than most writers of his time. The high value he ascribed to the domestic virtues, and his respect for marriage, gave him an esteem for womanhood as the cement of society and a principal source of the civilizing emotions. He considered it insulting to 'talk down' to them after the common fashion of so-called 'women's men', and in No. 158 Steele makes a lady write begging for the company of men of sense rather than 'Fribbles':

> You cannot imagine but that we love to hear Reason and good Sense better than the Ribaldry we are at present entertained with . . .

but she warns Mr Spectator that 'we shall not part with the Men we have at present till the Men of Sense think fit to relieve them'. And so Addison declares his desire

> to contribute to make Woman-Kind, which is the most beautiful Part of the Creation, entirely amiable, and wear out all those little Spots and Blemishes that are apt to arise among all the Charms which Nature has poured out upon them (57).

Addison may fairly be said, I think, to have begun to substitute, for the cynical or victimized Restoration lady, the tender and not unintelligent spouse of the next century. But there remains an accompanying archness, of the kind that is still found in Dickens a hundred and fifty years later. He advises 'the dear creatures' to 'eschew politics', since

> there is nothing as bad for the Face as Party-Zeal. It gives an ill-natured Cast to the Eye, and a disagreeable Sourness to the Look, besides that it makes the Lines too strong, and flushes them worse than Brandy. . . . I would therefore advise all my Female Readers, as they value their Complexions, to let alone all Disputes of this Nature (57).

Addison was a populariser; the first of a long line of purveyors of culture to the wider public. When, many years ago, the B.B.C. began its educational Talks and published a pamphlet called 'New Ventures in Broadcasting', it very appropriately took as motto for the title-page:

> It was said of Socrates that he brought philosophy down from heaven to inhabit among men; and I shall be ambitious to have it said of me, that I have brought philosophy out of closets and libraries, schools and colleges, to dwell in clubs and assemblies, at tea-tables and in coffee-houses (10).

(pp. 233-47)

Basil Willey, "Joseph Addison (1672-1719),"

in his The English Moralists, *W. W. Norton & Company, Inc., 1964, pp. 233-47.*

Robert Halsband (essay date 1966)

[*Halsband was an American educator and critic who specialized in the writings of Lady Mary Wortley Montagu and other eighteenth-century literary figures. In the following excerpt, he delineates what he perceives as the legacy of the* Spectator—*a "felicitous" style and universal appeal.*]

Mention The **Spectator** to an alert modern reader, and he probably thinks you mean the British weekly of that name. Founded in 1828 as an organ of "educated radicalism" (quite different from its right-of-center position today), the contemporary *Spectator* borrowed its name from a far more universal paper, and, paradoxically, one that prided itself on being apolitical. The original **Spectator** dominated the London literary scene from 1711 to 1714, and one would have to think long and probably in vain to name any periodical before or since matching it in popularity and influence. One can even claim, as Joseph Addison's recent biographer does, that its ultimate contribution exceeds that of any other work except the Bible.

Addison (previously known as a poet) and his friend, the playwright Richard Steele, began to issue the **Spectator** only two months after their **Tatler** had ended. The fact that their political party, the Whigs, was out of office allowed them freedom in time and imagination to project their new paper. It was more ambitious than *The Tatler:* as its title implied, it would thoughtfully observe and not merely tattle; and it appeared six times a week, instead of three—selling first for a penny, later for twopence. By the time it finally came to an end (635 essays later) it had reflected and affected almost every aspect of 18th-century life, manners, morals and thought. (p. 2)

"Mr. Spectator," a fictional creation assumed interchangeably by both men, avowed that his main purpose was to instruct his readers; but in setting down his thoughts, he obeyed the precept of Horace—*dulce et utile*—by liberally mixing delight with his instruction. As a reformer his scope was limitless. He criticized and ridiculed such things as dueling, gambling and superstition; fanaticism, whether political, religious or pedantic; Italian opera, sexual vice, and women's silly fashions; marital infidelity and brides' dowries. He dealt with abstract topics like immortality and love of glory, and concrete ones like snuff and petticoats; nothing was outside his ken.

His advice ranged from the most exalted moral problem to calisthenics with dumbbells ("the brandishing of two short Sticks grasped in each Hand, and loaden with Plugs of Lead at either end"). His essays on manners, if put together, make up a "conduct book" to teach an etiquette more fundamental than that of any mere Emily Post. Whether he preached, scolded or teased, he made his points clear, and he adorned them with good-natured wit and humor.

One of the features of *The Spectator,* delectable in its own time (and still there today, of course), was its unexpected variety. When the reader unfolded the daily essay, crisply printed on a single sheet, or opened a volume at random in the collected edition, almost any subject met his eye. This was Mr. Spectator's deliberate strategy, as he candidly explained to his readers: "The sprightly Reader, who takes up my Paper in order to be diverted, very often finds himself engaged unawares in a serious and profitable Course of Thinking; as on the contrary the Thoughtful Man, who perhaps may hope to find something Solid, and full of deep Reflection, is very often insensibly betrayed into a Fit of Mirth. In a word, the Reader sits down to my Entertainment without knowing his Bill of Fare, and has therefore at least the Pleasure of hoping there may be a Dish to His Palate." Moreover, Mr. Spectator avoided the monotony of straightforward essays by embodying his ideas in such literary forms as allegory, fable, visions, tales and (frequently) letters from correspondents, either actual or fictitious.

It was Macaulay who, a century later [in the *Edinburgh Review,* July 1843], pointed out that Addison, in *The Spectator,* was a forerunner of the great English novelists. Indeed, fiction played an important part in the periodical, its fictional "Club" being one of its engaging and memorable features. Its members, described in the second issue of the paper, are a modest microcosm of the English gentry and middle-class. Highest in rank is a baronet, Sir Roger de Coverley. We meet him not only in the Club but at home, when Mr. Spectator visits him for a month at his country seat. He is so fully and imaginatively created, in fact, that the essays in which he appears have been collected under the title of *The Roger de Coverley Papers.*

A critic of the day compared Sir Roger to Falstaff and to Don Quixote, so subtle is his characterization. Because Addison feared that with the termination of *The Spectator* the character would be stolen by other periodical writers, he swore: "By G-d, I'll Kill Sir Roger, that no Body else may Murder him." Accordingly, the Club members receive a letter from his butler, Edward Biscuit, reporting Coverley's death.

Historically, the most significant Club member is Sir Andrew Freeport, city knight and merchant. As his name suggests, he represents the rising mercantile class, a group despised in the drama and satire of the previous age. He is both advocate and exemplar of trade as a useful and dignified part of English society.

The remaining members of the Club are a barrister who frequents the theaters rather than the law courts, a military gentleman named Captain Sentry, a clergyman whose visits are rare, and Will Honeycomb, a super-annuated beau who ridicules women's vanities and exhibits his own. The Club adds human interest to the papers by the most obvious means—the depiction of human characters.

Addison was not averse to using the direct method in instructing readers. Early in the progress of the paper he outlined his goal: "It was said of Socrates, that he brought Philosophy down from Heaven, to inhabit among Men; and I shall be ambitious to have it said of me, that I have brought Philosophy out of Closets and Libraries, Schools and Colleges, to dwell in Clubs and Assemblies, at Tea-Tables, and in Coffee-Houses."

Unafraid to expound a complicated subject at length and in depth, he contributed a series of 11 essays on the Pleasures of the Imagination, which were influential in popularizing the theories of John Locke. In another long series of 18 essays he explored and expounded the beauties of *Paradise Lost,* tactfully publishing them on successive Saturdays so that his readers would have them for solemn contemplation on the following day.

His other essays—on English tragedy, on true and false wit, on the ballad as epic, on language, on genius—show that he did not write *down* to his audience; he expected them to read *up* to him. We know that they did, because the paper's circulation and advertising continued to flourish; it even survived a newspaper tax that thinned the ranks of competitors.

If all these attractions helped to win and keep the paper's readers, the negative virtue of steering clear of politics kept it from losing readers of either Whig or Tory persuasion, no trivial advantage in that day of violent political differences. Addison boasted: "As, on the one Side, my Paper has not in it a single Word of News, a Reflection in Politicks, nor a Stroke of Party; so, on the other, there are no fashionable Touches of Infidelity, no obscene Ideas, no Satyrs upon Priesthood, Marriage, and the like popular Topicks of Ridicule; no private Scandal, nor any thing that may tend to the Defamation of particular Persons, Families, or Societies."

Nothing dies so quickly as political controversy, which is why the Spectator papers retain their interest when political ones, even by such a great writer as Swift, do not. Addison steadfastly refused to be drawn into controversy with other papers because (he wrote) "they are like those Imperceptible Insects which are discover'd by the Microscope, and cannot be made the Subject of Observation without being magnified." Perhaps the Spectator's political chastity was not so pure as Addison boasted, for Sir Roger is depicted as an old-fashioned Tory, out of touch with the Whig wave of the future; but he is satirized ever so gently and sympathetically.

The achievement of *The Spectator,* if seen in perspective, was threefold. Through its dramatis personae, particularly Sir Roger de Coverley, it contributed to the close-grained realism of the future novel. Characters in prose fiction could no longer be statuesque, rhetorical figures or two-dimensional adventurers; they had to live and breathe, and perform actions that grew out of their characterization. Secondly, in its long sequence of varied papers *The Spectator* established the genre of the periodical essay, a felicitous blend of expository and personal writing, so durable that it remained in the ascendant for the rest of the century. Not until Charles Lamb's personal, quirky essays did The *Spectator* lose its pre-eminence as a model.

Finally, The *Spectator* established the "middle style" in writing. This was a happy compromise between the baroque complexity of the 17th-century writers (Milton and Sir Thomas Browne, for example) and the "naked" way of writing recommended by the Royal Society. It is an informal and easy style, luminous without blazing, neither too formal nor too skittish, its sentences neither too ample nor too brief. Dr. Johnson, who defined and extolled it, ends his praise with a recipe: "Whoever wishes to attain an English style, familiar but not coarse, and elegant but not ostentatious, must give his days and nights to the volumes of Addison" [*Lives of the Poets,* 1781]. One would think that most 18th-century writers took his advice.

This house-style was perfectly suited to Mr. Spectator's purpose and subject-matter. He was calm and reasonable, distrustful of enthusiasm of any sort. He avoided crudeness in tone as well as in subject-matter, and met the needs of his predominantly middle-class readers by subtly flattering and directing them.

It may be suggested, if we wish to see a contemporary parallel, that **The Spectator** is one of the ancestors of *The New Yorker.* The supercilious Eustace Tilley, monocle in hand, who appears like a reincarnated deity on the cover of a February issue every year, is a 20th-century Spectator; and what he sees throughout the year he sets down in a house-style that is as poised and urbane (allowing for a 200-year change in idiom) as that of Mr. Spectator. He is consummately and effortlessly "civilized"; slightly skeptical and slightly smug, perhaps, but always in favor of an enlightened and sweet reasonableness.

When readers today enter these five volumes, what will they find enjoyable in them—besides their historical interest? Has **The Spectator,** like other classics deserving of the label, retained its viability? Aside from its freshness and variety, its play of wit and humor, it illustrates the neoclassic doctrine that man's essential nature has remained unchanged since at least the days of Greece and Rome, when great writers described it, and that man still enjoys—or suffers—the same passions (as the 18th century called all the emotions).

The universality of **The Spectator** was proved in its own day by its appeal to both sexes, and to all classes, ages and professions. It seems as universal today because of what one reader called its "Spectatorial wisdom" and because of its emphasis not on how men differ but on how they agree. (pp. 2, 26)

> Robert Halsband, "*Speaking of Books: The Spectator,*" *in* The New York Times Book Review, *July 24, 1966, pp. 2, 26.*

Peter Gay   (essay date 1967)

[*Gay is a German-born American historian whose work is highly regarded by scholars and popular among general readers. His writings include detailed analyses of the Englightenment, nineteenth-century middle-class culture, and the art and politics of Imperial and Weimar Germany. His interpretation of primary source material is, according to many reviewers, characteristically well-balanced, insightful, and innovative, exposing distortions in long-accepted accounts and offering a new foundation for future studies. In the following excerpt, he portrays eighteenth-century London as a particularly brutal and coarse place, and contends that Addison's focus on civility was a much braver stance than modern readers might imagine.*]

This is not Addison's century. Addison's reasonableness strikes us as bland, his civility as genteel, his unfailing cheerfulness as downright fatuous. Forty years ago, Bonamy Dobrée called him "the first Victorian" [*Essays in Biography: 1680-1726,* 1925]—no compliment—and nearly everyone has adopted the label and accepted the verdict it implies. Certainly C. S. Lewis, though compelled by his perspicacity to recognise that Addison is neither a solved puzzle nor an open book, accepted it:

> Almost everything which my own generation ignorantly called Victorian, seems to have been expressed by Addison. It is all there in the **Spectator**—the vague religious sensibility, the insistence on what came later to be called Good Form, the playful condescension towards women, the untroubled belief in the beneficence of commerce, the comfortable sense of security which, far from excluding, perhaps renders possible the romantic relish for wildness and solitude. If he is not at present the most hated of our writers, that can only be because he is so little read. Everything the moderns detest, all that they call *smugness, complacency,* and *bourgeois ideology,* is brought together in his work and given its most perfect expression. ["Addison," in James L. Clifford, ed., *Eighteenth Century English Literature,* 1959].

We hold it against Addison that he never reached for the heights of sublimity, never probed the depths of despair.

There is much justice in these criticisms. Addison was indeed an amiable patronising champion of "the fair sex"; he was indeed a bland defender of social privilege: women, Mr. Spectator tells his readers, deserve to be well treated, for they can profit from gentle instruction, but it must be conceded that they are flighty creatures, empty-headed, affected, hopelessly addicted to triviality and self-display—and lovable. And the present class structure is right and unalterable:

> Since it is necessary, in the present Constitution of things, that Order and Distinction should be kept up in the World, we should be happy if those who enjoy the upper Stations in it would endeavour to surpass others in Vertue, as much as in Rank, and by their Humanity and Condescention make their Superiority easy and acceptable to those who are beneath them: and if, on the contrary, those who are in meaner Posts of Life, would consider how they may better their Condition hereafter, and by a just Deference and Submission to their Superiors make them happy in those Blessings with which Providence has thought fit to distinguish them [*Spectator* 219].

For a journalist with such views, the Stock Exchange may well serve as a model for civilised intercourse: "There is no place in the Town," Mr. Spectator muses,

> which I so much love to frequent as the *Royal-Exchange.* It gives me a secret Satisfaction, and, in some measure, gratifies my Vanity, as I am an *Englishman,* to see so rich an Assembly of Country-Men and Foreigners consulting together

upon the private Business of Mankind, and making this Metropolis a kind of *Emporium* for the whole Earth. I must confess I look upon High-Change to be a great Council, in which all considerable Nations have their Representatives. . . . As I am a great Lover of Mankind, my heart naturally overflows with Pleasure at the sight of a prosperous and happy Multitude, insomuch that at many publick Solemnities I cannot forbear expressing my Joy with Tears that have stolen down my Cheeks. For this reason I am wonderfully delighted to see such a Body of Men thriving in their own private Fortunes, and at the same time promoting the Publick Stock; or in other Words, raising Estates for their own Families, by bringing into their Country whatever is wanting, and carrying out of it whatever is superfluous.

This is scarcely heroic stuff. As C. S. Lewis concludes: Addison is, "above all else, comfortable." What, in our uncomfortable time, makes us more uncomfortable than that?

Emphatically, this is not Addison's century; if we must like an 18th-century figure—it seems like an unwelcome assignment, considering that the 17th century had Hobbes and Pascal, the 19th century, Kierkegaard and Nietzsche—we prefer, to Addison, Jonathan Swift or Samuel Johnson, with their savage indignation, their open-eyed pessimism, their fearless confrontation of the human condition. Still, it is odd: though Swift had his doubts, Johnson admired Addison without embarrassment and without reservations, admired him for his delicacy, his authentic elegance, his wit, admired him above all for his willingness to use his abundant talent in a cause as important as it was just:

> He not only made the proper use of wit himself, but taught it to others; and from his time it has been generally subservient to the cause of reason and of truth. He has dissipated the prejudice that had long connected gaiety with vice, and easiness of manners with laxity of principles. he has restored virtue to its dignity, and taught innocence not to be ashamed. This is an elevation of literary character, *above all Greek, above all Roman fame.* No greater felicity can genius attain than that of having purified intellectual pleasure, separated mirth from indecency, and wit from licentiousness; of having taught a succession of writers to bring elegance and gaiety to the aid of goodness; and, if I may use expressions yet more awful, of having *turned many to righteousness*" [*Lives of the English Poets,* 1781].

This, for Johnson, who chooses his words carefully, is high praise; his judgment introduces a new dimension into the common view of Addison. Dobrée's first Victorian and Johnson's classical moralist hardly seem to be the same man.

If anything can reduce the puzzle to its proper proportions—though for its solution we must go outside Addison's writings to the history of his times—it is Donald F. Bond's splendid new edition of *The Spectator,* in which most of Addison's best work appeared. (pp. 27-8)

But, eloquent as it is, the *Spectator* does not speak to us directly; we must know something of its time before we know something of its significance. And that is why we must welcome the opportunity to read the complete *Spectator* once again, and not those interminably reissued selections which concentrate on that lovable Tory eccentric, Sir Roger de Coverley, with his irresistible impulse to sleep in church, and omit so much that is valuable, in fact revolutionary, in Addison's journal.

The *Spectator* dealt with many subjects—that was its formula, and one reason for its success. Sir Roger was part, and an important part, of Addison's world, and so were the *Spectator's* rather repetitive criticisms of Italian opera or female affectations. But, as the specialist—and, I suspect, only the specialist—knows, Addison's world was wider and more varied than this. The *Spectator's* most interesting papers are its essays on literary criticism: the essays on wit, the appreciations of the popular ballad "Chevy Chase" and the august poetry of John Milton, and above all the celebration of the Imagination. In these papers, Addison was the radical, subversive of the prevailing rationalism and the dominant academicism of cultivated literary and artistic circles. As Pope's *Essay on Criticism* "belongs to the age and to the past," Professor Clarence Thorpe has argued in a persuasive essay on Addison's literary criticism, Addison's critical essays belong "to the age and to the future. . . . Unlike Pope, Addison's peculiar service to aesthetics and criticism was not to utilise the old—though he did some of that, too—but to accept and adapt and transmit the new, and in such a way and to such a degree that he became thereby one of the chief constructive forces in the literary theory of the century that followed" ["Addison's Contribution to Criticism," in R. F. Jones and others, *The Seventeenth Century,* 1951].

Addison, to be sure, was not an inventor; he articulated and extended tendencies already implicit in the scattered writings of his intellectual ancestors. Those tendencies were from rules to freedom, from reliance on objective criteria of beauty (like the theory of proportions) to the subjective appreciation of the work of art, from the academic to the passionate. But while these tendencies had been hidden in treatises or debates held in circumscribed circles of professionals, Addison, with his customary elegance, clarity, and good sense, brought the new ideas before a general public of amateurs: while the precise number of *Spectator*s sold remains a mystery, it must have been at least 3,000, and each issue had many readers—no daily paper before, and few daily papers after the *Spectator* reached so wide an audience; certainly none influenced so many, and such influential people.

Now this aesthetic radicalism, and this effectiveness, suggest that the modern view of Addison as a bland ideologist of the Establishment must be, if not mistaken, at least incomplete. Indeed, there is nothing new in Professor Bond's claim that Addison, vigorously aided by Steele, "helped to bring about" a "revolution in morals and manners." His contemporaries were certain of it; Samuel Johnson and, almost a century later, Lord Macaulay confirmed it. What Bond's edition does, with its authoritativeness, is to compel us to re-examine these early judgments, to take them seriously. If we do, I suggest, we will come to see Addison, the silent Mr. Spectator, as a leading actor in a great moral drama, and to recognise in Addison, the genteel journalist who wanted nothing more than to please the ladies and amuse the gentlemen, the serious moralist.

Before we can appreciate Addison's important role in the drama of the Western conscience, I must say some obvious things about manners. Today, the word *manners* is applied mainly to ritual polite gestures—to the way one addresses an elderly aunt or helps oneself to dinner; good manners, if they are anything, are a mark of having been to the right school, they are grace notes to conduct pleasing but by no means indispensable. It is no accident that the word *mœurs* should give the modern translator so much trouble: it means what we mean by *manners,* but it means far more than that. In the 18th century, manners were *mœurs,* and manners mattered; they were an essential element holding together a society undergoing rapid change. It was a society in which life was precarious, in which epidemics continued to threaten all segments of the population, in which the streets of the cities were dark, filthy, and unsafe, in which the lower orders were sunk in near-animal torpor and many of the privileged displayed their rank by coarseness and sheer violence. "In the early 18th century," so J. H. Plumb begins the first volume of his *Sir Robert Walpole,* "English politics were influenced by the smallness of the population, by the difficulty of communication and by the prevalence of disease." In such a world, to have manners meant to reduce the amount of violence, to increase the amount of rational intercourse; to "give the wall" while walking in the streets of London, or to call an adversary in debate "Sir," was to avoid physical combat—and more, it was to recognise others as human beings with rights of their own. In Addison's day, then, manners and morals were co-ordinate, allied, almost synonymous terms. [Gay adds in a footnote, "Thus, Addison can write in the **Spectator:** 'There are no Authors I am more pleased with than those who show Human Nature in a variety of Views, and describe the several Ages of the World in their different Manners. A Reader cannot be more rationally entertained, than by comparing the Virtues and Vices of his own Times, with those which prevailed in the Times of his Fore-fathers' (No. 209.)."] To speak about manners, therefore, in the **Spectator** and elsewhere, was to speak about the way one dealt with women and children and social inferiors, the way one conducted one's business or served one's country, the way one behaved and, almost, what one believed in church. In a time when much was new and almost everything was uncertain, a time when a modern civilisation was slowly, painfully arising out of the Christian millennium, men needed guidance in all things, and few things, not even one's taste in dress or in opera, could be dismissed as a triviality. The **Spectator** is a vast miscellany, moving with ease and without plan from attacks on superstitions to attacks on French fashions, from a little sermon on humanity to a serious discussion of Milton, and much of this variety, as I have said, is simply a journalist's stratagem to keep his readers' attention. But it is also symptomatic of the task of the moralist, the critic of manners, in the last years of the Stuart dynasty.

Addison had the wit—I am tempted to say, the genius—to perceive this. He was writing in a time, and in a place, when two intersecting cycles in the history of conscience—one, in Great Britain, short-term and local, the other, in the Christian West, long-term and general—were approaching a critical moment. Civilisation rests on many things, but one thing that is indispensable to it (as we, the heirs of Freud, can no longer doubt) is the internalisation of aggression. As long as all men freely act out their impulses, say what they want, take what they crave, kill whom they hate, and rape whom they desire, there is no civilisation, but the war of all against all, and the life of man, solitary, poor, nasty, brutish, and short. That is why, from the time of the most primitive tribe, societies have sought to curb impulse and direct it to the service of a larger whole. Agencies of socialisation—domestic training, formal schooling, rites celebrating stages in the life cycle, festivals recalling victories, saints, or heroes—have always been agencies aiding repression. But, as cynics in ancient Rome and 17th-century Europe alike recognised, these attempts to induce individuals to deny free range to their passions have never been adequate, or been adequate only with exceptional individuals: that is why, when Bayle offered the radical suggestion that a society of atheists could live happily and in peace, most of his contemporaries scoffed and Voltaire, a great student of Bayle, amended it to say that such a society could survive only if it were a society of philosophers. Religion, with its threats of hell and bait of heaven, was admittedly an efficacious agency in keeping public order, but the secular arm never could afford to discard the agency of force which repressed by physical compulsion the aggression that had not been successfully repressed by psychological manipulation.

It would be absurd to maintain that Christianity succeeded where other religions had failed: the Middle Ages, even in its most civilised centuries and most civilised centres, was an age of coarseness and irrepressible brutality. But Christianity, especially as it associated itself with the institutions of feudalism, offered some impressive models of obedience, self-abnegation, acceptance of one's role. The master metaphor of medieval life, the hierarchy, assigned to man his proper place in this world and the next, told him precisely where he belonged in his family, in his society, in his profession, in the legal structure, in his relation to religious authority, and even in the solar system. The hierarchy was a model distributing rights and duties; it legitimised the gratification of some impulses and denied the gratification of others. And it was an authoritative model because it rested on religious prescriptions and could call on religious sanctions: God, the apex of the hierarchy, was also its inventor and its guardian.

By the time of Addison, the authority of the hierarchy had been severely shaken. In some unforgettable pages, Burckhardt has pictured the consequences of individual freedom, at once exhilarating and dreadful, in the Italian Renaissance. And elsewhere and later, over and over again, in the realm of politics as much as in the realm of astronomy, degree had been shaken, and while discord had followed, the old order had never been fully restored anywhere. By the 18th century, hierarchies remained as social realities, but their religious authority had been undermined forever. Educated men were for the most part still devout Christians, but their devotion was rational; they were certain that the discoveries of modern science and the criticisms of modern philology must be, and could be, incorporated into a faith that they, as reasonable men, could accept.

This gradual and partial secularisation of life called for new justifications of self-denial, and so, in literature and in political theory, the 17th century developed secular canons for settling the conflicts and determining the respective spheres of reason and passion. The great neoclassical tradition was, among other things, precisely this: a set of rules governing the decorous expression and reasonable control of elemental emotional forces. Denham spoke for this tradition when he voiced his wish to be like the river Thames:

> Though deep, yet clear; though gentle, yet not
> dull;
> Strong without rage, without o'erflowing full.

The political theorists of the time were neo-Classicists in their own way; they went back to the Romans of antiquity to restate the theory of sovereignty: man must obey the authority of the state not because he is a member of a tribe, or placed into a cosmic hierarchy, but because he has the legal duty to keep order in the commonwealth.

In England, the struggle to secularise repression had spe-

Addison in the last years of his life, in a portrait by Sir Godfrey Kneller.

cial poignancy. For most Englishmen, the reign of the Puritans had been a trauma: an orgy of gloomy self-abnegation, of fanatical oppression crowned by parricide. The return of Charles II in 1660 thus permitted the explosive expression of long-suppressed grievances, and the defiant, almost ritualistic subversion of the moral rigour which the Puritans had imposed upon the country. The immorality of Restoration society has been greatly exaggerated; the court wits and titled rakes made up a small, if conspicuously brilliant segment of English society, and even they, for all their exhibitionism, turn out on historical scrutiny to have been rather less vicious and less immoral than gossip made them out to be. Still it is true that in the court of Charles II, and therefore among the fashionable, wit and morality were long regarded as antithetical, manner—not manners—was separated from content. Yet, as Joseph Wood Krutch said long ago, "The orgy of dissipation into which the ruling class plunged after the Restoration could not possibly last. England was not, like the Roman Empire, decadent and hence destined to wear itself out and die." Thus, "as the effects of the reaction passed, English moderation naturally reasserted itself" [*Comedy and Conscience after the Restoration,* 1924]. Some of this reassertion, to be sure, took rather immoderate forms: in particular the attempts to purge the stage seemed ready to discard the wit with the immorality. Yet, whatever the excesses of the moderates, their historical role was plain enough: it was part of a long, difficult, subtle process of creating a new civilisation. Most men continued to evoke God and the Church, but more and more, whether in discussions of the theatre or the family, new words began to make themselves heard: reason, experience, humanity. Dedicating a book to his wife—itself a remarkable sign of the new manners—Steele fondly wrote:

> That I think them [his children] preferable to all
> other children, I know, is the effect of passion
> and instinct. That I believe you the best of wives,
> I know proceeds from experience and reason.

The time to moralise wit was at hand.

The *Spectator*'s share in constructing the tradition of modern civility was considerable, but its precise measurement must remain uncertain. Students of literature are apt to overestimate the effect of the written word in society: it is often less a cause of social change than an expression of social change already under way. Surely Addison's journal was such a success because a wide public was ready to applaud, and perhaps to apply, its ethical teachings. Yet there is abundant evidence that the *Spectator* made its readers more aware of themselves than they had been before, that its gentle ridicule encouraged many to reform conduct, or discard opinions, that made them vaguely uneasy before. Professor Bond quotes the diary entry of young Dudley Ryder, who later became a distinguished judge:

> Read the 38th *Spectator,* was extremely pleased
> because I felt everything I read [in] it was de-
> signed against the fault that I find myself ex-
> tremely guilty of, and that is a too great desire
> and love of applause in things which are in them-
> selves the least commendable. I have continually
> a desire of pleasing in my eye and this gives birth

and life to every pursuit or engagement, whatever I do carries an air of affectation along with it.

There were many like Dudley Ryder, uncomfortable with their ways, uncertain of what the right way was, and thus "extremely pleased" to be so wittily seduced into virtue.

It is in this light, I think, the light of history, that we must read the *Spectator.* Its tone (which often seems insipid), its attacks on affectation, or petty superstitions, or Italian opera (which hardly seem worth troubling with), were parts of a great campaign on behalf of civilisation, appropriate to its own time if not to ours. [Gay adds in a footnote: "Though, given the beastliness, the shallow religiosity, the cant and brutality of our century, I'm not sure that we should feel above the need for Addison's moralising."] Addison's moderation—his deliberate avoidance of wounding personal allusions, his light-hearted mockery— was itself didactic, designed to teach civility by example. Mr. Spectator was demonstrating to his public that one could ridicule absurdities and oppose vice without retailing libels or using vicious language, that one could praise virtue without indulging in embarrassing rhapsodies. Besides, Addison's tone cast an air of reasonableness over all of Mr. Spectator's favourite causes; if Addison and his associates were ahead of the general public, they made sure they were no more than one step ahead, for they saw little point in persuading a mere handful of philosophers (who were in any event already persuaded) and leaving the wider public baffled or bored. "It was said of *Socrates,*" Addison observed quite early in the *Spectator,* "that he brought Philosophy down from Heaven, to inhabit among Men; and I shall be ambitious to have it said of me, that I have brought Philosophy out of Closets and Libraries, Schools and Colleges, to dwell in Clubs and Assemblies, at Tea-Tables, and in Coffee-Houses." No commentator has expressed the *Spectator*'s social programme more forcefully and more clearly than this: the time to diffuse the blessings of civilisation was now.

Mr. Spectator's tears at the sight of merchants in pacific assembly, therefore, calls not for the acid of the satirist but the understanding of the historian. Addison's was a coarse age, and, as Hogarth's work testifies, coarseness survived Addison's most strenuous efforts. But the way from coarseness to civility was open. To ridicule superstitions was to lend prestige to the scientific mode of thinking. To treat women with affection and to urge that they be raised by degrees to full human status was to offer a radical proposal; condescension is better than brutality. To romanticise the Stock Exchange was to assist in the burial of aristocratic martial values that had dominated European life for so long and served it so badly; Addison was not a Philistine, but he preferred a peaceful merchant to a brawny hero, a greedy shopkeeper to a stupid general. "There are not more useful Members in a Commonwealth," Addison wrote, "than Merchants. They knit Mankind together in a mutual Intercourse of good Offices, distribute the Gifts of Nature, find work for the Poor, add wealth to the Rich, and Magnificence to the Great." I need not demonstrate that this is a sentimental view of merchants, a fine specimen of what C. S. Lewis had already noted in Addison— bourgeois ideology. If we were to take it literally, we would have on our hands a hero only slightly less repulsive

than, and perhaps as destructive as his aristocratic predecessor. But there is good evidence that we need not so take him, and some of this evidence comes, strikingly enough, from a passage not in Addison, but in Voltaire. In the late 1720s, the decade after Addison's death, Voltaire lived in England for more than two years, learned English, steeped himself in English culture, and turned incurable Anglomaniac. He admired the "illustrious M. Addison," and obviously knew the *Spectator,* for in his celebrated report on England, the *Lettres philosophiques,* there appears this paragraph:

> Enter the London stock exchange, that place more respectable than many a court. You will see the deputies of all nations gathered there for the service of mankind. There the Jew, the Mohammedan, and the Christian deal with each other as if they were of the same religion, and give the name of infidel only to those who go bankrupt; there, the Presbyterian trusts the Anabaptist, and the Anglican accepts the Quaker's affirmation. On leaving these peaceful and free assemblies, some go to the synagogue, others go to drink; this one goes to have himself baptised in the name of the Father, the Son, and the Holy Ghost; that one has his son's foreskin cut off and Hebrew words mumbled over the child which he does not understand; others go to their church to await the inspiration of God, their hats on their heads, and all are content.

Here Voltaire fully develops the cultural implications of Addison's sentimental report: the stock exchange becomes an extended metaphor for a rational, pacific, secular civilisation which encourages diversity, protects dissent, chooses profit over bloodshed, and celebrates traders instead of heroes. We have had enough heroics in our day to recognise that Voltaire's—and Addison's—choice was eminently sensible.

Addison's moral preaching then, like his literary criticism, was an attempt to find the proper place for passion and to find that place by appealing not to some higher authority, or to caprice, but to a reasonable consideration of the evidence at hand. In the end, what allows us to patronise Addison is that he did what he did so well: "I sometimes wonder," even the critical C. S. Lewis was moved to ruminate, "whether the very degree of their success does not conceal from us the greatness of the undertaking." Precisely. We patronise Addison at the peril of surrendering our historical perspective. (pp. 28-32)

> *Peter Gay, "The Spectator as Actor: Addison in Perspective," in* Encounter, *Vol. XXIX, No. 6, December, 1967, pp. 27-32.*

Leopold Damrosch, Jr. (essay date 1979)

[*Damrosch is an American educator and critic who has published works about Samuel Johnson and eighteenth-century literature. In the following essay, he defends Addison's critical practice, describing his essays on John Milton's* Paradise Lost *(1667) as treatments of the poem that were sensitive to the needs of Addison's readership.*]

Joseph Addison is one of those writers whose reputation,

which once seemed established for all time, has fallen so drastically that literate people feel no shame in admitting complete ignorance of him. His poems and his **Cato** lost favor rapidly as the eighteenth century went forward, and even the **Spectator,** which readers like Benjamin Franklin pored over as a guide to culturally approved language and manners, long ago passed into eclipse. Since Addison has lost all authority as poet and moral censor, it would be surprising if his criticism had survived intact. But its historical influence is still conceded to have been immense, and I shall argue that the full implications of that influence have not had adequate recognition. Addison's role in the history of aesthetics is familiar enough, but I want to distinguish criticism from aesthetics and to propose that his critical *example* is what calls for our attention and respect. In an age when criticism prides itself on its rigor, and when poetics enjoys greater prestige than criticism, such a project may seem beside the point. But Addison himself was no stranger to the claims of criticism to be rigorous and theoretical, and it is possible that we can still learn something from his suspicion of those claims.

Writing sixty years after Addison's death, Johnson approached our topic in these words: "Addison is now to be considered as a critick; a name which the present generation is scarcely willing to allow him. His criticism is condemned as tentative or experimental rather than scientifick, and he is considered as deciding by taste rather than by principles" [*Lives of the Poets,* 1781]. Johnson's defense of Addison rests on two points: that later critics ought to acknowledge the debt they owe their superseded master, and that critics like Dryden had written for apprentice poets, so that a guide was still needed for the common reader.

> An instructor like Addison was now wanting, whose remarks being superficial, might be easily understood, and being just might prepare the mind for more attainments. Had he presented *Paradise Lost* to the publick with all the pomp of system and severity of science, the criticism would perhaps have been admired, and the poem still have been neglected; but by the blandishments of gentleness and facility he has made Milton an universal favourite, with whom readers of every class think it necessary to be pleased.

Johnson's defense is forthright and yet ambiguous: it raises some crucial doubts. First of all, what is the real value of a master who has been superseded, whether or not his successors owe him a debt? Next, how can criticism be "just" if it is also "superficial"? And finally, if Johnson is right—as I believe he is—to see the Milton papers as Addison's central achievement, can that achievement be separated from the cunning blandishments that seduce an uncritical audience into liking an author whom it becomes socially obligatory to like? Johnson's parrot-critic Dick Minim found Milton the only author whose books he could "read for ever without weariness" (*Idler* 61); Johnson himself said that *Paradise Lost* is a poem which one lays down and forgets to take up again. Is Addison a mere pander to the Dick Minims of the world?

Every one of these doubts has real substance. If they did not, Addison might still be a living critic. But a critic's in-

fluence depends as much on the way he approaches literature as on the things he says about it, and here Addison has not received the praise he deserves. Let us briefly consider his great predecessor Dryden. Dryden's essays are not only directed, as Johnson says, to aspiring writers who want to learn the technique of their art, but are also designed as propaganda to recommend the poems or translations to which they are attached. Even the *Dramatic Poesy* is oriented to Dryden's career: Are rhyming plays good or bad? Should one imitate the ancients or the French or the Elizabethans? Already, then, his criticism is complicated by motives which Addison, writing for the ordinary reader, can ignore. And more important still, Dryden is obsessed with the fear that the tough-minded French and their tough-minded English disciples will expose his criticism as casual or even shallow. Hence the endless casting about for arguments and precedents when he states an opinion; hence the otherwise inexplicable deference he shows the ferocious but silly Rymer.

It is immensely suggestive that Addison, a generation later, was contemptuous rather than impressed when John Dennis claimed to be a rigorous theorist basing his theories on French neoclassicism.

> The marks you may know him by are, an elevated eye, and dogmatical brow, a positive voice, and a contempt for every thing that comes out, whether he has read it or not. . . . He hath formed his judgment upon Homer, Horace, and Virgil, not from their own works, but from those of Rapin and Bossu. He knows his own strength so well, that he never dares praise any thing in which he has not a French author for his voucher [*Tatler* 165].

Dennis was a much more powerful critic than Rymer, more powerful in some respects than Addison, but his authoritarian air represents the critic as judge or even prosecutor, arraigning each work of literature by the standards of a code of law. Addison's originality lies in his conviction that the reader is more important than the prosecutor or judge, and should not let himself be bullied by authority. It is not simply as a pose that Addison appears as the reader's companion rather than his master.

Though I shall not examine Addison's contribution to aesthetic theory, it is significant that his emphasis there is affective or psychological, rather than formalist and systematic. Meyer Abrams [in his *The Mirror and the Lamp,* 1953] speaks of his "eclectic, but endlessly suggestive, papers on 'the Pleasures of the Imagination.' " They are eclectic because Addison is not afraid of gathering interesting ideas from a wide range of sources; they are suggestive because he stresses the openness of imaginative experience rather than any single doctrine about the nature of art. As he writes in the paper that introduces the series, "I could wish there were authors . . . who, beside the mechanical rules which a man of very little taste may discourse upon, would enter into the very spirit and soul of fine writing, and show us the several sources of that pleasure which rises in the mind upon the perusal of a noble work" (*Spectator* 409). Addison is firmly neoclassical; even humor "should always lie under the check of reason," and the humorist should possess "a certain regularity of thought which must discover the writer to be a man of sense" (*Spectator* 35). But the tendency of this aesthetic is, as Johnson said, experimental rather than scientific, deciding by taste rather than principles. Addison wants to know what readers feel and why they feel that way, not to dictate what their feelings must be or to analyze literary structure in narrowly formalist terms as the French neoclassicists had been doing.

A good illustration is furnished by Addison's famous defense of plays that violate poetic justice. Without doubt he sought to prepare the public mind for his own *Cato,* in which poetic justice would be violated, but he rests his case on audience response rather than the structure of the drama or the moral order of God's universe.

> We find that good and evil happen alike to all men on this side the grave; and as the principal design of tragedy is to raise commiseration and terror in the minds of the audience, we shall defeat this great end, if we always make virtue and innocence happy and successful. . . . Terror and commiseration leave a pleasing anguish in the mind; and fix the audience in such a serious composure of thought, as is much more lasting and delightful than any little transient starts of joy and satisfaction [*Spectator* 40].

In a fine phrase Addison says that the dramatist should not obstruct "the tide of sorrow." The attack on poetic justice, then, is empirically based: life is not like that, and tragedies wouldn't be moving if playwrights pretended it was. And although Dennis later stung Addison to further reflections on the suffering of the innocent, he never abandoned this essential orientation toward the audience rather than the artist or the art abstractly considered.

As soon as we turn to Addison's practical criticism, we are faced once more with the question, How can it be "just" if it is also "superficial"? Addison has been called a great popularizer; is he then a parasitical writer who simplifies other men's ideas in order to convey them to a large and not very thoughtful audience? It is worth quoting at some length from George Watson, who has sought to write the history of descriptive criticism and has found Addison grievously wanting.

> The book-by-book analysis [of *Paradise Lost*] . . . only confirms how very far from the text Addison is. At a glance, its abundance of quotations looks impressive. But Addison's comments on his quotations have all the vagueness of a schoolboy's ("wonderfully poetical," "truly sublime"), and he almost never ventures a strictly descriptive or interpretative statement. Casual value-judgements are the only mode of proceeding. For the Augustan Man of Taste, it soon appears, intelligent inquiry concerning the meaning of a passage is barely a possibility. Whatever is obscure is merely bad; the critic's function is simply to point and enthuse: "to point out its particular beauties, and to determine wherein they consist" (no. 369), as Addison explains in his concluding paper. And "wherein," for Addison, means only "under what preconceived category" (the Sublime, the Soft, the Natural). Much of the awful glibness of

the Augustan aesthetic, its pathetic readiness to take shelter behind a modish terminology of criticism, is plainly visible in the language of this ambitious but complacent critic [*The Literary Critics,* 1964].

Watson has more than enough complacency of his own, but the indictment needs to be faced, and it is well to have it stated so openly. Addison does not analyze, and his survey of *Paradise Lost* does fall, despite his interest in reader response, under a series of conventional categories drawn from neoclassical epic theory and specifically from René Le Bossu, the very writer he mocks Dennis for following.

My defense of Addison will take two parts. He fails to analyze because he holds a consistent, if modest, view of the scope and uses of criticism; I shall return to this point later. And he adopts conventional categories largely for tactical reasons: they help to organize one's impressions of a work, and may help to persuade a hostile reader who can only see the work plainly if he can see it through categories which he already knows. Consider, for instance, Addison's praise of the popular ballad by comparison with Homer and Virgil. As C. S. Lewis and Albert Friedman have shown, this discussion forms part of Addison's larger account of "true wit" and participates in a general European reaction against the metaphysical mode. If the neoclassical principle of universality is valid, then it should apply to works outside the canon of classical literature. The ballads offer a suitable test case, and Addison selects his examples, *Chevy Chase* and *The Two Children in the Wood,* precisely because their popularity was longstanding and widespread. In these terms, Addison is not particularly interested in the ballad at all, but in a neoclassical principle which he illustrates in the ballad, not without sly amusement at turning the term "Gothic" against the very poets who called the ballads Gothic.

This account is a fair statement of the theoretical impulse behind Addison's ballad papers, and of his use of the ballads to argue a neoclassical point. But it does an injustice to his genuine sense of what the ballads are and why people would want to read them. Consider his treatment of *The Two Children in the Wood:*

> This song is a plain simple copy of nature, destitute of all the helps and ornaments of art. The tale of it is a pretty tragical story, and pleases for no other reason, but because it is a copy of nature. There is even a despicable simplicity in the verse; and yet, because the sentiments appear genuine and unaffected, they are able to move the mind of the most polite reader with inward meltings of humanity and compassion. The incidents grow out of the subject, and are such as are the most proper to excite pity. For which reason the whole narration has something in it very moving; notwithstanding the author of it (whoever he was) has delivered it in such an abject phrase, and poorness of expression, that the quoting any part of it would look like a design of turning it into ridicule [*Spectator* 85].

Watson is right: Addison does not analyze here, evading analysis with phrases like "has something in it very moving." But he sees no reason to analyze; his purpose is to cajole the reader into rethinking his *attitude* toward ballad. Though the ballads are specifically invoked in the argument about true wit, Addison's esteem is none the weaker for that. Their simplicity is the true, permanent simplicity that readers have been taught to admire in Homer and Virgil, and if the best way to make them see it is to place parallel passages together, then Addison is glad to do so. If it seems incongruous to us to measure the ballads against Virgil, that is because we have learned a historical relativism that allows us to value them in their uniqueness. Addison writes for readers who see their simplicity as "despicable" and their language as "abject"; for them the Virgilian comparison is essential. Its strategic success is shown by the praise of another classically-trained reader a century later: Macaulay says that Addison "raised his voice against the contempt with which our fine old ballads were regarded, and showed the scoffers that the same gold which, burnished and polished, gives lustre to the *Aeneid* and the *Odes* of Horace, is mingled with the rude dross of *Chevy Chase*" [*"The Life and Writings of Addison,"* first pub. in the *Edinburgh Review,* July 1843.] And, as always, Addison is concerned with affective response: though the ballads are unsophisticated, they are above all moving.

Addison's major critical achievement, the eighteen **Spectator** papers on *Paradise Lost,* confirms these observations: he wants to help the reader open his sensibility to the poem, and his tactic is to relate the poem to the classical epics whose status was firmly established as the best poems in the highest genre. He is not really measuring *Paradise Lost* by the standards of Aristotle and Le Bossu, but is using their categories as a convenient means of opening up the poem. It was original to give so much space to a single work. As contrasted, say, with Dryden's spare, rigorous "examen" of *The Silent Woman* after the model of Corneille, Addison conveys an expansive sense of open-minded attentiveness and of the critic as reader, not judge. In his youth he seems to have been impressed by Dryden's view of Milton as a literary as well as political rebel; in the **Spectator,** twenty years later, he has not forgotten that Milton often exhibits "the wantonness of a luxuriant imagination" (No. 315), but he wants to emphasize control and order rather than anarchic licence. He sets out, then, by proposing an undogmatic classicism: whether the epic (or "heroic poem") can be rigorously defined or not, he will consider the relation of *Paradise Lost* to epic poems of admitted excellence.

> I shall therefore examine it by the rules of epic poetry, and see whether it falls short of the *Iliad* or *Aeneid* in the beauties which are essential to that kind of writing. The first thing to be considered in an epic poem, is the fable, which is perfect or imperfect, according as the action which it relates is more or less so. This action should have three qualifications in it. First, it should be but one action. Secondly, it should be an entire action; and thirdly, it should be a great action.
> [**Spectator** 267]

The terms come straight from Le Bossu, but are used in a notably relaxed manner. Addison's intention is to show that *Paradise Lost* is at least as great and unified as the

Iliad and *Aeneid,* not to find fault with it by some abstract standard of epic theory. And if parts of the poem cannot be strictly defended on these terms, then, as he cheerfully admits, he is prepared to drop the terms. "Milton's complaint of his blindness, his panegyric on marriage, his reflections on Adam's and Eve's going naked, of the angels eating, and several other passages in his poem, are liable to the same exception [of being extraneous], though I must confess there is so great a beauty in these very digressions, that I would not wish them out of his poem" (No. 297).

As with the ballads, the principal tactic is to emphasize the classical element in Milton's epic. Even the epigraphs are shrewdly chosen: of the eighteen, nine are from Horace—all but one from the *Ars Poetica,* insinuating Milton's conformity to received Augustan notions—and seven are from Virgil, mostly in the *Aeneid,* insinuating that *Paradise Lost* can be properly compared with the most "regular" of the epics. The first epigraph of all is from Propertius (who alludes to the *Aeneid*), "Give way, ye Greek and Roman writers!", and the papers that follow are designed to show that they must give way to Milton on their own ground. Addison of course recognizes how often Milton draws on the Bible rather than the classics, but he is at pains to demonstrate Milton's judgment "in duly qualifying those high strains of eastern poetry, which were suited to readers whose imaginations were set to an higher pitch than those of colder climates" (No. 339). While this points to a real quality in *Paradise Lost,* Milton himself must have thought of it as operating in the other direction—Biblicizing the epic, not classicizing the Bible. And at times Addison shows something like embarrassment about his tactic. He defends Milton's style, for instance, by asserting that Homer does similar things (No. 285), but later confesses that he has been making the best of a dubious business for the sake of argument. "Our language sunk under him, and was unequal to that greatness of soul, which furnished him with such glorious conceptions" (No. 297).

This last observation points to the true tendency of the *Paradise Lost* papers, which is to celebrate the poem for what it is, not to worry much about its classical credentials. It is only a debating point, as Addison says, whether an epic can be allowed to end unhappily or not. The deeper truth is that this poem turns upon a *felix culpa* whose religious basis distinguishes it from the happy or unhappy endings of traditional epics. "Our two first parents are comforted by dreams and visions, cheered with promises of salvation, and, in a manner, raised to a greater happiness than that which they had forfeited: in short, Satan is represented miserable in the height of his triumphs, and Adam triumphant in the height of misery" (No. 369). By emphasizing the sublime in Milton, as Dennis had done before him and as Johnson would do after him, Addison invokes a quality of greatness that transcends the ordinary preoccupations of prescriptive criticism.

It remains true that Addison's critical remarks are informal and, in Johnson's term, superficial. But we must not forget that Addison himself knew they were; in an important sense, he believed they had to be. He introduces his hesitant account of Milton's faults with the observation that it can only be useful to a reader who is fully at home with the poem.

> It is in criticism, as in all other sciences and speculations; one who brings with him any implicit notions and observations which he has made in his reading of the poets, will find his own reflections methodized and explained, and perhaps several little hints that had passed in his mind, perfected and improved in the works of a good critic; whereas one who has not these previous lights, is very often an utter stranger to what he reads, and apt to put a wrong interpretation upon it.

The critic's role is to help the reader clarify what he thinks about a poem he already knows well or should seek to know well, not to create meaning for him. The critic is, first and foremost, a reader himself, whose special qualification is a rigorous training in the art of logical thinking—Addison goes on to invoke Locke—and whose own style must prove his competence to judge the work of others. And after the critic has finished, the reader must be left alone with the poem. Having examined, for instance, the subject of epic simile, Addison concludes, "If the reader considers the comparisons in the first book of Milton, of the sun in an eclipse, of the sleeping Leviathan, of the bees swarming about their hive, of the fairy dance, in the view wherein I have here placed them, he will easily discover the great beauties that are in each of those passages" (No. 303). After the critic has placed the general issue in what he thinks is the proper light, the reader must go on to consider specific passages for himself.

Watson, we remember, disliked the smugness of Addison's Augustan notion of taste. Perhaps it was smug. But it derives from a strong humanist tradition of openness to literature. When Addison defines taste as "that faculty of the soul, which discerns the beauties of an author with pleasure, and the imperfections with dislike" (No. 409), he goes on to say that although this faculty must be based on some inborn potentiality, it can only be developed through years of thoughtful reading and conversation.

> Notwithstanding this faculty must in some measure be born with us, there are several methods for cultivating and improving it, and without which it will be very uncertain, and of little use to the person that possesses it. The most natural method for this purpose is to be conversant among the writings of the most polite authors. A man who has any relish for fine writing, either discovers new beauties, or receives stronger impressions from the masterly strokes of a great author every time he peruses him: besides that he naturally wears himself into the same manner of speaking and thinking.

Believing this, Addison must trust the reader to make his own application of general conceptions. And if he is complacent, his assumptions are a valuable challenge to the modern complacency that assumes literary experience to be a technique that can be easily taught. As the pages of our professional journals all too bleakly attest, our criticism is a machine that can run on any fuel. Turn it upon the *Divine Comedy* or *King Lear* and it generates splendid structures of imagery and meaning. Turn it upon the most insignificant poem that ever fell still-born from the press and it will still generate magnificent structures. Addison urges the humanist view that reading must precede analysis and that the habit of analyzing can often get in the way of intelligent reading. What is Ned Softly, who interprets metaphors and explains the "gliding" of a line free of consonants (*Tatler* 163), but a New Critic striving to be born?

I maintain, then, that Addison was immensely influential in developing a criticism that could deal directly with individual works of literature and make them more fully available to potential readers. He does not classify works by species like Aristotle or Frye, or rank them in order of merit like Arnold or the Scrutiny school, or deconstruct their inner contradictions; he helps the reader to understand and appreciate them, and so inaugurates a long line of later critics, however divergent their theoretical principles—Johnson and Hazlitt and Bradley and so on to the present day. If Johnson was right to call Dryden the father of English criticism, then Addison is at least its uncle, and like other uncles he enjoys a privileged status: one can be fond of him without the more turbulent emotions of competitive love and ritual defiance that a father calls forth. If later critics have surpassed him—and they certainly have—it is in large measure because they learned what he had to teach, which lay not so much in particular judgments or aesthetic theory as in a wise and humane conception of the function of criticism itself. (pp. 421-30)

> *Leopold Damrosch, Jr., "The Significance of Addison's Criticism," in* Studies in English Literature, 1500–1900, *Vol. XIX, No. 3, Summer, 1979, pp. 421-30.*

FURTHER READING

Alsop, J. D. "New Light on Joseph Addison." *Modern Philology* 80, No. 1 (August 1982): 13-34.
  Claims that the papers of Charles Spence, third Earl of Sunderland, contain information essential to a comprehensive understanding of Addison's life. These papers reveal Addison as an "industrious," "competent," and "evenhanded" administrator.

Bateson, F. W. "The *Errata* in The Tatler." *The Review of English Studies* V, No. 18 (April 1929): 155-66.
  Argues that all but one of the seventeen errata embodying stylistic corrections in the *Tatler* are by Addison, a statistic that suggests that he was "painfully conscientious in revising and correcting everything he wrote."

Beljame, Alexandre. "Joseph Addison." In his *Men of Letters and the English Public in the Eighteenth Century: 1660-1744, Dryden, Addison, Pope,* edited by Bonamy Dobrée, translated by E. O. Lorimer, pp. 212-316. London: Kegan Paul, Trench, Trubner & Co., 1948.
  Discusses Addison's role in fostering the growth of an enlightened and interested public and the influence of this public on Addison's writing and position in society.

Blair, Hugh. *Lectures on Rhetoric and Belles Lettres,* Vol. I. Carbondale, Ill.: Southern Illinois University Press, 1965, 496 p.

Reprints four of Blair's lectures, dated 1783, analyzing essays by Addison line-by-line to elucidate the "good sense, and good writing, the useful morality, and the admirable vein of humour which abound in [the *Spectator*]."

Bloom, Edward A., and Bloom, Lillian D. "Addison's 'Enquiry after Truth': The Moral Assumptions of His Proof for Divine Existence." *PMLA* LXV, No. 2 (March 1950): 198-220.

Avers that "Joseph Addison as one of the foremost popularizers of rational inquiry represents, in a large measure, the eclectic religious temper of his times." The Blooms contend that the structure of the universe indicated to Addison the existence of God.

———. "Addison on 'Moral Habits of the Mind'." *Journal of the History of Ideas* XXI, No. 3 (July-September 1960): 409-27.

Identifies Addison as an exponent of a movement during the Augustan period to assimilate the intellectual into the moral and religious nature of human existence. The Blooms maintain that Addison advanced the notion of a "happy man" as "a practical moralist who fitted rational intelligence with probity and subjected secular activity to ethical examination."

———. *Joseph Addison's Sociable Animal.* Providence, R.I.: Brown University Press, 1971, 276 p.

Study of Addison's essays on London society, consisting of three sections: "In the Market Place," "On the Hustings," and "In the Pulpit."

Brown, John Mason. "Invitation to Learning." *The Saturday Review,* New York XXVII, No. 13 (31 March 1945): 24-6.

Favorably compares Addison's essays to Steele's and views him as a progenitor of the columnists in the *New Yorker* magazine in the twentieth century.

Chambers, Robert D. "Addison at Work on the *Spectator.*" *Modern Philology* LVI, No. 3 (February 1959): 145-53.

Studies the manuscript versions of Addison's essays.

Chandler, Zilpha E. "An Analysis of the Stylistic Technique of Addison, Johnson, Hazlitt, and Pater." In *University of Iowa Humanistic Studies: Volume IV, 1927-1931,* pp. 20-35, edited by Franklin H. Potter. Iowa City: University of Iowa, 1931.

Statistical and technical analysis of Addison's style, which is determined to be "simple," "natural," "familiar," and "unaffected." His writing, however, is also described as deficient in "variety," "clearness," "strength," and "energy."

Dobrée, Bonamy. "The First Victorian (Joseph Addison)." In his *Essays in Biography: 1680-1726,* pp. 197-345. 1925. Reprint. Freeport, N.Y.: Books for Libraries Press, 1967.

Influential sketch of Addison suggesting that his emphasis on propriety shares much with Victorian ideology. "To us," he writes, "in rebellion with the Victorian view, with more faith in the human being, and much less in his ideals, approaching as we do indeed a nihilism in values, a character such as Addison must seem unsatisfactory. . . . We may not admire; but are we sure we do not a little, now and again, with reservations, envy the tranquility, the certitude?"

Drake, Nathan. *Essays, Biographical, Critical, and Historical, Illustrative of the "Tatler," "Spectator," and "Guardian,"* Vol. 1. London: John Sharpe, 1805, 468 p.

Notes the influence of the *Tatler, Spectator,* and *Guardian* and the founders of these periodicals on the literature and manners of England.

Dwyer, John. "Addison and Steele's Spectator: Towards a Reappraisal." *Journal of Newspaper and Periodical History* IV, No. 1 (Winter 1987-88): 2-11.

Concurs with Peter Gay ["The Spectator as Actor," *Encounter* 29 (December 1967)] that modern opinions of the *Spectator* lack the proper historical perspective, but dissents from Gay's assertion that Addison was too complacent.

Elioseff, Lee Andrew. *The Cultural Milieu of Addison's Literary Criticism.* Austin: University of Texas Press, 1963, 252 p.

Comprehensive exploration of Addison's critical writings.

Engell, James. "The Creative Impulse: Addison through Akenside and the 1740s." In his *The Creative Imagination: Enlightenment to Romanticism,* pp. 33-50. Cambridge, Mass.: Harvard University Press, 1981.

Depicts the *Spectator* series on "the pleasures of the imagination" (Nos. 409, 411-21), as a significant popularization of and expansion upon Locke's theories of ideas.

Epstein, Joseph. "Piece Work: Writing the Essay." In his *Plausible Prejudices: Essays on American Writing,* pp. 397-411. New York: W. W. Norton & Co., 1985.

Discusses the history of the essay, ascribing to Addison the change to "straightforward, flexible, and conversational" English prose and an advance in the form of the essay over Montaigne.

Frazer, James George. Preface to *Essays of Joseph Addison,* Vol. I, by Joseph Addison, edited by James George Frazer, pp. v-xxv. London: Macmillan and Co., 1915.

Evokes the vivid, lasting impression made upon Frazer by the fictional world of Sir Roger de Coverley. Frazer recounts his own "journey" to the grounds of Coverley Hall and claims he will see Sir Roger again at Staple's Inn "or somewhere in the land of dreams."

Freeman, Phyllis. "Who Was Sir Roger de Coverley?" *The Quarterly Review* 285, No. 574 (October 1947): 592-604.

Speculates on the identity of an historical prototype for Addison's Sir Roger. Freeman suggests that a friend of Steele and Addison's, William Walsh, was the model.

Furtwangler, Albert. "Mr Spectator, Sir Roger, and Good Humour." *University of Toronto Quarterly* XLVI, No. 1 (Fall 1976): 31-50.

Describes the fictional characters of Mr Spectator, a Whig, and Sir Roger de Coverley, a Tory, observing that though one would expect a clash, "a fast friendship between them served to enlarge both these characters."

———. "Addison among the Quidnuncs." *English Studies in Canada* VI, No. I (Spring 1980): 13-21.

Argues that Addison "consciously shaped the successes and technologies of news publishing, in order to make traditional literature inviting to a public of common readers" and "effected a solid integration between popular and lasting literature."

———. "Cato at Valley Forge." In his *American Silhouettes: Rhetorical Identities of the Founders,* pp. 64-84. New Haven, Conn.: Yale University Press, 1987.
    Describes the historical setting in which Addison's *Cato* was performed for the American revolutionary army at Valley Forge in 1778, observing that "[General George] Washington was all that Cato had been—as unbending in his virtues and as heroic in his stature among Americans."

Gilfillan, George. "Life of Joseph Addison." In *The Poetical Works of Joseph Addison: Gay's Fables; and Somerville's Chase,* edited by George Gilfillan, pp. xi-xxxiii. Edinburgh, Scotland: James Nichol, 1859.
    Account of Addison's life. Gilfillan states that Addison admired and imitated the poetry of the Bible and that, though "not a Shakespeare or a Milton," he ranks "high on the list of Christian poets."

Hazlitt, William. "On the Periodical Essays." In his *English Comic Writers,* pp. 91-105. New York: E. P. Dutton & Co., 1910.
    Judges Steele's essays in *The Tatler* superior to Addison's in *The Spectator,* remarking, "Addison seems to have spent most of his time in his study, and to have spun out and wire-down the hints, which he borrowed from Steele, or took from nature, to the utmost."

Horn, Robert D. "Addison's *Campaign* and Macaulay." *PMLA* LXIII, No. 3 (September 1948): 886-902.
    Detailed analysis of Macaulay's treatment of Addison's *Campaign.*

Kay, Donald. *Short Fiction in "The Spectator."* University: University of Alabama Press, 1975, 145 p.
    Examines the prose fiction pieces that are found throughout *The Spectator* and assesses their place in the development of the English short story.

Kelsall, M. M. "The Meaning of Addison's *Cato." The Review of English Studies* XVII, No. 66 (1966): 149-62.
    Contends that Addison's *Cato* was essentially intended to examine the nature of heroic virtue, particularly the noble stoicism valued in ancient Rome, rather than to establish the political parallel perceived by Whigs and Tories.

Kenney, William. "Addison, Johnson, and the 'Energetick' Style." *Studia Neophilologica* XXXIII (1961): 903-14.
    Contends that most eighteenth-century comparisons between the diametrically opposed styles of Samuel Johnson and Addison are "based on a fundamental confusion: critics simply fail to take into consideration the varying purposes of the two essayists that lead them to select styles that are essentially different."

Kingsley, Henry. "Addison." *Temple Bar* XLI, No. U (June 1874): 319-37.
    Encomium of Addison, who is reputed to be the modeler of the "school of essayism."

Lannering, Jan. *Studies in the Prose Style of Joseph Addison.* Essays and Studies on English Language and Literature, edited by S. B. Liljegren, vol. IX. Cambridge, Mass.: Harvard University Press, 1951, 203 p.
    Detailed study of the prose style of Addison in which Lannering asserts that Addison represents the first stage of maturity of neoclassical prose style.

Messenger, Ann. "Educational *Spectators:* Richard Steele, Joseph Addison, and Eliza Haywood." In her *His and Hers: Essays in Restoration and Eighteenth-Century Literature,* pp. 108-47. Lexington: University Press of Kentucky, 1986.
    Compares and contrasts the essays in the *Spectator* and those in the *Female Spectator* by Haywood, finding that Haywood "reveals a far deeper sense of the tragedy of the human condition . . . than anything Addison and Steele ever expressed. They were fairly comfortable in the world they perceived, despite its shortcomings. Mrs. Haywood was not."

Morris, Mowbray. "About Joseph Addison." *Temple Bar* LX, No. D (January 1879): 33-52.
    Sympathetic portrayal of Addison that examines the attacks of such critics as Alexander Pope and John Dennis and dismisses Addison's reputed troubles with alcohol.

Nussbaum, Felicity A. "Enemies and Enviers: Minor Eighteenth-Century Satires." In her *The Brink of All We Hate: English Satires on Women, 1660-1750,* pp. 117-36. Lexington: University Press of Kentucky, 1984.
    Discussion of the representative female image in eighteenth-century literature. Addison's writings in the *Spectator* and his translation of Semonides's version of the creation story are cited as the beginnings of a willingness to include the ideal woman rather than the whore, infidel, or Amazon in satire.

Otten, Robert M. *Joseph Addison.* Boston: Twayne Publishers, 1982, 182 p.
    Biographical and critical overview of Addison's life and career.

Pritchett, V. S. Review of *The Life of Joseph Addison* by Peter Smithers. *The New Statesman and Nation* XLVII, No. 1206 (17 April 1954): 504-05.
    Qualifies his praise for Addison and Addison's literary style: "Even . . . if we grant his great influence on society, he remains a meritorious functionary, and far less than the dominant figure in the literature of his time."

Quiller-Couch, Arthur. "The Bi-Centenary of Addison." *The Living Age* 302, No. 3916 (26 July 1919): 210-13.
    Praises Addison's journalism, adding: "Until we rediscover a passion for prose, Addison must wait; . . . his writing—being of cloth-in-grain and woven for wear—will outlast many fashions, and in the end securely come to its own."

Robertson, J. G. "The Beginnings of a New Aesthetics in England: Addison." In his *Studies in the Genesis of Romantic Theory in the Eighteenth Century,* pp. 235-49. Cambridge: Cambridge University Press, 1923.
    Maintains that Addison, much like Lodovico Antonio Muratori in Italy, helped develop a modern aesthetic theory based on the instinctive, creative forces of the imagination that bridged the literary gap between the classic taste of the upper class and the unpolished, nationalistic taste of the working class.

Salter, C. H. "Dryden and Addison." *The Modern Language Review* 69, No. 1 (January 1974): 29-39.
    Argues that Addison derived his theory of imagination,

as well as the ideas in his papers on drama, wit, ballads, and *Paradise Lost,* from John Dryden.

Scott, R. McNair. "An Aspect of Addison & Steele." *The London Mercury* XXVII, No. 162 (April 1933): 524-29.

Criticizes Addison's style as emotionless and observes: "It is difficult to believe that Addison is as great a reformer as this essay might well have shown him to be. Sometimes . . . the doubting spirit questions whether the *Tatler* and *Spectator* did not rather express than lead public opinion."

Smithers, Peter. *The Life of Joseph Addison.* Oxford: Clarendon Press, 1958, 499 p.

Considered the definitive biography.

Stephen, Leslie. "Joseph Addison." In *The Dictionary of National Biography: From the Earliest Times to 1900. Volume I: Abbadie—Beadon,* pp. 122-31, edited by Leslie Stephen and Sidney Lee. London: Oxford University Press, 1917.

Biographical and critical summary of Addison's life and works.

Stephens, John C., Jr. "Addison as Social Critic." *The Emory University Quarterly* XXI, No. 3 (Fall 1965): 157-72.

Notes that the originality of Addison's social criticism lies in its manner of expression rather than in its content.

Strahan, J. A. "Swift, Steele, and Addison." *Blackwood's Edinburgh Magazine* CCVIII, No. MCCLX (October 1920): 493-510.

Cites examples which contradict the common portrait of Addison as "the just man made perfect."

Summers, Silas E. "Addison's Conception of Tragedy." *College English* 8, No. 5 (February 1947): 245-48.

Attempts to determine Addison's conception of tragedy, observing that, according to Addison, the tragic hero is " 'A Man of Virtues mixt with Infirmities'." Summers

continues: "Addison insisted that tragedy must arouse terror and commiseration."

Tucker, William John. "Two Great Essayists." *The Catholic World* CL (January 1940): 445-51.

Discussion of Addison and Steele contending that "it is as a master of lucid and urbane prose that Addison lives. Judged by any strict standard, his morality, his political dissertations, and his critical comments are shallow enough."

Wendell, Barrett, and Greenough, Chester Noyes. Introduction to *Selections from the Writings of Joseph Addison,* by Joseph Addison, edited by Barrett Wendell and Chester Noyes Greenough, pp. xi-xlvi. Boston: Ginn and Co., 1905.

Highlights the writings responsible for Addison's political and literary success, concluding: "What Addison approved was the test of right to the generation that loved him; and to this day traditional criticism can pay no higher compliment to a prose style than to call it Addisonian."

Woodberry, George Edward. "Addison and Steele Newly Revisited." In his *Studies of a Litterateur,* pp. 113-25. New York: Harcourt, Brace and Co., 1921.

Notes Addison's debt to Steele although Addison was a "master of a literary manner usually finer than Steele's." Woodberry adds that Addison's cultural contributions in the areas of taste, manners, and good sense were instrumental but "passing."

Youngren, William H. "Addison and the Birth of Eighteenth-Century Aesthetics." *Modern Philology* 79, No. 3 (February 1982): 267-83.

Asserts that Addison ushered in a new literary aesthetic by reintroducing the idea that the imagination is intermediate between sense and understanding and by stressing "the way literature makes its impact on the mind and . . . the way the mind responds to that impact."

Bābur

1483-1530

(Full name Zahir ud-Dīn Mohammed Bābur Pādshāh Ghāzī; also transliterated as Bābar and Bāber) Afghan memoirist and poet.

A descendent of Genghis Khan and Tamerlane, Bābur was the first Moghul emperor of India. Known primarily as a formidable military leader, he is also recognized as an important author in the history of premodern Eastern literature. His memoirs, known as the *Bābur-nāma,* chronicle his efforts to conquer and occupy desirable territories, relate his observations and impressions of those regions, and reveal the author's personal nature to a degree that prefigures European autobiographies. Literary scholar Stephen Frederic Dale has stated that "it is possible to say that [Bābur] represents for Islamic civilization what his Italian contemporary Benvenuto Cellini represents for European civilization: the most completely revealed individual of the 16th century."

The son of Umar Shaikh Mirza, ruler of Ferghana (a region located north of present-day Kabul), and of the daughter of the head of the Mongol Khanate, Bābur was born on 14 February 1483 in Akhsi, site of Ferghana's strongest fort. Few particulars of Bābur's early childhood are known, but his later activities indicate that he was greatly influenced by tales of his ancestors' conquests and power. Upon the death of his father in 1494, Bābur succeeded to the throne of Ferghana. His uncles Sultan Ahmad and Sultan Mahmud immediately attempted to depose Bābur but were unsuccessful. Ahmad died shortly afterwards, leaving Mahmud in control of the wealthy neighboring kingdom of Samarkand. A lengthy power-struggle following Mahmud's death in 1495 ended when fifteen-year-old Bābur invaded and gained control of Samarkand, a region he had coveted since his father's death.

Bābur's reigns were short-lived, however. When a revolt broke out in Ferghana, he left Samarkand to try and restore peace in the region. Reaching the town of Andijan, he found that his home territory had been lost to rebel forces. Within days he also lost Samarkand to Sultan Ali, a cousin who usurped the throne during Bābur's absence. Ali transferred control of Samarkand to Shaibani Khan, an aggressive Uzbeg warrior who committed atrocities against members of the Timurid family (descendants of Tamerlane) and ultimately murdered Ali. Until around 1513, Bābur's career consisted of attempts to regain and maintain control of this rich territory. Suffering several major military setbacks in 1513, he lost Samarkand completely, never to regain dominion there. These defeats convinced Bābur to focus his attentions elsewhere, and he established himself in Kabul in 1504.

Using Kabul as his base of operations, Bābur planned and executed several raids that increased his area of authority in the direction of India. In 1525 he occupied Lahore, the capital of Punjab, and the following year succeeded to the

throne of Delhi after winning the battle of Panipat. Upon defeating the Rajputs at Khanua and dissident Afghan nobles in Bihar and Bengal between 1527 and 1529, practically all of northern India belonged to Bābur. Much of the territory he occupied was placed under the regional governance of longtime friends of his. The conqueror settled in Agra and died in his favorite garden there on 26 December 1530.

Bābur's most important work is his autobiography, the *Bābur-nāma.* He aroused an interest in the use of dialectical language among later Eastern writers by writing his memoirs in the Čaghatāy Turkish language instead of the more formal Persian. Beginning with Bābur's ascent to the throne of Ferghana, the *Bābur-nāma* records his actions and thoughts over the course of a quarter century, ending abruptly on 7 September 1529. It is an incomplete account of his life, however, as several significant lacunæ exist within the text. One such textual gap is between 1508 and 1519, and another between 1520 and 1525. The years encompassed by these lacunæ were full of important events for Bābur, and early scholars believed that the gaps were purposeful omissions meant to avoid reference to episodes Bābur found shameful or embarrassing. Present-day literary historians disagree on the reasons for these lapses in the *Bābur-nāma;* some propose that Bābur simply neglected to complete certain sections, while others hypothesize on Bābur's part and accidental loss or destruction of these portions as possible explanations.

Written in a simple, matter-of-fact style, the *Bābur-nāma's* modern autobiographical elements have often been commented on by literary scholars. Whereas other Eastern authors do not allow glimpses of their private selves in their writing, Bābur, though not often introspective, reveals his personality throughout the *Bābur-nāma.* As M. Fuad Köprülü stated, "it cannot be said that Bābur is impartial in his picture of himself, his friends, or his enemies. For example, we can see that his feelings got the better of him in his evident desire to belittle . . . Shaybāni Khān." Bābur's exceptional observational and analytical abilities are revealed by his descriptions and explanations of art, his surroundings, and of other people and their temperaments. Bābur's stylistic similarities to Cellini have led scholars such as Roy Pascal to propose that the memoirist was a precursor of Renaissance autobiographers. In his study of Bābur's autobiographical writings, Dale offers support for this theory, suggesting that Bābur "offers a coherent portrait of himself as an idiosyncratic personality whose life was . . . shaped by a driving force in his own psychology. In the course of his narrative he also maintains . . . an artistic balance between retrospective certainty and the indeterminacy of the moment."

Bābur is an important figure in the history of Eastern literature, having chronicled, in the *Bābur-nāma,* events and reflections in a clear, lucid style that allows modern readers to enjoy his adventures and ponder the observations of an emperor. As E. M. Forster commented, the *Bābur-nāma* leaves "an ambiguous and exquisite impression behind. We are admitted into the writer's inmost confidence. . . . And since to his honesty, and energy, and sensitiveness, Babur added a warm heart, since he desired empire chiefly that he might advance his friends, the reader may discover a companion uncommon among the dead and amongst kings."

PRINCIPAL WORKS*

Mubayyan (poetry) 1521-22
'Arud risālesi (treatise) 1525-28
Risāle-i Wālidiyya (translation) 1528-29
Bābur-nāme (autobiography) 1530
  [*The Bābur-nāme in English,* 2 Vols., 1722]
†*Dīwān* (poetry) 1530

*The dates given are approximate dates of completion.

†This work has been dated using Bābur's death date.

Stanley Lane-Poole   (essay date 1899)

[*In the excerpt below, Lane-Poole discusses the textual history of the* Bābur-nāma *and its believability as auto-*

biography, *claiming that* "the utter frankness of self-revelation, the unconscious portraiture of all [Bābur's] virtues and follies, his obvious truthfulness and fine sense of honour, give the* Memoirs *an authority which is equal to their charm."]

'In the month of Ramazán of the year eight hundred and ninety-nine [June, 1494], I became King of Farghána.' Such are the opening words of the celebrated *Memoirs* of Bábar, first of the 'Moghul' Emperors of Hindústán. (p. 9)

His permanent place in history rests upon his Indian conquests, which opened the way for an imperial line; but his place in biography and in literature is determined rather by his daring adventures and persevering efforts in his earlier days, and by the delightful *Memoirs* in which he related them. Soldier of fortune as he was, Bábar was not the less a man of fine literary taste and fastidious critical perception. In Persian, the language of culture, the Latin of Central Asia, as it is of India, he was an accomplished poet, and in his native Turki he was master of a pure and unaffected style alike in prose and verse. The Turkish princes of his time prided themselves upon their literary polish, and to turn an elegant *ghazal,* or even to write a beautiful manuscript, was their peculiar ambition, no less worthy or stimulating than to be master of sword or mace. In some of the boldly sketched portraits of his contemporaries which enliven the *Memoirs,* Bábar often passes abruptly from warlike or administrative qualities to literary gifts; he will tell how many battles a king fought, and then, as if to clinch the tale of his merits, he will add that he was a competent judge of poetry and was fond of reading the *Sháh Náma,* yet had such a fist that 'he never struck a man but he felled him.' Of another dignitary he notes regretfully that 'he never read, and though a townsman he was illiterate and unrefined'; on the other hand 'a brave man' is commended the more because he 'wrote the *nasta'lík* hand,' though, truly, 'after a fashion.' Wit and learning, the art of turning a quatrain on the spot, quoting the Persian classics, writing a good hand, or singing a good song, were highly appreciated in Bábar's world, as much perhaps as valour, and infinitely more than virtue. Bábar himself will break off in the middle of a tragic story to quote a verse, and he found leisure in the thick of his difficulties and dangers to compose an ode on his misfortunes. His battles as well as his orgies were humanized by a breath of poetry.

Hence his *Memoirs* are no rough soldier's chronicle of marches and countermarches, 'saps, mines, blinds, gabions, palisadoes, ravelins, half-moons, and such trumpery'; they contain the personal impressions and acute reflections of a cultivated man of the world, well read in Eastern literature, a close and curious observer, quick in perception, a discerning judge of persons, and a devoted lover of nature; one, moreover, who was well able to express his thoughts and observations in clear and vigorous language. 'His autobiography,' says a sound authority, 'is one of those priceless records which are for all time, and is fit to rank with the confessions of St. Augustine and Rousseau, and the memoirs of Gibbon and Newton. In Asia it stands almost alone.' There is no doubt a vast deal of dreary chronicle in the *Memoirs,* much desultory trifling, some repetition, and needlessly minute descriptions of secondary characters and incidents; the first part is infinitely better than the end; but with all this, the shrewd comments and lively impressions which break in upon the narrative give Bábar's reminiscences a unique and penetrating flavour. The man's own character is so fresh and buoyant, so free from convention and cant, so rich in hope, courage, resolve, and at the same time so warm and friendly, so very human, that it conquers one's admiring sympathy. The utter frankness of self-revelation, the unconscious portraiture of all his virtues and follies, his obvious truthfulness and fine sense of honour, give the *Memoirs* an authority which is equal to their charm. If ever there were a case when the testimony of a single historical document, unsupported by other evidence, should be accepted as sufficient proof, it is the case with Bábar's *Memoirs.* No reader of this prince of autobiographers can doubt his honesty or his competence as witness and chronicler.

Very little is known about the mode in which they were composed. That they were written at different dates, begun at one time and taken up again after long intervals, as leisure or inclination suggested, is to be inferred from the sudden way in which they break off, generally at a peculiarly critical moment, to be resumed without a word of explanation at a point several years later. The style, moreover, of the later portions is markedly different from that of the earlier, whilst the earlier portions bear internal evidence of revision at a later date. The natural (though conjectural) inference is that the *Memoirs* were written at various dates; that the earlier part was revised and enlarged after Bábar's invasion of India, though memory failed or time was wanting to fill the gaps; and that the later part remains in its original form of a rough diary because its author died before he had leisure or energy to revise it. The *Memoirs* were written in Turki, Bábar's native tongue. A copy of the work was in his cousin Haidar's hands, who probably obtained it during his visit to India within ten years of its author's death. Another copy, which appears to be the original of all the existing manuscripts, was transcribed from an original in Bábar's own handwriting by his eldest son, the Emperor Humáyún, in 1553, as is stated in an interpolation by Humáyún in the body of the work. That the son was a faithful copyist is evident, for he has not suppressed several passages in which his own conduct is censured by his father.

The *Memoirs* were more than once translated from Turki into Persian; notably, with scrupulous accuracy, by the illustrious Mirzá Abdu-r-Rahím, son of Bairam Khán, in 1590, by the desire of the Emperor Akbar. The close agreement, even in trifling details, of the various Turki and Persian manuscripts preserved in several collections, shows that the original text has been faithfully respected, and such variations as exist do not affect the essential accuracy of the document. Even the gaps in the narrative unfortunately occur at the same places and for the same intervals in all the manuscripts, Turki and Persian, with the exception of two or three short but interesting passages which one Turki text alone presents. This text was printed at Kazan by M. Ilminski in 1857, and was translated into French by M. Pavet de Courteille in 1871. Long before this, a translation into vigorous English, by John Leyden

and William Erskine, based upon a collation of Persian and Turki manuscripts, and enriched with a valuable introduction and copious notes, appeared in 1826, and has ever since held its place as the standard version. It represents the Persian more than the Turki text, but how little the two differ, and how trifling are the emendations (save in Turki words and names) to be gained from the Turki version, may be seen by a comparison of the French and English translations.

This comparison of two versions founded upon several manuscripts written in two languages brings us to the remarkable conclusion that Bábar's *Memoirs* have come through the ordeals of translation and transcription practically unchanged. We possess, in effect, the *ipsissima verba* of an autobiography written early in the sixteenth century by one of the most interesting and famous men of all Asia. It is a literary fact of no little importance. The line of Emperors who proceeded from Bábar's loins is no more. The very name of Mongol has lost its influence on the banks of Iaxartes; the Turk is the servant of the Russian he once despised. The last Indian sovereign of Tímúr's race ended his inglorious career an exile at Rangoon; a few years later, the degenerate descendants of Chingiz Kaán submitted to the officers of the Tsar. The power and pomp of Bábar's dynasty are gone; the record of his life—the *littera scripta* that mocks at time—remains unaltered and imperishable. (pp. 10-16)

> *Stanley Lane-Poole, in his* Rulers of India: Bábar, *Oxford at the Clarendon Press, 1899, 206 p.*

E. M. Forster (essay date 1922)

[*Forster was a prominent English novelist, essayist, and literary critic whose works reflect his liberal humanism. In the following excerpt from an essay originally published in 1922, he praises the style of the* Bābur-nāma, *stating that the work, "fresh, yet mature. . . . [leaves] an ambiguous and exquisite impression behind."*]

[Sanguine] and successful conquerors generally have defects that would make them intolerable as companions. They are unobservant of all that does not assist them towards glory, and, consequently, vague and pompous about their past; they are so busy; when they have any charm, it is that of our Henry V—the schoolboy unpacking a hamper that doesn't belong to him. But what a happiness to have known Babur! He had all that one seeks in a friend. His energy and ambition were touched with sensitiveness; he could act, feel, observe, and remember; though not critical of his senses, he was aware of their workings, thus fulfilling the whole nature of man. His admirers—and he has many—have called him naïf, because they think it somewhat silly of an emperor to love poetry and swimming for their own sake, and to record many years afterwards that the first time a raft struck, a china cup, a spoon, and a cymbal fell into the water, whereas the second time the raft struck, a nobleman fell in, just as he was cutting up a melon. Charming and quaint (they say), but no more: not realizing that Babur knew what he was about, and that his vitality was so great that all he had experienced rang and glowed, irrespective of its value to historians. It is the temptation of a cultivated man to arrange his experiences, so that they lose their outlines; he, skilled in two languages and all the arts of his day, shunned that false logic, and the sentences in his *Memoirs* jostle against one another like live people in a crowd:

> Zulnun Arghun distinguished himself among all the other young warriors in the presence of Sultan Abusaid Mirza by the use of the scimitar, and afterwards, on every occasion on which he went into action, he acquitted himself with distinction. His courage is unimpeached, but certainly he was rather deficient in understanding. . . . He was a pious and orthodox believer, never neglected saying the appointed prayers, and frequently repeated the supererogatory ones. He was madly fond of chess; if a person played at it with one hand he played at it with his two hands. He played without art, just as his fancy suggested. He was the slave of avarice and meanness.

No one of the above sentences accommodates its neighbour. The paragraph is a series of shocks, and this is characteristic of Babur's method, and due to the honesty of his mind. But it is not a naïf paragraph. He desires to describe Zulnun Arghun, and does so with all possible clearness. Similarly, when he is autobiographical. No softening:

> When, from the force of youthful imagination and constitutional impulse, I got a desire for wine, I had nobody about my person to invite me to gratify my wishes; nay, there was not one who suspected my secret longing for it. Though I had the appetite, therefore, it was difficult for me, unsolicited as I was, to indulge such unlawful desires. It now came into my head that as they urged me so much, and as, besides, I had come into a refined city like Heri, in which every means of heightening pleasure and gaiety was possessed in perfection, in which all the incentives and apparatus of enjoyment were combined with an invitation to indulgence, if I did not seize the present moment I never could expect such another. I therefore resolved to drink wine.

Here is neither bragging nor remorse; just the recording of conflicting emotions and of the action that finally resulted. On a subsequent page he does feel remorse. On still a subsequent he drinks himself senseless. Fresh, yet mature, the *Memoirs* leave an ambiguous and exquisite impression behind. We are admitted into the writer's inmost confidence, yet that confidence is not, as in most cases, an enervating chamber; it is a mountain stream, arched by the skies of early manhood. And since to his honesty, and energy, and sensitiveness, Babur added a warm heart, since he desired empire chiefly that he might advance his friends, the reader may discover a companion uncommon among the dead and amongst kings. Alexander the Great resembles him a little, but Alexander is mystic and grandiose, whereas there are neither chasms nor fences in Babur, nothing that need hinder the modern man if he cares to come.

Nevertheless . . . old books are troublesome to read, and it is right to indicate the difficulty of this one.

Those awful Oriental names! They welter from start to finish. Sometimes twenty new ones occur on a page and never recur. Among humans there are not only the Turki descendants of Tamerlane and the Moghul descendants of Genghis Khan, all royal, and mostly in motion; long lists of their nobles are given also. Geography is equally trying; as Babur scuttles over the earth a mist of streams, and villages, and mountains arises, from the Jaxartes, in the centre of Asia, to the Nerbudda, in the centre of India. Was this where the man with the melon fell overboard? Or is it the raft where half of us took spirits and the rest *bhang,* and quarrelled in consequence? We can't be sure. Is that an elephant? If so, we must have left Afghanistan. No: we must be in Ferghana again; it's a yak. We never know where we were last, though Agra stands out as the curtain falls, and behind it, as a tomb against the skyline, Kabul. Lists of flowers, fruits, handwritings, headdresses. . . . We who are not scholars may grow tired.

The original manuscript of the *Memoirs* was in Turki, and this brings us to our concluding point, that Babur belongs to the middle of Asia, and does not interpret the mind of India, though he founded a great dynasty there. (pp. 301-03)

> *E. M. Forster, "The Emperor Babur," in his* Abinger Harvest, *Harcourt Brace Jovanovich, 1936, pp. 300-04.*

S. M. Edwardes (essay 1926)

[*In the excerpt below, Edwardes examines the literary style of Bābur's poetry and prose, concentrating on the* Bābur-nāma.]

[Stanley] Lane-Poole has stated [in his *Rulers of India: Bābar,* 1899] that

> Babur's place in history rests upon his Indian conquests, which opened the way for an imperial line; but his place in biography and in literature is determined rather by his daring adventures and persevering efforts in his earlier days, and by the delightful *Memoirs* in which he related them. Soldier of fortune as he was, Babur was not the less a man of fine literary taste and fastidious critical perception. In Persian, the language of culture, the Latin of Central Asia, as it is of India, he was an accomplished poet, and in his native Turki he was master of a pure and unaffected style alike in prose and verse.

His faculty for literary composition was, no doubt, partly inherited: for Timur himself wrote annals in Turki; Timur's grandson, Ulugh Beg, was the author of two works; Ulugh Khan's two sons were distinguished, the one as a poet, the other as a prose-writer. Moreover, he had before him the example of Sultan Husain Baiqara, the Timurid ruler of Herat, a great patron of art and letters, whose court was thronged by the intellectual spirits of the age. Yet it is questionable whether any previous member of the Timurid family possessed literary talents equal to Babur's, or acquired an equal mastery of Turki prose. Great natural intelligence, an enquiring mind, a sense of humour, and good taste combined to render Babur's work unique; and when we remember that his literary activity was cultivated amid an unending series of military and political vicissitudes, we are fain to subscribe wholeheartedly to his cousin Mirza Haidar's eulogy of Babur's "many virtues and numberless excellences."

Considering his strenuous and adventurous life the volume of his written works is no less remarkable than their quality. They include, according to the list prepared by Mrs. Beveridge, the miscellaneous verse quoted in the *Babur-nama;* a *divan* or collection of poems sent to Pulad Sultan in 1519; a diary for 1519-20; the *Mubin,* a treatise on Moslem Law in 2,000 lines of Turki verse, composed in 1522 for the benefit of his son Kamran; a treatise on prosody written in 1524; poems written in Hindustan; the *Babur-nama,* his autobiographical *Memoirs;* and the *Walidiyyah-risala,* a metrical translation of Khwaja Obaidullah Ahrari's *Parental Tract,* composed in 1528-29. The genesis of the last-named work is ascribed by Babur in his *Memoirs* to an attack of fever which laid him low in November, 1528.

> I trembled less on Sunday. During the night of Tuesday it occurred to me to versify the *Walidiyyah-risala* of His Reverence Khwaja Obaidullah. I laid it to heart that if I, going to the soul of His Reverence for protection, was freed from this disease, it would be a sign that my poem was accepted, just as the author of the *Qasidatu'l-burda* was freed from the affliction of paralysis, when his poem had been accepted. To this end I began to versify the tract, using the metre of Maulana Abdur Rahim Jami's *Subhatu'l-ahrar*

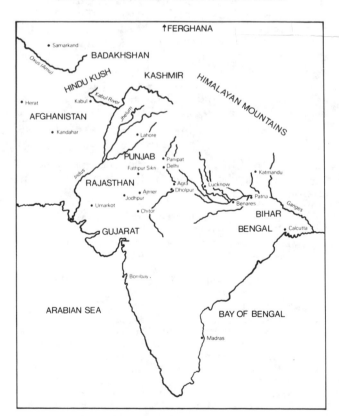

Map showing the areas associated with Bābur.

(Rosary of the Righteous). Thirteen couplets were made in the same night. I tasked myself to make not fewer than ten a day; in the end one day had been omitted."

The *Babur-nama* or autobiography, which has been described as "fit to rank with the confessions of St. Augustine and Rousseau and the memoirs of Gibbon and Newton," is unfortunately not wholly complete, the annals and diary of the years 1508 to 1519 having disappeared. The loss of the relevant sheets may, as Mrs. Beveridge suggests, have occurred during the vicissitudes of Humayun's fourteen years of exile from the throne of Delhi; and some pages may perhaps have been destroyed during the monsoon storm of 1529, which Babur describes as follows:—

> That same night . . . such a storm burst, in the inside of a moment, from the up-piled clouds of the Rainy Season, and such a stiff gale arose that few tents were left standing. I was in the Audience-tent, about to write: before I could collect papers and sections, the tent came down with its porch, right on my head. The *tungluq* (flap in tent-roof) went to pieces. God preserved me! No harm befell me! Sections and book were drenched under water and gathered together with much difficulty. We laid them in the folds of a woollen throne-carpet, put this on the throne, and on it piled blankets. . . . We, without sleep, were busy till shoot of day drying folios and sections.

The salient feature of the *Babur-nama* is its honesty. The conviction grows, as we read it, that it contains the truth, the whole truth, and nothing but the truth. In describing the favours he had bestowed upon his Chaghatai relatives and the sorry manner in which they were requited, he remarks:—

> I do not write this in order to make complaint; I have written the plain truth. I do not set down these matters in order to make known my own deserts; I have set down exactly what happened. In this history I have held firmly to it that the truth should be reached in every matter, and that every act should be recorded precisely as it occurred. From this it follows that I have set down of good and bad whatever is known concerning father and elder brother, kinsman and stranger; of them all I have set down carefully the known virtues and defects.

Again, when he pens a few words of pardonable pride on his capture of Samarkand at the age of nineteen, he repudiates any idea of magnifying his own achievement. In his own phrase "the truth is set down;" and our acceptance of that statement is amply justified by the fact that in the course of the work he never excuses his own mistakes and failures, nor slurs in the smallest degree over his own lapses from grace.

Babur's prose style was suited to his blunt and open nature. The flowery phraseology and hyperbole, so common in Eastern literature, find no place in his autobiography, which is written in clear, simple, terse language, void of superfluous words. His descriptions of the countries in which his lot was cast—their climate, fauna, flora, products, water-supply, population, trade and so forth, are models of what such compositions should be—never pro-lix, but containing all the details that a stranger, traveller, or student might wish to know. The following extract from a letter which he wrote to Humayun proves that he aimed at simplicity of expression and disliked slipshod composition:—

> Thou hast written me a letter, as I ordered thee to do. But why not have read it over? If thou hadst thought of reading it, thou couldst not have done it, and, unable thyself to read it, wouldst certainly have made alterations in it. Though by taking trouble it can be read, it is very puzzling, and who ever saw an enigma in prose? Thy spelling, though not bad, is not quite correct. . . . Although thy letter can be read if every sort of pains be taken, yet it cannot be quite understood because of that obscure word-ing of thine. Thy remissness in letter writing seems to be due to the thing which makes thee obscure, that is to say, to elaboration. In future, write without elaboration; use plain clear words. So will thy trouble and thy reader's be less.

Could a modern educationist have given better advice than this on epistolary style? Incidentally the letter re-minds us that Babur was no mean calligraphist. The art of fine writing has always been highly esteemed in India, Persia, and China; and the penmanship of a manuscript was often considered more valuable and more important than its illustrations. The dictum of Horace—*Poeta nasci-tur non fit*—aptly expresses the view prevalent in Asiatic lands of the genius of the *Khushnavis* or fine writer, whose handiwork was collected and preserved in albums as care-fully as the finest specimens of pictorial art. Broadly speaking, the various modes of writing were distinguished from one another by differences in the proportions of the straight and curved lines, and one mode at least was a combination of two of the older styles. Babur invented a new handwriting, which he calls *Baburi Khatt,* and wrote a copy of the Koran in it, which he afterwards sent to Mecca. He mentions that he showed the script and ex-plained its special features to one of the Kazis at Herat, who then and there wrote some sentences in it.

The **Babur-nama** reveals its author's talent for delineating character in a few words. The portrait of Sultan Husain Mirza of Herat, for example, is admirable: two short para-graphs lay bare his personal appearance, his virtues and his failings. Equally illuminating are the accounts of Sul-tan Ahmad Mirza and the Amirs of Umar Shaikh's court. One of the latter was "a good-natured and simple person, who used to improvise very well at drinking-parties;" an-other was "worthless by nature and habit, a stingy, severe, strife-stirring person, false, self-pleasing, rough of tongue and cold of face;" of a third he writes, "in management and equipment excellent, and took good care of his men. He prayed not, he kept no fasts, he was like a heathen, and he was a tyrant." There were also Mir Ghyas, "a laugher, a joker, and fearless in vice," and Qambar Ali the Mug-hal—"Till he was a made man, his conduct was excellent. Once he arrived, he was slack. He was full of talk and of foolish talk—a great talker is sure to be a foolish one—his capacity was limited and his brain muddy." A brief sketch

of Jani Beg, one of Ahmad Mirza's nobles, throws a side-light upon the rude manners of the times:—

> While he (Jani Beg) was governor in Samarkand, an envoy came to him from the Uzbegs, re-nowned for his strength. An Uzbeg is said to call a strong man a bull (*bukuh*). 'Are you a *bukuh?*' said Jani Beg to the envoy; 'if you are, come, let's have a friendly wrestle together.' Whatever ob-jections the envoy raised, he refused to accept. They wrestled, and Jani Beg gave the fall. He was a brave man.

There is many a happy touch in his picture of Husain Bai-qara's court. One noble was mad on chess; "he played it according to his own fancy, and, if others play with one hand, he played with both. Avarice and stinginess ruled in his character." Another wrote verse of all sorts, filled "with terrifying words and mental images;" when he recit-ed one of his couplets to Jami, the latter "asked him whether he was reciting verse or frightening people." Then there was the athletic spirit, who could take a flying leap over seven horses side by side, and "the curiously humble, disconsolate and harmless person, who seems to have had no equal in making riddles and to have given his whole time to it." Yet another, who was a Chief Justice, wrote a book which in the preface he declared to be Sultan Husain's "own written word and literary composition," while in the body of the book he wrote "all by the sub-signed author" above odes and verses well known to be his own. "A singularly absurd procedure," comments Babur, who clearly did not approve of "literary ghosts." He tells us also of Ali Sher, who besides being the best Turki poet of his day, was a fine soldier and leader of fashion. "When-ever anyone produced a novelty, he called it Ali Sher's, in order to give it credit and vogue. Some things were called after him in compliment, e.g., when he had ear-ache and wrapped his head in one of the blue triangular kerchiefs women tie over their heads in winter, that kerchief was called Ali Sher's comforter." Banai the poet, critic, and calligraphist, whose jokes sometimes got him into trouble, raised a laugh by inventing a new pad for his ass and call-ing it "the Ali Sher donkey-pad."

Babur's sense of humour must have been equally tickled by the tale which he recounts of the Sultan of Bajaur and his mother's corpse:—

> All through the hill country above Multa-Kundi . . . it is said that when a woman dies and has been laid on a bier, she, if she has not been an ill-doer, gives the bearers such a shake, when they lift the bier by its four sides, that against their will and hindrance her corpse falls to the ground; but if she has done ill, no move-ment occurs. This was heard not only from Ku-naris, but again and again in Bajaur, Sawad, and the whole hill-tract. Haidar Ali Bajauri—a Sul-tan who governed Bajaur well—when his moth-er died, did not weep or betake himself to lamen-tation, or put on black, but said 'Go! lay her on the bier! if she move not, I will have her burned!' (i.e. treated like an infidel). They laid her on the bier; the desired movement followed; when he heard this was so, he put on black and betook himself to lamentation.

Many and diverse were the occasions which prompted Babur to commit his thoughts to verse. He would write an ode during a halt in camp; in the brief respite after his capture of Samarkand, he amused himself by writing Turki poems; he composed verses just before battle, or when enjoying a peaceful excursion by river with his comrades, or when lying ill with fever. The conjunction of New Year's Day with the *Id-ul-fitr,* during a return march to Kabul, formed the subject of a neat quatrain; while his failures and disasters often served as the occasion for a well-turned couplet. After the battle of Panipat, when Nizam Khan of Biana seemed indisposed to surrender, Babur sent him "royal letters of promise and threat," and drove his meaning home with an *extempore* Persian quatrain:—

> Strive not with the Turk, o Mir of Biana!
> His skill and his courage are obvious.
> If thou come not soon, nor give ear to counsel,—
> What need to detail what is obvious?

Babur's poetry, like his prose, was usually marked by good taste. He admits to having composed frivolous and jesting verse in his younger days, but the composition of the **Mubin** cured him of this weakness. "A pity it will be," he declares, "if the tongue which has treasure of utterances so lofty as these are, waste itself again on low words; sad will it be, if again vile imaginings find way into the mind, which has made exposition of these sublime realities." After that declaration he was guilty of only one lapse, when he wrote a somewhat improper couplet on Mulla Ali Jan: but, believing that an illness which attacked him a few days later was sent as a punishment for his backsliding, he broke his pen in token of repentance and thenceforth faithfully avoided anything approaching ribaldry. Thus he was neither hypocritical nor insincere, when he openly condemned the poet Hilali for composing an ode on the immoral love of a darwesh for a king. Babur was greatly incensed at the thought that anyone "for the sake of a few elegant quatrains should describe a young man, and that young man a king, as resembling the shameless and immoral." (pp. 103-17)

> *S. M. Edwardes, in his* Babur: Diarist and Despot, *A. M. Philpot Ltd., 1926, 138 p.*

Sir E. Denison Ross (essay date 1937)

[*In the following excerpt, Ross praises the* Bābur-nāma *as "among the most enthralling and romantic works in the literature of all time."*]

While inheriting a savagery common to all the Mongols and Turks, and a total disregard for human life, [Bābur] was capable of great generosity in forgiving those who had behaved ill towards him. Like all his family he was strongly addicted to intemperance, though his drinking bouts were always followed by very sincere repentance. He had a love for the beauties of nature probably rare in his day, something apart from a delight in the artificial beauties of poetry, which was common to all his co-religionists whether Turks or Persians. His careful descriptions of the animals and plants of India reveal great powers of observation. These portions of his memoirs read like the notes of a peace-loving naturalist rather than those of a restless warrior.

The **Memoirs** of Bābur must be reckoned among the most enthralling and romantic works in the literature of all time. They were written in that form of Turkish known as Turkī, which was Bābur's mother-tongue. As we possess them they are not complete; all the copies known to us contain gaps from 1508 to 1519, from 1520 to 1525 and from 1529 to 1530. A more complete copy was apparently known to his cousin Mīrzā Haidar, the author of the *Tārīkh-i-Rashīdī;* but the translation into Persian made in 1589 by Khān Khānān 'Abdur-Rahīm, the son of Bairam Khān, contains the same gaps as the Haidarabad Codex, from which Mrs Annette Beveridge made her admirable English translation.

Bābur was a real poet, and apart from the incidental verses introduced in his memoirs we have from his pen a small collection of Turkī lyrics, which bear comparison with the best poetry of his day. He also wrote a religious poem called the **Mubayyin,** and about two years before his death he wrote a versified rendering of the *Risāla-i-Wālidiyya,* a pious tract written by the famous Khvāja Ahrār in honour of his parents. (pp. 19-20)

> *Sir E. Denison Ross, "Bābur," in* The Cambridge History of India: The Mughul Period, *Vol. IV, edited by Sir Richard Burn, Cambridge at the University Press, 1937, pp. 1-20.*

M. Fuad Köprülü (essay date 1960)

[*In the excerpt below, Köprülü provides a survey of Bābur's works, including brief commentaries on his literary style.*]

1. **Bābur-nāme.** In this famous autobiography, written in Čaghatāy Turkish, Bābur tells his story from childhood to the last years of his life, with no attempt to conceal his weaknesses, his mistakes, or his defeats. It is in no sense an *apologia pro vita sua;* indeed, so matter-of-fact and unemotional is the tone of the work that the casual reader might not recognise it as the memoirs of a skilful and valiant soldier and the founder of a dynasty, which closer study reveals it to be. It cannot be said that Bābur is impartial in his picture of himself, his friends, or his enemies. For example, we can see that his feelings got the better of him in his evident desire to belittle the important and worthy Shaybānī Khān. But despite occasional injustices of this nature, the **Bābur-nāme** is far more reliable than the general run of such works. The author's keen powers of observation and his analytical mind are apparent in his descriptions and explanations of works of art, of flora and fauna, of the group-psychology of peoples, and the characters of individuals. As a literary work, the simple and chaste language of the **Bābur-nāme,** its natural style, its colourful and lively descriptive passages, are some of the reasons which justify our regarding it as one of the finest examples not only of Čaghatāy but of Turkish prose generally.

2. **'Arūḍ risālesi.** It was known that Bābur had written a Čaghatāy treatise on prosody, from the **Bābur-nāme,** cer-

tain copies of his *Dīwān,* and the *Muntakhab al-Tawārīkh* of Badā'ūnī but the work did not come to light till 1923, when it was discovered by M. Fuad Köprülü in a Paris manuscript. It does not differ greatly from similar works in Persian; its chief importance is that on certain *'arūd* verse-forms used by the Turkish poets its information is fuller than that given by Nawā'ī in his *Mīzān al-Awzān.* Bābur gives both Persian and Turkish examples of metres in general use, including some from his own poems, but only Turkish examples of metres of his own invention. At the end of his *Dīwān* he states that the *'Arūd risālesi* was finished 2 or 3 years before the completion of the conquest of India; i.e., between 932 and 934/1525-8.

3. *Mubayyan.* A *mathnawī* in *khafīf* trimeter catalectic (*fa'ilatun mafā'ilun fa'ilun*), completed, according to a reference in the *'Arūd risālesi,* in 928/1521-2. It deals with some problems in Hanafī law, together with some matters relating to campaigning. This simple didactic work is of no artistic importance, but it does show that Bābur was interested in *fikh* and was a sincere Hanafī. Till recently it was known to Orientalists as *Mubīn;* A. S. Beveridge so refers to it, even though she mentions that the Indian historians Abu 'l-Fadl and Badā'ūnī read the title as *Mubayyan* (and that Sprenger called it *Fikh-i Bāburī*). *Mubīn* is in fact the name of a commentary on this work, written by Bābur's secretary, *Shaykh* Zayn.

4. Translation of *Risāle-i Wālidiyya.* The author of this work on Sūfī ethics was Khwāja 'Ubayd Allāh Ahrārī, the great Central Asian Sūfī and spiritual aide of the Tīmūrids. As the title implies, he wrote it at his father's insistence. Bābur's Caghatāy translation was made in 935/1528-9, and forms part of his *Dīwān.* It is a *mathnawī* of 243 lines in *Ramal* trimeter catalectic (*fa'ilātun fa'ilātun fa'ilun*). Though pleasantly and simply written, it has no aesthetic merit, but is of interest as showing Bābur's Sūfī leanings.

5. The *Dīwān.* The bulk of this is in Turkish, but some of the poems are in Persian. The verse-forms represented include the *ghazal, mathnawī, rubā'ī, kit'a, tuyugh, mu'ammā,* and *mufrad.* We find in it the various verses whose composition he mentions in the *Bābur-nāme.* The existing copies are not arranged in the classical *Dīwān* manner; the poems are set down in no apparent order. In the technique of versification Bābūr was not inferior to any of the 15th-century Caghatāy poets, not even Nawā'ī, and he expresses his thoughts and feelings in an unaffected language and style. Side by side with Sūfī songs of love and wine there are poems on everyday themes. Signs of the influence of earlier poets, especially Nawā'ī are not wanting, but there are no slavish imitations. Though Bābur had a taste for literary artifices and poetic *tours de force* (there are 29 of the latter in the *Dīwān*), and though, in obedience to the fashion prevailing at the time in both Persian and Turkish literature, he wrote numerous *mu'ammās* (the *Dīwān* includes 52), the greater part of his work is simple, sincere, and natural. He wrote a number of *tuyughs,* a verse-form peculiarly Turkish, as well as some *rubā'īs* of great beauty. Among his *türküs,* which belong to popular poetry, we find one poem in syllabic metre. He was capable of writing Persian poems—there are over 20

in the *Dīwān*—but his affection for his mother-tongue is evident in the preponderance of Caghatāy. Further, in his poems he often refers to the valour of the Turks, and the fact that he is one of them. In this respect he was following the intellectual and literary trend which had begun with Nawā'ī in the previous century and which prevailed not only in Khurāsān but at all the Tīmūrid courts. The literary influence of Bābur was responsible for the subsequent rise of poets writing in Caghatāy both among his descendants and among their courtiers. Certainly the literary historian must assign Bābur a leading position among the Caghatāy poets after Nawā'ī. (pp. 848-49)

> *M. Fuad Köprülü, "Babur," in* The Encyclopaedia of Islam: A-B, Vol. I, *edited by H. A. R. Gibb and others, E. J. Brill, 1960, pp. 847-50.*

Mohibbul Hasan (essay date 1985)

[In the following excerpt, Hasan discusses the inspirations for and the stylistic influences on Bābur's poetry and prose.]

Babur is mostly remembered as a conqueror and an empire builder. It is often forgotten that he was extremely versatile, interested not only in constructing gardens and palaces, but also in music, Persian and Turki poetry, *su-fism, fiqh* and calligraphy. He was a cultured prince and enjoyed the society of poets and scholars. Some of the poets and learned men who adorned his court were: Shaikh Abul Wajd, Maulana Ali Jan, Maulana Ali Khan, Tardi Beg Khaksar, Maulana Shamsud-Din Farghari, Maulana Shams Talib and Shaikh Zain, the author of *Ta-baqati Baburi.* Some other learned men were: Maulana Baqai, a poet, Maulana Shihabud-Din, who was skilful in the composition of enigmas and Mir Jamalud-Din, the Traditionist.

Babur was a good calligraphist, and invented a style known as *Khatt-i Baburi* in which he edited the Quran, and whose artistic rules were fixed by Qazi Ikhtiyarud-Din when he visited Murghab in 1506. He also excelled in music and other arts.

Babur was also a poet in Persian and Turki. His first poetical inspiration came in 1500 when he fell in love with Baburi, a boy belonging to the camp bazaar, and tried to express his feelings in Persian verse. Later, he composed many Persian verses, some of which are fairly good, but they cannot be compared with those of the masters. Babur at best remained a minor Persian poet. It is, however, as a poet in Chaghtay Turki, his mother tongue, that he achieved excellence. He probably composed Turki verse for the first time in 1498 and by 1500 he began to write with confidence. Turki poets before him had written in servile imitation of Persian poets, whom they regarded as their models. They had hardly ever composed anything original, but Ali Shir Navai and then Babur led a movement to get rid of Persian influence on Turki poetry and strike out a new literary trend. Babur's Turki poetry is characterised by "spontaneity." It is written in a simple, unaffected style, and covers every field of life—wine, war, love, religion and *sufism,* and experiments with various verse-forms—*ghazal, masnavi, rubai,* etc, In some of the poems he refers to the valour of the Turks and to his belonging to that race. He was influenced by the early Turki poets, especially Ali Shir Navai, whom he greatly admired and with whom he was in correspondence. According to Mirza Haidar, "in the composition of Turki poetry he was second only to Amir Ali Shir." Fuad Korpulu also thinks that Babur possessed a leading position among the Chaghatay poets after Navai, and adds that his poetry influenced the poets who wrote in Chagh'ay Turki. However at another place Korpulu remarks: "In the technique of versification he (Babur) was not inferior to any of the 15th century Chaghatay poets not even Navai, and he expresses his thoughts and feelings in an unaffected style."

Babur completed in 1521-2 the **Mubayyan,** a poem of 200 lines, dealing with some problems of Hanafi law, together with some matters relating to campaigning. It is a didactic work with no artistic importance, but it shows Babur's interest in *fiqh*, and that he was a sincere Hanafi.

Babur translated Ubaidullah Ahrar's *Risala-i Walidiyya,* a work on *Sufi* ethics, in Chaghatay Turki verse in 1528-29. It is a *masnavi* of 243 lines showing Babur's Sufi leanings but, like the **Mubayyan,** it has no artistic value. Babur also wrote **Risala-i aruz,** a tract on prosody in Turki, between 1526 and 1528. It shows that Babur was not only interested in various poetical forms, but also in classical rythms and modes of versification.

It is not different from similar works in Persian, except that it provides more information than is given by Navai on certain verse-forms, used by the Turki poets. He gives both Persian and Turkish examples of metres in general use, including some Turkish examples of metres of his own innovation.

Babur achieved great distinction as a prose writer. However, his reputation as a prose writer rests on his **Babur-Nama** which, according to Mirza Haidar, "is written in a simple unaffected and yet very pure style," According to Fuad Korpulu: "As a literary work, the simple and chaste language of the **Babur-Nama,** its natural style, its colourful and lively descriptive passages, are some of the reasons which justify our regarding it as one of the finest examples not only of the Chaghaty but of Turkish prose generally." (pp. 192-93)

Mohibbul Hasan, in his Babur: Founder of the Mughal Empire in India, *Manohar, 1985, 235 p.*

Stephen Frederic Dale   (essay date 1990)

[*In the excerpt below, Dale examines the stylistic and autobiographical elements of the* Bābur-nāma, *asserting that Bābur "humanizes the steppe, Afghanistan and the north Indian plain as effectively as Chaucer animates 14th-century England or Cellini invigorates Renaissance Italy."*]

In his essays on "Self-Expression" and "The Human Ideal" in the medieval Islamic world, the late Gustave E. von Grunebaum argued that both expressions and portrayals of individuality were a comparative rarity in the literature of pre-modern Islamic civilization. Von Grunebaum concluded from reviewing both autobiographical and biographical works written by Muslims that the social customs, religious values, and literary conventions of pre-modern Islamic society combined to discourage evocations or depictions of idiosyncratic personalities in favor of representations of impersonal stereotypes. He found that such bias characterized the autobiographies of scholars, biographies of saints, and lives of poets to the extent that religious autobiographies, such as that of the theologian, al-Ghazzali, represented little more than "confessional monologues," while the biographies of sufi saints routinely "obliterated peculiarities of character" and those of literary historians, such as the Iranian Dawlatshah, concentrated on features that revealed their subjects to share the characteristics of a literary stereotype, the poet.

When viewed against the backdrop of this depersonalized literary landscape, works of Muslim authors that either evoke or depict individuality compel attention because they offer humanistic insights into premodern Islamic civilization. One rare example of such a work—and an important, unacknowledged exception to von Grunebaum's characterization of the literature of Islamic societies—is the autobiographical memoir of Zahir al-Din Muhammad Babur, the founder, in 1526, of the Mughal Empire of India. Babur, who was born in 1483 in the Ferghana Valley, east of Samarqand, was a Turkic Muslim of impeccable lineage, descended from both Timur and Chingiz Khan. He composed his principal work, now known as the **Baburnama,** as well as a separate diwan of Turkic poetry and a treatise on Turkic prosody, during his tumultuous 47-year life in Transoxiana, Afghanistan, and northern India. In the **Baburnama** and in his poetry, Babur distinguished himself as an exceptional figure in premodern (or precolonial) Islamic literature, by vividly conveying a sense of himself as a unique personality. Indeed, he wrote so directly, so openly, and so extensively of himself that it is possible to say that he represents for Islamic civilization what his Italian contemporary Benvenuto Cellini represents for European civilization: the most completely revealed individual of the 16th century.

While much of Babur's poetry remains untranslated and little known, the **Baburnama** has long been recognized as a text that contains remarkably modern autobiographical elements. The text, that is, resembles the individualistic self-statements characteristic of European autobiographies of the Renaissance and the 18th century rather than the stereotypical portraits that typify premodern autobiographical writings of the Islamic world. Annette Susannah Beveridge, who has translated into English Babur's original Turkic prose, introduces her translation by observing that "what has kept interest in it [the **Baburnama**] alive through some four centuries is the autobiographic presentment of an arresting personality [which] its whole manner, style and diction produce." These qualities also captivated E. M. Forster, who writes in "The Emperor Babur":

> Fresh yet mature, the **Memoirs** leave an . . . exquisite impression behind. We are admitted into the writer's inmost confidence, yet that confi-

dence is not, as in most cases, an enervating chamber; it is a mountain stream, arched by the skies of early manhood. And since to his honesty, energy and sensitiveness, Babur added a warm heart, since he desired empire simply that he might advance his friends, the reader may discover a companion uncommon among the dead and amongst kings. Alexander the Great resembles him a little, but Alexander is mystical and grandiose, whereas there are neither chasms nor fences in Babur, nothing that need hinder the modern man if he cares to come.

More recently, Roy Pascal, the author of a seminal modern analysis of the autobiographical genre, *Design and Truth in Autobiography,* comments that the **Baburnama** "would occupy a significant place in the history of autobiography had it belonged to Europe." He implies that Babur's text possesses some of those same qualities that characterize the works of the European autobiographical tradition, extending from St. Augustine through Cellini and Cardano to what Pascal describes as the "classical" autobiographies of Rousseau and Goethe.

Despite Pascal's cultural condescension, he is the only scholar to recognize the modern, or modern European, autobiographical qualities of the **Baburnama** who has offered a conceptual framework for studying this aspect of the text. Forster's approach is more typical, in that he fails to act as a literary critic but writes instead as a publicist, a kind of intellectual "boon companion" of the monarch. He typifies the response that readers generally have to persuasive autobiographers; they are, as Pascal remarks, "won over . . . by being admitted to his [the autobiographer's] intimacy." Pascal enables readers to move beyond this natural but intellectually debilitating infatuation to a more critical understanding of autobiographers in general, and of Babur in particular. He does so just by identifying those qualities that are common to most modern European autobiographers. Studying the **Baburnama** with these commonalities in mind, it is easier to identify the elements of the text that shape Babur's self-portrayal, elements that make it seem so remarkably contemporary to 20th-century Western readers. Equally important, Pascal also alerts readers to the necessity of resisting Babur's considerable charm and, instead, attempting to analyze his text with an awareness that autobiographical writings are self-interpretations: they are crafted or designed self-revelations rather than objective analyses of personalities and events. If such a sensibility has become commonplace since Pascal wrote in 1960, it has not yet altered discussions of the **Baburnama,** nor has it been a very conspicuous feature of studies of Islamic autobiographical literature as a whole.

Pascal characterizes autobiography as the retrospective presentation of a life in which the author is primarily concerned with the development of the self, that is, with the evolution of his or her own intellect and personality. Writing from the perspective of maturity or old age, the autobiographer does not just describe his or her life but interprets it from a particular viewpoint, be it a social or political position, literary or artistic accomplishment, or philosophical outlook. "Autobiography means, therefore, discrimination and selection in face of the endless complexity of life, selection of facts, distribution of emphases, choice of expression." The most compelling autobiographies are distinguished from the generality of recorded lives by the author's ability to convey a sense that one's own life has a coherence, that it represents a triumph of personality over circumstance, that the personality is marked by a "driving force" which represents its "master" form. Yet, while autobiographers select from and interpret the experiences of their lives, if they do so too narrowly and logically, suggesting an inevitability and predestination, their work will suffer by failing to convey the indeterminacy of life. "The problem for the autobiographer is to establish some sort of balance between various types of meaning, a balance that will vary according to his character and intention. Something of the contemporary and perhaps aberrant meaning of an experience must be given as well as something of its ultimate retrospective significance. The autobiography is an artistic failure if . . . 'its end is assumed from the beginning'."

Autobiography emerged as an explicit, distinct literary genre only in the 18th century, and Pascal's characterization of the form is derived largely from his reading of works that were written then. While he believes that the texts of Rousseau, Goethe, Franklin, and Wordsworth were presaged by earlier autobiographical writings—most notably those of the Italian Renaissance writers, Petrarch, Cellini, and Cardano—he argues that these earlier writers were not, for different reasons, fully autobiographical. Cellini, he says, "presents" but does not analyze himself; Cardano, at the opposite end of the introspective spectrum, rigorously examines his intellect and emotions but fails to convey, "directly and imaginatively," his personality. By implication, Pascal would place Babur in the same category as Renaissance autobiographers; Babur can be regarded, that is, as one who wrote autobiographically but did not produce a fully realized life of the 18th-century type. As an autobiographer Babur does resemble Cellini more than Rousseau, for he is not often introspective and much of the **Baburnama** is a memoir, containing detailed narratives of a seemingly endless series of military skirmishes, interspersed with catalogues of arcane genealogies. Nonetheless, Babur—like Cellini—conveys a vivid and plausible individuality. He offers a coherent portrait of himself as an idiosyncratic personality whose life was, indeed, shaped by a driving force in his own psychology. In the course of his narrative he also maintains, whether he intended to do so or not, an artistic balance between retrospective certainty and the indeterminacy of the moment.

Unlike Cellini's *Vita,* Cardano's *De propria vita,* and other familiar autobiographical works of the Italian Renaissance, little is known about the genesis of the **Baburnama.** Nowhere in the extant Turkic text does Babur state what prompted him to write what he himself refers to, in traditional Islamic historiographical terms, as a *tārīkh.* Nor does he discuss his reasons for keeping the diary, now lost, that apparently provided the basis for the finished sections of the **Baburnama,** which he wrote between 1526 and 1529. The uncertainty both as to how the book came to be written and the audience for whom it was intended probably is due to the incompleteness of the extant Turkic manuscript. It lacks both an introduction and a conclusion; it begins with Babur describing how, in 1494, at the age of 12, he had inherited his father's small state of Ferghana: "On Tuesday, 5 Ramadan 899 [10 June 1494] in Ferghana Province, at the age of twelve, I became Badshah." It ends, equally abruptly, on 7 September 1529, 15 months before his death in December 1530. There are also major gaps within the text, most significantly, an 11-year lacuna between 1508 and 1519 and 5 years of unrecorded events between 1520 and 1525. Annette Beveridge concludes in her meticulous study of the ***Baburnama*** that some gaps resulted from Babur's failure to complete certain sections, and that other pages were lost or destroyed by such accidents as the collapse of his tent during a monsoon rainstorm in May 1529. As Babur describes that incident:

> I was in the audience-tent, about to write . . . before I could collect papers and sections, tent came down with porch, right on my head. God preserved me! No harm befell me! Sections and book were drenched under water and gathered together with much difficulty.

Most of the book's missing pages probably disappeared, though, during the wandering exile of Babur's son and heir Humayun. He was forced from India in 1540 by the Afghan Shir Shah and only regained his Indian throne in 1555.

Despite gaps in the ***Baburnama*** and the consequent ambiguity surrounding Babur's original reasons for keeping a diary and then composing this work, the surviving text is itself persuasive evidence that Babur was, first of all, chronicling the life of a Timurid prince. More particularly, he was recording the life of the last independent mirza of Timur's lineage. His writing is suffused with a profound, unselfconscious sense of political legitimacy deriving from his Timurid descent—the source of his self-described "ambition for rule and desire of conquest." From the vantage point of Agra and his Indian conquests, he interpreted his life as a continuing struggle to establish a new Timurid state. It began with two abortive occupations of Timur's capital of Samarqand in 1497 and 1500 and reached its climax with his victories in northern India, conquests that he justified by citing the precedent of Timur's brief occupation of Delhi in 1398. Babur was also convinced that his military feats rivaled those of any other Timurid offspring, as he made unmistakably clear when he favorably compared his second capture of Samarqand, with 240 men, to the seizure of Herat in 1470 by his Timurid kinsman Sultan Husayn Mirza Bayqara. While he concluded this passage by insisting that "In writing these things, there is no desire to magnify myself . . . ," he was doing just that. Husayn Bayqara was the greatest Timurid ruler of the late 15th and early 16th century. He died in 1506, just two years after Babur became an independent ruler in Kabul. Husayn Bayqara created the cultural oasis in the Khurasanian city of Herat of which Babur himself wrote, "The whole habitable world has not such a town as Herī had become under Sl. Husain Mīrzā, whose orders and efforts had increased its splendour and beauty as ten to one, rather, as twenty to one." By demonstrating that his own military exploits surpassed those of his illus-

trious relative, Babur was laying claim to recognition as the seal of the Timurid dynasty. He presumably intended the ***Baburnama*** to be read by members and supporters of various Timurid factions as well as by individuals within his own immediate family.

If the composition of the ***Baburnama*** may be attributed, in general terms, to the driving force of Babur's personality—his Timurid identity—it is much more difficult to identify specific literary or historical texts that Babur may have used as models. His dynastic sensibilities must have been heightened, and his desire to record his own life, stimulated, by awareness of such Timurid historical works as the *Zafarnama* (the Book of Victory) of Sharaf al-Din "Sharaf" Yazdi, cultural tutor and close personal friend of Babur's maternal grandfather, the Mughal Yunus Khan. However, profound differences of style and content distinguish the ***Baburnama*** from Yazdi's work and from other Timurid court histories, such as Khvandamir's *Habīb al-siyar,* whose author became one of Humayun's court historians. Babur wrote in his native Turkic language, now known as Chagatay; he expressed himself in a direct, unadorned prose that seems closer in style to the freshness and informality of the diary or court memoir than to any standard literary or historical format. Both Yazdi and Khvandamir wrote in Persian, freely using the allusive and metaphorical language that marked most court-patronized historical writing.

A sense of the difference between these contrasting styles can be gained by comparing narratives of the same events in the ***Baburnama*** and the *Habīb al-siyar.* The comparison is especially telling since Khvandamir used Babur's work to revise the *Habīb al-siyar.* When, for example, Babur describes how he reacted to the desertion of his own supporters in 1498, following a series of disastrous military reverses, he wrote: "It came very hard on me; I could not help crying a good deal. . . . " Khvandamir, who presumably took his account of this episode directly from the ***Baburnama,*** observed that "when this news [of the defections] reached the presence of the highly esteemed Padshah he was saddened at the discord of the perfidious times." That Babur deliberately chose his language and style is suggested by the contrasting preferences shown by his young cousin Mirza Muhammad Dughlat, when he wrote his own personally informed history of his ancestors and relatives, the Mughals of Central Asia. Muhammad Haydar not only chose to write the *Tārīkh-i Rashīdī* in Persian, the prestigious literary language which he probably knew no better than Babur, who composed competent Persian poetry, but he also expressed his preference for the ornate literary style of court historians. Thus, in the introduction he apologized for his "inability to write an elegant and ornate preface" and stated that to give his book "an auspicious opening" he had actually "transcribed the Prolegomena to the *Zafarnāma* of Sharaf-ud-Din Ali Yazdi."

In content, the ***Baburnama*** is a remarkably variegated text. Babur's assertion of his Timurid identity certainly constitutes the leitmotif of the narrative. The presence of certain didactic passages suggest that Babur composed the work not merely to inform Timurids, and posterity, of his genealogy and accomplishments but also to serve his heirs as a political guide, a mirror for Timurid princes. The latter purpose seems suggested when he reflects upon his decision, taken in 1499, to allow his troops to strip a group of captured Mughals who had earlier rebelled against him and plundered his men:

> In truth this seemed to be reasonable; our men were ordered to take what they knew to be theirs. Reasonable and just though the order was, [I now] understand that it was a little hasty. . . . In conquest and government, though many things may have an outward appearance of reason and justice, yet 100,000 reflections are right and necessary as to the bearings of each one of them. From this single incautious order of ours, what troubles! What rebellions arose.

Yet, many sections of the **Baburnama** have little evident connection with the dynastic history and genealogy of the Timurids. Some resemble treatises on geography and natural history, and others seem to be modeled on the memoirs of poets. Although Babur does not display strikingly original insight in his discussions of flora and fauna of Kabul and northern India, in his ad hoc experiments with flying squirrels, or in his often scathing criticisms of poets, his inquisitiveness and catholicity of interests led him to compose a work that ranges far beyond the usual subjects of the *tārīkh* format. The seeming modernity of the **Baburnama** is partly due to the precision with which Babur describes the natural world. In this regard, the work resembles some of the more intelligent European traveler's accounts, such as Alexander Burnes' classic, *Travels into Bokhara.* Still, Babur seems atypically modern for a Muslim author of his time primarily because he so persuasively conveys a sense of his own individuality. (pp. 37-42)

Babur's wistful longing for his Afghan territories or his Central Asian homeland appropriately concludes an autobiographical memoir that contains what is probably the most fully realized self-portrait in the literature of the premodern Islamic world. Writing both poetry and prose in styles that convincingly convey his own individuality, Babur successfully imparts a sense of aging; the uninhibited emotions of his youth in Ferghana give way to the reflective melancholy of his last days in India. His achievement can be understood most easily when his self-portrait is compared to the treatment of his personality by court historians. They strip him of his individuality with metaphor and ornamentation and depict him as a type: the charismatic conqueror, the pious, ascetic Muslim, and the great king. Abu al-Fazl, the court historian of Babur's grandson Akbar, mythologizes Babur in this way:

> His pearl-like nature was a station for the marks of greatness and sublimity; freedom and detachment together with lofty restraint and majestic power flashed forth in his nature; in asceticism and absorption (*faqr ū fanā*) a Junīd [sic] and Bāyazīd; while the magnificence and genius of an Alexander and of a Farīdūn shone from his brow.

Abu al-Fazl's prose, while an exaggerated example of hyperbolic court style, reflects prevailing literary norms that shaped the composition of dynastic histories in premodern Indo-Persian culture.

The **Baburnama**'s place in the intellectual history of the Islamic world appears to be analogous to that of Ibn Khaldun's *Muqaddima,* an anomalous exception to established literary norms and social interests of society. Just as modern readers find the autobiographical content of Babur's writing remarkably contemporary, so European and American scholars have generally regarded the *Muqaddima* as a modern work, albeit for the distinct reason that it posits civilizational laws from social relationships. In their own times, though, neither Ibn Khaldun nor Babur stimulated the development of new historical or literary genres. Babur, at least, did inspire imitators, most notably his great-grandson Jahangir, who also narrates his life in the first person; the book, the *Tūzuk-i Jahāngīrī,* possesses little of the ingenuous charm and vitality that distinguishes the **Baburnama.**

The failure of the **Baburnama** to trigger an epidemic of literary egotism is probably directly due to the influence of those cultural values that von Grunebaum identified as responsible for discouraging portrayals of individuality in premodern Islamic culture. Apart from the implicit but persuasive testimony of extant literature, an unusually ex-

A seventeenth-century painting of a melon seller.

plicit indication that these values persisted into the 19th century is Alexander Burnes's anecdote about an encounter he had while traveling from Kabul to Bukhara in 1832. Burnes, who seems to have had a good command of colloquial Persian, met a

> Khwaja . . . both a priest and a merchant. . . . I gave him the perusal of a small Persian work, the "Memoirs of King Shooja of Cabool." The book was written by the King himself; and gives a detail of his life and adventures free from the extracts of the Koran, metaphors and other extravagancies of oriental authors. . . . The work was, in fact, what would be called an interesting detail of events. The Khwaja returned it to me a few days after, saying that it was a dry production, not enlivened by the fear of God or a remembrance of the Prophet, but entirely occupied with matters of a personal nature.

While the opinion of a Central Asian alim and trader should not necessarily be taken to represent the attitudes of all Muslims, the khvaja's negative reaction to the Afghan monarch's memoirs makes it easier to understand the cultural significance of works such as the **Baburnama.** They were valued as sources of information or dynastic pride for a ruler's descendants or as mines of information for professional historians such as Khwandamir rather than as literary models for a type of self-expression that departed from prevailing social and religious norms.

If the **Baburnama** is properly regarded as an anomaly in Islamic literary culture then the question of its genesis remains unanswered. It may not be possible to trace the stylistic and autobiographical characteristics of the work to specific genres or particular texts, but it still may be hypothesized that certain aspects of Babur's political and social environment fostered its composition. Babur was, of course, compelled to become self-reliant at a very young age. It would have been surprising if his life had not forced him into a greater degree of self-awareness than he might have evolved if he had matured within the protective confines of his father's court. His decision to keep a diary may have been influenced by just such self-awareness—or perhaps he wrote it because he believed that in the prevailing turmoil of his early life it would be up to him to record his own dynastic history. In his early years at least, his camps—the roughly constituted courts of an aspiring emperor—usually lacked the scribes, portrayed in Mughal miniature paintings, who recorded every public utterance of his descendants ruling from Agra and Delhi. Babur's clear, concise style may well have been derived directly from the diary format, but it also seems possible that it was influenced by his situation as a man of affairs operating in confused and unstable circumstances that would have placed a premium on direct, succinct expression. He forcefully expressed his preference for clear, spare prose in personal communications when he reprimanded his son Humayun for writing him an ambiguously worded letter: "Although thy letter can be read if every sort of pains be taken, yet it cannot be quite understood because of that obscure wording of thine. . . . In future write without elaboration; use clear, plain words. So will thy trouble and thy reader's be less."

Babur's preference for lucid private correspondence, however, does not explain why he should retain a similar style in the polished sections of his text. Literate Muslims easily distinguished between styles that were appropriate for distinct genres or situations. Babur's distinctive autobiographical style and content may have been facilitated by his seminomadic life, which freed him from the influences and dictates of court literary etiquette. He spent nearly all of his life on campaign, as he recalled in 1527 when he wrote, "Since my 11th year I had not kept the Ramẓān feast for two successive years in the same place." In consequence his Turkic prose manifested the vigor and particularity of a vernacular language, remaining largely unaffected by courtly *adab* culture of Muslim states that, in von Grunebaum's view, combined with social norms and religious values to militate against portrayals of individuality. The literature of this refined, aristocratic court culture had gradually evolved into a belles-letters tradition. Regard for specificity, simplicity, and precision, which is said to have shaped premodern Islamic Iranian *adab* composition, had given way to a preference for elaborate, stylized expression and indirection of speech. Babur, who strove throughout his life to refine his own verse style in both Chagatay and Persian, was to a certain extent a part of this largely secular court culture. However, he represented the tradition at its most vigorous; his compositions showed little evidence of its increasingly stultifying restrictions.

The influence of camp life may by itself have been partly responsible for the openness with which Babur discusses both his own feelings and the individual characteristics of others—including, significantly, the personalities of women. His willingness to depict women—not simply as individuals, but as persons with negative as well as positive traits—offers an important clue to the source of his atypical social candor, for women are rarely treated at length in premodern Islamic literature, except as stereotypical objects of romantic love. Rarely are they accorded genuine personalities, as is Khadija Begum, one of Husayn Baiqara's wives. This woman, Babur writes, "took herself for a sensible woman but was a silly chatterer [and] may also have been a heretic [a Shica]." It seems likely that Babur's frankness derived in some measure from his experience in the Turco-Mongol *ordū,* the relatively fluid, unstructured camp society in which he usually lived. While both Turkistan and Afghanistan had cities whose society was clearly stratified, religiously conservative, and strongly influenced by Persian literary norms, the Central Asian and Afghan countryside and Babur's immediate entourage were still dominated by Turkic, Mughal, and Afghan tribes and tribal fragments. Kabul and Ghazni, Babur wrote, "were full of a turbulent and ill-conducted medley of people and hordes, Turks and Mughūls, clans and nomads (*aīmāq u aḥsham*), Afghāns and Hazāra. . . . " Social relations within this milieu were strikingly casual, unpretentious, and egalitarian. Babur's description of his return march from Qandahar in 1506-1507 and the revel near Kabul in 1519 reveal how open and informal were the relations of his immediate social environment. The cameraderie of common endeavor was still fundamentally important, and even an obscure Turkic woman, the troublesome Hul-hul

Aniga, could drink openly and raucously with a padshah, the title Babur had assumed after taking Kabul in 1504.

During most of his life in Ferghana and Afghanistan Babur lived in a frontier society, but the frontier was not defined primarily in terms of its location—"at the extreme north of the fashionable world," as Forster wittily characterized the geography of Babur's homeland—but it was a boundary that distinguished societies of the Central Asian and Afghan countryside—including the small towns of Andijan, Kabul, and Ghazni—from the more hierarchical, socially, and religiously conservative urban populations of Samarqand, Bukhara, and Herat. Viewed from a slightly different perspective, the **Baburnama** may be partly explained or regarded as the work of a man who represented an intermediate stage in Ibn Khaldun's scheme of evolution from "Bedouin" savagery and dynamism to urban, cultured decadence. Social groups that represented all of Ibn Khaldun's generations or stages could be found coexisting in Central Asia and Afghanistan of the late 15th century. Shaybani Khan's ferocious, untutored Uzbeks were one group personifying the first stage; Babur's Timurid cousins in Herat embodied characteristics of the decadent, concluding evolutionary phase. The Herat Timurids had lost their savagery and group feeling; they could socialize but their taste, training, and organization for battle had atrophied. When Uzbek armies threatened Herat in 1506,

> Three months it took the Mīrzās to get out of Herī, agree amongst themselves, collect troops and reach Murgh-āb. The Mīrzās were good enough as company and in social matters, in conversation and in parties, but they were strangers to war, strategy, equipment, bold fight and encounter.

Babur himself might be perceived as a member of the Timurid lineage who represented an atypical reversal of Ibn Khaldun's cycle of inevitable dynastic decline. His intellect had been stimulated and his personality had been polished by the refined Persian culture of the Central Asian steppe—or by that which had been brought to the area directly from Iran by his Mughal grandfather Yunus Khan. By composing Persian love lyrics he showed his partial assimilation to that civilization. At the same time Babur had been compelled by force of circumstance to retain a degree of "Bedouin" savagery, the "natural" vigor possessed by tribes of the desert and steppe. His Turkic and Mughal companions remained largely untouched by the social constraints and debilitating influences that had contributed to the fall of Timurid Herat. Mughals among them still exhibited the casual rapacity of the truly savage "Bedouin." Babur's untutored military boldness, his unaffected social openness, and the direct simplicity of his prose might all be regarded in some measure as attributes of his arrested state of social and cultural evolution. Yet, if Ibn Khaldun's thesis offers clues to his success as an autobiographer, it also suggests a general explanation for his failure to reestablish a Timurid empire in Turkistan or western Afghanistan. However personally brave and capable, Babur never possessed a coherent tribal following that had social cohesion—Ibn Khaldun's "group feeling," that would have enabled him to defeat the genuinely nomadic

Uzbeks. In these circumstances an urban-based, agrarian empire in Hindustan represented the last, best hope for the restoration of Timurid fortunes.

It is ultimately unlikely that it will be possible to offer more than an hypothesis to explain the **Baburnama** and the intensely personal verse of Babur's Indian diwan, any more than it has been feasible to assign precisely satisfactory reasons for Ibn Khaldun's composition of the *Muqaddima*. The exact sources or influences of Babur's inspiration may remain hypothetical, but that ambiguity should not detract from the significance of his writings as works that help to humanize Islamic civilization. The **Baburnama** populates 15th- and 16th-century Islamic society with genuine personalities, not just that of Babur himself, but also the dozens of others whose individuality he conveys as precisely as he describes the natural world. When, for example, Babur observes of Husayn Bayqara that he "could not perform the prayers on account of a trouble in the joints," he immediately transforms the abstracted, mythic figure of the Timurid pantheon into a memorable, idiosyncratic individual. In fact, Babur resembles certain Italian Renaissance literary figures not merely because he composed an autobiography but because of his "appreciation of the concrete, the specific and the unique" in people and nature, a cultural attitude and literary taste usually associated with the "social and intellectual climate of Renaissance Florence."

Babur's work represents an important literary legacy for students of pre-modern Islamic civilization. His writings offer an antidote to counteract the Orientalists' depersonalized vision of Muslim societies. This vision treats Muslims as categories rather than as individuals, although the stereotypes are not always Western preconceptions, but sometimes reflect conventional representations found in Islamic literature. The example of Babur's work is more likely to be effective in nullifying such misleading generalizations than is Edward Said's powerful but unrelenting polemic. Standing within an Islamic society, Babur reveals individual Muslims to be emotional and intellectual, pious, ambitious, depraved, eccentric, manic chess players, verbose poets, loyal friends, untrustworthy followers, sensitive naturalists, aggressive women, inept military tacticians, recovered alcoholics, and nostalgic conquerors. He humanizes the steppe, Afghanistan and the north Indian plain as effectively as Chaucer animates 14th-century England or Cellini invigorates Renaissance Italy. His writings ought to be regarded as fundamentally significant texts of Islamic civilization, even if the events he describes occur in an area that many may think of as an obscure and insignificant frontier region of the Islamic world. (pp. 49-53)

Stephen Frederic Dale, "Steppe Humanism: The Autobiographical Writings of Zahir Al-Din Muhammad Babur, 1483-1530," in International Journal of Middle East Studies, *Vol. 22, No. 1, February, 1990, pp. 37-53.*

FURTHER READING

Beveridge, Annette Susannah. Preface to *The Bābur-nāma in English* (*Memoirs of Bābur*), by Zahiru'd-dīn Muhammad Bābur Pādshāh Ghāzī, translated by Annette Susannah Beveridge, pp. xxvii-lxi. London: Luzac & Co., 1922.
    Traces the history of the *Bābur-nāma,* concentrating on the difficulties posed by the lacunæ in interpreting Bābur's motivation for writing the memoirs.

Gascoigne, Bamber. "Babur." In his *The Great Moghuls,* pp. 15-46. New York: Harper & Row, 1971.
    An informative essay focusing on the political upheaval of Bābur's time and his family history.

Jena, Krusnachandra. *"Baburnama" and Babur.* Delhi: Sundeep Prakashan, 1978, 128 p.
    Personal reflection on Bābur's life as related in the *Bābur-nāma.*

Kellett, E. E. "A Sixteenth-Century David." *London Quarterly Review* CXXXIX (April 1923): 225-37.
    Biographical sketch relating several of Bābur's military adventures and conquests.

Lal, Muni. *Babar: Life and Times.* New Delhi: Vikas Publishing House, 1977, 126 p.
    Biographical study focusing on Bābur's military exploits.

Rice, Stanley. "A Hero of Asia." *The Asiatic Review* XIX, No. 57 (January 1923): 155-62.
    Examines Bābur's place in fifteenth- and sixteenth-century Asian history.

Sir Francis Bacon

1561-1626

English philosopher, essayist, politician, and historian.

A towering figure in European intellectual history, Bacon was a statesman, scientist, jurist, and one of the supreme masters of English prose. Although widely considered a herald of the modern scientific and philosophical world view, he owes a significant portion of his fame to literary works such as his incisive and aphoristic *Essays,* which have fascinated readers for almost four centuries.

Born in London in 1561 into a prominent family, Bacon studied at Cambridge from 1573 to 1575, commencing legal studies at Gray's Inn the following year. In 1576 he temporarily left Gray's Inn to perform diplomatic duties in Paris, where he served until 1579. Bacon completed his studies in 1582, advancing in the legal profession with extraordinary speed. Two years later he became a member of Parliament, retaining his seat until 1621. Bacon incurred the wrath of Queen Elizabeth in 1593 by opposing a proposal for higher taxes backed by the Crown. Without powerful patrons, he turned to the earl of Essex, the queen's young favorite, who unsuccessfully sought to ensure high government office for his protegé. In 1597 he gained some renown by publishing a volume which included his early *Essays, Colours of Good and Evil,* and *Meditationes sacrae.* Following Essex's abortive rebellion against Elizabeth in 1601, Bacon turned against his protector, playing a crucial role, as queen's counsel, in obtaining Essex's conviction for treason. Despite his absolute loyalty to her, Bacon never won the queen's favor. Upon the accession of James I in 1603, he was knighted, but his prospects for high government office remained unclear. In 1605 he published the *Advancement of Learning,* the first part of his "Instauratio Magna," a grandiose project of classifying and interpreting all knowledge. He married the following year and in 1607, having attained some influence at court, received the post of solicitor general. During this period Bacon worked on his grand scheme to reformulate the study of natural science and also published important legal and political tracts. Having found a new and successful patron—the king's favorite, George Villiers—Bacon became lord chancellor and Baron Verulam in 1618. Despite his many duties, which included the prosecution of Sir Walter Raleigh in 1618, Bacon published his philosophical magnum opus, *Novum organum,* in 1620. The following year he was created Viscount St. Albans. A high point in his career as a courtier, the year 1621 also marks Bacon's political downfall. Accused of accepting bribes from clients in a law suit, Bacon was tried, convicted and sentenced by the House of Lords to a fine of 40,000 pounds and imprisonment in the Tower during the king's pleasure. Although he paid no fine, remained in prison only three or four days, and benefited from a general pardon later that year, Bacon was ruined as a politician. Furthermore, he was forced to leave office without having gained the respect of either monarch he served so faithful-

ly: neither Elizabeth nor James ever seemed interested in Bacon's suggestions concerning statecraft. Nevertheless, he continued working with great energy. In 1623, he published *De augmentis scientiarum,* a Latin translation of the *Advancement of Learning;* two years later, the final edition of his *Essays* appeared. Bacon died on 9 April 1626, of a chill, following an outdoor experiment with a dead chicken to determine whether snow can retard the decay of flesh.

According to literary critics, Bacon's fame rests upon his literary writings in English, a judgment that would have baffled and disappointed the man who wished to be remembered as a seminal European thinker and Latin author. Accessible to readers who might find his philosophical works daunting, the *Essays* address a wide variety of topics, ranging from the mundane to the momentous, as titles such as "Of Studies," "Of Death," "Of Friendship," and "Of Atheism" indicate. George Philip Krapp wrote that the "basis of the style of the *Essays* is the compact, aphoristic sentence, weighted with thought and finished, but not elaborate, in form." The classical model of Bacon's essayistic prose is the concise style of the Silver Age Roman writers Seneca and Tacitus. Having borrowed the term "essay" from Michel de Montaigne's *Essais* (1580), Bacon, as Krapp observed, may "have been the first to use the word in this sense in English." But critics affirm that though Bacon mentions him in the essay "Of Truth," Montaigne did not exert a significant influence on his style. Unlike the discursive French essayist, Bacon struggled to express his ideas in finely chiselled, gnomic phrases. Although widely praised for their aphoristic suggestiveness, the *Essays* have not earned universal critical acclaim. According to some critics, Bacon's stylistic brilliance is not matched by content. As Anthony Quinton observed, the "contrast between the richness of his style and the plainness of his message is not by any means the largest paradox about Bacon, if it is a paradox at all. In his age to write well and to write strikingly well were much the same. . . . " In a similar vein, C. S. Lewis described Bacon's *Essays* as "a book for adolescents," maintaining that there is no wisdom to be found in this work. "What makes young readers think they are learning," Lewis remarks, "is Bacon's manner; the dry, apophthegmatic sentences, in appearance so unrhetorical, so little concerned to produce an effect, fall on the ear like oracles and are thus in fact a most potent rhetoric. In that sense the *Essays* are a triumph of style, even of stylistic illusion." Nevertheless, early seventeenth-century English essayists generally referred to Bacon as a model; it was only later, in the second half of the century, that the additional influence of Montaigne becomes perceptible, as evidenced by Abraham Cowley's writing. Bacon's influence on the English essay persisted into the late seventeenth century, until the advent of the periodical essay, which was brought to its apogee by Sir Richard Steele and Joseph Addison.

Bacon's principal philosophical works are fragments of his Instauratio Magna. In addition to the *Advancement of Learning,* part of which represented the first segment of Bacon's grand scheme, the Instauratio also included, as part two, the unfinished *Novum organum,* which appeared in 1620. Two years later, he published the *Historia naturalis et experimentalis,* which also remained incomplete. The *New Atlantis,* Bacon's utopian novel, was published in 1626. His other writings include legal and political tracts, philosophical polemics and commentaries, descriptions of natural phenomena, historical treatises, translations, eulogies, stage monologues, sacred compositions, and translations. Possessing an impeccable classical education, Bacon was in many ways a typical Renaissance man of letters, despite his declared intention to build a new foundation for philosophical thinking and scientific methodology. For example, he believed culture was the province of Latin-speaking European elites. Consequently, he valued his Latin writings, such as the *Novum organum,* much higher than the *Essays.* But his philosophical writings, though deemed of great importance, have not withstood the test of time as successfully as have the *Essays.*

Although hailed as a herald of the modern spirit, Bacon

was essentially a traditional philosopher. For Bacon, as for Aristotle, all knowledge was the domain of philosophy. However, Bacon's definition of knowledge is modern, for he excluded metaphysics and theology from philosophical inquiry. Knowledge of nature can be attained, he affirmed, only when humans rid themselves of *idols,* or distorting mental mechanisms. For example, idols of the tribe (*idola tribus*) prevent humanity from differentiating between egocentric illusions and reality; idols of the cave (*idola specus*) hinder one from transcending a personal point of view; idols of the market (*idola fori*) are the misconceptions caused by the ambiguity inherent in human communication; and the idols of the theater (*idola theatri*) stand for received opinions, which are accepted uncritically. According to Bacon, scientific thinking should be inductive, proceeding from particular to general statements and methodically avoiding empirically unsubstantiated, general statements. Bacon believed that the new method, as expounded in his *Novum organum*—the title paraphrasing Aristotle's *Organon,* or "instrument," indicating writings on logic—in effect replaced the Greek philosopher's system of deductive reasoning. Aristotle's deductive logic is based on the syllogism, an argument which allows a conclusion, valid or invalid, following two statements describing one term. (In a well-known example of Aristotelian deduction, the premises "All men are mortal" and "Socrates is a man" yield the valid conclusion "Socrates is mortal.") It was this deductive reasoning, moving from general to particular statements, that Bacon considered inappropriate to natural science. Bacon's inductive procedure includes the search for the form, or essence, of a natural phenomenon, culminating in the scientist's complete understanding of objective reality. However, as Wilhelm Windelband explains, Bacon's induction "is certainly no simple enumeration, but an involved process of abstraction, which rests upon the metaphysical assumptions of the scholastic Formalism; the presage of the new is still quite embedded in the old habits of thought." Ironically, Bacon's method was never accepted by modern scientists. In Bertrand Russell's opinion, "Bacon's inductive method is faulty through insufficient emphasis on hypothesis. He hoped that mere orderly arrangement of data would make the right hypothesis obvious, but this is seldom the case. . . . Usually some hypothesis is a necessary preliminary to the collection of facts, since selection of facts demands some way of determining relevance. Without something of this kind, the mere multiplicity of facts is baffling." Unsuitable for the development of natural science, which involves theoretical suppositions, Bacon's philosophy and his deep thirst for knowledge nevertheless faithfully reflect the expansive and aggressive spirit of the seventeenth century. As an eminently practical thinker and a career politician, Bacon clearly understood the nature of power in the modern world. By identifying power with the accumulation of information—he coined the expression "Knowledge is power"—Bacon formulated one of the axiomatic rules of the dynamic and technological modern world launched by the renewed interest in science in the seventeenth century.

Bacon's intellectual acumen, originality, and sense of purpose also come to the fore in his political, legal, and historical writings, exemplified by his *History of the Reign of*

Henry VII. According to the noted historian Hugh Trevor-Roper, Bacon was the seventeenth century's foremost analyst of the monarchy. It seems, furthermore, that Bacon's intellect, which busied itself with an exhaustive and exhausting plethora of disciplines and problems, truly shines in the field of history. In fact, as Quinton asserts, "Bacon was the first analytic or explanatory English historian, since Polydore Vergil, the only possible earlier competitor, was an Italian." Bacon's interest in intellectual history is of particular significance for the student of literature, since literature is traditionally viewed as an intellectual discipline. "Bacon in his *Advancement of Learning,*" René Wellek has written, "formulates the ideal of literary history. It has been doubted whether Bacon included poetry in his scheme, or whether he did not think merely of a history of learning. But, even if one grant that he looked at literature mainly as a record of intellectual advance, his suggestions seem scarcely less important. . . . Bacon, for the first time in England, clearly conceived of literature as an expression of an age, and sketched even the methods by which such an evocation of the 'spirit of an age' could be achieved: observation of the argument, style and method of presentation of individual books, and the 'flourishings, decays, depressions, oblivions, and removes' of schools, sects, and traditions."

Although Bacon misunderstood, or ignored, the seminal accomplishments of other seventeenth-century scientists, including the discoveries of William Harvey, Nicolaus Copernicus, and Johannes Kepler, he was highly respected by younger English scientists. In addition, his ideas influenced a variety of thinkers. For instance, the fundamental thesis of John Locke's work *An Essay Concerning Humane Understanding* (1690), that all knowledge is apprehended through the senses, is a Baconian idea. Moreover, the seventeenth-century Czech philosopher and educational reformer John Comenius based his educational reforms on Baconian principles of empirical practicality. In the eighteenth century, Bacon's classification of intellectual disciplines was emulated by the creators of the French *Encyclopedie.* His devotion to positive scientific facts found an admirer in the early nineteenth-century French thinker Auguste Comte, founder of sociology, who developed positivism into a system of thought. Additional evidence of his widespread influence can be seen in John Stuart Mill's attempts, in his *System of Logic* (1843), to refine Bacon's methodology of inductive reasoning.

Twentieth-century thinkers, however, particularly analytical philosophers, have found little to admire in Bacon's system. According to Quinton, this can be explained by the fact that contemporary analytical philosophers view inductive reasoning as probable inference, a radical departure from Bacon's conception of induction as a road to certain knowledge. As a writer he is esteemed, but not universally admired. Quinton justifies his assertion that "Bacon's main claim to importance must rest on his role as a prophet and critic" by summarizing Bacon's principal accomplishments: the separation of science from religion; the liberation of natural investigation from medieval prejudices; and his grand program for increasing human knowledge and power. Critics have also identified Bacon as the quintessential embodiment of the modern spirit. As

Charles Whitney writes, "Freedom, reason, discovery, progress: Francis Bacon focuses these ideals in a distinctively modern call to search for knowledge as power over nature, knowledge for the benefit and use of life."

Yet Bacon, the herald of modernity, was a true Renaissance man in terms of his un-modern possession of a classical education, rhetorical virtuosity, and an encyclopedic erudition. He fully employed his prodigious rhetorical skills to expound his ideas, including his anti-rhetorical injunction that thinkers turn their attention to fact instead of searching for the right word. Although he condemned magic and alchemy, he entertained certain beliefs that appear in the writings of magicians and alchemists. For example, as Paolo Rossi noted, "in the *New Organon* and in the *History of Life and Death* Bacon declares that a spirit or spiritual (pneumatic) body is contained in all substances." Bacon was a man of many paradoxes and mysteries, and his oeuvre remains a rich mine for interpretation and misinterpretation. A notable distortion is the theory, which arose in the nineteenth century, that Bacon wrote the works attributed to William Shakespeare. Championed by researchers who believed that only a man of Bacon's superb education, general knowledge, and sophistication could have written the literary masterpieces that the world knows as Shakespeare's, this theory is now rejected by most scholars. For instance, in *The Life and Times of William Shakespeare* (1988), Peter Levi explains that Shakespeare's contemporaries—including John Marston and Ben Jonson—knew him as a writer. "The Bacon theory," Levi asserts, "was dreamed up by a dotty lady visitor and by a cuckoo vicar of Barton on the Heath. Shakespeare's education, if it was the normal one for his time and class, was adequate to make him a poet or a great poet; he learned to be a dramatist in the theatre." Scholars agree that Bacon is a fascinating figure, but not all find his world view admirable. The "whole drift of his scientific and ethical thought," Douglas Bush has written, "was toward empirical, irreligious naturalism. He wished, with a reverent acknowledgment of faith, to exclude theological and intuitional idols from the temple of science and in doing so he virtually denied the validity of a religious view of the world. If religion was outside the sphere of knowledge, it was outside the sphere of reality. Thus, while not condemning inquiry into first cause, Bacon left such problems to be settled by revelation and applied himself to the study of things. To machinery and material progress he sacrificed . . . that scale of spiritual and ethical values which the best minds of antiquity, the Middle Ages, and the Renaissance had striven to make prevail. He not only brought philosophy down to earth, he confined it within the four walls of a laboratory in which Plato and Aquinas, and Shakespeare and Milton, would have suffocated. That is why, though we recognize Bacon's intellectual power and our vast debt to him, we do not go back to his works for vital nourishment."

PRINCIPAL WORKS

Essays (prose) 1597; revised edition, 1612; also published as *Essays or Counsels, Civil and Moral* [enlarged edition], 1625

The Twoo Bookes of Francis Bacon. Of the Proficience and
   Advancement of Learning (prose) 1605
De sapientia veterum (prose) 1609
   [Of the Wisdom of the Ancients, 1619]
Novum organum (prose) 1620
   [The New Organon, 1878]
The History of the Reign of King Henry the Seventh
   (prose) 1622
Apophthegms New and Old. Collected by the Right Hon-
   ourable Francis Lo. Verulam, Viscount St. Alban
   (prose) 1624
New Atlantis (prose) 1624
Translation of Certain Psalms into English Verse (poet-
   ry) 1624
Sylva Sylvarum: Or a Natural History. In Ten Centuries
   (prose) 1626
*De interpretatione naturae proemium (prose) 1653
   [On the Interpretation of Nature. Proem published in
   The Works of Francis Bacon, 1857-74]
*Temporis partus masculus (prose) 1653
   [The Masculine Birth of Time; or, The Great Instaura-
   tion of the Dominion of Man over the Universe pub-
   lished in The Works of Francis Bacon, 1857-74]
*Valerius Terminus of the Interpretation of Nature
   (prose) 1734
† The Works of Francis Bacon (1857-74)

*These works were composed in approximately 1603.

† The standard edition of Bacon's works in 14 volumes, edited by
James Spedding, R. L. Ellis, and D. D. Heath; reprinted in 1968.
This edition includes Philosophical Works (vols. 1-4), Literary and
Professional Works (vols. 5-7), and The Letters and the Life of Fran-
cis Bacon, Including all His Occasional Works.

Francis Bacon   (essay date 1605)

[In the following excerpt from the preface to his Advancement of Learning (1605), Bacon expounds his philosophy of learning, observing that his method, in con-
tradistinction to the methods of earlier thinkers, encourages researchers to fully utilize their intellectual powers
in probing the nature of things.]

It appears to me that men know neither their acquirements nor their powers, but fancy their possessions greater
and their faculties less than they are; whence, either valuing the received arts above measure, they look out no further; or else despising themselves too much, they exercise
their talents upon lighter matters, without attempting the
capital things of all. And hence the sciences seem to have
their Hercules' Pillars, which bound the desires and hopes
of mankind.

But as a false imagination of plenty is among the principal
causes of want, and as too great a confidence in things
present leads to a neglect of the future, it is necessary we
should here admonish mankind that they do not too highly value or extol either the number or usefulness of the
things hitherto discovered; for, by closely inspecting the
multiplicity of books upon arts and sciences, we find them

to contain numberless repetitions of the same things in
point of invention, but differing indeed as to the manner
of treatment; so that the real discoveries, though at the
first view they may appear numerous, prove upon examination but few. And as to the point of usefulness, the philosophy we principally received from the Greeks must be
acknowledged puerile, or rather talkative than generative—as being fruitful in controversies, but barren of effects.

The fable of Scylla seems a civil representation of the present condition of knowledge; for she exhibited the countenance and expression of a virgin, while barking monsters
encircled her womb. Even thus the sciences have their specious and plausible generalities; but when we descend to
particulars, which, like the organs of generation, should
produce fruits and effects, then spring up loud altercations
and controversies, which terminate in barren sterility.
And had this not been a lifeless kind of philosophy, it were
scarce possible it should have made so little progress in so
many ages, insomuch, that not only positions now frequently remain positions still, but questions remain questions, rather riveted and cherished than determined by disputes; philosophy thus coming down to us in the persons
of master and scholar, instead of inventor and improver.
In the mechanic arts the case is otherwise—these commonly advancing toward perfection in a course of daily
improvement, from a rough unpolished state, sometimes
prejudicial to the first inventors, while philosophy and the
intellectual sciences are, like statues, celebrated and
adored, but never advanced; nay, they sometimes appear
most perfect in the original author, and afterward degenerate. For since men have gone over in crowds to the opinion of their leader, like those silent senators of Rome, they
add nothing to the extent of learning themselves, but perform the servile duty of waiting upon particular authors,
and repeating their doctrines.

It is a fatal mistake to suppose that the sciences have gradually arrived at a state of perfection, and then been recorded by some one writer or other; and that as nothing
better can afterward be invented, men need but cultivate
and set off what is thus discovered and completed; whereas, in reality, this registering of the sciences proceeds only
from the assurance of a few and the sloth and ignorance
of many. For after the sciences might thus perhaps in several parts be carefully cultivated; a man of an enterprising
genius rising up, who, by the conciseness of his method,
renders himself acceptable and famous, he in appearance
erects an art, but in reality corrupts the labors of his predecessors. This, however, is usually well received by posterity, as readily gratifying their curiosity, and indulging
their indolence. But he that rests upon established consent
as the judgment approved by time, trusts to a very fallacious and weak foundation; for we have but an imperfect
knowledge of the discoveries in arts and sciences, made
public in different ages and countries, and still less of what
has been done by particular persons, and transacted in private; so that neither the births nor miscarriages of time are
to be found in our records.

Nor is consent, or the continuance thereof, a thing of any account, for however governments may vary, there is but one state of the sciences, and that will forever be democratical or popular. But the doctrines in greatest vogue among the people, are either the contentious and quarrelsome, or the showy and empty; that is, such as may either entrap the assent, or lull the mind to rest; whence, of course, the greatest geniuses in all ages have suffered violence; while out of regard to their own character they submitted to the judgment of the times, and the populace. And thus when any more sublime speculations happened to appear, they were commonly tossed and extinguished by the breath of popular opinion. Hence time, like a river, has brought down to us what is light and tumid, but sunk what was ponderous and solid. As to those who have set up for teachers of the sciences, when they drop their character, and at intervals speak their sentiments, they complain of the subtilty of nature, the concealment of truth, the obscurity of things, the entanglement of causes, and the imperfections of the human understanding; thus rather choosing to accuse the common state of men and things, than make confession of themselves. It is also frequent with them to adjudge that impossible in an art, which they find that art does not affect; by which means they screen indolence and ignorance from the reproach they merit. The knowledge delivered down to us is barren in effects, fruitful in questions, slow and languid in improvement, exhibiting in its generalities the counterfeits of perfection, but meagre in its details, popular in its aim, but suspected by its very promoters, and therefore defended and propagated by artifice and chicanery. And even those who by experience propose to enlarge the bounds of the sciences, scarce ever entirely quit the received opinions, and go to the fountainhead, but think it enough to add somewhat of their own; as prudentially considering, that at the time they show their modesty in assenting, they may have a liberty of adding. But while this regard is shown to opinions and moral considerations, the sciences are greatly hurt by such a languid procedure; for it is scarce possible at once to admire and excel an author; as water rises no higher than the reservoir it falls from. Such men, therefore, though they improve some things, yet advance the sciences but little, or rather amend than enlarge them.

There have been also bolder spirits, and greater geniuses, who thought themselves at liberty to overturn and destroy the ancient doctrine, and make way for themselves and their opinions; but without any great advantage from the disturbance; as they did not effectively enlarge philosophy and arts by practical works, but only endeavored to substitute new dogmas, and to transfer the empire of opinion to themselves, with but small advantage; for opposite errors proceed mostly from common causes.

As for those who, neither wedded to their own nor others' opinions, but continuing friends to liberty, made use of assistance in their inquiries, the success they met with did not answer expectation, the attempt, though laudable, being but feeble; for pursuing only the probable reasons of things, they were carried about in a circle of arguments, and taking a promiscuous liberty, preserved not the rigor of true inquirers; while none of them duly conversed with experience and things themselves. Others again, who commit themselves to mechanical experience, yet make their experiments at random, without any method of inquiry. And the greatest part of these have no considerable views, but esteem it a great matter if they can make a single discovery; which is both a trifling and unskilful procedure, as no one can justly or successfully discover the nature of any one thing in that thing itself, or without numerous experiments which lead to further inquiries. And we must not omit to observe that all the industry displayed in experiment has been directed by too indiscreet a zeal at some prejudged effect, seeking those which produced fruit rather than knowledge, in opposition to the Divine method, which on the first day created time alone, delaying its material creations until the sun had illumined space.

Lastly, those who recommend logic as the best and surest instrument for improving the sciences, very justly observe, that the understanding, left to itself, ought always to be suspected. But here the remedy is neither equal to the disease, nor approved; for though the logic in use may be properly applied in civil affairs, and the arts that are founded in discourse and opinion, yet it by no means reaches the subtilty of nature; and by catching at what it cannot hold, rather serves to establish errors and fix them deeper than open the way of truth.

Upon the whole, men do not hitherto appear to be happily inclined and fitted for the sciences, either by their own industry, or the authority of authors, especially as there is little dependence to be had upon the common demonstrations and experiments; while the structure of the universe renders it a labyrinth to the understanding; where the paths are not only everywhere doubtful, but the appearances of things and their signs deceitful; and the wreaths and knots of nature intricately turned and twisted; through all which we are only to be conducted by the uncertain light of the senses that sometimes shines, and sometimes hides its head; and by collections of experiments and particular facts, in which no guides can be trusted, as wanting direction themselves, and adding to the errors of the rest. In this melancholy state of things, one might be apt to despair both of the understanding left to itself, and of all fortuitous helps; as of a state irremediable by the utmost efforts of the human genius, or the often-repeated chance of trial. The only clew and method is to begin all anew, and direct our steps in a certain order, from the very first perceptions of the senses. Yet I must not be understood to say that nothing has been done in former ages, for the ancients have shown themselves worthy of admiration in everything which concerned either wit or abstract reflection; but, as in former ages, when men at sea, directing their course solely by the observation of the stars, might coast along the shores of the continent, but could not trust themselves to the wide ocean, or discover new worlds, until the use of the compass was known; even so the present discoveries referring to matters immediately under the jurisdiction of the senses, are such as might easily result from experience and discussion; but before we can enter the remote and hidden parts of nature, it is requisite that a better and more perfect application of the human mind should be introduced. This, however, is not to be understood as if nothing had been effected by the immense labors of so many past ages; as the ancients have performed surprisingly in subjects that required abstract meditation, and force of genius. But as navigation was imperfect before the use of the compass, so will many secrets of nature and art remain undiscovered, without a more perfect knowledge of the understanding, its uses, and ways of working.

For our own part, from an earnest desire of truth, we have committed ourselves to doubtful, difficult, and solitary ways; and, relying on the Divine assistance, have supported our minds against the vehemence of opinions, our own internal doubts and scruples, and the darkness and fantastic images of the mind; that at length we might make more sure and certain discoveries for the benefit of posterity. And if we shall have effected anything to the purpose, what led us to it was a true and genuine humiliation of mind. Those who before us applied themselves to the discovery of arts, having just glanced upon things, examples, and experiments; immediately, as if invention was but a kind of contemplation, raised up their own spirits to deliver oracles: whereas our method is continually to dwell among things soberly, without abstracting or setting the understanding further from them than makes their images meet; which leaves but little work for genius and mental abilities. And the same humility that we practice in learning, the same we also observe in teaching, without endeavoring to stamp a dignity on any of our inventions, by the triumphs of confutation, the citations of antiquity, the producing of authorities, or the mask of obscurity; as any one might do, who had rather give lustre to his own name, than light to the minds of others. We offer no violence, and spread no nets for the judgments of men, but lead them on to things themselves, and their relations; that they may view their own stores, what they have to reason about, and what they may add, or procure, for the common good. And if at any time ourselves have erred, mistook, or broke off too soon, yet as we only propose to exhibit things naked, and open, as they are, our errors may be the readier observed, and separated, before they considerably infect the mass of knowledge; and our labors be the more easily continued. And thus we hope to establish forever a true and legitimate union between the experimental and rational faculty, whose fallen and inauspicious divorces and repudiations have disturbed everything in the family of mankind.

But as these great things are not at our disposal, we here, at the entrance of our work, with the utmost humility and fervency, put forth our prayers to God, that remembering the miseries of mankind, and the pilgrimage of this life, where we pass but few days and sorrowful, he would vouchsafe through our hands, and the hands of others, to whom he has given the like mind, to relieve the human race by a new act of his bounty. We likewise humbly beseech him that what is human may not clash with what is divine; and that when the ways of the senses are opened, and a greater natural light set up in the mind, nothing of incredulity and blindness toward divine mysteries may arise; but rather that the understanding, now cleared up, and purged of all vanity and superstition, may remain entirely subject to the divine oracles, and yield to faith, the things that are faith's: and lastly, that expelling the poisonous knowledge infused by the serpent, which puffs up and swells the human mind, we may neither be wise above measure, nor go beyond the bounds of sobriety, but pursue the truth in charity.

We now turn ourselves to men, with a few wholesome admonitions and just requests. And first, we admonish them to continue in a sense of their duty, as to divine matters; for the senses are like the sun, which displays the face of the earth, but shuts up that of the heavens: and again, that they run not into the contrary extreme, which they certainly will do, if they think an inquiry into nature any way forbid them by religion. It was not that pure and unspotted natural knowledge whereby Adam gave names to things, agreeable to their natures, which caused his fall; but an ambitious and authoritative desire of moral knowledge, to judge of good and evil, which makes men revolt from God, and obey no laws but those of their own will. But for the sciences, which contemplate nature, the sacred philosopher declares [in *Proverbs* 25:2], "It is the glory of God to conceal a thing, but the glory of a king to find it out." As if the Divine Being thus indulgently condescended to exercise the human mind by philosophical inquiries.

In the next place, we advise all mankind to think of the true ends of knowledge, and that they endeavor not after it for curiosity, contention, or the sake of despising others, nor yet for profit, reputation, power, or any such inferior consideration, but solely for the occasions and uses of life; all along conducting and perfecting it in the spirit of benevolence. Our requests are—1. That men do not conceive we here deliver an opinion, but a work; and assure themselves we attempt not to found any sect or particular doctrine, but to fix an extensive basis for the service of human nature. 2. That, for their own sakes, they lay aside the zeal and prejudices of opinions, and endeavor the common good; and that being, by our assistance, freed and kept clear from the errors and hindrances of the way, they would themselves also take part of the task. 3. That they do not despair, as imagining our project for a grand restoration, or advancement of all kinds of knowledge, infinitely beyond the power of mortals to execute; while in reality, it is the genuine stop and prevention of infinite error. Indeed, as our state is mortal, and human, a full accomplishment cannot be expected in a single age, and must therefore be commended to posterity. Nor could we hope to succeed, if we arrogantly searched for the sciences in the narrow cells of the human understanding, and not submissively in the wider world. 4. In the last place, to prevent ill effects from contention, we desire mankind to consider how far they have a right to judge our performance, upon the foundations here laid down: for we reject all that knowledge which is too hastily abstracted from things, as vague, disorderly, and ill-formed; and we cannot be expected to abide by a judgment which is itself called in question. (pp. 11-19)

Francis Bacon, in a preface to his Advancement of Learning, *edited by Joseph Devey, American Home Library Company, 1902, pp. 11-19.*

Voltaire   (essay date 1733)

[*A French philosopher and man of letters, Voltaire was among the seminal figures of the Enlightenment, an eighteenth-century intellectual movement which saw the principles of reason as the necessary alternative to religious and monarchical authority. A versatile and prolific writer, Voltaire is best known for his philosophical novels* Candide (1759) *and* Zadig (1747). *In the following excerpt from his* Lettres philosophiques (1734; Letters Concerning the English Nation, 1733), *he comments on Bacon's writings and ideas, praising the English philosopher's scientific and literary accomplishments but comparing him unfavorably to Montaigne and La Rochefoucauld.*]

The best and most remarkable of his works is the one which is the least read today and the least useful: I refer to his **Novum Scientiarum Organum.** It is the scaffolding by means of which modern scientific thought has been built, and when that edifice had been raised, at least in part, the scaffolding ceased to be of any use.

Chancellor Bacon did not yet understand nature, but he knew and pointed out the roads leading to it. He had very early scorned what the Universities called Philosophy, and he did everything in his power to prevent these institutions, set up for the perfection of human reason, from continuing to spoil it with their *quiddities,* their *abhorrence of a vacuum,* their *substantial forms* and all the inappropriate expressions which not only ignorance made respectable, but which a ridiculous confusion with religion had made almost sacred.

He is the father of experimental philosophy. It is true that some amazing secrets had been discovered before his time. Men had invented the compass, printing, engraving, oil-painting, mirrors, the art of restoring to some extent sight to the aged by glasses, called spectacles, gunpowder, etc. (pp. 58-9)

[However,] nobody before Chancellor Bacon had grasped experimental science, and of all the practical applications made since, scarcely one is not foreshadowed in his book. He had made several himself; he made a kind of pneumatic machine by means of which he guessed at the elasticity of the air, and he circled all round the discovery of its weight, indeed he almost had it, but the truth was seized upon by Torricelli. Not long afterwards experimental physics was suddenly taken up simultaneously in almost all parts of Europe. It was a hidden treasure the existence of which Bacon had suspected and which all the scientists, encouraged by his promise, strove to dig out.

But what has surprised me most has been to see in his book, in explicit terms, this new law of attraction for the invention of which Newton has the credit.

'We must try to discover,' says Bacon, 'whether there might not be a kind of magnetic force operating between the earth and things with weight, between the moon and the ocean, between the planets, etc.'

Elsewhere he says:

> It must either be that heavy bodies are impelled towards the centre of the earth, or that they are

mutually attracted by it, and in the latter case it is evident that the nearer these falling bodies get to the earth the more strongly they are attracted to each other. We must see whether the same clock with weights will go faster at the top of a mountain or at the bottom of a mine; it is probable, if the pull of the weights decreases on the mountain and increases in the mine, that the earth has a real attraction.

This precursor of science was also an elegant writer, a historian and a wit.

His ***Essays*** are very well thought of, but they are intended to instruct rather than to please, and being neither a satire on human nature like the *Maxims* of La Rochefoucauld, nor a school for sceptics like Montaigne, they are less often read than those two ingenious books. (pp. 60-1)

> *Voltaire, "On Chancellor Bacon," in his* Letters on England, *translated by Leonard Tancock, Penguin Books, 1980, pp. 57-61.*

William Enfield   (essay date 1791)

[*Enfield was an English clergyman and educator whose writings include* Natural Philosophy (1783) *and* The History of Philosophy (1791), *which was based on Brucker's* Historia Critica Philosophiae (1742-44). *In the following excerpt from the second-named work, Enfield lauds Bacon's philosophical method for its effectiveness in removing hindrances to clear thinking.*]

[The] reformation in philosophy, which had been unsuccessfully attempted by Bruno, Cardan and others, was happily accomplished by that illustrious English philosopher, Lord Bacon, who did more to detect the sources of former errors and prejudices, and to discover and establish the true method of philosophising, than the whole body of philosophers which many preceding ages had produced. (p. 584)

Possessing by nature a strong and penetrating judgment, and having inured himself from his childhood to a habit of close attention and deep thinking, Bacon was capable of taking an accurate and comprehensive survey of the regions of knowledge, and of thoroughly examining the foundations of those structures which had hitherto been honoured with the title of systems of philosophy. His first great attempt in philosophy was his incomparable treatise **On the Advancement of Learning,** first published in English, and afterwards translated by himself, with the assistance of some friends, into Latin.

The great design of this work was, to take an accurate survey of the whole extent of the intellectual world; to review the state of knowledge, as it then stood, in its several branches, in order to discover how far science had been successfully prosecuted, and what improvements might still be made for the benefit of mankind; and to point out general methods for the correction of error, and the advancement of knowledge. The author, following the division of nature into the three faculties of the soul, memory, imagination, and understanding, classes all knowledge under three general heads, corresponding to these faculties, history, poetry, philosophy. Philosophy he considers as the universal science, which is the parent of all others, and divides it into three branches; that which treats of God, or natural theology; that which treats of nature, or natural philosophy; and that which treats of man, or human and civil philosophy. Natural philosophy he distributes into speculative and operative; including under the former head, physics, which treat of the general principles of nature, of the frame of the world, and of distinct bodies, and their common or peculiar properties; and metaphysics, which treat of form and final causes: and comprehending under the latter, mechanics, as deduced from general physical causes; and magic, or the knowledge of peculiar properties and powers in nature, and of their application to produce unusual effects. Mathematics he considers as an appendage to natural philosophy. The philosophy of human nature he views generally and specially; generally, as it respects the whole man, liable to miseries, or possessing prerogatives, and as regarding the mutual connexion and influence of the mind and body; specially, as it respects human nature divided into body, the subject of medicinal, cosmetic, athletic, and voluptuary arts; and soul, whether rational or sensible, with its various faculties, their use and objects; and, as it respects civil life, comprehending conversation, negotiation, and government. Under the head of **"The Use and Objects of the Faculties of the Mind,"** he includes logic, comprehending inquiry or invention, examination or judgment, custody or memory, and elocution or tradition, in all the forms of speech and writing; and ethics, treating of the nature of good, simple, or comparative, and of the culture of the mind, respecting its natural or accidental characters, and its affections and distempers. To all this the author adds a discourse concerning the limits and use of human reason in matters Divine.

From this brief analysis of this excellent work, the reader may in some measure perceive, with what compass of thought and strength of judgment Bacon examined the whole circle of sciences; and if the treatise be carefully perused, as it ought to be by every one who is desirous of methodising and enlarging his conceptions on the general objects of science, the reader will not fail to admire the active and penetrating genius of the author, who could alone discover so many things, of which former ages had been ignorant, and hold up to posterity a light by which they have been so successfully guided into new fields of science. The numerous *desiderata,* which he has suggested in almost every branch of science, have furnished hints to succeeding philosophers, which have greatly contributed towards the leading object of all his philosophical labours, the advancement of learning.

Bacon was now desirous of becoming a faithful and useful guide to others in the pursuit of knowledge, by pointing out to them the best method of employing their reasoning faculties on the several objects of philosophy; and for this purpose wrote his **Novum Organon,** a treatise which the author himself esteemed the most valuable of his works. Rejecting the syllogistic method of reasoning, as a mere instrument of Scholastic disputation, which could not be applied with any advantage to the study of nature, he attempts, in this work, to substitute in its stead the method of induction, in which natural objects are subjected to the test of observation and experiment, in order to furnish certain facts as the foundation of general truths. By this expedient he hoped to remove those obstructions to the progress of knowledge, the prejudices (called by our author *Idolæ*) arising from ancient authority, from false methods of reasoning, or from the natural imbecility of the human mind. Physical experiment, the ORGAN or instrument which he proposed for the investigation of nature, he considered as the only effectual method of drawing men off from those uncertain speculations, which, contributing nothing towards discovering the true nature of things, only serve to bewilder the imagination, and confound the judgment. For the particular precepts which Bacon prescribed for this purpose, we must refer the reader to the work itself, which will amply repay the labour of a diligent perusal. The great number of new terms which the author introduces, and the complex mode of arrangement which he adopts, cast indeed some degree of obscurity over the work, and have perhaps rendered it less useful than it would otherwise have been: but the reader who has the courage to overcome these difficulties will meet with many excellent observations, which may materially contribute, even in the present advanced state of natural knowledge, to the improvement of science. But the principal value of this work is, that it represents in the most lively colours, the nature, the strength, and the mischievous effects of prejudice, and lays open the various circumstances which have, in all ages, hindered the free and successful pursuit of knowledge. (pp. 587-88)

The only thing to be regretted in the writings of Bacon is, that he has increased the difficulties necessarily attending his original and profound researches, by too freely making use of new terms, and by loading his arrangement with an excessive multiplicity and minuteness of divisions. But an attentive and accurate reader, already not unacquainted with philosophical subjects, will meet with no insuperable difficulties in studying his works, and if he be not a wonderful proficient in science, will reap much benefit as well as pleasure from the perusal. In fine, Lord Bacon, by the universal consent of the learned world, is to be ranked in the first class of modern philosophers. He unquestionably belonged to that superior order of men, who, by enlarging the boundaries of human knowledge, have been benefactors to mankind; and he may not improperly be styled, on account of the new track of science which he explored, the Columbus of the philosophical world. (p. 589)

> *William Enfield, "Of Francis Bacon, Lord Verulam," in his* The History of Philosophy, from the Earliest Periods: Drawn up from Brucker's Historia Critica Philosophiae, *Thomas Tegg and Son, 1837, pp. 584-89.*

Samuel Taylor Coleridge   (lecture date 1819)

[*One of the greatest poets and critics in English literature, Coleridge was a leading representative of the English Romantic movement. He is known for such poetic masterpieces as "The Rime of the Ancient Mariner" (1798) and "Kubla Khan" (1816). Presented in his* Biographia Literaria *(1817), Coleridge's critical ideas reflect his interest in German idealistic philosophy. In the*

*following excerpt from a lecture delivered in 1819, Cole-
ridge praises Bacon for developing a method of philosophical research which purifies the mind from errors
due to habit.*]

[When] the downfall of the scholastic philosophy and the
emancipation from the superstition in at least the Northern parts of Europe, had left the mind open and almost impelled it to real silence, there arose our great Lord Bacon,
and at the same time nearly with him, the famous Kepler;
two men, one of whom we all know as the beginning of
truly scientific astronomy, of that science which possesses
power and prophecy and which will for ever remain the
greatest monument of human greatness, because by laws
demonstrably drawn out of his own mind he has, in that
mind, not only light, but as far as his own purposes require
it, controlled the mighty orbs of nature; and Lord Bacon,
who appeared not for any one purpose but to purify the
whole of the mind from all its errors by having given first
that compleat analysis of the human soul without which
we might have gone on for ever weighing one thing after
another in scales which we had never examined, and thus
constantly, perhaps, mistaking as existing in the thing
weighed that which was really owing to the scales themselves. (p. 331)

Lord Bacon has been commonly understood as if, in his
system itself, he had deduced the propriety of a mode of
philosophizing of which, indeed, there are found in his
own writings not any specimens but some recommendations which it is difficult to suppose that he himself could
have been in earnest with. His own philosophy is this: he
demands, indeed, experiment as the true groundwork of
all real knowledge, but what does he mean by experiment?
He himself strongly contrasts it with the "gossiping with
nature", as he calls it, of the Alchymists, the putting one
thing to another in order to see if anything would come
out of it. No, he requires some well-grounded purpose in
the mind, some self-consistent anticipation of the result,
in short the *prudens* [*quaestio*], the prudent forethought
and enquiry which he declares to be [*dimidium scientiae*],
the one half of one science. He expressly says, "We do not
aim at science either by the senses or by instruments so
much as by experiments; for the subtility of experiments
is far greater than that of the sense though aided with the
most exquisite instruments. For we speak of those experiments which have been preconceived and knowingly
placed, and arranged, to the intention and for the purpose
of that which is sought for according to art. Therefore,"
says he, "we do not attribute much to the immediate and
proper perception of the sense, but we deduce the matter
to this point, that the sense can judge only of the experiment, but it is the experiment which must inform us of the
law which is the thing itself." In this instance Lord
Bacon's fondness for [verbal antitheses] has perhaps rather obscured his meaning; but the sense is this, that our perception can apprehend through the organs of sense only
the phenomena evoked by the experiment, but that same
power of mind which out of its own laws has proposed the
experiment, can judge whether in nature there is a law correspondent to the same. In order, therefore, to explain the
different errors of men, he says that there is a power which
can give birth to the question; *this* he calls the *lux intellec-*

tus, the *lux maxime*, the pure and impersonal reason freed
from all the personal idols which this great legislator of
science then enumerates, namely the idols of the den, of
the theatre, and of the market place; he means, freed from
the passions, the prejudices, the peculiar habits of the
human understanding, natural or acquired; but above all
pure from the delusions which lead men to take the forms
and mechanism [of their own mere reflective faculty] as
a measure of nature and the deity. In short, to use the bold
but happy phrase of a late ingenious French writer, he
guards you against the man particular, as contrasted with
the general man, and most truly and in strict consonance
in this with Plato, does the immortal Verulam [teach that
the human understanding, even independent of the causes
that always, previously to its purification by philosophy,
render it] more or less turbid or uneven, not only reflects
the object subjectively, [that is, substitutes for the inherent
laws and properties of the objects the relations which the
objects bear to its own particular constitution; but that in
all its conscious presentations and reflexes, it is itself only
a phenomenon of the inner sense, and requires the same
corrections as the appearances transmitted by the] outward senses. But that there is potentially, if not actually,
in every rational being a somewhat, call it what you will,
the purest reason, the spirit, true light, intellectual [intu-
ition, etc. etc.; and that in this are to be found the indispensable conditions of all science, and scientific research,
whether meditative, contemplative, or experimental; is
often] expressed and everywhere supposed by Lord Bacon.
And that this is not only the right but the [possible] nature
of the human mind, to which it is capable of being restored, is implied in the various remedies prescribed by
him for its diseases, [and in the various means of neutraliz-
ing or converting into useful instrumentality the imperfections which cannot be removed. There is a sublime truth
contained in his favourite phrase—*Idola intellectus*. He
tells us that the mind of man is an edifice not built with
human hands, which needs only to be purged of its idols
and idolatrous services to become the temple of the true
and living light. Nay, he has shown and established] the
true criterion between the ideas of the mind and the idols,
namely that the former are manifested by their adequacy
to those ideas in nature which in and through them are
contemplated.

This therefore is the true Baconic philosophy. It consists
in this, in a profound meditation on those laws which the
pure reason in man reveals to him, with the confident anticipation and faith that to this will be found to correspond
certain laws in nature. If there be aught that can be said
to be purely in the human mind, it is surely those acts of
its own imagination which the mathematician avails himself of, for I need not I am sure tell you that a line upon
a slate is but a picture of that act of the imagination which
the mathematician alone consults. That it is the picture
only is evident, for never could we learn the art of the
imagination, or form an idea of a line in the mathematical
sense, from that picture of it which we draw beforehand.
Otherwise how could we draw it without depth or
breadth? It becomes, evidently, too, an act of the imagination. Out of these simple acts the mind, still proceeding,
raises that wonderful superstructure of geometry and then
looking abroad into nature finds that in its own nature it

has been fathoming nature, and that nature itself is but the greater mirror in which he beholds his own present and his own past being in the law, and learns to reverence while he feels the necessity of that one great Being whose eternal reason is the ground and the absolute condition of the ideas in the mind, and no less the ground and the absolute cause of all the correspondent realities in nature—the reality of nature for ever consisting in the law by which each thing is that which it is.

Hence, and so has Lord Bacon told us, all science approaches to its perfection in proportion as it immaterializes objects. For instance, in the motion of the heavenly bodies, we in reality consider only a few obstructions of mass, distance, and so forth. The whole phenomenon of light, the materiality of which itself has been more than once doubted of, is nothing but a sublime geometry drawn by its rays; while in magnetism, the phenomenon is altogether lost and the whole process by which we trace it is the power of intellect. We know it not as visible but by its powers. If instead of this we are to substitute the common notion of Lord Bacon, that you are to watch everything without having any reason for so doing, and that after you have collected the facts that belong to any subject, if any person could divide them and tell what could be contradicted, then you may proceed to the theory, which must necessarily be false if you omit any one term; and consequently, (as in all physical things the difference between them and the mathematical is that in the mathematical you can control them because they are the things of your will) it follows necessarily, then, there can be no such thing as a physical theory. Nothing remains, therefore, but either an hypothesis, which if it is a thing is part of the problem, or the discovery of some law, by which our knowledge proceeds from the centre and diverges towards, by a constant approximation, an ever distant circumference, but feeling its progress as it moves and still increasing in power as it travels onward. (pp. 331-34)

> *Samuel Taylor Coleridge, "The Reformation, Bacon, Experimental Science," in his* The Philosophical Lectures of Samuel Taylor Coleridge: Hitherto Unpublished, *edited by Kathleen Coburn, Philosophical Library, 1949, pp. 312-38.*

William Hazlitt   (lecture date 1820)

[*An influential English critic and essayist, Hazlitt is known for his significant contribution to historical criticism. His writings include* Lectures on English Philosophy *(1812),* Lectures on the English Poets *(1818), and* The Spirit of the Age *(1825). In the following excerpt from a lecture delivered in 1820, he describes Bacon as a profound thinker who expresses his ideas in a powerful and concise style.*]

Lord Bacon has been called (and justly) one of the wisest of mankind. The word *wisdom* characterizes him more than any other. It was not that he did so much himself to advance the knowledge of man or nature, as that he saw what others had done to advance it, and what was still wanting to its full accomplishment. He stood upon the high 'vantage ground of genius and learning; and traced,

"as in a map the voyager his course," the long devious march of human intellect, its elevations and depressions, its windings and its errors. He had a "large discourse of reason, looking before and after." He had made an exact and extensive survey of human acquirements: he took the gauge and metre, the depths and soundings of human capacity. He was master of the comparative anatomy of the mind of man, of the balance of power among the different faculties. He had thoroughly investigated and carefully registered the steps and processes of his own thoughts, with their irregularities and failures, their liabilities to wrong conclusions, either from the difficulties of the subject, or from moral causes, from prejudice, indolence, vanity, from conscious strength or weakness; and he applied this self-knowledge on a mighty scale to the general advances or retrograde movements of the aggregate intellect of the world. He knew well what the goal and crown of moral and intellectual power was, how far men had fallen short of it, and how they came to miss it. He had an instantaneous perception of the quantity of truth or good in any given system; and of the analogy of any given result or principle to others of the same kind scattered through nature or history. His observations take in a larger range, have more profundity from the fineness of his tact, and more comprehension from the extent of his knowledge, along the line of which his imagination ran with equal celerity and certainty, than any other person's whose writings I know. He however seized upon these results, rather by intuition than by inference: he knew them in their mixed modes and combined effects, rather than by abstraction or analysis, as he explains them to others, not by resolving them into their component parts and elementary principles, so much as by illustrations drawn from other things operating in like manner, and producing similar results; or, as he himself has finely expressed it, "by the same footsteps of nature treading or printing upon several subjects or matters." He had great sagacity of observation, solidity of judgment and scope of fancy; in this resembling Plato and Burke, that he was a popular philosopher and philosophical declaimer. His writings have the gravity of prose with the fervour and vividness of poetry. His sayings have the effect of axioms, and are at once striking and self-evident. He views objects from the greatest height, and his reflections acquire a sublimity in proportion to their profundity, as in deep wells of water we see the sparkling of the highest fixed stars. The chain of thought reaches to the centre, and ascends the brightest heaven of invention. Reason in him works like an instinct; and his slightest suggestions carry the force of conviction. His opinions are judicial. His induction of particulars is alike wonderful for learning and vivacity, for curiosity and dignity, and an all-pervading intellect binds the whole together in a graceful and pleasing form. His style is equally sharp and sweet, flowing and pithy, condensed and expansive, expressing volumes in a sentence, or amplifying a single thought into pages of rich, glowing, and delightful eloquence. He had great liberality from seeing the various aspects of things (there was nothing bigotted, or intolerant, or exclusive about him), and yet he had firmness and decision from feeling their weight and consequences. His character was then an amazing insight into the limits of human knowledge and acquaintance with the landmarks of human intellect, so as to trace its past history or point out the path to future inquirers, but when he quits the ground of contemplation of what others have done or left undone to project himself into future discoveries, he becomes quaint and fantastic, instead of original. His strength was in reflection, not in production; he was the surveyor, not the builder of the fabric of science. He had not strictly the constructive faculty. He was the principal pioneer in the march of modern philosophy, and has completed the education and discipline of the mind for the acquisition of truth, by explaining all the impediments or furtherances that can be applied to it or cleared out of its way. In a word, he was one of the greatest men this country has to boast, and his name deserves to stand, where it is generally placed, by the side of those of our greatest writers, whether we consider the variety, the strength, or the splendour of his faculties, for ornament or use.

His *Advancement of Learning* is his greatest work; and next to that I like the *Essays;* for the *Novum Organum* is more laboured and less effectual than it might be. I shall give a few instances from the first of these chiefly, to explain the scope of the above remarks.

The Advancement of Learning is dedicated to James I., and he there observes, with a mixture of truth and flattery, which looks very much like a bold irony—

> I am well assured that this which I shall say is no amplification at all, but a positive and measured truth: which is, that there hath not been, since Christ's time, any king or temporal monarch which hath been so learned in all literature and erudition, divine and human (as your majesty). For let a man seriously and diligently revolve and peruse the succession of the Emperors of Rome, of which Cæsar the Dictator, who lived some years before Christ, and Marcus Antoninus, were the best-learned; and so descend to the Emperors of Grecia, or of the West, and then to the lines of France, Spain, England, Scotland, and the rest, and he shall find this judgment is truly made. For it seemeth much in a king, if by the compendious extractions of other men's wits and labour, he can take hold of any superficial ornaments and shows of learning, or if he countenance and prefer learning and learned men; but to drink indeed of the true fountain of learning, nay, to have such a fountain of learning in himself, in a king, and in a king born, is almost a miracle.

To any one less wrapped up in self-sufficiency than James, the rule would have been more staggering than the exception could have been gratifying. But Bacon was a sort of proselaureate to the reigning prince, and his loyalty had never been suspected.

In recommending learned men as fit counsellors in a state, he thus points out the deficiencies of the mere empiric or man of business, in not being provided against uncommon emergencies.—"Neither," he says,

> can the experience of one man's life furnish examples and precedents for the events of another man's life. For, as it happeneth sometimes, that the grand-child, or other descendant, resembleth

the ancestor more than the son; so many times occurrences of present times may sort better with ancient examples, than with those of the latter or immediate times; and lastly, the wit of one man can no more countervail learning, than one man's means can hold way with a common purse.

This is finely put. It might be added, on the other hand, by way of caution, that neither can the wit or opinion of one learned man set itself up, as it sometimes does, in opposition to the common sense or experience of mankind.

When he goes on to vindicate the superiority of the scholar over the mere politician in disinterestedness and inflexibility of principle, by arguing ingeniously enough—

> The corrupter sort of mere politiques, that have not their thoughts established by learning in the love and apprehension of duty, nor never look abroad into universality, do refer all things to themselves and thrust themselves into the centre of the world, as if all times should meet in them and their fortunes, never caring, in all tempests, what becomes of the ship of estates, so they may save themselves in the cock-boat of their own fortune; whereas men that feel the weight of duty, and know the limits of self-love, use to make good their places and duties, though with peril.

I can only wish that the practice were as constant as the theory is plausible, or that the time gave evidence of as much stability and sincerity of principle in well-educated minds as it does of versatility and gross egotism in self-taught men. I need not give the instances, "they will receive" (in our author's phrase) "an open allowance:" but I am afraid that neither habits of abstraction nor the want of them will entirely exempt men from a bias to their own interest; that it is neither learning nor ignorance that thrusts us into the centre of our own little world, but that it is nature that has put man there!

His character of the school-men is perhaps the finest philosophical sketch that was ever drawn. After observing that there are "two marks and badges of suspected and falsified science; the one, the novelty and strangeness of terms, the other the strictness of positions, which of necessity doth induce oppositions, and so questions and altercations"—he proceeds—

> Surely like as many substances in nature which are solid, do putrefy and corrupt into worms; so it is the property of good and sound knowledge to putrefy and dissolve into a number of subtle, idle, unwholesome, and (as I may term them) *vermiculate* questions; which have, indeed, a kind of quickness and life of spirit, but no soundness of matter or goodness of quality. This kind of degenerate learning did chiefly reign amongst the school-men, who, having sharp and strong wits, and abundance of leisure, and small variety of reading; but their wits being shut up in the cells of a few authors (chiefly Aristotle their dictator) as their persons were shut up in the cells of monasteries and colleges, and knowing little history, either of nature or time, did out of no great quantity of matter, and infinite agitation of

wit, spin out unto us those laborious webs of learning which are extant in their books. For the wit and mind of man, if it work upon matter, which is the contemplation of the creatures of God, worketh according to the stuff, and is limited thereby; but if it work upon itself, as the spider worketh his web, then it is endless, and brings forth indeed cobwebs of learning, admirable for the fineness of thread and work, but of no substance or profit.

And a little further on, he adds—

Notwithstanding, certain it is, that if those school-men, to their great thirst of truth and unwearied travel of wit, had joined variety and universality of reading and contemplation, they had proved excellent lights to the great advancement of all learning and knowledge; but, as they are, they are great undertakers indeed, and fierce with dark keeping. But, as in the inquiry of the divine truth, their pride inclined to leave the oracle of God's word, and to varnish in the mixture of their own inventions; so in the inquisition of nature, they ever left the oracle of God's works, and adored the deceiving and deformed images which the unequal mirror of their own minds, or a few received authors or principles did represent unto them.

One of his acutest (I might have said profoundest) remarks relates to the near connection between deceiving and being deceived. Volumes might be written in explanation of it. "This vice, therefore," he says,

brancheth itself into two sorts; delight in deceiving, an aptness to be deceived, imposture and credulity; which, although they appear to be of a diverse nature, the one seeming to proceed of cunning, and the other of simplicity, yet certainly they do for the most part concur. For, as the verse noteth, *Percontatorem fugito, nam garrulus idem est;* an inquisitive man is a prattler: so upon the like reason, a credulous man is a deceiver; as we see it in fame, that he that will easily believe rumours will as easily augment rumours, and add somewhat to them of his own, which Tacitus wisely noteth, when he saith *Fingunt simul creduntque,* so great an affinity hath fiction and belief.

I proceed to his account of the causes of error, and directions for the conduct of the understanding, which are admirable both for their speculative ingenuity and practical use:

The first of these . . . is the extreme affection of two anxieties: the one antiquity, the other novelty, wherein it seemeth the children of time do take after the nature and malice of the father. For as he devoureth his children, so one of them seeketh to devour and suppress the other; while antiquity envieth there should be new additions, and novelty cannot be content to add, but it must deface. Surely, the advice of the prophet is the true direction in this respect, *State super vias antiquas, et videte quenam sit via recta et bona, et ambulate in ea.* Antiquity deserveth that reverence, that men should make a stand thereupon, and discover what is the best way, but

when the discovery is well taken, then to take progression.

And to speak truly," he adds,

"*Antiquitas seculi juventus mundi.* These times are the ancient times when the world is ancient; and not those which we count ancient *ordine retrogrado,* by a computation backwards from ourselves.

Another error, induced by the former, is a distrust that anything should be now to be found out which the world should have missed and passed over so long time, as if the same objection were to be made to time that Lucian makes to Jupiter and other the Heathen Gods, of which he wondereth that they begot so many children in old age, and begot none in his time, and asketh whether they were become septuagenary, or whether the law *Papia* made against old men's marriages had restrained them. So it seemeth men doubt, lest time was become past children and generation; wherein, contrary-wise, we see commonly the levity and unconstancy of men's judgments, which, till a matter be done, wonder that it can be done, and as soon as it is done wonder again that it was done no sooner, as we see in the expedition of Alexander into Asia, which at first was prejudged as a vast and impossible enterprise, and yet afterwards it pleaseth Livy to make no more of it than this, *nil aliud quam bene ausus vana contemnere.* And the same happened to Columbus in his western navigation. But in intellectual matters it is much more common; as may be seen in most of the propositions in Euclid, which till they be demonstrate, they seem strange to our assent, but being demonstrate, our mind accepteth of them by a kind of relation (as the lawyers speak,) as if we had known them before.

Another is an impatience of doubt and haste to assertion without due and mature suspension of judgment. For the two ways of contemplation are not unlike the two ways of action, commonly spoken of by the ancients. The one plain and smooth in the beginning, and in the end impassable; the other rough and troublesome in the entrance, but, after a while, fair and even; so it is in contemplation, if a man will begin with certainties, he shall end in doubts; but if he will be content to begin with doubts, he shall end in certainties.

Another error is in the manner of the tradition or delivery of knowledge, which is for the most part magistral and peremptory, and not ingenuous and faithful; in a sort, as may be soonest believed, and not easiliest examined. It is true, that in compendious treatises for practice, that form is not to be disallowed. But in the true handling of knowledge, men ought not to fall either on the one side into the vein of Velleius the Epicurean: *nil tam metuens quam ue dubitare aliqua de re videretur;* nor, on the other side, into Socrates his ironical doubting of all things, but to propound things sincerely, with more or less asseveration; as they stand in a man's own judgment, proved more or less.

Lord Bacon in this part declares, "that it is not his purpose to enter into a laudative of learning or to make a hymn to the Muses," yet he has gone near to do this in the following observations on the dignity of knowledge. He says, after speaking of rulers and conquerors:—

> But the commandment of knowledge is yet higher than the commandment over the will: for it is a commandment over the reason, belief, and understanding of man, which is the highest part of the mind, and giveth law to the will itself. For there is no power on earth which setteth a throne or chair of estate in the spirits and souls of men, and in their cogitations, imaginations, opinions, and beliefs, but knowledge and learning. And therefore we see the detestable and extreme pleasure that arch-heretics and false prophets and impostors are transported with, when they once find in themselves that they have a superiority in the faith and conscience of men; so great, as if they have once tasted of it, it is seldom seen that any torture or persecution can make them relinquish or abandon it. But as this is that which the author of the Revelations calls the depth or profoundness of Satan; so by argument of contraries, the just and lawful sovereignty over men's understanding, by force of truth rightly interpreted, is that which approacheth nearest to the similitude of the Divine rule. . . . . Let us conclude with the dignity and excellency of knowledge and learning in that whereunto man's nature doth most aspire, which is immortality or continuance: for to this tendeth generation, and raising of houses and families; to this tendeth buildings, foundations, and monuments; to this tendeth the desire of memory, fame, and celebration, and in effect the strength of all other humane desires; we see then how far the monuments of wit and learning are more durable than the monuments of power or of the hands. For, have not the verses of Homer continued twenty-five hundred years and more, without the loss of a syllable or letter; during which time infinite palaces, temples, castles, cities, have been decayed and demolished? It is not possible to have the true pictures or statues of Cyrus, Alexander, Cæsar, no, nor of the kings or great personages of much later years. For the originals cannot last: and the copies cannot but lose of the life and truth. But the images of men's wits and knowledge remain in books, exempted from the wrong of time, and capable of perpetual renovation. Neither are they fitly to be called images, because they generate still, and cast their seeds in the minds of others, provoking and causing infinite actions and opinions in succeeding ages. So that, if the invention of the ship was thought so noble, which carrieth riches and commodities from place to place, and consociateth the most remote regions in participation of their fruits, how much more are letters to be magnified, which, as ships, pass through the vast seas of time, and make ages so distant to participate of the wisdom, illuminations, and inventions the one of the other.

Passages of equal force and beauty might be quoted from almost every page of this work and of the ***Essays.*** (pp. 174-81)

William Hazlitt, "Character of Lord Bacon's Works," in his Lectures on the Dramatic Literature of the Age of Elizabeth, *1845. Reprint by Lemma Publishing Corporation, 1972, pp. 174-94.*

Georg Wilhelm Friedrich Hegel   (lecture date 1825-26)

[*A German philosopher and educator, Hegel is one of the central figures of the Western philosophical tradition. His philosophical system, known as absolute idealism, attempts to transcend the dualism of traditional metaphysics—manifested by such opposites as nature and spirit, reality and ideality—by subsuming both nature and the creations of the human intellect under an absolute spirit, or* Geist. *Hegel explained the development of spirit as a dialectical process whereby an idea, or a thesis, and its antithesis yield an entirely new idea, or synthesis, which in turn becomes the thesis of a higher dialectical cycle. Hegel's philosophy of spirit, present in such works as* Die Phänomenologie des Geistes *(1807;* The Phenomenology of Mind, *1961), exerted a tremendous influence on subsequent historians, political theorists, and jurists, who sought practical applications for his ideas. In the following excerpt from a lecture delivered in Berlin as part of an 1825–26 series on the history of philosophy, Hegel assesses Bacon's importance as an early representative of modern philosophy. He also analyzes Bacon's method, explaining that the English philosopher rejected teleological thinking in his writings about nature and instead concentrated on identifying efficient causes of phenomena.*]

Many cultivated persons have spoken and thought about matters of human interest—affairs of state, the mind, the heart, external nature, and so on—according to experience or a cultured knowledge of the world. Bacon was such a man of the world, who thrived on affairs of state and who dealt with actuality in a practical manner, observing human beings, their circumstances and relationships, and working effectively with and within them: he was a cultured and reflective man of the world. After his career in the state had ended, he turned to scientific activity and treated the sciences in the same manner, according to concrete experience and insight, particularly in the way a practical man of the world considers their use. Value is accorded to what is present at hand. He repudiated the Scholastic method of reasoning or philosophizing from quite remote abstractions—the blindness for what lies before one's eyes. What constitutes the [philosophical] standpoint now is the sensible appearance as it comes to the cultivated person and as such a person reflects on it, on its utility and the like.

So what is noteworthy is that Bacon applied himself to the sciences in a practical manner, apprehending phenomena in a reflective fashion and considering first "their utility." He pursued this course methodically; he did not put forward mere opinions or sentiments and did not express his views on the sciences in the way a fine gentleman would, but proceeded meticulously and established a method for scientific cognition and general principles for cognitive procedure. The methodical character of the approach that he introduced is just what makes him noteworthy in the history of the sciences and of philosophy, and it was through this principle of methodical cognition that he had great influence [on others] too.

Bacon ranks as the commander in chief of the philosophy of experience; he will always be referred to in this sense. Speculative knowing, or knowing from the concept, stands opposed to knowing from experience or argumentation on the basis of experience. This opposition is indeed often grasped so harshly that cognition from the concept is ashamed of cognition from experience just as, on the other side, cognition from experience boasts of its own worth over against the concept. We can say about Bacon what Cicero said about Socrates: that he brought philosophy down into the mundane affairs and the homes of human beings. To that extent cognition from the concept or from the absolute can look down its nose on this [experiential] cognition. But it is necessary to the scientific idea for the particularity of the content to be developed. The idea is concrete, it determines itself inwardly, it has its development, and complete cognition is always more developed cognition. When we say that the idea is still limited, we mean only that the working out of its development is not yet far advanced. What we are dealing with here is the working out of this development; and in order for this working out of the determination of the particular from the idea to take place, and for cognitive knowledge of the universe or of nature to develop, knowledge of the particular is necessary.

It is the special merit of the modern era to have produced and fostered this cognitive knowledge of the particular. Empiricism is not sheer apprehension by the senses. To the contrary, it is essentially concerned to discover the universal, the laws or species; and in bringing them forth it begets the sort of thing that belongs to the region of the idea or of the concept, or that can be taken up into the region of the concept. When science is mature, it no longer begins from the empirical at all, although for it to come into existence science requires passage from what is singular, or what is particular, to the universal. Without the development of the sciences of experience on their own account, philosophy could not have advanced beyond the point that it reached among the ancients.

This passage of the idea into itself is something we must deal with; the other aspect is its beginning, the passage by which the idea comes to existence. In every science we begin from fundamental principles. At first, however, these abstract determinations themselves are results of the particular; it is when the science is mature that we begin from them. The same point applies to philosophy: the working out of the empirical aspect has been a necessary condition for the idea coming to existence and advancing toward more detailed development. For example, in order for the history of modern philosophy to occur, there had to be behind it the general history of philosophy, the course of philosophy through so many millennia; spirit had to have taken this long route in order to produce modern philosophy. Once it is mature, philosophy can burn its bridges behind it, but we must not overlook the fact that philosophy itself would not have come into existence with-

out them. This then is the spirit of the Baconian philosophy.

Bacon is especially famous for two works. ***De augmentis scientiarum*** is a classification or systematic encyclopedia of the sciences—an outline that must have excited much attention among his contemporaries. It classifies the sciences according to memory, imagination, and reason. Then it proceeds through the individual sciences (history, poetry, general science) in the style of the day; the interest that it held for its time lay in its ordering of knowledge in this intelligible way. One of its principal features is that positions are made plausible through examples, such as those from the Bible. When Bacon discusses kings, popes, and so on, then he brings up Ahab, Solomon, and the like. It was, after all, the custom of the medieval and even later ages to employ the Bible as a means of proving points. For example, just as the Jewish forms were normative in the current laws (the marriage laws), so they were models of the same sort in philosophy. Even "theology" is brought into Bacon's presentation, and magic as well; he speaks about alchemy, the transmutation of metals, the rejuvenation of the body, and the prolongation of life, and he discusses all of this material in an intellectually rational way. Bacon remains on the whole within the perspectives of his age.

More striking is the method that he expounded copiously in his second writing, his ***Organon.*** He declares himself opposed to deduction, to the syllogistic method of deduction that proceeds from a presupposition or from some Scholastic abstraction, and he insists upon induction, which he sets in opposition to deduction. But induction is a kind of deducing too, as Aristotle was well aware. Induction means making observations, performing experiments, and taking note of experience, and from this experience deriving general characteristics [of things]. He then calls these general characteristics *formae* and insists on the point that these forms are to be discovered and known; and these *formae* are none other than universal characteristics, species, or laws. He says, "Although in nature nothing truly exists but bodies, which of themselves produce individual acts, yet in science nature's law and the knowledge of that law is regarded as the foundation for knowledge as well as for activity." This law and its articles or more precise specifications Bacon calls "forms." "Whoever is cognizant of the forms thoroughly grasps the unity of nature in what are seemingly the most dissimilar materials." He goes over this point extensively and adduces many trivial examples of it. He says that the question arises whether the warmth of the sun, by which we see grapes ripen, is a specific warmth or a universal warmth. We must let grapes ripen by a wood fire and learn from this experiment that it is only a universal (and not a specific) warmth by which grapes ripen—a method that to us appears tedious.

One chief characteristic of his method is that Bacon spoke out against treating nature teleologically, or considering things according to final causes, which contributes nothing to cognitive knowledge. For that knowledge we must stick to treatment according to *causae efficientes.* Considering things in terms of final causes includes, for example, explaining the thick coat of animals as serving the purpose of warding off heat and cold, or hair on the head for the sake of warmth, or lightning as God's punishment, or leaves on the tree for the purpose of preventing harm to the fruit and sap. Bacon says that both ways of treating things can very well coexist. Treatment in terms of final causes refers principally to outer purposiveness, as Kant's apt distinction has shown us; whereas inner purposiveness constitutes the foundation "of the organic," [it is an] end in itself. External ends, however, are heterogeneous to these [ends in themselves], they are not connected [directly] with the objects under consideration. This is the sum and substance of what we have to say about Bacon. (pp. 111-17)

> *Georg Wilhelm Friedrich Hegel, "The Third Period: Modern Philosophy," in his* Lectures on the History of Philosophy: The Lectures of 1825-1826, Vol. III, *edited by Robert F. Brown, translated by R. F. Brown, J. M. Stewart, and H. S. Harris, University of California Press, 1990, pp. 105-274.*

Ralph Waldo Emerson   (lecture date 1835)

[*Emerson was one of the most influential figures of the nineteenth century. An American essayist and poet, he founded the Transcendental movement and shaped a distinctly American philosophy which embraces optimism, individuality, and mysticism. This philosophy stresses the presence of ongoing creation and revelation by a God apparent in everything and everyone, as well as the essential unity of all thoughts, persons, and things in the divine whole. In the following excerpt from a lecture delivered in 1835, Emerson admires Bacon's encyclopedic mind, clarity of purpose, and literary prowess, and comments approvingly on the English philosopher's interest in nature. In Emerson's view, Bacon is right to define "the perfect man" as "the interpreter of Nature and the priest of the world."*]

The most obvious trait in the genius of Bacon, is, the extent combined with the distinctness of his vision. Not less than Shakspear, though in a different way, he may claim the praise of Universality. He had a right to pass the censure upon others which he is fond of quoting from Heraclitus, that, "Men rather explore their own little worlds, than the great world which God made," for he is free from that fault himself. His expansive Eye opened to receive the whole system, the whole inheritance of Man. He did not appreicate only this or only that faculty, but all the divine energy that resides in him, and sought to make it all productive. None ever hoped more highly of what man could do.

It is inferior men who think meanly of human nature. Great men think greatly of it. In our age Goethe has summed up in an admirable sentence the powers of man:

> From the first animal tendency to handicraft attempts, up to the highest practising of intellectual art; from the inarticulate tones and crowings of the happy infant, up to the polished utterance of the orator and singer; from the first bickerings of boys, up to the vast equipments by which

countries are conquered and retained; from the slightest kindliness and the most transitory love, up to the fiercest passion and the most earnest covenant; from the merest perception of sensible Presence up to the faintest presentiments and hopes of the remotest spiritual future: all this and much more also lies in man, and must be cultivated, yet not in one but in many.

This sphere of life and power Bacon beheld. He saw what all saw and also what few see and what none understand.

All these powers he looked upon as productive. Truth was not barren. The perfect man was, to use his expression, "the interpreter of Nature and the priest of the world" and so he went over nature to make an inventory of man's kingdom. There in the great magazine of beings his genius finds room and verge enough.

He has not like others any favorite views into which as into a mould he is ever forcing all objects. He is content to view them where they lie and for what they are. He does not magnify the facts that make for his view and conceal or neglect all others. The system grinder hates the truth. Every object had some interest for him as a fact for he was wise enough to know that every object had value could he find its place. He as readily cites what is sordid as what is great. This he has nobly declared in his works:

> But for impolite or even sordid particulars which as Pliny observes require even an apology for being mentioned even these ought to be received into a natural history no less than the most rich and delicate; for natural history is not defiled by them any more than the sun by shining alike upon the palace and the privy. And we do not endeavor to build a capital or erect a pyramid to the glory of mankind; but to found a temple in imitation of the world and consecrate it to the human understanding so that we must frame our model accordingly. For whatever is worthy of existence is worthy of knowledge, which is the image of existence. Nay as some excrementitious matters, for example, musk, civet, etc. sometimes produce excellent odours so sordid instances sometimes afford great light and information.

Thence he is omnivorous and his keen eye pierces all nature and society and art for facts. He is greedy of truth and of fancies and of falsehoods.

He conceived more highly than perhaps did any other of the office of the Literary Man. Believing that every object in nature had its correlative in some truth in the mind he conceived it possible by a research into all nature to make the mind a second Nature, a second Universe. The perfect law of Inquiry after truth, he said, was, that nothing should be in the globe of matter, which should not likewise be in the globe of crystal; i.e. nothing take place *as event*, in the world, which did not exist *as truth*, in the mind.

Nothing was so great, nothing so small, nothing so vile but he would know its law. The literary man should know the whole theory of all that was done in the world whether by nature or by men and this in no general and vague way but with sufficient particularity to make him if need be master of the practice also. He would have the literary man master of the whole theory of business, of courts, of trades, of arts, of armies, of navigation, of luxury, and also of cunning, of dissimulation, of fraud, of poison. He seems to have taken to heart the taunts which are thrown out against speculative men as unfit for business, sharpened no doubt by his remembrance that Cecil had objected this to Bacon's qualification for office in the ear of the Queen, and aimed in his own Scheme of an Education to make the Scholar not only equal to useful oversight and direction of business, but to outshoot the drudge in his own bow, and even to prove his practical talent by his ability for mischief also. [According to ***The Advancement of Learning***]:

> To teach men how to raise and make their fortune is an unwonted argument, but the handling thereof concerneth learning greatly both in honor and in substance: in honor because pragmatical men may not go away with an opinion that learning is like a lark that can mount and sing and please herself and nothing else; but may know that she holdeth as well of the hawk that can soar aloft and can also descend and strike upon the prey. In substance, because there should not be anything in being and action which should not be drawn and collected into contemplation and doctrine.

This last sentence contains the theory of his life and labors as a philosopher: "There should not be anything in being and action which should not be drawn and collected into contemplation and doctrine." It is not an occasional expression but his settled creed. This happy constitution of mind, this Universal Curiosity determined undoubtedly his election of his literary task. He would not dedicate his faculties to the elucidation of the principles of law, though his law tracts are highly commended. He would not found a sect in moral, or intellectual philosophy, though familiar with these inquiries; nor in natural nor in political science; but he would put his Atlantean hands to heave the whole globe of the Sciences from their rest, expose all the gulfs and continents of error, and with creative hand remodel and reform the whole. In the execution of his plan there is almost no subject of human knowledge, especially none of human action, whereto he has not directed some attention and some experiment in the manner of one who was in earnest by acting to learn the facts.

Lord Bacon is surely not an author who can be rashly disposed of, in a superficial sketch. His massive sentences and treatises slowly collected and consolidated from year to year must be studied with a humble mind from year to year if we would apprehend the scope of his philosophy. Without attempting any minute analysis I shall content myself with an enumeration of his works, to intimate the ambition of his genius.

His great literary labor considered collectively is called the Instauration of the Sciences and consists of several parts.

The Advancement of Learning is one of the principal books in the English language, one on which the credit of the nation for wisdom mainly depends. The treatise itself is a survey of the literature of the world, the Recorded Thinking of Man, to report its sufficiency and its defects, but it is the survey as of a superior being so commanding, so prescient. As if the great chart of the Intel[lectual] world lay open before him, he explores every region of human wit, the waste and the cultivated tracts, and predicts departments of literature that did not then exist. It is made up of passages each of sufficient merit to have made the fame of inferior writers. Its style is an imperial mantle, stiff with gold and jewels. It is full of allusion to all learning and history. The meaning is everywhere embodied or pictured to the eye by the most vivid image. No man has done with this book who has read it but once. The sentences are so dense with meaning that the attention is withdrawn from the general views to particular passages.

Though the book is one stream of sense and splendor so that a passage selection cannot without injustice be made yet I am tempted to read the concluding sentences of the first book:

> Lastly leaving the vulgar arguments that by learning man excelleth man in that wherein man excelleth beasts; that by learning man ascendeth to the heavens and their motions, where in body he cannot come, and the like; let us conclude with the dignity and excellency of knowledge and learning in that whereunto man's nature doth most aspire which is immortality or continuance; for to this tendeth generation and raising of houses and families; to this tend buildings, foundations, and monuments; to this tendeth the desire of memory, fame, celebration and in effect the strength of all other human desires. We see then how far the monuments of wit and learning are more durable than the monuments of power or the hands. For have not the verses of Homer continued 2500 years or more without the loss of a syllable or letter; during which time infinite palaces, temples, castles, cities have been decayed and demolished? It is not possible to have the true pictures or statues of Cyrus, Alexander, Caesar: no nor of the Kings and great personages of much later years, for the originals cannot last and the copies cannot but lose of the life and truth. But the images of men's wits and knowledges remain in books exempted from the wrong of time and capable of perpetual renovation. Neither are they fitly to be called images because they generate still and cast their seed in the minds of others provoking and causing infinite actions and opinions in succeeding ages. So that if the invention of a ship was thought so noble which carrieth riches and commodities from place to place, and consociateth the most remote regions in participation of their fruits, how much more are letters to be magnified which, as ships, pass through the vast seas of time, and make ages so distant to participate of the wisdom, illuminations, and inventions, the one of the other.

The second part of the Instauration was designed to invigorate the powers of the mind by a juster application of its reasoning faculty to the works of nature.

Bacon was forcibly impressed with the vagueness and uncertainty of all the physical speculations then existing, and the entire want of connexion between the sciences and the arts.

Knowledge he said, was barren. From a few facts they rush to general propositions which are of no use to the arts, but very fruitful of debate. He proposed a new method, Novum Organon, namely a slow Induction which should begin by accumulating observations and experiments and should deduce a rule from many observations, that we should like children learn of nature and not dictate to her. His favorite maxim was "Command Nature by obeying her."

And before laying down the rules to be observed he enumerates the Causes of Error under the name of Idols, intimating that the mind of man is an edifice not built with human hands which needs only to be purged of its idols and idolatrous services to become the Temple of the true and living light. These are

1. The Idols of the Tribe, or the causes of error founded on human nature in general or on principles common to all mankind, as the Spirit of System.

2. Idols of the Den, those that spring from the character of the Individual. Each individual has his own dark cavern or den into which the light is imperfectly admitted and to some error there lurking truth is sacrificed.

3. Idols of the Forum, those that arise from commerce or intercourse of society and especially from language.

4. Idols of the Theatre, those which arise from the dogmas of different systems of philosophy.

Having exposed the causes of error he proceeds to expound the method in which a true History of Nature should be formed and to show how by a rigorous exhaustive method an answer might be extorted from nature to every inquiry of man.

This book was a new logic not to supply arguments for dispute but arts for the use of mankind, not to silence an academical antagonist but to subdue nature by experiment and inquiry.

To test his logic he began to show himself its use by making collections of facts in Natural History, and instituted thousands of experiments so costly and so minute as to be fit for the laboratory of the alchemist. And to these he added observations on all parts of nature. Some of these observations are of greatest value. He anticipated by happy conjecture some great astronomical discoveries. Some of them are of no value and have exposed him to the derision of very inferior men, especially those investigations which were favorite speculations in his age.

His curiosity was attracted by all parts of nature, those which are occult not less than those which are manifest. The whole mass of facts that stand on the confines of the spiritual and material world and which for want of name are sometimes called Natural Magic he studied with equal calmness though I think with no success, the influence of the Eye in love, in envy; the supposed virtues of amulets.

This obscure class of facts, coincidences, auguries, dreams, animal magnetism, omens, sacred lots, etc. have great interest for some minds. They run eagerly into this twilight and cry to the unwilling beholder, there's more than is dreamed of in your philosophy. Certainly these facts are interesting and are not explained. They deserve to be considered. A theory of them is greatly to be desired.

But they are entitled only to a share of our attention and that not a large share. Let their value as exclusive subjects of attention be judged by the infallible test of the state of mind in which much notice of them leaves us. They savour of nothing great or noble. Read a page of Cudworth or Milton and we are exhilarated and armed to manly duties. Read Cornelius Agrippa or Scott's Demonology or Colquhon's Report on Animal Magnetism and you are only bewildered and perhaps a little besmirched. We grope and stumble. They who love them say they shall reveal to us a world of unknown and unsuspected truths. No doubt; all nature is rich but these are her least valuable and productive parts. If a diligent collection and study of these occult facts were made they could never do much for us. They are merely physiological, pointing at the structure of man, opening to our curiosity how we live but throwing no light and no aid on the superior problem why we live and what we do. It is wholly a false view to couple them in any manner with the religious nature and sentiments and a most dangerous superstition to raise them to the lofty place of motives and sanctions. This is to prefer haloes and rainbows to the sun and moon.

Lord Bacon's speculations (and) proposed experiments on this class of facts have no scientific value whatever; they are only material as they show his all-seeing curiosity.

Newton, Davy, and Laplace have put in execution the plan of Bacon. The whole history of Science since the time of Bacon is a commentary and exposition of his views.

The book of Lord Bacon that gets out of libraries into parlors and chambers and travelling carriages and into camps, is his ***Essays.*** Few books ever written contain so much wisdom and will bear to be read so many times. Each reader is struck with the truth of the observations on that subject with which he happens to be most familiar. Yet almost all the topics are such as interest all men. They are clothed meantime in a style of so much splendor that imaginative persons find sufficient delight in the beauty of expression.

They delight us by the dignity of the sentiments whenever he surrenders himself to his genius, as when he writes in the first Essay ["**On Truth**"], "Certainly it is heaven upon earth to have a man's mind move in charity, rest in Providence and turn upon the poles of truth." How profound the observation in this passage!

> This same truth is a naked and open daylight that doth not show the masks and mummeries and triumphs of the world half so stately and daintily as candle lights. Truth may perhaps come to the price of a pearl that showeth best by day, but it will not rise to the price of a diamond or carbuncle that showeth best in varied lights. A mixture of a lie doth ever add pleasure. Doth any man doubt that if there were taken out of men's minds vain opinions, flattering hopes, false valuations, imaginations as one would and the like, but it would leave the minds of a number of men poor shrunken things, full of melancholy and indisposition and unpleasing to themselves?

And let us believe that the following sentence [from "**On**

Great Place"] contains his own apology to himself for submitting to the mortifications of ambition. "Power to do good is the true and lawful end of aspiring; for good thoughts though God accept them yet towards men are no better than good dreams except they be put in act, and that cannot be, without power and place, as the vantage and commanding ground."

How noble is the view which he takes of personal deformity as being more a spur to virtue than a cause of malevolence: "Because there is in man an election touching the frame of his mind and a necessity in the frame of his body, the stars of natural inclination are sometimes obscured by the sun of discipline and virtue; therefore it is good to consider of deformity not as a sign which is most deceivable but as a cause which seldom faileth of the effect."

The uses of Friendship are nobly set forth: "Certain it is that whosoever hath his mind fraught with many thoughts, his wits and understanding do clarify and break up in the communicating and discoursing with another; he tosseth his thoughts more easily; he marshalleth them more orderly; he seeth how they look when they are turned into words; finally he waxeth wiser than himself and that more by an hour's discourse than by a day's meditation."

The defects of this book stand in glaring contrast to its merits. Out breaks at intervals a mean cunning like the hiss of a snake amid the discourse of angels. But these passages need no index and no brand. The finger of a child can point them out.

What wisdom is shown in the essay on Travel and in that of Studies! What criticism on manners in that on Ceremonies and Respects! What nicety and curiosity of taste in those on Gardens and Masks and Buildings!

If I may adventure a criticism upon Lord Bacon's writings, it would be to remark a fault not easily separable from so colossal undertakings. His works have not that highest perfection of literary works, an intrinsic Unity, a method derived from the Mind. If a comparison were to be instituted between the Instauration and the Epic of Milton or the Hamlet of Shakspear I think the preference must remain with these last as the production of higher faculties. They are the mind's own Creation and are perfect according to certain inward canons which the mind must always acknowledge. But Bacon's method is not within in the work itself, but without. This might be expected in his *Natural History* but not in his elaborated compositions. Yet in his Essays it is the same. All his work lies along the ground, a vast unfinished city. He did not arrange but unceasingly collect facts. His own Intellect often acts little on what he collects. Very much stands as he found it—mere lists of facts material or spiritual. All his work is therefore somewhat fragmentary. The fire has hardly passed over it and given it fusion and a new order from his own mind. It is sand without lime. It is a vast collection of proverbs, all wise but the order is much of it quite mechanical, things on one subject being thrown together; the order of a shop and not that of a tree or an animal where perfect assimilation has taken place and all the parts have a perfect unity. The *Novum Organon* has taken

this form of separate propositions and the *Essays* would bear to be printed in the form of Solomon's proverbs, that is, in total disconnection.

So loose a method had this advantage, that it allowed of perpetual amendment and addition. And every one of his works was a gradual growth. Three times he published the *Essays* with large additions. Twelve times he wrote over the *Novum Organon,* that is once every year from 1607. Many fragments remain to us among his works, by which we may see the manner in which all his works were written. Works of this sort which consist of detached observations and to which the mind has not imparted a system of its own, are never ended. Each of Shakspear's dramas is perfect, hath an immortal integrity. To make Bacon's works complete, he must live to the end of the world.

Two reflections are forced upon the mind by this hasty retrospect of Bacon's achievement.

1. A new courage and confidence in the powers of man at the sight of so great works done under such great disadvantages by one scholar. This he has himself suggested in a passage in the *Novum Organon:*

"If any one should despair, let him consider a man of as much employment in civil affairs as any other of his age; a man of no great share of health, who must therefore have lost much time, and yet in this undertaking he is the first that leads the way, unassisted by any mortal, and steadfastly entering the true path that was absolutely untrod before, and submitting his mind to *things,* may have thus somewhat advanced the design."

2. The other moral of his history, is, the insufficiency we feel in his mighty faculties to varnish the errors of his life. We are made sensible, in his example, of the impossibility of welding together vice and genius. The first will stand out like a loathsome excrescence in its old deformity, nor wit, nor eloquence, nor learning will whiten ingratitude, or dignify meanness. There in the stream of Time he rears his immortal front nor seems "less than Archangel ruined, and the excess of glory obscured," dividing our sentiments as we pass from point to point of his character, between the highest admiration and the highest pity. (pp. 326-36)

> *Ralph Waldo Emerson, from a lecture delivered on December 24, 1835 in his* The Early Lectures of Ralph Waldo Emerson: 1833-1836, Vol. I, *edited by Stephen E. Whicher and Robert E. Spiller, Cambridge, Mass.: Harvard University Press, 1959, pp. 320-36.*

Thomas Babington Macaulay   (essay date 1837)

[*An English politician, essayist, and historian, Macaulay was an accomplished prose stylist whose three-volume* History of England *(1849; 1855; 1861) influenced historical studies as late as World War II. In the following excerpt from an article originally published in 1837, Macaulay approvingly reviews Bacon's philosophical thought and literary style. He concludes that, except for certain faults, Bacon's method of inquiry is fundamentally sound. While admiring Bacon's intellect, how-*

ever, Macaulay questions the philosopher's personal sense of morality.]

The chief peculiarity of Bacon's philosophy seems to us to have been this, that it aimed at things altogether different from those which his predecessors had proposed to themselves. This was his own opinion. "Finis scientiarum," says he, "a nemine adhuc bene positus est." And again, "Omnium gravissimus error in deviatione ab ultimo doctrinarum fine consistit." "Nec ipsa meta," says he elsewhere, "adhuc ulli, quod sciam, mortalium posita est et defixa." The more carefully his works are examined, the more clearly, we think, it will appear that this is the real clue to the whole system, and that he used means different from those used by other philosophers, because he wished to arrive at an end altogether different from theirs.

What then was the end which Bacon proposed to himself? It was, to use his own emphatic expression, "fruit." It was the multiplying of human enjoyments and the mitigating of human sufferings. It was "the relief of man's estate." It was "commodis humanis inservire." It was "efficaciter operari ad sublevanda vitæ humanæ incommoda." It was "dotare vitam human amnovis inventis et copiis." It was "genus humanum novis operibus et potestatibus continuo dotare." This was the object of all his speculations in every department of science, in natural philosophy, in legislation, in politics, in morals.

Two words form the key of the Baconian doctrine, Utility and Progress. (pp. 212-13)

In the temper of Bacon,—we speak of Bacon the philosopher, not of Bacon the lawyer and politician,—there was a singular union of audacity and sobriety. The promises which he made to mankind might, to a superficial reader, seem to resemble the rants which a great dramatist has put into the mouth of an Oriental conqueror half-crazed by good fortune and by violent passions.

> He shall have chariots easier than air,
> Which I will have invented; and thyself
> That art the messenger shall ride before him,
> On a horse cut out of an entire diamond,
> That shall be made to go with golden wheels,
> I know not how yet.

But Bacon performed what he promised. In truth, Fletcher would not have dared to make Arbaces promise, in his wildest fits of excitement, the tithe of what the Baconian philosophy has performed.

The true philosophical temperament may, we think, be described in four words, much hope, little faith; a disposition to believe that anything, however extraordinary, may be done; an indisposition to believe that anything extraordinary has been done. In these points the constitution of Bacon's mind seems to us to have been absolutely perfect. (pp. 244-45)

Closely connected with this peculiarity of Bacon's temper was a striking peculiarity of his understanding. With great minuteness of observation he had an amplitude of comprehension such as has never yet been vouchsafed to any other human being. The small fine mind of Labruyère had not a more delicate tact than the large intellect of Bacon.

The Essays contain abundant proofs that no nice feature of character, no peculiarity in the ordering of a house, a garden, or a court-masque, could escape the notice of one whose mind was capable of taking in the whole world of knowledge. His understanding resembled the tent which the fairy Paribanou gave to Prince Ahmed. Fold it; and it seemed a toy for the hand of a lady. Spread it; and the armies of powerful Sultans might repose beneath its shade.

In keenness of observation he has been equalled though perhaps never surpassed. But the largeness of his mind was all his own. The glance with which he surveyed the intellectual universe resembled that which the Archangel, from the golden threshold of heaven, darted down into the new creation.

> Round he surveyed,—and well might, where he
> stood
> So high above the circling canopy
> Of night's extended shade,—from eastern point
> Of Libra, to the fleecy star which bears
> Andromeda far off Atlantic seas
> Beyond the horizon.

His knowledge differed from that of other men, as a terrestrial globe differs from an Atlas which contains a different country on every leaf. . . . On the globe we shall not find all the market towns in our own neighborhood; but we shall learn from it the comparative extent and the relative position of all the kingdoms of the earth. "I have taken," said Bacon, in a letter written when he was only thirty-one, to his uncle Lord Burleigh, "I have taken all knowledge to be my province." In any other young man, indeed in any other man, this would have been a ridiculous flight of presumption. There have been thousands of better mathematicians, astronomers, chemists, physicians, botanists, mineralogists, than Bacon. No man would go to Bacon's works to learn any particular science or art, any more than he would go to a twelve-inch globe in order to find his way from Kennington turnpike to Clapham Common. The art which Bacon taught was the art of inventing arts. The knowledge in which Bacon excelled all men was a knowledge of the mutual relations of all departments of knowledge.

The mode in which he communicated his thoughts was peculiar to him. He had no touch of that disputatious temper which he often censured in his predecessors: He effected a vast intellectual revolution in opposition to a vast mass of prejudices; yet he never engaged in any controversy: nay, we cannot at present recollect, in all his philosophical works, a single passage of a controversial character. All those works might with propriety have been put into the form which he adopted in the work entitled *Cogitata et visa:* "Franciscus Baconus sic cogitavit." These are thoughts which have occurred to me: weigh them well: and take them or leave them.

Borgia said of the famous expedition of Charles the Eighth, that the French had conquered Italy, not with steel, but with chalk; for that the only exploit which they had found necessary for the purpose of taking military occupation of any place had been to mark the doors of the houses where they meant to quarter. Bacon often quoted this saying, and loved to apply it to the victories of his own intellect. His philosophy, he said, came as a guest, not as an enemy. She found no difficulty in gaining admittance, without a contest, into every understanding fitted by its structure and by its capacity, to receive her. In all this we think that he acted most judiciously; first, because, as he has himself remarked, the difference between his school and other schools was a difference so fundamental that there was hardly any common ground on which a controversial battle could be fought; and secondly, because his mind, eminently observant, preëminently discursive and capacious, was, we conceive, neither formed by nature nor disciplined by habit for dialectical combat.

Though Bacon did not arm his philosophy with the weapons of logic, he adorned her profusely with all the richest decorations of rhetoric. His eloquence, though not untainted with the vicious taste of his age, would alone have entitled him to a high rank in literature. He had a wonderful talent for packing thought close, and rendering it portable. In wit, if by wit be meant the power of perceiving analogies between things which appear to have nothing in common, he never had an equal, not even Cowley, not even the author of Hudibras. Indeed, he possessed this faculty, or rather this faculty possessed him, to a morbid degree. When he abandoned himself to it without reserve, as he did in the **Sapientia Veterum,** and at the end of the second book of the **De Augmentis,** the feats which he performed were not merely admirable, but portentous, and almost shocking. On these occasions we marvel at him as clowns on a fair-day marvel at a juggler, and can hardly help thinking that the devil must be in him.

These, however, were freaks in which his ingenuity now and then wantoned, with scarcely any other object than to astonish and amuse. But it occasionally happened that, when he was engaged in grave and profound investigations, his wit obtained the mastery over all his other faculties, and led him into absurdities into which no dull man could possibly have fallen. We will give the most striking instance which at present occurs to us. In the third book of **De Augmentis** he tells us that there are some principles which are not peculiar to one science, but are common to several. That part of philosophy which concerns itself with these principles is, in his nomenclature, designated as *philosophia prima.* He then proceeds to mention some of the principles with which this *philosophia prima* is conversant. One of them is this. An infectious disease is more likely to be communicated while it is in progress than when it has reached its height. This, says he, is true in medicine. It is also true in morals; for we see that the example of very abandoned men injures public morality less than the example of men in whom vice has not yet extinguished all good qualities. Again, he tells us that in music a discord ending in a concord is agreeable, and that the same thing may be noted in the affections. Once more, he tells us, that in physics the energy with which a principle acts is often increased by the antiperistasis of its opposite; and that it is the same in the contests of factions. If the making of ingenious and sparkling similitudes like these be indeed the *philosophia prima,* we are quite sure that the greatest philosophical work of the nineteenth century is Mr. Moore's *Lalla Rookh.* The similitudes which we have cited are very happy similitudes. But that a man like

Bacon should have taken them for more, that he should have thought the discovery of such resemblances as these an important part of philosophy, has always appeared to us one of the most singular facts in the history of letters.

The truth is that his mind was wonderfully quick in perceiving analogies of all sorts. But, like several eminent men whom we could name, both living and dead, he sometimes appeared strangely deficient in the power of distinguishing rational from fanciful analogies, analogies which are arguments from analogies which are mere illustrations, analogies like that which Bishop Butler so ably pointed out, between natural and revealed religion, from analogies like that which Addison discovered, between the series of Grecian gods carved by Phidias and the series of English kings painted by Kneller. This want of discrimination has led to many strange political speculations. Sir William Temple deduced a theory of government from the properties of the pyramid. Mr. Southey's whole system of finance is grounded on the phænomena of evaporation and rain. . . . It is curious that Bacon has himself mentioned this very kind of delusion among the *idola specus;* and has mentioned in language which, we are inclined to think, shows that he knew himself to be subject to it. It is the vice, he tells us, of subtle minds to attach too much importance to slight distinctions; it is the vice, on the other hand, of high and discursive intellects to attach too much importance to slight resemblances; and he adds that, when this last propensity is indulged to excess, it leads men to catch at shadows instead of substances.

Yet we cannot wish that Bacon's wit had been less luxuriant. For, to say nothing of the pleasure which it affords, it was in the vast majority of cases employed for the purpose of making obscure truth plain, of making repulsive truth attractive, of fixing in the mind forever truth which might otherwise have left but a transient impression.

The poetical faculty was powerful in Bacon's mind, but not, like his wit, so powerful as occasionally to usurp the place of his reason, and to tyrannize over the whole man. No imagination was ever at once so strong and so thoroughly subjugated. It never stirred but at a signal from good sense. It stopped at the first check from good sense. Yet, though disciplined to such obedience, it gave noble proofs of its vigor. In truth, much of Bacon's life was passed in a visionary world, amidst things as strange as any that are described in the *Arabian Tales,* or in those romances on which the curate and barber of Don Quixote's village performed so cruel an *auto-de-fe,* amidst buildings more sumptuous than the palace of Aladdin, fountains more wonderful than the golden water of Parizade, conveyances more rapid than the hippogryph of Ruggiero, arms more formidable than the lance of Astolfo, remedies more efficacious than the balsam of Fierabras. Yet in his magnificent day-dreams there was nothing wild, nothing but what sober reason sanctioned. He knew that all the secrets feigned by poets to have been written in the books of enchanters are worthless when compared with the mighty secrets which are really written in the book of nature, and which, with time and patience, will be read there. He knew that all the wonders wrought by all the talismans in fable were trifles when compared to the wonders which might reasonably be expected from the philosophy of fruit, and that, if his words sank deep into the minds of men, they would produce effects such as superstition had never ascribed to the incantations of Merlin and Michael Scot. It was here that he loved to let his imagination loose. He loved to picture to himself the world as it would be when his philosophy should, in his own noble phrase, "have enlarged the bounds of human empire." We might refer to many instances. But we will content ourselves with the strongest, the description of the House of Solomon in the *New Atlantis.* By most of Bacon's contemporaries, and by some people of our time, this remarkable passage would, we doubt not, be considered as an ingenious rodomontade, a counterpart to the adventures of Sinbad or Baron Munchausen. The truth is, that there is not to be found in any human composition a passage more eminently distinguished by profound and serene wisdom. The boldness and originality of the fiction is far less wonderful than the nice discernment which carefully excluded from that long list of prodigies everything that can be pronounced impossible, everything that can be proved to lie beyond the mighty magic of induction and of time. Already some parts, and not the least startling parts, of this glorious prophecy have been accomplished, even according to the letter; and the whole, construed according to the spirit, is daily accomplishing all around us.

One of the most remarkable circumstances in the history of Bacon's mind is the order in which its powers expanded themselves. With him the fruit came first and remained till the last; the blossoms did not appear till late. In general, the development of the fancy is to the development of the judgment what the growth of a girl is to the growth of a boy. The fancy attains at an earlier period to the perfection of its beauty, its power, and its fruitfulness; and, as it is first to ripen, it is also first to fade. It has generally lost something of its bloom and freshness before the sterner faculties have reached maturity; and it is commonly withered and barren while those faculties still retain all their energy. It rarely happens that the fancy and the judgment grow together. It happens still more rarely that the judgment grows faster than the fancy. This seems, however, to have been the case with Bacon. His boyhood and youth appear to have been singularly sedate. His gigantic scheme of philosophical reform is said by some writers to have been planned before he was fifteen, and was undoubtedly planned while he was still young. He observed as vigilantly, meditated as deeply, and judged as temperately when he gave his first work to the world as at the close of his long career. But in eloquence, in sweetness and variety of expression, and in richness of illustration, his later writings are far superior to those of his youth. (pp. 244-50)

We will give very short specimens of Bacon's two styles. In 1597, he wrote thus:

> Crafty men contemn studies; simple men admire them; and wise men use them; for they teach not their own use: that is a wisdom without them, and won by observation. Read not to contradict, nor to believe, but to weigh and consider. Some books are to be tasted, others to be swallowed, and some few to be chewed and digested. Reading maketh a full man, conference a ready man,

and writing an exact man. And therefore if a man write little, he had need have a great memory; if he confer little, have a present wit; and if he read little, have much cunning to seem to know that he doth not. Histories make men wise, poets witty, the mathematics subtle, natural philosophy deep, morals grave, logic and rhetoric able to contend.

It will hardly be disputed that this is a passage to be "chewed and digested." We do not believe that Thucydides himself has anywhere compressed so much thought into so small a space.

In the additions which Bacon afterwards made to the *Essays,* there is nothing superior in truth or weight to what we have quoted. But his style was constantly becoming richer and softer. The following passage, first published in 1625, will show the extent of the change:

> Prosperity is the blessing of the old Testament; adversity is the blessing of the New, which carrieth the greater benediction and the clearer evidence of God's favor. Yet, even in the Old Testament, if you listen to David's harp you shall hear as many hearse-like airs as carols; and the pencil of the Holy Ghost hath labored more in describing the afflictions of Job than the felicities of Solomon. Prosperity is not without many fears and distastes; and adversity is not without comforts and hopes. We see in needle-works and embroideries it is more pleasing to have a lively work upon a sad and solemn ground, than to have a dark and melancholy work upon a lightsome ground. Judge therefore of the pleasure of the heart by the pleasure of the eye. Certainly virtue is like precious odors, most fragrant when they are incensed or crushed; for prosperity doth best discover vice, but adversity doth best discover virtue.

It is by the *Essays* that Bacon is best known to the multitude. The *Novum Organum* and the *De Augmentis* are much talked of, but little read. They have produced indeed a vast effect on the opinions of mankind; but they have produced it through the operation of intermediate agents. They have moved the intellects which have moved the world. It is in the *Essays* alone that the mind of Bacon is brought into immediate contact with the minds of ordinary readers. There he opens an exoteric school, and talks to plain men, in language which everybody understands, about things in which everybody is interested. He has thus enabled those who must otherwise have taken his merits on trust to judge for themselves; and the great body of readers have, during several generations, acknowledged that the man who has treated with such consummate ability questions with which they are familiar may well be supposed to deserve all the praise bestowed on him by those who have sat in his inner school.

Without any disparagement to the admirable treatise *De Augmentis,* we must say that, in our judgment, Bacon's greatest performance is the first book of the *Novum Organum.* All the peculiarities of his extraordinary mind are found there in the highest perfection. Many of the aphorisms, but particularly those in which he gives examples of the influence of the *idola,* show a nicety of observation that has never been surpassed. Every part of the book blazes with wit, but with wit which is employed only to illustrate and decorate truth. No book ever made so great a revolution in the mode of thinking, overthrew so many prejudices, introduced so many new opinions. Yet no book was ever written in a less contentious spirit. It truly conquers with chalk and not with steel. Proposition after proposition enters into the mind, is received not as an invader, but as a welcome friend, and though previously unknown, becomes at once domesticated. But what we most admire is the vast capacity of that intellect which, without effort, takes in at once all the domains of science, all the past, the present, and the future, all the errors of two thousand years, all the encouraging signs of the passing times, all the bright hopes of the coming age. Cowley, who was among the most ardent, and not among the least discerning followers of the new philosophy, has, in one of his finest poems, compared Bacon to Moses standing on Mount Pisgah. It is to Bacon, we think, as he appears in the first book of the **Novum Organum,** that the comparison applies with peculiar felicity. There we see the great Lawgiver looking round from his lonely elevation on an infinite expanse; behind him a wilderness of dreary sands and bitter waters, in which successive generations have sojourned, always moving, yet never advancing, reaping no harvest, and building no abiding city; before him a goodly land, a land of promise, a land flowing with milk and honey. While the multitude below saw only the flat sterile desert in which they had so long wandered, bounded on every side by a near horizon, or diversified only by some deceitful mirage, he was gazing from a far higher stand on a far lovelier country, following with his eye, the long course of fertilizing rivers, through ample pastures, and under the bridges of great capitals, measuring the distances of marts and havens, and portioning out all those wealthy regions from Dan to Beersheba.

It is painful to turn back from contemplating Bacon's philosophy to contemplate his life. Yet without so turning back it is impossible fairly to estimate his powers. He left the University at an earlier age than that at which most people repair thither. While yet a boy he was plunged into the midst of diplomatic business. Thence he passed to the study of a vast technical system of law, and worked his way up through a succession of laborious offices, to the highest post in his profession. In the mean time he took an active part in every Parliament; he was an adviser of the Crown: he paid court with the greatest assiduity and address to all whose favor was likely to be of use to him; he lived much in society; he noted the slightest peculiarities of character, and the slightest changes of fashion. Scarcely any man has led a more stirring life than that which Bacon led from sixteen to sixty. Scarcely any man has been better entitled to be called a thorough man of the world. The founding of a new philosophy, the imparting of a new direction to the minds of speculators, this was the amusement of his leisure, the work of hours occasionally stolen from the Woolsack and the Council Board. This consideration, while it increases the admiration with which we regard his intellect, increases also our regret that such an intellect should so often have been unworthily employed. He well knew the better course, and had, at one time, resolved to pursue it. "I confess," said he in a letter

written when he was still young, "that I have as vast contemplative ends as I have moderate civil ends." Had his civil ends continued to be moderate, he would have been, not only the Moses, but the Joshua of philosophy. He would have fulfilled a large part of his own magnificent predictions. He would have led his followers, not only to the verge, but into the heart of the promised land. He would not merely have pointed out, but would have divided the spoil. Above all, he would have left, not only a great, but a spotless name. Mankind would then have been able to esteem their illustrious benefactor. We should not then be compelled to regard his character with mingled contempt and admiration, with mingled aversion and gratitude. We should not then regret that there should be so many proofs of the narrowness and selfishness of a heart, the benevolence of which was yet large enough to take in all races and all ages. We should not then have to blush for the disingenuousness of the most devoted worshipper of speculative truth, for the servility of the boldest champion of intellectual freedom. We should not then have seen the same man at one time far in the van, at another time far in the rear of his generation. We should not then be forced to own that he who first treated legislation as a science was among the last Englishmen who used the rack, that he who first summoned philosophers to the great work of interpreting nature, was among the last Englishmen who sold justice. And we should conclude our survey of a life placidly, honorably, beneficently passed, "in industrious observations, grounded conclusions, and profitable inventions and discoveries," with feelings very different from those with which we now turn away from the checkered spectacle of so much glory and so much shame. (pp. 251-54)

Thomas Babington Macaulay, "Lord Bacon," in his Critical, Historical, and Miscellaneous Essays and Poems, Vol. II, *Estes and Lauriat, 1880, pp. 142-254.*

H. A. Taine　(essay date 1863)

[*Taine was a French philosopher, critic, and historian who studied the influence of environment and heredity on the development of human character. In his well-known work,* Histoire de la littérature anglaise *(1863-64;* History of English Literature, *1871), he analyzed literature through a study of race and milieu. In the following excerpt from that work, Taine describes Bacon as "a great and luminous intellect" who clothed "his ideas in the most splendid dress." In Taine's opinion, Bacon is unique in his ability to use opulent imagery as a catalyst for thinking. Taine remarks, however, that Bacon's actual understanding of science does not match his enthusiasm as a reformer of science.*]

[Among the poets, scholars, dreamers, and inquirers of the English Renaissance appears] the most comprehensive, sensible, originative of the minds of the age, Francis Bacon, a great and luminous intellect, one of the finest of this poetic progeny, who, like his predecessors, was naturally disposed to clothe his ideas in the most splendid dress: in this age, a thought did not seem complete until it had assumed form and colour. But what distinguishes him from the others is, that with him an image only serves to concentrate meditation. He reflected long, stamped on his mind all the parts and relations of his subject; he is master of it, and then, instead of exposing this complete idea in a graduated chain of reasoning, he embodies it in a comparison so expressive, exact, lucid, that behind the figure we perceive all the details of the idea, like liquor in a fine crystal vase. Judge of his style by a single example [from *De Augmentis Scientiarum*]:

> For as water, whether it be the dew of Heaven or the springs of the earth, easily scatters and loses itself in the ground, except it be collected into some receptacle, where it may by union and consort comfort and sustain itself (and for that cause, the industry of man has devised aqueducts, cisterns, and pools, and likewise beautified them with various ornaments of magnificence and state, as well as for use and necessity); so this excellent liquor of knowledge, whether it descend from divine inspiration or spring from human sense, would soon perish and vanish into oblivion, if it were not preserved in books, traditions, conferences, and especially in places appointed for such matters as universities, colleges, and schools, where it may have both a fixed habitation, and means and opportunity of increasing and collecting itself.
>
> The greatest error of all the rest, is the mistaking or misplacing of the last or farthest end of knowledge: for men have entered into a desire of learning and knowledge, sometimes upon a natural curiosity and inquisitive appetite; sometimes to entertain their minds with variety and delight; sometimes for ornament and reputation; and sometimes to enable them to victory of wit and contradiction; and most times for lucre and profession; and seldom sincerely to give a true account of their gift of reason, to the benefit and use of men: as if there were sought in knowledge a couch whereupon to rest a searching and restless spirit; or a terrace, for a wandering and variable mind to walk up and down with a fair prospect; or a tower of state, for a proud mind to raise itself upon; or a fort or commanding ground, for strife and contention; or a shop, for profit or sale; and not a rich storehouse, for the glory of the Creator, and the relief of man's estate.

This is his mode of thought, by symbols, not by analysis; instead of explaining his idea, he transposes and translates it,—translates it entire, to the smallest details, enclosing all in the majesty of a grand period, or in the brevity of a striking sentence. Thence springs a style of admirable richness, gravity, and vigour, now solemn and symmetrical, now concise and piercing, always elaborate and full of colour. There is nothing in English prose superior to his diction.

Thence is derived also his manner of conceiving things. He is not a dialectician, like Hobbes or Descartes, apt in arranging ideas, in educing one from another, in leading his reader from the simple to the complex by an unbroken chain. He is a producer of conceptions and of sentences. The matter being explored, he says to us: "Such it is; touch it not on that side; it must be approached from the other." Nothing more; no proof, no effort to convince: he affirms, and does nothing more; he has thought in the manner of artists and poets, and he speaks after the manner of prophets and seers. *Cogitata et visa* this title of one of his books might be the title of all. The most admirable, the ***Novum Organum,*** is a string of aphorisms,—a collection, as it were, of scientific decrees, as of an oracle who foresees the future and reveals the truth. And to make the resemblance complete, he expresses them by poetical figures, by enigmatic abbreviations, almost in Sibylline verses: *Idola specûs, Idola tribûs, Idola fori, Idola theatri,* every one will recall these strange names, by which he signifies the four kinds of illusions to which man is subject. Shakspeare and the seers do not contain more vigorous or expressive condensations of thought, more resembling inspiration, and in Bacon they are to be found everywhere. On the whole, his process is that of the creators; it is intuition, not reasoning. When he has laid up his store of facts, the greatest possible, on some vast subject, on some entire province of the mind, on the whole anterior philosophy, on the general condition of the sciences, on the power and limits of human reason, he casts over all this a comprehensive view, as it were a great net, brings up a universal idea, condenses his idea into a maxim, and hands it to us with the words, "Verify and profit by it."

There is nothing more hazardous, more like fantasy, than this mode of thought, when it is not checked by natural and strong good sense. This common sense, which is a kind of natural divination, the stable equilibrium of an intellect always gravitating to the true, like the needle to the pole, Bacon possesses in the highest degree. He has a preeminently practical, even an utilitarian mind, such as we meet with later in Bentham, and such as their business habits were to impress more and more upon the English. At the age of sixteen, while at the university, he was dissatisfied with Aristotle's philosophy, not that he thought meanly of the author, whom, on the contrary, he calls a great genius; but because it seemed to him of no practical utility, incapable of producing works which might promote the well-being of men. We see that from the outset he struck upon his dominant idea: all else comes to him from this; a contempt for antecedent philosophy, the conception of a different system, the entire reformation of the sciences by the indication of a new goal, the definition of a distinct method, the opening up of unsuspected anticipations. It is never speculation which he relishes, but the practical application of it. His eyes are turned not to heaven, but to earth, not to things abstract and vain, but to things palpable and solid, not to curious but to profitable truths. He seeks to better the condition of men, to labour for the welfare of mankind, to enrich human life with new discoveries and new resources, to equip mankind with new powers and new instruments of action. His philosophy itself is but an instrument, *organum,* a sort of machine or lever constructed to enable the intellect to raise a weight, to break through obstacles, to open up vistas, to accomplish tasks which had hitherto surpassed its power. In his eyes, every special science, like science in general, should be an implement. He invites mathematicians, to quit their pure geometry, to study numbers only with a view to natural philosophy, to seek formulas only to calculate real quantities and natural motions. He recommends moralists to study the soul, the passions, habits, temptations, not merely in a speculative way, but with a view to the cure or diminution of vice, and assigns to the science of morals as its goal the amelioration of morals. For him, the object of science is always the establishment of an art, that is, the production of something of practical utility; when he wished to describe the efficacious nature of his philosophy by a tale, he delineated in the *New Atlantis,* with a poet's boldness and the precision of a seer, almost employing the very terms in use now, modern applications, and the present organisation of the sciences, academies, observatories, air-balloons, submarine vessels, the improvement of land, the transmutation of species, regenerations, the discovery of remedies, the preservation of food. The end of our foundation, says his principal personage, is the knowledge of causes and secret motions of things, and the enlarging of the bounds of human empire, to the effecting of all things possible. And this "possible" is infinite.

How did this grand and just conception originate? Doubtless common sense and genius too were necessary to its production; but neither common sense nor genius was lacking to men: there had been more than one who, observing, like Bacon, the progress of particular industries, could, like him, have conceived of universal industry, and from certain limited ameliorations have advanced to unlimited amelioration. Here we see the power of connection; men think they do everything by their individual thought, and they can do nothing without the assistance of the thoughts of their neighbours; they fancy that they are following the small voice within them, but they only hear it because it is swelled by the thousand buzzing and imperious voices, which, issuing from all surrounding or distant circumstances, are confounded with it in an harmonious vibration. Generally they hear it, as Bacon did, from the first moment of reflection; but it had become inaudible among the opposing sounds which came from without to smother it. Could this confidence in the infinite enlargement of human power, this glorious idea of the universal conquest of nature, this firm hope in the continual increase of well-being and happiness, have germinated, grown, occupied an intelligence entirely, and thence have struck its roots, been propagated and spread over neighbouring intelligences, in a time of discouragement and decay, when men believed the end of the world at hand, when things were falling into ruin about them, when Christian mysticism, as in the first centuries, ecclesiastical tyranny, as in the fourteenth century, were convincing them of their impotence, by perverting their intellectual efforts and curtailing their liberty. On the contrary, such hopes must then have seemed to be outbursts of pride, or suggestions of the carnal mind. They did seem so; and the last representatives of ancient science, and the first of the new, were exiled or imprisoned, assassinated or burned. In order to be developed an idea must be in harmony with surrounding civilisation; before man can expect to attain the dominion over nature, or attempts to improve his condition, amelioration must have begun on all sides, industries have increased, knowledge have been accumulated, the arts expanded, a hundred thousand irrefutable witnesses must have come incessantly to give proof of his power and assurance of his progress. The "masculine birth

of the time" (*Temporis partus masculus*) is the title which Bacon applies to his work, and it is a true one. In fact, the whole age co-operated in it; by this creation it was finished. The consciousness of human power and prosperity gave to the Renaissance its first energy, its ideal, its poetic materials, its distinguishing features; and now it furnishes it with its final expression, its scientific doctrine, and its ultimate object.

We may add also, its method. For, the end of a journey once determined, the route is laid down, since the end always determines the route; when the point to be reached is changed, the path of approach is changed, and science, varying its object, varies also its method. So long as it limited its effort to the satisfying an idle curiosity, opening out speculative vistas, establishing a sort of opera in speculative minds, it could launch out any moment into metaphysical abstractions and distinctions: it was enough for it to skim over experience; it soon quitted it, and came all at once upon great words, quiddities, the principle of individuation, final causes. Half proofs sufficed science; at bottom it did not care to establish a truth, but to get an opinion; and its instrument, the syllogism, was serviceable only for refutations, not for discoveries: it took general laws for a starting-point instead of a point of arrival; instead of going to find them, it fancied them found. The syllogism was good in the schools, not in nature; it made disputants, not discoverers. From the moment that science had art for an end, and men studied in order to act, all was transformed; for we cannot act, without certain and precise knowledge. Forces, before they can be employed, must be measured and verified; before we can build a house, we must know exactly the resistance of the beams, or the house will collapse; before we can cure a sick man, we must know with certainty the effect of a remedy, or the patient will die. Practice makes certainty and exactitude a necessity to science, because practice is impossible when it has nothing to lean upon but guesses and approximations. How can we eliminate guesses and approximations? How introduce into science solidity and precision? We must imitate the cases in which science, issuing in practice, has proved to be precise and certain, and these cases are the industries. We must, as in the industries, observe, essay, grope about, verify, keep our mind fixed on sensible and particular things, advance to general rules only step by step; not anticipate experience, but follow it; not imagine nature, but interpret it. For every general effect, such as heat, whiteness, hardness, liquidity, we must seek a general condition, so that in producing the condition we may produce the effect. And for this it is necessary, by fit rejections and exclusions, to extract the condition sought from the heap of facts in which it lies buried, construct the table of cases from which the effect is absent, the table where it is present, the table where the effect is shown in various degrees, so as to isolate and bring to light the condition which produced it. Then we shall have, not useless universal axioms, but efficacious mediate axioms, true laws from which we can derive works, and which are the sources of power in the same degree as the sources of light. Bacon described and predicted in this modern science and industry, their correspondence, method, resources, principle; and after more than two centuries, it is still to him that we go even at the present day to look for the theory of what we are attempting and doing.

Beyond this great view, he has discovered nothing. Cowley, one of his admirers, rightly said that, like Moses on Mount Pisgah, he was the first to announce the promised land; but he might have added quite as justly, that, like Moses, he did not enter there. He pointed out the route, but did not travel it; he taught men how to discover natural laws, but discovered none. His definition of heat is extremely imperfect. His *Natural History* is full of fanciful explanations. Like the poets, he peoples nature with instincts and desires; attributes to bodies an actual voracity, to the atmosphere a thirst for light, sounds, odours, vapours, which it drinks in; to metals a sort of haste to be incorporated with acids. He explains the duration of the bubbles of air which float on the surface of liquids, by supposing that air has a very small or no appetite for height. He sees in every quality, weight, ductility, hardness, a distinct essence which has its special cause; so that when a man knows the cause of every quality of gold, he will be able to put all these causes together, and make gold. In the main, with the alchemists, Paracelsus and Gilbert, Kepler himself, with all the men of his time, men of imagination, nourished on Aristotle, he represents nature as a compound of secret and living energies, inexplicable and primordial forces, distinct and indecomposable essences, adapted each by the will of the Creator to produce a distinct effect. He almost saw souls endowed with latent repugnances and occult inclinations, which aspire to or resist certain directions, certain mixtures, and certain localities. On this account also he confounds everything in his researches in an undistinguishable mass, vegetative and medicinal properties, mechanical and curative, physical and moral, without considering the most complex as depending on the simplest, but each on the contrary in itself, and taken apart, as an irreducible and independent existence. Obstinate in this error, the thinkers of the age mark time without advancing. They see clearly with Bacon the wide field of discovery, but they cannot enter upon it. They want an idea, and for want of this idea they do not advance. The disposition of mind which but now was a lever, is become an obstacle: it must be changed, that the obstacle may be got rid of. For ideas, I mean great and efficacious ones, do not come at will nor by chance, by the effort of an individual, or by a happy accident. Methods and philosophies, as well as literatures and religions, arise from the spirit of the age; and this spirit of the age makes them potent or powerless. One state of public intelligence excludes a certain kind of literature; another, a certain scientific conception. When it happens thus, writers and thinkers labour in vain, the literature is abortive, the conception does not make its appearance. In vain they turn one way and another, trying to remove the weight which hinders them; something stronger than themselves paralyses their hands and frustrates their endeavours. The central pivot of the vast wheel on which human affairs move must be displaced one notch, that all may move with its motion. At this moment the pivot was moved, and thus a revolution of the great wheel begins, bringing round a new conception of nature, and in consequence that part of the method which was lacking. To the diviners, the creators, the comprehensive and impassioned minds who

seized objects in a lump and in masses, succeeded the discursive thinkers, the systematic thinkers, the graduated and clear logicians, who, disposing ideas in continuous series, lead the hearer gradually from the simple to the most complex by easy and unbroken paths. Descartes superseded Bacon; the classical age obliterated the Renaissance; poetry and lofty imagination gave way before rhetoric, eloquence, and analysis. In this transformation of mind; ideas were transformed. Everything was drained dry and simplified. The universe, like all else, was reduced to two or three notions; and the conception of nature, which was poetical, became mechanical. Instead of souls, living forces, repugnances, and attractions, we have pulleys, levers, impelling forces. The world, which seemed a mass of instinctive powers, is now like a mere machinery of cogwheels. Beneath this adventurous supposition lies a large and certain truth: that there is, namely, a scale of facts, some at the summit very complex, others at the base very simple; those above having their origin in those below, so that the lower ones explain the higher; and that we must seek the primary laws of things in the laws of motion. The search was made, and Galileo found them. Thenceforth the work of the Renaissance, outstripping the extreme point to which Bacon had pushed it, and at which he had left it, was able to proceed onward by itself, and did so proceed, without limit. (pp. 347-58)

H. A. Taine, "The Pagan Renaissance," in his History of English Literature, *revised edition, translated by H. Van Laun, Edinburgh, Edmonston and Douglas, 1873, pp. 227-359.*

Leslie Stephen   (essay date 1881)

[*Stephen was an English man of letters whose writings include* History of English Thought in the 18th Century *(1876),* English Literature and Society in the Eighteenth Century *(1904), and numerous articles and essays. In the following excerpt from an article originally published in 1881, he analyzes Bacon's* Essays, *admiring "the literary genius which has coined so many pregnant aphorisms, and stamped even truisms with his own image and superscriptions."*]

The essay writer is the lay preacher upon that vague mass of doctrine which we dignify by the name of knowledge of life or of human nature. He has to do with the science in which we all graduate as we grow old, when we try to pack our personal observations into a few sententious aphorisms not quite identical with the old formulæ. It is a strange experience which happens to some people to grow old in a day, and to find that some good old saying— "vanity of vanities," for example—which you have been repeating ever since you first left college and gave yourself the airs of a man of the world, has suddenly become a vivid and striking impression of a novel truth, and has all the force of a sudden discovery. In one of Poe's stories, a clever man hides an important document by placing it exactly in the most obvious and conspicuous place in the room. That is the principle, it would sometimes seem, which accounts for the preservation of certain important secrets of life. They are hidden from the uninitiated just because the phrases in which they are couched are so familiar. We

fancy, in our youth, that our elders must either be hum-
bugs—which is the pleasantest and most obvious theory—
or that they must have some little store of esoteric wisdom
which they keep carefully to themselves. The initiated become aware that neither hypothesis is true. Experience
teaches some real lessons; but they are taught in the old
words. The change required is in the mind of the thinker,
not in the symbols of his thought. Wordly wisdom is
summed up in the familiar currency which has passed
from hand to hand through the centuries; and we find on
some catastrophe, or by the gradual process of advancing
years, that mystic properties lurk unsuspected in the domestic halfpenny.

The essayist should be able, more or less, to anticipate this
change, and make us see what is before our eyes. It is easy
enough for the mere hawker of sterile platitudes to imitate
his procedure, and to put on airs of superhuman wisdom
when retailing the barren *exuviæ* of other men's thought.
But there are some rare books, in reading which we slowly
become aware that we have to do with the man who has
done all that can be done in this direction—that is, redis-
covered the old discoveries for himself. Chief, beyond rivalry, amongst all such performances, in our own language, at least, is Bacon's *Essays.* Like Montaigne, he represents, of course, the mood in which the great aim of the
ablest thinkers was precisely to see facts for themselves instead of taking them on trust. And though Bacon has not
the delightful egotism or the shrewd humour of his predecessors, and substitutes the tersest method of presenting
his thought for the discursive rambling characteristic of
the prince of all essayists, the charm of his writing is almost equally due to his unconscious revelation of character. One can imagine a careless reader, indeed, skimming
the book in a hurry, and setting down the author as a kind
of Polonius—a venerable old person with a plentiful lack
of wit and nothing on his tongue but "words, words,
words." In spite of the weighty style, surcharged, as it
seems, with thought and experience, we might quote
maxim after maxim from its pages with a most suspicious
air of Polonius wisdom; and though Polonius, doubtless,
had been a wise man in his day, Hamlet clearly took him
for an old bore, and dealt with him as we could all wish
at moments to deal with bores. "He that is plentiful in expense of all kinds will hardly be preserved from decay."
Does it require a "large-browed Verulam," one of the first
"of those that know," to give us that valuable bit of information? Or—to dip into his pages at random—could we
not have guessed for ourselves that if a man "easily par-
dons and remits offences, it shows"—what?—"that his
mind is planted above injuries"; or, again, that "good
thoughts are little better than good dreams except they be
put in act"; or even that a man "should be sure to leave
other men their turns to speak." "Here be truths," and set
forth as solemnly as if they were calculated to throw a new
light upon things in general. But it would be hard to demand even of a Bacon that he should refrain from all that
has been said before. And the impression—if it ever crosses the mind of a perverse critic—that Bacon was a bit of
a windbag, very rapidly disappears. It would be far less
difficult to find pages free from platitude than to find one
in which there is not some condensed saying which makes
us acknowledge that the mark has been hit, and the defini-

tive form imposed upon some hazy notion which has been
vaguely hovering about the mind, and eluding all our attempts to grasp it. We have not thought just that, but
something which clearly ought to have been that. Occasionally, of course, this is due to the singular power in
which Bacon, whatever his other merits or defects, excels
all other philosophic writers; the power which springs
from a unique combination of the imaginative and speculative faculties, of finding some vivid concrete image to
symbolise abstract truths. It is exhibited again in the perverted, but often delightful, ingenuity with which he reads
philosophical meanings into old mythological legends, entirely innocent, as a matter of fact, of any such matter;
which often makes us fancy that he was a new incarnation
of Æsop, able to construct the most felicitous parables at
a moment's notice, to illustrate any conceivable combination of ideas; a power, too, which is connected with his
weakness, and helps to explain how he could be at once
an almost inspired prophet of a coming scientific era, and
yet curiously wanting in genuine aptitude for scientific inquiry. It is, perhaps, the more one-sided and colourless intellect which is best fitted for achievement, though incapable of clothing its ambition in the resplendent hues of
Bacon's imagination.

In the *Essays* the compression of the style keeps this
power in subordination. Analogies are suggested in a pregnant sentence, not elaborated and brought forward in the
pomp of stately rhetoric. Only, as we become familiar with
the book, we become more aware of the richness and versatility of intellect which it implies, and conscious of the
extreme difficulty of characterising it or its author in any
compendious phrase. That has hardly been done. . . .
Perhaps a thorough study of the *Essays* would be enough
by itself to make us really intimate with their author. For
we see as we read that Bacon is a typical example of one
of the two great races between whom our allegiance is generally divided. He would be despised by the Puritan as
worldly, and would retort by equal contempt for the narrow bigotry of Puritanism. You cannot admire him heartily if the objects of your hero-worship are men of the Cromwell or Luther type. The stern imperious man of action,
who aims straight at the heart, who is efficient in proportion as he is one-sided, to whom the world presents itself
as an internecine struggle between the powers of light and
darkness, who can see nothing but eternal truths on one
side and damnable lies on the other, who would reform by
crushing his opponents to the dust, and regards all scruples that might trammel his energies as so much hollow
cant, is undoubtedly an impressive phenomenon. But it is
also plain that he must have suppressed half his nature;
he has lost in breadth what he has gained in immensity;
and the merits of a Bacon depend precisely upon the richness of his mind and the width of his culture. He cannot
help sympathising with all the contemporary currents of
thought. He is tempted to injustice only in regard to the
systems which seem to imply the stagnation of thought.
He hates bigotry, and bigotry alone, but bigotry in every
possible phase, even when it is accidentally upon his own
side. His sympathies are so wide that he cannot help taking all knowledge for his province. The one lesson which
he cannot learn is Goethe's lesson of "renouncing." The
whole universe is so interesting that every avenue for

thought must be kept open. He is at once a philosopher, a statesman, a lawyer, a man of science, and an omnivorous student of literature. The widest theorising and the minutest experiment are equally welcome; he is as much interested in arranging a masque or laying out a garden, as in a political intrigue or a legal reform or a logical speculation. The weakness of such a man in political life is grossly misinterpreted when it is confounded with the baseness of a servile courtier. It is not that he is without aims, and lofty aims; but that they are complex, far-reaching, and too wide for vulgar comprehension. He cannot join the party of revolution or the party of obstruction, for he desires the equable development of the whole organisation. The danger is not that he will defy reason, but that he will succeed in finding reasons for any conceivable course. The world's business, as he well knows, has to be carried on with the help of the stupid and the vile; and he naturally errs on the side of indulgence and compliance, hoping to work men to the furtherance of views of which they are unable to grasp the importance. His tolerance is apt to slide into wordliness, and his sensibility to all manner of impulses makes him vulnerable upon many points, and often takes the form of timidity. The time-serving of the profligate means a desire for personal gratification; the time-serving of a Bacon means too great a readiness to take the world as it is, and to use questionable tools in the pursuit of vast and elevated designs.

The *Essays* reflect these characteristics. They are the thoughts of a philosopher who is not content to accept any commonplace without independent examination; but who is as little disposed to reject an opinion summarily because it has a slightly immoral aspect as to reject a scientific experiment because it contradicts an established theory. We must hear what the vicious man has to say for himself, as well as listen to the virtuous. He shows his tendency in the opening essay. The dearest of all virtues to the philosophic mind is truth, and there is no sincerer lover of such truth than Bacon. But he will not overlook the claims of falsehood. "Truth may, perhaps, come to the price of a pearl, that showeth best by day; but it will not rise to the price of a diamond or carbuncle, that showeth best in varied lights. A mixture of a lie doth ever add pleasure." That famous sentence is just one of the sayings which the decorous moralist is apt to denounce or to hide away in dexterous verbiage. Bacon's calm recognition of the fact is more impressive, and, perhaps, not really less moral. The essay upon **"Simulation and Dissimulation"** may suggest more qualms to the rigorous. Dissimulation, it is true, is condemned as a "faint kind of policy and wisdom"; it is the "weaker sort of politicians that are the great dissemblers." But this denunciation has to be refined and shaded away. For, in the first place, a habit of secrecy is both "moral and politic." But secrecy implies more; for "no man can be secret except he give himself a little scope of dissimulation; which is, as it were, but the skirts or train of secrecy." But if secrecy leads to dissimulation, will not dissimulation imply downright simulation—in plain English, lying? "That," replies Bacon, "I hold more culpable and less politic, except it be in rare and great matters." He enumerates their advantages, and their counter-balancing disadvantages; and the summing-up is one of his characteristic sentences. "The best composition and temperature is to love

openness in fame and opinion; secrecy in habit; dissimulation in seasonable use; and a power to feign if there be no remedy."

How skilfully the claims of morality and policy are blended! How delicately we slide from the virtue of holding our tongues to the advisability of occasional lying! "You old rogue!" exclaims the severe moralist, "your advice is simply—don't lie, unless you can lie to your advantage, and without loss of credit." . . . I fancy that the student of recent history would admit that the art of dexterous equivocation had not fallen entirely out of use, and is not judged with great severity when an opponent asks an awkward question in Parliament. A cynic might even declare the chief difference to be that we now disavow the principles upon which we really act, and so lie to ourselves as well as to others; whereas Bacon was at least true to himself, and, if forced to adopt a theory of expediency, would not blink the fact. It is this kind of sincerity to which the *Essays* owe part of their charm to every thoughtful reader. We must not go to them for lofty or romantic morality—for sayings satisfactory to the purist or the enthusiast. We have a morality, rather, which has been refracted through a mind thoroughly imbued with worldly wisdom, and ready to accept the compromises which a man who mixes with his fellows on equal terms must often make with his conscience. He is no hermit to renounce the world, for the world is, after all, a great fact; nor to retire to a desert because the air of cities is tainted by the lungs of his fellows. He accepts the code which is workable, not that which is ideally pure. He loves in all things the true *via media*. He objects to atheism, for religion is politically useful; but he is quite as severe upon superstition, which is apt to generate a more dangerous fanaticism. He considers love to be a kind of excusable weakness, so long as men "sever it wholly from their serious affairs and actions of life"; but he is eloquent and forcible in exalting friendship, without which a man may as well "quit the stage." In this, indeed, Bacon . . . seems to have spoken from his own experience; and in spite of the taint of wordliness, the feeling that there is something tepid in their author's nature, a certain want of cordiality in the grasp of his hand—we feel that the *Essays* have a merit beyond that which belongs to them as genuine records of the observation of life at first hand by a man of vast ability and varied and prolonged experience. They show, too, a marvellously rich and sensitive nature, capable of wide sympathies, with all manner of interests, devoted to a grand and far-reaching ambition, though not sufficiently contemptuous of immediate expediency, and fully appreciative of the really valuable elements in human life. If he has the weaknesses—he has also, in a surpassing degree, the merits—of a true cosmopolitan, or citizen of this world, whose wisdom, if not as childlike as the Christian preacher requires, is most certainly not childish. When we add the literary genius which has coined so many pregnant aphorisms, and stamped even truisms with his own image and superscription, we can understand why the *Essays* have come home to men's business and bosoms. (pp. 47-55)

Leslie Stephen, "The Essayists," in his Men, Books, and Mountains, *edited by S. O. A. Ull-*

mann, University of Minnesota Press, 1956,
pp. 45-73.

W. Windelband (essay date 1892)

[*Windelband was an eminent German Neo-Kantian
philosopher whose writings include the influential*
Geschichte der Philosophie *(1892;* A History of Philosophy, *1893). In the following excerpt from that work,
Windelband reviews Bacon's philosophy, emphasizing its
main principles and concluding that in "his hand philosophy was in danger of falling from the rule of a religious
end under that of technical interests."*]

All beginnings of modern philosophy have in common an
impulsive opposition against "Scholasticism," and at the
same time a naïve lack of understanding for the common
attitude of dependence upon some one of its traditions,
which they nevertheless all occupy. This fundamental op-
positional character brings with it the consequence, that
in all cases where it is not merely wants of the feelings, or
fanciful views that are set over against the old doctrines,
reflection on *new methods* of knowledge stands in the fore-
ground. Out of the insight into the unfruitfulness of the
"syllogism," which could merely set forth in proof or refutation that which was already known, or apply the same
to a particular case, arises the demand for an *ars inveniendi,* a *method of investigation,* a sure way to the *discovery of the new.*

If now nothing was to be accomplished with the help of
rhetoric, the nearest expedient was to attack the matter by
the reverse method, proceeding from the particular, from
the facts. This had been commended by Vives and San-
chez, and practised by Telesio and Campanella. But they
had neither gained full confidence in experience nor
known afterwards how to make any right beginning with
their facts. In both lines *Bacon* believed that he could
point out new paths for science, and in this spirit he set
up his "New Organon" as over against the Aristotelian.

Every-day perception—he confesses, admitting the well-
known sceptical arguments—offers, indeed, no sure basis
for a true knowledge of Nature; in order to become an experience that can be used by science it must first be purified from all the erroneous additions which have grown together with it in our involuntary way of regarding things.
These perversions or falsifications of pure experience
Bacon calls *idols,* and presents his doctrine of these fallacious images in analogy with the doctrine of the fallacious
conclusions in the old dialectic. There are first the "idols
of the tribe" (*idola tribus*), the illusions that are given in
connection with human nature in general, following
which we are always suspecting an order and an end in
things, making ourselves the measure of the outer world,
blindly retaining a mode of thought which has once been
excited by impressions, and the like; then the "idols of the
cave" (*idola specus*), by reason of which every individual
by his natural disposition, and his situation in life, finds
himself shut into his cave; then the "idols of the market"
(*idola fori*), the errors which are everywhere brought
about by intercourse among men, especially by language,
and by adherence to the word which we substitute for the

idea; finally, the "idols of the theatre" (*idola theatri*), the
illusory phantoms of theories which we credulously receive from human history and repeat without subjecting
them to any judgment of our own. In this connection
Bacon finds opportunity to direct a most violent polemic
against the word-wisdom of Scholasticism, against the
rule of authority, against the anthropomorphism of earlier
philosophy, and to demand a personal examination of
things themselves, an unprejudiced reception of reality.
Nevertheless he does not get beyond this demand; for the
statements as to how the *mera experientia* is to be gained
and separated from the enveloping husks of the idols are
extremely meagre, and while Bacon teaches that one must
not limit himself to accidental perceptions, but must set
about his observation methodically, and supplement it by
experiment which he thinks out and makes for himself,
this also is but a general designation of the task, and a theoretical insight into the essential nature of experiment is
still wanting.

Quite similar is the case with the method of *Induction,*
which Bacon proclaimed as the only correct mode of elaborating facts. With its aid we are to proceed to general cog-
nitions (axioms), in order that we may ultimately from
these explain other phenomena. In this activity the human
mind, among whose constitutional errors is over-hasty
generalisation, is to be restrained as much as possible; it
is to ascend quite gradually the scale of the more general,
up to the most general. Healthy and valuable as these prescriptions are, we are the more surprised to find that with
Bacon their more detailed carrying out is completed in
conceptions and modes of view which are entirely scholastic.

All knowledge of Nature has for its end to understand the
causes of things. Causes, however, are—according to the
old Aristotelian scheme—formal, material, efficient, or
final. Of these only the "formal" causes come into consideration; for all that takes place has its grounds in the
"Forms," in the "natures" of things. Hence when Bacon's
Induction searches for the "Form" of phenomena, *e.g.* for
the Form of heat, Form is here understood quite in the
sense of Scotism as the abiding essence or nature of phenomena. The Form of that which is given in perception
is composed out of simpler "Forms" and their "differences," and these it is important to discover. To this end
as many cases as possible in which the phenomenon in
question appears, are brought together into a *tabula
præsentiæ,* and in like manner, those in which the phenomenon is lacking are brought together into a *tabula
absentiæ;* to these is added, in the third place, a *tabula
graduum,* in which the varying intensity with which the
phenomenon appears is compared with the varying intensity of other phenomena. The problem is then to be solved
by a progressive process of exclusion (*exclusio*). The Form
of heat, for example, is to be that which is everywhere
present where heat is found, which is nowhere where heat
is lacking, and which is present in greater degree where
there is more heat, and in lesser degree where there is less
heat. What Bacon presents accordingly as Induction is
certainly no simple enumeration, but an involved process
of abstraction, which rests upon the metaphysical assump-

tions of the scholastic Formalism; the presage of the new is still quite embedded in the old habits of thought.

It is accordingly comprehensible that Bacon was not the man to bring to the study of Nature itself methodical or material furtherance: but this derogates nothing from his philosophical importance, which consists just in this, that he demanded the general application of a principle, to which he yet was unable to give any useful or fruitful form in the case of the most immediate object for its use: namely, the knowledge of the corporeal world. He had understood that the new science must turn from the endless discussion of conceptions back to things themselves, that it can build only upon direct perception, and that it must rise from this only cautiously and gradually to the more abstract, and he had understood no less clearly that in the case of this Induction, the point at issue was nothing other than the discovery of the simple elements of reality, from the "nature" of which, in their regular relation and connection, the whole compass of what we perceive is to be explained. Induction, he thought, will find the Forms by which Nature must be interpreted. But while in his cosmology he did not get far beyond an adherence to the traditional atomism, and even shut himself up against the great achievement of the Copernican theory, he demanded that his *empirical principle* should be applied also to *knowledge of man.* Not only the bodily existence in its normal and abnormal vital processes, but also the movement of ideas and of activities of the will, especially also the social and political system,—all these should be examined as to their moving forces ("Forms") by the method of natural science, and explained without prejudice. The *anthropological and social naturalism* which Bacon announces in the encyclopædic remarks of his work **De Augmentis Scientiarum,** contains examples of programmes for many branches of knowledge, and proceeds everywhere from the fundamental purpose to understand man and all the activities of his life as a product of the same simple elements of reality which also lie at the basis of external Nature.

Still another element comes to light in this anthropological interest. To understand man is not, for Bacon, an end in itself, any more than it is such to understand Nature. His entire thought is rather subordinated to a practical end, and this he conceives in the grandest form. All human knowledge has ultimately for its sole task to procure for man dominion over the world by his knowledge of the world. *Knowledge is power,* and is the only lasting power. While therefore magic with fantastic arts sought to make itself master of the working forces of Nature, this blind endeavour became clarified with Bacon to the insight that man can owe his mastery over things only to a sober investigation of their true essence. For him, therefore, the *interpretatio naturæ* is only the means of *subjecting nature to the human mind,* and his great work for the "Renovation of the Sciences"—*Instauratio Magna,* "*Temporis Partus Maximus*"—bears also the title *De Regno Hominis.*

In this, Bacon expressed what was moving the heart of thousands at his time, under the impress of great events. With that series of discoveries beyond the seas, where through mistakes, adventures, and crimes, man had at last

for the first time taken complete possession of his planet, with inventions such as those of the mariner's compass, of gunpowder, and of the art of printing, a mighty change had been introduced within a short time into the greater as well as the lesser life of man. A new epoch of civilisation seemed to be opened, and an exotic excitement seized upon men's fancy. Unheard-of things should succeed; nothing was to be impossible any longer. The telescope disclosed the mysteries of the heavens, and the powers of the earth began to obey the investigator. Science would be the guide of the human mind in its victorious journey through Nature. By her inventions, human life should be completely transformed. What hopes in this respect set free the fancy for its flights we see from Bacon's Utopian fragment of the **Nova Atlantis,** and also from Campanella's *Civitas Solis.* The English Chancellor, however, held that the task of the knowledge of Nature was ultimately to make of invention, which had hitherto been for the most part a matter of chance, a consciously exercised art. To be sure, he gave life to this thought only in the fantastic picture of Solomon's house, in his Utopia; he guarded himself from seriously carrying it out; but this meaning which he attributed to the *ars inveniendi* made him an opponent of purely theoretical and "contemplative" knowledge; just from this point of view did he combat Aristotle and the unfruitfulness of monastic science. In his hand philosophy was in danger of falling from the rule of a religious end under that of technical interests. (pp. 383-87)

> *W. Windelband, "The Problem of Method," in his* A History of Philosophy with Especial Reference to the Formation and Development of Its Problems and Conceptions, *revised edition, translated by James H. Tufts, The Macmillan Company, 1901, pp. 383-98.*

G. K. Chesterton   (essay date 1907)

[*Regarded as one of England's premier men of letters during the first half of the twentieth century, Chesterton is best known as a colorful bon vivant, a witty essayist, and creator of the Father Brown mysteries and the fantasy* The Man Who Was Thursday (1908). *In the following excerpt from an essay originally published in 1907, Chesterton touches upon the controversy concerning Bacon's putative authorship of Shakespeare's works, remarking that the argument for Bacon's authorship relies on numerous facts which, though seemingly plausible when taken separately, do not constitute a credible hypothesis.*]

The discussion touching whether Bacon wrote Shakspere is only important because it happens to be the battleground of two historical methods, of two kinds of judgment. In itself it matters little whether Bacon was Shakspere or whether Shakspere was Bacon. Shakspere, I fancy, would not much mind being robbed of his literary achievements; and I am sure that Bacon would be delighted to be relieved of his political history and reputation. Francis Lord Verulam would have been a happier man, certainly a better and more Christian man, if he also had gone down to drink ale at Stratford; if he had begun and ended his story in an inn. As far as the individual glory of the two men goes, the two men had this, and perhaps only this, in common: that they both at the end of their lives seem to have decided that all glory is vanity. (p. 413)

The two arguments that often clash in history may be called the argument from detail and the argument from atmosphere. Suppose a man two hundred years hence were writing about London cabmen. He might know all the details that can be gathered from all the documents; he might know the numbers of all the cabs, the names of all the cabmen, the single and collective owners of all the vehicles in question, the fixed rate of pay and all the Acts of Parliament that in any way affected it. Yet he might not know the rich and subtle atmosphere of cabmen; their peculiar relations to the comfortable class who commonly employ them. He would not understand how paying the plain fare to a cabman is not the same as paying the plain fare to a tram-conductor. He would not understand how when a cabman overcharges it is not quite the same as if a butcher or a baker had overcharged. He would not grasp to what extent these men regard themselves as the temporary dependents, the temporary coachmen of the wealthy; he would not understand how even their bad language is an expression of that idea of dependence on the historic generosity of gentlemen. He would not comprehend how this strange class of man contrived to be insolent without being independent. It is just such atmospheres as this that history only exists in order to make real; and it is just such atmospheres as this that nearly all history neglects. But those who say that Bacon wrote Shakspere are, so to speak, the maniacs of this method of detail against atmosphere which is the curse of so many learned men. As a matter of fact the Bacon-Shakspere people really are learned; they do really know an enormous amount about the period with which they are concerned. But it is all detail; and detail by itself means madness. The very definition of a lunatic is a man who has taken details out of their real atmosphere.

Here is an example. I remember long ago debating with a Baconian, who said that Shakspere could not have written the plays because Shakspere was a countryman, and there was in the plays no close study of Nature in the modern sense—no details about how this bird builds its nest, or that flower shakes its pollen—as we get them in Wordsworth or in Tennyson. Now, the man who said this knew far more about Elizabethan literature than I do. In fact he knew everything about Elizabethan literature except what Elizabethan literature was. If he had had even the smallest glimpse of what Elizabethan literature was he would never have dreamed of expecting any Elizabethan to write about Nature because he was brought up in the middle of it. A Renascence poet brought up in a forest would not have written about trees any more than a Renascence poet brought up in a pigsty would have written about pigs; he would have written about gods or not written at all. It was not a Renascence idea to write about the homely natural history which was just outside the door. To say that Shakspere, if he was really born at Stratford, would have written about birds and meadows, is like saying that Keats, if he was really born in London, would have written about omnibuses and drapers' shops. I was bewildered by this incapacity in a more learned man than I to capture the obvi-

ous quality of a time. Then somebody made it worse by saying that Shakspere could describe Nature in detail because he described in detail the appearance and paces of a horse—as if a horse were some shy bird that built its nest in dim English woodlands and which only a man born in Stratford could see. If there is one thing more certain about an Elizabethan gentleman than the fact that he would know nothing about Nature, it is the fact that he would know all about horses.

I merely quote this old example as an instance of the entire absence of a sense of historical atmosphere. That horse who built his nest in the high trees of Stratford is typical of all this unnatural criticism; the critic who found him did indeed find a mare's nest. Of the same kind is the argument that Shakspere must have been a learned man like Bacon, because he had heard so much about learning, about law and mythology and old literature. This is like saying that I must be as learned as the Master of Balliol because I have heard of most of the things that he talks about; because I have heard of the debate of Nominalists and Realists, or because I have heard of the Absolute and the Relative being discussed at Balliol. Again the man misses the whole mood and tone of the time. He does not realise that Shakspere's age was an age in which a fairly bright man could pick up the odds and ends of anything, just as I, by walking along Fleet Street, can pick up the odds and ends of anything. A man could no more live in London then and not hear about Pagan Mythology than he could live in London now and not hear about Socialism. The same solemn and inhuman incredulity which finds it incredible that a clever lad in London should pick up more than he really knew is the same that finds it incredible that he should have had his portrait painted for fun by some foolish painter in a public-house.

The truth is, I fear, that madness has a great advantage over sanity. Sanity is always careless. Madness is always careful. A lunatic might count all the railings along the front of Hyde Park; he might know the exact number of them, because he thought they were something else. A healthy man would not know the number of the railings, or perhaps even the shape of the railings; he would know nothing about them except the supreme, sublime, Platonic, and transcendental truth, that they were railings. There is a great deal of falsehood in the notion that truth must necessarily prevail. There is this falsehood to start with: that if a man has got the truth he is generally happy. And if he is happy he is generally lazy. The incessant activity, the exaggerated intelligence, generally belong to those who are a little wrong and just a little right. The whole advantage of those who think that Bacon wrote Shakspere lies simply in the fact that they care whether Bacon wrote Shakspere. The whole disadvantage of those who do not think it lies in the fact that (being folly) they do not care about it. The sane man who is sane enough to see that Shakspere wrote Shakspere is the man who is sane enough not to worry whether he did or not. (pp. 414-16)

G. K. Chesterton, "Shakspere, Bacon, and Historical Method: A Misaimed Letter to Chesterton," in his The Collected Works of G. K. Chesterton: "The Illustrated London News,"

1905-1907, *Vol. XXVII, edited by Lawrence J. Clipper, Ignatius Press, 1986, pp. 412-17.*

Lytton Strachey   (essay date 1908)

[*Strachey was a prominent English literary figure whose writings include* Landmarks in French Literature *(1912),* Eminent Victorians *(1918), and* Elizabeth and Essex: A Tragic History *(1928). In the following excerpt from an essay originally published in 1908, he offers a minute stylistic analysis of Bacon's* Essays, *asserting that the author's style clearly reflects his utilitarian philosophy and progressive outlook.*]

Besides being a great lawyer, [Bacon] was a great statesman and a great philosopher, so that his memory deserves honour, not only from the benchers of Gray's Inn, but from Members of Parliament and from the Fellows of the Royal Society. And if none of these claims to distinction had been his—if he had passed his life in private obscurity and had never written a word of his 'Instauratio Magna'—he would still fill a unique place among great Englishmen by virtue of his consummate mastery of the English language. Indeed, such is the strange power of the art of writing that it is through the *Essays* alone that Bacon's fame is today something more than a vague recollection in the minds of his countrymen. He himself would have been the last to be surprised at this. 'As for my *Essays,*' he says, 'I count them but as the recreations of my other studies, and in that sort purpose to continue them; though I am not ignorant that those kind of writings would, with less pains and embracement, perhaps, yield more lustre and reputation to my name than those others which I have in hand.' Bacon belongs to the very small band of our prose writers of whom it can be said with certainty that their popularity is as great as their achievement. Other writers of equal merit—Sir Thomas Browne, for instance, and Gibbon, and Burke—though they are widely read, are not read universally; none of their works is popular in the sense in which *The Pilgrim's Progress* is popular, and *Gulliver's Travels,* and *The Essays or Counsels, Civil and Moral.* And Bacon, no less than Bunyan and Swift, is read primarily for his matter. 'The King,' he says of Henry VII, 'to speak of him in terms equal to his deserving, was one of the best sort of wonders: a wonder for wise men'; and the words apply with singular exactness to the author of the *Essays.* Everyone must feel, after a reading in that fascinating book, that there indeed is 'a wonder for wise men', that there is the very soul of wisdom, the very embodiment of clear, profound, and powerful thought. 'Some books are to be tasted, others to be swallowed, and some few to be chewed and digested.' Who can doubt into which of these classes the *Essays* fall? Let us take a single example of their concentration of meaning. In the essay on **"Simulation and Dissimulation"** Bacon discusses with wonderful subtlety and judgment the various shades of concealment and deceit, the precise circumstances in which [in his opinion] they are permissible, and the rules which [he holds] should guide a good man in his use of them. He concludes in a sentence which sums up within itself his view of the whole philosophy of the subject: 'The best composition and temperature is, to have openness in fame and opinion; secrecy in habit; dissimulation in seasonable use; and a

power to feign if there be no remedy.' [We may not like his conclusion—for ourselves, we repudiate it as immoral and ignoble—but who can deny that it is an epitome of the worldly wisdom on the matter under consideration?]

Yet, in spite of the amazing force and weight of Bacon's matter, it is clear that the fascination of his work depends no less upon his style. If it is true that the generality of readers explore him for the sake of what he has to tell them, it is equally certain that they would never have troubled to find that out if he had not taken care to tell it them with exquisite art. To the lover of fine prose his writing brings a pleasure which no other English master quite succeeds in producing, and which, in its precise flavour, is called up by only one or two other writers in the literature of the world. In some ways the temper of his art is rather French than English. He is a supreme master of the sententious style—a style which has been practised by only one other English writer of the first rank, Burke, and by him only, as it were, incidentally, while in France the greatest writers have made it their own. Certainly the best of his aphorisms are worthy to take rank beside the most brilliant of La Rochefoucauld's and the most beautiful of La Bruyère's. How many of them one can recall with joy! 'Revenge is a kind of wild justice'; 'He that hath wife and children hath given hostages to fortune'; 'We take cunning for a sinister or crooked wisdom'; 'Men fear death as children fear to go in the dark'; 'There is no excellent beauty that hath not some strangeness in the proportion.' But it is easier to begin making such quotations than to stop. Yet we must remember that there is this important difference between the epigrams of Bacon and those of his French rivals—his form part of a related whole, while the others are detached jewels separately set. Thus the true charm of Bacon's writing cannot be revealed in single sentences; it lies in the elaboration, the interconnexion, the orderly development, the gradual exposition of a series of subtle and splendid thoughts. Of modern writers, Montesquieu, perhaps, comes nearest to him, but Montesquieu lacks the rich colouring which distinguishes Bacon's style. It is this characteristic—this combination of colour and of thought—which gives Bacon his unique position among prose writers. The great colourists—witness Sir Thomas Browne—have as a rule no very definite thoughts to show us, only gorgeous imaginations; while, on the other hand, the great thinkers—Swift, for instance—content themselves with clarity and vigour of expression. We must go back to the ancients—to some of the glowing pages of Thucydides or the sombre meditations of Tacitus—to find a parallel with what is finest in the prose of Bacon. As Taine admirably says, 'ce qui distingue celui-ci des autres, c'est que chez lui l'image ne fait que concentrer la méditation.' A famous passage from the first of the essays—**"Of Truth"**—affords an example of this rare concatenation of qualities:

> This same truth is a naked and open daylight, that doth not show the masques, and mummeries, and triumphs of the world, half so stately and daintily as candle-lights. Truth may perhaps come to the price of a pearl, that showeth best by day; but it will not rise to the price of a diamond or carbuncle that showeth best in varied lights. A mixture of a lie doth ever add pleasure.

Doth any man doubt that if there were taken out of men's minds vain opinions, flattering hopes, false valuations, imaginations as one would, and the like, but it would leave the minds of a number of men poor shrunken things, full of melancholy and indisposition, and unpleasing to themselves?

There is a happy valiancy in many of Bacon's phrases, which, while they betray the lover of words, yet never show a trace of mannerism of affectation. Thus his style is always unmistakable. Who but Bacon, for instance, could have written sentences at once as sober and as racy as these?—'Suspicions that the mind of itself gathers are but buzzes; but suspicions that are artificially nourished, and put into men's heads by the tales and whisperings of others, have stings.' And—'Beauty is as summer fruits, which are easy to corrupt and cannot last; and, for the most part, it makes a dissolute youth and an age a little out of countenance.' Who but Bacon would have described the flattering of counsellors as 'a song of *Placebo*'? Who but he could have invented that memorable maxim, so splendid and so bold in its concentration: 'To be master of the sea is an abridgment of monarchy'?

Bacon was, in the best sense of the expression, a man of the world. There can be no doubt that he was sincere in his religion, and that he was a genuine lover of the arts. But these things were not fundamental to him. He was not essentially spiritual like Pascal, nor essentially an artist like Keats. His philosophy was utilitarian, and his deepest interests were fixed upon the workings and the welfare of human society. His style reflects his character. It has no poetical mystery, no power of vague suggestion and romance. It never reaches the heights, nor explores the depths; but it is strong, subtle, clear, and it glows with an intellectual beauty. It comes nearest to passion when it touches upon the two greatest of worldly goods—virtue and truth. 'This is the strength and blood to virtue, to contemn things that be desired, and to neglect that which is feared.' That is a sublime sentence; and this is another: 'Certainly it is heaven upon earth to have a man's mind move in charity, rest in providence, and turn upon the poles of truth.' And when in the **New Atlantis** Bacon describes the journeys of the Fellows of Solomon's House, his writing becomes invested with an unwonted eloquence. ' "But thus you see we maintain a trade, not for gold, silver, or jewels; nor for silks; nor for spices; nor any other commodity of matter; but only for God's first creature, which was light: to have light, I say, of the growth of all the world." And when he had said this, he was silent; and so were we all.' It is difficult to remember that he who wrote thus could turn his mind without an effort to the exposition of the most effective arrangements for gardens, the best means of frustrating curiosity, or the surest methods of obtaining despatch in business; but Bacon's mind was universal in its comprehensiveness; there was nothing in the world of which he could not write. And this must be his praise—that while other men have shown us the spirit of an age in their writings, or the spirit of a cause or a belief, or the spirit of their own dreams and their own desires, Bacon has compressed into his immortal pages nothing more nor less than the spirit of the world itself. (pp. 82-7)

Lytton Strachey, "Bacon as a Man of Letters," in his Spectatorial Essays, Harcourt, Brace Jovanovich, 1965, pp. 82-7.

Rudolf Steiner   (essay date 1914)

[*Known as the founder of Waldorf education, Steiner was a noted Austrian philosopher, literary scholar, educator, social reformer, and critic. Many of his writings, which deal with a variety of subjects, elucidate the principles of Steiner's anthroposophy, or spiritual science. In the following excerpt from his* Die Rätsel der Philosophie *(1914;* The Riddles of Philosophy, *1961), he discusses Bacon's philosophy, maintaining that the English philosopher's search for certain knowledge does not amount to a valid world view.*]

The rise of natural science in modern times had as its fundamental cause the same search as the mysticism of Jakob Boehme. This becomes apparent in a thinker who grew directly out of the spiritual movement, which in *Copernicus* (1473-1543), *Kepler* (1571-1630), *Galileo* (1564-1642), and others, led to the first great accomplishments of natural science in modern times. This thinker is *Giordano Bruno* (1548-1600). When one sees how his world consists of infinitely small, animated, psychically self-aware, fundamental beings, the monads, which are uncreated and indestructible, producing in their combined activity the phenomena of nature, one could be tempted to group him with Anaxagoras, for whom the world consists of the "homoiomeries." (p. 63)

A comparison shows how different the ways are in which Aristotle and Giordano Bruno arrive at the conception of God. Aristotle contemplates the world; he sees the evidence of reason in natural processes; he surrenders to the contemplation of this evidence; at the same time, the processes of nature are for him evidence of the *thought* of the "first mover" of these processes. Giordano Bruno fights his way through to the conception of the monads. The processes of nature are, as it were, extinguished in the picture in which innumerable monads are presented as acting on each other; God becomes the power entity that lives actively in all monads behind the processes of the perceptible world. In Giordano Bruno's passionate antagonism against Aristotle, the contrast between the thinker of ancient Greece and of the philosopher of modern times becomes manifest.

It becomes apparent in the modern philosophical development in a great variety of ways how the ego searches for means to experience its own reality in itself. What *Francis Bacon* of Verulam (1561-1626) represents in his writings has the same general character even if this does not at first sight become apparent in his endeavors in the field of philosophy. Bacon of Verulam demands that the investigation of world phenomena should begin with unbiased observation. One should then try to separate the essential from the non-essential in a phenomenon in order to arrive at a conception of whatever lies at the bottom of a thing or event. He is of the opinion that up to his time the fundamental thoughts, which were to explain the world phenomena, had been conceived first, and only thereafter were the description of the individual things and events arranged to fit these thoughts. He presupposed that the thoughts had not been taken out of the things themselves. Bacon wanted to combat this (deductive) method with his (inductive) method. The concepts are to be formed in direct contact with the things. One sees, so Bacon reasons, how an object is consumed by fire; one observes how a second object behaves with relation to fire and then observes the same process with many objects. In this fashion one arrives eventually at a conception of how things behave with respect to fire. The fact that the investigation in former times had not proceeded in this way had, according to Bacon's opinion, caused human conception to be dominated by so many *idols* instead of the true ideas about the things.

Goethe gives a significant description of this method of thought of Bacon of Verulam.

> Bacon is like a man who is well-aware of the irregularity, insufficiency and dilapidated condition of an old building, and knows how to make this clear to the inhabitants. He advises them to abandon it, to give up the land, the materials and all appurtenances, to look for another plot, and to erect a new building. He is an excellent and persuasive speaker. He shakes a few walls. They break down and some of the inhabitants are forced to move out. He points out new building grounds; people begin to level it off, and yet it is everywhere too narrow. He submits new plans; they are not clear, not inviting. Mainly, he speaks of new unknown materials and now the world seems to be well-served. The crowd disperses in all directions and brings back an infinite variety of single items while at home, new plans, new activities and settlements occupy the citizens and absorb their attention.

Goethe says this in his history of the theory of color where he speaks about Bacon. In a later part of the book dealing with Galileo, he says:

> If through Verulam's method of dispersion, natural science seemed to be forever broken up into fragments, it was soon brought to unity again by Galileo. He led natural philosophy back into the human being. When he developed the law of the pendulum and of falling bodies from the observation of swinging church lamps, he showed even in his early youth that, for the genius, one case stands for a thousand cases. In science, everything depends on what is called, *an aperçu*, that is, on the ability of becoming aware of what is really fundamental in the world of phenomena. The development of such an awareness is infinitely fruitful.

With these words Goethe indicated distinctly the point that is characteristic of Bacon. Bacon wants to find a secure path for science because he hopes that in this way man will find a dependable relationship to the world. The approach of Aristotle, so Bacon feels, can no longer be used in the modern age. He does not know that in different ages different energies of the soul are predominantly active in man. He is only aware of the fact that he must reject Aristotle. This he does passionately. He does it in such a way that Goethe is lead to say, "How can one listen to him

with equanimity when he compares the works of Aristotle and of Plato with weightless tablets, which, just because they did not consist of a good solid substance, could so easily float down to us on the stream of time."

Bacon does not understand that he is aiming at the same objective that has been reached by Plato and Aristotle, and that he must use different means for the same aim because the means of antiquity can no longer be those of the modern age. He points toward a method that could appear fruitful for the investigation in the field of external nature, but as Goethe shows in the case of Galileo, even in this field something more is necessary than what Bacon demands.

The method of Bacon proves completely useless, however, when the soul searches not only for an access to the investigation of individual facts, but also to a world conception. What good is a groping search for isolated phenomena and a derivation of general ideas from them, if these general ideas do not, like strokes of lightning, flash up out of the ground of being in the soul of man, rendering account of their truth through themselves. In antiquity, thought appeared like a perception to the soul. This mode of appearance has been dampened through the brightness of the new ego-consciousness. What can lead to thoughts capable of forming a world conception in the soul must be so formed as if it were the soul's own invention, and the soul must search for the possibility of justifying the validity of its own creation. Bacon has no feeling for all this. He, therefore, points to the materials of the building for the construction of the new world conception, namely, the individual natural phenomena. It is, however, no more possible that one can ever build a house by merely observing the form of the building stones that are to be used, than that a fruitful world conception could ever arise in a soul that is exclusively concerned with the individual processes of nature. (pp. 64-6)

> *Rudolf Steiner, "The World Conceptions of the Modern Age of Thought Evolution," in his* The Riddles of Philosophy, *The Anthroposophic Press, 1973, pp. 63-90.*

George Philip Krapp (essay date 1915)

[*In the following excerpt, Krapp discusses the stylistic and technical features of Bacon's prose, describing the philosopher as one of the creators of modern English prose.*]

Bacon's philosophy is by no means popular in the narrower sense of that term. A lofty purpose, which he prosecuted with the most profound conviction, gives dignity to the general outlines and to the form of presentation of his system. He took, as he declares, all knowledge for his province, and in the acquisition of this knowledge, he purposed to employ a method hitherto unknown to mankind, whereby to make "philosophy and sciences both more true and more active." . . . [As he wrote in ***Novum Organum,*** his] plan was to "commence a total reconstruction of sciences, arts, and all human knowledge, raised upon the proper foundations." He felt that he had had the good fortune to happen upon a wonderful discovery, that his work was "the child of time rather than of wit," and he was filled with wonder that "the first notion of the thing, and such great suspicions concerning matters long established, should have come into any man's mind." He compares himself to Columbus, and like an explorer, he travels in his course "altogether a pioneer, following in no man's track, nor sharing these counsels with any one." He insists often that he is not to be compared with the ancients, that as he does not compete with them, he cannot detract from their greatness—"my object being to open a new way for the understanding, a way to them untried and unknown." But though he declares that he "leaves the honour of the ancients untouched," the whole habit of his mind was exalted above them. He accuses the Greek philosophers of leaning "too much to the ambition and vanity of founding a sect and catching popular applause," and he agrees with the characterization of the Greeks "by the Egyptian priest," that they were always boys, without antiquity of knowledge or knowledge of antiquity. "Assuredly they have," he adds, "that which is characteristic of boys; they are prompt to prattle, but cannot generate; for their wisdom abounds in words but is barren of works. And therefore the signs which are taken from the origin and birthplace of the received philosophy are not good."

It is this magnificence of purpose, this bold confidence in himself as a modern and as a discoverer which gives to Bacon's philosophizing its characteristic largeness and dignity of manner. His seriousness is so great that he feels no need for the slighter graces of speech or of learning.

> First then, away with antiquities and citations or testimonies of authors . . . everything in short which is philological . . . And for all that concerns ornaments of speech, such like emptinesses, let it be utterly dismissed. Also let all those things which are admitted be themselves set down briefly and concisely, so that they may be nothing less than words. For no man who is collecting and storing up materials for shipbuilding or the like, thinks of arranging them elegantly, as in a shop, and displaying them so as to please the eye; all his care is that they be so arranged as to take up as little room as possible in the warehouse. And this is exactly what should be done here.

These counsels of perfection fairly describe Bacon's own endeavors in his philosophical writing. Though his schemes may have been grandiose, his language is never so. Ever serious, lofty, dignified, it never loses itself in the fields of flowery eloquence. The reader who is attracted by its promising title to Bacon's *History of Life and Death* with the expectation of finding there a display of oratory will be disappointed, for Bacon never plays the part of the popular preacher, never forgets the proprieties of his subject. This *History of Life and Death* was designed to form a part of the *Great Instauration,* and as one "labouring for the perfection of arts," Bacon says he naturally took thought of the ways in which life is maintained and how it ceases, as well as "about the means of prolonging the life of man." An Elizabethan Nietzsche or Strauss might have found in this theme vast possibilities for poetic treatment, but with Bacon all passes under his gaze in the dry light of reason. Apparently he was never even tempted to yield

to the allurements of the more purely literary possibilities of his subject—at least he makes no apology for neglecting them. And yet, despite the dry and scientific treatment, the reader is constantly aware that Bacon was keenly alive to the elemental grandeur of his undertaking, that he could have treated it as poetry if he had not preferred to treat it as science. In the titles and names of divisions of the discussion his imaginative grasp of the whole is specially apparent, as for example, to choose one of a number, the title "the porches of death," a section which treats of "the things which happen to men a little before and a little after the point of death."

This happy faculty in choosing titles and catchwords is illustrated throughout Bacon's philosophical writings. His imagination often lends color and warmth to detail, but especially to structural detail like nomenclature. The designation of the impediments to sound thinking as Idols of the Tribe, of the Cave, of the Market Place, of the Theatre, are perhaps the best known and have been most frequently imitated, but other inventions in terminology are equally felicitous. The first general conclusion in the interpretation of nature he calls the First Vintage, and other bits of picturesque nomenclature are his Instances of the Twilight, Instances of the Lamp, "they are those which aid the senses," Instances of the Door or Gate, "this being the name I give to instances which aid the immediate actions of the senses."

When one comes to examine Bacon's philosophical writings singly, one discovers that they consist mainly of a collection of fragments. Bacon realized that his scheme implied more than one man or one generation of men could accomplish. "I was desirous," he says, "to prevent the uncertainness of my own life and times, by uttering rather seeds than plants." His purpose in the *Advancement* he declares to have been "to ring a bell to call other wits together," and in the *Novum Organum* he explains his willingness to publish incomplete parts of his work as due to the fact that "he knew not how long it might be before these things would occur to any one else, judging especially from this, that he has found no man hitherto who has applied his mind to the like." In consequence of this method of publication, one finds much repetition of thought and even of phrasing in the various works. The well-known figure in the *Advancement* of "the golden ball thrown before Atalanta, which while she goeth aside and stoopeth to take up, the race is hindered," used to illustrate the activities of those who by applying knowledge "to lucre and profession" interrupt the advancement of knowledge, occurs twice with the same application in *Valerius Terminus,* and perhaps elsewhere. And the figure of time like a river carrying down the light things but letting the heavy sink occurs a number of times. This repetition of thought and phrasing, partly due to the fact that Bacon preserved preliminary drafts of his writings, is indicative of a certain lack of literary finish and completeness in the philosophical works. The scheme was too vast, apparently, to permit the rounding out of even small sections of the whole. *The Advancement of Learning* is the most finished of the minor philosophical writings, but even here there are evident signs of haste in composition. . . . Of the great philosophical work, the *Magna Instauratio,* only the general outlines were broadly sketched. The most important part of this work in Bacon's plan was the second division which he entitled the *Novum Organum.* For this section, the most carefully written of all Bacon's philosophical works, the language chosen was Latin, which indeed was the intention for all the parts of the *Magna Instauratio.* As the *Novum Organum* presents the method by which Bacon hoped to bring about a reform of sciences and knowledge, it occupies the place of prime importance among the philosophical writings. The third part of the *Magna Instauratio* was to consist of a collection of separate histories of the phenomena of the universe, a stupendous undertaking represented only by the *Historia Ventorum,* the *Historia Vitae et Mortis,* and the *Historia Densi et Rari.* (pp. 525-30)

Similar in character to these histories of the *Magna Instauratio* was the last work upon which Bacon was engaged, his *Sylva Sylvarum,* a collection of experiments on many subjects, written in English and full of quaint misinformation. As an appendix to his *Sylva Sylvarum,* Bacon wrote his most popular philosophical work, the *New Atlantis,* a summary in the form of fiction of some of the principles of the Baconian philosophy. One of the latest of Bacon's writings, the *New Atlantis* remained a fragment and was not published until after his death. The story is that of an ideal commonwealth, the New Atlantis, reports of which are brought back by travelers who have met with it on a journey from Peru to China and Japan, by way of the South Sea. Like most accounts of imaginary voyages since More's time, the *New Atlantis* owes something to the *Utopia.* Concrete and minute descriptions of costume and similar details are introduced to lend verisimilitude to the narrative. One of the distinguished citizens of the New Atlantis "had on him a gown with wide sleeves, of a kind of water chamolet, of an excellent azure colour, far more glossy than ours; his under apparel was green; and so was his hat, being in the form of a turban, daintily made, and not so huge as the Turkish turbans; and the locks of his hair came down below the brims of it." Bacon's belief in the wealth and luxury which would result from the application of his philosophic method enabled him to indulge in the *New Atlantis* in characteristically Elizabethan opulence of description. But the main point of the treatise centers in the account of Solomon's House, a house of knowledge combining the characteristics of a museum of natural history, a scientific laboratory, and a modern university. An account of the method of experimentation in Solomon's House is given, and the experiments are of the same general kind as those collected by Bacon in the *Sylva Sylvarum.* The great quest of the New Atlantis, in the words of one of its citizens, was "only for God's first creature, which was Light: to have *Light* (I say) of the growth of all parts of the world." "The end of our Foundation" (he is speaking of Solomon's House) "is the knowledge of Causes, and secret motions of things; and the enlarging of the bounds of Human Empire, to the effecting of all things possible." The sublime simplicity of this Gargantuan curriculum reminds one of the Oriental stories of the philosopher who inscribed the *omne scibile* upon the walls of his pupil's chamber and then gave him seven days in which to learn it. But Bacon's New Atlantis was not all visionary romance, and though the possible

"bounds of Human Empire" seem now narrower than Bacon thought them, the task of slowly widening these bounds in Bacon's way has been assumed as its distinctive obligation by the modern world. (pp. 530-32)

Bacon wrote no other literary works of any extent in English except his *History of Henry VII.* . . . A very popular work in Bacon's day was his *De Sapientia Veterum,* allegorical interpretations of classic myths and legends. But this book, though not without a charm of its own, was originally written in Latin and never turned into English by Bacon. His remaining literary works are either fragmentary or of very brief extent. Among them may be mentioned translations of seven psalms into English verse, not notable in any respect except as the only verse written by Bacon now extant, and as illustrating a skill in the management of a variety of metrical forms which could have been the result only of considerable practice. Other verses he composed, but seems to have considered none of them deserving of preservation. He wrote an occasional poem when Elizabeth once dined with him at Twickenham, but saves himself with the apologetic remark, "I profess not to be a poet." (pp. 533-34)

Though the *Essays* were but the recreation of his other studies, they are nevertheless the completest exemplification of Bacon's aims and methods as a writer. They are the striking instance in which Bacon permitted technic to occupy as important a place as content, and the study of the technic of the essays is the study of the formation of Bacon's style.

Though for mere literary virtuosity, for technic as technic, Bacon frequently expressed utter disregard, it goes without saying that he did not arrive at his command over English prose without long and exacting preliminary exercise. The basis of the style of the *Essays* is the compact, aphoristic sentence, weighted with thought and finished, but not elaborate, in form. Since Bacon regarded ornament as padding, he consistently reduced it to a minimum in the *Essays.* In the first edition the separate essays are much shorter than in the later editions, and the thoughts are expressed more concisely and epigrammatically. They bear markedly the indications of being "dispersed meditations," as loosely put together as the Orphic passages of Emerson. As Bacon revised the *Essays,* however, he amplified them, supplied connecting links in thought, and in general gave much greater rotundity and fluency to the phrasing; and in these later forms the *Essays* consequently read more easily and currently. But they never become discursive treatments of the topics they consider, the fancy and imagination are not allowed to play freely. Bacon never permits the feeling for the solidity and reality of his intellectual world to weaken. The *Essays* remain, even in their elaborated forms, compact summaries of observations. The meditations of which they were composed are the essence of Baconian wisdom, put up in neat capsules and enclosed within labeled boxes.

"The word is late," says Bacon, commenting on the title of his *Essays,* "but the thing is ancient. For Seneca's epistles to Lucilius, if one mark them well, are but essays, that is, dispersed meditations, though conveyed in the form of epistles." Bacon seems to have borrowed the word from the *Essais* of Montaigne and to have been the first to use the word in this sense in English. Montaigne's *Essais* had appeared in 1580, seventeen years before Bacon's first edition, which in turn antedated Florio's translation of Montaigne by six years. But Bacon's indebtedness to Montaigne was not extensive. Neither the impulse which led to the composition of the essays nor the general spirit in which they were written owed much to the garrulous Frenchman. It is not necessary to look beyond Bacon's own mind and the fashion of the times to account for his interest in collecting "dispersed meditations." Among Renascence scholars the favorite medieval method of summarizing experience and doctrine, the narrative exemplum, had been to a large extent replaced by the aphorism and wise saying. The writings of the ancients were ransacked for pithy moral observations, and these, no matter how commonplace, seemed to acquire dignity by reason of their classical origin and by virtue of the fact that they had never before been succinctly formulated in vernacular phrases. (pp. 534-36)

Bacon's earliest writings contain many illustrations of his fondness for compact epigrammatic expression. In his ***Letter of Advice to Queen Elizabeth*** he distinguishes neatly between discontent and despair: "for it sufficeth to weaken the discontented; but there is no way but to kill the desperate . . . for among many desperate men, it is like some one will bring forth a desperate effort." And some of the following might be extracts from the ***Essays:***

> Laws, not refreshed with new laws, wax sour. Without change of the ill, a man cannot continue the good. To take away abuses supplanteth not good orders, but establisheth them. A contentious retaining of custom is a turbulent thing, as well as innovation.

> He seeketh not unity, but division, which exacteth in words that which men are content to yield in action.

These generalizations were doubtless in large part the fruits of that solitariness at his place at Twickenham Park which "collecteth the mind, as shutting the eyes doth the sight," of which Bacon on one occasion speaks. After they were excogitated, they were put down in note-books and preserved until an appropriate time for using them appeared. In fact they were collected very much in the same way that Bacon collected his observations of the phenomena of natural science in the external world. The thoughts were not merely spun out of Bacon's inner consciousness, but they have a kind of objective reality which results from the fact that their wisdom springs from the combination of reflection with experience.

Examples of these "forms," or thoughts neatly expressed to be employed later, together with a great variety of other detail indicative of Bacon's methods of self-discipline, may be found in one of Bacon's note-books which happens to have been preserved. It was made in 1608 and bears the title ***Comentarius Solutus.*** A somewhat similar work is the ***Promus of Formularies and Elegancies,*** a miscellaneous collection probably representing Bacon's reading and his reflections during the Christmas vacation of 1594. This latter collection consists of phrases to be used in conversation, of quotations from the Latin poets, a few natural history observations, several of Erasmus's *Adagia,* and a number of neat epigrammatic turns of thought—for example, "Ceremonies and green rushes are for strangers." To the student of Bacon as a writer, these collections are of great interest as containing suggestions for trains of thought, exercises in composition and conversation, in short all the minutiæ of self-discipline to which the literary artist must subject himself.

The methods which Bacon followed in practice he also preached by precept. "I hold the entry of commonplaces," so he writes in the ***Advancement of Learning,*** "to be a matter of great use and essence in studying; as that which assureth copie of invention and contracteth judgment to a strength. But this is true, that of the *methods* of common-places that I have seen, there is none of any sufficient worth; all of them carrying merely the face of a *school,* and not a *world,* and referring to vulgar matters and pedantical divisions without all life or respect to action." The method by which one was to avoid the arid deserts of the school and to cultivate the rich fields of the world of life and action, Bacon has detailed elsewhere. In his ***Letter of Advice to the Earl of Rutland on his Travels,*** Bacon recommends "writing or meditation or both" as aids to remembrance; and by writing he means not merely summaries of what one has read, but "notes and abridgements of that which you would remember." For the making of summaries or epitomes, Bacon expresses the greatest scorn. "I hold collections under heads and commonplaces of far more profit and use," he writes to Sir Fulke Greville, counseling him on his studies, "because they have in them a kind of observation without which neither long life breeds experience, nor great reading great knowledge." Then in detail Bacon shows how from particular narratives, general ideas may be deduced. From the story of Alexander in Plutarch, after observing "the variety of accidents he met withal in the course of his life," under the head of Conqueror one may note "that to begin in the strength and flower of his age; to have a way made to greatness by his father; to find an army disciplined, and a council of great captains; and to procure himself to be made head of a league against a common enemy, whereby both his quarrel may be made popular and his assistance great, are necessary helps to great conquests." In the same way Bacon shows how general ideas may be derived from particular narratives under the topics War and Periods or Revolutions of States. In short, what Bacon recommends is the combination of reading with thinking, to be followed by the crystallization of the thought in the forms of language. When one recalls Bacon's eloquent defense of learning and scholarship, his own statement that he has "rather studied books than men," and then the form which his writing took, one may confidently believe that Bacon's wisdom was in no small degree attained by the method he has described. And when one considers further the solidity and reality of Bacon's thought, qualities which make it still interesting and significant, perhaps one may conclude that the "school" and the "world" are not as far apart as they are usually supposed to be. It is true that, mingled with Bacon's profounder meditations, many aphorisms occur which are obvious in thought. But it was never Bacon's endeavor to astonish by the novelty or remoteness of his ideas. Apt expression when coupled with just thinking seemed to him to satisfy all reasonable demands. Aphorisms which sound trite in the sophisticated speech of the twentieth century seem not so facile in the language of the sixteenth century. Words inevitably abate their power after long use, but around Bacon's wise sayings there still lingers much of the freshness of first efforts.

The preference which Bacon gave to Latin over English, in his later years, has often been regarded as indication of a deplorable lack of understanding on Bacon's part of the possibilities of his native tongue and lack of faith in the great literature which was then being written in it. But Bacon's choice of Latin was both less significant and more reasonable than it is often made to seem. In his professional activities he was of course thoroughly accustomed to the use of Latin, which thus came to him not merely as a dead literary language, but as a speech fit for affairs and business. Nevertheless in his earlier writings he used English almost exclusively, employing Latin only where the proprieties and conventions of the situation required it. Nor did he descend to the shallow pedantry of Latinizing his English in an ostentatious way. His style is a highly Latinized style—he was no advocate of Saxon simplicity—but his vocabulary is made up in the main of words which had become legitimized in the learned use of the language. Compared with some of the more extravagant literary Latinizers, Bacon's vocabulary seems quite simple and modern.

When he came to carry out the project of the *Magna Instauratio,* it was almost inevitable that Bacon should turn to Latin. For this work was addressed not merely to the British nation, but to the world of scholars and thinkers. International communication was still to a large extent carried on in Latin, which was extensively used in the reign of James in theological controversy. In making use of Latin, Bacon was merely taking advantage of an opportunity the lack of which scientists and scholars to-day are vainly trying to supply artificially by the invention of theoretical languages. Latin in Bacon's time was still "the general Language," as he describes it in justifying the Latin translation of the *Advancement of Learning.* His purpose in putting this book into Latin was "to free it in the language" so that it might be read everywhere. In sending forth one of the presentation copies of this Latin translation, he expresses the conviction that the book "will live, and be a citizen of the world, as English books are not."

In the last years of his life, however, these good and reasonable motives for the use of Latin became mingled with others of baser character. As Bacon saw the prospect of realizing in any considerable degree the plans of his *Magna Instauratio* growing more remote, he turned his thoughts more and more towards the generations that were to follow him. As he saw not only present fame but also contemporary good name and reputation slipping from him, he desired more eagerly to leave something behind him at his death which should last and which men might recall with words of praise after they had forgotten his weaknesses. "For my name and memory," so he writes in his last will, "I leave it to men's charitable speeches, and to foreign nations and the next ages." Writing in 1623 to his friend Tobie Matthew, Bacon says that his chief occupation was then to have those works which he had formerly published, "as that of *Advancement of Learning,* that of *Henry 7th,* that of the *Essays,* being retractate and made more perfect, well translated into Latin by the help of some good pens which forsake me not. For these modern languages will at one time or other play the bankrowtes with books; and since I have lost much time with this age, I would be glad as God shall give me leave to recover it with posterity." With the help of these "good pens," who did most of the work, the task was carried to completion—an unnecessary task, as time has shown, since the interest of posterity in Bacon's English writing has not been kept alive by the Latin translations of them, nor have these translations sufficient interest or distinction to make them important in their own right. They have done no harm, however, and Bacon's weakness with respect to them must simply be cast, in Sir Walter Raleigh's phrase, in the sum of human error. (pp. 537-43)

Though [Bacon] takes his place among the writers of classic English prose largely by virtue of one book, his position there is secure. His *Essays* are the earliest original writing in English prose which has held a place in the general, one might almost say in the popular, interest of readers of English since the time of their composition. But whatever Bacon's relative rank may be, whether he was the greatest prose writer in his time or not, he takes an important place in the history of English prose as marking the close of the age of experiment and discovery. With him English prose has definitely found itself, has been not merely discovered but conquered. It is true that Bacon did not realize the varied possibilities of English prose as amply as some of its later masters have done, but his limitations were those which his nature, not the command of the technic of his art, imposed upon him. His profundity of thought, his poet's imagining of abstractions, above all the sense of the reality and truth of the intellectual world in which he moved and had his being, all these Bacon has adequately transferred to the forms of English speech. His writing, perhaps, lacks warmth and feeling, but in emphasizing the virtues of prose composition he also brought into relief its characteristic weakness. Bacon's endeavor was to be honest and clear in writing, to avoid the self-deception and the floundering to which human nature is prone. He takes his stand with the moderns upon a platform of independent thinking and an independent and intelligent mastery of his art. . . . [Like John Wiclif], to attain freedom Bacon became something of an iconoclast. Wiclif scorned to quote "holy doctors," and Bacon would away with the intellectual support of the ancients so dearly loved of all Renascence writers and scholars, away also with their superficial ornament. Both were moderns in their day, though Wiclif's reaction against medievalism and scholastic authority naturally seems much more remote from present interest than Bacon's rejection of philosophical abstractions in favor of truth as realized in experience, and of classical oratorical authority in favor of less literary and external standards of expression.

Bacon is distinctly with the moderns in his attitude toward the technic of writing. For technical skill as a means to a reasonable end, he had the highest respect. But technical skill as an exercise in virtuosity, or employed merely to realize the dream of an English style as good as that of Cicero, or of Cæsar or of Tacitus, seemed to him worthless and even reprehensible. The message came first in his estimation, and the arts of style were to be employed to make the message clear and effective, never to make it more pleasing than in justice it should be. This distrust of fine writing in English prose has not grown weaker with the passing of time. Prose has been, as Bacon would have it be, the servant of mankind, not merely an ornament of his state or a solace for his idler moments. As it has had various tasks to perform, so English prose has been made flexible to its different applications. Bacon had no theory of a fixed and standard form of prose, of an elaborated professionally literary style such as the Euphuists and Arcadianists, or such even as learned writers like Hooker, set up as their ideal. With Bacon prose took its place among the practical, not the theoretical virtues. It was not something to be imposed upon English life and culture, it was an inherent and changing element in that developing life and culture, an emanation not an acquisition. Time alone, it is true, could have made possible such opinions as Bacon held. He could rest satisfied with the product of the life of his day because English culture had at least reached the age of maturity. It had assimilated much in the generations since Wiclif and Chaucer, and it had learned by many errors as well as by some successes. Bacon's wisdom was manifested in his realization of the riches which lay at his very door. He saw himself not as a dæmonic being, rapt with a divine frenzy into the fiery clouds of inspiration and speaking and writing a language, not of men but of the gods. His Pegasus was his intelligence, a well-disciplined and governed intelligence. He placed English prose where English writers ever since have labored to keep it, in the everyday world of established experience, of good order, and of sound sense. The source of eloquence in prose he found not in the elevation of art above nature, but in the just expression of all that is best and most worthy of expression within the heart and mind of man. (pp. 543-46)

> *George Philip Krapp, "Bacon," in his* The Rise of English Literary Prose, *Oxford University Press, Inc., 1915, pp. 516-46.*

Émile Legouis   (essay date 1924)

[*Legouis was an eminent French scholar specializing in the field of English literature. His books include the acclaimed* Histoire de la littérature anglaise, *(1924; A* History of English Literature, *1926) written with Louis Cazamian. In the following excerpt from that work, Legouis appraises Bacon's philosophical and literary oeuvre, with special critical emphasis on prose style. He singles out Bacon's* Essays *as an outstanding literary accomplishment, concluding that by this work "Bacon proved himself a great writer of his own language."*]

Side by side with the religious literature [of the Elizabethan period], a secular literature, distinct from although not in conflict with it, was coming into existence and was concerned with philosophy and morals. Francis Bacon (1561-1626) never speaks of religion except with respect,

and seems himself to have been religious, for he wrote several very beautiful prayers for his own use and professed the Anglican faith. But his work had no connection with theology or even with Christian morality. It is the product of a free spirit, of thought which adventures in new paths discovered by itself. He is the first in date of the English philosophers and one of the most eminent and characteristic of them. Moreover, he is one of the pioneers of modern philosophy in all countries.

The contrast between his great intellect and his mediocre character is one of the commonplaces of history. This client and friend of Essex who directed the legal proceedings against him, this lord chancellor of James I who was obliged to acknowledge himself guilty of corrupt and abusive exercise of his office, could be summed up by Pope as 'the wisest, brightest, meanest of mankind.' While it may be admitted that there were extenuating circumstances to excuse him, it is impossible to deny that he made friendship and uprightness subordinate to his career. This low ambition was, however, redeemed and ennobled by another, the desire to serve mankind by the search for truth. Very early, while still at Cambridge, Bacon realized the sterility of the scholastic studies which lead to verbal controversy but never to reality. He then conceived the idea of a mission beside which all the acts of his practical life sank almost to insignificance:

> I found in my own nature a special adaptation for the contemplation of truth. For I had a mind at once versatile enough for that most important object—I mean the recognition of similitudes—and at the same time sufficiently steady and concentrated for the observation of subtle shades of difference. I possessed a passion for research, a power of suspending judgment with patience, of meditating with pleasure, of assenting with caution, of correcting false impressions with readiness, and of arranging my thoughts with scrupulous pains. I had no hankering after novelty, no blind admiration for antiquity. Imposture in every shape I utterly detested. For all these reasons I considered that my nature and disposition had, as it were, a kind of kinship and connection with truth.

His first object was to acquire the knowledge which increases man's empire over the earth. At thirty years old he wrote to Burleigh: 'I have as vast contemplative ends as I have moderate civil ends; for I have taken all knowledge to be my province.'

Little by little, he elaborated the doctrine which he formulated in 1620 in his ***Novum Organum.*** He declared science to be one, and to have a practical object.

> We are concerned not with pure skill in speculation, but with real utility and the fortunes of the human race. . . . For man is no more than the servant and interpreter of Nature; what he does and what he knows is but that which he has observed of the order of Nature in act or in thought; beyond this he knows nothing and can do nothing. For the chain of causes cannot be relaxed or broken by any force, and Nature cannot be commanded except by being obeyed.

Since the obstacles to the attainment of this power, which depends on science, are ignorance and error, the causes are analysed of error or the tendencies to error existing in the human mind, and here given the Platonic name of idols of the intelligence. Bacon takes pleasure in subdividing these idols into those of the tribe, the cave, the market-place, and the theatre, using a curious symbolism which bears the mark of the Elizabethan age. Then he determines the true method, establishing the importance of an objective attitude to nature, and the necessity of systematic experiment, and of caution against precipitate conclusion, 'for the subtlety of nature is many times greater than the subtlety of our logic.' The passage from particular facts to general laws should always be made by prudent and successive degrees.

True science is the knowledge of causes, which Bacon, like Aristotle, divides into material and efficient causes in the physical, and formal and final causes in the metaphysical, sphere. The search for the final cause leads to the corruption, rather than the progress, of science. Form is the true object of search, and is found in the fixed laws which rule bodies. It is the thing itself, the object in its relation to man and to his senses and understanding, as opposed to the object considered in its relations to the universe. These forms are limited in number and are the alphabet of nature. Therefore it is possible to hope that science and philosophy will in the future be complete. The great matter is to collect instances, that is facts, after which the inductive method can be followed with security. A beginning can be made with the hypothesis which yields the first 'vintage.'

Although Bacon may often go astray in his scientific researches while attempting to put his own method in practice, it remains none the less certain that his glorification of facts, the search for them and their classification, had a powerful effect on English thought, not, however, immediately, but after half a century. The Royal Society for Improving Natural Knowledge emanated from Bacon and was the means of the establishment of the Baconian spirit in the heart of the nation.

In the meanwhile, this man, who opened up new horizons to the understanding of his fellow-countrymen, who broke with the Middle Ages and made so bold a step forward into modern times, was chained to the past by his language. He was convinced that 'these modern languages will at one time or other play the bankrowtes with books,' and he entrusted his philosophy to Latin. His capital work *Instauratio Magna* (1620-3) is written in Latin, as are the numerous scientific and philosophical pamphlets appended to it. Even when he wrote in English his *Essays,* which soon became popular, it was the Latin translation of them, 'being in the universal language,' which might, he judged, 'last as long as books last.'

It is therefore only in spite of himself that Bacon ranks among English prose-writers, and only in virtue of the least of his works, his *Essays,* his *Advancement of Learning,* his *History of Henry the Seventh,* his *Apophthegms New and Old,* his unfinished novel, the *New Atlantis,* and various treatises and pamphlets. One hundred years after Thomas More, whose masterpiece also was in Latin, he continued this tradition, but his attitude had less justifica-tion, since in his time every literary *genre* was exemplified in the national literature. It is the more surprising because he could handle English prose so surely and vigorously that he became, in spite of himself, one of the first prose-writers of his country.

He cannot be said to owe this place to his *New Atlantis,* a painfully didactic and awkwardly written description of a new Utopia inhabited by scholars after Bacon's own heart. The most characteristic monument of the imaginary island is 'Salomon's House,' or the 'College of the Six Days' Works,' which is a sort of anticipation of the Royal Society and similarly destined to 'the producing of great and marvellous works for the benefit of men.' In its turrets for observing depth and height, and in its dissecting and vivisecting halls, audacious researches were conducted, some of which were afterwards realized, although the fantastic nature of others has become apparent. This novel is, in fact, Bacon's philosophy of science presented in romantic form by a writer without the gift for romance of which Thomas More received so fortunate a share.

The *History of Henry the Seventh* is stylistically much more remarkable. It was written, to please James I, in praise of his ancestor, the first Tudor sovereign, but it had all the gravity suited to an historical work. Bacon's sagacity often appears in it, and was to show itself more clearly in the portraits of Henry VIII and Elizabeth which he left behind him. No other favourable and admiring picture of the queen is as good.

It was, however, by his *Essays* that Bacon proved himself a great writer of his own language. Their title, although not their spirit, recalls Montaigne's masterpiece. While Montaigne is copious, familiar, prodigal of confidences, interested in everything, prone to philosophize on whatever relates to man, Bacon is curt, almost sibylline, entirely impersonal, and averse from pure speculation. He deduces general maxims only from the observations he has himself been able to make. He writes only for courtiers and statesmen like himself. His manner is intermediate between that of Montaigne's essays and that of the maxims of La Rochefoucauld. He supplies short dissertations wholly sententious in form, supported by quotations from the ancients but founded on direct observation. The construction is stiff and formal. Like a good lawyer, Bacon, with an air of complete impartiality, balances opposing arguments before he draws his conclusion.

Their essential merit lies in the density of the thought and expression, the frequent brilliancy of the poetic images, inserted never as ornaments but always to emphasize an idea, and the impressive loftiness of the oracular tone.

The moral is that set forth in the *Novum Organum,* and the design is practical and utilitarian. There are in fact two morals rather than one. Good for Bacon has a double character, according to whether it be considered relatively to the individual or to the state. He is strongly imbued with Machiavellism, and praises Machiavelli for describing what men do, not what they should do. He is doubtless aware of the difference between virtue and interest. He declares that he is so, and that nothing is of as much worth as virtue. But it is the art of success among men which is the subject of his *Essays.* He points man to the part he should play on the stage of social life, as is indicated in the subtitle of his book: *Counsels Civil and Moral.* Baudouin, its first French translator, was right to call it *L'Artisan de la Fortune.*

Within these limits the *Essays* have singular force and weight. No one has ever produced a greater number of closely packed and striking formulas, loaded with practical wisdom. Many of them have become current as proverbs. Other maxims, either coined by Bacon directly or translated from his Latin, can be extracted from all his works and added to those in the *Essays.* The value of some depends entirely on their wisdom and its forcible expression:

> He that hath wife and children hath given hostages to fortune, for they are impediments to great enterprises, either of virtue or mischief.

> Children sweeten labours, but they make misfortunes more bitter. They increase the cares of life, but they mitigate the remembrance of death.

> Lookers-on many times see more than the gamesters.

Others are remarkable by their images, at once large and terse:

> Men fear death as children fear to go in the dark, and as that natural fear in children is increased with tales, so is the other.

To show that religion is degraded by the shedding of blood, he says:

> Surely this is to bring down the Holy Ghost, instead of the likeness of a dove, in the shape of a vulture or raven, and to set out of the barque of a Christian Church a flag of a barque of pirates and assassins.

These *Essays* are the first in date of the classics of English prose, in the proper sense of the word. They are used as class-books almost as much as Shakespeare's plays. Schoolchildren learn from them to analyse their thoughts, to investigate the etymological sense of words—Bacon's words are weighted with their Latin meaning—and to formulate condensed reflections. The *Essays* also constitute a handbook of practical wisdom, enclosing in their shortest maxims an astonishing treasure of insight. There has been no more active stimulant to wit and the understanding. As compared with Hooker's great dialectical work [*The Laws of Ecclesiastical Polity*], with its vast, developed argument and concentration on temporary and local disputes, the *Essays* are a compendium of precepts, or rather of reflections, which are true of all men, for all time and in all places. (pp. 367-72)

> *Émile Legouis, "Prose from 1578-1625," in A History of English Literature: The Middle Ages and the Renascence (650-1660) [and] Modern Times (1660-1970) by Émile Legouis, translated by Helen Douglas Irvine, [and] Louis Cazamian, and Raymond Las Vergnas, revised edition, J. M. Dent and Sons Ltd., 1971, pp. 338-73.*

Alfred North Whitehead   (essay date 1925)

[*Whitehead was a prominent English philosopher and mathematician whose writings include* Principia Mathematica, *written with Bertrand Russell, (1910),* Science and the Modern World *(1925), and* Adventure of Ideas *(1933). In the following excerpt from the second-named work, he identifies Bacon as one of the earliest figures of the seventeenth-century intellectual revolution which culminated in the triumph of science over other fields of research. Whitehead notes, however, that in his attempts to define nature in terms of qualitative relations, Bacon misunderstood the quantitative spirit of modern science.*]

The men of [the seventeenth century] inherited a ferment of ideas attendant upon the historical revolt of the sixteenth century, and they bequeathed formed systems of thought touching every aspect of human life. It is the one century which consistently, and throughout the whole range of human activities, provided intellectual genius adequate for the greatness of its occasions. The crowded stage of this hundred years is indicated by the coincidences which mark its literary annals. At its dawn Bacon's *Advancement of Learning* and Cervantes' *Don Quixote* were published in the same year (1605), as though the epoch would introduce itself with a forward and a backward glance. The first quarto edition of *Hamlet* appeared in the preceding year, and a slightly variant edition in the same year. Finally Shakespeare and Cervantes died on the same day, April 23, 1616. In the spring of this same year Harvey is believed to have first expounded his theory of the circulation of the blood in a course of lectures before the College of Physicians in London. Newton was born in the year that Galileo died (1642), exactly one hundred years after the publication of Copernicus' *De Revolutionibus.* One year earlier Descartes published his *Meditationes* and two years later his *Principia Philosophiae.* There simply was not time for the century to space out nicely its notable events concerning men of genius. (pp. 39-40)

My discussion of the [seventeenth century] will be best introduced by a quotation from Francis Bacon, which forms the opening of Section (or 'Century') IX of his *Natural History,* I mean his *Silva Silvarum.* We are told in the contemporary memoir by his chaplain, Dr. Rawley, that this work was composed in the last five years of his life, so it must be dated between 1620 and 1626. The quotation runs thus:

> It is certain that all bodies whatsoever, though they have no sense, yet they have perception; for when one body is applied to another, there is a kind of election to embrace that which is agreeable, and to exclude or expel that which is ingrate; and whether the body be alterant or altered, evermore a perception precedeth operation; for else all bodies would be like one to another. And sometimes this perception, in some kind of bodies, is far more subtile than sense; so that sense is but a dull thing in comparison of it: we see a weatherglass will find the least difference of the weather in heat or cold, when we find it not. And this perception is sometimes at a distance, as well as upon the touch; as when the loadstone draweth iron; or flame naphtha of

Babylon, a great distance off. It is therefore a subject of a very noble enquiry, to enquire of the more subtle perceptions; for it is another key to open nature, as well as the sense; and sometimes better. And besides, it is a principal means of natural divination; for that which in these perceptions appeareth early, in the great effects cometh long after.

There are a great many points of interest about this quotation. . . . In the first place, note the careful way in which Bacon discriminates between *perception,* or *taking account of,* on the one hand, and *sense,* or *cognitive experience,* on the other hand. In this respect Bacon is outside the physical line of thought which finally dominated the century. Later on, people thought of passive matter which was operated on externally by forces. I believe Bacon's line of thought to have expressed a more fundamental truth than do the materialistic concepts which were then being shaped as adequate for physics. We are now so used to the materialistic way of looking at things, which has been rooted in our literature by the genius of the seventeenth century, that it is with some difficulty that we understand the possibility of another mode of approach to the problems of nature.

In the particular instance of the quotation which I have just made, the whole passage and the context in which it is embedded, are permeated through and through by the experimental method, that is to say, by attention to 'irreducible and stubborn facts', and by the inductive method of eliciting general laws. Another unsolved problem which has been bequeathed to us by the seventeenth century is the rational justification of this method of Induction. The explicit realisation of the antithesis between the deductive rationalism of the scholastics and the inductive observational methods of the moderns must chiefly be ascribed to Bacon; though, of course, it was implicit in the mind of Galileo and of all the men of science of those times. But Bacon was one of the earliest of the whole group, and also had the most direct apprehension of the full extent of the intellectual revolution which was in progress. Perhaps the man who most completely anticipated both Bacon and the whole modern point of view was the artist Leonardo Da Vinci, who lived almost exactly a century before Bacon. Leonardo also illustrated the theory . . . that the rise of naturalistic art was an important ingredient in the formation of our scientific mentality. Indeed, Leonardo was more completely a man of science than was Bacon. The practice of naturalistic art is more akin to the practice of physics, chemistry and biology than is the practice of law. We all remember the saying of Bacon's contemporary, Harvey, the discoverer of the circulation of the blood, that Bacon 'wrote of science like a Lord Chancellor.' But at the beginning of the modern period Da Vinci and Bacon stand together as illustrating the various strains which have combined to form the modern world, namely, legal mentality and the patient observational habits of the naturalistic artists.

In the passage which I have quoted from Bacon's writings there is no explicit mention of the method of inductive reasoning. It is unnecessary for me to prove to you by any quotations that the enforcement of the importance of this method, and of the importance, to the welfare of mankind, of the secrets of nature to be thus discovered, was one of the main themes to which Bacon devoted himself in his writings. Induction has proved to be a somewhat more complex process than Bacon anticipated. He had in his mind the belief that with a sufficient care in the collection of instances the general law would stand out of itself. We know now, and probably Harvey knew then, that this is a very inadequate account of the processes which issue in scientific generalisations. But when you have made all the requisite deductions, Bacon remains as one of the great builders who constructed the mind of the modern world.

The special difficulties raised by induction emerged in the eighteenth century, as the result of Hume's criticism. But Bacon was one of the prophets of the historical revolt, which deserted the method of unrelieved rationalism, and rushed into the other extreme of basing all fruitful knowledge upon inference from particular occasions in the past to particular occasions in the future. I do not wish to throw any doubt upon the validity of induction, when it has been properly guarded. My point is, that the very baffling task of applying reason to elicit the general characteristics of the immediate occasion, as set before us in direct cognition, is a necessary preliminary, if we are to justify induction; unless indeed we are content to base it upon our vague instinct that of course it is all right. Either there is something about the immediate occasion which affords knowledge of the past and the future, or we are reduced to utter scepticism as to memory and induction. It is impossible to over-emphasise the point that the key to the process of induction, as used either in science or in our ordinary life, is to be found in the right understanding of the immediate occasion of knowledge in its full concreteness. It is in respect to our grasp of the character of these occasions in their concreteness that the modern developments of physiology and of psychology are of critical importance. . . . We find ourselves amid insoluble difficulties when we substitute for this concrete occasion a mere abstract in which we only consider material objects in a flux of configurations in time and space. It is quite obvious that such objects can tell us only that they are where they are.

Accordingly, we must recur to the method of the school-divinity as explained by the Italian medievalists. . . . lecture. We must observe the immediate occasion, and *use reason* to elicit a general description of its nature. Induction presupposes metaphysics. In other words, it rests upon an antecedent rationalism. You cannot have a rational justification for your appeal to history till your metaphysics has assured you that there *is* a history to appeal to; and likewise your conjectures as to the future presuppose some basis of knowledge that there *is* a future already subjected to some determinations. The difficulty is to make sense of either of these ideas. But unless you have done so, you have made nonsense of induction.

You will observe that I do not hold Induction to be in its essence the derivation of general laws. It is the divination of some characteristics of a particular future from the known characteristics of a particular past. The wider assumption of general laws holding for all cognisable occasions appears a very unsafe addendum to attach to this limited knowledge. All we can ask of the present occasion is that it shall determine a particular community of occasions, which are in some respects mutually qualified by reason of their inclusion within that same community. That community of occasions considered in physical science is the set of happenings which fit on to each other—as we say—in a common space-time, so that we can trace the transitions from one to the other. Accordingly, we refer to *the* common space-time indicated in our immediate occasion of knowledge. Inductive reasoning proceeds from the particular occasion to the particular community of occasions, and from the particular community to relations between particular occasions within that community. Until we have taken into account other scientific concepts, it is impossible to carry the discussion of induction further than this preliminary conclusion.

The third point to notice about this quotation from Bacon is the purely qualitative character of the statements made in it. In this respect Bacon completely missed the tonality which lay behind the success of seventeenth century science. Science was becoming, and has remained, primarily quantitative. Search for measurable elements among your phenomena, and then search for relations between these measures of physical quantities. Bacon ignores this rule of science. For example, in the quotation given he speaks of action at a distance; but he is thinking qualitatively and not quantitatively. We cannot ask that he should anticipate his younger contemporary Galileo, or his distant successor Newton. But he gives no hint that there should be a search for quantities. Perhaps he was misled by the current logical doctrines which had come down from Aristotle. For, in effect, these doctrines said to the physicist *classify* when they should have said *measure.*

By the end of the century physics had been founded on a satisfactory basis of measurement. The final and adequate exposition was given by Newton. (pp. 41-5)

> *Alfred North Whitehead, "The Century of Genius," in his* Science and the Modern World, *The Macmillan Company, 1925, pp. 39-56.*

Alfred Noyes (essay date 1926)

[*Noyes was an English poet, playwright, and novelist known for his traditionalist views of literature. His writings include* Drake *(1908),* Tales of the Mermaid Tavern *(1913), and* Two Worlds for Memory *(1953). In the following excerpt from an article originally published in 1926, he questions the literary and scientific importance of Bacon's work, remarking that his "spurious philosophical reputation, by a vicious circle, has led to exaggeration of his literary merits."*]

"The worst thing of all," said Francis Bacon, "is the apotheosis of error." It is one of those "apophthegms" which have been acclaimed as among the most glorious jewels in the crown of Philosophy; and, whether the acclaim be deserved or not, the "apophthegm" has a special applicability to the tercentenary of Francis Bacon himself.

Macaulay rejoiced that the lot of the valetudinarian had been made easier by the results of the Baconian method.

Perhaps he had in mind that other remarkable utterance of the great Father of Modern Science:—

> It is said that the guts or skin of a wolf, being applied to the belly, do cure the colic. It is true that the wolf is a beast of great edacity and digestion and so, it may be, the parts of him comfort the bowels.

For Francis Bacon is the supreme instance in English history of a figure robed and crowned with error. Errors of every kind (from the hard, bright, shallow judgments of Macaulay to the pathetic futilities of those who believe that Bacon wrote the *Faërie Queene* and *Hamlet*), follies of every kind, fly to him as iron filings to a magnet. This may be an ironical judgment upon him for his dismissal of the real magnetic discoveries of Gilbert, whose real experiments led directly to the electrical world of to-day. A large section of the human race prefers hocus-pocus to reality; and, in a world where most people take their opinions at second-hand, their craving is easily satisfied. Nothing is easier than to avoid real thought by selecting a convenient figure to symbolise the achievements of an age.

By a kind of mental shorthand the scientific achievements of three centuries are attributed to the "Baconian method." In one passage of his famous essay in black and white, Macaulay does attribute every material benefit conferred upon mankind to the philosophy of Bacon, whether those benefits accrued before or after the great man's birth. Even Macaulay could not maintain, of course, that all useful inventions began in Bacon's lifetime. Science increases its wealth by compound interest; and progress was necessarily slower in the early ages. But the man who first made a wheel made a great contribution to the mechanism of civilisation. He achieved it by what is quite arbitrarily called the "Baconian method."

By suggesting that Bacon made no personal contribution to what was achieved by the "inductive method" (which he did not invent) Macaulay merely confuses any thoughtful reader who wishes to know exactly what it was that entitles Bacon to his apotheosis. The confusion thickens when Macaulay cheerfully points out that even Bacon's exposition of this method (our last hope) is quite useless. Bacon himself, indeed, did his best to demonstrate this. For what did he achieve, even as a mere logician, with the infallible new instrument which was to enable every man to arrive at the greatest results, without a spark of genius or imagination, provided that he followed the rules and never indulged in hypotheses (one of the most fruitful sources of discovery)?

Whenever he had an opportunity of advancing the august cause of which he has been proclaimed the leader he struck a direct blow at it. He not only rejected the Copernican theory with contempt, but he rejected it in the very face of the discoveries of Galileo. Lord Bacon, so eloquent in his dismissal of popular error, pointed to the popular conviction that the earth did not move as one of his chief reasons for that rejection. He asserted that the theory was due to a desire to make prettily rounded circles out of the movements of the heavenly bodies; and he did this in the very face of the discoveries of Kepler, who, with infinite patience, had worked out the true elliptical course of the planets.

To turn from the works of Bacon to those of Galileo is like passing from the crudities of a mediæval physician to the clear-cut efficiency of a Pasteur. In all his verbose attempts to put scientific thought and religious authority in their right places Bacon never rivalled the terse epigram of Galileo: *The Bible teaches us how to go to heaven. It does not teach us how the heavens go.* There speaks your true modern; and there, not in the ponderous ***Advancement of Learning,*** one hears the voice of the great new age.

Moreover, in his treatment of the discoveries of Galileo, Bacon contradicted all the rules of what is called his own method. So far from displaying caution at first, and then, after a process of testing, arriving by infallible steps at the truth, he did exactly the opposite. His first impulse was to welcome the discovery of the telescope. Nine years later he became suspicious of it. He was ready to attribute the things it revealed, for which an older contemporary had been facing the rack, to a flaw in the instrument. Surely, in those nine years, the Superhuman Father of Modern Science might at least have looked into the matter before he committed his adverse thoughts to paper.

Again, one of his most distinguished commentators praises him for the welcome he gave to the microscope. Any one who refers to the passage in the ***Novum Organum*** itself will observe that Bacon expressly dismisses the microscope as useless. He says that it would be a very fine invention *if it could do certain things;* but he takes it for granted that it cannot do these things (all of which it has since done, through the work of other men), and he therefore dismisses it for all practical purposes.

He rejected Harvey's great discovery of the circulation of the blood. To inquire into the functions of the body was erroneous, for his "new method" would have nothing to do with "final causes." He eliminated the teleological aspect of the universe entirely, and therefore forbade the most fruitful form of inquiry that practical science has ever used—from Aristotle to Darwin—the simple question, "What is this for?" "What purpose does this serve?" Such questions do not belong merely to the narrower sphere of dogmatic theology.

Macaulay dismisses Plato and the greatest of the Greeks as entirely fruitless. But Bacon's theories had no advantage over those of the medical school of Cos. His marvellous assertions that "the heart of an ape applied to the neck or head helpeth the wit, and is good for the falling sickness"; and that "there be divers sorts of bracelets fit to comfort the spirits, and they be of three intentions, refrigerant, corroborant, and aperient," can hardly be defended on the ground that they were "vulgar errors" of his time. Nobody doubts that. The tone is simply that of the intellectual humbug. Bacon was not proud of his Natural History; for he thought it the duty of the hodmen of science to collect "facts," while he played the intellectual Alexander. He was quite explicit about this. With amazing disingenuousness learned professors have tried to keep their hocus-pocus up by pretending that Bacon's lack of pride in the work meant that he disbelieved in it. His de-

scription of the way in which his own warts were healed purports to be a piece of first-hand observation. The warts were rubbed with fat. The fat was then nailed up in the open air and the warts diminished in proportion as the fat wasted away. It is simply a demonstration of the second-rate quality of his mind, in the age of Galileo and Kepler.

Macaulay's portrait of him is as monstrous as the impossible picture drawn by Pope of "the wisest, brightest, meanest, of mankind." The elements are mixed in every man; but they are not completely contradictory or the man would cease to exist. Macaulay depicts Bacon as an utterly black Devil, who is also a perfectly good God. He does, in sober earnest, compare him with the Eternal. "The beneficence of his philosophy resembled the beneficence of the common Father." But the great law-giver had also to be depicted as a torturer, taking down the evidence and listening to the shrieks of an old man upon the rack. It gives a sinister significance to Bacon's curiously mediæval remark that when Nature is placed on the rack all her secrets may be extorted. If philosophies are to be judged by their "fruits," these cannot possibly be limited to material fruits, even when the material fruits can really be attributed to the philosopher, as they cannot be attributed to Lord Bacon. Socrates, drinking the hemlock, with his eyes fixed upon his vision of eternal goodness, eternal beauty, and eternal truth, bequeathed to the world a spiritual heritage of inestimable value. There is nothing in the ascending process of Bacon's logic that can be compared for precision of method and result with that sublime ascent of the mind of Plato from form to form until it arrived at the unity of a "Beauty, wonderful in its nature."

The aims of Plato and the aims of applied science are not mutually exclusive, as Macaulay appeared to think. Bacon himself did not think so. He likens knowledge to a pyramid of which the basis is natural history; the second stage "physic"; and the stage next the vertical point "metaphysic." The peak he regards as unattainable, but the three stages climb to it like the three acclamations *"Sancte, sancte, sancte."* This is the ascent of Plato translated into the atmosphere of scholasticism, with the final ecstasy expressed through a chant of the Church. It is a dim vision of the truth from a great distance. But it is in such passages that the literary merits of Bacon are to be found. It is on literary merits of the less imaginative kind that his spurious reputation as a philosopher has been founded. He is often eloquent, but it is nearly always the eloquence of a man "philosophising like a Lord Chancellor."

His spurious philosophical reputation, by a vicious circle, has led to exaggeration of his literary merits. The ***Novum Organum,*** in its unfinished and fragmentary condition, is hardly more than a collection of detached apophthegms. Some of his worshippers appear to think it can be compared with the *Principia* of Newton. Occasionally Bacon makes a really wise detached observation, as in his remark that a little philosophy leads to atheism but much philosophy to religion. Yet always it is an observation *about* profound thoughts rather than a revelation of profundity in himself. When, instead of orating about the glories of thought, he attempts to think philosophically on his own account, he fails disastrously. His doctrine of "forms" is vitiated through and through by the fact that he uses the word "form" in a dozen different senses. If his treatment of his "forms" be compared with Plato's treatment of his "ideas," the difference between a third-rate and a first-rate mind is at once evident.

He desires to impose himself on the world as its greatest philosopher, without any real originality of his own. It was the *Utopia* of More that cast the little shadow of the *New Atlantis;* and almost any two pages of the notebook of Leonardo contain more fruitful ideas. If it be true that the Royal Society was born of that slight fable, one can only say that, in this case, a very small mouse brought forth a mountain. It is Polonius, not Shakespeare, that speaks in those crafty world-wise essays. "Neither a borrower nor a lender be"—the very tone is there; and one thinks that Shakespeare must have gone to life for some of the details in his portrait of a statesman. It is the wooer of the rich widow of Hatton who speaks in the essay on Love. Historians have defended his acceptance of bribes on the ground that, after all, he would betray the briber, and probably take a bribe from the other side as well. He had learned enough from Machiavelli to subdue all his affections to his personal advantage. He was able to superintend the execution of his best friend, and to send Raleigh to the scaffold. It is not necessary for historians to accuse the Cecils of jealousy because Burghley so steadfastly refused to promote the young Bacon. It was at least possible that they distrusted his character. He employed Hobbes as his secretary. The author of the *Leviathan,* afterwards, when he was writing on logic, never once mentioned the "new instrument" which had enabled his former employer to reject the greatest scientific discoveries of his age. For Hobbes knew well what the best minds in Italy knew.

But it is the eye that gives the finishing touch to the portrait. Harvey, a real scientific discoverer, and an acute observer, had seen Lord Bacon; and he left us his record in a single biting sentence, *"He had an eye like a viper."* (pp. 85-96)

> *Alfred Noyes, "The Tercentenary of Francis Bacon," in his* New Essays and American Impressions, *Henry Holt and Company, 1927, pp. 85-96.*

Charles Williams   (essay date 1933)

[*Williams was an English writer and critic known for his interest in supernatural and theological subjects. His writings include* War in Heaven (1930), Descent into Hell (1937), *and a poetical cycle on the Arthurian legend,* Taliesin through Logres (1938). *In the following excerpt, he presents Bacon as a multi-faceted genius— poet, scientist, dreamer—who dedicated his life to the pursuit of perfect knowledge.*]

The *Essays* which the Lord St. Alban sent to the French Ambassador, the last edition in his own life of his first book, had nothing directly to do with the Great Instauration. Bacon does not seem, perhaps for that reason, to have thought very highly of it, yet it has been his most popular. That is natural, for it is about man. At the beginning of the seventeenth century three books concerning

man were created from and received into English literature—the Authorized Version of the Bible, the collected First Folio of Shakespeare's plays, the *Essays Moral and Civil* of Francis Bacon. The first differed from the others, for it contained as an hypothesis and endeavoured to explore and imagine in words the secret place in man's being where the supernatural dwells, and to discover clearly the operation of that supernatural both in the world and in the soul. The second differed from the others, for it endeavoured to measure by the rule of the decasyllabic line the utmost pits and the farthest heights apprehensible by the natural human mind. The third differed from the others, for it implied as an ideal a certain self-possession and self-knowledge where they had accepted self-destruction; it considered rather man in society than man in solitude. Bacon has been called "the Father of English prose." It is true in the sense that he was among the first to make direct and easy communication of his private meditations, but the prose of solitude is hardly his. That, even during his lifetime, was being shaped again by one who in past years had been secretary to Sir Thomas Egerton, afterwards the Lord Ellesmere whom Bacon succeeded, and had in York House itself known an experience of young love which Bacon (it seems) never knew, by the interpreter of death whose name was John Donne. Donne's public sermons at Paul's Cross were more private than Bacon's secret meditations; they were more private because they entreated, and agonized, and wrestled with God, and because in such a wrestling God imparts something of his infinite secrecy to each ardent combatant. God, in Bacon, is the father of lights. He may be secret in himself but his concern with man is manifestation. Man has to strive with nature to discover truth, but nature is passive to his endeavours. Donne and the Authorized Version knew of no such passivity; they pursued God into His recesses; they fled into the mountain alone to see the rearward of His glory.

Mankind in action, then, is the subject of the *Essays,* and mankind in action in the world. Mankind in the desert was not Bacon's business. It is the sense of the desert indeed, and only the desert, which is lacking in his writing. The wilderness into which Christ was driven, the heath upon which Lear underwent dissolution, are not in that other prose. It would be rash and foolish to assert that there is any moment in Bacon's life when any other man can certainly say he himself would have acted differently. It would be rash and foolish to assert that he more than any of his—or of any—time and place sought preservation at the expense of perfection, or magnificence at the expense of magnanimity. It is still rash, but not quite so foolish, to assert that men have seemed to feel in him a certain cheapening of integrity, a lack of capacity for detachment. He did not make haste to deny himself everything but finality; he lingered in the world and the Court. He had even so the best of reasons; God, he thought, meant him to be a summons to men, and whom could he summon in the wilderness? But we, with St. John Baptist pre-eminent in our minds, are anxious to see him feeding on locusts and clothed in camel's skin; we expect so great a wind of marvel to come to us rather from the deserts than the towns. Certainly those warring and persecuted Puritans and Papists moved, one feels, to a mightier dance than he until he rode out to Gorhambury from the Tower, until (after five years of separation and neglect) he sent his last appeal to the King's Majesty. Yet he must have known more of the desert than we easily guess. His mother knew how he lay awake at night thinking strange things. We know how all those busy years he hid his vocation in his heart; the letters that are full of so much remind us that he could never release his mind to any of the men he wished to serve and to use; the prose itself witnesses that such sentences come only from thought intensely concentrated in loneliness. He also knew—*"neque eum fugit quanta in solitudine versetur hic experimentum,"* "my soul has been a stranger in her pilgrimage." But there is a distinction even in solitudes, and Bacon's loneliness, however lonely, was yet for society; he purposed to do social good to man. It was not loneliness that pursued farther loneliness; it did not presume to imagine Gethsemane or Dunsinane, where credible supernatural Good or imagined natural evil walked in their separate and self-chosen exile. It was neither his need nor his privilege; in that sense he is indeed the first of the modern world, the first great English mind fully escaped from the paths of the hermitages, the doors of the convents, or the mystical sepulchres of the saints. Shakespeare, though he called them by other names—Hamlet or Lear or Imogen—knew more of them than he. He has none of the irrational transcendencies which mark the poets nor the sharp and terrible comforts of the holy ones. To the lights and heats of youth, as of spiritual seers, the wisdom of the *Essays* often seems a poor thing. Blake dashed down "Atheist!" as he read, and scribbled that if what Bacon said was true what Christ said was false. But greater men even than Blake have hastily supposed they knew what Christ meant and what He did not, and Blake's negations are not as certain as his affirmations. He was wrong; he himself wrote that Creation was the Mercy of God, and the Mercy of God is a wider thing than Blake supposed. Poets do not write like Bacon nor perhaps do the prophets read him. But, poets and prophets having gathered their congregations, there still remain some who listen to that other bell calling men to know themselves as they are to know all other natural things.

In the *Novum Organum,* speaking of his beloved Forms, he had defined their nature. "In nature nothing really exists beside individual bodies, performing pure individual acts according to a fixed law." But "in philosophy this very law, and the investigation, discovery, and explanation of it, is the foundation as well of knowledge as of operation. And it is this law, with its clauses, which I mean when I speak of Forms." Mankind also consists of individual bodies performing pure individual acts, and though Bacon and his great religious contemporaries would alike have denied that man always acted according to a fixed law, yet in the generality of his actions man does so act. It is man in his actions, and the law that controls them, which are the continual subject of the *Essays;* they investigate and discover the law which is the Form, and determines knowledge and operation. Neither here nor in the *Novum Organum* is the Form anything like the great Platonic archetypes. Bacon himself had told us in the *Advancement of Learning* how Plato—he said "erred"; let us rather say, "differed." Plato had half-freed his Forms from matter; he had mingled theology with physics, and into his

theology his physics had escaped, nobly but unreliably transmuted on the way. Those Forms were after the style of the poets; because things in their nature disappointed Plato, he too would exalt the mind of man to some sphere outside known facts. It is not surprising that Platonism has so attracted and affected the English poets. But that Elizabethan Englishman would have nothing of these fantasies. Theology and the supernatural set aside, man was subject to his Form. "I form a history and tables of discovery for anger, fear, shame, and the like; for matters political; and again for the mental operations of memory, composition, and division, judgment and the rest; not less than for heat and cold, or light, or vegetation, and the like." For as regards man also he was concerned to build in the human mind a model of the world as it truly is, "and not such as man's own reason would have it to be." "Atheist!" wrote Blake. Bacon need not even write his comment; the works of his antagonist supply it. He has but to point to those shadowy giants, Los and Enitharmon, Orc and Rintrah, Thel and Palambron, Urizen and Oothoon; hardly with such companions is a man led accurately to know his preservation and perfection, the contemplation of true knowledge and the operation of true power. It is impossible to play hide and seek with such ghosts.

The *Essays,* then, are the definition of the Form, of the law, which controls the pure individual actions of the individual bodies of men. It is the sudden and compressed statement of some clause or other of that law which makes their greatness; it is the misapprehension of a clause of that same law which allows their mistakes. But the mistakes are few, and the successes many, and the final success of all those successes is greater still. Experience of the *Essays* is something more than the separate experiences of their many detached phrases. It seems to grow within us to something like a discovery of man's nature; to define something which is "present where man is present, absent when man is absent, and yet has a specification of a more generic nature"—perhaps the creative energy of the word. In the strength of the word it is possible, reading the *Essays,* to feel that we stand at some centre where, by the application of their knowledge and power, we can alchemize one kind of man into another, purifying, debasing, transmuting. The style which produced that sense of knowledge and power presents itself to us as itself a universal form. Its author is characteristic of man's knowledge; he is a principle of life, and in his sentences there is a definition of mankind. This is what we do; this is how we carry ourselves among our fellows. It may not be noble—it looks at man as he is. But neither is it ignoble; never, assuredly, while goodness, that is, the affecting of the weal of men, "of all virtues and dignities of the mind, is the greatest"; while envy "is the vilest affection and the most depraved"; while "truth, which doth only judge itself, teacheth that the inquiry of truth, which is the lovemaking or wooing of it, the knowledge of it, which is the presence of it, and the belief of truth, which is the enjoying of it, is the sovereign good of human nature. . . . Certainly, it is heaven upon earth, to have a man's mind move in charity, rest in providence, and turn upon the poles of truth." Nowhere perhaps has man been more accurately yet more generously defined, with more intelligence and charity at once, a sometimes victorious, often defeated, but always excelling wonder of the universe.

It is his possession by the word in action that has imposed him on us, directly and indirectly. His reputation has been affected by the accidents of his concern. The six parts of the **Natural History** which he proposed to issue separately were to be called: **Of Winds; Of Density and Rarity; Of Heaviness and Lightness; Of the Sympathy and Antipathy of Things; Of Sulphur, Mercury, and Salt; Of Life and Death.** Almost in the old alchemical method he named them; almost the great titles sound as if something more than **Natural History** were there investigated, as if he hid under veils the making of the *nova creatura* which he seemed to himself to have become. But it would be doing Bacon ill service to pretend he was occupied with such solemn occultisms, however saintly. The fascination of his person and devotion has drawn around him the wildest clouds of fable. Men have made him royal in his birth, the son of Elizabeth; they have clothed him with the more awful sovereignty of the poetic genius of Shakespeare; they have cast on him all miracles of words in that age, as in the Middle Ages the tales of many miracles were cast about one saint; they have attributed to him the knowledge of antediluvian wisdom and the foundation or nourishment of schools of secret science and spiritual mysteries. In his honour they have wrested, not insincerely, things to their thoughts; in his who all his life declared the necessity of submitting the thought of man to the fact of things.

Even when they have despised they have magnified him; if they cannot name him John they will call him Judas. There is imposed on them the fact of himself. Pope touched him with superlatives—"the wisest, brightest, meanest of mankind" ("the meanest"—Pope!). Macaulay—so unnecessarily—lamented over him as over a fallen archangel; even Lytton Strachey, in the midst of his dainty jests at the Trinity and the Earl of Essex, at the death-agony of Philip of Spain and the life-agony of Elizabeth of England—even Lytton Strachey, in a phrase perhaps caught from Macaulay, who perhaps caught it from Bacon himself, was compelled to turn him into an exquisite and terrible evil. He must be beyond belief subtle in wickedness, lest he should be merely honest, and, on one side, human. The other side, we know, is that of a god; touched with immortality, diffusing light. By a myth more terrible than that of any Greek legend they will have his divine clarity interfused with putrefying flesh and cancerous sores. He has been made to want what he never wanted, to believe what he never believed, to transpose his own professed fidelities, to deny his profoundest decisions, in order that he may be suitably denounced by an outraged world. They have made a myth out of a man who desired nothing but to keep myth in its small and remote place, so great has been the sorcerous glamour of his labour and his vision. But glamour was not for him. Something more or less than glamour is in the **New Atlantis.** There beyond the ocean, in the country of Bensalem, lies the College of the Six Days' Work of God, the house of Salomon, where justice and simplicity dwell, with its galleries and furnaces and gardens and libraries and terraces and cellars, its laboratories and studies, its halls and places of statuary;

whence the ships go out to the rest of the wide world to bring back all knowledge, all merchandise of truth, and for ever the experimentalists labour and the rationalizing students toil, and the Masters of the whole work judge and decree, and for ever the Father whom the travellers met declares to ages and peoples their great purpose—"the knowledge of the secret causes of things and the extending of human empire over all things possible." The Lord St. Alban was Chancellor of England and held great place, but his greater place is that in which he is one with the Father of Salomon's House and the visionary master of man's mortal scope.

It must be admitted that he took his revelation solemnly, and perhaps himself solemnly as its means. How he might have lived and written without the Great Instauration it is, unfortunately, impossible to judge. That solemnity may have been one of the elements which rendered him capable of the Great Instauration; a too vivid self-mockery would have thwarted his energy and blinded his vision. Yet sometimes a little would be grateful. Of pretended laughter, of mock humility, of the detestable mannerism by which a man fawns on the self he adores, Francis Bacon was incapable; prophets are not made of such metal. But of that other irony which thrives on the impossibility both of workman and of work, the laughter in the midst of labour at a complete overthrow of the labour, the enjoyment of universal absurdity, of this too he was senseless. There again is that little extra reach of Shakespearean greatness; could the playwright ever have taken *Macbeth* quite as solemnly as the Chancellor took the **Novum Organum?** This extra reach, this doubling in upon itself of genius, this beholding of their proper worlds from an infinite depth of sceptical delight, is not in the founders of missions. It was not in Milton or in Wordsworth; it is not in Bacon. He, as they were, is a dedicated soul, and such an experience of dedication, excluding scepticism, tends to exclude laughter also. If Bacon was indeed a concealed poet, it was not *Twelfth Night* and *Antony and Cleopatra* and *A Winter's Tale* that he wrote, but *Paradise Lost* and *Paradise Regained.*

Nevertheless, laughter and irony were not lacking; the universe took the burden of those enjoyments upon itself. In the preface to the **Novum Organum** Bacon had chanced upon a rare lightness—"Even as though the divine nature took pleasure in the innocent and kindly sport of children playing at hide-and-seek, and vouchsafed of his kindness and goodness to admit the human spirit for his playfellow at that game"—"*non aliter ac si divina natura . . . puerorum ludo delectaretur . . . atque animam humanam sibi collusorum in hoc ludo . . . cooptaverit.*" (The kindness and goodness of the divine nature might perhaps have excluded medicine from its play; we should have enjoyed the rest of it so much better.) The unusual sweetness of the metaphor makes one wonder if the universe or perfection or the divine nature or his Fortune—whatever name we give to that perpetual otherness—wrote that sentence for him; and with a peculiar appropriateness. For such a game of hide-and-seek it assuredly played with Bacon. The amusement which, it seems likely, he never found in his great task, it discovered for itself at his expense. It produced him in fortunate circumstances, a child of a man close by the Throne; it gave him in his early years every prospect of a satisfying career. It allowed him to take the first necessary steps of that career, and before they were ended it communicated the vision of something of its own perfection to his mind and heart. It showed him "what he was born for," and having shown him that, which was itself, it hid itself. At first it seemed to be immediately before him, but suddenly his father died and there was no direct way. He supposed it had fled to the Cecils, and sought it there, himself the while diligently recording the vision in the *Temporis Partus Maximus.* But the years passed, and after having diligently examined all the Lord Treasurer's purposes he determined that it was not hidden there. Again it seemed to be with the brilliant and intellectual Essex, and to Essex Bacon went, to see if he could discover there both preservation which is the search for perfection, and perfection which is the end of the search. Anthony returned, and the rooms of Essex House and the corridors of the royal palaces became full of much business; and Francis toiled patiently and drafted instructions and was quarrelled over and waited in antechambers and heard loud voices within and saw the raging exodus of the Favourite, and feared that if perfection had ever hidden there it had fled, and found himself gradually dropped. Then for some months perfection altogether disappeared, while the Queen talked to him and rumours were spread and Cecil deprecated hostility to the Earl, and Francis saw his very preservation in danger; until the Earl went mad altogether and the whole episode closed in blood, and there was a clear world again with only Cecil and Coke and a strange King. Perfection this time might, he thought, be hidden in retirement, not after all in great place, and thither he proposed to follow her. But, lest he should believe his early assignation false, she suddenly showed herself in the House of Commons, and ran in front of him to the royal throne, and sat at the table of the Commissioners for the Union. She even let herself leave the *Advancement of Learning* with him for encouragement, before she gleamed at the window of the office of the Solicitor and then of the Attorney. And now the game was very near an end; preservation and perfection were almost one. In York House and Gorhambury she waited for him, sat with him, talked with him, watched over the final revision of the *Novum Organum*—the second part of the great work; how much more remaining yet to do! And then, when he thought he had securely found her, when his interest and his advancement and his loyalty and his duty and his vision were almost one, she vanished in the days of a sudden March, and he found that he had been tricked again. His accusers were everywhere; in that moment he accused himself, but not of earthly corruption, only that he had not sought rightly for Perfection, he had not followed quickly enough on the flying feet of that divine nature, he had misspent his talent. As if in recompense, when the noise was over and he flung away, while he still looked back and thought she lingered in London, she came to him, quietly, almost secretly. She renewed his energies, she thrilled his style, she preserved in him the vision of the *New Atlantis* and the secret causes of things. In the time of his humiliation he had still believed in truth—

> This
> Stands as a child laughing to see the sun,

Immortal, incorruptible, sovereign truth;
Blessed be God who hath made our souls for
 truth!

The vitality of truth remained with him. As if in a wild symbolism his Fortune closed upon him, meeting him on Highgate in the experiment of preservative snow. By some such coldness she had preserved him, because through all mistakes and faults his own preservation had sought her; in a celestial and happy irony she sent, as it were, from his dying form, during that final Holy Week, a message such as he himself dictated to his secretary, and while the Lord Arundel read his letter, future ages and other nations turned to hear the lofty cry of the perfection that had summoned and charmed and eluded and led him: "The experiment succeedeth excellently well." (pp. 302-13)

> *Charles Williams, in his* Bacon, *A. Barker Ltd., 1933, 313 p.*

Bertrand Russell   (essay date 1945)

[*Considered one of the great thinkers of the twentieth century, Russell is known for his enduring contributions to the field of mathematical logic. In addition, he wrote on numerous philosophical, political, ethical, and social issues, becoming famous as a champion of pacifism and of other progressive causes. His writings include* Principles of Mathematics *(1903),* Principia Mathematica *(1910)—the classical treatise on mathematical logic written with A. N. Whitehead—*The Analysis of Mind *(1921),* An Inquiry into Meaning and Truth *(1940), and* Human Knowledge, Its Scope and Limits *(1948). In the following excerpt from his* History of Western Philosophy *(1945), Russell evaluates Bacon's method of inquiry, observing that Bacon may have underestimated the power of deduction in science because he did not grasp the potential—recognized by modern science—of mathematical deduction for formulating empirically verifiable consequences of scientific hypotheses.*]

Francis Bacon . . . , although his philosophy is in many ways unsatisfactory, has permanent importance as the founder of modern inductive method and the pioneer in the attempt at logical systematization of scientific procedure. (p. 541)

Bacon's most important book, *The Advancement of Learning,* is in many ways remarkably modern. He is commonly regarded as the originator of the saying "Knowledge is power," and though he may have had predecessors who said the same thing, he said it with new emphasis. The whole basis of his philosophy was practical: to give mankind mastery over the forces of nature by means of scientific discoveries and inventions. He held that philosophy should be kept separate from theology, not intimately blended with it as in scholasticism. He accepted orthodox religion; he was not the man to quarrel with the government on such a matter. But while he thought that reason could show the existence of God, he regarded everything else in theology as known only by revelation. Indeed he held that the triumph of faith is greatest when to the unaided reason a dogma appears most absurd. Philosophy, however, should depend only upon reason. He was thus an advocate of the doctrine of "double truth," that of reason and that of revelation. This doctrine had been preached by certain Averroists in the thirteenth century, but had been condemned by the Church. The "triumph of faith" was, for the orthodox, a dangerous device. Bayle, in the late seventeenth century, made ironical use of it, setting forth at great length all that reason could say against some orthodox belief, and then concluding "so much the greater is the triumph of faith in nevertheless believing." How far Bacon's orthodoxy was sincere it is impossible to know.

Bacon was the first of the long line of scientifically minded philosophers who have emphasized the importance of induction as opposed to deduction. Like most of his successors, he tried to find some better kind of induction than what is called "induction by simple enumeration." Induction by simple enumeration may be illustrated by a parable. There was once upon a time a census officer who had to record the names of all householders in a certain Welsh village. The first that he questioned was called William Williams; so were the second, third, fourth, . . . At last he said to himself: "This is tedious; evidently they are all called William Williams. I shall put them down so and take a holiday." But he was wrong; there was just one whose name was John Jones. This shows that we may go astray if we trust too implicitly in induction by simple enumeration.

Bacon believed that he had a method by which induction could be made something better than this. He wished, for example, to discover the nature of heat, which he supposed (rightly) to consist of rapid irregular motions of the small parts of bodies. His method was to make lists of hot bodies, lists of cold bodies, and lists of bodies of varying degrees of heat. He hoped that these lists would show some characteristic always present in hot bodies and absent in cold bodies, and present in varying degrees in bodies of different degrees of heat. By this method he expected to arrive at general laws, having, in the first instance, the lowest degree of generality. From a number of such laws he hoped to reach laws of the second degree of generality, and so on. A suggested law should be tested by being applied in new circumstances; if it worked in these circumstances it was to that extent confirmed. Some instances are specially valuable because they enable us to decide between two theories, each possible so far as previous observations are concerned; such instances are called "prerogative" instances.

Bacon not only despised the syllogism, but undervalued mathematics, presumably as insufficiently experimental. He was virulently hostile to Aristotle, but thought very highly of Democritus. Although he did not deny that the course of nature exemplifies a Divine purpose, he objected to any admixture of teleological explanation in the actual investigation of phenomena; everything, he held, should be explained as following necessarily from efficient causes.

He valued his method as showing how to arrange the observational data upon which science must be based. We ought, he says, to be neither like spiders, which spin things out of their own insides, nor like ants, which merely collect, but like bees, which both collect and arrange. This is somewhat unfair to the ants, but it illustrates Bacon's meaning.

One of the most famous parts of Bacon's philosophy is his enumeration of what he calls "idols," by which he means bad habits of mind that cause people to fall into error. Of these he enumerates five kinds. "Idols of the tribe" are those that are inherent in human nature; he mentions in particular the habit of expecting more order in natural phenomena than is actually to be found. "Idols of the cave" are personal prejudices, characteristic of the particular investigator. "Idols of the market-place" are those that have to do with the tyranny of words and the difficulty of escaping from their influence over our minds. "Idols of the theatre" are those that have to do with received systems of thought; of these, naturally Aristotle and the scholastics afforded him the most noteworthy instances. Lastly there are "idols of the schools," which consist in thinking that some blind rule (such as the syllogism) can take the place of judgement in investigation.

Although science was what interested Bacon, and although his general outlook was scientific, he missed most of what was being done in science in his day. He rejected the Copernican theory, which was excusable so far as Copernicus himself was concerned, since he did not advance any very solid arguments. But Bacon ought to have been convinced by Kepler, whose *New Astronomy* appeared in 1609. Bacon appears not to have known of the work of Vesalius, the pioneer of modern anatomy, or of Gilbert, whose work on magnetism brilliantly illustrated inductive method. Still more surprising, he seemed unconscious of the work of Harvey, although Harvey was his medical attendant. It is true that Harvey did not publish his discovery of the circulation of the blood until after Bacon's death, but one would have supposed that Bacon would have been aware of his researches. Harvey had no very high opinion of him, saying "he writes philosophy like a Lord Chancellor." No doubt Bacon could have done better if he had been less concerned with worldly success.

Bacon's inductive method is faulty through insufficient emphasis on hypothesis. He hoped that mere orderly arrangement of data would make the right hypothesis obvious, but this is seldom the case. As a rule, the framing of hypotheses is the most difficult part of scientific work, and the part where great ability is indispensable. So far, no method has been found which would make it possible to invent hypotheses by rule. Usually some hypothesis is a necessary preliminary to the collection of facts, since the selection of facts demands some way of determining relevance. Without something of this kind, the mere multiplicity of facts is baffling.

The part played by deduction in science is greater than Bacon supposed. Often, when a hypothesis has to be tested, there is a long deductive journey from the hypothesis to some consequence that can be tested by observation. Usually the deduction is mathematical, and in this respect Bacon underestimated the importance of mathematics in scientific investigation.

The problem of induction by simple enumeration remains unsolved to this day. Bacon was quite right in rejecting simple enumeration where the details of scientific investigation are concerned, for in dealing with details we may assume general laws on the basis of which, so long as they are taken as valid, more or less cogent methods can be built up. John Stuart Mill framed four canons of inductive method, which can be usefully employed so long as the law of causality is assumed; but this law itself, he had to confess, is to be accepted solely on the basis of induction by simple enumeration. The thing that is achieved by the theoretical organization of science is the collection of all subordinate inductions into a few that are very comprehensive—perhaps only one. Such comprehensive inductions are confirmed by so many instances that it is thought legitimate to accept, as regards them, an induction by simple enumeration. This situation is profoundly unsatisfactory, but neither Bacon nor any of his successors have found a way out of it. (pp. 542-45)

> *Bertrand Russell, "Francis Bacon," in his* A History of Western Philosophy, and Its Connection with Political and Social Circumstances from the Earliest Times to the Present Day, *Simon & Schuster, 1945, pp. 541-45.*

Douglas Bush (essay date 1945)

[*Bush was a Canadian-born American literary scholar whose writings include* Mythology and the Renaissance Tradition in English Poetry *(1932),* English Literature in the Earlier Seventeenth Century *(1945), and* English Poetry: The Main Currents from Chaucer to the Present *(1952). In the following excerpt from the second-named work, he summarizes Bacon's literary and philosophical accomplishments, concluding that the philosopher's materialistic and scientific world view lacks the spiritual power of great poetic and philosophical traditions.*]

While Bacon has always occupied a throne, the extent of his realm and authority has been subject to many mutations. He outshines the normal scientific recluse by virtue of his literary, legal, and political eminence, the dramatic quality of his career, and the real or apparent puzzles in his character which have attracted so many biographers. Then when we look at the philosopher and his monumental collected works Bacon seems to bestride his age like a Colossus. Standing between the medieval and the modern world, he pointed along the road civilization was to take in the following centuries. His scientific ideals had been proclaimed and practised by other Englishmen, of whom Gilbert was the most influential, but they did not stand in the Baconian pulpit under the Baconian sounding-board. If he himself was the father of no important specific contributions to science, he was the godfather of many, and his strictly scientific thought has more significance than the conventional estimate allows.

While Bacon's predominant passion was natural science, he was a man of the Renaissance who, unlike many of his critics, never lost sight of the whole range of knowledge. *The Advancement of Learning* is the most attractive of his philosophic works because it is the most broadly comprehensive and humane, because its strength and vision are least impaired by dead technicalities, and because it is,

with the *Essays,* the great example of his English prose. The other major work, the *Novum Organum,* though confined to the philosophy and methods of science, embodies, like the *Advancement,* a criticism of the past and a programme for the future, and we may consider Bacon's ideas under these two headings rather than in relation to particular books or to his own elaborate classification of knowledge. The *Instauratio Magna,* as he outlined it in the *Distributio Operis* prefixed to the *Novum Organum,* was to comprise six parts. The first was fulfilled with relative adequacy in *De Augmentis Scientiarum,* the enlarged Latin version of the *Advancement.* The *Novum Organum,* though incomplete, represents the second part, which was to teach the right method of investigating nature, a combination of the empirical and the rational; the title was a challenge to the Aristotelian tradition. For the rest we turn from torsos to *disjecta membra.* In the third part, which includes the natural histories and the *Sylva Sylvarum,* observations of natural phenomena were to be assembled as material for the new method of study. The fourth part, represented by a preface, was to give examples of its operation. In the fifth part, again represented by a preface, Bacon intended to report what he had himself discovered by more conventional methods, without the help of his special induction. This fifth part would lose its value with the completion of the sixth, which was to expound the new philosophy and methodology in full and describe the results of its application to all the natural phenomena of the universe. The fulfilment of this part Bacon left to posterity. Thus the *Instauratio Magna* is linked with *The Fairy Queen* and *The History of the World* as the partial accomplishment of an impossibly vast design.

As a destructive critic, a mouthpiece for the modern world's declaration of independence, Bacon has only one rival, Descartes (1596-1650), and Bacon, in addition to his priority, is more compendious and arresting. The *loci classici* are, next to the *Essays,* probably the best-known parts of Bacon's writings. The first is the discussion, in the first book of the *Advancement,* of the three principal vanities or distempers of learning (along with a series of 'peccant humours'). Bacon arraigns in turn the rhetorical discipline of medieval and Renaissance humanism, the study of words instead of matter; the medieval scholastic discipline, still dominant in the universities, which has also ignored nature and kept mankind in a desert of barren rationalism; and, thirdly, fallacious pseudo-sciences like astrology and alchemy. Then in the first book of the *Novum Organum* Bacon classifies the four kinds of 'idols' which colour what ought to be the dry light of the scientific mind and interfere with the true investigation of nature. Idols of the tribe are the erroneous modes of thought and feeling instinctive in the human race; idols of the cave arise from an individual's temperament and background; idols of the market-place from the loose language of common intercourse, which perpetuates traditional errors; and idols of the theatre from false systems of philosophy and wrong demonstrations. These categories are not entirely distinct; one notion, or one person, might appear in them all. Bacon is always a great phrase-maker, but here he is something more. His analysis of the permanent sources of uncritical credulity may now seem simple, and historically it was novel in its philosophic breadth rather than in its particular ideas, yet it is a landmark in the intellectual development of mankind, and to the individual reader in any age it gives that sense of illumination and growth which is the proof of great writing.

Like most men, Bacon is more vulnerable in his plans for the future than in his criticism of the past. We have been made so familiar with his defects that it might be idle to rehearse the common charges against him, however valid some of them are, if the case of Bacon did not, *mutatis mutandis,* illustrate that of many other philosophic minds of his 'crepuscular' age. In the first place he did not recognize the degree to which his own mind was affected (not wholly for ill) by the several 'distempers' of learning. Without the rhetorical tradition Bacon's prose would not be the powerful instrument it is; rhetorical and scholastic ways of thought lie behind his dream of a scientific *Summa* and run through his terminology and technique; and, finally, he was not untouched by the pseudo-scientific attitudes he condemned. In the **Novum Organum** Bacon is inspired by such sublime confidence in the novelty and rightness of his ends and methods that he drives his triumphal chariot forward over all Aristotelians and others (including Gilbert) who stand in his way, yet many illustrations for his idols can be found in his own writings, the natural histories in particular. However, as we have seen, most leaders of science retained uncritical notions along with their scientific obedience to observed fact, and in this age it was both inevitable and wise that the body of traditional lore should be preserved until it could be properly sifted.

In the second place Bacon did not know enough. We should never guess from his survey of knowledge that the preceding century had witnessed a scientific advance on all fronts. In medicine, for instance, he either did not know or did not appreciate the work of his personal physician, Harvey; Harvey was not unaware of the Lord Chancellor's philosophy. In astronomy Bacon was intelligent enough to criticize existing theories and ignorant enough to accept a pre-Aristotelian idea of spiral motion revived by Telesio. Yet he can hardly be blamed for his hostility to the Copernican hypothesis; even in later years a choice among the three major cosmological patterns, Ptolemaic, Copernican, and Tychonic, might be difficult not only for non-mathematical laymen but for a mathematician like Pascal. Here we approach a realm which Descartes ruled but which was *terra incognita* on Bacon's intellectual map; in some other realms superiority is reversed. An Aristotelian by the accident of training if not by inclination, Bacon missed that Platonic mathematical tradition which was such a fertilizing current in Renaissance thought. Besides, the deductive character of mathematics was repugnant to him. These are only a few items from the list of his blind spots, a list which would provide a fair set of topics for a history of science in the Middle Ages and Renaissance. But we should not forget that if Bacon had never read or written a word of natural philosophy, his achievements in other fields, from literature to the law of equity, would have made him a great figure, and we who find disparagement so easy appear beside him as anaemic pygmies.

Thirdly, there are the weaknesses of the inductive method which was to revolutionize civilization. The method starts from Bacon's doctrine of 'forms' and 'simple natures'. Simple natures are the relatively few physical properties, heat, colour, and the like, possessed by the heterogeneous bodies which make up the natural world. Behind each simple nature is a more generic form, residing in the constituent elements of bodies; and the discovery of these fundamental forms, the learning of the alphabet of nature, is the great end of science. As for the method, Bacon rejects deduction and 'simple enumeration' of affirmatives. To discover the form of heat he first assembles tables of positive, negative, and variable examples. The problem then is to find such a nature as is always present or absent with heat, always increases or decreases with it, and is a particular case of a more general nature. By progressive elimination of false alternatives from his tables Bacon arrives at the one remaining *sine qua non* which must be the form desired, that is, motion. The more difficult part of the inductive process, the establishment of exact scientific criteria for the method of exclusions, he recognized but never described. In general, he is not always clear or explicit and, since his views changed on some points, not altogether consistent. The experimental method in itself was of course very old and Bacon's elaborate superstructure, it is customary to say, was to prove more significant in the history of inductive logic than in the history of science, and was not of much value for Bacon's own end, the discovery of forms. Modern philosophic critics stress the fallacious ideas of card-indexing all nature, of uncontrolled experimentation, of co-operative research which can be carried out by mechanical industry and leaves no room for individual inspirations, inspirations, moreover, which have generally sprung from a very few experiments or even deductions. But many working scientists of Bacon's century, like Robert Hooke, praised the intellectual 'Engine' of 'the incomparable Verulam', and thought, as some men of science do now, that he had made a notable statement of the principles of scientific method. The reading of his works is enough to qualify the conventional charges. Bacon does not ignore hypothesis, for example, in the 'First Vintage concerning the Form of Heat' (his imaginative labels reveal both the scholastic and the poet), and elsewhere he frequently suggests experiments for the testing of hypotheses. And these facts with others—such as his consciousness that his method must be perfected as discovery advanced, or his very effort to guard the scientific mind from idols—imply allowance for the work of individual genius.

Blanket dismissals of Bacon's positive scientific thought are in part the result of misplaced emphasis, in part they are reactions against the panegyrical tradition of the French Encyclopaedists, Macaulay, and other laymen, and in part they are inherited from an age which accepted a strictly mechanical and materialistic view of the universe as the *ne plus ultra* of scientific philosophy. Tried, rather hastily, by this standard, Bacon seemed to belong to another world than Galileo and Descartes and to deserve banishment to the medieval lumber-room. More recent scientific thought has retreated, or advanced, from that mechanical absolutism, and some eminent philosophers of our time, including Whitehead, who have given Bacon serious and unprejudiced study, treat him with respect. This renewed but more intelligent admiration does not rest merely on the innumerable soundly scientific precepts scattered through Bacon's works, but rather on the scientifically prophetic penetration exhibited in his doctrine of forms and simple natures. The conception is not nullified by errors in the inductive method. A form is both an essence and a structural law, the mechanical condition or means of producing the physical property. Hence to discover forms is to understand the unity underlying diverse aspects of matter and also to have the power of intelligently producing the simple natures corresponding to the forms. Then by different combinations of simple natures, based on a knowledge of forms and latent structure, the scientist can transmute one substance into another, can ultimately control all the phenomena of nature. Bacon condemns the theories and methods of the alchemists but not their object, and modern science, with truer knowledge, has gone far in the same direction. If, as some writers say, the control of phenomenal recurrence is the only concern, the very definition, of the scientist, Bacon, whatever his particular shortcomings, is one of the pioneers of modernism. Further, as these summary remarks have indicated, Bacon represents a transitional phase of escape from the medieval qualitative conception of matter, and from the teleological animism of Renaissance thinkers, to something like the kinematical view. At the same time, whether from 'Aristotelian' insight or want of mathematical capacity, he generally stops short of the chief pitfall of 'classical' mechanism, the identification of reality with a kinematical pattern. If Bacon is not altogether in the direct line which leads from Kepler and Galileo to Newton, he is, by his fusion of a limited mechanism with dynamism, a link between Campanella and Leibniz.

Bacon is not, then, historically negligible as a scientific thinker, but his great claims upon us are more familiar. His scientific deficiencies did not essentially weaken the force of his message for his time, the substitution of humble, critical interrogation of nature for the arbitrary concepts of traditional authority, abstract reason, and the unaided senses. It was not an insignificant thing that a great lawyer, judge, and statesman should take up the cause of natural science, and Bacon did more than any other individual except Descartes to create a favourable intellectual climate. He not only summoned men to research, he brought the Cinderella of science out of her partial obscurity and enthroned her as the queen of the world. No one any longer could be deaf to the scientific and humanitarian gospel of experiment, invention, utility, and progress. The traditional view of human history was static or deteriorationist; Bacon made it dynamic and optimistic. He transferred the Golden Age from the mythical infancy of man to an attainable future. He was the chorus of the scientific drama, the Moses, in Cowley's great image, who led his people to the edge of the promised land. If we say that such changes would have occurred without Bacon, we must say also that the discoveries of Galileo and Newton would have been made if those men had never lived.

And the office of spokesman required gifts no less distinctive than the practical discoverer's. The works of Gilbert and Harvey, if we read them, may make some of Bacon's technical discussions look immature, but to whom other than Bacon can we go for a comparable synthesis of the forces and motives which were changing the character of civilization? His voice, moreover, would have lost much of its power if he had not been one of the great masters of the language whose permanence he doubted. His deliberate aim, set forth in the *Parasceve* and elsewhere, Dr. Rawley summed up when he said that Bacon 'did rather drive, at a Masculine, and clear, Expression, than at any Finenes, or Affectation, of Phrases'. Happily Bacon's conception of scientific and philosophic prose did not run to drab bareness. He was able to combine the homely and pithy stock of pure English idiom and diction with the pointed pregnancy of Tacitus, without losing the massive dignity of the Ciceronian period. His virtues are not of course a mere matter of word and rhythm. Shelley, who manifested his devotion from *The Necessity of Atheism* to *The Triumph of Life,* coupled Bacon and Plato as poet-philosophers, citing especially the *Filum Labyrinthi* and the essay **"Of Death"**; and he might have added such passages as the conclusion of the first book of the **Advancement.** Bacon is a scholar and a poet, a thinker and a wit, a realist and a dreamer. His noble eulogies of learning and the quest of truth, his infinite faith in the power of man, his vision of a new era and of himself as the torch-bearer, these things still quicken even the unsympathetic reader's pulse.

We may be unsympathetic because three centuries of progress have made it clear that the conquest of external nature is an inadequate goal, that, as Shelley said in one of his un-Baconian moods, 'man, having enslaved the elements, remains himself a slave'. Not that Bacon contemplated such an end. 'Only let the human race recover that right over nature which belongs to it by divine bequest, and let power be given it; the exercise thereof will be governed by sound reason and true religion.' Such words fall on our ear as a piece of tragic irony. But if scientific power was to override the assumed safeguards, Bacon himself cannot be cleared of all responsibility. His separation of the realms of knowledge and faith, and of external and internal morality, was all the more damaging for not being cynical. His personal religion, whatever its limitations, inspired some beautiful and sincere utterances, and he would have been shocked at a hint that he was less than a good Christian, but the whole drift of his scientific and ethical thought was towards empirical, irreligious naturalism. He wished, with a reverent acknowledgement of faith, to exclude theological and intuitional idols from the temple of science, and in doing so he virtually denied the validity of a religious view of the world. If religion was outside the sphere of knowledge, it was outside the sphere of reality. Thus, while not condemning inquiry into first causes, Bacon left such problems to be settled by revelation and applied himself to the study of things. To machinery and material progress he sacrificed, in a large and noble way, to be sure, that scale of spiritual and ethical values which the best minds of antiquity, the Middle Ages, and the Renaissance had striven to make prevail. He not only brought philosophy down to earth, he confined it within the four walls of a laboratory in which Plato and Aquinas, and Shakespeare and Milton, would have suffocated. That is why, though we recognize Bacon's intellectual power and our vast debt to him, we do not go back to his works for vital nourishment. (pp. 261-68)

Douglas Bush, "Science and Scientific Thought," in his English Literature in the Earlier Seventeenth Century, 1600-1660, Oxford at the Clarendon Press, 1945, pp. 258-93.

C. S. Lewis   (essay date 1954)

[*Lewis is considered one of the foremost Christian and mythopoeic authors of the twentieth century. Indebted principally to George MacDonald, G. K. Chesterton, Charles Williams, and the writers of ancient Norse myths, he is regarded as a formidable logician and Christian polemicist, a perceptive literary critic, and—perhaps most highly—as a writer of fantasy literature. Also a noted academic and scholar, Lewis held posts at Oxford and Cambridge, where he was an acknowledged authority on medieval and Renaissance literature. A traditionalist in his approach to life and art, he opposed the modern critical movement toward biographical and psychological interpretation, preferring to practice and propound a theory of criticism that stresses the author's intent rather than the reader's presuppositions and prejudices. In the following excerpt, Lewis comments on Bacon's philosophical writings, remarking that the philosopher excels as an "exposer of fallacies," but not as a "discoverer of truths." In Lewis's opinion, Bacon's Essays amount to brilliant rhetorical exercises without much content.*]

The work of Francis Bacon . . . falls almost entirely outside [the sixteenth century], but the little volume which he published in 1597 contains things worthy of notice. It consists of the ten earliest *Essays,* the *Meditationes Sacrae,* and the *Colours of Good and Evil:* in the second edition (1598) an English version, probably not by Bacon himself, was substituted for the Latin text of the *Meditationes.* This neglected work contains things very much more like 'essays' (in the ordinary sense of that word) than Bacon ever gave us again: the sections **"Of Moderation of Cares"** and **"Of earthly Hope,"** both on characteristically Johnsonian themes, are like the best *Ramblers*. The *Colours* is work of quite a different kind, a precursor almost of Miss Stebbing's *Thinking to Some Purpose*. By 'coulers' Bacon means not rhetorical colours but what we should call stock arguments: he is constructing a 'defence to the minde' by showing under what conditions such arguments are invalid. Here, as in the great passage about Idols in the *Novum Organum,* we see Bacon at his best: not as a discoverer of truths but as an exposer of fallacies. From these two works, diversely excellent, it is a shock to turn to the *Essays.* Even the completed *Essays* of 1625 is a book whose reputation curiously outweighs any real pleasure or profit that most people have found in it, a book (as my successor [Douglas Bush, author of *English Literature in the Earlier Seventeenth Century: 1600-1660* (1945)] admirably says) which 'everyone has read but no one is ever found reading'. The truth is, it is a book for adolescents. It is they who underline (as I see from the copy before me) sentences like 'There is little friendshipe in the worlde, and least of all betweene equals': a man of 40 either disbelieves it or takes it for granted. No one, even if he wished, could really learn 'policie' from Bacon, for cunning, even more than virtue, lives in minute particulars. What makes young

readers think they are learning is Bacon's manner; the dry, apophthegmatic sentences, in appearance so unrhetorical, so little concerned to produce an effect, fall on the ear like oracles and are thus in fact a most potent rhetoric. In that sense the *Essays* are a triumph of style, even of stylistic illusion. For the same reason they are better to quote than to re-read: they serve (in Bacon's own phrase) 'for ornaments'. But in these ten first essays, as they stand in the 1597 text, that style overshoots the mark: they are altogether too jejune, too atomic. And many good touches were left to be added to them in the later editions. Their connexion with Montaigne's work is quite unimportant. If Bacon took his title from Montaigne, he took nothing else. His earliest essays resemble essays by Montaigne about as much as a metallic-looking cactus raised on the edge of a desert resembles a whole country-side of forest, filled with light and shade, well stocked with game, and hard to get out of. It is only in the *Meditations* that Bacon is at all like his predecessor; and even there, of course, briefly. Nor had he any successors. The cactus remains unique; interesting, curious, striking, worth going to see once, but sterile, inedible, cold and hard to the touch. (pp. 537-38)

C. S. Lewis, "Epilogue: New Tendencies," in his English Literature in the Sixteenth Century, Excluding Drama, Oxford at the Clarendon Press, 1954, pp. 536-58.

Paolo Rossi   (essay date 1958)

[*In the following excerpt from a translation of his Francesco Bacone: Dalla magia alla scienza (1958), Rossi comments on Bacon's views on magic and occult science, remarking that his writings are not free from occult influences. Bacon's desire to attain perfect knowledge is definitely in tune with the efforts of Renaissance magicians and occultists, but what sets the English philosopher apart, Rossi explains, is his idea of scientific collaboration, which occult science excludes by definition.*]

Bacon spent the last years of his life compiling a great encyclopedia of nature and of arts (or nature modified by man). It was to provide the material for a study of the New Science, and Bacon was convinced that its publication would finally establish his fame and his reputation. Assisted only by his secretary Rawley he worked for many years at a *Primal History (Historia prima)* to include material for all particular histories, which was published as the *Sylva silvarum (Forest of Forests)* only after his death. But the particular histories came to assume an ever increasing importance for Bacon who made a 'sort of vow' to publish one each month for six consecutive months. Only two of these six histories were ever published in their entirety: the *History of Winds (Historia ventorum)* and a year later the *History of Life and Death (Historia vitae et mortis)* which was to have been the sixth.

Bacon believed that a meticulous and exhaustive compilation of natural and experimental histories would rapidly change the destinies of mankind, so he discarded his logic and gave up all his time to the realisation of this fantastic project, the greater part of which was never to be completed.

Thus the *Sylva silvarum* (a vast forest providing materials for future constructions) was written by a man who knew that he was working against time and who had besides to accomplish single-handed a job requiring a team of investigators and a complicated scientific equipment which he did not possess. These factors are mainly responsible for the dismissal of this work as unimportant and absurd. It is true that Bacon, pressed by time, resorted to ransacking existing texts for his material: the *Sylva silvarum* includes borrowings from Aristotle's *Meteorological Problems (Problemata meteorologica),* Pseudo-Aristotle's *Of the wonders of accoustics (De mirabilibus auscultationibus),* Pliny's *Natural History,* Della Porta's *Natural Magia (Magic naturalis),* Sandys' *A Relation of a Journey,* Cardano's *Of Subtlety (De subtilitate)* and Scaliger's *Against Cardano (Adversus Cardanum);* indeed the influence of magic and alchemical traditions on Bacon is nowhere more obvious. Thus the decomposition of bodies is explained by the tendency of the volatile spirits inhabiting them to escape and make merry in the sunshine; because dogs like bad smells their olfactory organs are said to be different from those of other animals; salamanders are described as being gifted with 'extinctive virtues'. This work also includes the theory of sympathies, and such beliefs as lunar influences, the evil eye, and the transmutation of metals. But such notions were widely held in those days even among the educated classes, and they survived for a long time; in 1646 the *Vulgar and Common Errors* by Sir Thomas Browne (himself a firm believer, in a number of these errors) was an attack aimed not at popular superstitions, but at beliefs similar to Bacon's which were still current in cultured circles.

However, of far greater significance is the fact that Bacon adopted certain fundamental theories of Renaissance natural philosophy. This is particularly evident in the *Sylva silvarum* where they are applied to individual cases but they are not absent from his earlier works. According to these theories all substances are gifted with the power of discrimination, and when two substances are placed in contact a selection takes place by which what is pleasant is accepted and what is painful is rejected; if a substance is altered by another or alters it, discrimination invariably precedes the operation. A universal link exists between all beings perceived either as attraction or as repulsion (all the examples in the tenth Century of the *Sylva silvarum* are based on this theory). The powers of the imagination are of the utmost importance. Though Bacon had violently attacked Paracelsus for such notions, he proposed to test the powers of the imagination by trying to arrest the fermentation of beer and prevent churned milk from turning into butter. Indeed he exalts the occult powers of the imagination more than many a Renaissance naturalist.

These theories, besides being typical of Renaissance vitalism, are a first step towards acknowledging the magical ideal that underlies it. Thus one of the major difficulties confronting the Baconian scholar is the presence of both mechanist and dynamic vitalist conceptions of reality in Bacon's physics.

However, we are more concerned with the recurrence of vitalist, magical, and alchemical themes in Bacon's earlier works which were written under more leisurely circumstances than the *Sylva silvarum* and with more clearly defined aims. For instance, in the *New Organon* and in the *History of Life and Death* Bacon declares that a spirit or spiritual (pneumatic) body is contained in all substances. As the concept of decomposition originates in the spirit the only antidote to this process is the *detentio* or retaining of the spirit. Greasy, compact substances are better able to resist decomposition because they are less porous than others. In the *History of Life and Death* Bacon specifies that by spirit he means neither a virtue, a power, an entelechy 'nor any other such trifle' but a body, subtle and invisible yet situated in actual space. And this is more or less the meaning alchemists gave to the term. The spirit, as vital source of nourishment that must be retained in order to preserve life and that penetrates like a watery vapour into each elemental particle, forms the basis both for a mystical theory of reality and for the doctrine of the transmutation of metals. For a given metal differs from other metals by virtue of a specific spirit which is no more than a variant or condition of the common metallic spirit; this in turn is an emanation of *anima mundi* or world spirit derived from the *spiritus universi* or universal spirit and, in the last analysis, from God. I do not think it is possible to find in Bacon either an explicit or an implicit espousal of these mystical aspects of alchemical tradition, but the influence of the hermetic doctrine of the transmutation of metals is clear. This last is based on the belief in a common metallic spirit entirely homogeneous except for unspecified impurities. To free a metal from these impurities is tantamount to making it perfect. This can be achieved by introducing into a basic metal the spirit of another metal. The process induced in the basic metal is called digestion.

Bacon's vocabulary bears the distinctive mark of this tradition: he speaks of the assimilation, nourishment, generation, and irritation of substances in the process of conservation or mutation; he makes frequent use of the term fixation with its traditional alchemical connotations. These linguistic affinities reflect an ingrained affinity of outlook, especially pronounced where Bacon's physics are concerned. Here, however, Bacon's atomist and materialist leanings have sometimes led him to use certain alchemical terms in a context that alters their original meaning, and it [is necessary] to determine the extent of these alterations. For the moment we need only remember that alchemical research was always related in some way to Aristotle's doctrine of matter. The alchemists saw it as a *continuum* or stream and also made use of the concepts of matter and form. Indeed, the transmutation of metals could only be possible if copper and gold, for instance, were not considered as two different matters but as different manifestations of the same matter; and Aristotle's theory of vapours with its implications of a total homogeneous identity for all metals gave further substance to this doctrine.

In fact there was little connection between alchemy and traditional atomism, and the atomistic revival to which Bacon largely contributed completely redirected the course of alchemical research. But here again Bacon's attitude is characteristic: his reappraisal of Democritean philosophy is known and he accepted most of the atomistic doctrine. However, his reservations were motivated by his alchemical allegiances; it was the problem of transmutation of metals which weighed the scales in favour of Democritus who believed in various forms of atoms, and against Pythagoras who maintained their absolute similarity. Bacon accepted Democritus' theory in so far as it stipulated an indirect transition from one substance to another in opposition to Pythagoras' theory of direct transition. Research should, besides, be diverted from the *queta principia rerum* (passive principles of substances) to their appetites and inclinations.

Bacon's attitude to the problem of vacuum was equally ambiguous. This may have been due to his uncertainty in the related problem of the continuity of matter, which brings us back to his interest in alchemy. For his whole theory of 'primal natures' (or simple natures), of 'latent configurations' and 'latent processes' stems from his belief in the transmutation of substances; thus his use of Aristotelian terms and of the distinction between matter and form are no mere coincidence. However, Aristotle's influence on Bacon was not direct; it affected him through the alchemists, so that the efforts of some scholars to find an absolute similitude between Bacon's texts and Aristotle's have rarely been crowned with success.

Bacon analysed substances to determine their primal natures or irreducible qualities, so that gold becomes a combination of yellowness, specific weight, a degree of pliancy, malleability and so forth. This process is akin to that of reducing a word to its component letters, and so these primal natures are 'nature's alphabet' and constitute the ultimate elements to which the whole of nature can be reduced. If one could discover a method for 'superinducing' upon a certain substance the correctly graduated natures of yellowness, specific weight, pliability and fluidity one could transmute it into gold. The method would be identical if one or more natures were to be superinduced but, adds Bacon, the difficulties would be greater in the second case, as it is not easy to assemble in a single substance a number of natures usually only assembled under natural circumstances. But there remains the fact that operations such as these are based on the constant, eternal and universal elements of nature and that they can immeasurably increase the powers of mankind.

Indeed for Bacon mankind appears to have no greater purpose than to 'generate or superinduce' new natures on a given substance, and he tries to find a 'true and perfect rule of operation' for discovering primal natures for this end.

Bacon's link with alchemical traditions is particularly evident here where he makes use of two typically alchemical notions; namely that transmutations from one substance to another can only be achieved by superinducing foreign elements upon a given substance—thus the alchemists often presented the transmutation of substance as a more pervasive form of dye; and that the attributes of a substance are seen as 'specific beings' or separate independent 'natures', to be added, removed, or exchanged at will. And when Bacon stresses the difficulty of introducing more than one nature into a single substance at one time, he

does no more than echo a characteristic alchemical problem. He declares that fire can produce previously non-existent substances and this belief was also shared by the alchemists. Further, he himself admits that, apart from their erroneous use of fire, their enquiries were directed towards the same ends as his own.

Now that we have seen how greatly Bacon was involved with the alchemical tradition it will be easier to understand some of the better-known aspects of his alchemical tendencies such as his assumption that matter could be reduced to two elements: mercury and sulphur. Also the notion of the convertibility of air to water. His bent for astrology—an interest he would not give up though he condemned its effect. And his belief in the possibility of prolonging human life indefinitely.

Two other basic theories of Bacon's philosophy can also be traced to Renaissance magical and alchemical sources: the ideal of man's scientific domination of nature, and the idea of man as nature's 'servant and interpreter', as opposed to the traditional definition of man as 'reasoning animal'; though he reshaped these concepts so that they assumed a very different significance in his philosophy. However, to appreciate their difference as well as their similarity we must recall the position held by magic in the Renaissance. Most of the important magical texts were based on older writings: thus Agrippa's *Occult Philosophy (Philosophia occulta)* was indebted to *Picatrix*. Yet the evaluation of magic and of its human and social function underwent a radical change at this time. Cornelius Agrippa, one of the foremost Renaissance magical writers, describes this change in his *Dedicatory letter to Johannes Trithemius:*

> The outstanding question was this: why is it that although magic originally occupied the pinnacle of excellence in the judgement of all the ancient philosophers and was always held in the highest veneration by those great sages and priests of antiquity, subsequently (from the beginning of the rise of the Catholic Church) it became an object of hatred and suspicion to the holy Fathers, and was at last hissed off the stage by the theologians, condemned by the sacred canons and, in fine, outlawed by the judgement of all laws?
>
> (pp. 11-17)

Indeed as Eugenio Garin has said, the magician of the Middle Ages was hunted and persecuted as the heretical disturber of godly order and reason; he was looked upon as a being who dwelt beyond the boundaries of the rational in contact with demons and the powers of evil.

Such accusations led to the confusion of magic with necromancy, of judicial with mathematical astrology and of ritualistic with experimental alchemy. Only the complete revaluation of man's significance in the world and of his relation to nature could reinstate magic as a 'human science' worthy of mankind and to be practised without shame. Thus magic ceased to be the disturber of universal order and of a fixed celestial structure when order and structure began to be contested from all sides; and in the Renaissance it acquired the status of an intellectual achievement praised by Ficino, Pico, Bruno, and Campanella. This status was to be maintained till the beginning of the modern era of Kepler, Bacon, Gassendi, and even Descartes.

One of the basic theories of Renaissance philosophy was the absence of a specific nature in man and his ability to acquire the nature of his choice. This theory was adopted by Pico and Bovillus among others, yet it never took a substantial hold on Bacon. For him man's powers were not infinite but always subject to the laws of nature (*obsessus legibus naturae*) and he cannot break or loosen the causal ties that govern it. Man's portion is neither to praise his infinite freedom nor to preserve his essential unity with the whole, but to realise that, in order to consolidate his limited power he must adapt himself to nature, submit to its commands and assist in developing its operations. Only thus can he achieve the true mastery of nature, because to dominate nature man must be its servant and interpreter. That is why it is not only harmful but foolish to imagine that man can penetrate the divine spheres with his senses and his reason, for the possibility of freely operating upon nature does not in any way imply the possibility of doing so how and when he pleases, but only of knowing no limits to those operations that observe the laws of nature and are essentially no more than a development of natural operations.

This idea of man's position in the world gives a clue to Bacon's concept of science and to his interest in the objective aspects of ethical life, his interest in reading faces and in the art of personal success and his partiality to Machiavelli's naturalism.

Yet Bacon's idea of a science serving nature by speeding or delaying operations should not be seen as an historical novelty; if we open one of the most popular texts of Renaissance magic—a text on which Bacon certainly meditated—we read:

> Therefore natural magic is that which having contemplated the virtues of all natural and celestial things and carefully studied their order proceeds to make known the hidden and secret powers of nature in such a way that inferior and superior things are joined by an interchanging application of each to each; thus incredible miracles are often accomplished not so much by art as by nature, to whom this art is as a servant when working at these things. For this reason magicians are like careful explorers of nature only directing what nature has formerly prepared, uniting actives to passives and often succeeding in anticipating results so that these things are popularly held to be miracles when they are really no more than anticipations of natural operations; as if someone made roses flower in March or grapes ripen, or even more remarkable things such as clouds, rain, thunder, various species of animals and an infinite transformation of things . . . therefore those who believe the operations of magic to be above or against nature are mistaken because they are only derived from nature and in harmony with it.

This passage from Cornelius Agrippa shows clearly that the so-called miracles of magic are not, like the miracles of saints, a violation of natural laws, but the result of developing natural powers. They are miracles only in the et-

ymological sense: things worthy of admiration. And this definition of natural magic is akin to Bacon's concept of an art following faithfully in the footsteps of nature, incapable of miracles because it is a human art with human limitations. (pp. 17-19)

[We know] that the metaphysical aspects of magic and alchemy had little or no influence on Bacon; but he did borrow from this tradition the idea of science as the servant of nature assisting its operations and, by stealth and cunning, forcing it to yield to man's domination; as well as the idea of knowledge as power. In fact Bacon's definition of magic is an almost literal repetition of Agrippa's words in the passage quoted earlier:

> I however understand it as the science which applies the knowledge of hidden forms to the production of wonderful operations; and by uniting (as they say) actives with passives displays the wonderful works of nature.

In a long list in the ***Great Works of Nature for the Particular Use of Mankind (Magnalia naturae praecipue quoad usus humanos)*** Bacon also includes examples of 'anticipations' used by Agrippa:

> Acceleration of time in maturation.
> Acceleration of germination.
> Impressing of air, and raising of tempests.
> Making of new species.
> Altering of complexions, and fatness and leanness.

It is not difficult to see why, in the fifth aphorism of the ***Day of Preparation (Parasceve),*** Bacon gives such prominence to the art of operating on bodies and altering substances to force nature into various unnatural forms. In the second chapter of the ***De augumentis,*** Book II, we are again confronted with the notion of a natural history assisting the passage 'from the wonders of nature to the wonders of art' (all that is required of the natural historian, however, is to observe the spontaneous development of nature so as to master it and use it for his own ends). And the opening paragraphs of the ***New Organon*** acquire a new significance beside the Renaissance texts quoted above:

> Man being the servant and interpreter of Nature can do and understand so much and so much only as he has observed in fact or in thought of the course of Nature: beyond this he neither knows anything nor can do anything.

> Towards the effecting of works all that man can do is put together or part assunder natural bodies. The rest is done by Nature working within.

Bacon's partiality to magic and alchemy, his wish to see them reinstated as the ultimate aims of human effort, are proofs of the influence of this tradition:

> The aim of magic is to recall natural philosophy from the vanity of speculations to the importance of experiments. Alchemy aims at separating and extracting the heterogeneous elements latent and implicit in natural substances, purifying what is polluted, releasing what is obstructed and bringing to maturation the unripe.

If Bacon had reservations about magic and alchemy they were not concerned with the experimental nature of their enquiries, for the idea of an active, inventive science was basic to his own method.

If we study the historical sources of a given idea and the recurrence of traditional concepts in even the more revolutionary contexts we may avoid the pitfall of taking all past philosophers for innovators or precursors, but we run the risk of making the opposite mistake and ignoring the novelty of traditional concepts refashioned by new interpretations to meet new demands. In this way scholars have successfully proved that Bacon was not the prodigy of the Encyclopedists but a product of his age, and then, without further investigation, have classed him among medieval or Renaissance thinkers. However, Bacon definitely detached himself from Renaissance alchemical and scientific traditions when he set up as a model for his New Science the mechanical arts with their progressive collaborative procedures. For he wanted science to depart from arbitrary uncontrolled personal research and turn instead to organised collaborative experiment, and he believed his logic would make the conquest of new truths possible. He was not interested in transmitting acquired truths and therefore refuted contentious Scholastic learning; because he saw science as a collaboration of seekers he stressed the importance of strict methods clearly and simply stated to provide rules for further experiments and ensure progress. (pp. 21-3)

Bacon pursued his plan of scientific reform with astonishing perseverance and very little success. Apart from the actual reorganisation of research on a practical, collective basis he wanted to see it supported by the State or some public organisation, and he also dreamt of an international brotherhood of scientists. (p. 23)

Bacon's efforts, as we know, were unsuccessful—'My zeal was taken for ambition', he wrote in 1603. But that same year his hopes were rekindled when James I came to the throne. In 1605 in the *Advancement of Learning* Bacon invoked the sovereign's aid once again. His programme had now assumed new proportions, for he not only clamoured for new institutions of learning but also for the reorganisation of the principal existing ones: the universities. He wrote:

> All works are overcomen by amplitude of reward, by soundness of direction and by conjunction of labours. The first multiplieth endeavours, the second preventeth error and the third supplieth the frailty of man.

But in the universities scholars were content with new editions and more accurate reprints of classical works, and ever more abundant glossaries and notes. While students became expert at debating and formal reasoning they were wholly ignorant of vast spheres of knowledge. The art of argumentation was reduced to 'childish sophistry and ridiculous affectation' and study restricted to a handful of texts, or even to no more than those of Aristotle. There were few facilities for experiment and botanical gardens only grew plants for medicinal purposes. Responsible persons would have to be engaged by the universities to report on progress in all branches of learning and to encourage

interest in unpopular branches. Finally relations should be established with scientific organisations all over Europe for an exchange of results and other information. Thus a brotherhood of scientists would develop, similar to the natural brotherhood in families.

When Bacon finally realised the impossibility of reorganising the universities to suit his purpose he still hoped to obtain the personal control of certain colleges: Westminster, Eton, Winchester; Trinity and St John's Colleges, Cambridge; and Magdalen College, Oxford.

There is an outline of Bacon's programme in the private *Free Commentaries (Commentarius solutus)* of 1608 and, under a slightly different form, in the long unpublished *Refutation of Philosophies (Redargutio philosophiarum)* and *Thought and Vision (Cogitata et visa).* It recurs with further alterations in the *New Organon* and *De augmentis,* but he did not set it down in its final consistent form till the *New Atlantis,* in a passage describing Solomon's house, where it is no longer presented as a project but as a Utopian dream. Indeed this plan, never realised during Bacon's lifetime, marked the birth of scientific humanism for the founders of the Royal Society and later for the Encyclopedists; and through humanism it has inspired some of the more progressive forms of European culture.

Bacon's plan for the reform of science was his great contribution to culture. It inspired the Encyclopedists' notion of the aims and purpose of man. . . . [For example,] Bacon's influence can be detected in d'Alembert's objections to the 'superiority of the liberal arts' and in his programme for a history of the arts 'a history of the uses to which man has put the products of nature to satisfy his needs or his curiosity'.

For Bacon science was not a luxury to be indulged in after human needs were satisfied, a detached contemplation, or an aspiring towards truth. This, however, was the picture which had come down through the centuries, and if the paint had worn a little thin in places it was still basically the same. Aristotle was the most coherent exponent of this view of science which stemmed from the economic structure of a society where slaves made mechanical devices unnecessary or even useless, and where contempt for the worker was extended to the work itself, depriving it of all cultural value. . . . For Aristotle the aims of artisan and merchant alike are degrading because their occupations are base and require no special skill. Thus the contrasts between slave and free citizen, artisan and scientist, practical and theoretical knowledge became merged during the classical and medieval eras for most of civilised Europe.

But Bacon saw the development of the mechanical arts as a new and exciting cultural event, and his reappraisal of their social and scientific significance and of their aims enabled him to disprove some of Aristotle's theories concerning the relation of nature to art.

For Bacon the 'history of arts' was but a section of natural history; by asserting this view he departed radically from the traditional opposition of art and nature where the former is only a vain attempt to imitate the latter. According to this tradition nature includes principles of infinite motion while the products of art, moved by exterior principles, can never successfully imitate the spontaneity of natural motion. Bacon exposed the relation of this doctrine to Aristotle's theory of 'species' where a natural product such as a tree is defined as possessing a 'primal form' while an artificial product such as a table possesses only a 'secondary form'. For Bacon natural and artificial objects possessed the same kind of form and essence, and differed only in their cause. Art was man added to nature, and if in one phenomenon the necessary conditions for its existence were naturally conjoined and in another they were conjoined by the art of man this did not make them incongruous. Man could only affect nature by joining or separating natural bodies. By distinguishing art from nature philosophers were led to consider art as a mere adjunct to nature and the consequences of this attitude were fatal, causing man to despair of ever being able to influence and improve the conditions of his existence.

Bacon voices his misgivings as to the practical consequences of Aristotle's theory in the *Masculine Birth of Time (Temporis partus masculus),* violently attacking Galen:

> Baleful star! Plague of the Human race! You would have us believe that only Nature can produce true compound. You snatch at the notion that the heat of the sun and the heat of fire are different things and parade this opinion with the malicious intention of lessening human power wherever you can and bolstering ignorance to all eternity through dispair of any improvement.

For Bacon science had a public, democratic and collaborative character, individual efforts contributing to its general success and the common good of all.

> Further it will not be amiss to distinguish the three kinds and as it were grades of ambition in mankind. The first is of those who desire to extend their own power in their native country; which kind is vulgar and degenerate. The second is of those who labour to extend the power of their country and its dominion among men. This certainly has more dignity, though not less covetousness. But if a man endeavours to establish and extend the power and dominion of the human race itself over the Universe his ambition (if ambition it can be called) is without doubt a both more wholesome thing and a more noble than the other two.

And if, he said, there are some men who take up science out of idle curiosity, and some to acquire a reputation, and others still to distinguish themselves in argument, there are yet a few who take it up for its real end which is the benefit of the entire human race. Thus there are men who see science as a bed to rest upon, or an arcade wherein to stroll, or a tall tower to satisfy their pride, or a fortress for warring, or a market place, but very few see it as it really is: a rich store for the glory of God and the good of humanity.

Thus Bacon implicitly refuted the traditional image of the enlightened sage and the conception of scientific collaboration as a meeting of *illuminati* jealously guarding their precious, mysterious discoveries. The distinction between ordinary mortals and the enlightened genius is prevalent in all European cultures from the Pythagoreans to the Gnostics, from Averroes to Ficino, and is even to be found at the dawn of modern civilisation together with the new ideals of scientific technology, co-operative progressive science and the union of knowledge and action. (pp. 24-7)

Bacon attacked pitilessly [occultist] attitudes and the ideals they implied. In the *Temporis partus masculus* he describes Paracelsus as a monster and a fanatical breeder of phantasms whose inquiries are surrounded by the trumpets of ostentation, the subterfuge of darkness, and connivance with religion. He describes Agrippa as a clown who turned everything into a futile joke, and Cardano as an untiring weaver of cobwebs, for ever in contradiction with all things and with himself. In the *Redargutio philosophiarum* his attacks are more explicit: if magic, encompassed in a framework of lies, is put to any use, it is only for its novelty or to provoke admiration, never for its real worth. A peculiarity of philosophical demonstrations, continues Bacon, is that they make everything seem less admirable than it is; but to make things appear more admirable is a form of deceit.

Bacon's target here was an attitude typical of all magic, but of Renaissance magic in particular. Della Porta among others describes the magician's aims:

> The magician who has an understanding of these matters mingles inferior things with superior qualities and extracts in this way from the very heart of nature the secrets enclosed therein—then he makes public the things he has found to be true so that all may know of them—and be full of good will towards the Artificer and praise him and honour his great powers.
>
> . . . And if you should wish for more magnificent results and to be considered truly admirable . . . then take up the study and the understanding of causes.

This is what Bacon had termed vulgar and degenerate ambition, the attitude to science which he compares to building a tall tower to satisfy one's pride. For the ethics of his new scientific research were inspired from the much despised mechanical arts:

> We have also houses of deceits of the senses; where we represent all manner of feats of juggling, false apparitions, impostures and illusions and their fallacies. And surely you will easily believe that we that have so many things truly natural which induce admiration, could in a world of particulars deceive the senses, if we would disguise those things and labour to make them seem more miraculous. But we do hate all impostures and lies; in so much as we have severly forbidden it to all our fellows under pain of ignominy and fines, that they do not shew any natural work or thing adorned or swelling; but only pure as it is and without all affectation of strangeness.

Bacon's reservations and his censures of magical and alchemical tradition concerned this one aspect only.

> Astrology, natural magic, and alchemy, of which sciences nevertheless the ends and pretences are noble . . . but the derivations and

prosecutions to these ends both in theories and in practices are full of error and vanity.

According to Bacon, magic endeavours to dominate and to improve nature; and for this it should be imitated. Where it needs revising is in its claim to use one man's inspiration instead of the organised efforts of the human race, and to make science serve individual ends rather than mankind.

Bacon condemned magic on ethical grounds. He accused it of fraud, of a craze for genius, and of megalomania; he refuted its non-progressive, non-co-operative methods and especially its attempts to replace human sweat by a few drops of elixir or an easy combination of substances. He was convinced that only infinite patience could unravel the 'riddles of nature'. Out of humility towards his Creator, affection for his fellows, pity for the sufferings of mankind, loathing of ignorance and love of truth, man should abandon or at least set aside those absurd philosophers who have trampled the works of God underfoot and claimed, on the grounds of a few hurried experiments, to have created a complete natural philosophy that no scholar could possibly take seriously. The pages of nature's great book should be read with patience and reverence, pausing and meditating over each one and discarding all easy interpretations. The language of nature must be learnt anew: it had suffered the confusion of the Tower of Babel and man must come to it again, not searching for marvels and surprises but handling, like a little child, each letter of its alphabet.

Bacon explicitly declared that his new scientific method would leave little scope for individual talent for it was to be a leveller of intelligences. Some scholars, showing a remarkable lack of insight, have taken this to indicate Bacon's optimistic faith in his method: that owing to its mechanical nature it would run, as it were, on its own steam once it had been instituted; and there have been violent objections to his so-called endeavours to make thought 'run on pre-established tracks'. However, it suffices to set Bacon's statement in its historical context for it to appear as no more than a reaction against magical and alchemical methods of research where results were entrusted to mysterious individual operations. Bacon opposed to this lack of method a system based on the division of labour and on a progressive continuity and it is to this aspect of his method that he alludes when he compares it to a ruler or a compass. In the absence of instruments we must rely on a steady hand and a sharp eye, qualities which are subjective and uncontrollable.

> For my part I am emphatically of the opinion that man's wits require not the addition of feathers and wings, but of leaden weights. Men are very far from realising how strict and disciplined a thing is research into truth and nature, and how little it leaves to the judgement of men.

What debars magic and alchemy from the status of science, continues Bacon, is precisely the burden they entrust to individual judgement and skill. Alchemical and magical research make use of a minimum of rules that have never been properly integrated into the methods because their essential communicability has not been stressed. They are expressed in symbols—not to be confused with the symbols used in modern chemistry with which they have nothing in common—referring by analogy and correspondence either to the Whole or to a Universal Spirit, or to God.

In the *New Organon,* Book II, paragraph four, Bacon made a deliberate attempt to modify alchemical rules to meet the needs of technical science. Here he acknowledges the aims of the alchemist and uses almost exactly their own vocabulary, but he refutes their subjective methods with decisive arguments. Suppose we wish to induce a new nature upon a given substance, he says, let us see how to set about it: we must be provided with a set of well defined rules because for an operation such as this a method is required that is reliable and comprehensible and that uses only the materials of which one disposes and is less complex than the operation undertaken: an abstract model, in fact, reduced to its simplest expression. The alchemists instead refer to supposedly sacred texts. Thus they can only accuse themselves for their inevitable failure, and with increasing self-reproach they repeat the experiment over and over again, convinced that they have misinterpreted the wilfully equivocal instructions in some minute detail.

Such were the views which distinguished Bacon from the great Renaissance thinkers. It is true that Della Porta, Cardano, Paracelsus and so many others stressed the importance of experiment, and, like Bacon, acknowledged the revolutionary significance of sixteenth-century discoveries and insisted on the practical aspect of every enquiry. However, they persisted in seeing scientific realisations as the fruit of individual efforts, the privilege of exceptional gifts or the result of a secret collaboration between *illuminati.* These theories exclude Bacon from their ranks.

Bacon's attitude to science and nature finds its expression in a tone of quiet modesty prevalent in much of his writing:

> My motives in publishing are the following: I wish to spread among men all that makes intellectual relationships and freedom of thought possible, so that it may be passed from mouth to mouth; the rest, with discernement and common sense will be accomplished by hand. Verily, I am setting in motion something with which others shall experiment. Indeed it is not in my nature to be always preoccupied with external events, I am no pursuer of fame, neither do I wish to establish a sect like an heretic, and I consider that it would be despicable and ridiculous to try and obtain personal advantage from so noble an enterprise. It is enough to know that I have worked for a good cause and written my books—with this last, Fortune herself cannot interfere.

It is only by wrenching this passage from its historical context that scholars have managed to give it an appearance of political scheming. The following is one of the many portraits Bacon draws of the scientist according to his own ideal:

> There were some fifty men there, all of mature years, not a young man among them, all bearing the stamp of dignity and probity . . . At his entry they were chatting easily among themselves but sitting in rows as if expecting some-

body. Not long after there entered to them a man of peaceful and serene air, save that his face had become habituated to the expression of pity. They all stood up in his honour, and he looked around and said with a smile: 'It is more than I can understand as I recognize you one by one, how you can all be at leisure at the same time. How is it to be explained?' Then one of the company replied: 'You yourself are the explanation, for we all put what you have to tell us above any other business.' 'Then', said he, 'I am incurring a heavy responsibility for the total of time that will be lost here, during which you might be all going about your several tasks serving I know not how many men. I must not keep you waiting any longer.' Which said, he took his seat, not on a platform or pulpit, but on a level with the rest and delivered the following address.

The scientist represented here is certainly more like Galileo or Newton than Paracelsus, Cardano, or Agrippa, who was known as 'philosopher, genius, hero, God and all'. Such classical composure—reminiscent of the early humanist conversations—is very different from the titanic bearing of the Renaissance magician; and there is, besides, a quiet confidence that comes from knowing the unlimited powers made available to man by technology and collaboration. The theatre of human endeavours is no longer only the city but the whole world. This portrait is inspired by a totally new idea of science. It is no longer the haphazard jotting of random ideas but methodical, systematic thought; it is more than experience, observation and a rejection of authority; it is not the solitary inspiration of the individual genius, but collaborative research institutionalised in specific social and linguistic forms. Above all scientific knowledge is not the fruit of enlightened, exceptional wisdom; it is a human product and tends to improve both the intellectual and the material conditions of the human race. Bacon's contribution to the expansion of these ideas was considerable; they are strikingly illustrated in his image of science as a relay race of torch-bearers where no single runner can ever be a substitute for the whole team. The aim of each participant is to free the world from the domination of magic, and though Bacon was finally entangled once again in its snares, the manner and rules of the race had been changed for ever. (pp. 31-5)

Paolo Rossi, in his Francis Bacon: From Magic to Science, *translated by Sacha Rabinovitch, The University of Chicago Press, 1968, 280 p.*

Lewis Mumford   (essay date 1961)

[*Primarily known for his works about cities and architecture, Mumford gained critical acclaim for his writings on a variety of disciplines. His works include* The Condition of Man *(1944),* The City in History *(1961), and* Interpretations and Forecasts: 1922-1972 *(1973). In the following excerpt from a 1961 paper included in the last-named work, Mumford discusses Bacon's conception of science as a technological endeavor, questioning the philosopher's glorification of technology. In Mumford's view, the current domination of technology over science, which seemingly confirms Bacon's predic-*

tions, leads to a narrow and impoverished conception of science.]

The title of this paper, 'Science as Technology,' would not have surprised or shocked Francis Bacon, for perhaps his most original contribution to the enlargement of the province of science was his understanding of its great future role in transforming the physical conditions of life. But I am sure that the conclusions that I shall finally present—conclusions in the form of doubts, challenges, and questions—would have shocked him quite as much as it will, I fear, shock many [readers], for his faith in science as a source of technology, and in technology itself as the final justification of science must now, after four centuries, be submitted to an historic evaluation and the pragmatic test. When Bacon's assumptions are rigorously examined, this should, I submit, lead to a modification of Bacon's original hopes and even a radical change in our own attitude toward many Baconian beliefs we have, somewhat blindly, taken to be axiomatic.

Doubtless it is natural, in celebrating Bacon's anniversary, that we should out of piety overemphasize those aspects of modern civilization that have confirmed his predictions and surpassed his none-too-cautious expectations. This is particularly true when we consider science as technology, for it is precisely in this department that his most extravagant intuitions have been realized. Three centuries before Jules Verne and H. G. Wells, to say nothing of later writers of science fiction, Bacon anticipated the multifold uses that technology would make of science.

Though Bacon was undoubtedly expressing, as a sensitive artist often does, the changing temper of his age, long before it was visible in the streets, his very predictions gave confidence in the new orientation toward the physical world as the only area in life sufficiently detached from subjective fantasies and emotional urges to serve as a common meeting ground for minds otherwise ideologically separated. Men who could not agree upon the nature of God, could come to terms by making a god out of nature, once they had hit upon a method that ruled out all experience that could not be experimentally repeated or independently verified. By following through the practical consequences of science, Bacon sought to show even those who were engaged in the most abstract calculations and experiments that they might ultimately confer greater benefits upon the race than those who were laboring to improve it by law, by morals, or by government, or who sought to change the environment solely by manual labor and art.

Now the notion that the scientific observation of air, earth, water, and fire might lead to fruitful applications in technology, must have occurred to many minds, Archimedes for one, Hero of Alexandria for another, and Bacon's medieval namesake for a third, before Francis Bacon himself elaborated the idea. But Bacon helped mightily to close the gap between the spheres of science and technology, one long considered liberal but exquisitely useless, except perhaps in medicine, the other, however useful, cursed by its servile and debasing nature. Bacon held that the advancement of knowledge depended upon more than the abstract, logic-disciplined exercises of mind. He felt that science in future would rest increasingly on a collective organization, not just on the work of individuals of ability, operating under their own power; and he held, further, that instruments and apparatus were as necessary in the technology of systematic thought as they were in mining or bridge-building.

"The unassisted hand," observed Bacon, "and the understanding left to itself possess little power." This was an even more revolutionary conception than Leonardo da Vinci's aphorism: "Science is the captain, practice the soldiers"; for it implied that the captain himself had something to learn from the men in the ranks. And it was no less revolutionary, no less effective, because, from the standpoint of a mature scientific method it was, by overcompensation, too one-sided. Bacon's very overemphasis on the collective apparatus of science, his close concern for the operational and instrumental aspects of scientific thought, were probably needed to overcome the bias of traditional leisure-class culture, theological and humanistic, operating by choice in a social vacuum. That was a necessary contribution in his own day—as necessary as the opposite position may become in our own time.

The timeliness and significance of Bacon's contribution here should have saved him from a little of the patronizing deflation that he has been subject to in recent years. Without doubt, he was blandly indifferent to the actual procedures of successful scientists in his own time, like Gilbert and Galileo; and, further, it is no doubt true that Bacon grossly overestimated the fruitfulness of mere fact-collecting and fumbling empirical observation, though there are still areas where this kind of systematic preparatory effort yields a certain reward. By the same token, Bacon seriously underestimated, one might almost say he entirely ignored, the immense liberation that would be effected in both science and technics through the audacities of pure mathematics, dealing with possibilities and probabilities that are, until experimentally verified, outside the field of direct observation and sensory experience.

On his own terms Bacon could not and did not anticipate the sweeping transformations of the entire framework of thought effected by single minds, almost destitute of apparatus, like Newton, Clerk Maxwell, or Einstein. Even Galileo's scientific world, a world conceived solely in terms of primary qualities and measurable quantities, was almost unthinkable to Bacon. But to offset these disabilities, which plainly reduced Bacon's importance as a philosopher of science, he had a strong sense of the sociological context of science, and of the appeal that this would make to scientists, to inventors, to engineers, and to their countless human beneficiaries. He foresaw that science would become a corporate enterprise, subject to deliberate organization; and that the social goal of science, as he phrased it in the *New Atlantis,* would be "the enlargement of the bounds of humane empire, to the effecting of all things possible."

Curiously, what is most fresh and original in Bacon, his conception of the role of science as the spiritual arm, so to speak, of technology, is the hardest part for our contemporaries to appreciate fully today. Partly they are put off by the fact that he absurdly arrayed these new conceptions in an elaborate metaphorical court dress; but even more they are alienated, or to speak more frankly, bored, because the ideas themselves have become so engrained in our life that most of us can hardly realize that they had a specific point of origin. But if Bacon failed miserably in interpreting the methodology of science, as it was actually taking shape in his own time, he leaped ahead four centuries to the mode and milieu in which science and technics both flourish, in their peculiar fashion, today. When Benjamin Franklin founded the American Philosophical Society, he felt it necessary to stress its aim of promoting "useful knowledge": but if he had been even closer to Bacon's spirit he would have realized that usefulness is implicit in every kind of scientific knowledge, almost it would seem in proportion to its degree of abstraction and its isolation from the immediate practical concerns. The singular mission of science, as a technological agent, is to suggest uses and outlets, issuing from purely theoretic and experimental discoveries, that could not have been conceived until the scientific work itself was done.

In the past, certain branches of science, like geometry, had developed out of practical needs, like the Egyptian need for surveying anew the boundaries that had been effaced in flooded fields; and some of that interplay between practical needs and scientific investigation of course still goes on, as in the classic instance of Pasteur's researches on ferments in response to the pleas of French wine growers. But the enormous advances of science in every field have not waited for such direct stimuli, though it may very well be that they are indirect responses organically connected with the needs and purposes of our society at a hundred different points. Thus, it is quite probably not by accident that the electronics of radar location have coincided with coordinate advances in the physics and technology of high-speed flight. Increasingly, however, it is the advance of science that suggests a new technological application: indeed the technological by-products seem to multiply in direct relation to the scope and freedom of scientific research.

Bacon's interest in the practical applications of science naturally endeared him to Macaulay and the other utilitarians of the nineteenth century, for in his *Novum Organum* Bacon boldly asserted that the "legitimate goal of the sciences is the endowment of human life with new inventions and riches." This is a more questionable goal than Bacon thought: but it is because of the accelerated fulfillment of these promises by the sciences, especially during the last half-century, that national governments and great industrial corporations have vastly augmented their financial contributions to scientific research. Bacon's merit was to make plain that there was no aspect of nature that would not lend itself to transformation and improvement through the unrestricted application of the experimental method. Necessity had always been the most reluctant mother of invention: Bacon understood that curiosity was a far more fertile parent, and that the inventions so promoted would become the mother of new necessities.

But Bacon went further: he saw that curiosity, to be fully effective, must enlist, not solitary and occasional minds, but a corps of well-organized workers, each exercising a specialized function and operating in a restricted area. By the technological organization of science as he portrayed it in the *New Atlantis,* he proposed to fabricate an engine capable of turning out useful knowledge in the same fashion that a well-organized factory would, shortly after Bacon's prediction, turn out textiles or shoes. Bacon's description of this division of labor strikes us as quaint and finicking, because of its static, ritualistic assignment of tasks; but those who would dismiss it altogether are wider of the mark than Bacon; for part of the immense quantitative output of contemporary science is surely due to its ability to make use, not only of a few great directive minds, but of a multitude of specialized piece workers, narrowly trained for their tasks, deliberately denied any individual opportunity to explore a wider field; whose part in the whole process increasingly resembles that of a factory worker on an assembly line. The corporate personality has taken over the attributes of the individual thinker; and as science comes more and more to rely for its results upon complicated and extremely expensive apparatus, like electronic computers and cyclotrons, no work along present lines can be done without close attachment to a corporate organization. The dangers that this technological advance offers to science have not yet been sufficiently canvassed; but they will perhaps nullify no small part of its rewards.

Bacon's conception of the organization of science as a technology did not altogether overlook the part played by individual creative minds: he even had a name for such seminal investigators, for he called them "Lamps," and indicated that their function was to "direct new experiments of a Higher Light, more penetrating into nature." But his peculiar contribution was to sense that, if the illuminations and insights of creative minds were to have the widest kind of application, they would need abundant collective support: state aid, corporate organization, systematic conferences and publications, liberal rewards and honors, and finally, public exhibition and celebration in museums of science and industry. It was these features of collective organization and state regimentation, not perhaps entirely unknown in pre-Christian Alexandria, that Bacon so presciently recognized, advocated, and exalted. So it was not only the Royal Society or the American Philosophical Society that Bacon anticipated: his quaint account of the future in the *New Atlantis* did ample justice to the new functions of our foundations for scientific research, and our specialized institutes and laboratories that utilize hundreds and even thousands of workers in what has increasingly become—with great rapidity since the national state itself became the main patron—factories for the mass production of knowledge, technologically exploitable and financially profitable.

In looking back over the fulfillment of Bacon's anticipations, it is plain that there were two critical points. The first occurred in the first half of the nineteenth century, when for the first time purely theoretic researches in physics, by Volta, Ohm, Henry, and Faraday, resulted, almost within a generation, in the invention of the electric telegraph, the dynamo, the electric motor; and within two generations in the invention of the telephone, the electric lamp, the x-ray, and the wireless telegraph: all of these being inventions that were not merely impracticable but

technically inconceivable until pure scientific research made them live possibilities. The methods that were so fruitful in mechanics and electronics were then applied, with growing success, in organic chemistry and biology; though significantly enough the parts of technology with the longest accumulation of purely empiric knowledge, like mining and metallurgy, remained almost impervious to the advances of science.

The second critical point came during the first half of the twentieth century, along with a change of scale and magnitude partly brought about, almost automatically, by the expansion of the facilities for communication and the exploitation of new sources of power. This change lifted hitherto inviolable limits on human activities: a shot could be heard around the world by means of radio more than eleven times faster than it could be heard by the unaided ear a mile away. At this point, science itself became the technology of technologies; and as the mass production of scientific knowledge went hand in hand with the mass production of inventions and products derived from science, the scientist came to have a new status in society, equivalent to that earlier occupied by the captains of industry. He, too, was engaged in mass production. (pp. 159-64)

Not merely have the sciences, then, become technologies, but the scientist himself, caught in the corporate process, is fast becoming the model of a docile, standardized, organization man, imprisoned by his own obsolete premises, incapable of making his escape without altering those premises. . . . As an agent of technology, science no longer has the immunities or the irresponsibilities that it claimed for itself during its great quarrels with the Church. Today, the greatest danger to science comes not from the hostility of traditional institutions but from the patronage of contemporary ones.

Now if the fulfillment of Bacon's dream deserves our respectful recognition of his prophetic insights, it also imposes upon us a special duty—that of dissociating ourselves from the mythology he so largely helped to promote, so as to appraise, in the light of historic experience, his unexamined premises. These premises are now so thoroughly institutionalized that most of our contemporaries continue to act upon them without even a quiver of doubt. But observe: science as technology presents a series of problems that science, as the disinterested examination of nature in search of rational understanding, never confronted; for already it shows the same deep irrationalities and absurdities that mass production in other fields has brought about. The chief premise common to both technology and science is the notion that there are no desirable limits to the increase of knowledge, of material goods, of environmental control; that quantitative productivity is an end in itself, and that every means should be used to expand the facilities for quantitative expansion and production.

This was a defensible position in the seventeenth century when an economy of scarcity still prevailed everywhere. Then, each new facility for production, each fresh increment of energy and goods, each new scientific observation or experiment, was needed to make up the terrible deficiencies in consumable goods and verifiable knowledge.

But today our situation is precisely the opposite of this. Because of the magnificent, awe-inspiring success of the sciences in widening the domain of prediction and control, in penetrating the hitherto inviolable mysteries of nature, in augmenting human power on every plane, we face a new predicament derived from this very economy of abundance: that of starvation in the midst of plenty. (pp. 164-65)

Our society has already reached the paradoxical state wherein our massive additions to the corpus of scientific knowledge have, through mere quantitative excess, lowered our capacity to make rational use of any part of it. In the exploding universe of science, the scattered parts are traveling at an accelerated rate even farther from the human center. Because of our concentration on speed and productivity, we have ignored the need for integration and assimilation, and continuity. The dubious morals of an acquisitive society have caught the once-disinterested promoters of science, along with their strange irrational compulsions. In practice this results in an inability to use more than a small fragment of the existing corpus of knowledge—namely that which is fashionable or immediately available, because it is being commercially exploited. This has already worked havoc in medicine, as any honest physician will tell you, and the results are visible in every other professional activity.

We are now faced, accordingly, as both Norbert Wiener and I have pointed out more than once, with the situation Goethe foresaw in the fable of the Sorcerer's Apprentice: we have achieved the magic formula for automatically increasing the supply of scientific knowledge; but we have forgotten the Master Magician's formula for regulating or halting the flood, and so are on the point of drowning in it. Science as technology gets its main financial support, and therefore its overall direction, from the national government, or from great industrial corporations like those engaged in exploiting new pharmaceutical preparations, chemical pest controls, or atomic energy, and from quasi-public philanthropic foundations exerting almost equally large powers. Though the professed aim of these organizations is truth and human welfare, they are governed in perhaps an ever greater degree by the Baconian goals of riches and power. On these premises they have no concern with ordering science in accordance with some human measure, toward the fulfillment of broader human goals: for this means altering the method of mass production and slowing down the whole process. Our schools and universities are helpless to restore an organic balance, because they themselves have accepted the same ideology and rely for a large part of their activities upon endowments that are scaled to the prospects of continued expansion and quick turnover: indeed the very possibilities for professional promotion depend more upon the number of scientific papers published than upon long-term results that may not be visible for a generation or more.

Is it not time, then, that we began to ask ourselves certain questions about science as technology that Bacon, by reason of his historic position, was too uninformed to put to himself? Are we sure that the control of all natural processes by science and technics is by itself an effective way of relieving or improving man's estate? Is it not possible to have a surfeit of knowledge no less that a surfeit of food—with similar distress to and derangement of the organism? Have we not already evidence to show that science as technology may, through its inordinate growth, become increasingly irrelevant to any human concerns whatever, except that of the technologist or the corporate enterprise: that, indeed, as in the form of nuclear or bacterial weapons, it may be not merely coldly indifferent but positively hostile to human welfare?

Just because science as technology has begun to dominate every other aspect of science, we are bound, if only in self-preservation, to correct the mistakes Bacon unwittingly fostered or sanctioned. Science now makes all things possible, as Bacon believed: but it does not thereby make all possible things desirable. A good technology, firmly related to human needs, cannot be one that has a maximum productivity as its supreme goal: it must rather, as in an organic system, seek to provide the right quantity of the right quality at the right time and the right place for the right purpose. To this end deliberate regulation and self direction, in order to ensure continued growth and creativity, must govern our plans in the future, as indefinite expansion and multiplication have done during the last few centuries. The center of gravity is not the corporate organization, but the human personality, utilizing knowledge, not for the increase of power and riches, or even for the further increase of knowledge, but using it, like power and riches, for the enhancement of life. On these terms it may be that all the work that has been turned out by Solomon's Houses these last four hundred years will have to be done over again, or at least be revised and amplified and integrated and made humanly more adequate in order to do justice to all the dimensions of life.

The greatest contribution of science, the most desirable of all its many gifts, far surpassing its purely material benefits, has been its transformation of the human consciousness, through its widening illumination of the entire cosmic and historic process, and its transfer to man of the power to participate, with his whole being, in that process. Has the time not come, then—in technology as in every other aspect of the common life—to re-examine our accepted axioms and practical imperatives and to release science itself from the humanly impoverished and underdimensioned mythology of power that Francis Bacon helped to promote? (pp. 165-67)

> *Lewis Mumford, "Bacon: Science as Technology," in his* Interpretations and Forecasts: 1922-1972, Studies in Literature, History, Biography, Technics, and Contemporary Society, *Harcourt Brace Jovanovich, Inc., 1973, pp. 159-67.*

Fulton H. Anderson (essay date 1962)

[*Anderson discusses Bacon's philosophy in the context of European rationalist thought. He explains that Bacon's inductive method, although not without scientific value, essentially excludes the possibility of certain knowledge.*]

Bacon is an original and originating philosopher. He propounds, in the first place, a distinctive pluralistic philosophy by which the science of nature is rendered free from overt invasions by revealed theology and from covert incursions by the same in the guise of theologico-metaphysics. Secondly, Bacon puts "mind" out of metaphysics. Thirdly, he reorganizes natural knowledge by assigning its recognized divisions new places and functions in a new classification of the sciences. Fourthly, he sets down the principles of a distinctive metaphysical naturalism, materialistic in character. Fifthly, he undertakes to establish metaphysics through a purely inductive procedure. Sixthly, he attempts to do for induction what Aristotle did for deduction, namely, to describe in detail its principles and to exemplify its operation. Seventhly, he regards logic, not as reason in operation, not as the alignment of terms in propositions, but as a "machine" for controlling the human faculties, including both sense and reason—an instrument which operates in exacting fashion between the empirical collecting of particulars and the asserting of general axioms. Eighthly, without a lapse into deduction, he makes the observation of induced causal processes in nature, that is, of operative works, including those of art, the test of every axiom or scientific principle, from the highest—erroneously called "first" in traditional logic—to the lowest.

Let us consider, partly by way of review, some of these achievements. . . . It is Bacon's opinion that the "Prerogative of God comprehends the whole man." Man's lot, under God's dispensing, lies within the three kingdoms: the Kingdom of God—known through Revelation—in which through Divine Grace man is saved from his sin and receives his moral rule of charity; the civil kingdom, where God—as the Scriptures teach—bestows political initiative upon rulers, who are the creatures of His own making; and the kingdom of nature—known through inductive science—whose dominion has been given to man by the Creator. These three areas of knowledge are not brought by Bacon under a single classification of sciences. They have no common categories. They cannot become parts or aspects of one integrated system. Bacon's philosophical thinking—to use this phrase in a most comprehensive sense—remains pluralistic in character. The author will not permit the weakening of the placets of Revelation by any accommodation to a "unity of truth" in which the several truths of theology, metaphysics, politics, ethics, and natural philosophy are made components of a system organized either according to a principle of equality or to a scale of ascent in a hierarchy.

Attempts by thinkers of the past to bring differing kinds of truths into a single system have, in Bacon's opinion, resulted in the reduction of all. Plato made knowledge and virtue dependent on the contemplation of abstract forms divorced, beyond reconciliation, from the world of particulars. As these abstract entities became the more removed from matter and actualities, they became for this author, in an absurdity, the objects of inquiry in natural philosophy, the ends of dehumanized human desire in ethics, the foundation of rule and sovereignty in politics, the components of a dialectically constructed universe in metaphysics, and in theology the mind and power of God, now reduced to a dialectical entity.

Aristotle, in turn, laid some stress on actual particulars, but not for long. He was not content to dissect these, but must abstract them. Then he went on to define his abstractions, and not physical nature as it is, nor ethical and political motives as they are, nor metaphysical operations of specified scientific significance, nor God as Creator, for the so-called First Cause of what Aristotle calls nature is but the crowning abstraction in a system of abstractions. Aristotle's philosophical system was supposedly held together by a teleological principle, which pervaded all things from the "first bodies" to the highest and first cause. But as a comprehending, unifying principle, governing all areas of being and operation, Aristotle's teleology was of a questionable sort: for it contained a contradiction, because by definition the Stagirite had already rendered completely segregate the several regions over which it was to prevail, his metaphysics or theology, physics, ethics and politics, and the poietical sciences or arts.

Later writers under Stoic influence made an attempt to overcome Aristotle's discontinuities by bringing the operations of physical nature, human conduct, political rule, even the mind of God, within the orbit of an all-comprehending Law of Reason. However, as the extension of this principle increased, and the attempt was made to tie physical nature and God together as subjects under one law and rule, the terms and clauses became the more incomprehensible and illusory. The distinctions and exclusions required in such a case as this must of necessity dissipate any unity and authority within a law.

Bacon is a pluralist. Of philosophical opinions which make for pluralism Bacon recognizes three sorts. One of these, of which Aristotle is a supporter, affirms that nature is composed of individual substances, or entities. In this opinion Bacon agrees, but only up to the point where he argues that the objects of philosophical investigation are not particular substances, but common forms, or natures. In the *New Organon* he writes, "Though in nature nothing really exists beside individual bodies, performing pure individual acts according to a fixed law, yet in philosophy this very law, and the investigation, discovery, and explanation of it, is the foundation as well of knowledge as of operation. And it is this law, with its clauses, that I mean when I speak of *Forms;* a name which I rather adopt because it has grown into use and become familiar." It is Bacon's contention that philosophy is not concerned with particulars or individuals as such, but moves in the realm of universals. The universals which the investigator of nature seeks are forms or laws or causes, constitutive of and operative within material bodies.

A second kind of philosophical pluralism, which is also to be found in Aristotle, rests on a plurality of segregate sciences, each with distinctive principles and concepts, notions, terms, whose only bond of union is a rationale called analytic, or logic. With this, Bacon disagrees. It is his opinion that the natural sciences can be brought together through informing general axioms which are inherent within the subject matter of each and all of them. These principles are to be established inductively by a method not hitherto employed, a method which is not "logical" in character, and which operates only after the rejection of what hitherto have been received as the "first" and commanding principles of reason and the founding and segregating axioms of independent sciences.

A third sort of pluralism issues from a regard for the distinctive sources and appropriately distinctive knowledges of truly different subject matters. This is Bacon's kind of pluralism. His theology treats of the nature and will of God, the knowledge of which is given to man by Divine Revelation—a knowledge unto which man by use of his own faculties cannot attain. Bacon's political doctrine is premised on the principle of divinely bestowed sovereignty and initiative which comprehends rule by justice and law. This principle he finds in the repeated affirmations of Holy Writ, which are not to be weakened or reduced by any philosophical reconstruction of their placets. Bacon's philosophy of nature is discovered through natural inquiry. In this there is no legitimate place for a doctrine of a First Cause, which Aristotle accommodates through the services of a teleological metaphysics. The principles of nature as a body, or system, are not to be confused with what in tradition are taken to be the subjects of metaphysics, such as the four causes and matter and form. They belong only to the physics of materiate things. They are the very axioms of nature itself, and do not apply to God, nor to political sovereignty and subjection of political subjects under sovereign rule.

In the next place, Bacon rejects mind as a metaphysical principle, or entity. Mind has been made inherent within the intelligible world by Plato. In one of his latest dialogues, the *Philebus,* Plato assigns four "concauses" to the objects of inquiry: the indeterminate, the determinate, the "mixture" of these two, and *nous,* or reason—the determining principle within whatever is knowable. Plato also, in his last dialogue, the *Laws,* finds *nous,* or reason, within the elements, laws, and the cosmos generally. Aristotle, in turn, makes *nous* a kind of divine reason which actualizes in intelligence logical forms; he also makes logic a rational thing, the normal function of reason in demonstration; and he finds a *logos,* or rational principle, as something pervasive within each area of science. The Stoics identify the *nous* with their *logos,* and make this *logos* a reason within nature, man, and God. This reason they employ as an explanatory principle in three conjunctions, as the judgment of the knower, as the formal statement of judgment in the scientific proposition, and as the objective counterpart of judgment in the rational structure of the universe. With the theological Platonists, the *logoi*—the *logos* pluralized—become both ideas in the mind of God and seminal principles in nature. Causes are now reasons, and the world, as intelligible order, contains the rational principles of the Creator's mind. These several meanings of the *nous* and the *logos* and varied offices of reason are put into employment by a succession of Platonists, Peripatetics, and eclectic philosophers.

In the ***Advancement of Learning,*** a work written when the author is embarking on his "voyage of discovery"—to use his own metaphor—and mentioning doctrines which he will later amend, he includes the statement that metaphysics handles "that which supposeth . . . in nature a reason, understanding, and platform." Then, almost immediately,

Bacon goes on to say that "the natural philosophy of Democritus and some others, who did not suppose a mind or reason in the frame of things . . . seemeth to me . . . in particularities of physical causes more real and better enquired into than that of Aristotle and Plato." This qualifying of the earlier statement is what we should expect, if we bear in mind that metaphysics is being regarded by the author as universalized physics. In the Latin translation of the ***Advancement of Learning,*** the *De augmentis,* of 1623, Bacon lays stress on the greater "penetration" into nature by Democritus, the philosopher who "removed God and Mind from the structure of things, and attributed the form thereof to infinite essays and proofs of nature . . . and assigned the causes of particular things to the necessity of matter." In the same reference the author maintains that God in his wisdom has not "communicated to all natural figures and motions the characters and impressions of His providence [or knowledge]." In the early ***Valerius Terminus*** the author states that "God hath framed the mind of man as a glass capable of the image of the universal world, joying to receive the signature thereof "—"signature" and not mind of nature or of God. In the ***New Organon,*** which contains his mature philosophy, Bacon states explicitly that what are sometimes taken to be the ideas of God in nature are properly to be regarded as the Creator's "seals" or "signets" on His creation. These are not, in manner or degree, divine ideas. The seals of nature are not reasons. The laws, processes, and structures of nature are not "logical" in the traditional meaning of the term. What is logical for Bacon belongs to a method which, he says, is a "machine" to control reason as a human faculty, and not to show a rationale inherent within nature. Bacon holds that the forms, or causes, or natures of philosophy are materiate, subject to the materiate laws of matter in motion. The structures and processes which scientific axioms embody are not of a rational or a mental, let alone a divine, order. The Creator has not put into nature His own mind, or any other sort of mind.

Bacon is so impressed by the greatness and majesty of God that he cannot entertain the opinion that the forms of matter are in any manner or degree participant in or even "imitative" of the ideas of the Creator. In the ***Valerius Terminus*** he writes: "If any man shall think by view and inquiry into . . . sensible and material things, to attain to any light for the revealing of the nature or will of God, he shall dangerously abuse himself. . . . God is only self-like, having nothing in common with any creature, otherwise than as in shadow and trope. Therefore attend His will as Himself openeth it, and give unto faith that which unto faith belongeth." Man at his creation "being a spirit newly inclosed in a body of earth, he was fitted to be allured with appetite of light and liberty of knowledge," yet, through his "intruding" by natural faculties "into God's secrets and mysteries," through his "presuming to come within the oracle of [Divine] knowledge, man transgressed and fell."

For Bacon there can be no "similitude" between man and God in the matter of knowledge, but only in goodness or charity, which "is nothing else but goodness put into action or applied." The rule of charity, which "comprehends and fastens all virtues together," is given in Revelation for the governing of that part of man which is made in the Divine Image. In the *De augmentis* Bacon explains:

> We are bound to obey the divine law though we find a reluctation in our will, so are we to believe His word though we find a reluctation in our reason. . . .

> And this holds not only in those great mysteries which concern the Deity, the Creation, and the Redemption; but it pertains likewise to a more perfect interpretation of the moral law, "Love your enemies"; "do good to them that hate you," and so on. . . . To which words this applause may well be applied, "that they do not sound human"; since it is a voice beyond the light of nature.

> The use of human reason in matters of religion is of two sorts; the former in the explanation of the mystery, the latter in the inferences derived from it. With regard to the explanation of the mysteries, we see that God vouchsafes to descend to the weakness of our apprehension, by so expressing his mysteries that they may be most sensible to us. . . .

> But with regard to inferences . . . after the articles and principles of religion have been set in their true place, so as to be completely exempted from the examination of reason, it is then permitted us to derive and deduce inferences from them. . . . the first propositions are not only self-existent and self-supporting; but likewise unamenable to that reason which deduces consequent propositions. Nor yet does this hold in religion alone. . . . we see in games, as chess or the like, that the first rules and laws are merely positive, and at will; and that they must be received as they are, and not disputed; but how to play a skilful and winning game is scientific and rational. . . .

> But as the use of the human reason in things divine is of two kinds, so likewise in the use there are two kinds of excess; the one when it inquires too curiously into the manner of the mystery; the other when the same authority is attached to inferences as to principles.

When we bear in mind that Bacon has put reason, even as rationale, out of nature as system and has placed questions respecting the supreme rule of ethical conduct, the basis of political sovereignty, and the being, knowledge, and providence of God within revealed theology, we can the more readily comprehend some of the naturalistic implications of his classification of the parts of human knowledge obtainable by the exercise of human powers. This classification, which we have already stated in outline, is undoubtedly modelled on that of Aristotle. But Bacon's originality becomes immediately evident when we consider his radical modifications of the traditionally accepted Peripatetic system. According to Aristotle, there are three main sorts of science, the theoretical, the practical, and the "poietical"—the third having to do with the making of things. Each science, of whatever sort, has its own distinctive determining axioms, by which it is rendered separate from and independent of all the others. The

sciences of the theoretical group include metaphysics, mathematics, and physics; these manifest several degrees of abstraction. Metaphysics is the most abstract and most universal of all the sciences, having to do with being *qua* being, which may be regarded, in several contexts of explanation in turn, as Pure Form, the First Cause, the First Mover, and God—the object of whose thought is Himself. This supreme science is founded on the metaphysical—as distinct from the logical—principle of identity: What is, is. From this principle is derived both being and unity, the latter convertible with being, as is also goodness which is being in act. The second of the theoretical sciences, mathematics, treats of quantity in abstraction from motion and matter, while the subject matter of the third, physics, consists of materiate things in motion. The motions of physics may be classified in a general way as generation and decay, augmentation, change in character, and local motion. Of the practical sciences, Aristotle names two, ethics and politics—in which ethics attains its end. While in the theoretical sciences the objects concerned cannot be other than they are, in those called practical the subject matter includes adventitious factors, such as choice and deliberate willing on the part of human agents. The third general sort of science includes the arts: medicine, cooking, architecture, husbandry, navigation, poetry, rhetoric, and so on. When describing these "poietical" sciences—those which have to do with making—Aristotle draws a distinction between nature and art. In the case of the latter, a secondary form is imposed on a primary, natural form—the form of a table, for example, or of a house, or the form of a tree. Some of the Peripatetics divide the arts into those of a higher, an "intellectual," sort, such as poetry and music, and those which are "manual," and lower, such as cooking, shoemaking, and husbandry. Aristotle recognized a science or art, namely analytic, later called logic, with its induction and deduction, which he did not place in any one of the divisions of his sciences because, in his view, it was assumed by all.

Aristotle's universe consists of fifty-five concentric spheres, with the earth at the centre. The outermost sphere is the *Primum Mobile*—the First Moved by the Prime Mover. This transmits motion to the remaining spheres in turn. The earth and terrestrial bodies are composed of four elements: fire, earth, air, and water. Terrestrial motion is rectilinear in character. Through this, the elements or "first bodies" tend to take up their respective appropriate places. Actually, the "first bodies" are never found in isolation, and the motions of earthly bodies are always combinations of several rectilinear motions. The element assigned by Aristotle to celestial bodies is a fifth essence, or quintessence, the "ether." Celestial motion is circular, without end or variation, as befits spheres near the First Mover. Their motions may appropriately be regarded as "imitations" of the motion of the *Primum Mobile,* the First Moved by God.

Materiate things are composed of matter and form. Matter in and by itself is formless, indeterminate, meaningless, deprived, potential. It is made significant when activated through the agency of form. In the motion of materiate bodies, four causes are to be distinguished: the material, that out of which something becomes; the formal, which brings what becomes out of privation into existence and significance; the efficient, which brings into act what without its operation remains potential; and the final, which is the actuality achieved when something becomes what it had had in it to become. Because the form is the activating agent upon matter, and also marks the end achieved through passage from potency to act, Aristotle sometimes reduces his four causes to two: the formal and the material.

Such is the system in part which Bacon learned at Cambridge. He was not taken with it. Soon he began to regard its logic . . . as fruitless, and became unhappy over its divisions, its abstractions, and its interpretations of natural processes and causation. In a rebellion against the teaching of the Peripatetics, Bacon turned to Plato and the Pre-Socratics. He also began to acquaint himself with some more immediate predecessors and contemporaries. In Plato he found to his liking a system of truth wherein things ascended from multiplicity to unity, and also a principle of determination by which infinite particulars were brought within intelligible bounds. But to his disliking he also found in Plato a doctrine by which forms were set in opposition to an indeterminate matter. Going back beyond Plato, Bacon discovered that "almost all the ancients, as Empedocles, Anaxagoras, Anaximenes, Heraclitus, and Democritus, though in other respects they differed about the first matter, agreed in this, that they set down matter as active, as having some form, as dispensing that form, and as having the principle of motion in itself." Of these early thinkers, Democritus impressed him most of all. "The philosophy of Democritus," he said, "seems worthy to be rescued," both because of its freedom from final causes and its assertion of a formed and determinate matter, causal in its motion.

By the time Bacon prepares his first philosophical publication, the ***Advancement of Learning,*** he has rejected from his thinking the main parts and principles of the Peripatetic philosophy and has chosen alternatives of his own conceiving. These he cultivates during the next fifteen years. He will have nothing to do with any metaphysics or other natural science which professes to deal with the nature and the mind of God, with abstract being as such, with a First Cause or with a Prime Mover. Metaphysics is for him generalized physics, the science of formed matter in motion.

Bacon will not agree in the separation of fields of inquiry by means of axioms. He regards the principle of abstraction, on which the Peripatetics rely in aligning the sciences, as the source of "infinite error" and as one of the impediments in the way of scientific advancement. Aristotle's several motions are reduced by Bacon, as a philosophical materialist, to one, local motion. He will not countenance a separation of matter from form. Rejecting Aristotle's formal and final causes, he recognizes one efficient materiate cause active within formed matter. Bacon dismisses as useless things the four terrestrial elements and also the fifth element, the celestial quintessence. He regards the separation of the respective elements and motions of celestial and terrestrial bodies as a calamity in the history of astronomy. He notes that this separation is still

being retained by some of those who profess a "new," heliocentric, theory.

In Bacon's classification of the sciences, mathematics is reduced in status from an independent science to an instrument of metaphysics and physics. The "poietical" sciences are merged with physics. Art and nature become one, both the products of the operation of common material causes. The practical sciences are put within "the Prerogative" of revealed theology. Political initiative and sovereignty are divine bestowals on rulers; the source of the governing principle and rule of ethics is Divine Revelation; all so-called principles of ethics are but "inferences" from this rule.

Bacon is extremely critical of Aristotle's teaching on the subject of ethics. It does not, in his opinion, touch the springs of human action. "We may," Bacon says, "discourse as much as we please," after the manner of Aristotle, "that the moral virtues are in the mind of man by habit, and not by nature, and we may make a formal distinction that generous spirits are won by doctrines and persuasions, and the vulgar sort by reward and punishment; or we may give it in precept that the mind like a crooked stick must be straightened by bending it the contrary way, and the like scattered glances and touches; but they would be very far from supplying the place of that which we require."

For an understanding of human motives, we could find more wisdom, says Bacon, if we turned from the philosophy of Aristotle to poetry and history. Machiavelli also has written informatively in this regard. In the works of poets and historians "we find painted forth with great life and dissected, how affections are kindled and excited, and how pacified and restrained, and how again contained from act and further degree; how they disclose themselves, though repressed and concealed; how they work; how they vary; how they are enwrapped one within another; how they fight and encounter one with another; and many other particularities of this kind amongst which this last is of special use in moral and civil matters."

Bacon has been attacking the Universities continuously for their employment in instruction of the Peripatetic logic and the doctrines and writings of Aristotle. His pleas for alternatives to these were often addressed directly to James and sometimes to Prince Charles. These entreaties produced no discernible effect in the reign of either of these sovereigns. However, during the days of the Commonwealth, Bacon's scheme for learning became the subject of common and vigorous debate. University curricula and exercises were made the objects of attack by pamphleteers and others who repeated what Bacon had written, often in the very words of the ***Advancement of Learning,*** the ***New Organon,*** and the ***New Atlantis.*** No less a person than a renowned Oxford professor, Seth Ward—a member of the experimental "philosophical college" which became the Royal Society—found it necessary to publish a vindication of university practices in answer to the writings of William Dell and John Webster, who had stated in vehement language what others again had presented, in keeping with Bacon's criticism of learning, as "humble advices" to the Universities and Petitions to Parliament. Before long, plans for a new sort of institution of learning, which would give effect to Bacon's principles, were drawn up by such men as William Petty, Abraham Cowley, John Evelyn, and Robert Hooke. These innovators were one in thinking what Evelyn said, that "Solomon's House . . . however lofty, and to appearance Romantic, hath yet in it nothing impossible to be effected." John Amos Comenius was invited to England mainly for the purpose of reforming the schools of the kingdom according to Bacon's design. Oliver Cromwell warned the Universities that unless they adopted Baconian methods they would be closed. Plans were made to sequester cathedral funds for a "new" public education. Cromwell tried to place the Baconian Samuel Hartlib in the headship of an Oxford College. None of these plans came to fruition. Cromwell's attention was diverted by troubles in Ireland and at Westminster. The Universities refused to provide Hartlib with a post or to bring their curricula into conformity with what was now generally known as the "new learning." (pp. 318-31)

[However, by] the end of the century the opinion was general that, largely through the influence of Bacon and his disciples, the physical and metaphysical doctrines of Aristotle were no longer entertained by learned men in England. (p. 333)

The scientific search which Bacon had begun was to be carried forward outside the Universities from the middle of the century. Members of the Royal Society undertook a "work," as their first historian said, "becoming the largeness of Bacon's wit to devise." These inquirers, at the bidding of the author whom their President, Robert Boyle, called "that profound naturalist . . . Verulam," took for their ambitious aim the investigation of every area of nature available to human observation and experiment. John Locke, whose scientific environment as a member of the Royal Society and whose study of the works of his philosophical progenitor made him one of the most thoroughly Baconian writers of the seventeenth century—specifically in doctrine, illustration, problem, and method—undertook the "historical" recording of the operations and structures of the human mind. Locke became, in turn, the progenitor of an ambitious family of epistemologists of a "psychologically" historical sort.

Not a few historians of philosophy would undoubtedly take issue with our placing of Locke in the Baconian tradition. Because of Locke's concern with "ideas" and "intuition" and his attempt to cope with the body-mind problem, he is often regarded as a disciple of Descartes (1596-1650), and his philosophy as a part of "Cartesianism." This is one of the causes of the contention that Descartes is the source of everything that is distinctively modern in the questions and methods of modern philosophy. (pp. 333-34)

The progeny of Descartes is a succession from generation to generation of a priori rationalists. Descartes, after entertaining doubt about the offices of sense and reason, takes refuge in mathematically clear and determined ideas. Having applied quantity to geometric forms, he rests his case on an ontology dialectically established. His philosophy emerges as a sort of Stoical, Augustinian Platonism. Its structures are not the products of the activities

of a knowing *anima,* or soul, but the noetic content of a nonorganic *mens,* or mind. This content, so far as it serves science, is composed of innate ideas, mathematically coördinated. This content Descartes divides according to two categories, *res cogitans* and *res extensa,* thinking "substance" and extended "substance," by a defining which forbids intercourse between the two things defined. And while he states the former of his two "substances" in the form of the active participle, this "thinking" thing actually performs no operation; its "acts" are specified in terms of its structure—as in the later case of Kant's transcendental mind. By his establishment of a noetic content, Descartes solves to his own satisfaction the problem—a concern of Augustine and Francisco Suarez before him—of making available to human comprehension the *logoi* inherent within the principle of divine omniscience. Descartes' treatment of this question, we may add, is motivated not by an epistemological requirement, but rather by a theological preoccupation.

Thought's content, having been elevated by Descartes into the structure of the "universe," is bequeathed in this form to his philosophical heirs, the Continental rationalists. By them it is specified in such terms as divine attributes, transcendental ideas, transcendental categories, schemata of thought, all of which they find innate, as it were, certainly inherent, within a transcendental mind. Descartes, therefore, may properly be regarded as a "modern" who introduces into inquiry that epistemological puzzle whose solution is said to lie, by the Spinozists, the Kantians, and the logical idealists respectively, in the intellectual knowledge of God, the identification of human thought-structures with a transcendental understanding, the possession within human logic, in "degree" at least, of the Eternal Mind.

Bacon, following a thoroughly different line of thought, denies that man has capacity by natural inquiry to know in range or degree what God thinks or is. The assumption that man could do so is for Bacon the presumption and sin whereby Adam fell and forfeited his rule over the kingdom of nature. Bacon banishes from philosophy the *logos* and *logoi* of the Stoics and the Augustinians. He sees in philosophical objects only the structures and motions of formed matter. He reduces the transcendental status assigned by Plato and some sorts of Platonist to mathematics, making it an instrument in physical discovery. He relegates ontology to the verbal limbo of dialectic, and expels metaphysical theology from science achieved through human faculties. He puts distinctively human powers to work on the investigation of the created world for the recapturing of man's dominion over Nature.

After rejecting the dialectic procedures of the rationalists Bacon calls for "a true and lawful marriage between the empirical and the rational faculty," whose ill-starred divorce and separation have brought "confusion" into the philosophical life of mankind. He asks for a new sort of philosophy, whose "end, scope, office" will lie not in plausible, resolved, and admired discourse and argument, but in the understanding of particulars and the production of operative works for "the better endowment and help of man's life." The new philosopher will recognize that the subtlety of nature is greater than the subtlety of subtle words and arguments. His discoveries will not "float in air," but will "rest on the solid foundation of experience of every kind, and the same well examined and weighed." He will be satisfied with the recapture of that "parcel of the world . . . fitted to the comprehension of man's mind." His aim will be "the restitution and reinvesting (in great part) of man to the sovereignty and power [over Nature] which he had in his first state of creation."

The descendants of Descartes, because of the recognition by academics of the continuity of their thinking with *philosophia perennis,* were readily assimilated by learned institutions. Bacon's progeny, when looked at by academics in the "old way," were regarded as little more than mechanics. They were long to be denied admittance to the Universities. Their laboring faithfully, fearlessly, and fruitfully beyond the walls of learning, their industrious example, and the report of undeniable discoveries, eventually caused learned academics to relent. Finally the Baconians were reluctantly invited to enter the portals of the Universities. They arrived with vigor and authority. Step by step they brought about a great modification of university studies. The scientific curricula of modern universities—and modern research foundations; the varieties of and the relations among scientific subject matters; the sciences which employ induction and not simply speculation, experimentally and not verbally defined terms; the philosophies which hang upon the methods and discoveries of the inductive science; the adjusting of new means to new ends for the betterment of the lot of man as an inhabitant of the kingdom of nature with the status of ruler, but not yet in full control—these were to be some of the offspring of the greatest thinker of the English Renaissance. No Telesio, no Campanella, Descartes, Spinoza, Hume, Kant, Schopenhauer, or Hegel has ever produced, or ever could have produced, a like progeny. The more these philosophers, and their kinds, have meditated and have contemplated their concepts and definitions, the less, according to the disciples of Bacon, have they furthered the understanding and the conquest of nature. The more some of them have attempted to elevate to the realm of the a priori and transcendental what, the Baconians say, does not there belong, the more have they hindered man's exercise of his original birthright and his religious duty, the rule over the kingdom of nature. (pp. 335-39)

Bacon, of course, never succeeds in providing a full inductive philosophy of nature; but he does, at every stage of his endeavor, resist the temptation to invent a speculative alternative which might pass for such a philosophy. Bacon does not succeed in preparing works in representation of the Fourth Part of the Great Instauration, which is to consist of exemplary Tables of axioms inductively discovered, and consequently can provide nothing of the Sixth Part, which is to contain a systematic philosophy. What this philosophy is to be, and not to be, the author of the ***New Organon*** can do no more than indicate, because inquiry has only begun. Its subject matter will, he says, comprehend all the structures and processes of nature. Its aim is to discover the forms, causes, and laws of natural operation and, having established these, to control nature in the production of operative works. This philosophy will not become a reality until the immense history on which it

must be founded has been fully gathered, and until the axioms—whether lowest, middle, or highest—which sustain it have been inductively secured. No matter how properly its general axioms may be established, these are not at any stage to be considered an all-comprehensive and complete statement of the operations of God's whole natural creation. Nature can never be fully known until inductive inquiry is finally complete. There is to be no premature constructing of a theoretical system.

"God forbid," says Bacon, "that we should give out a dream of our own imagination for a pattern of the world; rather may He graciously grant to us to write an apocalypse or true vision of the footsteps of the Creator imprinted on His creatures." Care must be taken to see that the universe of nature is not endowed by investigators with final causes or with mind. There is in nature no mind or reason, logical, universal, or divine. Such appellations can properly mean nothing more than the "seals" or "signets" which the Creator has stamped upon his material creation, where they appear as material, and not rational, forms. The material universe is not divine in nature, but only in origin. Only from the placets of Divine Revelation—and not through inductive philosophy—does man learn that God is nature's Creator and that nature as a kingdom lies under man's dominion. Inductive science provides no basic rule for human conduct. Human rules for the use of nature's operative works are but inferences from a divinely originated and divinely imposed rule of charity, which is the foundation and the supreme principle of all human virtue. (pp. 351-52)

> *Fulton H. Anderson, in his* Francis Bacon: His Career and His Thought, *University of Southern California Press, 1962, 367 p.*

Etienne Gilson and Thomas Langan (essay date 1963)

[*Gilson was a leading French Neo–Thomist philosopher and a historian of philosophy who wrote widely on medieval thought. Langan is a philosopher and educator whose writings include* The Meaning of Heidegger *(1959). In the following excerpt, the authors offer a systematic analysis of Bacon's scientific and philosophical ideas. They explain that modern scientists, though influenced by the Baconian spirit, never accepted the English philosopher's inductive-axiomatic method as a foundation.*]

The fact that Francis Bacon . . . was neither a cleric nor even a professional philosophy teacher is in itself a measure of the change that had overtaken philosophy since the Middle Ages. Previously, practically all philosophers were both clerics and professors. Then in the fifteenth and sixteenth centuries lay professors of philosophy started to appear, especially in Italy (one thinks, for example, of Peter Pomponazzi at Padua and Bologna). In the seventeenth century, no philosopher of great note, with the exception of Malebranche, will be a priest, and none at all a teacher! As to Bacon—he was no less than Lord Chancellor of England, and so little the cloistered type that he managed to get himself fired for accepting bribes.

Like Montaigne, he is a brilliant essayist, a figure with as secure a place in the history of literature as in the history of philosophy, and a man of "experience." In other respects, he contrasts markedly with the sixteenth-century French aristocrat. In Bacon we feel the product of a slightly less troubled time—there seems more room for confidence. Nor is the quest for truth held up by him as a monopoly of the noble soul; it now seems, we might say, something accessible even to the middle bourgeoisie, provided they can arm themselves with the proper method. Method is enthroned in the place of authority, genial intuition, and virtuous exaltation. And method knows no class.

The planning to be done in view of assuring the future progress of the sciences requires a sort of map of the territory already covered in order to project our course into still uncultivated zones. A good classification, or division, of the existing sciences is necessary for the advancement of learning. Bacon divides the sciences, or intellectual disciplines, according to a threefold division of the faculties, or powers, of the human soul: memory, imagination, and reason.

Memory gives rise to history, both natural and civil. Natural history includes the observation and recording of all facts and beings, normal or otherwise, to be found in nature. Normal beings express the "liberty" of nature; abnormal beings represent "errors" of nature. What man makes of nature represents still a third order of facts, which are also "natural." Given the importance this third order of facts was to assume in the future, Bacon was not likely to overlook it. He calls it nature in bondage to man, or chained nature: *naturae vincula*. Here as everywhere in his work, the best of Bacon is found in the details of his discussion, so that no conspectus can begin to do it full justice. For instance, in his description of "civil history," he includes, along with two well-recognized types, church and political history, a third one, practically non-existent in his own time, but destined to a brilliant future: literary history. In the nineteenth century, the great French literary critic, Sainte-Beuve, will pay Bacon homage and claim him for one of his predecessors. Except for a few scattered fragments, Bacon considered this *historia literarum* as not yet existent. So far, nobody has attempted to do for "letters"—meaning all the written monuments left behind by the human mind during the course of centuries—what has been often done for the works of nature and for civil and ecclesiastical institutions; yet without it "the history of the world seems to me to be as the statue of Polyphemus with his eye out; that part being wanting which does most show the spirit and life of the person."

Just as history corresponds to the "cell of the mind" called memory, poetry corresponds to imagination. Bacon speaks of poetry as a philosopher. To him it is a "feigned history" which describes things such as we would like them to be or to have been, that they might give us the satisfaction refused us by reality. Poetry is either *narrative, representative,* or *allusive* (i.e., *parabolical*). Narrative poetry is nothing but an imitation of real history, the only difference being that it recounts an imaginary past. Representative poetry "is as a visible history"; it represents actions as if they were happening before us. Allusive or parabolical poetry is destined to express such ideas as deserve or require to be expressed in a refined and subtle way, as well as to be illustrated by fit examples. By and large, this kind of poetry does not mind obscurity; in fact, it uses it to its own end; but there is another kind of parabolical poetry, which, instead of obscuring its object, aims to demonstrate and to clear up the meaning of what it teaches. Such is the case when "the secrets of and mysteries of religion, policy, or philosophy are involved in fables or parables." Bacon is not complaining about the condition of poetry. Like all natural and free-growing products of the soil, it has always been abundant. We actually owe more to it than to philosophy for our knowledge of man, and nearly as much as we owe to orators in the matter of "wit and eloquence." This is in fact so true that we should not tarry in its company! Let us now pass to the third and most important of the three main parts of learning, philosophy, which properly belongs to the faculty of reason.

Philosophy divides into *divine philosophy,* or theology, *natural philosophy,* and *human philosophy.* Bacon observes that there might be still another kind of philosophy; namely, a "prime philosophy," which would be a sort of universal and common science anterior to the point where philosophy begins to divide into the three above-mentioned ways. Bacon is not quite sure whether or not there *really ought* to be such a *philosophia prima,* conceived as the common spring from which all sciences flow. Anyway, it is at best a desideratum, for it certainly does not in fact exist.

Divine philosophy, still called natural theology, is the rudiment of knowledge about God that can be obtained by reason from the consideration of his creatures. Bacon aptly defines its nature and determines its limits: This knowledge "may be truly termed divine in respect of the object, and natural in respect of the light"; as to its bounds, they are "that it suffices to convince atheism, but not to inform religion."

Natural philosophy (or science, or theory) divides into *physics* and *metaphysics.* Obviously, Bacon is careful to retain ancient names while conscious of giving them new, or renovated, meanings.

By "metaphysics" Bacon does not mean to signify that "prime philosophy," the common source of all knowledge, of which we have only rudiments. That *philosophia prima* should deal with the principles and axioms common to all sciences, as well as with the secondary characters of essences (quantity, similitude, diversity, possibility, etc.), conceived not as logical notions but as real properties of things. Nor is metaphysics to be confused with natural theology such as it has just been described. Then what is metaphysics concerned with? This much should be retained of its ancient notion, that "physics should contemplate that which is inherent in matter, and therefore transitory; and metaphysics that which is abstracted and fixed." In more concrete terms, metaphysics handles the formal and final causes; physics handles the material and efficient causes.

The inquiry into formal causes, which belongs to metaphysics, in no way resembles the traditional speculations about the specific forms of beings and things (man, oak, gold, water, air, etc.). What Bacon has in mind seems to be something like the generalities of physics or, in other terms, the knowledge of the properties that enter the common position of the essences of all actually existing things or beings. What are gravity and levity, density and tenuity, heat and cold; in short, all the natures and qualities, limited in number like the letters of the alphabet, that enter the composition of all particular beings as letters enter the composition of innumerable words? We will discover later when we look with some care into Bacon's theory of induction both *that* the notion of form has by then become very obscure and *why*. For the moment, it suffices to realize that what he is thinking of has little to do with traditional metaphysics, and that his notion of "formal cause" would have more affinity with the general laws of physics than with Aristotelian essential "forms."

The consideration of *final* causes is definitely to be excluded from physics, but metaphysics is to continue to interest itself in ends. This kind of inquiry, says Bacon, "I am moved to report not as omitted but as misplaced." The physicists' concern with final causes worked in the past to block the effort required for the investigation of the "real and physical causes." Final causes in physics, he says elsewhere, are like unto virgins consecrated to God. They bear no children. They can serve in making the wisdom of God more admirable, but final causes cannot teach us anything as to the nature of things; so metaphysics is the place for them.

Mathematics also receives a new stature in the Baconian division of sciences. It was traditionally conceived as dealing with "quantity as such." Were it so, its object would be one of those general properties "relative" to essences which Bacon has attributed to that as yet not existent "prime philosophy" we described above. The true object of mathematics is quantity, not undetermined and in a state of complete abstraction, but determined by its proportions. As such, it is found in things, where it causes many effects. Thus understood, quantity "appears to be one of the essential forms of things." Since metaphysics is the science of forms, mathematics should be counted as a distinct part of natural philosophy and as a special branch of metaphysics. Mathematics is either pure, as arithmetic and geometry, or mixed, as when it is used in connection with various orders of physical phenomena, such as light (optics), sound (music), etc. Bacon casually mentions astronomy, cosmography, and engineering without giving any evidence that he suspected the prodigious development of mathematical physics then about to take place. The reason for this blindness we shall see later.

All the above-named sciences are speculative, and each one of them is attended by a corresponding operative science. Speculative sciences are concerned with the investigation of causes; operative sciences are concerned with the production of effects. The operative parts of philosophy, however, are, according to Bacon, still to be invented, as the knowledge of nature they presuppose is still deficient in his time.

After divine philosophy and natural philosophy, the third main part of philosophy is the *human,* which divides into the knowledge (*scientia*) of body and that of mind. The knowledge of body further divides into *medicine,* concerned with health, *athletics* with strength, and *arts voluptuary*. The knowledge of mind, in its turn, divides into two main parts: that of the substance or nature of the soul, which, in the last analysis, loses itself in religion, and the knowledge of the faculties or functions of the soul, which, although it already exists, could be very seriously bettered.

The faculties of man divide into rational and moral. The study of the rational faculties constitutes what is commonly called *logic*. As Bacon conceives it, this science includes the four intellectual arts, distinguished by their diverse ends: the art of *inventing* that which is sought; that of *judging* that which has been invented; that of *retaining* that which has been judged; and that of *delivering* that which has been retained.

The art of invention in the order of arts and sciences was lacking as yet in Bacon's day, which explains why, he says, so few discoveries are made in the sciences, "the art itself of invention and discovery having been passed over." Bacon would certainly be disappointed to learn that in the twentieth century we are still waiting for logic to invent any new science.

The art of examination or judgment will be dealt with in describing scientific method. The arts of custody or memory and that of elocution or tradition provide Bacon with opportunities to display his talents as essayist, which are far from being despicable but which result in developments of unequal interest. At any rate, his treatment of the art of elocution and tradition (transmission) of knowledge is very personal, and debaters could learn something from it.

After the rational faculties of man come his moral faculties; hence, after logic, *moral philosophy*. All the disciplines related to it deal with the human will. Bacon complains that, so far, moralists have rather accumulated examples and models of moral life than taught the way to achieve it. Here again, concrete problems have been neglected by men eager to jump at conclusions. Yet his own handling of the nature and division of the good is certainly not of a sort to remedy the defect. A more original contribution, however, is Bacon's intention of setting up as a distinct branch of moral philosophy the *cultura animi,* or cultivation of the mind. In attempting to say something about it, he may have realized why that most useful art was still a desideratum and not an accomplished fact. With his remarkable perspicacity in such matters, Bacon observes that here again men want to solve a problem before collecting its data. The starting point is going to have to be "sound and true distributions and descriptions of the characters and tempers of men's natures and dispositions." Once again we know today from the sad state of the much-talked-about science of characterology that Bacon is destined to be disappointed. His remarks on the subject are clever and often of the highest interest, but what he says of others on this occasion also applies to himself: "The distinctions are found (many of them) but we conclude no precepts upon them." In such cases one can always wonder if precepts can possibly be concluded.

In order not to leave any department of learning unclassified, Bacon concludes his division of the sciences with a few remarks concerning the knowledge of man as a social animal, thereby giving what is today called the "social sciences" their due consideration.

This "civil knowledge," as Bacon calls it, has three parts according to the three general activities of social life: *conversation,* or the art of social intercourse, which, perhaps too optimistically for once, he considers competently handled by the moralists; *negotiation,* or the art of conducting business, a most useful art, Bacon says, but which, shamefully enough, remains to be created; thirdly, *government,* of which the Romans were once good professors, although, in that order, nothing compares with the precepts laid down by King Solomon and received among the divinely inspired writings. So, although as a proper science this branch of learning is deficient, the example of Solomon constitutes for it an illustrious precedent. In handling it, one point should be kept uppermost in mind; to wit, "that all those which have written of laws, have written either as philosophers or as lawyers, and none as statesmen."

With this last branch of human philosophy, the description of philosophy has reached its term. By way of conclusion, Bacon comes back to an examination of divinity; that is, of sacred theology. As a rule, he finds no serious lacuna in the way this branch of learning has been handled by theologians, although his personal preferences are in favor of a "positive" theology as free as possible from useless controversies. Sacred theology ultimately rests upon faith in the divine revelation; but there is no harm in letting reason investigate the meaning of revelation, first in order to achieve some understanding of it, next in order to infer from it speculative consequences and practical directions. This is the point where Bacon finds a good project even in that field: an adequate inquiry into, and competent handling of, "the true limits and use of reason in spiritual things, as a kind of divine dialectic." Definitely, Bacon had an unfailing flair for sniffing out difficult problems!

Bacon's free-flowing mode of exposition makes it difficult to do justice to his philosophical positions, but for all that, few doctrines illustrate better the state of mind obtaining at the dawn of modern times. He himself has felicitously described his work when he wrote at the conclusion of his English treatise on the **Advancement of Learning:** "Thus have I made as it were a small globe of the intellectual world, as truly and faithfully as I could discover." In writing his book, Bacon was the spokesman for countless contemporaries who, like himself, could see in front of them a world of knowledge that had been explored only in part and in which marvelous discoveries remained to be made. The case of Bacon is the more remarkable as personally he had very little to contribute to the promotion of scientific learning. He himself was no scientist, but rather contented himself with standing on the sidelines lustily cheering on those who might follow his grand strategy.

The proper prelude to the unfolding of his great design is a final attack on the accumulations of the past. This is carried out in three movements: (a) an attack on the debilities and misuse of human reason which have cluttered the path of inquiry with false "idols"; (b) a destruction of extant philosophical systems; (c) a criticism of the traditional logic of demonstration, which Bacon would replace with a new logic, with a **Novum Organum,** no less, methodically correcting all the kinds of errors envisioned in these attacks and leading to "the Great Instauration of Human Control in the Universe."

The most popularly remembered part of all this is probably the theory of the causes of error. Already sketched in the **Advancement of Learning,** it was given full treatment in the **De augmentis.** One of the less worthy reasons it is still remembered is that Bacon gave the four general causes of error rhyming Latin names: *idola tribus, idola specus, idola fori, idola theatri.* He had not forgotten his own remarks on the art of mnemonics! He calls these causes of error *idola* because they are false images which, coming between us and objects, cause in us a distorted view of reality, becoming rooted in the mind until they are to it almost like objects of worship.

Bacon first attacks the idols that result from the inherent weaknesses of human reason. Prominent among these *Idols of the Tribe* is the inclination to conceive the world in a way that would make it handy and cozy for the likes of us. Hence the mind's inclination to "suppose the existence of more order and regularity in the world than it finds"—we think at once of the Aristotelian universe, with man stationed in the ideal center, its perfect spheres and circular motions, turning by means of anthropomorphic attractions and repulsions—a singularly comprehensible and hospitable place for man. The trouble is that science is bogged down by the interference of the will and the affections, which have been allowed too free reign in describing things not the way they are, but as one would have them be. A second disastrous trend of the human intelligence is its readiness at a moment's notice to fly off into the wildest generalization on the flimsiest experiential pretext, which is all the more catastrophic, given the inherent "dullness, incompetency and deceptions of the senses." These are both reasons for more, not less, careful attention to the data of these senses—for a will to observe, classify, experiment.

Bacon next acknowledges a problem already wonderfully developed by Montaigne—that of idols born of peculiarities of the individual judgment, arising from particularities of background. We are chained in the Cave of our own imaginations, condemned like Plato's spectator to seeing reflections of our own phantasy because we fail to see the need to turn to the things themselves. Our worst tyrants are our own creations: a Democritus can see nothing any more but his marvelous atoms. Aristotle must recast everything in the categories of his "Logic." We can also be blinded by our special gifts: those minds that are stronger in distinguishing things never synthesize, and the synthesizers never seem ready to acknowledge real differences; just as those who love what is new refuse honor to what is old, and the reverse. The list, Bacon suggests, could be extended *ad nauseam.*

The third class of idols is the most troublesome of all, the *Idols of the Market Place,* the obstacles placed in the path of the understanding by words. "Men believe that their reason governs words; but it is also true that words react on the understanding." Philosophers in the modern tradition, from Montaigne, with his sarcastic remark that more books are written on books than on things, all the way to Heidegger, with his insistence that reliance on words worn out by usage in the market place is an essential part of inauthenticity, have pointed to the fact that while in language alone we conceive, reliance on the already-formed language of the past can become a block to our access to things. Bacon's contribution to this tradition is a remarkably precocious one.

The names of things that do not exist (resulting from fantastic suppositions) and the names of things which exist, but which, as the result of faulty and unskillful abstraction, are less helpfully named than misleadingly, constitute, according to Bacon, the two principal categories of Market-Place Idols. "Fortune," "the Prime Mover," "Planetary Orbits," "Elements of Fire" are good examples of the first. As an example of the second, Bacon cites the word *humid*, which actually signifies a whole variety of actions loosely and confusingly lumped together: "It signifies that which easily spreads itself round any body; and that which in itself is indeterminate and cannot solidize; and that which readily yields in any direction; and that which easily divides and scatters itself . . . " Bacon's list goes on and on, showing his reader as concretely as possible how a word can become the lazy substitute for assiduous observation.

The three classes of Idols thus far considered hold influence over all men; and against them the thinking man, the man of science, will have to conduct a by no means hopeless but still never-ending battle. The fourth group, however, those *Idols of the Theater* which are produced by the prancings and pretensions of the philosophers, are not so widespread among humanity and are subject to complete neutralization by a right application of method. These constitute the subject of a new area of attack.

In confronting the *Idols of the Theater,* we move to the second aspect of the three-pronged attack on the old cobwebs. Here we can gain precious indications of the kind of general philosophical atmosphere in which Bacon wants the new endeavor to unfold. The first of the three kinds of traditional philosophy to be considered is of course the fashionable butt of all sarcasm, the "sophistical," of which Aristotle's "fashioning the world out of categories" is a good example. The destruction of the other Idols, especially the Idols of the Cave, takes care of this kind, as far as Bacon is concerned, well enough to excuse the need to develop the point any further.

The second sort of philosophy taken to task requires more comment; namely, the *empirical.* At first it might seem strange that the great prophet of close observation of nature should attack "empirical philosophy." The *empiricists,* sneers Bacon, are like ants: They store up observations and then live off them all winter without making anything out of them. That's almost as bad as the *rationalists,* who occupy the other extreme in this regard—they are like spiders, spinning fine systematic webs out of their own substance. What, then, does Bacon propose as an alternative? That the new philosophers gather like bees the nectar from flower and field and, passing it through the organ of the mind, transform it into the most highly usable "honey and wax" of knowledge.

Bacon's position here is complex and extremely interesting because, in an effort to react against a number of extremes in contemporary intellectual trends, he ends up outlining an epistemological position both original and subtle. Looking back on later developments like the actual successes of science, we can now point out both valid and erroneous elements in this epistemology. That he is right in his insistence on the need for a great deal more detailed, accurate observation and in his attack against the overly deductive and verbalistic philosophers of the universities, no one would care to dispute; that he is right, too, in some respects in attacking "empiricism" is also clear: it is true that nature will not yield up its secrets to mere observation. (Bacon goes so far as to suggest that there is no such thing really as sheer observation.) In this regard, Bacon makes a singularly important remark: Nature, he says, yields up her secrets best when "vexed" by experiments, just as a man will show his real mettle best when caught in a difficult situation. He does not elaborate on the remark, but its sense is fairly obvious. To work an experiment, one must have some sort of plan; this directs us deeply into the phenomenon and helps guide our regard. Hobbes will develop the psychology underlying this position, suggesting the guiding role of "desire" in giving a unity to a train of impressions. How true Bacon's idea can be in some cases is illustrated by the example of Bacon's contemporary, William Harvey, who in his anatomical experimenting proceeded almost as though he were using Bacon as a laboratory manual. Not only did he excel in clinical observation and in the invention of ingenious experiments, but he followed another Baconian suggestion for transforming the "nectar" through the mind's intervention: *comparison.* As we shall see in considering the positive program of the "new logic," Bacon attacks the "empiricist" tendency merely to enumerate positive instances; we must, he insists, seek out negative instances, deviations, variations, before we can arrive at a rule of constancy with any hope of exactness and certitude. Harvey was careful to compare his anatomical observations on the human body with results obtained from dissecting apes and other animals. In his work of 1628, *De motu cordis et sanguinis,* he is careful to point out that he had been confirming his views "for more than nine years" by "multiple demonstrations."

As an example of the wrong sort of empiricist, the kind who is suffering especially from that "Idol of the Cave" which consists in remaining too tied up with his own little observation, Bacon cites William Gilbert. This worthy had in 1600 published a work, based on his experiments with the magnet, in which he daringly attempted to explain the cohesion of the whole universe in terms of the one phenomenon of magnetism. Such a philosophy has its foundations, declares Bacon, "in the narrowness and darkness of a few experiments. To those who are daily busied with these experiments, and have infected their imagination with them such a philosophy seems probable and all but certain; to all men else, incredible and vain." The alchemists are cited as nefarious examples in the past, as Gilbert is in the present.

Yet history looks back rather kindly on Gilbert; in fact, to many he now seems a predecessor of Newton in the discovery of universal gravitation. Bacon, as we saw above, was aware of the importance of the challenge of practical imagination—what Hobbes will later term "desire"—in any search for knowledge. But what he failed to see—and this mistake cost him a good chunk of reputation in the history of science—was the extraordinary role the mathematical imagination could and would play in the conquest of nature. Gilbert's invention was in the line of the discoveries to follow; in tending to concentrate on a single, simple force, the scientist's imagination produced a manageable concept, potentially translatable into mathematical terms. Galileo and Kepler were the first actually to make such translations. The mathematically gifted Kepler was able to make order out of the rich harvest of astronomical observations he inherited from Tycho Brahe, because he followed a hunch that order could be achieved through conceiving the planetary orbits as ellipses. Bacon particularly disliked Galileo's method of turning the problem of motion into the problem of geometrical bodies moving in geometrical space. He rebelled against the tendency to leave out complications, like air resistance and the tensions that occur within the moving bodies themselves. He did not sufficiently appreciate the overriding value of mathematical exactness and projection, and failed to realize that, by first leaving out every secondary consideration, the mathematical philosophers would discover simple unifying rules and would then be able to add in later the temporarily set-aside complications. The actual methods followed by the Keplers, Galileos, and Newtons turned out to far outstrip any philosopher's prophetic epistemology; no one really foresaw their actual follow-your-nose development. Bacon does say, "If physics be daily improving, and drawing out new axioms, it will continually be wanting fresh assistance from mathematics," and again, even more strongly, "The investigation of nature is best conducted when mathematics are applied to physics." But the philosophy of nature underlying his detailed program of "new logic" never went more than halfway toward the point where such sentiments could become realities. Mathematics was not Bacon's forte and so remained in his estimation just an instrument.

Before turning to the details of the "new logic" itself, there remains a third sort of traditional philosophizing to be demolished: the "superstitious" or "theological," the kind that freely invents "abstract forms and final causes and first causes, with the omission in most cases of causes intermediate," an "unwholesome mixture of things human and divine." Bacon cites Pythagoras and Plato "and his school" as examples, evidently wishing to make certain that he has fully covered the lot of Christian scholasticisms, whether Platonic or Aristotelian. What is interesting in this regard is Bacon's tremendous narrowing of the field of "philosophy" through the exclusion, not only of mysteries knowable by faith alone, but of all consideration whatever of the nature of God; all finality beyond that necessary for the conduct of human affairs, this finality itself being narrowed to a purely naturalistic and materialistic scope; and all proofs for the existence of a first mover.

Bacon's attitude to religious truth is quite complex. Perhaps we had better say a word more about it before we go on, particularly as his point of view in this regard is often misrepresented. To oppose scholastic philosophy and even scholastic theology, as Bacon very vehemently did, does not, in his view, necessarily entail any opposition to theology as such, much less to religion. Bacon acknowledged that God himself possesses the highest knowledge, knowledge which, since it is not acquired, must not, like ours, be called "learning," but rather wisdom or "sapience." We, however, in our struggle to acquire knowledge, must turn to his works to learn of God. Creation witnesses to the *power* of God, by showing it at work in the creation of matter, and to the *wisdom* of God, by showing it as the cause of the beauty to be observed in the disposition of the form.

Actually the world of creation as Bacon conceived it is not so different from the Middle Ages' notion of a world dependent on God, even to the point of including the "celestial hierarchy" of the pseudo-Dionysius. The patristic tradition has a place in his own notion of learning, and although he thinks the Reformation was willed by God, he does not consider the Church of Rome past mending. On the contrary, Bacon sees the revival of learning and the revival of religion as destined by God to take place together, so that even Roman Catholicism ultimately benefits by it. The eminent part taken by the Society of Jesus in this revival does not escape his attention: "We see the Jesuits, who partly in themselves and partly by the emulation and provocation of their example, have much quickened and strengthened the state of learning, we see (I say) what notable service and reparation they have done to the Roman see." At any rate, far from finding any opposition between science and Christianity, Bacon thinks that, although a drop of philosophy may invite atheism, a strong dose of it will bring man back to religion. In order not to form a distorted image of Bacon, let us not forget the full title of one of his major works: *Of the Proficience and Advancement of Learning Divine and Human.* The first book is entirely devoted to the consideration of divine learning.

The method that is to achieve "a true and lawful marriage in perpetuity between the empirical and rational faculty" and thereby become "the mind's machine" for conquering nature must attack first the problem of gathering the nectar from the fields through the weak instruments at our disposal. Heretofore "no search has been made to collect a store of particular observations sufficient either in number, kind, or in certainty to inform the understanding, or in anyway adequate." This is not to say that natural histories have not been gathered—the "great Aristotle," for instance, supported by the wealth of Alexander, composed an "accurate history of animals." But natural histories composed for their own sake are not like those collected with the precise purpose to supply the understanding with information intended to help build up a philosophy. The strength of the new observation, which attempts to achieve this, lies in its alliance with modern mechanical arts. We have seen that just as a man's deep character is best revealed under trying circumstances, "so likewise the secrets of nature reveal themselves more readily under the vexations of art than when they go their own way." If nature has to be tampered with to be made to give up her secrets, why then, we might ask, have not the "mechanics," who have worked practically with her, discovered more material of genuine scientific interest? Because they are just the opposite of those philosophers who take wing on the slightest empirical pretext and fly to the most universal conclusions; "for the mechanic, not troubling himself with the investigation of truth, confines his attention to those things which bear upon his particular work, and will not either raise his mind or stretch out his hand for anything else."

The method usually followed by philosophers should be inverted. Instead of coming down from axioms to particular conclusions, as in syllogistic deduction, the scientist should go instead from particular experiments and observations up to axioms—induction, in other words, should replace deduction.

But scientific induction should be "learned induction," not the hasty inductions of everyday life. Bacon's description of this induction relates it to the logic of the invention of sciences, classified by him among the operations of the rational faculties. Instead of proceeding by simple enumeration of favorable cases, it proceeds by the due rejections and exclusions: *per rejectiones et exclusiones debitas.* The instances to be excluded are often the first ones to catch the eye; they must be rejected if, after careful investigation, they appear as being related to the fact under discussion by a merely accidental tie. The true sign that a supposed cause is the real one is that it alone successfully resists all attempts to eliminate it. Socrates had applied this method of progressive elimination to the determination of ethical notions. This is why Aristotle attributes to him general definition and induction as personal contributions to philosophy; but, concerning nature, Socrates said nothing. Plato applied the same method to the investigation of physical reality, but he did it in a still incomplete way. The method remains to be perfected and generalized.

This result is obtained by subjecting induction to precise rules. Hence the Baconian theory of the *tables of induction.*

In observing facts, the observer should set up three tables. First, a *table of existence,* or *presence.* On it are listed all the instances in which the property under consideration is present; the more varied the circumstances amid which that property is found to be present, the better. The colors of the rainbow, for instance, are found, it should be noted, not only in clouds but also in drops of water or in certain crystals. A second table should list all the observable cases in which facts similar among themselves do not exhibit the property at stake; let us call it the *table of absence.* The third table, or *table of degrees,* should list the variations of the property under discussion; that is to say, all the observable cases in which it can be said to be more intense or less intense. John Stuart Mill will make use of a similar system of tables in his *Logic,* III, viii, but will considerably improve it.

A proper, balanced induction based in rich observation solidly disposed in artful Tables of Discovery, and sufficiently "vexing" to reveal inner secrets: this, then, would be the right kind, the balanced kind of "stretching out the hand." The really central point in Bacon's exposition is that instead of flying from a few particulars to so-called first principles—axioms of the highest generality—and from these deducing the middle axioms, one should proceed "by successive steps, not interrupted or broken," rising from particulars to middle axioms, then from these to wider and wider principles. The lowest axioms are not yet the most fruitful, differing only slightly from bare experience, but they provide a firm base for the middle axioms, which, though not so general as to be "notional and abstract and without solidity," are rather the "living axioms, on which depend the affairs and fortunes of men."

The middle axioms embody the mind's grasp, not of the particulars, but of the universal forms to be found in a real class of particulars. The still more general principles abstract beyond the level of those forms which are real fixed laws of action.

But what exactly does Bacon mean by "form"? Quite obviously final comprehension of the method being offered us depends on a correct answer to this question. Here we touch on a central difficulty in Bacon's positive conception of nature. Central to any scientific philosophy is a sound conception of causality. In routing Aristotelianism, Bacon, as we have already suggested, while retaining the terminology, has really put the four causes in their traditional sense straight to the door. In describing the realm of natural philosophy, we saw that he excludes from its consideration "final" and "efficient" causality, which he would leave, he says, to that "metaphysics" which is concerned with "immutable causes." Bacon conceives of efficiency as a mechanistic shove, and finality—barely mentioned and then explicitly labeled a menace to physics—drops out of sight.

Natural philosophy is concerned only with the material and formal causes. But these fare in Bacon's hands little better than the immutable causes. Bacon seems always to conceive of matter as "some definite kind of stuff," and he has great trouble clarifying his notion of form; this is not too surprising, although, given the centrality of the notion to his whole "logic," it is most unfortunate. The notion of form had been through quite an ordeal during the days of waning scholastic thought. The conception that seems to have impressed itself on Bacon as "the" scholastic conception—and one, therefore, to be avoided at all costs—was that of a formal principle so real in itself that it could exist independently of the realm of concrete things. To distinguish his doctrine from any vestige of tired Renaissance Platonism, Bacon likes to insist that "in nature nothing really exists besides individual bodies," and he suggests that the "form" is somehow a principle of unity—"a fixed law"—accounting for whatever uniformity there is in the operation of a thing and for our ability to induce a primordial unity under the manifold of operations, but without being something that can either be grasped immediately in itself or exist by itself. Bacon is trying to retain the advantages of a scholastic notion of form without being obliged to accept a medieval philosophy of form—an untenable combination of desires that leads to great difficulties in working out a clear and consistent doctrine.

Philosophy for the next one hundred fifty years will continue to be concerned with the problem of reconceiving the relationship of the substance to its qualities and of arriving at a satisfactory description of the "formal" unity underlying consistency in phenomena. The deeper dimensions and the ultimate roots of the problem must be gradually disengaged through the course of our narrative. As a beginning, Bacon's early, rather ambiguous efforts to formulate a modern doctrine of "natures" and forms is quite instructive.

The senses, he declares, are confronted immediately with "natures" through which science is to seek to know the "forms"; that is, the "fixed laws" underlying these natures and responsible for the constancy of their manifestation. There are two types of natures: the simple and the complex; simple natures being qualities like yellowness, transparency, opacity, tenacity, malleability, fixity, etc.; and complex natures constituting substances, like "oak," "gold," "water," "air," etc. To inquire into the form of "complex natures," says Bacon, would be "neither easy nor of any use," for they are infinite in number; besides, they are just complexes of simple natures, and these latter can be studied more easily, as they fortunately "are not many and yet make up and sustain the essences and forms of all the substances." Not only does the reality confronting the scientist thus seem to reduce to a kind of qualitative atomism reminiscent of Anaxagoras and prophetic of Berkeley, but the fact that the number of simple natures is very limited is encouraging; Bacon even contends that among the simple natures some are more primitive than others, and therefore constitute in turn *their* forms, which means that the inductive method has only to happen ultimately upon this small crowd of ultimate notions in order to possess the world!

All of which seems clear enough. But then we encounter a passage like this, in the fifteenth Aphorism of the First Book of the **Novum Organum:**

> There is no soundness in our notions whether logical or physical. Substance, Quality, Action, Passion, Essence itself, are not sound notions: much less are Heavy, Light, Dense, Rare, Moist, Dry, Generation, Corruption, Attraction, Repulsion, Element, Matter, Form and the like; but all are fantastical and ill-defined.

One is forced to admire the range with which this critical mind lashes out; but it must be said, after such an attack, we are not left with much to work with. Where does one turn now? The fourteenth Aphorism would encourage and direct the seeker of truth: Hope lies in obtaining notions that are not "confused and over-hastily abstracted from the facts"—which is to be accomplished by "true induction." But the trouble is that, other than the undeveloped hint about the need to "vex" and "constrain" nature and a few examples of his own efforts at clarification, Bacon has left no systematic program assuring the proper acquisition of sound general notions. The **New Organon's** positive program lays down some basic rules governing the in-

duction of axioms; i.e., of universal principles. But these axioms themselves are composed of terms the soundness of which has to be presupposed before the axioms can be of any value. How are we to come by such notions?

When the Cartesians take up the problem of securing a foundation in certain clear notions, they will proceed by a road altogether different from Bacon's vaguely indicated "induction." The clear and distinct idea analysis will be based, as we shall see, on a conception of "idea" that is far more successful in shaking the dust of peripatetic pathways from its feet than Bacon ever was.

What is perhaps more ironic is the fact that the ultimately most successful scientific tradition, the Galilean-Newtonian, never will share the "father of science's" concern for conceptual and axiomatic induction, nor, as we have already suggested, even his concern for exhaustive observation and enumeration. Instead of securing a base in carefully inducted notions of qualities and states, mathematical physics in the seventeenth and early eighteenth centuries will dispense with them altogether, pinning its well-justified hopes instead on a mathematical system which confines itself to constructions whose clarity and simplicity are assured by its restricted nature.

Where Bacon's remarks will turn out to have the most validity is in the area of the classificatory life sciences. We could suspect that already from the way Bacon understood and appreciated the physician Harvey and completely missed the significance of Gilbert's speculations with magnetism. Be this as it may, men should be appreciated for their positive contributions rather than for their deficiencies. *Non omnia possumus omnes*—we cannot all do everything—and the fact that Bacon himself has often failed to recognize the positive contributions of his predecessors does not justify us for making the same mistake.

He himself was no scientist, so he could speak of scientific research really from hearsay only, yet he correctly weighed the transformation of the philosophical notion of scientific knowledge brought about by the recent development of the methods of observation. Incomplete as it is, his epistemology contains sound elements, particularly concerning the respective merits of deduction and induction as methods of discovery in natural sciences. It has become customary to say that no scientist ever made a single discovery by merely applying the famous three tables of Bacon. This is probably true, but the object of epistemology is not to teach men the art of making discoveries, it is to give a correct description of the way discoveries are made. Bacon has noted this all-important fact, that scientists had begun to make new discoveries at the precise moment they had replaced the *Organon* of Aristotle by a new one. His own task was simply to describe it, and if there is much more in the method of science than the three tables, they certainly are included in it.

Above all, perhaps, Bacon was what Carlyle was to call a "representative man." He epitomizes the boundless ambition to dominate and to exploit the material resources of nature placed by God at the disposal of man. From this very important point of view, it must be observed that the seventeenth century, at the same time as it witnessed the birth of modern science, has seen the beginning of the age of the machines in which we are living still today. Science, mechanics, engineering, and a progressive industrialization of human life were inseparably connected from the very beginning of these events.

In the thirteenth century, the Franciscan Roger Bacon had clearly anticipated the future transformation of human life in consequence of the limitless possibility to invent new machines. In his own utopia, the *New Atlantis,* Francis Bacon was in a position to go much farther than his medieval predecessor along this line. For page after page, this unfinished treatise describes life such as it is on the unknown continent of Bensalem and as it will be in the cities of the future when they all possess "engine-houses, where are prepared engines and instruments for all sorts of motions," flying machines, "ships and boats for going under water," and numbers of such marvels. His dream city had "two very long and fair galleries," one sheltering "patterns and samples of all manner of the more rare and excellent inventions," the other containing "the statues of all principal inventors." There now are many such galleries; their existence should help us to understand what was a new and living force in the message of Francis Bacon. (pp. 25-44)

> *Etienne Gilson and Thomas Langan, "Francis Bacon," in their* Modern Philosophy: Descartes to Kant, *Random House, 1963, pp. 25-44.*

Frances A. Yates   (essay date 1972)

[*Yates was an eminent English scholar known for her significant contributions to Renaissance studies. Her books include* The French Academies of the Sixteenth Century *(1947),* Giordano Bruno and the Hermetic Tradition *(1964),* The Art of Memory *(1966), and* The Rosicrucian Enlightenment *(1972). In the following excerpt from the last-named work, Yates argues that Bacon absorbed many Rosicrucian ideas into his system of thought. Identifying certain parallels between Bacon's philosophy and Rosicrucianism, an occultist movement which supposedly flourished in the seventeenth century, she focuses on the* New Atlantis *as the example of a genuine Rosicrucian utopia.*]

The great Rosicrucian furore seemed to arouse little or no public attention in Britain. No floods of pamphlets addressed to the R. C. Brothers poured from the printing presses, as in Germany from 1614 to 1620. No Invisibles put up placards, arousing frantic interest and storms of abuse, as in Paris in the 1620s. The trumpet sounds of the *Fama* [the first Rosicrucian manifesto], announcing a new era and vast new advances in knowledge impending for mankind, seem to have been muffled in these islands.

There were, however, other trumpet sounds, making a striking announcement, not with the Rosicrucian wild excitement but in measured and reasonable terms. These were the manifestos concerning the advancement of learning issued by Francis Bacon. These manifestos were dedicated to James I, the same monarch as he to whom the Ro-

sicrucian movement in Germany so vainly pinned its hopes.

The Advancement of Learning, published in 1605, is a sober survey of the present state of knowledge, drawing attention to those areas of learning which are deficient, where more might be known if men would give their minds to research and experiment, particularly in natural philosophy which Bacon finds deplorably deficient. Such improved knowledge of nature could and should be used for the relief of man's estate, the betterment of his position in this world. Bacon demands that there should be a fraternity or brotherhood in learning, through which learned men might exchange knowledge and help one another. The universities do not at present promote such exchange, for there is not sufficient mutual intelligence between the universities of Europe. The brotherhood of learning should transcend national boundaries.

> Surely as nature createth brotherhood in families, and arts mechanical contract brotherhoods in communities, and the anointment of God superinduceth a brotherhood in kings and bishops, so in learning there cannot but be a fraternity in learning and illumination, relating to that paternity which is attributed to God, who is called the father of illumination or lights.

In reading this passage, after our explorations in this book, one is struck by the fact that Bacon here thinks of learning as 'illumination', light descending from the Father of Lights, and that the brotherhood in learning which he desires would be a 'fraternity in learning and illumination'. These expressions should not be passed over as pious rhetoric; they are significant in the context of the times.

Nine years later, in Germany, the Rosicrucian *Fama* was to present the Brothers R. C. as a fraternity of illuminati, as a band of learned men joined together in brotherly love; it was to urge that learned magicians and Cabalists should communicate their knowledge to one another; and it was to proclaim that the time was at hand of a great advance in knowledge of nature. This parallel may suggest that comparison of the Baconian movement with the Rosicrucian movement might be revealing for both, and particularly, perhaps, for Bacon.

Recent scholarship has made it abundantly clear that the old view of Bacon as a modern scientific observer and experimentalist emerging out of a superstitious past is no longer valid. In his [*Francis Bacon: From Magic to Science,* 1968], Paolo Rossi has shown that it was out of the Hermetic tradition that Bacon emerged, out of the Magia and Cabala of the Renaissance as it had reached him via the natural magicians. Bacon's view of the future of science was not that of progress in a straight line. His 'great instauration' of science was directed towards a return to the state of Adam before the Fall, a state of pure and sinless contact with nature and knowledge of her powers. This was the view of scientific progress, a progress back towards Adam, held by Cornelius Agrippa, the author of the influential Renaissance textbook on occult philosophy. And Bacon's science is still, in part, occult science. Amongst the subjects which he reviews in his survey of learning are natural magic, astrology, of which he seeks a reformed version, alchemy, by which he was profoundly influenced, fascination, the tool of the magician, and other themes which those interested in drawing out the modern side of Bacon have set aside as unimportant.

The German Rosicrucian writers hold similar views about the return to the wisdom of Adam and the millennial character of the advance in knowledge which they prophesy. After study of their writings in comparison with those of Bacon, one has the strong impression—when the fantastic Rosencreutz myth is set aside as a *ludibrium*—that both these movements are concerned with magicoscientific advance, with illumination in the sense of enlightenment.

Nevertheless, though one can see both these movements as belonging naturally to the same times, both ultimately products of the Renaissance Hermetic-Cabalist tradition, both leading out of Renaissance into seventeenth-century advance, there are profound differences between them. Bacon is anxious to emphasize his disapproval of the pride and presumption of the Renaissance magus. He warns particularly against Paracelsus, who . . . was a prophet for the German Rosicrucian movement. Bacon had studied the system of Paracelsus 'reduced into a harmony by Severinus the Dane', and had decided that 'the ancient opinion that man was *microcosmus,* and abstract or model of the world hath been fantastically strained by Paracelsus and the alchemists'. This attacks the macrocosm-microcosm philosophy, so basic for Fludd and the Rosicrucian theories of world harmony.

Another great difference in outlook between Baconian and Rosicrucian schools of thought is Bacon's deprecation of secrecy in scientific matters, his attack on the long tradition of the alchemists of concealing their processes in incomprehensible symbols. Though the Rosicrucian manifestos advise, as does Bacon, an exchange of knowledge between learned men, they are themselves couched in mystifications, such as the story of the cave in which Rosencreutz's body was found, and which was full of geometrical symbols. That symbolism *may* conceal abstruse mathematical studies by members of a group, leading in advanced directions, but, if so, such studies are not announced but concealed in language which whets the appetite to know more of the mathematical or scientific secrets hidden in the Rosicrucian cave. This atmosphere is the opposite of that in which the Baconian manifestos move, and it is precisely his abandonment of magico-mystical mystification technique which makes Bacon's writings sound modern.

The Advancement of Learning was published in 1605. The *Novum Organum,* which Bacon wrote in Latin to facilitate its diffusion in Europe and which he regarded as the most important statement of his philosophy and programme, was published in 1620. The *De augmentis,* the Latin translation and revision of the *Advancement,* was published in 1623. Thus the Baconian philosophy had begun to appear several years before the first Rosicrucian manifesto; its major statement was published in the year of destiny, the year of the brief reign in Bohemia of the Winter King and Queen; the Latin translation of the *Advancement* appeared at the time of the Rosicrucian scare in Paris. It is important to realize that the Rosicrucian movement is

contemporary with the Baconian philosophy, that the strange Rosicrucian excitements were going on in Europe during the years in which the works of Bacon were appearing in England.

There are, I believe, undoubtedly connections between the two movements, though these are difficult to trace and to analyse. On the one hand, the close connections between England and the Palatinate would have facilitated a Baconian influence on the German Rosicrucian movement. On the other hand the differences between Rosicrucianism and Baconianism have to be carefully considered.

The reign of a daughter of the King of Great Britain in the Palatinate made communications easy between England and that part of Germany and led to an influx of English influences, amongst which should be included an influence from Bacon's *Advancement.* We may speculate on how the influence may have been imported. Both Frederick and Elizabeth were readers and interested in intellectual movements. That they had books from England with them is proved by the fact that they took a copy of Raleigh's *History of the World* with them to Prague, where it fell into the hands of the conquerors, but eventually found its way back to London and the British Museum, where it now reposes. They are therefore likely to have had works by Bacon with them at Heidelberg. We know that in later life Elizabeth was interested in the works of Bacon; in her early life before her marriage she would have known Bacon in England; he composed one of the entertainments for her wedding. Perhaps another transmitter of Baconian influence might have been Michael Maier who was in close contact with England during the reign of Frederick and Elizabeth in the Palatinate. Maier transmitted works by early English alchemical writers to the German alchemical movement, and he may well have also carried books by Bacon to Germany. Maier was deeply interested in philosophical interpretation of mythology and that side of Bacon's thought, expressed in his philosophical interpretation of myth in *The Wisdom of the Ancients* (1609), may well have had a fascination for Maier and his school. That his alchemical philosophy was hidden in the ancient myths was a basic tenet for Maier, and Bacon, too, had sought for his own natural philosophy in mythology. However we need not particularize too much as to what the points of contact may have been. It will suffice to say that the Anglophil movement in the Palatinate and surrounding Protestant states at the time when so much was hoped for from James I would have included an interest in the great philosopher of the Jacobean age, Francis Bacon.

There are, however, as already mentioned, obviously basic differences between Baconianism and German Rosicrucianism. The latter is more profoundly Hermetic, more deeply magical than Bacon's more soberseeming outlook. [There is] in the German movement a strong undercurrent of influences from Giordano Bruno and, above all, from John Dee. We [know] that Dee's *Monas hieroglyphica,* the symbol in which he summed up his philosophy, recurs in the Rosicrucian literature. Bacon nowhere mentions Dee, and nowhere cites his famous *Monas hieroglyphica.*

It has been a well-known objection to Bacon's claim to be

an important figure in the history of science that he did not place sufficient emphasis on the all-important mathematical sciences in his programme for the advancement of learning, and that he showed his ignorance of these sciences by his rejection of the Copernican theory and of William Gilbert's theory of the magnet. In [a 1968 article, "The Hermetic Tradition in Renaissance Science"] I argued that Bacon's avoidance of such topics might have been due to a desire to keep his programme as free as possible from implications of magic. Dee had been heavily suspected as a magician and 'conjuror'; Giordano Bruno, the Hermetic Magus, had associated the Copernican theory, in a work published in England, with a forthcoming return of 'Egyptian' or magical religion; William Gilbert was obviously influenced by Bruno in his work on the magnet. I suggested that Bacon's avoidance of mathematics and the Copernican theory might have been because he regarded mathematics as too closely associated with Dee and his 'conjuring', and Copernicus as too closely associated with Bruno and his extreme 'Egyptian' and magical religion. This hypothesis is now worth recalling because it suggests a possible reason for a major difference between German Rosicrucianism and Baconianism. In the former Dee and his mathematics are not feared, but Bacon avoids them; in the former Bruno is an influence but is rejected by Bacon. In both cases Bacon may have been evading what seemed to him dangerous subjects in order to protect his programme from witch-hunters, from the cry of 'sorcery' which, as Naudé said, could pursue a mathematician in the early seventeenth century.

In thinking about Bacon's attitude to science, and his way of advocating scientific advancement, we ought always to remember the character and outlook of the monarch whom Bacon had to try to propitiate and to interest in his programme for the advancement of learning. In this he was not successful; as D. H. Wilson has pointed out [in *King James VI and I*], James 'did not understand or appreciate Bacon's great plan', nor did he respond with any offer to help Bacon's projects for scientific institutions. When he was sent the *Novum Organum* in 1620 he was heard to remark that this work was like the peace of God which passeth all understanding.

It has never, I think, been suggested that James's doubtful attitude towards Baconian science might be connected with his very deep interest in, and dread of, magic and witchcraft. These subjects had a fascination for him which was tied up with neuroses about some experiences in his early life. In his *Demonology* (1597) James advocated the death penalty for all witches, though he urges care in the examination of cases. The subject was for him a most serious one, a branch of theology. Obviously James was not the right person to examine the—always rather difficult—problem of when Renaissance Magia and Cabala were valuable movements, leading to science, and when they verged on sorcery, the problem of defining the difference between good magic and bad magic. James was not interested in science and would react with fear from any sort of magic.

It is not surprising that when old John Dee appealed to James for help in clearing his reputation from charges of conjuring devils, James would have nothing to do with him. Dee's fruitless appeal to James was made in June 1604. The old man to whose learning the Elizabethan age was so infinitely indebted was disgraced in the reign of James and died in great poverty in 1608. Bacon must have taken good note of James's attitude to Dee, and he must also have noted that survivors from the Elizabethan age of mathematics and magic, of navigational boldness and anti-Spanish exploits, were not sure of encouragement under James, as they had been under Elizabeth. Northumberland and Raleigh pursued their studies in prison in the Tower under James, working at mathematics and alchemy with their learned associate, Thomas Hariot.

Obviously, Bacon would have been careful to avoid, in works intended to interest James, anything savouring of Dee and his suspicious mathematics. Even so, Bacon did not succeed in allaying James's suspicions of scientific advancement, however carefully presented.

And even more obviously, it was not the way to influence James in favour of his son-in-law's plans and projects in the Palatinate and Bohemia to associate him with a movement which wrapped its designs in enchanted vaults and invisible R. C. Brothers, who could easily be turned into sorcerers by witch-hunters. Among the many mistakes made by the friends of the unfortunate Elector Palatine, the Rosicrucian manifestos may have been one of the worst. If any rumour of them came to James's ears, and any rumour of their being associated with Frederick, this would certainly have done more than anything else to turn him against Frederick, and to destroy any hope that he would countenance his projects.

Thus Francis Bacon as he propagated advancement of learning, and particularly of scientific learning, during the reign of James I was moving amongst pitfalls. The old Elizabethan scientific tradition was not in favour, and some of its major surviving representatives were shunned or in prison. The late Queen Elizabeth had asked John Dee to explain his *Monas hieroglyphica* to her; King James would have nothing to do with its author. Bacon, when he published **The Advancement of Learning** in 1605, would have been aware that James had repulsed Dee in the preceding year. And moreover the exported Elizabethan traditions, which had gone over to the Palatinate with James's daughter and her husband, were not in favour either. Francis Bacon was one of those who regretted James's foreign policy and urged support of the Elector Palatine. Here, too, the writer of English manifestos for the advancement of learning would have to walk warily, lest he might seem too much implicated in movements in the Palatinate.

Bacon had to steer a cautious course through many difficulties and dangers as he pleaded for advancement of scientific learning in those years of the early seventeenth century when the witchcraft hysteria was mounting throughout Europe.

We too have been moving cautiously through this chapter, struck by the idea that there might be a certain parallelism between the Rosicrucian and the Baconian movements, that these might be, so to speak, differently developing halves of the same problem, that it might be illuminating for both to study them together. Up to now we have had no evidence to give the reader as to what Bacon himself may have thought about the Rosicrucian manifestos. But now comes evidence of a most striking kind, from the *New Atlantis.*

Bacon died in 1626. In 1627 there was published from his papers an unfinished and undated work in which he set forth his Utopia, his dream of an ideal religious and scientific society. It takes the form of an allegory, about the discovery by storm-tossed mariners of a new land, the New Atlantis. The inhabitants of the New Atlantis had built there the perfect society, though remaining entirely unknown to the rest of the world. They were Christians; Christianity had been brought to them in early times, an evangelical Christianity which emphasized brotherly love. They were also in an advanced state of scientific knowledge. In their great college, called Salomon's House, an order of priest-scientists pursued researches in all the arts and sciences, the results of which they knew how to apply for the benefit of men. This fiction sums up the work and aims of Bacon's whole life, the advancement of learning to be applied for the use and benefit of mankind.

This fiction, parable, or *ludibrium,* reflects at several points themes from the Rosicrucian manifestos in such a way as to make it certain that Bacon knew the Rosencreutz story.

Before the travellers landed they were handed a scroll of instructions by an official from New Atlantis. 'This scroll was signed with a stamp of cherubin's wings, not spread, but hanging downwards, and by them a cross.' So was the Rosicrucian *Fama* sealed at the end with the motto 'Under the shadow of Jehova's wings', and the wings, as we have seen, often appear as characteristic emblems in other Rosicrucian literature.

On the following day the travellers were conducted with great kindness to the Strangers' House and here their sick were cared for. The travellers offered payment for these services but this was refused. The *Fama,* it will be remembered, lays it down as a rule for the R. C. Brothers that they are to heal the sick *gratis.*

A few days later, another official of New Atlantis came to visit the strangers in the Strangers' House. He wore a white turban 'with a small red cross on the top', further proof that Bacon's shipwrecked travellers had come to the land of the R. C. Brothers.

On a following day a governor of the country called on them and kindly explained to them all that they asked to know about the history and customs of the country, how Christianity was brought to it, and about the 'house or college' of Salomon's House with its staff of wise men. The travellers were permitted to ask questions about any matter which might still puzzle them. Whereupon they said that what surprised them most was that the inhabitants of New Atlantis knew all the languages of Europe, and seemed also to know all about the affairs of the outside world and the state of knowledge in it, yet they themselves were quite unknown and unheard of outside their own country:

that they should have knowledge of the languages, books, affairs, of those that lie at such a distance from them, it was a thing we could not tell what to make of; for that it seemed to us a condition and propriety of divine powers and beings, to be hidden and unseen to others, and yet to have others open, and as in a light to them.

At this speech the Governor gave a gracious smile and said that we did well to ask pardon for this question we now asked, for that it imported, as if we thought this land a land of magicians, that sent forth spirits of the air into all parts, to bring them news and intelligence of other countries. It was answered by us all, in all possible humbleness, but yet with a countenance taking knowledge, that we knew he spoke it but merrily; that we were apt enough to think that there was somewhat supernatural in this island, but yet rather as angelical than magical.

Further on, it is explained how it was that the wise men of New Atlantis knew all that went on in the outside world though themselves remaining invisible to it. It was because travellers were sent out from New Atlantis to collect information; they dressed in the dress of the countries they visited and adopted their habits, and so passed unperceived. In terms of a Rosicrucian manifesto, this means that they followed one of the rules of the R. C. Brothers, to wear no special habit or distinguishing mark but to conform in dress and appearance with the inhabitants of whatever country they were visiting. The ordinance laid down in New Atlantis was that every twelve years 'three of the fellows or brethren of Salomon's House' should go forth on a mission to collect knowledge of the state of arts and sciences, to bring back books, instruments and news. This trade, it was explained, was not a commerce in ordinary material commodities, but only a seeking 'for God's first creature, which was light; to have light, I say, of the growth of all the parts of the world'.

Thus, though the name Rose Cross is nowhere mentioned by Bacon in the *New Atlantis,* it is abundantly clear that he knew the Rose Cross fiction and was adapting it to his own parable. New Atlantis was governed by R. C. Brothers, invisibly travelling as 'merchants of light' in the outside world from their invisible college or centre, now called Salomon's House, and following the rules of the R. C. Fraternity, to heal the sick free of charge, to wear no special dress. Moreover the 'cherubin's wings' seal the scroll brought from New Atlantis, as they seal the *Fama.* The island had something angelical about it, rather than magical, and its official wore a red cross in his turban.

Modern students of Bacon are not familiar with Rosicrucian literature, which has not been included in their studies nor recognized as a legitimate branch of history of thought or science. But those who read the *New Atlantis* before the *Fama* and the *Confessio* were forgotten would have immediately recognized the R. C. Brothers and their Invisible College in the denizens of New Atlantis. One such reader recorded his recognition. This was John Heydon whose *Holy Guide,* published in 1662, is largely based on adaptation of the *New Atlantis.* When the man in the white turban with the red cross on it comes to visit the sick, Heydon quotes this as follows: 'I am by Office Governour of this House of Strangers, and by vocation I am a Christian priest, and of the Order of the Rosie Cross'. When Bacon speaks of one of the wise men of the House of Salomon, Heydon quotes this as, 'one of the wise Men of the Society of the Rosicrucians'. Heydon speaks explicitly of the House of Salomon in New Atlantis as the same as the 'Temple of the Rosie Cross'. There are very many other points at which Heydon associates *New Atlantis* with the *Fama;* in fact he is reading Bacon's work as practically the same as the Rosicrucian manifesto.

Heydon's significant Rosicrucian interpolations into *New Atlantis* should be studied in more detail than is possible here, but one other of his points must be mentioned. When Bacon says that they have some of the lost works of Solomon in New Atlantis, Heydon expands this into a statement that they have 'the book M', which was written by Solomon, in New Atlantis. The book M was one of the sacred objects found in the tomb of Christian Rosencreutz, according to the *Fama.*

The fact that Bacon's *New Atlantis* shows knowledge of the *Fama,* and that Heydon confirms the parallel, is most certainly not a proof that Bacon belonged to some Rosicrucian or masonic secret society. The historical evidence is spoiled and distorted if it is used to support unverifiable claims of this kind. It is perhaps justifiable reaction against such fanciful theories which has prevented serious historians from taking proper note of the fact that there are undeniably influences from the *Fama* in the *New Atlantis.*

This fact will have to be studied very seriously in the future by historians of thought, and studied in connection with the German Rosicrucian movement. The religion of *New Atlantis* has much in common with that of the Rosicrucian manifestos. It is intensely Christian in spirit, though not doctrinal, interpreting the Christian spirit in terms of practical benevolence, like the R. C. Brothers. It is profoundly influenced by Hebraic-Christian mysticism, as in Christian Cabala. The inhabitants of New Atlantis respect the Jews; they call their college after Solomon and seek for God in nature. The Hermetic-Cabalist tradition has borne fruit in their great college devoted to scientific enquiry. There is an unearthly quality in the world of New Atlantis. Though it may be prophetic of the advent of the scientific revolution, this prophecy is made, not in a modern spirit, but within other terms of reference. The inhabitants of New Atlantis would appear to have achieved the great instauration of learning and have therefore returned to the state of Adam in Paradise before the Fall—the objective of advancement both for Bacon and for the authors of the Rosicrucian manifestos. One of the most revealing moments in *New Atlantis* is when the travellers wonder whether they are not in the presence of divine powers and beings, whether the invisibility of the Brothers (whom we now know to have been R. C. Brothers) may not have in it something supernatural, 'yet rather angelical than magical'. Though the Governor treats this doubt 'merrily' (or as a *ludibrium*), and gives rational reason for their invisibility, yet the *New Atlantis* is poised on a knife edge, depending for its favourable reception by the reader on whether that reader accepts the scientific influences in it

as 'almost angelical', or as diabolically inspired. (pp. 118-29)

Frances A. Yates, "Francis Bacon 'Under the Shadow of Jehova's Wings'," in her The Rosicrucian Enlightenment, *Routledge & Kegan Paul, 1972, pp. 118-29.*

Anthony Quinton   (essay date 1980)

[*In the following excerpt, Quinton surveys Bacon's scientific, philosophical, and literary works, concluding that the "completeness of [Bacon's] vision of a human future dominated by natural science was a speculative and wholly non-inductive leap of the mind which is none the less admirable for its uneasy conformity with his own ideas about the growth of knowledge."*]

[Bacon] did not effectively develop his professed principle that the same empirical and inductive method should be applied to man and society as to nature. The account he gives of logic, ethics and 'civil knowledge' in *The Advancement of Learning* represents them as arts, or even technologies, as operative or practical disciplines. There is no exposition of the theoretical sciences on which, for conformity with his doctrine about the two aspects of natural philosophy, they ought to rest.

He was, of course, quite right to see logic, ethics and 'policy', the art of prudent conduct in private life and politics, as practical or normative disciplines. Where his inventiveness failed him was in the matter of delineating in the abstract the theoretical correlates on which they should be based. The interesting thing is that he did better, from the point of view of his own principle of the comprehensiveness of the inductive method, in his practice as a student of human affairs than as a detached anatomist of the possible and desirable varieties of that practice.

Thus, when he was actually engaged in writing history or about politics and law or, again, in the worldly moralising of the *Essays,* a grimly realistic and empirical spirit prevails. Recommendations about how to deal with human beings are firmly founded on a thoroughly unsentimental conception of human motives and characters. He was, indeed, a distinguished practitioner of some of the social studies: history, politics and jurisprudence. He made a much more significant addition to the stock of first-order knowledge about the world in the human sphere than he did in the domain of non-human nature.

His chief historical work is his *Reign of the History of Henry VII,* written very quickly after his fall from glory in 1621, presumably from previously assembled materials. It has been established with the utmost Teutonic thoroughness, by the German historian of the early Tudors, Heinrich Busch, that Bacon's materials were not his own original discoveries, and that he relied for them almost entirely on the *English History* of Polydore Vergil, a protégé of Henry VII, published in 1533, nearly a quarter of a century after that monarch's death, and to a lesser extent on various Tudor chroniclers. More important is the fact that Bacon, for all his professions of scientific objectivity, used his materials very selectively and sometimes dishonestly.

Nevertheless, to suppose that if he is not an original source his sole importance as a historian derives from the excellence of his style betrays a pitiable kind of academic philistinism. What judgement would the egregious Busch have passed on Gibbon? In Bacon's time the writing of history in England was no longer the monopoly of monastic chroniclers. Their place had been taken by urban and lay chroniclers, culminating in Holinshed. Undigested material also accumulated in the work of a great generation of antiquaries. Thomas More's book on Richard III is a denigratory pamphlet. Bacon was the first analytic or explanatory English historian, since Polydore Vergil, the only possible earlier competitor for the description, was an Italian.

Bacon represents Henry VII as a cautious, suspicious and rational man, anxious to achieve his aims as cheaply and safely as possible. The reconstruction of the thinking that lay behind his manner of presenting himself to his new subjects after his victory in 1485 is nakedly and convincingly prudential. The prose of this book, incidentally, is much plainer and less ornamented than that of the *Advancement,* let alone that of the *Essays.* It is a working illustration of statecraft rather than an item of polite literature.

Bacon's political opinions are dispersed around various very different genres of writing. Half of the *Essays,* at their final count, deal with public affairs. There are also letters of advice to monarchs and ministers. He comes forward, not surprisingly, as the theorist of Tudor monarchy, but not as a supporter of the absolutism favoured by the Stuarts and above all by the first of them, James I. Bacon believed in a strong monarchy; advised but not in any way dominated by parliament; respectful of, but not exposed to the arbitrament of, the courts. Judges, as he said in a famous phrase, should be lions, 'but yet lions under the throne'.

He saw great accumulations of wealth as unfavourable to the stability of the nation. He wanted the king, in accordance with a traditional idea, to be rich enough 'to live of his own', reserving serious taxation for public emergencies. There is an echo of the Machiavelli of the *Discorsi* in his belief that the highest life for a citizen is military, that there should be a citizen army and never mercenaries. He saw war, in a moderately unattractive analogy, as the exercise of states, a kind of bodily exertion essential to their health.

His hostility to lawyers, at least in their more overweening, politically ambitious aspect, was more than a by-product of his long-drawn-out quarrel with Coke. It is entirely in keeping with his rational progressivism, his dismissal of the presumption of the greater wisdom of the past, that he should scorn the retrospective obsession of lawyers with precedent. In the same way his exclusion of religion from the serious life of the intellect is congruous with his Erastian attitude to the church. C. D. Broad described him as 'a sincere if unenthusiastic Christian of that sensible school which regards the church of England as a branch of the Civil Service'. He advised Queen Elizabeth to water down the oath of allegiance so as not to compel

reasonable Roman Catholics into treason, while agreeing that they should be excluded from office.

Bacon's animus against lawyers was in no way the expression of a sense of personal inadequacy as a lawyer. He was proud of his own abilities in his pre-eminently professional sphere, predicted he would in due time be seen as a better lawyer than his enemy, Coke, and received, in the end, an endorsement of this claim from the great historian of English law, Sir William Holdsworth, who said of him that he was 'a more complete lawyer than any of his contemporaries'. Holdsworth goes on to say of chapter 3 of the eighth book of *De Augmentis,* which is the most articulate presentation of Bacon's theory of law, that it was 'the first critical, the first jurisprudential, estimate of English law which had ever been made'.

Bacon lays characteristic stress on the need for certainty in law, seeing its absence as sometimes the result of there being no law in some area, sometimes of the obscurity of the law that there is. Obscure law leads to insecurity and to delay. The whole inherited mystery of the common law, with its immensely variegated constituents and its professional priesthood of devotional interpreters, suffered from what Bacon saw as the worst of vices in any human construction: inefficiency. He did not go so far as to recommend the complete codification of law. But he believed that English law should be digested, should have all obsolete, overruled and repetitive matter excised from it.

In his usual programmatic way this projected digest of the law should be accompanied by other works: a register of precedents, to be treated with respect, but not as binding authorities; a dictionary of legal terms; a volume of Institutes; and a volume, *De Regulis Juris,* listing fundamental legal principles, which he sketched himself in his *Maxims of the Law,* written in 1597 and published shortly after his death.

Bacon believed that the law should be efficient and cheap. He did not share the almost religious sentiments of many Englishmen towards their common law inheritance, and it was this attitude, incarnated in Coke, that was in the end to prevail, so that Bentham would react to the law of England in much the same way as Bacon two hundred years later. In the seventeenth century the common law was seen to be, and was, an obstacle to the arbitrary extension of the powers of the crown, something that was in part made inevitable by new circumstances, in part a matter of the Stuart dynasty's appetite for absolute power. Bacon, brought up under the more measured and cautious Elizabeth, did not see that danger, and was not minded to see absolutism as much of a danger anyway.

The historian Hugh Trevor-Roper regards Bacon as the clearest-sighted discerner of the critical problems of the monarchy in the early seventeenth century, above all the financial one of securing sufficient revenuc to operate effectively. But his efforts to lead the crown to economic rationality, to curb its wastefulness, failed in face of the frivolous extravagance of James I and the jewelled catamites he ennobled. Bacon, Trevor-Roper writes, 'diagnosed the evil—no man perhaps so completely'. In law and in politics, then, his good advice was not taken: unthinking traditionalism prevailed in the one, foolish and wasteful arbitrariness in the other. But, as Trevor-Roper goes on to show, he still exerted an important social influence through his ideas about education.

Bacon did not have much to say about education directly. As regards schools he does little more in explicit terms than recommend imitation of the Jesuits. He has more to say about universities, the objects of some lively invective in **The Advancement of Learning,** where he disparages the ancient scholastic exercises of wordy disputation, and proposes a style of education fit to produce capable statesmen in which history and politics take the place of logic and Latin. It was not until a couple of decades after his death that a Baconian educational doctrine was colourfully propounded by the Bohemian John Comenius, a somewhat mystical version of Bacon's views, as it turned out, derived from **New Atlantis** more than less fanciful works, and associating apocalyptic prophecy with such Baconian ideas as the need to attend to things rather than words.

But if Bacon himself said little directly about education as an institution, much is obviously implied by his writings, above all the need for the perceptual study of natural objects instead of unmitigated book-learning. For all his own religious indifference, his opposition to contemplative, aristocratic uselessness and his consequent concern with usefulness in the actual world were highly attractive to the growing spirit of moderate, non-fanatical Puritanism, for which sober productiveness and not millenial frenzy was the proper rule of life.

A general survey of Bacon's work cannot end without some reference to his more narrowly literary qualities and convictions. The contrast between the richness of his style and the plainness of his message is not by any means the largest paradox about Bacon, if it is a paradox at all. In his age to write well and to write strikingly were much the same; the self-effacingly 'natural' prose of Swift, the most perfect linguistic vehicle ever used for the conveyance of thought, was still far away. It should be remembered that Sir Thomas Browne was to some extent a Baconian chastener of superstitious error and an even more colourful and ornate writer.

It is not just their somewhat artificial air of being exemplary exercises that makes Bacon's **Essays** less attractive than other, more earnest-seeming works that he wrote in English. Their aphoristic style of construction, a string of epigrammatic felicities printed as continuous prose, is tiresome. The impersonality which is brought into vivid relief by the comparison with Montaigne is, we feel, inappropriate to the form: impersonality is for the treatise or paper; the essay proper should be more confessional and intimate. Douglas Bush memorably said of Bacon's **Essays,** 'everyone has read them, but no one is ever found reading them'.

Inevitably Bacon's are not the very first essays in English literature, but they are the first to have become famous, and they have always remained so. Most people, one may well suppose, know more of them than they realise. As a quarry for anthologists of memorable sayings Bacon's **Essays** cannot rank far behind *Hamlet.* The first ten, which

were published in 1597, were simply sequences of aphorisms and might have benefited from being printed on separate lines in the familiar style of the proverbs and psalms of the Old Testament. In the final edition of 1625 the number of essays had risen to fifty-eight and the senior members of the collection had been often considerably enlarged. The staccato series of aphorisms had been modulated into a much more continuous discursive flow by the inclusion of illustrative anecdotes and citations from classical literature, by digressive embroideries on the original theme, and by the provision of simple verbal devices of connection.

The insistently aphoristic nature of the original essays tends to reveal itself, despite these changes, in their arrestingly memorable first sentences: 'What is truth? said jesting Pilate; and would not stay for an answer', 'Men fear death, as children fear to go in the dark', 'Revenge is a kind of wild justice', 'The joys of parents are secret; and so are their griefs and fears. They cannot utter the one; nor will they not utter the other. Children sweeten labours; but they make misfortunes more bitter', 'He that hath wife and children hath given hostages to fortune', 'It is a miserable state of mind to have few things to desire and many things to fear; and yet that commonly is the case of kings', 'Suspicions amongst thoughts are like bats amongst birds, they ever fly by twilight', 'God Almighty first planted a garden. And it is indeed the purest of human pleasures.'

Bacon's fondness for an aphoristic mode of expression is not just a bare idiosyncrasy of taste. He offers a defence of it in principle in the **Advancement of Learning** as particularly suitable for the presentation of tentative opinions ('broken knowledges') and, in conformity with that idea, it is clear that he took the word *essay* in his first use of it in an etymologically primitive way, as meaning *attempt* or *experiment.* In later editions the more discursively expressed book was called **Essays or Counsels.**

The essays as a whole can be roughly divided into three main kinds: those which deal with public affairs, those which deal with particular aspects of private life, and those which deal with large abstract topics like truth and death, beauty and studies, revenge and the vicissitudes of things. The first group are comparatively practical and humdrum. At times, notably in the essay on usury, a lucid and competent piece of economic reasoning, they anticipate the impersonally rational style of exposition of the empirical social theorists of the eighteenth century. Bacon has sensible, only mildly unedifying views to communicate about the aristocratic order and social stability, the causes and cures of sedition, factions and negotiations, atheism and superstition, arrived at by careful and clearsighted reflection on an ample experience of the matter in hand.

The cynical, reptilian side of Bacon is more evident, perhaps because less appropriate from the point of view of twentieth-century moral tastes, in the essays on such private topics as children and marriage (seen mainly as obstacles to worldly advancement), friendship and expense (friends are useful as receptacles for one's emotional overflow and as better critics of one's deeds than one is oneself), riches and ambition. An unusually sad experience of life is suggested by the remark, 'There is little friendship in the world and least of all between equals, which was wont to be magnified.'

It is the essays of the third group, dealing with large abstract ideas, that are deservedly the best-known. In them Bacon is freed from the fussy preoccupations of a high public official serving a third-rate despot, and from the obsession with advancement in the world that corrupts his thoughts about relations with other human beings. He said of himself that he had concerned himself more with studies than with men, and in these solitary, almost transcendental, meditations his prose is at its most free, rich and energetic. This is baroque prose, much closer to the language of Thomas Browne and Robert Burton, of John Aubrey, Jeremy Taylor and the Authorised Version, than it is to the plain expository style which the Royal Society, inspired by Bacon's *New Atlantis,* sought to make the vehicle of scientific thought.

Figures and conceits abound in these essays, resonant, mysterious, sometimes sinister.

> Truth may perhaps come to the price of a pearl, that sheweth best by day; but it will not rise to the price of a diamond or carbuncle, that sheweth best in varied lights. . . . Groans and convulsions, and a discoloured face, and friends weeping, and blacks, and obsequies, and the like, shew death terrible. . . . And at first let him practise with helps, as swimmers do with bladders or rushes; but after a time let him practise with disadvantages, as dancers do with thick shoes. . . . For the helmet of Pluto, which maketh the politic man go invisible, is secrecy in the counsel and celerity in the execution. For when things are once come to the execution, there is no secrecy comparable to celerity; like the motion of a bullet in the air, which flieth so swift as it outruns the eye.

In a well-known essay on Bacon and the 'dissociation of sensibility' L. C. Knights has argued that the pervasively rich imagery of Bacon's prose is externally applied ornament, deliberately put on for illustrative purposes and not part of the actual fabric of his thought. He goes on to connect this with the new attitude to nature proclaimed in Bacon's writing, one in which nature is seen as a field of uses and manipulations, something alienated from the self, to be mastered, tricked, 'put to the question'. Certainly Bacon's view of nature would make such a stylistic consequence plausible. One may agree that there is not the same delight in the visible world in a Baconian view of it as in the attitude of the pagan Renaissance. But in the middle ages nature was from an orthodox point of view a snare, appropriately mentioned in the same breath as the flesh and the devil. It could well be that the dissociation of sensibility is rather to be attributed to the way in which people lived, to the change from a comparatively natural to a comparatively artificial environment, than to any formal doctrines about the character of the natural world.

The kind of specialised pursuit of inductive natural science with a view to its technological application that Bacon heralded has come to be culturally estranged from art and the imagination. Bacon himself, indeed, while allocating a dignified place to the imagination in the life of the mind

as the basis of 'poesy', acknowledged that 'imagination hardly produces sciences' and that poesy is 'rather a pleasure or play of wit than a science'. In the same spirit is his mechanisation of scientific inquiry and the associated principle that no special gifts are needed to make profitable use of his method in that inquiry. Bacon, then, honoured art and the imagination but was emphatic about the difference between art and science.

In his own brief but significant remarks on beauty, above all in his one-page essay on the subject, Bacon adopts a more or less romantic view of the essential creativeness of the artist. Against the idea of there being canons of art he says, 'a painter may make a better face than ever was; but he must do it by a kind of felicity, . . . and not by rule.' The same attitude is expressed in his best-known aesthetic observation: 'there is no excellent beauty that hath not some strangeness in the proportions.' These explicit remarks and the high position he accorded poesy and the imagination led such apparently un-Baconian figures as Shelley to admire him. The richness and colour of his own prose is, indeed, less in harmony with his main message about natural knowledge and the relief of man's estate than the plain style deliberately adopted by the members of the Royal Society in pursuit of his intellectual ends. (pp. 70-8)

It is a commonplace about Bacon that he was remarkably blind to the important scientific work that was going on in his own time. To start with things near at hand, he ignored the brilliant work of his own doctor, William Harvey, on the circulation of the blood. By interpreting the crucial aspect of human vitality in hydraulic terms as a pumping system, Harvey prepared the way for another of Bacon's associates, Thomas Hobbes, to develop an account of man as a wholly natural object. Bacon dismissed another instance of major scientific advance in his own immediate environment, Gilbert's theory of magnetism, as a kind of occultist fantasy. Going further afield, he disdained Copernicus and ignored Kepler and Galileo.

Nevertheless there is no question about the degree of respect in which he was held by British scientists of the succeeding generation. Robert Hooke and Robert Boyle praised him without qualification and he became the patron saint or presiding deity of the Royal Society. Hobbes, the great scientific philosopher of the period after Bacon's death, took an absolutely opposed view of the nature of science and made no acknowledgement of Bacon. But he was no scientist, only an incautious amateur mathematician, and an object of scorn to the Baconians of the Royal Society. On the other hand, the grand culmination of British science in the seventeenth century, the work of Newton, contains the puzzling, but highly Baconian, phrase *hypotheses non fingo.*

In the eighteenth century the glorification of British science of the immediately preceding period, first by Voltaire and, following him, by all the great figures of the French Enlightenment, unhesitatingly included Bacon, seen as the great originator of the whole process. The more specific detail of Bacon's work as a classifier of the sciences was the most admired and authoritative exemplar for the work of the creators of the *Encyclopédie,* the great collaborative work in which the leading thinkers of the French Enlightenment expressed their comprehensive liberal ideology in the light disguise of a reference book. Grateful praise is offered him in the *Discours préliminaire* by Jean d'Alembert, the great mathematician who was Diderot's coeditor.

The special regard of this particular party in the intellectual life of France explains two later, and directly opposed, attitudes to him. It is not surprising that Comte should have admired the most distinguished and unwavering prophet of positive science. On the other side, the most extreme and resonant of French conservatives, de Maistre, devoted a whole book of fierce criticism to Bacon and refers to him from time to time in more familiar works such as the *Soirées de Saint-Pétersbourg* as the initiator of the infidelity of the Enlightenment. For him Bacon is the first and most undisguised of those induced by satanic pride to reject the revealed knowledge judged by God to be sufficient for man and to turn from it to knowledge they have acquired on their own.

De Maistre's critique contains some knockabout philosophy of uncomplicatedly polemical intent. Bacon's belief that all causes are physical, he says, ignores the fact that laws of physical causation only describe. For explanation and real causes we must go behind nature to its transcendent source of motion. 'Full of an unconscious rancour, whose origin and nature he did not himself recognise, against all spiritual ideas, Bacon fastened the general attention with all his might upon the physical sciences in such a way as to turn men away from all other branches of learning. . . . In conformity with this system of philosophy, Bacon urges men to seek the cause of natural phenomena in the configuration of constituent atoms or molecules, the most false and gross idea ever to have stained the human understanding.'

If Bacon no longer elicits that sort of hostility, he does not excite the kind of enthusiasm among philosophers that he did from Comte and other nineteenth-century positivists such as G. H. Lewes, in whose *Biographical History of Philosophy* he occupies a position of honour. John Stuart Mill, indeed, pays Bacon the sincerest of compliments, that of rather exact imitation, encumbered with some muddle-headed complications. But he makes hardly any reference to him in the *System of Logic.* Macaulay admired the prophet of utility and progress, despised the man and cast some inept aspersions on the inductive logician. (Macaulay objects that the inductive procedure Bacon systematises is natural to men and does not need to be formulated. That is an irrelevant objection to start with. It may be 'natural' to reason in a certain way as a matter of habit or custom. It is quite another thing to give explicit verbal expression to the rules embedded in that practice. It is also a false objection. Many thinking men no doubt reasoned in an eliminatively inductive way before Bacon came on the scene. It is still a somewhat exceptional and sophisticated style of inductive thinking. Simple enumeration, the logical equivalent of the formation of conditioned reflexes, is vastly more usual).

The Scottish philosophers of common sense of the late eighteenth and early nineteenth centuries, exponents of the official academic philosophy of Britain and America until the 1850s and 60s, were the last professionals to be really devoted admirers of Bacon as a philosopher, apart from a couple of rather obscure figures swimming against the prevailing idealist tide of late Victorian Oxford: Thomas Fowler and Thomas Case. The greatest of the pragmatists, C. S. Peirce, wrote that 'superior as Lord Bacon's conception is to earlier notions, a modern reader who is not in awe of his grandiloquence is chiefly struck by the inadequacy of his view of scientific procedure'. He goes on to argue that any mechanical system, such as Bacon's tables of exclusion, cannot produce significant scientific knowledge.

Bacon has been almost wholly neglected by the analytic philosophers of the twentieth century. Von Wright . . . tried to do him justice in some brief historical asides in his writings on induction. But the major figures—Russell, Moore, Wittgenstein and Carnap—have next to nothing to say about him. This is partly because the treatment of induction by analytic philosophers has concentrated on the conception of it as *probable inference,* and the notion of probability has no place in Bacon's thinking, convinced as he was that his method was capable of yielding certain knowledge of the laws of nature. More generally, in their eyes Bacon lacks the right sort of rigour. Where his exposition is reasonably exact, as in his theory of elimination, it is the philosophically uncontroversial aspect of the field with which it is concerned and, where noticed at all, it is remitted to textbooks. But for the most part the admixture of rhetoric with argument is too strong for currently austere philosophical tastes.

The one important exception to this is the attention given to Bacon by Sir Karl Popper in his influential books on the philosophy of science. Popper sees the imaginative speculation, condemned by Bacon as the intellectual vice of scholasticism, as the nerve of scientific progress. Bacon's idea of scientific theorising as a mechanisable business, owing nothing to the special gifts of those who pursue it, is something it has been his main task to repudiate. It is interesting that he uses to undermine Bacon's position the very logical feature of general statements, the greater force of the negative instance, which Bacon relied on to demonstrate the weakness of simple enumeration. Popper would claim that by developing the full potential of the idea he has shown how little Bacon succeeded in making of it. Nevertheless he counts Bacon as an ally on the very broadest front, in opposition to the kind of purely verbal speculation which never puts its findings to the test of experience, recognising Bacon as a fellow-rationalist in the good, nineteenth-century sense of that word. On a particular point he suggests persuasively that there is less difference between what Bacon understood by true induction and what Aristotle did, the procedure now labelled 'intuitive induction,' than is usually supposed. Bacon himself thought that Aristotelian induction was simply enumerative, so he was in no position to acknowledge the identity of view, even if Popper is right about what he means by 'the interpretation of nature'.

Popper's, and for that matter Peirce's, criticisms are only particularly thorough and sophisticated versions of one of the two main and persistent objections to Bacon's theory of science, that it wholly fails to accord an adequate place to hypothesis, the imaginative construction of novel theories. As a result he neglected the importance of scientific creativity and, in his ideas about the levelling of men's wits, of the very marked inequality with which it is distributed. The other leading objection is that, unlike the Italian philosophers of nature who preceded him, he failed altogether to understand the importance of mathematics for the natural science of the new age.

This second deficiency—and it is, of course a real one—stemmed largely from the fact that he did not know much about mathematics anyway. But there is a more philosophical, or at any rate ideological, factor involved, namely the close association between mathematics and occultism, shown in numerology, astrology, the measuring of pyramids and the calculating of millennia. An analogous factor was at work in his attitude to imaginative speculation, namely his identification of it with the cobweb-spinning verbalism of the more dismally repetitive kind of academic Aristotelian.

A third weakness which is large enough to be mentioned alongside the two just considered is his dogmatism, his failure to conceive that the price of substantial general beliefs is uncertainty, that we cannot do more than confirm, render more or less rationally credible, the theories about the world in which science consists. It is not an objection of principle, but it is still an objection, that he made such an insensitive response to the real scientific advances of his own age.

He is sometimes defended on grounds of being too early on the scene, since, it is said, his methods, although not those of the great physicists of the seventeenth century, were very much those of the biologists of the nineteenth, as the greatest of them, Charles Darwin, explicitly testifies. If that is so, the same could be said of his ideas about the connection between science and technology. Science contributed negligibly to economic production before the nineteenth century and the emergence of industrially applicable chemistry. What it did do was help in the production of more science by making possible new scientific instruments.

Bacon's main claim to importance must rest on his role as a prophet and a critic. It remains a very large claim. His firm separation of science from religion and religious metaphysics; his transformation of the status of natural investigation from that of the forbidden, when seen as sorcery, or the despised, when seen as low drudgery; his intoxicating programme of a vast increase in human power and pleasure through inquiry in a great array of clearly and colourfully delineated fields—all these add up to a major turning-point in the history of the European mind. For it is the empirical natural science which Bacon called for and the technology that eventually sprang from it that have been the main contribution, an incalculably great and irrevocably ambiguous one, that Europe has made to the world, first by political mastery, now, more subtly, by mastery of thought. The completeness of his vision of a human future dominated by natural science was a speculative and wholly non-inductive leap of the mind which is

none the less admirable for its uneasy conformity with his own ideas about the growth of knowledge. (pp. 79-84)

Anthony Quinton, in his Francis Bacon, *Hill and Wang, 1980, 90 p.*

Charles Whitney   (essay date 1986)

[*In the following excerpt, Whitney identifies Bacon as a true precursor of the modern spirit. Even Bacon's inability to finish his extensive projects appears, in Whitney's opinion, to result from a Freudian "repetition obsession," a manifestation of guilt feelings resulting from the "primal sacrifice."*]

Freedom, reason, discovery, progress: Francis Bacon focuses these ideals in a distinctively modern call to search for knowledge as power over nature, knowledge for the benefit and use of life. Bacon's work has often been a focus for discussion about the what and why and how of modern ideas and institutions. His astonishingly diverse reception over the past 350 years brings out tensions or discontinuities that are basic to modern culture and that his own work also suggests—those between faith and reason, authority and freedom, participation and dominion, feeling and intellect, rhetoric and logic, and, perhaps above all, tradition and innovation. Jonson praises Bacon's learning, Swift censures Baconian philistinism. But then Rousseau praises Bacon's courageous iconoclasm; Kant, Macaulay, and writers of the left and of the moderate right praise his progressivism and humanitarianism, yet many condemn his godlessly narrow quest for power. Seventeenth-century scientists find inspiration in Bacon's specifically Christian science—although later freethinking ones also hail Bacon as an ancestor. Over the objections of others, some literary scholars in our century have ignored Shelley's discovery of Bacon the prophetic poet by their assessments of Bacon's reptilian style, while some communications experts find important answers through analyzing how Bacon functioned as Master Rhetorician.

If Bacon has occasionally been seized upon merely to provide a setting for his readers' conceptions or critiques of secular society, this is nevertheless because of his provocativeness: interest in him has originated in questions about the nature, validity, and direction of modern culture that his work still prompts us to ask. This paradigmatic character of Bacon has been illuminated in Hans Blumenberg's subtle work *The Legitimacy of the Modern Age.* Blumenberg, a leading philosopher and intellectual historian of Germany, does not simply try to justify the inevitable. He wishes to understand, defend, and help successfully carry forward certain Western values of the modern epoch that began in the Renaissance. Thus Bacon becomes one of his book's many "unfashionable heroes" of intellectual history. (pp. 1-2)

The modern age is a specific historical epoch beginning in the Renaissance, but the word *modern* itself is relative. It suggests, however, a fruitful way to begin understanding Bacon and the modern epoch. *Modernus* simply designates "now" as distinct from "then," that is, marks a recognition of the difference between conditions in the present and those in the past. Not surprisingly, it first appeared in a period when such differences were extreme: that following the dissolution of the Roman Empire. The word tends to denote the historical self-consciousness of a particular person or era. The relativity of the word also extends to the value set upon the present era. An innovator can be said to assert his modernity, denying the relevance of the past to his life; the experience of many Modernist writers, such as T. S. Eliot, author of *The Wasteland,* has been, on the contrary, to discover an inescapable condition of modern belatedness. But innovating moderns are often restorers, rejecting only the recent past; in 1550 the new age was called "modern" by Giorgio Vasari in his *Lives of the Painters, Sculptors, and Architects* because it revived the "antique" style; by Bacon's time the element of revival was not nearly so strong a connotation of the word, and today it is lost completely. (pp. 8-9)

Indeed, it was in the Renaissance that, once the discontinuity between present and past was established, the interpenetration of tradition and innovation was most exuberantly and consciously fostered; in comparison our traditions often seem burdensome and our originality trivial. Lawyer, teacher, divine, courtier all made daily and pragmatic application of the content and style of Latin classics. A Michelangelo, Montaigne, or Spenser could seem most strongly original when most subtly imitating or emulating others; for such artists, to realize oneself was also to realize the past in oneself. Modern science began when ancient scientific texts were collected and edited: the spirit of exploration that brought the New World was first directed toward antiquity. The printing press made the past much more available, yet it also made the communal meanings and values of tradition less important and the private judgment of the solitary reader more important. (pp. 9-10)

Bacon's work grows out of this fertile exchange of old and new in the Renaissance. With his assertion of independence from the past he begins to pull apart the elements of what had usually been a dynamic, if paradoxical, tension; therefore in him the tension becomes unusually intense, though often covert. Bacon was one of the most learned men of his age. He did not really master scientific lore, but rather the classics that could provide the best models for the shape of his own thought. Partly because of his courtroom experience, Bacon the writer kept his learning ready; he never approached it as an amorphous pile of research needing extensive reworking before presentation. His often repeated aphorism, "Time is like a river, which has brought down to us things light and puffed up, while those which are weighty and solid have sunk," suggests that he approached learning as a vast salvage operation or, as he says, "like a general who means to take possession."

Yet there is, beyond the apparent limits he sets on the past's influence, a deep, pervasive coloration of tradition to his prose and thought, an intertextuality suggesting both unspoken commitment and unspoken bondage. "He was a great reader of books," reports his chaplain and biographer William Rawley, "yet he had not his knowledge from books, but from some grounds and notions from within himself." Between the act of reading and the birth

of these "grounds and notions" a complex process of transformation and exchange occurs. (p. 10)

As if resisting his commitment to the past, Bacon centers his philosophy on discovery. Perhaps only certain philosophes responded appropriately to Bacon's inspiring call to intellectual revolution, a call comprising his claims to originality; his demands for new beginnings, knowledge by direct experience, original invention, and discovery, and even pervading his scientific method. This call does not jibe with the moderate rationality celebrated by many recent historians of science; it is radical and uncompromising. Certainly there has been no wide recognition of the cumulative effect of Bacon's different emphases on discovery and the degree to which these emphases anticipate the more single and explicit declarations of Descartes over a generation later. Knowledge-as-power means humanity's freedom from the authority of the past so that it can invent new principles and works, thereby fulfilling its destiny.

Bacon's philosophical works all set out to practice innovation: whether like **The Advancement of Learning** by surveying each area of knowledge and suggesting how it can progress, like the *Instauratio Magna* by presenting a philosophy and a method of scientific discovery as well as a refutation of established schools of thought, or like the **Essays** where, as in much of Bacon's work, traditional allusions suggest intriguing dissonances with the asserted meaning. In the *Instauratio Magna* and many other writings Bacon insists that he himself is launching a totally new enterprise; at the same time the requirement of his scientific method is that nature must be seen anew, as if for the first time, "with minds washed clean from opinions . . . becoming again as little children."

Bacon's program would thus appear to be absolutely modern: Bacon expresses his historical self-consciousness by insisting on his own and his age's independence from the past, and by calling for the invention of novelties that will further distinguish present from past, and the future from both. Certain characteristic difficulties of modernity stem from this assertion of discontinuity. What existence can new and original things have apart from the resources that compose them, and how can truly novel ideas be presented to uninitiated readers without heavy, distorting dependence on all-too-familiar language? After he finally got there, Columbus immediately had to make the strange familiar by declaring that he had found only a new route to an old place, the East Indies. At the most general level, Bacon's opposite, more difficult problem of definition parallels that of anyone seeking, in life or in art, to "make it new," as Pound says; Bacon and Columbus represent two extremes of an almost existential level of modernity. As aspects of historical consciousness, problems of modernity had been latent, of course, in the Renaissance exploration of the past from the perspective of a newly established present; they were bound to become more acute and multifarious in an advanced capitalist society like ours, where the ideal of individualism, the constraints of mass society, and the ideology of advertising together impel many to find and assert their unique ever-freshness through the frantic pursuit of novel artifacts and experiences. Blumenberg defines the paradox well when he speaks of the problem of legitimacy. It "is bound up with the very concept of an epoch. . . . [It] is latent in the modern age's claim to carry out a radical break with tradition, and in the incongruity between this claim and the reality of history, which can never begin entirely anew." This problem of modernity is perfectly illustrated by juxtaposing Bacon's presentation of his ideas in the *Instauratio Magna* as "quite new, totally new in their kind" with the contradictory conclusions about him offered by the distinguished scholar Paolo Rossi [in *Francis Bacon: From Magic to Science,* 1968]:

> Bacon was voicing the general opinion of his age, defining some of its essential demands, when he strove to rehabilitate the mechanical arts, denounced the sterility of Scholastic logic, and planned a history of arts and sciences to serve as a foundation for the reform of knowledge and of the very existence of mankind.

At issue here is not the existence of this modern discontinuity, but rather its nature, depth, and implications. Bacon, as we have just seen, reflects the nature and problems of the modern not only because he claims novelty but because he claims it for inventing a philosophy of invention. The major discontinuity in this new philosophy of the new thus actually lies between two ideals of innovation: between an emerging philosophy of discovery and its traditional matrix. I shall call the matrix change as reform; the emergence, change as revolution. Though Bacon does not use either of these terms significantly, they are the most appropriate for designating the two implicit but distinct perspectives yoked together in the title of Bacon's project of discovery, "The Great Instauration." Bacon's modern discontinuity (oversimplifying for now) results from this circumstance: in places Bacon calls clearly for a revolution in thinking that will lead to radical changes in culture, but in the process of definition and elaboration the call comes to be opposed by the recalcitrant older ideas of change as reform that are used to grasp at it.

In part because Bacon left it deliberately inexplicit, the importance of his key concept of instauration in the history of modern ideas of change, especially of revolution, has been entirely overlooked. But because he builds meaning powerfully from traditional contexts and because his power had such a lasting influence, exploring the nature of the modern discontinuity expressed in Bacon's instauration becomes exploration of the dynamic tension of past and present that has formed Western ideologies of change. The Great Instauration encompasses Christian ideas of reform related to biblical prophecy (to which classical ideas of recurrence have become assimilated) as it gropes toward a secular idea of revolution and as it drafts a discourse of secular prophecy. On the one hand biblical prophecy and exegesis, and the visionary tradition of literature springing from them, are profoundly recuperative. Each prophecy validates a tradition of prophecies, applying a series of general expectations to specific historical situations. But in its call to commitment and action prophecy can be subversive and revolutionary. The Book of Revelation, for instance, which was so intensely studied and discussed in the English Renaissance, carries an idea of revolution implicit in its prophecy of an apocalypse that

fulfills history, synthesizes a broad range of genres, and at the same time makes all things new. James I appealed to it and so did the revolutionaries who beheaded his son. Bacon's *Instauratio Magna* exemplifies the doubleness of prophecy.

Reform, for which Augustine provides a classic definition and example, is a purposefully evolving change, one that, at least as much as it revises and discards, builds upon the past toward fulfillment, toward redemption or mending of the fallen world. The discontinuity upon which historical self-consciousness rests is less extreme here than with revolution. Traditional models offer rich possibilities for imitation and emulation: reform is a process by which something (or someone) progresses toward fulfillment through better likenesses of itself. The idea of intellectual revolution exemplified in the seventeenth and consolidated in the eighteenth century more unequivocally suggests a new beginning and reliance on individual or collective powers of judgment. Even though this revolutionary stance appeals to ancient or God-given rights, it tends to uphold spontaneity, originality, or human reason's autonomous powers.

To alter or create anything, of course, is also to assert some form of power. Ideologies of change supply frameworks within which innovators, a category including artists, scientists, businesspeople, and in one way or another all members of society, assert humanity's present dominion over itself and nature as well as over tradition. Bacon's appeals to James for leadership and financial backing show his realization that even discovering new knowledge requires not only a new learning establishment but also a new relationship between learning and political power. Indeed ideologies of change supply legitimation for whatever group holds political power, guiding but also obscuring its exercise, transfer, and succession. If, as Marx says, the prevailing concepts of revolution that developed in the seventeenth and eighteenth centuries represent bourgeois ideologies in that they tended to further the interests of this rising class, the *Instauratio Magna* represents the conflicting class interests involved in both old and new ideologies of change. Bacon's relationship to James underscores the identities of both English absolutism and the *Instauratio Magna* as representations of and responses to class conflict.

Bacon's discourse on change encompasses two contradictory views of truth and its representation in language, and it is as functions of his dominant philosophy of change that these two epistemologies can best be understood. Reform invites analogy and multiple levels of meaning as it variously connects old and new; it exposes the poverty of brute facts by, for one thing, fixing knowledge in a hierarchy of literary kinds or genres. Reformative visions of history grow in part out of biblical exegesis, which distinguishes literal and figurative meanings, and out of classical contexts in which the word *mimesis* signifies at once imitation of traditional models and imitation of reality. With Bacon, revolution reduces and unmasks; it is not dialectical but, like many other "bourgeois" concepts of revolution, seeks direct encounter with "things as they are" and plain, denotative language for this encounter. Bacon the reformer masters the subtleties of metaphor and allegory in *The Wisdom of the Ancients,* the iconography of the *New Atlantis,* his rich legal and philosophical rhetoric, and in his views of nature's laws, which clearly depend on mechanical metaphors or models; in many ways his scientific method itself is a kind of reform or fulfillment of rhetorical ideals and practices, while his ideal of discovery is modeled on prophetic revelation. At the same time, however, Baconian discovery is revolutionary in that it aims to grasp a fully present reality unmediated by models. Bacon's metaphorical discourse of reform draws much from the older ideas of the world united by a chain of correspondences and similitudes that make all things potentially symbols or likenesses of all other things. But his aspirations toward what he conceives to be the precise language of revolution help formulate emerging views that dissolve, as do those of Descartes and the Port-Royal logicians, likeness into identity and difference.

Dividing the presentation of Bacon's thought according to reform and revolution reflects my conclusions not only that ideas of change are central to his thought but also that discontinuity runs to its core. Whether or not Bacon was aware of the fissure in his writing—and he could hardly have measured it fully—it seems unmendable. In Latin *instauratio* means both fulfillment and new beginning; with his new sense of revolution Bacon strains this wonderful ambiguity to the breaking point. To be self-consistently original, Bacon has to conceal the connections of revolution to revelation. This denial is his response to the problem of modernity, to the dilemma of tradition and innovation with which his aims and his historical moment present him.

Bacon's case, then, does not seem to add up to a pragmatic modernity any more than it adds up to the triumph of objective reason over the forces of superstition. And with Descartes an idea of secular revolution similar to Bacon's swam through terrible swamps of radical doubt, breathlessly seeking a new foundation as firm as that prophetic conviction. But more fundamentally, Bacon's case suggests that even to look for identifiable qualities of modernity can be misleading, for his modernity lies not so much in his vision of revolution as in the very discontinuity between new and old ways of conceiving visions. Modernity becomes not so much a condition or a stance as the incomplete or deferred attempt to fix a stance. In this view, the subversiveness implicit in Bacon's demand for total novelty acts first on the vision of novelty itself, for that must find articulation in the cultural matrix that is the target of subversion. The vision thus releases tradition's still powerfully daemonic, unpredictable forces, which in the play of differences between new and old can disarm and translate meaning as well as amplify and empower it. Tradition means handing on, but by that handing on it threatens the recipient's sovereignty over sense.

By what criteria can one judge such a modernity? It certainly possesses an inherent weakness, but what if some of the peculiar strengths of the modern condition emerge from such contradictions? Paul de Man, who has dealt usefully with the inherent contradictions of modernity, is most interested in the sense of *modern* not as designating a particular period of history or as historical selfcon-

sciousness per se, but as designating part of the "specificity of literature" of any period, though more intensely part of literature since the Renaissance. He points to an impulse within literature to break out of the confines of language and form in order to achieve "immediacy"—to present, rather than merely to represent, its subject. This goal of immediacy, I take it, can range from Archibald MacLeish's Modernist credo that the poem should not mean but be, to the common desire of writers to burst the confines of their media and speak and act directly. The modern frustration is that in order to envision what is unique, immediate, and original one must depend on, that is, be envisioned by, existing styles, ideas, and language. (pp. 10-16)

Bacon's works gain a kind of sputtering power precisely because Bacon the revolutionary pits his strongly referential vision of novel truth in Bacon the reformer's rich matrix of language and tradition. Bacon's call is displaced and enlarged by its rich contexts. His assertion of modernity hides a predicament of modernity; his romance of reason suffers a kind of hermeneutic tragedy in its textual career, reflecting Bacon's own deeply ambivalent relationship to his training and talents.

If modernity suggests a standard of evaluation in its discontinuity, the most modern writer would be not the one who achieves the greatest independence and originality, but the one whose work offers the most breathtaking strain between vision and matrix, who, like certain *hommes d'avant-garde,* meets the greatest risks of incoherence. Absolute monarchs cannot be well disposed to such exercises, if only because they can hint at the contradictions of absolutism. King James was impatient with the *Instauratio Magna,* but perhaps he saw the impossibility of joining Bacon's revolutionary stance to the Christian ideology of change while feeling the impossibility of construing the work's meaning apart from that context. Of Bacon's work he jested, "It is like the peace of God, which passeth understanding." Rightly understood, Bacon becomes one of history's most modern figures, more so, perhaps, than a speeding Rimbaud or locomotive Descartes, the latter having both consolidated the revolutionary stance and repressed its contexts more fully than Bacon.

Such consolidation and repression has helped produce the partial readings that make it difficult for us to understand Bacon. For the reformer and literary artist is clearly the literary historian's subject, while the call to a triumphant modernity of knowledge and power comprise the subject of a historian of ideas or science. Though Bacon inveighed against overspecialization, his influential distinction between disciplines that cultivate knowledge (that is, what we call the humanities) and those that discover it (the sciences) plays a role here. Bacon's own modern blindness has thus led to the blindness of his readers. Further, our perspective on the *Instauratio Magna* is so contaminated by a formula for boredom, a Whig reading that too easily finds Bacon's prophecies everywhere fulfilled in modern science and technology, that we see only with difficulty how uncanny the work is.

De Man's delight in finding discontinuity and contradiction can be a kind of Midas touch which, as some have complained, tends to render any text an absurdist, quivering mass of canceled signifiers that finally discourages both the search for meaning and the will to action. This need not be so. De Man's approach to literary modernity provides useful suggestions for analysis, but need not be pursued with the fine enthusiasm that ends in resignation to the frustrations of modernity, to confinement in literature as an institution and, therefore, implicitly, to writer's and reader's confinement in the institutions of society, however unjust. Bacon continues to be read (unfashionably) partly because his utopian, refreshingly antiliterary prophecies are not fully contained by the frustrations of literary institutionalization.

Bacon suggests, in fact, a qualifying and enriching context for the most subversive of contemporary modernities. Here I can best explain the insight Bacon affords in this respect by briefly considering his relationship to Nietzsche, a major factor in contemporary views of modernity, including de Man's. In *On the Genealogy of Morals,* delivering the broadest possible critique of modern culture as mere secularization, Nietzsche argues that philosophy, modern science, scholarship, and much of art and literature represent covert manifestations of the "ascetic ideal" invented by ancient priests in order to ruin the wonderful meaninglessness of life and introduce "spiritual" values. By becoming interpreters of meaning priests gained power over others and the exquisite sadomasochistic pleasures the administration of spiritual suffering can afford. In the modern age the ideal of truth, Nietzsche argues, is the ascetic illusion that has grown with, evolved from, and finally replaced God; modern science, art, and scholarship have only intensified this reverent asceticism or "will to truth" actually underlying Western culture from the beginning. Ideal truth, further, has come to be defined by priestly philosophers like Plato as the knowledge of Being, that is, knowledge of a "real" world or self beyond the apparent world or self; the realm of Being has been defined as timeless, always present to itself, and therefore different from the constant whirl of appearances. Calling it the "metaphysics of presence," others have elaborated and updated Nietzsche's diagnosis, asserting that an oppressive metaphysics continues to define the fundamental Western orientation toward the world and to complement society's authoritarian and patriarchal mechanisms of control.

Bacon displays not just a will to truth but a kind of spontaneous lust for reality (I call it "visionary realism" to distinguish it from its Scottish cousin and to emphasize its genealogy) that is simply not sophisticated enough for any twentieth-century philosophy. On top of what is sometimes seen as his crude or naive realism Bacon holds a crudely referential view that language is meant to mirror reality, and that it can be made to do so without distortion. Here then is a macho philosophy clearly exemplifying the metaphysics of presence, a philosophy expressed with the help of little sacred innuendos that bespeak the hidden, ascetic impotence of Nietzsche's priest-philosopher.

Understanding the literary politics of affiliation and genealogy in Bacon will make clear some of the ways the ideal of truth can mask the assertion of power. But this is an insight that Bacon's work also leads us to. Nietzsche admires Shakespeare tremendously because the dramatist has "the strength required for the vision of the most powerful reality"—reality far different, obviously, from the scholar's priestly ideal. But Nietzsche was never a great reader of the English. Nothing reveals this more clearly than that this sensitive critic could apparently believe (if the sublime posturing of *Ecce Homo* signifies) that Bacon wrote Shakespeare's plays. Nietzsche concludes this, he tells us, because of Bacon's own pursuit of reality: "We are very far from knowing enough about Lord Bacon, the first realist in every great sense of that word." Just as Bacon's authorship remains secret, so, Nietzsche remarks, might his own if he had published under Wagner's name. Rather than membership in a line of profound and devious priests of reason, Nietzsche seems to suggest that Bacon and he are members of a line of skeptical visionaries, those open to the play of differences beyond the myth of Being. His distant admiration of Bacon the realist leads us to the only apparently odd conclusion that Bacon's will to truth is at once that part of him most vulnerable to deconstruction and most robustly liberating.

Bacon's instauration of learning calls our attention to an essential discontinuity of modernity. That instauration embraces polarities of faith and secular reason, hegemony and subversion. In its light, twentieth-century modernism, avant-garde, and postmodernism become a bit more movements grounded in Western history, and a bit less horizons of absolute novelty: these movements find precedent as symptoms of our alienation and isolation expressed in successive cults of the new, or as (coopted) gestures of revolution. But Bacon also affirms the possibility of an instauration that, even though it has an aspect of blindness, fuses writing and action, tradition and discovery. (pp. 16-19)

．．．．．

Much of the force of Bacon's aphorisms, natural histories, and essays depends on their prospective quality as beginnings or representations of beginnings. But Bacon's philosophical work, and much of his other work as well, seems always to be just getting started. Its revolutionary character is manifested mainly in claims, statements of intention, and in exhortation. One assumes that Bacon would have liked to finish more than he did, but works that inadequately realize their projected plans are in such a majority that they must be viewed as fulfilling some unstated (and perhaps unconscious) pattern—one that reveals the modernity of his project.

Bacon's written contributions to the instauration of learning are syntheses of earlier, incomplete works, and yet the Instauration itself is decisively incomplete. The portion of the Instauration published in 1620 could be called a reformation of earlier, mostly unfinished works, although the 1620 volume exploits them piecemeal for apt phrases as much as it builds and elaborates their patterns. The *Valerius Terminus* is Bacon's earliest mapping of existing knowledge and its deficiencies, and includes sweeping suggestions for improvement. It is fragmentary, and part of it gets expanded in *The Advancement of Learning* and taken up again in the fragmentary *Descriptio Globus In-*

tellectualis of 1612. The *De Dignitate et Augmentis Scientiarum* is the Latin revision of the *Advancement* meant to fulfill part one of the six-part *Instauration*—and remains its only complete part. Part 2, the *Novum Organum,* also has origins in the *Valerius Terminus,* and echoes some of the early work's passages. Portions of many earlier works are included in the texture of the *Novum Organum* and in the *Instauratio Magna* prefaces. Part 3 of the Instauration, the natural histories, finds representation in the 1620 volume in an introduction (the *Parasceve*), which is again distilled from past work, and a list of subjects for histories. It was to collect data for this part that Bacon abandoned both his studies on method and, if we can believe his chaplain and biographer William Rawley, the unfinished *New Atlantis.* Parts 4, 5, and 6 are only mentioned in the 1620 volume; 4 and 5 are elsewhere represented by brief introductory fragments, *Scala Intellectualis* and *Prodromi sive Anticipationes Philosophiae Secundae,* respectively, each of which finds a few echoes in 1620.

In the whole body of Bacon's work, part 3 is represented by fragments, sketches, or beginnings of collections of facts on motion, heat and cold, minerals, compounding of metals, light, weight, sound, and magnetic attraction; and more formidable but still incomplete histories of density and of winds, the latter published together with prefaces to five other natural histories never undertaken. The fragmentary *Abecedarium Naturae* attempts to define simple natures, a basic problem in trying to conceptualize or narrate scientific observations. Robert Ellis pronounces the *Historia Vitae et Mortis* "more or less complete"; he cannot mean, of course, that Bacon considers himself to have given the last word on this subject: it is far less faithful to experience than others of Bacon's natural histories. The posthumous, popular *Sylva Sylvarum* stands complete. But since it derives its structure not from nature but from the preconceived plan of providing ten general headings with exactly one hundred observations each, it conforms least of all Bacon's histories to the ideal of the scientific text. The *Essays,* which have an oblique but important relationship to part 3, are incomplete by their very nature and went through two processes of revision and expansion.

Other works cannot be precisely assigned to a stage in the Instauration, and most of Bacon's other works were not intended as contributions. But the six-part scheme includes all knowledge, and many of these other works have some relevance to it; many of them are also incomplete. Bacon proposed a vast "History of England from the Union of the Roses to the Union of the Crowns." The first book, the *History of Henry VII* is complete; the second, on Henry VIII, is an introductory fragment; the other books are nonexistent. A "History of Great Britain" exists in an introductory fragment. The *Maxims of the Law,* Bacon's most important legal work, is complete, but only a remnant of the general review and recompilation of English law that he proposed. Of the two myths concerned with natural philosophy to be discussed in the *De Principiis atque Originibus* only one is studied, and not fully; the *Temporis Partus Masculus* is one chapter of a projected work of three books; the **"Letter and Discourse to**

Henry Savill Touching Helps for the Intellectual Powers" is not finished.

Whatever all this incompleteness may suggest about Bacon's temperament, it also suggests that Bacon finds existing knowledge and forms of discourse inadequate to grasp his revolutionary goals. Further, that his approach to a problem is open-ended; what he cannot determine he comes back to later or leaves for others, since discovery to him is a collective enterprise. Brian Vickers says [in his *Bacon and Renaissance Prose*], "Bacon's constant drive to revise and improve was not a fussy expression of indecisiveness, rather the sign of an intellectual horizon which was always expanding, of a reach which invariably exceeded the grasp and left not over-written books but unfinished ones." Bacon is impulsive, not indecisive. But I suggest that his typical incompleteness also conceals a protective turning away, a conscious or unconscious recognition that elaborating the plan will compromise its freshness and originality, and expose it as a function of knowledge already institutionalized. Incompleteness shows the vulnerability as well as the robustness of Bacon's modernity.

Many of Bacon's writings are only beginnings, a preface here, a few chapters there. Passages are often repeated in these fragments. The *Instauratio Magna* of 1620 distills some of this material, though that work went through "at least twelve" revisions of its own, according to Rawley. This idiosyncratic genre of beginnings includes the following:

Phaenomena Universi
"Filum Labyrinthi sive Formula Inquisitionis"
Prodromi sive Anticipationes Philosophiae Secundae
Partes Instauratio Secundae Delineatio et Argumentum
Temporis Partus Masculus
"De Interpretatione Naturae Proemium"
Scala Intellectualis sive Filum Labyrinthi
De Interpretatione Naturae Sententiae XII
Aphorismi et Consilia, de Auxiliis Mentis, et Accensione Luminis Naturalis
"Letter and Discourse to Henry Savill Touching Helps for the Intellectual Powers"

These works are in a sense all the same work. They comprise a gesture of beginning, a deliberate moment of self-assertion that defines the central theme of Bacon's work. Other works not necessarily incomplete but essentially fragmentary in thought and form could be added here:

Valerius Terminus
Redargutio Philosophiarum
Cogitationes de Natura Rerum
Cogitationes de Scientia Humana

They center on an arresting and sweeping declaration of independence. For instance: "Francis Bacon thought in this manner. The knowledge whereof the world is now possessed, especially that of nature, extendeth not to magnitude and certainty of works" (**"Filum Labyrinthi"**).

Along with this challenger's stance comes the hope for progress through emancipation from the past. These works in sum explore the nature of the fresh beginning, yet forever repeat the frustration of finding a truly fresh beginning. They express again and again the will behind the choice of vocation in one of their most distinguished examples, the three-page **"De Interpretatione Naturae"**: "Believing that I was born for the service of mankind, and regarding the care of the commonwealth as a kind of common property which like the air and the water belongs to everybody, I set myself to consider in what ways mankind might be best served, and what service I myself best fitted by nature to perform" (*Letters and Life*).

Bacon's abandonment of the *Novum Organum,* from this point of view, must indicate more than openness to development. Book I begins with some of the finest examples of aphorisms ever written. By the end of this book, the units have lengthened and have become more like paragraphs. Book II begins with shorter paragraphs composed of a high proportion of aphoristic sentences. At the point where book II is abandoned, the organizational unit is the length of a short chapter, several pages long. Book II gives an example of induction and begins what promises to be a long and detailed account of ways in which the observer can discern more significant facts from the limitless breach of natural perceptions (the Prerogative Instances). Then Bacon stops writing, embarks on a program of experiment and observation, and never goes on again to the eight other "helps to the understanding" besides the Prerogatives. Two ironies present themselves here. The prerogative instances, not to mention the other "helps," seem to be becoming too complex and unmanageable themselves, and they are qualifying the ideal of pure induction. The opening vision must be salvaged by incompleteness.

In general there seems to be a regulated cycle in Bacon's philosophical works producing a kind of contentious balance of new and old. Perhaps an unconscious awareness of his almost total dependence upon tradition and rhetoric helped produce the extremity of Bacon's rejection of cultivated knowledge. How remarkable, especially in view of Harvey's remark that Bacon's was the philosophy of a Lord Chancellor, that an attempt to set aside "speech and argument" should form the basis of a Lord Chancellor's philosophy. Yet the contradictory impulses go together, for the dependence upon rhetoric as appropriate ornament and manipulative tool required by lawyer, politician, and diplomat can produce both the mastery and the devaluation of rhetoric and erudite tradition that Bacon the scientist shows. Bacon declares "I have taken all knowledge to be my province" (*Letters and Life*); he did so at a time when such a goal had substantial meaning. His erudition could not have produced writing that is more than commentary without a tremendous effort to control and define the meaning of that erudition from an independent vantage in the present. Perhaps his jealously guarded independent vantage is at once a bold assertion and a retreat, a defensive attempt to cope with engulfment. On the other hand, the very strictness of Bacon's definition of truth demands a paradoxical proliferation of device. The eloquence of old for new is more insistently demanded the more insistent the demand for novelty beyond eloquence becomes.

The psychology of Freud and the aesthetics of tragedy revel in such vicious and virtuous circles and supply ready "explanations" for Bacon's condition, although we were better to treat such interpretations simply as illuminating analogies. Under the influence of what Freud diagnoses as the "repetition compulsion," for instance, a person performs acts that seem spontaneous and original but that, if examined in the light of past actions and experiences, fall into a pattern of unconsciously determined behavior that keeps acting out in different terms some devastating trauma of the past. Continual failure, while in every case attended by circumstances that appear to be beyond the individual's control, can add up to a pattern that finally must be ascribed to an unconscious will to repeat some overwhelming frustration. Repetition occurs in order to harden the nervous system against the shock of the traumatic experience and its possible recurrence. Understanding the forces behind such repetition—if that can be done—obviously becomes the first step toward ending the chain. But it is just such understanding that Bacon the revolutionary denies to himself or cannot achieve. Rather, his slogans and repeated beginnings aim at the perfected sharpness of the departure from tradition. His claims of originality protect his fragile independence from the profound and giddy literary universe of similitudes in which he was educated. This *paideia* imposed a repressive set of power relationships over his will and imagination. Yet his self-consciously revolutionary position further isolates him and renders him more vulnerable. Thus while the "purpose" of the repetition compulsion is to protect the psyche from the possible recurrence of some traumatic experience, it also works against the wishes and needs of the individual. No progress of understanding is made through repetition, nor is any made through Bacon's repeated beginnings.

Freud's myth of the revolt against the "primal father" also explains a kind of compulsive act involving ritual repetition and attitudes toward tradition and authority that plausibly represents the antithetical forces operating in Bacon's work. Freud's primal horde story is in fact a powerful symbolic representation of the characteristic limitations facing explicit moderns like Bacon. The ritual of the sacrifice, in Freud's hypothesis, is a symbolic repetition of the killing of the primal father, who controlled all the women of his tribe and denied sexual access to the sons. The attitude of the sons after their acts of murder and incest is ambivalent: they are glad to be free from the oppression of the father but are guilty about what they have done, revere the father because they believe he wields power from the beyond, and recognize the practical need for incest prohibitions. The ritual sacrifice of an animal, as a repetition of the murder, affirms the sons' own independence and power to act but also provides a means of both propitiating the ancestral father and securing benefit from him in return for sacrificial meat. In the sacrifice the revolt is affirmed—but so is the dependency. Thus at each sacrifice the father is again killed but buried respectfully.

So also Bacon lays to rest the figures of the past not by attacking but by attempting to define the limits of their power and hence preserving his reverence for them at the same time. Just as the sacrificial killing is symbolic, so Bacon's continual beginnings seldom get beyond generalities and intentions, and never overcome the presence of the "fathers" in the text. Bacon's burials of the fathers in his manifestos actually provide ritualized memorials that keep the memory of tradition alive, pointing to an as yet undisplaced adversary.

It is not just Bacon the writer who displays the fertile agonies of modernity: his image of the heroic scientist also embodies this condition. In discussing Bacon's concept of the scientist as hero, John Steadman concludes that Bacon's view of heroism is traditional. Unlike most "contemplative" philosophic and poetic heroes, such as Lucretius's Epicurus, Bacon's hero fits into the "mixed" category. Like the Moses to whom Cowley compares Bacon in his "Hymn to the Royal Society," this hero combines action and contemplation. But Bacon's method of science reflects his radical stance of originality achieved through humility. The scientist emulates his stance by opening himself to revelation of natural truth. If one considers this reflection of stance in method, it becomes clear that Bacon's image of the scientist is as paradoxical as his claims to originality.

The hero battles against fortune and fate as the representative of human will and accomplishment. The opposition of heroic *virtus* with fortune, mutability, or destiny is common in Renaissance thought and art, as it is in classical epic and tragedy. But with his particular assertion of modernity Bacon proposes a solution to the opposition of virtus and mutability that is extreme, if not unique. By making his ideas the product of time rather than wit, and by claiming that he is not really controverting any other natural philosophy, the speaker in the *Instauratio Magna* himself achieves heroic stature by a peculiar reconciling, or rather collapsing, of heroic passion into mutability. Bacon extends his stance of priority to the strict method that limits the scientist-hero's virtus (as intellectual and emotional richness) radically by substituting for it the mechanical process of induction by negation. He presents himself as a paradoxically ascetic hero, and recommends asceticism to his readers: for Bacon, humanity realizes itself through the scientist's disciplined denial of self.

Such Freudian processes are pertinent to Bacon's *New Atlantis,* where modern consciousness is symbolized by the island of Bensalem, "a land unknown." The *New Atlantis* is different. Surprisingly, because it is a fable, this utopia's relationship to reality is easier to grasp than that of any of the nonfiction works of Bacon we have considered in this chapter. For since Bacon's special problem is the relation of text-bound to text-free truth, an explicitly fictional story offers a relief. The *New Atlantis*'s fictionality and representational simplicity center on the proposition that one civilization in the world never needed cultural and social instauration, because it discovered the secret of scientific instauration long ago. This civilization aims not to match itself to its true identity using a series of figurations and surmises that are inaccurate in as yet indeterminate ways; rather, it becomes for its readers such a surmise. The island of Bensalem is isolated from the rest of the world, but in striking contrast to More's Utopia, Bensalem has a history that relates it to the rest of the world, indeed makes it the flower and realization of human history. For while the world experienced catastrophic wars and natural

disasters that ruined the high level of civilization that prevailed three thousand years ago (and that has yet to be matched even in the European Renaissance), Bensalem escaped through luck, compassion toward enemies, and wisdom. The wise King Solamona established a program of scientific discovery based in the laboratory complex Solomon's House, and controlled and limited the contact between Bensalem and the rest of the world (which in its reduced state could probably offer only corruption anyway).

The *New Atlantis* represents an end run around the originary utopias of Western political philosophy, Plato's *Republic* and *Critias,* back to the greater time of which Plato and the readers of the *New Atlantis* are remnants. The problem that preoccupied or limited so many political theorists from Plato to Machiavelli to Bodin—how to overcome the flux of historical change and achieve stability, or how to achieve development in the face of historical degeneration—is answered in the fictional portrait of a society that has achieved its strength partly by ignoring the ages of civil and moral philosophy, instead preserving continuity with the ages before that, when natural philosophy dominated.

For all its conservatism, Bensalem's success is far from being the fulfillment and realization of Europe's long history. Its goals of preservation, isolation, and discovery come from a "revolutionary" urge (in the sense defined here) to achieve liberation from the compromising tension between tradition and innovation in the timeless presence of the moment of discovery ever repeated. Central planning buffers peaceful Bensalem from the shock of the new that must be constantly generated from the research complexes, and turns innovation to uses at once constructive and conservative; the continual production of new knowledge, Bacon asserts in the *New Atlantis* just as he asserts in his interpretation of the Orpheus myth, can neutralize history and so overcome its natural cycles of florescence and decline. Successful resistance to historical process through continuous discovery is thus really triumph over the necessity of having an historical consciousness, which must struggle with the fact that present conditions are different from past ones, and yet exist in a living relationship with them.

This modern goal of narrowing and intensifying consciousness finds reflection also in Bensalem's curious international relations. As Bacon attempts to manipulate the traditional and familiar from an autonomous vantage point in the present, and as he attempts to make the scientist's encounter with nature supremely disinterested, so the researchers of Bensalem send out spies to the rest of the world to gather information for their scientific programs. "We know, and are ourselves unknown" could be their motto, for the Bensalemites have become the world's intellectual imperialists. As Bacon aims to dominate and control the past for present use, so conditions for Europe's economic and political exploitation of the world find precedent in Bensalem's relationship to its intellectual "colonies"—the rest of the world. The dangers to the mother country of such a relationship are suggested by the ominous echo of "We know, and are ourselves unknown" in the Delphic oracle's ancient premise for civil and moral wisdom, "Know thyself." Such knowledge requires the introspection that is invigorated by a sense of ourselves in others' eyes. But Bacon's stance prevents such insights.

If a measure of a classic is that it continues to be timely, Bensalem's modernity, its resistance to historical process partly through its one-way commerce in ideas, also offers parallel, if not precedent, for neo-colonial industrial development today, that is, the kind of "modernization" programs that benefit a tiny segment of third-world populations and preserve a one-way flow of profit and the sovereignty of transnational capital over nations. And as we can imagine the horror with which the good subjects of Bensalem contemplate a more balanced commerce in powerful knowledge, so we see the malevolence many good citizens of the United States today direct at third-world struggles to be free of neo-colonialism. Possibly our sophisticated colonizers have yet to enjoy the kind of introspection Bacon's Bensalem also denies to itself.

On the personal level Bacon, whom one historian has called "the one solitary figure of the Jacobean world," admits to this kind of blindness: "My soul hath been a stranger to me in the course of my pilgrimage" (**Letters and Life**). Poignant, but Bacon kept this line from the Psalms handy, using it at appropriate moments over years. Such self-fashioning makes him vulnerable to Walter Savage Landor's stereotyping in an imaginary conversation between Bacon and Richard Hooker.

> *Bacon.* But we who care nothing for chants and cadences, and have no time to catch at pleasures, push forward over stones and sands straightway to our objects. I have persuaded men, and shall persuade them for ages, that I possess a wide range of thought unexplored by others, and first thrown open by me. . . . Few [subjects] that occurred to me have I myself left untouched or untried: one however hath almost escaped me, and surely one worth the trouble.
>
> *Hooker.* Pray my Lord, if I am guilty of no indiscretion, what may it be?
>
> *Bacon.* Francis Bacon.

The **New Atlantis** is much less a narration of events than it is a narration of procedures, culminating in that of Solomon's House's scientific procedures. Before that culmination comes the detailed description of the ritual called the Feast of the Family, which epitomizes the society of Bensalem and itself is full of symbols celebrating nature and scientific discovery. At its worst the Baconian search for truth is a furious, compulsive, and ascetic "ritual" (as Karl Popper calls induction by negation) of life-negation. Bacon's utopia and the community of truth-seeking intellectuals at its core thus represent the blind or the secret will to domination and control that ideologies of both reform and revolution can harbor. At its best, Bacon's utopia represents an affirmative and healing ritual of life that attempts to encompass both reformative and revolutionary possibilities for human realization.

If a utopia governed by reason is like a family of many generations gathered lovingly to share their abundance and do honor to their progenitors in a ritual celebration at

once magnificent and intimate, the attainment of knowledge as power, Bacon says in the *Instauratio Magna,* is like the bridal song or epithalamium sung at that marriage of the mind and the universe.

> The explanation . . . of the true relation between the nature of things and the nature of the mind is as the strewing and decorating of the bridal chamber of the mind and the universe, the divine goodness assisting, out of which marriage let us hope (and be this the prayer of the bridal song [epithalamium]) there may spring helps to man, and a line and race of inventions that may in some degree subdue and overcome the necessities and miseries of humanity.

The metaphor of marriage is used elsewhere by Bacon to describe the goal of his science: he wishes to correct "an unkind and ill-starred divorce": he hopes that "knowledge may not be as a courtesan, for pleasure and vanity only, or as a bond-woman, to acquire and gain to her master's use; but as a spouse, for generation, fruit, and comfort." Mind is groom, universe bride, but the objectification of the feminine implied by these metaphors does not necessarily invalidate the use of the marriage ritual as a metaphor for discovery or promise of fulfillment. With its allegory of a (male) deity's marriage to his congregation of worshippers, the Bible's epithalamium, the Song of Solomon, provides the reformative background for Bacon's ideal of redemptive intellectual marriage (with erotic anticipation in the Song of Solomon being divided about evenly). Spenser's poem *Epithalamion* assimilates this biblical background and displays a complex orderliness that parallels the kind of systematic knowledge Bacon hopes for. The twenty-three stanzas plus one envoy and the 366 long lines suggest that *Epithalamion* is a microcosm of all time, a metaphorical attempt to enclose time in a human ritual lasting twenty-four hours and representing a harmonious cosmos.

Of the ritual element of poetry in general, Northrop Frye says,

> Poetry imitates human action as total ritual, and so imitates the action of an omnipotent human society that contains all the powers of nature within itself. . . . The impetus of the magical element in ritual is clearly toward a universe in which a stupid and indifferent nature is no longer the container of a human society, but is contained by that society, and must rain or shine at the pleasure of man.

Bacon's (and perhaps Frye's) rituals are orderly rather than carnivalesque. The **New Atlantis** solemnly celebrates the knowledge that may be all people's power, but this popular power unfortunately finds inadequate correlatives in the narrative. For the general population of Bensalem is not part of the economy of knowledge production, nor do the fragments of ethnography in the **New Atlantis** show how the dissemination and application of knowledge has sustained the utopia. Since humanity's earthly goal is laboring to produce and then enjoying the knowledge that is power, most of the people in Bensalem must be working and living in varying degrees of alienation. And they represent the scientific ideology of their rulers in their allegorical feast. The wife of the patriarch, for instance, must sit alone, concealed in a special loft. She represents, probably, Nature, the feminine object of scientific study (whose "summary law" can never be disclosed), cheerfully validating the benevolent system that alienates her. Clearly Bacon understands how custom and belief can make authority seem legitimate, like his ancient Greek mythmakers grasping intuitively and experientially what Gramsci and Althusser have studied more systematically.

It has recently been suggested, however, that the feasting family is a model for "incorporated families," royally chartered family businesses that became important in early English capitalism. In this reading the family *would* play an active part in technical innovation (the *New Atlantis,* after all, is unfinished). Bacon may then have been working toward suggesting a closer relationship between the sons of science and the ordinary citizens, whether or not he would have envisioned the extended families as in some ways free of the patterns of exploitation in which incorporated families actually participated.

But if scientists are clearly privileged in utopia, scientific language is not necessarily privileged in Bacon's utopian discourse. We have seen how Bacon demotes rhetoric in favor of inductive logic, excluding the former from the new science and assigning it to a popular rather than a learned audience. But if isolation of the discourse of science from the rest of discourse creates a new class of elite speakers and writers, this isolation may also have the effect (everywhere except in utopia) of separating, and demoting, the producers of knowledge from the institutional processes that maintain them. Since they lack control of management, the producers cannot really represent an elite. For instance, scientists need not understand the theological nuances of *instauratio,* but if they need funding from a theologically learned king, they certainly could use an agent who understands these matters. The Feast of the Family, which offers an allegorical version of scientific investigation preceding the literal version to follow in the description of Solomon's House, would represent an aristocratic, allegorical use of language in comparison with the bourgeois clarity of scientific language: the figured speaking would have a status that the plain speaking does not. Is the otherness of nature's secrets best preserved by a social other, as in pastoral and georgic, a technocratic group admired for its honest diligence? This question shows the degree to which the paradoxes of modernity (here of traditional and innovative language) can represent social conflict. In Bacon the ideologist and the scientist contend.

In the *New Atlantis* Bacon offers biblical sanctions for his ambivalent ideal of dominion: the wise and devout (for a time) rule of the Bible's King Solomon. Intellectual and technological dominion in the *New Atlantis* appears with biblical sanction: Solomon's Temple of worship has become Solomon's House of truth, which builds a model of the universe in the mind. Solomon himself hoped that the dominion of Israel and the dominion of the Hebrews over themselves would be achieved through faith in the dominion and omniscience of God over all. Thus his people's penitent recognition of their own sins would make prayerful appeals to Solomon's Temple effective:

> If there be in the land famine, if there be pestilence, blasting, mildew, locust, or if there be caterpillar; if their enemy besiege them in the land of the cities; whatsoever plague, whatsoever sickness there be; What prayer and supplication soever be made by any man, or by all the people Israel, which shall know every man the plague of his own heart, and spread forth his hands toward this house: Then hear thou in heaven thy dwelling place, and forgive, and do, and give to every man according to his ways, whose heart thou knowest; (for thou, even thou only, knowest the hearts of all the children of men).

Like that of Solomon's Temple, the magic of Solomon's House can only work if the "petitioners," that is, the scientists, have insight into and control over selfishness and pride, and the competition and inequity pride breeds.

But it is not really so much the self-knowledge of the righteous that Bacon's new Temple recapitulates as the omniscience and omnipotence of God that Solomon himself so deeply admires in the prayer above, that he emulates as God's anointed ruler, and that finally results in his ruin amid strange gods. Thus the high point of the *New Atlantis,* the description of the wondrous achievements of Solomon's House, where hieratic garb and ritual adorn the priestlike members who work secretly to benefit men, hearkens back to its literary original, the [biblical] description of Solomon's Temple. There the Temple is lavishly adorned with the symbols of divine power and dominion and of the wondrous order of the universe conceived, made, understood, and owned exclusively and totally by God. But now text threatens to undercut context rather than vice versa: it casts a shadow back on its precursor, and suggests that the Bible's vision of power and order itself remains necessarily blind to its full nature. We know, for instance, as Bacon did not, that the Bible in its glorification of God suppresses its enormous debt to prior religions' beliefs, practices, and revelations. Paul Ricoeur calls this suppression another kind of demythologization, the vast and necessarily covert and unauthorized demythologizing project of the Bible in its imagining of an exclusive god. This great Judaic demythologization aims, like that of the classical Greek philosophers, to free humanity's encounter with transcendence from the glittering veils of polytheism and ritual. Bacon's reliance on Solomon's Temple thus represents not simply a brilliant and somewhat opportunistic appropriation of a sacred symbol but to some degree a validation and continuation of complex power relationships between text and predecessor. With the Bible as with Bacon, such relationships function in illuminating complex ideological roles.

The heterogeneous sample readings above explore the possibilities of meaning latent in the conflicting forces of Bacon's work. On the one hand Bacon's theme of liberation is pursued by calling into play traditional, compromising authorities and standards of interpretation; on the other this theme comes to be partly contained in a new bourgeois ideology. Bacon's account of how tradition and discovery interact in utopia reveals issues of authority and dominion in Bacon's own cultural and social world and in our own. The *New Atlantis* and the other subjects . . . —the frustration of aphoristic assertion by aphoristic implication or allusion, the indeterminate realism of the natural histories, the "surrealism" of the *Essays,* and incompleteness—all point to struggles between rhetoric and reason, representation and truth, and tradition and innovation. But they may also lead through these to questions about authority and legitimation, to an awareness of how struggles between text and context in the creation of meaning illuminate the operation of power in society.

Paolo Rossi's article "Baconianism" in the *Dictionary of the History of Ideas* is one of the strongest pieces ever written on Bacon. The institutionalizing dictionary format is significant. Rossi defines and defends Bacon's place in a canon of modern thinkers. He views modernity as a project and concludes, "The liberation of man—and in this too [Bacon] is modern—can be painfully achieved (by ways far more complicated than he was able to imagine) only through the labor, the works, the well-being of the whole of humanity." The necessarily abstract form of this conclusion may make it suitable for fervent or apathetic adoption by neoconservatives, liberals, and radicals alike. The conclusion is part of Rossi's response to Horkheimer's and Adorno's criticism of Bacon in *Dialectic of Enlightenment* for his instrumentalization of nature and language and for his multifarious will to power. Despite the one-sidedness of much of this criticism, acknowledging its strengths, learning from it, and continuing to read in a resolutely critical spirit can contribute to the meaningfulness of Rossi's conclusions. My reading of Bacon as a modern has attempted to do this. Bacon's two mutually qualifying discourses on change form a vitally antithetical modern discourse. Combined with Bacon's own critical bent and his concern for the roles learning plays in society, this modernity criticizes from within and points beyond its constituent ideologies, which are in many ways still the ones that inform our life. (pp. 189-204)

> *Charles Whitney, in his* Francis Bacon and Modernity, *Yale University Press, 1986, 234 p.*

Harry Levin   (essay date 1988)

[*In the following excerpt, Levin argues that Bacon, though primarily a prose writer and a rationalist not particularly inclined toward poetry, nevertheless exhibited a peculiar kind of intellectual passion which could be defined as poetic.*]

Since Francis Bacon was both willing and able to play the Renaissance man in so many other respects, it may be significant that he professed "not to be a poet." He could hardly have been blamed if the sonnet that prompted this admission, composed in a last-minute effort to heal the breach between the earl of Essex and Queen Elizabeth, had been as uninspired as it would prove ineffectual. The single lyric from his prolific pen that sometimes turns up in anthologies, a paraphrase from the Greek with the comprehensive Latin title **"In vita humana,"** seems to be no less coolly detached nor sweepingly sententious than his *Essays.* His metrical translations from the Psalms seem much more prosaic than those of his contemporaries who rendered them, without benefit of meter, for King James's Authorized Version. One of his *Apophthegms* records the "opinion touching poets" of Sir Henry Savile, who had been the queen's tutor and would be one of the king's translators: "He thought them the best writers, next to those that write prose." Such was Bacon's preference, or at least his priority, which may well have suited his own temperament. Thus he shows "a lack of poetic instinct" in his mythological commentaries, according to a modern commentator, the late Jean Seznec. Yet D. G. James, in some paradoxical Oxford lectures, placed him at the other extreme—a position complementary rather than antithetical to Shakespeare's—as, "by nature and endowment, more a poet than a scientist or a philosopher."

Bacon's reputation, over the centuries, has zigzagged strikingly between such extremes. Attacks upon it by uneasy poets have ranged from the damning superlatives of Alexander Pope to the prophetic denunciations of William Blake. Yet, for every detractor, Bacon has had an admirer. By the most cerebral among the English Romantics, Samuel Taylor Coleridge and Percy Bysshe Shelley, he could not have been evaluated more highly. But, having done his utmost to repudiate the scholastic authority of Aristotle, he never fitted into the speculative part that they both assigned him as "the British Plato." From a more empirical standpoint, he had personified—in Abraham Cowley's simile—a new Moses, preparing for if not staking out those promised lands of seventeenth- and eighteenth-century science, the Royal Society and the *Encyclopédie.* His only noteworthy experiment—noteworthy because the chill was fatal to him—had been a problem in domestic technology, which involved deep-freezing an eviscerated hen, and which is so easily solved and so abundantly replicated through the supermarkets today. Had it succeeded, it would have been classified among his *experimenta fructifera* rather than *lucifera,* experiments bearing fruit rather than bringing light. Most of the projects he mentions would have come under the former rubric, involving the procedures of observation, collection, classification, application, and organization. At this distance, his programmatic description of Salomon's House, in *The New Atlantis,* may sound more like a museum than a laboratory.

Generally speaking, Baconianism has served as a confident ideology for progress, enlightenment, and utilitarianism—for main historical currents no longer looked upon as inevitable or even indisputably auspicious. And, since his all-too-worldly career had conveyed him from the very summit of England's legal hierarchy—the Lord Chancellorship—into the professional disgrace of impeachment, Bacon's advocacy has exposed discussions of his outlook to *ad hominem* considerations. The metaphorical mascot that trails him through critical arraignment and novelistic biography, from Lord Macaulay to Lytton Strachey, could not have been anything less ambiguous than a serpent. Though this beast is evoked conventionally as an emblem of the subtle wisdom enjoined by Jesus upon his disciples, together with a lamblike innocence, no one could have forgotten its underlying activity as the persistent agent of man's fall. But, when Bacon himself looks back to the very beginning of the beginning, the first chapters of Genesis, his overwhelming symbol is the primordial image of light—if indeed that can be viewed as an image and not an effulgence. "God's first creature" he liked to phrase it, and it dominates his imagery from first through last. The Deity is "the Father of lights," as venerated by the Epistle of James; a "dry light [*lumen siccum*]" formulated by Heraclitus, is precisely that which philosophers should cultivate; and "the light of nature" would account for much that had been hitherto ascribed to divine revelation. His neo-Atlantic voyagers are "merchants of Light." [In her *Shakespeare's Imagery and What It Tells Us*] Caroline Spurgeon has graphically demonstrated how "Light, indeed, to Bacon, very noticeably represents all good things."

Its Manichaean adversary was darkness, inert, chaotic, encircling, and stubbornly grounded in the past. Bacon shared, with the lesser projectors of his age, an acute sense of timing; innovation was always opening up, obsolescence always closing in. His most resounding titles are advertisements for renewal: *The Advancement of Learning, De Augmentis Scientiarum, Novum Organon, Instauratio Magna.* If he was acknowledged as the herald—literally the trumpeter—of modernity (*buccinator novi temporis*), it was because he deliberately presented himself in that part. Given an intellectual heritage heavily overloaded with dogmatic presuppositions and farfetched deductions, it would be his contribution to propose the farthest-reaching critique. Once the diagnostic analogue was admitted, treatment could be dealt with as a matter of curing distempers or purging the peccant humors. He had started from, and often returned to, polemics; a favorite mode of discourse, perhaps for lawyerly reasons, was *redargutio* or refutation. He pounced upon elenchs (or exposable sophistries) with the collector's zeal of a Sir Thomas Browne compiling vulgar errors. Among the four classes of Idols that had bemused men's minds with erroneous notions, he attacked his final set with a special iconoclasm. In calling them *Idola Theatri,* he linked together his own skeptical attitudes toward traditional philosophy and toward theatrical illusion. "In my judgment," he redargued, "all the received systems are but so many stage-plays, representing worlds of their own creation after an unreal and scenic fashion."

Voltaire likened Bacon's achievement to a scaffolding, essential for the construction of New Philosophy but soon to be outmoded by the edifice itself. Probably Bacon had contributed less to the actual building than to the preliminary demolitions and excavations. Outdating was a normal aspect of the continuous process he contemplated, in viewing scientific advance as a "conjunction of labours," the collective accumulation of an institutional enterprise. In his much-trumpeted letter to Lord Burghley, wherein he spoke of taking "all knowledge to be [his] province," he had momentarily considered giving up his public and personal ambitions in order to retreat into research, "to be a true pioneer [a digger in the earth, as originally construed] in that mine of truth"—if only some supporting institution could be established. But royal patronage was otherwise disposed, and individualism guided his subsequent course to its compromised outcome. His collected works, which badly need reediting, were by-products from

unsought and unpredictable moments of leisure. In spite of their methodological catchwords and frequent calls to order, they tend to be somewhat rambling, repetitious, and anecdotal, albeit redeemed again and again by memorable phrases, eloquent fragments, pithy outlines, and fascinating lists of unwritten treatises. The clearest plans among them are seldom the most promising; they are the ones that run to inventories and taxonomies more than to inventions or discoveries. But the tone is charged with that inherent feeling for greatness which, transcending mundane complications, seeks to sponsor grand designs.

Bacon's declared purpose in *The Advancement of Learning,* amplified and Latinized in *De Augmentis Scientiarum,* was to put together "a small Globe of the Intellectual World." His starting point, the intellect itself, could unfortunately not be typified as a sheer illuminating transparency: "Nay, it is rather like an enchanted glass, full of superstition and imposture, if it be not delivered and reduced." And science was deliverance and reduction from enchantment, from the magical pretensions of alchemy and astrology, from the benighted sphere of idols and "false appearances." Anatomy was still vague in relating the functions of the mind to the lobes of the brain. Phrenology would be unduly specific, two centuries afterward, in attaching psychological traits to cranial organs. Descartes did not resolve his metaphysical dualism by singling out the pineal gland as the abode of the soul. Bacon took little interest in the material basis of the mental processes that he delineated; yet Freudian psychoanalysis, after all, offers no organic evidence for the existence of the Ego, the Superego, and the Id. Bacon was content to draw his conceptual triad from the ancient apparatus of faculty psychology: Memory, Imagination, Reason. (Albertus Magnus would have located them at the back, the middle, and the front of the head respectively.) Moreover, the Baconian universe, though more open than most of its precursors, remained anthropocentric, corresponding neatly to his tripartite pattern of human understanding. Each of those three faculties correlated with an appropriate domain of knowledge: memory with history (storage and arrangement for the mind's perceptions), reason with philosophy (the dynamics and consequences of the mind's operations), and—somewhere between them—poesy (an inner, darker, yet freer area of speculation and recombination, harboring both illusory and creative potentialities). Bergson, less rationalistically, would locate his *fonction fabulatrice* between the spheres of cognition and intuition.

Bacon's deepest commitment is to the comprehensive span of the whole, and to unifying the paradigms that he sought through an intrinsic *philosophia prima*. Among the ternary branches of learning, the one that clearly interested him most was philosophy. Within that sphere, as within the others, there may still reside a theological component, which can be bracketed—if not taken for granted—by his profession of Fideism. By keeping religion in a separate category, he is enabled to isolate it from his other categories. His credo, "*Da fidei quae fidei sunt* (Give to faith what belongs to faith)," carries an unspoken corollary: "And be careful not to take anything else on faith—above all, never mix up faith with reason." Hence he is free to pursue his central concern, the augmentation of the sciences through Natural Philosophy. On the subject of history, Bacon can speak both as a participant and as a chronicler. Having accorded due notice to Natural, Civil, and Ecclesiastical History, he goes on to enumerate a fourth kind, not yet existent but seriously desiderated. This, termed "Literary History," seems to reach beyond belles lettres to broader conceptions of cultural movement: what the Germans term *Geistesgeschichte* or the French *histoire des mentalités*. Its absence from the records of civilization would be like the blinded eye in a statue of Polyphemus, "that part being wanting which doth most shew the spirit and life of the person." This similitude is so grotesquely striking that we forget to wonder why civilization itself should be likened to, of all creatures, a Cyclops.

Comparably, Aristotle's *Poetics* had situated its theme between history and philosophy. On the grounds of probability—the difference between the particulars of some immediate happening and the universals of widely tested experience—it had asserted that poetry was more philosophic than history. [In his *Aristotle's Theory of Poetry and Fine Art,* H. S. Butcher] begs a serious question by quoting Bacon in support of that view. Actually, Bacon made no appeal to philosophy in this connection, and had referred to history only by way of an invidious comparison: his concept of Poesy, apart from its more formal characteristics, was "nothing else but Feigned History." This could be both better and worse than straightforward historical verity. It could improve upon the status quo by offering "some shadow of satisfaction to the mind of man in those points wherein the nature of things doth deny it." It can depart from ordinary events to envisage more heroic adventures; it can intervene, when providence does not, to bring about poetic justice; and consequently it surpasses "true history" in conducing to "magnitude, morality, and to delectation." But that last effect is problematic, inasmuch as it invokes the pleasure principle. Setting aside his fideistic reserve, Bacon is even ready to align poetry with religion, at a lofty but nebulous height, before he presses on to an incisive distinction: "And therefore [poesy] was ever thought to have some participation of divineness, because it doth raise and erect the mind, by submitting the shews of things to the desires of the mind; whereas reason doth buckle and bow the mind to the nature of things." The mind exalted by its subjective desires may find itself living with shadows that darken its light; the mind that faces objective realities will be constrained to buckle and bow; but critical realism allows no choice. Many a scientist must have encountered a guiding presumption, as B. F. Skinner attests, in the Baconian aphorism: "Nature, to be commanded, must be obeyed." As between the shows or shadows of things (*umbrae rerum*) and the nature of things (*rerum natura*), Bacon had already made a prolegomenal decision: "Those however who aspire not to guess and divine, but to discover and know; not to devise mimic and fabulous worlds of their own [*simiolas et fabulas mundorum*], but to examine and dissect the very nature of this world itself; must go to facts themselves for everything."

In other words, in words less ornate and more up-to-date, the pleasure principle (*Lustprinzip*) must yield to the reality principle (*Realitätsprinzip*). Freud's terminology can be rather too glibly superimposed upon some of his predecessors; but, in this case, it is Bacon whose ideas are reflected, refracted, and virtually parodied by Freud. In a crowded paragraph concluding one of his *Introductory Lectures,* the latter speculated about the workings of the artistic imagination. He saw the artist as an introvert, ineffectually and hence neurotically longing for honor, power, riches, fame, and the love of women. Though there must be large numbers of ungifted people who also have such daydreams, the artist has a talent for sublimating and projecting these fantasies out of the libido into art. In that guise they are enjoyed vicariously by the others, and he is thereupon honored by the rewards he has longed for, having, as Freud would put it, "won—through his phantasy—what before he could only win in phantasy." This reductive and philistine case history seems quite unworthy of its searching proponent. (pp. 3-8)

Bacon is far less concerned than Freud with the individual; yet they seem agreed in their willingness to equate fantasy with wish fulfillment. Both the Greek $\phi\rho\alpha\nu\tau\alpha\sigma\iota\alpha$ and the Latin *imaginatio* have a similarly modest origin, rooted in visual perception, implying little more than the mind's ability to visualize again what the eyes have seen before. Since that second sight is no longer controlled by literal circumstance, it is through this area of reproduction and variation that the possibilities for novelty and creativity can enter the picture; and that is why Joseph Addison dwelt upon what he described as "the secondary imagination." Only God may be presumed to create *ex nihilo,* but through the senses He has provided mankind with materials for something like creation. Naturally, young persons are more receptive than their elders: "Imaginations stream into their minds better, and as it were more divinely," Bacon says in his essay **"Of Youth and Age."** In general, he has much more to say from a positive angle than Montaigne, whose essay *"De la force de l'imagination"* is a series of warnings against being led astray. Most of the Elizabethan testimony is equally negative, stressing the distortions, delusions, and dangers of so wayward a faculty. So is Dr. Johnson's caveat in *Rasselas* on the dangerous prevalence of imagination. Shakespeare's purple passage in *A Midsummer Night's Dream* grants full recognition to the unconscious and irrational elements:

> Lovers and madmen have such seething brains,
> Such shaping fantasies that apprehend
> More than cool reason ever comprehends.

But the poet's function is counterbalanced. On the one hand, his eye rolls "in a fine frenzy," the *furor poeticus.* On the other, those inchoate fancies are shaped and named and localized by his pen. This internalizes, at all events, the primitive notion of genius (as a tutelary spirit) or inspiration (as a supernatural incitement) or a Muse (as a goddess feeding the poet his lines), which had metaphorically implied that his poetic expression somehow originated outside of himself.

More than once Bacon, who was no prolocutor for the Church Fathers, cites the patristic suspicion that poetry may be a diabolical intoxicant (*vinum daemonum*), "because it filleth the imagination; and yet it is but with the shadow of a lie" (here again the votary of light recoils from shadow). This is cited from his essay **"On Truth,"** where lies are obviously inadmissible, though they "make for pleasure as with poets," and on occasion sustain flagging spirits with "flattering hopes . . . and the like." It remained for Addison to expatiate on "the pleasures of the imagination." The perennial quarrel between poetry and philosophy can be traced to the pre-Socratic imputation that poets—by instinct, habit, and vocation—were liars. The duplicity of their role was bound up with the double meaning of their craft: in Greek ποιησισ, in late Latin *fictio,* in plain English *making.* All of these synonyms cast the poet as, in George Puttenham's Elizabethan phrase [in his *The Arte of English Poesie*], "both a maker and a counterfaitor." Making can be reduced to make-believe: the craftsman, *homo faber,* is one who fabricates. Fiction, though it begins as something solidly formed or convincingly shaped, ends by acquiring an overtone of fictitiousness. Bacon's key word underlies this equivocal implication. The modifying participle in "feigned history" goes back to the *fingo* in *"historia conficta."* This, in turn, is cognate with what Isaac Newton seems to have meant by his repeated declaration, *"hypotheses non fingo."* The English verb he used at one point ("feign," not "frame") signalized not so much a refusal to make hypotheses as a denial that he was making them up as he went along.

Insofar as hypothesis consisted of heuristic theory unsupported as yet by inductive fact, Bacon put even less trust in it than Newton. And Newton must have been following Bacon's example when he dismissed conjecture as "romance." But he had never undertaken, though Bacon implicitly had, to consider romance upon its own ground—or, at least, within its own stratosphere. Significantly, Bacon turned from **The Advancement of Learning** to **The Wisdom of the Ancients** (**De Sapientia Veterum**) and, when he came back to **De Augmentis Scientiarum,** he emphasized and enlarged his discussion of Parabolical Poesy, illustrating with detailed interpretations from the earlier mythographical treatise: with parables on Pan, or Nature; Perseus, or War; and Dionysus, or Desire. Along with the march of intellect, he predicated a rediscovery of the secret lore that darker ages had embodied through myths: "as hieroglyphics were before letters, so parables were before arguments." (The Latin version adduces the instance, so dear to the Elizabethans, of Menenius Agrippa's fable about the belly and the members, used by Shakespeare in *Coriolanus* to draw a rather sophistical analogy.) Classical mythology furnished Bacon, as it did so many European writers, with a typology of human nature. However, he went far beyond allusion into hermeneutics, allegorizing morals and rationalizing meanings out of the fabulous improbabilities that he reinterpreted. Myth could be assimilated to science if, "Under the Person of Proteus, Matter, the most ancient of all things next to God, is meant to be represented."

As a mythographer Bacon was the acknowledged forerunner of Giambattista Vico, whose *Scienza Nuova* would present a synchronic method for recovering prehistory by rereading Homer, the ancient lawgivers, and other archetypal sources of prelogical knowledge—in short, a reinterpretation of poetic wisdom. (Among the many fables, inevitably, would be that of Menenius Agrippa.) Bacon's surveys reported "no other deficiency in Poesy" beyond the one he had attempted to fill with **The Wisdom of the Ancients.** Poetry was like a plant, or possibly a weed (*"herba luxurians"*), that had "sprung up" from the spontaneous richness of the soil and "spread abroad more than any other kind." That lack of deliberate cultivation, the notion of running wild, applies to its content and not its form, since it is said to be restrained in wording (*"verbis astrictum"*) but "free and licensed [*solutum et licentiosum*]" in other matters. Poetic license is more affirmatively treated in **A Description of the Intellectual Globe (Descriptio Globi Intellectualis).** Knowledge, in dealing with individuals, usually exercises itself, but sometimes it sports. *Historia* "is the exercise and work of the mind"; *poesis* "may be regarded as its sport [*lusus*]. In philosophy the mind is bound to things; in poesy it is released from that bond, and wanders forth, and feigns what it pleases [*fingit quid vult*]." Bacon here reverts to his triple scheme for the understanding, while relieving the imagination of all responsibilities. What is left, to be positively developed by Kant and Schiller, is the aesthetics of *der Spieltrieb,* the impulse to play.

This is confirmed when Poesy is described by **The Advancement of Learning** as "rather a pleasure or play of imagination, than a work or duty thereof." It has therefore produced no science, though there could be a science about it. But Imagination turns out to be Janus-faced, looking toward Reason, "which hath the print of Truth," and likewise toward—not Memory, but on another plane apparently—Action, "which hath the print of Good." Rhetoric is the intermediate province of "Imaginative or Insinuative Reason" ("insinuative," I suppose, because it works not directly nor explicitly), whereas Religion, on the other side, sets Imagination over Reason. On both sides the inquiry shades off into ethics: in Delphic terms, *"the knowledge of ourselves."* With regard to emotional conduct, "the passions" and "the affections," poets have more to teach than philosophers. Bacon is less mindful of other poetic genres than the parabolical, though he expatiates on two of them more fully in **De Augmentis Scientiarum.** Narrative poems aspire to be heroical, and to celebrate "the dignity of human nature." Drama, which has the advantage of making a direct impression on a social group, could become a sort of plectrum for playing upon their minds. This influence, among the ancients, acted as a discipline, whereby they could be educated to virtue. Such aims, among the moderns, have fallen off into corruption. Writing in the heyday of Shakespeare and Ben Jonson, Bacon recorded his measured opinion that "play-acting is esteemed but as a toy (*pro re ludicra*)." His consistent suspicions of the drama would work, if nothing else did, against the attempts to identify him as Shakespeare's ghostwriter.

The deprecatory English monosyllable, *toy,* was common usage for the Jacobeans. To them it did not signify a child's plaything but stood more broadly for any trifle or else for dallying, with a possible touch of sexual innuendo. "These things are but toys"—so Bacon apologized for, and rapidly dismissed, the subject matter of his late and slight essay, **"Of Masques and Triumphs."** He himself had participated in one such courtly entertainment, the up-roarious *Gesta Grayorum,* enacted by fellow lawyers for the queen at Gray's Inn, where elaborate spectacle was combined with politic counsel. As for dramatic action, that was then supplied by the afterpiece, Shakespeare's *Comedy of Errors,* appropriately or not. Bacon's own distrust of plays comes out again, in defining the Idols of the Theater, when he criticizes wishful thinking. When *The Advancement of Learning* moves on from literary to philosophical exposition, his satisfaction is proclaimed by his tropes: "But it is not good to stay too long in the theatre. Let us now pass on to the judicial place or palace of the mind, which we are to approach and view with more reverence and attention." During the next generation Henry Reynolds would be outraged by this dictum; and, in his Neoplatonic tract *Mythomystes,* he accuses Bacon of inconsistency for expressing such positivistic impatience after having devoted other studies to the allegorical exegesis of myths. But the dismissive contrast is strengthened by Bacon himself in his Latin continuation, when he takes his leave from Poesy's "dream of learning (*doctrinae somnium*)" and awakens to Science's clear air.

Leonardo da Vinci, a century before, had deprecated poetry from the vantage point of painting. That was a bolder step, since visual art had been played down by the humanistic authorities, who categorized it among the mechanical rather than liberal arts. Furthermore, or so Leonardo contended it outranked its verbal counterpart by qualifying as a science. Pictorial representation came much closer to nature than written texts could do because it dealt with facts and not with words. (pp. 8-12)

Undoubtedly Bacon was well acquainted with Sir Philip Sidney's *Defence of Poesie,* which was not only the most influential of Elizabethan critical statements but—as J. E. Spingarn pointed out [in *A History of Literary Criticism in the Renaissance*]—"a veritable epitome of the literary criticism of the Italian Renaissance." Its posture of defense, or the *Apologie* of its alternate title, had been provoked by Puritan attacks, and may help to account for its moralistic premises. Yet it is really a panegyric or eulogy, a teeming survey and sprightly appraisal, a large-minded synthesis of conventions and improvisations, not excluding the familiar—if dubious—object lesson of Menenius Agrippa. In Sidney's perspective, as in Bacon's, Poesy is flanked by Philosophy and History, but the relations that Sidney works out are based upon the original Aristotelian poetics. Philosophy has its precepts, history its examples; and, if the poet can derive precepts from the historian's examples, he can also devise examples for the philosopher's precepts. He can universalize the particular, as Aristotle had more or less observed; Sidney would add that he can particularize the universal. Turning to Plato, who is warmly welcomed as "our Patron, and not our adversarie," Sidney's approach is less defensive than conciliatory. To the Platonic charge that poetry is falsehood, he responds: "Now for the *Poet,* he nothing affirmeth, and therefore never lieth." Why, then, should we be expecting him to tell the factual truth? Yet, though poetic truth may be a paradox, it has aesthetic canons and ethical standards. These "should be εἰκαστική, . . . figuring foorth good things," rather than "φανταστική: . . . which doth

contrariwise infect the fancie with unwoorthy objects." Sidney was nothing if not an idealist. (pp. 12-13)

Bacon was heavily pledged to discriminate substance from shadow, and authentic brass from the gold of the alchemists. To the idealism of Sidney he would have counterpoised the realism of "Machiavel and others, that write what men do and not what men ought to do." Not that Bacon, as a practising advocate and parliamentary orator, was unconcerned with telling men what they ought to do. Just as language was the field of his greatest mastery, so rhetoric was the middle ground between his professional and his intellectual interests. His *Table of Colours or Appearances of Good and Evil,* demonstrating how the art of persuasion could put the best face upon any cause, is well versed in the uses of the optative mood. This invites a moral skepticism and is posited upon a relativistic sense of values; yet Bacon's juridical training had accustomed him to entertaining opposite points of view, and his dialectical habit was flexible enough to hold them in ambivalent suspension. Future generations would have to oscillate, wavering between a tough and bleak materialism and a sensitive and elusive transcendence, between Thomas Hobbes's mechanistic definition of Fancy and Coleridge's ineffable mystery of Imagination. Ever since the seventeenth century, culture as a whole has been suffering—in the diagnosis of T. S. Eliot—from a "dissociation of sensibility." Bacon has been accused of fostering, if not of having initiated, that mutually detrimental rift disjoining what C. P. Snow has taught us to call the two cultures.

To Bacon such an allegation would have been inconceivable. Knowledge was for him an indivisible totality, though—in his timely endeavors to make room for scientific experimentation and to cut down on verbalistic tradition—he did much to animate a reversal of that imbalance, a shift to the other side. It has been claimed that he became perfunctory and derivative whenever he theorized about literature, and that he would never have bothered to do so if he had not engaged himself to complete an undertaking of encyclopedic scope. As it happened, though many of his undertakings stand uncompleted, he did leave a substantial and interesting sequence of literary animadversions. He took some pains—as we have just noted—to reconsider the arguments of the leading previous English critic, disparate from his own outlook as they were, and to meet them halfway. At that midpoint the romancer of the *Arcadia* and the science-fiction writer of *The New Atlantis* seem to unite in attesting the value of imagination, and of hypothetical constructs as a means of adjustment between the human psyche and the physical universe. Philosophy might not be so austerely remote from Poesy, in the long run, as Baconian rigor had presupposed. Jeremy Bentham would sketch a theory of fictions; Hans Vaihinger would systematize a "philosophy of as if [*als ob*]"; more recent philosophers would concern themselves with the accommodations of thought to language. The continuing presence of myth as an active force in history, even when unmasked as "the big lie," could be deplored but not ignored. As Wallace Stevens would conclude in *Notes toward a Supreme Fiction:*

> the bride
> Is never naked. A fictive covering

Weaves always glistening from the heart and mind.

Bacon had ample occasion to distinguish the fictive from the real in courts of law, as well as to confound them at the courts of royalty. During the five final years that he spent in the shadows, he must have felt the fullest rigors of the *rerum natura*. Forced at last to give up the civil for the contemplative life, he may have come to believe more fully in the existence of worlds beyond worldliness, in a plurality of those not-quite-impossible worlds which had been conceived as fables or romances. He could scarcely have lived up to the motto *plus ultra* by sticking to known facts. Stimulated by the "feigned commonwealth" of a less worldly lord chancellor, he had briefly indulged in his own dream of learning. That posthumous fragment, with its glistening vision of Salomon's House, "enlarging the bounds of Human Empire, to the effecting of all things possible," would have greater influence on the future than the wide shelf of Bacon's more discursive prospectuses. Its story begins—in spite of, or else because of, its author—with a scriptural miracle, "a pillar of light." *The New Atlantis* would be, for Joseph Glanvill and his colleagues, "a Prophetick Scheam of the ROYAL SOCIETY." A. G. Baumgarten, the rationalistic philosopher who would introduce the study of aesthetics, redefined a poem as a heterocosmic version of actuality. Sidney had long before pleaded that Plato's model commonwealth, *The Republic,* and Xenophon's portrait of a model ruler, Cyrus the Great, along with More's *Utopia,* should be accepted as poetry. If a poet may be characterized as a designer of models, then it is hard to think of any poet whose imaginings have reverberated farther than Bacon's. His involvements with reason and memory remain significant; and he would be restless and skeptical in any of his three spheres; but if one of them accords with his disposition better than the others, shadowy and precarious though it may be, it is imagination. And today we can observe what Addison foresaw, that "there are none who more gratifie and enlarge the Imagination, than the Authors of the new Philosophy." (pp. 13-15)

Harry Levin, "Bacon's Poetics," in Renaissance Rereadings: Intertext and Context, *Maryanne Cline Horowitz, Anne J. Cruz, Wendy A. Furman, eds., University of Illinois Press, 1988, pp. 3-17.*

FURTHER READING

Anderson, F. H. *The Philosophy of Francis Bacon.* Chicago: University of Chicago Press, 1948, 312 p.
Exhaustive study of Bacon's philosophy, including the historical background of his ideas. Focuses on the role of logic in Bacon's system.

Babbit, Irving. "Two types of Humanitarians: Bacon and Rousseau." In his *Literature and the American College,* pp. 32-71. Boston: Houghton Mifflin, 1908.

Includes a discussion of Bacon's ideas about humankind. Babbit defines Bacon as a typical Renaissance elitist who also responded to the Christian notion of humanitarian sympathy.

Balfour, Arthur James. "Francis Bacon." In his *Essays Speculative and Political,* pp. 137-50. New York: George H. Doran, 1921.
Summarizes Bacon's intellectual accomplishment, concluding that his efforts at building philosophical and scientific systems is secondary to his role as a prophet and a seer.

Church, R. W. *Bacon.* London: Macmillan, 1884, 227 p.
Comprehensive study of Bacon's life and works, including discussion of his philosophical ideas and literary style.

Cranston, Maurice. "A Founder of Modern Science." *The Listener* LXV, No. 1661 (26 January 1961): 185-86.
Credits the benefits of modern technology to the Baconian revolution in science.

Eisley, Loren. *The Man Who Saw through Time.* New York: Scribner's, 1973, 125 p.
Revised and enlarged edition of the author's 1961 work *Francis Bacon and the Modern Dilemma.* Interprets Bacon as an innovative philosopher, arguing that he foresaw many future scientific and philosophical developments.

Farrington, Benjamin. *Francis Bacon: Philosopher of Industrial Science.* New York: Henry Schuman, 1949, 202 p.
Traces Bacon's intellectual development and literary work, with particular emphasis on the relevance of Baconian ideas to modern science and technology.

———. *The Philosophy of Francis Bacon.* Liverpool: Liverpool University Press, 1964, 139 p.
Surveys Bacon's philosophical thought, focusing on the crucial points of his intellectual development.

Fish, Stanley. "Georgics of the Mind: The Experience of Bacon's *Essays.*" *The Critical Quarterly* 13, No. 1 (Spring 1971): 45-68.
Analyzes Bacon's prose, with special emphasis on the *Essays.* Fish argues that Bacon, in his *Essays,* nourishes and "at the same time exposes definitions and schematizations that have been accepted without sufficient validation."

Fowler, Thomas. *Bacon.* New York: Putnam, 1881, 202 p.
Detailed analysis of Bacon's social, scientific, philosophical, and religious ideas by an eminent Baconian scholar.

Fuller, Jean Overton. *Francis Bacon.* London: East-West Publications, 1981, 384 p.
Detailed biography of Bacon, focusing on the background of his literary, scholarly, and political activities.

Green, A. Wigfall. *Sir Francis Bacon.* Twayne: New York, 1966, 200 p.
Overview of Bacon's life and work which includes an extensive discussion of his principal works.

Harrison, John L. "Bacon's View of Rhetoric, Poetry, and the Imagination." *The Huntington Library Quarterly* XX, No. 2 (February 1957): 107-25.
Disputes the claims of critics who interpret Bacon's view of poetry as fundamentally negative.

Jameson, Thomas H. *Francis Bacon: Criticism and the Modern World.* New York: Praeger, 1954, 72 p.

Examines Bacon's views on such subjects as the mind, imagination, and ethical judgment in relation to modern perceptions.

Jardine, Lisa. *Francis Bacon: Discovery and the Art of Discourse.* Cambridge: Cambridge University Press, 1974, 267 p.

Discusses a variety of issues central to Bacon's work, including his theory of knowledge, interpretation of nature, ethical thought, view of rhetoric, and literary method, with emphasis on the *Essays.*

Knights, L. C. "Bacon and the Seventeenth-Century Dissociation of Sensibility." In his *Explorations,* pp. 92-111. London: Chatto & Windus, 1946.

Discussion, originally published in 1943, of Bacon's influence on modern sensibility. Knights argues that Baconian rationalism, although responsible for some beneficial scientific and cultural development, does not capture the totality of human experience.

Kotarbinski, Tadeusz. *Gnosiology: The Scientific Approach to the Theory of Knowledge.* Oxford: Pergamon Press, 1966, 548 p.

Includes a discussion of Bacon's philosophy of knowledge in the the socio-political context of his time.

Lang, Andrew. *Shakespeare, Bacon, and the Great Unknown.* London: Longmans, Green, 1912, 314 p.

Revisits the controversy surrounding Bacon's putative authorship of Shakespeare's work.

Moore, Marianne. "Sir Francis Bacon." In her *Predilections,* pp. 115-18. New York: Viking Press, 1955.

Reprint of an essay originally published in 1944; Moore praises Bacon as an ingenious observer and connoisseur of human nature.

Patrick, J. Max. *Francis.* London: Longmans, Green, 1961, 43 p.

Concise review of Bacon's life and works.

Pitcher, John. Introduction to *The Essays,* by Francis Bacon, pp. 14-45. New York: Penguin Books, 1985.

Discusses Bacon's *Essays* in the context of his philosophical and literary ideas.

Rowse, A. L. "Bacon: 'All Knowledge Was His Province'." *The New York Times Magazine* (22 January 1961): 20, 56, 58.

Reviews Bacon's monumental intellectual accomplishments, asserting that he contributed a vital impulse to the development of scientific knowledge.

Shera, Jesse H. "Dignity and Advancement of Bacon." In *College and Research Libraries* 23, No. 1 (January 1962): 18-23.

Explains the importance of Bacon's classification of knowledge for the practice and theory of library science.

Taylor, A. E. "Francis Bacon." *Proceedings of the British Academy* (1926): 273-94.

Praises Bacon's efforts to build a unified system of knowledge, arguing that Bacon, despite the materialistic stance attributed to him by commentators, stands as a bridge between the great metaphysical traditions of Plato and Baron Gottfried Wilhelm Leibnitz.

Trevor-Roper, Hugh. "Francis Bacon." *Encounter* XVIII, No. 2 (February 1962): 73-7.

Discusses Bacon's multi-faceted genius, focusing on the relevance of his political ideas.

Vickers, Brian. *Francis Bacon and Renaissance Prose.* Cambridge: Cambridge University Press, 1968, 313 p.

Study of Bacon's literary style, technique, imagery, and argumentation in the context of Renaissance literature and culture.

——. *Francis Bacon.* London: Longman, 1978, 41 p.

Concise study of Bacon's life and work, with particular emphasis on how Renaissance rhetoric and culture in general influenced the philosopher's ideas and style.

Wallace, Karl R. *Francis Bacon and the Nature of Man.* Urbana: University of Illinois Press, 1967, 202 p.

Discusses Bacon's interpretation of basic philosophical and psychological concepts, including understanding, reason, will, and memory.

Warhaft, Sidney. "Science against Man in Bacon." *Bucknell Review* VII, No. 3 (March 1958): 158-73.

Considers the less beneficial consequences of the Baconian scientific revolution, concluding that "if we owe much to Bacon for the method and inventions of our age, so too do we owe him much for our world of telegrams and anger."

——. "The Providential Order in Bacon's New Philosophy." In *Francis Bacon's Legacy of Texts,* edited by William A. Sessions, pp. 151-67. New York: AMS Press, 1990.

Comments on the idea of order in Bacon's thought, arguing that his philosophy, though basically secular, shows distinct traces of a sacral world view.

White, Howard B. *Peace among the Willows: The Political Philosophy of Francis Bacon.* The Hague: Martinus Nijhoff, 1968, 266 p.

Presents Bacon's political thought in the context of the European philosophical tradition.

Wiley, Basil. "Francis Bacon." In his *The English Moralists,* pp. 124-47. New York: Norton, 1964.

Examines the ethical underpinnings of Bacon's philosophy, maintaining that the pursuit of knowledge, as envisioned by the English philosopher, does not necessarily obviate Christian charity.

Williamson, George. "Bacon and the Stoic Rhetoric." In his *The Senecan Amble,* pp. 150-85. Chicago: University of Chicago Press, 1951.

Analysis of the classical background of Bacon's prose style.

St. John of the Cross

1542-1591

(Born Juan de Yepes y Alvarez; also known as San Juan de la Cruz) Spanish poet, philosopher and prose writer.

The most important writer in the Christian mystical tradition, St. John of the Cross is also one of the foremost poets in Hispanic literature. The essence of St. John's mystical doctrine is captured in his three major poems, "Noche oscura del alma" ("The Dark Night of the Soul"), "Cántico espiritual" ("The Spiritual Canticle"), and "Llama de amor viva" ("The Living Flame of Love"). Renowned for their power, musicality, and evocative imagery, these intense lyrics symbolize the process of purgation, illumination, and union with God: the ultimate goal of the contemplative life. St. John rigorously schematized the steps of the mystic ascent in his prose treatises, which take the form of line-by-line exegeses of his three major poetic works: *The Spiritual Canticle, The Living Flame of Love, The Dark Night,* and *Subida del Monte Carmelo (Ascent of Mount Carmel)*—the last two named works commenting on the same poem, "The Dark Night." While his prose has been characterized by critics as prolix and obscure, his poetry is universally lauded for its deft construction and vivid rendering of abstract metaphysical concepts through concrete physical imagery, as well as for its religious ardor.

John was born Juan de Yepes in Fontiveros in 1542, the youngest of three brothers. His father, a nobleman who had been repudiated by his family, died when John was two, leaving the family in extreme poverty. As a boy, John helped his mother, a weaver, support his family by working for a carpenter, a tailor, and a painter. The family eventually moved and settled in Medina del Campo, where John attended a Jesuit grammar school. At the age of fourteen, he began working in a hospital, where he attracted the attention of the hospital supervisor, who offered to put John through the Jesuit college at Medina in return for his services begging for alms in the streets to support the hospital—an offer John accepted. He remained at the hospital until he was twenty, when he declined the chance to become chaplain of the hospital and chose to enter the Carmelite monastery in Medina as a novice. After two years there, his superiors sent him to the University of Salamanca in 1564, where he completed a three-year program in the Arts. He was ordained a priest in 1567, taking the name Juan de San Matías. Soon after his ordination, the reformer and mystic Teresa de Jesús, then fifty-two, visited John's monastery in Medina looking for a young friar to help her extend her ideas of reform to the male branch of the Carmelite Order; their meeting would prove the most important event in John's career. He found Teresa's emphasis on increased prayer and contemplation particularly appealing, and the two developed a lifelong friendship. In 1558, after another year at the University of Salamanca, John helped found the first Reformed (Discalced) Carmelite monastery in a humble

farmhouse in Duruelo, taking the vows of the reform on 28 November as Juan de la Cruz, or John of the Cross.

The reformed order grew rapidly over the next decade, and John served in turn as a master of novices at Pastrana, teacher at the Carmelite college at Alcalá, and confessor to the nuns of Teresa's priory at Avila, where he remained for five years. During that time, tensions between the Discalced and Calced monasteries escalated, and in 1575 the Calced kidnapped John in an effort to halt the reform movement. Released by order of the Papal Nuncio in 1576, he was abducted again a year later and imprisoned for nine months at the Calced priory in Toledo. Confined in a small, windowless cell, John was subjected to daily punishment including the circular discipline, in which his bare back was scourged with leather whips by each brother in turn. He was offered immediate release and a high position in the order if he would renounce the reform, but John refused, despite the threat of excommunication. In

May 1568 a new jailer, fearing for the frail man's health, mitigated John's punishment and allowed him a pen and paper to pass the time. Thus, in the prison cell in Toledo, John began to record his major poetic works, including the first half of "The Spiritual Canticle" and possibly "The Dark Night." The jailer also permitted John to walk about the monastery during the daily siesta; during these walks he was able to familiarize himself with the grounds and plan an escape. In August he carried out his scheme, escaping by night from an upper window, using a rope made from strips of his blanket and tunic.

For his own safety, John was sent to a remote retreat in Andalusia, where he served as vicar, completed the last half of "The Spiritual Canticle," and began his *Ascent of Mount Carmel.* When the strife between the Discalced and Calced monasteries lessened and the two orders were officially divided, John was elected Prior of Los Mártieres in Granada. He remained there from 1581 to 1588, completing "The Living Flame of Love" and his major treatises despite constant travel and official duties, including the establishment of five new monasteries. He eventually was elected councillor to the provincial in 1588 and reelected to the post in 1590. However, conflict with the innovative provincial led to John's removal from office in June 1591. Exiled to a solitary house in Peñuela, he learned soon after that the decision to strip him of office had been revoked, but he was content to live out his days in solitude and prayer as a simple friar. A few months later, stricken with fever, John was removed to Ubeda for medical treatment. He died there at midnight on 14 December 1591, after weeks of excruciating pain. He was beatified in 1675, canonized in 1726, and pronounced a Doctor of the Church in 1926.

The mystical works of St. John of the Cross were not collated and published until 1618, some twenty-seven years after his death. The profusion and possible destruction of the original manuscripts and copies raises several questions about the texts' composition dates, order of composition, and completeness. Yet scholars and critics agree that the extant works of St. John provide among the world's richest and most comprehensive accounts of the soul's mystic ascent from the distractions of the world to spiritual communion with God. His greatest literary legacy is undoubtedly derived from his three major poems, "The Dark Night," "The Spiritual Canticle," and "The Living Flame of Love." Viewed against the theological paradigm of purgation, illumination, and union, these works symbolize the various stages and goals of the ascetic and contemplative life. In "The Dark Night," perhaps his best known work, St. John depicts the initial stages of the soul's mystic journey: the purgation of earthly desires in a terrifying yet ecstatic process of purification symbolized by the Dark Night. The poem represents the soul's yearning for God, depicting the journey of a person through the dark of night in search of his or her beloved. As the night enshrouds the searcher's senses, it becomes symbolic not only of self-abnegation and detachment, but of faith itself; only in total darkness could God shine so brightly. At the poem's conclusion the intense imagery of heat and light at the revelation of the beloved gives way to the union of the seeker and the one sought for, imagery central to "The Spiritual

Canticle." A pastoral poem drawing its inspiration from the biblical *Song of Songs,* the "Canticle" comprises a loosely allegorical framework in the form of a dialogue between a lover and her beloved to illustrate the entire mystical journey of the soul to God. The couple's wedding preparations prefigure the spiritual marriage and beatific vision that mark the highest levels of the mystic experience. The four exclamatory songs of "The Living Flame of Love" focus exclusively on the experience of communion between the soul and God, every verse ringing with transcendant joy.

Although the number of his poems is rather small, his only other verses being a few allegorical ballads and glosses, St. John's profound lyrics have earned him consideration as one of Spain's greatest poets. The melodious meter, vivid imagery, and artful technique of his verse are together recognized as a standard of lyrical accomplishment by modern critics; as poet and critic Jorge Guillén states, "San Juan de la Cruz has found the supreme equilibrium between poetry of inspiration and constructed poetry." Yet the verses pose many problems for the reader, with their rigorous logic and complex symbolism, in which, for example, the same word may have multiple meanings. Textual and thematic studies of St. John's poetry have explored eucharistic, conjugal, and sensory imagery, as well as such recurring symbols as nature and the dark night. The relationship the poems bear to St. John's overall mystic doctrine constitutes another aspect of critical study; however, while commentators may differ on the theological implications of his poetry, they are unanimous in their praise of St. John's ability to capture abstract metaphysical and theological concepts in a poem suffused with erotic imagery.

Critical discussions of St. John's poetry often lead naturally to examinations of his prose commentaries, which thoroughly rationalize the progress of the mystic experience depicted in his poems. He devised these commentaries at the specific request of the nuns and friars under his spiritual direction, to help explicate the poetry and serve as a practical guide to ascetic contemplation. The concept of these prose works as together forming a spiritual guidebook or map is elucidated by St. John's own graphic representation of the mystic journey: a diagram which served as the frontispiece of his *Ascent of Mount Carmel* and which he apparently hoped would be included with the manuscripts of all of his treatises. In its final version, the engraving depicts a mountain whose summit represents the highest spiritual plane and whose base marks the starting point of contemplation. Wide, winding paths representing imperfect methods of prayer end far from the top of the mountain, while the initially narrow but very steep path marked "Spirit of Perfection" leads directly to the summit; on this road is the inscription "Nothing, nothing, nothing, nothing, nothing," signifying the ascetic purgation of desires necessary for union with the divine. In the *Ascent* and *The Dark Night,* both of which comment on the poem "The Dark Night," St. John rigorously details this process of purification and detachment necessary to prepare the soul for the experience of the divine. *The Living Flame of Love,* centering on the poem of the same title, focuses entirely on the spiritual marriage with God that culminates the mystic vision. The mystic journey is detailed in its entirety only in *The Spiritual Canticle,* where the process of purgation, illumination, and union is comprehensively described. While direct, powerful, and scrupulously logical, the style of St. John's prose works has been characterized by some critics as redundant, tedious, and obscure. Furthermore, many scholars allege that the poet's own commentaries ignore the complex and shifting symbolism of the poems by forcing them into an overly restrictive allegorical framework. Yet most critics acknowledge a debt to the prose treatises for their exposition of the fundamental mystic doctrine and the insights they lend to the poems, noting that the author was attempting to construct neither a conscious work of art nor a work of literary criticism, but a series of instructional tools for a highly specialized audience, his fellow Carmelites. St. John himself attests to the limitations of his prose analyses to elucidate the ineffable concepts of his poetry, asserting in the prologue to his *Spiritual Canticle* that his verses "cannot be fairly expounded, nor shall I attempt to expound them, but only to throw upon them some light of a kind."

The critical history of these mystical works has been lively and varied, despite critic Menéndez y Pelayo's exclamation that St. John's poetry "scarcely seems to belong to this world at all; it is hardly capable of being assessed by literary criteria." Beyond stylistic and thematic issues relevant to the poetry and prose, and the relationship between the two forms, critics have speculated on the possible sources and influences of St. John's works as well as the order and date of their composition. The autobiographical nature of his writings has proved a point of departure for many critics, as has the question of whether his poetry was divinely inspired. The overall metaphysical and theological conception of St. John dominates much of the critical corpus, which often centers on his emphasis on asceticism and self-denial. Viewed by many critics as overly harsh and austere, St. John's teachings on the purgation of the senses and the will have been characterized as fanatical, inhuman, and even heterodox, as they seem to imply self-annihilation and quietism. The majority of scholars, however, attest to the humanity and orthodoxy of St. John's views. They assert that such censorious interpretations result from critical overemphasis on the *Ascent of Mount Carmel* and *The Dark Night,* which detail only the initial preparation for mystic communion. Furthermore, commentators maintain that St. John does not insist on the total annihilation of reason and will, but rather a recognition of the overwhelming superiority of God, which transcends these faculties. The uncompromising stance of this Carmelite saint testifies to the "unwavering devotion to Christ" cited by Edgar Allison Peers as the overarching theme of St. John's writings. Reflecting rigorous logic and a lifelong study of theology, the works of St. John of the Cross occupy a preeminent place in the Christian mystic tradition, just as the sensitivity, beauty, and clarity of his phrasing mark him as one of the world's most accomplished poets. "It is perhaps not an exaggeration," asserts Peers, "to say that the verse and prose works combined of St. John of the Cross form at once the most grandiose and the most melodious spiritual canticle to which any one man has given utterance."

PRINCIPAL WORKS

*"Noche oscura del alma" (poetry) 1581
[*"The Dark Night of the Soul,"* 1864]
Subida del Monte Carmelo (treatise) 1582
[*Ascent of Mount Carmel,* 1864]
*"Cántico espiritual" (poetry) 1583
[*"The Spiritual Canticle,"* 1864]
Noche oscura del alma (treatise) 1583
[*The Dark Night of the Soul,* 1864]
Cántico espiritual (treatise) 1584; revised 1590
[*The Spiritual Canticle,* 1864]
*"Llama de amor viva" (poetry) 1584
[*"The Living Flame of Love,"* 1864]
Llama de amor viva (treatise) 1585; revised 1587
[*The Living Flame of Love,* 1864]
Obras espirituales que encaminan a una alma a la perfecta unión con Dios (poetry, treatises) 1618
The Complete Works of St. John of the Cross (poetry, treatises) 1864
Obras de San Juan de la Cruz. 5 vols. (poetry, treatises) 1929-31
The Complete Works of Saint John of the Cross (poetry, treatises) 1932

*Represents completion of manuscript version; dates are approximate. The English translations were first published in *The Complete Works of St. John of the Cross,* 1864.

Arthur Symons   (essay date 1899)

[*Symons was a critic, poet, dramatist, short story writer, and editor who first gained notoriety in the 1890s as an English decadent. Eventually, he established himself as one of the most important literary critics of the modern era with his book* The Symbolist Movement in Literature *(1899). Here, Symons examines* "The Dark Night," Ascent of Mount Carmel, *and* The Living Flame of Love *to discuss St. John of the Cross's depiction of abstract metaphysical concepts through sensory imagery.*]

The poetry of San Juan de la Cruz is metaphysical fire, a sort of white heat in which the abstract, the almost negative, becomes ecstatically realised by the senses. Here, in a translation as literal as I can make it, line for line, and with exactly the same arrangement and repetition of rhymes, is his most famous poem, **"En una Noche escura,"** a poem which is the keystone of his whole philosophy:

> Upon an obscure night,
>   Fevered with love in love's anxiety,
> (O hapless—happy plight!)
>   I went, none seeing me,
> Forth from my house where all things quiet be.
>
> By night, secure from sight,
>   And by the secret stair, disguisedly,
> (O hapless—happy plight!)
>   By night, and privily,

Forth from my house where all things quiet be.

Blest night of wandering,
    In secret, when by none might I be spied,
Nor I see anything;
    Without a light or guide,
Save that which in my heart burnt in my side.

That light did lead me on,
    More surely than the shining of noontide,
Where well I knew that one
    Did for my coming bide;
Where he abode might none but he abide.

O night that didst lead thus,
    O night more lovely than the dawn of light,
O night that broughtest us,
    Lover to lover's sight,
Lover with loved in marriage of delight!

Upon my flowery breast,
    Wholly for him, and save himself for none,
There did I give sweet rest
    To my beloved one;
The fanning of the cedars breathed thereon.

When the first moving air
    Blew from the tower, and waved his locks
        aside,
His hand, with gentle care,
    Did wound me in the side,
And in my body all my senses died.

All things I then forgot,
    My cheek on him who for my coming came;
All ceased, and I was not,
    Leaving my cares and shame
Among the lilies, and forgetting them.

The greater part of the prose of San Juan de la Cruz is built up out of this poem, or condensed into it: the *Noche Escura del Alma* is a line-by-line commentary upon it, and the *Subida del Monte Carmelo,* a still longer work, takes this poem for starting-point, and declares that the whole of its doctrine is to be found in these stanzas. The third and last of the three contemplative books, the *"Llama de Amor Viva,"* is, in a similar way, a commentary on the poem which follows:

O flame of living love,
That dost eternally
Pierce through my soul with so consuming heat,
Since there's no help above,
Make thou an end of me,
And break the bond of this encounter sweet.

O burn that burns to heal!
O more than pleasant wound!
And O soft hand, O touch most delicate,
That dost new life reveal,
That dost in grace abound,
And, slaying, dost from death to life translate.

O lamps of fire that shined
With so intense a light,
That those deep caverns where the senses live,
Which were obscure and blind,
Now with strange glories bright,
Both heat and light to his beloved give.

With bow benign intent

Rememberest thou my breast,
Where thou alone abidest secretly,
And in thy sweet ascent,
With glory and good possessed,
How delicately thou teachest love to me!

Thus the whole *Obras Espirituales,* 614 quarto pages in my copy of the original edition of 1618, are but a development of these two poems; the poetry, as it should be, being at the root of the philosophy.

In that strange, pedantic "figure" which stands at the beginning of the *Subida del Monte Carmelo,* the narrow way which leads to the mount is inscribed, "Nothing, nothing, nothing, nothing, nothing," and above, "and in the mount nothing"; but above that begin higher heights, inscribed with the names of the ultimate virtues, and above that the "divine silence" and the "divine wisdom," and the dwelling of the soul with God Himself. With San Juan de la Cruz the obscure night is a way, the negation of all earthly things, of the earthly senses even, a means, to the final union with God; and it is in this union that darkness blossoms into the glittering delights of the poems. Pierce the dark night to its centre, and you will find light, for you will find God. "And so," he tells us, "in this soul, in which now no appetite abides, nor other imaginings, nor forms of other created things; most secretly it abides in so much the more inner interior, and more straitly embraced, as it is itself the more pure, and single of all things but God." This rapture of negation becomes poetry, and poetry of the highest order, because it is part of a nature to which, if God is what Vaughan calls a "deep but dazzling darkness," He is also the supreme love, to be apprehended humanly by this quality, for which, and in which, He put on humanity. To San Juan de la Cruz the idea of God is an idea which can be apprehended mentally only by a series of negations; the person of God can be apprehended only emotionally, and best under the figure, which he accepts from the "Song of Solomon," of earthly marriage, the marriage of the soul and Christ. At once the door is opened in the seventh heaven of metaphysics for all the flowers in which the earth decks itself for lovers; and this monk can give lessons to lovers. His great poem of forty stanzas, the **"Cancion entre el Alma y el Esposo,"** once or twice becoming almost ludicrous in the liveliness of its natural images, as when the Spouse drinks in the "interior bodega" of the Beloved, has a peculiar fragrance, as of very strong natural perfumes, perfumes really made honestly out of flowers, though in the fieriest of alcohols. Here, and in the two mystical love-poems which I have translated, there is an abandonment to all the sensations of love, which seems to me to exceed, and on their own ground, in directness and intensity of spiritual and passionate longing, most of what has been written by the love-poets of all ages. These lines, so full of rich and strange beauty, ache with desire and with all the subtlety of desire. They analyse the sensations of the soul, as lovers do, that they may draw out their sweetness more luxuriously. In a merely human love they would be almost perverse, so learned are they in sensation. Sanctified to divine uses, they do but swing a more odorous incense, in censers of more elaborately beaten gold, in the service of a perpetual Mass to the Almighty.

Of the **"Canciones"** there are but five; and of these I have translated another, somewhat more abstract, less coloured, than the rest.

> Well do I know the spring that doth abound,
> Although it is the night.
>
> That everlasting spring, though hidden close,
> Well do I know whither and whence it flows,
> Although it is the night.
>
> Beginning know I not, for none there is,
> But know that all beginning comes from this,
> Although it is the night.
>
> I know there is not any fairer thing,
> And that the heavens and earth drink of this
>   spring,
> Although it is the night.
>
> I know that end within it is not found,
> Nor is there plummet that its depths can sound,
> Although it is the night.
>
> Upon its brightness doth no shadow come:
> Well know I that all light cometh therefrom,
> Although it is the night.
>
> I know its currents are so hard to bind,
> They water hell and heaven and human-kind,
> Although it is the night.
>
> The current that from this deep spring doth
>   flow,
> How mighty is its flowing, well I know,
> Although it is the night.
>
> This everlasting spring is occulted,
> To give us life within this living bread,
> Although it is the night.
>
> Here it doth speak to man, and say to him:
> Drink of this living water, although dim,
> Although it is the night.
>
> This living spring, I have desired of old,
> Within this bread of life do I behold,
> Although it is the night.

But, besides the **"Canciones,"** there are five "Coplas" and "Glosas," still more abstract than this poem, but brimfull of what I have called metaphysical fire, "toda ciencia transcendiendo"; the ecstasy striving to find immediate, and no long mediate, words for its revelation. Finally there are ten "Romances," of which all but the last are written in quatrains linked by a single rhyme, the accommodating Spanish rhyme in "ia." They are Biblical paraphrases and statements of theological doctrine, and reverence has not permitted them to find any fine, wild liberties for themselves, like the other, more instinctive, more emotionally inspired poems. They have the archaic formality of the fourteenth-century paintings of the Madonna, stiffly embroidered with gold, and waited on by formal angels. Some personal sentiment yet remains, but the personal form is gone, and they might seem to have been really written in an earlier century. (pp. 544-47)

> *Arthur Symons, "The Poetry of Santa Teresa*
> *and San Juan De La Cruz," in* Contemporary
> Review, *Vol. LXXV, April, 1899, pp. 542-51.*

Rev. Benedict Zimmerman, O. C. D. (essay date 1907)

[*In the excerpt below from an essay originally published in 1907, Zimmerman provides "a short sketch of the experiences a soul generally makes on its journey through the realms of Mysticism." He focuses on the* Ascent of Mount Carmel *and* The Dark Night *to describe the "active purgation" of the senses and the "passive purgation" of the spirit deemed necessary by St. John of the Cross for mystical union with God.*]

It may be useful for some readers of St. John's works to find here a short sketch of the experiences a soul generally makes on its journey through the realms of Mysticism. Let us suppose that it has been unexpectedly struck by a ray of divine grace. It may never really have been estranged from God since the day of baptism, or it may have strayed: no essential difference would result therefrom, because motion is determined not so much by the direction whence it proceeds but whither it tends. Such a soul, then, finds a delight, hitherto unknown, in spiritual matters; a new chord has been touched and set vibrating, the whole world seems transfigured, God's work becomes visible and palpable in every blade of grass, His interests absorb all earthly pursuits; the human heart has found and holds fast a treasure of incomparable value; heaven has descended upon earth. 'This is he that heareth the word and immediately receiveth it with joy.'

Such an experience is indeed a great grace, but it does not last. True spirituality consists not in sentiments but in the exercise of virtue. The first impulse is not strong enough to carry the soul very far in its flight heavenwards. The question arises how best to utilise this initial motive power? St. John gives the answer in the **Ascent.** Almost ruthlessly he tears off the brilliant surface so as to save the substance. The first ray has indeed transfigured the heart but has not transformed it. There remain many dangerous germs, the weaknesses and shortcomings of human nature. The very warmth of paradise, the dew descending abundantly upon a tender heart, might develop these so that 'the last state of that man is made worse than the first.' They must, therefore, be destroyed by a long process of self-denial. St. John teaches the beginner how to mortify his senses and faculties, sacrificing even much that in itself is good, in order to strengthen the soul by the simple exercise of Faith, Hope, and Charity, and the four cardinal virtues. This is the active purgation.

But this represents only the smaller portion of the work to be done. However, it prepares the way for Him who 'searcheth the reins and hearts.' The passive purgation follows closely upon, and sometimes accompanies the former. The passive purgation of the sense is not merely a reaction from the exultation of the first awakening to spiritual life, it cuts far deeper. Were it only a reaction it would end in lukewarmness, but he who is being tried by God, so far from growing indifferent, becomes the more diligent in seeking God the more God appears to hide Himself, for he feels His absence keenly. (pp. ix-xi)

This purgation of the sense comes in different ways, such as reverses of fortune, loss of friendship, loss of one's reputation, ill success in one's undertakings, illness, and the whole train of temporal misfortunes. It is always accompanied by the loss of sensible devotion. To keep still under the chastising hand of God elevates the soul to the plane where the holy man Job stood. If we have received good things at the hand of God, why should we not receive evil? The active purgation through which the soul has passed under the guidance of St. John of the Cross is the best preparation for this passive purgation of sense, for there it has learnt utterly to despise all comfort.

Far more terrible, as our author tells us, is the passive purgation of the spirit which reaches 'unto the division of the soul and the spirit, of the joints also and the marrow.' Of course there are different degrees, all souls are not tried to the same extent, and St. John takes rather an extreme case. In the most acute form, then, positive satanic interference adds to the distress of a soul already weighed down by a feeling of the loss of God. Sometimes it takes the shape of a spirit of blasphemy, or of uncleanness or despair. The lives of the Saints furnish some remarkable instances of such trials. St. Mary Magdalen de Pazzi was subject to them for five years. St. Francis de Sales was, for a long time, haunted by the thought that he should be finally lost. The effect it had upon him was to render him extremely conscientious so that he should offend God not even in small matters, and that his loss should not come through his own fault. 'Although He should kill me I will trust Him; but yet I will reprove my ways in His sight.'

It stands to reason that a soul under such trials is absolutely dependent upon the guidance of a learned and experienced director. Otherwise the result might be fatal. In fact there is reason to think that some of the appalling falls from spiritual height to utter perversion should be attributed to the absence of proper direction during this most dangerous period.

The purpose of these trials is, however, not to throw the soul into despair but to wean it from all comfort so as to leave it with no other support than God Himself, as St. John says in one of his poems:

> My soul is detached
> From every thing created,
> And raised above itself
> Into a life delicious,
> Of God alone supported.
> And therefore I will say,
> That what I most esteem
> Is that my soul is now
> Without support, and with support.

Or, as it is expressed in some verses attributed to him:

> On Mount Carmel God alone and I,
> God alone in my spirit to enlighten it,
> God alone in my acts to sanctify them,
> God alone in my heart to possess it.

This is one of the objects of the passive purgation. Sooner or later every soul must pass through it. All that is of earth earthly will have to be left on one side before that which is of heaven heavenly shall appear. The process is under all circumstances a painful one, but it is unavoidable. St. John assists the soul in stripping itself, and allowing itself to be stripped here below. He calls this a purgatory, but

a very different one from what awaits the soul after death, inasmuch as there the soul is cleansed by fire, and here by love. Moreover, the perfect purgation of the soul in the present life leaves it free to act with infinitely greater power, and therefore to gain innumerable merits, whereas after death the account is closed before even the soul enters purgatory. No power on earth could resist a thoroughly detached soul—it might almost be said to participate in God's omnipotence. Here lies the secret of the marvellous deeds of so many Saints.

There is one other reason why the soul should pass through the trials of the Dark Night. Its ultimate destiny is union with God. Now the soul is finite, and God is infinite. The disproportion between the two is so enormous (being, in fact, infinite in itself) that the mere comparison must have a crushing effect upon the finite being. Every soul will have to pass through this experience, the minority already in this life in the Dark Night of contemplation, the vast majority on leaving this life, when they will suddenly find themselves encompassed by the infinite Majesty and Power of the Godhead. When the finite comes into contact with the infinite it realises its utter nothingness; it is humbled to the ground. The contrast causes it the most intense pain. This thorough humiliation makes it possible for the infinitesimal to be united to the infinite, for, as Christ says, 'he who humbleth himself shall be exalted.' (pp. xii-xvi)

Rev. Benedict Zimmerman, O. C. D., in an introduction to The Dark Night of the Soul *by Saint John of the Cross, revised edition, James Clarke & Co. Ltd., 1973, pp. vii-xix.*

James Fitzmaurice-Kelly (essay date 1924)

[*Fitzmaurice-Kelly was an English Hispanist who wrote and edited several works on Spanish literature, including* Chapters of Spanish Literature *(1908) and the biography* Cervantes *(1913). In the following excerpt, he compares the life and works of St. Teresa and St. John of the Cross, concluding that St. John "has not her caressing beauty of phrase in prose," but that he "is a far greater poet, and, in his own sphere, he has no equal in Spanish literature."*]

[Santa Teresa] was most fortunate in making the acquaintance of a Carmelite monk, whose name was Juan de Yepes, but who was known in his order, and is now famous the whole world overlong, as San Juan de la Cruz. She formed a redoubtable alliance with San Juan de la Cruz, a man of resplendent gifts, twenty-seven years younger than herself, consumed by the same reforming passion and endowed with a mystic fervour no less zealous and concentrated. It may be that St. John of the Cross had less diplomatic tact than Santa Teresa; it may be that harsher measures were deliberately adopted against him. Be that as it may, he suffered bitter persecution, and died in most distressing circumstances before he was fifty years of age. Santa Teresa's regard for St. John of the Cross, apart from her esteem for his eminent sanctity, was, as Churton observes, like that of an experienced mother for a son of the most splendid promise. That describes the position accurately. As she was the Mother, so is he in a sense the Father, of the great Carmelite reform; or, to word it differently, what she did for the Carmelite nuns, he did for the friars of the order.

Perhaps inferior to Santa Teresa in mundane experience, scarcely equal to her, it may be, in practical organizing talent, St. John of the Cross was much more copiously endowed with respect to absolute literary gifts. Santa Teresa would no doubt have felt flattered could she have known that in the 1912 edition of the **Llama de amor viva** the last five stanzas of her *letrilla* are described as an original poem by St. John of the Cross. This ascription cannot, however, be accepted. (pp. 84-6)

St. John of the Cross was not learned, if judged by any very high standard of learning. But he was more versed in mundane literature than Santa Teresa, and the very form of his poems betrays the influence of Garci Lasso de la Vega. It is one of art's little ironies that the form of the *lira,* first used by Garci Lasso for the very human purpose of softening an Italian beauty's heart, should have recommended itself above all others to St. John of the Cross, as the most appropriate form of expression for his ecstatic exaltations. There is an excellent version of his **Llama de amor viva** by Mr. Arthur Symons, which suggests a parallel between the amorous pleading of Garci Lasso and what has been daringly called the 'celestial eroticism' of St. John of the Cross:

> O Flame of living love,
> That dost eternally
> Pierce through my soul with so consuming heat,
> Since there's no help above,
> Make thou an end of me,
> And break the bond of this encounter sweet.
>
> O burn that burns to heal!
> O more than pleasant wound!
> And O soft hand, O touch most delicate,
> That dost new life reveal,
> That dost in grace abound,
> And, slaying, dost from death to life translate!
>
> O lamps of fire that shined
> With so intense a light
> That those deep caverns where the senses live,
> Which were obscure and blind,
> Now with strange glories bright,
> Both heat and light to His belovèd give!
>
> With how benign intent
> Rememberest thou my breast,
> Where thou alone abidest secretly;
> And in thy sweet ascent,
> With glory and good possessed,
> How delicately thou teachest love to me!

St. John of the Cross accompanies his poems by an elaborate and voluminous commentary in prose. This commentary—now scholastically ingenious in the manner of the mediaeval schoolmen and now exuberantly oriental owing to its wealth of Biblical reminiscence—is intended (we are told) as a guide to highly trained confessors, expert casuists, deeply versed in the baffling arcana of moral theology. It is a relief to know this. The prose commentary of St. John of the Cross is incomprehensible to at least one layman whom I, for obvious personal reasons, would wish to

regard as a person of average intelligence. And he is not alone. The prose of St. John of the Cross is of extreme obscurity to the profane. Quevedo and Estébanez Calderon pass as being two of the most difficult authors in Spanish literature; the difficulty of both the seventeenth- and the nineteenth-century authors is very real, but both are simpler than is St. John of the Cross in his prose commentary on himself. In the cases of Quevedo and Estébanez Calderon, the difficulties concerned with grammar and vocabulary, can, with application, be surmounted. St. John of the Cross moves on a lofty, inaccessible plane, breathing an atmosphere too rarefied for the ordinary mortal. In verse, unobscured by his too subtle commentary, he is infinitely more comprehensible than in his prose. It is customary to say that he sings with the voice of an angel. That may be. For me it is enough to describe his achievement in terms of literature. His poems are of irreproachable technique; they abound in daring oriental images; they stir you with their enchanting music, they are irresistible in the force of their emotional appeal. St. John of the Cross has not the romantic personality of Santa Teresa; he has not her caressing beauty of phrase in prose. But he is a far greater poet and, in his own special sphere, he has no equal in Spanish literature. (pp. 89-93)

> *James Fitzmaurice-Kelly, "Two Mystic Poets," in his* Some Masters of Spanish Verse, *Oxford University Press, 1924, pp. 73-93.*

Aubrey F. G. Bell　(essay date 1930)

[*An English writer, editor, and scholar, Bell was an acknowledged specialist in Spanish and Portuguese literature who asserted the dominance of the Castilian spirit in Spanish literature. In the excerpt below, Bell offers an overview of the life and works of St. John of the Cross, maintaining that the saint's artistic expression manifests his intense religious and personal experience.*]

To us, San Juan de la Cruz is at once a most elusive figure and radiantly clear. His mysticism was not a cold mistiness, but an intensity of heat and light. His few brief poems are one of the most individual things in literature. They resemble an Easter hymn rising triumphant out of the bonds of death and darkness in a church white with flowers, through the air heavy with the scent of lilies. (pp. 15-16)

In the prose works the reader may sometimes be blinded by excess of light, but he is always convinced that he is not walking in darkness. To suffer darkness, said San Juan de la Cruz, begets a great light. The very darkness becomes divine, a "deep but dazzling darkness." It is in the darkness that the "living flame of love" and the "lamps of fire" become visible and increase and glow, burning steadily upward until the night itself becomes light, "clearer than any light of noonday sheen," and "more kindly than clear morning-tide." It shines with a white heat through the soul, and the soul, bathed in divinity, strengthened with the fuel of the cross of Christ, passes on and upward along the gleaming hills and the gardens of lilies to the "asientos y sillas gloriosas" of Heaven. It was in the utter gloom of the Toledo prison, when "todo padecía, alma y cuerpo," that the spirit of San Juan de la Cruz, when he was thirty-six, found expression in song and his soul leapt up to union with its God. . . . (p. 17)

The verse flows forth, purely lyrical, from an inner intensity, moulded by the spirit without a thought of rhetorical effect. The prose works were built round the lyrics, just as some plays are built up out of a song. The poems soar above the eternal snows of the highest mountain-tops, yet in their whiteness and light concrete things retain their shape and even their colour—although it is rather a pervading fullness of colour, a great blueness or whiteness, green or purple, than any shades and gradations, which are merged in the conception of colour as differences of loveliness are merged in the word "hermosura" repeated twenty-three times in a single sentence of the *Cántico Espiritual.* The scented lilies of his song have been gathered on earth, even though they have been transferred to heaven. His imagination is the Castilian imagination, which always preserves a certain plastic and artistic concreteness. San Juan de la Cruz started from the visible world, and from it built up a symbolical world of the spirit. Even when divested of the things of earth, he never ceased to be at heart an artist, a spiritual carver of statuettes. In speaking of the things of the spirit, we are told, he was never dull or wearisome. He passes up through the world to a higher plane, where the sensible things are spiritualized and quiver in ecstasy, in an inner life, in light from the Light of Light. In this light the many become one, but they retain their individuality and remain real and evident even when blended in a reality more living and complete. Suffering and renunciation only made San Juan de la Cruz a more gracious figure, as the feet of the messengers are lovely on the mountains when they bring the glad tidings of peace. Building from within in the true spirit of the Renaissance, he returned to the visible world, fashioning it into a new region of beauty and of truth.

Study of the Bible, love of Nature, these were two of the main pillars of his genius. Luis de León's Spanish version of the "Song of Songs," made in 1561, although not published till 1798, must have become known to Fray Juan at Salamanca. It was a pure well of poetical thought and expression as well as of mystic longings. It tells us how "the nights and days in their changes and seasons speak aloud who God is." It tells how "the souls that love God, when by secret and invisible means He communicates to them the treasures of His grace, woo Him in an ecstasy of love with many soft and delicious words"; how those who love God "go out from the cities and delight in the desert places and the mountains, living among trees, apparently forgotten and alone, but in truth happy and joyous"; "God is everywhere, and all that we see of goodness and beauty in the sky and on the earth and in all other creatures is a ray of His divinity." From Luis de León Fray Juan learnt the mystic fervour of the divine poem, and learnt also the *lira's* effective metre, introduced by Garci-Lasso and marvellously adapted to the artistic expression of intense spiritual emotion.

Much of San Juan de la Cruz' life was spent in beautiful places, and he was never insensible to such beauty nor to the "imaginatio locorum." They cast a spell over his spirit.

He lived at Salamanca, Ávila, Granada, Segovia: four cities utterly different, yet all possessing a distinct spiritual individuality and containing treasures of art in regions of marked natural beauty. We see him in the Convento de los Mártires beneath the soft snows of the Sierra Nevada or in the gardens of the Generalife or wandering along the lonely banks of the Darro and Genil, that flow rapidly murmuring from the mountain snows; we see him at Duruelo, in sight of the Sierra de Gredos, beautiful among all the mountains of the earth, eating a crust of bread as he sits beside a spring; at Segovia he looks out at night over the surrounding country from a cell-window "donde se veía el cielo y el campo"; at Beas de Segura he loves to gaze from his cell at the green country of trees and plants, rocks and streams:

> the hills outspread,
> The lonely valleys where the woodland gleams.

"Lonely valleys," he says elsewhere, "are quiet, pleasant, fresh, and shaded, filled with sweet waters, and in their variety of trees and the musical song of the birds they plainly delight and revive the senses, yielding refreshment and rest in their solitude and silence."

From those long silent watchings in the concentration of his spirit he learnt to describe Nature in a few pregnant words, in a single expressive epithet.

As in his art, so in his character, there was a steadfast core of concreteness, a Castilian sobriety, loyalty and sincereness. "Ferme dans l'équilibre de sa pensée," says M. Jean Baruzi, who has penetrated further than any other commentator into the depths of San Juan de la Cruz's spirit, "Jean de la Croix apparaît d'autre part comme un caractère rigoureusement maître de soi." Master of himself, master of others. What a quiet mastery of himself is indicated when the young friar of twenty-five, in answer to Santa Teresa's invitation to join her new Order, says that he will do so "if the delay be not too great"! Perfect simplicity, a glowing love: these with San Juan de la Cruz had nothing to do with a watery sentimentalism or cold abstractions. It is because his mysticism springs from a direct vision and is based in definiteness that it is a pearl of exceeding price. There was nothing insipid in his selflessness, as there was nothing morbid in his love of beauty. His "nothingness" was full of divine treasures. At a time of keen disappointment and humiliation towards the end of his life, he wrote to a friend in reference to their victorious opponents: "Where there is no love put love, and you will find love" ("Y adonde no hay amor ponga amor y sacará amor"). That may be a perfection difficult of attainment, but it was reached by San Juan de la Cruz, not through any evasion or indifference, but through suffering and battling with the actual facts of life. He recreated the world of men and things in the light, the blinding light, of his spiritual intensity. . . . (pp. 19-21)

Aubrey F. G. Bell, "Saint John of the Cross: A Portrait," in Bulletin of Spanish Studies, *Vol. VII, No. 25, January, 1930, pp. 13-21.*

Jacques Maritain　(essay date 1932)

[*A French philosopher, writer, and educator, Maritain was the foremost spokesman for the Catholic Literary Revival in France as well as a vigorous proponent of the theology of Thomas Aquinas, which affirms the validity of Aristotelian philosophy and recognizes no conflict between reason and faith. His own philosophical system, which has been described as a modified form of Thomism, emphasizes the importance of rationality in theology, thereby opposing the intense mysticism of much nineteenth-century theology. In the following excerpt from a work originally published in French in 1932, Maritain summarizes the teachings of St. John of the Cross on the purification of the soul, recapitulating the saint's views on the role of the senses, reason, and discursive meditation in achieving union with God.*]

[To St. John of the Cross] man is no pure spirit making use of a body; his natural life, even in the world of the spirit, thrusts its roots down into the senses, and is only exercised in the shaping of images: which is why St. John the practician of human souls links together the senses, the work of the reason and discursive meditation. In regard to the being of God all these are the country of unlikeness.

He does not ask us to destroy the activity of the senses—no more than the Gospel, in speaking of those who have 'made themselves eunuchs for the kingdom of God', prescribes mutilation. He loved the beauty of the countryside which helped his prayer; he had an exquisite sensibility; he was one of the greatest poets of Spain and of the world; he was often depressed; he had a profound tenderness for his brother Francis the poor mason, and a deep delight in his spiritual children. But he wishes that in the use of notions as of sensible attractions our lack of possessiveness should be absolute. It is to use as though not making use. Later, on the mountain, all will be transfigured. Meanwhile it is necessary to begin by losing all; that is the rule of the road. In the order of physical and material being total renunciation is not possible, and the renunciation of particular possession by the vows of chastity, poverty and obedience is the privilege of a few, but in the order of spiritual realisation total renunciation is asked of all who seek after perfection. There is only one way out of the lamentable struggle of a spirit enracinated in the flesh, which communicates to it its infinitude of desire. Give everything, poor men: how much easier it is to give all than by halves! Everything that we keep is like a cancer gnawing at our entrails.

The senses bring two forms of impurity in their train: one which is contrary to the life of virtue, and over which the soul triumphs by the direct use of its faculties, of the senses themselves: and the other which is contrary to the contemplative union and over which the soul triumphs in surpassing the senses. For the cure of the former the ascesis of John of the Cross knows two remedies [according to Silverio, in *Testimony of Eliseus of the Martyrs*]:

> He used to say that a man could conquer the vices and acquire virtue in two ways. There is first of all the ordinary method and it is less perfect. It consists in combating a vice, a sin or a temptation by the direct opposition of acts of the contrary virtue. . . .

The second method . . . is at once easier, more fruitful and perfect. There the soul fights against and destroys the temptations of the adversary, and raises itself to the most perfect degree of virtue, by the sole use of spiritual acts and motions inspired by love, without any other exercises. How is this possible? He explained it in the following way.

As soon as the first motion or the first attack of some vice makes itself felt—luxury, anger, impatience or the spirit of vengeance for some injury, etc.—do not oppose to it an act of the contrary virtue, as is done in the first way, but immediately resist it by an act or movement of spiritual love which opposes itself to the assault and lifts the soul to union with God; because in so raising itself the soul absents itself from this life and is present with God and unites itself to him; and by the same fact the vice or temptation and the enemy are defeated of their end and remain frustrate, knowing not where to strike. The soul, in effect, which "is more where it loves than where it lives" divinely abstracts itself from the flesh and from temptation, and the enemy cannot find where to strike or to wound. . . . The soul has escaped. . . . Thus there is born in the soul that heroic and admirable virtue which the Angelic Doctor called the virtue of the perfectly purified soul.

To defeat the second form of impurity which is produced by the senses and which hinders union and the love of contemplation with a fog of creatures, there is only one remedy: night and emptiness. This purification, which is the particular interest of mystical theology, St. John of the Cross deals with in the fullest and most complete fashion in his doctrine of the Night of the Senses. It is a double night, at once active and passive, or rather perhaps a twilight, into which those souls penetrate who have received the call to contemplation (the Saint only addresses himself to these). On the one side the soul exercises itself on its own rightful initiative, thinning down the taste of the senses and the force of their attraction, putting the appetites to sleep. On the other side, God acts upon the soul and himself purifies it with an incomparably greater effectiveness. Without this divine decapitation of the passive night the soul would never be delivered from those all too visible blots which are imperceptible to it, from the desire for consolations, from the spiritual presumption, sensuality, impatience, avarice, gluttony, envy and sloth which are the common defects of the apprentices of perfection. In discerning the spiritual realities in the representations of the senses, in rising above phantasms, in beginning to understand and to comprehend that the Divine will fill it just in so far as it empties itself, the soul also begins to catch a glimpse of the peace of God, to enter into the prayer of quiet, that tiny beginning of infused contemplation. (pp. 440-43)

Jacques Maritain, "Conclusion: Todo y Nada," in his The Degrees of Knowledge, *translated by Bernard Wall and Margot R. Adamson, Charles Scribner's Sons, 1938, pp. 431-71.*

Charles Williams   (essay date 1942)

[*Williams was a writer of supernatural fiction and a poet whose best works treat the legends of Logres (Arthurian Britain). He was also a central figure in the literary group known as the Oxford Christians or "Inklings," whose members included C. S. Lewis and J. R. R. Tolkien. In the excerpt below, Williams discusses St. John's mystic approach to loving God, stressing the ideals of self-abnegation and "complete detachment."*]

There was born at Ontiveros, in Old Castile, on 24 June, 1542, a certain Juan de Yepes y Alvarez, called afterwards St John of the Cross. He became a Carmelite in 1563; he died in 1591; in 1726 he was canonized and in 1926 declared by the Apostolic See to be a Doctor of the Universal Church. His doctorate was deserved if delayed; he is one of the great masters of knowledge.

He wrote especially for those who are called to the Way of Rejection of Images; that is, for those "who can enter, and desire to enter, into this complete detachment and emptiness of spirit". "Few reach this state." He was of the tradition of Dionysius the Areopagite and of the author of the *Cloud of Unknowing.* "There is only one method, that which makes empty." It is, of course, to be recognized that this state, expressed in words, or considered by the mind, presents itself by means of an image. Detachment, solitude, the night of the soul—these words are as much images as Beatrice or Wordsworth's mountain. In discussing these things (not that they should be much discussed) we cannot help using images. But those who are concerned with those more natural images—of Dante, of Wordsworth, of Elizabeth Fry—ought at times to consider the darker metaphors. I do not know, in the last analysis, that there is so much difference between the two great methods as is sometimes thought. Mr Aldous Huxley assures us, in *Grey Eminence,* that one of them is quite useless and the other the only possible. But Mr Aldous Huxley's ignorance of the Christian revelation does not encourage us to believe him on the Christian life.

It is said of St John that at his first Mass he prayed that he might never commit mortal sin but might suffer the penance for those faults which he might have committed but for God's grace. The courtesy of our Lord acceded, as in so many cases it does, to his request; we are astonishingly given what we innocently ask. That our accumulated guilt, when we finally receive our request, generally causes us to repudiate the wish is irrelevant, except to cause us to remark that St John did not repudiate his. He fell into difficulties with his own Order; he was spoken against, arrested, imprisoned, beaten, deprived of the Sacrament. He suffered, that is, through the good intentions of the uncomprehending faithful. He was at other times Prior of Granada, Vicar-General of Andalusia, Prior of Segovia. He was tried both ways—"in all time of our tribulation, in all time of our wealth", says the Litany, and does not confine the word "wealth" to money. Afterwards he fell again into disgrace; also he fell ill, with a kind of physical corruption. That, distressing to him, was, it is reported, mysteriously lovely to others; the women who attended him said that the matter which came from him had the smell of flowers. Nothing, of course, could be more like

idle chat; nor anything more like mere fact. The courtesies of our Lord might easily happen so. The flesh St John did not affirm, affirmed itself beautifully in him.

"At eventide," he wrote, "they will examine thee in love." The Christian discovery that Love itself has the power to love, the Christian dogma that Love has the power unselfishly to love itself, is the fundamental of that examination. Everyone lives by that act; few care to live only in it. Most hope to escape with a few light questions: "Were you faithful to your wife? Did you do your duty to your country? Did you give alms, forgive those who lied about you, pray night and day, rejoice always?" Some are called—perhaps more than we think, for even the courtesy of our Lord admitted that of those called few chose the vocation—to something more. It is defined by St John (I quote from Dom Bede Frost's valuable work on him) thus: "All the movements and operations which the soul had aforetime, as belonging to the principle of its natural life, are now in this union changed into movements of God". The soul is not God, and never can become God; its substance, everlastingly and eternally, is created and not uncreated, but the created is united with the uncreated, by virtue of the will of the uncreated.

The Way, for St John, was the way of complete detachment. "The soul must be in darkness with regard to everything that enters through the eye and by the ear, or which can be imagined by the fancy (or imagination) and comprehended in the heart." It "must pass beyond all to unknowing". This is its spiritual exercise, and the recollection of it is to be present not only to those called to it but also to those called, for one reason or another, to the study of the images which that soul rejects. Even in that study there comes a point of difficult detachment; even images must in the end be loved only because God loves them. The first serious apprehension of this necessity is apt to be a shock; the first quick grasp of the abandonment of a personal love of—Beatrice, for an impersonal love of Beatrice shows only between the two a great gulf fixed, and then it is easy to become dizzy, and to confuse and lose the two in a mere self-meditation. Distraction is not detachment. But, of course, this loss of all images does not mean that the images do not exist. St John did not cease to acknowledge the Incarnation because the Incarnation seemed to mean nothing to him (if it did), or because (if he did) he turned his attention from it. The whole possibility of that great final examination in love depended on the Incarnation. If Love had not so loved man, man would not have been able to love Love—in any sense. The facts which dogma proclaimed are the conditions of experiment—the laboratory, the crucible, the acid, the fire. The soul is "transformed in the Three Persons of the Most Holy Trinity". The hasty answer to that is that St John was brought up as a Christian, and therefore wrote as a Christian; if (they say) he had been brought up as a Buddhist, he would have written as a Buddhist, but about the same experience. "Who deniges of it, Sairey?" Certainly St John would not have thought that his experience proved the reality of the Trinity; he took some trouble to say that it proved nothing of the sort. What he would have said would have been that no other philosophy had such authority or so satisfied with intellectual truth. If this was because he was what he was, then also Mr Huxley's neo-Buddhism (to use his name again apologetically) is what it is because he is what he is. I do not deny it altogether; but to affirm it altogether is to kill all discussion. We are then left not in the Night of the Intellect but in a void of intelligence—for which no serious "mystic" ever had the slightest use.

Those who are transformed "are moved by the Spirit of God, that is, are moved to divine actions in their faculties". The actions are secret movements in God and simple movements in the world. What is the difference between St John and anyone? only that all that St John thinks, says, or is, is a divine action. Should we, if we met him, notice it? only if we were already ourselves a little trained in the same school; if Love. . . .

At that point, still brooding, I casually picked up Mr William Saroyan's *The Time of Your Life*. The author, in an introduction, said: "The deepest and most general love is love of God, the defining of which I leave to you, as you please. ('As you please'? As you please.) Love of God includes regard of self. . . . The essence of my work is honour, honesty, intelligence, grace, good-humour, naturalness, and spontaneity, and these things do not appear to be nicely balanced in my critics." "Love of God?" Yes; I assure you, "love of God." It is this meaning or St John's; there is, in the end no other choice.

Charles Williams, "St. John of the Cross," in
Time & Tide, *Vol. 23, No. 26, June 27, 1942,
p. 522.*

Robert Sencourt (essay date 1944)

[*Sencourt was the literary pseudonym of Robert Esmonde Gordon George, a New Zealand-born critic, biographer, historian and educator. Here, he focuses on the works of St. John of the Cross to demonstrate the superiority of poetry over prose in conveying the mysteries of communion with God.*]

Poetry, said Fray Juan himself in his Prologue to **"The Song of the Spirit,"** has a greater power than reason. The soul which has known the raptures of love, and the riches of its dream, knows more than any genius can express: poets know those groanings of the spirit within us which cannot be uttered. "And it is for this reason," says San Juan, "that, by means of figures, comparisons, and similitudes, they allow something of that which they feel to overflow and utter secret mysteries from the abundance of the spirit rather than explain those things rationally. These similitudes, if they be not read with the simplicity of the spirit of love and understanding embodied in them, appear to be nonsense rather than expressions of reason, as may be seen in the Divine *Songs of Solomon* and in other books of the Divine Scripture, where, since the Holy Spirit cannot express this abundance of his meaning in common and vulgar terms, he utters mysteries in strange figures and similitudes. Whence it follows that no words of holy doctors, despite all they have said and yet may say, can ever expound these things fully, neither could they be expanded in words of any kind. *That which is expounded of them, therefore, is ordinarily the least part of that which they contain.*"

Let us, therefore, above all read and enjoy the poems. The indescribable communion which comes from song where music adds so much of its mystery to the pattern of words will teach us further "that love which comes from abounding mystical knowledge," under the influence of which these poems were composed.

There is, then, much that a poetic admirer like M. Baruzi can add to all the expositions of the theologians. He can point to a region of rapture where the soul learns by admiring beauty; what the soul feels and knows, it can suggest rather than convey, for the mysteries it knows are infinite. "Let no one believe," said Fray Juan himself, "that this thing is not more than what can be expressed of it." He has opened a window on a garden stretching beyond all human sight in beauty after beauty: and "to learn the immediacy of the things of God, the only fit language is to hear and feel it for oneself, and to enjoy it and to be silent as to what it tells."

Why is it that a song or a poem can convey what a prose treatise cannot convey of the deeper mysteries of the spirit? The answer is this: It is because when the soul is rapt in the contemplation of the eternal beauty, it admires both the splendour and the order of the universe. Beauty is in fact the delightful resplendence of a spiritual and intelligible perfection: *ordine di perfezione ammirate*—as Agosto Conti wrote in *Il Bello nel Vero*. And the spirit that enjoys this resplendence of the truth is stamped by and therefore mirrors it in the sense of order which the spirit enjoys, and which it conveys in composition, balance, harmony, or pattern. That is why Meredith set as a test for truth the question, "Is it accepted of song?" That is why St. Paul said that as we survey the mirror of perfection, we are changed from glory to glory as by the Spirit of the Lord. That is what San Juan meant in **"The Song of the Spirit,"** when, talking of the eyes he longed to meet, he wrote: "I always crave and limn them in my dreams"; that is why Dante said of Beatrice:

> *Negli occhi suoi ardeva un riso
> Tal ch'io pensai co' miei toccar lo fondo
> Della mia grazia et del mio Paradiso.*

As a man in love floods his whole life with his romance, so the artist, the musician, and the poet, if seeking for true beauty, are impregnating with it the deepest processes of the mind: "In the fresh years," wrote Conti, "when the heart unfolds to unaccustomed feelings, and the eyes wander in desire from beauty to beauty, and a mysterious instinct runs from fancy to fancy, and from sigh to sigh, and the ears crave for song and sound, all these appearances of Nature, being gathered together in the mind and heart, suddenly reappear to us in dreams—inspired, alive, at once like our previous experience and new, in an image of beauty, in a love never seen or experienced, with its own inward light and undefined harmony, so that on awakening the soul longs for the vanished dream: and this inward power—which arose from inspiration and yet was spontaneous—is the same which inspires verses in the poets, and statues and pictures and buildings in the designer, and in the musicians immortal melodies." (pp. 151-53)

The object of San Juan de la Cruz is to do away with meditation and lead the soul where it gives over its action in a wise passiveness to the operation of a power other than its own. *"In this state,"* says Fray Juan, *"the soul can perform no acts but it is the Holy Spirit that moves it to perform them."* His object is to lead men inward to the most sacred mystery of their being, to the centre of the soul, for "the centre of the soul is God." Now the more the soul approaches these inward and spiritual graces of the life God has given it, the more it moves from the discourse and analysis of reason. All the processes of the mind are accompanied by another sense, another quality of living. Even though the mind is busy, its impulsions and its secret are in a quiet communion when it knows, in a way that is dim to consciousness, and yet that is fixed with an authority of conviction which it regards as sovereign, that it is sustained by this communion: for the communion is a sharing with a power, with a wisdom, with a love that are all one, as the Three in One are God. (p. 156)

The more a life has experience of this communion, the clearer becomes its view that, though the communion can sustain and inspire thought, yet it is not thought. In it all thought, even the thought about God, seems to be exchanged for a more direct, a more intuitive knowledge: faith vanishes into darkness, a darkness lit by fires. And so, too, with memory and hope, for all that can be recalled and all that can be desired seem to be found, and are found, in a life which fills the whole capacity of desire, as it does of knowledge: hope, therefore, is fulfilled in this sense of immediacy, of timeless being. As San Juan puts it: "When the soul has attained to Him according to the whole capacity of its being, and according to the force of its operation, it will have reached the last and deep centre of the soul which will be when with all its powers it loves and understands and enjoys God." Understanding completes the work of faith: enjoyment satisfies the flights and eagerness of hope: both of these are merged in another activity in "the love which unites the soul to God," because love above all renders us like Him. It is the entry into Christ, who is the Way and the Life.

But we are still enquiring how this new act to move inwards, to strip oneself of created things, and to forego all intercourse with them can be not merely combined with the passion and beauty of the poet, but better expressed in the sensuous images of poetry than in the discourses of the theologian. With magisterial precision San Juan answers us in a great passage of **"Song of the Spirit."** He shows there that when the mystic race is finished, and a man attains to the wisdom which sees all things in God, he learns how God is in all things; and then all that was lost is found. Most people build up their knowledge of God by what He has created:

> and by those hid ascents climb up to Thee
> Who art in all things, though invisibly.

But the mystic, if by cultivating his gift of abstraction he communes with the transcendence merged in the deepest centre of the soul, can learn about creation more directly from God Himself; for in Him and with Him and through Him are all things.

While the outward world hints and stammers what He is, the soul, therefore, rapt into still communion, which transcends the imperfect offices of prayer and praise, under-

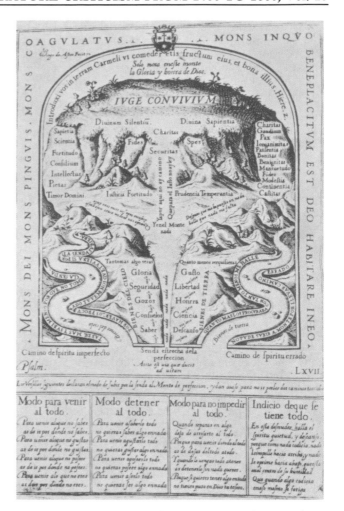

The graphic representation of the Mount, engraved by Diego de Astor from St. John's original hand drawing.

stands them all in Him, and sees, therefore, how He is in them. Both by searching God through creation and looking to creation from the heart of God can we come to wisdom; but Fray Juan insists that the way of interior prayer is the better and clearer.

> For when by this essential love, the soul is commingled with the Ineffable and so awakens to glory, although it is true that the soul is now able to see that these things are distinct from God, inasmuch as they have a created being, and it sees them in Him, with their force, root and strength, it knows equally that God, in His own Being, is all these things, in an infinite and preeminent way, to such a point that it understands them better in His Being than in themselves. And this is the great delight of this awakening: to know the creatures through God and not God through the creatures: to know the effects through their cause and not the cause through the effects: for the latter knowledge is secondary, and this other is essential. . . .
>
> But God, as the soul is enabled to see, is always moving, ruling, and giving to all creatures being and virtue and graces and gifts, containing them

all in Himself, by His power, by His presence and by their partaking in His reality. So that in one single glance the soul sees that which God is in Himself, and that which He is in the creatures. Even so, when a palace is thrown open, a man may see at one and the same time the eminence of the person who is within the palace and also what he is doing. And it is this, as I understand it, that happens in this awakening and glance of the soul. Though the soul shares the reality of God, as does every creature, *He draws back from before it some of the veils and curtains which are in front of it, so that it may see of what nature He is, and then there is revealed to it and it is able to see (though somewhat darkly, since not all the veils are drawn back) His countenance full of graces and beauties.*

At last the process is explained: God moves all things gently and according to their nature; and at times He gives flashes of His beauty through a sense of inward communion; and the more this power of communion is developed, the more will be seen. So that there are always two ways to the secret of the universe, the way which adores His transcendence and the way which cherishes His immanence. But these two ways interchange and intermingle as the universe exhibits a double movement, downward from God and upward towards Him, for all things are returning to perfection through Him from whom they took their origin.

The poet, therefore, who gives in music and beauty a hint of his delight in the perfection he has found, will always best convey the power of communion. Literature is not merely a decorative accompaniment to worship: it can be a spontaneous revelation of the mystery by which created things are a living, visible garment of God; and *everything, if looked at rightly,* is but a symbol, and therefore a disclosure, of things unseen, and of the underlying reality which is the mind of God.

Nowhere is this doctrine so clear as in San Juan de la Cruz; his thorough philosophical training was combined with an analytical psychology, which traced the process of knowledge to that region where images are perceived and felt: he had his peculiar power over this region of the memory and feeling of images, so that he could make certain words peculiarly evocative.

All these things were one with the passion of his temperament, and his experience of love as a violent magnetism, first of desire,

> If I see not thee,
> What use have eyes?

and then of rapture

> O night which to the side
> Of lover brought his bride,
> And then didst make them one.

He was not afraid of passion: he had learnt from the *Song of Songs* to welcome it: he was still more familiar with it in the works of Boscán and Garcilaso, and though he did not accept the contention of Luis de León that *The Song of Songs* was a human drama, yet its imagery was con-

stantly affecting him to reinforce all the instincts of his own prodigal temperament.

The crude Freudian would say that this passion for the unseen lover was but an ebullition or at best a sublimation of the carnal in his nature: San Juan had anticipated that contention; for he actually says that men who live by the impulses of physical sex will assess all motives accordingly. But the Freudian explanation is soon refuted by the technical treatises: they make it perfectly clear how the flesh of the mystic was subdued to the spirit: his impulses of love were both ordered and exalted. As San Juan himself says, "all the harmony and ability which the body gives to man's human nature served him for greater recreation and as a help towards a knowledge and love of God in peace and concord with his higher part." There, in the inward man, the ways of human love are outdone. In this inward communion in the hidden part of the soul, God, as the Very Being of Love, assails the faculties with His glory and greatness so loftily that the human side of the mind no longer understands, and the spirit "soars aloft through high and noble knowledge and through excesses of love most strange and singular." In this high and noble knowledge, theology enabled San Juan to be particularly clear and precise.

God's scheme is a hierarchy, for all things in the world are related to God in Christ, Who in His Incarnation exalts them all with Himself: the creatures, says San Juan, are as it were traces of the passing of God, for in them He has left pointers to His greatness, power, wisdom, and other perfections. But the creatures are the lesser works of God, Who made them as it were in passing. The greater works, wherein He revealed Himself most clearly and to which He paid most heed, are those of the Incarnation of the Word and the other mysteries of the Christian faith. Now, according to the faith, God and Man in the Incarnation are one Christ, not by conversion of the Being of God into flesh, but by taking the nature of man into the Divine. As Fray Juan read day by day in the Missal, God, Who had marvellously formed the nature of man, by ways yet more marvellous had redeemed it that man should be a partaker of the dominion and the glory of God. But, since man is within the realm of nature, and mirrors the realm of nature in his mind, and thus assimilates it, therefore, when Christ accepted human nature into His own, He raised all creation to take its part in his Divineness. In the words of San Juan, in uniting Himself with man, He united Himself with the nature of them all. This is expounded with precision in **"The Song of the Spirit"**: " 'The Son of God is the brightness of his glory and the express image of his substance.' It must be known, then, that God looked at all things in this image of His Son alone, which was to give them their natural being, to communicate to them many natural gifts and graces and to make them finished and perfect, as He says in *Genesis* in these words: 'God saw all the things that He had made, and they were very good.' To behold them and find them very good was to make them very good in the Word His Son. And not only did He communicate them their being and their natural beauties when He beheld them, but also in this image of His Son alone He left them clothed with beauty, *communicating to them supernatural being.*" This was when He became man, for when He thus exalted man into the beauty of God, and in uniting Himself with man He united Himself with the nature of all creatures, He consequently exalted them all into His Being and Glory. "And therefore this same Son of God said: *'I, if I be lifted up from the earth, will draw all things unto me.'* And thus in this lifting up through the Incarnation of His Son and in the glory of His resurrection according to the flesh, not only did the Father beautify the creation in part, but He can say He left them all clothed with dignity and beauty."

So much was Catholic philosophy: it was the logical conclusion to belief in the Incarnation and Ascension of the mysterious Second Person of the Infinite Trinity. But to this corollary mysticism immediately added something more. It added a revelation of God in nature by the communion of loving admiration of the excellence of creation. As San Juan said:

> After all the philosophical doctrine, I will go on and speak rather with the heart and faculties of a mystic: in the vivid contemplation and knowledge of the creatures, the soul sees with great clearness that there is in them such an abundance of graces and powers and beauty, with which God has endowed them, that, as it seems to the soul, they are all clothed with marvellous natural beauty, derived from and communicated by that infinite supernatural beauty of the image of God, whose beholding of Him clothes the world and the heavens with beauty and joy, just as does also the opening of His hand: *Thou openest thy hand and fillest all things living with blessing.* And therefore the soul, being wounded in love by this trace of the beauty of her Beloved which she has known in His creatures, yearns to behold the invisible beauty.

This passage explains with perfect precision both the mysticism of nature and the mysticism of love. It harmonizes Juan de la Cruz with Donne, with Vaughan, with Traherne, with Wordsworth, with Coleridge. But none of them ever approached such masterly precision.

That in the words which have both the rhythm of music and the pattern of art mysticism may be turned to poetry, so much we have known. It needed a poet's combination of mysticism with theology to make the Christian reasons for it clear and distinct. (pp. 157-63)

> *Robert Sencourt, in his* Carmelite and Poet: A Framed Portrait of St. John of the Cross, *The Macmillan Company, 1944, 278 p.*

Gerald Brenan   (essay date 1947)

[*In the excerpt below, Brenan analyzes "The Spiritual Canticle," "The Dark Night of the Soul," and "The Living Flame of Love" as the poetic expressions of union with God. The critic also explores the multiple symbolic meanings of Nature and the Dark Night.*]

San Juan de la Cruz's principal poems were written to express his mystical experiences. It follows, since we cannot form to ourselves any picture of these, that they are obscure. We shall not be able to go so far to meet them with our own experience as we can in the case of most other poetry. And . . . San Juan himself found them difficult to understand. But there are different kinds of obscurity in poetry; let us therefore, though we cannot hope to 'interpret' these poems in any complete sense, try to see what sort of meanings can and cannot be got out of them. If this can be done without entering too far into the jargon of mysticism, we may perhaps find that we have learned to appreciate them better.

I think it will help us in attempting this if we first look at the plot of one of the poems. The **"Cántico Espiritual"** is the one that presents most difficulties, so I will start with a brief précis of it. That in itself will provide a preliminary elucidation.

The **"Cántico"** is written in the form of a dialogue between a Lover and his Beloved. It starts with a cry of pain, in which the Beloved complains that her lover has wounded and then deserted her. Setting out to seek him, she inquires of the shepherds, the woods and the fields if they have seen him pass. They answer that he went by hurriedly, leaving them clothed in his beauty as he looked at them. She then, in another cry, recalling in its intensity an Andalusian *saeta,* complains once more of her abandonment, declares that everything in Nature reminds her of him, and begs him to show himself and kill her with his beauty. If only his eyes, she exclaims, could be reflected in that crystal fountain! The eyes appear and she is transported in an ecstasy.

The Lover now speaks, telling her that her transports have refreshed the wounded stag—that is himself. The Beloved answers him, saying . . . that her Lover *is* the mountains, valleys, strange islands, rivers, night, music, silence, refreshing feast and so forth.

Up to this moment the general drift of the poem has been clear enough, but from now on it becomes harder to follow. The action is slowed up and it is not easy to say at any given moment what point in the love story has been reached. San Juan was evidently aware of this, for in writing his prose commentary some years later, he altered the order of the next eighteen stanzas. The effect of the new arrangement is not so much, as M. Baruzi has said, to postpone the 'nuptials' (if by that word he means the consummation), as to allow the love-making that follows the 'espousals'—which is the point in the poem we have just reached—to develop more gradually and naturally. The alteration helps to clarify the action and therefore presumably the prose interpretation, but I agree with other critics that it does not improve the poem, because it spoils certain poetic effects. For this reason I shall follow here the original version.

To continue: the Beloved, in a passage full of reminiscences of the *Song of Songs,* describes the preparations for the nuptials. The marriage couch is ready, the bridegroom's procession is formed and the Lover leads her into his inner wine cellar (*in cellum vinarium* in the Vulgate) and gives her to drink: he takes her in his arms and teaches her a *ciencia muy sabrosa.* She promises to be his spouse and, going out into the fields, drunk with love, loses the sheep she had been tending. From now on, she declares, love will be her only trade. Some stanzas follow, describing how the lovers employ themselves, and the Beloved then calls on the South Wind to blow through her garden, that her Lover may feed among its flowers.

The Lover then speaks, and his words denote that the consummation of the marriage has taken place. After an allusion to the apple tree where her mother (Eve) was lost, in the shade of whose wood (the Cross) he had betrothed himself to her, he conjures the birds, lions, stags, mountains, valleys, river banks, waters, airs and wakeful fears of night not to disturb his Beloved who is sleeping in his arms.

The Beloved in her turn then commands the 'nymphs of Judah' not to disturb them and makes an obscure request to her Lover. In two wonderful stanzas, full of echoes of Andalusian folk poetry and of the Bible, the Lover replies to her, announcing that the white dove has returned to her mate and made her nest alone with him in solitude.

After this the Beloved begs him to take her to see the hills and forests and the fountain of pure water by the light of his beauty, and to go deeper with her into the thickets and rocky caverns. There he must show her what she longs to see and give her 'what the other day he gave her'. The freshness of the breeze, the song of the nightingale, the charm of the poplar grove, the clear night. No one to see. Aminadab (the Enemy) away, the siege (passions of the soul) relaxed and the horsemen (the senses) descending to the waters (to be purified in them).

Such, then, is the plot of the **"Cántico"**. Its general intention is clear enough. We scarcely need the Argument, which the poet gives us at the beginning of his Commentary, to see that is an allegory representing the mystical journey of the soul to union with God. Let us see what this programme has to tell us. According to it, the first twelve stanzas represent the 'purgative stage' of the *via mistica* and express the miseries and restlessness of the soul filled with an unsatisfied love for God. Then comes the 'illuminative stage', which begins with the appearance of the Lover's eyes in the water and contains the 'spiritual espousals'. This is followed by the 'united stage' (introduced in the second version by the line *Entrádose ha la Esposa,* and presumably so in the first version also) which starts, as one would expect, with the 'spiritual nuptials'. The last two stanzas represent the Beatific Vision, granted only to the perfect. Obviously the programme does not fit the poem very well. The confusion over the espousals, only partly rectified in the second version, mars its inner logic. Nor is any place found in the poem for the very severe 'purgation of the spirit', which should accompany the 'illuminative stage'. In this respect neither the poem nor the programme fit the experience, as described at great length in two of the prose works. Although this discrepancy does not strictly concern us here, I point it out because it shows how far the poems are from being the systematic representations of the mystical experience which, as we shall see in a moment, San Juan himself tried to make them.

In comparison to the **"Cántico,"** the plot of the **"Noche Oscura"** is very simple. It, too, is an allegory describing the journey of the soul to union with God. The first four stanzas describe the 'purgative stage' (purgation both of the senses and of the spirit), and in the fifth we reach the 'nuptials' or state of union. The eighth and last stanza presumably represents the Beatific Vision, but the Commentary does not tell us this, because the two prose works that set out to interpret it break off at the end of the second stanza. The **"Llama"** is simpler still: it deals with particular experiences at the moment of union. But when one tries for any of these poems to press the allegorical interpretation, one is at once in difficulties. The details do not fit. Many passages are obscure, whilst others, if not exactly obscure, appear to contain a greater wealth of meanings than is required by the allegory.

Let us look, then, at the prose commentaries. Here, if anywhere, we ought to be able to discover what these hidden meanings are, for in them San Juan takes his poems and interprets them, line by line, at considerable length. Yet the result is disappointing. Although now and then we come on something that throws light on a passage, most of the poet's 'interpretations' drag down the text and destroy its radiations. It does not add, for example, to the significance of the line *Iré por esos montes y riberas* to know that the *montes,* being high, represent the virtues and the *riberas,* being low, mortifications and penances. Nor do we find it easy to believe that meanings of this sort were in the poet's mind at the time of his writing the poem. And, as we read on, we realize that the reason why San Juan's interpretations have the effect of mutilating the poems is that he is treating them down to their smallest details as allegories, in which every important word or image must have some precise concept that corresponds to it and 'explains' it. But the very failure of his explanations proves to us what we had already guessed—that the poems are only allegorical in a very loose sense: their intimate structure is both deeper and more complex.

In fact, San Juan himself admits this. In his prologue to the prose *Cántico* he tells us that no gloss can fully interpret the stanzas and that we need not, therefore, feel bound to the explanation there offered. The *dichos de amor en abundante inteligencia mística,* inspired as they are by the spirit of the Lord, cannot be properly explained in words, any more than can the divine verses of the *Song of Solomon.* He feels before them the same thrilled surprise that other poets have felt on looking in the dead air of morning at their miraculous overnight productions. He feels this with particular force because he knows that these poems contain little ornament or incidental imagery; every word, every image, something tells him, has its roots deep in the soil, and is packed with significance. And then let us remember that in writing his commentaries he was not attempting a work of literary criticism. His aim was a series of guide books, for the use of a small circle of *almas enamoradas,* chiefly Carmelites, whom he was directing, which should instruct them on the various landmarks and hazards of the mystical road. It was merely as a matter of convenience that he wrote them in the form of commentaries on his own poems, instead of, as the Scholastic paraphrasers he was following had done in the past, in that of commentaries on the Scriptures. Whilst, therefore, we can learn much that will help us from these books, because they throw a light on the poet's mind and inner experience, we must not attempt to use them slavishly. (pp. 339-43)

San Juan de la Cruz's poetry springs from his experience as a practising mystic. This is a region very remote from our experience today and one of which I am quite unqualified to speak. But there are two themes in his poetry which are, I think, more approachable. One of them is his attitude to Nature, and the other is his great symbolic conception of the Dark Night. Although the latter is bound up with his mystical experience, its fringes descend to the ordinary world and are therefore to some extent palpable to us. And the number of feelings and images that gather round it make it the most important and characteristic thing in his writings.

The Nature passages to which I would like to draw attention occur in the first fifteen stanzas of the **"Cántico."** They contain a sort of philosophy of Nature, which was, I think, first suggested to him by a chapter in St. Augustine's Confessions, where he speaks of the beauty of all created things coming from God. This was amplified by the Thomist view, quoted by San Juan, according to which the creatures are 'substantially' united to God, because he created them. That is to say, the ideas expressed here by San Juan are not new: it is the use he made of them in his poetry that interests us.

Let us look at the poem. The forsaken soul is searching for her Lover. She sees the woods and thickets, the flowers and fields which he has planted. In lines of wonderful tenderness . . . she implores them to tell her where he has gone, and they reply that he passed by in haste, leaving them clothed with his beauty as he looked at them. In haste, because they belong to the lower orders of Creation. A glance was sufficient to stamp his image on them. But their beauty continues to remind her of his greater beauty. It wounds her, and, more than that, there is *un no sé qué*—a something, she cannot say what—that they go on murmuring, which kills her.

Then a little further on the 'Spiritual Betrothal' is announced by the Beloved in two rapturous stanzas which assert that her Lover *is* the mountains, valleys, rivers, islands, music, night, etc. This surprisingly pantheistic statement receives only the bald comment that 'these mountains are my lover for me'. But San Juan's orthodoxy cannot be questioned. The Beloved here is anticipating the state of the union and Beatific Vision represented in the later stanzas of the **"Cántico"** when the soul, purified of all sin, sees the whole of Creation flooded with God's presence. As in Dante's *Paradiso,* the poet's powers of apprehending beauty increase as he approaches the source of it.

In his prose Commentary San Juan has done his best to spoil these passages for us by telling us that the groves, woods, flowers and so forth, signify the Virtues, Elements, and Angels. He is here, of course, following those barbarously rationalizing tendencies of the early centuries of Christianity (that have their counterpart in the utilitarian tendencies of today) by which everything in the visible world must owe its virtue to being the symbol of some invisible higher entity. But in one case this passion for interpretation has added something to the poetry. Every reader

will have paused over those *ínsulas extrañas,* 'strange islands', which occur twice in the poem. Clearly they are an allusion to the newly discovered islands in the Indies. But San Juan adds more: they represent also those states, categories and modes of being that are comprehended in the nature of God—but are unknown to men. I think we may say that this meaning was almost certainly in the poet's mind at the time of his writing the line. San Juan, like Spinoza, was deeply impressed by the infinite range of the possibilities of being that are contained in the Divine Essence. In one place he remarks that those who knew God best—by which he means the angels and blessed souls in Heaven—were precisely those who knew how little they really know of Him. And in the last stanzas of the **"Cántico"** we find the soul in union with God asking to be taken further into his presence and shown new marvels and mysteries of the Divine Wisdom. San Juan's often-expressed repugnance for the vulgar type of 'supernatural revelation' or, indeed, for any *noticia* or communication that was not imageless and wordless, shows that no superstitious meaning should be attached to this passage. His aim in desiring further 'communications' was simply to draw closer, *más adentro,* to the object of his search.

In the **"Dark Night"** we come to the deepest and most comprehensive of San Juan de la Cruz's symbolic themes. (pp. 350-52)

But what exactly was San Juan's conception of the Dark Night? To explain this we must go to the starting point of his mystical philosophy. In the **Súbida del Monte Carmelo,** where one finds the best account of this, he lays it down as an axiom that, compared with the infinite being of God, all the being of the creatures is *nothing*. From this it follows that those who put their affections on them are nothing, and less than nothing, also. Man can only be *something* by allowing God, who alone has real existence, to fill him; but for this to happen, he must first have emptied himself of every attachment to the creatures. Two contraries cannot exist together in the same person, said Aristotle, and so, if the choice is to be God, the senses, imagination, understanding, memory and will must all be torn up and uprooted from their ordinary functions. It is this process of tearing up, known as purgation, which is the first meaning given to the term 'Dark Night'. For as night is a deprivation of light, so the deprivation of its faculties can be called night to the soul. (p. 353)

Less than all cannot satisfy man,' said William Blake, and to obtain all Fray Juan de la Cruz was prepared to follow the road of renunciation and mortification, as prescribed by the teaching of his day, to the end. For him no compromise was possible, and the account he has given in his best-known book, **The Dark Night of the Soul,** of the trials and sufferings experienced during the period of purgation, has helped, even among Catholics, to throw a harsh and forbidding light on his character. Both William James and Huysmans, for example, speak of him with horror as a sort of fakir.

Yet without seeking in any way to attenuate the severity of the course he prescribed or the enormous, obsessionary nature of his whole undertaking, we should note that there is nothing punitive in San Juan's ascesis. He did not hate the world and the senses, as so many religious people have done, but sought rather to escape from them and leave them behind him. His career, therefore, appears less as a struggle than a flight—a vertiginous ascent away from everything and towards God. (p. 354)

But one can only rise by throwing off ballast. And so the first series of images associated with the Dark Night are those that express deprivation. Solitude, silence, *desnudez*, poverty, emptiness, forgetfulness, detachment from self and from all things. These words have no painful associations. The sufferings of the Dark Night, especially in its second spiritual phase, come from the sense of unsatisfied love, mixed with self doubts and the fear of abandonment, which increase as the state of union draws near. They are the reverse side of that love, corresponding to what jealousy is to ordinary lovers. The work of purgation, on the other hand, gives peace. In it 'the soul finds its rest and quietude because, since it desires nothing, nothing fatigues it and, since it is in the centre of its humility, nothing can oppress it'. This night is *pacífica, dichosa*. And that is why, throughout his prose works, the words peace, solitude, emptiness, ignorance, forgetfulness and all the rest of that long series have an aura of happy and soothing connotations. Like Mallarmé, San Juan is the poet of the minus sign.

But the theme or symbol of the **Dark Night** has other meanings than those associated with the purgative process. It also signifies Faith. Now Faith is the intellectual aspect of the triple instinct that leads the soul towards God, but it is dark because to the mind it is inexplicable. And the end of the polar journey, where the compass needle points downwards—that is to say, God—is also inexplicable. He, too, therefore (borrowing a phrase from Dionysius the Areopagite), is 'dark night to the soul in this life'. San Juan uses the simile of a moth and a bat to explain this; their eyes being adjusted to the twilight, they cannot see when the light becomes too great. Thus the sun or a lamp can be said to look dark to them, because it makes their sense organs useless. In the same way God will appear dark to the human intelligence, because it lacks the organs to apprehend Him. It is here that the purgation of the intellect comes in. Being useless for the purpose, it must be discarded and new organs developed in its place. Whilst this is happening, the soul lives in a double obscurity, without either its new faculties or its old. Night has delivered it from the anarchy of apparent existence, and there has seeped in from the deep darkness around an obscure apprehension of the true.

But the **Dark Night** will not be properly understood unless it is felt to represent a state that precedes and heralds the day. A note of suppressed excitement and exhilaration rustles under the surface, recalling, in a quieter key, the thrilling tones of Donne's poem on his sickness. *Este noche*, San Juan says, *encubridora de las esperanzas de la luz del dia*—'This night, accomplice of the hopes of the light of day'. And although the two greatest of his prose works describe the Night, with its hushed suspense and its sharp stabs of longing, it is chiefly the coming of Day that the lyrics celebrate. The poet, emerging from the dim states that precede the ecstasy of composition, finds in the marvellous illumination of that ecstasy his best subject-matter. The poems are the explosions of a man whose ordinary condition had up till then been, if not *noche oscura*, then twilight.

The end of the night meant the satisfaction of the longings that had carried him forward—the final accomplishment of the work of love. 'To this end of love', he says, 'we were created.' 'The one means by which the Soul and all its faculties is moved is love.' It is here that one is struck by the difference from such modern mystics as Aldous Huxley. In all San Juan's books there is not a single word of disparagement, either for other people or for those human senses and faculties which he had felt it necessary to purge. But love for a Catholic mystic meant first of all love for God, because that embraced everything else. Such love could not be satisfied by anything short of 'union'. But what is union? It seems, a stage of great aloofness punctuated by trance or ecstasy, in which the moral values wither away because they have become useless and the æsthetic ones take their place. As in earthly love unions—but here we return to allegory—the Lovers become two mirrors reflecting one another's beauty. Or so San Juan describes it, commenting the line of the **"Cántico,"** *Y vámonos a ver en tu hermosura.*

> So I shall see thee in thy beauty, and thou shalt see me in thy beauty, and I shall see myself in thee in thy beauty and thou shalt see me in thyself in thy beauty; and so I shall appear to be thee in thy beauty and thou shalt appear to be me in thy beauty and my beauty will be thy beauty and thy beauty my beauty; and so I shall be thee in thy beauty and thou shalt be me in thy beauty; because thine own beauty will be my beauty and so we shall see one another in thy beauty.

For beauty is the flowering of love. *A la tarde te examinarán en el amor.* (pp. 354-56)

> *Gerald Brenan, "Studies in Genius, II: St. John of the Cross, His Life and Poetry," in Horizon, London, Vol. XV, No. 89, June, 1947, pp. 324-56.*

Edgar Allison Peers (essay date 1948)

[*Peers was an English Hispanic scholar and educator whose works focus on the Spanish mystics and Romantics. In 1923 he founded the quarterly* Bulletin of Spanish Studies, *now the* Bulletin of Hispanic Studies. *In the excerpt below, from an essay originally published in 1948, Peers chronicles the life of St. John of the Cross and refers to his three great poems: "The Dark Night," "The Spiritual Canticle," and "The Living Flame of Love."*]

Because of the curious way in which their lives were intertwined, St. John of the Cross is generally thought of side by side with St. Teresa. Her writings . . . touch great heights, and, if we consider with them her achievements as a reformer and her personality, it is probably no exaggeration to say that she was one of the most remarkable women who have ever lived. But, though she continually delights the reader, and sometimes, either by her versatile and flexible mind or by her sheer power, surprises him, she can hardly be compared as a writer with St. John of the Cross, who, besides the same native shrewdness and the same unerring instinct of sanctity, had at his command the fruit of a lifetime's reading, an aptitude for generalization, a technical skill in the presentation of a theme and the marshalling of arguments—in short, the mind and the gifts of a scholar. He, too, had a far wider vision of the entire range of the interior life: his works form nothing less than a contemplative's library, and a library stocked with works of such profundity that few readers can hope to assimilate it fully in a lifetime.

And, with all that, St. John of the Cross was one of Spain's greatest poets, and one of the greatest poets who wrote of the life behind the wall that the world has seen. He wrote so little that for a few pence you can buy all the poems which made him famous, and yet they contain all the essence and magic of poetry, and the poetry-lover can enjoy them to the full, quite independently of their allegorical meaning. His principal prose works take the form of commentaries on three of his own poems, grouped in a little collection entitled **Songs of the Soul,** so that if we study this collection we shall be at the very heart of his writing, both in verse and in prose. (pp. 127-28)

[He] was, above all, a man of God: that was both the initial and the lasting impression that he made upon everyone. "He was so *good* a man," was St. Teresa's first verdict upon him. "They take him for a saint," she remarked later, "and a saint, in my opinion, he is, and has been all his life."

"It always seemed that his soul was at prayer," wrote a nun who had a happy knack for description. That was as near as she could get to describing what she felt about him. Others, in speaking of his goodness, would use symbols and call him a "flaming torch" and a "white dove." The habit still persists; and a modern poet, Antonio Machado, has apostrophized him, most happily of all, as *espíritu de llama:* "spirit of flame."

And now let us turn to his three great "Songs of the Soul." The first of them is called **"Dark Night."** It tells about a girl who escaped from her house, much as John had escaped from prison, and journeyed through the darkness, "lit . . . only by heart's inmost fire ablaze," to seek her lover. She attains her goal, and then she sings this song to the darkness:

> O night that led'st me thus!
> O night more winsome than the rising sun!
> O night that madest us,
> Lover and lov'd, as one,
> Lover transform'd in lov'd, love's journey done!

A much longer poem is the **"Spiritual Canticle,"** packed with rich and daring imagery—a modern "Song of Songs," in which the Bride and the Spouse sing to each other in turn. Incidentally it illustrates the poet's love of the beauties of nature, to which various accounts of his life bear eloquent witness:

> My love is as the hills,
> The lonely valleys clad with forest-trees,
> The rushing, sounding rills,

> Strange isles in distant seas,
> Lover-like whisperings, murmurs of the
>   breeze . . .

The third of his great poems, **"Living Flame of Love,"** is a wonderful attempt to describe the deepest and most intimate communion with God. He piles image upon image as he strives to express the ineffable, but perhaps the most moving stanza is the last, the rhythm of which conveys so complete an impression of confidence and security:

> How tender is the love
> Thou wak'nest in my breast
> When thou, alone and secretly, art there!
> Whispering of things above,
> Most glorious and most blest,
> How delicate the love thou mak'st me bear!

Besides his **"Songs of the Soul,"** St. John of the Cross wrote some similar verses. A lovely poem, for example, on the Fountain of life, with a haunting refrain, "Although 'tis night," written in the Toledo prison. And a striking allegory of the Crucifixion in the form of a story about a shepherd boy. Here he uses the artless language of popular poetry. The love-inspired shepherd-boy is Christ; His love is the human soul; and the villain that comes between the two is the devil. Listen to the plaintiveness and simplicity of the last two stanzas:

> "Woe!" cries the shepherd-boy, "woe be in store
> For him that's come between my love and me,
> So that she wishes not to know or see
> This breast that love has stricken very sore!"

> Then climbs he slowly, when much time is o'er,
> Into a tree with fair arms wide outspread,
> And, clinging to that tree, forthwith is dead,
> For lo! his breast was stricken very sore.

In his four great prose treatises, St. John of the Cross built upon these three poems a comprehensive account of the interior life as he knew it in its fullness, the highest stages of which embody sublime experiences of divine intimacy. But he also gives a great deal of excellent advice to those who would follow him on his quest for God, much of which may be laid to heart by every Christian. His knowledge of humanity and understanding of human motives were extraordinary. As his poems suggest, one of his main themes is the twofold "Dark Night"—the Night of Sense, which means briefly the renunciation of all material things that may come between us and God, and the Night of Spirit, an "incomparably more awful" experience, in which it seems to the journeyer, as it once seemed to Christ, that God has forsaken him. It is noteworthy that this great "Doctor of the Church Universal," whose descriptions of the Uncreated Light of Union perhaps surpass any others, should have written with such clarity and force about the Dark Night as well.

But how, you may ask, can this sixteenth-century saint have anything to do with our busy, troubled, agonizing world of to-day? I believe he has everything to do with it and we need to learn a great deal that he can teach us.

First of all, there is the appeal of the man himself. Not for nothing was he, like St. Teresa, born and bred in the luminous, crystal-clear atmosphere of the Castilian plateau. He sees life sharply; calls a spade a spade; rejects pretence, euphemism, and compromise. And everything that he teaches he illustrates in his own character.

Then he restores, to a world which sometimes seems in danger of losing it, the Biblical conception of the overwhelming greatness of Almighty God. He cries, with St. Augustine, "What can any say who speaks of Thee?" He meditates, like Pascal, on "the infinitely great and the infinitely small." He draws us right out of the petty, imperfect existence with which our spirits are too often satisfied. He uplifts our hearts and desires, and yet he abases our pride. And, as we enter those deep caverns, lit by the lamps of the divine attributes, which he describes in his **"Living Flame,"** we are hushed into reverence and awe.

Once we begin to realize something of God's greatness and man's littleness, we begin to understand the necessity for self-stripping and self-purification if we would undertake the quest for Him. The standards of St. John of the Cross are high; his demands are severe; in the comfortable, easygoing nineteenth century, men called his teaching fanatical and repellent, even inhuman. But to-day we know that we shall never get the best things of life by living in an easy-chair. In recent years we have had to fight and struggle and suffer for things which our fathers and grandfathers took for granted; and we know that the prize has more than justified the sacrifice.

Much more so does this prize of which we read in St. John of the Cross; and what he demands of us is merely to be as severe with ourselves as we think the prize merits. He calls us from a hothouse religiosity into a keen, bracing air which is really the very atmosphere of the Gospels. And we can all find inspiration in those invigorating maxims of his, which ring out as clearly as the strokes of a church bell on the frosty air:

> Feed not thy spirit on aught beside God.
> Look not at the imperfections of others: keep silence, and have continual converse with God.
> Love consists not in feeling great things, but in having great detachment and in suffering for the Beloved.
> Keep the image of God clearly and simply in thy soul.

Renunciation, single-mindedness, and detachment: in those three words we shall find the secret of true religion, which is ever-giving, unexpecting love. (pp. 130-35)

> *Edgar Allison Peers, "St. John of the Cross: 'Songs of the Soul'," in his* Behind That Wall: An Introduction to Some Classics of the Interior Life, *1948. Reprint by Books for Libraries Press, 1969, pp. 125-35.*

M. C. D'Arcy, S. J.   (essay date 1951)

[*D'Arcy was an English Jesuit priest who lectured and wrote widely on philosophical and religious topics. In the following excerpt from his preface to Roy Campbell's translation of St. John of the Cross's poetry. D'Arcy analyzes St. John's motivation for recording his mystical experiences and describes his comparative facility with verse and prose.*]

For a long time interest in this country was so centered on St Teresa of Avila that St John stood in her shade. The nineteenth century was not seriously attracted to mysticism. Memories of its excesses still lingered: and St Teresa was read more because her character was irresistible than through a desire to follow her mystical way. As is well known, many leading Protestant divines refused to give mysticism a place within the Christian faith, and for a period Catholic spiritual writers advocated a vigorous practice of the virtues in preference to what savoured of illuminism or quietism. In the last fifty years this open or veiled hostility has changed in a marked degree to appreciation. The writings of Evelyn Underhill and Dean Inge stirred the interest of those outside the Catholic Church, while within the Church a host of writers, of whom I need mention only Baron Von Hügel, Abbot Butler, H. Bremond and P. Maréchal, gave a lead to a new and serious study of mystical writings. Among such writings those of St John of the Cross were bound to take a foremost place. They give what many consider the most complete and clear-cut description of the many stages in the mystical ascent.

St John of the Cross was far from any intention to describe his experiences. He was the humblest of men, tiny in body and most retiring of disposition. It was St Teresa who with her genius for reading souls saw through the exterior littleness into the greatness of his spirit, and she singled him out to do for men what she was heroically undertaking in the reform of the nuns of the Carmelite Order. His admiration for and love of St Teresa made him accept what was most repugnant to his nature, and the work he took on his shoulders brought him trials of every kind, many indignities, and even imprisonment by his outraged brethren. Without any preconceived idea of writing, he adopted the habit of jotting down maxims to help others, and at the request of those he thus helped he wrote out for their sake and guidance a treatise for souls entering on the mysterious paths of mystical prayer. Even when doing this he took care, as he thought, only to supplement what he felt St Teresa, with far greater sanctity and experience, was writing. It looks, however, as if the poems just escaped from him; they are stanzas of the spontaneous and semi-ecstatic love song he had always in his heart, once he had come to know God. Many of these poems seem to have been composed when he was imprisoned at Toledo. Others were written at Baeza, a place he loved because in the woods around and by the side of the river Guadalimar he could pass happy hours in union with God. Later, while Prior at Granada, between 1582 and 1585, he wrote the last parts of his prose works as a commentary on the stanzas of the poems.

From this it would appear that poetry was more natural to him than prose: and this is confirmed by the testimony of a nun at the process of his canonisation in 1618.

> One day he asked this witness in what her prayer consisted, and she replied: "In considering the beauty of God and in rejoicing that He has such beauty". And the Saint was so pleased with this that for some days he said the most sublime things concerning the beauty of God, at which all marvelled. And thus, under the influence of

this love, he composed five stanzas, beginning
"Beloved let us sing, and in Thy beauty see ourselves portray'd". (*Rejoice, my love, with me*).
And in all this he showed that there was in his
breast a great love of God.

In this artless but vivid account we see how St John was
taken out of himself by the simple words of another, and
so moved that at the end the ecstasy spilled over into stanzas of love, the Bride crying to the Beloved:

Rejoice, my love, with me
And in your beauty see us both reflected:
By mountain-slope and lea
Where purest rills run free
We'll pass into the forest undetected.

(pp. 1-3)

Mystical experience is caviare to the general: it is attained
only by the denial of all that we commonly call experience.
A new world is discovered which is so different from our
familiar one that all our words drawn from our ordinary
and familiar experience fail to describe it. They would
seem bound in fact to give a wrong impression, as they
make us think of what we know instead of this new unknown. In a sense, undoubtedly, mystical experience is ineffable: it would not be that experience if the words used
to tell of it were common to it and what we already know.
Even within the multiple experience which we all share it
is extremely hard to communicate what we may have felt.
A man may want to tell us what he felt when he was listening to some music or after meeting someone he loves, or
when he met death face to face for the first time; or he may
wish to tell us the effect on him of a drug or a spasm of
pain or the joy of an unexpected success. The experience
is to him unique and all the words he uses could be applicable to something else. It would be easy to argue that private experiences are quite incommunicable; and yet the
mysterious fact is that there is a human art of communication which somehow or other overcomes the seemingly insuperable obstacle. The good artist knows that sound and
taste, for instance, will help to tell the truth about sight,
that we can feel colour and transpose sight into sound.
Moreover, by assonances, and associations and by change
of rhythm and by heightening the power of words and enlisting our sympathy, he can enable us to relive his own
individual experience; and this is precisely what the poet
or the great artist does. This is his magic, his gift from
God. And this is why neither St John of the Cross nor a
translator, like Roy Campbell, refrains from putting into
the language of verse what is in itself far more difficult to
communicate than the most personal of ordinary human
experiences.

To appreciate intelligently the songs of a mystic like St
John of the Cross it is essential to grasp the nature of true
mysticism. Otherwise such words as

Reveal your presence clearly
And kill me with the beauty you discover,
For pains acquired so dearly
From love, cannot recover
Save only through the presence of the lover.

will in all likelihood be thought to be the description of an
intense and very human emotion of the love we know. The
truth is that this mystical love cannot even begin until the
emotions we are thinking of have been hushed and put to
sleep. In our everyday life we are both active and passive,
and this is seen very well in our relations with others. They
influence our thoughts and behaviour when we are in their
presence. A frightened man before an interview can dramatize to himself what he will do and what he will say; but
in the interview itself he feels the impact of the other and
despite himself may be overpowered by the other's character. Again, our love for the long dead must be very strong
for their influence to remain with us and touch us as if they
were still alive and present. Now normally we cannot feel
any contact with disembodied spirit, and if there be any
truth in the supposed communications with the dead, it
should be noticed that the contact is on the level of our
ordinary sight and by sensible words. In religion, as God
is supreme Spirit, our knowledge of Him is indirect, that
is to say, by faith or true report. But St John, following
the line of the great mystics, in his commentaries on his
poems explains how with the grace of God those who are
drawn to contemplation may experience the presence of
God in a way comparable to that which we enjoy when
our friends meet us. The way, however, is exceedingly arduous, so arduous, in fact, as to terrify all except the bravest of lovers. It comes to this, that we must surrender all
that is dearest to us in the enjoyment of the senses and go
through a dark night in which we live without their help
and comfort. Then when this is accomplished we have to
sacrifice the prerogative of our own way of thinking and
willing and undergo another still darker night in which we
have deprived ourselves of all the supports which are familiar to us and make us self-sufficient. This is a kind of
death, the making nothing of all that we are to ourselves;
but the genuine mystic tells us that when all has been
strained away our emptiness will be filled with a new presence; our uncovered soul will receive the contact of divine
love, and a new circuit of love will begin, when the soul
is passive to an indescribable love which is given to it.

This experience is as remote as can be from the hot life of
the senses or even the exalted sharing of human love. Nevertheless just because God is love and man was made in
the image of God, the symbolism of human love can be
turned to use and made to describe what are the effects of
mystical union. How this can be done only a Saint like St
John of the Cross can tell us, and he does so by so using
language that we know all the time how the images of
lover and beloved, bridegroom and bride, the *clichés* of
love we might almost say, are no more exact than pointer
readings; they are copper coins acting as currency for silver. The touch of God is entirely spiritual, and the soul
is touched at its source below the level of its activities of
thought and will. It is true that the love aroused by this
contact may overflow into the emotions and the body and
so charge any words used with a supernatural sense, but
all the same great artistry and holiness must combine to
etherialize the passionate words of sense and make us feel
that they have been dipped in some divine spring. There
are those who will refuse to believe that this mystical verse
is anything more than concealed human passion, and such
critics persuade themselves that saints, like St John of the
Cross, are victims of some pathological disorder. There is
not the slightest evidence for this, so far as I know, in the

life of St John, and we have his quiet and strong commentaries on his poems to prove to us what he had in mind when he wrote the poems. To those who have ears to hear, the accents of a genuine experience are unmistakable, and the unprejudiced reader must, I think, become conscious of an unearthly glow in the verse, a strange quality which invades the images and persuades him that there must be a love which is a secret between God and the soul. (pp. 4-7)

M. C. D'Arcy, S. J., in a preface to The Poems of St. John of the Cross, *translated by Roy Campbell, Pantheon Books Inc., 1951, pp. 1-8.*

Thomas Merton   (essay date 1953)

[*Merton was a religious writer and scholar. A naturalized American citizen born in France, he joined a Trappist monastery in Kentucky in 1941 and was later ordained as Father M. Louis. Here, Merton pays homage to St. John's life and artistic achievement, asserting that "of all the saints he was the greatest poet as well as the greatest contemplative."*]

If you have never seen El Greco's view of Toledo, you might take a look at it. It will tell you something about St. John of the Cross. I say it will tell you something—not very much. St. John of the Cross and El Greco were contemporaries, they lived in the same country, they were mystics, though by no means in the same degree. In other ways they were quite different. Father Bruno, in the best life of St. John of the Cross so far written, reminds his reader several times not to go imagining that St. John of the Cross looked like an El Greco painting. He was more like one of Zurbaran's Carthusians. Even that comparison is not altogether exact. The original and authentic portrait of the saint shows him to have an innocent and rather expressionless face. He does not look in any way ascetic. In fact you would think you were looking at the portrait of a Madrid shopkeeper or of a cook.

El Greco's view of Toledo is very dramatic. It is full of spiritual implications. It looks like a portrait of the heavenly Jerusalem wearing an iron mask. Yet there is nothing inert about these buildings. The dark city built on its mountain seems to be entirely alive. It surges with life, coordinated by some mysterious, providential upheaval which drives all these masses of stone upward towards heaven, in the clouds of a blue disaster that foreshadows the end of the world.

Somewhere in the middle of the picture must be the building where St. John of the Cross was kept in prison. Soon after the beginning of St. Theresa's reform he was kidnaped by opponents of the reform, and disappeared. No one had any idea where he had gone and, as St. Theresa lamented, nobody seemed to care. He was locked up in a cell without light or air during the stifling heat of a Toledan summer to await trial and punishment for what his persecutors seriously believed to be a canonical crime. The complex canonical and political implications of the Carmelite reform had involved the saints of that reform in the kind of intrigue for which they alone, of all Spain, had no taste. And even St. Theresa, whose dovelike simplicity was

supported by an altogether devastating prudence in these adventures, seems to have rather enjoyed them.

John of the Cross found little that was humanly speaking enjoyable in his Toledo jail. His only excursions from his cell came on the days when he was brought down to the refectory to be publicly scourged by his jailers, who were scandalized at his meek silence, believing it to be the sign of a reprobate conscience, hardened in rebellion. Why didn't the man do something to defend himself?

Here in Toledo, in what he called "the belly of the whale," the saint, wisely more silent than the prophet Jonas, dealt not with men but with God alone, waiting patiently for the divine answer that would end this dark night of his soul. No one knows when or how the answer came, but when St. John made his miraculous escape during the octave of the Assumption, in 1578, he carried in his pocket the manuscript of a poem which respectable critics have declared to be superior to any other in the Spanish language. These critics range from Menéndez y Pelayo, who may be deemed to be respectable in a rather stuffy sense, to more recent and more advanced writers. Even the London magazine *Horizon,* which has a certain rating among intellectuals, included two very competent articles on St. John of the Cross in a series of "studies of genius." As far as I know, John of the Cross was the only saint in the series.

El Greco was painting in Toledo when St. John of the Cross was in prison there. But the imprisonment of St. John of the Cross, and the **"Spiritual Canticle"** which bloomed miraculously in the closet where he was jailed, had little to do with the exiled Greek. The color scheme is quite different. The painter's view of the city must be a winter view, black, purple, green, blue, and gray. And the movement is a blind upheaval in which earth and sky run off the top of the canvas like an ebb tide in the Arctic Ocean. The color scheme of John's imprisonment is black and ochre and brown and red: the red is his own blood running down his back. The movement is centripetal. There is a tremendous stability, not merely in the soul immobilized, entombed in a burning stone wall, but in the depths of that soul, purified by a purgatory that those alone know who have felt it, emerging in to the Center of all centers, the Love which moves the heavens and the stars, the Living God.

The last place in the world where one would imagine the **"Spiritual Canticle"** to have been written is a dungeon!

I will try to translate a little of it:

> My Beloved is like the mountains.
> Like the lonely valleys full of woods
> The strange islands
> The rivers with their sound
> The whisper of the lovely air!
>
> The night, appeased and hushed
> About the rising of the dawn
> The music stilled
> The sounding solitude
> The supper that rebuilds my life
> And brings me love.
>
> Our bed of flowers
> Surrounded by the lions' dens

Makes us a purple tent,
Is built of peace.
Our bed is crowned with a thousand shields of
    gold!

Fast-flying birds
Lions, harts, and leaping does
Mountains, banks and vales
Streams, breezes, heats of day
And terrors watching in the night:

By the sweet lyres and by the siren's song
I conjure you: let angers end!
And do not touch the wall
But let the bride be safe: let her sleep on!

Only the saint and God can tell what distant echoes of an utterly alien everyday common life penetrated the darkness of the jail cell and the infinitely deep sleep of the peace in which his soul lay hidden in God. *Touch not the wall . . .* but the religious police could not disturb the ecstasy of one who had been carried so far that he was no longer troubled at the thought of being rejected even by the holy!

No one can become a saint without solving the problem of suffering. No one who has ever written anything, outside the pages of Scripture, has given us such a solution to the problem as St. John of the Cross. I will not speculate upon his answers. I will merely mention the fact that they exist and pass on. For those who want to read it, there is the *Dark Night of the Soul.* But this much must be said: Sanctity can never abide a merely speculative solution to the problem of suffering. Sanctity solves the problem not by analyzing but by suffering. It is a living solution, burned in the flesh and spirit of the saint by fire. Scripture itself tells us as much. "As silver is tried by fire and gold in the furnace, so the Lord trieth hearts." "Son, when thou comest to the service of God, stand in justice and fear and prepare thy soul for temptation. Humble thy heart and endure: incline thy ear and receive the words of understanding and make not haste in the time of clouds. Wait on God with patience: join thyself to God and endure, that thy life may be increased in the latter end. Take all that shall be brought upon thee, and in thy sorrow endure and in thy humiliation keep patience. For gold and silver are tried in the fire and acceptable men in the furnace of humiliation."

Sanctity does not consist in suffering. It is not even directly produced by suffering, for many have suffered and have become devils rather than saints. What is more, there are some who gloat over the sufferings of the saints and are hideously sentimental about sufferings of their own, and cap it all by a voracious appetite for inflicting suffering on other people, sometimes in the name of sanctity. Of such were those who persecuted St. John of the Cross in his last days, and helped him to enter heaven with greater pain and greater heroism. These were not the "calced" who caught him at the beginning of his career, but the champion ascetics of his own family, the men of the second generation, those who unconsciously did their best to ruin the work of the founders, and who quite consciously did everything they could to remove St. John of the Cross from a position in which he would be able to defend what he knew to be the Theresian ideal.

Sanctity itself is a living solution of the problem of suffering. For the saint, suffering continues to be suffering, but it ceases to be an obstacle to his mission, or to his happiness, both of which are found positively and concretely in the will of God. The will of God is found by the saint less in *manifestations* of the divine good-pleasure than in God Himself.

Suffering, on the natural level, is always opposed to natural joy. There is no opposition between natural suffering and supernatural joy. Joy, in the supernatural order, is simply an aspect of charity. It is inseparable from the love that is poured forth in our hearts by the Holy Ghost. But when sanctity is not yet mature, its joy is not always recognizable. It can too easily be buried under pain. But true charity, far from being diminished by suffering, uses suffering as it uses everything else: for the increase of its own immanent vitality. Charity is the expression of a divine life within us, and this life, if we allow it to have its way, will grow and thrive most in the very presence of all that seems to destroy life and to quench its flame. A life that blazes with a hundredfold brilliance in the face of death is therefore invincible. Its joy cannot fail. It conquers everything. It knows no suffering. Like the Risen Christ, Who is its Author and Principle, it knows no death.

The life of charity was perfect in the great Carmelite reformer, St. John of the Cross. It was so perfect that it can hardly be said to shine before men. His soul was too pure to attract any attention. Yet precisely because of his purity, he is one of the few saints who can gain a hearing in the most surprising recesses of an impure world. John of the Cross, who seems at first sight to be a saint for the most pure of the Christian élite, may very well prove to be the last hope of harlots and publicans. The wisdom of this extraordinary child "reaches from end to end mightily." Lost in the pure wisdom of God, like God, and in God, he attains to all things. This saint, so often caricatured as an extremist, is actually beyond all extremes. Having annihilated all extremes in the center of his own humility, he remains colorless and neutral. His doctrine, which is considered inhumanly hard, is only hard because it is superhumanly simple. Its simplicity seems to present an obstacle to our nature, which has sought to hide itself from God in a labyrinth of mental complexities, like Adam and Eve amidst the leaves of Paradise.

The hardest thing to accept, in St. John of the Cross, is not the Cross, but the awful neutrality of his interior solitude. After all, as he so reasonably points out, when the soul is detached, by the Cross, from every sensible and spiritual obstacle, its journey to God becomes easy and joyful: "The Cross is the staff whereby one may reach Him, and whereby the road is greatly lightened and made easy. Wherefore Our Lord said through St. Matthew: My yoke is easy and my burden is light, which burden is the Cross. For if a man resolve to submit himself to carrying his cross—that is to say if he resolve to desire in truth to meet trials and to bear them in all things for God's sake, he will find in them great relief and sweetness wherewith he may travel on this road, detached from all things and desiring nothing."

The two words "desiring nothing" contain all the difficulty and all the simplicity of St. John of the Cross. But no Christian has a right to complain of them. They are simply an echo of two words that sum up the teaching of Jesus Christ in the Gospel: *abneget semetipsum.* "If any man would come after me, let him *deny himself . . .* "

This total self-denial, which St. John of the Cross pursues into the inmost depths of the human spirit, reduces our interior landscape to a wasteland without special features of any kind whatever. We do not even have the consolation of beholding a personal disaster. A cataclysm of the spirit, if terrible, is also interesting. But the soul of the contemplative is happy to be reduced to a state of complete loneliness and dereliction in which the most significant renouncement is that of self-complacency. Many men are attracted to a solitude in which they believe that they will have the leisure and the opportunity to contemplate themselves. Not so St. John of the Cross:

> These times of aridity cause the soul to journey in all purity in the love of God, since it is no longer influenced in its actions by the pleasure and sweetness of the actions themselves, . . . but only by a desire to please God. It becomes neither presumptuous nor self-satisfied, as perchance it was wont to become in the time of its prosperity, but fearful and timid with regard to itself, finding in itself no satisfaction whatsoever; and herein consists that holy fear which preserves and increases the virtues . . . Save for the pleasure indeed which at certain times God infuses into it, it is a wonder if it find pleasure and consolation of sense, through its own diligence, in any spiritual exercise or action . . . There grows within souls that experience this arid night (of the senses) care for God and yearnings to serve Him, for in proportion as the breasts of sensuality, wherewith it sustained and nourished the desires that it pursued, are drying up, there remains nothing in that aridity and detachment save the yearning to serve God, which is a thing very pleasing to God.

The joy of this emptiness, this weird neutrality of spirit which leaves the soul detached from the things of the earth and not yet in possession of those of heaven, suddenly blossoms out into a pure paradise of liberty, of which the saint sings in his **"Spiritual Canticle:"** it is a solitude full of wild birds and strange trees, rocks, rivers and desert islands, lions and leaping does. These creatures are images of the joys of the spirit, aspects of interior solitude, fires that flash in the abyss of the pure heart whose loneliness becomes alive with the deep lightnings of God.

If I say that St. John of the Cross seems to me to be the most accessible of the saints, that is only another way of saying that he is my favorite saint—together with three others who also seem to me most approachable: St. Benedict, St. Bernard, and St. Francis of Assisi. After all, the people you make friends with are the ones who welcome you into their company. But besides this, it also seems to me that St. John of the Cross is absolutely and in himself a most accessible saint. This, to those who find him forbidding, will seem an outrageous paradox. Nevertheless it is true, if you consider that few saints, if any, have ever opened up to other men such remote depths in their own soul. St. John of the Cross admits you, in the *Living Flame,* to his soul's "deepest center," to the "deep caverns" in which the lamps of fire, the attributes of God, flash mysteriously in metaphysical shadows; who else has done as much? St. John reveals himself to us not in allegory, as does St. Theresa (in the *Mansions*) but in *symbol.* And symbol is a far more potent and effective medium than allegory. It is truer because it is more direct and more intimate. It does not need to be worked out and applied by the reason. The symbols that spring from the depths of the heart of St. John of the Cross awaken kindred symbols in the depths of the heart that loves him. Their effect, of course, is supported and intensified by grace which, we may believe, the saint himself has begged for the souls of those who have been called to love him in God. Here is a union and a friendship than which nothing could be more intimate, except the friendship of the soul with God Himself. Earth knows no such intimacies. Those who love St. Peter from the Gospels and react in vivid sympathy for his all too human experiences, do not come as close to Peter as the one who meets St. John of the Cross in the depths of prayer. We know St. Peter on a more exterior surface of life—the level of passion and emotion. But on that level there is less communion, and less effective communication, than in the depths of the spirit.

And thus St. John of the Cross not only makes himself accessible to us, but does much more: he makes us accessible to ourselves by opening our hearts to God within their own depths.

In the end, however, I may as well have the courtesy to admit one thing: St. John of the Cross is not everybody's food. Even in a contemplative monastery there will be some who will never get along with him—and others who, though they think they know what he is about, would do better to let him alone. He upsets everyone who thinks that his doctrine is supposed to lead one by a way that is exalted. On the contrary, his way is so humble that it ends up by being no way at all, for John of the Cross is unfriendly to systems and a bitter enemy of all exaltation. *Omnis qui se exaltat humiliabitur.* His glory is to do without glory for the love of Christ.

John of the Cross is the patron of those who have a vocation that is thought, by others, to be spectacular, but which, in reality, is lowly, difficult, and obscure. He is the patron and the protector and Master of those whom God has led into the uninteresting wilderness of contemplative prayer. His domain is precisely defined. He is the patron of contemplatives in the strict sense, and of their spiritual directors, not of contemplatives in the juridical sense. He is the patron of those who pray in a certain way in which God wants them to pray, whether they happen to be in the cloister, the desert, or the city. Therefore his influence is not limited to one order or to one kind of order. His teaching is not merely a matter of "Carmelite spirituality," as some seem to think. In fact, I would venture to say that he is the Father of all those whose prayer is an undefined isolation outside the boundary of "spirituality." He deals chiefly with those who, in one way or another, have been brought face to face with God in a way that methods cannot account for and books do not explain. He is in Christ the model and the maker of contemplatives wherever they may be found.

When this much has been said, enough has been said. St. John of the Cross was not famous in his own lifetime and will not be famous in our own. There is no need that either he, or contemplation, should be famous. In this world in which all good things are talked about and practically none of them are practices, it would be unwise to make contemplative prayer a matter for publicity, though perhaps no harm has been done, thus far, by making its name known. God Himself knows well enough how to make the thing known to those who need it, in His designs for them.

Let it suffice to have said that this Spanish saint is one of the greatest and most hidden of the saints, that of all saints he is perhaps the greatest poet as well as the greatest contemplative, and that in his humility he was also most human, although I have not said much to prove it. I know that he will understand that this article about him was written as a veiled act of homage, as a gesture of love and gratitude, and as a disguised prayer. He knows what the prayer seeks. May he grant it to the writer and to the readers of these words. (pp. 52-61)

> *Thomas Merton, "St. John of the Cross," in* Perspectives, U.S.A., *No. 4, Summer, 1953, pp. 52-61.*

Jorge Guillén   (essay date 1961)

[*One of Spain's best-known lyric poets, Guillén was a member of the so-called "Generation of 1927," a group of Spanish poets whose works were known for their untraditional rhyme schemes, powerful metaphors, and emphasis on pure aestheticism. A political exile after the Spanish Civil War, Guillén lectured at several universities in the United States while completing numerous volumes of poetry, including* Cantico *(1928) and* Clamor *(1960). Below, Guillén examines "The Dark Night of the Soul," "The Spiritual Canticle," and "The Living Flame of Love," asserting that "San Juan de la Cruz has found the perfect equilibrium between poetry of inspiration and constructed poetry." The critic also remarks on the complex symbolism in the saint's poems and the prose commentaries.*]

An increasingly intense religious concentration, in San Juan de la Cruz, turns into mystic experience. This experience is communicated in two ways: in doctrinal exposition and in poetic expression. Life, doctrine, and poetry are the three areas in which San Juan de la Cruz unfolds. A rather extensive explanation of the doctrine accompanies a poetic output which is very brief. San Juan de la Cruz is the briefest great poet in the Spanish language, perhaps in world literature. If we leave aside the compositions of doubtful authenticity and a few of minor interest, San Juan's poetic expression is condensed into seven poems: like the Pleiades, a small but brilliant constellation. No one could be less the professional rhymer than he. However, he must have written more poems than we know. It is not conceivable that the **"Noche oscura"** and the **"Cántico espiritual"** should be the early works of a novice. But poetry never

came to be his principal task; it was something extra, overflowing from a life consecrated to religious zeal, the true name for which is none other than "sainthood." The highest pinnacle in Spanish poetry is reached not by an artist who is primarily an artist, but by a saint, who ascends to this height by his most rigorous road to perfection; and the **"Noche oscura,"** the **"Cántico espiritual,"** and the **"Llama de amor viva"** are the work of a person who never wrote the word "poetry." This is curious: San Juan often has recourse to the terminology of the arts and trades, and uses the words "rhetoric," "metaphor," "style," "verses," and others of the literary craft. In one passage he applies the word "poet" to the author of the *Book of Proverbs.* Yet the word "poetry" never appears.

Three poems stand forth from the seven, unique. The three form a series which is perhaps the highest culmination of Spanish poetry: **"Noche oscura del alma" ("Dark Night of the Soul"), "Cántico espiritual" ("Spiritual Canticle"), "Llama de amor viva" ("Living Flame of Love").** In order to feel and understand these texts purely as poems, we must approach them directly, not as if they were anonymous, but still disregarding for the moment the supplementary information available about them, such as the historical circumstances of their origin and their transcendental interpretation. It will be a good exercise in "ascetic" criticism to leave until later the saint's own explanations, and to read the poems attentively as if we knew nothing about the author. (pp. 79-80)

In our reading of the three poems, let us pay no attention as yet to the titles, which incline us toward the author's interpretation. And the author at this point is not explaining: he is saying, telling, singing. They are three love poems. This love shapes a world with its atmosphere, its nights, its half lights, its days, its fields, its caverns; in a solitude that welcomes the lovers; in a remoteness where they reign over themselves and over Creation; and in the most secret way, protected by the most impregnable walls. The first poem is the poem of nocturnal adventure. . . .

> Upon a gloomy night,
> With all my cares to loving ardours flushed
> (O venture of delight!)
> With nobody in sight
> I went abroad when all my house was hushed.

A woman, moved by love, has slipped out of her house. And, before morning comes, in the hour between night and dawn, the lovers meet, and their love is consummated in the most profound fulfillment. . . .

> Lost to myself I stayed,
> My face upon my lover having laid,
> From all endeavor ceasing:
> And all my cares releasing,
> Threw them amongst the lilies there to fade.

This first poem is perhaps the purest of the three great poems. (And "pure" refers here to a quality devoid of any suspicion of rhetoric.) This is why the images appear in organic function. At first, between silence and solitude, moving through darkness to darkness, the amorous woman repeats her exclamation: "O venture of delight!" And we feel her whole being suspended, concentrated in eagerness—which holds itself back, tensely, when it is on the point of bursting forth: "O venture of delight!" Delight with adventure, with boldness, but without disorder. "I went abroad when all my house was hushed": this is the last line of both the first and second stanzas. The nocturnal departure depends on this sure repose, which opens toward love—with no light other than the light from the heart. ("Blessed is that secret place of the heart that is of such great price that it possesses everything." Letter to Mother María de Jesús, 1589.) This light illuminates so clearly that it is brighter, in the midst of darkness, than "the light of noonday" and "dawn." Never has dawn been suggested with more tender clarity than in this verse: . . .

> Oh night that is more kindly than the dawn!

And the deep peace of consummated love—*Allí quedó dormido,* "There he lay asleep"—abandons itself to the slow rhythm, in an atmosphere of beauty and rapture. The lover sleeps on the beloved's flowering breast. And she "regales" him, *regala.* No expression could be more delicately voluptuous. The decorative elements, robust and graceful—*el ventalle de cedros,* "the airs with which the cedars wave," oriental and Biblical; *el aire de la almena,* "Over the ramparts . . . the fresh wind," medieval and Castilian—are not limited to a decorative role and collaborate in the action: the airs with which the cedars wave act as a fan; the fresh wind from the ramparts is now a hand that suspends the senses, and even more, wounds the neck of the beloved. The violence of the verb "wounds," which might have destroyed the harmony of the moment, is made subject to this harmony, and everything is absorbed by a love absorbed in itself, consummated. This is shown in a crescendo of reiteration by the series of verbs of increasing negation: *quedéme, olvidéme, recliné, cesó, dejéme,* "stayed," "lost to myself," "laid," "ceasing," "releasing." *Dejéme,* literally "I abandoned myself," is followed immediately by *dejando,* "abandoning," in a lightly explanatory tone, less elevated, more prosaic. The level rises again with the oblivion among the lilies: a final picture that is precise, concrete, physically and spiritually pure. Seldom, very seldom has love's consummation been sung as it is in this final stanza, so compact, with its abandonment that is fulfillment.

The same story, passing through the same stages—seeking, finding, consummation—is told again in the second poem, which is considerably longer. (It has two hundred lines; the first, **"Dark Night of the Soul,"** has only forty.) A **"Canticle"**—eclogue. It was also called **"Canciones de la Esposa" ("Songs of the Bride"),** according to a letter to Mother Ana de San Alberto, 1586. The lovers here are shepherds, and the eagerness of the Bride takes her by sheep-folds and river banks, through woods and meadows. Finally the lovers are joined. . . .

> My Love's the mountain range,
> The valleys each with solitary grove.

Against this depth of great landscapes, and not just in immediate rural surroundings, the action unfolds, and its bucolic elements always manifest the most genuine states—spiritual and sensual—of love: absorption, abandonment, rapture, perfect union, perfect bliss. Nature allies herself with passion; and the pastoral details, borrowed from lit-

erary texts, are combined with a story that is very much alive. . . .

> O brook of crystal sheen,
> Could you but cause, upon your silver fine . . .

Everything here is symbolic: everything is what it is, and something more. The amorous Bride, in stanza 13, is a dove, and the Bridegroom calls her this, and with her flight—"fanned by the wind . . . of your flight"—she cools the Bridegroom, a wounded stag. This eclogue, then, is highly dramatic, full of movement, with gradations in intensity which have been superbly analyzed by Dámaso Alonso. Broad spaces, withdrawn and solitary,—with mountains, valleys, islands, streams—are followed by pictures of smiling, early morning brightness: garlands of flowers, flowers interwoven with strands of hair, dewy mornings, clusters of roses. The mountain, *montaña,* becomes a hillock, *montiña,* and not merely because of the exigencies of the rhyme. All is love: "And only now in loving is my duty" *(Que ya sólo en amar es mi ejercicio).* This exercise, or "duty," gives rise to audacious visions: "Which my Beloved browses with his mouth" *(Y pacerá el Amado . . .*). Everything takes place in the open, but without ever losing the reserve of intimacy. The Bride has now fallen asleep; the Bridegroom adores and watches over her sleep. (An admirable theme: to watch love sleeping.) Wishing to protect her sleep with a conjuration, the Bridegroom invokes and evokes the most seductive of all profane music: the song of poets and of sirens.

> By the sweet lyre and call
> Of sirens, now I conjure you to cease
> Your tumults one and all,
> Nor echo on the wall
> That she may sleep securely and at peace.

This wall, thick and solid, is the boundary and the barrier between the world at large and the other world created by love for itself. And the word *muro,* "wall," rises up with prodigious material density impregnated with spirit. No, let "the wall" not be touched, the complete wall protecting the complete couple, withdrawn as always into their fortified castle. Then the couple returns to the fields—the mountain slope, the fountain, the caverns—amid gentler elements: the nightingale, the grove. "The waving charm/ Of groves in beauty seen" *(El soto y su donaire),* with its incredible grace. It is now serene night, . . .

> With fire that can consume yet do no harm.

This line in the next to the last stanza of the **"Canticle"** announces the third poem (the shortest of the three, with twenty-four lines), which refers only to the final stage of the lovers' relationship. This poem is all astounded exclamation and fire, fire that illumines love while it burns in it. . . .

> Oh lamps of fiery blaze
> To whose refulgent fuel
> The deepest caverns of my soul grow bright,
> Late blind with gloom and haze,
> But in this strange renewal
> Giving to the belov'd both heat and light!

We are immediately fascinated by these forms that do not break with the laws of our world. And yet this is another universe, with its own autonomous harmony, sustained by passion and contemplated by the spirit, to the sound of a music that is at once image, feeling, and beauty. By the close interlocking of all these components we are made to feel with persuasive force the intensity of each word, each line, each stanza—without ever losing sight of the closely knit whole. In the poem it may be either night or day, but the language is always luminous, and this light illumines a mystery without making it any the less inaccessible. The melody rises above a silence of solitudes. In this way, with this restrained decorum, the absolute nature of the passion is brought into sharper relief—a passion that seeks, awaits, finds, and at last is fulfilled. Who are these lovers? They are given only generic names: the Bride, the Beloved. Where do they live? Here in these poems, in the world created by these words. The things that happen, throughout the **"Canticle"** and the **"Flame,"** are set before us in a very real present. This is not a past already concluded that the poet reconstructs. Nothing in the poems is alien to the burning actuality which here and now—within the compass of the poem—sets forth its present acts of love.

Poetry is achieved by means of art: the art of the poem. It must be pointed out that San Juan de la Cruz has found the supreme equilibrium between poetry of inspiration and constructed poetry, unlike so many modern writers for whom poetry and art represent an irreconcilable contradiction. (For them any voluntary attempt at fitting or adjustment, any effort to compose, would ruin or nullify the inspiration of the poet, who abandons himself with complete passivity to his muse, or, to say it with scientific pretensions, to his subconscious.) San Juan de la Cruz does not fall into the heresy of quietism either when searching for the treasure or when wishing to display his find. His poem is erected like the most subtle work of architecture, in which each piece has been worked with the most elaborate care in the hope of achieving perfection; and artistic perfection is joined to spiritual. "The soul that walks in love wearies not neither is wearied." Only thus, by loving, artful labor, could he create the marvel that is the **"Dark Night of the Soul,"** a poem of even greater purity perhaps than the **"Spiritual Canticle,"** which is a peerless epithalamium. Who can say at what invulnerable distance, on what heights or in what depths, the marriage of the sublime lovers takes place? Not for a moment does San Juan de la Cruz cease to insist on the three notes which he exalts as no one else has: remoteness, solitude, secrecy. Each word he uses is felt in all its crystalline purity, infinitely refined as the result of a thrusting up from unknown depths. But this deep rooting in no way obstructs or dulls the final accomplishment. Was not the fire sufficient to reach the diamond? Rapture, reserve, serene security . . . These are poems of great love, which has the extremely rare privilege of being happy love. "And where there is no love, put love, and you will find love," was the recommendation of that ardent man. Here there is nothing to do but to find love. As Pedro Salinas says so well: "Everything in San Juan de la Cruz presents an obvious case of clear mystery . . . The trajectory of San Juan's poetry is like that of a bright flash of lightning, shooting like an arrow from darkness to darkness, piercing it and disappearing, leaving the shadows dissipated behind it, and darkness illuminated. The mysterious will continue to be mysterious,

because San Juan in his poems does not explain anything logically, but it will now be clothed in the brightness of the light that pierced it like the light of grace." And Salinas adds: "The final impression is one of pure flame in which absolute poetic unity is attained." (pp. 81-9)

> *Jorge Guillén, "The Ineffable Language of Mysticism: San Juan de la Cruz," in his* Language and Poetry: Some Poets of Spain, *translated by Stephen Gilman and Ruth Whittredge, Cambridge, Mass.: Harvard University Press, 1961, pp. 77-121.*

Leo Spitzer   (essay date 1962)

[*In the following excerpt, Spitzer provides an overview and close analysis of "The Dark Night of the Soul," focusing upon the use of bodily imagery in describing the inner feelings engendered by the mystic experience of the divine. The critic explores St. John of the Cross's depiction of human love as a figuration of divine love as part of the poet's attempt to "express figuratively the spiritual by the physical."*]

[The] Jewish sensibility—and I believe this to be as true today as in the days of the patriarchs—admits the coexistence of the body and the soul in the presence of God, but with no attempt at fusing them. It is then not surprising that a sensuous Oriental epithalamium that had found access to the Jewish biblical canon, the *Song of Songs . . . ,* should have been, by Christian exegesis, transformed into an allegorical treatise of mystic union. And it is this mystical theme that we find in the Spanish poem **"En una noche escura"**—which might be described as a Catholic *Song of Songs* (for, indeed, it derives its inspiration from the reinterpreted Hebrew canticle). This poem, written about 1577 by the Carmelite monk San Juan de la Cruz, is a perfect example of the manner in which the body can be made artistically tributary to the mystic experience. The Catholic saint treats no lesser subject than the ecstatic union, not with a human being, but with the divine, in terms that constantly fuse soul and body. . . . (p. 153)

This poem, as has been recognized by its finest commentators, the Frenchman Baruzi [in his *Saint Jean de la Croix et le problème de l'expérience mystique*] and the Spaniard Dámaso Alonso, [in his *La poesía de San Juan de la Cruz*] falls into three parts: the beginning of the soul's pilgrimage, stanzas 1-4; the arrival and the announcement of the mystic union, stanza 5; and the scene of the union itself, stanzas 6-8. In order to gain insight into the poetic organism, let us begin again by a "list". . . . [We] shall start with an (at first glance) trivial linguistic detail: starting from the point of view of tense usage, let us draw up a list of the preterites used in our short narrative, because it is by these that the action is carried forward: they form, as it were, the dramatic framework, expressing an unbroken development. We shall see them increase at the end of the poem: in Part I there is only *salí,* "I started forth" (stanza 1); in Part II (stanza 5) only *guiaste,* "you [the night] led me," and *juntaste,* "you joined us"; in Part III, in addition to *allí quedó dormido,* "my love fell asleep," of stanza 6, we find five preterites in the last stanza, four of them verbs of bodily movement; the action, as I said, is conceived in bodily terms. This climactic increase in dramatic tenses toward the end coincides, strangely enough, with a decrease in voluntary or dynamic action on the part of the protagonist: the loving soul that in Part I started forth resolutely on its pilgrimage, is, in Part II, led forward by the night, and it is the night that joins the soul with its Beloved (who is himself passive: *quedó dormido*)—whereupon all striving ceases; and the activity of the soul in the last stanza is one of gradual self-extinction: *cesó todo*. This contrast between the accumulation of dramatic tenses and the *smorzando* of the activities they express is paradoxical: the climax of action is reached in non-action, in the receiving of the mystic invasion (which can be only a gift of divine grace), in self-annihilation. The first preterite *salí* was an élan motivated "con ansias en amores inflamada," by the burning anxiety of the flame of love; the *dejéme* of the end, though expressing self-abandonment, melts immediately into "dejando mi cuidado . . . olvidado" ("leaving my sorrow forgotten"): the cessation of all perturbation. The action of the Spanish poem, which begins with a movement dictated by pain and by the will to still pain, ends with the achievement of self-forgetfulness free from pain.

After having gained a bird's-eye view of the whole and of the salient features of its structure, let us now return to the beginning and seek to analyze in their turn the three parts we have isolated.

In the first stanza, as has already been said, the outstanding word which starts the movement of the poem is *salí*. But we may ask ourselves: who is it that started forth? Who is the protagonist of the poem? The participle *inflamada* (stanza 1), followed by *notada* and later by *amada* and *transformada* (stanza 5), would seem to indicate a feminine being; and since this being speaks of joining her Beloved *(Amado)*, we might be justified in seeing the action in terms of an earthly love. Or is this feminine aspect predicated only of that spiritual being, the soul (Spanish *alma*, a word never mentioned in our poem), eternally conceived as feminine? This ambiguity is obviously intended by the author not only because of his desire to express figuratively the spiritual by the physical: it is true also that, just because the identity of the protagonist is presented as self-evident, as needing no elucidation, we are drawn immediately into the atmosphere of the one who speaks of her love, and we can share, unquestioningly, in her experience, as this develops in the poem.

To return again to *salí*: whence was this departure? From what background does this sudden movement emerge? But it is only the first two stanzas *taken together* that give us this background; indeed, these two stanzas must, as Dámaso Alonso has pointed out, be taken as one sentence (not to be separated by a period, as is done in all the editions): they contain the same rhymes and, if considered as a unit, the opening period will show that *parellelismus membrorum* characteristic of the Hebrew model (the *Song of Songs*). . . . These musical, even dance-like cadences help situate our poem in the climate of Biblical mystery, in which movements that would seem erratic to the uninitiated are guided by Providence. In the stillness of the night we hear those mysterious accents, supported, as it were, by *word-motifs* which repeat themselves with a consistency suggestive of continuity of will and purpose. Here the repetitions are not destined to bring one concept to full clarity by ever-new similes . . .; instead, we find a few very simple word-motifs parsimoniously repeated with only slight variation: indeed "¡Oh dichosa ventura!" is repeated without change, as is also "estando ya mi casa sosegada": these establish the homology of the two stanzas. Again in the sequence "en una noche escura—a escuras y segura—a escuras y en celada" we find one word *(escuro)* thrice repeated—while in the sequence "sin ser notada—secreta escala disfrazada—en celada" we have only thematic affinity, but still affinity. Not that there is always a musical *echo*: gentle contrasts may be heard: it is a soul stirred by passion that leaves the house now wrapped in silence *(inflamada—sosegada);* the darkness of the night *(a escuras)* is in opposition to the sureness of the purpose *(segura).* And the rhyming of *ventura* with *segura* also suggests a contradiction—though this is softened by the fact that the adventure is called *dichosa* ("blessed"). The decision of the soul is, indeed, a *venture* into the unknown, an *adventure,* not in the trivial sense of today (a capricious interruption of everyday life), but in the sense in which it has been said that in the Middle Ages all of life was an adventure: man's venturesome quest for the *advent* of the divine. The soul that has here decided to meet the divine has engaged itself in an existential adventure, and we are assured of a response from the divine by the epithet *dichosa.* And the word *escala,* with its suggestion of height, is the symbol of the upward development of the soul (we may remember the mystic ladder of Bernard de Clairvaux).

The next two stanzas (which I would translate as follows: "In the happy night, in secrecy—for no one saw me nor saw I aught but the light of my heart—, this light, brighter than the noon-day sun, did guide me to the one whom I knew to be in a place accessible to none other") should also be taken together (though this suggestion has not been made by others) because of the same rhymes in *-ía* and also because of a discreet parallelism which runs through them. Here we find again the alternation of motifs which assures the continuous flow of the poem: the words *dichosa* and *secreta* of stanza 2 re-appear; *sin ser notada* of stanza 1 is continued by *nadie me veía*, and *en celada* of stanza 2 by *en parte donde nadie parecía*. We may also note that in this pair of stanzas the one main verb is the imperfect *guiaba*. Once the decision is made, announced dramatically by the preterite *salí*, the action may subside to a calm, steady, prolonged rhythm, suggestive of firm direction. And we sense a new note of serenity and clarity: *en una noche escura* has given way to *en la noche dichosa;* night has now become a familiar medium in which the soul knows its way. In this darkness a light appears which shines from the heart; and this light is first introduced negatively (*"without* a light . . . save that . . . "*), as if, thereby, made to emerge out of darkness. It is this radiance by which the soul is guided *(guía—guiaba)* more surely than by the brightness of noon-day. And with the first line of stanza 4 there is suggested an outburst of glad relief: *aquesta me guiaba,* "this, this was my guide." Out of the maze of the third stanza, which suggests the movement of the soul as it feels its way through the darkness, there emerges, like a clearing, the sure guide; the wondrous light, which was first suggested tentatively (negatively as we have said) in a dependent clause, is now, in the main clause, hailed openly: *aquesta. . . .* The sentence structure is thus allowed to translate the consistent progress of the soul that has striven, encouraged by an inner hope *(segura—dichosa),* until now the light within her shines around her, beyond her, toward the goal, now well discerned *(adonde),* toward that one *(quien)* whose dwelling-place is instinctively known to her ("one whom I knew to be in a place accessible to none other"). Here we have the idea of secret, exclusive knowledge, just as earlier there were suggestions of a secret, clandestine journey (the mystic ladder was "camouflaged," *disfrazada).* This motif of surreptitious love may be ultimately a remnant of the social-poetic conventions of the Troubadour love-poetry, but it has acquired with Juan de la Cruz a mystical sense; since Christian mysticism represents the highest development of the Christian belief in a personal God, Who conditions the immortal soul of man, as this, in turn, presupposes God—the *mystic* soul, then, is able to affirm its knowledge of that individual God, as it were, as its *personal* possession in isolation, even in secrecy. With these last lines the pilgrimage has come to an end: with the allusion to *quien* "one who" (that ambiguous pronoun which posits an individual without revealing his identity). Later, this beloved individual here alluded to by *quien* will appear as *amado* (line 4, stanza 5) and finally as *el Amado* (in the following line).

We have been led, by the technique of musical variation and of a gradual syntactical unfolding, from the *noche escura* to the light that is brighter than day, from loneliness to the meeting with Him who is the divine goal—from what the Greeks would call $\sigma\tau\epsilon\rho\eta\sigma\iota\delta$ ("privation") to $\epsilon\xi\iota\delta$ ("possession"). These are basically terms of logic and indeed we find the idea of privation, of absence of positive characteristics, rendered by such negative grammatical elements as *sin, nadie, ni . . . cosa, sin, nadie,* which lead to the positive *aquesta* and *quien,* to fulfilment: "seeing nothing" leads to seeing the Beloved. Mysticism, indeed, posits privation, renunciation, and purgation as the starting-point toward fulfilment: expanding the Christian tenet that to have-not is ultimately to have, that only by closing one's eyes to the outward world does one truly see (the eyes of the heart, *oculi cordis,* are keener than the eyes of the senses), and that the light of the heart shines brighter than any other light.

And now we understand the jubilant exclamations with which the next part (consisting of one stanza alone) begins:

> ¡Oh noche, que guiaste,
> Oh noche amable más que el alborada,
> Oh noche, que juntaste . . . !

Here, too, there is a paradox: "night that didst guide." It is more natural to think of the light that guides: but, then, as we know, the night has become light ($\sigma\tau\epsilon\rho\eta\sigma\iota\delta$ appears in the splendor of $\epsilon\xi\iota\delta$). And this radiant night has also "joined together" *(juntaste).* This *juntaste* is the climax of the sequence *guiaba—guiaste—juntaste;* we have already noted that in *aquesta me guiaba* there was a new note of tranquillity (the momentum of will-power, originally announced by *salí,* has subsided, as the soul yields

to the inner light); now with *¡oh noche que juntaste!* the guidance has become a successfully accomplished fact, and the initiative passes from the light of the heart to the *night* itself; and it is the night alone which brings about the union. This poetic symbol of the night, as the mediator of the spiritual marriage, is original with Juan de la Cruz, as Baruzi has pointed out—who would also distinguish between the *symbol* of the night as it is used in our poem, and the *allegory* of the night as we find this elaborated in the prose commentaries of our author. For whereas allegory consists of an intellectual play wherein a series of fixed qualities belonging to one realm are made to correspond to a series of fixed qualities belonging to another realm (so that a literal "translation" is possible at any stage), a symbol represents an emotional identification of a complex of feelings with one outward object which, once the initial identification has been achieved, produces itself ever-new images, with their own rhythm and their own development, not always translatable. The symbol continually unfolds before us in time, while the allegory once developed is fixed forever, as is the relationship of its details. The allegory of love in the *Roman de la Rose* can be translated step by step; for example, the rose is characterized by thorns, by a delightful odor, etc., the allegorical implications of all of which are obvious. But the cross of Christ is a symbol: once Christ's suffering has been symbolized by that particular wooden instrument of torture, once Christ has "taken the cross on Himself," this Cross may become, in time, the "balance" on whose scales the sins of the world are weighed, the "tree" of life that conquers death, the "lyre" of Orpheus, etc. And with Juan de la Cruz the night is a similarly untranslatable symbol, generative of new situations and emotions which must be grasped as they unfold in time: it was first only the medium in which the lonely soul started its venturesome journey; now it has become the guide and (here no "translation" is actually possible) even the mediator between the Lover and the Beloved. Indeed the night itself is drawn into the atmosphere of *amar: noche amable.* Perhaps there is suggested an equation between night and love; surely it is love which joins the lovers, and yet it has been said of the night: "¡oh noche que juntaste . . . !" Therefore night = love. And, together with *amado* and *amada,* our *noche amable* forms a triangle (implying the triune relationship). The three variations of the stem *amar* are symbolical of this mystic alchemy.

The *noche amable* which figures as the basic essence of the union, of the transformation of the *amada* into the *amado,* is actually referred to in line 2 of stanza 5 as "amable más que la alborada" (more lovely than the dawn). Here we may see a continuation of the motif (stanza 4), "más cierto que la luz del mediodía" (night more precious than day), in which the normal evaluation of night and day is reversed. The praise of the night at the expense of the day is also quite contrary to the tendency in the Christian hymns, of hailing the morning star or the crowing of the cock as signs of the defeat of the powers of darkness and evil by those of good. Nor, obviously, is our apostrophe: "¡oh noche amable más que la alborada!" to be compared to the "o vere beata nox!" of the Holy Saturday liturgy, which prepares the believer for the more important, the all-important resurrection of the Lord, which will take place on Easter Sunday. Perhaps the poetic inspiration may be traced here not only to the general tradition of Christian mysticism, but also (again) to the Troubadour genre called the *alba,* in which so often the glory of the night, the night of love, is extolled to the disparagement of dawn. Of course, the dramatic situation is not the same: there is no friendly guard posted on the tower to warn the lovers (often in vain) of the danger of approaching dawn—for here no danger need be feared by the lovers.

And here it should be remarked that the mystical metamorphosis as described by Juan de la Cruz . . . implies no complementary transformation . . . ; that is, no equality between the lovers. . . . If our Catholic poet is able to use human love as a figuration of love for the divine, this is because human love itself, according to age-old tradition, implies no equality: the bride submits to the bridegroom.

We have treated stanza 5 as representing the lyrical culmination of the poem, an interpretation borne out linguistically by the sequence of three apostrophes to the night. This exclamatory style has already been foreshadowed by the repetition of "¡oh dichosa ventura!", parenthetically inserted. But now the exultant note comes to full *épanouissement*—and is expressed in a pattern which, in Judeo-Christian liturgy . . . , was reserved for addressing the deity: a vocative, followed by relative clauses describing the triumphs or the favors of God, and usually followed in turn by a request for further favors (though, in our poem, no additional divine favor can be desired; the soul wishes only to pour forth its gratefulness to the charismatic power of love).

And now the scene of the *unio mystica:* with the first lines of stanza 6, we sense immediately a new stillness and composure—after the exultant, ringing notes of the preceding stanza. Let us note first the word *pecho* ("breast")—a word capable of both a moral meaning (here, perhaps, "the heart") and, of course, a physical meaning. It is surely in the moral sense that we must understand line 2: "que entero para él solo se guardaba" (which kept itself entire for Him alone), a line which makes explicit for the first time the motivation, the monogamic motivation, of the pilgrimage: of that *salí* which may have first appeared prompted by sudden passion, but is now revealed as springing from deep-set faithfulness to the divine. And yet with *pecho florido* of the first line, which means, no doubt, "flower-scented breast," a suggestion of the sensuous is inescapable; here the disembodied soul whose progress we have followed acquires a mystical body. The prepositional phrase "en mi pecho florido" may remind us of the similar phrases "en una noche oscura" and "en la noche dichosa": the framework of the background of the dark night gives way to that flower-scented breast on which the Beloved reposes: "En mi pecho florido . . . Allí quedó dormido."

But in this *allí* ("on my breast, *there* he rested"), in this logically superfluous, somehow idiomatic adverb, do we not feel an emotional insistence ("there, in this place") as if on the breast as a goal attained—by the Beloved? So far, we have treated the pilgrimage only as a striving of the soul toward her own goal. And in describing her expectation we have, perhaps, passed over too easily the reference, in stanza 4, to the Bridegroom who was waiting *(esperaba),* waiting at the trysting-place. By now, in this one word

allí we may catch the delicate suggestion of the quiet, steadfast yearning of the divine for the human soul—whose relief from longing is now declared in the gently climactic *allí* (surely an echo of that *aquesta,* that sigh of relief with which the Bride greeted the guiding light). There the divine sleeps. And it is while he sleeps that the soul knows its final mystic rapture (described only in the last stanza). This sleep of Christ, how is it to be understood? (The critics, all of them silent on this point, must have thought only of the Bridegroom of the *Song of Songs,* who is shown "as a bundle of myrrh, that lieth betwixt my breasts"; but it is not said there that he is sleeping.) The only suggestion that seems satisfactory to me is the hallowed medieval legend of the Unicorn, who, as the symbol of Christ, falls to sleep on the sweet-smelling breast of a virgin. Against this background, the *pecho florido* "that kept itself entire for Him alone" acquires a particular significance. And, in the idyllic scene centered about the quiescent divine, all activity is subdued, all the participants are hushed: divinity, the human soul, and Nature—the latter figured by the cedar trees (suggesting a Biblical landscape) gently fanned by the air. The idyllic quality of the scene is enhanced by the repetition of *and* which suggests never-ending tenderness: ("y yo le regalaba / y el ventalle de cedros aire daba"). The word *aire* is repeated in the first line of the next stanza; we seem still to be in the same gentle atmosphere lulled by a soft breeze—which perhaps plays with the hair of the Beloved as the Bride spreads it to the air. But let us not be deceived; it is "el aire del almena," the air from the battlement *(almena,* the Spanish word of Arabic origin, implies a medieval castle and its tower). Does this not suggest warfare, sudden attack, hostile arrows? Dámaso Alonso has not sensed this military note: to him the tower is a place of pleasant refuge to which the lovers have ascended, to enjoy, according to him, the air gently blowing between the turrets. But between these two contradictory pictures evoked by two interpreters let common sense decide: are even the cedars of Lebanon tall enough to reach up to the turrets? And the lilies of the last stanza—would they be growing on the tower? No, surely the lovers are at the *foot* of the tower (among the lilies), beneath the cedar trees.

And from this turreted tower, something strikes and wounds *(hería);* it must be, though this has been suggested by no other critic, *the arrow of love,* the arrow by which Saint Teresa was pierced, in the scene made graphically familiar to us by the statue of Bernini. Our scene, of course, is not to be visualized so concretely, so plastically, or with such harrowing effect; the arrow that strikes the unprotected neck is still only the air, and it strikes gently "con su mano serena"—but it finds its mark and leaves sweet death in its wake. This is the moment of ecstasy and annihilation ("todos mis sentidos suspendía"), the familiar "theopathic" state experienced by all mystics and often described by them as a blend of heavenly sweetness and piercing pain. And the gentle hand that wounds suggests a bold personification which does not, however, quite materialize: the "aire del almena" does not harden into a figure of definable contours (least of all into the figure of the gay archer Cupid of Bernini): it remains in the state of that *vaporoso* atmosphere of a Murillo. It is an intangible, an immaterial agent which, by an imperceptible activity, produces the climactic effect—while Christ sleeps. Is this air that wounds with serenity a symbol of the Holy Ghost, who is often compared, in Juan de la Cruz' commentaries, with air (cf. the relationship of Latin *spiritus* with *spirare,* "to breathe")? Perhaps we cannot hope to penetrate the veil of mystery with which the Spanish Saint has wished to conceal as well as to reveal the mystery of the inactive activity, the Nature-like activity of the deity.

And now the last stanza, which may be said to render acoustically the gradual extinction of life: a love-death. Even before we come to this stanza we have learned that all the senses are suspended—as ours too must be: the sensations which had been earlier aroused (the olfactory sense [the flowers], the sense of touch [the air]) by now are numbed; the life of the senses, which came to its highest intensity in the mystic union, recedes; these have been stimulated by the poet only to make us realize the *spiritual* eroticism experienced by the mystic soul that will *abandon* the life of the senses. And this condition of deprivation or στερησις is very aptly symbolized by the immaculately white lilies *(azucenas),* delicately profiled against the dawn, which lack a positive color (unlike the pomegranate of the love-scene in the *Song of Songs*); the Umbrian mystic Jacopone da Todi says of the mystic soul engulfed in the sea of God: "en ben sí va notando / belleza contemplando la qual non ha colore," "all its feeling swims in sweetness: it contemplates a beauty which has no color." The suggestion of beatific nothingness, of gradual Lethean self-forgetfulness, is achieved in our poem by a combination of two devices: we are offered a picture of bodily relaxation, leading to psychic extinction *(recliné mi rostro, dejéme),* together with an acoustic effect of lulling incantation, produced by the monotonous repetitions of sounds. As for the first, *el rostro recliné,* "I let my face fall," suggests clearly the physical; *dejéme,* "I abandoned myself," perhaps a blend of the physical and the spiritual; while, of course, *dejando mi cuidado,* "leaving my sorrow forgotten . . . ," describes purely a state of the soul. The psycho-physical and the active-inactive aspect of the mystic experience could not be better expressed than by this ambivalent *dejar.* As for the acoustic devices, we may note the two variations on the verb *dejar (dejéme—dejando)* and the two on *olvidar,* "to forget" *(olvidéme—olvidado),* and particularly the repetition of the rhyme in *-éme.* *(quedéme—olvidéme—dejéme),* which suggests a gradual sinking into the abyss of forgetfulness. And in the words "dejéme, / Dejando mi cuidado / Entre las azucenas olvidado," which offer a final, lingering cadence, we have a transition from the act of abandoning the world to the state resulting from this act: oblivion attained. In the final word *olvidado,* "already forgotten," this state is presented as an accomplished fact which must have taken place, somehow, before—so that when we actually come to the word *olvidado,* we know we have left it behind. The soul *is* already resolved in God. And this "already," the temporal adverb that I see implied in *dejando,* is the counterpart to the explicit *ya,* "already," of the first stanzas ("estando ya mi casa sosegada"): from the beginning to the end of the poem we are reminded of the progress in time of the mystic experience.

Juan de la Cruz has been able to transcribe the unbroken line, the parabola of that experience in its evolution from energetic pursuit to self-annihilation, from human to divine action—and this is a short poem of eight stanzas (as though the poet would suggest that what happened with such intensity cannot be measured by man-devised clock-time), a poem in which mystery is presented with the greatest clarity and simplicity (as though he felt that his experience, which may be given only to the elect, has nevertheless a limpid quality that even a child could understand).

For, unlike such a German mystic as Jacob Böhme, who resorts to new coinages in the attempt to express the inexpressible, adding the mystery of words to the mysterious experience, our poet, following the sober Latin tradition of all religious writing in Romance languages, is content with the stock of words already given by the language and, even here, limits himself to a restricted number. At the same time, however, he multiplies, by repetition, variation, and syntactical disposition, the density of the web of semantic interrelations, resuscitating the memories (memories of the soul and of the flesh) that are latent in popular terms. Thus, although the poem contains only familiar Spanish words which can be understood by the Spaniards of today as well as they were in the sixteenth century (perhaps with the exception of the Gallicism *ventalle,* "fan"), these words have become endowed with a mystical depth which makes them appear as new words (though they *are, pace* Mr. Shapiro, the old words). And we have again a suggestion of profundity coupled with simplicity in the easy, though far from trivial, musicality of our poem. This is written in the meter of the *lira,* that solemn, ode-like form which, however, becomes singable thanks to the predominance of *one* rhyme in each stanza—in our poem of a feminine rhyme by which the musicality of the Spanish verse is still more enhanced; nor do the consonants that occur in these bisyllabic rhymes, mainly evanescent spirants [-b- and -d-], detract from the vocalic character of this language, but rather suggest the soft breathing of the "aire del almena."

It could be said that, in Juan de la Cruz' mystic poetry, there is to be seen a development of Spanish Renaissance lyricism away from its learned, verbally ornate character—perhaps through the influence of the sublime Biblical poetry of the *Song of Songs,* which, in turn, we find with him desensualized: the sensual world of that epithalamium has become with him a borderland between the realm of the senses and that of the soul. Such a poetic blend was possible for a poet in whom the Renaissance poetic ideal of outward beauty and clarity has met with the tradition of medieval mysticism centered in inward contemplation.

But there is, perhaps, an important problem to be faced before we leave this poem: the expression of mystic experience in a manner that appeals to the sensuous realm, the presentation of mystic love in terms that could be taken as describing erotic pleasure—is this not sacrilegious? Is it not the pagan subsoil of Catholicism that comes here to the surface? Many of you, while listening to my explanation, must have asked yourselves, more or less explicitly, such questions—since, in our own age, to which few religious geniuses have been given, the Saint's psychophysic

A statue of St. John of the Cross in the Church of St. Teresa in Avila.

or theopathic experience is not self-evident. I would say simply that the description of the mystical event in physical terms gives a graphic effect of *actuality* which might not have been achieved otherwise. Here, too, though in another sense, the body serves as a necessary "alloy": that which gives concreteness to the elusive emotion. The documentary value of our poem we must accept with reverence. Here, truly, beauty is truth and truth beauty: the beauty of the mystic's description testifies to its veracity, and the evidence with which that concrete happening develops before us in time is undoubtable: we know that this event *has happened.* We may remember that the capacity of giving the evidence of the flesh and of temporal development to spiritual experience is first found with the greatest medieval poet, Dante, who, in the place of timeless allegories of the perfect Beloved, substituted the graphic image of a Beatrice who actually walks, smiles, sighs, within a poem that has a beginning, a middle and an end. . . . Modern lyricism, even of a worldly kind, is indebted to such religious poets as Dante and Juan de la Cruz for the evidence (evidence of the flesh and evidence of time) which they have given forever to the description of inner feeling. (pp. 155-71)

Leo Spitzer, "Three Poems on Ecstasy: John Donne, St. John of the Cross, Richard Wagner," *in his* Essays on English and American Literature, *edited by Anna Hatcher, Princeton University Press, 1962, pp. 139-79.*

Kieran Kavanaugh, O. C. D.   (essay date 1964)

[*Kavanaugh is a Roman Catholic priest of the Order of the Discalced Carmelites. A translator specializing in the works of the Spanish mystics, he prepared, along with Otilio Rodriguez, an English edition of* The Collected Works of St. John of the Cross *(1964); he also translated* The Collected Works of St. Teresa of Avila *(1976). In the excerpt below, Kavanaugh provides a brief overview of the writings of St. John of the Cross, touching on poetry and prose representative of his two key themes: "the way leading to union with God, and the life itself of divine union."*]

In considering the doctrinal-literary production of St. John of the Cross, it is at once obvious that it is not comparable in quantity and thematic variety to the works of many of the other doctors of the Church, of St. Augustine, for example, or St. Gregory, or St. Thomas Aquinas. Leaving aside those writings attributed to him without adequate foundation, and those which have never been found but of which there is testimony, we number only three major treatises: *The Ascent of Mount Carmel-The Dark Night; The Spiritual Canticle;* and *The Living Flame of Love.* The remainder of his writings comprise relatively few letters, various maxims and counsels, and his poems. All his works that have come down to us were written during the last fourteen years of his life, between the age of thirty-six and forty-nine, after he had attained an intellectual and spiritual maturity. A study of his doctrine discloses that his synthesis of the spiritual life was substantially complete in his mind once he began to write, and thus there is no essential change of thought in his teaching. A study of his writings does not reveal, as is the case with other writers, ideas representing an earlier period of thought which can then be contrasted with those of a later period. The themes with which he mainly deals are also constant: the way leading to union with God, and the life itself of divine union. (p. 33)

With the exception of the *Sayings of Light and Love* and some of his letters—whose autographs are conserved—St. John of the Cross's original writings have been lost, and thus his works have reached us only through numerous codices containing more or less faithful copies. (p. 34)

In the field of Spanish literature, St. John of the Cross has won a prominent place, particularly for his poetry. As a poet he is ranked among the greatest in the history of Spain. Such eminent critics as Menéndez Pelayo and Dámaso Alonso have confessed to a religious terror they felt before the beauty and the burning passion of his verses.

His prose style, on the other hand, has not gained such certain praise. It is in the main didactic and often discursive, especially in the *Ascent.* Concerned with the practical goals of teaching, of pointing out the way that leads to perfection, St. John obviously made no particular effort to phrase his ideas in graceful, stylish, and impeccable prose. We find it quite unpolished (he himself complained of his style), cluttered with repetitions, redundancies, ambiguities, split constructions that are often complicated and obscure, Latinisms, and so on. His long, labyrinthine sentences have not infrequently proved a challenge to his editors seeking clear punctuation. We have the fantastic example in a recent Spanish edition of his works in which one sentence has been buttressed with fifty commas, four semicolons, two uses of parentheses, and a use of the dash. In spite of all, however, there are not lacking prose passages in which the Mystical Doctor shows plainly his literary genius for expressing a thought in phrases of beauty, originality, and power.

In doctrine, there is no longer any doubt concerning the mark he has left in the area of ascetical and mystical theology. Manuals in spiritual theology more and more reflect the theologian's dependence upon St. John of the Cross in the arrangement of the subject-matter and the resolution of thorny problems. But wonderfully combining both the practical and the theoretical, his works, while appealing to psychologists, philosophers, and theologians, have never failed to appeal as well to a large number of the devout who are not specialists.

In the bull proclaiming St. John of the Cross a Doctor of the Church, placing the Church's highest approval upon his writings, Pius XI declared:

> Although they treat of difficult and profound matters, *The Ascent of Mount Carmel, The Dark Night of the Soul, The Living Flame of Love,* and several other shorter works and letters written by him, are nevertheless full of such sound spiritual doctrine and are so well suited to the reader's understanding, that they are rightly looked upon as a code and guide for the faithful soul endeavoring to embrace a more perfect life.

Subsequent to this declaration of Pius XI, Jacques Maritain, in his introduction to Pere Bruno's life of the Saint, has perhaps summed up as well as any scholar the significance of the Mystical Doctor in our age:

> The doctrine of St. John of the Cross is the pure Catholic doctrine of the mystical life. We may well believe that, if he has been proclaimed in our own days a Doctor of the Church, it is because, like Thomas Aquinas, he meets a special need of the age. At the present day, Naturalism has so ruined and subverted Nature that there is no possible healing for Nature itself, no possible return to the stable order of reason, save by a full and complete recognition of the rights of the supernatural, the absolute, the demands of the Gospel and of living faith.
>
> (pp. 34-5)

Kieran Kavanaugh, O. C. D., "General Introduction," The Collected Works of St. John of the Cross, translated by Kieran Kavanaugh and Otilio Rodriguez, 1964. Reprint by Thomas Nelson and Sons Ltd., 1966, pp. 15-38.

Benjamin Gibbs (essay date 1976)

[*Below, Gibbs summarizes the saint's doctrine of mystical contemplation. He outlines the steps St. John describes as essential to true union with God, elucidating the concept of the Dark Night.*]

St. John is regarded as one of the great Spanish poets, though his output was slight in quantity. His mystical treatises are commentaries on poems which he wrote in 1577 while imprisoned at Toledo by Carmelites of the Observance. *The Ascent of Mount Carmel* and *The Dark Night of the Soul* are parts of a single commentary on the first two stanzas of the poem **"Dark Night."** *The Spiritual Canticle* and *The Living Flame of Love* are commentaries on the poems of the same names. There are passages in these writings where St. John, like less sophisticated authors, seems to suggest that mystical contemplation is utterly inexpressible and incommunicable: but the suggestion is usually hedged with qualifications. He says the subject is 'extraordinary and obscure,' and that what he says will seem 'somewhat obscure and prolix' to persons without experience of contemplation. All he can give us is figures, comparisons and similitudes, not rational explanations; and these similitudes,

> if they are not read with the simplicity of the spirit of love and understanding embodied in them, appear to be nonsense rather than the expression of reason.

These warnings reflect St. John's adherence to a theory of meaning which derives from a crude empiricist epistemology alien to the mind of St. Thomas Aquinas. But it should be borne in mind also that his treatises were addressed primarily to particular groups of nuns in his own Carmelite Order, who were often only moderately well educated, ignorant of theology, and sometimes in the grip of superstitious misconceptions about mystical contemplation.

What is mystical contemplation? The neo-Platonists thought of it as a kind of esoteric knowledge gained by exercising the highest faculties. St. John of the Cross, however, is not a philosophical mystic; on the contrary, he ties natural knowledge to what is obtained from sensory experience. In this life, he says, the understanding can grasp nothing but what is contained within, and comes under the category of, forms and imaginings of things that are received through the bodily senses. We can understand clearly only what falls under genus and species. St. John's motive in depreciating the senses is not, as the neo-Platonists' motive was, to exalt the intellect. He thinks the poverty of the intellect in forming an idea of God follows directly from the inability of the senses to supply it with materials suitable for forming such an idea. We cannot comprehend God by our imagination or by our natural intelligence, and nothing that can be imagined or of which we can form a concept can serve as a means to union with him.

> All distinct images and kinds of knowledge, both natural and supernatural, that can be encompassed by the faculties of the soul, however lofty they be in this life, have no comparison with the Being of God.

In practice, like everyone else, St. John regularly uses terms such as 'good', 'true', 'similar', 'existence', 'not' and so on, which do not stand for anything perceptible or imaginable and are not definable *per genus et differentiam.* To recognize the indispensability of such terms, and the naivety of St. John's epistemology, is not of course to imply that we can after all form an adequate idea of the nature of God.

St. John would deny also that mystical contemplation is an experience which follows, as a natural sequel, programmes of physical and spiritual asceticism, or taking drugs. Contemplation is bestowed by God alone, and cannot be merited, let alone produced, by human efforts, however intricate or strenuous. He does not deny that philosophy, fasting or drug-taking may lead to thrilling experiences; but he denies that any experiences so got are genuine instances of contemplation. Moreover, he rejects the idea that true mystics are visionaries, persons who enjoy extraordinary experiences such as trances or levitations. He does not deny that such things happen, but he attributes them to imperfection or psychic disharmony in the subject. Perhaps he would have agreed with those many modern writers who claim that the intrinsic character of certain extraordinary experiences is the same whether they are produced by a lot of strenuous effort, such as fasting and meditation, or got easily, by taking a drug. Perhaps the study of all such so-called mystical experiences belongs properly to biochemistry and psychopathology.

According to St. John of the Cross, genuine mystical contemplation, in its purest form, is so hidden and secret that the subject may be unaware he is receiving it. Visions and hallucinations are a sign that the subject is spiritually imperfect, even if he has not striven to produce them. Raptures and torments of the body no longer exist among the perfect, because they are enjoying liberty of spirit and their senses are neither clouded nor transported. Even if a vision does come from God, it is less precious in his sight than a single act done in charity, because it calls for neither praise nor blame. Many souls who have known nothing of such things have made incomparably greater progress than others who have received many of them. If extraordinary experiences occur the subject should ignore them; for the only proximate and proportionate means whereby the soul is united with God is faith.

Nevertheless, it is possible, according to St. John, for a person who renounces the world and devotes himself in perfect detachment to the service of God, to come for short periods, even in this life, to a supernatural contemplation of God. This is not an anticipation of the Beatific Vision, but an 'obscure and general' knowledge of God, for the mystic like other men must walk by faith; yet it can prepare a man so perfectly that when he dies the light of glory will be bestowed on him at once. St. John defines mystical contemplation as

> an infused and loving knowledge of God, which enlightens the soul and at the same time enkindles it with love, until it is raised up step by step, even unto God its creator.

While in the way of nature it is impossible to love if one does not first understand what one is to love, nevertheless in the supernatural way God can readily infuse love and increase it without infusing or increasing distinct knowledge . . . And this is the experience of many spiritual persons, who often find themselves burning in the love of God without having a more distinct knowledge of him than before.

The loving knowledge which the soul receives passively from God is like heat-giving light, for the light of contemplation also enkindles the soul in love.

Contemplation cannot be secured by virtuous living and spiritual exercises; it is God's gift, which he bestows on whom he pleases. Not even half of those who embark upon a cloistered vocation are brought by God to contemplation. The subject may however dispose himself for the reception of the gift, by setting out to detach himself from every created thing. The one thing necessary is the ability to deny oneself, giving oneself up to suffering for Christ's sake, and to total annihilation. The soul will not be able to pass to union with God till it empties itself from desire of anything, natural or supernatural, which may hinder it. One must reject every pleasure presenting itself to the senses that is not purely for the honour and glory of God. This self-denial is so difficult as to be a kind of 'dark night' to the senses. But the dark night of sense has another aspect, more effective and important than what the subject's own efforts can achieve. God himself begins to act upon the soul. This is the beginning of mystical contemplation. In receiving it a person is completely passive, like someone who has his eyes open 'so that light is communicated to him passively without his doing more than keep them open.' A man may labour hard at purifying himself, but he will not be prepared for divine union unless God plunges him into that 'dark fire' which is contemplation. The novice should spend his time in discursive meditation, exercising his faculties; but eventually all such activity must cease, so that God may of his own accord unite the soul to himself. Just when the beginner is going about his spiritual exercises with the greatest delight and pleasure, and believes the sun of divine favour is shining brightly upon him, God turns all that light into darkness.

> He leaves them so completely in the dark that they know not where to go with their sensible imagination and meditation; for they cannot advance a step in meditation, as they used to do, their inward senses being submerged in this night, and left with such dryness that not only do they experience no pleasure and consolation in the spiritual things and good exercises wherein they used to find their delights and pleasures, but instead, on the contrary, they find insipidity and bitterness in the said things.

God is drawing near and paralysing the natural operation of the faculties, so that the subject will live by faith. The contemplative now fails to find pleasure in the thought of any creature; he thinks painfully of his failure to serve God, and is full of grief at his inability to pray effectively as (it seems to him) he used to do. God is transmitting a purely spiritual benefit to the soul, for the reception of which the sensual part has no capacity. Sense is left without savour and too weak for action; but the spirit goes forward in strength, the subject becoming more alert and solicitous not to fail God than he was before. St. John says that in time infused contemplation will be received as a subtle pleasure; but the refreshment of it is so delicate that ordinarily it will not be received if one desires it, like the air which, if one would close one's hand upon it, escapes.

A man may spend a long time, even years, in the dark night of sense. Eventually he comes forth as from an imprisonment, and goes about his spiritual duties with greater freedom and satisfaction. He no longer has to bother with the distracting activities of novices, and readily finds serene and loving contemplation without the labour of meditation. But subtle imperfections remain in the soul; and the person will not reach full union with God till he passes through a second 'night' worse than the first, 'horrible and awful to the spirit.' In the first 'night' the sensual part of the soul was subdued to the spirit. Now the spiritual part of the soul has to be purged and stripped and made ready for union in love. The night of sense is common, St. John says; but the night of the spirit is the portion of very few, and those that are already practised and proficient. This night is an intensified return of passive contemplation, aimed at freeing the soul from everything that holds it back from God; it is 'an inflowing of God into the soul.' It is called 'night' because divine things are dark and hidden to the faculties in their natural operation. If we look directly at the sun it overcomes and darkens our vision; similarly, when the light of contemplation assails the imperfect soul, it overwhelms and dislocates the intellect. Another reason for speaking of contemplation as 'dark night' is that the purity of God's wisdom causes misery in the sinful soul. The fire of divine love, in acting upon the soul, at first makes it seem black and evil and worse than it was. The person never realized so many faults were rooted in him, but now the light of contemplation illuminates them, and he fears that he will never be worthy and that all good things are over for him. But God is humbling the soul only in order that he may afterwards exalt it. The same fire which assails the soul in order to purge it will later be united with the soul to glorify it. Eventually the soul will be transformed, and take on something of the divine nature. When a person's will and God's will are 'conformed together in one,' God will possess all the faculties of the soul and will move them according to his Spirit, so that all the operations of the soul will be divine. (pp. 532-36)

> *Benjamin Gibbs, "Mysticism and the Soul," in*
> The Monist, *Vol. 59, No. 4, October, 1976, pp.*
> *532-50.*

George H. Tavard   (essay date 1988)

[*An ordained Roman Catholic priest, Tavard is a French-born educator, writer, poet, and theologian living in the United States. In the excerpt below, Tavard explores the theme of night in the poetry and prose of St. John of the Cross.*]

The poetic flowering that coincided with John of the Cross's imprisonment in Toledo did not dry out with his escape. One cannot know for certain how he employed his time during the month and a half he spent in hiding at the home of don Pedro Gonzalez de Mendoza, a canon of the cathedral of Toledo who was a friend and supporter of the Carmelite sisters. Yet in all likelihood the poem of the **"Dark Night,"** written before the end of 1578, was composed before his departure for Andalusia, which was decided by the chapter of the discalced in Almodovar in October 1578. As was apparent in the first **"Canticle,"** the poet willingly borrowed images from the simplest elements of his human experience in contact with nature, with his family, with people in general. He formulated his ineffable experience of God with the help of such images. Thus the poem of the **"Dark Night"** is a tale of his flight, in a warm August night, when he escaped through a window, lowered himself down to the wall of the city, above the river Tagus, with an improvised cord, climbed over the wall of a neighboring convent, and finally walked on top of the city wall till he was able to jump down into a dark alley.

> One dark night . . .
> I went out unseen . . .
> In darkness and secure,
> by the secret ladder, disguised . . .

Another of the so-called minor poems could well also refer to this experience of captivity. In the Sanlúcar manuscript, this bears the awkward title of "stanzas concerning an ecstasy of high contemplation." More simply, one may call it, from its first words, the poem **"Entréme."** There is no agreement on the probable date of this work. It has been dated from the time of the chaplaincy at the convent of the Incarnation, between 1572 and 1577, before John of the Cross was kidnapped. It has been included among the writings made in Granada, between 1582 and 1584. A third hypothesis may be proposed. For these stanzas start with what does sound like a scarcely veiled allusion to the author's imprisonment, with the difference that if the **"Dark Night"** is the poem of the prisoner's escape, **"Entréme"** would be the poem of his incarceration:

> I entered where I knew not . . .
>
> I knew not where I entered,
> yet when there I saw myself,
> without knowing where I was,
> great things I understood . . .

The theme is germane to that of the **"Dark Night":** it speaks of "perfect knowledge," which is "so secret a thing," and which transcends all knowledge. It is the poem of an unknowing that is truly knowing, of a noncomprehension that is truly comprehension. It also speaks the language of the night, with its " . . . dark cloud / which lit up the night." One of its verses seems to echo the famous line of the **"Spiritual Canticle,"** *"un no se qué que quedan balbuciendo"* (an I-know-not-what which they keep stammering):

> It was so secret a thing
> that I remained stammering,
> transcending all knowledge.

This last verse recurs at the end of each stanza, as in the envoy. The last but one, which is equally borrowed from the envoy, is slightly modified, yet keeps the hesitant assonance that is germane to the *no se qué* of the **"Canticle":**

que me quedé . . . (twice), *que se queda . . . , queda siempre . . . , hace quedar. . . .* Even the third stanza, as it changed the penultimate verse (*de un entender no entendiendo*), preserved the stammering effect by moving it: *que se quedo* appears in the third verse instead. Stanzas 6 and 7, which have also replaced the penultimate verse with phrases that are close to those of the third stanza, have kept the stammering by starting the verse with *que* and *quien:* there are two *que* in stanza 5, two *que,* one *quien,* one *aqueste,* and one *con* in stanza 6. The entire poem seems to be stammering on this *que*-sound as though on the ineffable unknowing that transcends all knowing. Moreover, the frequent recurrence of the verb *quedar* (to remain) gives the whole performance an aura of quiet: the "peace" of the second stanza has been contagious and marked the whole poem. This is no longer the form of the **"Canticle",** when the bride went searching for her Beloved. It may be that the poet now knows, after undergoing the terrible testing of Toledo, that he has been entirely carried by grace: even in the night all is light:

> this is the dark cloud
> which lit up the night . . .

Thus searching is really finding, unknowing is "supreme knowledge." By himself the poet was powerless:

> The one who truly arrives there
> from himself falls away . . .

But the hearing of "great things" relating to "the divine essence," has entirely been "the work of his mercy."

Indeed, if the first five stanzas are descriptive of John of the Cross's experience, as, "so enraptured, / so absorbed and withdrawn," he was initiated to transcendent unknowing, the last three have fallen into the didactic genre. They no longer place the reader face to face with an experience that can only be stammered out. Rather, one is listening to an instructor who explains and compares.

Undoubtedly, the poem originated in a rewriting *a lo divino* of stanzas on a secular topic, like other previous compositions of John of the Cross. Yet this does not alter its meaning or its intent. Whether it came from John's Toledan captivity, or earlier, the passage from description to didactic instruction highlights a dilemma that confronted the poet as soon as, having escaped his adversaries among the calced Carmelites, he picked up his activities among the discalced and with the sisters of Teresa of Jesus: how could he explain his mystical poems to those who wished to understand them yet recognized that they could not grasp their meaning? That the mystical moment of **"Entréme"** is followed by a didactic one detracts from the poetic purity of the whole. The solution that John of the Cross will soon adopt, or maybe simply stumble into, and that will be characteristic of his works in the eyes of posterity, will be different: he will write prose commentaries on his poems.

As is well known, John of the Cross began his treatise on the **Ascent of Mount Carmel,** which is a commentary on the first two stanzas of the poem of the **"Dark Night,"** in Andalusia, in the small house of the Calvario where he arrived at the end of 1578. As he was not too far from the Carmelite sisters of Beas de Segura, he visited them regu-larly and talked to them about contemplative life in the light of his poems, which thus came to function as his "text." At the same time, he began to elaborate orally on the **"Spiritual Canticle."** The *Ascent of Mount Carmel* was eventually left unfinished; the commentary on the **"Canticle,"** version (A), was terminated at Granada in 1584, at the time, or near the time, when the author started once more to comment on the **"Dark Night"** in another perspective.

These commentaries raise a special problem. The relation of each poem to its commentary is clear: it provides the basic text and the point of departure. The commentary at times—as is regularly the case in the *Ascent of Mount Carmel*—wanders a considerable distance from the text, which is then partially relegated to a role of "pretext." But what is the relation of the commentary to the poem? The poem is evidently not written for the commentary. Yet does not the commentary give the poem a new sense that it would not otherwise have? Is it possible, once the commentaries have been written, to read the poems as though the commentaries did not exist? Yet should one really believe that the theological commentator gave the only correct interpretation of the poet's insight? Some have studied the poetry with no or few references to the commentaries. Others—and theologians have usually been among these—have spoken of the tractates as though these constituted the heart of John of the Cross's works, with an ecclesial dimension instead of the subjectivity of the poems. The attitude that I feel bound to adopt is the following.

The poems generally stand by themselves, independently of the commentaries, which, in the case of the first **"Canticle"** and the **"Dark Night,"** were not foreseen when they saw the light. Yet self-evidently the additions to the **"Canticle"** that were made during the Andalusian phase of the poet's life, the first in 1582, the last between 1582 and 1584, were written with the awareness that they would be included in the commentary that was then under way. By the same token, the meaning of the latter may have impacted John's rereading of the poem. This is why version (A) of the **"Canticle"** should be identified as another poem than that of Toledo, the first **"Canticle."**

In the case of the **"Dark Night,"** the poem exists by itself before the author forms the project of a commentary. From this point of view it is similar to the poems from Toledo. And the fact that it occasioned two commentaries that are rather different shows that it constitutes an integral whole, independent of the *Ascent of Mount Carmel* and of the treatise on the **"Dark Night,"** even if one may be led to read it in the light of these.

Let us now read, after **"Entréme,"** the poem of the **"Night."** It follows the same general structure as the **"Spiritual Canticle,"** with the five-line stanza that Spanish stylistics calls a *lira.* But the poem, much shorter, has only five *liras.* Instead of a dialogue in three voices, it is a monologue in two moments. The poet remembers an event in his recent past. His escape from captivity has become the symbol of another adventure, of an escape out of self. No more sadness lurks under the words, no more anxiety serves as backdrop, even if it is with "anguish" that the author declares he fled; the tone is of joy. The adventure is "happy," the night that witnessed it is "happy." As in several passages of the **"Canticle,"** exclamations break the story with a recurring shout of joy: "Oh, happy adventure!" And stanza 5, at the center, is a sequence of exclamations, in which joy reaches its acme:

> O guiding night!
> O night more lovely than dawn!
> O night which united
> the Beloved with his beloved,
> the beloved transformed into her Beloved!

Joy is inseparable from the night. The night is featured in the poem in the guise of a friend, even the supreme friend: no longer like the creatures of the **"Canticle,"** which could no more than stammer, or the "nymphs of Judea," who, in their eagerness to celebrate the wedding, could awaken the Beloved by knocking at the threshold. On the contrary, night is now the agent of the union that is sung by the poet, the all-encompassing atmosphere of his adventure, the guide. This theme leads to the fifth stanza, which itself forms a hinge between the two halves of the poem. The first five stanzas celebrate the escape, the mystical movement toward the one whom she loves (for the poet puts himself in the feminine, facing the masculine of the Beloved). The night is evoked in many ways: by the night itself as it is directly named, by the "darkness," which appears both as a noun and as an adjective, by the secrecy of the staircase, which does not tell if the movement goes up or down the stairs, by the detail that no one noticed her, that no one saw her, by the "quiet" of the house. Along the same line, the poet specifies that he "did not look for anything," that there was no light, except within his heart, and that the place where the Beloved waited for her was in solitude: no one "appeared," not even, as one may note, the stag who, in the **"Canticle,"** was seen atop the mountain.

The theme of the night is not negative. For the night itself is, in the second moment of the poem, luminous, on the model of the Paschal vigil as celebrated in the *Exsultet* of the deacon: *nox illuminatio mea in deliciis meis* (night is my light in my delights). It is a "guide," surer than "the midday light." It is also accompanied by the flame of love (". . . inflamed with desires in loves"), by fire (". . . that burned in my heart"); and where it leads the poet, the one whom she "knows well" is waiting for her. Thus the night is entirely turned to a knowing, which is not, like sight by daylight, active, but rather passive; it leads, not really toward knowing, but toward being known. There is indeed unknowing; yet, within and beyond unknowing there is also being-known. This is the mystery of union, which is first summed up in the exclamations of stanza 5; it is the night of oneness, the night of love, in which union is transforming, since in their intimacy the "beloved" is "transformed into her Beloved."

John of the Cross does not let us know if we have reached a summit, up the stairs, or an abyss, down the stairs. Uncertainty pertains to the night in which he wishes to plunge us along with himself. What is condensed in stanza 5 unfolds more slowly later. The last three stanzas sound quite differently from the first four. When it sang the mutual love, the fifth stanza changed the orientation of the poem. The house being now left behind in its nocturnal quiet, we have arrived at what is better than dawn. The Beloved is asleep in his beloved's arms; she caresses him; the cedars—that is, nature, the creatures—like eolian harps, softly vibrate under the breeze that flows from beyond the walls. Although he borrows an image from Garcilaso, John of the Cross may also be thinking of the high walls of the castle that dominate the city of Medina del Campo: hence a scene of serenity, of the calm of two lovers beneath the castle walls, feeling the wind that makes the beloved shiver deliciously as she caresses her sleeping Lover and strokes his hair. Nothing else then counts; all her senses are suspended.

The last stanza brings back the theme of night, though at another level. Oblivion, abandonment, now dominate: self-oblivion, self-abandonment. Everything ceases to be, except the experience of love, for the beloved "remains." Forgetting herself, her "face" leaning over her Beloved, she reaches the high point of her glorious adventure. And the final image, of concern "forgotten among the lilies," is not without relation to a symbolism that John of the Cross must have known. The lilies, which are presumably borrowed, along with the walls, from the *Song of Songs,*—the walls and the coolness of the breeze being also inspired by some lines in Garcilaso—are, in Christian iconography, symbols of purity, of joyful renunciation. They signify oblivion and abandonment, the place where abandonment, transformed into self-offering, turned to promise, itself comes to bloom. The lilies on which the **"Dark Night"** ends recall pictures of the Annunciation, in which the dialogue between the angel and Mary, itself pointing to that between the Word and the Virgin, takes place near a vase with lilies. The paradox of mystical experience lies here. In most likelihood this was also, for John of the Cross, the paradox of the Christian Faith.

Was John of the Cross aware, as he was about to start his commentary, of the paradoxical aspect of the poem of the **"Dark Night"**? This seems to have been the case, given the unusual, not to say odd, structure of the two commentaries of it, the **Ascent of Mount Carmel** and the treatise of the **Dark Night.** Their redaction took place between 1578 and 1585, presumably in sequence, though one cannot rule out that they may have been written simultaneously. In 1582-84 John of the Cross was also commenting on the **"Spiritual Canticle."** He therefore worked at several levels, alternately, in keeping with the needs and requests of the sisters, chiefly those of Beas and of Granada, to whom he explained orally, in talks and homilies, the meaning of his poems and their connection with the inner life. The structure of the **Canticle** commentary is simple, even self-evident, as it follows the poem step by step. But the real structure of the others, patterned on John's own mystical experience and his theological understanding of it, remains far removed from the poem. For the **Canticle** John of the Cross proceeds verse after verse to the end. Although he commences the poem of the **Night** in the same way, no doubt with the intent of going through all the stanzas and verses in order, he leaves off long before the end. As regards the **Ascent,** the first stanza corresponds to Book One; yet as many as thirteen chapters cover the first verse, but only one chapter covers the second verse, and verses 3 to 5 come in the last chapter. Books Two and Three are presented as commentaries on the second stanza, but the verses are not examined one by one. The general theme of the stanza provides the point of departure for a development that apparently forgets the text. The remaining parts of the poem are not commented on at all, the author having interrupted his work, never to return to it.

As regards the *Dark Night,* Book One starts all over again with the first stanza, and again gives lopsided attention to the first verse. Being cited at the end of the prologue, and again at the end of chapter 7, this verse is the subject matter of the first ten chapters. The second verse, cited at the end of chapter 10, is commented on at the beginning of chapter 11, in which the third and fourth verses are also cited. The fifth verse appears toward the end of chapter 13, where it sums up the effects of the mystical night previously described.

Instead of continuing with the second stanza, as one would have expected it, Book Two, after three introductory chapters, picks up once more the first stanza, and gives it, counting the *Ascent,* a third commentary. Once again the first verse predominates, as it takes up the first ten chapters. The second verse is then cited and commented on until the end of chapter 13. Then the last three verses are quoted one after the other in a very brief space, at the end of chapter 13 and in chapter 14. Their commentary is only one chapter long. The commentary on the second stanza is more even: chapter 15 as introduction, chapter 16 for the first verse, chapters 17 to 21 for the second, then one chapter on each of the remaining verses. The third stanza is introduced in chapter 25; but the work ends unexpectedly after quoting the first verse, "In the happy night."

As one may see, John of the Cross, who binds himself to strict rules of versification as accepted in his time, is free from all structural regularity in his commentaries, despite their didactic and at times scholastic contents. The freedom of the poem lies in its images, not in its form, that of the commentary resides in the form, the content being dictated by the objective datum of the experience. Yet if one may understand the disjuncted aspect of these two books in their relation to their common text, one cannot help surmising that John of the Cross did find himself in a bind that he could not easily overcome. Really, the idea of a didactic discourse on a poetic text could hardly fit the requirements of a master in mystical theology (to speak like Teresa of Avila), in his project of teaching the Carmelite sisters who were called to the contemplative way. This demanded a progressive, at times elementary, manner. One may further wonder if the author's problem remained confined within the order of form and style, or spread to a wider domain. As regards form and style, John of the Cross, who was as free here as everywhere else, easily hit on a solution: a disorderly order, an unstructured structure, a holy chaos that organizes itself as it goes, in keeping with the needs of every moment and question. If there was a deeper problem, the solution was not so easy.

It is not necessary for our study to proceed to a thorough analysis of the commentaries on the poem of the **"Night."**

This has been done many a time. Yet an inquiry into selected themes of the *Ascent of Mount Carmel* and the *Dark Night* may throw light on our research. The chief theme is of course that of the night. This is a many-sided symbol: John of the Cross identifies the dark night of his escape with the purification of the soul, which itself has many aspects. There will be the successive purifications of sense, active and passive, and the active and passive purifications of spirit; and they will all bear on the three levels of the intellect, the memory, and the will. Moreover, there will be a comparison, even an identification, of nocturnal darkness and creaturely weakness, of the night and the nothingness (*nada*) that mark the only way to the whole (*todo*), as in the axioms on the *todo-nada* that frame the drawing of Mount Carmel and are repeated within the commentary. The night will be the nudity of spirit of those who have embarked on the ascent of the mountain. It will be faith, the only "blindman's guide" toward the light. It will be the "knowledge" given by faith to the Church Militant, "where it is still night." It will even be, paradoxically, God, of whom John of the Cross has said that he "is also for the soul a part, or the third cause, of this night," the first two causes being the blindness of sense and the obscurity of faith. Admittedly, the mystical doctor sees neither identity nor equivalence between these symbolic dimensions of night. Linguistically, the word is polysemic, with numerous connotations around a common core, the darkness. Philosophically, the meaning of the term is not univocal, but analogical. Theologically, according to a traditional image, God is "light," even "inaccessible light." In the Creed of Nicaea-Constantinople, God is *lumen,* and the divine Word, *lumen de lumine.* In relation to creatures, such as he is perceived, or rather unperceived, by them, God can only be darkness. The following text is of major importance for John of the Cross's doctrine of night as well as for an understanding of the problem that John had to face as he commented on his poetry:

> The third part, that period before dawn, approximates the light of day. The darkness is not like that of midnight, since in this third period of the night we approach the illumination of day. And this daylight we compare to God. Although it is true that God is for the soul, speaking naturally, as dark a night as faith is; yet since, these three parts of the night, which for the soul are naturally dark, having passed, God enlightens the soul supernaturally with the beam of his divine light, which is the principle of the perfect union which follows after the third night, this one may be said to be less dark.

John of the Cross explains that if the night of faith is darker than that of sense, this is because it deprives the soul of its own rational light. As the night of spirit, it is more deeply obscure than that of sensibility. It holds in itself "contraries." These are obstacles that one meets along the path of purification, contradictions that are more or less profound and more or less temporary. At another level contraries are not obstacles, but rather the very condition of the night. At this point the language of the mystical doctor is strictly exact: "For," says he, "we must prove now how this second part, faith, is night to the spirit just as the first is to the senses. Then we shall also discuss the contraries that it has. . . . " 'It' is the second night, the night of faith. The contraries in question are not in the first place the "impediments" that will be studied from chapter 10 on, after the treatise on faith that occupies chapters 3 to 9 of the second part of the *Ascent.* They are rather contraries that are within faith, contrasting yet inseparable dimensions of this night. The demonstration that faith is a night is the topic of chapter 3. The contraries immediately follow: the night gives light; "the night, being dark, illumines"; the soul "must be in darkness to have light along this way." This theme is continued in chapters 4 to 9, when the author shows how and in what way faith, which is at the same time light and darkness, acts at this time as the soul's guide. John of the Cross is thus aware of an apparent contradiction in this doctrine: faith-night is also faith-light; God is himself day and night. (pp. 53-63)

George H. Tavard, in his Poetry and Contemplation in St. John of the Cross, *Ohio University, 1988, 286 p.*

FURTHER READING

Bellport, Mary Fidelis. "The Healing Aesthetic: Fresh Patterns of Wholeness." *Studies in Formative Spirituality* IV, No. 1 (February 1983): 11-23.

Discusses the teachings of St. John of the Cross as part of an examination of the role of asceticism in spiritual life. Bellport decries "the dichotomy between asceticism and aesthetic in our age" and points to St. John as an exemplary combination of both personal austerity and creative artistic expression.

Brenan, Gerald. "Studies in Genius: II: St. John of the Cross, His Life and Poetry." *Horizon* XV, No. 88 (May 1947): 256-81.

Offers a detailed, comprehensive overview of the life of St. John of the Cross and provides a succinct analysis of the religious upheaval in sixteenth-century Spain. Brenan comments on the personal and political ramifications of St. John's role in the reform of the Carmelite Order and the autobiographical nature of his poetry.

Carmichael, Montgomery. *"The Spiritual Canticle* of St. John of the Cross." *The Dublin Review* 173 (October-December 1923): 194-209.

Compares three published versions of "The Spiritual Canticle" and its commentary. Carmichael notes significant differences between them and calls on scholars of the Carmelite Order to authenticate the texts.

Cummins, John G. "Aqueste lance divino: San Juan's Falconry Images." In *What's Past is Prologue: A Collection of Essays in Honour of L. J. Woodward,* edited by Salvador Bacarisse, Bernard Bentley, Mercedes Clarasó, and Douglas Clifford, pp. 28-32. Edinburgh: Scottish Academy Press, 1984.

Examines falconry imagery in "Tras un amoroso lance" ("On an Impulse of Love"), asserting that the process of spiritual fulfillment and self-denial is likened to the movement of a peregrine falcon and its prey.

Dicken, E. W. Trueman. *The Crucible of Love: A Study of the Mysticism of St. Teresa of Jesus and St. John of the Cross.* New York: Sheed and Ward, 1963, 548 p.

Extensive discussion of the mystical doctrines of St. Teresa and St. John of the Cross. Dicken expounds on the life and works of the two Carmelite saints, exploring their writings to detail the stages of the soul's progress toward union with God.

Domínguez, Carlos. "San Juan de la Cruz's 'Pastorcico' and the Obliteration of Origins." *Papers on Language and Literature* 21, No. 3 (Summer 1985): 317-23.

Compares St. John's pastoral poem "A Lone Young Shepherd" to its anonymous secular model. Domínguez argues that St. John of the Cross recast the original to complement and extend the themes of love, sacrifice, and forgetfulness into the realm of religious allegory.

Gosse, Edmund. "A Spanish Mystic." In his *Silhouettes,* pp. 43-9. New York: Charles Scribner's Sons, 1925.

Chronicles the life of St. John of the Cross, stressing the physical and moral hardships that inspired his greatest artistic works.

Graves, Robert. "A Lo Divino." In *The Poems of St. John of the Cross,* by St. John of the Cross, rev. ed., edited and translated by John Frederick Nims, pp. ix-xv. New York: Grove Press, 1968.

Remarks on the poetry of St. John of the Cross in light of *"duende,"* or "a spirit of ecstatic love caught and preserved in a poem, painting, or sculpture."

Green, Dierdre. "St. John of the Cross and Mystical 'Unknowing.'" *Religious Studies* 22, No. 1 (March 1986): 29-40.

Takes issue with the critical stance that the teachings of St. John of the Cross are anticognitive and reject all supernatural revelations. Green characterizes St. John's concept of "unknowing" as a higher type of knowledge that transcends reason and "must be experienced by the mystic to be fully known."

Maritain, Jacques. "Saint John of the Cross, the Practician of the Contemplative Life." In his *The Degrees of Knowledge,* rev. ed., edited and translated by Bernard Wall and Margot R. Adamson, pp. 382-429. New York: Charles Scribner's Sons: 1938.

Asseses the spiritual teachings of St. John of the Cross, comparing the complementary views on the contemplation of God held by St. John and St. Thomas Aquinas.

McInnis, Judy B. "Eucharistic and Conjugal Symbolism in *The Spiritual Canticle* of Saint John of the Cross." *Renascence* XXXVI, No. 3 (Spring 1984): 118-38.

Studies the use of eucharistic and conjugal imagery in *The Spiritual Canticle.* McInnis maintains that St. John "traces the soul's progress from the beginning of its search for God through union in the mystic marriage" and explores the work's debt to the biblical *Song of Songs.*

Merton, Thomas. Introduction to *Counsels of Light and Love of Saint John of the Cross,* by St. John of the Cross, pp. 9-20. London: Burns and Oates, 1953.

Outlines the ascetic doctrines of St. John of the Cross, defending them against the critical charge that they are overly harsh and austere. Merton recapitulates St. John's assertion that interior detachment and self-abnegation are the keys to finding communion with God.

Parker, Alexander A. "The Human Language of Divine Love." In his *The Philosophy of Love in Spanish Literature,* pp. 73-106. Edinburgh: Edinburgh University Press, 1985.

Discusses the relationship between St. John's mystical poetry and secular love poetry. Parker suggests that St. John incorporated "the language of human love to express divine love" and explores the use of analogy and symbolic language in the major poems.

Pax, Clyde. "Companion Thinkers: Martin Heidegger and Saint John of the Cross." *Philosophy Today* 29, No. 3/4 (Fall 1985): 230-44.

Contrasts the philosophies of Martin Heidegger and St. John of the Cross. Pax asserts that differences in background and religious orientation conceal fundamental similarities in reasoning.

Peers, E. Allison. "St. John of the Cross." In his *Studies of the Spanish Mystics,* Vol. I, pp. 229-88. London: Sheldon Press, 1927.

Surveys the life and works of St. John of the Cross. Peers offers a synopsis of St. John's mystical teachings and stresses that all of the saint's writings correspond to one overarching theme: "unwavering devotion to Christ."

———. "St. John of the Cross." In his *St. John of the Cross and Other Lectures and Addresses: 1920-1945,* pp. 11-53. London: Faber and Faber, 1946.

Examines the structure, themes, and imagery of St. John's major poems. Peers characterizes St. John of the Cross as "one of the most attractive, invigorating, and inspiring religious writers who have ever lived."

———. "The Source and Technique of San Juan de la Cruz's Poem 'Un Pastorcico . . . '." *Hispanic Review* XX, No. 3 (July 1952): 248-53.

Recapitulates the critical controversy surrounding possible sources for St. John's pastoral poem "A Lone Young Shepherd." Peers asserts that the inspiration for the work came from an anonymous sixteenth-century manuscript, but that St. John radically altered the source to dramatize the story of Christ's Redemption.

———. Introduction to *The Complete Works of Saint John of the Cross, Doctor of the Church,* Vol. I, by St. John of the Cross, rev. ed., edited and translated by Edgar Allison Peers, pp. xxi-lxiii. London: Burns and Oates, 1953.

An overview of the works and religious philosophy of St.

John of the Cross, focusing on his prose style. Peers also documents the publication history of St. John's various treatises, probing the diffusion and possible destruction of the original manuscripts.

Sanderlin, David. "Faith and Ethical Reasoning in the Mystical Theology of St. John of the Cross: A Reasonable Christian Mysticism." *Religious Studies* 25, No. 3 (September 1989): 317-33.

Appraises the role of reason in the mystical teachings of St. John of the Cross. Sanderlin declares that St. John's doctrines do not deny reason, for they emphasize scripture and the Christian virtues of faith, hope, and charity.

Sencourt, Robert. "St. Teresa and St. John of the Cross." *The Contemporary Review* (June 1954): 342-46.

Explores the enduring appeal of the works of St. Teresa and St. John of the Cross. Sencourt maintains that their "mystic theology" stresses communion with God "in the adoring calm of love."

Swietlicki, Catherine. "The Christian Cabala of San Juan de la Cruz and of the Mystical Union." In her *Spanish Christian Cabala: The Works of Luis de León, Santa Teresa de Jesus, and San Juan de la Cruz,* pp. 155-86. Columbia: University of Missouri Press, 1986.

Argues that St. John followed in the tradition of the Christian Cabala and utilized imagery from the Old and New Testaments to serve as an apologist for the Christian mystic tradition.

Taylor, A. E. "St. John of the Cross and John Wesley." *The Journal of Theological Studies* XLVI (1945): 30-8.

Points out the fundamental similarities and differences between the teachings of St. John of the Cross and Methodist founder John Wesley. Taylor asserts that while St. John found mystical experience "the very central truth of Christianity," Wesley regarded mysticism as "the most dangerous of all corrupters" of the soul.

Werblowsky, R. J. Zwi. "On the Mystical Rejection of Mystical Illuminations: A Note on St. John of the Cross." *Religious Studies* I, No. 2 (1966): 177-84.

Investigates St. John's distrust of illumination, prophecy, and revealed knowledge. St. John held that such phenomena could actually be detrimental to true mystic communion with God, asserts Werblowsky, affirming that self-negation and faith are far more important virtues.

Rise of the Essay in England

During a period spanning the late sixteenth through the eighteenth centuries, informal and discursive expository prose became a popular form of instruction and entertainment in England, and the essay emerged as a distinct genre in English literature. Best represented by the works of such authors as Sir Francis Bacon, Joseph Addison, and Sir Richard Steele, the essay, as it was practiced during this time, has been explored from both historical and literary perspectives. Commentators examining the development of the essay have focused on its formal characteristics, the merits of its chief contributors, and its significance in world literature.

The characteristic brevity and discursive style of the essay prompted Samuel Johnson to pronounce it "a loose sally of the mind . . . an irregular, undigested piece, not a regular and orderly performance." As the genre gained critical acceptance, attempts to arrive at a more functional definition of the essay proliferated, resulting in the division of essays into such categories as instructive, aphoristic, historical, and familiar. Modern critics, however, have often found these classifications inaccurate, and most commentators now agree that the term "essay," used indiscriminately for centuries in reference to philosophical, religious, political, and personal compositions, defies definition. In this context, Joseph Epstein has referred to the essay as "a pair of baggy pants into which nearly anyone and anything can fit." Ted-Larry Pebworth and O. B. Hardison, among others, have explored ways in which the essay is a protean literary genre, assuming forms that serve a variety of purposes, from personal reflections to philosophical pronouncements.

While William Paulet's *The Lord Marquess' Idleness* (1585) and the anonymous *Remedies against Discontentment* (1596) have been cited as the first essay collections published in English, Bacon is generally credited with introducing and popularizing the essay in England. Influenced by the works of the French essayist Michel de Montaigne, who, in 1580, first used the term "essais," or "attempts," to describe his prose reflections on commonplace topics and occurences, Bacon published *Essays, Religious Meditations, Places of Persuasion and Dissuasion* in 1597, taking its structure and subjects from Montaigne's work. While Montaigne addressed his readers in a casual, intimate tone, however, Bacon wrote in a prose style that has been consistently described as aphoristic. Offering pragmatic counsel in formal and concise language, such essays as "Of Friendship," "Of Regiment and Health," and "Of Atheism" appealed largely to readers of advanced education. Critics have noted, nevertheless, that Bacon's revisions and additions to his *Essays,* in editions published in 1612 and 1625, employ a more prosaic tone that brought Bacon, in the words of Bonamy Dobrée, "nearer the ordinary man."

For much of the seventeenth century, essay writing reflected Bacon's aphoristic style and incorporated elements of the commonplace book, the character sketch, and the personal letter. Such essayists as Sir William Cornwallis and Robert Johnson adopted Bacon's style to advise their readers on proper deportment and methods of education. Ben Jonson used quotations from works of classical Greek and Roman authors as the basis for his essays in *Timber: or, Discoveries Made upon Men and Matter* (1641). Sir William Temple and Abraham Cowley are regarded as England's most prominent essayists of the second half of the seventeenth century. Cowley has been credited by Dobrée as the "first really friendly essayist" who "never pretends to be more enlightened or more exquisite in feeling than the average man." While the essay continued to exhibit the influence of Bacon's aphoristic prose throughout much of the seventeenth century, it gradually became less abstract and more familiar, appealing to a wider audience.

The inception of the periodical magazine in the eighteenth century was instrumental to the development of the essay. Steele and Addison's *Tatler* and *Spectator,* as well as Johnson's *Rambler* and Daniel Defoe's *A Weekly Review of Affairs in France,* featured prose designed to entertain and instruct the English middle class. In his preface to the first issue of the *Tatler* in 1709, Steele wrote that the purpose of his essays was "to expose the false arts of life; to pull off the disguises of cunning, vanity, and affectation; and to recommend a general simplicity in our dress, our discourse, and our behavior." In addition to providing guidance in matters of wardrobe and proper behavior, Addison's and Steele's periodical essays discussed such popular subjects as witchcraft and duelling and satirized the aristocracy through fictional correspondents, the best known of whom are Isaac Bickerstaff and Sir Roger de Coverley. Immensely popular during their time, the early periodical essayists are esteemed for introducing humor and less formal diction into the English essay. In the early nineteenth century William Hazlitt commented that the essays of Addison and Steele "are more like the remarks which occur in sensible conversation, and less like a lecture. Something is left to the imagination of the reader." The periodical essay was modified by Hazlitt, Charles Lamb, Leigh Hunt, Thomas De Quincey, and other writers associated with the Romantic movement. By augmenting the essay's scope and length, and by developing a highly personal voice, these writers continued the development of the essay form, producing some of the most popular and skillfully rendered prose works in English literature.

DEFINITIONS AND ORIGINS

G. K. Chesterton

[*Regarded as one of England's most prominent scholars during the first half of the twentieth century, Chesterton is best known as a colorful bon vivant, a witty essayist, and creator of the Father Brown mysteries as well as the fantasy* The Man Who Was Thursday *(1908). His essays are characterized by their humor, frequent use of paradox, and chatty, discursive style. In the following excerpt, he describes the essay as an "attempt at writing" which results in circuitous and often entertaining discourse.*]

The essay is the only literary form which confesses, in its very name, that the rash act known as writing is really a leap in the dark. When men try to write a tragedy, they do not call the tragedy a try-on. Those who have toiled through the twelve books of an epic, writing it with their own hands, have seldom pretended that they have merely tossed off an epic as an experiment. But an essay, by its very name as well as its very nature, really is a try-on and really is an experiment. A man does not really write an essay. He does really essay to write an essay.

One result is that, while there are many famous essays, there is fortunately no model essay. The perfect essay has never been written; for the simple reason that the essay has never really been written. Men have tried to write something, to find out what it was supposed to be. In this respect the essay is a typically modern product, and is full of the future and the praise of experiment and adventure. In other words, like the whole of modern civilization, it does not know what it is trying to find; and therefore does not find it.

It occurs to me here, by the way, that all this applies chiefly to English essayists; and indeed that in this sense the essay is rather an English thing. So far as I remember, English schoolmasters tell a boy to write an essay, but French schoolmasters tell a boy to write a theme. The word theme has a horrid suggestion of relevancy and coherence. The theme is only too near to the thesis. The English schoolmaster profoundly understands his pupils when he assumes that they will not produce a theme but an essay at a theme, or a considerably wild cockshy or pot-shot at a theme. Mr. P. G. Wodehouse (the works of whose imagination do not fall strictly within either the tragic or the epic form) has described how the benevolent nobleman, burdened with a son of the name of Freddie, appealed to that youth to behave, if possible, like a sane and rational human being; to which Freddie replied, with a solemn fervour: "I'll have a jolly good stab at it, Governor." The essayist should be the reasonable human being; the philosopher, the sage with a judgment at once delicate and detached; the thinker considering a theme; the logician expounding a thesis. But England, expecting every man to do his duty, does not expect so much as all this. England knows that her beloved essayists will not be reasonable human beings; but will only have a jolly good stab at it. It is something of a symbol that, for the English schoolboy, an essay is an effort. The whole atmosphere of the thing is full of doubt, experiment and effort. I know not

if it is hell, or heaven, or perhaps merely a piece of earth that is for ever England; but anyhow all this field is paved with bad essays and good intentions.

Of course there are essays that are really themes and themes that are really theses. They represent what may be called the Extreme Right of rigid right reason and militant purpose, after the Latin model. A model of the militant or controversial essay (and all the more so because there is no mailed fist, but a very iron hand in a very velvet glove) is Alice Meynell's essay in defence of the despised wife of Dr. Johnson. The words are spoken in the softest accent of irony; the mere style preserves all the stylist's special pose of gliding over things easily; but the whole thing is constructed controversially; it is as argumentative as any argument in any law court or debating club. It is also very effective argument, for, until it was written, nearly everybody talked exactly that nonsense about poor Mrs. Johnson; and nobody I know of has talked it since. This theme really is a thesis; but when the same writer turns, let us say, to describing in the same elegant English the mere effect of blue twilight glowing in the cracks of the London streets, she is at most concerned with a theme. Even here a certain Latin logic in her made her stick to the theme. We all know, however, that there are English essays that are very English essays and yet very jolly essays; that are none the less beautiful because they twist and ramble like an English road. Of these are some of Thackeray's *Roundabout Papers* and some of Mr. Belloc's best essays; like that highly unscrupulous dissertation which promises to deal with a particular feature of seventeenth century architecture, proceeds to argue with itself about the respective ages of Charles the Second and Louis the Fourteenth, amplifies itself into a glowing panorama of the landscapes of the Pyrenees, and ends with a Rebuke to His Pen, chiding it for having taken him so far away from the mere title and topic of his essay. People are so prone to say that Mr. Belloc is French that it is worth noting that in this and many other matters he is extraordinarily English. By the true test of literary consistency and conscientiousness, there was much more that was French about Mrs. Meynell. Or perhaps it might be maintained that something of Latin lucidity, which leads the former writer to value the strict form of the sonnet, in itself enables him to perceive the essential formlessness of the essay. Anyhow, except when it is tightened by the militant relevancy of debate or propaganda, the essay does tend to be formless, or at the best to present a very bewildering variety of forms. But I cannot help thinking a man must be as English as Mr. Belloc to enjoy it in its most formless form.

This indefinite and indeterminate quality would at once appear if we tried to classify the subordinate type under the general type of the essay. The types are so many and the tests are so few. There is one kind of essay that consists of staring out of the window at the garden and describing what you see there; but from this I am inhibited by a complete ignorance of the names of all the plants that I see. I have sometimes wondered whether it would be possible to disguise my ignorance under an appearance of abstruse or specialized or purely localized knowledge, as by saying: "That torrid and almost terrible blossom which is called in Persia the Blood of Kings," or: "The shrub which, in spite of its new scientific name, I still love to call *Judæus Esuriens,* as did the dear old naturalists of the later seventeenth century," or: "The little flower that we in Westmoreland have always called Bishop's Buttonhook, though they have another name for it in the South." It is obvious that the same bright and rather breathless enterprise might be applied to another sort of essay; the rambling historical and archæological causerie, in which one name leads to another; and generally to very little else. Would it be safe to begin a paragraph: "I was dipping into Dio Cassius the other day . . ." or to go on: "To find a parallel to this, I imagine we should have to go as far afield as the second period of the Upanishads," and perhaps conclude: "But after all, is not all this to be found in Scotus Erigena?" Very few people have read Dio Cassius or Erigena; and it may be doubted if even the aged Theosophists, who can still be found stranded in drawing-rooms, could pass an examination in the Eastern documents I have named. If done as a skit, it would be a successful skit; for certainly it would expose many before it was itself exposed. If done as the foundation for a solid career of learning, it would be unwise; for though only two people in the world knew it was nonsense, those two would certainly turn up. This covers an excellent sort of essay; the solemn skit, such as Mr. Gilbert Norwood's immortal fancy called *Too Many Books.* Then there is another sort of essay that has lately become fairly common and frequently quite picturesque; that may be called the Historical Glimpse. It will be devoted to describing a day with Moses or an afternoon call on Mahomet or Marat, or a chance meeting with Nero or Mr. Gladstone. The special technique developed for this design generally involves the detailed description of the hero before he is introduced by name, and it ends with: "Fear not, you carry Cæsar," or: "You may be interested to know that you have given a glass of milk to Prince Albert." All these are bold and promising essays at the elusive nature of the essay; but in itself it remains somewhat elusive. And, if I may end this rambling article on the subject of rambling articles, and end it with a personal confession, I will own that I am haunted with a faint suspicion that the essay will probably become rather more cogent and dogmatic, merely because of the deep and deadly divisions which ethical and economic problems may force upon us. But let us hope there will always be a place for the essay that is really an essay. It is an old story that soldiers sing songs round the camp-fire; but I doubt if they are all about soldiering. Indeed they are sometimes so lively in their range over other topics, that respectable patriots have found a difficulty in including them in collections of patriotic songs. St. Thomas Aquinas, with his usual common sense, said that neither the active nor the contemplative life could be lived without relaxations, in the form of jokes and games. The drama or the epic might be called the active life of literature; the sonnet or the ode the contemplative life. The essay is the joke. (pp. xi-xviii)

G. K. Chesterton, "The Essay," in Essays of the Year, *The Argonaut Press, 1932, pp. xi-xviii.*

O. B. Hardison, Jr.

[*Hardison was an American educator and critic best known for his studies of medieval and Renaissance literature. In the following excerpt, he examines the nature of the essay as a literary genre and discusses its origins in the writings of Montaigne and Bacon.*]

The ancient god Proteus knew the secrets of the past and the future. Those who would learn them were required to bind him with chains before asking their questions. When bound, Proteus would change into all manner of shapes to escape. Menelaus visited Proteus when becalmed at Pharos and forced him to reveal the fates of Agamemnon and Odysseus. Aristaeus, a shepherd of Tempe, was told by his mother Cyrene to visit Proteus when his bees were dying. She advised: "The more he turns himself into different shapes, the more you, my son, must hold onto those strong chains."

Writing an essay on the essay is doubtless appropriate for an age that delights in strange loops and Gödelian recursions and that has announced, probably too often, that every art form is first and foremost a comment on itself. Since of all literary forms the essay is the one that resists most successfully the effort to pin it down, making that effort is like trying to bind Proteus.

Let me put one card on the table immediately. A rumor is going around that the essay is an endangered species. There have even been calls to "save the essay," as there are calls to save whales and condors. Nothing could be more absurd. The essay is not a sensitive species on the point of extinction. It is tough, infinitely adaptable, and ubiquitous. It has more in common with the German cockroach than with the Tennessee snail darter. The analogy has hidden relevance. The cockroach is a primitive creature that appears very early on the evolutionary chain. The essay is also primitive. Roland Barthes suggests that in the evolution of projections of the imagination, it may precede the formation of all concepts of genre. (pp. 610-11)

To return now to the myth I have invoked—the basic characteristic of Proteus is elusiveness. If there is no genre more widespread in modern letters than the essay, there is also no genre that takes so many shapes and that refuses so successfully to resolve itself, finally, into its own shape.

Francis Bacon concludes in *The Wisdom of the Ancients* that Proteus symbolizes matter and adds: "If any skillful servant of Nature shall bring force to bear on matter, and shall vex it and drive it to extremities as if with the purpose of reducing it to nothing" it will assume all shapes but return "at last to itself." I take heart from Bacon's *Wisdom.* In spite of the danger—that the essay may fight back—I propose to vex it and drive it to extremities in the hope that by the end it will return to itself and reveal something of its true nature.

The word *essay* derives from Old French *essai,* defined in Partridge as "a trial, an attempt." From this meaning comes English "to essay" in the sense of "to make a trial or an attempt," as in Emerson's statement "I also will essay to be." The word also comes into English via Norman French *assaier* as "to assay," meaning to try or test, as in testing the quality of a mineral ore.

German has two words for essay: *Abhandlung,* a "dealing with" something, and *Aufsatz,* a "setting forth." Herder's "Essay on the Origin of Speech" is an *Abhandlung;* Martin Heidegger's essay on thingliness—*Das Ding*—is an *Aufsatz. Abhandlungen* tend to be ponderous and, you might say, Germanic. *Aufsätze* have an altogether lighter touch—a touch, one imagines, like the touch of Goethe tapping out the rhythms of the hexameter on the back of his Roman mistress:

> Oftmals hab' ich auch schon in ihren Armen ge-
>   dichtet
> Und des hexameters Maas leise mit fingernder
>   Hand
> Ihr auf dem Rücken bezählt.

So far as I can learn, the first use of *essay* to refer to a literary composition was for the title of the most famous collection of such compositions ever published—Montaigne's *Essais.* If you look for the first English use of the term in this sense in the OED, you may be surprised at what you find. Instead of a majestic series of entries marching forward from the Middle Ages, you encounter this bald statement: "Essay. A composition of moderate length on any particular subject, or branch of a subject; originally implying want of finish . . . but now said of a composition more or less elaborate in style though limited in range. The use in this sense is apparently taken from Montaigne, whose *essais* were first published in 1580."

In other words Montaigne invented the term, and the English got it directly from him. Another surprise. The first English use of the term was on the title page of the *Essayes* Francis Bacon published in 1597. The second was on the title page of John Florio's translation of—you guessed it—Montaigne's *Essayes, or Morall, Politike, and Militarie Discourses* (1603). Thereafter the term was used with increasing promiscuity to refer to any composition that does not fall obviously into some other, better defined category. It has the same relation to literary criticism that the term *miscellaneous* has to budgeting.

Supplementing these lexicographical observations are three historical facts.

First, the essay did not appear ab ovo. Montaigne's principal guide and mentor in the art of the essay was Plutarch, whose *Moralia* consists of short compositions on topics of general interest, such as the cessation of oracles, whether fish or land animals are more crafty, whether water or fire is most useful, against running into debt, and the man in the moon. According to Montaigne, "of all the authors I know, [Plutarch] most successfully commingled art with nature and insight with knowledge." Another writer much admired by Montaigne and more so by Bacon is Seneca, whose unfailingly uplifting letters often come close to being essays.

Second, in spite of these and other precedents, the essay *is* something new. In the sixteenth century the standard prose form was the oration. Orations are utilitarian—their authors want to accomplish something. As the rhetoric books say, their object is to persuade. Montaigne calls this the *Hoc age*—the "Do this!"—impulse. To persuade efficiently, orators developed a standard kind of organization called *dispositio. Dispositio* is the literary equivalent of the foregone conclusion.

Dispositio remains familiar today. All rhetoricians, from Aristotle to Hughes and Duhamel, agree that a proper oration should begin with an *exordium* stating the main point and largest divisions of the argument. The body of the oration consists of arguments in favor (*confirmatio*), plus a demolition of arguments against (*refutatio*). The work should end with a *peroratio* that summarizes the argument and restates the main point.

Montaigne carefully disavows all such advance planning. In "On Education" he quotes with obvious relish the comment of the King of Sparta on a long speech by the ambassadors from Samos: "As for your beginning and exordium, I no longer remember it; nor consequently, the middle; as for the conclusion, I do not desire to do anything about it." In "On the Resemblance of Children" he asserts "I do not correct my first ideas by later ones. . . . I wish to represent the progress of my moods, and that each part shall be seen at its birth." In another context he adds: "I have no other drill-master than chance to arrange my writings. As my thoughts present themselves to my mind, I bring them together." So much for *dispositio.*

As Sir Philip Sidney's *Defence of Poesie* shows, orations can be impressive and informative. They can even, on occasion, be persuasive. There is not much room in them, however, for spontaneity. They move ahead with the elephantine thump of the *Abhandlung* rather than the butterfly tango of the *Aufsatz.* The point of orations is not to reveal private feelings but to make things happen.

In fact the essay is the opposite of an oration: it is a literary trial balloon, an informal stringing together of ideas to see what happens. From the point of view of the oration, the essay is feckless. It doesn't want to *do* anything, and it has no standard method even for standing around doing nothing. Montaigne calls essay-writing "that stupid enterprise" ("cette sotte entrepris"), and when Roland Barthes delivered an oration in which he accepted a chair at the Collège de France, he apologized for his literary philandering. "I must admit," he said, " . . . that I have produced only essays."

Third fact. Even in its infancy, the essay shows its protean heritage. Montaigne's essays are associative, discursive, informal, meandering, slovenly. Being the first of their kind, they ought at least to have become models for what followed, in the same way that even disreputable people—muggers, prostitutes, con men, etc.—will become models if they are really good at what they do. They did not. Bacon's essays were inspired by Montaigne's, but are, if anything, anti-Montaignian. Especially in their 1597 form they are aphoristic, staccato, assertive, hortatory, abrasive.

This brings us to style.

Morris Croll wrote the classic study of sixteenth-century prose style [*Attic and Baroque Style: The Anti-Ciceronian Movement,* 1969]. He calls Montaigne's style "libertine," and the style of Bacon "Tacitean." Libertine sentences slither along from phrase to phrase with no proper sense of an ending. They are just what you would expect from writing that refuses to get organized. Tacitus was curt to the point of churlishness, and his name has the same root as English "taciturn." That too is appropriate. In their first edition Bacon's *Essayes* are abrupt and businesslike. Not a word wasted. Time is money.

The fact is that both Montaigne and Bacon were reacting not only against the oration with its preordained *dispositio,* but also against the rhetorical exhibitionism of the periodic sentence. In the earlier Renaissance Cicero was the pre-eminent model for the periodic kind of writing. His sentences make language into a kind of sound-sculpture. The closest thing to them in English is the elegantly figured prose of John Milton's *Areopagitica.*

Montaigne and Bacon, however, were anti-Ciceronian. In "Of the Education of Children" Montaigne recalls: "At the height of Cicero's eloquence many were moved to admiration; but Cato merely laughed at it. . . . I would have the *subject* predominate, and so fill the imagination of him who listens that he shall have no remembrance of the words." And again, in "Of Books": "To confess the truth boldly . . . [Cicero's] manner of writing seems to me irksome. . . . If I spend an hour reading him . . . I find oftenest only wind."

Bacon put the same idea in terms of *res* and *verba*—in terms, that is, of meaning versus hot air. In the *Advancement of Learning* he observes that the Ciceronian humanists searched "more after wordes than matter, and more after the choisenesse of the Phrase, and the round and cleane composition of the sentence, and the sweet falling of the clauses . . . then after the weight of matter, worth of subject, soundnesse of argument, life of invention, or depth of judgement."

His style enacts this rejection of humanism. Its harshness is a way of announcing his contempt of Ciceronian flatulence—his commitment to weight of matter rather than choiceness of phrase.

Does this mean that the early essay abandons rhetoric? Absolutely not. It means only that the early essay substitutes one kind of rhetoric for another. Since the new kind of rhetoric is unconventional and thus unfamiliar, the early essay gives the impression of novelty. And since the impression of novelty depends on the use of formulas that are unfamiliar and therefore not obvious to the reader, the early essay creates the illusion of being spontaneous. It pretends to spring either from the freely associating imagination of the author or the draconian grammar of the world of things.

The formula for this kind of style is *ars celare artem*—art that conceals art. Montaigne announces: "The way of speaking that I like is a simple and natural speech, the same on paper as on the lips . . . far removed from affectation, free, loose, and bold." The statement is charming, but it is a palpable lie. Both Montaigne and Bacon revised their essays over and over again. The lack of artifice is the product of years of effort.

I think we have some chains around Proteus. Now let us begin to vex him.

The first edition of Montaigne's *Essais* (1580) lacked the present Book III. Another, moderately augmented edition appeared in 1582. A third version, with a new book (incorrectly labeled Book V) and with major revisions and additions, appeared in 1588. Finally Montaigne's famous *fille d'alliance* Marie de Gournay issued a posthumous edition in 1595 that has further major changes and that was the basis of standard editions of the *Essais* until the twentieth century.

The record shows that Montaigne was a familiar type—the literary neurotic who can never let his works alone even after they are published. In general, as he revised, the self-revelation of the essays became more overt. That is, the more clothes he put on, the more naked he became. And as his nakedness increased, the more he—and his readers—became aware that he was not a single consistent identity, but a boiling pot of conflicts and changes.

The first edition of Bacon's essays (1597) offers ten essays. That may be said to initiate literary minimalism. They seem to consist chiefly of sayings from Bacon's commonplace book. The Renaissance would have called the sayings "flowers" or "sentences." Bacon's strategy may owe something to the hugely successful collection of aphorisms made by Erasmus—the *Adagia*—but Erasmus could never resist gilding every aphorism with a commentary, whether it was a lily or a dandelion. In the first edition of the *Essayes* Bacon offers his flowers plain.

Like Montaigne, Bacon revised compulsively. By 1625 the 10 original essays had grown to 58, plus an incomplete 59th. The essays also grew obese over the years. "Of Studies," for example, roughly doubled in size between 1597 and 1625.

As Montaigne revised, his essays became richer. Bacon's revisions seem to me to have been less felicitous. As his essays enlarge, they lose the taciturnity—the aggressive minimalism—that is a principal source of their power. The sentences get more sequential, more official, more pontifical, more—shall I say it?—like sentences in an oration.

In addition to making the essays more official, Bacon tried to give them philosophical status by suggesting they are part of the grand philosophical scheme outlined in the *Novum Organum.* In the Renaissance classification of the sciences, ethics, economics, and politics occupy an area equivalent to what would today be called the social sciences. By calling his essays "civil and moral," Bacon was suggesting they are contributions to the social sciences—specifically to politics and ethics. In my own opinion, which goes against official wisdom in this case, relating the essays to the program of the *Novum Organum* was an afterthought intended to enhance their dignity.

Whatever the case, philosophy is directly relevant to the early history of the essay, and I now turn to it.

In *Representative Men* Emerson properly calls Montaigne "the skeptic." The first of the *Essais* to be composed is also the longest, most ponderous essay of the lot—Montaigne's

Apology for Raimond Sebond, which is essay 12 in Book II. Sebond was a late medieval theologian who wrote a *Theologia Naturalis* showing how design in Nature will convince even the most depraved agnostic of the truth of the Christian religion. Montaigne translated it from Latin into French at his father's request.

The work culminates a long tradition of pious fatuity about the Book of Nature. Once his father was safely in the ground, Montaigne deconstructed it. The deconstruction became so devastating that, by the end, very little basis remained for believing in God or design in Nature or anything else. Hamlet seems to have read the *Apology* since he quotes from it when he observes that the earth is a pestilent congregation of vapors and man a quintessence of dust.

Hamlet is quoting the right author. Montaigne had been forced by the controversies of the reformation and the collapse of traditional verities about nature to doubt every aspect of the received view of the world. This is what the *Apology for Raimond Sebond* is all about. The St. Bartholomew Day Massacre, which occurred just eight years before the first edition of the *Essais,* magnified the shock. If Christians who proclaim themselves models of piety can establish their position only by slaughtering those Christians who disagree with them, what evidence is there that reason has any place at all in religion? In short a world that had once seemed solid, reasonable, and self-evident had shown that it was none of the above. There were times when it looked like a pestilent congregation of vapors. John Donne reached the same conclusion:

> The new philosophy calls all in doubt,
> The element of fire is quite put out;
> 'Tis all in pieces, all coherence gone,
> All just supply and all relation.

Historians argue about whether Montaigne was a fideist or a skeptic. The terms are so close that we need not quibble. The fideist believes God and His ways are utterly beyond human comprehension. Therefore we must accept whatever law or custom or the local tyrant tells us to believe. The skeptic, as far as Montaigne and his contemporaries are concerned, is a follower of the ancient philosopher Pyrrho of Elis (fl. 300 B. C.) and of his disciple Sextus Empiricus, whose works were published with Latin translation by Henri Estienne around 1560. The skeptics developed a systematic demonstration that man is deceived both by sense-evidence and by reason.

If this is so, the proper stance for the philosopher is to doubt everything. This is not nihilism but a reserving of judgment, a determination to be a detached observer rather than a partisan. The Greek term for this sort of detachment is *ataraxia,* which means "calmness" and, by extension, a refusal to become involved. Montaigne explains in the *Apology:* "This attitude of [the skeptics] . . . accepting all objects without inclination and consent, leads them to their Ataraxy, which is a placid, settled condition of life, exempt from the emotions that we experience. . . . They are even exempted thereby from zeal about their own doctrine."

At its coolest, ataraxy produces the ideal of the scientist who welcomes refutation because it advances knowledge. Observers are, by definition, outsiders, however; and for outsiders detachment can become terrifying isolation. Hamlet's detachment is announced by his black suit and his refusal to be drawn into the *Gemütlichkeit* of the Danish court. It is closer to despair than freedom from passion, and its result is not a series of essays enacting the process of self-realization, but soliloquies in which the speaker alternates between murder and suicide.

This takes us to the dark outer edge of the early essay. It is a darkness acknowledged by Montaigne but, for the most part, beyond the emotional boundaries he set for himself.

Having been led by his own analysis to doubt the world as he had conceived it, Montaigne turned inward in the quest for certainty. The basic question of the *Essais* is "What do I know"—"Que sçais-je?" The question became Montaigne's official motto. In the *Apology* he explains that he inscribed it under a pair of scales. The scales symbolize ataraxy—the balancing of alternatives.

Montaigne's innumerable quotations are intended to be part of his answer. André Gide remarks in an often-quoted essay that they are there "to show that man is always and everywhere the same"—i.e., there *is* a stable, universal something that can be called "human nature." Unfortunately, as Michael Hall has demonstrated, the quotations are inconsistent. They show that when you collect several centuries' worth of wisdom on a topic, you do not get a philosophy: you get a chain of contradictory platitudes.

Turning inward was no more helpful than consulting the sages. When he turned inward, Montaigne discovered not universality but infinite variety. He was forced to conclude that the self is as various, as elusive, as many-shaped as the world.

Without fully understanding what he was doing, Montaigne was searching for a central "I"—what Descartes would later call the *cogito;* and as a matter of fact Montaigne powerfully influenced the Cartesian project. But he was more radical than Descartes. Descartes admitted we may be dreaming the world, but he insisted the *cogito* is beyond doubt—so solid, in fact, that it is the rock on which you can build everything else.

Montaigne concluded from his inquiry that there is no rock. There is only an endless series of illusions. Early in the *Essais* he announces: "We must remove the mask from things as from persons," and that "being truthful is the beginning of virtue"; but his great discovery is that man is as protean as the world: "Every man has within himself the entire human condition." Later still Montaigne uses metaphors of the a-rational to describe his discovery of himself: "I have seen no monster or miracle on earth more evident than myself . . . the better I know myself, the more my misshapenness astonishes me, and the less do I comprehend myself."

In the famous introduction to "Of Repenting," the second essay in Book III, we read:

> Others shape the man; I narrate him, and offer
> to view a special one, very ill-made, and whom,

could I fashion him over, I should certainly make very different from what he is; but there is no doing that. The world is but perpetual motion; all things in it move incessantly. . . . I can not anchor my subject; he is always restless and staggering with an unsteadiness natural to him. I catch him in the state that he is in at the moment when I turn my attention to him. I do not paint his being, I paint his passing—not the passing from one age to another . . . but from day to day, from moment to moment. . . . Writers commune with the world with some special and peculiar badge; I am the first to do this with my general being, as Michel de Montaigne.

Here we have the authentic note of the *Essais* and of the essay as a genre. The essay is the enactment of a process by which the soul realizes itself even as it is passing from day to day and moment to moment. It is the literary response to a world that has become problematic. The complexity of Montaigne's text works to disguise this fact, but it has always been an open secret.

Perseverance is also important. Each essay leads to another, and all of them have to be revised, and the job is never finished until Montaigne is dead. Cyrene's advice to Aristaeus was "Hold on, son." "Hold on" was also a motto of the skeptics. Montaigne explains in the *Apology:* "Their symbolic word is *epécho*—that is to say, 'I hold on, I do not budge.'"

Now let us return to Bacon. If Montaigne's essays give the feeling of the mind as it seeks by constant adjustments to find a path through a labyrinth, Bacon's method is to assert the existence of a path whether one is there or not. In the *De Argumentis Scientiarum* Bacon calls his method "initiative" in contrast to "magisterial." The magisterial method is used for teaching. It has a well-defined shape—the shape of an oration. The initiative method is, by contrast, suggestive. As Bacon explains, "the initiative intimates. The magisterial requires that what is told should be believed; the initiative that it should be examined."

Like Montaigne, Bacon was strongly attracted to skepticism. "The doctrine of those who have denied that certainty could be attained at all has some agreement with my way of proceeding," he admitted. Although he argued that empiricism offers an escape from uncertainty, he believed that most of the received knowledge of his age was false—the result of "errors and vanities," which he categorized by the metaphor of Idols: Idols of the tribe, Idols of the cave, Idols of the marketplace, Idols of the theater.

Bacon did not spend much time on religion; perhaps he felt it was above—or beneath—the reach of reason. He never attacked it, but his heavy-handed condescension looks like thinly disguised contempt. Conversely the collapse during the sixteenth century of scientific doctrines accepted as verities for thousands of years fascinated him. The prime example was the toppling of Ptolemaic by Copernican astronomy, but astronomy was only one of many areas in which received knowledge was crumbling when put to the test. Each failure of a traditional theory was a demonstration of the validity of the theory of Idols.

This kind of skepticism looks forward to a fully developed scientific method. It underlies Sir Thomas Browne's *Pseudodoxia Epidemica,* better known as *Vulgar Errors,* which systematically exposes many superstitions of the sort deconstructed in Montaigne's *Apology.* The *Pseudodoxia* appeared in six editions during Browne's lifetime. In matters of religion Browne was a fideist. Montaigne ends the *Apology* with the remark that man "will be lifted up if God by special favor lends him his hand; he will be lifted up, when abandoning and renouncing his own means, he lets himself be upheld by purely heavenly means." Browne writes in *Religio Medici:* "Me thinks there be not impossibilities enough in Religion for an active faith . . . I love to lose myself in a mystery, to pursue my reason to an *Oh Altitudo.* . . . I learned of *Tertullian, Certum est quia impossible est.*"

Bacon's dedication of the ten essays of 1597 claims only that they are "medicinable." The dominant meaning is that they are useful—they expose various errors and vanities and provide compass points for a world in flux. But the term *medicinable* is a metaphor, and its implications invite comment. According to the metaphor the reader needs to be cured. In other words there is some kind of metaphysical plague going around. It is a plague of doubt. Jimmy Carter felt the same thing about twentieth-century America and called it a malaise in one of his more disastrous orations. If Bacon had been present, he would have called it a failure of nerve and voted for Ronald Reagan. His essays are intended to be a cure for social malaise. They are "medicinable" because they distill wisdom gained from life in what Bacon's heirs have insisted ever since on calling "the real world." For that reason they often have the quality of a pep talk by the coach of a losing team.

The strategy is to create what might be called a "rhetoric of assurance." Accordingly, in the first edition, the sentences are chiefly commands and assertions. Omission of understood words (zeugma) gives the sentences a telegraphic quality reinforced by the paring away of modifiers, modifying phrases, and subordinate clauses. Further economy is achieved by parallelism and balance. The word order is standard. The speaker knows what he wants to say and says it directly. The main units are set off by paragraph marks—we would call them "bullets" today. The term is appropriate. Bacon wants each sentence to have the force of a pistol shot:

> •Reade not to contradict, nor to believe, but to waigh and consider. • Some books are to bee tasted, others to bee swallowed, and some few to bee chewed and digested. . . . • Reading maketh a full man, conference a readye man, and writing an exacte man. . . . • Histories make men wise, Poets wittie: the Mathematickes subtle, naturall Phylosophie deepe: Morall grave, Logicke and Rhetoricke able to contend.

The sentences often have an edge of cynicism, of *Realpolitik,* reminding us that Bacon had read his Machiavelli: "ambition is a winding stair"; "those who marry give hostages to fortune"; "the stage is more beholding to Love than the life of man"; "wounds cannot be cured without searching"; "a mixture of lie doth ever add pleasure."

You can hear a subtext under the words: "Son, I know things are rotten in Denmark. There is some sort of malaise going around. But look here. Life never was a bed of roses. You might even say it is an unweeded garden. That's no reason to whine. Remember, son, you can't weed a garden without getting dirt on your boots." Push the *Essayes* a little further, and you begin to hear the voice of King Lear on the heath: "Robes and furr'd gowns hide all; plate sin with gold and the strong lance of justice hurtless breaks; a dog's obeyed in office."

Is this *Realpolitik* or despair? Whatever it is, the message of the *Essayes* is "So be it." That's how things are in the real world, and that's how they always will be.

Let us recall one other legacy from Montaigne and Bacon. Both men were authors. Therefore it follows as the night the day that, having invented a form, both proceeded to muck it up. As we have seen, neither could let an essay alone once it had been written. We can argue this habit is a virtue in Montaigne and is not fatal in Bacon, but its implications are ominous. The constant revision implies a change in the concept of the essay from the enactment of a process to something that looks supiciously like literature—perhaps an oration propped up like a scarecrow on the scaffolding of its *dispositio*.

To turn the essay into literature is to domesticate it—to make it not very different from a letter by Seneca or one of Plutarch's *Moralia*. Recall Florio's use of the word *discourse* as a rough synonym for *essay*. The usage is pregnant with future confusion. John Locke's *Essay Concerning Human Understanding* is splendid philosophy. It might even be called an "essay" on the basis of being an exploration of its subject, but if so, any work of philosophy short of Nietzsche's *Thus Spake Zarathustra* can be called an essay. Its proper title is obviously discourse, maybe *Abhandlung*.

To turn the essay into literature is also to encourage authors to display beautiful—or delicately anguished, or nostalgic, or ironic, or outraged, or extraverted, or misanthropic—souls; or, alternately, to create prose confections, oxymorons of languid rhythms and fevered images.

I admit this sometimes happens to the essay, but I think the really surprising thing is that, in spite of all temptations, the essay has tended to remain true to its heritage. I do not mean that essays are products of what you might call "troubled times," but that the essay was born from a moment of profound, even terrifying doubt, and that its rhetoric has often been adopted by authors who have sensed the power of the forces of dissolution. Matthew Arnold entitled his most famous collection of essays *Culture and Anarchy,* and Joan Didion named her first collection from the apocalyptic image in Yeats's poem "Second Coming": *Slouching Towards Bethlehem.*

Essays are written on an infinite variety of subjects from infinitely various points of view. Time and time again, however, the essay reverts to its original forms—on the one hand to the Montaignian enactment of the process of self-realization in a world without order: "I do not paint [my subject's] being, I paint his passing . . . from day to day, from moment to moment." And on the other hand

to Baconian assertiveness in a world that threatens to reduce assertions to black comedy: "I will do such things. . . . what they are, I know not, but they shall be the terrors of the earth."

The eighteenth century approved the idea of cool detachment from the malaise of things. Addison and Steele are officially observers of life in the *Tatler*. Under the surface, however, runs the old motif of the search for the self. Steele concludes the *Tatler* with the image of the world as labyrinth: "I must confess, it has been a most exquisite pleasure to me . . . to enquire into the Seeds of Vanity and Affectation, to lay before my Readers the Emptiness of Ambition: In a Word, to trace Humane Life through all its Mazes and Recesses. . . .''

The *Spectator* has even more obvious relations to its ancestry. A spectator is an observer, an outsider—someone who withholds assent. This is exactly the point made by Addison in the introduction to the new journal: "I live in the World rather as a Spectator of Mankind, than as one of the species. . . . I have acted in all the Parts of my Life as a looker-on, which is the Character I intend to preserve in this Paper."

For the most part the *Spectator* preserves its detachment, but occasionally there is a powerful updraft of emotion. It is the terror—or the malaise—of the world that makes people want to be spectators; but as Werner Heisenberg has shown, spectators are always tangled up in the things they are observing. The following comment, from *Spectator* number 420, is directly traceable to the tangling of human motive with the world science has revealed. This is all the more striking because it is not what you expect from an eighteenth-century spectator:

> If . . . we contemplate those wide Fields of *Ether,* that reach in height as far from *Saturn* as to the fixt stars, and run abroad almost to an infinitude, our Imagination finds its Capacity filled with so immense a Prospect . . . [it] puts it self upon the Stretch to comprehend it. But if we yet rise higher, and consider the fixt Stars as so many Oceans of Flame . . . and still discover new Firmaments and new Lights, that are sunk further in those unfathomable Depths of *Ether,* so as not to be seen by the strongest of our Telescopes, we are lost in . . . a Labyrinth of Suns and Worlds, and confounded with the Immensity and magnificence of Nature. . . . Let a Man try to conceive the different bulk of an Animal, which is twenty, from another which is a hundred times less than a Mite, or to compare, in his Thoughts, a length of a thousand Diameters of the Earth, with that of a Million, and he will quickly discover that he has no . . . Measures in his Mind, adjusted to such extraordinary Degrees of Grandeur or Minuteness. The Understanding, indeed, opens an infinite Space on every side of us, but the Imagination, after a few faint efforts, is immediately at a stand, and finds her self swallowed up in the immensity of the Void that surrounds it.
>
> (pp. 611-27)

I do not think we live in a solid empirical world of the sort Bacon dangled tantalizingly before readers of *The Ad-*

vancement of Learning, even as he demonstrated that it was an illusion. We live in a world of changes and shadows, a world where the real dissolves even as we reach for it and meets us even as we turn away. It is a world of mazes and illusions and metaphors and idols and stairways that go upward and downward to infinity.

We live at a time much like the sixteenth century. It is a time of immense destructive and constructive change, and there is no way of knowing whether the destructive or the constructive forces are more powerful. It is a time when the world looks like an unweeded garden and doubt is a condition of consciousness. The essay is as uniquely suited to expressing this contemporary mode of being-in-culture as it was when Montaigne began writing the *Apology for Raimond Sebond.*

What *is* the essay? I come back to that tough question. If there is such a thing as an essential essay—a *real* Proteus—that same Proteus changes into so many shapes, so unlike the real Proteus, that it requires an act of faith to believe the shapes are all variations on a single underlying identity. That, of course, is why Proteus adopted the strategy of change in the first place. People who lack faith will turn away convinced nothing is there. *We,* however, will remember the advice of Cyrene: "The more he turns himself into different shapes, the more you, my son, must hold onto those strong chains."

Holding on may be important. If the essay enacts the creation of the self—if we must essay to be—and the essay does not exist, then you might legitimately ask whether that which the essay enacts can be said to exist. The epigraph of the last *Spectator* is from Persius: *Respue quod non es. . . .* : "Throw away what you are not." It is good advice, but it assumes that after you throw everything superfluous away, there is something left.

If you have bound Proteus and all the changes have occurred, and if he returns to his own shape, he will have already answered your first question: there is something there. But is there? Maybe what you are seeing is only another counterfeit, another Idol.

That's the way things are, and the essay is the most expressive literary form of our age because it comes closest to being what all literature is supposed to be—an imitation of the real. You can vex the essay and drive it to extremities. Maybe the result will be nothing. Your action will be dubious, but in the real world, to get a piece even of a dubious action, you have to follow advice: Hold on, son. (pp. 630-32)

> O. B. Hardison, Jr. "Binding Proteus: An Essay on the Essay," in The Sewanee Review, Vol. XCVI, No. 4, Fall, 1988, pp. 610-32.

Ted-Larry Pebworth

[Pebworth is an American educator and critic. In the excerpt below, he suggests that the essay may be defined as a chronicle of its author's mental processes.]

The essay as a distinguishable genre emerged concurrently with the anti-Ciceronian movements in prose style in the late sixteenth century; and the early essayists, both in France and in England, were all anti-Ciceronians of one kind or another. [In his *Attic and Baroque Prose Style: The Anti-Ciceronian Movement,* 1969] Morris Croll has reminded us that the anti-Ciceronian reformers of prose style had as their intention and goal the desire "to portray, not a thought, but a mind thinking." More cautiously stated, they sought to give the impression, often achieved through diligent revision, that they were essentially the secretaries of their minds in motion. The genres that these anti-Ciceronians embraced or created reflect the same impulse. Lengthy and overtly rhetorical forms gave way to briefer, more loosely constructed ones, the essay among them. But a mind can think in at least two directions: it can move toward a predetermined, albeit vague or general, goal; or it can wander at will. The first kind of thinking is discoverable in most prose genres of the late Renaissance. The latter freedom defines the essay.

The generic distinctions between the anti-Ciceronian "kinds" are distinctions of intention and structure. Generally, the meditation, the vow, and the resolve portray a mind thinking toward the making of a promise to God or to the writer himself, a resolution to better life or conduct in some way; or they show a mind thinking toward a consolation designed to make hardship or death easier to bear. The injunction moves toward an explicitly hortatory conclusion directed at its audience; the paradox and the problem aim toward the construction of specific arguments; and the character is pointed toward the painting of a full, though frequently one-sided, word picture. They are all anticipatory forms, with specific ends or conclusions in view. The essay, on the other hand, is essentially reflective. It is designed to give the impression of a mind thinking on a subject with no predetermined goal or formulaic conclusion toward which it need aim. It is the record of a mind apparently roaming freely—using the devices of definition, partition, contrast, antithesis, illustration, and example, to be sure, but calling upon them as they naturally suggest themselves in a free association of ideas.

This distinction between the early essay and its related forms is hinted at by many of the early English essayists and by their master Montaigne; it is suggested by the kind of titles that they characteristically give to their essays; and it is implied in what may be the earliest set of rules proffered in print for the writing of essays. In the piece which closes the first edition of his *Essais* (1580), Montaigne emphasizes immediacy and suggests that he has no interest in conclusions which can be known in advance: "Je ne corrige point mes premières imaginations par les secondes. . . . Je veux représenter le progrès de mes humeurs, et qu'on voie chaque pièce en sa naissance" ("I never correct my first imaginings by my second. . . . I want to represent the course of my humors, and I want people to see each part at its birth.") And in 1588, Montaigne made an even more revealing comment on the intention of the form that he had created: "Je ne puis assurer mon objet. Il va trouble et chancelant, d'une ivresse naturelle. Je le prends en ce point, comme il est, en l'instant que je m'amuse à lui. Je ne peins pas l'être. Je peins le passage" ("I cannot keep my subject still. It goes along befuddled and staggering, with a natural drunkenness. I take it in this condition, just as it is at the moment I give my attention to it. I do not portray being: I portray passing.") Montaigne created a form which was free to follow his mind as it thought ("represent the course of my humors"); and he allowed that mind to think in any direction that it chose, in its "natural drunkenness," with no particular conclusion in view. His kind of essay is not the picture of a result, it is the record of a passage.

Montaigne's first self-acknowledged English disciple, Sir William Cornwallis the younger, endorsed his master's conception of the new genre. In 1601, he excused what some critics, accustomed to the formal, overtly rhetorical pattern of the treatise, might consider a fault in his own prose writings. In characterizing the essay as "a maner of writing well befitting vndigested motions," Cornwallis betrayed his awareness that at the genre's core are process and progress. He, too, recognized that the new form's distinctive feature is the chronicling of the thought process wherever it might wander. Referring to his own essays, he writes: "Nor if they stray, doe I seeke to amende them, for I professe not method, neither will I chaine my selfe to the head of my Chapter."

Throughout the seventeenth century there are allusions to the kinetic nature of the essay and oblique references to the genre as the picture of a mind thinking. In the laudatory poem prefacing Nicholas Breton's *Characters upon Essays* (1615), "W. P." writes:

> Words are the pensils, whereby drawne we find
> The picture of the inward man, the mind.
> Such thoughts, such words; such words, such is
>   the man. . . .

In concluding one of his *Essayes Morall and Theologicall* (1609), Daniel Tuvill remarks: "I could adde more; but the humour of *Essaies* is rather to glaunce at all things with a running conceit; then to insist on any with a slowe discourse." And in 1628, Owen Felltham echoes Tuvill in noting that the essay is *"of all writing . . . neerest to a running* Discourse." To Cornwallis's "motions" and "stray," Tuvill and Felltham add "running." Clearly, all three saw the essay as progress and passage.

Another indication that the English prose writers of the late Renaissance saw a difference between the intention of the essay and the intentions of the vow, the resolve, the injunction, the paradox, and the problem can be discerned in the kinds of titles chosen for individual works in these various genres. The close-ended forms, when they have titles, generally indicate in them the conclusion or conclusions reached in the work, while the open-ended essay almost always indicates merely the subject thought upon, prefaced by that ubiquitous preposition "of." For example, Donne's paradoxes have such titles as "That Women ought to paint," "That good is more common then evill," and "That Nature is our worst Guide"; and his problems are headed with specific questions that call forth conclusions, such as "Why hath the common Opinion afforded Women Soules?" and "Why does the Poxe so much affect to undermine the Nose?" His one essay, on the other hand, is entitled "Of Valour." Similarly, Felltham gave to his resolves (1623) such titles as "Cowardice worthlesse," "Gouernment and Obedience the two causes of a Com-

mon Prosperitie," and "A good Rule in wearing of Apparell"; while to his essays (1661) he assigned such titles as "Of Memory," "Of Superstition," and "Of Conscience." Even more significantly, when Felltham late in life revised some of his early resolves, turning them into essays, he frequently modified their titles accordingly, making them less indicative of conclusions reached. Thus the resolve "A Rule in reading Authors" became the essay "Of reading Authors"; "Liberty makes Licentious" became "Of the danger of Liberty"; and "The great Euill that Neglect brings both to God and Soule" became "Of Neglect."

By the 1640's, the essay had become an officially recognized genre, sanctioned for use as a grammar school and university exercise. John Hall's essays, published in 1646 as *Horae Vacivae,* appear to have been assigned to him by his tutor at St. John's College, Cambridge; and by the mid-1660's, at least one handbook, *The Scholars Guide from the Accidence to the University* (1665), written by the schoolmaster Ralph Johnson, contained a definition of the essay and a set of rules for its composition. The definition and the instructions are illuminating:

> An Essay.
>
> An Essay is a short discourse about any vertue, vice, or other commonplace. Such be Learning, Ignorance, Justice, Temperance, Fortitude, Prudence, Drunkenness, Usury, Love, Joy, Fear, Hope, Sorrow, Anger, Covetousness, Contentation, Labour, Idleness, Riches, Poverty, Pride, Humility, Virginity, &c.
>
> RVLES for making it.
>
> 1.   Having chosen a Subject, express the nature of it in two or three short Definitions, or Descriptions.
>
> 2.   Shew the severall sorts or kinds of it, with their distinctions.
>
> 3.   Shew the severall causes, adjuncts, and effects of each sort or kinde.
>
> 4.   Be carefull to do this briefly, without tautology or superfluous words, in good and choice language.
>
> 5.   Metaphors, Allegories, Antithetons, and Paranomasia's do greatly adorn this kind of exercise.
>
> 6.   In larger and compleat Essays (such as *Bacon's, Felltham's, &c.*) we must labour compendiously to express the whole nature of, with all observables about our subject.

It is interesting to note that by 1665 the essay is beginning to allow comprehensiveness, paving the way for Locke twenty years later to call his rather exhaustive exploration of human understanding an essay. But what is more interesting about these rules for making an essay is what is omitted. The rules given for the writing of fables and characters in the same handbook specifically mention the kind of conclusion appropriate to each of these two forms, but Johnson does not concern himself with how the essay is to be concluded. The early essayists sometimes do reach summary conclusions, and they occasionally even mix forms by ending an essay with a resolve or a vow. But the essay is essentially passage for its own sake rather than for its destination alone; it exists for the totality of its irreducible motion.

The usual method of the early essayist is to begin with an axiomatic statement or series of statements. In thinking on the subject thus set up, he draws upon his reading and his personal experience, making use of those rhetorical devices which reflect natural thought processes: definition, division, contrast, example, illustration, etc. His great freedom lies in the fact that he can use as many or as few of these devices as he chooses, that he can employ them in any order that suggests itself to his wandering mind, that he need have no particular end in view when he commences his musings, and that he can even wander away from the announced subject if he chooses to do so. The early essayist, then, works within an extraordinarily free form.

The fullest and most explicit critical recognition of the unique freedom of the sixteenth- and seventeenth-century English essay is provided, though in a condescending context, by that master of a different kind of essay, Joseph Addison. In *The Spectator* for 5 September 1712, he writes: "Among my Daily-Papers, which I bestow on the Publick, there are some which are written with Regularity and Method, and others that run out into the Wildness of those Compositions, which go by the name of *Essays*." Addison comes close to seeing this "wilder" form of essay as portraying a mind thinking on a subject; but, as he continues the contrast, he does not quite make the distinction between thoughts and the thinking process, and he misses entirely the early essay's principle of organization: "As for the first, I have the whole Scheme of the Discourse in my Mind, before I set Pen to Paper. In the other kind of Writing, it is sufficient that I have several Thoughts on a Subject, without troubling my self to range them in such order, that they may seem to grow out of one another, and be disposed under the proper Heads." Addison's favorite kind of essay is controlled and organized by neo-classical rules of logic and rhetoric; and he ultimately fails to recognize the more subtle, though no less demanding, method of organization employed by the early essayists as they attempted to picture the mind in its natural wanderings, unfettered by textbook laws of exposition.

The recognition that the early essay's intention is to present a mind thinking allows us to apprehend the form's characteristic aesthetic effects. In addition, it enables us to see an artistic organizing principle controlling essays which may at first glance seem to be disjointed and lacking in focus, as, for example, the eighth essay in Cornwallis's 1600 collection. After announcing a double subject in its title, "Of Praise and Glorie," Cornwallis dismisses glory with a definition (seeing it as a response called forth only by ultimate perfection and therefore due only to God); and he concentrates on praise (the highest form of recognition that man can achieve). A consideration of the three "chiefest" virtues through which post-lapsarian man can earn praise is followed by a distinction drawn between fame (limited to time) and praise (as enduring as eternity); and

the essay ends in a contemplation of "eternal Contentment."

Neither from its title nor from its first paragraph can one reasonably predict this essay's progression or its final statement. Reflecting a kind of "wildness," it is not the carefully organized, methodical discourse that Addison most admires. In addition to lacking proportion, it is even self-contradictory. After concluding that patience is the one virtue to which all others are merely trappings, Cornwallis ostensibly has second thoughts and affirms that for the meriting of true praise a harmony of temperance, fortitude, and patience is necessary. After judging that virtue should not be pursued for its ultimate reward, an eternity in Heaven, he ends the essay with a contemplation of precisely that reward. But what "Of Praise and Glorie" lacks in methodical order and internal consistency, it makes up for in intimacy and immediacy. In it we do not find a finished thought, stripped of inconsistencies and set out in dignified proportion. Rather, we are allowed to participate in the thinking process of an interesting mind. We follow the "natural drunkenness" of a search for truth as that mind, through free association, attempts new combinations of ideas. We see old truths finding slightly new shapes as the essayist moves from generalities about glory and praise into considerations of specific virtues. Not only do we witness the discovery of a slightly different shape to truth, but we are also allowed an intimate glimpse into Cornwallis's personality as we see the sobriety of contemplation yield occasionally to irrepressible, youthful pride in wit, as when he suddenly notices a clever kinship between fortitude and temperance: the former is abstention from fear as the latter is abstention from excessive appetite. Even though we cannot predict the essay's final paragraph from its opening statement, we are satisfied by that final paragraph. It is not the satisfaction of a thesis proved, but the satisfaction of an exploration of old ideas which has discovered new relationships.

The method employed by Cornwallis is typical of that of most early English essayists. Bacon's procedure is occasionally different. But even when his essays are exceptional, they are so not in kind, but in the thought pattern which they picture. Bacon spent much of his literary and philosophical efforts in an attempt to reform the way men think. In particular, he sought to displace deductive reasoning with his own form of induction; and several of his essays reflect this major concern. As Fulton Anderson has noted [in *Francis Bacon: His Career and His Thought,* 1962], Bacon believed that the most productive kind of inquiry "starts . . . by subjecting to examination things which ordinary logic takes on trust." To carry out that inquiry, he developed a new form of induction. One feature of this new method is the questioning of accepted truths "through an examination of agreeing and disagreeing instances of particulars under observation and experiment." Although Stanley Fish exaggerates when he implies [in *Self-Consuming Artifacts: The Experience of Seventeenth-Century Literature,* 1972] that the Baconian essay is always inductive, many of the Lord Chancellor's essays do follow that pattern of reasoning. Being essays, they are only tentative and do not aspire to new generalizations; but they are concerned with testing the validity of axiomatic truths, not with illustrating or proving them. Like other essays of the late sixteenth and the early seventeenth centuries, they are attempts to portray a mind in the act of thinking; but the mind they chronicle is a mind thinking inductively.

Bacon's well-known "Of Marriage and Single Life" is a good example of his inductive approach to the essay. It exists in three versions, but since the revisions consist essentially of multiplying statements of qualification without changing the shape or the direction of the piece, the final state (1625) will serve as well as any to illustrate his method. Its opening statement is an axiom: "He that hath *Wife* and *Children,* hath giuen Hostages to Fortune; For they are Impediments, to great Enterprises, either of Vertue, or Mischiefe." The second sentence supports a part of the first, affirming that single or childless married men have been the most public-minded; but this assertion is immediately undercut by the consideration that those who have progeny "haue greatest care of future times" and by the observation that some single men are often self-centered and selfish. The essay proceeds in like manner. Arguments supporting marriage are opposed to equally strong arguments against it and to arguments which suggest that whether or not one marries is of no consequence. Al-

Title page of a 1632 volume of Sir William Cornwallis's essays.

though the essay ends differently in the different versions, in all cases it ends with a particular, not with a generalization. In none of the versions does Bacon state which of the two—marriage or single life—he considers to be better. He uses his essay not to make that point, but to show a mind thinking on the subject. His controlling connectives are "but" and "yet," and on one occasion even "but yet"; and such is the pattern of his kind of inductive thinking. In a Bacon essay, the process is frequently a major message.

Even though "Of Marriage and Single Life" differs from "Of Praise and Glorie" in the thought pattern it reflects, it is quite similar to Cornwallis's essay in more important respects. Bacon's piece most certainly was subjected to painstaking revision, but the final version nonetheless has an air of spontaneity about it. Indeed, the movement in the revisions from a predominantly epigrammatic to a more nearly conversational prose style parallels and helps achieve the greater immediacy and intimacy of the successive versions. The final revision gives the impression of a cultivated but pragmatic mind—one which knows much of life both through books and through direct activity and observation—proceeding among contradictory particulars on a subject as they naturally suggest themselves and ultimately refusing to generalize from those conflicting particulars. Through these details and this refusal we get a distinct notion of the essayist's personality. The overall impression may be that Bacon is detached and aloof, but we nevertheless witness a spark of playfulness in his personality as he moves from serious considerations of liberality, sternness, charity, impartiality, and gravity to a quotation from Thales which affirms that a young man should marry *"not yet, an Elder Man not at all."*

We can safely suppose that if a familiar essayist such as Cornwallis had written an essay entitled "Of Marriage and Single Life," we would be given in it some indication of whether or not the writer himself was married, or at least whether he considered that state to be better than the single life. But such personal details are not the only things that make an essay personal or familiar. Rosalie Colie [in *The Resources of Kind: Genre-Theory in the Renaissance,* 1973] sees the development of new genres such as the essay in the late Renaissance as the reflection of an awakened concern with "the concept of 'self,'" an interest which made itself manifest in the writer's "need to project himself as a personality on his world." In allowing us a fifteen-minute glimpse of his mind in action, Bacon has—in an important sense—projected his "self." Though in a different way, he has been just as "familiar" with us as Cornwallis was. Perhaps we do not warm to the personality reflected in "Of Marriage and Single Life," but we have an intimate experience of that personality as we participate in its thinking process, in its individualistic exploration of a complicated issue.

Stanley Fish has included Bacon's essays among several seventeenth-century works that he terms *Self-Consuming Artifacts,* arguing that they use themselves up in the reader's experience of them. I would like to expand Fish's argument to affirm that all early essays are "experience," process rather than being, both to the writer and to the reader. I would also prefer to look at the essay from a different perspective, seeing it as self-creating rather than self-consuming. One of the joys afforded by literature is that in reading a seventeenth-century essay we can re-create the process of a mind long since turned to dust. While the essayist may have used up his experience in writing it down, the genre within which he worked is one of the freest, most self-creating, literary types ever devised.

Literary critics no longer need excuse an interest in genre. Rightly applied, generic study is not merely an antiquarian interest of a narrowly defined scholarship divorced from criticism. As Rosalie Colie has argued, "a generic theory of literature is fundamentally comparative and therefore . . . fundamentally *critical.*" For examples of this one need go no further than recent Milton criticism where considerations of the generic intentions of the masque, the pastoral elegy, and the epic—to name only three forms—have significantly broadened our understanding and appreciation of the artistic achievements in *Comus,* "Lycidas," and the major poems. On a somewhat less exalted slope of Parnassus, a recognition of the generic intention of the early essay can be equally productive. Obviously, a realization of the essential intent of the early essay can narrow our critical focus, enabling us to distinguish more clearly than has heretofore been possible between the essay and the other short prose forms of the late Renaissance. More importantly, however, it can at the same time broaden our areas of inquiry. As has been noted often, the early English essayists for the most part wrote on the same handful of topics; and they dipped into the same body of historical, biographical, philosophical, and belletristic works for illustration and example. Their chief interest for us, what Douglas Bush calls their "capital," is personality and style. Personality can encompass more than simply the warmth or the aloofness reflected in an essayist's works, and style can concern itself with considerations beyond his preferences in tropes and in sentence structure. The fascination of these early essays lies finally in the mental processes which they chronicle. The questioning and pragmatism of Bacon, the toughness of Ben Jonson, the youthful sobriety of Cornwallis, the gentleness and charity of Felltham are qualities which emerge with vivid immediacy from the pictures of their minds ir passage; for the mind is the core of personality and the source of style. (pp. 17-27)

Ted-Larry Pebworth, "Not Being, But Passing: Defining the Early English Essay," in Studies in the Literary Imagination, *Vol. X, No. 2, Fall, 1977, pp. 17-27.*

Francis N. Zabriskie

[*In the following excerpt, Zabriskie contends that the essay is not defined by its content or the length at which it treats its subject, but rather by a discursive and familiar style.*]

I doubt whether any term in literary nomenclature is so indefinite as the word "essay." In histories of literature we rarely find the essayists classified by themselves, but under the head of moralists, critics, humorists, and the like; or, if used, the term is little more than a convenient mode of designating whatever may not very well be otherwise catalogued. As ordinarily understood, the essay is simply a comparatively short prose composition on a single theme.

The special object of this article is to protest against this confusion of thought, and to vindicate the essay proper as a distinct species of literary production, both in form and quality. History, criticism, philosophy, description, or any kind of information or research, may enter into its subject-matter. But these do not in themselves constitute a genuine essay, any more than swallows can make a summer, or piety and music are sufficient for a hymn.

An essay is *not,* as Worcester gravely defines it, "a short treatise or dissertation, a tract." The shortness is neither here nor there. And Worcester himself quotes Gilpin as follows:

> When we write a treatise, we consider the subject throughout; we strengthen it with arguments, we clear it of objections, we enter into details; and, in short, we leave nothing unsaid which properly belongs to the subject.

What a prodigious joke it would have been to Charles Lamb or Dick Steele to have any such thing as that expected of him! A tract is the product of the pamphleteer, who wants to preach, or to prove something. A dissertation is "an argumentative inquiry." Perish the thought that the essayist's pen should be guilty of tracts, even with the Miltonic suffix tract*ate!* And for him to "dissertate" is to be damned.

The essay is what the word implies, as set forth by, perhaps, the greatest master of the art. "To write just *treatises,*" says Lord Bacon, "requireth time in the writer and leisure in the reader, which is the cause that hath made me choose to write certain brief *notes,* set down rather *significantly* than *curiously,* which I have called *essays;* the word is late, but the thing is ancient." The reader will pardon my italics, because in these words we come at the heart of the whole matter. The essay is properly a collection of notes, indicating certain aspects of a subject, or suggesting thought concerning it, rather than the orderly or exhaustive treatment of it. It is not a formal siege, but a series of assaults—*essays,* or attempts upon it. It does not pursue its theme like a pointer, but goes hither and thither, like a bird to find material for its nest, or a bee to get honey for its comb. It is, in point of fact, a honeycomb, a thing which has unity and proportion, but which has its thousand separate cups of sweet suggestion and full of the distillations of fancy.

The essayist is not the commercial traveller nor the scientific explorer, but rather the excursionist of literature. There may be several ways of reaching a given point—as by railway, or steamboat, or turnpike stage with relays of horses. But there may also be such a thing as getting upon an ambling horse or into a family phaeton, and jogging on through bridle paths or through primrose and hawthorn lanes, going by the sun and not the guide-book, making *détours* to gather wild flowers, to gain a wider prospect, or to visit some old mansion or an old friend. Perhaps the way is worth more than the goal, and is an end in itself.

The essayist, in fact, is not apt to be burdened with the responsibilities of his theme. He will generally know what he is to write about when he begins, but not necessarily the "line of thought" he will pursue. He has ideas about it, and he is sure that others will suggest themselves as he goes on. He is interested in the thing, and thinks he sees it a little more vividly than most people; and he expects to interest others and make them see it more vividly. But he does not propose to argue the case with them, nor has he any pedagogic yearning to diffuse useful knowledge. The subject is the occasion rather than the efficient cause, or the end, of the essay. It may be said to liberate thought, rather than to limit it, in the mind of the writer. You never know what a genuine essayist will say next. It will not necessarily flow out of the last thing, nor have a logical connection with it. It may be suggested to him by what has gone before, but often by some subtle association unperceivable by the reader. And it is this surprise and unexpectedness which constitute a part of his peculiar fascination and perennial freshness.

Not that the true essay is a careless performance, the slouch or sloven of the literary sisterhood. On the contrary, no form of prose composition requires a more exquisite precision and felicity of expression. A genius for words is one of the essentials of the art. Hence it was the essayists, more than any others, who perfected prose style in England and France. Bacon re-wrote some of his works a dozen times. Pascal says that he sometimes took twenty days in perfecting a single piece, and it is affirmed that not a word of his *Provincial Letters* has become obsolete. "Point" is more absolutely essential than in any other kind of composition. Though leisurely and discursive in the general treatment, it must be sententious and exact in the expression of particular thoughts.

In short, it may be said that *the style is the essay,* so far, at least, as quality is concerned. It is not so much what is written about—all things are the essayist's spoil—as the way of saying it. While the most flexible and unfettered of literary products, it is one of the most distinctive. The mere outward semblance does not constitute it, nor can another literary form disguise it. Hence, as we shall find, essayism pervades every department of literature. We detect its essential attar in the histories and biographies of Carlyle, in the philosophy and science of Cousin and Max Müller, in the poetry of Shakespeare and Cowper, in the novels of Cervantes and Shorthouse, in the orations of Beecher and Phillips, in the devotional writings and homilies of Jeremy Taylor, Wickliffe, and Frederick W. Robertson. Even Augustine has the accent of the essayist in his *Confessions.* Bunyan's genius partakes of this quality quite as much as of the romance. (pp. 227-29)

On the other hand, things go by the name of essays which are merely "sermons," or reviews, or political tracts, or abridged histories. It was absurd for Burke to call his philosophical treatise on *The Sublime and the Beautiful* an "Essay." The same is true of many so-called essays of writers like Alison, Jeffrey, Brougham, and even Macaulay, which differ from histories and biographies only in length and in being of the nature of monographs. And so of a large proportion of the published "essays" of literary criticism. It is one thing to write book notices on an extended scale, or a minor treatise on rhetoric; and it is another thing to talk about books and authors with the rich poetic and humorous sympathy of Lowell, or, with Sainte-Beuve, to read the very soul of the writer in his book.

It does not seem an impossible task to formulate the chief characteristics of the essay, most of which must appear in each specimen in order to vindicate its title to the name.

And yet its very first feature is its informality and unconventionality of treatment. It is the child of freedom, and is shaped and guided simply by the selfhood of the writer. Hence it may proceed with the regularity of plan of a checker-board, or it may be as unmethodical as a crazy-quilt. It is not necessary to accept the suggestion that an essay is "a thing without beginning, middle, or end." But it is strictly true to say that it has no need of an introduction to "pave the way" or explain its appearance, nor of a "middle term" to "couple" the compartments together and constitute a legitimate "train of thought"; nor is the writer under stress either to continue on or to "conclude" at a definite stage of the process, but may stop whenever he has given enough of his thoughts to amuse himself or his readers. For this reason, if for no other, we claim Jean Paul Richter among the essayists. "He writes," says Doctor Hedge, "like one who enters on a journey with no determined end in view; or who, having one, forgets it in adventures by the way, in the pleasant company he falls in with, or strays into endless episodes." So also Rousseau, in his preface to *Émile* (the essay quality of which will be perceived at once on comparing it with Herbert Spencer's tractate on education), speaks of it as a "collection of observations and reflections without order and almost without sequence," and anticipates the objection that his book contains "rather a heap of reveries than a treatise." And Montaigne says of his essays, "As things come into my head, I heap them in; sometimes they advance in whole bodies, sometimes in single files."

There must, however, be an essential unity of subject. Informality is a different thing from formlessness, or chaos. The essayist may tack, and even drift, as much as he pleases, but it must be about the central buoy. Even Laurence Sterne, whose style may be described as a perpetual digression, never entirely lost his bearings.

It is sometimes taken for granted that the essay must be "brief," and this is one of the snares into which classifiers have fallen. But the nature of an essay is not a question of the yardstick. And yet it will transcend the limits of decided brevity at its peril. I do not think that Montaigne averaged two thousand words. The papers of Steele and Addison would hardly suffice for a two-page tract, and you could write most of Bacon's on a letter-sheet; the latter look ludicrously short when we compare them with the ten and even twenty-fold annotations of Whately upon them.

Maurice de Guérin wrote anxiously to his sister Eugénie, "I want you to reform your system of composition; it does not talk enough." The essayist is the man who chats. He is the club man of literature, standing at the club-house window and making his comments on the life that passes.

He takes down a book from the shelves, and talks about it to the group that gathers around him. Or he sits by the fire and tells unreservedly what he knows and thinks, and, in doing so, what he is. Some of the best essayists have written in the form of letters, which are the counterpart of conversation. The essay is spoiled if it gives us the feeling of going to school. Hence we can understand why Charles Lamb should class Gibbon, Robertson, Paley, and Soame Jenyns with "directories, statutes at large, and scientific treatises." And our own soul finds little of the genuine flavor in a long array of so-called essayists as able and elegant as John Foster, Harriet Martineau, Frances Power Cobbe, and W. R. Greg.

The essay, as has been said, treats its subject by a series of suggestions rather than by a chain of reasoning, or even of logical connection. This was the style, to an almost exaggerated degree, of the chief of the old masters, Bacon and Montaigne, and is specially characteristic of Plutarch. Emerson's essays were little else than the skilful boiling down of his commonplace-books and the ingenious jointing together of the contents of his scrap-books. His neighbor, Bronson Alcott, once found him down upon his library floor, which was strewn with these memoranda, and raking out from them the materials for his next essay.

The French mind has especially worked in this way. La Rochefoucauld of the "Maxims," and La Bruyère of the "Characters," are well-known examples; also Vauvenargues, "the Pascal of the eighteenth century," whose ideas lie around in seeming confusion, and are yet (as Vinet remarks) "the finished and fitted stones of an unbuilt palace." The series was "crowned," according to Sainte-Beuve, by Joseph Joubert, in his *Thoughts, Essays, and Maxims.* But it begins to look as if the end is not yet, for the unearthed *Pensées* of the Abbé Roux have already suggested a title for him as "the La Bruyère of to-day." I do not know a better illustration of the genuine essayist than this obscure parish priest. Here is a man of original, reflective, and observing mind, who is condemned to the isolation (which he carefully distinguishes from solitude) of a remote cure among the most uncongenial and uncultivated peasantry. He must find expression to relieve the numb pain of his heart and mind, and so talks to his paper as thoughts come to him or as things strike him. Under no constraint to convince an audience or to spread out his ideas for adaptation to "the public mind," he is in no temptation to fall into dissertation. He says what he has to say about the matter in hand in his own way, and in few or many words, as he happens to feel—and stops. He "essays" at a thousand topics, sometimes in one sentence, sometimes in a hundred, but never starts to "exhaust the subject," nor cares to ask afterward whether he has demonstrated it. He does not feel under the least obligation to his subject to "do justice" to it. His sole obligation is to himself, and to the fancy or the feeling that is in him.

Underneath all its sparkle, and even seeming *persiflage,* the essay is reflective. The essayist is the man who meditates, as distinct from the "thinker." He is the literary angler. We find no better example of this quality than in the thoughtfully devout pages of dear old Izaak Walton, whose pen was as true an angle as his fishingrod. There

is a fitness in such names as the *Spectator,* the *Rambler,* the *Idler,* applied to collections of these compositions. They are not voices from the crowd, vibrating with the strain and rush of life, but the observations of thoughtful and interested lookers-on. It was the opinion of Montaigne that "the sweets of life" were "peace, leisure, travel, and the writing of essays." But the first three are highly important to the fourth, in order to create the atmosphere of observing reflection. We might almost speak of the essay as a literary mood. Perhaps, with Montaigne, as with Rousseau and Chateaúbriand and Burton and Thoreau, it may amount to what has been called "the malady of reverie"; I had almost added Swift and Carlyle, but with them it is rather the essay "on the rampage," *rampant,* and not *couchant,* which latter is its true attitude and *pose.*

Not that the essay has any affinity with dulness or prosiness. Of all forms of composition, it can least afford that. The diamond could as well be without sparkle, or the mocking-bird without vocal range, as the essayist without vivacity and variety. An article whose design is information or investigation needs only to be clear, in respect to style. The essay must coruscate. Brightness and point are the breath of its life. A "labored" essay forfeits its claim to recognition.

The essay is marked by its scope and freedom of allusion. The essay mind does not run to abstractions, but tends constantly to the concrete in the way of examples and illustrations. It regards its subject not as a flower-cup into which to plunge for sweetness, but as a cell into which to convey the honey of a thousand blossoms, gathered in the farthest flights. It would be one of the best of rhetorical exercises to pick apart the tissue of an essay by Lowell or Holmes, and assign the multitudinous allusions to their originals. The great master whom the gentle Elia loved, and whose *Anatomy of Melancholy* is said to have been able to draw Doctor Johnson out of bed two hours earlier than any other book, is one mass and mosaic of anecdote, reference, and quotation. Of Jean Paul it is said that "his dominant principle in composition seems to have been to work in somehow, to lug in somewhere, all that he had ever read or thought of." Of the same school are the two undoubting Thomases—he of the *Urn Burial,* and he of the *Holy and Profane State*—whose pious learning was the oil that fed a thousand cressets of many-colored lights, which cast their rays on all things in heaven and on earth. Thomas Fuller has been called the founder of this "quaint school," which included also Donne and Taylor, but without their excess and exaggeration. He is at times as profound as Bacon, as imaginative as Milton, as witty as Sydney Smith. When he reasons, his logic unrolls a cloth of gold. Even Bacon cannot write a page on such a topic as "Fortune" without quoting or referring to Appius Claudius, Livy, Cæsar, Plutarch, Cato, Sylla, Timotheus, Timoleon, Agesilaus, and Epaminondas, and citing the customs of the Spaniards and Italians, the science of astronomy, and the verses of Homer.

Matthew Arnold has puzzled us all with his definition of poetry as a "criticism of life." It would be a far better definition of the essay. The essayist is the man who observes. Whether it be the social espionage of a *Spectator,* the amused sympathy of a "Geoffrey Crayon," the glare of a Swift, the scowl of a Carlyle, the sharp censorship of a Ruskin, the mousing and microscopic watch of a Thoreau, whether the glance comes from under the broad brow of Verulam, from the sad and eager eye of Rousseau, or the clear and sunny vision of Christopher North, the true essayist sees life in its manifold aspects as other men do not. He is in sympathy with M. Houssaye, who closes his *Confessions* by saying: "Whatever happens, and whatever befalls me, I thank the gods that I have been elected to behold the great spectacle of life!" So Maurice de Guérin, whose fragmentary relics are exquisite types of the essay, full of the most delicate perception and the subtilest sympathies, testifies: "I am neither philosopher nor naturalist, nor anything learned whatsoever; there is one word which is the god of my imagination, the tyrant (I ought rather to say) that fascinates it, lures it onward, gives it work to do without ceasing, and will finally carry it I know not where—the word *life.*" Théophile Gautier brought the faculty of describing the aspect of things to perfection. His *Caprices et Zigzags* and his *Voyage en Espagne* are the farthest possible from mere traveller's tours. They are absolute reproductions, by a marvellous word-artistry, of scenes and characters, with all their local color and atmosphere, their picturesqueness and humor. Professor Wilson, on the contrary, was an impressionist. The reader feels as if he were in Kit North's very company, breathing the mountain air, threading the perfumed woods, hearing his hearty voice, and helped by his strong hand over dangerous places; but without getting in a whole volume as definite a picture as Ruskin or George Sand will give in a page.

But, of course, the observation of nature is only a small part of the criticism of life. It is curious to note the topics which have engaged writers so different in mental *timbre* as Bacon, Burton, Emerson, and Leigh Hunt. You will find them all treating of the everyday sights and common life of men about them, precisely as did Steele and Addison in the high noon of the English essay, or as the Abbé Roux and the "Easy Chair" of *Harper's Monthly.*

The alcove of my library to which I turn as to its very heart and eyes, is that which contains the goodly fellowship of the essayists. The true essayist is intensely human. He dips his pen into the red ink of his heart and the violet ink of his fancy, rather than into the colorless fluid of the intellect. Nay, he employs all the variegated crayons of his moods and sentiments. His sympathies sound along his wire, from the fiery prejudice of a Teufelsdröckh to the jibe of a Jerrold, or the half-sigh and half-smile of the gentle Elia. His theme may be an abstract one, but he straightway brings it into the region of human interests. If historical, he produces not a Macaulayan pageant, in which the chief use of men is as parts of the procession, but a Carlylean drama of human passion and personality. If literary criticism, it is the man in the book that he discovers and analyzes. His sketches of out-door nature are not botanical or zoölogical calendars; he finds the man in the fields. His records of travel are not graphic and intelligent guidebooks like Henry James's, but in the mood and manner of Mr. Howell's Italian and suburban sketches, full of close and interested observation of people, charming specula-

tion as to their traits and histories, and minute study of the small incidents and details of his own and their surroundings—such, for example, as his sketches of a country store, of his door-step acquaintances, and of his fellow-passengers on the horse-cars.

Our final characteristic of the essay is a certain naïveté of self-expression. The essayist is not necessarily egotistical. He takes everybody into his confidence, and it does not occur to him that others are not as artless, or as interested in himself and his thoughts, as he is; or, if he admits it theoretically, or finds it out by harsh experience, he cannot remember it when the fit is on him. He is far from being a defier of critics or of canons. But he is born with a natural armor of ingenuousness, which protects the tender tissues of his genius from a rude and unsympathetic world. To the essayist, of the Montaigne type particularly, reticence is fatal, or the hesitancy which stops to ask whether people will pronounce him an egotist or a gossip. He is essentially autobiographic. Montaigne says of his essays: "In these fancies of my own I do not pretend to discover things, but to lay open myself." (pp. 229-35)

Francis N. Zabriskie, "The Essay as a Literary Form and Quality," in The New Princeton Review, *Vol. IV, No. 5, September, 1887, pp. 227-45.*

Virginia Woolf

[*An English novelist, essayist, and critic, Woolf is one of the most prominent figures of twentieth-century literature. Like her contemporary James Joyce, with whom she is often compared, Woolf employed the stream-of-consciousness technique in the novel. Concerned primarily with depicting the life of the mind, she rebelled against traditional narrative techniques and developed a highly individualized style. Her critical essays, which cover almost the entire range of English literature, contain some of her finest prose and are praised for their insight. In the excerpt below from an essay originally published in 1905, she comments on the proliferation of personal essays, advising essayists to confine their writing to subjects within their realm of direct experience.*]

The spread of education and the necessity which haunts us to impart what we have acquired have led, and will lead still further, to some startling results. We read of the over-burdened British Museum—how even its appetite for printed matter flags, and the monster pleads that it can swallow no more. This public crisis has long been familiar in private houses. One member of the household is almost officially deputed to stand at the hall door with flaming sword and do battle with the invading armies. Tracts, pamphlets, advertisements, gratuitous copies of magazines, and the literary productions of friends come by post, by van, by messenger—come at all hours of the day and fall in the night, so that the morning breakfast-table is fairly snowed up with them.

This age has painted itself more faithfully than any other in a myriad of clever and conscientious though not supremely great works of fiction; it has tried seriously to liven the faded colours of bygone ages; it has delved industriously with spade and axe in the rubbish-heaps and ruins; and, so far, we can only applaud our use of pen and ink. But if you have a monster like the British public to feed, you will try to tickle its stale palate in new ways; fresh and amusing shapes must be given to the old commodities—for we really have nothing so new to say that it will not fit into one of the familiar forms. So we confine ourselves to no one literary medium; we try to be new by being old; we revive mystery-plays and affect an archaic accent; we deck ourselves in the fine raiment of an embroidered style; we cast off all clothing and disport ourselves nakedly. In short, there is no end to our devices, and at this very moment probably some ingenious youth is concocting a fresh one which, be it ever so new, will grow stale in its turn. If there are thus an infinite variety of fashions in the external shapes of our wares, there are a certain number—naturally not so many—of wares that are new in substance and in form which we have either invented or very much developed. Perhaps the most significant of these literary inventions is the invention of the personal essay. It is true that it is at least as old as Montaigne, but we may count him the first of the moderns. It has been used with considerable frequency since his day, but its poularity with us is so immense and so peculiar that we are justified in looking upon it as something of our own—typical, characteristic, a sign of the times which will strike the eye of our great-great-grandchildren. Its significance, indeed, lies not so much in the fact that we have attained any brilliant success in essay-writing—no one has approached the essays of Elia—but in the undoubted facility with which we write essays as though this were beyond all others our natural way of speaking. The peculiar form of an essay implies a peculiar substance; you can say in this shape what you cannot with equal fitness say in any other. A very wide definition obviously must be that which will include all the varieties of thought which are suitably enshrined in essays; but perhaps if you say that an essay is essentially egoistical you will not exclude many essays and you will certainly include a portentous number. Almost all essays begin with a capital I—'I think', 'I feel'—and when you have said that, it is clear that you are not writing history or philosophy or biography or anything but an essay, which may be brilliant or profound, which may deal with the immortality of the soul, or the rheumatism in your left shoulder, but is primarily an expression of personal opinion.

We are not—there is, alas! no need to prove it—more subject to ideas than our ancestors; we are not, I hope, in the main more egoistical; but there is one thing in which we are more highly skilled than they are; and that is in manual dexterity with a pen. There can be no doubt that it is to the art of penmanship that we owe our present literature of essays. The very great of old—Homer and Aeschylus—could dispense with a pen; they were not inspired by sheets of paper and gallons of ink; no fear that their harmonies, passed from lip to lip, should lose their cadence and die. But our essayists write because the gift of writing has been bestowed on them. Had they lacked writing-masters we should have lacked essayists. There are, of course, certain distinguished people who use this medium from genuine inspiration because it best embodies the soul of their thought. But, on the other hand, there is a very large number who make the fatal pause, and the mechanical act of writing is allowed to set the brain in motion which should only be accessible to a higher inspiration.

The essay, then, owes its popularity to the fact that its proper use is to express one's personal peculiarities, so that under the decent veil of print one can indulge one's egoism to the full. You need know nothing of music, art, or literature to have a certain interest in their productions, and the great burden of modern criticism is simply the expression of such individual likes and dislikes—the amiable garrulity of the tea-table—cast into the form of essays. If men and women must write, let them leave the great mysteries of art and literature unassailed; if they told us frankly not of the books that we can all read and the pictures which hang for us all to see, but of that single book to which they alone have the key and of that solitary picture whose face is shrouded to all but one gaze—if they would write of themselves—such writing would have its own permanent value. The simple words 'I was born' have somehow a charm beside which all the splendours of romance and fairy-tale turn to moonshine and tinsel. But though it seems thus easy enough to write of one's self, it is, as we know, a feat but seldom accomplished. Of the multitude of autobiographies that are written, one or two alone are what they pretend to be. Confronted with the terrible spectre of themselves, the bravest are inclined to run away or shade their eyes. And thus, instead of the honest truth which we should all respect, we are given timid side-glances in the shape of essays, which, for the most part, fail in the cardinal virtue of sincerity. And those who do not sacrifice their beliefs to the turn of a phrase or the glitter of paradox think it beneath the dignity of the printed word to say simply what it means; in print they must pretend to an oracular and infallible nature. To say simply 'I have a garden, and I will tell you what plants do best in my garden' possibly justified its egoism; but to say 'I have no sons, though I have six daughters, all unmarried, but I will tell you how I should have brought up my sons had I had any' is not interesting, cannot be useful, and is a specimen of the amazing and unclothed egoism for which first the art of penmanship and then the invention of essay-writing are responsible. (pp. 24-7)

> *Virginia Woolf, in her* The Essays of Virginia Woolf: 1904-1912, Vol. I, *edited by Andrew McNeillie, Harcourt Brace Jovanovich, 1986, 411 p.*

INFLUENCES ON THE ESSAY

Charles E. Whitmore

[Below, Whitmore traces the literary sources of the essay and comments on its broad range of styles and subject matter.]

Of all the literary terms in common use, the word "essay" has perhaps the widest field and the most indeterminate content. Since the form to which it applies has taken on a fresh character in the hands of almost all its chief exponents, it has become in practice the designation for any piece of prose of moderate length, and has consequently embraced a bewilderingly various subject-matter. Moreover, the essayists themselves are by no means all of a piece. Bacon and Lamb, for instance, have little in common; and the type of 'essayist' represented by Macaulay and Carlyle has little in common with either. As a result of this wide extension, studies of the essay either include so much as to be very indefinite, or else are based on partial views, the upshot, in either case, becoming sufficiently vague. At the same time, the word "essay" goes on being used, and collections, of curiously assorted content, go on being made; and it therefore seems worth while to pass in review the different types represented in actual practice, in order to see just how much continuity is discernible among them.

I take it that the chief distinguishing marks of the essay would be held to be relative brevity and a prevailingly informal tone. The first requisite is certainly fulfilled by Bacon and Addison, and in the main by Lamb and his successors; but the second is certainly not fulfilled by Bacon, nor, on the whole, by Hazlitt, especially if we compare him with Addison and Lamb. Moreover, relative brevity no longer necessarily applies when we turn to critical and biographical work, as is at once obvious in the case of Macaulay. We here encounter a third connotation of our elusive term, that of experimental rather than exhaustive approach—the essay as opposed to the treatise, the biographical essay, for instance, as opposed to the full-length and voluminous life. This connotation, too, is not foreign to the Baconian essay; but if it is applied as a mediating factor between Bacon and Macaulay, the consideration of relative brevity is at once demolished. An essay of Macaulay's is more like a condensed book than an essay of Bacon's is like an essay of Macaulay's. Thus the attempt to keep these three criteria together shows us that they need not be, and in practice often are not, found in combination; so that any attempt to apply them systematically tends to split up the field into groups marked by one or two of them, but seldom by all three.

A similar cleavage is revealed if we consider the types of writing which essays represent. One type, formal argument, is obviously very rare; Bacon's *Of Usury* is unique in his collection, and the informal argument which appears in Addison is very different in procedure and in tone. Nowadays we should hardly look for explicit argument in anything properly to be called an essay, or, conversely, should think the appearance of such argument sufficient ground for denying the title. As Professor MacDonald observes [in "Charles Lamb, Greatest of the Essayists," *PMLA,* Vol. XXXII], "Throughout the history of the essay contemporary events and controversial questions have been excluded." The other three major types, however, are liberally represented. Bacon describes the ideal country-house and the ideal garden; such ampler collections as the *Spectator* and the *Sketch-Book* abound in instances of description and narration, easily classifiable under their respective forms. Closely united with these is the character-sketch, as distinguished from the formal bi-

ography. As for exposition, it is obvious that probably a majority of essays fall within it, and that much of the supposed 'essay-quality' resides precisely in them. We have formal exposition in Bacon, with a conclusion emphasized and enforced; we have informal in Addison, with the conclusion not insisted on, or even left for the reader to draw; we have the use of discussion and dialog to bring out and develop differences in point of view. Whatever our angle of approach, then, we find in the essay a mixture of types and of procedures; and our problem is to decide how this mixture is to be accounted for. To solve it, we must have recourse to the historical method.

If we look back well beyond the accepted beginnings of the modern essay in Montaigne and Bacon—back, indeed, to the beginnings of modern prose literature in the humanists of Italy—we shall find the genesis of a double literary development in which lies the clue we seek. The point of departure is the Latin letter which the humanists revived after the example of the younger Seneca, and which is shown in its first stage in the works of Petrarch and Coluccio Salutati. In their hands the letter was less a means of friendly intercourse than a medium of scholarly communication; it was carefully and conscientiously written, it often passed freely from hand to hand, it might attain a very considerable length. No sharp line was drawn between the letter of this type and the treatise; the ostensible recipient was often forgotten, and the treatment became lengthy and formal. Soon, however, a wider and exacter knowledge and appreciation of ancient models began to clarify this confusion, until we have, on the one hand, real letters, following the example of Cicero, and on the other genuine treatises, frankly designed for general circulation. The process has been excellently described by Professor Rossi [in *Il Quattrocentro,* 1900]:

> Long letters, which in their content may be compared to philosophical treatises, are frequently encountered in the correspondence of Petrarch and Coluccio, but less often in those of the humanists of the Quattrocento. For the example of Cicero, operating by a double path, favored the short and lively letter, and indicated a fitter form for the exposition of philosophical matters in the dialog. Treatises freed from that last relic of the epistolary arrangement, the superscription—the dedicatory letter might precede, independently—abound in the humanistic literature.

This influence of the Ciceronian (and ultimately Platonic) dialog also has its share in the subsequent development. Before long all these types were taken over by vernacular writers; a capital example of the developed treatise is Leon Battista Alberti's *Three Books on Painting,* of the dialog his discourse *On Tranquillity of Mind.* We must also, before quitting this period, mention the commentary—a conveniently inclusive term for any collection of observations which did not pretend to the formality of a treatise, and which covers, among other works, Vespasiano da Bisticci's lives of his distinguished contemporaries and Ghiberti's sketch of the history of the fine arts before and during his own time.

After wider and exacter literary training had brought about this differentiation, a new force was added by the invention of printing. Thus, the slighter and more casual treatise assumed the form of the pamphlet, of what Professor Schelling, in speaking of the Elizabethan development, has aptly called "the prose of contemporary comment;" later the periodical essays, their brevity strictly conditioned by the circumstances of their issue, take shape in the hands of Steele and Addison; later still, the development of journalism creates the article and the editorial, thereby, we may note, furnishing a channel for the argumentative stream which has flowed away from the essay as we now understand it. But the old connection with the letter is still visible. Some of Seneca's moral epistles would serve well enough as short editorials in a religious paper of to-day; certain letters of Petrarch and Salutati are easily conceived of as the ancestors of the modern review article; and conversely we still find numerous "letters to the editor" in newspaper and weekly.

Such, then, is the complex heredity which lies behind the essay in the sense of a short piece of prose. Its kinship with the letter is unmistakable, as is also its connection with the short treatise and the dialog. We may note in the *Spectator* the large part played by letters, real or imaginary; the discussions in which members of the Club, and others, participate; and the direct addresses to the public. But the kinship with the letter is the most important, and the longest to survive. In Lamb, for instance, the germs of several of the *Essays of Elia* can be found in his correspondence; and some of his letters are virtually indistinguishable from miniature essays, a statement also true of the letters of others. I can see no sense in which Gray's well-known letter on the laureateship differs in mood or style from an essay; it merely carries brevity to an extreme.

Yet another point of contact deserving mention is that between the essay and the journal or diary. We might conceive the *Spectator* as a series of detached leaves from the complete record of its author's observations and reading; and we know that various writers have actually used the journal as a repository for material later to be utilized for developed works. Joubert's *Pensées* are gleanings from the journal which he kept almost throughout his life; and the examples of Thoreau and Emerson are too familiar to need more than mention. The addition of a certain thread of plot gives such a record sufficient continuity to produce a type of story, in which the reflections of author and characters provide the main interests, as in Sterne's *Sentimental Journey* and Holmes' *Breakfast Table* series, the plot being merely a mechanism to keep the characters moving, and provide occasions for discourse—a device for avoiding formal presentation.

The upshot of all this is that when traits belonging to letter, informal dialog, or journal are discerned in a short piece of unclassified prose, the temptation to call it an "cssay" is ready at hand; and yet what is meant is not a form, but a tone or an attitude. This tone, this attitude, may appear in such different shapes as a letter, a *Spectator* paper, or *The Autocrat of the Breakfast-Table;* and it is therefore not surprising that the field to which the term "essay" is applied should be broad and indeterminate. Defining the essay on the basis of any collection, by one author or by several, is like trying to define a magazine on the basis of its contents; the only satisfactory account of a miscellany is just that it is a miscellany, and only a general labelling of content and intention is possible.

We thus seem brought to the conclusion that what we mean by "essay" is after all largely a matter of 'essay-quality,' and obliged to inquire whether we can give a satisfactory account of that quality. Even among the 'canonical' essayists the wide diversity of style and point of view is obvious. We can, however, limit our search by not carrying it back to Bacon; for his work, though it apparently stands at the beginning of the English essay, yet in a broader view represents the end, not the beginning, of a tradition—the tradition, that is, of humanism, clarified by experience, modified by the dawn of modern science, but unmistakable. This fact explains many traits of the *Essays,* and indeed of Bacon's general attitude. It explains his distrust of contemporary physical science, and of the vernacular as a permanent literary medium; it explains his contempt for romantic love, and his rather slighting attitude toward poetry; it explains why one of the longest and most highly finished of the essays is that on the stock humanistic theme of friendship; it explains his fondness for the younger Seneca, always a favorite with the humanists. When he refers us to Seneca as the source of his own conception of the essay he is absolutely right, and those who wonder at his silence touching Montaigne exhibit an oddly needless perplexity.

For all practical purposes, then, the essay in its modern aspect begins with Addison, and in his work we may first examine the adjustment of author's attitude to diversified material. We find in him, as already noted, description, narration, and informal discussion; and we also find a class of essays characterized by *the inversion of a normal expository process.* That is, they expound a matter seemingly too trivial or absurd for serious exposition, or they expound it in an unexpected and whimsical way. The paper on the Fan (*Spectator,* No. 102) is a mock explanation of a process, soberly setting forth the workings of the academy which offers systematic drill in the management of the "little modish machine." The paper on the Cat-call (*ibid.,* No. 361) in reply to a letter inquiring the origin of the instrument, gives the various theories on the subject offered by learned friends, and discusses its applications in the writer's own day. So the proposal (*ibid.,* No. 251) to appoint a comptroller-general of the street-cries of London, which are duly divided into vocal and instrumental, with their relative sub-groups, is perfectly regular in development. In papers such as these the essay assumes a radically new shape, and discharges a novel function.

The same inversion, under a more bewildering stylistic cloak, can be traced in much of the most characteristic work of Lamb. The "Dissertation on Roast Pig"—if classification of that delicious whimsey be needed—is a mock process; "The Two Races of Men" is a mock division; "Imperfect Sympathies" is a thesis supported by deliberately humorous examples. We have also the mock encomium—a form which can trace its ancestry well back into classical times, and which was also practised in the Renaissance—in "The Praise of Chimney-sweepers" and "A Complaint of the Decay of Beggars." In his hands this subdivision of the essay makes steady progress in unexpectedness of topic, treatment, and style, until the second and third of these elements decisively prevail over the first. It is a method which obviously admits large amounts of paradox and parody, and may indeed employ them in excess, in which case the 'essay-quality' inevitably suffers, as it does with Mr. Chesterton. In Lamb, however, serious views usually underlie the discourse, however whimsical its outer aspect; and so they do in most of his successors who have adopted the type.

This method of inversion, it must be noted, necessarily falls in the domain of exposition, that is, on the intellectual side of writing; for the perception of unlikeness on which it rests involves comparison. An absurdity is not an absurdity to one who is unconscious of its conflict with ordinary experience; and in literature the wildest record of emotion, the most fantastic narrative, is in *method* indistinguishable from any other piece of description or narration. A fanciful story may be sober and close-knit like *Through the Looking-Glass,* or diffuse and rambling like *Water-Babies;* but only the reflective intelligence can distinguish either from a tale of common fact. So in general with inversion, paradox, irony: to the unreflective they are something quite other than what they are intended to be, and as unreflective readers abound, the puzzlement and irritation often caused by such methods are easily accounted for.

The unity of the essay, then, so far as it exists, is that of the essayist's point of view and manner of approach, not that of the several pieces, often radically different in method and temper, grouped under the term. Hence only resemblances between authors enable us to equate groups. The effort to discover a single continuous 'essay-tradition' in English is vain; I can see no reason to suppose that Lamb's work would have been in the slightest degree altered if Bacon had never written a line. Kinships between authors we can find; but they are exceedingly likely to cut across accepted literary divisions. Lamb derived much from Burton and Sir Thomas Browne; but can either be called an essayist in the sense that he is one? Dr. Holmes and Dr. Crothers have much in common; but surely the narrative interest in *The Autocrat* distinguishes it from *The Pardoner's Wallet.* In other words, the principle of classification is less that of literary form than that of author's attitude and intention.

Is it, however, possible to use this last criterion as the basis of a sounder division? I believe that it is; and in conclusion I wish to point out the various main groups which have come to light in the course of our survey, and to suggest names for them, so far as reliable practice supplies them. We have three main classes, with some sub-divisions, the relations of which will be clearest if they are arranged in quasi-tabular form.

I. The non-exhaustive treatment of a historical, biographical, or critical topic, the best general term for which is *study,* as in Froude's *Short Studies in Great Subjects,* Lord Bryce's *Studies in Contemporary Biography,* or Mr. Symons' *Studies in Prose and Verse.* Sometimes, in purely critical work, the term *estimate* appears, as in Professor Mather's *Estimates in Art,* or Mr. Drinkwater's *Swinburne: An Estimate.* In biography the variations of scope

and treatment may justify the use of a separate term, the best, apparently, being *portrait,* as in Mr. Gamaliel Bradford's *Confederate Portraits* and *Union Portraits.*

II. The brief description of a place or a character, whether the latter be general, as in the older type, or specific. The best term for this is *sketch,* as in Irving's *Sketch-Book,* or Henry James' *Transatlantic Sketches.* The term *character,* however, will doubtless be retained in its technical sense with reference to the seventeenth-century type or to later work directly modelled on it.

III. The purely expository essay, of which we can distinguish three main types:

1) the essay which condenses the writer's experience and reading about a single topic, as in Bacon.

2) the essay which provides informal discussion of a point of manners or taste, as often in Addison and his successors.

3) the essay which inverts or whimsically applies a normal expository process, as in the examples cited from Addison and Lamb.

All three of these are sufficiently distinct to deserve separate names, especially the last; but I do not find that current practice justifies any. Certainly neither *informal* nor *familiar* can properly be restricted to either the second or the third class (neither fits the first); and there would seem to be a good opportunity for an inventor to supply us with the needed terms. Perhaps *commentary* might be revived to designate miscellaneous discussions of life in general; but it of course does not apply to any type of the essay proper.

It is now possible to see the lines by which the field of the essay is really divided. Brevity is at least highly desirable; informality has come to be largely taken for granted; tentativeness of approach and method, on the other hand, is a feature not necessarily restricted to the purely literary essay. As for the kinds of writing, the essayist's type of mind is most clearly reflected in the expository form, descriptive and narrative pieces being either subdued to it or given independent place, and argument given its own sphere in editorial or article. The literary essay as thus conceived has been well defined by Mr. D. T. Pottinger [in his *English Essays,* 1917] as "a written monologue or—in terms of another art—a personal letter addressed to the public." It might puzzle him to explain in what sense Pater's "Child in the House" (which he includes in his collection) is either. In truth, the portrait is obviously distinguished from the pure essay by the fact that it discards the direct approach of writer to reader, and confines itself to the presentation of its real or imaginary subject: and the style which it adopts, whether rich and full-textured as in Pater, or keenly analytical in Mr. Bradford, is necessarily far removed from that of the *causerie.*

Thus we conclude that the unifying personality of the essayist, if sufficiently strong, can bring together a great variety of themes, and that the individual essay has free scope for variation. "We have to admit," says Mr. Ernest Rhys [in his *A Century of Essays*], "that so long as it obeys the law of being explicit, casually illuminative of its theme, and germane to the intellectual mood of its writer, then it may follow pretty much its own devices." But when it becomes interested in depicting a character or narrating an event for their own sakes, it begins to pass from the circle of the essay proper to that of the sketch or the portrait; in Irving's *Sketch-Book* no long scrutiny is needed to separate the real essays from the tales, and the task is fairly easy in many other cases. But the true province of the essay is in the setting forth—directly or invertedly—of its author's moods, tastes, predilections, aversions, and all other reactions to experience. "We might end," says Mr. Rhys again, "by claiming the essayists as dilute lyrists, engaged in pursuing a rhythm too subtle for verse, and lifelike as common-room gossip." In a sense it is very true that the essay in the hands of such a writer as Lamb exemplifies the finest capacities of prose as a medium of self-expression precisely as lyric poetry expresses those of verse; but thereby an *Essay of Elia* and a pure lyric are as unlike as are the two media which they thus present at their most highly finished development; they are parallel, but unmistakably different, and neither could conceivably discharge the function of the other.

I do not suppose that any examination such as the present will result in a much more careful restriction of the term "essay"; the free and easy use has gone on too long to be easily discarded. None the less, the discrimination of the true essay from the study, the portrait, and the sketch is worth making, and a perception of the real distinctions between them may in time help to make usage a little more exact. (pp. 551-64)

> Charles E. Whitmore, "The Field of the Essay," in PMLA, *Vol. XXXVI, No. 1, March, 1921, pp. 551-64.*

Elbert N. S. Thompson

[*Below, Thompson surveys the literary precursors of the essay, commenting on the various sources of Francis Bacon's work and the contributions of Bacon's peers to the stylistic maturation of the essay.*]

Critics have often remarked that the prose essay is a direct product of the modern, scientific attitude of mind, and that it therefore necessarily made its first appearance late, in the time of the Renaissance. True, many of the thoughts that give body to the English essay could not have antedated the inquiring, restless mental activity of modern times, and many others would have been too hazardous for utterance before some freedom of speech was permissible. It is equally true that the great pioneer essayists, Montaigne and Bacon, were leaders in the rationalistic movement of the seventeenth century. Despite all that, however, the essay is really much older than the modern world. In the seventeenth century, the essay presented merely some reflections on conduct in public or private life, illustrated often by historical anecdotes or wise sayings of ancient philosophers. Such reflection must be as old as society itself. Doubtless, the roots of the essay lie far back in unrecorded oral discussions of conduct; for Caliban would talk on Setebos and other weighty topics. Then the flowering appeared, in whatever forms of literature chance or fash-

ion might supply—the discourse, the dialogue, the epigram, or what not. One and all convey the response of the human mind to the problems of life. The content of the essay, therefore, is as old as the race.

Throughout the sixteenth and seventeenth centuries, a widespread interest prevailed in all questions bearing on the right government of life. Guidance for the individual in his private life was called *sapientia,* and for the man in public station, *prudentia.* The emblem books alone sufficiently attest the popularity of short, practical homilies on conduct. The lessons there presented in picture and poem took moral philosophy, using Addison's phrase, from the "closets and libraries, schools and colleges," if it ever had suffered such confinement, and handed it over to the ordinary man. Is there a subject handled by Bacon or Montaigne that was not broached in these quaint emblems? The interest in statecraft was just as keen, especially in Italy. That an audience would listen patiently to the long, argumentative speeches of *Gorboduc,* and that Machiavelli was eagerly read at Oxford and Cambridge, show that it, too, was a matter of general concern among the cultured. Strange that the world to-day is no better after all this hungry search after wisdom and truth.

On both these moral and political concerns the ancient philosophers had spoken with authority, and leaders of the Renaissance hearkened with reverence to their teaching. To the domain of *sapientia* belonged much of the dialectic of Plato, some of the treatises of Aristotle, the discourses of Cicero on old age, friendship, and ethical duties, the dissertations of Plutarch, and the letters of Seneca. Their thoughts are rounded in a larger mold than that of the essay. But the matter of length is not a determining criterion; for many discourses, like Cicero's *De Finibus* and much later Alain de Lille's *De Arte Praedicatoria,* are broken into separate parts, each like a little essay, and few are steadily progressive to the end. Hence the common sixteenth-century discourse, loosely constructed in this way, furnished essayists with an abundance of material from which to draw their lessons on life.

It would be futile to attempt to gather all these discourses and dialogues written during the Renaissance. As specimens of the discourse, one might think of Bartoli's *La Poverta Contenta,* which extolled the virtue of contentment; Justus Lipsius's *De Constantia,* which drew up the doctrine of the Neo-Stoics; and Barnabe Rich's *Honestie of this Age,* published in 1614. The dialogue was just as popular, and was long used in books as diverse as the *Colloquies* of Erasmus, More's *Utopia,* Walton's *Compleat Angler,* and Dryden's *Essay of Dramatic Poesy.* To fix again on a single example, one might choose the dialogues of Jacques Tahureau. In the reasoning spirit of Montaigne, he criticized such social follies as dancing, duels, and affectations of speech. He censured the arrogance of the nobility, the injustice of the courts, and the greed of physicians. In general, he aimed to judge life in the light of reason, as the great Erasmus had done. Few of these Renaissance works, however, have the steady, stately progress of Drummond's *Cypresse Grove;* they disintegrate into parts, each part like an imperfect essay. Had it not been, however, that discourse and dialogue, as the sixteenth century used them, could do the work that later devolved on the essay, our modern Bacons and Montaignes would have appeared earlier and would have created more of a sensation.

There are numerous examples of this type of dissertation that breaks up easily into short, isolated parts. Thomas Churchyard's *A Sparke of Friendship and Warm Good-Will,* for example, has much the brevity and lightness of the essay. Its general style resembles that of Elizabethan narrative prose, and its rhythm, therefore, can hardly be that of the aphoristic essay. But Churchyard speaks in the fashion of a moralist and often in this close approach to the style of the essayist: "And now to proceed forward with this friendship, and shew the degrees thereof orderly, methinks that the first branch thereof is the affectionate love that all men in general ought to bear to their country: for the which Mutius Scævola, Horatius Cocles, Marcus Curtius, Marcus Regulus, and many more, have left us most noble examples." Such use of authority, presumably from some commonplace-book, is noteworthy; for later essayists were fond of it. Even more nearly in their style runs the sentence: "I can but wish their payment no worse nor better, but such as Tarpeia found of the Latins and Sabines, for selling unto them the capitol of Rome: a most notorious example, read it who pleaseth." Or here again the manner of the essayists appears: "If friends be chosen by election and privy liking, these open palterers may go whistle; for they neither know the bounds of a good mind, nor the blessedness that belongs to friendship."

Lodovick Brysket's *Discourse of Civill Life,* a translation of one of Giraldi's treatises, possesses no more structural unity than does the *Sparke of Friendship.* The author shows how a man can yield to vice, although the good is everywhere coveted, or he describes the ways of youth somewhat in the style of the character-writers. But a still better specimen of a treatise made up of brief, separate discourses, is Barnabe Rich's *Faultes, Faultes, and Nothing Else but Faultes.* As he passes from one subject to another in this exposure of the vices of the age, he dwells on at least some in the style of an essayist. Two quotations alone will show how the germs of the seventeenth-century essay lie imbedded in portions of these disjointed treatises of earlier days.

> I thinke Flatterie at this day be in as good request as Tobacco, two smokie vapours, yet the one purgeth wise-men of their witte, and the other fooles of their money. And no marvell though Flatterers are so acceptable, when men for the most part can flatter themselves with an over-weening, to be what they are not: this maketh them so willing to give care to Flatterers, of whom they think they are praysed, when they are but flattered, for so much as false praise is nothing else but flat mockerie. And we are growen to thinke so well of our selves, that we account him, either to be envious, or prowde, that will not soothe and smoothe us up in all our follies, so great is our vaine-glorie, that when we be commended farre aboue our desert, yet we rather attribute it to the aboundance of good will, then to the fraude of him that flattereth.

> Prosperity pampereth us in pleasure, it maketh us to forget God, and to repose our greatest con-

fidence in the vanities of the world. Adversity maketh us contemptible in the eye of the world, it is the meane whereby we are taught to know our selves, and to drawe us to God.

Material just as close to the content of the typical essay is presented in Peter de la Primaudaye's treatise translated in 1586 as the *French Academie.* In the form of dialogue, it deals with fortitude, idleness, friendship, pride, and other topics common to the later essays. The book shows plainly what thoughts were current at the time, and its illustrations are just those that appear and reappear in the essays. And where the speeches assigned to the different speakers are long, especially at the ends of chapters, the style crudely resembles that of the essay, especially those that end with direct exhortation introduced by "let us."

In crude discourses and dialogues of this kind, the habit of discussion was fostered in England, and the way was certainly prepared for Bacon and his successors. In another sort of book, even more popular during the Renaissance, a great deal of material was gathered that served the needs of the essayists. These were the encyclopedic commonplace-books that presented in handy form the wise sayings and the noble deeds of the ancients. Men in those days had an unbounded respect for the Classics and turned to them for lessons on all the common affairs of life. But few, comparatively, could read the Latin, and fewer still the Greek. Hence scholars laboriously compiled these volumes containing sentences, apothegms, and examples from classical literature. They may have remembered that Aristotle had approved the use of illustration, whether from history or fable, as an effective means of exposition, and that he considered it easier for even a clever man to invent a fable than to find, off hand, an apposite historical example. So these compilations were made, and from such books, dry as they were, many readers obtained their first, or even total, knowledge of ancient history, philosophy, and poetry. The fragments, of course, offered in these compilations, revealed only the word or bare deed, and lost entirely the beauty of the original. But they offered concrete matter that the essayist might use. What is more essential, the humanist may have asked, for effective exposition than stories from the Classics? The Song of Moses is nothing other than a series of examples of God's mercies. Plutarch had often resorted to the use of instances. Montaigne's first essays, especially, are little more than brief statements of abstract truth well substantiated by citations. And even Montaigne, greatest of the essayists, found his material in these huge collections of ancient wisdom.

For some essays, Cato's *Disticha de Moribus* supplied Montaigne with the material he needed. The book is made up of two-line poems, like the couplets of the emblem-books, presenting such thoughts or precepts as "Deo Supplica," "Diligentiam Adhibe," and "Pauea in Convivio Loquere." Schoolboys of the sixteenth century were made to memorize these brief moral lessons, and they are found in many a book to illustrate some abstract truth. Michael Drayton told his friend, Henry Reynolds, that, as a boy, he had been inspired to emulate the poets by reading these distichs and a similar collection, the *Sententiae Puerilis.* But the apothegms of Erasmus, with their greater fulness, suited much better the purposes of the essayists, and Montaigne used them, too, frequently. The author of the English translation demonstrated the utility of such sayings for those who, owing either to ignorance or lack of time, were unable to read the Classics. They seemed to him useful for preachers, also, "to quicken soche as at Sermones been ever noddyng." He translated, therefore, from Erasmus the wise sayings of Socrates, Diogenes, Alexander, Augustus, Pompey, and others, and so provided Montaigne and all who followed him with an abundance of apothegms for use in exposition.

Other scholars who thus garnered the wisdom of the ancients included in their compilations instances of noble conduct as well as helpful utterances. The *Factorum et Dictorum Memorabilium* of Valerius Maximus furnishes this twofold authority for virtues like bravery, patience, moderation, and liberality. These same virtues, side by side with the corresponding vices, form the staple of John Stobaeus's *Sententiae.* Examples and noble words were gathered also by Domenichi in *Detti et Fatti.* Compilations of this kind, if they were at all exhaustive in content, became virtually encyclopedias of all sorts of information. In his widely circulated *Officinae,* Ravisius Textor printed long lists of suicides, patricides, and infanticides, of both learned and unlearned men, of musicians, sculptors, and poets. He also offered a complete pharmacopoeia, an extensive atlas minus the maps, a long section on morals, and much other information, useful and useless, arranged in this topical way. The *Officinae,* in short, was both biographical dictionary and encyclopedia for readers of the sixteenth century.

Sir William Temple.

Almost all of these redoubtable pilferers from antiquity had a moral end in view; they would teach as well as instruct. Since this purpose led inevitably to the inclusion of some comment on the excerpts printed, something like the essay gradually emerged. Valerius Maximus prefixed to each group of examples a brief bit of exposition on the topic broached. To make more of this; to curtail the examples; and then to merge the two, would produce the typical essay of the seventeenth century.

Two collections of facts and wise words, in stressing the "lesson" as they do, made a notable advance toward the form of the genuine essay. One by Pedro de Mexia, *La Silva di Varia Leccion,* first appeared in 1542 and was later republished in enlarged form. Its English translator, Thomas Fortescue, gave it the name, *The Forest, or Collection of Historyes no lesse profitable, then pleasant and necessary.* It offers information on history, science, philosophy, and other branches of knowledge. Many topics are introduced briefly, as by Valerius Maximus, but others are more fully discussed, with only a few examples. Insistence on the lesson thus occasionally transformed a series of examples into the essay.

Writing in the first book "Of the Excellency of Secrets," Pedro de Mexia offered these reflections. "One of the perfectest notes to knowe a wise man, is if he well can cover the Secrets committed to him by an other, holding evermoore his owne affaires close and unknowen." Then, after a few words on God's hidden mysteries, the author resumed: "By means whereof the wise and sage in all ages have loved and learned to conceale and cover their secrets." Hereupon, the essay turns off to example. Again, Mexia wrote "Of the Excellency and Commendation of Travail, as also of the Damages that growe of Idlenes." The passage reads: "It lyeth us on of necessitie bothe by the lawes and commandments of God, to swinck and toile in this worlde continually." The curse of labor, in fact, is not only accepted but justified. Mexia's expression is here noticeably aphoristic; "To be short, no Vertue may any where be put in execution without the assistance of careful pain and dilegence." Authority is then adduced to prove that all things labor ceaselessly; but much of the argument comes from experience. "High waies and common paths not frequented or used are in short time closed and shut up against the passinger: whence it now is open manifest, that what soever lyeth unused and unlaboured, wasteth to nothing." Finally, after his examples, Mexia concludes with this paragraph: "For conclusion, in such honest exercises should we passe our few dayes, that we might reape the frute thereof in the kingdome of God, which is provided for those that are called into the Vineyard to laboure it, where they shall receive the det to them belonging." Scripture concludes the proof "that eche man shall receive his salery or payment, according to that he hath travailed in this worlde."

In this fashion, Mexia discusses topics of all kinds: on talking little, on diversity of language, or on the invention of letters. In paragraphs on the three unsolvable philosophic doubts and on man's never aspiring to perfection, his progress is by simple enumeration. But he closes the latter nicely with the thought: "We then must indevour by all meanes possible, for man that is reasonable and yeeldeth not unto reason, but dwelleth still as wedded to his owne fond appetite, is as he that would sail on the top of high Mountaines or build him houses on the restlesse and surging waves of the Sea, which bothe are lesse advised and fruteles immaginations.''

The same attention to exposition is found in Pierre Bouaystuau's *Theatrum Mundi,* translated by John Alday, in the third quarter of the sixteenth century, as *The Theatre or Rule of the World.* Bouaystuau had searched far and wide for his material; "I have left no Author sacred or prophane, Greeke, Latin, or in our vulgar tongue, but that I have bereft him of a leg or a wing, for the more sounder decking and furniture of my worke." But he wove his matter together, to represent "the running race and course of everye mans life, as touching misery and felicity, wherein is contained wonderfull examples, learned devises, to the overthrowe of vice, and exalting of vertue." In the first book, he showed by quotation that man has no right to exalt himself above the animals. Then, passing on, he considered more closely the miseries of mankind. He is especially interesting in what he said of the hardships endured by husbandmen, merchants, warriors, and even kings; for he here resorted less often to example. In the third book, he turned to those evils caused by war and pestilence and the passions of the heart, and he concluded all with a discourse "Of the Excellencie and Dignitie of Man." So again the essay emerged from the common-place-book.

Many of these popular books were soon translated into English. The *Garden of Pleasure,* or, as it was later called, *Hours of Recreation, containing Sayings and Deedes Notable, as well Grave as Pleasant,* contains matter gathered from earlier books of the kind. James Sandford, the compiler, discusses such propositions as: "That byting answeres are meete for sharpe demands," and "That covetousnesse blindeth men," and "That povertie doth not give anoye, but man's insatiable greedinesse." To these well-worn themes some more modern anecdotes are added of common people like the tricked husbands of the jest books. Another such book, the *Living Librarie,* which appeared in 1621, is a direct translation of Philip Camerarius's *Meditationes Historicae.* Some of its chapters deal with matters of fact, explaining, for example, why salt water does not quench fire and why there are no wolves in England. Others discuss ethical questions. Camerarius first states the question and then illustrates it, as Valerius Maximus had done; but the examples are joined by longer comments, and greater stress is laid on exposition. Both books simply bring the old volume of sayings and deeds somewhat up to date.

In the year of the Restoration another volume of the kind appeared. For his efforts, Thomas Forde offered the usual justification. The *Theatre of Wits, Ancient and Modern* comprises a great number of wise sayings, "ready dress'd and dish'd out to thy hand; like some Diamonds, which grow smooth and polished, and need no farther labour to fit them for use." He saw a real value in that kind of book, since "we have many things to learn, and but little time to live." Strangely enough, however, Forde, who seems so

conversant with the common opinion and content of such volumes, knew little of their history; for he asserted that only one work of the kind, a brief manual by Francis Bacon, had been published in English. There were many in fact, and resort to them was general. Indeed, their use had become such a matter of course that Lord Shaftesbury, late in the century, complained: "The most confused head, if fraught with a little invention, and provided with common-place book learning, might exert itself (in the essay) to as much advantage as the most orderly and well-settled judgment." Sir Henry Wotton could object that these books merely offered "a short course to those who are content to know a little, and a sure way to such whose care is not to understand much." But already when these words were published, the common-place book had long been a feeder for the essay, justified, to use Tom Fuller's quaint words, because it arrayed "many Notions in garrison, whence the owner may draw out an army into the field on competent warning." In these early discourses and dialogues, then, moralists found crude examples of the free discussion of ideas, and from the common-place books they derived many of the facts with which they illustrated their thoughts. The power, of course, of expressing those thoughts artistically, and of weaving in the illustrative matter neatly, was acquired gradually from the reading of Seneca, Plutarch, Epictetus, and other ancient masters. So the artistic essay slowly emerged.

The actual essay, however, as a distinct literary type did not make its appearance in England much before the time of Francis Bacon. One would like to accept as genuine the essays attributed by James Howell to Sir Philip Sidney and Sir Francis Walsingham. But Howell is not a trustworthy authority, and the piece, "Valour Anatomized in a Fancie," assigned to Sidney, made its appearance first in the eleventh edition of Overbury's *Characters,* in 1622, and was published as one of Donne's essays by his son in 1652. The three essays supposedly by Walsingham, the "Anatomizing of Honesty, Ambition, and Fortitude," have probably a similar origin. These pieces are even more aphoristic than Donne's. "Honesty is a quiet passing over the days of a man's life, without doing injury to another man." "As chastity is the honesty of women, so honesty is the chastity of men," and this honesty lies "in spinning on the delicate threads of life, though not exceeding fine, yet free from bracks, and staines." Of such thoughts the essay consists. The other two wander more. Only when his discussion is half done does the author settle down, in Bacon's fashion, in the words: "Ambition in itself, is no fault; but the most natural commendation of the soul, as beauty is of the body." But none of these pieces could one assuredly accept as Walsingham's; and they have too much the ring of the character or the aphoristic essay to belong to his early time.

Another apparent predecessor of Bacon was the Puritan clergyman, Richard Greenham. He published nothing himself, and, as far as is known, left no manuscript ready for the press. In 1599, however, some years after his death, a friend, Henry Holland, issued a collected edition of his works. The "Grave Counsels" which stand first in the volume, simply present brief thoughts on topics like anger, atheism, conscience, and censures. Since many of them are introduced by the words, "he said," the reader assumes that Holland himself was largely responsible for the form in which they appear. Even the longest discussions do not exhibit the structure of an essay. The "Godly Instructions" of Part II more nearly resemble the essay; but again the editor, who admits that he gathered the copy from many sources, may have given the paragraphs their final form. On topics like hypocrites and prosperity, the author, without any display of learning, drives right to his point. The essay-like titles were undoubtedly supplied by the editor; the themes discussed were so common that a parallelism here and there with Montaigne would justify no inference of indebtedness. But, although, one can hardly take them just as they stand as antedating Bacon, their early date makes them significant. The essay, "Of Murmuring" may relevantly be quoted.

> It is a common thing with men to grudge and murmur against God's true servants, and therefore Ministers and Magistrats and such like, must learne with patience to beare it, and to prepare themselves for it. For if the Israelites murmured against Moses, being so rare a man, how much more will men now grudge against such as have not obtained the like measure of graces? This is a sore temptation, and Moses himself did once offend, because of the murmuring of the people: yet was he said to be the meekest man upon the earth. But else always Moses overcomes evil with good: for he was so acquainted with that people, that he had (as it were) heardened his heart against them.

Many other discourses on practical morality may have taken on the qualities of an essay in this same way. The first known collection of actual essays, however, the *Remedies against Discontentment,* was published in 1596. The author refers to his paragraphs as "small discourses," and for their very brevity he believes that they will be more often available "to calme and appease our mind" than the longer, profounder discourses of ancient moralists. He wrote "Of the Choice of Affaires," "Of the Diversitie of Men's Actions," "Of Dissembling," "Of Vanitie," "Of Sorrow," and "Of Death." Some of these titles recall at once the essays of Montaigne. But such correspondence would be almost inevitable, and the author's pattern may just as well have been Seneca's *Epistles* or Plutarch's *Morals.* The essay, "How we ought to rule our life," is distinctly like Seneca, and the closing sentence has the true touch of the aphorism: "And to say the troth, Hee which taketh much uppon him, giveth fortune much power over him."

Greenham's essays may have been cast in their final form as early as 1597. The *Remedies against Discontentment* is a collection of genuine essays done unquestionably before Bacon's first venture in the field. Nevertheless, it is wrong to consider either one or the other as the first of their kind, and to speculate on the surprise that Bacon's first volume must have aroused. The earliest specimens of the essay are discoverable in discourse, dialogue, and common-place book. These writings may be crude and undeveloped; but their authors were doing just what the later essayists did, offering their opinions on matters of current interest, in a compound of reflection, anecdote, and example. Hence one sees why Bacon himself declared that, although the word, essay, might be unused in that particular sense, the thing designated was old and familiar. "Senecaes Epistles to Lucilius," he declared, "yf one marke them well, are but Essaies." And Seneca was only one of the most artistic of these ethical writers. Bacon could well have acknowledged the less artistic work of others in England who preceded him. So the essay made its beginning, and time only was needed for its full development and for the building up of a prose style suited to its needs. (pp. 10-21)

In 1597 Francis Bacon's first essays appeared. He had inherited the common sixteenth-century interest in moral and political philosophy, and simply discussed, in somewhat new form, matters directly pertaining to one or the other of them. The little volume, therefore, probably created no such sensation as imaginative critics have supposed.

The exact content of Bacon's first collection of essays is seldom stated definitely. There are in it three parts or divisions. In the first section, there are the ten pieces in English, gathered, according to his own statement, as the first fruit before they were properly matured. Here Bacon discussed such topics as Study, Discourse, Ceremonies and Respects, and Suitors and Expense—all having to do with the affairs of men in public life. The second section of the volume comprises the *Meditationes Sacrae,* written in Latin, but published again in an English translation in 1598. These meditations deal with more strictly religious themes, like "Of the Workes of God and Man," "Of Atheism," and "Of Heresie." With this special section for his more religious speculations, Bacon could restrict himself in the English essays to considerations of worldly prudence, as critics have often noted that he did. Thirdly, the volume contained a section called *Colours of Good and Evil.* Bacon defines them as "impressions perplexing and over ruling the Reason by the power of the Imagination." He was following, he professed, the example of Aristotle in making this analysis of popular sayings. On such proverbs as *"Quod bono vicinum, bonum: quod a bono remotum malum,"* he gathered all the evidence, pro and con; for such material, he later explained, is "of excellent use, especially for business and the wisdom of private discourse."

Critics have assumed that Bacon was prompted to write his essays by the example of Montaigne, whose work appeared first in 1580 and was added to in 1588 and was finally translated into English by Florio in 1603. The work of Montaigne had certainly come to Bacon's attention; for the term, essay, that Bacon adopted had been used up to that time only by Montaigne. Sir Anthony Bacon, moreover, his brother, was personally acquainted with the French writer. But Francis Bacon made no reference to Montaigne before he wrote on Truth, which was published first in 1625. In his earlier work he nowhere mentioned his predecessor, and his method is never that of Montaigne. Where the French writer is diffuse and informal, Bacon is terse and aphoristic; and Montaigne's early essays are tissues of examples where Bacon's first essays are absolutely without them. In fact, evidence of Montaigne's influence on Bacon is quite lacking, and a much more probable source can be more directly pointed out.

The early essays of Bacon, as compared with Montaigne's or even with his own later work, are terse and elliptical. They seem like jottings from a note book gathered together in brief paragraphs. Each thought is finely phrased; but one follows another without the marks of continuity usual in artistic prose, and amplifying material is wanting. In short, they are just what their author called them—"dispersed meditations." In these collections of concentrated thought, Bacon deals, moreover, with matters of prudence, the getting along in the world. The exclusion of a more religious trend of thought may be due to the presence in the same volume of the Religious Meditations. But the fact, at all events, remains, that Bacon in such essays as "Of Negotiating," "Of Faction," "Of Honour and Reputation," and "Of Followers and Friends," gathers his thoughts on the art of living in this world. If William Penn entitled his little book *Some Fruits of Solitude,* Bacon might have well called his *Some Fruits of Experience;* for his entire message bears on what is prudent, expedient, and creditable.

An abundant literature of this sort had been developed before Bacon's time, designated by the term, Maxim. Humanists remembered that Aristotle had sanctioned the use of these brief precepts on life, and their composition became a common diversion in sixteenth-century Italy. There in the little courts, where almost every gentleman had at least some opportunity to serve in civic or diplomatic affairs, the minds of the Humanists turned naturally to statecraft, and many collections of maxims were made. Bacon used to meditate as he walked, jotting down his thoughts as they came to him and never expecting that some of these reflections would be preserved. Other men like Sir Walter Raleigh and John Selden showed the same interest in maxims pertaining not to ethical concerns so much as to public life. Bacon's first English essays were only such maxims transfused with true artistic genius.

The leader in this school of Italian statecraft was Machiavelli. He himself made no formal collection of maxims bearing on political science; but his works are simply sown with them. The *Prince* is nothing more than a manual of statesmanship based on principles clearly expressed and on actual worldly experience, and the *Discourses* on Livy's history abound in scattered bits of such wisdom. Some of the chapters pertain exclusively to incidents in Roman history; but even from them lessons might be drawn. "Herein three points are to be noted," is Machiavelli's observation as he passes from fact to precept. Other sections are more general in significance, showing, for example, that new methods of modern warfare differ greatly from the old, or that "it was never judged a prudent course to peril your whole fortunes where you put not forth your full strength." Still others, coming closer to the field of the ethical essay, consider human nature. In matters of moment, good counsellors often judge amiss; taunts and abuse breed hatred toward the user and bring no advantage; promises made under compulsion need not be observed; the great man has a powerful control over the multitude. In all this, Machiavelli displays fully ripened knowledge of man in his world. His style in the *Prince,* especially, has more continuity than that of the typical series of maxims. But it was soon seen that both the *Prince* and the *Dis-*

courses depended largely on their tersely expressed theories of statecraft. So collections of maxims were gathered from them and published separately. Bacon, of course, was familiar with Machiavelli's works and sympathetic toward his rationalistic handling of facts. Professor Arber has called attention to the similarities between the essay, "Of Vicissitude of Things," and one section of the *Discourses.* These obvious reminiscences of the Italian statesman are found in the essays of 1614 and 1625; but Bacon must have known of these maxims when he first composed the ten essays.

The most notable collection of such maxims for the modern reader of Bacon was gathered by Francesco Guicciardini, a follower of Machiavelli. His work is preserved in two manuscripts, one composed before 1628 and consisting of 182 paragraphs, the other written somewhat later in 221 paragraphs. They were first published entire by Canestrini in 1857 as the *Ricordi Politici e Civili;* but partial collections, much mutilated by editors and printers, appeared in the late sixteenth century. Corbinelli published some of them in Paris in 1576, the *Più Consigli et Avvertimenti;* Sansovino edited the *Avvertimenti Politici* in 1583; and in 1585 a third collection, *I Precetti et Sententie Piu Notabile in Materia di Stato,* was issued. All these and others as well came before Bacon's time.

Guicciardini himself did not publish his maxims; but they were written with great care, as the manuscripts attest, and show a sagacious, vigorous mind. He proffered in the maxims his observations on wealth, courage, reputation, honor, and many other such topics. His mind may have lacked the imaginative reach of Machiavelli's. But his ideas on statecraft are as positive as they are sane, and his style is firm. Elsewhere as a historian, he used long, involved sentences just as Bacon did. But in his maxims he expressed his thoughts more tersely and with more care for emphasis. In style, therefore, as well as in his practical, empirical attitude toward life, his maxims resemble Bacon's essays. Even on friendship and the closest domestic relationships, both take the same worldly, unemotional point of view.

On the subject of prosperity, Guicciardini wrote much as Bacon did. Compare the familiar essay with this maxim: "Prosperity is often our worst enemy, making us vicious, frivolous, and insolent; so that to bear it well is a better test of a man than to bear adversity." Nor was Bacon's attitude toward dissimulation one whit more indulgent than his predecessor's:

> A frank and liberal Nature doth please universally, and it is in itself a generous thing; yet sometime it doth hurt a man; on the other hand, dissimulation is useful; but it is odious, and hath a taste of baseness, and is only needful through the evil Natures of others. Wherefore, I know not, which is to be chosen; I think, that the one may be used ordinarily, and yet the other not abandoned, that is, in thine ordinary and common course of living, to use the first in such wise, as that thou gainest the name of frankness; and, nevertheless, in certain cases of importance, to use dissimulation, which is so much the more useful, and doth succeed the better, to one who

doth thus live, inasmuch as, through having a name for the contrary, it is more easily believed in him. In conclusion, I do not applaud him who lives continually in dissimulation and with artifice; but I excuse him who doth sometime use it.

These maxims, which so closely resemble Bacon's, were popular in England, and Guicciardini's *History of Italy,* also, like Machiavelli's *Discourses,* was gleaned of its sentences, and an English collection was published by Robert Dallington in 1613. His method was to propound each maxim, illustrate it by a number of brief examples drawn from Plutarch, Aristotle, Lucan, Seneca, and other philosophers, and then clinch all by a longer story from Italian history. Some of the maxims resemble the lessons taught in the emblem-books; others were transferred by Guicciardini from the unpublished *Ricordi* to his history. More often, however, they touch on civic duties, where the resemblance to Bacon would be especially noticeable. "He that weareth his heart in his fore-head, and is of an ouvert and transparent nature, through whose words, as through cristall, ye may see into every corner of his thoughtes: That man is fitter for a table of good-fellowshippe, then a Councell table: For upon the Theater of publick imployment either in peace or warre, the actors must of necessity weare vizardes, and change them in everie Scæne." Another of these little essays begins: "Nothing rideth on swifter wings then fame and opportunitie: here is only the difference, that flieth still forward, this backward. She must therefore be taken by the fore-top, at the very instant of her coming." Another paragraph starts: "Custome to do well, is like the Dyers scouring, it cleanseth and purgeth the minde of vicious dregs, by Education: and then Reason and Exercise finding a subject so well prepared, giveth it the tincture of vertue in graine." Thus Dallington tried to give a somewhat new form to a type of book long familiar to readers. "The Method," he declared, "is not vulgar, for though bookes of Civill discourse be full of axiomes, Philosophers of proofes, and Historians of instances; yet shall ye hardly meete them all combined in one complement." This compilation offers just what Montaigne and Bacon, in his last essays, furnished in more artistic form.

One of the early editors of Guicciardini, Francesco Sansovino, was an ardent compiler of these maxims and a composer of them as well. One of his volumes was translated into English in 1590 by Robert Hichcock as the *Quintesence of Wit.* These maxims deal as usual with the affairs of public men, and are in general short and compact. The English translation, it may be worth noting, was dedicated to Robert Cecil, the cousin of Francis Bacon. Occasionally, Sansovino presented a topic of general interest; "a capable wit that knows how to make choise of time hath no occasion to lament himselfe that his life should be shorte, for he that can applye himselfe to infinite things and spend his time profitably dooth gaine time." But most of the maxims are simply commonplaces of political philosophy. "In publick affaires," one reads, "we ought diligentlye to consider of the beginnings, for that it is not after in the power of men, to part from the deliberations alreadye made, and in the which they have persevered long time, without dishonour and perill." A book of this type,

Sansovino believed, "breeds a lightsomenes in man, and puts away the wearines of time, and labour of the spirites." He derived most of his maxims from other authors, chiefly Machiavelli and Guicciardini, but some are his own.

In another collection of maxims, somewhat wider in scope, the *Avvedimenti Civili,* Giovanni Lottino arranged his material, just as Bacon arranged his in *Exempla Antithetorum,* under such topics as laws, adulation, ministers of state, and gratitude. His advice on public life is less commonplace than Sansovino's, and he more often handles general, ethical ideas. One paragraph is virtually a little essay on friendship. "There are many reasons that cause one man to be the friend of another. But the greatest of all is that which springs from friendship itself, which is of such force that it outweighs all others. True friendship, without any expectation of gain, desires to create it, for no other motive than good will, which extends to him who receives it. Hence there is great difference between good will due to friendship, and good will prompted by the expectation and hope of profit; because in one case men think of the profit, in the other case, of the friend." Another paragraph begins: "Ingratitude is naturally hated by all men, being directly contrary to humanity, which is inspired by benevolence, courtesy, and all that makes human intercourse possible." From this beginning a brief essay develops. There is much, in fact, in this collection that was available material for the English essayists.

A great many of the most notable maxims from the volumes of Pedro de Mexia, Sansovino, Anthony Du Verdier and others were assembled in a volume called the *Treasurie of auncient and moderne Times.* Some of the early divisions of the work are theological and religious, dealing with God and the Good Angels and the like. In the second volume, the topics are mainly historical and geographical. But in one portion of the first volume there are chapters "Of Manhood," "Of Wisedom," and "Of Prudence," that are closer in content to the ordinary English essay. Clearly, these maxims furnished much to the content as well as to the style of the essay, and Bacon, in jotting down thoughts for his first essays, had such a collection in mind. Not Montaigne at all, but Guicciardini, Sansovino, Lottino, and the other framers of maxims were his earliest models.

In the Latin essays of 1597, the *Meditationes Sacrae,* Bacon was less strongly indebted to this type of literature. For the average English reader, these pieces seem to want the trenchant phrase and the arresting thought that render the *Essays* notable. The original Latin, of course, shows a clarity and conciseness that the translation lacks; for some of the long English sentences are formed by the imperfect joining of several clear periods. But there is an absence of aphorism in the meditations, and the diction is not especially apt and is certainly wanting in the homely phrase and racy idiom that give color to the essays.

The general structure of the meditations is superior to the phrasing and that could not be spoiled to such a degree in translation. The first meditation is a clear-cut paragraph which presents the contrast between the excellence of God's work and the imperfection of man's. "Of Impostors," likewise, rests on a similar contrast between the actions of a hypocrite in the presence of his fellow men and his demeanor alone in the presence of God. "The Miracles of our Savior" sets the mercifulness of Christ over against the cruelty of Moses. One or two essays, in spite of their brevity, are developed by the method of division or classification. The thought is clear and well ordered; the close of the essays, like that on miracles, has force. And in the discussion of charity, there is less of the doctrine of expedience that mars the English essays and more of unselfish morality. This piece on charity and another on the mitigation of care, present subjects that appeared often in later essays. On the whole, therefore, the meditations less nearly resemble the maxims than do the essays, and come closer to the discourses of Seneca, Plutarch, and other moralists.

One late moralist whose work Bacon may have known was Giovanni Pontano, a prominent statesman at Naples during the early sixteenth century. He composed in Latin rather loosely formed dissertations on subjects like fortune, liberality, splendor, obedience, and prudence. Each is divided into several parts. For example, in discussing splendor, he wrote separately on ornaments, dress, precious stones, and gardens and villas. Each part is a short essay in itself, and on the last Bacon, it will be remembered, wrote most interestingly. In discussing another phase of the subject, which again Bacon handled, the matter of public games, Pontano showed that some festivals, like those proclaimed by victorious Roman generals or the sacred plays in honor of the Eucharist, given at Rome, Florence, and Naples, are prompted by piety. On the other hand, equestrian games and mock combats are purely secular in intent. Pontano then closed with a short account of Pompey and others who had been very fond of such pastime. In a much more philosophical spirit, Pontano discussed the trait of liberality. He would class it among the virtues, since many may use wealth either wisely or foolishly and merits praise or blame accordingly. But good fortune, he insisted in another essay, possesses none of the marks of a virtue. Good fortune is due to purely fortuitous circumstances, and has no connection with reason. Where reason sways, fortune is absent; and where fortune rules, reason is not to be considered. So on one topic after another, prudential, ethical, or purely worldly, Pontano marshalled his thoughts. Although his style is diffuse, the product is a collection of essays, and they were rather widely known in the sixteenth century.

In such essays as these by Pontano, Bacon could find late examples of brief discourse. Far more artistic examples of the same type of prose were familiar to him from his reading of Seneca and Plutarch. So that one small volume of Latin and English essays, published in 1597, represents the deep twofold interest in life that its author had inherited alike from antiquity and the Renaissance. The *Essays* bear more upon the conduct of public life, and the *Meditationes Sacrae* consider matters more intimately related to the inner life. For both, very direct sources other than Montaigne can be found. (pp. 22-30)

The gentlemen and statesmen of the Italian Renaissance who thus prompted Bacon's first efforts, inspired others as well. During his imprisonment in the Tower, Sir Walter Raleigh is supposed to have put together his *Prince, or Maxims of State*. It contains, first, short definitions or descriptions of monarchy, aristocracy, and other forms of government. Then three sections follow on the proper methods of founding, preserving, and altering a state. But there is no attempt at continuity in the work. Each part consists simply of a number of brief sentences, called "sophismes," bearing on the topic broached. The same criticism may be applied to the advice offered to his son. With more of the continuity of a treatise and less of the brevity of the maxim, King James traversed somewhat the same ground in the *Basilikon Doron,* a manual written for his son's instruction. It offers, among other things, some advice on study. There is first a brief essay on the subject in general, ending with the sentence: "for knowledge and learning is a light burthen, the weight wherof will never presse your shoulders." This is followed by several discussions of the reading of Scripture, law, and history. The book as a whole resembles the early treatises that have been already mentioned; but in places it broaches the same subjects that Raleigh handled in the form of maxims.

Saying really nothing of Bodenham's *Politeuphuia, Wits Commonwealth,* which illustrates the purely unliterary development of the maxim, one passes on to the *Timber* or *Discoveries* of Ben Jonson. The little book is made up of prose paragraphs about midway between the jottings of a commonplace-book and the finished essay. Its thoughts had come to Jonson at different times, many of them as the result of his reading; but most of them probably date from the later years of his life. Certainly, the fine reference to Bacon was penned after the Chancellor's disgrace. Some of the entries deal with moral questions, others touch the principles of literary criticism, while still others are concerned with statecraft. Jonson's prevailing manner corresponds to that of the writers of the Italian maxims, and in the essay, "Clementia," he mentions Machiavelli. But Jonson did not restrict himself to the narrow compass of the maxim. There is a really fine discussion of education, as complete and as well developed as the best of the genuine essays. Another like it handles the topic, "Ingeniorum Discrimina." In a number of cases, furthermore, brief paragraphs are arranged in groups, each devoted to the exposition of some one topic. The graphic arts, style, and government are handled in this progressive way. Jonson is clearly writing with some of the moral essayists in mind. And in his frank introduction of his own experience in many of his essays, he but follows the example of Montaigne. He talks of his failing memory, he confesses his admiration for Shakespeare, he chats of some of his acquaintances, and he speaks of certain orators whom he has known and respected for their earnest quest of knowledge. "Yet these men I could not but love and admire," he confesses, after speaking of their facile oratory. So in general he gave the color of his own personality to all that he touched. He may have borrowed from Seneca, or taken his critical opinions from Heinsius; but on all that he appropriated he left the impress of his own strong personality.

But there is a finer grain in Jonson's thought than was common to the Italian school of statecraft. "Nothing is a courtesy," he believed, "unless it be meant us; and that friendly and lovingly." Equally fine are these sentiments:

"Truth is man's proper good, and the only immortal thing was given to our mortality to use;" and "A good man will avoid the spirit of sin." Finally, in reference to Bacon's downfall, Jonson nobly remarked: "In his adversity I ever prayed that God would give him strength; for greatness he could not want."

Another great scholar of the century, John Selden, will belong among the writers of maxims only if one disregards the long and learned treatises that he composed on tithes, the freedom of the seas, and titles of honor, all of which he published himself, and considers simply the *Table Talk* that was put together thirty-five years after his death, in 1689, by Richard Milward. The topics unquestionably are Selden's, and the serious, almost oracular, tone in which they are presented doubtless reflects his style of conversation. Although they may express the ideas that passed through his mind from time to time, it would be unfair to say that they convey always the deliberate, settled judgments of the author, as the thoughts of a book are supposed to do. The *Table Talk,* however, consists of apothegms in the true sense of the word, confined not to statecraft, but ranging widely over the great scholar's unlimited field of interests, and expressed with the brevity and directness of the maxim.

Another writer who adhered to the terse, aphoristic style of these early maxims, even after the essay had reached its full development, was the conservative old knight, Sir Henry Wotton. This is especially true of the *Aphorisms of Education,* a collection of wise or witty maxims having little to do with education. "They who travel far, easily miss their way," he argues in one instance; "few men thrive by one onely Art, fewer by many," he argues in another. His style shows something of the antithesis and point of the conceited school of prose writers; but in general it corresponds well to the style of the maxim, with only a little more striving for literary display. "But these effects are not general, many receiving more good in their Bodies by the tossing of the Ship, than benefit in their Minds by breathing in a foreign Air, when they come to land." The maxims are interesting and reveal plainly, as does the essay on pedantry, the character of the courtly old provost of Eton College. It is but a characteristic revelation of himself and his mode of writing when he says in the Dedication of the *Survey of Education:* "I am old and childless; and although I were a Father of many, I could leave them nothing, either in Fortune or in Example."

But there were strong influences that kept the essay from developing further along these lines, at least until the latter part of the century when French influences were predominant. One of these forces that contributed largely to the maturing of the English essay along other lines was Florio's translation of Montaigne in 1603. Already a knowledge of the French philosopher was common in England, for the essays had appeared in 1580 and 1588; but Florio's version widened that knowledge immeasurably. Montaigne became one of the two great pioneers in the field, and his style and his habits of thought determined to a large extent the course of the essay in England. Henceforth, it is Bacon or Montaigne who seems to guide the hands of English essayists.

Of the writers immediately following Bacon who helped in the maturing of the English essay, Sir William Cornwallis holds the leading position. He was a man of note in the literary world, and a friend of Jonson and Donne. Naturally, then, his work reveals some of the prevailing fashions in prose. Since he was personally associated with Jonson, it may seem strange that he did not follow him and Bacon more nearly. To be sure, his first essays may have been composed before Bacon's were widely known; for Cornwallis published his first collection as early as 1600 and added the last pieces to it in 1610. Be that as it may, Montaigne, and not Bacon, was his guide. Cornwallis professed in the essay, "Of Censuring," never to have read the French essays in the original, but admitted that he had seen "divers of his pieces" in translation, and that before Florio's work was issued. One might suspect that he had somewhere read many, if not all, of them. Like Montaigne, he discussed anger, the education of children, perseverance, justice, and lying. He criticised Montaigne in his preface, and mentioned him in seven essays of the final edition, and, although he objected that Montaigne is a little too squeamish about the suffering of animals, and hardly positive enough in his remarks on Caesar, he in general was in full accord with Montaigne's thought. Professor Upham [in *French Influence in English Literature,* 1908] has pointed out the resemblances between the two. For example, in the essay, "Of Advise," Cornwallis recommended the lessons taught by experience, advocated an education that fits a man for active service in life, and enjoined moderation in all things. The number of such resemblances renders it certain that Cornwallis was thoroughly acquainted with his predecessor's work.

Directly dependent on Montaigne, as it seems, for his thought, Cornwallis was somewhat misled by his master's discursive style. Cornwallis boldly declares: "I professe not method, neither will I chaine my selfe to the head of my chapter." This is the clue to his method. He begins an essay with some thought remote from his topic, and progresses in a free, discursive fashion to the close. That he was conscious of this informality and freedom is plain from a second confession: "All this time I have built but the bridge I meane to travel upon, and not that annointed with a finical Exordium. I travaile where I list, & when I list, & will not bind my selfe to more then I list." But Cornwallis had little of Montaigne's genius for this expansive type of essay, and especially in some of the longer pieces of the second edition, he grew dull. And although he expressed some thoughts directly and emphatically, he more often constructed his sentences loosely. So he wrote: "It is a pretty soft thing this same Love, an excellent company keeper, full of gentlenesse, and affabilitie, makes men fine, and to go cleanly, teacheth them qualities, handsome protestations; and if the ground bee not too barren, it bringeth forth Rimes, and Songs full of passion, enoogh to procure crossed armes, and the Hat pulled down: yea, it is a very fine thing, the badge of eighteen, and upward, not to be disallowed; better spend thy time so at Dice." Such a sentence may be roughly in Montaigne's manner, but is destitute of Montaigne's art.

This informality in style accorded well with the attitude toward learning that Cornwallis assumed. Like Montaigne and many of the late essayists, he took his stand squarely against pedantry. He ridiculed the futility of the conversation of great men and the formality of academic disputants, whom "you undoe if you suffer them not to goe Methodically to worke." In his opinion, a gentleman's knowledge "ought to bee generall, it becomes him not to talke of one thing too much, or to be wayed downe with any particular profession." Hence he resolved "not to loose my selfe in my tale, to speake words that may be understood, and to my power to meane wisely, rather then to speake eloquently." This discussion of false eloquence is continued in the essay entitled "Of Vanitie." All this, also, is distinctly like Montaigne's philosophy. But since Montaigne was a great reader, as well, his disciple was free to admit that he, too, had led a bookish life, and that his essays were simply the unburdening of an overstored mind.

In some respects, nevertheless, Cornwallis differed from Montaigne. He was more dogmatic in the discussion of his subjects and was more swayed by prejudices and scruples. There is less complexity in his thought, and less originality, than in Montaigne's. He succeeded, however, in leaving the impress of his personality on what he wrote. "I would rather choose to rise by loving distressed virtue, then by adoring pompe," he remarked in one essay. On reason and affectation he wrote much less intimately; but even that essay contains the Senecan reflection: "I hold adversity nearer a kinne to vertue, then prosperity." Sometimes, a very general and commonplace truth diverts him to self-confession. Holding, for example, that all things have their use, he remembers his boyish delight in stories like John of Bordeaux and King Arthur, and his maturer tolerance of ballads and two-penny tracts even while he is conscious of the greater worth of Plutarch and the historians. Or again, when he sees the warning, "Feare God," woven in the hangings of an ale-house, his thoughts grow active. "Shall it be objected to me, that the respect of right ought to carrie me? I thinke so too, if my power might give Right the upper hand; but I do wrong to sinke with Right, for so Right looseth a Champion: & headlong to run into mischiefe is not zeale, but desperation." In such confessions there is neither profundity nor originality; but there is the touch of personality. Unfortunately, Cornwallis was never able to sustain this touch to the end, especially in his longer efforts; and he was forced to confess, as Montaigne never had any occasion to do, that his mind worked most actively on a subject at the start, and that he would "after fall and waxe lazie, and in truth shallow."

In addition to this volume of essays, Cornwallis published a number of paradoxes, which will be noticed later, and a long essay or "encomion," the *Prayses of Sadnesse,* and some other works that lie altogether remote from our subject. The long essay, the *Prayses of Sadnesse,* begins with a disparagement of mirth and a commendation of its opposite, a mood which connoted to Cornwallis both truth and sobriety. The two resemble the ladies, Virtue and Pleasure, he felt, who offered themselves to Hercules. And although he would not approve of "a rigid, soure, morose austerity" or of a sorrow that "eates his owne heart; that abandons the rudder in a storm, and dares not live for feare of dying," he saw in sadness an "outside . . . sober,

calme, constant, modest, and for the most part silent; her inside full of peace, industry, and resolution." Hence sadness, he believed, contributes most to that all important art, the governing of life. It defends youth from pleasures and the old man from grief; it is "the beame that keeps the cogitations of man even." The reader feels that Cornwallis here reveals himself better than in the essays—a thoughtful, retiring man, fond of nature, if the long description of a sunrise is to tell at all, and of his country environment, and of books.

If Sir William Cornwallis thus showed himself to be a disciple of Montaigne, Robert Johnson came forward almost as early as a follower of the other pioneer of the essay, Francis Bacon. In 1601, there appeared a small volume, entitled *Essaies, or Rather Imperfect Offers.* Later, when the work was reissued in 1638, it was called *Johnson's Essayes: expressed in Sundry Exquisite Fancies.* Possibly, as Oldys conjectured, the writer wished to convey the impression that the sixteen short essays were the work of Ben Jonson.

Both in thought and form, Johnson's essays are much like Bacon's. Like his forerunner, Johnson clearly shows a knowledge of character and the ways of the world. There is even a touch of Bacon's expediency in his doctrine. "To deny a suite," he wrote, "doth dismisse men discontented; therefore in some cases it is better to promise, although there appear no conveniency for the effectuating." He may have learned this truth from the maxims of Guicciardini or Sansovino, whom Bacon also had read. But Johnson realized that this advice "cannot stand with the strict precepts and square of honesty." Exactly in Bacon's style, also, Johnson depended on homely comparisons to color and enforce his thought. So he amplified one idea by this comparison: "A wit too pregnant & sharp is not good: It is like a rasor, whose edge the keener it is, the sooner it is rebated, or like soft wood, which is ready to receive the impression of the Limner, but for warping is unable to keepe." Bacon in his first volume used no historical illustrations; but Johnson, following possibly the example of Montaigne or of Plutarch, introduced them occasionally and dismissed them neatly and briefly. Johnson wrote on travel, as Bacon did, and displayed Bacon's attitude toward learning in the sentence: "If wee will know what wisedome is, let us lay aside the curious questions of Schoolemen, and such as are truelie Nominalles, and consider it in the frame of our Microcosme."

Just as directly, Bacon influenced the structure of Johnson's essays. They are apt to begin with a terse, definitive sentence, such as: "Education is a good and continuall manuring of the minde, the principall foundation of all humane happiness." Sometimes, one finds an accumulation of these definitive terms, as one finds them at the beginning of Lamb's "Poor Relations." One essay, for example, begins: "Discretion is the Governesse of vertue, the rule of our behaviour, the measure of our affections, the Mistresse of demeanour, that seasoning of our actions, which maketh them acceptable." The essay, "Of Jests," is terse and aphoristic throughout. Another on learning, somewhat longer, shows steady progress. "It is a happy thing," it begins, "to keepe a meane of Wisdome, least while wee thinke too much of doing, we leave undone the effect of thinking." Seldom does the thought run beyond control. In the essay, "Of Histories," Johnson may wander a little in the long critique of Tacitus; but, in the first part of even this essay, his phrasing is compact and forceful. Either of the following statements might be attributed to Bacon: that history "teacheth more then twentie men living, successively can learn by practise," and that "slow counsels are fit rather to preserve then increase a State, speedy and quicke doe rather encrease then preserve." The latter is nothing other than the old Italian maxim. At the close of his essays, finally, Johnson tries to give point to what he has written. One reads, therefore, such sentences as this: "Here wee may see ruines without feare, daungerous warres without perill, the customes of all nations without expence."

Nothing definite is known of the author of these essays. There was a Robert Johnson at court, a musician, and our author shows some knowledge of the art in two of his discourses. In one he wrote: "Neither can I more fitly compare these book-knights than to a Musician, who insisting onely upon the Theoricke, is not able to express any thing." In the other, he declares that "Affabilitie is like Musick, which is made by a judiciall correspondency of a sharpe and flat." Possibly Johnson, the essayist, was also Johnson, the musician, a lutenist and composer who took part in Lord Leicester's entertainment at Kenilworth in 1575, and who, as a member of Shakespeare's company, wrote the music for some of his songs. That Robert Johnson, as far as records show, had never had a university career; but a thoughtful man, familiar with the Italian maxims and Bacon, and provided with some commonplace-book, could easily have composed these sixteen short essays.

In conjunction with such men as Cornwallis and Johnson, Francis Bacon himself contributed to the maturing of the essay; for what he began in 1597 as the "first fruits of his invention," he added to in 1614 and again in 1625. Possibly, he was encouraged by the popularity of his first efforts; for his essays, of all his works he says, were "most current: For that, as it seems, they come home, to mens Businesse and Bosomes." Or he may have yielded to the ever-growing demand for such prose. At all events, he enlarged his collection twice, by adding new essays and expanding the old. But a change had come, and the outstanding differences between his earliest and latest essays have been often pointed out. The latter are longer and carry in solution, as it were, more modifying matter that gives color to the thought and greater ease and coherence to the style. These essays are less like jottings from a commonplace-book, or, in other words, less like the Italian maxims from which they proceeded, and more similar to the essays that had been written during the years intervening. Bacon, for example, resorted to historical illustrations now, just as Montaigne, Cornwallis, Johnson, and other essayists had been doing. Some of his most effective essays, like that on adversity, and some of the most often-quoted phrases from the older essays, are found first in the edition of 1625.

The change has often been ascribed to the enkindling of Bacon's cold and rigid habits of thought. Rather, the change seems due to the progress made by the essay in the years elapsing between 1597 and 1625. Bacon certainly had come to know what Montaigne and the English essayists had done; for he remarked that in their work it had "become the fashion to make, out of a few axioms and observations upon any subject, a kind of complete and formal art, filling it up with some discourses, *illustrating it with examples,* and digesting it into method." Just this he accomplished in his last essays. Moreover, in 1625 he mentioned Montaigne in his essay on truth and turned to subjects on which Montaigne had written, such as friendship, parents and children, truth, and vain glory. Nicholas Breton, furthermore, in 1615 dedicated his collection of essays to Bacon as his master, and Bacon could not have been ignorant of what he and other Englishmen were doing. Bacon was too great a man to swing his views on life into accord with theirs; where Montaigne found refuge in philosophic speculation, Bacon remained an empiric philosopher. But Bacon could, and did, alter his method. So, as he put the finishing touches to his first essays or composed new ones, he plainly showed the influence of what men like Cornwallis and Johnson had done.

A comparative study, therefore, of the various editions of Bacon's essays is highly interesting. The early essays were later expanded, often by the addition of fresh, subordinate material, and sometimes by the addition of a new conclusion. Where he formerly had used a colon and a comma in corresponding positions of a compound sentence, he in 1625 more consistently punctuated thus: "To spend too much Time in Studies, is Sloth; To use them too much for Ornament, is Affectation; To make Judgement wholly by their Rules is the Humour of a Scholler." In other cases, greater clarity is obtained by the expansion of some thought at first too tersely phrased. The abrupt sentence, "For expert men can execute, but learned men are fittest to judge or censure," becomes in its final form: "For Expert Men can Execute, and perhaps Judge of particulars, one by one; But the generall Counsels, and the Plots, and Marshalling of Affaires, come best from those that are learned." Or an entirely new illustration may be added to color the bare thought of the original. Of such a nature is the suggestion: "For Naturall Abilities are like Naturall Plants, that need Proyning by Study: And Studies themselves, doe give forth Directions too much at Large, except they be bounded in by experience." The fine close of this essay, "Of Studies," first appeared in 1625. The discussion of friendship in the volume of 1614 was entirely rewritten in 1625, and one sentence from "Of Nobility" was at that time transposed to the essay, "Of Envy." The latest version of the essay, "Of Expence," was considerably enlarged by the insertion of more precise and specific advice. Historical examples were frequently introduced in the latest essays. And finally, some of the sentences most often quoted from Bacon are found only in the last edition. In that edition, for example, first appeared the statement: "Therefore it doth much adde, to a Mans Reputation, and is (as Queene Isabella said) Like perpetuall Letters Commendatory, to have good Formes." Such alterations as these carry the essays away from the Italian maxim and bring them into accord with the style that had been developing in London during the reign of King James.

When Bacon's last essays were published, in 1625, that new literary form was fully matured. Through most of the subsequent work in that field, the influence of Bacon or Montaigne can be traced. Ben Jonson had too rugged a personality to yield to the new fashion and spoke his frank criticism of it; John Selden possessed too much learning to give his time to such trifles; and both held to the older style of the maxim. Lord Clarendon, also, preserved his own individual style in writing his essays. But most of these prose writers simply followed the general fashion, and in style and thought and general range of subject there is much sameness in what was done. By the year 1625, therefore, the essay as a genre was fully matured. (pp. 31-41)

> *Elbert N. S. Thompson, "Seventeenth-Century English Essay," in* University of Iowa Humanistic Studies, *Vol. III, No. 3, November 15, 1926, pp. 10-41.*

HISTORICAL BACKGROUND

H. V. Routh

[*In the following excerpt from an article comparing the origins of the English and the French essay, Routh outlines the social and cultural circumstances surrounding the rise of the essay in England.*]

The Renascence was the golden age of essay-writing and as English prose did not become academic or even formalised till the Revolution, the mere habit of keeping common-place books was bound sooner or later to end in the publication of essays. The first English collection is anonymous and is entitled *Remedies against Discontent,* but the writer was followed by Cornwallis, Robert Johnson, Tuvill, Stephens, Brathwaite, Mason, Peacham and others who all called their fragmentary productions essays and more or less followed or coincided with Montaigne in the choice of subjects. Though their desultory writings have the moralising and meditative manner which characterises the type, neither the style nor the opinions are remarkable. As the story of practically all their lives is unknown, we can form only the most general idea of the conditions which influenced their work. Its mediocrity proves that essay-writing had become a habit, if not a fashion. Fortunately there appeared another essayist, second only to Montaigne, and when we examine his life we find that his literary greatness is due to the same kind of impulses as those which actuated his prototype.

Bacon's first slim volume, which appeared in 1597, does not contain essays in the true sense of the word. The style is aphoristic and epigrammatic, but jejune and impersonal, and the thought is confined to the narrow and practical problem of success at Court. Whether or no these were suggested by Lord Burghley's *Precepts or Directions,* which at that time existed in MS., they read more like a

book of courtesy brought up to date than a collection of essays. They might almost be styled the manual of the opportunist. These limitations are not the result of inexperience. Bacon was thirty-seven years old when he published his first edition and the style, with all its faults, displays that concentration and control of thought which marks the born writer. The thought itself is not that of an essayist. Bacon was then full of ardour and of ambition. The glamour of a public career, which in that enterprising age hypnotised even poor Gabriel Harvey, had taken possession of his imagination. As a boy he had served in the British embassy at Paris. Since the age of twenty-three he had been a member of Parliament. Since 1591 he had intrigued with Essex. He believed in the promise of the future, and however much he had set his heart on scientific research, he intended also to be a man of action and not a penurious and secluded student. It is not out of such confidence and enthusiasm that an author can expect to rival Marcus Aurelius, Montaigne or Lamb. He had not, at this stage, the essayist's attitude of mind. By 1625 the final edition appeared 'enlarged both in number and weight, so that they are, indeed, a new work.' As compared with Montaigne, Bacon's essays at first sight seem fundamentally different. London had, at that epoch, developed far more rapidly than Paris. The forces of the nation were already centred in the capital, and the Court and Parliament had become not only the seat of political power but a laboratory for studying the science of government. So it is not surprising to find that Bacon's mind still runs on questions of statecraft and of courtiership. But when we start to re-read the volume, we find that Bacon's point of view has completely changed since 1597. Like Montaigne he is now an onlooker. He is no longer teaching himself or others how to succeed at Court; he is teaching his readers how to think, and the art of ruling happens to be uppermost in their minds. So he explains, exposes, unmasks. For this reason, again like Montaigne, Bacon is now impressed with the immense value of learning, especially of the classics. Fuller [in *Church-History of Britain,* 1655] describes him as 'a great honourer of antient authors, yet a great deviser and practiser of new waies of learning.' After drawing on his own experience or observations to discuss what is fittest, he refers to antiquity to decide what is best. Many of the most striking thoughts put forth without any acknowledgement are (to say the least) similar to passages in Greek, Latin or Italian authors. He even maintains that for a real grasp of business a knowledge of books is even more helpful than a knowledge of men. But as we become more familiar with the rather disconcerting mannerisms of Jacobean thought, we penetrate to the fundamental idea of Bacon's essays and realise how profoundly his purpose resembles that of his French prototype. Bacon's thought is the best equipment for a man engaged in the unavowed duel with himself. The ex-chancellor is never tired of warning his readers against trusting to appearances or admiring what is merely imposing. As if by accident, he is always discovering new and unexpected examples of self-deception and of meanness. While discussing topics of public interest, he is constantly turning one's eyes in upon oneself. While seeming to teach men how to mould their fortunes, he is really teaching them how to mould their characters. Thus in spite of an appearance of worldliness and of administrative capacity the tenor of Bacon's mind harmonises with the tenor of Montaigne's.

Their two styles are distinct but similar. Unlike Montaigne, Bacon lived in an age of conceits and cliches, and he could not escape the atmosphere of his time. But his epigrams are the illustrations of thought and not the triumphs of conversational wit. Ben Jonson declared that 'no man ever spoke more neatly, more presly, more weightily, or suffered less emptinesse, lesse idlenesse, in what he uttered.' Rawley concludes that his 'opinions and assertions were, for the most part, binding . . . rather like oracles than discourses.' . . . [The] influence of the *Salons* had seduced many French authors from the essay-writing for which they were gifted, and the sign of this defection will be found in the conversational *préciosité* of their style. But with Bacon the art of conversation ended in the precision of thought and he wrote in the style of soliloquy. There is all the difference in the world between describing children as 'hostages given to fortune' and describing chairs as 'les commodités de la conversation.' Bacon's is the style of a writer who is communing with himself, who is winning his way into other people's minds by showing the working of his own. It is only because his disposition is so reticent and his thought is so chastened and concentrated that its character is lost in the effect.

In fact Bacon, as an old man clinging to the emoluments and submitting to the humiliations of high office under a court favourite, or languishing in disgrace, is essentially one of the spiritual exiles who turn to study for the satisfying sense of reality which they cannot buy at the world's price. In some respects the Jacobean and Caroline ages were more congenial to men of this stamp than was the corresponding epoch in France, because the male portion of society was left to pursue culture in its own way. Women played a prominent part in the gay life of the capital, but if they influenced literature, it was only as a theme for cavalier lyrics. There were no *Salons* and there was little or none of the kind of literature which, as we have seen, *Salons* produced, Fuller, Sir Philip Warwick, Clarendon and Burnet did indeed write portraits of historical characters, modelled on Thucydides or Livy, but the reader will look in vain in our language for an encomium of social accomplishments such as the *portrait* of Cléomire (Mlle de Rambouillet) or of Parthénice (Mme de Sablé) in *Grand Cyrus.* Englishmen, such as Arthur Wilson, Weldon, Warwick and Richard Baxter, wrote more or less private histories from a personal point of view, yet Sir William Temple was the first to write anything even distantly comparable to the French *Mémoires.* On the other hand there were plenty of notable conversationalists, including, besides Bacon, Ben Jonson, Howell, Carew, Hampden, Vane, Hutchinson, Earle, Hales, Waller, Cowley; but they made their reputations among men in private symposia. Those who had inherited from the age of Euphuism the taste for conversational artistry succeeded in exercising their gifts by developing the Theophrastan character sketch. Aristotle in Bk II of his *Rhetoric* delineated a few human types as models for 'Middle Comedy,' and his disciple Theophrastus following the same idea created a much larger number of social types, suitable as *dramatis personae* for the 'new Comedy.' Jacobeans went further and described

any character and finally any institution which lent itself to humorous treatment. The art consisted in selecting for enumeration those traits which are common to all members of the class portrayed so that the type is at once recognised. At the same time the descriptions must have so much of the warmth and colour of conversation that the subject appeals to some emotion. The reader should be filled with amusement or contempt or admiration. This form of composition has little in common with the French *portrait,* but it amounts to a series of illustrations for the Essay. The character sketch embodies the same spirit as the Essay, but leaves out its erudition and its contemplation. In the hands of Overbury and his circle it became an appendix to Bacon's *Essays* and Peacham's *Compleat Gentleman.* In the hands of Earle it deals with the less conspicuous questions of conduct and of conscience and should be read with Jeremy Taylor's *Holy Living* and *Holy Dying.*

It is not of course to be expected that all humanists and moralists should write essays. Some, like Burton and Sir Thomas Browne, though admirably qualified, both by disposition and training, were more in love with the academic dignity of a connected treatise, and others, like Reginald Scot, Nashe, Dekker, Gifford, Cotta, Milton, Filmer, Ady, Wagstaffe and Webster, were too completely absorbed by the controversies of the time to miss opportunities of writing pamphlets. But a sufficiently large number of authors have produced essays and characters, to prove that the age was congenial to that form of self-expression. The period from the accession of James I to the outbreak of the Civil War is characterised by an ever-growing veneration for learning and by an ever-increasing spirit of reaction after the hopes of Elizabeth's reign. Erudition and disillusionment were the note of the time and, as we have seen, these were the chief features of Montaigne's immediate environment.

The Civil War suspended but did not abolish these conditions, and as no new literary form took possession of the field at the Restoration, it is not surprising that the Essay survived until the Revolution. With the succession of William and Mary, English culture was possessed by a new spirit. It became the function of literature not to mirror life but to recreate it. Almanzor was conceived to be more noble and imperious and Cato more virtuous and resigned than any real mortal. Even fraudulent prentices like Barnwell and dissolute gamesters like Beverley were expected to inspire tears of compassion. Vergil and Homer were translated, because they were supposed to depict a heroism and a gentility which no story of modern life could offer. Satire was to exhaust the arts of rhetoric in order that vice might be portrayed with all the disfigurements of a monstrosity. Genres which could have no pretensions to such creativeness were yet to civilise by adventitious excellencies. If the subject-matter was trivial, they could at any rate display their author's ingenuity and give the reader the pleasure of exercising his literary taste. These conceptions, which gradually took possession of the nation from the age of Dryden to the age of Johnson, were partly borrowed from Silver Latin and partly from the court of Louis XIV and expressed the nation's new felt desire for progress and culture. It was, in the language of Defoe, a projecting age. The atmosphere of the seventeenth century, in which the Essay flourished, had disappeared, and the type ought to have vanished from England as completely as it had vanished from France. Instead of that, it reappeared in a new form sufficiently important to inspire imitation in both France and Germany and so popular that Addison compared the genre to Ulysses's bow 'in which every man of wit or learning may try his strength.'

Though literature, since the Renascence, had become as imitative as the art of war, this development finds no parallel in other countries, and as a phenomenon it appears, at first sight, so contrary to the principles laid down in the foregoing inquiry, that a few words must be spent on its explanation. The cause will be found, not in any cult of the Essay of the Renascence, but in the peculiar social condition of England. While the compatriots of Richelieu and Mazarin were learning to think nobly in drawing-rooms, aloof from the friction of ordinary life, the contemporaries of Hampden and of Milton were realising their power as a class in politics. All through the Civil War, the Protectorate and the Restoration, this great body of citizens became more and more homogeneous and conscious of its destiny. They found their own literature in the enormous output of pamphlets, corrantos, diurnals and broadsides, and when the theatres were closed and the taverns were shut, they made coffee-houses their place of assembly. The absolutism of the Stuarts, the dissipation of the aristocracy, the schemes of Louis XIV, the intrigues of the Jesuits, whether real or imagined, continued to keep this class united and on its guard, and when the Revolution at last brought them security, there was little in the new and unpopular Court at Hampden to charm them out of their bourgeois culture. They cared little for Congreve's wit, Waller's sentimentality or Dryden's efforts at heroic drama, but they were very far from losing the habit of reading and discussing. To satisfy their interest, a new and multitudinous growth of fugitive literature came into existence and English journalism was established. In all the periodical publications from Pecke's *Perfect Diurnall* to Defoe's *A Review of France* the investigator will find nothing which foreshadows the recrudescence of the Essay. They were, for the most part, factious fly-sheets and broadsides engaged in an unequal contest with the restrictions of the censorship. But after the Licensing Act had collapsed in 1688 and periodicals appeared every year dealing with topics as different as etiquette and plague precautions in France, their immense importance was accidentally discovered by Richard Steele in 1709. The journalistic press of London was at that period the only means of catching a reader when he or she was in a natural mood. All other kinds of literature were imposing; their form or their subject-matter or their associations transcended the reader; they could be approached only after an interval of mental preparation. The newspaper was the one literary recreation which the average person could enjoy without sacrificing his ordinary self.

It was thus that the essayist of the eighteenth century was given his opportunity. The industrious and domesticated middle class was full of a practical and intelligent curiosity in life. They were interested in character, education, manners and morality. They had a sense of humour and a sense of pathos; above all they were determined to learn how to live well. Though no man could assimilate the culture of his age without absorbing its artificiality, the literature of the coffee-houses still kept open an approach to their common-sense. The same reader who perused a book of verse epistles for the pleasure of tracing analogies to Horace would welcome a friendly discussion of his own personal problems in so informal a publication as a news-sheet. Thus there was an eager and appreciative public waiting for the essayist; that is to say for the writer who could give intimate and confidential counsels on conduct, based on the experience of other ages. Once again a comparison will reveal the significance of these facts. France also had her popular press. Between 1649 and 1652 the Fronde occasioned a crop of *Courriers* and *Mercures* no less polemical than the Thomason tracts and no more lacking in merit. These were followed by a number of *Gazettes,* beginning with *La Muse historique* (1650-65), many of them couched in verse and all of them more elegant than their counterparts across the Channel. But the French middle class lacked a civilisation of its own and looked to the aristocracy for culture, so their journalism reached its goal in *Le Mercure Galant,* a lively record of high society in the form of a letter which, founded by Donneau de Visé in 1672, continued as *Mercure de France* till 1820, but reached its highest usefulness as the prototype of the 'petits journaux' and its greatest distinction when it was 'lu par le Roi.' The English middle class produced the *Tatler, Spectator, Examiner, Guardian, Freeholder, Onlooker* which contain some of the suavest humour, the most homely wisdom, and the least affected prose in the language. Many of the contributors were not essayists in the more scholarly sense of the word. Steele in spite of his flashes of insight and his touches of characterisation was never more than a social pamphleteer of genius. Defoe in his hundreds of contributions hovers between the rôle of a political agitator and the rôle of a sensationalist. Gay, Budgell, Arbuthnot, Wotton, Tickell display no particular talent for occasional writing. Pope lacked sympathy and Swift lacked every other feeling. But Berkeley with his fund of abstract knowledge which he knew how to distil into moral counsels would have developed into a great essayist if *The Minute Philosopher* had not claimed his energies.

The most complete type of the eighteenth century essayist is, of course, Addison, and it is instructive to notice that his education and temperament correspond to the qualities which we have laid down as being typical of the genre. Though he rose to be under-secretary of State and one of the lords commissioners of trades and married a countess, Addison had no reason to regard his public career or his wedded life as a success. He was shy, reticent and utterly inept at business. His timidity and self-suppression are well illustrated by his habit of ridiculing others with ironical praise. On the other hand, he had visited foreign countries and had observed men, and had acquired the faculty of divining other people's thoughts and peculiarities. His mind was so stored with erudition that his point of view was that of the classics. He had their sense of proportion, their eye for the fitness of things, their interest in moral questions and their urbane amusement at human frailty. Unpractical and reserved as ever, Addison had great difficulty in finding a field for these gifts. He tried Latin verse, then archæology, then a book of travels, then English verse and drama. At last Steele, by founding *The Tatler,* brought him into touch with his proper public. From 1710 till 1715, Addison succeeded in transforming his classical wisdom and insight into counsels, admonitions, and illustrations homely enough to suit the middle class, which inspired and responded to these efforts. Like the Grecian that he was, he frequently made a practice of symbolising his ideas, sometimes in allegories imitated from the Platonic *mythus,* and sometimes in character sketches, like the incomparable Coverly papers. At the same time it must not be forgotten that his genius was constrained by the necessity of attracting and holding a public that would buy his and Steele's daily issues. The Essay was already beginning to fall a victim to journalism. (pp. 143-51)

> *H. V. Routh, "The Origins of the Essay Compared in French and English Literatures," in* The Modern Language Review, *Vol. XV, No. 2, April, 1920, pp. 143-51.*

Michael L. Hall

[*In the following excerpt, Hall discusses ways in which the rise of the essay, represented by the works of Michel de Montaigne, Francis Bacon, Sir Thomas Browne, and others, reflects and responds to a spirit of scientific discovery prominent in the sixteenth and seventeenth centuries.*]

My thesis, simply stated, is that the essays of Michel de Montaigne and Francis Bacon as well as later examples by John Donne and Sir Thomas Browne—different as they are in their formal qualities—exhibit not only similar rhetorical strategies but also a common attitude, a spirit of exploration; that in certain important respects the essay emerged in the late sixteenth and early seventeenth centuries as a product of the Renaissance "idea" of discovery and in response to it.

But the "idea" of discovery is not the same thing as discovery itself. We have heard it said, for example, that in 1492 Columbus discovered America, but the event was not as simple as that statement suggests. We generally do not find something unless we have some "idea" of what we are looking for. Columbus was looking for a new trade route to the East, not a new world. It took other voyages and the insights of other explorers such as Amerigo Vespucci before the knowledge began to form and sink into the European consciousness that Columbus had found a "new world." And if we think for a moment, perhaps we can begin to comprehend with Edmundo O'Gorman the impact that this "discovery" must have had on European thought and on received notions not only about geography but about other kinds of knowledge as well.

Similarly, Copernicus did not immediately address the profound religious and cosmological implications of his hypothesis that the earth was not stationary but revolved around the sun. What he hoped to establish was a simpler (and certainly more aesthetically and mathematically pleasing) way of accounting for astronomical phenomena by taking the sun as the center around which the earth and the planets revolved. Only many years later (after contributions by others such as Kepler and Galileo) would astronomers regularly assume that the Copernican theory correctly represented the movement of the planets. Throughout the seventeenth century, laymen and philosophers alike disputed the mounting scientific evidence, and poets such as Donne and Milton seem to have had it both ways.

We should begin by recalling the familiar commonplace that the Renaissance was an age of discovery and invention—an age marked by the appearance of such new things as the mariner's compass, printing, the telescope, new lands, and new stars as well as by the recovery of much of the wisdom of the past, the restoration of lost languages, and the editing and dissemination of lost texts. A few key dates may be helpful. In addition to Columbus's voyage of 1492, we should remember that Gutenberg's Bible was published sometime after 1454, that Luther's ninety-five theses were nailed to a church door in 1517, and that Copernicus's *De Revolutionibus Orbium Coelestium* appeared in 1543. The full impact of these events, and of many other similar ones that accompanied them, was still being felt throughout the sixteenth century and well into the seventeenth. Not until 1580 did Francis Drake become the first Englishman to circumnavigate the world, and not until 1610 did Galileo publish his *Siderius Nuncius,* with its revelations of mountains and craters on the moon and spots that moved across the face of the changeless sun.

Even so, within a relatively brief span of time, the ancient model of an ordered universe, which for centuries had seemed unassailable, was challenged and overthrown by Renaissance astronomers; the face of the earth itself was altered by Renaissance voyages. Nor was this spirit of discovery limited to the sciences alone, to knowledge of earth and stars. In the late sixteenth and early seventeenth centuries, it manifested itself as a new mode of thought and discourse. Essayists as diverse as Montaigne and Bacon, or Donne and Browne, turned their attention to the examination of received opinions, to a search for inward truths as well as outward. The new discoveries in geography and astronomy required rethinking the past and reexamining old assumptions about the earth and the heavens, but they also made necessary a reassessment of the place of men (and women) in the new conception of the universe that was beginning to emerge from the ruins of the older order. Renaissance writers sometimes looked backward as well as forward. Discovery and recovery were often intertwined as philosophers and poets tried to put their world back together, to reestablish relation and coherence. When we turn to the literature of the Renaissance and seventeenth century, we detect something more than excitement over specific discoveries or inventions; we find a growing sense of discovery as an "idea" influencing a wide range of Renaissance thought and expression: from Thomas More's utopian vision to Francis Bacon's scientific method and, finally, to the emergence of the essay, a new genre written in a new style of prose.

One of the more unsettling and at the same time thought-generating discoveries was the New World. America, even before it was clearly recognized as a new world, captured the imagination of the Renaissance not simply with promises of wealth and empire, though these were strong inducements to exploration and settlement, but also with visions of the golden age and the earthly paradise. We can see this association even in the first letter of Columbus describing what he saw on his first voyage. He marveled that in the month of November trees were "as green and lovely as they are in Spain in May." And he continued, "the people of this island, and all the other islands which I have found and of which I have information, all go naked, men and women, as their mothers bore them." These inhabitants appear to Columbus totally innocent and guileless. Clearly, ideas both of the biblical paradise and of the classical golden age came to mind as he searched for familiar formulas to convey impressions of the tropical regions and native populations he encountered on his voyage.

Because of the association between the New World and paradise or the golden age, the discovery of America had a profound effect on Renaissance thought. Early accounts of the newfound land in Hakluyt's *Principal Navigations, Voyages, and Discoveries of the English Nation* and in Sir Walter Raleigh's *History of the World* abounded with references to "the golden age" and "the Paradise of Eden." The New World became an embodiment of an ancient ideal of human perfection. Montaigne's remarks in his essay "Of the Caniballes" are perhaps the clearest evidence of what I am suggesting. With his usual penetration and overstatement, Montaigne observes that the discovery of the New World has made the speculations of philosophers and poets obsolete: "For me seemeth that what in those nations we see by experience, doth not only exceed all the pictures wherewith licentious poesie hath proudly imbellished the golden age, and all her quaint inventions to faine a happy condition of man, but also the conception and desire of Philosophy. They could not imagine a genuitie so pure and simple, as we see it by experience; nor ever beleeve our societie might be maintained with so little art and humane combination."

The method of Sir Thomas More's *Utopia* (1516) had already, to some extent, supported Montaigne. The fictions with which More constructed his humanist fantasy rely heavily on details which link *Utopia* to the literature of discovery as much as to the dialogues of Plato. Raphael Hythloday, we recall, is a Portuguese navigator who has sailed with no less an explorer than Amerigo Vespucci himself. But the sense of the New World as an ideal vision is even stronger in Francis Bacon's *New Atlantis* (1627), written some 100 years after More's *Utopia*. Though the *New Atlantis* too is an island discovered by European voyagers, Bacon's fantasy world is very different from More's humanistic vision. The *New Atlantis* is more than a Utopia; it offers a glimpse of the kind of future which Bacon and his followers imagined—a world transformed by the discoveries of science and technology rather than by humanism.

We come, then, to the new philosophy. Bacon connects the New World and new sciences not only in *New Atlantis* but elsewhere. His essay "Of Plantations," for example, presents a practical program for planting colonies and for systematically exploiting the new American lands. And in his *Novum Organum,* which displayed on its title page an engraving of a galleon sailing through the pillars of Hercules (the limits of the ancient world), Bacon remarks: "We must, therefore, disclose and prefix our reasons for not thinking the hope of success improbable, as Columbus, before his wonderful voyage over the Atlantic, gave reasons of his conviction that new lands and continents might be discovered besides those already known; and these reasons, though at first rejected, were yet proved by subsequent experience and were the causes and beginnings of the greatest events." There is a similar use of the image of discovery in the concluding remarks to the *Advancement of Learning.* There Bacon observes; "Thus have I made as it were a small globe of the intellectual world, as truly and as faithfully as I could discover; with a note and description of those parts which seem to me not constantly occupate, or not well converted by the labour of men."

In these examples Bacon invokes the image of the voyage of discovery to describe scientific exploration; the "small globe of the intellectual world" resembles the larger globe then being mapped by Renaissance voyagers. Of course, not every Renaissance author was as optimistic as Bacon. For some the new discoveries, particularly in astronomy, were disturbing, as John Donne's well-known comments in the *First Anniversarie* attest:

> And new Philosophy cals all in doubt,
>   The Element of fire is quite put out;
>   The Sunne is lost, and th'earth, and no mans
>   wit
>   Can well direct him, where to looke for
>   it. . . .
>   Tis all in pieces, all cohaerence gone;
> All iust supply, and all Relation.

The new philosophy, more than the New World, offered a serious challenge to the Renaissance worldview. The new stars sighted by Tycho Brahe and Johann Kepler, the new cosmology of Copernicus, Kepler, and Galileo, destroyed more than the authority of Aristotle; they undermined the very nature of Renaissance science and religion. After Copernicus, and certainly after Kepler and Galileo, Renaissance scientists were no longer satisfied merely with "saving the phenomena" within traditional patterns of explanation: they were ready to alter the patterns themselves in light of new discoveries.

In fact, the idea of discovery looms large in Bacon's description of his new method of science. The new induction, as he called it, was intended to supplant the tautologous system of Aristotle and the scholastics, with its reliance on the logic of the syllogism, and to break away from the dominion of classical authority. Bacon proposed, instead, a mode of invention grounded in experience rather than argument. In the *Novum Organum* his indictment of the old philosophy is succinctly stated: "Even the effects already discovered are due to chance and experiment, rather than to the sciences; for our present sciences are nothing more than peculiar arrangements of matters already discovered, and not methods for discovery or plans for new operations" (I, 8). In a later aphorism he continues: "The present system of logic rather assists in confirming and rendering inveterate the errors founded on vulgar notions than in searching after truth, and is therefore more hurtful than useful."

I am suggesting that the discoveries of the New World and the new stars and all of the other new things which seemed to be coming to light in the sixteenth and seventeenth centuries helped inform an idea of discovery which obtained not only in the sciences but in other areas of knowledge as well. Truth in any realm is no longer something acquired by assimilating received views but something which one must seek out for oneself and experience, like an explorer charting new lands. The key word in this discussion, it seems to me, is "experience," and it applies to inward journeys of self-discovery as well as to the ventures of outward-bound exploration. In his essay "Of Experience," Montaigne asserts, "I study my selfe more than any other subject. It is my supernaturall Metaphisike, it is my naturall Philosophy," and goes on to add, "Out of the experience I have of my selfe, I finde sufficient ground to make my selfe wise, were I but a good proficient scholler." In the face of conflicting claims and uncertainty about the nature of human knowledge, there is a tendency among Renaissance and seventeenth-century authors to look inward, to explore the interior landscape, to seek paradise within, to move in true Renaissance fashion from macrocosm to microcosm. One thinks of Donne's remark in his *Devotions upon Emergent Occasions:* "Stil when we return to that Meditation, that *Man is a World,* we find new *discoveries.*"

If the main lines of this discussion seem clear, let me sketch in more clearly the links between the idea of discovery and the emergence of the essay during this same period as a distinct, new prose genre. It was surely no accident that this new genre, this new mode of inquiry, along with a new style of prose, should appear at this particular moment in European history. In an age fascinated by the implications of the new philosophy and the discovery of the New World, the essay provided a kind of prose composition particularly suited to the examination of conventional wisdom, the exploration of received opinion, and the discovery of new ideas and insights—a kind of written discourse which allowed the author to think freely outside the constraints of established authority and traditional rhetorical forms. We may also find the same idea in the background of the revolution in prose style which occurred in the late sixteenth and early seventeenth centuries, when Ciceronianism, long associated with the discredited doctrines of the old philosophy, was overthrown by writers such as Montaigne and Bacon, who sought a rhetorical style which would portray in language, as Montaigne put it, "the progress of my humours, that every part be seene or member distinguished, as it was produced."

Montaigne, who published his first book of *Essais* in 1580, tells us explicitly what he perceives to be the essential qualities of his new kind of prose composition, a genre which represents a definite break with the elaborate rhetorical conventions of other forms of writing. Essays, he says, are not supposed to be the products of art or study, but are intended to be spontaneous, tentative, open-ended, and even unfinished. For example, in his essay "Of Friendship," he describes his compositions as "antike workes, and monstrous bodies, patched and hudled up together of divers members, without any certaine or well ordered figure, having neither order dependencie, or proportion, but

casuall and framed by chance." The prose style of the essay also suggested tentativeness, openness, and spontaneity. Both in France and in England, the early essayists tended to reject the artificial symmetry of Ciceronian prose, its balanced clauses and studied formality, preferring to portray in language the actual process of the mind seeking truth. Such a style was ideally suited to the essay, itself a tentative and unstructured exploration of a topic in which matter, according to Montaigne, is more important than words: "It is for words to serve and wait upon matter, and not for matter to attend upon words. . . . I would have the matters to surmount, and so fill the imagination of him that harkneth, that he have no remembrance at all of the words." He then declares his preference for "naturall, simple, and unaffected speech . . . so written as it is spoken, and such upon the paper, as it is in the mouth, a pithie, sinnowie, full, strong, compendious and materiall speech, not so delicate and affected, as vehement and piercing. . . . Rather difficult than tedious, void of affection, free, loose and bold, that every member of it seeme to make a bodie."

The essay, then, was regarded as tentative and spontaneous, written in a style which reflected the movements of the author's mind as he meditated on a subject. But we should notice other qualities in the new genre. One is the frequent quotation from and allusion to authorities, a generic trait probably related to the practice, so popular among Renaissance humanists, of keeping commonplace books. These collections of favorite passages and familiar quotations from ancient and modern authors were often supplemented with personal observations by the collector and gathered together under topical headings as in Ben Jonson's *Timber; or, Discoveries Made upon Men and Matter,* in which we find headings such as *Fortuna* and *Consilia* and *De bonis et malis.* (It is worth noting that Seneca and Plutarch were among Jonson's favorite ancient authors, as they were for both Montaigne and Bacon.) Another related quality is the subversion of received opinion and even of accepted rational processes of thought, or at least of the deductive process which depends on established authority for its major premises and axioms. In fact, commonplace books often collected conflicting and even contradictory passages from the ancient authorities, a practice which Bacon recommends in his *De Augmentis Scientiarum* and often employs in his essays. Finally, there is the tension between the private, interior world of the essayist meditating on some topic and the public world of his audience or readers, the rhetorical tension between the writer and his book.

All of these qualities may be clearly observed in the essays of Montaigne. The many quotations from and allusions to classical authors, along with anecdotes from history and Montaigne's personal experience, are not deployed as proofs or as undisputed authority presented to confirm a single thesis but are assembled as conflicting cases and contradictory evidence. In the essay "Of Sadnesse or Sorrowe," for example, Montaigne begins by declaring himself free of this passion, describing it as a "foolish and base ornament" and agreeing with the Stoics who reject it as base and cowardly. But the examples and quotations which he cites no more support this thesis about the nature of passion than its opposite. He repeats the story of *Psamneticus* (Psammenitus), a king of Egypt who endures the degradation of his daughter and execution of his son without display of emotion but breaks into tears at the sight of "a familiar friend of his haled amongst the captives." Then he recounts the similar case of a prince who receives the news of the death of his elder and younger brothers with "unmatched countenance and exemplar constancie" but is transported when he learns of the death of a servant and abandons himself "to all manner of sorrow and grief." From these examples, Montaigne remarks, some have concluded that excess of grief leads to the passionate release of emotions. But in the case of Psammenitus we have the king's own testimony that he showed his sorrow at the sight of his friend held captive "because this last displeasure may be manifested by weeping, whereas the two former exceed by much, all meanes and compasse to be expressed by teares." Montaigne adds the examples of the painter who portrayed Agamemnon with a veil over his face at the sacrifice of Iphigenia, "as if no countenance were able to represent that degree of sorrow," and of the poets who say that Niobe was changed to stone from excess of grief. At the same time, quoting classical authority all the while, he dilutes the impact of these explanations by remarking that love may have a similar effect and, likewise, excess of pleasure and even excess of shame.

We quickly note that Montaigne does not stay close to his topic (sorrow and sadness), nor does he argue a thesis—that he is not subject to this passion. Instead, he explores the topic by presenting examples from lore and literature, but the examples prove nothing and are, in fact, contradictory, open to various interpretations. His conclusion, that he is "little subject to these violent passions" because he hardens his "apprehension" by daily doses of discourse, seems almost a nonsequitur. Certainly, it does not follow from his examples, though these may be the method of his physic. Instead, what we encounter when we read Montaigne are what Barry Weller [in "The Rhetoric of Friendship in Montaigne's *Essais*," *New Literary History* 9 (1978)] has called "repeated strategies of disorientation."

The relationship between the essayist and the reader is an important part of Montaigne's subversive rhetoric. He wants us to feel that we are reading his own private thoughts, presented as they occur to him without the intervention of art or design. In his preface, "The Author to the Reader," Montaigne expresses the desire to stand "naked" before us: "I desire therein to be delineated in mine owne genuine, simple and ordinarie fashion, without contention, art or study: for it is myself I pourtray." He even goes so far as to suggest that the reader will have no interest in so personal, "so frivolous and vaine a subject" and therefore dismisses us and bids farewell. But we recognize, of course, that all of this is part of Montaigne's rhetorical technique, the same technique which labels the essays themselves as tentative, spontaneous, and open-ended. He hopes to remove the barriers between author and reader, but he also wants us to lower our critical resistance, to forget ourselves for a moment and enter into the private world of the author. The sincerity, the honesty of his observations, like the roughness and openness of his

style, must be seen as part of the art which conceals "art or study."

In an often quoted passage from "Of Giving the Lie," Montaigne acknowledges the tension between the private and the public aspects of the essay, between the interior world of a mind meditating and the exterior world of books and readers: "In framing this pourtraite by my selfe, I have so often beene faine to frizle and trimme me, that so I might the better extract my selfe, that the patterne is thereby confirmed, and in some sort formed. Drawing my selfe for others, I have drawne my selfe with purer and better colours, then were my first. I have no more made my booke, then my booke hath made me." The notion that the essay is a record of spontaneous thought, an honest and even artless representation of the essayist thinking to himself, is a rhetorical fiction that Montaigne recognized more openly as he increasingly saw his essays in terms of a book and a reading public. Moreover, the nature of the genre creates this tension between private and public. The act of writing, even without publication, introduces art and rhetoric; as soon as an author commits his private thoughts to paper, they are no longer merely "antike workes" or the play of a mind thinking but literary artifacts with syntax, grammar, and rhetoric directed toward some reading "public," whether that public is limited to the author himself (and possibly to a small circle of intimate friends) or includes the vast unknown audience of readers who may walk in off the street and purchase his book. The introduction of an audience, however defined, implies, even necessitates, rhetorical strategy and posturing. As Montaigne acknowledges, in drawing himself for others he has drawn with "purer and better colours"; he has availed himself of art and rhetoric. But more than that, the act of writing itself has colored not only his words, but also his thoughts, his actions, his being: "I have no more made my booke, then my booke hath made me." He might almost have said, "I have no more influenced my readers, than my readers, through the prospect of my writing to them, have influenced me."

The rhetorical technique of the essay is somewhat dialectical in that it involves both author and reader in an implied dialogue—or at least in heuristic, cooperative exploration of a subject—that leads to moments of revelation though not necessarily to any final synthesis. And the shared experience of author and reader is central to the genre's rhetorical appeal; it is also an important part of all the other qualities we have observed: the tentativeness, openness, and spontaneity; the roughness of style; the reference to authority and persistent questioning of received opinion; the tension between private and public worlds. It is not sufficient to say that the essay is an explorative genre or that it is a form of meditation and discovery through discourse. We must also acknowledge that the essayist marshals rhetorical strategies with the intention of conveying to a reader the experience of personal exploration and discovery.

Francis Bacon's methods were different, but his intentions were similar. In the first book of *Advancement of Learning* (1605), Bacon appears to echo Montaigne: "Here therefore is the first distemper of learning, when men study words and not matter; . . . for words are but the images of matter; and except they have life of reason and invention, to fall in love with them is all one as to fall in love with a picture." In the second book he describes the object of his new inductive method: "Knowledge that is delivered as a thread to be spun on, ought to be delivered and intimated [insinuated], if it were possible, _in the same method wherein it was invented:_ and so is it possible of knowledge induced." He advocates the use of aphorisms, which "cannot be made but of the pith and heart of sciences" and which, "representing a knowledge broken, do invite men to inquire further," abjuring the examples and fluid transitions of connected discourse and presenting dispersed particulars.

More than any other seventeenth-century English author, Bacon demonstrates the direct relationship between the new mood of discovery in science and learning and the art of discourse, notably the part played by the new knowledge in the rejection of Ciceronianism and its replacement by an anti-Ciceronian style variously labeled plain, Senecan, or Attic. The new philosophical discourse for which he called was to be one that would imitate in writing not so much _the_ process of discovery as _a_ process of discovery, carefully re-presented to the reader, allowing the reader to experience the movement of the author's mind and to examine the premises upon which his conclusions are founded. In _Valerius Terminus, of the Interpretation of Nature,_ Bacon observes "that . . . it is not a thing so easy as is conceived to convey the conceit of one man's mind into the mind of another without the loss or mistaking, specially in notions new and differing from those that are received. That never any knowledge was delivered in the same order it was invented."

Scholars have long known that Bacon's essays, first published in 1597, then expanded and revised in 1612 and 1625, were a part of his scientific program, his Columbian voyage in quest of "new lands and continents," his description of the "small globe of the intellectual world." In them he attempts to reach a varied audience with writings on subjects of practical interest. Even essays on themes which from the titles ("Of Truth," "Of Death," "Of Atheism," and so forth) would appear more speculative than practical, Bacon writes in a pragmatic, if not a Machiavellian, manner. His philosophical statements about the nature of truth, for example, are a soft kernel of familiar platitudes surrounded by hard insights.

The essay "Of Truth" begins by describing the attraction of lies: "But it is not only the difficulty and labour which men take in finding out of truth, nor again that when it is found it imposeth upon men's thoughts, that doth bring lies in favor, but a natural though corrupt love of the lie itself." Later he adds, "this same truth is a naked and open daylight, that doth not show the masks and mummeries and triumphs of the world, half so stately and daintily as candlelights." Finally he remarks rather cynically: "Truth may perhaps come to the price of a pearl, that showeth best by day; but it will not rise to the price of a diamond or carbuncle, that sheweth best in varied lights. A mixture of a lie doth ever add pleasure." After such a beginning, the philosophical tone that follows seems somewhat sanctimonious: "But howsoever these things are thus in men's depraved judgments and affections, yet truth, which only doth judge itself, teacheth that the inquiry of truth, which is the presence of it, and the belief of truth, which is the enjoying of it, is the sovereign good of human nature." But these concessions to philosophy are pale indeed in the glaring daylight of the remarks that issue when Bacon passes from "theological and philosophical truth, to the truth of civil business": "It will be acknowledged, even by those that practice it not, that clear and round dealing is the honour of man's nature; and that mixture of falsehood is like allay in coin of gold and silver; which may make the metal work the better, but it embaseth it." Bacon's image of falsehood as the alloy used in coining gold and silver is interestingly ambiguous. Although the statement ostensibly supports truth over falsehood, the image itself undercuts that support and recalls the usefulness of "allay" which, though it "embaseth" the gold and silver, makes the coin more practical as currency. Rhetorically this assertion hidden in a statement suggesting the general acceptance of the high value placed on "clear and round dealing" casts a shadow of doubt upon those earlier philosophical platitudes. By remarking parenthetically that the truth is valued "even by those that practice it not," Bacon insinuates into the minds of his readers the suggestion that such high talk is the lip service that everyone, even the most corrupt, pays to the good. But there is a further rhetorical objective. Having brought us down to earth, Bacon has made us properly receptive to his final admonitions, which, though high, are also practical: "There is no vice that doth so cover a man with shame as to be found false and perfidious." This Bacon knew at first hand, and it is worth noting that he mentions specifically the shame that follows being "_found_ false and perfidious" (my emphasis). But furthermore, Bacon notes, the judgment of men will be followed by a final judgment hereafter. Here he quotes (or at least alludes to) Montaigne's "Of Giving the Lie": "If it be well weighed, to say that a man lieth, is much to say, as that he is brave towards God and a coward towards men." Bacon has shifted from arguing that truth is its own reward to arguing that falsehood can get us into serious trouble, both on earth and later on as well. The second proposition does not exclude the first, but by acknowledging, at least through implication, the conflicting values of accepted wisdom, Bacon manages to engage our attention and cause reflection, perhaps even further inquiry. Without ever stating it, the essay puts forward yet another platitude: honesty is the best _policy._

This unstated theme seems hardly accidental. We should recognize that policy, the prudent application of moral knowledge, most concerns Bacon in the _Essays._ His intention is not to discover the nature of truth but to "instruct and suborn action." Writings which instill practical wisdom, "Georgics of the mind," Bacon insists in _The Advancement of Learning,_ "are no less worthy than the heroical descriptions of virtue, duty, and felicity." Thus he detects two categories of moral knowledge: "the Exemplar or Platform of Good, and the Regiment or Culture of the Mind: the one describing the nature of good, the other prescribing rules how to subdue, apply, and accommodate the will of man thereunto." The essays clearly fall within the second category. As I have said, even an essay such as "Of

Death" illustrates such accommodation. Though his principal purpose appears to be to dispel the "natural" but otherwise "weak" and exaggerated fear of death by adducing contrary evidence and interjecting a good deal of gallows humor, Bacon's practical advice prescribes action: "He that dies in an earnest pursuit is like one that is wounded in hot blood; who for the time, scarce feels the hurt; and therefore a mind fixed and bent upon somewhat that is good doth avert the dolours of death." "Of Atheism" similarly "suborns" action rather than contemplation. Bacon begins with an expression of faith: "I had rather believe all the fables in the legend, and the Talmud, and the Alcoran, than that this universal frame is without a mind." But though he presents a series of strong arguments against it, his purpose is not wholly the refutation of atheism, and his conclusion avoids altogether the issue of *true* religion, asserting only the practical necessity for *some* religion.

We can see that Bacon's *Essays* are written in a rhetorical style which encourages us to examine them critically as aphoristic expressions of wisdom; but more important, the rhetoric is intended to move us to action, to subdue, apply, and accommodate our wills unto the good. The *Essays* display the interaction of rhetoric and the method of discovery. A truly philosophical discourse presents the actual movement of the mind in the process of thinking, searching for truth. The best method for expressing such a movement, according to Bacon, is the disjunctive method of dispersed aphorisms, the method of his *Novum Organum.* But the "duty and office of Rhetoric is to *apply Reason to the Imagination* for the better moving of the will." In the *Essays* the aphoristic method is subtly transformed into a rhetoric of discovery intended to challenge received notions and provoke examination of them, to recreate the experience of discovering truth. At the same time, these transformed aphorisms are also carefully ordered so that the good might appear reasonable and practical.

Bacon's practical and sometimes aphoristic essays have always seemed very different from Montaigne's loose, open-ended explorations. Yet though their styles and methods may seem different, both Montaigne and Bacon share a skeptical attitude toward received opinions and ancient authority, and both essayists employ in their essays a rhetoric of discovery intended to engage the reader in a personal journey of exploration. Both rely on rhetorical techniques which are subtly subversive, which purposely confound the reader and often lead to active and cooperative inquiry in the place of straightforward assertion or rational instruction, to open exploration and the discovery of new insights rather than to closed argument or resolved debate. Finally, both essayists often subvert their own arguments and call into question the familiar forms of human reason.

Montaigne and Bacon were not the only essayists to employ a rhetoric of discovery. That the essay might be considered a journey into the unknown, a voyage of discovery, John Donne makes clear in his *Essays in Divinity* (1611?) when he invokes images of journeys and voyages to describe the process of his discourse. In one instance, passing from meditation on God's mercy to a more difficult consideration of his power, Donne remarks: "For thus long we have been in the Harbour, but we launch into a main and unknown Sea, when we come to consider his *Power.*" And in another passage, when Donne finds himself entangled in a discussion of Moses as the "first Author," he resorts to an elaborate simile:

> Therefore, as in violent tempests, when a ship dares bear no main sayl, and to lie stil at hull, obeying the uncertain wind and tyde, puts them much out of their way, and altogether out of their account, it is best to put forth such a small ragg of sail, as may keep the barke upright, and make her continue neer one place, though she proceed not; So in this question, where we cannot go forward to make *Moses* the first Author.

In one sense Donne's was a journey among the Scriptures themselves, and he turns to the Bible for his authority: "Search the Scriptures because in them ye hope to have eternal life." But at the same time he is, somewhat in the manner of Montaigne and Bacon, conducting a "search of learning" through the commentaries of the church fathers and books by other learned men. And when he apologizes, with almost equal portions of wit and humility, for infringing on anyone's copyright, his imagery suggests the activities of Renaissance explorers and trading companies (like the Virginia Company, from which he had sought preferment in 1608/9): "But because to such as I, who are but Interlopers, not staple Merchants, nor of the company, nor within the commission of Expositors of the Scriptures, if any licence be granted by the Spirit to discover and possesse any part, herein, it is condition'd and qualified as the Commissions of Princes, that we attempt not any part actually possess'd before, nor disseise others." Donne's image here of the essayist as interloper captures something essential to the new genre, something we detect in Bacon and Montaigne as well—the essayist as amateur, though in this particular case, of course, Donne is thinking of himself as someone lacking a license to preach, someone who is merely essaying in the preacher's art.

[Let] me turn finally to Sir Thomas Browne. The idea of discovery and the image of the New World appear in yet another form in his *Hydrotaphia; or, Urne-Buriall* (1658). In the opening paragraph Browne remarks: "That great Antiquity *America* lay buried for thousands of years; and a large part of the earth is still in the Urne unto us." By describing America as an uncovered antiquity, similar to those ancient urns recently turned up in Norfolk, the ostensible occasion for his essay, Browne identifies the new-found land and the recently uncovered human remains, adding that there are further mysteries still to be discovered, or perhaps we should say "uncovered" or "recovered." Our concentration focuses on the urns and their contents: the unknown parts of the earth or the dust of some ancient men. The emphasis leads naturally into the essay, the next paragraph of which begins with the primordial man, Adam, "made out of an extract of the Earth." Browne's America metaphor is suggestive and consciously so, I would argue. He remarks that "Nature hath furnished one part of the Earth, and man another." If we make the proper associations when we read that "a large part of the earth is still in the Urne unto us," it takes only a small leap of the imagination to recognize that Browne is playing on two meanings of the word "earth": the world and man, "made out of an extract of the Earth."

It is appropriate for Browne to commence with an image of discovery, for his method of meditation relies on the process of discovery. His elaborate and often perplexing exploration of human attitudes toward death and immortality, of the rites and superstitions surrounding burial, is a necessary preparation for the revelations of the final chapter of *Urne-Buriall,* the often anthologized chapter 5. The first four chapters Browne characterizes as a record of vain hopes, empty ceremonies, and confused intimations which are finally replaced by the realized knowledge of the Christian resurrection: "The superior ingredient and obscured part of our selves, whereto all present felicities afford no resting contentment, will be able at last to tell us we are more than our present selves; and evacuate such hopes in the fruition of their own accomplishments." This is an interesting use of the word "evacuate," suggesting that the resurrection will somehow empty these vain hopes and leave only the experience of true immortality. There is no way to persuade us through reason, for reason itself has led men to such vanities. Thus Browne observes: "Happy are they, which live not in that disadvantage of time, when men could say little for futurity, but from reason." Therefore Browne relies on the experience of discovery. By articulating with nearly exhaustive completeness the vain hopes of the past, whether founded on reason or superstition, he intends to demonstrate the futility of such beliefs. And once we have been emptied of error, we are prepared to receive the truth revealed in his fifth chapter, the true belief of Christianity.

The method of discovery employed by Browne in *Urne-Buriall* approximates in many respects Bacon's method of philosophical discourse; the early chapters seem to be objective observations on the variety of human attitudes toward death and burial. But that objectivity is only apparent. What at first appears to be a process of exploration is actually an evacuation. The encyclopedic completeness of Browne's exposition purges the mind of moral vanity, a necessary preparation for the revelation of the final chapter. Both Bacon and Browne employ a rhetoric of discovery, though Bacon's discoveries are in the great world of scientific knowledge and civil affairs, Browne's in the little world of the human soul; one is an outward quest for truth, the other an inward, meditative quest. Browne evokes the image of discovery to turn our thoughts in, toward ourselves. In *Urne-Buriall* that great Antiquity *America* becomes an emblem of self-knowledge rather than knowledge of the world.

Let me conclude with a final example from Browne's earlier work *Pseudodoxia Epidemica* (1646), a vast collection of "Enquiries into Vulgar and Common Errors" which very probably began as a collection in commonplace books. In his preface, "To the Reader," Browne uses the image of America and discovery in a context even more reminiscent of Bacon's usage than in *Urne-Buriall.* He compares the great world of knowledge and vulgar errors that he is about to explore to a "Labyrinth" in which "we find no open tract, . . . but are oft-times fain to wander

in the America and untravelled parts of Truth." Interestingly, Browne also appears to invoke a pre-Copernican image of heavenly motion when he describes his inquiries into received notions: "and therefore in this *Encyclopaedie* and round of Knowledge, like the great and exemplary Wheeles of Heaven, we must observe two Circles: that while we are daily carried about, and whirled on by the swing and rapt of the one, we may maintain a natural and proper course, in the slow and sober wheel of the other." But despite his lapse regarding the new astronomy (a lapse borne out by his apparent reluctance to embrace the "hypothesis of Copernicus" in Book VI, chapter 5), Browne's collection of personal opinions and observations on the learning of his day are, as Robin Robbins has noted very definitely, in the tradition of Bacon's great plan in *The Advancement of Learning.* As Ted-Larry Pebworth has demonstrated rather convincingly ["Wandering in the America of Truth." In *Approaches to Sir Thomas Browne: The Ann Arbor Tercentenary Lectures and Essays,* 1982], *Pseudodoxia Epidemica* is indeed a collection of essays very much in the mode of Montaigne and Bacon and may, moreover, be an important step in the development of the more scientific essays of Robert Boyle.

I will bring my own exploration to a close by pointing out that Browne's collection of his own thoughts and various bits of information and misinformation in *Pseudodoxia Epidemica* is perfectly in keeping with the method of the seventeenth-century essay from Montaigne and Bacon onward. Certainly, the collections of minor English essayists belong to this tradition: the works of William Cornwallis, Robert Johnson, and Daniel Tuvill. But I would also include a work such as Robert Burton's *Anatomy of Melancholy,* where, despite the elaborate structure of his partitions, Burton's method and attitude are explorative, a mixture of digressions, allusions, and equivocations that finally leave his book as open-ended and unfinished as Montaigne's. In certain respects all of these essayists were responding to the idea of discovery, to the notion that the world was in flux and that knowledge was no longer fixed by authority but in a state of transition. Recent doubts about the quality of human knowledge had encouraged writers such as Montaigne and Bacon and others such as Donne and Browne (and even Burton) to make a small globe of their intellectual world and chart the progress of their humors as they attempted to experience the world anew, to discover what was known and yet unknown and, if not restore order and coherence, at least wander a bit in the America and untraveled parts of Truth. (pp. 73-89)

Michael L. Hall, "The Emergence of the Essay and the Idea of Discovery," in Essays on the Essay: Redefining the Genre, *edited by Alexander J. Butrym, The University of Georgia Press, 1989, pp. 73-91.*

THE ESSAY IN THE SEVENTEENTH CENTURY

Douglas Bush

[*Bush was a Canadian-born American educator, literary historian, and critic whose works include* Mythology and the Renaissance Tradition in English Poetry *(1932) and* Science and English Poetry *(1950). In the excerpt below, he traces the development of the English essay during the seventeenth century.*]

Since the essayists [of the early seventeenth century] as a group reveal an early and deliberate concern with style, we may take a preliminary glance at the nature of prose in general. Literary history has given currency to the notion that prose writing before 1660 was largely ornate and poetical, and that a plain, workaday, modern style was first inaugurated after the Restoration, chiefly through the efforts of the Royal Society to develop this along with other elements of its Baconian heritage. To correct that vulgar error we have only to think of the vast bulk of plain writing in books of travel, history, biography, politics, economics, science, education, religion, and much popular literature. Plain prose was the natural medium for most kinds of utilitarian writing, and most writing was utilitarian. That old and vigorous tradition was steadily reinforced, moreover, by the needs and demands of a rapidly expanding public. We may grant, to be sure, that the prose of the Restoration achieved a more coherent form and texture, a more civilized ease and urbanity, but we must acknowledge that Dryden and his fellows represented a culmination rather than a beginning. We must acknowledge, too, that the civilizing process, in prose as well as in poetry, was a levelling process which gained some virtues at the cost of some others, and we may be glad that it was not completed in our period.

Such a movement was necessary because Elizabethan prose, while it encouraged both poetic elevation and homely raciness, had not become a tempered and reliable instrument. Along with the general circumstances and purposes which nourished plain prose in the seventeenth century, one special and self-conscious motive, which came over from the Continent, left few intellectual writers untouched. Although by 1600 English prose, even in Hooker, had scarcely attained Ciceronian maturity, there ensued a repetition of the phenomenon which had taken place in imperial Rome, a reaction against the rotund, balanced, oratorical period and in favour of a concise, flexible, semi-colloquial style. If the ultimate theoretical sanction was derived from Aristotle, the stylistic models were Seneca and Tacitus and the editor of both, the chief reviver of Stoic thought, Justus Lipsius. The 'Attic' style of the anti-Ciceronians was not of course uniform; it ranged from the 'libertine' naturalness of Montaigne or Burton to the weighty condensation of Bacon and Jonson or the clipped, pointed sententiousness of Hall or Feltham. But with all its theoretical and individual differences the movement as a whole implied the recognition of a changing world in which the accepted verities were less secure than they had been, and it embodied a philosophic desire for a more realistic, arresting, and subtle expression of both general ideas and private experience. Hence the simplicity

Abraham Cowley.

of the new style or styles was not always simple. Like the parallel manifestation in verse, the Senecan style had its 'metaphysical' tricks of antithetical and epigrammatic patterns, abrupt surprises, and ingenious images, and it did not meet with unanimous approval. Breton's *Characters upon Essays* was commended for its 'Lipsian stile, terse Phrase', but Earle—though he later deleted a remark which did not leave his own withers unwrung—censured his 'selfe-conceited Man' as one who preferred 'Lipsius his hopping stile, before either Tully or Quintilian'. And Milton jeered at Hall for making 'sentences by the Statute, as if all above three inches long were confiscat'. Dr. Kettell's judgement of Seneca's style, recorded by Aubrey, was more critical than quotable. Senecan or Lipsian prose, loose or curt or a mixture of both, was frequently wedded to Stoic thought, and among the offspring of the marriage were the English essayists, whose moral didacticism and studied informality made them the natural exponents of the new modes.

We think of the essay as one of the late courses in the banquet of literature. It presupposes a class of readers who possess economic and social security and who can appreciate rational reflection upon civilized manners and morals. While Plato and Cicero and Horace have contributed to the spirit and sometimes to the form of the modern essay, the classical prototypes are the moral works of Seneca and Plutarch. Seneca's *Epistles to Lucilius,* as Bacon observed, 'are but Essaies,—That is dispersed Meditacons, thoughe conveyed in the forme of Epistles'. The essay absorbed many other tributaries, the formal treatises and often formal letters of medieval and Renaissance humanists and the academic exercises of generations of students, the private commonplace books which almost all serious readers kept, and the published collections, ancient and modern, of anecdotes, aphorisms, and didactic discourses. And behind all these things was the inexhaustible treasury of classical literature as a whole. Then although the essay tended in its very nature to be secular in tone, it long bore traces of the religious homily and devotional meditation. These various kinds of writing were themselves being carried on in our period, so that a working definition of the essay must be both comprehensive and arbitrary. The genre was at any rate a natural expression of the heightened self-consciousness of the seventeenth-century mind.

The essay was born when Montaigne retired to his tower to take stock of himself and thereby of all human experience, and the evolution of his essays epitomizes the general evolution of the form from the commonplace book to independent reflection. Bacon's went through a partly parallel development, though he never approached nor apparently wished to approach the spacious freedom and intimate personal candour of the first and greatest of modern essayists. While the two men naturally had some common roots, they were far apart in temperament and outlook, and Bacon, after borrowing Montaigne's title, seems to have gone his own way. To the general recognition of the tentative character of the essay Bacon added his special belief in the suggestive virtues of the aphoristic style. The ten 'Essays' of 1597 were merely groups of related apothegms transcribed from the commonplace book. That Bacon was aware of a more fluid form is sufficiently indicated by other early writings, and when his own and the public's interest in his book led to extensive revision and enlargement he inclined to the looser, more 'methodical' and persuasive style which he had brought to maturity in the *Advancement of Learning* and which was nearer to the established manner of the essay. Although in their final state (1625) his essays remained strongly aphoristic in texture, the discontinuity and abstract severity of the early *sententiae* had been increasingly unified and relieved by expatiation and by interpolated examples and quotations, and enriched by metaphor and cadence. There was, however, only a little relaxing of Bacon's cool objectivity. That, while partly inherited from his chosen models and the commonplace book, represents also the attitude of the scientific analyst who does not gossip and ramble, whose mind is a dry light. Even in his reflections on adversity the fallen Lord Chancellor's pen betrays no momentary quiver; the essay might have been written by a cloistered sage. It is Bacon's impersonality and Tacitean brevity, rather than grandiloquence, which make his style seem less familiar than it is. Though his name suggests full-dress stateliness, he was the theoretical and practical leader of the anti-Ciceronian movement in England, and the groundwork of his prose is reinforced homespun. And along with his genius for pithy and proverbial expression goes a full share of the 'wit' of his age; many of his opening phrases remain as arresting as those of Donne's poems.

Of the fifty-eight essays in the final edition, more than half deal with public life or public affairs, and the statesman or courtier has at least a finger in many others, including such varied pieces as those on truth, marriage, love, and friendship. In 'Of Vicissitude of Things', Bacon touches, greatly, the great Renaissance chord of mutability, and then shrinks back upon the actualities of religious strife and war. Of his countless biblical allusions many permit a political application and some have it forced upon them; the comparison of the kingdom of heaven to a mustard-seed illustrates the difference between extent of territory and real power. Bacon reveals to us the interests, problems, and modes of thought of the ruling class of his age, but the artist who is wedded to the mundane and temporal has given hostages to fortune. We are, to be sure, vaguely aware of some wholly admirable counsels of moral wisdom and public and private virtue (especially in the volume of 1612), but we are much more strongly impressed by an atmosphere of 'business', of cold-blooded expediency, and sometimes of unscrupulous self-interest. While Montaigne's chief concern is in man sitting upon his 'owne taile', Bacon's is in man sitting in an office chair. Obvious reasons for a degree of moral obtuseness are at hand in the facts of his own world and career and in the influence of his favourite authors. But a more fundamental explanation of Bacon's choice and treatment of themes appears in the second book of the *Advancement of Learning.* There he deplores philosophers' preoccupation with abstract ethics and their neglect of the basic material of morality and policy, that is, ordinary human nature as it operates in the various circumstances of the active life. The several lists of particular desiderata which he proceeds to give make a fair table of contents for the *Essays.* In spite of Bacon's disclaimer, in a dedicatory epistle to Andrewes, the essays were not merely the casual recreation of a busy life, they were to a great extent an integral part of the *Instauratio Magna,* an appendix—as innumerable borrowings remind us—to the *Advancement.* Bacon wished to fill a gap in practical psychology and ethics, to contribute to that realistic knowledge of the genus *homo* without which the individual cannot prescribe for his own needs nor the statesman for the needs of society.

Thus it is not simply the limitations of the essayist's mind and heart which lead him to see life so much in terms of tangible success and failure. Even when he reveals a Jonsonian world of politic knaves and gulls he can claim a philosophic purpose. In the *Advancement* he notes the lack of serious studies of professional frauds and vices, a kind of knowledge which is 'one of the best fortifications for honesty and vertue that can be planted', and he pays tribute to 'Macciavell & others that write what men doe and not what they ought to do'. At the same time, in his expert dissection of human egoism, Bacon may forget the ends of honesty and virtue, and the essays are, morally, something of a jumble. The two elements which appear in harmonious innocence in the title *Essays or Counsels, Civil and Moral* appear in Machiavellian or Hobbesian nakedness in the distinction made in the *Advancement:* 'Againe, morrall Philosophye propoundeth to it selfe the framing of Internall goodnesse: But civile knowledge requireth onelye an Externall goodnesse: for that as to societye sufficeth.' These psychological and utilitarian motives keep Bacon's *Essays* in the category of admired books rather than among the well thumbed and beloved. Everyone has read them, but no one is ever found reading them. Yet, if he is less generous and companionable than the other great essayists, we should remember what he was and was not trying to do. And we rejoice all the more when Machiavelli, or a Machiavellian Samuel Smiles, gives way to the Jacobean lover of beauty or royal magnificence in the loving particularity of the essays on gardens, building, or masques and triumphs, and much more still when flashes of poetic phrase and intuition light up Truth and Death and other noble themes. For all his narrowness or obliquity of vision, his tense, athletic prose reflects his unquenchable vitality and his eager curiosity about the earthly doings and experience of man.

Before we leave Bacon a less familiar collection of short discourses must be mentioned. That interest in allegorical mythology which is patent to every reader of the *Essays* and the *Advancement of Learning* received full expression in the popular *De Sapientia Veterum* (1609), which Sir Arthur Gorges translated as *The Wisdom of the Ancients* (1619). Here Bacon, not without a note of apology, allows his philosophic mind and poetic fancy to play around some thirty characters of classic myth. In part he takes over the methods and materials of the mythographers, but his interpretations, whether new or old, are adapted to his own special view of science and civil and moral knowledge. It is easy to guess what the herald of modern science makes of Prometheus or of Oedipus unriddling the Sphinx (Cupid is less obvious as the natural motion of the atom), or what the statesman makes of Cassandra and Typhon. Thus if *The Wisdom of the Ancients* represents Bacon's less modern side (though he was by no means the last exponent of allegory), it is also, except in the character of its initial texts, a twin volume to the *Essays*.

From the standpoint of general fame the early history of the essay is a picture of a whale followed by a school of porpoises, but before Bacon published the genuine essays of his second edition the form had been more or less ably handled by a number of men. We can take account of only one, the first exponent of the more personal and informal essay, Sir William Cornwallis (1579?-1614). Cornwallis's *Essays* (1600-1) were published when he was only a little past twenty and, if it were not for references to his youth, we might think so sage a moralist, so disillusioned a critic of society, was a lean and slippered pantaloon. He has got beyond adolescent follies but he is still only crawling through the darkness of 'Opinion' towards 'the Land of light'. 'I write therefore to my selfe, and my selfe profits by my writing.' In a decayed and corrupt world men must seek guidance and strength from within. To himself and others Cornwallis preaches a Stoicism which is really, if not very explicitly, Christian. But Stoic rigour is modified by compromises between abstract and practical morals, by the attitudes of an Elizabethan Englishman, and by the inconsistency of youth. How, for instance, is ambition to be shunned by a young man of his time, how is the contemplative life to be reconciled with the duty of public service? 'I must choose the active course, my birth commands me to that.'

The sources of Cornwallis's wisdom are largely classical. Plato (read in Latin) is the supreme philosopher, and he sometimes inspires flights above the Stoic level. But Cornwallis owes most to Seneca and Plutarch, and of their disciple Montaigne he had acquired some knowledge in a translation (probably Florio's unpublished manuscript). It is not the sceptical or naturalistic Montaigne who attracts him, but the man, the nobleman, who makes moral philosophy doff its gown and speak courageously, who puts 'Pedanticall Schollerisme' out of countenance and shows that 'learning mingled with Nobilitie, shines most clearly'. Along with aristocratic morality Cornwallis upholds aristocratic standards of culture, the amateur ideal of Montaigne and Renaissance courtesy books. And, though he is chiefly concerned with individual man, he expounds the traditional view of 'degree' as the frame of the social fabric. But he is aware that gentlemen's bodies may contain slavish minds and, standing between Diogenes and Carlyle, the apologist of order can imagine a naked assemblage from which pre-eminence has vanished with clothes.

Like other early practitioners Cornwallis has a critical consciousness in regard to the scope and spirit of the essay. Ancient writers of short discourses and even Montaigne, he thinks, went beyond the proper limits of the genre. He himself avoids both schematic and unduly loose writing and aims at the familiar level—'Montania and my selfe . . . doe sometimes mention our selves'. Though he respects Cicero the moralist he dislikes the tradition of Ciceronian rhetoric. In spite, however, of his attachment to the concise Tacitus and Seneca, he inclines to the discursive manner of Montaigne. His normal style is a colloquial but dignified 'plainenesse' (his own word), with occasional touches of both solemnity and journalism.

Cornwallis's two posthumous volumes, *Essays or Rather Encomions* and *Essays of Certain Paradoxes* (1616), represent a different genre. The facetious or ironical encomium was a classical device, analogous to the mock-epic, which the Renaissance revived, notably in Erasmus's *Praise of Folly*. This kind of encomium was related to the paradox, which also had a long and varied pedigree. A form sanctioned by Cicero was made witty and lively by Ortensio Lando, whose *Paradossi* (1543) were everywhere imitated. The paradox could not fail to attract men brought up on academic disputations and touched by the current of scepticism. It might be called the *enfant terrible* of the essay family. The author takes a holiday from truth and moral responsibility in order to amuse and stimulate his readers by a display of dialectical ingenuity and rhetorical wit in the proof of any thesis, however contrary to reason or convention. The paradox was especially alluring to disillusioned young intellectuals, in the grey time around 1600, as a counterpart in prose to the overworked satire and epigram. The brilliant exponent of the paradox and the somewhat similar 'problem' was Donne, whose chief activity in this field belongs to the years 1598-1602. His pieces, circulating in manuscript, were treasured by Wotton and other friends, though they were not published until 1633, after his death. The paradox was a weapon made to Donne's hand. His half-playful, half-serious questioning of accepted ideas about man and woman, society and the universe, is a link between the 'cynical' poet and the troubled preacher. Cornwallis knew Lando's work, and acquaintance with Donne, which probably began about 1600, may have stirred him to emulation of his more learned, acute, intense, and speculative friend. Though his *Essays* proper include some *jeux d'esprit,* Cornwallis lacks the light touch and edged wit that irony demands, and he cannot readily divest himself of his sober moral principles. Whereas Donne attacks some articles of the Stoic creed, Cornwallis's 'Prayse of Sadnesse' (that is, 'Seriousness') becomes another exposition of the Stoic ethical ideal; and his eulogy of debt—despite his painful experience—rises, with eloquence more restrained than that of Panurge, to contemplation of the ordered system of nature. Some of his paradoxical material was borrowed from abroad.

Possibly the paradox, and certainly the developing 'character', did something to relieve and diversify the gravity and abstractness of the moral essay. Some authors who used both forms, like John Stephens (1615) and Geffray Mynshul (1618), distinguished between the decorous plainness of the essay and the mannered wit of the character; others, like Nicholas Breton and Sir William Cavendish—the pupil of Hobbes and friend of Bacon—in his *Horae Subsecivae* (1620), made a conscious or unconscious fusion of the two. In Breton's *Fantastics* (1604?) the 'characters' of the seasons, months, and hours, for all their balanced itemizing, resemble the 'Nows' of Leigh Hunt. And Breton's *Characters upon Essays, Moral and Divine* (1615), though dedicated to Bacon, treat wisdom, learning, and similar themes in the pattern and pointed style of the character. Such variations, however, did not carry the essay very far towards informal flexibility. The *Horae Vacivae* (1646) of the young John Hall (1627-56), which received unusual commendations from the literary, was largely in the Baconian tradition. If any writer before 1660 fulfils our notion of the familiar essayist, it is that versatile ex-schoolmaster, Henry Peacham (1578?-1642?), in *The Truth of our Times: Revealed out of one Man's Experience, by way of Essay* (1638). Peacham has of course an eye to the good of the commonwealth, from manners to agriculture, and he is a preacher of moderation, but he writes to please himself. Whether his theme is God's providence or fashions in dress, schools or authorship or liberty or travel, he sets forth his serious convictions with easy, intimate discursiveness and with a store of reminiscence and anecdote—a Holborn sempster's report of the fantastic price of neck-bands, a boyhood memory of Tarlton's acting, the capture of a continental town. A 'character' of a plain country fellow reminds us of Earle's, but Peacham's farmer, in 1638, grudges the payment of ship-money. We are not reminded of Bacon's essay on friendship when we read of those acquaintances who, on a chance encounter, exclaim, 'Good Lord, are you alive yet?' The familiar essayist's capital is personality and style, and Peacham has something of both. His industrious and unprosperous career has given a touch of disillusionment to his wide experience and sturdy good sense. He is 'living in the last age of the world, wherein all iniquity and vice doth abound'. But Peacham's interest in life is not dulled by pessimism and is quickened by some special antipathies, for Nonconformists in particular. His book is a small landmark in the history of the essay and it remains enjoyable on its own account.

The didactic motives of so much secular prose make it hard to distinguish the essay from kindred forms, and it is almost impossible to separate the religious essay from its congeners. Even within fairly strict limits we find such various names as Breton and Brathwait, Joseph Hall and Fuller, and Drummond and Browne, but here we may pass by these men of many books for a less prolific author. If the essays of Cornwallis partake of the 'resolve', Owen Felltham's *Resolves, Divine, Moral, Political* (1623?) often approach the pure essay. Like Cornwallis and the rest, Felltham upholds wisdom and the amateur ideal of culture against mere knowledge and pedantry. He defends the practice Burton censured, quoting without naming one's authors; to do otherwise would be 'for a Gentleman . . . a little pedanticall', especially in an essay, 'which of all writing, is the neerest to a running Discourse'. Books are Felltham's delight and recreation, not his trade. His praise of poetry has an intimate warmth which reminds us that he was a poet in his own right. (Of late years he has regained his title to a lyric long ascribed to Suckling, 'When, Dearest, I but think on thee'.) As a devout Anglican and royalist, who could look back on Charles the First as 'Christ the Second', Felltham was a man of piety but not a pietist. His essay on Puritans illustrates his fundamental reverence for 'the beauty of order' in the Church, in society, and in the individual. Although he seeks the *via media* in all things—except the love of God and hatred of evil—and although the commonplaces of religion and morals are his staple article, he can, more than most didactic essayists, make virtue sound exciting and moderation adventurous. Felltham's harmony of Christianity and Stoicism is tempered and sweetened by a love of life and literature, by philosophic charity and undogmatic good sense. His moralizings on death and mutability and vainglory, as well as his Christian Stoicism, carry us forward, if not to *Urn Burial,* at least to *Christian Morals.* Thomas Randolph in his eulogy summed up the qualities of thought and style which the age increasingly admired:

> I mean the stile, being pure, and strong, and round,
> Not long but Pythy: being short breath'd, but sound.
> Such as the grave, acute, wise Seneca sings,
> That best of Tutours to the worst of Kings.
> Not long and empty; lofty but not proud;
> Subtile but sweet, high but without a cloud,
> Well setled, full of nerves, in briefe 'tis such
> That in a little hath comprized much.

But the pointed style does not exclude homeliness or metaphysical wit. 'A bounded mirth, is a Pattent adding time and happinesse to the crazed life of Man.' 'When the Husband and the Wife are together, the World is contracted in a Bed.' And with Felltham's Christian faith and pagan reason is blended a strain of the Platonism which we encounter everywhere in the period. Earthly music awakens thoughts of 'a higher Diapason'. For Felltham as for Marvell and others the soul is 'manacled' by the flesh. We are not surprised to find that Vaughan often echoed him, and it was the poet in Felltham who saw 'Eternities Ring' and the soul as 'a shoot of everlastingnesse'.

While the infant essay was taking its first uncertain steps in various directions, its parents, the aphorism and the commonplace book, were still moving along the familiar paths. The tradition of Machiavelli, Guicciardini, and Bacon was carried on in Robert Dallington's *Aphorisms Civil and Military* (1613) and Ralegh's posthumous *The Prince, or Maxims of State* (1642); the moral tradition of humanism in the *Aphorisms of Education* (1654) of Sir Henry Wotton (1568-1639); and both 'Piety and Policy' in the very popular *Enchiridion* (1640-1) of Francis Quarles, who borrowed a good deal from Bacon and Machiavelli. The aphorism usually remained impersonal but was handled somewhat loosely, perhaps because few men had Bacon's or Jonson's gift for massive compression. It was such a natural outgrowth of the commonplace book (or vice versa), entered so largely into the texture of the essay, and was itself treated in such various ways, that it can scarcely be distinguished as a special type of writing.

The commonplace book *par excellence* is Jonson's *Timber: or Discoveries,* which was posthumously published in the folio of 1640-1 edited by Sir Kenelm Digby. The collection was apparently made in Jonson's later years, since the fire of 1623 had destroyed 'twice-twelve-yeares stor'd up humanitie, With humble Gleanings in Divinitie'. He seems to have contemplated publication, though he left the material in no very clear arrangement. The longer pieces of the latter part constitute a sort of draft for a treatise on the art of writing and on types of literature. The first part is a much less homogeneous body of observations which range from isolated *sententiae* to miniature essays and which deal mainly with such aspects of life, thought, and learning as we find in the essayists—though Jonson damns that tribe, 'even their Master Mountaigne', for rushing into print with undigested reading. Thus *Timber* is a visible link between the commonplace book and the essay. It is also a link between a learned poet's reading and his method of poetic composition.

A commonplace book was not as a rule an original product, and the title-page of *Timber* indicated its character. Modern research has traced about four-fifths of the material to its sources. Jonson's chief creditors were the two Senecas and Quintilian (with Heinsius for a good deal of literary theory), but he drew more or less from other ancients and from such moderns as Vives, Erasmus, Machiavelli, Lipsius, John Hoskyns, and Bacon. The moving eulogy of the fallen Lord Chancellor apparently came almost verbatim from Hobbes's manuscript translation of the letters of the Italian scholar, Fulgenzio Micanzio, to the first Earl of Devonshire. Of the four passages on life and conduct cited in the standard edition of Jonson in proof of his sterling honesty and fearlessness, his searching insight and fine economy of words, three and a half are borrowed. Even ostensibly personal bits may be translated. Yet such facts by no means contradict such praise. Jonson's choice of authors and items reveals hardly less of his mind and temper than if the book were wholly original. 'He invades Authours like a Monarch, and what would be theft in other Poets, is onely victory in him.' Then, while there is much translation and paraphrase, there is also much recasting and condensed analysis, with comments and illustrations from Jonson's own store of experience. 'And such his wit,' as Falkland said in *Jonsonus Virbius,* 'He writ past what he quotes.' Finally, apart from occasional traces of Latin diction or idiom, Jonson's prose is no less masculine and pithy, and more naturally crisp and colloquial, than Bacon's. The writers he borrowed from had borrowed from others, and they often lacked the pregnant force which makes his moral reflections arresting.

The book may, therefore, be justly accepted as a portrait of the compiler, a man too independent and too sincere to put down what he has not weighed or does not believe. If, for instance, the wise remarks on the right attitude towards the ancients are derived from Vives, or those on 'Custome of speech' and good style from Quintilian, they none the less represent Jonson's own fundamental faith and practice. The tribute to Bacon's oratory, or the censure of Shakespeare's facility, gains rather than loses when we read the originals in Seneca, for we realize that Jonson's scale of values is not set by personal prejudice or by fashion, that he speaks with the authority of a central and living tradition. Everywhere we see the critical inheritor and the active exponent of the aristocratic and practical wisdom of Renaissance humanism, the poet who is not merely an artist but a philosophic citizen vitally concerned with questions of private and public conduct, with education and government, with the whole range of moral and cultural ideas. Jonson's moral utterances are less well known than his literary dicta, but the latter, with all their judicious breadth and good sense, were recorded by the neoclassical theorist, the former by the man and the strongly Stoic humanist. If the one group of observations explains the disciplined art of his poems and plays, the other explains their rational sobriety and weight.

To this heterogeneous but far from exhaustive survey of the essay family one important member is still to be added. From antiquity to the present the letter has been an elder sister, if not a twin, of the essay. During the Middle Ages and the Renaissance the art of letter-writing was assiduously cultivated as a branch of rhetoric. Writers in the vernaculars, like Guevara and Pasquier, inherited from the humanistic tradition a didactic aim and a rhetorical method. In England in the early seventeenth century the literary epistle, like the essay itself, was breaking away from didactic formalism and approaching the genuine familiar letter. Joseph Hall (1574-1656) invited Prince Henry to observe that his *Epistles in Six Decades* (1608-11) inaugurated 'a new fashion of discourse, by Epistles; new to our language, usuall to others'. But we cannot give heed to his clerical, anti-Romish, and Senecan exhortations when livelier authors are frisking before us.

Nicholas Breton's *Post with a Mad Packet of Letters,* published in 1602 and later enlarged, went through many editions. Breton was aware of 'Latine, French, Italian, and Spanish, Bookes of Epistles'—indeed he imitated one of Guevara's letters—and presumably also of the popular middle-class formularies of William Fulwood and Angel Day, but he changed 'the complete letter-writer' into literature. In his compound of moralizing, satire, and romantic love, and his euphuism, he was a sort of lighter and less didactic Lyly. But to these conventional elements Breton adds novel situations and motives and fresh bits of humorous realism in background, characterization, and expression. In fact, though he treats essay themes, from education and travel to love and marriage, he comes closer to epistolary fiction than to the essay. And, unlike the aristocratic and philosophic essayists, Breton makes a distinct appeal to the moral and mercantile interests of the middle-class reader. As late as the sixteen-seventies, when for a generation French preciosity had dominated the English letter-book, a compiler still found Breton worth pilfering.

The supreme epistolizer of the age was James Howell (1593?-1666). He 'came tumbling out into the World a pure Cadet, a true Cosmopolite; not born to Land, Lease, House or Office'. Both as a man of business, in connexion with Sir Robert Mansell's glass factory, and as a minor diplomatic envoy, Howell enjoyed—the word is not colourless—extensive travel; he became an expert linguist and an authority on foreign countries. He had a wide acquaintance among literary and public men, including Sir Kenelm Digby, who claimed to have cured him of a wound by his powder of sympathy. In 1626 he became secretary to Lord Scrope, Lord President of the North, and in 1627 a member of Parliament. Shortly after being sworn Clerk of the Council in August 1642, Howell was arrested by parliamentary order, probably because of royalist activity during the previous decade. The eight years of incarceration (1642-50) were, until his appointment as Historiographer Royal in 1661, the most settled period of his career and turned him into a professional author. He had already published a political allegory, *Dodona's Grove* (1640; enlarged later), and *Instructions for Foreign Travel* (1642). There followed dozens of political pamphlets and miscellaneous and philological works. Howell lives, of course, in the *Epistolae Ho-Elianae,* the four books of which appeared in 1645, 1647, 1650, and 1655. Whether or not he used actual letters, the necessitous and thrifty author drew freely upon his own and other men's works, and especially no doubt upon his note-books, for the more solid portions of his masterpiece, such as the virtual articles or essays on the religions, wines, and languages of the world, the unity of creation, and the theory of the habitable moon. Howell's Oxford education had never been 'any burden or encumbrance' to him, and the chances and changes of his life had provided him with one kind of capital, a fund of varied experience and observation.

The first letter, originally prefixed to the second book, indicates his knowledge of epistolary authors and manuals, and his dislike of neo-Latin commonplaces and French affectation and emptiness. The true familiar letter, he says (after Seneca), should have the naturalness of talk but should not lack substance and ideas. Howell's letters live up to his theory. Like Leigh Hunt, he was a tricksy sprite for whom stone walls did not a prison make. The bulk of his work deals with the course of English and continental affairs and with the life and manners of continental countries and cities. There are few names, events, or topics which do not come in somewhere and do not give an impression of immediacy. Howell's eager curiosity embraces ship-money, Platonic love at court, and the disease of witty preaching; Spinola and Galileo; the siege of Rochelle and the glories of Venice. Whatever charges of inaccuracy or shallowness the historian may lodge against him, it is to Howell that we owe our most vivid pictures of the Overbury trial, of Gondomar stalking in to King James to ejac-

ulate 'Pyrats, Pyrats, Pyrats', of Prince Charles's difficult courtship of the Infanta, of Buckingham rising on the fatal day and cutting a caper or two—these and many other incidents great and small are sketched with the dramatic instinct of a journalist. We see Ben Jonson at the supper table betraying his 'Roman infirmity' of self-praise, or Lord Leicester bearing up stoutly through thirty-five healths at a Danish banquet and departing, unlike his royal host, on his own legs. Something is always putting Howell in mind of a good anecdote, like the Earl of Kildare's ingenuous explanation that he would not have burned a church if he had not thought the bishop was in it. Then there are some famous and more serious tales, of the anchorite, the pied piper of Hamelin, and the white-breasted bird of the Oxenhams.

Like all good essayists, Howell reveals his own character. Our true cosmopolite is glad to return 'to the sweet bosom of England' and breathe again the smoke of London. His mercurial spirit has its saturnine moods, but misfortunes cannot submerge a man so interested in life—one who, moreover, looks back to that illustrious Armorican dynasty of the Howells. Mercurial and mundane gusto is carried, quite sincerely, into his religion, even if his devotional schedule does not suggest Celtic kinship with Henry Vaughan; he can address his Maker every day in a different language 'and upon Sunday in seven'. With Sir Thomas Browne Howell rather pities than hates Turk or infidel. If he hates any, it is those schismatics 'that puzzle the sweet peace of our Church, so that I could bee content to see an Anabaptist go to Hell on a Brownists back'. (pp. 181-97)

Douglas Bush, "Essays and Characters," in his English Literature in the Earlier Seventeenth Century, 1600-1660, *Oxford at the Clarendon Press, 1945, pp. 181-208.*

Hugh Walker

[In the following excerpt, Walker focuses on the essays of Francis Bacon in an examination of seventeenth-century prose writers.]

[Bacon] is the first of English essayists, as he remains, for sheer mass and weight of genius, the greatest. It is, then, of peculiar interest to consider what he had in mind when he wrote the papers to which he gave the name of essays, and how he regarded these products of his pen. Obviously the general conception was borrowed from Montaigne, whose essays had appeared seventeen years before the earliest of Bacon's. Bacon felt at once that the form was suitable to receive many thoughts of his own mind, and not merely his intellect but his whole disposition made such a form as that which Montaigne supplied valuable to him. Bacon was extraordinarily discursive in his interests: he took all knowledge for his province; and while several contemporaries surpassed him in depth of insight into subjects which he had specially studied, few in any age have rivalled him in the capacity to utter pregnant thoughts on almost any theme. We may accept the judgment of experts that Coke was a profounder lawyer, and we may believe that Harvey was justified in jeering at the Lord Chancellor's knowledge of science. But we have to go back to Aristotle to discover Bacon's superior in encyclopædic range of mind. Further, Bacon was thrifty of his thoughts and his literary material. Of material wealth he was careless, though he was by no means indifferent to it; but the treasures of his mind he felt to be a debt to posterity, and he willingly wasted none of them. The mass of papers which he left proves his extraordinary diligence, and the care with which he hived his wisdom. Macaulay has noted that the best collection of jests in the world—they are really something deeper than jests—was dictated by him on a day when illness had unfitted him for more serious work.

To a man thus endowed, and thus thrifty of time and of literary material, the essay was a godsend. Here could be preserved thoughts that would not, for the time at least, fit into any part of the *Instauratio Magna,* and yet were too well-developed and too coherent to be buried in a mere entry in a commonplace book. Bacon therefore takes the form from Montaigne, but fills it with material drawn from his own mind. There is all the difference in the world between the secluded and solitary French gentleman—once indeed a courtier and perhaps a soldier, but now merely the spectator of life and its shrewd critic—and the ambitious English lawyer and statesman, with one eye fixed upon the pole-star of philosophic truth, and the other watching the political weather-cock.

That Bacon regarded the essay as a receptacle for detached thoughts is evident both from the essays themselves and from his own words about them. He speaks of them as "dispersed meditations." He ranks them but as recreations in comparison with his more serious studies. Yet he is conscious of and pleased with their popularity. In 1612 he refers with satisfaction to "the often printing of the former" volume. In the "epistle dedicatory" to Andrewes, Bishop of Winchester, written in 1622, he says: "I am not ignorant that those kind of writings would, with less pains and embracement (perhaps), yield more lustre and reputation to my name, than those others which I have in hand." And in the epistle to the Duke of Buckingham prefixed to the edition of the essays of 1625, he says that of all his works they have been most current, "for that, as it seems, they come home to men's business and bosoms." Their popularity is shown by the fact that they were early translated into French, Latin and Italian; and they still retain the favour they so speedily won. Few books of the kind have been so widely read, and probably no volume of prose in the English language has furnished so many popular quotations. It would seem that Bacon was not only pleased with their popularity but convinced of their importance. In the dedicatory epistle to Buckingham he speaks of them as "of the best fruits that, by the good increase which God gives to my pen and labours, I could yield." Naturally, therefore, he was anxious to have them turned into Latin; and though the Latin translation which we possess was not published till after Bacon's death, it was prepared under his own direction, and probably contains touches of his pen, if not whole essays from it. With regard to the comparative value of the English original and the Latin version, Bacon made the mistake usual in his time. It was the latter which he anticipated might "last as long as books last."

By extracts from the essay "Of Studies", which was one of the ten published in 1597, and "Of Adversity", which first appeared in the edition of 1625, Macaulay illustrated what he calls the two styles of Bacon. The contrast is striking; but the soundness of Macaulay's inference, that in Bacon the judgment had grown faster than the fancy, may perhaps be questioned. Bacon wrote more than two styles; and, if the essay "Of Adversity" is more ornate than the essay "Of Studies", there are passages in *The Advancement of Learning*—for example, the peroration to the first part—not less richly adorned and far more stately in movement than the former essay. Now the *Advancement of Learning* was published in 1605. If, therefore, the change of style be attributed to the growth of Bacon's mind, it is necessary to suppose that within eight years of the first appearance of the essays he had reached a point of development in the imagination as high as that at which he stood at the close of his life. As this supposition is hardly tenable we must seek for some other explanation of the phenomenon. It is probably to be found in a change in Bacon's conception as to the function and the possibilities of the essay form. In the early essays the sentences are nearly all short, crisp, sententious. There are few connectives. Each sentence stands by itself, the concentrated expression of weighty thought. But this is not because Bacon's imagination was not yet developed, not because he could not have written in the richer and smoother style of later days, had he chosen to do so. It is because, at this period, the essay was, to him, literally and precisely an 'attempt' at a subject. It was something incomplete, something which ought to bear on its face the visible marks of its unfinished condition. It was a group of jottings, different from the memoranda of diaries and commonplace books inasmuch as they *were* a group. Such memoranda, too, may be "meditations," and they are certainly "dispersed." But they are apt to be dispersed over the universe, while the meditations of the essays are confined within the four corners of a single subject. The connexions are not worked out and expressed, but are implicit and can be supplied by the intelligence of an alert reader. Essays such as those "Of Studies" and "Of Suitors" are something of the nature of that running analysis of paragraphs which is occasionally printed on the margins of books. When, therefore, it is said that each sentence of Bacon's contains matter for a paragraph of an ordinary writer, the statement is true; but not so the implication that the Baconian sentence does the work of the paragraph. If Bacon had been treating the subject fully, he too would have written the paragraph. It would not have been the paragraph of an ordinary writer, but the extreme condensation would be found no longer.

If we turn to the essays of 1612, and still more to those of 1625, we observe, indeed, precisely the contrast which Macaulay points out. Bacon finds room for conjunctions and connective clauses. He does more, he imparts warmth and colour to the style. His keen sense of analogy enables him to discover illustrations everywhere. Metaphors and similes are frequent, and sometimes, though not very often, they have a poetical quality.

> Virtue is like precious odours, most fragrant when they are incensed or crushed; for prosperi-

ty doth best discover vice, but adversity doth best discover virtue.

It is heaven upon earth to have a man's mind move in charity, rest in providence, and turn upon the poles of truth.

It is a poor centre of a man's actions, himself. It is right earth. For that only stands fast upon his own centre; whereas all things that have affinity with the heavens move upon the centre of another, which they benefit.

Suspicions amongst thoughts are like bats amongst birds,—they fly best by twilight.

A great estate left to an heir, is as a lure to all the birds of prey round about to seize on him, if he be not the better established in years and in judgment. Likewise, glorious gifts and foundations are like sacrifices without salt, and but the painted sepulchres of alms, which soon will putrefy and corrupt inwardly.

Compositions in which such sentences as these occur are obviously a good deal more than mere jottings. Bacon's conception of the essay had developed, and therefore he clothed his "dispersed meditations" in a richer vesture. As essayist, it is true, he was still the philosopher in undress; but perhaps the popularity he had won had made him more fully conscious of the importance of the step he had taken in the little book of 1597. It was worth while spending time and taking trouble to weave together the *disjecta membra* of his meditations; for, as he must now have seen, he had naturalised in England a new species of literature, and he was showing the way to the development of a new style of English prose. For the end in view it is hard to conceive anything better than the essays "Of Truth", "Of Death", "Of Adversity". The general conception of the essay is still preserved. The subject is still treated incompletely. The essays are "loose thoughts, thrown out without much regularity." But though loose they are not disconnected, and for the irregularity there is compensation in the familiar ease and friendly confidence of the writer. Bacon is too stately, and his thought is too profound, to permit us to speak of the essays as the confidential chat of a great philosopher; but in them he comes as near that as his nature would permit.

Just here we detect the secret of Bacon's inferiority (of course merely *qua* essayist) to his model Montaigne or to the greatest English master of the form, Charles Lamb. The ideal essay seems to imply a certain lightness and ease, and a confidential relation between the author and the reader. That we find in *Oxford in the Long Vacation* and in *Mrs. Battle's Opinions on Whist.* But not in Bacon. Even where he most unbends Bacon is still stately and magnificent. The "toys" to which he descends in the essays are never more trivial than such things as masques and triumphs and gardens; and though of the former he says "it is better they should be graced with elegancy than daubed with cost," his taste for splendour appears conspicuously in the treatment, as it does also in his description of the garden. In Montaigne and in Lamb the subject is often unimportant. For such writers every road leads to the end of the world, and a title which promises only some grace-

ful triviality may cover deep feeling, if not profound thought. The praise of cannibals may conceal a satire on civilisation. But in Bacon the subject always is important, and however unsystematic he may be in his treatment of it, he never wanders beyond its bounds. Masques and triumphs are "toys," but they are discussed at nearly as great length, and with as strict adherence to the theme, as truth itself, or as atheism.

While it would be difficult if not impossible to make a satisfactory classification which should embrace all the essays of Bacon, it is easy to detect what are the prevailing sorts. Bacon was a moralist and a politician, and a large proportion, including many of the most interesting, of the essays deal either with the ethical qualities of men, or with matters pertaining to the government of states. His purely scientific interests make but little show. The conditions were not favourable, and besides, science was the subject of those serious works in comparison with which the essays were merely recreations.

As a moralist Bacon makes no pretence to system. To do so would have been to write something different from an essay as he conceived it. It would, moreover, have implied a disposition alien from that of the father of empirical philosophy. In this respect the modern mind is widely different from the ancient. Socrates advised the abandonment of physical investigations on the ground that they were too complicated; but on the other hand he undertook to inquire into the essential principle of justice in the belief that the investigation, though difficult, was by no means hopeless. The modern feeling is precisely the contrary, and no one did more to make it so than Bacon. By the aid of his method he hoped that the secret of nature might ere long be solved completely. He had no such hope with regard to the principles of morals. It is not clear that he was certain of the existence of principles of absolute validity. The *Essays* seem to be the work of an opportunist. Bacon admires truth, moral and well as intellectual. "Clear and round dealing is the honour of man's nature." But then falsehood is like alloy in gold and silver, which, though it debases the metal, makes it work the better. The impression here given is immensely strengthened by the essay "Of Simulation and Dissimulation". Bacon approves of secrecy: "nakedness is uncomely, as well in mind as in body." But to preserve secrecy dissimulation is often necessary, and in some cases even simulation, or the pretence to be what one is not. This last, indeed, is "more culpable, and less politic, except it be in great and rare matters." But by these steps we are led to the conclusion that "the best composition and temperature is: to have openness in fame and opinion; secrecy in habit; dissimulation in seasonable use; and a power to feign, if there be no remedy." It is not an elevated or an elevating ideal. A careful and candid reading of the essay will show that Bacon's morality is higher than that of average humanity, and perhaps as high as is easily practicable in a workaday world. But the framer of such maxims could never have felt that awe of the moral law within which Kant coupled with the awe of the starry heavens above; nor is there in any Baconian maxim a suggestion of the spirit of the saying, Let justice be done though the heavens should fall. The principle to be inferred is rather, let right be done, and let truth be told, if it be not too costly. As a man must be judge in his own case of what *is* too costly, the standard is not extravagantly high.

On the whole Bacon gives the impression of singular aloofness from moral considerations. His maxims are prudential. He appears to be looking down with absolute dispassionateness from a height, and determining what course of conduct pays best. He condemns cunning, not as a thing loathesome and vile, but as a thing unwise. Occasionally he even lays down the rules for immoral conduct without a word of overt disapproval. In the essay "Of Suitors" he recognises indeed the existence of right and wrong: "There is in some sort a right in every suit; either a right of equity, if it be a suit of controversy; or a right of desert, if it be a suit of petition." But he goes on: "If affection lead a man to favour the wrong side in justice, let him rather use his countenance to compound the matter than to carry it. If affection lead a man to favour the less worthy in desert, let him do it without depraving or disabling the better deserver." Was ever moralist so impartial between right and wrong? Let the wrongdoer be moderate. But he seems to be so advised, less in the interest of the sufferer, than because in pushing matters to an extreme there is danger to the perpetrator of the wrong.

This impression is confirmed by the tone and substance of a remarkable group of essays which deal neither with moral principles in the individual, nor with the interests of the state, but with domestic relations and with special ties between man and man. Few readers of Bacon can have been insensitive to the extraordinary coldness of the essays "Of Parents and Children", "Of Marriage and Single Life" and "Of Love". Perhaps the defects of the essay "Of Friendship" are less obtrusive, but a little consideration shows that they are cognate. The view is fundamentally utilitarian. Here certainly is the philosophy of fruit. Bacon values friendship highly, but mainly for the fruits to be gathered from it—comfort to the emotions, light to the understanding, aid in the affairs of life. "A friend is another himself," and something more. But it is always what a man receives from his friend, never for a moment what he gives, that is insisted on. He never hints that a man may be ennobled by a deed of pure unselfishness. Apparently the blessedness of giving had no place among Bacon's beatitudes.

So it is too with the essays on the domestic relations. Wife and children are "hostages to fortune," "impediments to great enterprises, either of virtue or mischief." Bacon's recognition of the moral development due to those relations is most inadequate. It is true he sees that "wife and children are a kind of discipline of humanity," but he seems hardly conscious of any wider influence. And apparently he thinks the balance of advantage swings to the other side; for he says that "unmarried men are the best friends, best masters and best servants," though he adds that they are "not always the best subjects." Evidently Bacon was both deficient in and disposed to underrate the emotional element. His own marriage was a marriage of convenience; and though his condemnation of the excesses of the passion of love is fully justified, the pronouncement that it is "the child of folly," and the advice to sever it

wholly from the serious affairs and actions of life, seem to indicate coldness of blood and heart. Contemporaries, uncharitably and perhaps unjustly, suspected him to be more susceptible of the meaner than of the more generous passions, and saw in the essay "Of Deformity", a covert satire on his cousin Robert Cecil, Earl of Salisbury.

An examination of Bacon's attitude towards religion leads to similar results. His belief in religion, like his belief in moral principles, was largely prudential and was destitute of fervour. It had its root in the understanding; the religion of saints and martyrs has its root in the heart. Bacon's declaration in the essay "Of Atheism" that he "had rather believe all the fables in the Legend, and the Talmud, and the Alcoran, than that this universal frame is without a mind," is perfectly sincere. But if circumstances had tempted him to sign a declaration to the contrary, his conscience would never have forced him, as Cranmer's did, to hold his right hand in the flames. The essay "Of Unity of Religion" is the work of a political opportunist. It views religion as "the chief band of human society," and Bacon's main preoccupation is to determine how it may be made most useful in that capacity. Most remarkable of all perhaps is the essay "Of Death"—remarkable not so much for what it says as for what it leaves unsaid. As Dr. Abbott points out, the hopes and fears of a second life are absent; for the bare remark that "the contemplation of death as the wages of sin and passage to another world, is holy and religious," can hardly be regarded as a recognition of them. Such a conventional acknowledgment, followed by nothing, is almost more striking than complete silence. It is a fair inference that such hopes and fears counted for little in Bacon's case. Though he could upon occasion compose grand prayers, religion seems to have played very little part in his life. The division he set up between faith and reason enabled him to relegate it to a world distant from that in which he lived.

When he can, Bacon loves to escape from the private and personal to the political aspect of the question with which he deals. This he does not only in the discussion of unity in religion, but in the treatment of marriage. Evidently he felt himself more at home in the character of statesman than in that of moralist, and among the weightiest of his essays are those which treat of political questions. Nowhere does his wisdom show to better advantage. The essay "Of Plantations" is a compendium of principles whose soundness has been gradually established by the experience of generations and centuries. Had they been accepted from Bacon the worst mistakes of England in her relations with the colonies might have been avoided. Modern humanitarianism seems to be anticipated in the remark, "I like a plantation in a pure soil, that is, where people are not displanted to the end to plant in others. For else it is rather an extirpation than a plantation." And the advice to use savages justly and graciously; to fight in their defence, but not to win their favour by helping them to invade their enemies; and frequently to send some of them to the colonising country, so that they may teach a higher civilisation on their return,—all this rises to the highest point attained by English opinion after an experience of three centuries. It is immeasurably superior to that which was lately exemplified in what was sardonically called the

Congo Free State. Of the essence of wisdom, as well as of humanity, is the denunciation of "the base and hasty drawing of profit in the first years," and the declaration that "it is a shameful and unblessed thing to take the scum of the people, and wicked condemned men, to be the people with whom you plant." Bacon's countrymen learnt this only when the colonies showed that they would no longer endure the treatment which he had condemned. We have to bear such facts in mind in order to do justice to the marvellous prescience and elevation of mind shown in this essay. In his capacity of political moralist Bacon seems to shake off the fetters which cramp him when he is dealing with individual morality; or rather, perhaps, it is the fact that he is always, at heart, a political moralist that lowers his tone in the other class of cases. The accepted standard of the ethics of public life is to this day, even outside Germany, lower than that of private life. In Bacon's time the difference was still wider—*how* wide may be gathered from the bitter irony of More's *Utopia;* for there had been no great improvement in the century intervening between More and Bacon.

There is no other of the political essays which shows Bacon so immeasurably superior to his time as that "Of Plantations". Mr. Reynolds, in his edition of the *Essays,* has shown that in the essay "Of Usury" Bacon has not only fallen into fallacies, but that they are fallacies some of which had been transcended by at least one contemporary, Mun. The subject of the essay "Of Empire", monarchs and their policy towards their subjects and towards rival monarchs, has lost much of its interest and importance. "Of the True Greatness of Kingdoms and Estates" is, to the modern mind, too exclusively concerned with war and military policy; and even the essay "Of Seditions and Troubles", full as it is of ripe wisdom, touches no principles so large or so generous as those which are expressed in the course of the discussion of colonies. Nevertheless, there is not one of these essays which does not show that Bacon had mastered some principle which probably no contemporary had grasped. The remark, for example, that "to be master of the sea is an abridgement of a monarchy," with the paragraph which follows, embodies a truth illustrated again and again in English history—a truth which, though it was familiar to Thucydides, was first adequately expounded by an American writer in the present generation, Captain, afterwards Admiral, Mahan.

Essays filled with thought so massive could only be written by a Bacon; and in this respect the earliest of English essayists still stands alone. It took Ulysses to draw the bow of Ulysses. But though it was impossible to rival Bacon, it was not difficult to take hints from him. He did more than introduce a new literary form: he took one of the longest steps ever taken in the evolution of English prose style; a step which set that style upon the road which it travelled, though not without divagations, down to the days of Swift and Addison. English prose was already, before Bacon, or independently of him, rich and sonorous. Hooker, the last book of whose *Ecclesiastical Polity* was published in the same year with Bacon's earliest essays, still ranks as one of our greatest stylists. So does Raleigh, who had written several things before that date, though his *History of the World* did not appear till seventeen years

later. But while these writers have majesty and strength, while in their hours of inspiration they were able to write as few have written since, while Raleigh's apostrophe to death remains absolutely unsurpassed, it cannot be said that they were masters of a style suited to all the purposes which prose must subserve. It was admirable for great themes and for moments of elevation, but ill adapted to the pedestrian passages which must link such themes and moments one to another. The sentences were inconveniently long, and even in the hands of the most skilful writers were frequently involved and obscure. Parentheses were extremely common. These faults were characteristic not only of scholars; and there is no need to go for illustration to the Euphuists. Even men who, like Richard Hakluyt, were primarily simple men of action, fall into similar vices, because no model of a style consistently simple and clear had yet been set. The same is true of Bacon himself in his larger and more sustained works. But in the *Essays* he *did* set the example, he *did* furnish the model. By the very plan and conception, almost of necessity the sentences had to be short. They are so even in the later essays. With shortness came lucidity. The essays of Bacon have to be read slowly and thoughtfully, not because the style is obscure, but because they are extremely condensed and the thought is profound. The grammatical structure is sometimes loose, but it is rarely ambiguous.

With shortness came also flexibility. The older style was cumbrous: it could rise, but it could not easily sink: to adapt Goldsmith's jest about Johnson, it might befit the mouths of whales, but hardly those of little fishes. The new style of Bacon fitted itself as easily to buildings and gardens, or to suitors and ceremonies, as to truth and death. It could sink to the familiarity of likening money to muck, not good unless it be spread, or rise to a comparison between the movements of the human mind and the movements of the heavenly bodies. To Bacon, in short, we are largely indebted for making good that which had hitherto been the chief defect of English literature. Till the closing years of the sixteenth century, except in translations, no one had shown a mastery of the principles of prose. Then Bacon showed such mastery, and Shakespeare in even higher degree than Bacon. Shylock's tremendous outburst in the first scene of the third act of *The Merchant of Venice,* and Antonio's letter in the scene following it, are models as superb in prose as are the lines on mercy in verse.

The example set by Bacon was followed by two men who have little in common with him and but a slender share of his gifts—Sir William Cornwallis, whose *Essays* were published in 1600, and Robert Johnson, who thought even essay too ambitious a name, and called his little volume *Essaies, or rather Imperfect Offers* (1601). Johnson took a special interest in education; Cornwallis was discursive in treatment and varied in his themes, though he showed a preference for abstract qualities, such as *Patience, Humility, Vanity, Ambition.* He had views of his own upon the art of essay-writing. "I hold," he says, "neither Plutarch's, nor none of these ancient short manner of writings, nor Montaigne's, nor such of this latter time to be rightly termed Essays, for though they be short, yet they are strong, and able to endure the sharpest trial: but mine are Essays, who am but newly bound prentice to the inquisition of knowledge, and use these papers as a painter's boy a board, that is trying to bring his hand and his fancy acquainted." His own reflections certainly are rather shallow—*not* strong, nor able to endure the sharpest trial. But for his historical position he would scarcely deserve mention. One of his gifts, however, may be noticed. He shows considerable critical insight. He was an admirer of Shakespeare, and allusions to *Hamlet, Othello* and other plays are scattered through the essays in the later editions. So too he warmly praises the English translation of Montaigne.

There was one writer who came near bending the bow of the English Ulysses—Ben Jonson. The great dramatist has received his full meed of praise and fame as a poet, and perhaps even more than his meed; but in spite of the warm eulogy of a few discerning critics his prose, which is quite worthy of comparison even with Bacon's, has been shamefully neglected. Dryden perceived Jonson's greatness as a critic, and declared that he had laid down "as many and profitable rules for perfecting the stage, as any wherewith the French can furnish us." Swinburne read him with characteristic discernment, and expressed his admiration, unfortunately with characteristic exaggeration. He compares Jonson with Bacon, very much to the disadvantage of the latter. "Donne's verses [the *Anniversaries*]," he says, "are as far above Gray's [the *Odes*] as Jonson's notes or observations on men and morals, on principles and on facts, are superior to Bacon's in truth of insight, in breadth of view, in vigour of reflection and in concision of eloquence." And again: "From the ethical point of view which looks merely or mainly to character, the comparison is little less than an insult to the Laureate; and from the purely intelligent or æsthetic point of view I should be disposed to say, or at least inclined to think, that the comparison would be hardly less unduly complimentary to the Chancellor." The exaggeration here carries its own corrective. Wide differences of opinion may legitimately be held as to the ethics of Bacon; but it is absurd to suggest that any man is so great as to be insulted by being compared with him intellectually. It is all the more absurd to exalt Jonson so greatly because, as is hinted in the subtitle, *Discoveries* is largely composed of extracts and adaptations from Jonson's reading. But though Swinburne has thus damaged his own cause, the high opinion he held of Jonson's *Discoveries* is (apart from the comparison with Bacon and the question of originality) essentially just. He is wrong rather in his needless depreciation of Bacon than in his panegyric of Jonson; but he is further wrong in that he has not made the necessary deduction from the credit of Jonson on the score of his inferior originality. Not merely did Jonson not introduce the essay, as Bacon may reasonably be said to have done, but it has been proved beyond dispute that he owed the substance of his thought in very great measure to other writers.

Timber, or Discoveries, is among the latest of Jonson's works. It was not printed till 1641, and internal evidence points to the conclusion that much of it was not written till after 1630. The extraordinary neglect from which it has suffered may be explained partly by the remissness of editors. Outwardly it has the appearance of a collection of loose jottings, 171 in number, varying in length from

merely a sentence or so to the dimensions of one of the shorter Baconian essays. But if we look to the substance, we find in several cases that the notes are not really disjointed but connected and, in some measure, systematic. Thus, there is an excellent group of four notes which constitute jointly an essay on the principles of art, or, as Jonson phrases it, 'picture.' Another group is seen to be a thoughtful and weighty essay on style; and a third should be read together as an essay on government. These notes, therefore, are considerably less discursive than, on the surface, they appear to be. If their real connexions were indicated, one hindrance to their popularity would be removed; for men are apt to shun such meditations as seem to them to be too 'dispersed.' They want a certain continuity of thought.

As Bacon's essays have been divided into moral and political, so may Jonson's notes be classed as mainly moral and critical. In the sphere of morals Swinburne's preference for him as against Bacon may be justified. There is a fervour and generosity in Jonson which cannot be paralleled from Bacon. Take for example the beautiful note, headed *Beneficia:*—

> Nothing is a courtesy unless it be meant us; and that friendly and lovingly. We owe no thanks to rivers, that they carry our boats; or winds, that they be favouring and fill our sails; or meats, that they be nourishing. For these are what they are necessarily. Horses carry us, trees shade us, but they knew it not. It is true, some men may receive a courtesy and not know it; but never any man received it from him that knew it not. Many men have been cured of disease by accidents; but they were not remedies. I myself have known one helped of an ague by falling into a water, another whipped out of a fever; but no man would ever use these for medicines. It is the mind, and not the event, that distinguisheth the courtesy from wrong. My adversary may offend the judge with his pride and impertinences, and I win the cause, but he means it not *me* as a courtesy. I scaped pirates by being shipwrecked, was the wreck a benefit therefore? No, the doing of courtesies aright, is the mixing of the respects for his own sake, and for mine. He that doth them merely for his own sake, is like one that feeds his cattle to sell them: he hath his horse well drest for Smithfield.

Or take the note on truth:—

> Without truth all the actions of mankind are craft, malice, what you will, rather than wisdom. . . . Nothing is lasting that is feigned; it will have another face than it had ere long. As Euripides saith, 'No lie ever grows old.'

Equally admirable for terse wisdom are the note on parasites; the group of six on envy; that which deals with good men and bad men; and the powerful discussion of the love of money. No one who reads these notes with care will deny to Jonson the title of a moralist, and a weighty one.

In the department of criticism it was hardly possible for Jonson to fail, for he had been thinking of the subject all his life. His own application of his principles in the drama prepares us to differ from him; and in his famous note on

Shakespeare there is a touch of condescension which makes it less surprising to discover that there are certain aspects of beauty to which he was blind. But no Englishman had at that date expressed so much critical truth as is condensed into the two essays on painting and on style. Even where we may think him wrong there is in Jonson's remarks a robust sense that makes us respect him as we respect his namesake of the following century. And as his sentences are invariably the expression of thought in himself, so they are the cause of thought in others. Few writers are more suggestive, few more sound and just. No one has written more judiciously on the proper mean between archaism and neologism:—

> Custom is the most certain mistress of language, as the public stamp makes the current money. But we must not be too frequent with the mint, every day coining, nor fetch words from the extreme of utmost ages; since the chief virtue of a style is perspicuity, and nothing so vicious in it as to need an interpreter. Words borrowed of antiquity do lend a kind of majesty to style, and are not without their delight sometimes. For they have the authority of years, and out of their intermission do win themselves a kind of grace—like newness. But the eldest of the present, and newest of the past language, is the best. For what was the ancient language, which some men so dote upon, but the ancient custom? Yet when I name custom, I understand not the vulgar custom; for that were a precept no less dangerous to language than life, if we should speak or live after the manner of the vulgar: but that I call custom of speech, which is the consent of the learned; as custom of life, which is the consent of the good.

No one, again, has a truer conception of the use of ornament in diction:—

> Some words are to be culled out for ornament and colour, as we gather flowers to strow houses, or make garlands; but they are better when they grow to our style; as in a meadow, where though the mere grass and greenness delight, yet the variety of flowers doth heighten and beautify.

Criticism of a somewhat different kind is to be found in the note entitled *Ingeniorum Discrimina,* which is justly praised by Swinburne for "its soundness of judgment, its accuracy of definition, and its felicity of expression." The remarks on the essayists, are, for the present purpose, peculiarly interesting. Although he was at the moment invading their sphere, Jonson thought but meanly of them, and declared that all of them, "even their master Montaigne," "turn over all books," and "write out what they presently find or meet, without choice."

Jonson was a man of wide range as well as of extraordinary power of thought, and although in the essay on government he is off his beat, even here he comes with credit through the ordeal of comparison with Bacon. The essay is as close-packed with thought as any of Bacon's own. The two notes on clemency are as honourable to Jonson's heart as they are to his head; that on an illiterate prince, and the one which follows it, are almost perfect; and there

is a very happy union of wisdom with wit in *Mores Aulici:*—

> I have discovered, that a feigned familiarity in great ones, is a note of certain usurpation on the less. For great and popular men feign themselves to be servants to others, to make these slaves to them. So the fisher provides bait for the trout, roach, dace, etc., that they may be food for him.

The quotations sufficiently illustrate Jonson's style. It combines lucidity, terseness and strength in a degree rivalling even Bacon's. It is capable of rising to eloquence, but a plain subject is treated in a plain and simple way. In his use of ornament Jonson obeys his own rule: his flowers of speech are such as "grow to" his style. He is absolutely free from the vice of euphuism. In the art of coining epigrammatic phrases he has had few equals. He speaks of a tedious person as "one that touched neither heaven nor earth in his discourse." The self-taught man, if he be proud of his tuition, is annihilated in a dozen words: "He that was only taught by himself, had a fool for his master." This mastery of epigram is a dangerous gift, as the character-writers of Jonson's time showed. But it was dangerous to them because they were men of third-rate power. They were perpetually straining after epigram; in Jonson's mind the epigram rose naturally and easily. Their flowers were culled; his grew in the meadow of his thought. They were proud when they could compose a piece wholly of epigrams; but Jonson knew that unmixed epigram was as unpalatable as a dish of pepper alone. In a word, his style is the expression of a genius which never ceases to be common sense; and *Discoveries* may be taken as one of the most trustworthy of guides upon almost any subject with which it deals.

If it be permissible to treat as literature a book which was not written by its author, then by virtue of *Table-Talk* John Selden (1584-1654) deserves a place beside Bacon and Jonson. More than thirty years passed after Selden's death before the book was published, but there is fair ground for concluding that it was put together within a short time after his death, and that not only the substance but a good deal of the phraseology is to be ascribed to Selden. At any rate, the credit of this remarkable book must be shared between him and the compiler, Richard Milward; and together they have produced a little volume which shows more mastery of the aphoristic style than anything else in English, except the works of Bacon and Jonson, which have just been commented on. The resemblance to Jonson is closer than the resemblance to Bacon; for Bacon's essays are in their own way finished works, and they underwent careful revision, while many sections of the *Discoveries* are merely jottings which the author would probably have expanded had he lived to issue the book himself. *Table-Talk* was never meant for publication at all, and is still less formal than the *Discoveries.* But it is the concentrated essence of immense learning and a life of thought. It is always weighty and often most felicitously expressed. Again and again it gives the ripe fruit of Selden's wisdom in reflections upon the subjects to which he had devoted his life. Spoken in the midst of civil strife, the opinions of Selden are characterised by a moderation and a judicial balance which would have been equally displeasing to the zealots of both parties. Thus Selden had far too high a conception of the power and rights of the State to please the High Church. "So [by the stronger party] religion was brought into kingdoms, so it has been continued, and so it may be cast out when the State pleases." And in speaking of religion, to the question whether the Church or the Scripture is judge of religion he answers, "In truth neither, but the State." On the other hand, he would have pleased the zealots of dissent if possible even less. The whole current of his thought, as the most casual reader must see, runs against them; but there is a homely vigour in his refutation of one of their contentions that makes it worth quoting: "The main argument why they would have two sermons a day is, because they have two meals a day; the soul must be fed as well as the body. But I may as well argue, I ought to have two noses because I have two eyes, or two mouths because I have two ears. What have meals and sermons to do one with another?" The zealot on either side would have torn asunder the man who said: "Religion is like the fashion, one man wears his doublet slashed, another laced, another plain; but every man has a doublet: so every man has his religion. We differ about trimming." Here surely is a mind as detached as even Hume's in his discussion of superstition and enthusiasm.

Selden has the power, invaluable in literature, of conveying suggestion in a few words: "The King himself used to eat in the hall, and his lords sate with him, and then he understood men." Possibly, if he had continued to sit in the hall and had still understood men, there might have been no Civil War. He has also a marked gift for felicitous illustration: " 'Twas an unhappy division that has been made between faith and works; though in my intellect I may divide them, just as in the candle, I know there is both light and heat. But yet put out the candle, and they are both gone, one remains not without the other: So 'tis betwixt faith and works; nay, in a right conception *Fides est opus,* if I believe a thing because I am commanded, that is *opus.*" If Selden had written more in the vernacular, and had devoted his powers to literature rather than to learning, he would have been unsurpassed in the union of instruction and entertainment. (pp. 15-37)

Hugh Walker, "The Aphoristic Essayists," in his The English Essay and Essayists, *J. M. Dent & Sons Ltd., 1915, pp. 15-37.*

Bonamy Dobrée

[*A highly regarded English historian and critic, Dobrée distinguished himself both as a leading authority of Restoration drama and as an author of biographical studies that seek, through vivid depiction and captivating style, to establish biography as a legitimate creative form. Dobrée is also known for his skillful editing of* The Oxford History of English Literature. *In the excerpt below, he analyzes differences in style and subject matter that distinguish the works of some early essayists, including Francis Bacon, Abraham Cowley, and William Temple.*]

Francis Bacon, Lord Verulam (1561-1626) was primarily a philosopher, and it is to this rather than to his essays or his place in political history as Chancellor, that he owes his universal fame. So it is not surprising that his earliest essays are wholly aphoristic; he is giving a picture not of himself, but of mankind. As he mellowed, however, and wrote more essays—they were added to in an edition of 1612, and reached the number of fifty-eight in his final edition of 1625—he came nearer the ordinary man because he talked of matters which interest the ordinary man. In one sense, certainly, his essays were still philosophical, but in them he was extending his scientific vision to include everyday affairs and the common emotions. In speaking of these, and of the things which happen to all men, he was filling the gap in his system; he was intent "to pass from theological and philosophical truth to the truth of civil business," that is, to what you and I do. Therefore his style relaxes; he becomes less stiffly formal. He seems just a little more to take you into his confidence, to be less concerned to make pronouncements, though it is still true, as has been well said, that "while Montaigne's chief concern is in a man sitting upon his 'owne taile,' Bacon's is a man sitting in an office chair." His personal likes and dislikes become visible, though they are veiled by his impersonal manner; we know, because we feel, that much of what he writes comes out of his personal experience, is an expression of his own feeling. You see the difference if you compare his early and his late essays on Death. The first begins:

> Men fear death as children fear to go in the dark;
> and as that natural fear in children is increased
> with tales, so is the other.

So it goes on, sprinkled with Latin quotations and examples drawn from the ancients, a discourse on a matter which scarcely affects him. But this is how his second essay begins:

> I have often thought about death, and I find it
> the least of all evils. All that which is past is as
> a dream; and he that hopes or depends upon
> time coming, dreams waking.

Yet he doesn't pretend that others do not mind the idea of dying, and he goes on through a variegated catalogue of people who have reasons for fearing death, and in one passage at least forgets the office chair and becomes almost a poet:

> Death arrives gracious only to such as sit in
> darkness, or lie heavy burthened with grief and
> irons; to the poor Christian that sits bound in the
> galley; to despairful widows, pensive prisoners,
> and deposed kings; to those whose fortune runs
> back, and whose spirits mutiny; unto such death
> is a redeemer, and the grave a place for retiredness and rest.

> These wait upon the shore of death, and waft
> unto him to draw near, wishing above all others
> to see his star, that they might be led to his place;
> wooing the remorseless sisters to wind down the
> watch of their life, and to break them off before
> the hour.

This essay is, one may think, his friendliest; but he rarely appeals so directly to the emotions, preferring to keep his style matter-of-fact.

His essays have large titles: they are "Of Truth," "Of Envy," "Of Wisdom," and so on; but his later ones are less abstract, dealing with such things as houses, gardens, the law, and a dozen matters of our daily lives, though sometimes they engage such abstract matters as, for instance, anger. The style is not difficult, but you must pay attention since his thought is very close-packed; you cannot afford to miss anything. He is still popular, because, however aloof he may seem, he every now and then comes close to our own feelings: friendship "redoubleth joys, and cutteth griefs in halves: for there is no man that imparteth his joys to his friend, but he joyeth the more; and no man that imparteth his griefs to his friend, but he grieveth the less." It must be confessed, however, that he is unduly hard on love!—though he is very wise on marriage, and on children and their education. As a good son of the Renaissance he believes in the greatness of man, saying in his essay "Of Parents and Children," "The perpetuity by generation is common to beasts; but memory, merit, and noble works, are proper to men." You find that he does not care for self-seekers, men whose thoughts are always concerned for their own good, and he is sharp on them: "Wisdom for a man's self is, in many branches thereof, a depraved thing: it is the wisdom of rats, that will be sure to leave a house somewhat before it fall." He has no use for pedantry, for the pride of barren book-knowledge: "Studies serve for delight, for ornament, and for ability. . . . Crafty men contemn studies, simple men admire them, and wise men use them." And he adds, "Some books are to be tasted, others to be swallowed, and some few to be chewed and digested." His essays belong to the last class—"to be read wholly, and with diligence and attention." Then they become invigorating and delightful.

About the same time that Bacon was writing, two other popular forms made their appearance, forms which were later to become fused with the essay, to relieve its purely thoughtful content—a kind of yeast in the dough—and to make us look at our fellow-creatures. First we may take what we might call the 'descriptive piece,' sometimes combined with conversations and stories: we can take as a fair sample of this kind of writing the works of Nicolas Breton (1548?-1625?), who may have been a relation of Bacon's. Among his many entertaining works, the one which concerns us most here is his *Fantastics* (1626), which has descriptions of the seasons, the months, and the hours of the day. A very short one, "Seven of the Clock," will give an idea of what he was trying to do, namely to give you the feel of life at any particular time or season by describing what was going on, with all its variety of bustle and noise:

> It is now the seventh hour, and time begins to set the world hard to work: the milk-maids in their dairy to their butter and their cheese, the ploughmen to their ploughs and their harrows in the field: the scholars to their lessons, the lawyers to their cases, the merchants to their accounts, shop-men to 'What lack you?,' and every trade to his business. Oh 'tis a world to see how life leaps about the limbs of the healthful; none but finds something to do: the wise, to study, the strong, to labour: the Fantastic, to make love: the poet, to make verses: the player, to con his part: and the musician to try his note: every one

in his quality, and according to his condition, sets himself to some exercise, either of the body, or the mind. And therefore since it is a time of much labour, and great use, I will thus briefly conclude of it: I hold it the enemy of idleness, and employer of industry. *Farewell.*

As Breton wrote them, such things are isolated pieces; but they soon became absorbed in the body of the essay, merged in the general flow of consciousness of the reader. The other form which was to lend an enormous amount of colour to the essay was the 'character,' a form which goes back a long way in literary history, to Theophrastus, who lived about three hundred years before Christ. Character writing was extremely popular in the early seventeenth century; many poets and playwrights tried their hands at it (there were, for instance, the Overbury *Characters* of 1614, by Overbury, Webster and others); but the most famous collection is that of John Earle, (1601?-1665), later Bishop of Worcester and then of Salisbury, whose *Micro-cosmography, or a Piece of the World Discovered* was first published in 1628. He said that his characters were written "especially for his private recreation, to pass away the time in the country," and they read so easily that one may well believe this to be true. Earle amused himself by drawing spirited pen-pictures of a large number of such people as he met casually and could imagine more about: a grave divine, a drunkard, a reserved man, a shark, a plain country fellow, a pot-poet, a surgeon, a contemplative man, a shy precise hypocrite, a cook. He wrote in short, sharp sentences, making types out of personalities. Here, for example, is part of "A Mere Alderman":

> He is venerable in his gown, more in his beard, wherewith he sets not forth so much his own, as the face of a city. You must look on him as one of the town gates, and consider him not as a body, but a corporation.

All the time he displays a certain critical wit, which becomes tiring after a while, but is enlivening in small snatches. "A plain country fellow is one that manures his ground well, but lets himself lie fallow and untilled." It cannot be said that the future bishop was full of the milk of human kindness; most of his characters are satirically drawn, but sometimes he is more humane and tender:

> A good old man is the best of antiquity, and which we may with least vanity admire. . . . The next door of death sads him not, but he expects it calmly as his turn in Nature: and fears more his recoiling back to childishness than dust.

This sort of writing became a common part of the essay: Earle's figures are the ancestors of Sir Roger de Coverley, Will Wimble, and scores of others; but the descendants came to be typical personalities rather than the abstract types the earlier writers aimed at presenting to the reader.

In the later half of the seventeenth century we find yet other elements creeping into the essay to give it its complete form; or perhaps, not so much new elements as variants of older ones, made easier, more likeable, more friendly. Instead of the philosophic epigram we find musing contemplation; instead of a statement implying finality, we get discussion of a general idea. These two ingredients are best represented in the writings of Abraham Cowley (1618-1667) and of Sir William Temple (1628-1699). These new elements do not stand out clearly separated, as though the two writers were deliberately importing some new discovery, but they are mingled, seeming to enter in through a natural process of evolution. The essays of these two men approximate to the essay as we know it, but the form is not yet fully fleshed.

Cowley's *Several Discourses by Way of Essays* (1668) seem very odd to us, being partly written in verse, and always concluding with poetry. Cowley is the intimate essayist . . . , nearer to Montaigne, to whom he sometimes refers, than he is to Bacon. He has nothing very new to say, but if his wisdom is largely drawn from the ancients, he divagates upon such stock themes as the deceit of ambition, the servitude of greatness and riches, and so on, with the conviction of a man who had been involved in great affairs, mixed with famous men, and had found that such a life was not one for him. They are personal, not abstract. He tells us in his "Essay of Myself":

> I met with several great persons, whom I liked very well, but could not perceive that any part of their greatness was to be liked or desired, no more than I would be glad, or content to be in a storm, though I saw many ships which rid safely, and bravely in it. A storm would not agree with my stomach, if it did with my courage.

Thus when he writes so charmingly about the delight of gardens, one knows that he himself is a gardener, whereas one is pretty certain that Bacon had never plied a hoe. Moreover Cowley is such pleasant reading because wherever he can he uses the homely image; he doesn't challenge your thought or argue with you, but makes you feel all the time how pleasant it is to agree with him, especially as he brings large ideas to the test of here and now. So he begins his essay on "The Shortness of Life" by asking:

> If you should see a man who were to cross from Dover to Calais, run about very busy and solicitous, and trouble himself many weeks before in making provisions for his voyage, would you commend him for a cautious and discreet person, or laugh at him for a timorous and impertinent coxcomb?

And he draws out the obvious moral without being portentous about it.

Cowley is, perhaps, our first really friendly essayist; he never pretends to be more enlightened or more exquisite in feeling than the average man, and he asks you to share his shy and rather long-winded jokes:

> The best kind of glory, no doubt, is that which is reflected from honesty, as was the glory of Cato and Aristides, but it was harmful to them both, and is seldom beneficial to any man whilst he lives. What it is to him after his death I cannot say, because I love not philosophy merely notional and conjectural, and no man who has made the experiment has been so kind as to come back to inform us. ("Of Obscurity.")

Temple, on the other hand, was plainly fond of conjectural

philosophy, and as a successful man of affairs who had been a great ambassador, liked to have notions about how things worked. Like Bacon, he attempted to bring the findings of philosophy and the discoveries of science into relation with life as we live it. Where Cowley tries to make you muse gently, Temple invites you to think rather more strenuously, about history, about Confucius, about civilisation generally: he liked the broad sweep, but he wrote for those who, as he did, judge a book for the pleasure it gives them rather than for the instruction it affords. Lamb called his style "plain natural chit chat, written in his elbow chair and undress." His gentle pessimism is attractive, best phrased perhaps at the conclusion of what is probably his best-known essay "Of Poetry," with which he brackets music " . . . Happy those that content themselves with these [pleasures], or any other so easy and so innocent; and do not trouble the world, or other men, because they cannot be quiet themselves, though nobody hurts them! When all is done, human life is, at the greatest and the best, but like a froward child, that must be played with and humoured a little to keep it quiet till it falls asleep, and then the care is over." (pp. 10-16)

> *Bonamy Dobrée, "The Essay Takes Shape," in his* English Essayists, *Collins, 1946, pp. 10-16.*

THE ESSAY IN THE EIGHTEENTH CENTURY

Edwin W. Bowen

[*Bowen was an American educator and critic. In the excerpt below, he offers an historical and critical overview of the essay's rise to prominence in the eighteenth century.*]

The essay was defined by Dr. Johnson as "a loose sally of the mind; an irregular, indigested piece; not a regular and orderly composition." This definition furnishes an accurate description of the periodical essay, which had its origin in the eighteenth century and became so popular a form of literature. Probably it was the contemporary essay that the lexicographer had in mind when he gave his definition. The term is still used in this sense, though it is also used to include a thorough and exhaustive treatment of a subject. It is the purpose of this paper to give, not a complete or full treatment of the periodical essay in the eighteenth century, but rather a brief sketch of its rise and its development in the hands of its leading practitioners during the period named.

It is presumably safe to consider Montaigne the father of the modern essay. Certainly he seems to have been the first modern practitioner of the literary art, practiced in ancient times by Seneca and Plutarch in their ethical and religious reflections. As a critic has observed, Montaigne was the first philosopher in an easy-chair. But difficult would be the task to trace step by step the influence of the French philosopher on English literature, and I do not propose here to attempt so minute an investigation. Suffice it to state that Montaigne's essays are said to have been diligently read by Bacon; but to what extent he was influenced by them, it were impossible to determine. Indeed, while, by the style and matter of his essays, Bacon may, in a certain sense, be regarded as a pioneer of the essay form, still he is clearly not entitled to rank as the inventor of the periodical essay. Dryden can perhaps offer a better claim to this distinction; for, though he wrote no formal essays, yet by his wholesome influence upon English prose, and by the literary criticisms of his prefaces, he did quite as much as, if not more than, Bacon in preparing the way for the form of the essay.

There existed originally a certain relation, in subject-matter at least, between the periodical essay and the drama. The relation concerns, however, only one phase of the drama—namely, the comedy of manners. When comedy came to be neglected and ceased to be presented on the stage, the public seemed to crave some form of literary entertainment that should take the place of comedy in reflecting contemporary manners. This followed as a natural sequence from the change that had taken place in social life during and immediately after the Restoration. Consequently, in the reign of Queen Anne the essay undertook to supply this demand, "to judiciously season culture with the requisite spice of scandal, and to exhibit the foibles of the time with a humor that should not be impure." As a result there sprang into existence such brilliant though short-lived periodicals as the *Tatler* and *Spectator,* the like of which had never been before. Their very names are suggestive of their character: they observed and gossiped—in a word, they criticised the foibles of the times, contemporary manners. Here then without any doubt we have the origin of the periodical essay; and the founders of these famous periodicals were Joseph Addison and Richard Steele.

There is another aspect of the problem which needs to be considered in tracing the origin of the periodical essay. It has just been suggested in the preceding paragraph. It is the relation of the essay to the press. To be sure, one must be on one's guard on this ground, lest the inviting problem of the history of the press lead one far afield. Only the briefest reference to this matter can here be made.

Three days after Queen Anne ascended the throne appeared the first regular daily newspaper, the *Daily Courant.* During the succeeding year (1703), Daniel Defoe, author of the immortal *Robinson Crusoe,* founded, within the walls of Newgate prison, an influential political newspaper which he called the *Review.* (It was not, however, a daily.) This paper had more effect in shaping the form and character of the nascent essay than any other of the many ephemeral newspapers of those times. But Defoe's journal, like other mushroom papers of his day, was not destined to a long existence, and ceased to appear after the passage of the Stamp Act imposing a penny a sheet. This chilling act, in the jesting language of the *Spectator,* produced a general "fall of the leaf." It is worthy of note, however, that in this *Review* of Defoe's, which lived only a decade, some are inclined to see the prototype of the *Tatler.* But if Defoe's *Review* can be considered the *Tatler in posse,* it most assuredly was not the *Tatler in esse.* The

motive that called the *Review* into being and fostered it was primarily a political affair. Yet it is true that Defoe read the signs of the times, and yielded so far to the pressure of the moment as to establish a column which he called the "Scandalous Club."

Now, it is quite within the range of the possible that Steele may have taken his cue from Defoe, and gotten from the "Scandalous Club" the suggestion for "using club life as a suitable framework for his essays." But there is a vast difference between the essays of Defoe and those of Steele. Defoe's essays lack that wit, gentle humor, and graceful ease which are conspicuous characteristics of Addison's and Steele's papers in the *Tatler* and the *Spectator.* Defoe had a different conception of an essay. His notion of an essay was that of a hastily written article upon some subject of passing interest. It never occurred to him to present the thought in the very best literary form at his command. Not regarding the essay as essentially literature, he did not take the pains to give his essays a creditable degree of finish and style. This he did for his novels, and thus became the author of the first great English novel. It follows, then, that Defoe's claim to be classed as the founder of the modern essay reposes on no basis of fact. This credit belongs to Richard Steele.

In April, 1709, the initial number of the *Tatler* appeared under the editorship of Isaac Bickerstaff, Steele's adopted pseudonym. The following division of its contents was arranged by the editor: "All accounts of gallantry, pleasure, and entertainment shall be under the article of White's Chocolate House; poetry under that of Will's Coffee-House; learning under the title of Grecian; foreign and domestic news you will have from St. James's Coffee-House; and what else I shall on any other subject offer shall be dated from my own apartment."

One doubtless notices with some degree of curiosity the repetition of "coffee-house" in the above announcement. This is significant as pointing out the prominence of the coffee-house in the social life of Queen Anne's time. Indeed, the periodical essay is very intimately connected in its history with club life. The clubs were the *rendezvous* of the men of letters, where literary gossip was exchanged. As Lobban well observes in the introduction to his *English Essays:*

> It was eminently natural for the early essayists, when they were on an outlook for a simple device by which to give some degree of unity to their loose sallies, to avail themselves of this predominating social feature. The atmosphere of the coffee-house pervaded the whole of the literature of the reign, and affected it in many obvious ways. Both Defoe and Swift conceived the idea of an English academy, and the coffee-house to a certain extent realized the conception. In the latter days of Johnson this becomes more apparent, but even in Queen Anne's time the literary taste of the town was almost entirely directed by the judgments of the chief coffee-house dictators. The first half of the eighteenth century witnessed a vast improvement in the manners and customs of society, a reformation in effecting which the essay was not the least powerful factor; but at the same time it is indubitable that

the coffee-house, and not the home, was the center of social life, and that the former was regarded as a kind of happy compromise between Restoration profligacy and Puritan domesticity.

When the *Tatler* began to appear curiosity was on tiptoe to identify the author of the papers. It is said that even Addison did not suspect Steele's authorship till the fifth number. As for the journal itself, it was a phenomenal success from the very start, and was far in advance of anything of the kind ever before attempted. Steele soon enlisted the active coöperation of Addison in his new enterprise, and the eighteenth number is from the latter's deft and graceful pen. But the *Tatler,* like all its predecessors from the periodical press of those times, was short-lived, being discontinued in 1711, after it had attained to its two hundred and seventy-first number. Of these two hundred and seventy-one numbers, Steele was the author of one hundred and eighty-eight, Addison of forty-two, and both joint authors of thirty-six. The remaining few were written by Hughes, a clever minor author of the day.

Steele seems to have been made of coarser clay than Addison. Steele's intellect was not so refined as Addison's; yet the former was of a more emotional nature than the latter, who appears to have been somewhat phlegmatic and cold. Indeed, it is Steele's prevailing tenderness of heart that serves as a touchstone to reveal his authorship in the *Tatler* papers. He is really one of the most pathetic of English writers. His style, too, as being less correct than Addison's, and sometimes even ungrammatical, is a good test of his authorship. He conceived the idea that, writing in the character of a tattler, he ought consistently to affect a certain "incorrectness of style and an air of common speech." His matter as well as his manner is much more extravagant and less elegant than is Addison's. In his own words: "The elegance, purity, and correctness in Addison's writings were not so much my purpose," said he, "as, in any intelligible manner I could, to rally all those singularities of human life, through the different professions and characters in it, which obstruct anything that was truly good and great."

In the dedication of the first collected papers of the *Tatler* to Arthur Maynwaring, Steele acknowledges his purpose "to publish a paper which shall observe upon the manners of the pleasurable as well as the busy part of mankind." Here, then, is stated Steele's avowed intention of establishing a paper which, through its articles, should exhibit contemporary manners. Now these articles were the essays which Steele himself and his collaborator contributed to the columns of the *Tatler.* Consequently we find the essay, in its very inception, used as an instrument for the exhibition of the manners and customs of contemporary social life. This is generally true of the periodical essay in the eighteenth century.

Two months after the suspension of the *Tatler* another joint enterprise of still more pith was projected by Addison and Steele. This was the famous *Spectator,* the first number of which appeared in March, 1711. The success of this journal was assured from the start. The paper was announced to appear daily, and to contain the reflections and impressions of the members of an imaginary club, of which "Mr. Spectator" was the soul and center. The purpose of this paper, as Addison boasted, was to bring "philosophy out of closets, libraries, schools, and colleges, to dwell in clubs and assemblies, at tea tables and coffee-houses." The paper continued to appear till December, 1712, when it was suspended; but it was afterwards revived, in 1714. It contained five hundred and fifty-five numbers, of which two hundred and thirty-six were from the pen of Steele, and a larger number from the pen of Addison; one, "The Messiah," from Pope; and the remainder from the minor authors of the day. The most famous character in these papers was the Worcestershire knight, Sir Roger de Coverley, who was the creation of Addison's inventive genius. Addison also contributed frequent critiques on *Paradise Lost,* on the opera, tragedy, and other topics. In the five hundred and seventeenth number he killed the amiable knight Sir Roger, as he said, "that nobody else might murder him."

The crowning feature of the *Spectator* papers was the character of Sir Roger, the English country gentleman. He is the hero of the book. I said a moment ago that we are indebted to Addison for the invention of this character. This is generally conceded. But the fact is, the knight is the product of the inventive genius of both Addison and Steele, for the former developed him after the latter had sketched him. Nor, indeed, do the two authors seem to have drawn his character consistent throughout. For example, Steele in his original sketch describes Sir Roger as having been formerly a fine gentleman who was acquainted with town life; Addison, on the other hand, represents him as a rather plain country squire who had come up to the great metropolis, and visits the chief places of interest there—the theater, the Temple, the Abbey, Vauxhall, etc. But despite this slight incongruity, arising, no doubt, from differences of conception, the character of the old knight is a most attractive sketch and thoroughly natural. Addison is at his best in his delineation of the knight's conduct at these places of attraction. Here, as nowhere else, we see Addison's humor, his subtle wit, his delicate grace, and withal his admirable lightness of touch.

If any one quality of Addison's were to be mentioned as being predominant in these essays, it would probably be his simplicity. Indeed, this quality is the peculiar merit of his prose, which is generally taken as a model. His style is thus described by Johnson, the imperious literary authority of his century:

> His [Addison's] prose is the model of the middle style; on grave subjects not formal, on light occasions not groveling, pure without scrupulosity, and exact without elaboration; always equable, always easy, without glowing words or pointed sentences. Addison never deviates from his track to snatch a grace; he seeks no ambitious ornaments, and tries no hazardous innovations. His page is always luminous, but never blazes with unexpected splendor. It was apparently his principal endeavor to avoid all harshness and severity of diction; he is therefore sometimes verbose in his transitions and connections, and sometimes descends too much to the language of conversation; yet if his language had been less idiomatical, it might have lost somewhat of its genu-

ine Anglicism. What he attempted, he performed; he is never feeble, and he did not wish to be energetic; he is never rapid, and he never stagnates. His sentences have neither studied amplitude nor affected brevity; his periods, though not diligently rounded, are voluble and easy. Whoever wishes to attain an English style, familiar but not coarse, and elegant but not ostentatious, must give his days and nights to the volumes of Addison.

Addison's style had a stimulating influence upon the development of English prose. Despite De Quincey's strictures upon Addison's superficiality, his essays, by reason of their admirable style and matter, produced the wholesome effect of diffusing a taste for learning and of quickening the feeble interest then existing in literary criticism. However, in this connection it would be better not to speak of Addison alone, but of the joint influence of Addison and Steele. Contemporary observers of manners bear evidence as to the moral influence exerted by the essays of these two mild reformers, affirming that many of the little immoralities and questionable social practices were put under the ban as a result of their criticism. "It is impossible," says Gay, "to conceive the effect Steele's writings have had on the town; how many thousand follies they have either quite banished or given a very great check to; . . . how entirely they have convinced our fops and young fellows of the value and advantage of learning." Such was the influence from a stylistic as well as a moral point of view of the essays of the *Spectator.*

The *Spectator* was succeeded by the *Guardian,* the first number of which appeared on the 12th of March, 1713. With the hundred and seventy-sixth number this paper, like its predecessors, suspended publication. Addison and Steele were likewise the chief contributors to this periodical. Subsequently the *Guardian* was reissued as the *Englishman* under the sole management of Steele, and conducted mainly as a political organ. But this reached only its fifty-seventh number, when it was discontinued, to be followed in quick succession by two other sheets, the *Lover* and the *Reader.* These in turn were doomed to early suspension. Meanwhile Addison published independently a paper of his own—the *Freeholder*—which was brought to an end with its fifty-fifth number, in 1716. It was through this channel that Addison gave to the world his interesting character of the Tory fox hunter. But political passion had now come to run so high that the essays published in the last-named journals degenerated into mere diatribes and caricatures. Addison and Steele threw themselves, without restraint and with all the warmth of their natures, into the political affairs of the times; and, sad to relate, the old friends, if they did not actually quarrel, at all events became estranged from one another. This estrangement Steele, with characteristic generosity of heart, bitterly lamented upon the premature death of Addison, which occurred shortly afterwards, in 1719.

It is quite evident that the periodical essay, through the zealous labors of Addison and Steele, had now become established as a definite form of English literature. But these authors not only invented the periodical essay and gave it a foothold in the literature; by the perfecting of their art they carried the essay to its acme of development. After their death the essay, it is true, was practiced, but chiefly by minor writers and imitators, and after awhile it seems to have fallen into disfavor with the public.

It remained for Johnson in the Georgian era to attempt a resuscitation of the periodical essay, so popular in Queen Anne's time. The result of his earnest effort was the establishment of the *Rambler.* This paper was first issued in 1750, and inaugurated a new epoch for the essay. Johnson's purpose, says Boswell, was "to come forth in the character for which he was eminently qualified—a majestic teacher of moral and religious wisdom." "The *Tatler, Spectator,* and *Guardian,*" continues the biographer of the great Cham, "were the last of the kind published in England, which had stood the test of a long trial; and such an interval had now elapsed since their publication as made him justly think that to many of his readers this form of instruction would in some degree have the advantage of novelty." The *Rambler* was therefore projected as a successor to the *Spectator,* of which it was designed to be an imitation. But Johnson's ponderosity was far removed from Addison's graceful elegance and lightness of touch, and was likely to pall on the public taste. It is not, therefore, surprising that the *Rambler* suspended publication in 1752, after a two years' existence. Johnson had probably grown weary in his effort to revive the public interest in the essay and to rival in brilliance of execution the famous papers of the *Spectator,* and consequently the death of his wife furnished him a suitable opportunity for bringing the *Rambler* to a close.

Johnson wrote all the numbers of the *Rambler* except five, which were contributed by several of his friends. At first it was not known who the author of the *Rambler* was; but at length Johnson's heavy, pedantic style betrayed his identity, and his authorship was no longer a secret. The publisher, in order to make Johnson more hopeful when the *clientèle* of the paper had begun to diminish appreciably, remarked that "the encouragement as to sale" was not in proportion "to the raptures expressed by the people who did read it." Indeed, the great dictator himself had the candor to confess that the *Rambler* was "too wordy." Johnson was not at his best in the *Rambler* papers, though he devoted much time and attention to their preparation. But while not happy as a whole, some of the papers, as, for instance, "Literary Courage" and the "Advantages of Living in a Garret," are quite readable. The latter is far the happier, the former being in the author's usual ponderous vein.

Johnson did not fail in the *Rambler* because he did not possess many of the essential qualities of an essayist. Humor, wit, judgment, and a rare knowledge of human nature—all these admirable qualities he had in no small degree. But the great moralist possessed, in addition, a pompous mannerism of which he was never quite able to divest himself. It was this that counteracted his other excellent qualities. It was this "sonorous grandiloquence" that Goldsmith had in mind when he said in jest that, if Johnson had occasion to make little fishes talk, he would make them talk like whales. Addison somewhere says: "No periodical writer, who always maintains his gravity

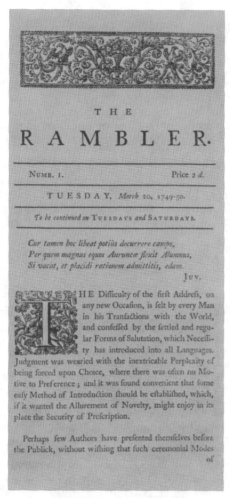

The first edition of Samuel Johnson's The Rambler.

and does not sometimes sacrifice to the Graces, must expect to keep in vogue any considerable time." It was just this bit of wisdom that Johnson never learned. He would never unbend, but was always on his dignity. He could never sacrifice to the Graces, and this is the secret of the failure of the *Rambler.*

However, simple justice demands that we should add that the great moralist was happier in his next venture, the *Idler.* These papers were published from 1758 to 1760, and they show more ease and lightness of touch than Johnson's early essays. These *Idlers* contain the author's character sketch of Dick Minim, and, as Mr. Saintsbury observes, "Johnson as an essayist is most happy when he analyzes a character, in the manner of La Bruyère, mingling criticism with narrative." Nor is Johnson so verbose or so pedantic in his *Idler* papers. His sesquipedalians he uses here very sparingly, as he does also in his *Lives of the Poets.* Prof. Minto maintains that in this latter work Johnson's style is not so Latinized as the average style of the present day, and that the proportion of Latin words here is not above half so great as in a leader of the London *Times.* Whether this be true or not, I am not prepared to

say; but the style of the *Idlers* and of the *Lives of the Poets* seems far less Johnsonese.

Whatever the failings and shortcomings of Johnson as an essayist may have been, assuredly his efforts at the revival of the essay must be pronounced an eminent success. Swarms of imitators sprang into existence after him, and this period of the history of the essay almost rivaled that of the Queen Anne in popularity. But most of the essayists of the Georgian period were mere imitators of the Johnsonese style, and even Johnson by no means maintained the tradition of excellence set by the founders. Indeed, the essay seems to have reached its high-water mark for the century under Addison and Steele.

Among the host of imitators of the Johnsonese style (they imitated the dictator's mannerism, but lacked his vigor and force) was one writer who was destined to break with the prevailing fashion and write according to the dictates of his own refined taste. This was Oliver Goldsmith. In that age of magnificence of phrase and swelling bombast he stands out as a conspicuous exponent of an easy, graceful, and almost faultless prose style. Abandoning the periodic sentence as unsuited to the essay, he adhered tenaciously to the loose sentence of Addison. It is true that in his formative period Goldsmith did conform to the dominant fashion of his day and "masqueraded in Johnsonian buckram." This was but natural, especially in view of the friendly and even intimate relation existing between the great literary autocrat and the improvident, good-natured Goldsmith, who as yet was a mere Grub Street hack writer. But Goldsmith soon abandoned his practice of imitation, a sin of his youth, and blazed out a path for himself. In learning to form his style he went back to Dryden, Temple, and Addison. Hence it came about that he developed in his essays that delicate, graceful style which commands universal admiration and is to-day held up as a model. A contemporary estimate of his genius is found in the epitaph (written by Johnson) upon his monument in Westminster Abbey: *"Nullum quod tetigit non ornavit"*— There was nothing he touched that he did not adorn.

Goldsmith continued the early tradition of the periodical essay as a criticism upon contemporary manners. For under the disguise of "Chinese Letters"—a series of essays which he contributed to Newbery's *Public Ledger*— he "assumed the person of a philosophic Chinaman, and criticised certain English customs and manners, such as the absurd form of dress, the practice of charging admission to the tombs of great men, the abuses in the administration of justice, and so forth." Goldsmith was well fitted by temperament and education to assume the point of view of a foreigner and to satirize, in his gentle way, the peculiar manners and customs of his nation, which, in his judgment, needed reforming. By nature a man of broad sympathies, he liked to regard himself as a citizen of the world. There was nothing insular about him—no national prejudice in his constitution. His judgment therefore was never warped by his narrowness of view, as was Johnson's. Goldsmith was so pleased with the cosmopolitan spirit of his essays that, when he subsequently collected them, he published them separately under the title of *The Citizen of the World.*

The conception of the "Chinese Letters" was by no means original. It had been adopted before, with much success, by Montesquieu in his "Persian Letters," and with these Goldsmith must have been acquainted, if we may judge from a reference he makes to them in an article he published in the *Monthly Review*. Moreover, Horace Walpole had published a pamphlet consisting of "A Letter from Xo Ho, a Chinese Philosopher in London, to his friend Lien Chi, at Pekin;" and Mr. Austin Dobson has endeavored to show that this was the source whence the author of the "Chinese Letters" borrowed his idea. The "Chinese Letters" are marked by their accurate criticism, their delicate satire, and their gentle humor. The foreign air which the author tried to impart to the "Letters" does not count for much, only to give them a thin disguise. Lien Chi Altangi, writing to his friend Fum Hoam, in Pekin, does not make the comments on European civilization which you would expect an Oriental to make. Lien Chi's strictures are rather those of an Englishman who sees much in his nation to inveigh against and to be reformed. I venture to quote for illustration a brief passage from the essay on "National Prejudice." Its humor is admirable and the satire is quite delicate:

> The English seem as silent as the Japanese, yet vainer than the inhabitants of Siam. Upon my arrival I attributed that reserve to modesty, which I now find has its origin in pride. Condescend to address them first, and you are sure of their acquaintance; stoop to flattery, and you conciliate their friendship and esteem. They bear hunger, cold, fatigue, and all miseries of life without shrinking; danger only calls forth their fortitude; they even exult in calamity; but contempt is what they cannot bear. An Englishman fears contempt more than death; he often flies to death as a refuge from its pressure, and dies when he fancies the world has ceased to esteem him.
>
> Pride seems the source not only of their national vices but of their national virtues also. An Englishman is taught to love the king as his friend, but to acknowledge no other master than the laws which himself has contributed to enact. He despises those nations who, that one may be free, are all content to be slaves; who first lift a tyrant into terror, and then shrink under his power as if delegated from Heaven. Liberty is echoed in all their assemblies, and thousands are ready to offer up their lives for the sound, though perhaps not one of all the number understands its meaning. The lowest mechanic, however, looks upon it as his duty to be a watchful guardian of his country's freedom, and often uses a language that might seem haughty even in the mouth of the great emperor who traces his ancestry to the moon.

(pp. 12-25)

As Addison and Steele in the *Spectator* created the character of Sir Roger de Coverley for our enjoyment, so Goldsmith, in his "Chinese Letters," brought into the world, as heirs of his invention, two extremely entertaining characters in his Man in Black and his Beau Tibbs. The Man in Black, with his helping hand and generous heart, is said to be a portrait of the happy-go-lucky, kind-hearted Oliver Goldsmith himself, who could never find it in his nature to turn a deaf ear to a call for need as long as he had a guinea in his pocket; and when his guineas failed and he was thrust into prison for debt, he could, even in these depressing surroundings, "turn a sentence on the humorous side of starvation." His own prodigal generosity seems reproduced in the Man in Black. When cast into prison he jestingly remarks that he is "now on one side of the door, and those who are unconfined are on the other; and that is all the difference between them." It was probably with such a stroke of wit that the real Goldsmith used to console himself when confined in no imaginary prison. His portrait of Beau Tibbs, that "prince of shabby-genteel gentlemen," who lodged in the first floor down the chimney, as he facetiously expressed it, is of its kind unsurpassed.

The essay on "A City Night Piece" is probably Goldsmith's tenderest and most pathetic production. Indeed, there are but few more touching pictures in English literature. As he contemplates the sad scenes of human misery in this picture, misery which he is unable to relieve, he cries out:

> Why, why was I born a man, and yet see the sufferings of wretches I cannot relieve? Poor houseless creatures! the world will give you reproaches, but will not give you relief. The slightest misfortunes of the great, the most imaginary uneasiness of the rich, are aggravated with all the power of eloquence, and held up to engage our attention and sympathetic sorrow. The poor weep unheeded, persecuted by every subordinate species of tyranny, and every law which gives others security becomes an enemy to them. Why was this heart of mine formed with so much sensibility; or why was not my fortune adapted to its impulse? Tenderness, without a capacity of relieving, only makes the man who feels it more wretched than the object which sues for assistance.

When we read this passage we feel that the author is unbosoming his own heart, wrung by the anguish of others. We feel that his breast was full of the milk of human kindness. It is this feeling which endears him to the world and has won for him its gratitude. Here lies the secret, in his deep humanity, of the perennial charm of his essays.

After the death of Goldsmith the essay began again to decline, just as it had done before upon the death of Addison and Steele. Not that writers were lacking in the last quarter of the eighteenth century who endeavored to continue it. Essayists there were, but they did not possess the essential qualities, ease and grace, and were therefore unable to maintain the standard of excellence set by Goldsmith. Other forms of literature, consequently, supplanted the essay in public favor. Fiction now took the lead. The tendency toward character-sketching has already been noticed in the history of the essay. This tendency soon developed into a distinct branch of literature and became merged into the novel, which now began to absorb the public interest. The taste of the reading public was completely captivated by the novel. Even Goldsmith, in his day, saw this and so far yielded to the demand of the age as to write his charming story of *The Vicar of Wakefield.*

Thus at the close of the eighteenth century the essay was eclipsed by the rising novel. However, during this century it had been the most enduring and characteristic form of literature, and had engaged the genius of the best writers. It was again revived, in the first quarter of the following century, by Hazlitt, and by Lamb in his inimitable *Essays of Elia.* But it seems to have lost, in the nineteenth century, its distinctive feature of being a criticism of contemporary manners. It has now, at the end of the century and beginning of a new, become almost altogether associated with literary criticism. It is, however, not within the scope of the present study to extend the survey beyond the eighteenth century. (pp. 26-7)

> *Edwin W. Bowen, "The Essay in the Eighteenth Century," in* The Sewanee Review, *Vol. X, No. 1, Winter, 1902, pp. 12-27.*

William Hazlitt

[*Hazlitt, an English critic and journalist, was one of the most renowned commentators of the Romantic age. He is best known for highly descriptive criticism in which he stressed that no motives beyond judgment and analysis are necessary on the part of the critic. Though he wrote on many diverse subjects, Hazlitt's most important critical achievements are his typically Romantic interpretation of characters from William Shakespeare's plays, influenced by the German critic August Wilhelm Schlegel, and his revival of interest in such Elizabethan dramatists as John Webster, Thomas Haywood, and Thomas Dekker. In the excerpt below from a lecture originally published in 1819, Hazlitt comments on the debt of the periodical essayists to Michel de Montaigne and assesses the strengths and weaknesses of essays published in such periodicals as the* Tatler *and the* Spectator.]

I now come to speak of that sort of writing which has been so successfully cultivated in this country by our periodical Essayists, and which consists in applying the talents and resources of the mind to all that mixed mass of human affairs, which, though not included under the head of any regular art, science, or profession, falls under the cognizance of the writer, and 'comes home to the business and bosoms of men.' *Quicquid agunt homines nostri farrago libelli,* is the general motto of this department of literature. It does not treat of minerals or fossils, of the virtues of plants, or the influence of planets; it does not meddle with forms of belief, or systems of philosophy, nor launch into the world of spiritual existences; but it makes familiar with the world of men and women, records their actions, assigns their motives, exhibits their whims, characterises their pursuits in all their singular and endless variety, ridicules their absurdities, exposes their inconsistencies, 'holds the mirror up to nature, and shews the very age and body of the time its form and pressure;' takes minutes of our dress, air, looks, words, thoughts, and actions; shews us what we are, and what we are not; plays the whole game of human life over before us, and by making us enlightened spectators of its many-coloured scenes, enables us (if possible) to become tolerably reasonable agents in the one

in which we have to perform a part. 'The act and practic part of life is thus made the mistress of our theorique.' It is the best and most natural course of study. It is in morals and manners what the experimental is in natural philosophy, as opposed to the dogmatical method. It does not deal in sweeping clauses of proscription and anathema, but in nice distinctions and liberal constructions. It makes up its general accounts from details, its few theories from many facts. It does not try to prove all black or all white as it wishes, but lays on the intermediate colours, (and most of them not unpleasing ones,) as it finds them blended with 'the web of our life, which is of a mingled yarn, good and ill together.' It inquires what human life is and has been, to shew what it ought to be. It follows it into courts and camps, into town and country, into rustic sports or learned disputations, into the various shades of prejudice or ignorance, of refinement or barbarism, into its private haunts or public pageants, into its weaknesses and littlenesses, its professions and its practices—before it pretends to distinguish right from wrong, or one thing from another. How, indeed, should it do so otherwise?

> Quid sit pulchrum, quid turpe, quid utile, quid
> non,
> Plenius et melius Chrysippo et Crantore dicit.

The writers I speak of are, if not moral philosophers, moral historians, and that's better: or if they are both, they found the one character upon the other; their premises precede their conclusions; and we put faith in their testimony, for we know that it is true.

Montaigne was the first person who in his Essays led the way to this kind of writing among the moderns. The great merit of Montaigne then was, that he may be said to have been the first who had the courage to say as an author what he felt as a man. And as courage is generally the effect of conscious strength, he was probably led to do so by the richness, truth, and force of his own observations on books and men. He was, in the truest sense, a man of original mind, that is, he had the power of looking at things for himself, or as they really were, instead of blindly trusting to, and fondly repeating what others told him that they were. He got rid of the go-cart of prejudice and affectation, with the learned lumber that follows at their heels, because he could do without them. In taking up his pen he did not set up for a philosopher, wit, orator, or moralist, but he became all these by merely daring to tell us whatever passed through his mind, in its naked simplicity and force, that he thought any ways worth communicating. He did not, in the abstract character of an author, undertake to say all that could be said upon a subject, but what in his capacity as an inquirer after truth he happened to know about it. He was neither a pedant nor a bigot. He neither supposed that he was bound to know all things, nor that all things were bound to conform to what he had fancied or would have them to be. In treating of men and manners, he spoke of them as he found them, not according to preconceived notions and abstract dogmas; and he began by teaching us what he himself was. In criticising books he did not compare them with rules and systems, but told us what he saw to like or dislike in them. He did not take his standard of excellence 'according to an exact scale' of Aristotle, or fall out with a work that was good for any thing, because 'not one of the angles at the four corners was a right one.' He was, in a word, the first author who was not a book-maker, and who wrote not to make converts of others to established creeds and prejudices, but to satisfy his own mind of the truth of things. In this respect we know not which to be most charmed with, the author or the man. There is an inexpressible frankness and sincerity, as well as power, in what he writes. There is no attempt at imposition or concealment, no juggling tricks or solemn mouthing, no laboured attempts at proving himself always in the right, and every body else in the wrong; he says what is uppermost, lays open what floats at the top or the bottom of his mind, and deserves Pope's character of him, where he professes to

> —pour out all as plain
> As downright Shippen, or as old Montaigne.

He does not converse with us like a pedagogue with his pupil, whom he wishes to make as great a blockhead as himself, but like a philosopher and friend who has passed through life with thought and observation, and is willing to enable others to pass through it with pleasure and profit. A writer of this stamp, I confess, appears to me as much superior to a common bookworm, as a library of real books is superior to a mere book-case, painted and lettered on the outside with the names of celebrated works. As he was the first to attempt this new way of writing, so the same strong natural impulse which prompted the undertaking, carried him to the end of his career. The same force and honesty of mind which urged him to throw off the shackles of custom and prejudice, would enable him to complete his triumph over them. He has left little for his successors to achieve in the way of just and original speculation on human life. Nearly all the thinking of the two last centuries of that kind which the French denominate *morale observatrice,* is to be found in Montaigne's Essays: there is the germ, at least, and generally much more. He sowed the seed and cleared away the rubbish, even where others have reaped the fruit, or cultivated and decorated the soil to a greater degree of nicety and perfection. There is no one to whom the old Latin adage is more applicable than to Montaigne, '*Pereant isti qui ante nos nostra dixerunt.*' There has been no new impulse given to thought since his time. Among the specimens of criticisms on authors which he has left us, are those on Virgil, Ovid, and Boccaccio, in the account of books which he thinks worth reading, or (which is the same thing) which he finds he can read in his old age, and which may be reckoned among the few criticisms which are worth reading at any age.

Montaigne's Essays were translated into English by Charles Cotton, who was one of the wits and poets of the age of Charles II; and Lord Halifax, one of the noble critics of that day, declared it to be 'the book in the world he was the best pleased with.' This mode of familiar Essay-writing, free from the trammels of the schools, and the airs of professed authorship, was successfully imitated, about the same time, by Cowley and Sir William Temple, in their miscellaneous Essays, which are very agreeable and learned talking upon paper. Lord Shaftesbury, on the contrary, who aimed at the same easy, *degagé* mode of communicating his thoughts to the world, has quite spoiled his matter, which is sometimes valuable, by his manner, in which he carries a certain flaunting, flowery, figurative, flirting style of amicable condescension to the reader, to an excess more tantalising than the most starched and ridiculous formality of the age of James I. There is nothing so tormenting as the affectation of ease and freedom from affectation.

The ice being thus thawed, and the barrier that kept authors at a distance from common sense and feeling broken through, the transition was not difficult from Montaigne and his imitators, to our Periodical Essayists. These last applied the same unrestrained expression of their thoughts to the more immediate and passing scenes of life, to temporary and local matters; and in order to discharge the invidious office of *Censor Morum* more freely, and with less responsibility, assumed some fictitious and humorous disguise, which, however, in a great degree corresponded to their own peculiar habits and character. By thus concealing their own name and person under the title of the Tatler, Spectator, &c. they were enabled to inform us more fully of what was passing in the world, while the dramatic contrast and ironical point of view to which the whole is subjected, added a greater liveliness and *piquancy* to the descriptions. The philosopher and wit here commences newsmonger, makes himself master of 'the perfect spy o' th' time,' and from his various walks and turns through life, brings home little curious specimens of the humours, opinions, and manners of his contemporaries, as the botanist brings home different plants and weeds, or the mineralogist different shells and fossils, to illustrate their several theories, and be useful to mankind.

The first of these papers that was attempted in this country was set up by Steele in the beginning of the last century; and of all our periodical Essayists, the Tatler (for that was the name he assumed) has always appeared to me the most amusing and agreeable. Montaigne, whom I have proposed to consider as the father of this kind of personal authorship among the moderns, in which the reader is admitted behind the curtain, and sits down with the writer in his gown and slippers, was a most magnanimous and undisguised egotist; but Isaac Bickerstaff, Esq. was the more disinterested gossip of the two. The French author is contented to describe the peculiarities of his own mind and constitution, which he does with a copious and unsparing hand. The English journalist good-naturedly lets you into the secret both of his own affairs and those of others. A young lady, on the other side Temple Bar, cannot be seen at her glass for half a day together, but Mr. Bickerstaff takes due notice of it; and he has the first intelligence of the symptoms of the *belle* passion appearing in any young gentleman at the West-end of the town. The departures and arrivals of widows with handsome jointures, either to bury their grief in the country, or to procure a second husband in town, are punctually recorded in his pages. He is well acquainted with the celebrated beauties of the preceding age at the court of Charles II.; and the old gentleman (as he feigns himself) often grows romantic in recounting 'the disastrous strokes which his youth suffered' from the glances of their bright eyes, and their unaccountable caprices. In particular, he dwells with a secret satisfaction on the recollection of one of his mistresses, who left him for a richer rival, and whose constant reproach to her husband, on occasion of any quarrel between them, was 'I, that might have married the famous Mr. Bickerstaff, to be treated in this manner!' The club at the Trumpet consists of a set of persons almost as well worth knowing as himself. The cavalcade of the justice of the peace, the knight of the shire, the country squire, and the young gentleman, his nephew, who came to wait on him at his chambers, in such form and ceremony, seem not to have settled the order of their precedence to this hour; and I should hope that the upholsterer and his companions, who used to sun themselves in the Green Park, and who broke their rest and fortunes to maintain the balance of power in Europe, stand as fair a chance for immortality as some modern politicians. Mr. Bickerstaff himself is a gentleman and a scholar, a humourist, and a man of the world; with a great deal of nice easy *naïveté* about him. If he walks out and is caught in a shower of rain, he makes amends for this unlucky accident by a criticism on the shower in Virgil, and concludes with a burlesque copy of verses on a city-shower. He entertains us, when he dates from his own apartment, with a quotation from Plutarch, or a moral reflection; from the Grecian coffee-house with politics; and from Wills', or the Temple, with the poets and players, the beaux and men of wit and pleasure about town. In reading the pages of the *Tatler,* we seem as if suddenly carried back to the age of Queen Anne, of toupees and full-bottomed periwigs. The whole appearance of our dress and manners undergoes a delightful metamorphosis. The beaux and the belles are of a quite different species from what they are at present; we distinguish the dappers, the smarts, and the pretty fellows, as they pass by Mr. Lilly's shop-windows in the Strand; we are introduced to Betterton and Mrs. Oldfield behind the scenes; are made familiar with the persons and performances of Will Estcourt or Tom Durfey; we listen to a dispute at a tavern, on the merits of the Duke of Marlborough, or Marshal Turenne; or are present at the first rehearsal of a play by Vanbrugh, or the reading of a new poem by Mr. Pope. The privilege of thus virtually transporting ourselves to past times, is even greater than that of visiting distant places in reality. London, a hundred years ago, would be much better worth seeing than Paris at the present moment.

It will be said, that all this is to be found, in the same or a greater degree, in the *Spectator.* For myself, I do not think so; or at least, there is in the last work a much greater proportion of commonplace matter. I have, on this account, always preferred the *Tatler* to the *Spectator.* Whether it is owing to my having been earlier or better acquainted with the one than the other, my pleasure in reading these two admirable works is not in proportion to their comparative reputation. The *Tatler* contains only half the number of volumes, and, I will venture to say, nearly an equal quantity of sterling wit and sense. 'The first sprightly runnings' are there; it has more of the original spirit, more of the freshness and stamp of nature. The indications of character and strokes of humour are more true and frequent; the reflections that suggest themselves arise more from the occasion, and are less spun out into regular dissertations. They are more like the remarks which occur in sensible conversation, and less like a lecture. Something is left to the understanding of the reader. Steele seems to

have gone into his closet chiefly to set down what he observed out of doors. Addison seems to have spent most of his time in his study, and to have spun out and wire-drawn the hints, which he borrowed from Steele, or took from nature, to the utmost. I am far from wishing to depreciate Addison's talents, but I am anxious to do justice to Steele, who was, I think, upon the whole, a less artificial and more original writer. The humorous descriptions of Steele resemble loose sketches, or fragments of a comedy; those of Addison are rather comments or ingenious paraphrases on the genuine text. The characters of the club not only in the *Tatler,* but in the *Spectator,* were drawn by Steele. That of Sir Roger de Coverley is among the number. Addison has, however, gained himself immortal honour by his manner of filling up this last character. Who is there that can forget, or be insensible to, the inimitable nameless graces and varied traits of nature and of old English character in it—to his unpretending virtues and amiable weaknesses—to his modesty, generosity, hospitality, and eccentric whims—to the respect of his neighbours, and the affection of his domestics—to his wayward, hopeless, secret passion for his fair enemy, the widow, in which there is more of real romance and true delicacy, than in a thousand tales of knight-errantry—(we perceive the hectic flush of his cheek, the faltering of his tongue in speaking of her bewitching airs and 'the whiteness of her hand')—to the havoc he makes among the game in his neighbourhood—to his speech from the bench, to shew the Spectator what is thought of him in the country—to his unwillingness to be put up as a sign-post, and his having his own likeness turned into the Saracen's head—to his gentle reproof of the baggage of a gipsy that tells him 'he has a widow in his line of life'—to his doubts as to the existence of witchcraft, and protection of reputed witches—to his account of the family pictures, and his choice of a chaplain—to his falling asleep at church, and his reproof of John Williams, as soon as he recovered from his nap, for talking in sermon-time. The characters of Will. Wimble, and Will. Honeycomb are not a whit behind their friend, Sir Roger, in delicacy and felicity. The delightful simplicity and good-humoured officiousness in the one, are set off by the graceful affectation and courtly pretension in the other. How long since I first became acquainted with these two characters in the *Spectator*! What old-fashioned friends they seem, and yet I am not tired of them, like so many other friends, nor they of me! How airy these abstractions of the poet's pen stream over the dawn of our acquaintance with human life! how they glance their fairest colours on the prospect before us! how pure they remain in it to the last, like the rainbow in the evening-cloud, which the rude hand of time and experience can neither soil nor dissipate! What a pity that we cannot find the reality, and yet if we did, the dream would be over. I once thought I knew a Will. Wimble, and a Will. Honeycomb, but they turned out but indifferently; the originals in the *Spectator* still read, word for word, the same that they always did. We have only to turn to the page, and find them where we left them!—Many of the most exquisite pieces in the *Tatler,* it is to be observed, are Addison's, as the Court of Honour, and the Personification of Musical Instruments, with almost all those papers that form regular sets or series. I do not know whether the picture of the family of an old college acquaintance, in the *Tatler,* where the children run to let Mr. Bickerstaff in at the door, and where the one that loses the race that way, turns back to tell the father that he is come; with the nice gradation of incredulity in the little boy, who is got into Guy of Warwick, and the Seven Champions, and who shakes his head at the improbability of *Æsop's Fables,* is Steele's or Addison's, though I believe it belongs to the former. The account of the two sisters, one of whom held up her head higher than ordinary, from having on a pair of flowered garters, and that of the married lady who complained to the Tatler of the neglect of her husband, with her answers to some *home* questions that were put to her, are unquestionably Steele's.—If the *Tatler* is not inferior to the *Spectator* as a record of manners and character, it is superior to it in the interest of many of the stories. Several of the incidents related there by Steele have never been surpassed in the heart-rending pathos of private distress. I might refer to those of the lover and his mistress, when the theatre, in which they were, caught fire; of the bridegroom, who by accident kills his bride on the day of their marriage; the story of Mr. Eustace and his wife; and the fine dream about his own mistress when a youth. What has given its superior reputation to the *Spectator,* is the greater gravity of its pretensions, its moral dissertations and critical reasonings, by which I confess myself less edified than by other things, which are thought more lightly of. Systems and opinions change, but nature is always true. It is the moral and didactic tone of the *Spectator* which makes us apt to think of Addison (according to Mandeville's sarcasm) as 'a parson in a tie-wig.' Many of his moral Essays are, however, exquisitely beautiful and quite happy. Such are the reflections on cheerfulness, those in Westminster Abbey, on the Royal Exchange, and particularly some very affecting ones on the death of a young lady in the fourth volume. These, it must be allowed, are the perfection of elegant sermonising. His critical Essays are not so good. I prefer Steele's occasional selection of beautiful poetical passages, without any affectation of analysing their beauties, to Addison's finer-spun theories. The best criticism in the *Spectator,* that on the Cartoons of Raphael, of which Mr. Fuseli has availed himself with great spirit in his Lectures, is by Steele. I owed this acknowledgment to a writer who has so often put me in good humour with myself, and every thing about me, when few things else could, and when the tomes of casuistry and ecclesiastical history, with which the little duodecimo volumes of the *Tatler* were overwhelmed and surrounded, in the only library to which I had access when a boy, had tried their tranquillising effects upon me in vain. I had not long ago in my hands, by favour of a friend, an original copy of the quarto edition of the *Tatler,* with a list of the subscribers. It is curious to see some names there which we should hardly think of, (that of Sir Isaac Newton is among them,) and also to observe the degree of interest excited by those of the different persons, which is not determined according to the rules of the Herald's College. One literary name lasts as long as a whole race of heroes and their descendants! The *Guardian,* which followed the *Spectator,* was, as may be supposed, inferior to it.

The dramatic and conversational turn which forms the distinguishing feature and greatest charm of the *Spectator* and *Tatler,* is quite lost in the *Rambler* by Dr. Johnson.

There is no reflected light thrown on human life from an assumed character, nor any direct one from a display of the author's own. The *Tatler* and *Spectator* are, as it were, made up of notes and memorandums of the events and incidents of the day, with finished studies after nature, and characters fresh from the life, which the writer moralises upon, and turns to account as they come before him: the *Rambler* is a collection of moral Essays, or scholastic theses, written on set subjects, and of which the individual characters and incidents are merely artificial illustrations, brought in to give a pretended relief to the dryness of didactic discussion. The *Rambler* is a splendid and imposing common-place-book of general topics, and rhetorical declamation on the conduct and business of human life. In this sense, there is hardly a reflection that had been suggested on such subjects which is not to be found in this celebrated work, and there is, perhaps, hardly a reflection to be found in it which had not been already suggested and developed by some other author, or in the common course of conversation. The mass of intellectual wealth here heaped together is immense, but it is rather the result of gradual accumulation, the produce of the general intellect, labouring in the mine of knowledge and reflection, than dug out of the quarry, and dragged into the light by the industry and sagacity of a single mind. I am not here saying that Dr. Johnson was a man without originality, compared with the ordinary run of men's minds, but he was not a man of original thought or genius, in the sense in which Montaigne or Lord Bacon was. He opened no new vein of precious ore, nor did he light upon any single pebbles of uncommon size and unrivalled lustre. We seldom meet with any thing to 'give us pause;' he does not set us thinking for the first time. His reflections present themselves like reminiscences; do not disturb the ordinary march of our thoughts; arrest our attention by the stateliness of their appearance, and the costliness of their garb, but pass on and mingle with the throng of our impressions. After closing the volumes of the *Rambler,* there is nothing that we remember as a new truth gained to the mind, nothing indelibly stamped upon the memory; nor is there any passage that we wish to turn to as embodying any known principle or observation, with such force and beauty that justice can only be done to the idea in the author's own words. Such, for instance, are many of the passages to be found in Burke, which shine by their own light, belong to no class, have neither equal nor counterpart, and of which we say that no one but the author could have written them! There is neither the same boldness of design, nor mastery of execution in Johnson. In the one, the spark of genius seems to have met with its congenial matter: the shaft is sped; the forked lightning dresses up the face of nature in ghastly smiles, and the loud thunder rolls far away from the ruin that is made. Dr. Johnson's style, on the contrary, resembles rather the rumbling of mimic thunder at one of our theatres; and the light he throws upon a subject is like the dazzling effect of phosphorus, or an *ignis fatuus* of words. There is a wide difference, however, between perfect originality and perfect common-place: neither ideas nor expressions are trite or vulgar because they are not quite new. They are valuable, and ought to be repeated, if they have not become quite common; and Johnson's style both of reasoning and imagery holds the middle rank between startling novelty and vapid commonplace. Johnson has as much originality of thinking as Addison; but then he wants his familiarity of illustration, knowledge of character, and delightful humour.—What most distinguishes Dr. Johnson from other writers is the pomp and uniformity of his style. All his periods are cast in the same mould, are of the same size and shape, and consequently have little fitness to the variety of things he professes to treat of. His subjects are familiar, but the author is always upon stilts. He has neither ease nor simplicity, and his efforts at playfulness, in part, remind one of the lines in Milton:—

> —The elephant
> To make them sport wreath'd his proboscis
>   lithe.

His Letters from Correspondents, in particular, are more pompous and unwieldy than what he writes in his own person. This want of relaxation and variety of manner has, I think, after the first effects of novelty and surprise were over, been prejudicial to the matter. It takes from the general power, not only to please, but to instruct. The monotony of style produces an apparent monotony of ideas. What is really striking and valuable, is lost in the vain ostentation and circumlocution of the expression; for when we find the same pains and pomp of diction bestowed upon the most trifling as upon the most important parts of a sentence or discourse, we grow tired of distinguishing between pretension and reality, and are disposed to confound the tinsel and bombast of the phraseology with want of weight in the thoughts. Thus, from the imposing and oracular nature of the style, people are tempted at first to imagine that our author's speculations are all wisdom and profundity: till having found out their mistake in some instances, they suppose that there is nothing but commonplace in them, concealed under verbiage and pedantry; and in both they are wrong. The fault of Dr. Johnson's style is, that it reduces all things to the same artificial and unmeaning level. It destroys all shades of difference, the association between words and things. It is a perpetual paradox and innovation. He condescends to the familiar till we are ashamed of our interest in it: he expands the little till it looks big. 'If he were to write a fable of little fishes,' as Goldsmith said of him, 'he would make them speak like great whales.' We can no more distinguish the most familiar objects in his descriptions of them, than we can a well-known face under a huge painted mask. The structure of his sentences, which was his own invention, and which has been generally imitated since his time, is a species of rhyming in prose, where one clause answers to another in measure and quantity, like the tagging of syllables at the end of a verse; the close of the period follows as mechanically as the oscillation of a pendulum, the sense is balanced with the sound; each sentence, revolving round its centre of gravity, is contained with itself like a couplet, and each paragraph forms itself into a stanza. Dr. Johnson is also a complete balance-master in the topics of morality. He never encourages hope, but he counteracts it by fear; he never elicits a truth, but he suggests some objection in answer to it. He seizes and alternately quits the clue of reason, lest it should involve him in the labyrinths of endless error: he wants confidence in himself and his fellows. He

dares not trust himself with the immediate impressions of things, for fear of compromising his dignity; or follow them into their consequences, for fear of committing his prejudices. His timidity is the result, not of ignorance, but of morbid apprehension. 'He runs the great circle, and is still at home.' No advance is made by his writings in any sentiment, or mode of reasoning. Out of the pale of established authority and received dogmas, all is sceptical, loose, and desultory: he seems in imagination to strengthen the dominion of prejudice, as he weakens and dissipates that of reason; and round the rock of faith and power, on the edge of which he slumbers blindfold and uneasy, the waves and billows of uncertain and dangerous opinion roar and heave for evermore. His *Rasselas* is the most melancholy and debilitating moral speculation that ever was put forth. Doubtful of the faculties of his mind, as of his organs of vision, Johnson trusted only to his feelings and his fears. He cultivated a belief in witches as an out-guard to the evidences of religion; and abused Milton, and patronised Lauder, in spite of his aversion to his countrymen, as a step to secure the existing establishment in church and state. This was neither right feeling nor sound logic.

The most triumphant record of the talents and character of Johnson is to be found in Boswell's [*The Life of Samuel Johnson*]. The man was superior to the author. When he threw aside his pen, which he regarded as an incumbrance, he became not only learned and thoughtful, but acute, witty, humorous, natural, honest; hearty and determined, 'the king of good fellows and wale of old men.' There are as many smart repartees, profound remarks, and keen invectives to be found in Boswell's 'inventory of all he said,' as are recorded of any celebrated man. The life and dramatic play of his conversation forms a contrast to his written works. His natural powers and undisguised opinions were called out in convivial intercourse. In public, he practised with the foils on: in private, he unsheathed the sword of controversy, and it was 'the Ebro's temper.' The eagerness of opposition roused him from his natural sluggishness and acquired timidity; he returned blow for blow; and whether the trial were of argument or wit, none of his rivals could boast much of the encounter. . . . He had faults, but they lie buried with him. He had his prejudices and his intolerant feelings; but he suffered enough in the conflict of his own mind with them. For if no man can be happy in the free exercise of his reason, no wise man can be happy without it. His were not time-serving, heartless, hypocritical prejudices; but deep, inwoven, not to be rooted out but with life and hope, which he found from old habit necessary to his own peace of mind, and thought so to the peace of mankind. I do not hate, but love him for them. They were between himself and his conscience; and should be left to that higher tribunal, 'where they in trembling hope repose, the bosom of his Father and his God.' In a word, he has left behind him few wiser or better men.

The herd of his imitators shewed what he was by their disproportionate effects. The Periodical Essayists, that succeeded the Rambler, are, and deserve to be, little read at present. The *Adventurer,* by Hawksworth, is completely trite and vapid, aping all the faults of Johnson's style, without any thing to atone for them. The sentences are often absolutely unmeaning; and one half of each might regularly be left blank. The *World,* and *Connoisseur,* which followed, are a little better; and in the last of these there is one good idea, that of a man in indifferent health, who judges of every one's title to respect from their possession of this blessing, and bows to a sturdy beggar with sound limbs and a florid complexion, while he turns his back upon a lord who is a valetudinarian.

Goldsmith's *Citizen of the World,* like all his works, bears the stamp of the author's mind. It does not 'go about to cozen reputation without the stamp of merit.' He is more observing, more original, more natural and picturesque than Johnson. His work is written on the model of the Persian Letters; and contrives to give an abstracted and somewhat perplexing view of things, by opposing foreign prepossessions to our own, and thus stripping objects of their customary disguises. Whether truth is elicited in this collision of contrary absurdities, I do not know; but I confess the process is too ambiguous and full of intricacy to be very amusing to my plain understanding. For light summer reading, it is like walking in a garden full of traps and pitfalls. It necessarily gives rise to paradoxes, and there are some very bold ones in the Essays, which would subject an author less established to no very agreeable sort of *censura literaria.* Thus the Chinese philosopher exclaims very unadvisedly, 'The bonzes and priests of all religions keep up superstition and imposture: all reformations begin with the laity.' Goldsmith, however, was staunch in his practical creed, and might bolt speculative extravagances with impunity. There is a striking difference in this respect between him and Addison, who, if he attacked authority, took care to have common sense on his side, and never hazarded any thing offensive to the feelings of others, or on the strength of his own discretional opinion. There is another inconvenience in this assumption of an exotic character and tone of sentiment, that it produces an inconsistency between the knowledge which the individual has time to acquire, and which the author is bound to communicate. Thus the Chinese has not been in England three days before he is acquainted with the characters of the three countries which compose this kingdom, and describes them to his friend at Canton, by extracts from the newspapers of each metropolis. The nationality of Scotchmen is thus ridiculed:—'*Edinburgh.* We are positive when we say, that Sanders Macgregor, lately executed for horsestealing, is not a native of Scotland, but born at Carrickfergus.' Now this is very good; but how should our Chinese philosopher find it out by instinct? Beau Tibbs, a prominent character in this little work, is the best comic sketch since the time of Addison; unrivalled in his finery, his vanity, and his poverty.

I have only to mention the names of the *Lounger* and the *Mirror,* which are ranked by the author's admirers with Sterne for sentiment, and with Addison for humour. I shall not enter into that: but I know that the story of La Roche is not like the story of Le Fevre, nor one hundredth part so good. Do I say this from prejudice to the author? No: for I have read his novels. Of the *Man of the World* I cannot think so favourably as some others; nor shall I here dwell on the picturesque and romantic beauties of *Julia de Roubigné,* the early favourite of the author of *Rosamond Gray;* but of the *Man of Feeling* I would speak with

grateful recollections: nor is it possible to forget the sensitive, irresolute, interesting Harley: and that lone figure of Miss Walton in it, that floats in the horizon, dim and ethereal, the day-dream of her lover's youthful fancy—better, far better than all the realities of life! (pp. 91-105)

William Hazlitt, "Lecture V: On the Periodical Essayists," in his Lectures on the English Comic Writers and Fugitive Writings, *Dent 1963, pp. 91-105.*

A. P. Peabody

[*In the following excerpt, Peabody examines the evolution of the periodical essay, commending compositions by Joseph Addison and Richard Steele as sources of instruction and entertainment influential in the style and content of nineteenth-century expository writing.*]

There are adequate reasons why the periodical essay should have flourished as a form of literature precisely in the eighteenth century, and neither earlier nor later. English literature can in no sense have become popular till the reign of James I. Prior to the standard version of the Scriptures, the language had been too indefinite and fluctuating in its forms for the growth of so much as a style, which should blend precision, beauty, harmony, and adaptation to the general taste. The reading of an author of a previous generation must have demanded either scholarly habits, or arduous and often ungrateful toil; and we can find little evidence of intellectual activity or curiosity among the mass of the people, or even of the privileged classes. When a popular literature became possible, there commenced forthwith the series of political agitations, fanned by the despotism of the Stuarts, aroused to internecine strife under Charles I., prolonged through successive revolutions, and allayed only by the settlement of the powers of the realm and the balancing of parties toward the close of the reign of William of Orange. During this entire period, the whole nation was in intense and never-flagging excitement on the most momentous subjects, involving the dearest earthly rights and immortal hopes. The termination of the long struggle in the consolidation of a constitutional government left the general mind alert, vigorous and earnest, intent on the current of public affairs and of social life, keenly critical of opinions, and craving objects of fresh interest. The troubled condition of the realm, than which the generation then living had known no other state, had of course nourished the appetency for novelty in every kind,—for racy and stimulating condiments to the mind and the passions. The entire people had been less spectators than actors in a series of wild and complicated tragedies, and they could not now retire from the stage, without longing to be spectators at least at the more comic after-piece of party countermarches, literary rivalries, and fashionable frivolities. The newspaper of the day did more to feed than to appease this craving. Giving only the names of the *dramatis personæ* and the most meagre playbill possible, it prompted more questions than it answered. The *Gazette,* as a form of publication, was indeed imported with the name from Italy into England in the latter part of the sixteenth century; but periodical papers were not regularly issued till during the civil war, when they were employed mainly to disseminate political dogmas or to arouse military zeal. They must, we think, have subsequently declined in the interest of the people with the dearth of stirring incident; for on the accession of Queen Anne to the throne, there was but one daily paper printed in the kingdom. This, and still more its weekly contemporaries, must have been too scantily sustained, to furnish remunerating employment for genius or erudition. So little satisfaction did they give as to certain portions of what would be now deemed their sphere, that they were outrivalled in the provincial towns by manuscript news-letters from London, written by some of the number, not even then small, of cultivated men who sought a precarious living by penwork, and *despatched* (if the word be not too gross an anachronism) to the principal cities,—each copy there circulated, and perhaps recopied for more rapid circulation, among the gentry and the rural nobility. These letters, giving sketches of London life, aptly prepared the way, and generated the taste, for the periodical essay, which, with two or three generations, filled an essential place in the public demand, which there was nothing else to occupy.

Thus was there fitness in the birth-time of this form of literature. Its decline was equally necessitated by the progress of the age. With the multiplication of newspapers and their readers, competition enlisted, and growing patronage retained, in their service a higher order of talent. The editorial columns and the regular literary contributions covered the ground that had been occupied by the daily essay. News was served up with the condiments which Steele and Addison had first rendered essential to the public appetite. The daily paper was no longer an arid journal, but a spicy commentary on its own records; while, so far as the essays had discussed topics of ethical and religious philosophy and general literature, they were superseded by the accumulated literary productions of a prolific century, by the now teeming issues of the press, by the older magazines, and, at a later period, by the *Edinburgh Review* and the other quarterlies to which its success gave birth.

Among the results of the essays [in eighteenth-century British periodicals], we must give a prominent place to the simplification of style. With a very few noble exceptions, English prose had been lumbering, obscure, pedantic, deformed by quotations from the ancient languages, and fit for the perusal only of readers equally learned and long-suffering. Authorship had for its object display, rather than conviction, persuasion, or instruction,—the ventilation, rather than the transfer, of the writer's acquisitions,—the reputation of learning, rather than the wielding of intellectual power. The daily sheet excluded such recondite labor. The event, the rumor, the mood, the fashion of the current time, the book last read, the theme last discussed in private, must needs furnish the material for the next morning's issue. And the work must be wrought in hot haste. The expressed vintage of a life's study might indeed be poured out upon the paper, but it could not hold the crude clusters that had been awkwardly jammed in between the covers of ponderous quartos. The recoil was therefore sudden and entire to the extreme of simplicity and *naïveté;* and compositions of this type, daily before the public, and by authors of unsurpassed ability and repute,

remodelled the general taste, and were the chief agency in creating the directness, transparency, and purity of diction, which characterized English literature through the whole of the last century, and till Coleridge and Carlyle, each in his way, and for his numerous imitators, flooded the fountains of "English undefiled" from turbid sources of transcendental metaphysics and foreign tongues.

Here we crave liberty to speak of what we deem the false estimate of the two greatest names among the Essayists. It has been fashionable to cite Addison as a master of style. This rank is a tradition rather than a fact. Its basis lies in the age that preceded him. He has indeed one crowning merit for all times. It is impossible to misapprehend a sentence of his on the first reading. His words were always the most obvious drapery—that nearest at hand—for the thoughts they covered. And it is a graceful and elegant attire; for the mind that wove it has had no superior, few equals, in native taste and in liberal culture. But the shuttle flew so rapidly, that the texture often will not bear close inspection. Addison is apt to be loose and repetitious. His choice of words is better than their collocation. His sentences are seldom deficient in euphony; but his offences against syntax are neither few nor small. His essays often have a slipshod air, not by any means unbecoming in one whose fine proportions give comeliness even to a *dishabille,* but which can be imitated only at the risk of copying the carelessness without the grace that relieves and adorns it. At this risk, and with this almost invariable result, has it been imitated, especially by cultivated men who have been occasional, rather than professional authors; and there has never been wanting in England a class of writers, who, no doubt under shelter of this high example, seem to have rejoiced in grammatical solecisms, and a lax, off-hand treatment of the parts of speech, as betokening the aristocratic ease of pencraft.

Johnson, on the other hand, has had much more than his due laid to his charge on the score of verbosity and pompousness. The high appreciation in which Addison was held placed him at a disadvantage with his immediate public; and criticisms, level with the standard of the times, have perpetuated themselves under a standard which makes them obsolete. Johnsonese is the severest simplicity by the side of Carlylese. Johnson is not so much turgid, as thought-full. His sentences are plethoric, not with wind, but with condensed meaning. They are packed full; but it is with their legitimate freight. They groan with heavy epithets; but it is with actual *epi*-thets, each adding its subsidiary idea, to define or modify the scope of the phrase laden with it. His style is not *verbose,* if by that word is denoted *superfluous* verbiage. He gives his readers, indeed, on topics that come within the range of lighter literature, an amount of analytic thought, an exactness and careful limitation of statement, and a thoroughness of mental elaboration, which hardly have precedent elsewhere; and it is this which sustains his unbending stateliness of movement. To him no literature was light,—authorship was a solemn work, performed under the goading of an imperious conscience, and beneath the forecast shadow of Divine retribution.

Here, no doubt, we are to seek the cause of his preference

for words of Latin derivation. There can be no question that this part of our language is best adapted to serve the scrupulous accuracy of a morbidly conscientious writer. Saxon words, with their quick, sharp ring upon the auditory nerve, pulse upon the inward ear with a stronger *ictus;* they are more suggestive; and, because they set the reader's mind into action to find a meaning for them, it is inferred that they minister to greater precision than the portions of our vocabulary derived from the classical tongues. But, in fact, Saxon roots are traced with great difficulty and still greater uncertainty; the words thence drawn have no ultimate standard of signification; not a few of them have without any assignable cause changed, in some instances reversed, their meaning within the last two or three centuries; and there are some cases, (that of *let,* for instance,) in which in the same book a word appears in two opposite senses, with nothing to indicate in which sense it is intended. On the other hand, words of classic origin acquire only such significations as can be readily deduced from, traced back to, and verified by, their parentage; and there are no instances in which such a word has now a sense that is not involved in its *etymon,* and hardly an instance in which such a word is employed in opposite significations, or in senses differing otherwise than as a metaphorical must differ from a literal sense. The word *prevent,* though used sometimes by the same author to denote both *hinderance* and *help,* does not furnish an exception to our remark; for both senses are included in *prevenio,*—one may *come before* another either to thwart or to second his purposes.

To return to Johnson. His strongly Latinized style, while it no doubt impairs the electric impulse, the quickening power, of his diction, enhances its *impressiveness* in the literal sense of the word; for it makes every sentence like a motto cut on a gem by the point of a diamond, and forced down upon the recipient surface by a compact, heavy weight. Thus it is that, though he is hard to read, he is easy to understand. It may require effort to take in all that he means to convey, but it is impossible to mistake his meaning. And while we can conceive of a diminished affluence and a less painful precision of thought as adding grace and beauty to not a few of his works, yet we doubt whether the same amount of thought can be expressed with equal exactness in fewer or less sonorous words than he was wont to employ. We have tried the experiment, not only upon sentences and paragraphs, but on the definitions in his Dictionary,—some of them made ludicrous by their seeming inflation, but, when they are most so, unfailingly justifying themselves by the sharpness with which they limit the sense and use of the word defined. Thus, for instance, one can hardly read without mirthfulness his definition of *network:* "Anything reticulated or decussated with interstices between the intersections"; and the definition can be of no possible use except to some studious recluse who has abjured women and all their works, but to such a one it would be impossible to impart the idea of network in fewer or simpler words. Indeed, this is beyond measure preferable to Webster's shambling definition, which seems to have been diluted from Johnson's, and which substitutes for seeming pedantry real vagueness and obscurity: "A complication of threads, twine, or cords, united at certain distances, forming meshes, interstices, or open spaces, between the knots or intersections."

We have said that the essayists of the [eighteenth] century exercised a decisive and lasting influence on the current style of English prose. It is impossible to say how large was their agency in the diffusion of knowledge and literary taste. There is hardly one among the numerous subjects of common interest in the last and the present century, on which may not be found in the collection under review at least a single treatise which still remains unequalled for clearness, comprehensiveness, and sound judgment. From these volumes one might derive a better knowledge of the Greek and Latin classics, than in any other way is open to the merely English reader; and this remark applies not only to the authors with whom every scholar is conversant, but equally to a considerable number of writers of secondary merit, yet typical and representative of their respective times, whose works are much less read now than they were a hundred years ago. In turning over the general index, which occupies the last volume of the edition before us, we have been struck with the idea that the entire series might almost serve the purpose of a classical dictionary, so copious are the references under all the prominent titles of such a work, and so numerous are the extended discussions, the anecdotes, and the versions under titles which the dictionary despatches in half a dozen lines. Then, of recondite items of history, of quaint morsels of biographical incident, of the curiosities of literature, the various series together constitute a rich repertory, each in its peculiar vein extracting from seams now closed specimens which the learned world cannot afford to part with. Of criticisms of English literature there are here found not a few, which it were well for us, critics of a later day, to ponder diligently as models, at once of patient labor, exhaustive treatment, and the amenities which constitute the sadly neglected ethics of our craft. We would here refer to the incomparable analysis of the *Paradise Lost* in the *Spectator,* and to numerous elaborate essays on different plays of Shakespeare in the *Rambler,* the *Adventurer,* the *Connoisseur,* the *Mirror,* the *Lounger,* and the *Observer.* These papers contain many brilliant specimens of a type of comparative criticism, now infrequent, in which an English author is placed by the side of one or more of the ancient classics, (as, for instance, Shakespeare by the side of Æschylus,) analogous passages are cited, resemblances and contrasts traced, and the underlying principles or fundamental canons of the kind of composition deduced from the collation. We cannot over-estimate the efficacy of an instrumentality like this in an age when books were costly, when there were few libraries accessible to the majority of readers, and when popular editions, translations, compends, lexicons, and cyclopædias were not so much as dreamed of. It was a privilege of the highest order for a family to have almost forced upon its perusal a daily paper, which in the course of a year might cover nearly the entire ground of a university curriculum, and that not with superficial, second-hand smatterings of learning, but with solid and thorough, though brief and miscellaneous, treatises by the very writers who were the best fitted to impart sound knowledge and just views, to awaken and direct curiosity, and to point out the sources for its gratification. It is not too much to say that the popular literature of the present day, the manuals for general use in every department of knowledge, the means of a truly liberal culture within the reach of all who can read, are the direct and inevitable result of the intellectual habits formed, the tastes nurtured, the demands created, by the British Essayists.

Not less important was their influence as critics of life and manners, of fashions and of morals, of popular fallacies and aristocratic absurdities. No phasis of the times escaped their keen cognizance; no folly, their lash of silken but knotted cords; no pretension, their delicate yet withering irony. Dress and diet, modes of reception and table manners, shops and taverns, theatres and concerts, city coteries and country neighborhoods, vulgar wealth and showy poverty, poor relations and country cousins, despotic masters and insolent servants, all came in turn under the Argus-eyed censorship. Multitudes must have felt that they were dwelling in houses of glass, nay, that their soul-dwellings were but a transparent medium, so accurately did they find depicted in the daily sheet the transactions of their households, the habits of their families, their own inmost and unuttered thoughts. Never before nor since has the mirror been so held up to life. And, while among the series of papers to be found only in the collections of antiquaries there were undoubtedly (as there are reported to have been) some that pandered to inferior tastes and even to vicious passions, among those that had an extensive currency and an established reputation, and that have taken their places among the classics of the English tongue, there is not one whose moral standard was not just, high, unyielding, and exacting. There was intense need of such a continuous force as was thus applied for the emendation of manners and morals. The restoration of the Stuarts inaugurated the carnival of profligacy. Never can British society have been more corrupt than during the last two reigns of that dynasty; nor do we find reason to suppose that the succeeding generation made any essential progress in those civic and social virtues, which were the only possible support and safeguard of the constitutional government, or rather which alone could so vitalize the forms of the constitution, that they should not stiffen into members of a more complex but not less oppressive despotism than that which had been overthrown and exiled. In this progress, the *Tatler* and the *Spectator* took the initiative; the *Rambler* and the *Adventurer* bore a prominent part; and all the leading series of essays have left permanent records of their quiet working in the renovation of the social order, in the creation of a high tone of domestic morality, and in the sentence of ban and outlawry upon excesses once fashionable, and vices which it was once prudery to condemn. (pp. 503-11)

A. P. Peabody, in an originally unsigned review of "The British Essayists: With Prefaces, Historical and Biographical," in The North American Review, *Vol. LXXXIV, No. 175, April, 1857, pp. 502-14.*

FURTHER READING

Baldwin, Edward Chauncey. "The Relation of the Seventeenth-Century Character to the Periodical Essay." *PMLA* XIX, No. 1 (December 1904): 75-114.
    Discusses the periodical essay as the vehicle through which character-writing reached its apex in English letters.

Binkley, Harold C. "Essays and Letter-Writing." *PMLA* XLI, No. 2 (June 1926): 342-61.
    Argues for the existence of "a definite and deliberate indebtedness on the part of essay writers for elements which belong primarily to the familiar letter."

Burton, Richard. "The Essay as Mood and Form." *The Forum* XXXII (September 1901): 119-26.
    Comments on the contributions of Francis Bacon, Joseph Addison, Richard Steele, and Oliver Goldsmith to the development of the English essay.

Chalmers, Alexander, ed. *The British Essayists; with Prefaces, Historical and Biographical,* Vol. 1. London: Longman & Rees, 1808, 288 p.
    Selected essays by Joseph Addison and Richard Steele, prefaced by Chalmers' discussion of biographical and historical events surrounding the publication of the *Tatler.*

Croll, Morris W. "Essay Four. Attic Prose: Lipsius, Montaigne, Bacon." In his *Style, Rhetoric, and Rhythm,* edited by J. Max Patrick and Robert O. Evans, pp. 167-202. Princeton, N. J.: Princeton University Press, 1966.
    Examines the contributions of essayists Justus Lipsius, Michel de Montaigne, and Francis Bacon to seventeenth-century Anti-Ciceronian or "Attic" philosophy, in a study of seventeenth-century prose style.

Dobson, Henry Austin. "Eighteenth-Century Periodical Essayists." In *Toward Today: A Collection of English and American Essays Presenting the Earlier Development of Ideas Fundamental in Modern Life and Literature,* edited by Erich A. Walter, pp. 339-42. Chicago: Scott, Foresman and Co., 1938.
    Assesses the strengths and weaknesses of the eighteenth-century periodical essayists, emphasizing "the supremacy of [Joseph] Addison and [Richard] Steele" and observing that "in native purity of tone, moreover, they were far in advance of their age and were certainly not excelled by any of those who followed them."

Drake, Nathan. "General Observations on Periodical Writing," pp. 15-40. In his *Essays, Biographical, Critical, and Historical, Illustrative of the 'Tatler,' 'Spectator,' and 'Guardian.'* London: C. Whittingham, 1805.
    Surveys the history of the essay's rise to prominence in English society, praising the periodical essayists for their commitment to education and literary excellence.

Dunham, W. H. "Some Forerunners of the *Tatler* and the *Spectator.*" *Modern Language Notes* XXXIII, No. 1 (January 1918): 95-101.
    Discusses Joseph Addison's and Richard Steele's literary debt to the style and technique of the character sketch made popular in such periodicals as the *Athenian Gazette* and Daniel Defoe's *Review.*

Epstein, Joseph. "Piece Work: Writing the Essay." In his

Plausible Prejudices: Essays on American Writing, pp. 397-411. New York: W. W. Norton & Co., 1985.

Surveys the history of the essay in an exploration of its enduring appeal.

Fadiman, Clifton. "A Gentle Dirge for the Familiar Essay." In his *Party of One: The Selected Writings of Clifton Fadiman,* pp. 349-53. Cleveland: The World Publishing Co., 1955.

Attributes the familiar essay's decline in popularity to the limitations of its subject matter and perspective.

Freeman, Edmund L. "Jeremy Collier and Francis Bacon." *Philological Quarterly* VII, No. 1 (January 1928): 17-26.

Discusses the influence of Francis Bacon's prose on that of Jeremy Collier, concluding that "by Bacon's conception of the essay form and his feeling for rich colour of phrase and economy of epithet Collier was moved to full admiration and we may almost safely say to discipleship."

Freeman, John. "The English Essay—Francis Bacon to George Saintsbury." *The Bookman* LXV, No. 387 (December 1923): 149-52.

Offers an overview of works by the more prominent English essayists, including Sir Thomas Browne, John Dryden, Joseph Addison, and others.

Lobban, J. H. "Introduction." In *English Essays,* edited by J. H. Lobban, pp. ix-lxi. London: Blackie & Son, 1903.

Traces the development of the English essay through the nineteenth century.

MacDonald, W. L. *Beginnings of the English Essay.* Toronto: The University Library, 1914, 122 p.

Offers analyses of the nature of the essay, its ancient and medieval prototypes, and associated prose forms.

Matthews, Brander. "A Note on the Essay." *The Book Buyer* XVI, No. 3 (April 1898): 201-04.

Appreciative overview of the essay as a catalyst in the development of the novel and the field of literary criticism.

Routh, H. V. "The Origins of the Essay Compared in French and English Literatures." *The Modern Language Review* XV (January 1920): 28-40.

Compares the French essay with the English essay, exploring style and technique, developmental influences, and significance in literary history.

Squire, John. "The Essay." In his *Flowers of Speech: Being*

Lectures in Words and Forms in Literature, pp. 108-15. 1935. Reprint. Freeport, New York: Books for Libraries Press, 1967.

Discusses the essay as "a particular kind of wandering, personal thing which has flourished in England as nowhere else."

Thomas, Sidney. "*The Lord Marquess' Idleness:* The First English Book of Essays." *Studies in Philology* XLV, No. 4 (October 1948): 592-99.

Contends that the passages in William Paulet's *The Lord Marquess' Idleness* (1585) contain significant stylistic improvements on the "commonplace sketches" prevalent during Paulet's time, suggesting that his work is worthy of consideration as the earliest published volume of English essays.

Thompson, Francis. "The Essay: Ancient and Modern." *The Academy and Literature,* No. 1624 (20 June 1903): 611-12.

Offers a general discussion of the most esteemed English essayists in a review of William Peacock's *Selected English Essays.*

Turner, Margaret. "The Influence of La Bruyère on the 'Tatler' and the 'Spectator'." *The Modern Language Review* XLVIII, No. 1 (January 1953): 10-16.

Suggests that "the debt of the *Tatler* and the *Spectator* extends . . . to the imitation and adaptation of La Bruyère's methods of characterization, and to some borrowing of subject-matter."

Watson, E. H. Lacon. "The Essay Considered from an Artistic Point of View." *The Westminster Review* 141, No. 5 (May 1894): 559-65.

Considers the merits of English and American essay-writing, finding that "the ideal essayist . . . has yet to be evolved, the man who shall combine in his own person the original power of Bacon, the grace of Addison, the transcendental insight of Emerson, the gay fancy of Charles Lamb, with any unconsidered trifles that he may chance to pick up from other essayists."

Watson, Melvin R. "The Tradition Established." In his *Magazine Serials and the Essay Tradition, 1746-1820,* pp. 1-18. Baton Rouge: Louisiana State University Press, 1956.

Discusses ways in which the familiar essay developed under the auspices of magazine serials such as the *Tatler, Spectator,* and *Guardian.*

Sir Richard Steele

1672-1729

(Also wrote under the pseudonym Isaac Bickerstaff)
Irish-born English poet, journalist, essayist, pamphleteer,
and dramatist.

Considered by many critics the father of the periodical
essay, Steele is best known for his famous literary partnership with Joseph Addison, with whom he wrote and edited
the *Tatler* and the *Spectator*. Printed from 1709 to 1712,
these influential periodicals promoted the reformation of
manners and morals through light, entertaining, and satirical essays. Perhaps less known, but no less vigorous in
their advocacy of morality, are Steele's comedies. Steele
took a stand against what he perceived as excessive debauchery in Restoration comedy and attempted to write
plays which championed virtue and inspired benevolence.
According to critics, his most successful drama was *The
Conscious Lovers,* a work many critics consider the premier representative of the genre of sentimental comedy.
Steele's reputation has declined since his own day; his essays are not widely read and his comedies are no longer
fashionable. Nevertheless, commentators emphasize his
influence on the development of the periodical essay and
sentimental comedy. For example, Calhoun Winton, one
of Steele's biographers, maintains that his mark "was set
principally as a literary innovator. . . . He invented *The
Tatler* and the rest followed. He did not invent exemplary
drama but his influence and the example of *The Conscious
Lovers* gave it a mighty push."

Steele was born in Dublin in 1672. Orphaned at age six,
he was raised by his paternal aunt and her husband, Henry
Gascoigne, the private secretary to the Duke of Ormonde.
When he was 12 years old, Steele was sent to Charterhouse
School, where he first met Addison. In 1687 he entered
Christ Church College, Oxford, and then transferred to
Merton College in 1691. Some scholars contend that
Steele wrote his first comedy at Oxford, but destroyed it
at the suggestion of a fellow student who considered the
play seriously flawed. He left school in 1692 to pursue a
military career, enlisting as a gentleman trooper in service
of the Duke of Ormonde. In 1695 he dedicated his first poetic work, "The Procession," an elegy honoring Queen
Mary, to Lord John Baron Cutts, and earned an appointment to Cutts's Coldstream Guards. Five years later, he
was promoted to captain of a foot regiment. During this
period, several failed investments and the birth of an ille-
gitimate daughter brought Steele greater expenses; he
turned to writing as a means of paying his increasing
debts. One of Steele's first works was *The Christian Hero*
(1701), a moralistic treatise which denounced dueling and
urged soldiers to practice virtue. The work was immensely
popular and went through ten editions in Steele's lifetime,
but his fellow officers ridiculed it. Eager to redeem himself
with his peers, Steele wrote *The Funeral,* a comedy produced at Drury Lane in 1701. The play met with great success and elevated him to London's leading literary and in-

tellectual circles. Some scholars believe that shortly afterward Steele became one of the earliest members of the Kit
Cat Club, a group of Whig intellectuals dedicated to en-
suring a Protestant succession to the throne of England.
During this period, he wrote two more comedies. *The
Lying Lover,* produced in 1703, was roundly condemned
by critics and theater-goers; Steele claimed that the play
was "damned for its piety" or for its emphasis on virtue
rather than depravity. Two years later, with Addison's
help, Steele wrote *The Tender Husband,* which was much
more successful than *The Lying Lover* and re-established
his popularity as a playwright.

Steele left the army in 1705 with little money and few social connections that might lead to desirable appoint-
ments. After much searching, he eventually acquired a position as gentleman waiter to Queen Anne's consort,
Prince George. His good fortune continued when, in that
same year, he married Margaret Ford Stretch, a wealthy

widow. Her death one year later brought Steele a sizable inheritance and considerable property in Barbados. In 1707 he married Mary Scurlock, to whom, over the next eleven years, he wrote hundreds of letters which have become valuable to scholars for their insights into Steele's intemperate character as well as his sincere love of his wife. Later that year, he was appointed editor of the *London Gazette*. This official government newspaper provided Steele with first-hand access to major news events of his day. Although this important position strengthened his ties with Whig leaders, it failed to provide an outlet for Steele's literary talent.

On 12 April 1709, Steele launched the first issue of the *Tatler*, a tri-weekly journal offering news and moral edification under the guise of entertaining social commentary. Writing under the pseudonym "Isaac Bickerstaff "—a figure already made famous in Jonathan Swift's satirical writings—Steele enjoyed phenomenal success. The witty, satirical nature of his essays was immensely popular, particularly among women. Steele compiled the majority of the *Tatler*'s 271 issues, with Addison collaborating on the last forty-six. In 1710 Steele's fortunes took a turn for the worse when the Tory party gained political power. He lost his post as gazetteer, and the next year he discontinued the *Tatler*, probably because of pressure from Tories who resented the periodical's political innuendos and sympathy toward Whigs. The *Spectator*, Steele's next journalistic venture, first appeared on 11 March 1711. This periodical was less politically oriented than the *Tatler*, but proved even more successful, mainly due to Addison's highly polished contributions. Although he wrote in Addison's shadow, Steele used the *Spectator* as another vehicle for promoting moral reform through witty essays, principally those composed in the popular and highly influential personas of Mr. Spectator and the old country baronet Sir Roger de Coverley.

In the years following the final issue of the *Spectator* in 1712, Steele's other journalistic ventures included the *Guardian* in 1713, his last joint effort with Addison, and the *Englishman*, issued sporadically from 1713 to 1715. During this time, Steele was elected to Parliament, only to be expelled a year later for what the Tories considered "seditious" paragraphs in his controversial tract *The Crisis* and certain numbers of his *Englishman*. Steele's expulsion from Parliament in 1714 occasioned his *Apology for Himself and His Writings*, an essay that critics value for the biographical and critical insight it provides into his early works. When the accession of George I to the English throne returned the Whigs to power in 1714, Steele regained political favor, earning a knighthood, re-election to Parliament, and royal appointment as the Supervisor of the Theatre Royal at Drury Lane. In 1717, he invested heavily in the Fish-Pool project, a scheme intended to transport live fish from the coast of Ireland for sale in London markets. He lost all his money, however, when the venture failed. Steele's *The Account of the Fish-Pool*, offers an account of these events. This financial fiasco preceded a series of unfortunate events: in 1718 his second wife, Mary Scurlock, died during pregnancy, and in 1719 he waged a bitter pamphlet war with Addison over a controversial bill before Parliament. The rift between the two

friends remained unreconciled when Addison died later that year.

Steele enjoyed a literary victory in 1722 with the production of his last comedy, *The Conscious Lovers*. The play was a great success with London critics and audiences, and remained in Drury Lane's repertory for decades. Records indicate that it was one of the most highly regarded dramas of the eighteenth century. Although gout and intemperance contributed to a decline in his health, Steele continued to serve as an elected official and manager of Drury Lane. In 1723 he left London to escape mounting debts and find relief for his worsening physical condition. Steele never returned to the city, spending his last years in retirement on his wife's estate in Carmarthen, Wales. At the age of fifty-four, Steele suffered a paralytic stroke that left him in broken health until his death in 1729.

The partnership between Steele and Addison is one of the most famous in English literature. Their names have become synonymous with the English periodical essay, and critics have made their respective contributions to the genre a central point of debate. While Steele's literary reputation has suffered in comparison to Addison's, he is nevertheless credited as the originator of the periodical essay. Although the pieces that appeared in Daniel Defoe's *Review* (1704-1713) and Michel de Montaigne's *Essays* (1580) are acknowledged as forerunners of periodical literature, Steele's contributions provided a central focus for this emerging genre. In the *Tatler*, Steele implemented a unique device, structuring the various news sections around the different coffee houses in London—White's Chocolate House served as the locale for the entertainment section, Will's Coffee-House for poetry, the Grecian Coffee-House for learning, and the St. James's Coffee-House for foreign and domestic affairs. Scholars also consider Steele the first commentator to recognize the full significance of Milton's works, and they note that he was the creator of the *Spectator*'s immensely popular character Sir Roger de Coverley. Addison refined Steele's contributions to this journal, and thus many critics have given him credit for developing them. There is little disagreement, however, that Steele was the primary editor of the *Tatler*, completing 188 of the periodical's 271 issues.

Steele's description of the *Tatler*'s objectives also applies to those of the *Spectator*: "The general purpose of the whole has been to recommend truth, innocence, honour, and virtue, as the chief ornaments of life." His ethical writings advocated the importance of friendship, benevolence, frankness, and the simple virtues of married and family life above all other things. These ideas appealed to the growing English middle class, whose Puritanism was in direct opposition to aristocratic notions of morality. Critics have also observed that Steele devoted a significant number of his essays to writing about women, whom he viewed as worthy and intelligent beings whose capabilities could be further developed through education. Because he presented his ideas on women with tact, sincerity, and good humor, as Rae Blanchard notes, Steele was able "to disseminate ideas which contributed to the evolution of feminist thought in England." Steele also attempted to reform the theater, which, in his opinion, had degenerated since the Restoration. He was heavily influenced by Jeremy Collier's *Short View of the Immorality and Profaneness of the English Stage* (1689), a tract which expressed Puritanical outrage at the loose morality of plays that Collier felt "rewarded debauchery," "ridiculed virtue and learning," were "disserviceable to probity and religion," and made vice attractive. In his comedies, Steele attempted to restore virtue as the focus of the dramatic action and provide audiences with moral instruction. Although his plays were hailed by theatrical reformers, they generally met with limited success among critics and audiences.

In examining Steele's compositional style, critics tend to compare his work with that of Addison, usually to Steele's disadvantage. Most commentators contend that Addison was a more adept essayist than Steele, not only because he had an excellent classical education, but also because his style was more refined. Lacking his friend's aesthetic polish, Steele instead exhibited immense originality and enthusiasm. The simplicity of his essays made them highly popular with his middle class readers. His ability to translate the mundane elements of the human experience into a literary form was a gift that Addison lacked. In addition, Steele wrote with a rare sympathy and immediacy perhaps best exemplified in his moving account of the death of his father in *Tatler,* 181. Steele's attempts to imitate the natural human voice in his periodical essays found at least one detractor, however; according to the early nineteenth-century critic Nathan Drake, Steele's attempts to write in a tone of common conversation "must surely be considered as one of the most preposterous conceptions that ever entered the brain of an author." While to some critics his essays seem unpolished, most commentators agree that Steele truly and heartily recorded the life around him with love and reverence for humankind.

While most of Steele's comedies met with moderate success in his day, he built his literary reputation chiefly as the editor and contributor to the *Tatler,* the *Spectator,* and the *Guardian.* These journals served as influential models for the evolving genre of periodical literature, a literary form that has continued to evolve over the centuries. For several years after his death, many noteworthy critics actually preferred Steele's essays to Addison's. William Hazlitt, for example, in a lecture on the evolution of the periodical essay, described Steele's works as "less artificial and more original" than those of Addison. Steele's literary reputation gradually declined in favor of his partner, however, culminating in Thomas Babington Macaulay's depreciation of Steele in his 1843 essay, "Life and Writings of Addison," where he compared Steele's essays for the *Tatler* to "light wines which, though deficient in body and flavor, are yet a pleasant small drink if not kept too long or carried too far."

Steele's literary reputation has never fully recovered from critical attacks such as Macaulay's. His comedies are today more popular with scholars than with stage directors, and many modern critics rank his essays as second-rate at best. Nevertheless, commentators generally recognize Steele as an important catalyst in the evolution of the English periodical essay. He possessed the originality and wit necessary to define the new genre, while Addison had

the refinement and insight to transform it into an effective literary form. Although his plays are presently denigrated as sententious and poorly-constructed, scholars nevertheless agree that they played a pivotal role in the emergence of sentimental comedy and that Steele's *The Conscious Lovers* represents the epitome of that genre.

(See also *Dictionary of Literary Biography,* Vols. 84 and 101.)

PRINCIPAL WORKS

The Procession: A Poem on Her Majesty's Funeral (poetry) 1695
The Christian Hero: An Argument Proving that no Principles but Those of Religion Are Sufficient to make a Great Man (essay) 1701
The Funeral; or, Grief à-la-Mode (drama) 1701
The Lying Lover; or, The Ladies Friendship (drama) 1703
The Tender Husband; or, The Accomplish'd Fools (drama) 1705
*The Tatler. 6 vols. [with Joseph Addison and others] (essays) 1709-11
†*The Spectator. 5 vols. [with Joseph Addison and others] (essays) 1711-12
‡*The Guardian. 2 vols. (essays) 1713
§*The Englishman* (essays) 1713-15
The Crisis; or, A Discourse Representing, from the most Authentick Records, the just Causes of the late Happy Revolution: and the several Settlements of the Crowns of England and Scotland on Her Majesty; and on the Demise of Her Majesty without Issue, upon the Most Illustrious Princess Sophia, Electress and Dutchess Dowager of Hanover, and The Heirs of Her Body Being Protestants . . . With Some Seasonable Remarks on the Danger of a Popish Successor (essay) 1714
Mr. Steele's Apology for Himself and His Writings; Occasioned by his Expulsion from the House of Commons (essay) 1714
The Account of the Fish-Pool (essay) 1718
//*The Plebeian* (essays) 1719
#*The Theatre* (essays) 1720
The Conscious Lovers (drama) 1722
The School of Action, and the Gentleman (unfinished drama) 1809

*Originally published as individual numbers from 12 April 1709 to 2 January 1711.

†Originally published as individual numbers from 1 March 1711 to 6 December 1712.

‡Originally published as individual numbers from 12 March to 1 October 1713.

§Originally published as two separate series and one issue: *The Englishman: Being the Sequel of the Guardian* (6 October 1713 to 11 February 1714), *The Englishman: Being the Close of the Paper so called* (15 February 1714), and *The Englishman, second series* (11 July 1715 to 21 November 1715).

//Originally published as individual numbers from 14 March to 6 April 1719.

#Originally published as individual numbers from 2 January to 5 April 1720.

John Gay   (essay date 1711)

[*Gay was a skillful and popular eighteenth-century poet and dramatist who specialized in humorous and satiric works. He is primarily remembered today for his* Beggar's Opera *(1728), which was adapted by Bertolt Brecht as* The Threepenny Opera *in 1928. In the excerpt below from an essay originally published in 1711, Gay surveys various British periodicals, reserving the highest praise for the* Tatler *and the* Spectator, *and judging Steele "the greatest Scholar and best Casuist of any Man in England."*]

[At] the beginning of the Winter, to the infinite surprize of all Men, Mr. Steele flung up His *TATLER,* and instead of Isaac Bickerstaff Esq; Subscrib'd himself Richard Steele to the last of those Papers, after an handsome Compliment to the Town for their kind acceptance of his Endeavours to divert them. The Chief Reason he though fit to give for his leaving off writing, was, that having been so long look'd on in all publick Places and Companies as the Author of those Papers, he found that his most intimate Friends and Acquaintance were in Pain to Act or Speak before him. The Town was very far from being satisfied with this Reason; and most People judg'd the true cause to be, either that he was quite spent, and wanted matter to continue his undertaking any longer, or that he lay'd it down as a sort of Submission to, and Composition with the Government for some past Offences; Or lastly, that he had a Mind to vary his Shape, and appear again in some new Light.

However that were, his disappearing seem'd to be bewailed as some general Calamity, every one wanted so agreeable an Amusement, and the Coffee-houses began to be sensible that the Esquires Lucubrations alone, had brought them more Customers than all their other News Papers put together.

It must indeed be confess'd, that never Man threw up his Pen under Stronger Temptations to have imployed it longer: His Reputation was at a greater height than, I believe, ever any living Author's was before him. 'Tis reasonable to suppose that his Gains were proportionably considerable; Every one Read him with Pleasure and Good Will, and the Tories, in respect to his other Good Qualities, had almost forgiven his unaccountable Imprudence in declaring against them.

Lastly, It was highly improbable that if he threw off a Character, the Ideas of which were so strongly impress'd in every one's mind, however finely he might write in any new form, that he should meet with the same reception.

To give you my own thoughts of this Gentleman's Writings, I shall in the first place observe, that there is this noble difference between him and all the rest of our Polite and Gallant Authors: The latter have endeavour'd to please the Age by falling in with them, and incouraging

Frontispiece from the first collected edition of The Tatler *(1709-1711), entitled* The Lucubrations of Isaac Bickerstaff Esq. *(1710-1711).*

them in their fashionable Vices, and false notions of things. It would have been a jest, sometime since, for a Man to have asserted, that any thing Witty could be said in praise of a Marry'd State, or that Devotion and Virtue were any way necessary to the Character of a fine Gentleman. Bickerstaff ventur'd to tell the Town, that they were a parcel of Fops, Fools, and vain Cocquets; but in such a manner, as even pleased them, and made them more than half enclin'd to believe that he spoke Truth.

Instead of complying with the false Sentiments or Vicious tasts of the Age, either in Morality, Criticism, or Good Breeding, he has boldly assur'd them, that they were altogether in the wrong, and commanded them with an Authority, which perfectly well became him, to surrender themselves to his Arguments, for Vertue and Good Sense.

'Tis incredible to conceive the effect his Writings have had on the Town; How many Thousand follies they have either quite banish'd, or given a very great check to; how much Countenance they have added to Vertue and Religion; how many People they have render'd happy, by shewing them it was their own fault if they were not so;

and lastly, how intirely they have convinc'd our Fops, and Young Fellows, of the value and advantages of Learning.

He has indeed rescued it out of the hands of Pedants and Fools, and discover'd the true method of making it amiable and lovely to all mankind: In the dress he gives it, 'tis a most welcome guest at Tea-tables and Assemblies, and is relish'd and caressed by the Merchants on the Change; accordingly, there is not a Lady at Court, nor a Banker in Lumbard-Street, who is not verily perswaded, that Captain Steele is the greatest Scholar, and best Casuist, of any Man in England.

Lastly, His Writings have set all our Wits and Men of Letters upon a new way of Thinking, of which they had little or no Notion before; and tho' we cannot yet say that any of them have come up to the Beauties of the Original, I think we may venture to affirm, that every one of them Writes and Thinks much more justly than they did some time since.

The vast variety of Subjects which he has treated of in so different manners, and yet All so perfectly well, made the World believe that 'twas impossible they should all come from the same hand. This set every one upon guessing who was the Esquires Friend, and most people at first fancied it must be Dr. Swift; but it is now no longer a Secret, that his only great and constant assistant was Mr. Addison. (pp. 2-4)

It may be observ'd, That when the Esquire laid down his Pen, tho' he could not but foresee that several Scriblers would soon snatch it up, which he might, one would think, easily have prevented, he Scorn'd to take any further Care about it, but left the Field fairly open to any Worthy Successor. Immediately some of our Wits were for forming themselves into a Club, headed by one Mr. Harrison, and trying how they could shoot in this Bow of Ulysses; but soon found that this sort of Writing, requires so fine and particular a manner of Thinking, with so exact a Knowledge of the World, as must make them utterly Despair of Success.

They seem'd indeed at first to think, that what was only the Garnish of the former *TATLERS,* was that which recomended them, and not those Substantial Entertainments which they every where abound in.

According they were continually talking of their Maid, Night-Cap, Spectacles, and Charles Lillie. However there were now and then some faint endeavours at Humour and Sparks of Wit, which the Town, for want of better Entertainment, was content to hunt after, through an heap of Impertinencies; but even those are at present, become wholly invisible, and quite swallow'd up in the Blaze of the *SPECTATOR.*

You may remember I told you before, that one Cause assign'd for the laying down the *TATLER* was, want of Matter; and indeed this was the prevailing Opinion in Town, when we were Surpriz'd all at once by a Paper called The *SPECTATOR,* which was promised to be continued every day, and was writ in so excellent a Stile, with so nice a Judgment, and such a noble profusion of Wit and Humour, that it was not difficult to determine it could come

from no other hands but those which had penn'd the Lucubrations.

This immediately alarm'd these Gentlemen, who (as 'tis said Mr. Steele phrases it) had The Censorship in Commission. They found the new *SPECTATOR* come on like a Torrent and swept away all before him; they despaired ever to equal him in Wit, Humour, or Learning; (which had been their true and certain way of opposing him) and therefore, rather chose to fall on the Author, and to call out for help to all Good Christians, by assuring them again and again, that they were the First, Original, True, and Undisputed Isaac Bickerstaff.

Mean while The *SPECTATOR,* whom we regard as our shelter from that Flood of False Wit and Impertinence which was breaking in upon us, is in every ones Hand, and a constant Topick for our Morning Conversation at Tea-Tables, and Coffee-Houses. We had at first indeed no manner of Notion, how a Diurnal Paper could be continu'd in the Spirit and Stile of our present *SPECTATORS;* but to our no small Surprize, we find them still rising upon us, and can only wonder from whence so Prodigious a Run of Wit and Learning can proceed; since some of our best Judges seem to think that they have hitherto, in general, outshone even the Esquires first *TATLERS.*

Most People Fancy, from their frequency, that they must be compos'd by a Society; I, with all, Assign the first places to Mr. Steele and His Friend.

I have often thought that the Conjunction of those two Great Genius's (who seem to stand in a Class by themselves, so high above all our other Wits) resembled that of two famous States-men in a late Reign, whose Characters are very well expressed in their two Mottoes (viz.) Prodesse quam conspici, and Otium cum Dignitate. Accordingly the first was continually at work behind the Curtain, drew up and prepared all those Schemes and Designs, which the latter Still drove on, and stood out exposed to the World to receive its Praises or Censures.

Mean time, all our unbyassed well-wishers to Learning, are in hopes, that the known Temper and Prudence of one of these Gentlemen, will hinder the other from ever lashing out into Party, and rend'ring that wit which is at present a Common Good, Odious and Ungrateful to the better part of the Nation. (pp. 5-6)

> *John Gay, "The Present State of Wit, &c.," in his* The Present State of Wit, *Augustan Reprint Society, 1947, pp. 1-7.*

Richard Steele   (essay date 1714)

[*In the excerpt below from* Mr. Steele's Apology for Himself and His Writings *(1714), which gives an account of the trial proceedings and of Steele's three-hour speech in defense of charges of sedition, the author shows how such works as his* Christian Hero *and his comedies demonstrate his efforts to promote morality.*]

It ever was my Sentiment . . . that Respect to Clergymen and their Prosperity are essential to the Good of Society. Give me Leave, Mr. *Speaker,* on this Occasion, to read to you a Passage out of a little Tract called **The Christian Hero;** the 58th Page, speaking of the Enemies to the Christian Name, and Persons who envied the Clergy, runs thus:

> But alas! its State is as much Militant as ever; for there are earthly and narrow Souls as deeply scandall'd at the Prosperity the Professors and Teachers of this Sacred Faith enjoy, and object to them the Miseries and Necessities of the Primitive Believers. Light and superficial Men! not seeing that Riches is a much more dangerous Dispensation than that of Poverty. This we oppose as a Foe, that we run to as a Friend; and an Enemy does his Business more successfully in an Embrace than a Blow. But since the Necessaries, Conveniencies, and Honours of Life which the Clergy enjoy, are so great an Offence to their Despisers, they are the more engaged to hold them dear; for they who envy a Man what he has, would certainly scorn him without it. When therefore they are both in good and bad Fortune irreconcileable to them, may they always offend with their Happiness: For it is not to be doubted, but that there are Bishops and Governours in the Church of *England,* whose decent Hospitality, Meekness, and Charity to their Brethren, will place them in the same Mansions with the most heroick Poor, convince the Mistake of their Enemies, and shew that the eternal Pastor has given his worldly Blessings into Hands by which he approves their Distribution; and still bestows upon us great and exemplary Spirits, that can conquer the Difficulties and Enchantments of Wealth it self.

I have carried this Inclination to the Advancement of Virtue so far, as to pursue it even in things the most indifferent, and which, perhaps, have been thought foreign to it. To give you an Instance of this, Sir, I must mention a comedy called **The Lying Lover,** which I writ some Years ago, the Preface to which says,

> Tho' it ought to be the Care of all Governments, that publick Representations should have nothing in them but what is agreeable to the Manners, Laws, Religion, and Policy of the Place or Nation wherein they are exhibited; yet it is the general Complaint of the more learned and virtuous amongst us, that the *English* Stage has extremely offended in this Kind. I thought therefore it would be an honest Ambition to attempt a Comedy, which might be no improper Entertainment in a Christian Common-wealth.

Mr. [Jeremy] *Collier* had, about the Time wherein this was published, written against the Immorality of the Stage [in his *Short View of the Immorality and Profaneness of the English Stage,* 1698]. I was (as far as I durst for fear of witty Men, upon whom he had been too severe) a great Admirer of his Work, and took it into my Head to write a Comedy in the Severity he required. In this Play I make the Spark or Heroe kill a Man in his Drink, and finding himself in Prison the next Morning, I give him the Contrition which he ought to have on that Occasion. 'Tis in Allusion to that Circumstance that the Preface further says as follows:

> The Anguish he there expresses, and the mutual

Sorrow between an only Child and a tender Father in that Distress, are perhaps an Injury to the Rules of Comedy, but I am sure they are a Justice to those of Morality: And Passages of such a Nature being so frequently applauded on the Stage, it is high Time that we should no longer draw Occasions of Mirth from those Images which the Religion of our Country tells us we ought to tremble at with Horrour.

> But Her most excellent Majesty has taken the Stage into Her Consideration; and we may hope, from her gracious Influence on the Muses, that Wit will recover from its Apostacy; and that by being encouraged in the Interests of Virtue, 'twill strip Vice of the gay Habit in which it has too long appeared, and cloath it in its native Dress of Shame, Contempt and Dishonour.

I can't tell, Sir, what they would have me do to prove me a Churchman; but I think I have appeared one even in so trifling a thing as a Comedy: And considering me as a Comick Poet, I have been a Martyr and Confessor for the Church; for this Play was damn'd for its Piety. (pp. 310-12)

> *Richard Steele, "Mr. Steele's Apology for Himself and His Writings," in his* Tracts and Pamphlets, *edited by Rae Blanchard, The Johns Hopkins Press, 1944, pp. 275-346.*

Alexander Chalmers   (essay date 1803)

[*Chalmers was a Scottish critic and biographer who edited many editions of works by well-known authors. His most ambitious and widely acclaimed work is* A General Biographical Dictionary, Containing an Historical and Critical Account of the Most Eminent Men of Every Nation *(1812-17). Here, in an essay originally published in 1803, Chalmers discusses Steele's earlier works and his essays written for the* Tatler *and comments on Steele's literary partnership with Addison.*]

[**The Christian Hero**] consists chiefly of a review of the characters of some celebrated Heathens, contrasted with the life and principles of our blessed Saviour, and of St. Paul, from which it is his object to prove, that none of the heroic virtues, or 'true greatness of mind,' can be maintained, unless upon Christian principles. The language is far from being regular, and, perhaps, he may seem deficient in powers of argument: but his address has much of that honest zeal and affection which comes from the heart. It has been often reprinted and circulated among the middling class of readers, but in his own time probably redounded more to his honour as an author, than to his advantage as a man; for he informs us that the rebuffs he met with, instead of encouragements for his declarations in regard to religion, laid him under a necessity of enlivening his character; and with this view, he wrote his first play, called **The Funeral, or Grief Alamode,** which was very successfully performed the same year, and is yet a favourite with the publick. This play is said to have procured him the regard of KING WILLIAM, who intended to have bestowed some mark of favour upon him, which the death of that monarch prevented. . . . ADDISON is said also to have assisted him in the comedy of the **Tender husband,** *or the Accomplished Fools,* which was acted with great success in 1704. The friendship between these two illustrious characters commenced when they were school-fellows at the Charterhouse. 'I remember,' says STEELE, 'when I finished the *Tender Husband,* I told him (ADDISON) there was nothing I so tenderly wished, as that we might, some time or other, publish a work written by us both, which should bear the name of the MONUMENT, in memory of our friendship.'

His next play was *The Lying Lover,* which, he tells us, 'was damned for its piety;' a fate which it does not appear to deserve on that, or any other account more within the province of a dramatic tribunal. There is great regularity in the fable of all his plays, and the characters are well sketched and preserved; but in the dialogue he is sometimes tedious. He wants the quick repartee of CONGREVE; and though possessed of humour, falls into the style rather of an essay than a drama. Much of that point which appears in his *Tatlers* may be discovered in his Comedies. (pp. xlii-xliii)

The *Tatler,* like many other eminent superstructures, rose from small beginnings. It does not appear that the author foresaw to what perfection this method of writing might be brought, when he should by the aid of his illustrious colleague be able to reject his first plan. By dividing each paper into compartments, he appears to have consulted the ease with which an author may say a little upon many subjects, who has neither leisure nor inclination to enter deeply on a single topic. This, however, did not proceed either from distrust in his abilities, or in the favour of the public; for he at once addressed them with confidence and familiarity; but it is probable that he did not foresee to what the continued practice of writing will frequently lead a man whose natural endowments are wit and eloquence, superadded to a knowledge of the world, and a habit of observation. (pp. l-li)

In the selection of a name for the work, STEELE affords an early instance of delicate raillery, by informing us that the name *Tatler* was invented in *honour* of the fair sex; and that in such a character he might indulge with impunity the desultory plan he first laid down, with a becoming imitation of the tattle and gossip of the day. His paper professed to embrace 'accounts of gallantry, pleasure, and entertainment,' under the head 'White's Chocolate-house;' 'poetry' under that of 'Will's Coffee-house;' and 'learning' under that of 'the Grecian:' 'foreign and domestic news' from 'St. James's Coffee-house;' 'and other articles' 'from his own apartment,' and sometimes 'from Shire-lane.' This plan was preserved for a considerable time, until his pen became more accustomed to essay-writing, and the assistance of his friend ADDISON enabled him to adopt a more regular method.

The Dramatic articles are numerous, and are said to have been serviceable to the theatre. CIBBER acknowledges the force and influence of the *Tatler* in filling the playhouses; yet STEELE had no share in the management of the playhouse in Drury-Lane for several years after this period. We have seen however that he was a dramatic writer, and was always anxious for the improvement of the stage; and that, with ADDISON and other writers, he wished to hasten

the time, all hope of which seems now given up, when the morals of the age should be reformed by what they called 'a well regulated theatre.' (pp. li-liii)

STEELE appears to have begun the paper without any concert, or hope of other assistance than what might come spontaneously. His chief dependence was on his intelligence, which gave him a superiority over his contemporaries, who were merely news-writers, and had never discovered that a periodical paper might furnish instruction of a better and more lasting kind. In the other parts of the *Tatler,* he was at first less careful; his style had a familiar vulgarity not unlike that of the journalists of the age, which he adopted either in compliance with the prevailing manner, or by way of disguise. In one paper he acknowledges 'incorrectness of style,' and writing 'in an air of common speech'. All this however became a *Tatler,* and for some time he aimed at no higher character. But when associated with ADDISON, he assumed a tone more natural to a polished and elegant mind, and dispersed his coarser familiarity among his characteristic correspondents. If he did not introduce, he was the first who successfully employed the harmless fiction of writing letters to himself, and by that gave a variety of amusement and information to his paper, which would have been impracticable had he always appeared in his own character. All succeding Essayists have endeavoured to avail themselves of a privilege so essential to this species of composition, but it requires a mimickry of style and sentiment which few have been able to combine. (pp. lv-lvi)

Such an assistant [as Addison] was of incalculable value to STEELE, who began to sacrifice his original plan by degrees, and as his views became enlarged and public attention more generally drawn to the paper, soon rose to the dignity of a teacher of wisdom and morals. (p. lvi)

It appears that some part of the popularity of the *Tatlers,* during their first publication, was owing to a very prevalent opinion, that the characters described in an unfavourable light, and held up to ridicule or contempt, were real. Of this many hints are given; and the question is very artfully obscured in every attempt to decide it. That some of the characters, both good and bad, were real, has been ascertained beyond all doubt: allusions to the *events* of the times are so frequent as to render it necessary to introduce the *actors.* We may instance the Bangorian controversy, which in itself however was perhaps too serious for the kind of ridicule employed. Religious controversy, when conducted with asperity and calumny, might often afford a proper subject of ridicule; but the attempt is dangerous, and we must never forget that the *matter* or object of all religious controversy, however misrepresented, is of eternal importance. The peevishness of Bishop BLACKALL, it must notwithstanding be confessed, is parodied with great humour in the letters of the Puppet-shew man, which have been admired by many readers who looked no farther than to the affected consequence of a vagrant of that mean employment. In No. 51, STEELE has apologised for his interference in this controversy with considerable shrewdness.

Besides the gamblers, many of whom were certainly real characters, a few of a more harmless cast are introduced, as RATCLIFF and ARNE; but in general, the allusions to living characters, not of the depraved kind, are free from asperity or malevolence. (pp. lviii-lix)

The general opinion, however, that all the characters delineated or alluded to, were real, certainly kept up the public attention to these papers; and the authors, being aware that nothing can render a work more popular than the supposition that it contains a proportion of scandal or personal history, were not very anxious to deprive themselves of a hold on the public mind which they could, and had the virtue to turn to the best of purposes. In writings of this kind, it is essential that vice and folly should be illustrated by characters; it is this which distinguishes them from dissertations of the more serious cast: and to readers of a certain description, it is a delightful employment to reduce fictitious to real names, conjecture wisely on place and person, and find resemblances where none were meant. Our authors cannot therefore be very severely blamed if they occasionally played with this species of self-deception, and, knowing the perverted taste of some of their customers, sold them lawful goods as contraband.

The chief design of all these papers is briefly expressed by Hughes in No. 64, to be 'a wholesome project of making wit useful,' a project the more to be commended as of all talents wit is the most liable to be abused; and as for many years preceding the date of the *Tatler,* the most celebrated wits had prostituted their pens in the service of the grosser vices. Few men could be better qualified than STEELE to employ this endowment in useful designs. Notwithstanding his personal failings, he appears to have uniformly entertained the purest principles of religion and morals: a strong sense of propriety in words as well as in action: and an abhorrence of gross vices, as offensive to the Deity, and dangerous to the eternal welfare of man. When betrayed by liveliness of temper into an expression inconsistent with piety or decency, he was ever ready to apologize and to revoke: if he committed errors, he certainly defended none. In manners he had a quick sense of what was ridiculous, and exposed it with easy playfulness, or humorous gravity. Availing himself of the many shapes an ESSAYIST may assume, he exposed levity of conduct, absurd fashions, improprieties of dress and discourse, in every various light; and laid the foundation for a change in the public mind, which has contributed beyond all calculation to the refinement of society.

[He] is not to be accounted the writer of every paper to which his name has been prefixed or appended. Those which appear in the regular form of ESSAY are certainly his; those consisting of letters, &c. were sometimes the contributions of correspondents. With respect to his able coadjutor, we are less liable to mistake. ADDISON's papers have been correctly ascertained, yet the frequent resemblance between these two writers in style and manner is a circumstance which deserves particular notice. We have seen that STEELE was the original author of the *Tatler,* that he was the first who prescribed a mode of periodical writing, new to the world from the nature of its subjects, and that he had made some progress before he received or appears to have expected assistance from ADDISON, who was then in a distant country, and in an official situation not likely to afford him the requisite leisure. Yet from the

time they began to write in conjunction, if the reader will attentively compare those papers which are certainly the respective productions of STEELE and ADDISON, he will meet with a surprising similarity of humour. In many instances STEELE imitates what has been since called the ADDISONIAN manner with a closeness which would have rendered it very difficult to assign the papers to their proper authors, if we had been left without any authority but a supposed knowledge of the style. Of this happy coincidence of talent, there are many striking instances in the *Spectator,* to which we shall have occasion to advert hereafter. In the mean time, we may remark that it contributed to preserve the uniformity and consistency of character, or the personal identity of ISAAC BICKERSTAFF. 'Throughout the whole work,' says an author who well knew how to appreciate its merits, 'the conjuror, the politician, the man of humour, the critic; the seriousness of the moralist, and the mock dignity of the astrologer; the vivacities and the infirmities peculiar to old age, are all so blended and contrasted in the Censor of Great Britain, as to form a character equally complex and natural, equally laughable and respectable.' (pp. lix-lxii)

STEELE'S manner of taking leave of the public, as *Mr. Bickerstaff,* is characteristic and not ungraceful. 'The general purpose of the whole,' it is said in the last paper,

> has been to recommend truth, innocence, honour, and virtue, as the chief ornaments of life; but I considered that severity of manners was absolutely necessary to him who would censure others, and for that reason and that only, chose to talk in a mask. I shall not carry my humility so far as to call myself a vicious man; but at the same time must confess, my life is at best but pardonable. And with a greater character than this, a man would make but an indifferent progress in attacking prevailing and fashionable vices, which Mr. Bickerstaff has done with a freedom of spirit, that would have lost both its beauty and efficacy, had it been pretended to by Mr. STEELE.

From a scarce pamphlet in the Lambeth library supposed to be written by [John] GAY ["The Present State of Wit "], we have authority to add, that STEELE'S disappearing was bewailed as some general calamity: every one wanted so agreeable an amusement: and the coffee houses began to be sensible that his Lucubrations alone had brought them more customers than all their other newspapers put together. Never man threw up his pen under stronger temptations to have employed it longer; for his reputation was at a greater height, says this writer, than ever any living author's was before him. There was this difference between him and all the rest of the polite and gallant authors of the time; the latter endeavoured to please the age by falling in with them, and encouraging them in their fashionable vices, and false notions of things. It would have been a jest some time since, for a man to have asserted that any thing witty could be said in praise of a married state; or that devotion and virtue were any way necessary to the character of a fine gentleman. Bickerstaff ventured to tell the town, that they were a parcel of fops, fools, and vain coquettes: but in such a manner, as even pleased them, and made them more than half-inclined to believe that he spoke truth. (pp. lxxxii-lxxxv)

Alexander Chalmers, "Historical and Biographical Preface to 'The Tatler', 1803," in his The British Essayists with Prefaces, Historical and Biographical, Vol. I, *J. Johnson and Others, 1808, pp. xiii-lxxxv.*

Nathan Drake   (essay date 1805)

[*Drake was an English physician who built a reputation as an essayist, critic, and anthologist. He also served as the editor of the* Speculator *(1790). In the following excerpt from an essay originally published in 1805, Drake provides an in-depth analysis of Steele's compositional style, asserting that the editor's attempt to write in a tone of common conversation "must surely be considered as one of the most preposterous conceptions that ever entered the brain of an author."*]

At the period when Steele commenced his labours as a writer of periodical Essays, little attention had been paid to accuracy of style or beauty of composition. To study the structure of a sentence, its harmony, compactness, or strength, and its relative connection as to variety and perspicuity with the surrounding text, were employments, however important, usually neglected, and, if pursued at all, generally deemed pedantic.

Swift, perhaps our earliest prose writer who made correctness and purity his peculiar province, had not, when Steele began his literary career, acquired that influence over the diction of his country in the departments of accuracy and precision which he afterwards obtained. Composition remained, with few exceptions, loose, disjointed, and slovenly; without choice of phrase or vigour of arrangement; and if occasionally exhibiting melody, richness, and force, these are to be attributed not to analysis, scientific acquirement, and design, adapting the powers of a copious language to the nature of the theme, but to the strength of momentary feeling, to the casual felicities of genius.

I am afraid it cannot be affirmed, that our author contributed much to improve or embellish the art of composition. He found it incorrect, and left it so. He is seldom, however, unintelligible; and though he can establish few claims to dignity or elegance, his pages are never deficient in vivacity and ease. Yet of these, I imagine, it must be allowed that his vivacity is more the result of thought than of expression; and his ease the consequence rather of feebleness and relaxation, than of tasteful and assiduous cultivation.

It was the opinion of Mr. Addison, that "there is as much difference between comprehending a thought clothed in Cicero's language, and that of an ordinary writer, as between seeing an object by the light of a taper and the light of the sun."

It had been fortunate for the literary reputation of Steele had he entertained a similiar idea, and composed accordingly. Nothing has contributed so much to depreciate him in the estimation of the public as the evident inferiority of his style, when compared with that of his friend and coadjutor. It is given to few to judge of the accuracy of informa-

tion, or the strength and concatenation of argument; but many, in the present age, are competent to decide on the accuracy and selection of language, on the modulation and cadence of a period; and where one individual may rise offended from a volume by the want of depth in reasoning, or of authenticity in subject, twenty shall be disgusted by negligence and harshness of style, by irregular construction, or vulgar phraseology.

That the reflection, good sense, and knowledge of character, which Steele every where displays in his writings, would have made a greater impression on the mind had they been clothed in diction of a sweeter and more graceful cast, will not be denied by any who have felt the seductive and enchanting powers of harmonious composition. But, unhappily, purity in the selection of words, and a curious felicity in their arrangement, were never, according to his own confession, the ambition or object of our author. The very title of his first series of papers seems to have warped and led astray his judgment; and he idly conceived that, having assumed the appellation of the ***Tatler,*** his language should resemble the chit-chat and common conversation of the day. "The nature of my miscellaneous work," says he,

> is such, that I shall always take the liberty to tell for news such things (let them have happened never so much before the time of writing) as have escaped public notice, or have been misrepresented to the world; provided that I am still within rules, and trespass not as a tatler any farther than in *incorrectness of style, and writing in an air of common speech* [***Tatler,*** 5].

That this was not an hasty decision, the product of the moment, and then laid aside, but acted upon in some degree throughout the whole of his periodical works, and avowed at a period long subsequent to their completion, is evident from the following passage in his dedication of the Drummer to Mr. Congreve: "The elegance, purity, and correctness in his writings (speaking of Addison's) were not so much my purpose," he observes, "as in *any intelligible manner as I could,* to rally all those singularities of human life, through the different professions and characters in it, which obstruct any thing that was truly good and great."

To imagine that essays addressed to the people at large, intended to improve their morals, correct their taste, and ridicule their frailties, should be written in the tone of common conversation, not only without any research after purity and elegance, but even rendered *purposely incorrect* in point of style, must surely be considered as one of the most preposterous conceptions that ever entered the brain of an author. Nothing, without doubt, could be contrived better calculated to depress the powers of a writer, and to render his efforts to instruct and please totally useless and inefficient, than this extraordinary plan, which, had Sir Richard fully acted upon and carried into execution, would long ago have consigned his works to merited oblivion.

It will readily be granted, that elaborate diction and profuse ornament, majesty of cadence and intricacy of collocation, are foreign to the nature of a popular essay. But between this excessive brilliancy and colloquial barbarism the distance is immense. In the interval there may be found a simplicity not careless and languid, but graceful, sweet, and unaffected, admitting of a due degree of embellishment, and yet speaking the very language of nature, and bringing forward without disguise the character and feelings of the author. Of a style thus simple, chaste yet elegant, the acquisition is not of easy purchase, but requiring much taste, much cultivation, and much acquaintance with the best models. . . . (pp. 185-90)

There is no doubt that Steele, had he chosen to bestow the necessary application, might have attained considerable proficiency in this mode of composition. He knew its value, we find, by terming it pure, correct, and elegant; and he had perpetually before his eyes, in the productions of his accomplished friend, a specimen of its appropriation to every popular and pleasing topic. It is probable, therefore, that the dissipation and hurry in which the greater part of his life was consumed, precluded that attention to the *limæ labor,* to those repeated and finishing touches, without which it is scarcely possible to reach excellence. Wanting time, therefore, and perhaps inclination, for the labours of revision, he endeavoured to render his style familiar, not by a correct and graceful plainness, but by the wretched expedient of systematic negligence.

To be *intelligible,* the first virtue of composition, was, however, the laudable aim of Steele, and he soon found, as he advanced, that negligence and incorrectness were of all means the least adapted to his purpose. His style, consequently, improves as he proceeds; and though seldom entitled to high commendation, either for its melody, its purity, or strength, it is in the latter volumes of his **Tatler,** and especially in his **Spectators** and **Guardians,** for the most part clear and animated.

To dwell upon the careless composition and grammatical inaccuracies of a writer, who, in almost every other respect, is highly meritorious, appears to be an invidious, and is certainly a very ungrateful task. Were these faults, nevertheless, of a nature subtle and obscure, or covered with any seductive charm, it might be highly useful and necessary to point them out with peculiar precision; but as the errors of Steele are, in general, of a kind too glaring to escape the detection of any person tolerably acquainted with our best and latest masters of style, I shall content myself with barely producing a few of the transgressions most commonly occurring in his works.

The following instances of awkward involution and violated grammar, and of what may, with propriety, be termed colloquial vulgarisms, will indicate with sufficient amplitude the usual blemishes of Sir Richard's style.

> 1. "Eucrate—enjoyed this part of the royal favour so much without being envied, that it was never enquired into, by whose means what no one else cared for doing, was brought about." **Spectator,** No 84.

> 2. "Others you shall find so obsequious, and so very courteous, *as there is* no escaping their favours of this kind." **Spect.** No 259.

> 3. "It is not *Me* you are in love with." **Spect.** No 290.

> 4. "Were any one to see Mariamne dance, let him be *never* so sensual a brute." **Spect.** No 466.

> 5. "I came to the knowledge of the most epidemic ill of this sort, by *falling into* a coffee-house, where I saw my friend the upholsterer, whose *crack* towards politics I have heretofore mentioned." **Tatler,** No 178.

> 6. "It is certain, there are many thousands like the above-mentioned yeoman and his wife, who are never highly pleased or *distasted* in their whole lives." **Tatler,** No 188.

> 7. The misapprehensions people themselves have of their own state of mind, *is* laid down with *much discerning* in the following letter." **Spect.** No 79.

> 8. "This excellent young woman has nothing to *consolate* herself with." **Tatler,** No 199.

Errors and defects such as these, which too frequently disfigure some of the most valuable productions of our author's pen, can only be ascribed to habitual carelessness. To a similar cause, likewise, is it owing that numerous passages, which a little attention to arrangement and verbal selection, might have raised to energy and elegance, remain flat, nerveless, and involved.

The ensuing lines, which are taken neither from his worst nor happiest effusions, present a fair specimen of the usual style in which Sir Richard chose to clothe his thought.

"In conversation," observes he,

> the medium is neither to affect silence *or* eloquence; not to value our approbation, and to endeavour to excel us who are of your company, are equal injuries. The great enemies, therefore, to good company, and those who transgress most against the laws of equality, which is the life of it, are, the clown, the wit, and the pedant. A clown, when he has sense, is conscious of his want of education, and, with an aukward bluntness, hopes to keep himself in countenance by overthrowing the use of all polite behaviour. He takes advantage of the restraint good-breeding lays upon others not to offend him, to trespass against them, and is under the man's own shelter while he intrudes upon him. The fellows of this class are very frequent in the repetition of the words 'rough and manly.' When these people happen to be by their fortunes of the rank of gentlemen, they defend their other absurdities by an impertinent courage; and, to help out the defect of their behaviour, add their being dangerous to their being disagreeable. This gentleman (though he displeases, professes to do so; and, knowing that, dares still go on to do so) is not so painful a companion, as he who will please you against your will, and resolves to be a wit [**Tatler,** 244].

This passage, which is throughout somewhat feeble and entangled, exhibiting little modulation, and where not a sentence can be termed vigorously or beautifully constructed, a few alterations from the hand of taste would have rendered lucid and harmonious.

Had Steele possessed either the cultivated critical powers or the unwearied assiduity of Addison, who was minute even to excess in polishing and retouching his pieces, this and every other part of his works requiring no particular elevation of style, would have been neat, correct, and graceful; qualities indispensable to almost every species of composition, and without which the utility of writing cannot be carried to its full extent.

Though on topics involving no particular interest, nor exciting any strong feelings, our author was very apt to be remiss and slovenly in his style; yet when, warmed by the nature of his subject, his sensibility was appealed, to or his passions roused, it will generally be found, on examination, to flow with considerable spirit and perspicuity.

I could, with equal ease and pleasure, produce several passages from the essays of Steele in confirmation of this remark, and which are alike creditable to his heart and taste. Two, however, after having severely censured his *general* mode of composition, I think myself compelled in justice to quote.

The first contains some natural and touching reflections on the loss of a beloved object by premature death.

"In such a humour as I am now in," exclaims our author, "I can the better indulge myself in the softnesses of humanity, and enjoy that sweet anxiety which arises from the memory of past afflictions.—

> Here, were there words to express such sentiments with proper tenderness, I should record the beauty, innocence, and untimely death, of the first object my eyes ever beheld with love. The beauteous virgin! how ignorantly did she charm, how carelessly excel! Oh death! thou hast right to be bold, to the ambitious, to the high, and to the haughty; but why this cruelty to the humble, to the meek, to the undiscerning, to the thoughtless? Nor age, nor business, nor distress, can erase the dear image from my imagination. In the same week I saw her dressed for a ball, and in a shroud. How ill did the habit of death become the pretty trifler [*Tatler,* 181].

The second contrasts with much eloquence and effect the virtuous and the vicious of the female sex.

"The ill," says he,

> are employed in communicating scandal, infamy, and disease, like furies; the good distribute benevolence, friendship, and health, like angels. The ill are damped with pain and anguish at the sight of all that is laudable, lovely, or happy; the virtuous are touched with commiseration towards the guilty, the disagreeable, and the wretched. There are those who betray the innocent of their own sex, and solicit the lewd of ours. There are those who have abandoned the very memory, not only of innocence, but shame. There are those who never forgave, nor could ever bear being forgiven. There are those also who visit the beds of the sick, lull the cares of the sorrowful, and double the joys of the joyful. Such is the destroying fiend, such the guardian angel, woman [*Tatler,* 201].

The energy, perspicuity, and modulation of these extracts sufficiently prove that when animated by his theme Sir Richard had selection of language, and felicity of arrangement, adequate to every demand which periodical composition could bring forward. How highly is it to be regretted then, that in adopting a style for the majority of his essays, he should have suffered his judgment so far to be misled, as avowedly to prefer the tone of common speech, with all its negligences, to a pure and chastely ornamented diction, in which the attainment of excellence was perhaps only wanting to render his otherwise valuable productions perfect and imperishable. (pp. 190-97)

After the observations that we have now given on the style of Steele, . . . it may be asserted without fear of contradiction, that among the numerous obligations which Sir Richard has conferred on his country, through the medium of his writings, the improvement of its language and composition cannot with propriety be enumerated. He will be found in purity and simplicity inferior to Tillotson; to Temple in elegance and harmony; to Dryden in richness, mellowness, and variety. To the two former, however, he is equal in correctness; to the latter in vivacity; and with all he is nearly on a level as to ease and perspicuity.

Steele's great misfortune has ever been the comparison so perpetually drawn with regard to style between himself and Addison. The proximity of their productions has naturally led to the consideration of their respective merits in point of composition; and though it must be allowed that from the best manner of Addison Steele stands widely apart, yet are there several papers which, having been written by Sir Richard with more than usual care, and with evident marks of emulation, appear to have imbibed a portion of Addisonian grace. It is, therefore, by no means an easy task, as has been affectedly pretended, to distinguish accurately, and without hesitation, their respective papers, merely from the contrast of style. Addison is not always equal to himself in diction or construction; he is now and then feeble and remiss, and were the initials of designation withdrawn, those most familiar with the differences of style, with the shades of idiom and expression, might sometimes be foiled in the attempt.

We shall conclude this subject with remarking, that Steele is, perhaps, under this head, an exception to a general rule. It is style which usually embalms for posterity the effusions of elegant literature. Such however are the various merits of Steele in every other respect, and such the popularity of his topics, that, notwithstanding his negligent and frequently inelegant diction, he has attained, and still preserves, the rank of a British Classic. (pp. 201-02)

> *Nathan Drake, "Observations on the Style of Steele," in his* Essays, Biographical, Critical and Historical, Illustrative of the "Tatler," "Spectator," and "Guardian," Vol. I, *1805. Reprint by Johnson Reprint Corporation, 1968, pp. 185-202.*

Leigh Hunt   (essay date 1810)

[*Hunt was a prominent English poet, essayist, and literary critic who was instrumental in influencing several young poets, including John Keats and Percy Bysshe Shelley. Here, in a drama review originally published in the* Examiner *in 1810, Hunt praises Steele's* Conscious Lovers *not for its strong writing or wit, but for its "unaffected knowledge" and its "insights into human nature."*]

To witness the **Conscious Lovers,** after being pestered with all the *new* nonsense at the Lyceum, is like going out of a tavern-cellar into an elegant company. Taste and improvement breathe again: you have a respect for yourself and your society; and are prepared once more to venerate the use and beauty of social dialogue. The play is not remarkable either for strong writing or for wit; but its best scenes are in a charming strain of unaffected knowledge, the sentiments as delicate as rational, and the insights into human nature of that nice and feeling discrimination which is the first characteristic of Steele's writings. It is this talent, exemplified throughout the **Tatler** and **Spectator** in so many nice varieties of character and so many touches of pathos exquisitely careless, which certainly gives him the palm of invention in those admirable works, though his genius has been overpowered by the wit and the more dignified wisdom of Addison. The characters of the play are kept up with truth and pleasing contrast to the last—the gentlemanly authority of *Sir John Bevil* and the less prejudiced plain sense of *Mr. Sealand,* who had seen the world—the accomplished sensibility of *Indiana* and the freer though innocent spirit of *Lucinda*—the young coxcomb servant of *Bevil,* and the old staid servant of his father—and lastly, the high gentlemanly rationality and pure manliness of *Bevil* opposed to the intemperate enthusiasm of his friend *Myrtle.* The challenge-scene between these two gentlemen is well known to everybody from childhood, and is one of the best practical arguments that ever were furnished against duelling, since the person challenged has at the same time warmth enough to be worked into momentary provocation, yet philosophy enough to conquer by explanation. It was a delicate point to shew the hero of a play withstanding a challenge and at the same time preserving his character with the audience, and yet this is what Steele has done by the mere force of his hero's solid consistency of character. If we except the coarse character of *Cimberton,* into whose mouth, as satirists are too apt to do, the author put more than was needed, all the scenes are of a piece with this instruction, not omitting the playful follies of *Mr. Tom* and *Mrs. Phillis,* who shew us in what rank of life the coxcomb and flippant coquet ought to be found. The translations of this comedy sufficiently prove its estimation on the Continent, where the imitation of Terence and of nature is still reckoned a mark of taste, and the modern English drama is known only to be despised. (pp. 35-7)

> *Leigh Hunt, "The Conscious Lovers," in his* Dramatic Criticism, 1808-1831, *edited by Lawrence Huston Houtchens and Carolyn Washburn Houtchens, Columbia University Press, 1949, pp. 35-7.*

William Hazlitt   (essay date 1819)

[*An English essayist, Hazlitt was one of the most important critics of the Romantic age. Below, in an essay originally published in 1819, the author contends that he prefers Steele's writing for the* Tatler *to that of the* Spectator, *on which Steele and Addison collaborated. "I am far from wishing to depreciate Addison's talents," Hazlitt asserts, "but I am anxious to do justice to Steele, who was . . . a less artificial and more original writer."*]

[Periodical essay composition] is the best and most natural course of study. It is in morals and manners what the experimental is in natural philosophy, as opposed to the dogmatical method. It does not deal in sweeping clauses of proscription and anathema, but in nice distinctions and liberal constructions. It makes up its general accounts from details, its few theories from many facts. It does not try to prove all black or all white as it wishes, but lays on the intermediate colours, (and most of them not unpleasing ones,) as it finds them blended with 'the web of our life, which is of a mingled yarn, good and ill together.' It inquires what human life is and has been, to shew what it ought to be. It follows it into courts and camps, into town and country, into rustic sports or learned disputations, into the various shades of prejudice or ignorance, of refinement or barbarism, into its private haunts or public pageants, into its weaknesses and littlenesses, its professions and its practices—before it pretends to distinguish right from wrong, or one thing from another. . . . The writers I speak of are, if not moral philosophers, moral historians, and that's better: or if they are both, they found the one character upon the other; their premises precede their conclusions; and we put faith in their testimony, for we know that it is true.

Montaigne was the first person who in his Essays led the way to this kind of writing among the moderns. The great merit of Montaigne then was, that he may be said to have been the first who had the courage to say as an author what he felt as a man. And as courage is generally the effect of conscious strength, he was probably led to do so by the richness, truth, and force of his own observations on books and men. He was, in the truest sense, a man of original mind, that is, he had the power of looking at things for himself, or as they really were, instead of blindly trusting to, and fondly repeating what others told him that they were. (pp. 91-2)

The ice being thus thawed, and the barrier that kept authors at a distance from common sense and feeling broken through, the transition was not difficult from Montaigne and his imitators, to our Periodical Essayists. These last applied the same unrestrained expression of their thoughts to the more immediate and passing scenes of life, to temporary and local matters; and in order to discharge the invidious office of *Censor Morum* more freely, and with less responsibility, assumed some fictitious and humorous disguise, which, however, in a great degree corresponded to their own peculiar habits and character. By thus concealing their own name and person under the title of the **Tatler, Spectator,** &c. they were enabled to inform us more fully of what was passing in the world, while the dramatic contrast and ironical point of view to which the whole is subjected, added a greater liveliness and *piquancy* to the descriptions. The philosopher and wit here commences newsmonger, makes himself master of 'the perfect spy o' th' time,' and from his various walks and turns through life, brings home little curious specimens of the humours, opinions, and manners of his contemporaries, as the botanist brings home different plants and weeds, or the mineralogist different shells and fossils, to illustrate their several theories, and be useful to mankind.

The first of these papers that was attempted in [England] was set up by Steele in the beginning of the last century; and of all our periodical Essayists, the *Tatler* (for that was the name he assumed) has always appeared to me the most amusing and agreeable. Montaigne, whom I have proposed to consider as the father of this kind of personal authorship among the moderns, in which the reader is admitted behind the curtain, and sits down with the writer in his gown and slippers, was a most magnanimous and undisguised egotist; but Isaac Bickerstaff, Esq. was the more disinterested gossip of the two. The French author is contented to describe the peculiarities of his own mind and constitution, which he does with a copious and unsparing hand. The English journalist good-naturedly lets you into the secret both of his own affairs and those of others. A young lady, on the other side Temple Bar, cannot be seen at her glass for half a day together, but Mr. Bickerstaff takes due notice of it; and he has the first intelligence of the symptoms of the *belle* passion appearing in any young gentleman at the West-end of the town. The departures and arrivals of widows with handsome jointures, either to bury their grief in the country, or to procure a second husband in town, are punctually recorded in his pages. He is well acquainted with the celebrated beauties of the preceding age at the court of Charles II.; and the old gentleman (as he feigns himself) often grows romantic in recounting 'the disastrous strokes which his youth suffered' from the glances of their bright eyes, and their unaccountable caprices. In particular, he dwells with a secret satisfaction on the recollection of one of his mistresses, who left him for a richer rival, and whose constant reproach to her husband, on occasion of any quarrel between them, was 'I, that might have married the famous Mr. Bickerstaff, to be treated in this manner!' The club at the Trumpet consists of a set of persons almost as well worth knowing as himself. The cavalcade of the justice of the peace, the knight of the shire, the country squire, and the young gentleman, his nephew, who came to wait on him at his chambers, in such form and ceremony, seem not to have settled the order of their precedence to this hour; and I should hope that the upholsterer and his companions, who used to sun themselves in the Green Park, and who broke their rest and fortunes to maintain the balance of power in Europe, stand as fair a chance for immortality as some modern politicians. Mr. Bickerstaff himself is a gentleman and a scholar, a humourist, and a man of the world; with a great deal of nice easy *naïveté* about him. If he walks out and is caught in a shower of rain, he makes amends for this unlucky accident by a criticism on the shower in Virgil, and concludes with a burlesque copy of verses on a city-shower. He entertains us, when he dates from his own apartment, with a quotation from Plutarch, or a moral reflection; from the Grecian coffee-house with politics; and from Wills', or the Temple, with the poets and players, the beaux and men of wit and pleasure about town. In reading the pages of the *Tatler,* we seem as if suddenly carried back to the age of Queen Anne, of toupees and full-bottomed periwigs. The whole appearance of our dress and manners undergoes a delightful metamorphosis. The beaux and the belles are of a quite different species from what they are at present; we distinguish the dappers, the smarts, and the pretty fellows, as they pass by Mr. Lilly's shop-windows in the Strand; we are introduced to Betterton and Mrs. Oldfield behind the scenes; are made familiar with the persons and performances of Will Estcourt or Tom Durfey; we listen to a dispute at a tavern, on the merits of the Duke of Marlborough, or Marshal Turenne; or are present at the first rehearsal of a play by Vanbrugh, or the reading of a new poem by Mr. Pope. The privilege of thus virtually transporting ourselves to past times, is even greater than that of visiting distant places in reality. London, a hundred years ago, would be much better worth seeing than Paris at the present moment.

It will be said, that all this is to be found, in the same or a greater degree, in the *Spectator.* For myself, I do not think so; or at least, there is in the last work a much greater proportion of commonplace matter. I have, on this account, always preferred the *Tatler* to the *Spectator.* Whether it is owing to my having been earlier or better acquainted with the one than the other, my pleasure in reading these two admirable works is not in proportion to their

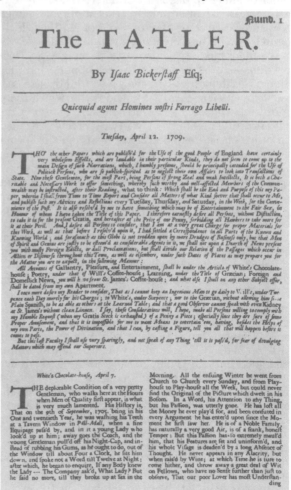

Title page of the Tatler *from its first number, 12 April 1709.*

comparative reputation. The *Tatler* contains only half the number of volumes, and, I will venture to say, nearly an equal quantity of sterling wit and sense. 'The first sprightly runnings' are there; it has more of the original spirit, more of the freshness and stamp of nature. The indications of character and strokes of humour are more true and frequent; the reflections that suggest themselves arise more from the occasion, and are less spun out into regular dissertations. They are more like the remarks which occur in sensible conversation, and less like a lecture. Something is left to the understanding of the reader. Steele seems to have gone into his closet chiefly to set down what he observed out of doors. Addison seems to have spent most of his time in his study, and to have spun out and wire-drawn the hints, which he borrowed from Steele, or took from nature, to the utmost. I am far from wishing to depreciate Addison's talents, but I am anxious to do justice to Steele, who was, I think, upon the whole, a less artificial and more original writer. The humorous descriptions of Steele resemble loose sketches, or fragments of a comedy; those of Addison are rather comments or ingenious paraphrases on the genuine text. The characters of the club not only in the *Tatler,* but in the *Spectator,* were drawn by Steele. That of Sir Roger de Coverley is among the number. Addison has, however, gained himself immortal honour by his manner of filling up this last character. Who is there that can forget, or be insensible to, the inimitable nameless graces and varied traits of nature and of old English character in it—to his unpretending virtues and amiable weaknesses—to his modesty, generosity, hospitality, and eccentric whims—to the respect of his neighbours, and the affection of his domestics—to his wayward, hopeless, secret passion for his fair enemy, the widow, in which there is more of real romance and true delicacy, than in a thousand tales of knight-errantry—(we perceive the hectic flush of his cheek, the faltering of his tongue in speaking of her bewitching airs and 'the whiteness of her hand')—to the havoc he makes among the game in his neighbourhood—to his speech from the bench, to shew the *Spectator* what is thought of him in the country—to his unwillingness to be put up as a sign-post, and his having his own likeness turned into the Saracen's head—to his gentle reproof of the baggage of a gipsy that tells him 'he has a widow in his line of life'—to his doubts as to the existence of witchcraft, and protection of reputed witches—to his account of the family pictures, and his choice of a chaplain—to his falling asleep at church, and his reproof of John Williams, as soon as he recovered from his nap, for talking in sermon-time. The characters of Will. Wimble, and Will. Honeycomb are not a whit behind their friend, Sir Roger, in delicacy and felicity. The delightful simplicity and good-humoured officiousness in the one, are set off by the graceful affectation and courtly pretension in the other. How long since I first became acquainted with these two characters in the *Spectator!* What old-fashioned friends they seem, and yet I am not tired of them, like so many other friends, nor they of me! How airy these abstractions of the poet's pen stream over the dawn of our acquaintance with human life! how they glance their fairest colours on the prospect before us! how pure they remain in it to the last, like the rainbow in the evening-cloud, which the rude hand of time and experience can

neither soil nor dissipate! What a pity that we cannot find the reality, and yet if we did, the dream would be over. I once thought I knew a Will. Wimble, and a Will. Honeycomb, but they turned out but indifferently; the originals in the *Spectator* still read, word for word, the same that they always did. We have only to turn to the page, and find them where we left them!—Many of the most exquisite pieces in the *Tatler,* it is to be observed, are Addison's, as the Court of Honour, and the Personification of Musical Instruments, with almost all those papers that form regular sets or series. I do not know whether the picture of the family of an old college acquaintance, in the *Tatler,* where the children run to let Mr. Bickerstaff in at the door, and where the one that loses the race that way, turns back to tell the father that he is come; with the nice gradation of incredulity in the little boy, who is got into Guy of Warwick, and the Seven Champions, and who shakes his head at the improbability of Æsop's Fables, is Steele's or Addison's, though I believe it belongs to the former. The account of the two sisters, one of whom held up her head higher than ordinary, from having on a pair of flowered garters, and that of the married lady who complained to the *Tatler* of the neglect of her husband, with her answers to some *home* questions that were put to her, are unquestionably Steele's.—If the *Tatler* is not inferior to the *Spectator* as a record of manners and character, it is superior to it in the interest of many of the stories. Several of the incidents related there by Steele have never been surpassed in the heart-rending pathos of private distress. I might refer to those of the lover and his mistress, when the theatre, in which they were, caught fire; of the bridegroom, who by accident kills his bride on the day of their marriage; the story of Mr. Eustace and his wife; and the fine dream about his own mistress when a youth. What has given its superior reputation to the *Spectator,* is the greater gravity of its pretensions, its moral dissertations and critical reasonings, by which I confess myself less edified than by other things, which are thought more lightly of. Systems and opinions change, but nature is always true. It is the moral and didactic tone of the *Spectator* which makes us apt to think of Addison (according to Mandeville's sarcasm) as 'a parson in a tie-wig.' Many of his moral Essays are, however, exquisitely beautiful and quite happy. Such are the reflections on cheerfulness, those in Westminster Abbey, on the Royal Exchange, and particularly some very affecting ones on the death of a young lady in the fourth volume. These, it must be allowed, are the perfection of elegant sermonising. His critical Essays are not so good. I prefer Steele's occasional selection of beautiful poetical passages, without any affectation of analysing their beauties, to Addison's finer-spun theories. The best criticism in the *Spectator,* that on the Cartoons of Raphael, of which Mr. Fuseli has availed himself with great spirit in his Lectures, is by Steele. I owed this acknowledgment to a writer who has so often put me in good humour with myself, and every thing about me, when few things else could, and when the tomes of casuistry and ecclesiastical history, with which the little duodecimo volumes of the *Tatler* were overwhelmed and surrounded, in the only library to which I had access when a boy, had tried their tranquillising effects upon me in vain. I had not long ago in my hands, by favour of a friend, an original copy of the quarto edition of the *Tatler,* with a list of the subscribers. It is curious to see some names there which we should hardly think of, (that of Sir Isaac Newton is among them,) and also to observe the degree of interest excited by those of the different persons, which is not determined according to the rules of the Herald's College. One literary name lasts as long as a whole race of heroes and their descendants! (pp. 95-9)

William Hazlitt, *"Lecture V: On the Periodical Essayists," in his* Lectures on the English Comic Writers and Fugitive Writings, *Dent, 1963, pp. 91-105.*

William Makepeace Thackeray   (essay date 1853)

[*Thackeray is one of the most important English novelists of the nineteenth century. Although some commentators argue that his criticism—collected in* The English Humorists of the Eighteenth Century *(1853) from lectures he delivered in Europe and the United States—is of mixed quality, it reveals interesting aspects of Thackeray's character and the literary taste of his time. In the following excerpt from that work, Thackeray comments on the admiration and respect for women evident in Steele's works, and compares his natural writing style with those of Swift and Addison.*]

[Women] . . . are bound to be grateful to Steele, as he was the first of our writers who really seemed to admire and respect them. Congreve the Great, who alludes to the low estimation in which women were held in Elizabeth's time, as a reason why the women of Shakspeare make so small a figure in the poet's dialogues, though he can himself pay splendid compliments to women, yet looks on them as mere instruments of gallantry, and destined, like the most consummate fortifications, to fall, after a certain time, before the arts and bravery of the besieger, man. There is a letter of Swift's, entitled "Advice to a very Young Married Lady," which shows the Dean's opinion of the female society of his day, and that if he despised man he utterly scorned women too. No lady of our time could be treated by any man, were he ever so much a wit or Dean, in such a tone of insolent patronage and vulgar protection. In this performance, Swift hardly takes pains to hide his opinion that a woman is a fool: tells her to read books, as if reading was a novel accomplishment; and informs her that "not one gentleman's daughter in a thousand has been brought to read or understand her own natural tongue." Addison laughs at women equally; but, with the gentleness and politeness of his nature, smiles at them and watches them, as if they were harmless, half-witted, amusing, pretty creatures, only made to be man's playthings. It was Steele who first began to pay a manly homage to their goodness and understanding, as well as to their tenderness and beauty. In his comedies, the heroes do not rant and rave about the divine beauties of Gloriana or Statira, as the characters were made to do in the chivalry romances and the high-flown dramas just going out of vogue; but Steele admires women's virtue, acknowledges their sense, and adores their purity and beauty, with an ardor and strength which should win the good-will of all women to their hearty and respectful champion. It is this ardor, this respect, this

manliness, which makes his comedies so pleasant and their heroes such fine gentlemen. He paid the finest compliment to a woman that perhaps ever was offered. Of one woman, whom Congreve had also admired and celebrated, Steele says, that "to have loved her was a liberal education." "How often," he says, dedicating a volume to his wife, "how often has your tenderness removed pain from my sick head, how often anguish from my afflicted heart! If there are such beings as guardian angels, they are thus employed. I cannot believe one of them to be more good in inclination, or more more charming in form than my wife." His breast seems to warm and his eyes to kindle when he meets with a good and beautiful woman, and it is with his heart as well as with his hat that he salutes her. About children, and all that relates to home, he is not less tender, and more than once speaks in apology of what he calls his softness. He would have been nothing without that delightful weakness. It is that which gives his works their worth and his style its charm. It, like his life, is full of faults and careless blunders; and redeemed, like that, by his sweet and compassionate nature. (pp. 14-16)

The great charm of Steele's writing is its naturalness. He wrote so quickly and carelessly, that he was forced to make the reader his confidant, and had not the time to deceive him. He had a small share of book-learning, but a vast acquaintance with the world. He had known men and taverns. He had lived with gownsmen, with troopers, with gentlemen ushers of the Court, with men and women of fashion; with authors and wits, with the inmates of the spunging-houses, and with the frequenters of all the clubs and coffee-houses in the town. He was liked in all company because he liked it; and you like to see his enjoyment as you like to see the glee of a boxful of children at the pantomime. He was not of those lonely ones of the earth whose greatness obliged them to be solitary; on the contrary, he admired, I think, more than any man who ever wrote; and full of hearty applause and sympathy, wins upon you by calling you to share his delight and good humor. His laugh rings through the whole house. He must have been invaluable at a tragedy, and have cried as much as the most tender young lady in the boxes. He has a relish for beauty and goodness wherever he meets it. He admired Shakspeare affectionately, and more than any man of his time; and, according to his generous expansive nature, called upon all his company to like what he liked himself. He did not damn with faint praise: he was in the world and of it; and his enjoyment of life presents the strangest contrast to Swift's savage indignation and Addison's lonely serenity. Permit me to read to you a passage from each writer, curiously indicative of his peculiar humor: the subject is the same, and the mood the very gravest. We have said that upon all the actions of man, the most trifling and the most solemn, the humorist takes upon himself to comment. All readers of our old masters know the terrible lines of Swift, in which he hints at his philosophy and describes the end of mankind:

Amazed, confused, its fate unknown,
The world stood trembling at Jove's throne;
While each pale sinner hung his head,
Jove, nodding, shook the heavens and said:
'Offending race of human kind,

By nature, reason, learning, blind;
You who through frailty stepped aside,
And you who never err'd through pride;
You who in different sects were shamm'd,
And come to see each other damn'd;
(So some folk told you, but they knew
No more of Jove's designs than you;)
The world's mad business now is o'er,
And I resent your freaks no more;
I to such blockheads set my wit,
I damn such fools—go, go, you're bit!'

Addison, speaking on the very same theme, but with how different a voice, says, in his famous paper on Westminster Abbey (*Spectator,* No. 26):—

> For my own part, though I am always serious, I do not know what it is to be melancholy, and can therefore take a view of nature in her deep and solemn scenes with the same pleasure as in her most gay and delightful ones. When I look upon the tombs of the great, every emotion of envy dies within me; when I read the epitaphs of the beautiful, every inordinate desire goes out; when I meet with the grief of parents on a tombstone, my heart melts with compassion; when I see the tomb of the parents themselves, I consider the vanity of grieving for those we must quickly follow.

(I have owned that I do not think Addison's heart melted very much, or that he indulged very inordinately in the "vanity of grieving.") "When," he goes on,

> when I see kings lying by those who deposed them: when I consider rival wits placed side by side, or the holy men that divided the world with their contests and disputes,—I reflect with sorrow and astonishment on the little competitions, factions, and debates, of mankind. And, when I read the several dates on the tombs of some that died yesterday and some 600 years ago, I consider that Great Day when we shall all of us be contemporaries, and make our appearance together.

Our third humorist comes to speak upon the same subject. You will have observed in the previous extracts the characteristic humor of each writer—the subject and the contrast—the fact of Death, and the play of individual thought, by which each comments on it, and now hear the third writer—death, sorrow, and the grave being for the moment also his theme. "The first sense of sorrow I ever knew," Steele says in the *Tatler,*

> was upon the death of my father, at which time I was not quite five years of age: but was rather amazed at what all the house meant, than possessed of a real understanding why nobody would play with us. I remember I went into the room where his body lay, and my mother sat weeping alone by it. I had my battledore in my hand, and fell a beating the coffin, and calling papa; for, I know not how, I had some idea that he was locked up there. My mother caught me in her arms, and, transported beyond all patience of the silent grief she was before in, she almost smothered me in her embraces, and told me in a flood of tears, 'Papa could not hear me, and would play with me no more: for they were

going to put him under ground, whence he would never come to us again.' She was a very beautiful woman, of a noble spirit, and there was a dignity in her grief amidst all the wildness of her transport, which methought struck me with an instinct of sorrow that, before I was sensible what it was to grieve, seized my very soul, and has made pity the weakness of my heart ever since.

Can there be three more characteristic moods of minds and men? "Fools, do you know anything of this mystery?" says Swift, stamping on a grave, and carrying his scorn for mankind actually beyond it. "Miserable, purblind wretches, how dare you to pretend to comprehend the Inscrutable, and how can your dim eyes pierce the unfathomable depths of yonder boundless heaven?" Addison, in a much kinder language and gentler voice, utters much the same sentiment: and speaks of the rivalry of wits, and the contests of holy men, with the same sceptic placidity. "Look what a little vain dust we are," he says, smiling over the tombstones; and catching, as is his wont, quite a divine effulgence as he looks heavenward, he speaks, in words of inspiration almost, of "the Great Day, when we shall all of us be contemporaries, and make our appearance together."

The third, whose theme is death, too, and who will speak his word of moral as Heaven teaches him, leads you up to his father's coffin, and shows you his beautiful mother weeping, and himself an unconscious little boy wondering at her side. His own natural tears flow as he takes your hand and confidingly asks your sympathy. "See how good and innocent and beautiful women are," he says; "how tender little children! Let us love these and one another, brother—God knows we have need of love and pardon." So it is each man looks with his own eyes, speaks with his own voice, and prays his own prayer.

When Steele asks your sympathy for the actors in that charming scene of Love and Grief and Death, who can refuse it? One yields to it as to the frank advance of a child, or to the appeal of a woman. A man is seldom more manly than when he is what you call unmanned—the source of his emotion is championship, pity, and courage; the instinctive desire to cherish those who are innocent and unhappy, and defend those who are tender and weak. If Steele is not our friend he is nothing. He is by no means the most brilliant of wits nor the deepest of thinkers: but he is our friend; we love him, as children love their love with an A, because he is amiable. Who likes a man best because he is the cleverest or the wisest of mankind; or a woman because she is the most virtuous, or talks French, or plays the piano better than the rest of her sex? I own to liking Dick Steele the man, and Dick Steele the author, much better than much better men and much better authors. (pp. 22-6)

William Makepeace Thackeray, "Steele," in his English Humorists of the Eighteenth Century, *The Century Co., 1907, pp. 1-42.*

John Forster   (essay date 1855)

[*Forster was an English biographer and critic whose works include* The Life and Times of Oliver Goldsmith *(1854),* Historical and Biographical Essays *(1858), and one volume of* The Life of Jonathan Swift *(1876). In the following excerpt, the critic takes exception to various remarks of Thomas Babington Macaulay, who depreciates Steele's writing as inferior to Addison's. Forster contends that Steele's literary wit was established long before he and Addison collaborated on the* Tatler, *and deems the editor the "sprightly father of the English Essay."*]

In forming his most celebrated literary project, we are told [in Thomas Babington Macaulay's *The Life and Writings of Addison,* 1852], Steele was far indeed from seeing its consequences; and Mr. Macaulay proceeds to give us his own description of the aim and design of the *Tatler.* Suggested by Steele's experience as Gazetteer . . . , it was to be on a plan quite new, and to appear on the days on which the post left London for the country, which were, in that generation, the Tuesdays, Thursdays and Saturdays. Mr. Macaulay thinks it immaterial to mention that De Foe's *Review,* with not a few points of resemblance, had already for five years travelled by the country posts on those days; but indeed the resemblance could hardly be expected to suggest itself, with such a low opinion of Steele's purpose in the *Tatler* as he seems to have formed. It was to contain, he says, the foreign news, accounts of theatrical representations, and the literary gossip of Will's and of the Grecian. It was also to contain remarks on the fashionable topics of the day, compliments to beauties, pasquinades on noted sharpers, and criticisms on popular preachers. 'The aim of Steele does not appear to have been at first higher than this.' Mr. Macaulay's manifest object is to convey the impression that the *Tatler* had no real worth until Addison joined it.

Now the facts are, that, with the exception of very rare occasional hints embodied in papers indubitably by Steele, and of the greater part of one essay which appeared in May and of another published in July, Addison's contributions to the *Tatler* did not begin until his return from Ireland in the middle of October, 1709, when eighty numbers had been issued. If, therefore, what Mr. Macaulay would convey be correct, Steele's narrow and limited design must have lasted at least so long; and that which gives the moral not less than the intellectual charm to these famous essays, which turned their humour into a censorship of manners at once gentle and effective, and made their wit subservient to wisdom and piety, could not have become apparent till after the middle of the second volume. Up to that time, according to Mr. Macaulay, Steele must have been merely compiling news, reviewing theatres, retailing literary gossip, remarking on fashionable topics, complimenting beauties, pasquinading sharpers, or criticising preachers, and could not yet have entered the higher field which the genius of Addison was to open to him. Nevertheless this is certain, that in dedicating the first volume of the work to Maynwaring he describes in language that admits of no misconstruction, not only his own intention in setting it on foot, but what he calls 'the sudden acceptance,' the extraordinary success, which immediately followed; and he further explains the character of his design

as precisely that attempt 'to pull off the disguises of cunning, vanity, and affectation, and to recommend a general simplicity in our dress, our discourse, and our behaviour,' which Johnson marks as its happy distinguishing feature, and the very drift of all its labour in teaching us the minuter decencies and inferior duties, in regulating the practice of our daily conversation, in correcting depravities rather ridiculous than criminal, and in removing, if not the lasting calamities of life, those grievances which are its hourly vexation.

But the papers themselves are before us, if we want evidence more conclusive. Where are the commonplaces described by Mr. Macaulay? How shall we limit our selection of examples in disproof of the alleged compiling, gossiping, complimenting, pasquinading? Why, as we turn over the papers preceding that number 81 which must be said to have begun the regular contributions of Addison, there is hardly a trait that does not flash upon us of the bright wit, the cordial humour, the sly satire, the subtle yet kindly criticism, the good nature and humanity, which have endeared this delightful book to successive generations of readers. There is, indeed, not less prominent at the outset than it continued to the close, the love of theatrical representations, and no doubt actors are criticised and preachers too; but we require no better proof than the very way in which this is done, of the new and original spirit that entered with it into periodical literature. In both the critic finds means of detecting countless affectations; and no one acquainted with the Pulpit of that day need feel surprise at the hints he gives of the service the Stage might render it, or that Mr. Betterton should have borrowed from Mr. Bickerstaff the answer to Sancroft's question—why it was that actors, speaking of things imaginary, affected audiences as if they were real; while preachers, speaking of things real, could only affect their congregations as with things imaginary? 'Why, indeed, I don't know; unless it is that we actors speak of things imaginary as if they were real, while you in the pulpit speak of things real as if they were imaginary.' An admirable paper to the same effect among the early *Tatlers* is that wherein he tells us that in tragical representations of the highest kind it is not the pomp of language, or the magnificence of dress, in which the passion is wrought that touches sensible spirits, 'but something of a plain and simple nature which breaks in upon our souls by that sympathy which is given us for our mutual good will and service.' And he illustrates his position by the example of Macduff when he hears of the murder of his children, and of Brutus when he speaks of the death of Portia.

There is no criticism of Shakspeare in that day at all comparable to this of Steele's, at the outset and to the close of the *Tatler.* With no set analysis or fine-spun theory, but dropped only here and there, and from time to time, with a careless grace, it is yet of the subtlest discrimination. He ranks him as high in philosophy as in poetry, and in the ethics of human life and passion quotes his authority as supreme. None but Steele then thought of criticizing him in that strain. The examples just quoted, for instance, are used as lessons in art, but also as experiences for patience under actual sorrow; and he finely adds, that it is in life itself exactly as at one of his plays, where we see the man overwhelmed by grief yet struggling to bear it with decency and patience—'we sigh *for* him, and give him every groan he suppresses.'

In this mode of eliciting, not merely canons of taste, but moral truths and rules of conduct, from the plays he sees acted, or the books he has been reading, Steele enriched his earliest and his latest *Tatlers* with a style of criticism which he must be said to have created. Nor is he satisfied with less than the highest models; delighting not more to place the philosophy above the poetry of Shakspeare, than to discover the sweetness and grace that underlie the majesty of Milton. The sixth *Tatler* begins the expression of his reverence for the latter poet, and not till the last line of the last *Tatler,* on which Shakspeare's name is imprinted, does it cease in regard to either. It was he, and not his friend, who, in that age of little faith, first raised again the poet of Paradise; his allusions to him, from the very commencement, are incessant; and a *Tatler* of but a few days earlier than that just quoted contains not only the noble lines in which Adam contemplates the sleeping Eve, but, by way of comment on its picture of manly affection made up of respect and tenderness, throws out this delightful remark. 'This is that sort of passion which truly deserves the name of love, and has something more generous than friendship itself; for it has a constant care of the object beloved, abstracted from its own interests in the possession of it.'

At a time in no way remarkable for refinement, Steele's gallantry to women, thus incessantly expressed in *The Tatler* to the last, was that of a Sir Tristan or Sir Calidore; and in not a small degree, to every household into which it carried such unaccustomed language, this was a ground of its extraordinary success. Inseparable always from his passion is the exalted admiration he feels; and his love is the very flower of his respect. But as, unhappily, a woman's education was then sunk to the lowest ebb, there is also no subject to which he has occasion so often and so eagerly to return, as a comparison of the large amount of care bestowed on her person with the little given to her mind. You deliver your daughter to a dancing-master, he says in one of these papers, you put a collar round her neck, you teach her every movement, under pain of never having a husband if she steps, or looks, or moves awry; and all the time you forget the true art which 'is to make mind and body improve together, to make gesture follow thought, and not let thought be employed upon gesture.' As he says in another paper to the like effect, a woman must think well to look well. He is never weary of surrounding her form with hosts of graces and delights; in her mind, how unused and uncultivated soever, he yet always recognises a finer and more delicate humanity; and all the fascinating things ever uttered in her praise by poet or romancer must yield to what is said of Lady Elizabeth Hastings in the 49th *Tatler.* 'Though her mien carries much more invitation than command, to behold her is an immediate check to loose behaviour, and *to love her is a liberal education.*'

As we have turned to this charming passage, we meet another of his illustrations from Shakspeare, in which, rebuking the author of a new tragedy for relying too much

on the retinue, guards, ushers, and courtiers of his hero to make him magnificent, 'Shakspeare,' he exclaims, 'is your pattern. In the tragedy of Cæsar he introduces his hero in his nightgown.' The resemblance of Addison's 42nd *Spectator* to this 53rd *Tatler* need not be pointed out; and we shall be excused for saying, with all our love and respect for Addison, that he might with good effect have taken, now and then, even a hint of conduct as well as of criticism from his friend. As to modes of dying, for example. The 11th *Tatler,* with a truth and spirit not to be surpassed, remarks that any doctrine on the subject of dying, other than that of living well, is the most insignificant and most empty of all the labours of men. A tragedian can die by rule, and wait till he discovers a plot, or says a fine thing upon his exit; but in real life, and by noble spirits, it will be done decently, without the ostentation of it. Commend me, exclaims Steele, to that natural greatness of soul expressed by an innocent and consequently resolute country fellow, who said, in the pains of the colic, 'If I once get this breath out of my body, you shall hang me before you put it in again.' Honest Ned! And so he died.

And what hints of other characters, taken from the same portion of the *Tatler,* need we, or shall we, add to honest Ned's, in proof that Steele did not wait for Addison's help before stamping his design with the most marked feature that remained with it? The difficulty is selection. Shall we take the wealthy wags who give one another credit in discourse according to their purses, who jest by the pound, and make answers as they honour bills; and who, with unmoved muscles for the most exquisite wit whose banker's balance they do not know, smirk at every word each speaks to the other? Shall we take the modest young bachelor of arts, who, thinking himself fit for anything he can get, is above nothing that is offered, and, having come to town recommended to a chaplain's place but finding none vacant, modestly accepts that of a postilion? Shall we introduce the eminent storyteller and politician, who owes the regularity and fluency of his dullness entirely to his snuff-box? Shall we make acquaintance with the whimsical young gentleman, so ambitious to be thought worse than he is, that, in his degree of understanding, he sets up for a freethinker, and talks atheistically in coffee-houses all day, though every morning and evening, it can be proved upon him, he regularly at home says his prayers? Shall the well-meaning Umbra take us by the button, and talk half an hour to us upon matters wholly insignificant with an air of the utmost solemnity, that we may teach ourselves the charity of not being offended with what has a good intention in it, by remembering that to little men little things are of weight, and that, though our courteous friend never served us, he is ever willing to do it, and believes he does it? Or, while Mr. Bickerstaff thus teaches us that impotent kindness is to be tolerated, shall Mrs. Jenny Distaff show us that impotent malice is not, and that society should scout the fool who cannot listen to praise without whispering detraction, or hear a man of worth named without recounting the worst passage of his life?

Shall we follow into Garraway's or the Stock Exchange those two men, in whom so striking a contrast appears of plain simplicity with imposing affectation, and learn that the sort of credit which commerce affects is worthless, if but sustained by the opinions of others and not by its own consciousness of value? Shall we let the smallest of pedants, Will Dactyle, convince us that learning does but improve in us what nature endowed us with; for that not to have good sense with learning is only to have more ways of exposing oneself, and to have sense is to know that learning itself is not knowledge? Shall the best-natured of old men, Senecio, prove to us that the natural, and not the acquired man is the companion; that benevolence is the only law of good breeding; that society can take no account of fortune; and that he who brings his quality with him into conversation, coming to receive homage and not to meet his friends, should pay the reckoning also? Shall we listen to Will Courtly, saying nothing but what was said before, yet appearing neither ignorant among the learned nor indiscreet with the wise, and acknowledge, so long as Will can thus converse with the wittiest without being ridiculous, that, if ceremony is the invention of wise men to keep fools at a distance, good-breeding must be its opposite expedient of putting wise men and less wise on equality? Shall we make ourselves easy in the company of Sophronius, who, when he does a service, charms us not more by his alacrity than, when he declines one, by his manner of convincing us that such service should not have been asked? Or shall we fidget ourselves in a room with Jack Dimple, who, having found out that what makes Sophronius acceptable is a natural behaviour, in order to the same reputation makes his own entirely artificial, meditates half an hour in the ante-room to get up his careless air, and is continually running back to the mirror to recollect his forgetfulness?

Such are among a few of the characters and essays which, while Mr. Macaulay would represent the *Tatler* as yet given up to sheer commonplace, with a prodigal wit and exuberant fancy Steele was pouring out upon its readers. We touch but slightly these few, and only hint at their purport and design; entering into no more detail than may carry with it the means of outweighing an assertion advanced on authority too high to be met by mere assertion of our own. We leave fifty things unnamed, and take from those named only a sentence here and there: but is it not enough? Not to speak of what will better be described hereafter of social colouring and individual expression, have we not here what gave life to the *Tatler?* Have we not the sprightly father of the English Essay, writing at the first even as he wrote to the last; out of a true and honest heart sympathizing with all things good and true; already master of his design in beginning it, and able to stand without help, if the need should be? In his easy chair we shall hereafter see Mr. Bickerstaff, amid the rustling of hoop-petticoats, the fluttering of fans, and the obeisance of flowing perukes: but what here for the present we see is the critic and philosopher Steele, more wise and not less agreeable; who, in an age that faction brutalized and profligacy debased, undertook the censorship of manners, and stamped at once upon the work he invented a genius as original as delightful. Here we have ourselves the means of judging if it was gossip, and compliments, and pasquinades, in the midst of which Addison found his friend; or whether already he had not struck out the thought by which both must be famous for ever, of enlivening morality with wit and tempering wit with morality?

But another fact is not less manifest in the examples given, and with it perhaps something of excuse for the half contemptuous tone that has done him such injustice. There is nothing so peculiar to his manner as the art of getting wisdom out of trifles. Without gravely translating his humorous announcement, that, when any part of his paper appeared dull, it was to be noted that there was a design in it, we may say with perfect truth that he had a design in everything. But a laugh never yet looked so wise as a frown; and, unless you are at pains to look a little beneath it, the wisdom may now and then escape you. The humorous old gentleman who is always prying into his neighbours' concerns, when he is not gossiping of his own; to whom the young beau is made responsible for wearing red-heeled shoes, and the young belle for showing herself too long at her glass; who turns the same easy artillery of wit against the rattling dice-box and the roaring pulpit; who has early notice of most of the love-affairs in town, can tell you of half the domestic quarrels, and knows more of a widow with a handsome jointure than her own lawyer or next of kin; whose tastes take a range as wide as his experience, to whom Plutarch is not less familiar than a pretty fellow, and who has for his clients not only the scholars of the Grecian, but the poets at Will's, the men of fashion at White's, and the quidnuncs of the St. James's,—this old humourist, one would say, is about the last man to pass for a Socrates. And yet there was something more than whim in his ambition to have it said of his lucubrations, that, whereas Socrates had brought philosophy down from heaven to inhabit among men, he had himself aimed to bring philosophy out of closets and libraries, schools and colleges, to dwell in clubs and assemblies, at tea-tables and in coffee-houses. For it is his actual and marked peculiarity that neither more nor less than this may be generally detected in Steele. One of the sincerest of men, he was the most natural of writers; and, living in the thick of the world, he could not write but with a vivid and ever present sense of it. The *humanitas humanissima* is never absent from him. If he takes up a book, it is not for a bookish purpose; he is always thinking of the life around him. Never yet, we think, has he had the due and distinctive praise for this, which in some sort separates him from every humourist and satirist of his time. Wit more piercing and keen, a reflective spirit of wider scope, a style more correct and pure, even humour more consummate than his own, will be found, in the way of comment upon life, among his friends and fellow-labourers; but for that which vividly brings actual Life before us, which touches the heart as with a present experience, which sympathizes to the very core of all that moves the joy or sorrow of his fellows, and which still, even as then, can make the follies of men ridiculous and their vices hateful without branding ridicule or hate upon the men themselves,—we must turn to Steele. In his little pictures of the world, that open new and unexpected views of it; in his wonderfully pathetic little stories, that fill our eyes with tears; in those trivial details by which he would make life easier and happier, in those accidents the most common and familiar out of which he draws secrets of humanity; what most, after all, impresses us, is a something independent of authorship. We like him the more for being nearer and more like ourselves, not for being higher or standing apart; and it is still the *man* whom his writings make pleasant to us, more than the author, the wit, the partizan, or the fine gentleman.

And a great reason for this we take to be, that he founded his theory and views of life rather on the realities that men should bravely practise, than on the pretences to which for the most part they shamefully submit. To be a man of breeding was with him to be a man of feeling; to be a fine gentleman, in his own phrase, was to be a generous and brave man; he had a proper contempt for the good manners that did not also imply the good morals; and it was the exalting and purifying influence of love for Lady Betty Modish, that made his Colonel Ranter cease to swear at the waiters. Be his theme, therefore, small or great, he brings it still within rules and laws which we find have not lost their interest for ourselves; and to which in truth we are in all respects still as amenable as if the red-heeled shoe, the hooped petticoat, or the flowing peruke, were yet potent and predominant in our century. As an instance which at once will explain our meaning, let us take what he says of vulgarity. It is also in one of these early *Tatlers.* There is, perhaps, no word so misused, none certainly of which the misuse is so mischievous; and not unfairly, by the opinions held of it, we may take the measure of a code of ethics and philosophy.

Steele's view of the matter is, then, that it is to him a very great meanness, and something much below a philosopher, which is what he means by a gentleman, to rank a man among the vulgar for the condition of life he is in, and not according to his behaviour, his thoughts, and his sentiments in that condition. For, as he puts it, if a man be loaded with riches and honours, and in that state has thoughts and inclinations below the meanest workman, is not such a workman, who within his power is good to his friends and cheerful in his occupation, in all ways much superior to him who lives but to serve himself? He then quotes the comparison, from Epictetus, of human life to a stage play; in which the philosopher tells us it is not for us to consider, among the actors, who is prince or who is beggar, but who acts prince or beggar best. In other words, the circumstance of life should not be that which gives us place, but our conduct in that circumstance. This alone can be our solid distinction; and from it Steele proceeds to draw certain rules of breeding and behaviour. A wise man, he says, should think no man above him or below him, any further than it regards the outward order or discipline of the world; for if we conceive too great an idea of the eminence of those above, or of the subordination of those below, it will have an ill effect upon our behaviour to both. With a noble spirit he adds, that he who thinks no man his superior but for virtue, and none his inferior but for vice, can never be obsequious or assuming in a wrong place; but will be ready as frequently to emulate men in rank below him, as to avoid and pity those above. Not that there was anything of the democrat or leveller in Steele. He knew too well that the distinctions of life, if taken at their true worth, would never fail to support themselves; and it was his knowledge of the quite irrepressible influence of wealth and station that urged him to such repeated enforcement of the social charities and duties to which he held them bound. It was no easy part, in his opinion, that the man of rank and wealth had to

play. It was no easy thing, in friendly intercourse, to check the desire to assume *some* superiority on the ground of position or fortune. It is not every man, he said with an exquisite felicity of phrase, that can entertain with the air of a guest, and do good offices with the mien of one that receives them.

And as Steele thus held, in the great commerce of the world, that a man must be valued apart from his circumstances, in like manner he also held, that, in his relations with it, he must regulate what he would appear to be by nothing other than actually becoming it. He must not hope to pass for anything more than he is worth; he must take care of his own wisdom and his own virtue, without minding too much what others think; and in what he knows he has, can be his only safe pledge at any time for its acknowledgment by others. It will be a useful hint in all cases, Steele says, for a man to ask himself whether he really *is* what he has a mind to *be thought,* for if he is, he need not give himself much further anxiety; nor is there, in this mode of reasoning, anything too little or too great not to yield as its result to his philosophy the value of reality beyond appearance.

Neither philosophy nor good writing, however, can Mr. Macaulay bring himself to recognise in Steele. All he admits is, that his style was easy and not incorrect; and though his wit and humour were of no high order, his gay animal spirits imparted to his compositions an *air of vivacity* which ordinary readers could hardly distinguish from comic genius. 'His writings have been well compared to those light wines which, though deficient in body and flavour, are yet a pleasant *small drink,* if not kept too long, or carried too far.' It is sufficiently clear, at least, that they have survived too long for Mr. Macaulay. Vinegar is not more sour than the pleasant small drink, kept now too long by nearly a century and a half, is become to him. (pp. 516-25)

At the outset of [Steele's *Christian Hero*] he tells you that men of business, whatever they may think, have not nearly so much to do with the government of the world as men of wit; but that the men of wit in that age had made a grave mistake in disregarding religion and decency. He attributes it to classical associations, that, being scholars, they are so much more apt to resort to Heathen than to Christian examples; and to correct this error he proposes to show, by a series of instances, how inadequate to all the great needs of life is the Heathen, and how sufficient the Christian morality. Anticipating and answering Gibbon, he looks upon it as the special design of Providence that the time when the world received the best news it ever heard was also that when the warriors and philosophers whose virtues are most pompously arrayed in story should have been performing, or just have finished, their parts. He then introduces, with elaborate portraiture of their greatness, Cato, the younger Brutus, and other characters of antiquity; that he may also display them, in their moments of highest necessity, deprived of their courage, and deserted by their gods. By way of contrast, he next exhibits, 'from a certain neglected Book, which is called, and from its excellence above all other books deservedly called, The Scripture,' handling it with no theological pretension, but as the common inheritance vouchsafed to us all, what the Christian system is. He finds in the Sermon on the Mount 'the whole heart of man discovered by him that made it, and all our secret impulses to ill, and false appearances of good, exposed and detected;' he shows through what storms of want and misery it was able to bear unscathed the early martyrs and apostles; and, in demonstration of the world's present inattention to its teaching, he tells them that, after all they can say of a man, let them but conclude that he is rich, and they have made him friends, nor have they utterly overthrown him till they have said he is poor. In other words, a sole consideration to prosperity has taken, in their imaginations, the place of Christianity; and what is there that is not lost, pursues kind-hearted Steele, in that which is thus displaced? 'For Christianity has that in it which makes men pity, not scorn, the wicked; and, by a beautiful kind of ignorance of themselves, think those wretches their equals.' It aggravates all the benefits and good offices of life by making them seem fraternal, and its generosity is an enlarged self-love. The Christian so feels the wants of the miserable, that it sweetens the pain of the obliged; he gives with an air that has neither oppression nor superiority in it, 'and is always a benefactor with the mien of a receiver.'

In . . . the *Tatler* we have . . . a paraphrase of these last few words, but indeed Mr. Bickerstaff's practical and gentle philosophy, not less than his language, is anticipated by Captain Steele. The spirit of both is the same. The leading purpose in both is a hearty sympathy with humanity; a belief, as both express it, that 'it is not possible for a human heart to be averse to anything that is human;' a desire to link the highest associations to the commonest things; a faith in the compatibility of mirth with virtue; the wish to smooth life's road by the least acts of benevolence as well as by the greatest; and the lesson so to keep our understandings balanced, that things shall appear to us 'great or little as they are in nature, not as they are gilded or sullied by accident and fortune.' The thoughts and expressions, as may be seen in these quoted, are frequently the same; each has the antithetical turns and verbal contrasts, 'the proud submission, the dignified obedience,' which is a peculiarity of Steele's manner; in both we have the author aiming far less to be author than companion; and there is even a passage in this *Christian Hero* which brings rustling about us the hoops and petticoats of Mr. Bickerstaff's Chloes and Clarissas. He talks of the coarseness and folly, the alternate rapture and contempt, with which women are treated by the wits; he desires to see the love they inspire taken out of that false disguise, and put in its own gay and becoming dress of innocence; and he tells us that 'in their tender frame there is native simplicity, groundless fear, and little unaccountable contradictions, upon which there might be built expostulations to divert a good and intelligent young woman, as well as the fulsome raptures, guilty impressions, senseless deifications, and pretended deaths, that are every day offered her.' Captain Steele dedicates his little book to Lord Cutts, dates it from the Tower Guard, and winds it up with a parallel between the French and the English king, not unbecoming a Christian soldier. But surely, as we thus read it on to its close, the cocked hat, the shoulder-belt, the jackboots disappear; and we have before us, in gown and slip-

pers, the Editor of the *Tatler.* Exit the soldier, and enter the wit. (pp. 538-40)

The *Funeral, or Grief à la Mode,* Steele's first dramatic production, was played at Drury Lane in 1702. Very sprightly and pleasant throughout, it was full of telling hits at lawyers and undertakers, and, with a great many laughable incidents, and no laugh raised at the expense of virtue or decency, it had one character (the widow on whom the artifice of her husband's supposed death is played off) which is a masterpiece of comedy. Guardsmen and Fusileers mustered strong on the first night; in the prologue, 'a fellow soldier' made appeal to their soldierly sympathies. . . . One can imagine the enjoyment of the scene where the undertaker reviews his regiment of mourners, and singles out for indignant remonstrance one provokingly hale, well-looking mute. 'You ungrateful scoundrel, did not I pity you, take you out of a great man's service, and show you the pleasure of receiving wages? Did not I give you ten, then fifteen, now twenty shillings a week, to be sorrowful. *And the more I give you, I think the gladder you are!*' But this was a touch that should have had for its audience a company of Addisons rather than of gay Fusileers and Guardsmen. Sydney Smith, indeed, who delighted in it, used to think it Addison's; but certainly Steele's first comedy had no insertion from that masterly hand. When it was written he was in Italy, when it was acted he was in Geneva, and he did not return to England, after an absence of more than four years, till towards the close of the following autumn. (pp. 540-41)

[It is not difficult] to trace Addison's hand in the *Tender Husband.* There is a country squire and justice of the quorum in it, perhaps the very first the stage had in those days brought from his native fields for any purpose more innocent than to have horns clapped on his head, and in the scenes with him and his lumpish nephew, there is a heightened humour we are disposed to give to Addison. But Steele's rich invention, and careless graces, are also very manifest throughout; and in the dialogues of the romance-stricken niece and her lover, from which Sheridan borrowed, and in that of the niece and her bumpkin of a cousin, to which even Goldsmith was somewhat indebted, we have pure and genuine comedy. The mistake of the piece, as of its predecessor, is the occasional disposition to reform morals rather than to paint manners; for the rich vein which the *Tatler* worked to such inimitable uses, yielded but scantily to the working of the stage. But the *Tender Husband,* . . . well deserved its success. Before its production there had arrived the glorious news of Blenheim, and Steele flung in some Whiggish and patriotic touches. Addison wrote the prologue, and to Addison the piece was dedicated: the author taking that means of declaring publicly to the world that he looked upon this intimacy as the most valuable enjoyment of his life, and hoping also to make the Town no ill compliment for their kind acceptance of his comedy by acknowledging, that this had so far raised his own opinion of it as to make him think it no improper memorial of an inviolable friendship. To Addison he addressed at the same time a more private wish, which lay very near his heart. 'I told him there was nothing I so ardently wished, as that we might sometime or other publish a work written by us both, which should bear the name of The Monument, in memory of our friendship.' Such a work, under a livelier title, not planned with that view by either friend, was soon to perpetuate, and inseparably to connect, the names of both. (pp. 542-43)

John Forster, "Sir Richard Steele," in The Quarterly Review, Vol. 96, No. CXCII, March, 1855, pp. 509-68.

H. B. Baker   (essay date 1872)

[*In the excerpt below, Baker states that although Steele's comedies are practically unknown to the modern reader, they were the "pioneers of a purer drama," the sentimental comedies of the early seventeenth century.*]

[In 1701, Steele] produced his first acted comedy—**The Funeral, or Grief à la Mode,** a satire directed against lawyers and undertakers. King William was so much pleased with the work that he conceived a great regard for the author, which would doubtless have led to handsome patronage, had not the death of the monarch put an end to all such hopes. (pp. 519-20)

In 1704 was produced the comedy of **The Tender Husband,** which proved a great success. In the composition of this work he was in some way assisted by Addison, whose services he thus generously acknowledged: "When the play above-mentioned was last acted, there were so many applauded strokes in it which I had from the same hand, that I thought very meanly of myself that I had never publicly acknowledged them." This was written after the death of Addison, and consequently after that unhappy estrangement which sundered the friends during the latter portion of their lives. Steele's next comedy was **The Lying Lover,** which proved a failure.

Although greatly admired in their day, and although containing much wit and humour, and many capitally-drawn characters—of which materials succeeding dramatists unscrupulously availed themselves—Steele's comedies are almost unknown to the modern reader. Their tone is too professedly moral; they read too much like sermons in dialogue. This is especially the case in **The Lying Lover,** which was composed after reading Jeremy Collier's book upon the immorality of the stage with a view to embody that writer's opinions, and as an effort towards the reform of that licentiousness which disfigured the dramatic literature of the age.

This was the age when ladies—and not over-prudish ladies—thought it necessary to appear at the theatre in masks, which hid blushes (?) evoked by the prurient dialogue of the play. "Some ladies," says the **Spectator,** "wholly absent themselves from the playhouse, and others never miss the first night of a new play, lest it should prove too luscious to admit of their going with any countenance to a second." It was the age of the brilliant but vicious comedies of Congreve, Farquhar, and Wycherley. Never has poor humanity cut so sorry a figure as in those eighteenth-century mirrors of nature, more especially in the mirror held up by the first of the illustrious trio. Connubial love and constancy, every domestic virtue, were held up

to ridicule: all the male characters were profligates, all the women shameless wantons; every plot turned upon deluded husbands and lawless gallantry.

Such was the stage that Steele endeavoured to purge of its grossness—such the characters that he desired to replace by beings actuated by moral impulses. And he did not labour in vain. Those old forgotten comedies of his were the pioneers of a purer drama, the true progenitors of the sentimental comedy—the origin of which is usually ascribed to a much later period—a species of composition which, however distasteful it may be to us of the nineteenth century, was at least cleanly and healthy in its moral tones; and those same old comedies led the way for the nobler works of Goldsmith and Sheridan, in which we have wit without ribaldry, humour without indecency. Hazlitt says: "The comedies of Steele were the first that were written expressly with a view, not to imitate, but to reform the manners of the age." But he adds: "It is almost a misnomer to call them comedies; they are rather homilies in dialogue, in which a number of very pretty young ladies and gentlemen discuss the fashionable topics of gaming, duelling, &c."

Thackeray, a by no means warm friend to Steele, writing of these comedies, gives him a yet higher praise [in his *English Humorists of the Eighteenth Century,* 1853]: "It was Steele who first began to pay a manly homage to their (women's) goodness and understanding, as well as to their tenderness and beauty. In his comedies his heroes do not rant and rave about the divine beauties of Gloriana or Statira. Steele admires women's virtue, acknowledges their sense, and adores their purity and beauty, with an ardour that should win the goodwill of all women to their hearty and respectful champion." (pp. 520-21)

His last literary work was the comedy of **The Conscious Lovers,** produced in 1722. It was an immense success. The King was so pleased with it that he presented the author with five hundred pounds. He commenced two other comedies, but they were never finished. (p. 531)

As a writer—although he was not gifted with the genius of Swift, and did not possess the polished philosophic vein of Addison; although many of our humourists possessed a keener spirit of satire, and a profounder knowledge of the heart—he is more human and less bookish than any other writer of the eighteenth century. His essays more resemble the gossip of a friend than the elaborations of an author. There is no scent of the midnight oil, nor of Russia, calf, nor printer's-ink about his lucubrations. The man has stepped out of Fleet Street, with the hum of traffic and the voices of the crowd in his ears, to write down what he has seen and heard. His library was the coffee-house and the street—his books men and women. If he describes a deathbed scene, or tells a pathetic story, it is not with the trickery of an author striving for effect, but with the simple unconscious pathos of a man who has witnessed the scene, and is still under its saddening influences. Turn to one of his essays after reading Addison, and it is like emerging into the woods and fields after the perusal of some fine pastoral poem: the poem was very beautiful, very vivid, but it lacked the fresh breeze, the freedom, the vigorous reality of life. (p. 532)

*H. B. Baker, in an originally unsigned essay ti-
tled "Richard Steele," in* Temple Bar, *Vol.
XXXIV, March, 1872, pp. 518-32.*

John Dennis   (essay date 1876)

[*In the following excerpt, the critic praises Steele's natural compositional style in his periodical essays, but finds
his dramas uninspiring in their artificial construction
and absurd plots.*]

Among the Queen Anne writers there is no figure which
we seem to see more vividly than that of Sir Richard
Steele. The man was by no means a hero. He wanted
strength of will and the invincible determination that
struggles successfully with evil. He was always sinning, always repenting; and there was no doubt a want of backbone in a nature that could thus lightly yield to temptation. There are many persons whose characters are so
firmly knit that the compassion they may feel for a man
like Steele is closely allied to contempt; there are others,
more generous and perhaps more wise, whose sorrow for
the failings of such a life is largely blended with sympathy.
They will feel that, if there be much to regret in the story
of Steele's career, there is much also which gives us a
higher opinion of humanity and claims the noblest kind
of charity. Steele frequently acted like a fool and suffered
bitterly for his folly; but we forget and forgive the moral
weakness of the man in our admiration of his virtues and
genius.

The period at which he lived and the men of letters with
whom he associated have an interest for us which has increased rather than diminished with the lapse of time.
Half a century ago these writers were in less repute than
they are now; fifty years hence it may be pretty safely asserted their reputation will not have waned. "A time
comes," it has been well said, "to most readers when in
the literature of the eighteenth century the mind finds its
best repose;" and it is surely well to turn aside occasionally
from the absorbing interest and often irritating suggestiveness of modern literature to a period that can be surveyed
with the complacency and calmness with which we look
upon the portrait of a venerable ancestor. Defects there
may be in the picture, but they are viewed without annoy-
ance; and we feel no inclination to quarrel with the critic
who may point out a mole upon the cheek or a cast in the
eye.

The Queen Anne essayists and poets, with one or two
doubtful exceptions, do not impress us with a sense of
greatness. They are pigmies by the side of the Elizabethan
heroes; they are inferior in the highest literary qualities to
many illustrious men who have lived and died in our own
century. The names of Tickell, Prior, Gay, Thomson, and
Steele may readily be matched by some second-rate modern authors; and even the noble trio Addison, Swift, and
Pope, each of whom in his own department we are accustomed to regard as unrivalled, cannot be justly compared,
for breadth of intellect and splendour of imagination, with
the poets and men of letters who stand in the front rank
of our literature.

A great man, however, is not necessarily the most pleasant
of companions. Milton is a sublime poet, but we are not
quite sure that a week spent in his company would have
been remembered with unalloyed pleasure. Coleridge, it is
just possible, might have wearied us with his unceasing
talk; and Wordsworth, though a good man and a noble
poet, did not, we must believe, always act the part of a host
with entire satisfaction to his guests. It is not given to
every distinguished man to make himself, like Sir Walter
Scott, as much beloved as he is admired; and it is not every
writer, however admirable and accomplished, who can
make his readers his friends, and bring them, as it were,
into cousinly relationship with himself. This is what Addison and Steele have done, and this is why we feel so much
at home in their company. Goodness, Milton tells us, is
awful; but Addison's goodness has in it a grace and sweetness, a gentleness and almost womanliness of tone which
forbid the sense of awe.

Steele, who, to quote Johnson's felicitous phrase, was "the
most agreeable rake that ever trod the rounds of indulgence," was far from being the model of a Christian hero;
but he was one of the most humane of men, most lovable,
most tender-hearted. If he hurt himself by his follies, he
did his best to help others by his wisdom; and that wisdom
of a genial kind blends with the humour of his essays no
one will doubt who has learnt to enjoy them thoroughly.

Sir Richard Steele—or let us style him Dick Steele, for a
title sits awkwardly upon his affectionate and loosely-built
man—calls up a host of memories in readers conversant
with his age. A literary artist who would represent him
properly requires a large canvas. He is himself a striking
personage; and it is scarcely possible to picture him alone,
so closely is he associated with the wits of the time. His
figure is seen in every variety of position as we examine the
literary and dramatic history of the period. Nor are his familiar features wanting in the political world. His talents
were of the most varied description, and his intellectual
energy was to be matched only by the amazing persistence
and courage of his contemporary De Foe.

The late Mr. Forster [in *The Quarterly Review,* vol. 96,
March 1855], borrowing the phrase apparently from
Leigh Hunt, has termed Steele "the sprightly father of the
English Essay." This, beyond question, is his highest literary honour. He created a new kind of literature, and
proved himself a master of the happy style which he invented. He did far more than this. It is scarcely too much
to say that we owe Addison to Steele. If Steele had not hit
upon this mine, Addison might never have displayed his
exquisite skill in converting the rough ore into delicate and
lovely specimens of workmanship. Without **The Tatler**
and **Spectator** Addison would be to us in the present day
little better than a name. We could not read his English
poetry; we could not tolerate his *Cato,* or applaud his *Rosamond;* and, although competent scholars might still admire his Latin verses, he would have secured no permanent place in literature. Had Steele possessed a less generous nature he must have felt jealous of his powerful auxiliary; but he was too true a friend, and had a disposition
too healy, to be the victim of so mean a passion. It is only
in recent days that the attempt has been made to praise
one of the friends at the expense of the other. In his well-

known and admirably-written essay on Addison ["The Life and Writings of Addison," 1852], Lord [Thomas Babington] Macaulay did his utmost, many years ago, to detract from the merit of Steele; and considering that everybody in that day read Macaulay's Essays, and that few comparatively read the essays of Steele, the latter came to be spoken of by those who knew nothing about him in a half-indulgent, half-contemptuous manner. Steele was regarded as a poor sort of fellow, whose chief honour in life was the friendship of Addison. That great moralist, it was said, might justly have renounced such a scapegrace, but he was too generous to cast off his old schoolfellow "when he diced himself into a sponging-house or drank himself into a fever." It was inevitable, according to these critics, that so good and wise a man as Addison should feel a contempt for Steele; and it is to his honour that he clung to him notwithstanding, and tried, though with little success, to keep him out of scrapes, for the sake of their early friendship at the Charterhouse. An exquisite humourist and great novelist of our day has also, we regret to say, taken the view of Steele which is allied to pity. In Mr. [William Makepeace] Thackeray's [*English Humorists of the Eighteenth Century,* 1853] Steele is no doubt represented with the utmost good humour and with much appreciation; but he is alluded to as "poor Steele," or "poor Dick Steele," is patted kindly on the back, and has his frailties exposed so as to awaken the feeling of compassion.

Now we do not think that this is quite the way in which this remarkable man should be regarded. We doubt greatly whether he needed pity in his lifetime, for he was blessed with a hopeful courageous nature, which no disappointment could for long depress and no difficulty daunt; and we doubt still more, considering his achievements and how much Englishmen owe to him, whether we should write of Sir Richard now as of one to be remembered with commiseration. In some respects, indeed, Addison deserves far more of our pity. He lacked the confidence in himself felt by his friend; he was painfully shy . . . he suffered the torture shy men feel in general society; and he had the misfortune to marry a countess. Steele had many failings, and his life witnessed many failures; but he was free from morbid tendencies, and, we venture to think, enjoyed existence more heartily than Addison. (pp. 408-10)

His earliest work was the result of a conflict in his mind similar to that which has been so vividly pictured by John Bunyan. The flesh and the spirit were at war within him, and the flesh got the upper hand. In his desire for amendment, he wrote for his private use *The Christian Hero,* a little treatise not without some literary merit. . . . The result of the publication was not altogether salutary. Captain Steele could not follow his own precepts, and the contrast between the printed page and the living hero called forth the mirth of his companions. On the other hand, it taught Steele that his true weapon was the pen rather than the sword, for the public liked the book, and within a few years several editions of the work were called for. About the close of the seventeenth century, Collier produced his celebrated attack on the immorality of the stage. The publication was well timed, and the arguments urged by the Jacobite clergyman were based upon facts too well known to be denied. Steele, whatever might be the vices of his life,

never transgressed propriety, or failed to uphold whatever is lovely and of good report, when he pursued his calling as a man of letters. There are, no doubt, passages in his plays and essays that cannot with propriety be read aloud in the family; but this is due to the change of manners which forbids our using plain language for plain subjects. Steele is occasionally coarse, and may repel readers who can tolerate, perhaps enjoy, the more alluring pictures of vice painted for them in verse and prose by some living writers; but Steele is never immoral, and his first comedy, *The Funeral; or, Grief à-la-Mode,* has the merit of affording a striking contrast to the licentious dramas of the Restoration. (pp. 411-12)

[On April 12, 1709] Steele published the first number of *The Tatler.* The significance of this event could have been foreseen by no one. Steele did not know, and none of his readers knew, that from this small seed would spring many a goodly tree, bright with flowers and wealthy in fruit, and that foliage, blossoms, and fruit would be unlike aught that had been grown hitherto in the garden of our literature. . . . The paper was published three times a week, the days on which the post left London, and contained, besides amusing sketches of character, "accounts of gallantry, pleasure, and entertainment," and poetical criticisms, a portion devoted to foreign and domestic news. This variety of plan suited the habits of Steele, and afforded scope for his genius. His versatility and his mercurial nature made prolonged labour distasteful; but he had wit, and readiness, and lively fancy, a quickness of perception and a facility in composition, which eminently fitted him for the task he had selected. Addison detected Steele's hand in the sixth number, and afforded him some slight assistance from that time; but it was not until about eighty numbers had appeared that he became a frequent contributor. For some months almost all the writing, as well as the editing, of the work devolved upon Steele. It would seem that he was not a little careless about the revision of the proofs; but readers in those days were easily satisfied, and the niceties of composition were as much disregarded as a uniform system of spelling. Pope in verse, and Addison in prose, were the literary reformers of the age; and the latter, after a century and a half, retains his fame not only as a moralist and humourist, but as a consummate master of language. Steele wrote with strong feeling and healthy enthusiasm, with much pathos and a varied knowledge of life; but he often wrote incorrectly, and his sentences are sometimes so oddly put together as to obscure the meaning. The depreciation he has received from some critics is due, we believe, in great measure, to the looseness of his style; but it may be observed, while acknowledging Steele's weakness in this respect, that frequently and almost always when moved by the pathos of his subject, the writer's language is simple, forcible, and appropriate. The best of Steele's papers in *The Tatler* are excelled by Addison alone, and there is a sprightliness and simplicity of tone about them which make them delightful reading. Steele came to his work well furnished, he carried it on with infinite vivacity, and in spite of the help rendered him by his illustrious friend, the colour of the work, if the term may be allowed, comes from the hand of Steele. As the teller of slight and pathetic tales he is superior to

Addison, and in criticism he takes a place by Addison's side. (pp. 418-20)

Steele was impulsive and given to change, but he was not lazy, and two months after the exit of *The Tatler* appeared the first number of *The Spectator.* Addison was consulted this time. The two friends formed the plan of the papers in concert, and, according to Bishop Hurd, the characters that comprise the celebrated club were the common work of both. This may be true; but it is certain that the second number, in which the different characters of the club are sketched, was written by Steele, and that we are indebted to his pen for our first introduction to the immortal Sir Roger de Coverley. Miss Aikin, with the curious habit of depreciating Steele in vogue amongst writers, regards it as "a singular circumstance" that the first hints of this character should have been thrown out by him; as if the versatile fancy and happy art of character-drawing that had so long sustained *The Tatler* were incapable of picturing the humourous knight! The portrait is a mere sketch, but the few lines that form it show the hand of a master. There was a time when every one who reads at all was perfectly familiar with *The Spectator,* and when an allusion to a paper would have sufficed without quotation. But time, though it cannot destroy our finest literature, is apt to rust it. Even Sir Roger himself is known by name only to many well-informed readers, and the short passage we shall quote may have the recommendation of novelty:—

> It is said he keeps himself a bachelor by reason he was crossed in love by a perverse beautiful widow of the next county to him. Before this disappointment Sir Roger was what you call a fine gentleman, had often supped with my Lord Rochester and Sir George Etherege, fought a duel at his first coming to town, and kicked Bully Dawson in a public coffee-house for calling him youngster. But being ill-used by the above-mentioned widow, he was very serious for a year and a half; and though, his temper being naturally jovial, he at last got over it, he grew careless of himself, and never dressed afterwards. He continues to wear a coat and doublet of the same cut that were in fashion at the time of his repulse, which, in his merry humours, he tells us, has been in and out twelve times since he first wore it. . . . He is now in his fifty-sixth year, cheerful, gay, and hearty; keeps a good house both in town and country; a great lover of mankind; but there is such a mirthful cast in his behaviour that he is rather beloved than esteemed; his tenants grow rich, his servants look satisfied; all the young women profess love to him, and the young men are glad of his company; when he comes into a house, he calls the servants by their names, and talks all the way upstairs to a visit. I must not omit that Sir Roger is a justice of the quorum; that he fills the chair at a quarter session with great abilities, and three months ago gained universal applause by explaining a passage in the Game Act.

The art with which Addison afterwards treats the knight is inimitable; but it should be always remembered that the first representation of Sir Roger is due to Steele. who seems throughout Addison's career to have paved the way

for his successes. *The Spectator* was wonderfully popular. All the town became familiar with it; it was found on every breakfast table; fine ladies who knew nothing of literature followed the prevailing fashion, and learnt to talk about Will Honeycomb and Will Wimble, and to laugh at the eccentricities of Sir Roger. The circulation was enormous for an age in which books and papers were usually the food of a circle of wits, instead of being, as in our day, a common necessary of life. Both in numbers and in volumes the famous essays sold by thousands, and the surprise of Steele must have been as great as his pleasure. Nevertheless, after a while he grew restless and impatient, and at the close of 1712 brought his journal to an end. This was done, as in the former case, without consultation with Addison; and when two or three months later Steele commenced *The Guardian,* he did so without communicating with his friend. The reasons for this reticence are not obvious, but the fact is noteworthy as exhibiting Steele's confidence in his own judgment and resources. He was always glad to receive literary aid from Addison, but in no instance does he seem to have acted as if dependent upon it. Addison was at work upon his *Cato,* and contributed nothing to the first volume of *The Guardian;* but Steele's name and reputation were now established, and the first men of the day were glad to fight under his banner. Bishop Berkeley, one of the noblest and purest of characters in an age that was far from being noble or pure, wrote fourteen papers; Pope, whose *Essay on Criticism* had lately placed him in the front rank among the writers of his time, contributed eight essays, one of which on the pastorals of Philips acquired no small notoriety; Philips himself wrote a paper upon song-writing; Gay, Parnell, Rowe, Hughes, Budgell, and Tickell also contributed; and after a time Addison was able to return to his alliance, and to write above fifty numbers, while upwards of eighty came from the prolific pen of the editor. For a third time Steele had achieved a great literary success, and for a third time he suddenly put an end to his work before it had exhibited any symptoms of decay. (pp. 420-21)

As an essayist, [Steele] was the most natural of writers; as a dramatist, he is the most artificial; his plots are absurd, and his characters possess no verisimilitude. There is not one of them for which it is possible to feel the remotest interest; not one that has acquired a living place in literature. It is a bore to read his dramas, and we are inclined to believe that the author was mistaken when he said that *The Lying Lover* was damned for its piety; it must have been for its dulness. A writer of Steele's genius was not likely, indeed, to produce any kind of literary work that should be wanting in ability; and the artful construction of his comedies pleased the playgoers of his age, who cared much more for art than nature. His purpose as a moralist is good throughout, and occasionally, as in *The Funeral,* we find a happy display of humour; but the principal impression left upon the mind after reading Steele's four plays is one of painful weariness. (p. 425)

How much Steele accomplished for English literature will be best understood by those who are familiar with the age in which he lived; and the more we become acquainted with it, the higher will be our estimation of the man who, with the help of his friend Addison, reformed the morals and manners of society, and showed how possible it was to employ the wit and humour that had been so often prostituted to vice in the service of virtue and religion. (p. 426)

John Dennis, "Sir Richard Steele," in The Cornhill Magazine, *Vol. XXXIV, October, 1876, pp. 408-26.*

W. J. Courthope   (essay date 1884)

[*Courthope was an English educator, poet, literary critic, and biographer whose most notable work is his six-volume* History of English Poetry *(1895-1910). Here, in an excerpt from his* Addison *(1884), Courthope discusses the development of the* Tatler, *maintaining that Steele bridged "the chasm between irreligious licentiousness and Puritanical rigidity" through his meditations on virtue in various periodical essays.*]

Richard Steele . . . was, above all things, "a creature of ebullient heart." Impulse and sentiment were with him always far stronger motives of action than reason, principle, or even interest. . . . Vehement in his political, as in all other feelings, he did not hesitate to resign the office he held under the Tory Government in 1711 in order to attack it for what he considered its treachery to the country; but he was equally outspoken, and with equal disadvantage to himself, when he found himself at a later period in disagreement with the Whigs. He had great fertility of invention, strong natural humour, true though uncultivated taste, and inexhaustible human sympathy.

His varied experience had made him well acquainted with life and character, and in his office of Gazetteer he had had an opportunity of watching the eccentricities of the public taste, which, now emancipated from restraint, began vaguely to feel after new ideals. That, under such circumstances, he should have formed the design of treating current events from a humorous point of view was only natural, but he was indebted for the form of his newspaper to the most original genius of the age. Swift had early in the eighteenth century exercised his ironical vein by treating the everyday occurrences of life in a mock-heroic style. Among his pieces of this kind that were most successful in catching the public taste were the humorous predictions of the death of Partridge, the astrologer, signed with the name of Isaac Bickerstaff. Steele, seizing on the name and character of Partridge's fictitious rival, turned him with much pleasantry into the editor of a new journal, the design of which he makes Isaac describe as follows:—

> The state of conversation and business in this town having long been perplexed with Pretenders in both kinds, in order to open men's minds against such abuses, it appeared no unprofitable undertaking to publish a Paper, which should observe upon the manners of the pleasurable, as well as the busy part of mankind. To make this generally read, it seemed the most proper method to form it by way of a Letter of Intelligence, consisting of such parts as might gratify the curiosity of persons of all conditions and of each sex. . . . The general purposes of this Paper is to expose the false arts of life, to pull off the disguises of cunning, vanity, and affectation, and to

recommend a general simplicity in our dress, our discourse, and our behaviour [*Tatler,* 1].

The name of the **Tatler,** Isaac informs us, was "invented in honour of the fair sex," for whose entertainment the new paper was largely designed. It appeared three times a week, and its price was a penny, though it seems that the first number, published April 12, 1709, was distributed *gratis* as an advertisement. In order to make the contents of the paper varied it was divided into five portions, of which the editor gives the following account:—

> All accounts of Gallantry, Pleasure, and Entertainment, shall be under the article of White's Chocolate-House; Poetry under that of Will's Coffee-House; Learning under the title of Grecian; Foreign and Domestic News you will have from Saint James' Coffee-House; and what else I have to offer on any other subject shall be dated from my own apartment. [*Tatler,* 1]

In this division we see the importance of the coffee-houses as the natural centres of intelligence and opinion. Of the four houses mentioned, St. James's and White's, both of them in St. James's Street, were the chief haunts of statesmen and men of fashion, and the latter had acquired an infamous notoriety for the ruinous gambling of its *habitues.* Will's in Russell Street, Covent Garden, kept up the reputation which it had procured in Dryden's time as the favourite meeting-place of men of letters; while the Grecian in Devereux Court in the Strand, which was the oldest coffee-house in London, afforded a convenient *rendezvous* for the learned Templars. At starting the design announced in the first number was adhered to with tolerable fidelity. The paper dated from St. James' Coffee-House was always devoted to the recital of foreign news; that from Will's either criticised the current dramas, or contained a copy of verses from some author of repute, or a piece of general literary criticism; the latest gossip at White's was reproduced in a fictitious form and with added colour. Advertisements were also inserted; and half a sheet of the paper was left blank, in order that at the last moment the most recent intelligence might be added in manuscript after the manner of the contemporary newsletters. In all these respects the character of the newspaper was preserved; but in the method of treating news adopted by the editor there was a constant tendency to subordinate matter of fact to the elements of humour, fiction, and sentiment. In his survey of the manners of the time Isaac, as an astrologer, was assisted by a familiar spirit, named Pacolet, who revealed to him the motives and secrets of men; his sister, Mrs. Jenny Distaff, was occasionally deputed to produce the paper from the wizard's "own apartment;" and Kidney, the waiter at St. James' Coffee-House, was humorously represented as the chief authority in all matters of foreign intelligence.

The mottoes assumed by the **Tatler** at different periods of its existence mark the stages of its development. On its first appearance, when Steele seems to have intended it to be little more than a lively record of news, the motto placed at the head of each paper was—

> Quidquid agunt homines,
> nostri est farrago libelli.

It soon became evident, however, that its true function was not merely to report the actions of men, but to discuss the propriety of their actions; and by the time that sufficient material had accumulated to constitute a volume, the essayists felt themselves justified in appropriating the words used by Pliny in the preface to his *Natural History:*—

> Nemo apud nos qui idem tentaverit: equidem sentio peculiarem in studiis causam eorum esse, qui difficultatibus victis, utilitatem juvandi, protulerunt gratiæ placendi. Res ardua vetustis novitatem dare, novis auctoritatem, obsoletis nitorem, fastidits gratiam, dubiis fidem, omnibus vero naturam, et naturæ suæ omnia. Itaque NON ASSECUTIS *voluisse,* abunde pulchrum atque magnificum est.

The disguise of the mock astrologer proved very useful to Steele in his character of moralist. It enabled him to give free utterance to his better feelings without the risk of incurring the charge of inconsistency or hypocrisy, and nothing can be more honourable to him than the open manner in which he acknowledges his own unfitness for the position of a moralist: "I shall not carry my humility so far," says he, "as to call myself a vicious man, but at the same time must confess my life is at best but pardonable. With no greater character than this, a man would make but an indifferent progress in attacking prevailing and fashionable vices, which Mr. Bickerstaff has done with a freedom of spirit that would have lost both its beauty and efficacy had it been pretended to by Mr. Steele" [*Tatler,* 271].

As Steele cannot claim the sole merit of having invented the form of the *Tatler* so too it must be remembered that he could never have addressed society in the high moral tone assumed by Bickerstaff if the road had not been prepared for him by others. One name among his predecessors stands out with a special title to honourable record. Since the Restoration the chief school of manners had been the stage, and the flagrant example of immorality set by the Court had been bettered by the invention of the comic dramatists of the period. Indecency was the fashion; religion and sobriety were identified by the polite world with Puritanism and hypocrisy. Even the Church had not yet ventured to say a word in behalf of virtue against the prevailing taste, and when at last a clergyman raised his voice on behalf of the principles which he professed, the blow which he dealt to his antagonists was the more damaging because it was entirely unexpected. Jeremy Collier was not only a Tory but a Jacobite, not only a High Churchman but a Nonjuror, who had been outlawed for his fidelity to the principles of Legitimism; and that such a man should have published the *Short View of the Immorality and Profaneness of the English Stage,* reflecting, as the book did, in the strongest manner on the manners of the fallen dynasty, was as astounding as thunder from a clear sky. Collier, however, was a man of sincere piety, whose mind was for the moment occupied only by the overwhelming danger of the evil which he proposed to attack. It is true that his method of attack was cumbrous, and that his conclusions were far too sweeping and often

unjust; nevertheless the general truth of his criticisms was felt to be irresistible. (pp. 89-94)

Collier, however, did nothing in a literary or artistic sense to improve the character of English literature. His severity, uncompromising as that of the Puritans, inspired Vice with terror, but could not plead with persuasion on behalf of Virtue; his sweeping conclusions struck at the roots of Art as well as of Immorality. He sought to destroy the drama and kindred pleasures of the Imagination, not to reform them. What the age needed was a writer to satisfy its natural desires for healthy and rational amusement, and Steele with his strongly-developed two-fold character was the man of all others to bridge over the chasm between irreligious licentiousness and Puritanical rigidity. Driven headlong on one side of his nature towards all the tastes and pleasures which absorbed the Court of Charles II., his heart in the midst of his dissipation never ceased to approve of whatever was great, noble, and generous. He has described himself with much feeling in his disquisition on the *Rake,* a character which he says many men are desirous of assuming without any natural qualifications for supporting it:—

> A Rake . . . is a man always to be pitied; and if he lives one day is certainly reclaimed; for his faults proceed not from choice or inclination, but from strong passions and appetites, which are in youth too violent for the curb of reason, good sense, good manners, and good nature; all which he must have by nature and education before he can be allowed to be or to have been of this order. . . . His desires run away with him through the strength and force of a lively imagination, which hurries him on to unlawful pleasures before reason has power to come in to his rescue.

That impulsiveness of feeling which is here described, and which was the cause of so many of Steele's failings in real life, made him the most powerful and persuasive advocate of Virtue in fiction. Of all the imaginative English essayists he is the most truly natural. His large heart seems to rush out in sympathy with any tale of sorrow or exhibition of magnanimity; and, even in criticism, his true natural instinct, joined to his constitutional enthusiasm often raises his judgments to a level with those of Addison himself, as in his excellent essay in the **Spectator** on Raphael's cartoons. Examples of these characteristics in his style are to be found in the **Story of Unnion and Valentine,** and in the fine paper describing two tragedies of real life; in the series of papers on duelling, occasioned by a duel into which he was himself forced against his own inclination; and in the sound advice which Isaac gives to his half-sister Jenny on the morrow of her marriage. Perhaps, however, the chivalry and generosity of feeling which make Steele's writings so attractive are most apparent in the delightful paper containing the letter of Serjeant Hall from the camp before Mons. After pointing out to his readers the admirable features in the serjeant's simple letter, Steele concludes as follows:—

> If we consider the heap of an army, utterly out of all prospect of rising and preferment, as they certainly are, and such great things executed by

them, it is hard to account for the motive of their gallantry. But to me, who was a cadet at the battle of Coldstream in Scotland when Monk charged at the head of the regiment now called Coldstream, from the victory of that day—I remember it as well as if it were yesterday, I stood on the left of old West, who I believe is now at Chelsea—I say to me, who know very well this part of mankind, I take the gallantry of private soldiers to proceed from the same, if not from a nobler, impulse than that of gentlemen and officers. They have the same taste of being acceptable to their friends, and go through the difficulties of that profession by the same irresistible charm of fellowship and the communication of joys and sorrows which quickens the relish of pleasure and abates the anguish of pain. Add to this that they have the same regard to fame, though they do not expect so great a share as men above them hope for; but I will engage Serjeant Hall would die ten thousand deaths rather than that a word should be spoken at the Red Lettice, or any part of the Butcher Row, in prejudice to his courage or honesty. If you will have my opinion, then, of the Serjeant's letter, I pronounce the style to be mixed, but truly epistolary; the sentiment relating to his own wound in the sublime; the postscript of Pegg Hartwell in the gay; and the whole the picture of the bravest sort of men, that is to say, a man of great courage and small hopes [*Tatler* 87].

With such excellences of style and sentiment it is no wonder that the *Tatler* rapidly established itself in public favour. It was a novel experience for the general reader to be provided three times a week with entertainment that pleased his imagination without offending his sense of decency or his religious instincts. (pp. 96-8)

A comparison of the amount of material furnished to the *Tatler* by Addison and Steele respectively shows that out of 271 numbers the latter contributed 188 and the former only 42. Nor is the disparity in quantity entirely balanced by the superior quality of Addison's papers. Though it was, doubtless, his fine workmanship and admirable method which carried to perfection the style of writing initiated in the *Tatler,* yet there is scarcely a department of essay-writing developed in the *Spectator* which does not trace its origin to Steele. It is Steele who first ventures to raise his voice against the prevailing dramatic taste of the age on behalf of the superior morality and art of Shakespeare's plays.

"Of all men living," says he in the eighth *Tatler,*

> I pity players (who must be men of good understanding to be capable of being such) that they are obliged to repeat and assume proper gestures for representing things of which their reason must be ashamed, and which they must disdain their audience for approving. The amendment of these low gratifications is only to be made by people of condition, by encouraging the noble representation of the noble characters drawn by Shakespeare and others, from whence it is impossible to return without strong impressions of honour and humanity. On these occasions distress is laid before us with all its causes and con-

sequences, and our resentment placed according to the merit of the person afflicted. Were dramas of this nature more acceptable to the taste of the town, men who have genius would bend their studies to excel in them.

Steele, too, it was who attacked with all the vigour of which he was capable the fashionable vice of gambling. So severe were his comments on this subject in the *Tatler* that he raised against himself the fierce resentment of the whole community of sharpers, though he was fortunate enough at the same time to enlist the sympathies of the better part of society. (pp. 102-03)

The practice of duelling also, which had hitherto passed unreproved, was censured by Steele in a series of papers in the *Tatler,* which seemed to have been written on an occasion when, having been forced to fight much against his will, he had the misfortune dangerously to wound his antagonist. The sketches of character studied from life, and the letters from fictitious correspondents, both of which form so noticeable a feature in the *Spectator,* appear roughly, but yet distinctly, drafted in the *Tatler.* Even the papers of literary criticism, afterwards so fully elaborated by Addison, are anticipated by his friend, who may fairly claim the honour to have been the first to speak with adequate respect of the genius of Milton. In a word, whatever was perfected by Addison was begun by Steele; if the one has for ever associated his name with the *Spectator,* the other may justly appropriate the credit of the *Tatler,* a work which bears to its successor the same kind of relation that the frescoes of Masaccio bear, in point of dramatic feeling and style, to those of Raphael; the later productions deserving honour for finish of execution, the earlier for priority of invention. (p. 104)

> *W. J. Courthope, in his* Addison, *1884. Reprint by Macmillan and Co., Limited, 1911, 197 p.*

Austin Dobson   (essay date 1886)

[*Dobson, an English verse-writer and man of letters, wrote a number of biographical prose works that show a close knowledge of eighteenth-century society and literature. He is best remembered for his series* Eighteenth Century Vignettes *(1892-96) and for his* Poems on Several Occasions *(1899). In the following excerpt, Dobson discusses the moral intentions of Steele's* Funeral, Lying Lover, *and* Tender Husband.]

Finding himself, [Steele] says in the *Apology,* 'slighted, instead of being encouraged, for his Declarations as to Religion . . . it was now incumbent upon him to enliven his Character, for which Reason he writ the Comedy called *The Funeral,* in which (tho' full of Incidents that move Laughter) Virtue and Vice appear just as they ought to do.' The full title of the play referred to is *The Funeral; or, Grief à la Mode.* (pp. 29-30)

The stress laid by Steele upon the part which virtue and vice play in his piece indicates a certain difference in his aims from those of his predecessors. The *Funeral,* indeed, appeared at a time when an appreciable reaction in stage morality was in progress. In some of the higher literary qualities, the comedy which had preceded the production of Congreve's *Way of the World* in 1700 has never since been equalled. But Wycherley's robustness and Vanbrugh's gay frivolity, the brisk and bustling vivacity of Farquhar, the dazzling brilliancy even of Congreve himself, had rendered little service to the purification of manners. Marriage as the sacrament of adultery, infidelity and libertinism as the indispensable equipment of the fine gentleman, pruriency and unchastity as the prevailing characteristics of the fine lady, ridicule of all that is honest and of good report as a general proposition,—these were the chief things which the later drama of the Stuarts had offered for the imitation of its audiences. Side by side, however, with the uncontrolled lawlessness of the anti-Puritan spirit, a spirit of righteous repugnance was also beginning to assert itself. . . . In his *Short View of the Immorality, and Profanity of the English Stage* Jeremy Collier framed an indictment against the existing drama which his arguments made unanswerable and his energy resistless. The Wits might have pricked a meaner man to death with epigram; but the terrible Nonjuror in the armour of his fearless indignation was invulnerable. He remained master of the field. Dryden, soon to die, declined the combat; Congreve answered feebly; Vanbrugh (whose *Relapse* was specially dissected), Settle, and Dennis, all replied in vain. Gradually a new spirit of decency began to manifest itself, at least ostensibly, in the works of contemporary playwrights, and by 1702, Charles Gildon could write in his *Comparison between the Two Stages,* that 'Our Audiences are really mended in their tast of Plays, and notwithstanding all the Raillery we have put upon Mr. *Collyer,* it must be confest that he has done the Stage good Service in correcting some of their Errors.' That he should correct them all was not to be expected; still less can it be said that the drama became pure by reason of his impeachment of it; but it may fairly be affirmed that licence received a definite check, and that the proclamation of a moral purpose became henceforth the conventional ensign of the popular dramatist.

Steele's *Funeral* came upon the wave of this new order of things, and we have seen that the moral purpose of making 'Virtue and Vice appear just as they ought to do' was not absent from his programme. Moreover, his play has a great deal of fresh vivacity, and not a little originality of conception. An old nobleman, Lord Brumpton, believed to be dead, although he is only in a fit, is persuaded by his servant Trusty—one of the earliest examples of the trusty servant on the English stage—to continue to feign death in order to observe the effect of his loss upon the members of his household, in particular upon his young wife, who is by no means unwilling to become a young widow. The idea is not without some obvious improbabilities; and as Gildon did not fail to point out in his excellent contemporary criticism, much of the subordinate intrigue between Lord Brumpton's wards and their soldier-admirers is out of keeping in the house where the head of the family is lying dead, while the escape of one of the heroines to her lover in the very coffin itself, although justified by stage precedent, certainly implies a liberal allowance of *bonne volonté* on the part of the spectator. Indeed Steele's negligence in this respect can only be explained by the supposition that, knowing himself Lord Brumpton was not dead,

Steele's second wife, Mary Scurlock, in a portrait by Sir Godfrey Kneller.

he forgot to remember that several of his *dramatis personæ* were not equally well informed. But if the plot be open to question on this score, the characters are less assailable. Those belonging to the legal and funereal class, at whom the main assault of the satire is directed, are certainly exceedingly diverting. Mr. Sable, the undertaker, drilling his mutes, and expostulating, more in sorrow than in anger, with the unfortunate man, who, engaged at first upon the strength of his wobegone countenance, has provokingly grown haler and gladder with each week's access of unhoped-for prosperity,—Mr. Puzzle, the lawyer and 'last great prophet of tautology,' instructing his clerk in the *longæ ambages* of testamentary phraseology, and the barbarous Law-Latin, the *Barnos, Outhousas, et Stabulas,* which Fielding ridiculed long after in the *Champion,*—fairly foreshadow the best character sketches in the **Spectator** and **Tatler.** The scene of the ragged recruits, too, one of whom has made his way from Cornwall by being whipped from constable to constable, and another who, in justification of his tattered condition, explains that, in his last regiment, 'the Collonel had one Skirt before, the Agent one behind, and every Captain of the Regiment a Button'—must have been hugely relished by the 'gentlemen of the Army,' who packed the house on the first night, and gallantly applauded their comrade's maiden effort. But Steele's most notable achievement in the **Funeral** is to be found in the freshness with which he has managed to invest his younger female characters. Lady Brumpton's woman Tattleaid administering mock consolation to her mistress with her mouth full of pins is a humorous picture which might be matched from earlier writers; but the dialogue between Lady Harriot and Lady Sharlot, with a little modernisation, would easily fit into a chapter by Trollope:—

> LADY HARRIOT. Nay, good Sage Sister, you may as well talk to [*Looking at herself as she speaks*] me, as sit Staring at a Book which I know you can't attend——Good Dr. *Lucas* may have writ there what he pleases, but there's no putting *Francis* Lord *Hardy*, now Earl of *Brumpton,* out of your Head, or making him absent from your Eyes, do but look at me now, and Deny it if you can——
>
> L. SH. You are the Maddest Girle——[*Smiling.*]
>
> L. H. Look'e you, I knew you could not say it and forbear Laughing—[*Looking over* Sharlot] Oh I see his Name as plain as you do—F..r..a..n Fran..c..i..s, cis Francis 'Tis in Every line of the Book.
>
> L. SH. [*Rising*] Tis in Vain I see to mind any thing in such Impertinent Company—but Granting 'twere as you say, as to my Lord *Hardy*——'Tis more excuseable to admire another than One's self——
>
> L. H. No I think not—Yes I Grant you than really to be vain at One's person, But I don't admire myself—Pish! I don't believe my Eyes have that Softness—[*Looking in the Glass*] They A'n't so piercing: No 'tis only a Stuff the Men will be talking—Some People are such admirers of Teeth—What signifies Teeth? [*showing her Teeth*] A very Blackamore has as White Teeth as I—No Sister, I Don't admire my self, but I've a Spirit of Contradiction in me: I don't know I'm in Love with my self, only to Rival the Men——
>
> L. SH. Ay, but Mr. *Campley* will gain Ground ev'n of that Rival of his, your Dear self——
>
> L. HA. Oh! what have I done to you, that you should name that Insolent intruder—A Confident Opinionative Fop—No indeed, If I am, as a Poetical Lover of mine Sigh'd and Sung, of both Sexes,
>
> *The Publick Envy, and the Publick Care,*
>
> I shan't be so easily Catch'd—I thank him——I want but to be sure, I shou'd Heartily Torment H·m, by Banishing him, and then consider whether he should Depart this Life, or not.
>
> L. SH. Indeed Sister to be serious with you, this Vanity in your Humour does not at all become you!
>
> L. HA. Vanity! all the Matter is we Gay People are more Sincere than you wise Folks: All your Life's an Art—Speak your soul—Look you there——[*halling her to the Glass*] Are not you Struck with a Secret Pleasure, when you view that Bloom in your Looks, that Harmony in your Shape, that Promptitude of your Mein!
>
> L. SH. Well Simpleton, if I am, at First so Silly,

> as to be a little taken with my self, I know it a Fault, and take Pains to Correct it.
>
> L. HA. Psaw! Psaw! talk this Musty Tale to Old Mrs. *Fardingale,* 'tis too soon for me to think at that Rate——
>
> L. SH. They that think it too soon to Understand themselves, will very soon find it too Late—But tell me honestly don't you like *Campley?*
>
> L. HA. The Fellow is not to be Abhorr'd, if the Forward thing did not think of Getting me so easily——Oh—I hate a Heart I can't break when I please——What makes the Value of Dear China, but that 'tis so Brittle——were it not for that, you might as well have Stone-Mugs in your Closet.

(pp. 30-6)

There is no doubt that the play was a success, and that it would have been so without the countenance of the Duke of Devonshire, who witnessed its rehearsal, or the friendly military *claque.* Gildon, who examines it minutely, begins by a half-apology for criticising what so many good judges have approved, and he winds up with a high compliment to the character of the author, who, he says, is 'indued with singular Honesty, a noble Disposition, and a conformity of good Manners; and as he is a Soldier, these Qualities are more conspicuous in him, and more to be esteemed.' He also commends the loyalty of his expressions,—a characteristic which, taken in connection with that timely reference to his Majesty in the **Christian Hero,** no doubt played its part in those 'Particulars enlarged upon to his Advantage,' which obtained for him the notice of William the Third, in whose 'last Table-Book,'—the *Apology* tells us,—the name of the author of the **Funeral** was noted for promotion. (pp. 36-7)

Strangely enough, [Steele's] next play, **The Lying Lover; or, the Ladies' Friendship,** was in its profession much more what might have been expected from the author of the **Christian Hero** than was the **Funeral.** The **Funeral,** though unobjectionable enough in the days of Farquhar and Vanbrugh, was still far from deserving the reproachful title of 'homily in dialogue,' hastily given by Hazlitt to all Steele's comedies, and, it may be added, applied with greater reason to the first essays of sentimental comedy in France, the *drames sérieux* of La Chaussée. Nevertheless its tone was infinitely more 'cleanly and beneficial' than the Restoration Comedy which Collier had assailed. Steele's second play, however, according to his own account in the **Apology,** was a deliberate attempt to put the precepts of Collier, whose work he greatly approved, into practice, and 'to write a Comedy in the Severity he required.' He took for basis the *Menteur* of Corneille, which Corneille in his turn had adapted from the Spanish of Ruiz de Alarcon. In many of the passages, the Old and Young Bookwit of the **Lying Lover,** who correspond to the Geronte and Dorante of the elder play, closely follow their originals; but Steele's chief moral interpolation was a prison-scene, in which young Bookwit, who is supposed to have killed a man in his cups, is shown overwhelmed with remorse. This deviation from the recognised practice of contemporary comedy, heightened by the fact that the added passages were written in blank verse, while the rest of the play was in prose, accounts in some measure for the comparative failure of the piece. When it was produced in December, 1703, it was performed but six times, or in its author's summary words, 'damned for its Piety.'

There were, however, other reasons for its misfortune, and among the rest, inferiority to its predecessor. The character of the hero seems better suited to the Spanish or French stage than the English; and Steele did not improve Corneille by the needless extension of certain of the speeches. Yet the *Lying Lover* is not without its happy pages. Some of young Bookwit's mendacious romancing is highly successful; and there is a group of gaol-birds in Act iv. who suggest certain chapters of Fielding's *Amelia.* One of these, Mr. Charcoal, the chemist, who is described as never cheating a fool, but 'still imposing on your most sprightly Wits and Genius—Fellows of Fire, and Metal, whose quick Fancies, and eager Wishes, form'd Reasons for their undoing'—almost seems to glance indirectly at certain chemical misadventures of Steele's own. . . . There is also a clever scene in Act iii., not borrowed from Corneille, where the two heroines, both anxious to do execution upon the hero, endeavour, by perfidiously patching each other, to mitigate the effect of their respective charms; while the second Act contains a pleasant vignette of that popular eighteenth-century resort, well known, no doubt, to Captain Steele of Lucas's,—the new Exchange:—

> YOUNG BOOKWIT. No Faith, the New Exchange has taken up all my Curiosity.
>
> OLD BOOKWIT. Oh! but, Son, you must not go to Places to stare at Women. Did you buy any thing?
>
> Y. BOOK. Some Bawbles.—But my Choice was so distracted among the pretty Merchants and their Dealers, I knew not where to run first.—One little lisping Rogue, Ribbandths, Gloveths, Tippeths.—Sir, cries another, will you buy a fine Sword-knot; then a third, pretty Voice and Curtsie,—Does not your Lady want Hoods, Scarfs, fine green silk Stockins.—I went by as if I had been in a Seraglio, a living Gallery of Beauties—staring from side to side, I bowing, they laughing—so made my Escape, and brought your Son and Heir safe to you, through all these Darts and Glances.—To which indeed my Breast is not impregnable.

The *Funeral* had been dedicated to the Countess of Albemarle; and its preface had contained a handsome compliment to John, Earl Somers. The *Lying Lover* was inscribed to the Duke of Ormond, in whose grandfather, the first duke, Steele gratefully recognised the patron of his childhood. When the preface which follows the dedication was written, the fate of the play must already have been decided; and Steele probably glances at contemporary criticism when he admits that the prison scene, notwithstanding its moral aspect, is perhaps 'an Injury to the Rules of Comedy.' 'But,'—he continues,—and the words deserve quotation for the reference they contain, 'Her Most Excellent Majesty has taken the Stage into Her Consideration; and we may hope, by Her gracious Influence on the Muses, Wit will recover from its Apostacy; and that by

being encourag'd in the Interests of Virtue, 'twill strip Vice of the gay Habit in which it has too long appear'd, and cloath it in its native Dress of Shame, Contempt, and Dishonour.' The allusion here is obviously to Queen Anne's proclamation of the 17th of January, which had appeared only a few days before the *Lying Lover* issued from the press. Reverting to the orders already given to the Master of the Revels and the Comedians that 'Nothing be Acted in either of the Theatres (i.e. Drury Lane and Lincoln's Inn Fields) contrary to Religion or Good Manners,' it went on to forbid the wearing of Vizard masks by women (a practice which had given rise to great irregularities), and the presence of strangers behind the scenes or upon the stage. Other proclamations followed this timely one; but from the notices in the newspapers for several years later, it seems that going behind the scenes had become too inveterate a custom to be summarily discontinued.

By the earlier biographers the failure of the *Lying Lover* to keep the stage has generally been held to account for Steele's long intermission of his dramatic efforts. Whatever may be the explanation of this misconception, it is clear that it is a misconception, based upon the belief that the *Lying Lover* was the third of Steele's acted plays. In reality it was the second, being succeeded by another, which, until lately, has usually been placed before it. This was the *Tender Husband; or, The Accomplished Fools,* produced at Drury Lane in April, 1705, with scarcely more success than its forerunner. . . . [Apart] from the equivocal character of some of the intrigue, which nevertheless can scarcely have caused any scruple of conscience to an eighteenth-century audience, it is brightly and effectively written. Moreover, several of the subordinate personages, if they do not actually stand *in loco parentis* to certain well-known dramatic figures of later date, are distinctly among their ancestors. There is a country gentleman, clearly of the race of Squire Western and the Tory Foxhunter, while his booby son, who is heir to fifteen hundred a year, who has been kept in ignorance that he has attained his majority, and who 'boggles a little at Marrying his Own Cousin,' is more than a mere indication of the future Tony Lumpkin. But the closest anticipation of a later personage is that of the romance-reading Biddy Tipkin, whose head is stuffed with *Pharamond* and the *Grand Cyrus,* who sighs to be called 'Parthenissa,' objects 'to go out at a Door to be Married' instead of out of a window, and hungers for the indispensable accompaniments of a courtship,—'Disguise, Serenade and Adventure,'—like the veriest Lydia Languish. 'Had *Oroondates* been as pressing as *Clerimont*'—she tells her impatient suitor—'*Cassandra* had been but a Pocket-Book,'—a fact which is undeniable, and is also in Molière. '*La belle chose que ce seroit,*' says Mademoiselle Magdelon of the *Précieuses ridicules, 'si d'abord Cyrus épousoit Mandane, et qu'Aronce de plain-pied fût marié à Clélie!*' Dennis, indeed, years afterwards, taunted Steele with taking Biddy Tipkin direct from this source. He would have shown more sagacity if he had pointed out another and more unmistakable debt to Molière. The episode of Parthenissa's lover, who disguises himself as a portrait painter, is plainly adapted, and in some places translated, from the *Sicilien; ou, l'Amour Peintre,* of the same author, a piece which must be held to have been unusually suggestive, since it is also supposed to have afforded hints both to Sheridan and Beaumarchais.

Addison, having by this time returned from Italy, and written the *Campaign,* contributed a rather colourless prologue to his friend's play; and there were also, Steele tells us in a later **Spectator,** 'many applauded Stroaks' in the piece itself from the same already eminent hand. Except upon the principle of assigning to Addison generally all the good things which it contains,—a plan which has been adopted by some of his admirers,—it is of course impossible to estimate the exact measure of this indefinite assistance. With the recolleciton of Addison's 'Will Wimble' fresh in one's mind, one might indeed be disposed to suspect that Captain Clerimont's definition of the vocation of a younger brother as consisting in 'Calling over this Gentleman's Dogs in the Country, Drinking his Stale-Beer in the Neighbourhood, or Marrying a Fortune,' must have proceeded from Addison's pen. Unfortunately Will Wimble has a nearer prototype in 'Mr. Thomas Gules' of **Tatler,** No. 256, one of those vague joint productions which cannot with certainty be assigned to one or other of the two colleagues. But if speculation upon this question is fruitless, the dedication to Addison of the play itself affords pleasant illustration of Steele's chivalrous attachment to his old schoolfellow, with whom, at this date, he declares himself to be in 'daily and familiar Conversation.' 'I look' (he says) 'upon my Intimacy with You, as one of the most valuable Enjoyments of my Life. At the same time I hope I make the Town no ill Compliment for their kind Acceptance of this Comedy, in acknowledging that it has so far rais'd my Opinion of it, as to make me think it no improper Memorial of an Inviolable Friendship. I should not offer it to you as such,' he goes on, 'had I not been very careful to avoid everything that might look Ill-natured, Immoral, or prejudicial to what the Better Part of Mankind hold Sacred and Honourable.'

These last words were no doubt perfectly sincere, although the modern reader who turns to the play itself, and opens upon the dubious *rôle* of the elder Clerimont's mistress, Mrs. Fainlove, may be forgiven a certain amount of astonishment. But a very slight acquaintance with the stage-literature of the Augustan age, and especially with the stage-literature of the Augustan age while it still bore about it the half-cleansed stains and smirches of Restoration drama, will not fail to convince him that the practice indicated by Steele's precepts still fell far short of the practice which would be expected to follow such precepts now. Its chief merit, in fact, consisted rather in refraining from rewarding and glorifying vice, than in positively inculcating and rewarding virtue. Regarded in this light, and making fair allowance for contemporary laxity of expression, Steele's three comedies may be justly described as moral in their intention. That this intention is more apparent in one case than another, is due to the conditions under which they were produced. In the **Funeral** the author of the **Christian Hero** went as far as he dared in the way of stage reformation. That is to say, he had to bear in mind both the imputation of sanctimoniousness which the book had brought upon him, and the probable opposition of the Wits at Will's, upon whom, as he admits in the **Apology,**

Collier 'had been too severe.' Direct moral sentiment plays but a small part in the first piece although it is undoubtedly there. In the **Lying Lover** the case is different. Steele had the **Funeral** behind him; and the Queen, at no time a lover of Theatres, was known to be opposed to the license of the stage. Writing a play—as was then possible—'in the severity Collier required,' he not only interpolated a long serious passage in Corneille's plot; but he bracketed it off, by writing it, after the mistaken fashion of the day, in blank verse. As a result, the piece was, as he puts it, 'damned for its Piety,' although the errors of its construction have quite as much to do with its failure. In the **Tender Husband** he seems to have contented himself with the more modest aim of being harmless, instead of didactic,—in other words, he tried to be simply amusing. Nevertheless, the **Tender Husband,** which certainly is amusing, was effectively acted, and, as the author says in . . . his dedication, was 'kindly accepted by the Town,' seems to have lived exactly as long as its predecessor,—the space of about seven nights. The case for the useful as against the agreeable, when Steele, according to tradition, intermitted his labours as a playwright, was therefore fairly equal. (pp. 37-45)

Austin Dobson, in his Richard Steele, *1886. Reprint by Scholarly Press, 1970, 240 p.*

George A. Aitken   (essay date 1889)

[*Aitken is primarily remembered for numerous essays on eighteenth-century literature that he contributed to various journals. He also wrote book-length studies of Jonathan Swift and John Arbuthnot, and edited Swift's* Journal to Stella. *Here, Aitken considers Steele's contributions to the* Tatler, *the* Spectator, *and the* Guardian, *deeming him "the originator of nearly every new departure in the periodicals Steele and Addison produced."*]

The first number of the **Tatler** appeared on Tuesday, April 12, 1709, and it was published three times a week—on Tuesday, Thursday, and Saturday, the post days. . . . The teaching accomplished by the new paper was to be unobtrusive; the first step was to get at the hearts of the people. In No. 26, after some grave remarks upon duelling, Steele adds: "Pacolet was going on in this strain, when he recovered from it, and told me, it was too soon to give my discourse on this subject so serious a turn; you have chiefly to do with that part of mankind which must be led into reflection by degrees, and you must treat this custom with humour and raillery to get an audience, before you come to pronounce sentence upon it." Steele had the serious end in view from the very beginning, but at first it was not wise to make it too prominent. He called his paper simply **The Tatler,** published, like the rest, "for the use of the good people of England." The tastes of all classes were to be met, and the nature of the topic discussed was indicated by the name of the place from which the article was supposed to have come, which was printed at the head. "All accounts of gallantry, pleasure, and entertainment shall be under the article of White's Coffee House; Poetry, under that of Will's Coffee House; Learning, under the title of Grecian; Foreign and Domestic news you will have from Saint James's Coffee House; and what else I have to offer on any other subject shall be dated from my own Apartment." The earlier numbers contained short papers from all or several of these addresses; but as the periodical progressed it became more and more usual to confine a number to one subject; and the article of news gradually disappeared entirely. No doubt Steele thought that his position of Gazetteer would enable him to give fresh items of news, which, he says, brought in a multitude of readers, and the idea of increasing his income by a paper above the ordinary may have first led him to turn his thoughts to such an enterprise; but as the *Tatler* grew the support of the paragraphs of news was felt to be unnecessary, and they were practically discontinued after the eightieth number. (p. 243-44)

From the beginning Steele professed that he was writing for the people, and that he expected to be paid by the public for his work. Unlike the mountebank who pretended that he sold his nostrums from purely disinterested motives, "we have," he says,

> all along informed the public, that we intend to give them our advice for our own sakes, and are labouring to make our lucubrations come to some price in money, for our more convenient support in the service of the public. It is certain that many other schemes have been proposed to me; as a friend offered to show me a treatise he had writ, which he called 'The Whole Art of Life; or, The Introduction to Great Men, illustrated in a Pack of Cards.' But, being a notice at all manner of play, I declined the offer" [*Tatler,* 4].

We have here, in brief, a true representation, in his own words, of Steele's relation to the people throughout his life. Addison, on the other hand, played an honest and successful game through the aid of great men, but it was only when he came to work with Steele, and in Steele's fashion, that he wrote the papers by which alone he will always live.

The *dramatis personæ* in the *Tatler* do not hold a position in any way so important as that occupied by their successors in the *Spectator.* Isaac Bickerstaff, Esq., aged sixty-four, "an old man, a philosopher, an humourist, an astrologer, and a Censor," is alone essential to the plan of the work. . . . Besides Isaac Bickerstaff we hear of other members of his family, especially his half-sister, Jenny Distaff, and her husband, and his three nephews, and they are the subjects of some of the most charming sketches. In the last number Steele wrote: "It has been a most exquisite pleasure to me to frame characters of domestic life." There is, too, a familiar named Pacolet. Quite late in the periodical we have a description of some of the members of Isaac Bickerstaff's club, the Trumpet, in Shire Lane; Sir Geoffery Notch, a gentleman of an ancient family, who had run through his estate in his youth, in hounds, horses, and cock-fighting, and called every thriving man a pitiful upstart; Major Matchlock, Dick Reptile, and the Bencher who was always telling stories of Jack Ogle, with whom he pretended to have been intimate in his youth.

In the Dedication to Maynwaring of the first volume of the collected edition . . . Steele states in a few words the aim

of the *Tatler:* "The general purpose of this paper is to expose the false arts of life, to pull off the disguises of cunning, vanity and affectation, and to recommend a general simplicity in our dress, our discourse, and our behaviour." And in another place, referring to a letter from a country correspondent, he says: "As for my labours, which he is pleased to enquire after, if they but wear one impertinence out of human life, destroy a single vice, or give a morning's cheerfulness to an honest mind; in short, if the world can be but one virtue the better, or in any degree less vicious, or receive from them the smallest addition to their innocent diversions; I shall not think my pains, or indeed my life, to have been spent in vain." At the close, speaking in his own name, Steele says: "The general purpose of the whole has been to recommend truth, innocence, honour, and virtue, as the chief ornaments of life; but I considered, that severity of manners was absolutely necessary to him who would censure others, and for that reason, and that only, chose to talk in a mask. I shall not carry my humility so far as to call myself a vicious man, but at the same time must confess my life is at best but pardonable."

In the Preface to the first collected edition of the *Tatler,* Steele acknowledged with his usual large-hearted generosity the assistance in his work which he received from others, especially Swift and Addison. Of the latter he says:

> I have only one gentleman, who will be nameless, to thank for any frequent assistance to me, which indeed it would have been barbarous in him to have denied to one with whom he had lived in an intimacy from childhood, considering the great ease with which he is able to dispatch the most entertaining pieces of this nature. This good office he performed with such force of genius, humour, wit and learning, that I fared like a distressed prince, who calls in a powerful neighbour to his aid; I was undone by my auxiliary; when I had called him in I could not subsist without dependence on him.

In the last number of the *Tatler,* Steele repeated that "the most approved pieces in it were written by others," especially by one who "is a person who is too fondly my friend ever to own them; but I should little deserve to be his, if I usurped the glory of them." And years afterwards, still speaking of Addison's share in the *Tatler,* Steele said, in the Preface to the second edition of the *Drummer,* "That paper was advanced indeed! for it was raised to a greater thing than I intended it! For the elegance, purity and correctness which appeared in his writings were not so much my purpose, as (in any intelligible manner, as I could) to rally all those singularities of human life, through the different professions and characters in it, which obstruct anything that was truly good and great." There have always been some admirers of Addison who have seized upon such ungrudging utterances of his friend to aid them in raising Addison's fame at the sacrifice of Steele's. . . . Lord [Thomas Babington] Macaulay, than whom no one has done more reckless injustice to Steele's reputation, says that at the close of 1709 the *Tatler* was more popular than any periodical had ever been, and that it was known that Addison was a contributor, but that it was not known that almost everything good in it was his; and adds that his fifty or sixty numbers were the best, so much so that any five of them were of more value than all the two hundred numbers in which he did not assist [*The Life and Writings of Addison,* 1852]. It is not necessary, after the noble defence of Steele set up by John Forster in the *Quarterly Review* [vol. 96, March 1855], to refute Macaulay at length; and in what follows I can do little more than sum up what previous writers have said. Of the whole 271 numbers of the *Tatler,* Steele wrote—approximately— 188, Addison 42, and about 36 were written by them jointly. Steele started the paper without consulting his friend, who did not know who was the author until he read some remarks upon Virgil in the sixth number, which were the result of a discussion he had himself had with Steele. Addison's first contribution appeared in No. 18, but it was not until the autumn of 1709 that Steele received any substantial aid from him. Steele was entirely responsible for the paper, and if some numbers are of unequal merit, it must never be forgotten that Steele was compelled to write whenever he had no article by his friends ready to hand, whereas they only wrote when they found some subject which specially interested them. Swift contributed only one entire paper to the *Tatler,* and a few letters and shorter articles; and contributions from other writers are so few that they need not be noticed here. It is fortunately not necessary nowadays to argue as to the comparative merits of the papers by Steele and Addison, and such a discussion would be the last thing that Steele would wish; but this may be said, that Steele was the originator of nearly every new departure in the periodicals which the two friends produced; and if Steele had not furnished Addison with the opportunity for displaying his special power, Addison would in all probability have been known to us only as an accomplished scholar and poet of no great power. The world owes Addison to Steele. "I claim to myself," says Steele, "the merit of having extorted excellent productions from a person of the greatest abilities, who would not have let them appear by any other means." And although many of Addison's papers are so perfect and polished, yet the very care bestowed upon them frequently makes them come home to us with less force than the often hastily composed papers of Steele, who wrote from his heart, full of impulse and kindly feeling. It is just because the *Tatler* is more thoroughly imbued with Steele's spirit than the *Spectator,* that many competent judges have confessed that they found greater pleasure in the earlier periodical than in its more finished and more famous successor. [William] Hazlitt [in his *Lectures on the English Comic Writers,* 1818-19] said that the *Tatler,* with half the number of volumes in the *Spectator,* contained "at least an equal quantity of sterling wit and sense."

It is curious how generally the subjects discussed in the *Spectator* had been already made the topics of papers in the *Tatler.* Gamesters and swindlers are unsparingly attacked; brutal pastimes are condemned; the habits of the drunken "roarers," "scourers," and other boon companions of the day are satirised; a constant warfare is maintained against the practice of duelling. Follies and minor evils of all descriptions are ridiculed, but without one touch of malice. . . . The lesson is generally instilled unostentatiously by a vivid sketch of some individual, so full of life that a very few words suffice to make the character remain fixed in our memories. In the number and variety of such portraits Steele is unrivalled. (pp. 244-49)

Steele stands apart from and above all the writers of his time, except Defoe, in the humanity which is everywhere found in his work. "If things were put in a true light, and we would take time to consider that man, in his very nature, is an imperfect being, our sense of this matter would be immediately altered, and the word imperfection would not carry an unkinder idea than the word humanity." And again: "It is to me a great meanness, and something much below a philosopher, which is what I mean by a gentleman, to rank a man among the vulgar for the condition of life he is in, and not according to his behaviour, his thoughts and sentiments in that condition. . . . This sense of mankind is so far from a levelling principle, that it only sets us upon a true basis of distinction, and doubles the merit of such as become their condition." "The appellation of gentleman is never to be affixed to a man's circumstances, but to his behaviour in them."

One way in which Steele strove to raise the tone of his contemporaries was by inculcating a purer and more chivalrous feeling towards women. "As charity is esteemed a conjunction of the good qualities necessary to a virtuous man, so love is the happy composition of all the accomplishments that make a fine gentleman." And in this same paper, No. 49, Steele observes of Lady Elizabeth Hastings what has passed into a proverb: "Though her mine carries much more invitation than command, to behold her is an immediate check to loose behaviour, and to love her is a liberal education." "Wife," he says, "is the most amiable term in human life." But women must be educated in a right fashion if they are to be treated by and to influence men as they should; and Steele constantly urges the need for bestowing true graces on the mind as well as on the body. "Flavia is ever well dressed, and always the genteelest woman you meet, but the make of her mind very much contributes to the ornament of her body. . . . Her distinction is owing to her manner, and not to her habit. . . . Howsoever she is apparelled she is herself the same; for there is so immediate a relation between our thoughts and gestures that a woman must think well to look well."

Another way in which Steele aimed at raising the minds of his readers was by maintaining a friendly touch with those who provided the popular amusements. Himself a successful dramatist, he always took a keen interest in the fortunes of the stage, and he did his utmost to aid actors who strove to improve its condition. "How often," said Cibber years afterwards, "have we known the most excellent audiences drawn together at a day's warning, by the influence or warrant of a single *Tatler,* in a season when our best endeavours without it could not defray the charge of the performance!" One result of Steele's love for the drama was, that he was acquainted with Shakespeare, and criticised his plays in a way adopted by no other writer of the time. He quotes Shakespeare naturally as a great authority on many topics, without any attempt at subtlety, and he urges that Shakespeare must be followed if the stage and the plays acted are to be reformed. He maintained the same high standard of criticism in speaking of other forms of literature, and it is especially noteworthy how he refers to Milton. As early as the sixth number of the *Tatler* he contrasts the treatment of the same subject by Milton and Dryden, and in subsequent papers he frequently quotes from Milton with reverence and admiration. In this he led the way to Addison's papers on "Paradise Lost" in the *Spectator,* which were infinitely more elaborate, but sometimes not so natural and appreciative. (pp. 250-52)

None of the papers in the *Tatler,* as originally issued, bore any indication of their author's name, and it is occasionally difficult and even impossible to determine who wrote a paper or portion of a paper. The reliable information that we have is furnished, firstly, by Steele's Preface to the *Tatler,* in which he announced the authorship of certain papers; and, secondly, by the list of papers by Addison which Steele supplied to Tickell. But that list was not complete, because, as Steele says in the Preface to the second edition of the *Drummer,* "What I never did declare was Mr. Addison's, I had his direct injunctions to hide." . . . "Many of the writings now published as his, I have been very patiently traduced and calumniated for, as they were pleasantries and oblique strokes upon certain the wittiest men of the age." It is well known, too, that Swift would not confess all he wrote. There are, therefore, a few papers respecting which a doubt remains. (pp. 257-58)

. . . . .

The first number of the *Spectator* appeared on the 1st March 1711, with the announcement, "To be continued every day," and the paper was issued without intermission until the 6th December 1712, when No. 555, the last of the original series, was published. . . . Machinery such as had hardly been used at all in the *Tatler* was introduced at the very beginning in the *Spectator.* Addison wrote the first number, which contains a light sketch of the Spectator himself. This "looker-on" had shown remarkable gravity and silence as a child, and whilst at school and college. A thirst for knowledge led him to travel after his father's death; but he had passed his latter years in London, where he was frequently to be seen in public places, though there were not above half-a-dozen of his select friends that knew him. He now resolved, however, although he never opened his lips but in his own club, to publish a sheet full of thoughts every morning, for the benefit of his contemporaries. In No. 2 Steele described the club where, as the Spectator had said, the plan of the work, as all other matters of importance, were laid and concerted. The first of the Society was a gentleman of Worcestershire, of ancient descent, and a baronet, Sir Roger de Coverley. Besides Sir Roger the paper contains sketches of the Templar; the Merchant, Sir Andrew Freeport; the Soldier, Captain Sentry; the Fine Gentleman, Will Honeycomb; and the Clergyman. Several of these characters hardly ever come to the front in the subsequent working-out of the original plan. The Clergyman and the Templar are never conspicuous; Sir Andrew Freeport makes sensible remarks on trade and thrift, and on giving alms to beggars, but he has not any very distinct personality in papers subsequent to the second number. Captain Sentry, "a man of good sense but dry conversation," appears hardly more frequently; and even Will Honeycomb, the fine gentleman about town,

who, after pursuing every belle for thirty years, marries a farmer's daughter when he is sixty, occupies comparatively little space. Sir Roger de Coverley alone retains a prominent place in the paper, and the development of his character we owe chiefly to Addison. But Steele drew the first sketch, and wrote several papers containing touches worthy of comparison with Addison's best efforts. I need only particularise Steele's description of Sir Roger's love for the perverse widow. We have no evidence as to the manner in which Addison and Steele arranged the work between them except that of Tickell, who says that "the plan of the *Spectator,* as far as regards the feigned person of the author, and of the several characters that compose his Club, was projected in concert with Sir Richard Steele," and he accordingly printed No. 2, which was by Steele, in his edition of Addison's Works, in order to render subsequent papers more intelligible. "As for the distinct papers," he adds, "they were never or seldom shewn to each other by their respective authors; who fully answered the promise they had made, and far outwent the expectation they had raised, of pursuing their labour in the same spirit and strength with which it was begun." (pp. 309-11)

The *Spectator* has remained to this day, as Steele hoped, the most lasting monument of his friendship with Addison. In No. 555 Steele wrote, with his usual noble generosity, of "the gentleman of whose assistance I formerly boasted in the Preface and concluding leaf of my *Tatlers.* I am indeed much more proud of his long-continued friendship, than I should be of the fame of being thought the author of any writings which he himself is capable of producing. I remember when I finished the *Tender Husband,* I told him there was nothing I so ardently wished, as that we might some time or other publish a work written by us both, which should bear the name of *The Monument,* in memory of our friendship." It was of this friendship that Addison wrote in a verse of his well-known hymn, which was first printed in No. 453:—

> Thy bounteous hand with worldly bliss
> Has made my cup run o'er,
> And in a kind and faithful friend
> Has doubled all my store.

In No. 532 Steele said: "I claim to myself the merit of having extorted excellent productions from a person of the greatest abilities, who would not have let them appear by any other means; to have animated a few young gentlemen into worthy pursuits, who will be a glory to our age; and at all times, and by all possible means in my power, undermined the interests of ignorance, vice and folly, and attempted to substitute in their stead learning, piety and good sense."

Addison was certainly at his best in the *Spectator.* He wrote 274 out of the 555 numbers, while Steele contributed 236, leaving only 45 for Budgell, Hughes, Pope, and other occasional contributors. Addison had, indeed, been little more than an occasional contributor to the *Tatler,* and although some of his articles in that periodical take rank among his finest work, yet it was only in the *Spectator* that he found opportunity to show fully all his powers. Steele, on the other hand, was at his best in the *Tatler,* in which there is a certain sense of freedom and freshness which we can hardly expect to find always in its more stately successor. Yet, as Forster says in comparing Steele's work in the *Spectator* with that in the *Tatler,*

> there was the same inexpressible charm in the matter, the same inexhaustible variety in the form; and upon all the keen exposure of vice or the pleasant laugh at folly, as prominent in the life-like little story as in the criticism of an actor or a play, making attractive the gravest themes to the unthinking, and recommending the lightest fancies to the most grave, there was still the old and ineffaceable impress of good-nature and humanity—the soul of a sincere man shining out through it all. . . .

A contemporary writer, speaking of the periodicals started by Steele, said [in "An Essay sacred to the memory of Sir Richard Steele," *British Journal, or the Censor.* September 13, 1729]:

> This was laying the axe to the root of vice and immorality. All the pulpit discourses of a year scarce produced half the good as flowed from the *Spectator* of a day. They who were tired and lulled to sleep by a long and laboured harangue, or terrified at the appearance of large and weighty volumes, could cheerfully attend to a single half-sheet, where they found the images of virtue so lively and amiable, where vice was so agreeably ridiculed, that it grew painful to no man to part with his beloved follies; nor was he easy till he had practised those qualities which charmed so much in speculation.

(pp. 311-15)

There is nothing to show what determined Steele and Addison in bringing the *Spectator* to a close in December 1712. All we know is, that the decision was not one taken suddenly. On the 12th November Steele told Pope that he had a new design—the *Guardian*—which he proposed to open in a month or two; and in the agreement with Buckley of the 10th November it is stated that it was proposed to continue the *Spectator* to the end of November. The members of the Club were gradually disposed of; and a new Club was to be formed, where the Spectator would alter his character and be loquacious. The ceremony of opening the Spectator's mouth was to be on the 25th March next. The date, however, might be altered, but of this public notice would be given. (p. 358)

· · · · ·

The *Guardian,* [begun in 1713], was published daily, and extended to 175 numbers, the last of which appeared on the 1st October. Addison, occupied with the preparation of *Cato* for the stage, took little part in the earlier numbers of the *Guardian,* but afterwards he was a frequent contributor. Pope, Berkeley, and Tickell all assisted Steele with excellent papers. . . . Budgell, Hughes, and others also helped, but Steele himself wrote 82 out of the total of 175 papers. (p. 363)

The Guardian was a certain Mr. Nestor Ironside, and his relations with the various members of the Lizard family, who are introduced to us by Steele in Nos. 2, 5, and 6, form the machinery used throughout the periodical. The main purpose of the work was, "to protect the modest, the industrious; to celebrate the wise, the valiant; to encourage the good, the pious; to confront the impudent, the idle; to contemn the vain, the cowardly; and to disappoint the wicked and profane." It aimed at the advancement of the conversation of gentlemen, the improvement of ladies, the wealth of traders, and the encouragement of artificers. After speaking, in No. 21, of the aid rendered by Raphael's paintings to the cause of religion, Steele says: "It is with this view that I presume upon subjects of this kind, and men may take up this paper, and be catched by an admonition under the disguise of a diversion." Everything published on a Saturday, as was the case during the greater part of the career of the *Spectator,* bore some relation to the duties of the following day. "It is an unspeakable pleasure to me, that I have lived to see the time when I can observe such a law to myself, and yet turn my discourse upon what is done at the play-house. I am sure the reader knows I am going to mention the tragedy of Cato." There is the same variety of topics discussed in the *Guardian* as in its predecessors, and as in the earlier papers, here too Steele expressed opinions on many subjects which were far in advance of the time. In No. 34 he gave another excellent character of a fine gentleman,—"a man completely qualified as well for the service and good as for the ornament and delight of society." In No. 61, by Pope, the writer plainly showed his opinion of sanguinary sports, and in particular hunting, great as were the authority and custom which supported the diversion. In No. 98, while announcing the erection of a Lion's Head at Button's Coffee-house, into whose mouth letters and papers for the *Guardian* could be conveyed, Addison reviewed the course of periodical writing, and said that above a hundred authors, some of them writers of great eminence in other paths, had endeavoured after Bickerstaff and Nestor Ironside's way of writing, but that none of them had hit upon the art; though several had acquitted themselves well in single papers.

In the first number of the *Guardian* Steele observed that parties were too violent to make it possible to pass them by without observation; but that as to these matters he would be impartial, though he could not be neuter. "I am, with relation to the government of the church, a tory, with regard to the state, a whig. . . . I am past all the regards of this life, and have nothing to manage with any person or party, but to deliver myself as becomes an old man with one foot in the grave, and one who thinks he is passing to eternity." But before the close of April, when the paper had reached its fortieth number, Steele was drawn into a quarrel with the *Examiner,* and the contest was continued in subsequent papers. . . . [The] introduction of politics was the ruin of the *Guardian,* a periodical which, so far as it went, contained work in no way unworthy of being placed by the side of Steele's contributions to the *Tatler* or *Spectator.* (pp. 364-66)

George A. Aitken, in his The Life of Richard Steele, Vol. I, *1889. Reprint by Greenwood Press, 1968, 419 p.*

Rae Blanchard (essay date 1929)

[*In the excerpt below, Blanchard examines Steele's*

views on the status of women in society. The critic concludes that although Steele was aware of the "innovating feminist ideas" of his day, he did not necessarily approve of them.]

Whether Steele writes of the "fine lady," the "notable woman," or the "witty female," his reforming intention is unmistakable. Frequently, however, this emphasis on feminism as an important social problem has been misconstrued as unlimited praise of woman's sense and virtue and as a constructive reforming program ahead of the time. We need the perspective of a synthesis which will correlate his views of woman with those of his contemporaries. I propose to examine Steele's views as expressed in his essays, periodicals, and plays from the **Christian Hero** to the **Conscious Lovers** and to construe them in the light of contemporary thought on the subject.

There appear to have been, from about 1650 to 1725, three fairly distinct groups of writers interested in the subject of woman. The first was comprised of the conservatives—clergymen, educators, and moralists—whom Steele would have called the "men of sense." Although their opinions were tempered by moderation and affection for their own wives and daughters, they had no genuine respect for woman as a self-directing individual and, in all matters relating to her status in society, were wholly on the side of law and custom. The second group, chiefly men of letters from whose pens came the literature of "wit and gallantry," toyed half-gallantly, half-scornfully, in poetry and essay, with ideas concerning woman. The third group were reformers, more or less consciously attempting to bring about social conditions rising above custom and conformable to reason. They wrote in the spirit of rationalism on a subject which they considered of importance to the welfare of society and humanity. They believed in the justice of educating woman, modifying the old conception of her subordinate position in marriage, and accepting her as an individual with rights and responsibilities.

I shall consider the various reactions of these groups—the conservatives, the wits, and the reformers—to the chief points of contention, with the purpose of placing Steele among them and of evaluating his contribution to feminism. The four subjects for consideration are: the nature of woman, that is the quality of her mind and the stability of her character; her education; her status in marriage; and her rôle in society.

The conservative view of the nature of woman, expressed by seventeenth-century moralists and such writers of courtesy literature as Richard Brathwaite in the *English Gentlewoman* (3rd. ed., 1641), Gervase Markham in the *English House-wife* (8th. ed., 1676), Richard Allestree in the *Ladies' Calling* (1671), Fénelon in *De l'éducation des filles* (1687), and Halifax in *Advice to a Daughter* (1688) was that, in mind and in morals as well as in body, she is weaker than man. This is attested, they maintained, by "the law of nature," custom, and Biblical authority. (pp. 325-26)

Steele's ideas concerning the mind and character of woman should be considered against this background of current opinion. When we look for ideas which combat the doctrine of inferiority as squarely as the logic of Poulain de la Barre or the intellectual conviction of Defoe, we have to admit that Steele did not express them. He was aware of innovating ideas, if one may judge from his casual references, here and there, to the subjects of sex-distinction in souls and woman's claim to reason or to the comparison of the faculties in man and woman. But he avoided taking sides. His most liberal statements were non-committal. As the following conspicuous passage in the **Tatler** [172] indicates, he apparently wished to pacify woman and by increasing her self-respect to gain his reforming objective:

> . . . a Creature formed with a Mind of a quite different Make from his own. I am sure, I do not mean it an Injury to Women, when I say there is a Sort of Sex in Souls. I am tender of offending them, and know it is hard not to do it on this Subject; but I must go on to say That the Soul of a Man and that of a Woman are made very unlike, according to the Employments for which they are designed. The ladies will please to observe, I say, our Minds have different not superior Qualities to theirs. The Virtues have respectively a Masculine and a Feminine Cast. What we call in Men Wisdom is in Woman Prudence. It is a Partiality to call one greater than the other. A prudent Woman is in the same Class of Honour as a Wise man, and the Scandals in the Way are equally dangerous. . . . To manage well a great Family is as worthy an Instance of Capacity, as to execute a great Employment; and for the Generality, as Women perform the considerable Part of their Duties, as well as Men do theirs; so in the common Behaviour, those of ordinary Genius are not more trivial than the common Rate of Men.

But Steele's tactful generosity, here as elsewhere, is not to be construed as whole-hearted acceptance of the views held by the rationalistic reformers. He was not at all interested in giving woman a more responsible and respected position in society; in fact there is nothing to indicate that he had confidence in her ability to hold such a position. His reforming intention, like that of the conservative moralists, was merely to eradicate selfishness and the vices of idleness and to hold before her dignified ideals of conduct. He differed from the other moralists only in his magnanimous admission that woman, in matters of morality, is more handicapped than man from the lack of a trained understanding and judgment:

> If we grant an Equality in the Faculties of both Sexes, the Minds of Women are less Cultivated with Precepts, and consequently may, without Disrespect to them, be accounted more liable to Illusion in Cases wherein natural Inclination is out of the Interest of Virtue [**Tatler,** 79].

Frequent censure of the licentious wits is further evidence of Steele's purposes of effecting woman's moral reform by increasing her self-respect. The **Christian Hero** (1701), addressed to soldiers and wits, was designed to reform their social attitudes, among others that toward woman. Careful not to antagonize his readers, he approaches the subject tactfully and meets them on their own ground. But the jaunty gallantry and sentimental phrasings of the man of fashion do not conceal his serious intention. Here he praises rational courtship and the dignity of marriage. Important, also, is the relatively long digression on Portia's loyalty to Brutus, obviously meant to defend woman against the charges of inconstancy, pettiness, and self-love. Portia has left behind her "an everlasting Argument, how far a Generous Treatment can make that tender Sex go even beyond the Resolution of Man." There are other indications in his early years of authorship of more or less conscious censure of cynicism. Among these is his portrayal of women in the early plays. Young Bookwit in the **Lying Lover** is probably voicing Steele's opinion when he says: "a woman, methinks, is a being between us and angels . . . and I swear to you I was never out in't yet, but I always judged of men as I observed they judged of women." Steele condemned especially "affecting a superior Carriage" toward woman from "a false Notion of the Weakness of a Female Understanding"; and valuing her as "mere Woman"—that is, having "but one Reason for setting any Value on the Fair Sex." And in later years, as this quotation from the **Guardian** [26] shows, he continued to make the same criticism:

> A set of fops, from one generation to another, has made such a pother with "bright eyes, the fair sex, the charms, the air" and something so incapable to be expressed but with a sigh, that the creatures have utterly gone out of their very being, and there are no women in all the world. If they are not nymphs, shepherdesses, graces, or goddesses, they are to a woman, all of them "the ladies."

But it would be misrepresenting the facts to maintain that Steele, on this question of woman's mind and character, entirely separated himself, in literary style or in ideas, from the man of wit. Both his denunciation and his defence of woman are similar to those in the gallant tradition. An amazing number of "characters" in the periodicals are dominated by the egoism, pride, vanity, indolence, and wantonness "of the thoughtless Creatures who make up the Lump of that Sex." Conspicuous among them, from the **Tatler** to the **Theater,** are Cleomira, whose vanity lies in concealment of her age; Flavia and Lucia, the mother and daughter jealous of each other; Castabella, the prude, and Lydia, the coquette, equally culpable in their "affectation of pleasing men"; the Pict, notorious for her vanity and ill humor; Sempronia, a go-between in love intrigues; Jenny Lipsy, Madame Twilight, and Clidamira Dustgown, women of the town; and Leucippe, the celebrated wanton. Steele also very often follows the current literary device of balancing, for purposes of contrast, a virtuous character with a faulty one: for example Daphne with Laetitia, and Emilia with Honoria. Women are either furies or angels:

> The Ill are employed in communicating Scandal, Infamy, and Disease like Furies; the Good distribute Benevolence, Friendship, and Health, like Angels. The Ill are damped with Pain and Anguish at the Sight of all that is laudable, lovely, or happy. The Virtuous are touched with Commiseration towards the Guilty, the Disagreeable, and the Wretched. . . . Such is the destroying Fiend, such the Guardian Angel, Woman [**Tatler,** 201].

Steele's ideal women, moreover, like those praised by the men of wit, are suffused with what is perilously near mawkish sentimentality. Eve, in the **Christian Hero,** heads the list! She is described as "softened into sweetness" and "tempered into smiles," a beautiful creature over whom Adam claimed superiority in "Strength and Wisdom," but acknowledged inferiority in "Affection." Similar are Emilia, the meek and long-suffering wife, Fidelia, the self-effacing daughter, and Eucratia, the pattern of beauty, who possesses "an Inferiority that makes her still more lovely." The portrayal of his last heroine, Indiana, in the **Conscious Lovers** shows the persistence of this ideal of feminine beauty, set forth most vividly, perhaps, in the character of Eucratia in the **Spectator** [144]:

> In like manner if you describe a right Woman in a laudable Sense, she should have gentle Softness, tender Fear, and all those parts of Life, which distinguish her from the other Sex; with some Subordination to it, but such an Inferiority that makes her still more lovely. Eucratia is that Creature, she is all over Woman. Kindness is all her Art and Beauty all her Arms. Her Look, her Voice, her Gesture, and whole Behaviour is truly Feminine. A Goodness mixed with Fear, gives a Tincture to all her Behaviour. It would be Savage to offend her, and cruelty to use Art to gain her. Others are Beautiful, but Eucratia thou art Beauty!

Thus Steele, although unwilling to commit himself unequivocally on the subject of woman's inferiority, was otherwise at one with the moralists, who aimed at personal reform only. The general tenor of his writings indicates, however, that he followed the denunciation and defence convention of the wits. In the former, his characterization of woman is worldly and cynical; in the latter, sentimental, her inferiority to man and dependence upon him constituting her chief charm. He indicated little more than awareness of a movement of ideas which related rational womanhood to the larger question of social welfare.

The question of woman's education provoked expression of diverse views—prejudiced, conventional, or thoughtful. Is woman educable? If so, is it desirable to educate her? What should be the nature of her training? Although all were agreed that she should have some training beyond that of pretty accomplishments to serve as an antidote against her natural moral unsteadiness, there was disagreement as to the nature and extent of it. The conservative moralists and the men of wit marshalled the same arguments and discussed the problem in the same current commonplaces, only now and again differing in temper and tone. Such women as Mrs. Katherine Philips and Lady Winchilsea shrank alike from the "raillery of the Wits" and the "severity of the Wise." The chief arguments against learning for woman, except that necessary for reading books of house-wifery, and piety, were that it would unfit her for household duties; that her pride would become insufferable; that the sovereignty of man would be shaken; and that, on account of her mental instability, anything like learning would "turn her brain"—an enigmatic phrase on everyone's pen. The "learned woman" or "witty female" became a literary anathema, and everyone interested in any aspect of the subject had something to say against romance reading. (pp. 331-36)

There is no assumption in Steele's work, expressed or suggested, that woman's brain would be turned by knowledge. "The fair sex are as capable as men of the liberal sciences," he stated in the ***Guardian*** [172]; and he implied at every point that he believed it. He thought that much social disorder proceeded from "an unaccountable wild Method in the Education of the better half of the World, the Women." Parents' neglect of their daughters and complete ignoring of their education aroused his indignation:

> I am apt to believe, there are some Parents imagine their Daughters will be accomplished enough, if nothing interrupts their Growth or their Shape. According to this Method of Education, I could name you Twenty Families, where all the Girls hear of in this Life is, That it is Time to rise and to come to Dinner; as if they were so insignificant as to be wholly provided for when they are fed and cloathed.
>
> It is with great Indignation that I see such Crowds of the Female World lost to humane Society [*Tatler,* 248].

He also criticized the tendency to consider a woman educated if she were taught drawing-room decorum and pretty feminine graces:

> To make her an agreeable Person is the Main Purpose of her Parents . . . The Management of a young Lady's Person is not to be overlooked, but the Erudition of her Mind is much more to be regarded. . . . The true Art in this Case is, To make the Mind and Body improve together [*Spectator,* 66].

But curiously enough if Steele had any definite ideas about a course of training, he never expressed them, not even in the ***Guardian,*** where he had ample opportunity to discuss the education of the five daughters in the Lizard family. When a correspondent in the ***Tatler*** asked for advice concerning the education of his daughter, Steele's comment was:

> I am as serious on this Subject as my Correspondent can be, and am of Opinion That the great Happiness or Misfortune of Mankind depends upon the Manner of Educating and Treating that Sex [*Tatler,* 141].

He said that he intended later to turn his thoughts more particularly to an answer; but he did not return to the subject. The fullest expression of his opinion is that women should have "Talents and Accomplishments without Respect to their Sex"—such qualifications as would make them pleasing were they not women; and that they should have such training as "would furnish them with Reflections and Sentiments proper for the Companions of reasonable Men."

Acting on these principles, he avowedly made his contribution to woman's education by publishing in 1714 a three volume treatise called the ***Ladies' Library,*** which was advertised as "consisting of general rules for conduct in all the circumstances of the Life of Women." This project,

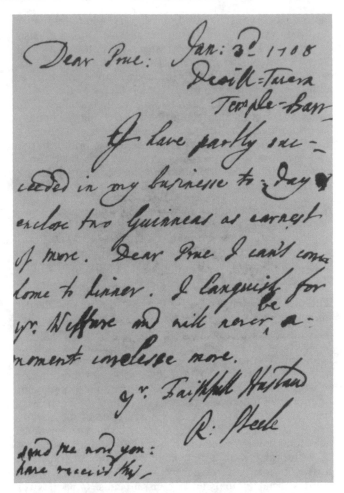

Letter to Steele's second wife, Mary Scurlock Steele, whom he called his "Dear Prue."

which he had been considering for several years, appeared as "Written by a Lady, Published by Mr. Steele"; and, as he explained in the preface, is a compilation "out of several writings of our greatest divines." What Steele did, apparently, was to select suitable excerpts and dovetail them together with transitional passages of his own. The borrowings comprise selections from Taylor's *Holy Living;* Fleetwood's *Relative Duties of Parents and Children;* Richard Allestree's *The Whole Duty of Man, The Ladies' Calling,* and the *Government of the Tongue;* Locke's *Treatise on Education;* Richard Lucas's *Practical Christianity* and *Enquiry after Happiness;* John Scott's *Christian Life;* Tillotson's *Sermons;* Halifax's *Advice to a Daughter;* Fénelon's *L'éducation des filles;* and Mary Astell's *Serious Proposal to the Ladies.* This makes curious reading for the present-day reader. There are passages from the conservative writers, which are in direct contradiction to what Steele professed to believe: for instance Fleetwood's very strong assertion of the inferiority of woman, according to reason, usage, custom, and God's decree in the Bible. There are others, from Mary Astell for example, which indicate his agreement with the idea that social schemes in the realm of woman should rise above custom and conform to reason. In the main the compilation assumes the capability of woman's mind, the dignity of her personality, and the desirability of giving her morals a rational basis. It does not, however, in any respect, share the new speculative spirit or the purpose of the reforming group. Instead, it fits definitely into the conservative tradition, its unmistakable prototypes being such books as the *English Gentlewoman* and the *Ladies' Calling*. It resembles them in its assumption that the interests of woman are chiefly in domestic affairs and in religion. Its general design—with chapters on chastity, prudence, envy, pride, charity, and meekness—is like theirs. And it shares their aim of offsetting the peculiarly feminine vices of vanity and idleness by inculcating lessons of piety.

We are obliged to conclude, then, that whatever may have been Steele's attitude toward the feasibility and the desirability of educating woman, his constructive efforts did not go beyond producing another moral treatise for her perusal in the vein of the seventeenth-century conservative tradition.

The prevailing conception of marriage in the seventeenth and eighteenth centuries was not that of an idealistic partnership, based on mutual respect and love and purposing to serve society by rearing a family, but rather a social and economic contract, designed to protect private property and male inheritance. The social and legal subordination of woman was a necessary aspect of the conception, being bound up in a complex of ideas including the doctrine of her natural inferiority, a rigid observance of distinctions in social status, and a belief that social institutions must have final power vested in a head. The first duty, therefore, of the moral, law-abiding woman was to submit graciously to the authority of her parents or her husband (a widow being a social anomaly and a constant cause of perplexity). Such subordination was an ethical principle, and deviation from it was regarded as mutiny against law and religion. (pp. 340-43)

It is obvious, of course, to the most casual reader of Steele that his reform was particularly directed toward marriage. . . . [His] ideas followed the channels of rationalism. Much of his propaganda was consciously opposed to social attitudes established by the literature of wit. From his very first writings—the *Christian Hero* and the early plays—he endeavored to dignify courtship and marriage. A passage on rational courtship in the *Christian Hero,* in which he exonerates woman from the conventional charges, forecasted the position which he was to maintain during the next two decades:

> Indeed it is, among other Reasons, from want of Wit and Invention in our Modern Gallants, that the beautiful Sex is absurdly and vitiously entertained by 'em: For there is in their tender Frame, native Simplicity, groundless Fear, and little unaccountable Contradictions, upon which there might be built Expostulations to divert a good and Intelligent Young Woman, as well as the fulsome Raptures, guilty Impressions, senseless Deifications, and pretended Deaths that are every Day offer'd her.

Lord Hardy and Mr. Campley in the *Funeral* made love according to this principle; and Young Bookwit in the

Lying Lover came to grief because of his lies to Penelope. Steele paid the highest possible tribute to his doctrine, as the following letter to Mary Scurlock attests, by adhering to it in his own courtship:

> As I know no reason why difference of Sex should make our Language to each other differ from the ordinary rules of right reason, I shall affect plainnesse and sincerity in my discourse to you, as much as other Lovers do perplexity and rapture. Instead of saying "I shall die for you," I professe I should be glad to Lead my life with you.

Steele continued to make a point of this until he overdid it in the *Conscious Lovers* by having Bevil Junior and Indiana exult in the fact that the understanding and not the passions is the spring of their love! Usually, however, his emphasis was sensible. A man should bring his "Reason to support his Passion." Marriage is an everyday matter, and women should not be "treated as if they were designed to inhabit the happy Fields of *Arcadia,* rather than be Wives and Mothers in old *England.*"

His effort to dignify the conception of marriage prevailing in the fashionable world was very thoroughgoing. Contemporary drama, he maintained, was to some extent responsible for the banter and ridicule to which marriage was subjected. "The Theater, in some late Reigns owed its chief Support to those Scenes which were written to put Matrimony out of Countenance." He undertook, therefore, to point out not only its social value but the dignified happiness which it affords. The connotation of wife should be changed. Indeed he found this word to be "the most amiable Term in Humane Life." And in order to make it seem agreeable and delightful to his polite readers, he made conspicuous use in one *Tatler* paper of letters from Pliny to Calphurnia; in another, of a letter from Cicero to Terentia; and in a *Spectator* paper, of a translation of an epigram by Martial in honor of his wife Cleopatra. Marriage, he maintained, is a rational contract based on mutual love and respect. His emphasis on the idea that "love is a union of minds" was directed pointedly toward the gallant tradition, which emphasized the sensual element. "Wedlock is but a more solemn Prostitution, where there is not an Union of Mind," he asserted. The position of the wife in the contract should be one of companionship rather than of subjection: "It is the glory of woman to be her husband's friend and companion." There was never any suggestion of servile subordination or of domestic slavery.

He was rigorously opposed to any basis for marriage except mutual love; and consideration of it as an economic contract aroused his indignation. Parents who arrange mercenary marriages for their children were made the subjects of satire and invective in both plays and periodicals. The custom of marriage settlements, whereby a generous jointure was secured to the bride on the death of her husband and "pin-money" allowed her during her lifetime, was particularly distasteful to him, not because it gave more economic freedom to woman, but because it implied that marriage is not a union of mutual confidence: "Thus is Tenderness thrown out of the Question; and the great Care is, what the young Couple shall do when they come to hate each other?" "Pin-money," he denounced as something invented "to intimate to the young People, that they are very soon to be in a State of War with each other." It might be argued that Steele's own marriages showed an inclination to worldliness, because his wives were both wealthy women. Of the first wife, Margaret Stretch, little is known except that on her death Steele inherited her estate in the Barbados. His second wife, Mary Scurlock, was also an heiress; but no one who reads the remarkable series of four hundred notes and letters which Steele wrote to her during their courtship and married life of eleven years can believe there was a worldly motive in Steele's choice.

Considering the social customs of his age, Steele's persistent efforts to bring about one standard of sex morality and matrimonial fidelity were remarkable. The *Tatler* [33] denounced the "Tyrant Humour," which condemns woman for what is condoned in man; and affirmed "it is certain, that Chastity is . . . as much to be valued in Men as in Women." Later, in the *Guardian* [45], in a systematic discussion of the matter, Steele arraigned the social usages which "instead of avenging the cause of an abused woman, will proclaim her dishonor; while . . . he who did the wrong sees no difference in the reception he meets with." There is a chasm between Steele's ideal of wifehood and that presented by Halifax and other conservatives, who praised woman for an infinite capacity to forgive infidelity in her husband and beguile him back to virtue.

Steele's conception of marriage and wifehood, consistently idealistic, identifies him—if not in principle, at least in reforming objective—with the rationalistic innovators. Unlike theirs, his views are never polemical and are not clearly related to a system of feminist propaganda. They are, however, consciously directed against fashionable opinion, which degraded marriage by ridicule; and they are out of sympathy with the essentially ignoble view held by conservative moralists. One is grateful to know that his ideas were not mere theories but living principles exemplified in his marriage and regard for his wife. His letters to Mrs. Steele extending from August 1707 to May 1717 are charming and convincing evidence that theirs was a happy marriage. Barring a little undercurrent of anxiety about money affairs, partly due to Prue's tendency to over-value money, partly to Steele's impecuniosity, there is nothing to suggest that he did not find his views demonstrable.

On the question of the rôle of woman in society, all three groups were of the same mind. The goal of woman is marriage. The characteristic position of such conservative treatises as the *Ladies' Calling* was very much like that of Overbury's exasperating smugness [in *The Wife*]:

> Marriage their object is; their *being* then
> And now perfection, they receive from men.

Their contribution to society, therefore, must come from within the home. . . . All contemporary plans for woman's education . . . were designed to give her a happier and more efficient life in the administration of home. The boldest plea of those advocating reform in her education was that she be given an equal chance with men to develop her reason and will for the more complete understanding and mastery of life. (pp. 347-51)

What was Steele's idea of the social rôle of woman? It should be stated at the outset that he did not regard the question lightly, nor as an isolated problem, but seriously, as one bearing greatly on the whole problem of public welfare. His most direct statement of this point of view is given in the *Englishman* (first series), designed he stated in the first number, for serious discussion of public matters, which he hoped to lay before English citizens "like a Man of Experience and a Patriot." Accordingly, when he came to the subject of woman in the ninth number, he wrote in a tone of earnestness, attempting to show the far-reaching effects involved in the treatment of women:

> In all Nations their public Affairs are conducted with more or less Elegance, Dexterity, and Success, as they respectively restrain or give Freedom to their Women. . . . Where the fair Sex are treated with Gallantry and superior Civility, that Treatment has its visible Effect to the Advantage of all publick and private Transactions. I will take upon me to say, the *French* principally owe their Greatness to it. . . . *Holland* by the same Rule, . . . also owe their Prosperity to their Treatment of their Women. . . . It is indeed a senseless Imagination, to suppose the Business of humane Life is to be carried on with an Exclusion of half the Species [*Englishman* (first series) 9].

But the "Business of humane life" which Steele allotted to the other "half of the species" did not lie outside the walls of home. This bias may be inferred from his occasional comment on the learned ladies of the age. Approbation was conspicuously wanting. Swift's satiric presentation of Mary Astell—Madonella—and her college for women must have had Steele's editorial approval. He himself mentioned her in other *Tatler* papers with slight though unmistakable satiric intention—in one as "Mrs. Comma, the great scholar." Elizabeth Elstob was cited in a *Tatler* paper [63] by Swift as "a certain lady who is now publishing two of the choicest Saxon novels." Steele's name was not one of the subscribers to her *English-Saxon Homily* (1709). His literary quarrel with Mrs. Manley lasted from 1709 to 1717; and in the course of these years there were unsavoury remarks on his side as well as on hers. Lady Elizabeth Hastings, as Aspasia, received sincere and beautiful praise from Steele, but not as a woman who was in the public eye. Neither are there evidences in any of his dedications to women that he praised them for work which carried them into the realm of man.

For Steele was entirely in agreement with his age and not beyond it in considering marriage as the one goal for woman and the home as her only province. Surprisingly like Overbury's is his couplet in the *Funeral:*

> And woman's happiness, for all her Scorn,
> Is only by that side whence she was born.

Nestor Ironsides, in the *Guardian* [15], voices Steele's opinion when he says anxiously of the "Sparkler," one of the Lizard daughters, who shows signs of being a wit: "I should be loth to have a poetess in our family." Steele was half-apologetic to Mrs. Steele in the graceful dedication of the third volume of the *Ladies' Library* for bringing her into the public view at all: "You are so great a Lover of

Home, that I know it will be irksome to you to go into the World even in an Applause." It was Steele's belief that the only service which women can render to society lies entirely within the circle of home. One clear expression of this position, as extreme as that of the dyed-in-the-wool conservatives, is found in the *Spectator* [342]:

> We have indeed carried Women's Characters too much into public Life, and you shall see them now-a-Days affect a sort of Fame: but I cannot help venturing to disoblige them for their Service, by telling them, that the utmost of a Woman's Character is contained in domestick Life: She is Blameless or Praiseworthy according as her Carriage affects the House of her Father or her Husband. All she has to do in the World, is contained within the Duties of a Daughter, a Sister, a Wife, and a Mother . . . when they consider themselves as they ought, no other than an additional Part of the Species (for their own Happiness and Comfort as well as that of those for whom they were born) their Ambition to excel will be directed accordingly; and they will in no Part of their Lives want Opportunities for being shining Ornaments to their Fathers, Husbands, Brothers, or Children.

Steele's views, then, on the status of women did not coincide with those of any one group of contemporary writers. He did not agree wholly with the opinion held by conservative moralists of woman's intellectual and social inferiority, and he objected vigorously to their view of her servile subordination in marriage. But, on the question of her education, not only his perfunctory discussions, but also his *Ladies' Library,* designed to embody his principles, indicate that his ideal, like theirs, was merely to give woman conventional ethical instruction. Neither was he in complete agreement with the literary group. He strongly opposed their tendency to emphasize one aspect of woman's nature and to sneer at courtship and marriage; and toying with the subject according to the rules of a literary mode was not to his taste. He had, however, a very decided affinity with the group. From the first, he was in sympathy, through temperament and conviction, with the literary and social ideals of the wits, and it is obvious that he conformed to the fashionable tradition in the *Christian Hero,* in the plays, and—with the exception of the *Guardian* and the *Englishman*—in the periodicals. This accounts for his frequent gallant tone, which in comparison with the earnestness of the reformers, seems flippant. It may account for some aspects of his disparaging "characters." Very likely a remnant of the flowery descriptions of woman in the gallant tradition lingered on in the sentimentality with which he was inclined to invest virtuous woman.

The conservatism and the superficiality which Steele shared, respectively, with the moralists and the wits make it impossible to identify him with the reformers. It is plain that his reforming intention, although sincere and persistent, was not in the confident spirit of the rationalistic group, who, assailing custom and opinion, affirmed belief in woman as a rational being and advocated training which would make her a self-directing individual. His inability to accept such an optimistic doctrine and to use it as a basis for constructive reform should be connected with his acknowledgment of the irrationality of human nature—a fundamental element in his moral theory which has been obscured by persistent overemphasis on his confidence in the "excellency of human nature." In woman as in man, he believed, egoism and the power of the passions are basic. The irrational and selfish women portrayed by Steele far outnumber those whose conduct is motivated by reason; his ideal women—the Lady Sharlots, Eucratias, and Indianas—exemplify the aspect of his "anti-rationalism" which expressed itself, in this particular as in others, in a concept of sentimental virtue.

Thus Steele's zeal for improving woman's morals should not be mistaken for unqualified reverence. His awareness of innovating feminist ideas should not be construed as approval of them. He never expressed his reforming principles in a manner even approaching the controversial spirit of Poulain de la Barre, the intellectual conviction of Defoe, or the daring of Mary Astell. But probably for this very reason he had more influence and a far larger reading public than they. Tactful, sincere, avoiding overearnestness, he continued for twenty years to disseminate ideas which contributed to the evolution of feminist thought in England. (pp. 352-55)

> *Rae Blanchard, "Richard Steele and the Status of Women," in* Studies in Philology, *Vol. XXVI, No. 3, July, 1929, pp. 325-55.*

Bonamy Dobrée   (essay date 1929)

[*A highly regarded English historian and critic, Dobrée distinguished himself both as a leading authority of Restoration drama and as a creator of vivid biographical studies. Below, he compares the writing styles of Addison and Steele and examines the* Tatler's *appeal to women of the time.*]

The single grudge that we feel against [Steele] is that he should have been so self-abasing; his itch to confess is a trifle exaggerated; his humility seems a perversion of his riotous generosity: it would be mean to appear more virtuous than one's friends. Yet it is his faculty for wearing his heart upon his sleeve, as a true creature of impulse, that makes him so vivid a figure to-day. He knew, of course, that if his instincts were not always of the most respectable they were shared by most healthy men. It was no doubt his careless dash, his spontaneity, which made him attractive to Addison, just as it may have been Addison's somewhat chilly self-control which caused Steele to admire him. He was optimistic in the extreme, almost gullible, involving himself in later years in the wild "fish-pools" scheme of bringing salmon alive to London, just as in his earlier days he had dabbled in alchemy: he even thought he could reconcile warring Churches. If he could live gaily, as well as live hard, there is this of peculiar about him—that though he liked to be popular, though he loved the good opinion of his friends and basked in the praise of his wife, he always went his own way. He was sometimes ridiculous; but, as Stevenson remarked, "God help the man who is afraid of making a fool of himself!" He was, no doubt, in a strict view, a little sentimental—that is, he felt his emotional experiences more than is consistent with a wholesome balance; but it is largely this capacity for acute feeling that gave him the sympathy which makes him the first of our intimate essayists. He never forgot the hideous experience of nearly killing his man in a duel, so never ceased to inveigh against duelling: he always remembered the distresses of fathering a natural child, so always insisted upon the difference between love and lust. He could not have seen the higher had he not pursued the lower, but he need not have insisted so much on his falls from grace. . . . It may be true that it is the fool who learns only from his own experience, but the wisdom which grows from the experience of others is shallow and disagreeable. Better to err with Steele than shine in rectitude with Addison.

To belittle Addison is the rock every writer on Steele must seek to avoid; yet it is almost impossible. He can only sigh with Hazlitt [in his *Lectures on the English Humorists,* 1818-19], "I am far from wishing to depreciate Addison's talents, but I am anxious to do justice to Steele." That we cannot do the latter without now and then drifting upon the former is to some extent Steele's own fault, as he himself realized with some bitterness after Addison's death, when Tickell, Addison's literary executor, went to show that Steele had sought to build up his reputation on Addison's writings. The truth was that Steele had been "very patiently traduced and calumniated for" certain papers Addison had not wished to own. Indeed it was his wholesale and admiring acknowledgment to Addison in the preface to the *Tatler* which caused generations to give him less than was fair. He would not mind; he sought his friend's weal much more than his own; and even at the end it was his bountiful heart which made him rush in to the attack of the meddlesome Tickell. It is the result of his own selflessness that, like his Sir Roger, he has been "rather loved than esteemed"; a happy state of affairs, perhaps, which Steele would have welcomed; but the critic who attempts to estimate him at the bicentenary of his death must strive to give him his due.

Here we are on healthier ground, for though the writings of the two men are sometimes so alike as to make it hard to distinguish between them, there are certain qualities to be rendered to Steele and others to Addison. On the whole, the originality is Steele's: it was he who began the *Tatler* without saying a word to Addison about it, so it was he who conceived the plan, the drawing in of a certain number of "characters," just as it was he who later sketched in Sir Roger de Coverley and his group. His was the idea to civilize London life in a way different from, more humane and more effective than, that of the Society for the Reformation of Manners, as well as the tactful method of the dangerous procedure. The first letters, anecdotes and allegories are his. It is often forgotten that out of the 271 *Tatlers,* 188 are by Steele, only forty-two by Addison, while thirty-six are by them both. The *Tatler* improved as it progressed, partly through Steele's widening experience, but partly, no doubt whatever, because of Addison's help and stimulation; in the *Spectator* it was Addison who took the lion's share. The fact is that both throve in collaboration. Addison's papers are certainly more polished, perhaps because he had more leisure, but more likely because he was the finer craftsman. Certainly the mind

at work is no better, but the erudition is greater, the finish more perfect; the most delicious literary toys are from his pen. Yet in some ways Steele's papers are more delightful— . . . because they are more friendly, less removed; there is more of the street and the open air in them. With Addison the gusto is too refined down; it all smells a little of the study, whereas we feel that Steele's things were written in the coffee-house as a direct reaction to life. We have a sense of this also in their prose; there is more nerve and vivacity in Steele's, while Addison's is a little dulcet, the movement something too slow and urbane. There is rather much of the looker-on in Addison; indeed (he need not have confined his statement to parties) he never espoused anything with violence.

Though the end at which both men aimed was the same— namely, to make mankind better, wiser, and therefore happier—the motives were different. Steele was urged by a "great benevolence," Addison by an abstract love of virtue. The difference between the two men, in attitude and in prose style, is beautifully illustrated by their statements as to the impulses which made them write. Thus Steele in the last *Tatler*:—

> I must confess it has been a most exquisite pleasure to me to frame characters of domestic life, and put those parts of it which are least observed into an agreeable view; to inquire into the seeds of vanity and affection, to lay before the readers the emptiness of ambition: in a word, to trace human life through all its mazes and recesses, and show much shorter methods than men ordinarily practise to be happy, agreeable and great.

And thus Addison, in a famous passage of the tenth *Spectator*:—

> It was said of Socrates that he brought philosophy down from heaven, to inhabit among men; and I shall be ambitious to have it said of me, that I have brought philosophy out of closets and libraries, schools and colleges, to dwell in clubs and assemblies, at tea-tables and in coffee-houses.

It is the joy of doing as opposed to the ambition for praise; the thing for its own sake rather than for the result; the delight in life as it is, as against the pleasure of life as it ought to be: on the one hand, vitality ending on a firm note; on the other, the drawing-room manner slowing down to a trochee.

Steele's genius is most apparent in his bold launching out into the new venture of journalistic literature, in his conception both of the form it was to take and of the audience it was to appeal to. In form, the nearest approach so far had been Defoe's admirable *Review,* which was too polemical; while cognate descriptive writing of the time, such as Ned Ward's the *London Spy* or "The Amusements Serious and Comical" of Tom Brown, "of facetious memory," were far too heavy to provide breakfast-table fare. Essayists also there had been, but of the more studious variety, such as Cowley and Temple; while the philosophic writers, Shaftesbury for instance, wrote that sterner stuff which it is the province rather of philosophers than of the town to read. Well-timed, above all, was the revival of the "character," a form practised by many in this country—Sir Thomas Overbury, Samuel Butler—though his were not published till much later—and others, most notably John Earle, who in "Microcosmography" reveals much of the gentle humour, the general kindliness, which is the mark of Steele's and to a lesser degree, since a certain pointed and agreeable malice creeps in, of Addison's. La Bruyère also had his influence. But it was the combination of these elements into a whole, which would be delectable to the audience which Steele sought to attract, that led to the immediate success of the *Tatler.*

A deal has been made of the appeal to the "fair sex"; but the emergence of reading women cannot be separated from the change which was coming over society, a society which the theatre was beginning to attract, but for which most other writing, apart from more or less scurrilous romances, was far too abstract and literary. It was the rise of a middle class with enough education to wish to read, and enough leisure to gratify the wish, which made up the new audience ready to be captured by such a journal, an audience larger than the comparatively small class of University men and their families. Thus Mr. Sealand in *The Conscious Lovers* remarks:—

> I know the town and the world; and give me leave to say that we merchants are a species of gentry that have grown into the world this last century, and are as honourable, and almost as useful, as you landed folks, that have always thought yourselves so much above us.

He knew the town and the world, and he wanted literature which dealt with the town and the world that he knew; his wife and daughters would also want it, for most did not have the chance of being the good type of gentlewoman, with her especial responsibilities, and did not on the whole want to imitate the bad type, with her routs and masquerades, her quadrille, her chair and her patches—in short, all the dull frivolity of mode.

Since it was to this large new class that the paper was to appeal, it was to be light and amusing: it would rely upon the middle-class prejudice against the fashionable world and would glorify trade. Above all, it would be moral, for when a class rises to power it is always upon its superior morality that it insists as a justification for its search after position. The morality and the conventions, therefore, were commonplace enough—what oft was thought but hardly ever expressed, at least in popular writing: there could hardly be any of the upsetting notions of that forerunner of Nietzsche, Bernard Mandeville. Addison wished to make it serve also to cool the heats of faction; but, though Steele might have desired this, his passions were too strong to permit him to remain permanently out of the political turmoil. It was no use Addison being "in a thousand troubles for poor Dick"; he could only stand on the bank ready to pull him out of the current whenever he was in risk of drowning; he could not prevent him from plunging into the stream. When Whig principles were at stake he would infallibly embroil himself. It was this sad propensity which led to the abrupt termination of the *Tatler,* to Steele's non-participation in the last volume of the *Spectator,* his writing of the *Englishman* and the fatal *Crisis,* and eventually the *Plebeian,* which brought about his final rupture with Addison.

Yet if it was not the "fair sex" apart from its males which determined the form of the paper, it is obvious that the improvement of the position of women was one of its real objects, for Steele realized that it is women who determine the niceties of civilization. And since it was clear that they were to play an important part in society, it was necessary that they should become more serious, more enlightened—in a word, emancipated. Steele had a livelier sympathy for women than Addison had, and Thackeray was right to make Esmond say, "There's not a writer of my time of any note, with the exception of poor Dick Steele, that does not speak of a woman as of a slave, and scorn and use her as such." But here it was not altogether Steele's "benevolence" that was at work; it was his Bohemian nature. He had, certainly, no use for the intelligent—but not too intelligent—household drudge, which was Addison's ideal; true, he did not want women to be wasteful, silly and vain; but then, dreadful alternative, they might develop into household autocrats. The problem was, and perhaps still is, not how women may be happiest, but how men may be happiest with women. If it was bad to be married to a foolish dependent little creature, it was even worse to be held in leash by a would-be ruler. Thus in Steele's first comedy [*The Funeral*], written as early as 1701, Lord Hardy declares that he expects his felicity from his wife "in her friendship, her constancy, her piety, her household cares, her maternal tenderness." Friendship comes first; and it led to the question which crops up in the periodicals, "Can a wife be to her husband as a friend?" The answer was "Yes"; but it was born of Steele's hopes rather than of his experience. (pp. 657-58)

[Steele] left his mark upon his generation, not by his plays, for these, drawn largely from Corneille, Molière and Terence, have the broad vivacity of Vanbrugh and the irony of Farquhar only in a lesser degree, but by the personality operant in his papers.

> It is incredible to conceive the effect his writings have had on the town ([John] Gay wrote in "The Present State of Wit", [1711]); how many thousand follies they have either quite banished, or given a very great check to . . . his writings have set all our wits and men of letters upon a new way of thinking . . . we may venture to affirm that every one of them writes and thinks much more justly than they did some time since.

This is perhaps to rate the effect of one man too high. Steele, brilliant journalist that he was, sensed what was in the air—reform of manners, the education of women, the change in the drama—and led the public the way its best elements wanted to go. He was himself of its very best elements. There is no need to pity "poor Dick"; he died, as he had lived, with an aura of good nature and sympathy around him; and if he attained to no great position, largely owing to his reckless honesty, there are few who can have enjoyed life so fully and yet left an enduring monument behind them. (p. 658)

Bonamy Dobrée, in an originally unsigned essay titled "Richard Steele," in The Times

Literary Supplement, *No. 1439, August 29, 1929, pp. 657-58.*

Gilbert Thomas   (essay date 1929)

[*Thomas was an English poet and prose author. In the following excerpt, he discusses Steele and Addison's complementary literary partnership, arguing that "Addison was the greater scholar, Steele the better man of affairs. Addison excelled in refinement of taste; Steele had the warmer heart."*]

"It was said of Socrates," wrote Addison, "that he brought philosophy down from heaven to inhabit among men; and I shall be ambitious to have it said of me that I have brought philosophy out of closets and libraries, schools and colleges, to dwell at clubs and assemblies, at tea-tables and in coffee-houses." The epitaph which Addison coveted can certainly be assigned to him; but we must not forget that he owed an immeasurable debt to his friend and collaborator, Sir Richard Steele, the bicentenary of whose death we are now celebrating. Attempts to weigh the relative merits of Steele and Addison are apt to reflect merely the critic's own temperament. There were surely never two literary partners who were more ideally each other's complement. Not only in character, but by the circumstances of their lives, they were perfectly adapted for the double harness in which they worked. (p. 268)

[Steele's] *The Christian Hero,* save for its excessive adulation of William III., whom the author idolized, is a sensible, well-written pamphlet, condemning laxity of morals and placing Christ on a higher plane of courage than Cato or Brutus. But Steele's military friends made fun of it, and, to show what a gay fellow he could be if he liked, he wrote his earliest comedy. *The Funeral,* produced in the same year, is true comedy. But already the moralist in Steele was too sincere to be quenched. The play is wholly free from the coarseness of Wycherley, Congreve, and the other Restoration dramatists. The reaction against lewdness had been voiced in 1698 by Collier's *Short View of the Profaneness and Immorality of the English Stage;* and Steele followed precept by example. His next comedy, *The Lying Lover,* was too explicitly didactic and won the unique distinction for its age of being "damned for its piety." But *The Tender Husband* was more successful. It was equally pure in tone; but its humour was spontaneous and its characters—stage forerunners of Squire Western, Tony Lumpkin, and Lydia Languish—really alive. Seventeen years later, in 1722, Steel produced *The Conscious Lovers,* the best of all his plays. In the meanwhile, he had found another medium than the drama for his cherished purpose of reconciling wit and good breeding with virtue. On April 12th, 1709, the first number of the *Tatler* appeared. (pp. 268-69)

When, in the eighteenth number, Addison began to write for the *Tatler,* Steele modified the paper so as to give greater scope to his brilliant collaborator, and the "diversion" became the essential feature. Steele himself remained the more regular contributor to the *Tatler.* But the *Spectator* which succeeded it in 1711 and lived for two years . . . belongs rather to Addison's career. The *Guardian,* started

in 1713, was a mutual enterprise, while Steele later ran other journals of his own. Among these were the *Englishman,* the *Reader,* and the *Plebeian,* in which last he engaged in a political controversy with Addison. Estrangement ensued between the two friends, though there was never real personal bitterness. Steele's generous heart was filled with remorse when Addison died, in 1719, before a reconciliation had been effected.

The *Tatler* and *Spectator*—both in their own day and since—have had countless imitators. But, though the essay was to develop under Lamb and other writers into something more intimate and whimsical, Steele and Addison remain unmatched for the expression of sheer good breeding and good sense in pure, simple language. Their genius, however, can only be fully appraised when we remember the period in which they lived. They were no mere reflectors of public opinion. They created standards of manners and morals in an age that lamentably lacked them. The Revolution had brought political stability and tolerance. But, beneath the surface, society was still split by old antagonisms. The spirit, if not the letter, of Puritanism survived, causing its followers to frown upon innocent pastimes; while, on the other hand, as a legacy from Charles II., the notion still persisted in aristocratic circles that a "gentleman" must necessarily be an atheist or a roué. With a deliberate effort of sweet reasonableness, Steele and Addison bridged the gulf. Dealing with serious matters in a light and urbane manner, they showed, with faultless balance of judgment and with exquisite tact and persuasion, that religion has its place for joy, and, on the reverse side of the shield, that true breeding cannot be divorced from morality. English literature has always acted as a reconciling social leaven. It was never more so than in the hands of Steele and Addison.

To these inseparable names the honours must be awarded evenly. Addison was the greater scholar, Steele the better man of affairs. Addison excelled in refinement of taste; Steele had the warmer heart. Addison dressed ideas impeccably; but the ideas themselves were often Steele's. Steele set the pace for Addison in the revolt against impure drama. Steele—"a Kind of Guardian to the Fair"—inspired the nobler conception of womanhood; and Steele germinated the idea of the Club and gave the bare bones to Sir Roger de Coverley, though it was Addison's finer touch that turned him into a garrulous, ridiculous, but immortally lovable creature of flesh and blood. Steele was the better editor, Addison the better writer; though even as a writer it is only to the consumate Addison that Steele himself, in the same genre, comes second. . . .

Steele found it easier to teach than to follow his own instructions. Not only was he irresponsible in financial matters; in other ways he failed to live up to his own standards. But, mercurial, impetuous, and generous, he erred always in warm blood, and never fell into the final sin of mistaking evil for good. His ideals, at least, were kept untarnished. As a writer, he survives by intrinsic virtue of his dignity and charm. The good sense and fine feeling of his best work are applicable for all time. But to appreciate the full stature of the man we must, again, remember his period and setting. His ideals flowered, not in a ready-made garden, but in a wilderness. A creator, not a crystallizer, of public opinion, he was among the most potent builders of the eighteenth century, which, as historians are increasingly recognizing, was, beneath its undramatic exterior, a time of quiet but solid reconstruction. (p. 269)

Gilbert Thomas, "Sir Richard Steele," in The Spectator, *Vol. 143, No. 5279, August 31, 1929, pp. 268-69.*

Edmund Blunden   (lecture date 1929)

[*Blunden was an English essayist and literary critic. In the following text of a lecture originally given in 1929, he examines Steele's literary standing in his partnership with Addison, and comments on the style of his personal letters to his wife.*]

Into a world where as yet the arrival of the weekly newspaper was an event, and where the frequenters of the coffee-house listened with an attentive passion to the clear-voiced gentleman selected to read it all out, the genius of Steele and of Addison brought a richness of rapid ideas and constant style; to those two conscientious originators we have long acknowledged our indebtedness through the honourable history of periodical literature in England. Had we lost all intimate acquaintance with their own journals it would scarcely be possible for us to speak coldly of their influence on the range of topics, the diversity of treatment, the nicety of judgment, and enthusiasm for what is happiest in human society, which have been subsequently the expected standards of regular essayists. But the great name of these two colleagues is by no means extant only in a retrospect of former power and importance. The humanists of the *Tatler* and *Spectator,* after more than two hundred years, address us in lively friendship; they are authors not by tradition but by endurance in the battle of the books; the characters, situations, and scenes which their genial industry depicted for instant amusement and instruction maintain their gay liberty. Sir Roger is coeval with Elia and Mr. Pickwick.

If, in the process of applauding the excellence of Addison and his intellectual light, there has been some tendency to lose sight of the full merits of Steele, it would be well should the bicentenary of Steele's death produce a better reckoning. A recurrence to the letter of Bishop Rundle anticipating the posthumous character of Steele, and almost claiming for him more disciples than Socrates had, would freshen the general opinion:

Steele would have been what he was, had Addison never been born; but Addison would have died with narrow fame had he never had a friendship with Sir R., whose compositions have done eminent service to mankind. To him we owe that swearing is unfashionable, and that a regard to religion is become a part of good breeding. . . . Let thy faults, O Sir R., be buried in thy grave, and thy virtues be imitated by all! Let thy writings be beloved; for whoever doth that sincerely will, before he thinks of it, become a lover, if not a practiser, of virtue; and the world may owe to thee the removal of fopperies, that are to be born again in centuries to come.

Probably only the most inveterate bookmen are prepared to explore anew everything that the British Censor wrote. Steele had a fertile pen. His generous disregard of economy obliged him to make the most of it. His verse, to be sure, is not voluminous. As the Bishop of Derry, already quoted, observes, "He had no genius for rhyme; and he knew that he had not, and therefore but seldom attempted it." His drama is more substantial and more to the purpose. The editorial zeal of Mr. G. A. Aitken for Steele did not stop short of those plays, **The Funeral, The Tender Husband, The Lying Lover, The Conscious Lovers,** through which the resolute purity of Steele's principles gleams finely, and out of which we hear the notes of his social satire.

Yet Steele is not in the memory of his country on account of the plays, nor to any considerable degree because he gave the world a treatise on **The Christian Hero,** nor again on the strength of his pamphlets. We love him all the more for collaborating in an **"Account of the Fish-pool, consisting of a Description of the Vessel so called, lately invented and built for the Importation of Fish alive, and in good health, from parts however distant"**; but we do not inquire actively into that relic of a pleasant speculation, in its bearings upon literature. *The Crisis,* once so intense and ominous, a "scandalous and seditious libel," has died away.

Steele's series of activities in the sphere of periodical writing, too, is longer than is commonly apprehended. The two immortal titles, the *Tatler* and *Spectator,* occur in the course of an imposing catalogue of enterprise, from which at random arise such other titles as the *Guardian,* the *Lover,* the *Reader,* the *Plebian,* the *Theatre;* and wherever Steele appeared as a journalist he infallibly deserved a following and received it. The *Guardian,* in particular, continued to be reprinted, and may be dipped into at this date with assurance of agreeable discoveries; Johnson even calls it "a continuation of the *Spectator,* with the same elegance and the same variety." In its pages you are invited to sit in your easy chair and smile at the entertainment offered by the genuine spirit of Steele; there Jack Lizard returns from the University, a precocious philosopher, "to pinch one of his sister's lap-dogs, and afterward prove he could not feel it"; or Nic Hawthorn writes enticingly, "I have a pack of pure slow hounds against thou comest into the country, and Nanny my fat doe shall bleed when we have thee at Hawthorn hall"; or the Terrible Club meets in the Tower under oath to cut its beef with bayonets instead of knives and to drink no liquor but rack-punch, quickened with brandy and gunpowder. The *Guardian,* however, is an overflowing of that spring of charming and enlightening faculties which runs most brilliantly in the *Tatler* and *Spectator.*

It is Steele's distinction to have been first in the field with the notion and achievement of the *Tatler*—the creation of an Isaac Bickerstaff, Esq., a personality fitted to observe and annotate the tricks of the town without offence or selfish ambition. The *Tatler,* in which Steele has by much the greatest share of composition, is a microcosm, abundant in comic paintings and serious intimations. From White's Chocolate-House, or Will's, or Bickerstaff's "own Apartment," we are made to see the fantastic show of which we are a part. Lady Fidget and Will Voluble, Harry Spondee and Tom Wildair, Tom Courtly and Jack Gainly, Ralph Nab the hatter, and Ralph Incense the chaplain—these and scores besides come on the stage for our fond ridicule. We laugh ourselves out of court under the art of Bickerstaff in his lucubrations. Nor will those *Tatler* essays be neglected, or set down as dull exceptions, in which our merry moralist is found in a mood of definite doctrine. Steele attained at once a high beauty of style and glory of sympathy when he produced in the England of 1710 that paper challenging cruelty to animals and, above all, blood sports. In another way he triumphed that summer when he contrasted with the mere hobby of tulip-growing his "visits to a spot of daisies or a bank of violets" and "reflected on the bounty of Providence, which has made the most pleasing and most beautiful objects the most ordinary and most common."

After the *Tatler* the *Spectator* rose in its elaborate symmetry, and the *Spectator* is Addison's in its total effect and principal honours; yet, even here, Steele not only vies with his old schoolfellow in the number and resourcefulness of his contributions, but takes the lead in one matter of significance to generations of booklovers. Addison, in the first number, with perfect delicacy and harmony introduces us to that reticent being whose character is the unity of the *Spectator.* In the second number it is the fancy of Steele which, building upon the suggestion of a club made in Addison's paper, conjures up the rare spirits who form that "sweet society," and begins without hesitation at "a gentleman of Worcestershire, of an ancient descent, a baronet, his name Sir Roger de Coverley." Before he has done, we know, among several beings more vividly present than our neighbours, another masterpiece, the gallant Will Honeycomb. Later on, when Addison has devoted to these characters his own grace and truth, Steele courteously and wisely contents himself with a very few additions to his own first sketches; again he displays his diversity in the imagining of other figures and groups.

Reluctantly enough, one leaves the good ground of the inimitable partnership between Steele and Addison in the two journals which set the standard for our periodical prose; but there remains another body of writings, in which Steele is by himself, has put off the author, and yet wins from us who read a tribute which might please him best of all. The work is the collection of letters and notes surviving from the profusion which he wrote to his wife Mary. Ordinarily, though he was a good letter-writer, and his manner and meaning support the fine opinions which he won as "Isaac Bickerstaff, Esq.," he scarcely stands on the level of Cowper and Keats and Fitzgerald. But in the correspondence with his wife ("dear Ruler"), brief and insignificant-seeming though so much of it is, he was recognised from the time when John Nichols published the text (1787) as having given his fellow-men a kind of testament of most touching and lasting sensibility. The lady, it is too probable, did not rise to Steele's exalted simplicity of love; we have, in these letters, the invincible courtesy of the man meeting all the minor and major difficulties which her nature put in his way.

It is in this idyll, this brave constancy and frankness, that

Steele may be perhaps viewed by us with our most eager admiration. Nothing that he wrote in public could repay more subtly a close gaze than these little memorials. There is humour in them as well as honour and love.

> Tennis-Court Coffee-House, May 5, 1708.
>
> DEAR WIFE,—I hope I have done this day what will be pleasing to you; in the mean time shall lie this night at a barber's, one Leg, over against the Devil tavern at Charing-cross. I shall be able to confront the fools who wish me uneasy, and shall have the satisfaction to see thee chearful and at ease. . . .

The veritable laconic occurs: "Dear Prue, Sober or not, I am ever yours." The letters often have the fragrance of a particular thoughtfulness, whether it is seven pennyworth of walnuts or a pound of green tea that he is sending or some guineas which he no doubt might have kept himself with avoidance of discomfort. The signatures are endlessly pretty and spontaneous. Before her marriage the contentious Prue had written of Richard Steele to her mother that he had "a mind so richly adorned as to exceed an equivalent to the greatest estate in the world." "His temper," she reported, "is what I am sure will make you, as well as myself, perfectly happy." First and last Steele as an author and as a man was worthy of that confidence; the last word on him is our general agreement with Prue on the occasion. (pp. 107-12)

> *Edmund Blunden "Richard Steele," in his* Votive Tablets: Studies Chiefly Appreciative of English Authors and Books, *Harper and Brothers, 1932, pp. 107-12.*

Rae Blanchard   (essay date 1932)

[*In the following excerpt from her introduction to a 1932 edition of* The Christian Hero, *Blanchard reconsiders Steele's essay, exploring its emphasis on Christian morality and its anti-Stoicism.*]

The **Christian Hero** was . . . related in a general way to the vast output, at the turn of the century, of reforming tracts on every possible subject. In particular, it was related to those tracts whose purpose was reform of the 'Universal and Destructive Torrent of Error and Pleasure' among the 'Men of Wit and Gallantry'. But it was not in the vein of the numerous contemporary manuals of prayer and piety for young men, used so extensively as propaganda by the Society for the Reformation of Manners and by the religious societies. (pp. ix-x)

Steele's model had more dignity than these manuals of piety. It is to be found, rather, in the moral and psychological essay with religious colouring, which inquired into the principles of morality: into the nature of reason and the passions, the motives of conduct, and the relation of Christianity to right conduct. (p. x)

From the very first, Steele's essay has been criticized for weaknesses in both subject-matter and style. The first critic, writing in 1702 in *A Comparison between the Two Stages,* was very severe:

'Tis a Chaos, 'tis a confusion of Thoughts, rude and indigested; . . . 'Tis Dated from the Tower-Guard, as a present to his Colonel, that his Colonel might think him even in time of Duty a very contemplative Soldier, and I suppose by the roughness of the Stile, he writ it there on the Butt-end of a Musquet.

The reading public of the nineteenth century almost forgot it. At best it was remembered only as 'a valuable little manual'; it was apologized for as the writing of 'a theologian in liquor', and it was even vaguely referred to by one historian as a poem. In recent years it has suffered the fate of a minor essay overshadowed by its author's more famous works.

But in spite of the fact that it belongs to a genre of slight literary value and that it is marred in places by careless writing, the **Christian Hero** is worth reconsideration. There are fine passages in it which admirers of Steele regard as being among his best. It is interesting because it contains the initial expression of some of the ideas—for example, the defence of women and the denunciation of false honour and duelling—which he elaborated in his periodicals, and because his moral theory, his starting-point for two decades of corrective propaganda, is first outlined here. Moreover, the **Christian Hero** is historically important in that it contains a notable early discussion of benevolence, its origin and nature, a subject prominent in eighteenth-century thought. But the question of originality and intrinsic value apart, Steele's essay, which ran into twenty editions during the eighteenth century, cannot be ignored in the history of ideas. Steele himself thought well of it. In July, 1701, after its appearance in April, he published a second edition enlarged and carefully revised; and in 1710 he took the pains to revise it again for a third edition. From time to time, also, he incorporated portions of it in his periodicals. (pp. xi-xii)

The general theme of the essay, as the title implies, is the superiority of religion over pagan philosophy as a moral guide for men of affairs. Steele was on the defensive. Aware of prejudices among his readers given to 'the Fashionable Vice of Exploding Religion', he inquired tactfully into the reason why the 'Christian sneaks' in the imagination while the 'Heathen struts'. In spite of the 'Pompous Look Elegant Pens' had given pagan heroes, he hoped to prove that the early Christians were the 'most truly Gallant and Heroick that ever appeared to Mankind'. In the first chapter he discussed the lives of Cato, Caesar, and Brutus in order to demonstrate that their philosophy failed them in times of crisis. In the second, he told of the heroic elements in the life of Christ. The third eulogized the precepts and lives of the early Christians, especially of Saint Paul, whose heroism Steele contrasted with the false heroism of the pagans. The fourth endeavoured to show the value of religious motives to all men who aspire to greatness; and the conclusion was a tribute to a modern hero, William the Third. Such is the general design of the essay. The various strains of thought in it require a more detailed analysis.

Steele's view of human nature was on the whole pessimistic. In the first place, natural depravity is fundamental. Pride and vanity caused the fall. Later, as social life grew more complex, the egoistic passions, 'Self-opinion' and 'Self-admiration', continued to become stronger, until 'from the desire of Superiority in our deprav'd Natures' there were bred 'Envy, Hatred, Cruelty, Cunning, Craft, and Debate' to be our 'bosom Companions'. Thus egoism, a 'false and unreasonable Fondness of ourselves', became firmly rooted in human nature.

A second point in Steele's analysis of human psychology was that the passions are 'the Springs of Human Action', whose important function it is to motivate conduct. But not all of them are evil. For example, love and the desire for fame, universal passions, are responsible for virtuous as well as evil actions. Revenge produces evil; but pity, an altruistic passion, produces highly virtuous conduct. Every action has its origin in a passion; and the passions are, therefore, the seeds of virtue as well as of vice. Although Steele's emphasis was on the primacy of the passions, he granted that reason is important as a check on them. But he lacked confidence in its power. 'The Living Conscience, or the Knowledge and Judgment of what we are doing' was intended to be a guide. It has not sufficient power, however, to control the passions; and it cannot be trusted to define ethical standards. Steele's opinion was that

> Whatever Law we may make to ourselves, from the Greatness of Nature or the Principles of Philosophy for the Conduct and Regulation of Life is it self but an Artificial Passion, by which we vainly hope to subdue those that are Natural.

Thus human nature, weak in reason and ridden by passions, must have support and guidance. Christianity is effective, he believed, where pagan morality fails. It operates to save man, first through grace—that is, through the vicarious atonement by Christ, a mediator—and second through the precepts and examples of Christ and the early Christians. Christianity is able to control and direct the passions, to supply incentives of reward and punishment, and to define virtuous conduct. Steele emphasized the fact that it does not attempt to destroy the passions: God 'claims not an utter Extirpation, but the Direction only of our Passions'. Accepting even the unruly ones as natural and useful, Christianity directs them into virtuous channels. Love is moralized by the Christian institution of marriage. Fame is given a wider scope—the undertaking of great deeds for the glory of God rather than for personal renown. And compassion, an altruistic passion, becomes the origin of charity, which is the supreme Christian duty, the 'reiterated Abridgment of all His Law'—the 'Command of Loving one another'. Thus Steele arrived at his criterion of virtue: that which contributes to 'The Good and Welfare of others'. And he found that Christianity was superior to any other system of morality in its power to develop this social virtue:

> For the neglected and despised Tenets of Religion are so Generous, and in so Transcendent and Heroick a manner disposed for publick Good, that 'tis not in a Man's power to avoid their Influence; for the Christian is as much inclined to your Service when your Enemy, as the moral Man when your Friend.

But in spite of the fact that it was his lack of confidence in the rational faculty which caused him to advocate moral guidance by a system with supernatural sanctions, Steele made a special point of the approval of Christian doctrines by reason. Christ's teachings, he insisted, were directed to 'the Reason and Judgment' and must be received by '*Arduous* and *Indisputable Conviction*'. Religious incentives are the 'reasonable terms of Reward and Punishment'. Saint Paul's preaching 'strikes all along at the Reason'.

Steele's interest in reason, however, was perfunctory; his confidence in it, slight. Indeed one particular emphasis in his moral theory, as he outlined it in this essay, was its anti-rationalism. All men are moved primarily by passions, which are, in the main, egoistic; depravity and irrationality must be taken for granted. But Steele was unwilling to draw completely pessimistic conclusions. He saw nothing in human nature that precluded virtue—under the corrective influence of Christianity. And he declared that side by side with depravity is a natural 'Temper of Mind' hospitable to virtue; that by the 'Force of their Make' men are 'framed for mutual Kindness'.

This idealism concerning man's innate tendency to good nature is one element in Steele's sentimentalism. But the sentimentalism in the *Christian Hero* lies chiefly in his conception of virtue, which he defined as Christian benevolence, insisting on its affinity with good nature, its origin in compassion, its association with humility, meekness, a forgiving spirit, and submission to the will of God, its amiability, and finally its appeal to the sensibilities. A pronounced fervour pervades his discussion of charity. Forgiveness is 'the most arduous Pitch human Nature can arrive at'; reconciliation with one's enemies, 'consummate Bliss'; meekness, a 'Sublime and Heroick Virtue'; pity, 'a beautiful kind of Ignorance' which men have of their own selfish affairs; charity, 'a noble Spark of Celestial Fire'.

These three prominent emphases in Steele's moral theory—his anti-rationalistic analysis of human nature, his refusal to accept the pessimistic implications of such an analysis, and his sentimentality—are all related to the dominant intention of the essay, an attack on the claims of neo-Stoicism. Every element in his belief has anti-Stoic colouring. His disparagement of the reason as an ethical guide, his defence of the passions, his appeal to the sensibilities, and his insistence that morality must be Christian—all support the claim that his system is not a 'Stoical Rant'. (pp. xiii-xvii)

[Steele's] central theme, 'No principles but those of religion are sufficient to make a great man,' expressed disapproval of the claims of neo-Stoicism that reason is a trustworthy moral guide and that pagan precepts and examples constitute an adequate moral system. Such a system was ineffective, he insisted with other Christian moralists, because of man's natural depravity—his impotent reason and selfish passions. This analysis of human nature agreed, of course, with the views of anti-Stoic moralists; it was supported by Augustinian theology; and up to a certain point, it harmonized with the egoistic theory.

Steele, however, did not accept the gloom of Augustinian theology or the cynicism of the egoistic analysis. The first element in his optimism was his confidence, shared with many anti-Stoic moralists, in the passions as natural—hence defensible—and manageable. The Stoic doctrine of insensibility was as distasteful to him as it was to his fellow moralists. He regarded the Stoic wise man, governed entirely by reason, without sensibilities, and invincible to pleasure and pain, not only as an unattainable human ideal but also as an undesirable one. The passions were to be defended as the springs of action; benevolence itself sprang from pity. Steele also found cause for optimism, as did others who disapproved of the egoistic theory, in a strong belief that human nature has a natural inclination towards benevolence. And finally, he was completely confident of the power of revealed religion. With the Augustinians, he relied on the saving element of grace and the invaluable check on depravity of reward and punishment. With the anti-Stoic moralists he believed religion capable of giving ethical direction to the passions. The reasonableness of Christianity, which the Latitudinarians stressed, he believed was also in its favour. And with all Christian moralists, he insisted that benevolence, the supreme virtue, is in its origin and nature peculiarly Christian. However seemingly inconsistent were his views, they were unified by his belief that Christianity, and no other moral system, will ensure right conduct.

Thus altruism and egoism, rationalism and anti-rationalism, natural and supernatural sanctions were intermingled in Steele's thought. But such contradictions were not peculiar to him. It is obvious that they existed also in the doctrines of contemporary Christian moralists who, like Steele, sensed danger both in the exaltation and in the denial of reason. The effort to combat in one synthesis both of these dangerous extremes accounts for the fact that in their doctrines, side by side with an element of pessimism conceding man's irrationality and depravity, there was an element of idealism praising his natural goodness. One fact should be emphasized: the strain of idealism in Steele's moral theory was not completely flattering to human nature—his was not a facile optimism.

The *Christian Hero* did not make any important new contribution to the ethical thought of the age. Steele's ideas were all ideas widely diffused among his contemporaries. There is no new single element in his essay and nothing original in his synthesis. And in fairness, it should be said that others writing in a similar vein . . . set forth their position much more thoroughly and clearly than Steele did. His essay, however, is more appealing. The reader turns gratefully from seventeenth-century sermons, reforming tracts, moral essays, and manuals of piety to the *Christian Hero,* which has, in addition to the earnestness characterizing them all, an appealing generosity of spirit and persuasive grace.

The principles which Steele laid down in the *Christian Hero* he adhered to, in the main, in his later reforming designs. As Isaac Bickerstaff and the Spectator, addressing a larger social group, he still regarded it as the chief duty of the moralist 'to look out for some Expedient to turn the Passions and Affections on the Side of Truth and Honor'. Religion he continued to praise as the most noble expedient—'the most honourable Incentive to good and worthy Actions'. And he continued to urge upon the fine gentleman the compatibility of religion and good breeding. The 'Word Christian', the *Spectator* admonished, should carry with it 'All that is Great, Worthy, Friendly, Generous, and Heroick' [356]. The *Guardian* [21] reaffirmed the purpose of Captain Steele:

> However, I will not despair but to bring men of wit into a love and admiration of the Sacred Writings; and, old as I am, I promise myself to see the day when it shall be as much in fashion among men of politeness to admire a rapture of Saint Paul, as any fine expression in Virgil or Horace; and to see a well-dressed young man produce an evangelist out of his pocket, and be no more out of countenance than if it were a classic printed by Elzevir.

Nevertheless it is apparent that, as the years passed, Steele's ideas about what could and what should motivate right conduct came to be modified, probably as a result of the insistence of many of his contemporaries that the reason can furnish a basis for a moral life. He increasingly emphasized the nobility of rational motives—'conscious virtue' and 'conscious goodness'. And unlike the Christian hero, his last hero, Bevil Junior of the *Conscious Lovers,* is first of all a rational being, whose 'actions are the result of thinking', who believes that 'there is nothing manly but what is conducted by reason'.

In his mature writings, as in this first essay, Steele exalted benevolence as the supreme virtue. At the centre of all of his corrective propaganda was the principle that 'the good of others' is the 'most generous motive of life'. He continued to identify benevolence with the Christian virtue, charity. And as an extract from a famous political pamphlet written at the height of his career will serve to indicate, his discussions of this virtue were pervaded by an emotional fervour similar to the sentimentalism of the *Christian Hero:*

> . . . tho I may be ridiculous for saying it, I hope I am animated in my Conduct by a Grace which is as little practised as understood, and that is Charity. . . . The greatest Merit is in having social Virtues, such as Justice and Truth exalted with Benevolence to Mankind. . . . He who has warmed his Heart with Impressions of this kind, will find Glowings of Good-will, which will Support him in the Service of his Country against all Calumny, Reproach and Invective, that can be thrown upon him. Riches and Honours can administer to the Heart no Pleasure, like what an Honest Man feels when he is contending for the Interest of his Country, and the Civil Rights of his Fellow-Subjects.
>
> (pp. xxv-xxix)

> *Rae Blanchard, in an introduction to* The Christian Hero *by Richard Steele, edited by Rae Blanchard, 1932. Reprint by Octagon Books, 1977, pp. ix-xxix.*

Cambridge History of English Literature (essay date 1933)

[*In the following excerpt, the unsigned critic examines Steele's promotion of virtue in* The Christian Hero, *his early comedies, and the* Tatler. *The critic also notes how several of Steele's periodical essays anticipate the short story and the novel.*]

[*The Christian Hero*] is an attempt to persuade educated men into accepting the Bible as a moral counsellor. Steele describes how Cato, Caesar, Brutus and Cassius died, and argues that heathen philosophy failed each in the great crisis of his life. He then tells over again the story of the creation of Adam and Eve, and how, after their fall, men became corrupt and so a prey to ambition and the love of ostentation. This dependence on the applause of the world is, to Steele, the root of all evil; even the tales which young fellows tell of debauches and seductions are prompted by "fame"; even "heathen virtues, which were little else but disguised or artificial passions (since the good was in fame) must rise or fall with disappointment or success." Christ, and then St. Paul, by their labours and death, first brought men help, teaching them that the true guide in conduct is conscience. Man sins or suffers through dependence on the world; he is saved by the inwardness and self-effacement of Christianity. In the spiritual distress which drove Steele to write this pamphlet, he had learnt to think for himself. The description of Eve's creation shows that he had studied Milton, then an unfashionable author; the passage on chivalrous respect for women's virtue was a defiance to the conventionality which regarded immorality as a sign of high spirits; the advice that a man should do a kindness as if he would "rather have his generosity appear an enlarged self-love than a diffusive bounty" was a new ideal for good taste; in his contention that the false ideals of society led men to err, he touched the true weakness of his times.

Thus, *The Christian Hero* is important because it foreshadows Steele's message to his age. But, though the book passed through a second edition within the same year and continued to be popular with readers of a certain religious temperament, it was not otherwise a success. The prosperous middle class, busy with the peaceful round of city life, did not need to be warned against choosing Caesar or Brutus for their model or Seneca for their spiritual pastor. Nor, again, if they ever opened this little manual of meditations, would they find it clearly explained how the self-sacrifice of St. Paul and the divinity of Christ could guide them amid the thousand little perplexities of their growing social system. Steele sermonised on heroism to readers who were interested in manners, and deserved the fate "that from being thought no undelightful companion, he was soon reckoned a disagreeable fellow."

This missionary spirit, when roused, impelled him to other forms of expression. Having not yet found his peculiar bent, he was inevitably attracted to the drama. During a century, comedy and tragedy, with intervals of repression, had been one of the most popular outlets for an author and must have seemed exactly the medium for a man with Steele's sense of humour and knowledge of character. Besides, the moral movement among the people, which had been influencing Steele, had also caught the theatre. Sir Richard Blackmore and Jeremy Collier were calling for a pure and reformed drama, and so Steele's conscience, as well as his tastes, urged him to put his ideas on the stage. Since the restoration, writers of comedies had aimed at brilliance and cleverness. As the court was amused at cuckoldry, they represented seducers and seduced as endowed with all the wit, ingenuity, or beauty which society admired, while intrigues leading to adultery could always be rounded off into a well-constructed, if somewhat unoriginal, plot. Steele went over the same ground—love, courtship, married life, intrigue; his purpose, however, was avowedly to paint virtue and vice in their true colours. Following the example of Molière, from whom he borrowed freely, he covered his bad characters with ridicule and confusion. But he was not content to let them occupy the front of the stage, as Molière had done. He wished to champion virtue; so his villains, for the most part, are minor characters, dismissed with humiliation at the *dénouement,* while his leading figures are quite ordinary people, whose careers begin and end in the triumph of homely virtues. Such characters, however desirable in a book of devotions, lack true comic interest, and Steele was obliged to lead his heroes and heroines through a series of domestic calamities and surprises, in order to sustain sympathy. In *The Funeral, or Grief-à-la-mode* (1701), his first and best constructed comedy, the defunct Lord Brumpton has to be kept secretly alive all through the play, in order to shame his worldly widow's enjoyment of affluence and freedom, and to reward his daughters' two suitors. In *The Lying Lover* (1703), copied from Corneille's *Menteur,* young Bookwit becomes drunk, then fights and appears to kill his rival, is arrested, suffers all the pangs of remorse and the horrors of Newgate and, after this gruesome lesson against intemperance and duelling, learns that his victim still lives and ends by marrying the sweetheart whom he had courted with a fidelity rare on the stage. In *The Tender Husband* (1705), the third and last of Steele's plays at this period of his career, he rises to one of Molière's leading ideas, in the conception that a son tyrannised till manhood in a boorish home will end by deceiving his father and contracting a foolish marriage, and that a girl, left to the companionship of French romances, will become a "Quixote in petticoats." But, when the elder Clerimont is presented as despatching his mistress, disguised as a gallant, to tempt the virtue of his wife and then, on the failure of the seducer, tearfully seeking a reconciliation, all dramatic propriety is sacrificed, in order to give a by no means convincing picture of conjugal tenderness. Such was the tone which the moral movement of queen Anne's reign introduced into the theatre, and, since succeeding dramatists came under this influence, Steele may be regarded as the founder of sentimental comedy. Unhappily, as in the case of most comedies with a purpose, plots are sacrificed to the moral, and, apart from improbability of incident, Steele's plays show but little of that correctness of construction which the age exacted.

If Steele's dramatic work added scant laurels to his reputation, it was of the first importance in forming his mind. He had come to his task with the same stock of ideas as had served him in composing *The Christian Hero.* But, as a playwright, he had to make these ideas talk and act. He

had to penetrate beneath the surface of life, and to show how often a profession or training degrades a man; how servants inevitably become mimics of their masters' excesses and frivolities; how women, who are untrained in the serious responsibilities of life, fall victims to fulsome adulation and often end in a marriage of convenience; how the best of them, for lack of moral sense, become tyrannical and fastidious before wedlock, and how others prey like vampires on their deluded husbands. Thus, Steele had learnt to look inside the domestic circle and to note how fashion and conventionality were warping the natural goodness of his fellow-creatures. Here and there, he hints at the conception of the purer and simpler, though rather emotional, family life which he was afterwards to depict. But, as we have seen, comedy was not a suitable medium for teaching of this nature. Although an atmosphere of earnest inquiry and reflection had formed itself in London, and had reached the stage, the public of the playhouse was not yet in a mood for social and moral speculation. It still expected wit and amusement. Steele had yet to discover where the world of thought that embodied the qualities which he had in mind was to be found, and how he was to approach it. (pp. 31-4)

Steele certainly did not perceive into what a world of thought and sentiment he was penetrating when he ventured, in *The Tatler,* to appeal to coffee-houses. After writing *The Tender Husband,* he seems to have relinquished the theatre for the more lucrative career of a court favourite. He, probably, never lived within his income and, after losing, in 1708, his position of gentleman-waiter to prince George of Denmark and failing to obtain two other posts, he returned to literature in order to meet his debts. Since the censorship had been removed from the press, journalism had become a profitable enterprise, and Steele's chief motive in starting *The Tatler* on 12 April, 1709, was, undoubtedly, the fear of bankruptcy. However, the desire to improve his fellow-creatures was as strong as in the days of *The Christian Hero.* Steele was himself a frequenter of coffee-houses. He knew how confused and misguided their political discussions often were, thanks to the irresponsible news-sheets which flooded London; and he also realised how many other topics were wrongly or superficially canvassed in those daily and nightly gatherings. So, he set himself to enlighten, as well as to entertain, his fellow-talkers. As gazetteer, he could give the most trustworthy foreign news, and, as a man of culture and society, he could tell them what to think concerning other matters which occupied a discursive and critical generation. The paper came out three times a week, and each issue (unlike *The Spectator*) contained several essays, dated, according to their subjects, from particular coffee-houses.

Thus, in its original conception, *The Tatler* was hardly more than an improved imitation of Defoe's *Review* and *The Athenian Mercury.* From the first, Steele aimed at making his paper more comprehensive. He perceived that different coffee-houses stood for widely different interests, and he laid them all under contribution. He persevered in finding instruction or amusement for every taste, till *The Tatler* became almost as diversified as the opinions of its readers. In the hands of most editors, so undiscriminating a policy would soon have reduced a journal to a periodical miscellany, and Steele the essayist is certainly not free from charges of inconsistency and confusion. But it must be remembered that his long struggle after a sober, scholarly existence, though hardly successful in his personal life, had rendered him keenly responsive to kindred influences around him, and enabled him to discover and give expression to the spirit of humanised puritanism which existed beneath the babel of coffee-houses. Like all originators, he had to feel his way. He began by making a feature of foreign intelligence and theatrical news and, full of middle-class disgust at frivolity and incompetence, exposed the vagaries of prominent social characters, apparently convinced that offenders would mend, if pilloried under a pseudonym. Inspired by the same respect for order and regularity, he gave expression, in some rather commonplace articles, to the public antipathy against gambling, and argued, in a series of papers, that duelling was a senseless, guilty practice, observed by exquisites as an affectation of bravery but secretly condemned by level-headed burghers. He warned his readers against swindlers, pointing at certain well-known sharpers as dogs, but without a touch of the old English amusement at roguery. Indeed, except for two jestbook stories, a mock testament and a few sentimental extravagances in the style of seventeenth century romances, his earlier attempts in a lighter vein consist of coffee-house discussions on literary questions and talks on current topics of city life such as changes in slang and the abuse of the title esquire

These and similar performances were half-hearted, because Steele was finding his true level in the alleged lucubrations of Isaac Bickerstaff. He had borrowed this pseudonym from Swift's famous pamphlet, as being the best known type of intellectual detective and watchman. Soon, coffee-houses began to make their influence felt, and, as he gradually marked out as his province the intimate world of conduct and courtesy, he tended more and more to invest his figurehead with a new personality. The literature of coffee-houses must be as light and informal as their discussions; so, he puts his moral counsels into the mouth of Bickerstaff, in order to preserve a conversational style and an air of persuasive authority quite acceptable to men who looked up to a self-constituted oracle in all their debates. As his readers were interested in eccentricity, Bickerstaff becomes an aged recluse living a lonely and mysterious life, surrounded, as Swift had suggested, by the old-fashioned paraphernalia of astrology and attended by his familiar Pacolet, like the now discredited magicians of the previous century. And yet this atmosphere of unreality gives effectiveness to Bickerstaff's character. His isolation enables him to study his fellow creatures dispassionately, and Pacolet, like the *diable boiteux* of Lesage, reveals to him the inaccessible secrets of other people. As the numbers of *The Tatler* increased, he developed into the first, and rather roughdrawn, portrait of eighteenth-century civilisation. He has the reasonableness and insight of coffee-houses, a sympathy with common things, out of which the domestic novel was to come, and a spirit of independent thought, coupled with respect for order and religion, such as the seventeenth century never knew.

In this thin disguise, Steele touched on all those questions of breeding, good taste, courtesy and chivalry where the middle class had discarded old aristocratic ideals, without having yet learnt to trust entirely to their own. No wonder *The Tatler* became immensely popular when its readers found their half-formed notions confirmed and proclaimed. One of their perplexities centred round the ideal of what they called a gentleman. In aristocratic circles, men still emulated the type set forth by Jacobean essayists and affected "warmth of imagination, quick relish of pleasure and the manner of becoming it." Such lubricity and self-assertion would be intolerable where friendly intercourse was the foundation of culture, and Steele points out that the first quality of a gentleman is not brilliance but forbearance and the art of accommodating another's susceptibilities without sacrificing one's own. Many recognise this ideal, but have not the tact to combine compliance with self-respect, and become "pretty fellows" or even "very pretty fellows," or, again, affect an unwarrantable familiarity and merely succeed in becoming "whisperers without business and laughers without occasion." Society being now a mosaic of different units, all of them seeking some common ground of intellectual fellowship, men of one interest, such as are many scholars and soldiers, are shown to be as superficial as those who think that boisterous good humour will make up for a lack of ideas. But, again and again, Steele insists that a man's first duty is to please his hearers, showing how often the "wag" and the "wit" of the old school still abuse the privileges of acquaintanceship merely to gain a reputation for smartness and satire.

The puritan desire to see the seriousness of life in every word and deed was now being humanised into a standard of good taste, and, if Londoners refused to admire cleverness devoid of charity, they were even more ready to be warned against coarser methods of self-advertisement. Affectation in dress and manner, such as the manipulation of the snuffbox or the wearing a cane on the fifth button, is mercilessly ridiculed; the man who uses expletives to make his conversation forcible is declared to be merely empty-headed; the whole fraternity of fops is characterised as "the order of the insipids"; but the severest strictures are passed on the pretence of viciousness which was part of the dandies' pose. Thus, the two nations pass before us. On the one hand, the degenerate imitators of Jacobean cavaliers and restoration courtiers, with the underworld of sharpers and gamesters; on the other, the middle-class coffee-houses, where citizens learnt to become urbane without ceasing to be pious. Steele belonged to both classes and traces the conflict between them. In many of his papers, after gibbeting the false ideal, he presents the true model, and it is not surprising that his own moral struggle, which gave him this insight, is sometimes recorded. In one paper, he pleads for the rake, claiming that he sins, repents and sins again only because his natural passions are too strong for him. Later, in a fit of self-humiliation, he confesses that good nature is often laziness, and, towards the end of *The Tatler,* he denounces his own besetting sin, declaring that the drunkard cannot be either a friend, a gentleman, a master or a subject, and is especially dastardly when he has a virtuous wife.

If, however, the middle classes had much to reform in the manners of men, they had far more to criticise in the social position of women. When Madame de Rambouillet brought together in her *salon* the most cultured men and the most beautiful women in France, she created a new standard of social refinement for Europe. The management of intimate relations between the two sexes became a proof of good breeding, and the civilisation of any court could almost be measured by the influence which ladies enjoyed in it. In the earlier Stewart times, the English aristocracy readily adopted this cult, and all people of quality practised the art of inspiring or suffering the passion of love. But, so soon as this accomplishment became a fashion, it was perverted to most ignoble uses. The coarser types of the restoration gained caste by affecting the same delicacy of sentiment and purity of devotion, while they really gratified their lusts. Immorality was invested with a ritual of compliments, odes, assignations and addresses, and, when the rising middle class came into touch with the *beau monde,* many well-intentioned young people were too inexperienced to detect the baseness which underlay this glitter and polish. Steele had primarily designed **The Tatler** to be an organ of the coffee-houses, and his first few papers on women are hardly anything but what one might expect from the gossip of the smoking-room. But, in the stage of social evolution thus reached, the follies of men and women were so inextricable that Steele could not satirise rakes and fops without penetrating into the lives of their victims or deceivers. So far back as the protectorate, moralists had begun to abandon the savage invective which Elizabethan and Jacobean misogynists had affected, and filled pamphlets with more humane, but none the less searching, ridicule of female frivolities. Steele is continuing a puritan tradition as well as breaking new ground, when he allows us to catch sight of the treachery and dishonour hidden beneath these hypocritical observances; sometimes, dwelling on the persecutions and outrages to which girls unwittingly exposed themselves and, at other times, revealing the jealousies and intrigues of more experienced matrons who looked on marriage, for all its euphemisms, as a game of skill or a masque of vanity. Now and then, he gives us glimpses of the amours of those who shrink from matrimony or dwells upon the more horrible tedium and disillusionment of marriages made without love. Had Steele lived in an age of decadence, he would, like most satirists in such periods, have confined himself to invective. But, if he helped to push one social order into the grave, he also helped to bring another to the light. As in his papers on men's manners, so now, after exposing vice, he holds up to admiration virtue, especially in his well-known portrait of Lady Elizabeth Hastings, whose passion is so high-souled and graceful that "to love her is a liberal education."

Such portraits would have had but little effect if Steele had not also pointed out the change which must inevitably befall the moral training of youth. While showing that vice was often concealed under a veil of refinement and liberality, he argued that the young give way to its allurements from a false idea of manliness or by way of revolt against parental tyranny. The old puritan methods of education had to be softened and humanised. He argued that children could be kept from extravagance and sensuality only by a sense of self-respect and by awakening in them tender memories of a father or mother whom they had learnt to love. He then explains how the parent or guardian must be their companion, and encourage their confidence if he is to understand their characters, ending with the portrait of a perfect father, Dr. Lancelot Addison, the one man "among all my acquaintances, whom I have thought to live with his children with equanimity and good grace."

In his charming papers on childhood, as well as in his moral essays on men and women, Steele writes like a man at one with his audience. He does not feel the need to argue or convince; it is enough to appeal to the sense of right and wrong. As he said himself, when exposing the tyranny of husbands, "touching upon the malady tenderly is half way to the cure; and there are some faults which need only to be observed, to be amended." His business was not so much to create sentiments as to awaken them by a vivid description, and teach his readers to recognise their own principles in some poignant situation. As civilisation became complex and peaceful, the affairs of daily life assumed greater importance; men concerned themselves with little things, and Steele found himself enabled to play on the deeper springs of thought and emotion, by describing an everyday episode. In this way, he discovered the modern "short story," that is to say, a tale which suggests fundamental ideas or convictions. Among the problems of social life which he thus illumined with imagination or even with emotion, none lay nearer Steele's own heart than questions of family life. To heighten and illustrate such reflections, he invented a lady editor, Jenny Distaff, Bickerstaff's half-sister, a typical middle class girl, who, from time to time, gives her views on women's affairs. But, as he returned again and again to this congenial theme, Jenny's personality grew upon him till she became the heroine of his domestic sketches. When reminding his female readers that matrimony is not a flight of romance, but a resolve to stake one's happiness on union with a partial stranger, he makes Jenny's marriage with Tranquillus the occasion for counsels based on this view, and gives a lively description of the wedding festivities. From time to time, the young couple reappeared to illustrate the experiences of married life. We have the first inevitable passing cloud which is happily smoothed over and forgotten. Like sensible *bourgeois,* they learn to understand one another, and Steele gives a picture of the lady's character maturing in wedlock. She and her husband dine with her half-brother, and she enters the room "with a decent and matronlike behaviour." The household thrives, and the perils of prosperity are dwelt on. Jenny calls on the astrologer, and, this time, he notices "in her manner and air, something . . . a little below that of the women of first breeding and quality but at the same time above the simplicity and familiarity of her usual deportment." Bickerstaff then discovers that his sister had fallen a victim to the love of display and writes to warn her husband of the folly of aiming above their station in life. Thus, besides discovering the short story, Steele might well have invented the serial domestic novel, if only the conditions of his work had permitted more continuity of application. For, in his writing, we find, for the first time, the temperament which is drawn to the pathos, and even the tragedy, of family life. He gave up one paper to a picture of perfect domestic happiness, describing it as "a complication of all the pleasures of life and a retreat from its inquietudes"; and, five weeks later, he introduces us to the same family plunged in the deepest woe as they gather round the death-bed of their mother. In these and other fugitive papers of like nature, we may notice the rise of that sentimentality which dominated the taste of the mid-eighteenth century and survives so late as Thackeray's novels. Steele, thanks to his double character, was one of the first to find that he could combat his own wayward, bohemian nature by cultivating a tenderness for home affections. The next generation either followed his example or discovered the same secret, fleeing from the crudity of their own civilisation by exaggerating the softer side of life, till lachrymose sensibility became the mark of refinement. He tells us himself how he was often driven to seek a steadying force in solemn and melancholy thoughts, and admits that he reserved certain times "to revive the old places of grief in our memory and ponder step by step on past life." Thus, out of distant memories, Steele recalled many intimate and pathetic scenes which a less effusive writer would have shielded from public gaze. Had it occurred to him to weave such incidents as the oft-quoted description of his father's death and of his mother's passionate grief into the history of Jenny Distaff, the domestic novel would, in a rudimentary form, have been invented. As it was, he ended the story with a sequel in which an unexpected hamper of wine vanishes among boon companions.

Steele touched on many more topics. As was to be expected from the mouthpiece of the coffee-houses and from the self-appointed "Censor of Great Britain," he is full of contempt for feudal prejudices and the arrogance of the rich. He sided with Hoadly, bishop of Winchester, against Blackall, bishop of Exeter, on the doctrine of passive obedience. He worked up Roger Grant's supposed healing of a blind boy into an enthusiastic description not unlike a broadside. He criticised the lack of pulpit eloquence. He composed, or published, some charming letters on the pleasures of country life. Just as John Dunton had constituted himself an oracle for all questioners in *The Athenian Mercury,* so Steele, sometimes, filled whole numbers with the correspondence he received or pretended to receive. In his constant endeavour to "extirpate . . . all such as are either prejudicial or insignificant to society," his characterisation is often onesided and becomes caricature. But, now and then, he pierced beneath the superficiality almost inseparable from satire, and hinted at the profound complexity of the civilised mind, showing, in several papers, how the ordinary human character is inextricably interwoven with the social fabric to which it belongs and becomes as particoloured as the woof itself. While society grows more heterogeneous, conflicting principles exist side by side, and, as men are bound, in some measure, to think according to their environment, they misunderstand each other on the commonest topics, fluctuate between opposite ideals and often end by distrusting their own instincts and mistaking their own emotions. These more complex and impressionable personalities are distinguished from simpler types: first, society nonentities, subordinate characters of men such as Tim Dapper, who are "like pegs in a building, they make no figure in it but hold the structure together," and, then, the vast workaday world, which steadfastly performs the tasks of its rulers, and "cannot find out that they are doing nothing."

These reflections are accidental and were probably shared by many another coffee-house critic of men and manners. Steele had neither the talent nor the opportunity to work them up into a philosophy. The same lack of system impairs his interpretation of literature. At a time when the most enlightened critics admired a poet for his rhetoric, Steele discovered in Shakespeare and Milton the sublime moralists of middle-class life, quoting from their pages to show where the everyday virtues of fidelity, pity and conjugal love have found their purest and noblest expression. He does not, however, seek to impress this view on his public. Beyond retelling the Bible story of Joseph and his brethren, to illustrate how, in moments of despondency, he "turns his thoughts to the adversities of persons of higher consideration in virtue and merit to regain tranquillity," he never taught his readers how to look for moral and spiritual guidance in literature. They are left to glean what they can from chance utterances. Had it been otherwise, these papers would have been the most remarkable critical production of Steele's generation. (pp. 37-47)

> *"Steele and Addison,"* in The Cambridge History of English Literature, *Vol. IX, 1933, pp. 29-72.*

Willard Connely   (essay date 1934)

[*Connely was an American biographer whose works include* Young George Farquhar *(1949), and* Count D'Orsay *(1952). In the following excerpt from his biography of Steele, the critic explores both the circumstances surrounding Steele's writing of, and the critical reception to,* The Funeral, The Lying Lover, *and* The Tender Husband.]

[In Steele's *The Funeral,*] undertakers, "a set of people who live in impatient hopes to see us out of the world, a flock of ravens that attend this numerous city for their carcases," the whole tribe were to be ridiculed; but Steele used this caricature only to introduce his plot, in which a Lord Brumpton pretended to be dead in order to weigh the loyalty of his second wife against that of Lord Hardy his son. Hardy by way of sub-plot was in love with bashful young Lady Sharlot, in ward to his father, while Hardy's friend Campley was in love with Lady Sharlot's unbashful sister, Lady Harriot. "Pish—the familiar coxcomb frets me heartily," said Lady Harriot, loud enough for Campley to hear. But she was to marry him. Her sister on the other hand could only stammer to Hardy, "Your lordship, I think, has travelled those parts of Italy where the armies are." Steele caused love to emerge equally from that. The step-mother, Lady Brumpton, sinister, scheming, and bigamous for good measure, was to be elaborately foiled in her ambitions to be a widow for the benefit of Cabinet, her lover.

Writing the part of Lord Hardy, a young captain who had to recruit a company, Steele perhaps drew upon what he had himself observed as a guardsman. [The Drury Lane stage manager Christopher] Rich gave this part to Colley Cibber, first comedian of the day, a man with thick legs and a clumsy figure, whose voice when raised went shrill as a whistle. Acting of the period demanded a touch of coxcombry, at which Cibber was deft; also a sharp sense of character, and Cibber at once so lived any character he played that audiences grew a bit languid at his exits; finally, since Lord Hardy was a bashful lover, Cibber's lack of grace quite sealed the rôle. Hardy's friend Campley on the contrary had to be easy, glib, a conqueror of fashionable ladies, to which requirements Rich wisely invited Robert Wilks, famous as Prince Hal, puffed in society as a model of deportment, and known as the most adaptable actor in London since the Restoration. Always conscious of his walk, Wilks stepped with chin up, brows lofty, mouth confident, "beseeching gracefully, approaching respectfully," dispensing hauteur rather like a bird of important plumage. He needed small humour, for he had infinite form.

A chit of a girl who had lately been a reciter of verses whilst she served as barmaid was to try the critical character of Lady Sharlot. Only eighteen, unfinished and amateurish, Anne Oldfield was not ill qualified to enact the bashful maiden. She was vivacious, tall, and of good figure. Between the lines she read she spoke with her eyes, which she half closed when stressing a crisp phrase. But perhaps a rarer charm, beyond her eyes, beyond her swan neck, her imperious nose, and a crescent of hair on either side her forehead, was her silvery voice, as fresh and as natural as water on a hill, a voice which improved, too, as a stream from a spring on its course, and was even so

Illustration of a dapper young Captain Steele.

early far enough cultivated to deepen the fun of *The Funeral.*

Yet with regard to the personal life of Dick Steele and its bearing upon his first play, the most reminiscent character was none of these, but Will Trim, servant to Hardy, and described as "the young man that attended him at Christ Church, in Oxford, and followed him ever since." Will Trim is almost certainly identifiable with Steele's man Will, whose character the Captain in his letter to Revett disclosed only two months before the play opened, that Will whom Steele's landlady called "as pretty a well-spoken gentleman as ever she saw." In this part, Rich cast the oblong-faced William Pinketham, veritable successor of Joe Haynes as prince of the drolls. "Pinkey" was beloved of the pit. He could give a most eloquent shrug, devour a cold chick right merrily, shake the house over the dextrous way he got under a table, and to the whole add a pinch of that spice of vulgarity which all of the audience liked a taste of and most of them hungered for.

Steele the Captain toiled without shame to "pack the house" on the first night. In old Drury Lane the pit was an amphitheatre of backless benches covered with green cloth. Beaux and soldiers, ladies and harlots, all sat together, chattered, toyed, played, groaned, whooped, heard and heard not. Against the wall under the first balcony another amphitheatre shut off "the quality," mostly women. But there were two galleries, and in them the opening performance of *The Funeral* disclosed a population of Coldstream troopers; Captain Dick well reckoned that such a following, to say nothing of officers in the pit who might at least be open to conviction, could save his play, and when the debonair Wilks had come on to speak the prologue the guardsmen heard him finish with these lines:

> No, in old England nothing can be won,
> Without a faction, good or ill be done;
> To own this our frank Author does not fear,
> But hopes for a prevailing party here;
> He knows he's numerous friends; nay, knows
>   they'll show it,
> And for the fellow soldier, save the poet.

What should incline that mob of troopers to save him? What should soften the late resentment of the officers below? "Nothing can make my heart ache but a dun," Steele had confided to Colonel Revett. . . . Suiting the ache to the cure in hand, the author, as if imagining himself the young Lord Hardy (also a captain in the Guards) introduced Hardy in Act II, in his lodgings:

"But methinks this is a calm midnight; I've heard no duns today. . . . "

"Duns, my lord?" replied Will Trim.

> I shall grow a little less upon the smooth with 'em than I have been. Why, friend, says I, how often must I tell you my lord is not stirring? His lordship has not slept well; you must come some other time. Your lordship will send for him when you are at leisure to look upon money-affairs; or if they are so saucy, so impertinent as to press to a man of your quality for their own—there are canes, there's Bridewell, there's the stocks for your ordinary tradesmen. But to a

haughty, thriving Covent Garden mercer, silk or laceman, your lordship gives your most humble service to him, hopes his wife's well. You have letters to write, or you'd see him yourself; but you desire he would be with you punctually such a day, that is to say the day after you are gone out of town.

In that scene alone there was a plain story from the barrack-room, almost enough to dispel the blight of the **Christian Hero.** But Steele had another card to conquer with. When in Act IV the play threatened to sag from the weight of interwoven intrigues the author transcribed the approximate experience of any fellow officer and his man in recruiting:

> LORD HARDY (*reading an order*). Gentlemen soldiers quartered in and about Guy Court in Vinegar Yard . . . belonging to the honourable Captain Hardy's Company of Foot—So, answer to your names. . . . John Horseem, corporal, march easy, that I may view you as you pass by men. Drums, Simon Ruffle, Darby Tattoo— there's a shilling for you—Tattoo be always so tight; how does he keep himself so clean?
>
> TRIM. Sir, he's a tragedy drum to one of the playhouses.
>
> LD. H. Timothy Ragg! O Ragg! I thought when I gave you your discharge just afore the peace we should never have had you again. How came you to list now?
>
> RAGG. To pull down the French king.
>
> LD. H. Bravely resolved! But pull your shirt into your breeches in the meantime. Jeoffrey Tatter—what's become of the skirts and buttons of your coat?
>
> TATTER. In our last clothing in the regiment I served in afore, the colonel had one skirt before, the agent one behind, and every captain of the regiment a button.
>
> LD. H. Hush, you rogue. You talk mutiny. (*Smiling.*)
>
> TRIM. Ay, sirrah, what have you to do with more knowledge than that of your right hand from your left? (*Hits him a blow on the head.*)
>
> LD. H. Hugh Clump—Clump, thou growest a little too heavy for marching.
>
> TRIM. Ay, my lord, but if we don't allow him the pay he'll starve, for he's too lame to get into the hospital.
>
> LD. H. Richard Bumpkin! Ha! A perfect country hick. How came you, friend, to be a soldier?
>
> BUMP. An't please your honour, I have been crossed in love, and am willing to seek my fortune.

Here was a scene almost equal to the immortal picture of Falstaff pricking down soldiers before Shallow's house in Gloucestershire. Captain Steele's own man Will was a perfect example of "gentleman soldier"; in sketching character Steele had drawn with sure strokes from the life; he

caught the applause, the acknowledgment, the enthusiasm of an audience critically military. As for Hardy, Colley Cibber though acting to the high approval of the Coldstreamers was full of fears; he owned that **The Funeral** won "more than expected success." So dizzy with joy was Christopher Rich that he paid all the actors for nine days in one week. (pp. 59-63)

[Steele's next play, **The Lying Lover,**] proved to be a thing wholly new to the London stage—a "sentimental" comedy. Young Lord Hardy, the soldier-lover in **The Funeral,** now became Young Bookwit, soldier and "lying lover." Having run away from Oxford to loves and wars, Bookwit (the elegant Wilks) spent the whole first scene telling his friend Latine (the comic Cibber) the factors in his conquering formula: first catch your lady, then lie to her about your exploits until she surrenders. Partly at the instigation of Cibber, Steele heaped up the sentiment from the beginning:

"I . . . can see when the soul is divided," said Bookwit, "by a sparkling tear that twinkles and betrays the heart. A sparkling tear's the dress and livery of love—of love made up of hope and fear, of joy and grief." And Bookwit thought his Oxford manner would help: "Were it not a taking compliment with my college face and phrase to accost a lady: Madam, I bring your ladyship a learned heart, one newly come from the university." And war talk: " 'Tis but looking big, bragging with an easy grace, and confidently mustering up an hundred hard names. . . . "

Picking up a pair in the Mall (Penelope and Victoria), Bookwit through several acts lied swimmingly, until the young women caught him out, jeered at him, and ran off. He got a little drunk, then sought to soothe himself by fighting a duel with a jealous rival, Lovemore. As the rival fell, Bookwit believed forever, guards rushed in and packed the lot off to Newgate prison.

This gave Steele a chance to agitate his pet reform, to cry down the custom of duelling. Green in his memory still was the harrowing affair of Captain Kelly in Hyde Park; in the present play, on an excuse for a duel equally indefensible, the author caused Bookwit and Lovemore to cross swords with a result in appearance fatal. But a scene in Newgate perhaps reflected Steele's experience of life yet a little more vividly: when the Captain on behalf of Lord Cutts had visited the prison to talk with a man under sentence of death he had no doubt kept eyes and ears alert. Coming to write the end of Act IV in **The Lying Lover** the author put Bookwit amidst a crowd of gaol-birds, such as Storm, a highwayman, and—was not Richard Steele still smarting from being gulled and defrauded?—Charcoal, an alchemist. To Storm, Steele gave the honour of introducing the quack to Bookwit:

> STORM. This gentleman, Mr. Charcoal the chemist, was our secret correspondent, and as we never robbed a poor man, so he never cheated a fool, but still imposed on your most sprightly wits and genius—fellows of fire and metal, whose quick fancies and eager wishes formed reasons for their undoing. He is a follower of the great Raimundus Lullius; the public think to

frighten him into their own purposes. But he'll leave the ungrateful world without the secret.

CHARCOAL. You know, sir, he that first asserted the Antipodes died for that knowledge; and I, sir, having found out the melioration of metals, the ignorant will needs call it coining: and I am to be hanged for it, would you think it?

BOOKWIT. When, pray sir, are you to be immortal?

CHAR. On Friday next. I'm very unhappy our acquaintance is to be so short. I'm very sorry your business is not over, sir, that, if it must be, we might go together.

BOOK. I'm highly obliged to you, sir.

CHAR. Yet let me tell you, sir, because by secret sympathy I'm yours, I must acquaint you, if you can obtain the favour of an opportunity and a crucible, I can show projection—directly Sol, sir, Sol, sir, more bright than that high luminary the Latins called so—wealth shall be yours; we'll turn each bar about us into golden ingots. Sir, can you lend me half a crown?

"Pinkey" and Bullock, masters in small character parts, acted to the queen's taste this scene, which Steele from bitter memory was able to inform with all the jargon of alchemy.

But what dedicated *The Lying Lover* to the decline of English comedy was its lachrymose culmination. Steele had to bring alive his dead man, marry him to Penelope, who had been faithful to this Lovemore until Bookwit lured her away with lies, then marry off Victoria to Bookwit, and so end all with "mirth and fiddles." As the dead Lovemore in disguise paced the stage the author almost saturated the scene with sorrow, with characters wailing in blank verse when he desired the sorrow to drip fast. Thus Penelope on Lovemore:

> Oh, could I see him now, to press his livid lips,
> And call him back to life with my complaints,
> His eyes would glare upon my guilt with horror,
> That used to gloat and melt in love before
> me. . . .
>
> LOVEMORE (*skulking about unrecognized*).
> This is worth dying for indeed. I'll follow her.

At last he had his fill of moaning, especially from Bookwit, and flinging off his disguise cried "Lovemore still lives to adore your noble friendship, and begs a share in't. Be not amazed! But let me grasp you both, who, in an age degenerate as this, have such transcendant virtue—"

> BOOKWIT. Oh, Lovemore! Lovemore! How shall
> I speak my joy at thy recovery—
>
> I fail beneath the too ecstatic pleasure,
> What help has human nature from its sorrows,
> When our relief itself is such a burthen?

He "spoke his joy," that is, in verse. Bookwit's emotion was so supremely melting that his prose and his poetry fused in the same speech. This character, needless to say, added little to the standing of Robert Wilks, nor did the vapid part of Victoria, "the other lady," elevate Anne Old-

field. After running for six performances, the last for the benefit of the needy author, *The Lying Lover* rose to the surface once more on December 15, and the waters closed over it.

If Steele intended "a generous pity of a painted woe," he found his audience cared neither for the generosity nor for the paint, nor yet for his dimpled didacticism. If his concoction was in part Alarcon filtered through Corneille, his residue was a mixture akin to saccharine. "I can't tell, Sir, what they would have me do to prove me a churchman," he afterward protested, "but I think I have appeared one even in so trifling a thing as a comedy; and considering me as a comic poet, I have been a martyr and confessor for the Church; for this play was damned for its piety." It was poor Dick's second damnation. Remembering that after the rather sodden piety of the *Christian Hero* he had had to write *The Funeral* to apologize for it, he now became aware that in some similar fashion he should have to warm anew the cold shoulder of Drury Lane. Had he read *The Lying Lover* to friends before it was staged? Had any one but Cibber applauded it in private? A not too kind contemporary said that "Captain Steele was constant at teatable, and used to break through his taciturnity by moving with a great deal of volubility his lips and all other muscles of his short face, when he was reading out of a comedy a love part, to show how sensible he could be of that passion."

Although Steele confessed that this play did "injury to the rules of comedy," the manuscript of *The Lying Lover* as something quite new in Drury Lane did not go begging for a publisher, since Bernard Lintot, rival of Tonson, thought the rights to it worth £21.10*s*. On January 26, 1704, it appeared, dedicated to the Duke of Ormond, "out of gratitude to the memorable and illustrious patron of my infancy, your Grace's grandfather." (pp. 78-82)

[In Steele's *The Tender Husband,*] the work of Addison amounted almost to collaboration by the time the play stood completed in March, 1705. "When I finished *The Tender Husband,* the Captain recorded his enthusiasm, "I told him there was nothing I so ardently wished as that we might some time or other publish a work written by us both, which should bear the name of 'The Monument,' in memory of our friendship." The important fact was that when writing dialogue in company with so highly disciplined a master of letters Steele got his first inkling that he and Joseph Addison as a team might labour much further to the literary advantage of both.

Late in March Christopher Rich, "the waspish ignorant pettifogger in law," accepted *The Tender Husband* in lieu of the unfinished *Election of Gotham*. Steele with all speed urged the manager to rehearse his "chief actors" in the play, which on the face of it continued to draw upon the author's own career for its main action: the protagonist a young army captain, and the theme—more marked than hitherto—fortune-hunting. As he had taken warning to cover the *Christian Hero* with *The Funeral,* so now with *The Tender Husband* he thought to wipe away the stigma of *The Lying Lover.* A year and a half had elapsed. Had his life as an officer of the Guards in town and the commander of a garrison in the country revealed to him more truly the nature of a comedy?

There was something dependable, if not unfamiliar, about the story: A country cousin (Humphry Gubbin) was brought by his father to London to marry a city cousin (Biddy Tipkin), neither one wishing the match. Farmer and banker sires argued ludicrously about the settlement. A second city gentleman (Clerimont) set his mistress (Fainlove), disguised as a fop, to spy on a gambling wife (Mrs. Clerimont). (Thus Steele ventilated another of his aversions, gambling, as in **The Lying Lover** he had exposed duelling) But Clerimont's younger brother, Captain Clerimont of the army, set cap at Biddy Tipkin, the heiress, with connivance of a lawyer (Pounce). In spite of a spinster aunt (Mrs. Tipkin) who proved more coquettish than sagacious, Pounce in turn secured Humphry Gubbin as husband for his own sister, who was none other than Fainlove. Here was a good tight plot, with not a few devices from Congreve and Wycherley. (pp. 87-8)

The first night [of the play] was on April 23, Shakespeare's birthday. Captain Steele, himself at the moment a penniless lover, himself an army officer on the trail of an heiress, had certainly a vested interest in watching the effect of a flirtation between his stage army officer Captain Clerimont and his stage heiress Biddy Tipkin. Steele had Pounce contrive to introduce Clerimont to Biddy in the park:

> CLER. We enjoy here, madam, all the pretty landscapes of the country without the pains of going thither.
>
> BIDDY. Art and nature are in a rivalry, or rather a confederacy, to adorn this beauteous park with all the agreeable variety of water, shade, walks, and air. What can be more charming than these flowery lawns?
>
> CLER. Or these gloomy shades—
>
> BIDDY. Or these embroidered valleys—
>
> CLER. Or that transparent stream—
>
> BIDDY. Or these bowing branches on the banks of it, that seem to admire their own beauty in the crystal mirror?
>
> CLER. I am surprised, madam, at the delicacy of your phrase. Can such expressions come from Lombard Street?
>
> BIDDY. Alas, sir! what can be expected from an innocent virgin that has been immured almost one-and-twenty years from the conversation of mankind, under the care of an Urganda of an aunt?
>
> CLER. Bless me, madam, how have you been abused! Many a lady before your age has had an hundred lances broken in her service, and as many dragons cut to pieces in honour of her.
>
> BIDDY. (aside). Oh, the charming man!
>
> CLER. Do you believe Pamela was one-and-twenty before she knew Musidorus?

> BIDDY (aside). I could hear him ever.
>
> CLER. A lady of your wit and beauty might have given occasion for a whole romance in folio before that age.
>
> BIDDY. Oh, the powers! Who can he be?—Oh, youth unknown—but let me, in the first place, know whom I talk to. . . . You seem, indeed, by your deportment . . . to have been in a conflict. May I not know what cruel beauty obliged you to such adventure till she pitied you?
>
> CLER (aside). Oh, the pretty coxcomb!—Oh, Blenheim, Blenheim! Oh, Cordelia, Cordelia!
>
> BIDDY. You mention the place of battle. I would fain hear an exact description of it. . . . Were there not a great many flights of vultures before the battle began?
>
> CLER. Oh, madam, they have eaten up half my acquaintance.
>
> BIDDY. Certainly never birds of prey were so feasted. . . .
>
> CLER. Had we not fought near a wood we should never have got legs enough to have come home upon. The joiner of the Foot Guards has made his fortune by it.
>
> BIDDY. I shall never forgive your general. . . . But your own part in that action?
>
> CLER. Only that slight hurt, for the astrologer said at my nativity, nor fire, nor sword, nor musket shall destroy this child, let him but avoid fair eyes—But, madam, mayn't I crave the name of her who has captivated my heart?

They told each other their names, but Biddy asked to be called Parthenissa, heroine of a romance, while Clerimont speedily offered to bestow upon her his own name as well:

> CLER. If you will give me leave, I'll put you in possession of it. By a very few words I can make it over to you, and your children after you.
>
> BIDDY. O fie! Whither are you running? You know a lover should sigh in private, and languish whole years before he reveals his passion; he should retire into some solitary grove, and make the woods and wild beasts his confidants. . . . And yet besides—to talk to me of children! Did you ever hear of a heroine with a big belly?

Whether Dick Steele in this vein of 'Lysistrata' had written with or without the help of Addison, he had it appeared within recent date profited by the works as well as the friendship of Will Congreve. Clerimont of course was not greatly unlike Steele himself, quite up to the farce of the beaux in the Mall; but Biddy Tipkin, carried away by romance yet no fool, was the best character part so far written by Steele, and her lines showed her creator lengths ahead of his earlier plays in sparkle of dialogue.

Biddy was ably set off further by the rustic Humphry and the urban Pounce. Humphry, goaded by his father to marry Biddy, objected to the dictates of old Gubbin, whom he described to Pounce as "a weasel-faced cross old gentleman with spindle-shanks . . . a creb-tree stick in his hand":

> HUMP. Why, sir, would it not vex a man to the heart to have an old fool snubbing a body every minute afore company?
>
> POUNCE. Oh fie, he uses you like a boy.
>
> HUMP. Like a boy! He lays me on now and then as if I were one of his hounds. You can't think what a rage he was in this morning because I boggled a little at marrying my own cousin.
>
> POUNCE. A man can't be too scrupulous, Mr. Humphry—a man can't be too scrupulous.
>
> HUMP. Sir, I could as soon love my own flesh and blood; we should squabble like brother and sister. . . . Pray, gentlemen, may I crave the favour of your names? . . .
>
> POUNCE. My name, sir, is Pounce, at your service.
>
> HUMP. Pounce, with a P?
>
> POUNCE. Yes, sir, and Samuel, with an S.
>
> HUMP. Why, then, Mr. Samuel Pounce, do you know any gentlewoman that you think I could like? . . .
>
> POUNCE. I have a thought just come into my head—Do you see this young gentleman? (*indicating his sister Fainlove in man's dress*). He has a sister, a prodigious fortune. Faith you two shall be acquainted. . . .
>
> HUMP. If I had your sister, she and I should live like two turtles.

While with two such drolls Steele naturally accelerated from comedy toward farce, best of all he had taken care to thin out the sentimentalism which "damned" him earlier. *The Tender Husband* propped the Captain's shaken repute in Drury Lane. (pp. 89-92)

With *The Tender Husband* Steele was aware of a debt, a debt of the kind he did pay: to the nice skill of Addison he owed many telling lines, to say nothing of the prologue; upon Addison his choice rested. "You'll be surprised," the Captain worded his dedication, "in the midst of a daily and familiar conversation, with an address which bears so distant an air. . . . My purpose in this application is only to show the esteem I have for you, and that I look upon my intimacy with you as one of the most valuable enjoyments of my life. . . . I hope I make the town no ill compliment for their kind acceptance of this comedy, in acknowledging that it has so far raised my opinion of it as to make me think it no improper memorial of an inviolable friendship." (p. 93)

> *Willard Connely, in his* Sir Richard Steele, *1934. Reprint by Kennikat Press, 1967, 462 p.*

William John Tucker   (essay date 1940)

[*In the excerpt below, Tucker favorably compares*

Steele's importance in the development of The Tatler *to that of his better-known collaborator, Addison.*]

Richard Steele has had but scant justice done him at the hands of biographers, essayists, and historians; even his friends have treated him but scurvily, damning him with faint praise; while his critics have denied to him the possession, not only of every respectable quality, but almost of all literary talent. In the forefront of these is that brilliant but most partial and untrustworthy of writers, where individual character or political bias is concerned, Lord [Thomas Babirston] Macaulay, whose vicious attack upon the memory and fame of a great writer [in his *The Life and Writings of Addison,* 1852] seems to have been dictated by no other motive than the desire to array his idol Addison in poor Steele's stolen raiment. But while numbering among his defenders such celebrated authors as [William] Hazlitt, [in his *Lectures on the English Comic Writers,* 1818-19], Leigh Hunt [in *Leigh Hunt's Dramatic Criticism: 1808-1831,* 1949] and Charles Lamb, the character and work of Steele may claim a hearing even after judgment has been pronounced by the omniscient Victorian. (p. 445)

We owe to Steele the beginnings of the periodical literature which was to develop into the magazines and journals with which we are familiar today. Steele and his followers avoided questions of religion, science, and philosophy in the strictest sense, and devoted their attention to the "more immediate and passing scenes of life," to "temporary and local matters." They made it their aim to exhibit the whims, characterize the pursuits, ridicule the absurdities, and expose the inconsistencies of men and women. The periodical essay gives us an excellent picture of the times. It shows us English city life during the eighteenth century; the men and their attire, the professions, the theaters, the trades, the interior of private houses, the prevailing ideas about education and criticism. We have every condition of life, and almost every kind of opinion, conversation, taste, fashion, folly, vice. In Hazlitt's words, the periodical essay "takes minutes of our dress, air, looks, words, thoughts, and actions; shows us what we are, and what we are not; plays the whole game of human life before us."

The society which was congenial to Steele, congregated at the coffee-houses, where men would sit for hours, discussing politics, literature, and the world at large. People went to the coffee-houses to pick up the latest news, and to garner the latest ideas. They wished to peep behind the political scenes; they also wished to be up-to-date in culture and in art, to follow the best fashion in criticism and in conversation, to adopt the new principles of manners and the new canons of taste. It occurred to Steele that the written gossip of the coffee-houses would be acceptable to the man about town; and it was under this inspiration that *The Tatler* was conceived.

Throughout the paper Steele keeps to his intention of rallying "all those singularities of human life, through the different professions and characters in it which obstruct anything that was truly good and great." The rallying is often done with humor, sometimes more gravely, and occasionally, as in his attacks on dueling and gaming, with an earnestness which makes it no longer rallying at all. The plan of the paper was Steele's invention alone. Just before the appearance of the first number, Addison had gone to Ireland, and was not aware of his friend's connection with the new venture, until, upon reading one of the essays, he discovered a criticism, which had been previously communicated to him by Steele. Though Addison began to contribute after the sixth number, he was not a regular contributor until after the eightieth. Of the two hundred and seventy-one numbers of which *The Tatler* is composed only forty-one are ascribed to Addison, thirty-four to the two friends jointly, twelve to Swift, and the remainder to Steele alone. (pp. 446-47)

There is a considerable difference of opinion as to the relative merits of the two authors. Much misunderstanding has arisen from a too liberal interpretation of the generosity with which Steele praised his friend's assistance in the following passage: "This good office he performed with such force of genius, humor, wit, and learning, that I fared like a distressed prince who calls in a powerful neighbor to his aid; I was undone by my auxiliary. When I had once called him in, I could not subsist without dependence upon him." After Addison's death he reiterates: "I rejoiced in being excelled, and made those talents—whatever they are—which I have, give way and be subservient to the superior qualities of a friend whom I loved." Such self-denying generosity was taken too literally, and belittled Steele in the eyes of the world. No doubt, Steele's contributions to *The Tatler* were often hastily written, and they lack the grace and polish which distinguish the articles of Addison. Indeed Steele admitted that he was not particularly interested in "the elegance, purity, and correctness" of Addison's style, since they were not so much to his purpose. But he possessed a gift of pathos and a depth of feeling almost entirely absent from Addison. Besides, he originated ideas which were afterwards developed by his friend. Of all Addison's writings, those upon which his fame most securely rests are the papers on Sir Roger de Coverley, and his criticism on Milton; and for the idea of these he was indebted to Steele. The share of each writer is accurately indicated by Hazlitt: "Steele seems to have gone into his closet chiefly to set down what he had observed out-of-doors. Addison seems to have spent most of his time in his study, and to have spun out and wiredrawn the hints *which he borrowed from Steele,* or took from nature to the utmost." And with this judgment [W. J.] Courthope [in his *Addison,* 1884] agrees: "Though it was doubtless Addison's fine workmanship and admirable method which carried to perfection the style of writing initiated in *The Tatler,* yet there is scarcely a department of essay writing developed in *The Spectator* which does not owe its origin to Steele."

The effect produced by *The Tatler* must have been extraordinary. "It is incredible," says [John] Gay [in his "The Present State of Wit," 1711], "to conceive the effect Steele's writings have had upon the town; how many thousand follies they have either quite banished, or given a great check to; how much countenance they have added to virtue and religion; how many people they have rendered happy, by showing that it was their own fault if they were not so; and, lastly, how entirely they have convinced

our fops and young men of the advantage of learning." Such an effect is clear evidence that Steele's periodical essay was a civilizing force in an age of newly-acquired comfort and of rapid fusion which yet needed urbanity and culture. His type of writing was welcomed as a device for reconciling fashion and virtue, industry and civil demeanor, philosophy and coffee-house tatlerdom. Steele diagnosed the malady of the hour and proposed to remedy it, not with moral declamation, but by good sense, good taste, sympathetic banter, and good-humored morality disguised beneath an easy and fashionable style.

Though Steele was not gifted with the genius of Swift, and did not possess the polished philosophic vein of Addison, he is more human and less bookish than any other writer of his time. His essays are more like the gossip of a friend than the elaborations of an author. He has stepped out of the busy thoroughfare, with the hum of traffic and the voices of the crowd in his ears, to write down what he has seen and heard. His library was the coffee-house and the street—his books men and women. He was pre-eminently a man of sentiment. His convivial life, and constant intercourse with the world in relations far from friendly to the temper, had no power to blunt the delicacy of his affections. Sweetness and love breathe through his moral speculations. The beauty of his sentiment consists not in a philosophical or imaginative meditation on human life, but in a gracious warmth and almost childlike facility of feeling. "There may have been," says Andrew Lang, "wiser, stronger, greater men. But many a strong man would have been stronger for a touch of Steele's indulgent sympathy; many a great man has wanted his genuine largeness of heart; many a wise man might learn something from his deep and wide humanity."

The essays of Steele abound in wit, humor, common sense, and pathos; in narrative, description, and character; in the inculcation of sublime truths, and correction of humblest faults. He never writes as if he had a literary character to support, or indeed any character but that of the kind old gentleman who has taken our morals into his keeping. And though he knows very well how to exaggerate in a quiet, grave style, which looks like truth, yet there is no writer who is less driven to literary artifices to relieve himself from the trouble of thinking. (pp. 447-48)

William John Tucker, "Two Great Essayists," in The Catholic World, *Vol. CL, January, 1940, pp. 445-51.*

John Loftis (essay date 1952)

[*Loftis is an American educator whose works include* Steele at Drury Lane *(1952),* Comedy and Society from Congreve to Fielding *(1959), and* Sheridan and the Drama of Georgian England *(1977). Here, the critic considers Steele's theory of comedy as exemplified in* The Conscious Lovers *and the critical controversy surrounding its initial production.*]

The restoration of Steele to Drury Lane prepared the way for the production, in November, 1722, of *The Conscious Lovers,* in Benjamin Victor's phrase, the "last blaze of Sir Richard's glory." His acute political entanglements back of him, Steele was free to appear again as a playwright—to offer to London audiences a dramatization of a number of ideas and precepts with which, in only slightly different forms, they were already familiar. Knowing that the comedy was written by Steele, few well-read play-goers could fail to associate it with the *Tatler,* the *Spectator,* and the *Guardian,* to which in ideological content it bears a close resemblance.

Like many of the earlier essays, the play is obviously didactic in intent: it presents a pattern for virtuous living, and particularly a pattern for the conduct of the "fine gentleman," a character in whom Steele had long been interested. Rejecting in *The Conscious Lovers,* as he did in the periodicals, the satirical theory of comedy implicit in the plays of the principal Restoration dramatists, Steele provides in Bevil, Jr., a direct model for emulation, endowing him with the qualities of filial obedience, faithfulness and generosity in love, nobility in friendship, and reasonableness in affairs of honor, all of which were recommended time and again in the *Tatler,* the *Spectator,* and the *Guardian.* Steele avoided the error into which he believed many of the earlier dramatists had fallen—that of making vice agreeable—by presenting his single degraded character, Cimberton, in so ridiculous a light as unquestionably to arouse contempt. Nor are the resemblances between the ideas in *The Conscious Lovers* and those in the earlier essays restricted merely to matters of characterization. In the play, as earlier, the problem of dueling is reviewed; Bevil, Jr., and Indiana discuss the opera in familiar terms; Bevil, Jr., discusses the relations between masters and servants in a manner that suggests the *Spectator;* Bevil, Jr., meditates on Addison's "Vision of Mirza." In writing the comedy, Steele was clearly under the influence of the opinions that led to many of his earlier lubrications.

These similarities between the play, first produced in 1722, and the essays, published between 1709 and 1713, have always been common knowledge; they are almost inescapable; but it has not been generally known that *The Conscious Lovers* was planned and perhaps in part written while Steele was writing the essays that appear in the major periodicals. Though modern scholars have known that Steele worked on the play for a long time, they have not known that he was working on it almost certainly by 1713 and was probably planning it as early as 1710. The great similarities between the periodicals and the comedy have been accounted for merely by the supposition that Steele was actively interested in approximately the same ideas for a number of years—and indeed there is no reason to assume that he was not. (pp. 183-84)

The *Tatler,* No. 182 (June 8, 1710), is one of Steele's many essays devoted almost entirely to the theater: Bickerstaff acknowledges his delight in plays and he praises the actors, especially Robert Wilks and Colley Cibber. Of particular interest, he speaks paternally of a young playwright now working on a comedy who can probably be identified as Richard Steele:

> I have at present under my tutelage a young poet, who, I design, shall entertain the town the ensuing winter. And as he does me the honour to let me see his comedy as he writes it, I shall

endeavor to make the parts fit the genius of the several actors, as exactly as their habits can their bodies: and because the two I have mentioned [Cibber and Wilks] are to perform the principal parts, I have prevailed with the house to let "The Careless Husband" be acted on Tuesday next, that my young author may have a view of the play which is acted to perfection, both by them and all concerned in it, as being born within the walls of the theatre, and written with an exact knowledge of the abilities of the performers. Mr. Wilks will do his best in this play, because it is for his own benefit; and Mr. Cibber, because he writ it. Besides which, all the great beauties we have left in town, or within call of it, will be present, because it is the last play this season. This opportunity will, I hope, inflame my pupil with such generous notions from seeing this fair assembly as will be then present, that his play may be composed of sentiments and characters proper to be presented to such an audience. His drama at present has only the outlines drawn. There are, I find, to be in it all the reverent offices of life, such as regard to parents, husbands, and honourable lovers, preserved with the utmost care; and at the same time that agreeableness of behaviour, with the intermixture of pleasing passions as arise from innocence and virtue, interspersed in such a manner, as that to be charming and agreeable shall appear the natural consequence of being virtuous. This great end is one of those I propose to do in my Censorship; but if I find a thin house, on an occasion when such work is to be promoted, my pupil shall return to his commons at Oxford, and Sheer Lane and the theatres be no longer correspondents.

There are several reasons for believing that Steele here alludes to his own composition of *The Conscious Lovers,* the principal one being his description of the young playwright's plan for the play. Like the comedy projected by the young man, *The Conscious Lovers* portrays "all the reverent offices of life, such as regard to parents, husbands, and honourable lovers . . . ," exhibiting a preoccupation with these "offices" almost to the exclusion of everything humorous. Young Bevil's relations with his father, as previously noted, provide a major theme in the play, a theme that offers some justification to John Dennis's charge that "the filial Obedience of young *Bevil* is carried a great deal too far." And young Bevil, supporting Indiana but rigorously refusing to acknowledge his own love for her or to take advantage of her dependent position, is an extreme type of the honorable lover. Less is made in *The Conscious Lovers* of a wife's regard for her husband—in Mrs. Sealand, Steele presents a woman who is not entirely respectful toward her spouse—but the tone of the comedy is unmistakably one of conjugal fidelity; the indifference toward the marriage tie exhibited in many of the earlier comedies is noticeably absent here. Certainly in intention and design *The Conscious Lovers* resembles the play that Bickerstaff's protégé was writing.

The young man's play, it appears, like *The Conscious Lovers,* is to be an exemplary comedy: its moral precepts are to be conveyed primarily by providing models for conduct rather than by making folly ridiculous. Bickerstaff explains that "agreeableness of behaviour, with the intermixture of pleasing passions which arise from innocence and virtue," are to be "interspersed in such a manner, as that to be charming and agreeable shall appear the natural consequences of being virtuous," an explanation suggesting the theory of comedy of which *The Conscious Lovers* is a preeminent example; it was precisely this theory that was debated most heatedly in the literary controversy precipitated by the acting of the play. "How little do they know of the Nature of true Comedy, who believe that its proper Business is to set us Patterns for Imitation . . . ," wrote John Dennis in opposition (in an essay immediately occasioned by *The Conscious Lovers*). The comedy projected by Bickerstaff's protégé, then, was one planned in accordance with the theory of comedy of which *The Conscious Lovers* was a controversial example. Though it would not be accurate to describe it as the first exemplary comedy, *The Conscious Lovers* was the play that was first generally recognized as such—it first brought into the open the clash between the proponents of the two different comic theories. To Steele the play represented a studied attempt at providing the English stage with a comic form that could be an effective stimulant to virtuous action. Hence, when Bickerstaff describes an exemplary comedy (a form of comedy that Steele thought to be his own innovation), there is strong reason to believe that he is referring to the one on which it is known that Steele was working some three years later. (pp. 186-89)

[*The Conscious Lovers*] was not a product of his middle age, of the years after his health had broken and he had encountered serious personal reverses; rather it was conceived, and perhaps in part written, during the vigorous years when he was writing the essays on which his fame rests. *The Conscious Lovers* was planned under the stimulus of the ideas that led to the many essays on the character of the fine gentleman and to the essays denouncing the type of comedy represented by *The Man of Mode*. It was planned, at the time Steele was writing about comic theory, as an example of the new type of comedy he was advocating—exemplary rather than satirical comedy. What is new and most significant about *The Conscious Lovers*— its exemplary characters—thus represents a bond with the essays he conceived contemporaneously. (p. 193)

To the modern student *The Conscious Lovers* belongs to the number of plays that are rather more interesting as dramatic landmarks than as drama. It is usually read not because of any dramatic excellence but because it illustrates an important change in the history of comedy. Nor is this modern reputation of the play as a landmark without strong eighteenth-century precedent. Steele himself and his contemporaries considered it a pronounced departure from English comic tradition—as something new, as a studied attempt to break away from the pattern of earlier comedies. This conviction explains partly, of course, the magnitude of the critical commentary evoked by the play; Steele's long campaign in preparation for it let everyone know that it was to be different, and put them on their guard to look for innovations. His prominence and his controversial career, moreover, added intensity to the interest in comic theory; other authors had written plays

embodying critical principles more original than those in *The Conscious Lovers*, only to be greeted by complete indifference. But a play by the celebrated Richard Steele on principles enunciated in the *Spectator*, a play some ten or twelve years in preparation, was one precisely calculated to bring to public attention conflicting views about comedy that previously had lacked articulate statement.

The Conscious Lovers is generally considered the prime exemplar of "sentimental comedy," the name usually applied to the form of comedy that emerged in association with the early-eighteenth-century reform movement. Yet, as applied to *The Conscious Lovers*, the term "sentimental comedy," implying an emphasis on appeal to the emotions of sympathy, is inadequate to explain what Steele and his contemporaries found to be new and most controversial about the play. Steele did, in his preface, defend the inclusion of pathetic incident in comedy, and John Dennis and Benjamin Victor, among others, debated its propriety. The quality of *The Conscious Lovers* that was felt to be most original and that proved to be most controversial, however, was not the appeal to pathos but the employment of admirable characters providing models for conduct— notably Bevil, Jr., the "fine gentleman"—rather than the traditional witty yet debauched characters familiar in Restoration comedy. It is the insistence on the exemplary characters that most conspicuously differentiates *The Conscious Lovers* from Steele's earlier plays (though *The Funeral* possesses such characters less fully developed) and from the plays, for example, of Cibber, who shares with Steele in popular opinion the leadership of the movement toward sentimental comedy; and it is assuredly the nature of the characters that was responsible for the frequent comparisons of Dorimant and Bevil, Jr., during the critical controversy stirred up by the play. This is not to say that Steele inaugurated exemplary comedy . . . but it remained for Steele in his periodicals to make the principles of exemplary comedy the current coin of dramatic criticism, and in *The Conscious Lovers* to provide an embodiment, at once successful and controversial, of those principles.

I would recognize three different, though related, aspects of Steele's comic theory as finally embodied in *The Conscious Lovers:* the employment of exemplary characters; the appeal to the emotion of sympathy; the self-conscious avoidance of licentious dialogue. (The third is, of course, a negative quality that was scarcely controversial.) These are the qualities that in combination represent the dramatic formula Steele evolved, and only one of them (the appeal to sympathy) was a uniform characteristic of earlier "sentimental" comedy. Charles Harold Gray's remark [in his *Theatrical Criticism in London to 1795*, 1931], "Over the production of . . . *The Conscious Lovers* . . . arose the first open discussions of the antagonism between the dominant tradition of the comedy of manners set by Wycherley and Congreve and the new sentimental comedy," is somewhat misleading, because what chiefly was discussed was not the "sentimental" (pathetic) element— though it received attention—but the exemplary characters.

Consider, as a demonstration of the inadequacy of the

term "sentimental comedy" to describe what was distinctive about *The Conscious Lovers,* the sharp differences between it and Cibber's *The Careless Husband*—the most conspicuous of the earlier sentimental plays. In Cibber's play the humanity of Lady Easy's concern for her husband's health is, of course, abundantly evident, and the strong appeal it makes to the sympathy of the audience is perhaps not different in kind from the emotion evoked by Indiana's distresses. But here alone—in the pathetic appeal—have the plays anything in common. *The Careless Husband* has in spirit much in common with the Restoration tradition. The play exhibits licentious characters (slightly subdued) preoccupied with adulterous sexual relations; it was censured for its lasciviousness—by, among others, the author of the *Anti-Theatre.* Far from employing characters who provide models for conduct, Cibber supports explicitly in the dialogue of the play the satirical theory, to which Steele so strongly took exception, by which Restoration dramatists sought to defend their employment of depraved characters. "'Tis Hard, indeed, when People won't Distinguish between what's Meant for Contempt, and what for Example," Lady Easy observes, in a direct thrust at the reformers. Dennis would have agreed completely with Lady Easy—witness *A Defence of Sir Fopling Flutter,* written in opposition to *The Conscious Lovers.* In short, to identify *The Conscious Lovers* as merely a preëminent exemplar of the type of comedy represented by *The Careless Husband* is to ignore differences that are quite as important in the evolution of drama as the similarities.

In the contemporary controversy over *The Conscious Lovers* the two distinct principles—employment of exemplary characters and appeal to sympathy—were debated, no one assuming that they were indivisible; and of these two principles, the one that differentiates *The Conscious Lovers* from most earlier "sentimental" comedies received decidedly the larger share of attention.

There is, of course, a logical relationship between these two principles, one that was acknowledged in some of the contemporary discussions of the play. It is not merely by chance that exemplary characters so frequently appear in "sentimental" action. A moment's consideration will reveal that an exemplary character cannot, without damage to his effectiveness as a model for conduct, be placed in a ridiculous situation; if he appears in hilarious action at all, not he but someone else must have the experiences that arouse the spectators' laughter. The anonymous author of a pamphlet in defense of Steele explained the matter:

> [Dennis] tells us, that the Principal Characters of Comedy should be always ridiculous, and gives some Instances to prove it: But if this were granted, where the finest Gentleman is to be expos'd to View in a Character upon the Stage, how ridiculous must it make a Fine Gentleman appear to the World. To my Understanding, a Fine Gentleman, and a Ridiculous Character, are wholly inconsistent; so that this Character must be banish'd the Stage: Or you may as well make a Buffoon a Fine Gentleman, as a Fine Gentleman a Buffoon ["Sir Richard Steele, And . . . *The Conscious Lovers,* Vindicated", 1723].

If the playwright, then, desires to present a fine gentleman, he must find some means other than the traditional resource of comedy—ridicule—by which to interest his audience. That substitute was, of course, frequently found in pathos.

Pathetic situations, moreover, provide a means of demonstrating the benevolence and humanity of exemplary heroes. A man is tried not by prosperity and its attendant gaiety but by misfortune, his own or another's, and its attendant sorrow. By emphasizing a character's magnanimous response to his own adversity or generous response to the adversity of someone else, a playwright could show him to be a fit subject for the spectators' emulation.

Though there are thus cogent reasons why exemplary characters and the appeal to sympathy are frequently associated, the exemplary and the sentimental by no means always appear together. Exemplary characters cannot, as I have already said, be made to appear ridiculous. Yet ridiculous characters can assuredly be employed to elicit a sympathetic response—Young Bookwit in *The Lying Lover,* for example. To state the relationship another way, "sentimental" comedy is by no means always exemplary comedy; but exemplary comedy can scarcely be laughing comedy without loss of didactic effectiveness. In short, sentimental comedy and exemplary comedy are frequent companions, but they are not identical.

Perhaps the relationship between these two principles—the sentimental and the exemplary—in *The Conscious Lovers* can best be perceived in terms of the critical controversy precipitated by the play. In the development of this controversy, as I believe will become apparent, the two principles remained substantially independent.

Steele had expressed long before *The Conscious Lovers* the rationale of laughterless comedy—as in the epilogue to *The Lying Lover:*

> For laughter's a distorted passion, born
> Of sudden self-esteem and sudden scorn;
> Which, when 'tis o'er, the men in pleasure wise,
> Both him that moved it and themselves despise;
> While generous pity of a painted woe
> Makes us ourselves both more approve and
>   know.

An appropriate epilogue to a play that had so freely called on the spectators' sympathy. In *The Funeral* also Steele had exploited the sober appeal of magnanimous altruism—as in the loyalty of the old servant Trusty—though he subordinated pathos to the merriment of two pairs of young lovers. John Hughes, himself an active literary theorist who had probably discussed the play with Steele, praised especially the humanity of Trusty's reflections when alone at the lodgings of the disinherited young Lord Hardy. "Everyone will own," Hughes added, "that in this Play there are many lively Strokes of Wit and Humour; but I must confess I am more pleas'd with the fine Touches of Humanity in it, than with any other Part of the Entertainment" [*The Lay Monk,* No. 9]. In Steele's own periodicals there are expressions of a similar preference for sober emotions, as in his praise in the *Tatler,* No. 68, of manly tears as a mark of humanity, and in his disparagement in the *Tatler,* No. 219, of misdirected ridicule. Addison too distrusted laughter, associating it in the *Spectator,* Nos. 47 and 249, with a selfish contempt for and feeling of superiority over the person provoking it (he acknowledged his debt to Hobbes).

It was consistent with Steele's defense of pathos in comedy that he admired Terence, believing, as Professor Krutch has pointed out [in his *Comedy and Conscience After the Restoration*], that in Terence he had found a precedent for his own comic theory, in which laughter was relegated to a subordinate position. Praising *The Self-Torturer* in the *Spectator,* No. 502, he found it a merit in the play that it did not provoke laughter; rather it was remarkable for "worthy Sentiments." Such admiration for the Roman dramatist's humanity doubtless led to his selection of *The Andria* as the source for *The Conscious Lovers,* the Roman play providing ample incident for displaying tender emotions.

The Conscious Lovers was indeed but a modernization of Terence's play, the major characters, the relationships between them, and the plan of action being derived from it—a fact of which Steele's contemporaries were acutely aware. When reproached for following Terence so closely, Steele insisted [in his Preface to *The Conscious Lovers*] that he considered the faithfulness of his adaptation a merit. "I am extremely surprised to find . . . that what I valued myself so much upon—the translation of him [Terence]—should be imputed to me as a reproach." In an age of authoritarian criticism, the good name of the Roman dramatist was welcome support in literary controversy.

Steele's desire to gain respectability for his inclusion of pathos in comedy perhaps accounts also for the presence on the title page of the first edition of *The Conscious Lovers* of a quotation from Cicero [in his *Rhetor. ad Herenn.* Lib. I.] in which the dramatic formula Steele employed is described with surprising accuracy.

> Illus genus narrationis, quod in personis positum est, debet habere sermones festivitatem, animorum dissimilitudinem, gravitatem, lenitatem, spem, metum, suspicionem, desiderium, dissimulationem, misericordiam, rerum varietates, fortunae commutationem, insperatum incommodum, subitam letitiam, jucundum exitum rerum.

No distinction is here made between tragedy and comedy, a distinction that became a central issue in the controversy over *The Conscious Lovers.* But Steele did not ignore the distinction. Meeting the charge that he had confused the two genres, he argued, in a famous statement appearing in his preface, that anything with "its foundation in happiness and success must be allowed to be the object of comedy; and sure it must be an improvement of it to introduce a joy too exquisite for laughter, that can have no spring but in delight. . . ." This was an extension of the subject matter of comedy not acceptable to orthodox critics in that it confounded the laughing reaction evoked by traditional comedy with a benevolent participation in the happiness of the dramatic characters. . . . (pp. 195-201)

So much for Steele's theoretical justification of the pathos in *The Conscious Lovers,* a quality that was present in all

his earlier plays and one that he had publicly defended as early as 1703. Consider now his exposition of the principle of exemplary comedy.

Bevil, Jr., the exemplary hero of the play, is a direct descendant of Steele's Christian hero of 1701 and of the many fine gentlemen in the *Tatler,* the *Spectator,* and the *Guardian;* and, as I have already said, he is a close relation of Lord Hardy of *The Funeral.* He is, and was recognized to be by Steele's contemporaries, an embodiment of precisely the contrary moral qualities of those exhibited by the Restoration gallants who people the comedies of Etherege, Dryden, Wycherley, and Congreve; he owes his existence to Steele's conviction (shared with a multitude of other reformers) that, theory to the contrary, the display of debauched characters on the stage was damaging to the morals of the spectators.

Steele had, of course, employed a modified exemplary method in at least one of his early comedies, a method in which he was anticipated by a number of dramatists led by Shadwell; but apart from affirming his desire to write morally inoffensive plays, he had not, before he began his periodicals, insisted on the exemplary method. Rather, it was while he conducted his major periodicals (and in all likelihood he then planned *The Conscious Lovers*) that he self-consciously evolved the exemplary theory. His method was both negative and positive: he denounced characters of Restoration plays, Dorimant of *The Man of Mode* most conspicuously, and praised the display in comedy of "all the reverent offices of life." Dennis openly charged that in condemning Etherege's play he was purposely preparing the way for *The Conscious Lovers.* "The Knight certainly wrote the fore-mention'd *Spectator* (No. 65), tho' it has been writ these ten Years, on Purpose to make Way for his fine Gentleman, and therefore he endeavours to prove, that Sir *Fopling* is not that genteel Comedy, which the World allows it to be." In all essentials Dennis's charge seems to have been just. Steele's papers in the *Spectator* on the characters proper to comedy were, as I have previously argued, written under the stimulus of the ideas responsible for *The Conscious Lovers.*

Not until the *Theatre,* however, did Steele openly associate the theory of exemplary comedy with his forthcoming play; and nowhere is he more explicit about his didactic method than in the *Theatre,* No. 19, in which he explains that the play would already have been produced had not "some accidents" prevented.

> The third act of this Comedy . . . has a scene in it, wherein the first character bears unprovoked wrongs, denies a duel, and still appears a man of honour and courage. This example would have been of great service; for since we see young men are hardly able to forbear imitation of fopperies on the Stage, from a desire of praise, how warmly would they pursue true gallantries, when accompanied with the beauties with which a Poet represents them, when he has a mind to make them amiable!

This puff represents, of course, an early stage of the publicity campaign that preceded the play's production, a campaign in which the admirable nature of the leading character was uniformly insisted on—it is significant that the play was called, before it appeared, "The Fine Gentleman." Everyone in London remotely interested in the theater knew before the play was first acted, in November, 1722—if he knew nothing else about it—that its leading character was a young man of extraordinary virtue. Such was the popular reputation of the play (deliberately fostered by Steele in the *Theatre*) responsible for the conviction that it represented a new kind of comedy; the advance talk about sober comedy (receiving no direct support from Steele as applied to *The Conscious Lovers*) was subordinated to discussion of characters proper to comedy. (pp. 201-03)

It was five days before *The Conscious Lovers* was first acted that Dennis, honestly contemptuous of Steele's theory of comedy and of his publicity campaign, in an effort to curb the enthusiasm for the new play, published *A Defence of Sir Fopling Flutter*. Because Dennis had not read *The Conscious Lovers*—his information about it was gained only from the newspaper reports and from friends who had heard it read—he could attack only the dramatic principles upon which the play was based. His arguments, however, are not for that reason the less compelling, because it was, of course, the principles—which Dennis already understood with perfect clarity—that were chiefly at issue. Dennis could not be misled here, as he was in a portion of his later *Remarks on . . . The Conscious Lovers,* by relatively unimportant considerations of detail. In *A Defence of Sir Fopling Flutter* he puts unequivocally the case against exemplary comedy, and conversely the case for satirical comedy. Freely acknowledging the degeneracy of characters in *The Man of Mode,* he insists, citing Aristotle and Horace as authorities, that such characters are the proper subjects of ridicule and that ridicule alone is the proper concern of comedy. " 'Tis its [comedy's] proper Business to expose Persons to our View, whose Views we may shun, and whose Follies we may despise; and by shewing us what is done upon the Comick Stage, to shew us what ought never to be done upon the Stage of the World." Virtuous characters presented as models for imitation are out of place in comedy, he explains, "For all such Patterns are serious Things, and Laughter is the Life, and the very Soul of Comedy." Comedies of Molière and Ben Jonson are the ones he finds most admirable, laughing comedies in which the principal characters are absurd and ridiculous by reason of faults exhibited as admonitions to the spectators.

Dennis insists on instruction by laughter, and he implies, in no uncertain terms, that Steele's new comedy will be deficient in laughter; but he does not discuss the inclusion of pathos in comedy. He acknowledges that exemplary comedy must necessarily be deficient in laugh-provoking characters, but he says nothing, in this essay that articulates the contemporary critical expectations of Steele's new play, about the pathetic elements in it. His attitude is negative, not positive: he anticipates the absence of laughter, not the presence of pathos. In short, what Dennis was led to expect as the distinguishing feature of *The Conscious Lovers* was its exemplary characters rather than its sentimentality (or pathos).

Far from prejudicing the town against *The Conscious Lovers* and decreasing its popularity as he intended, Dennis's attack, a few days before the play was first presented, increased public interest and contributed indirectly to its success. *A Defence of Sir Fopling Flutter* contains much sound criticism—the objections to Steele's comic theory are cogent ones—but critical arguments were not in themselves sufficient to counteract the widespread curiosity to see the play.

Because of this curiosity it is understandable that the play attracted a large amount of attention in three of the newspapers, the *Freeholder's Journal,* the *Weekly Journal* (Mist's), and the *St. James's Journal.* The two former were mainly hostile, the *Freeholder's Journal* even more than the *Weekly Journal,* whereas the *St. James's Journal* assumed the position of a neutral, sometimes defending, sometimes attacking the play. In the *Freeholder's Journal* and the *St. James's Journal* there were serious attempts at critical appraisals of *The Conscious Lovers;* personal animosity, though sometimes evident, was subordinated to reasoned critical argument. In the *Weekly Journal* criticism of the play, except in a single "letter" printed in the paper, provided merely a medium for further attacks on the group in charge of Drury Lane.

Like Dennis, the *Freeholder's Journal* began its comments on the play before its production; and, also like Dennis, the newspaper emphasized the importance to Steele's design of his leading character. "We flatter ourselves," the unidentified author wrote on October 31, "that the Drama we expect will . . . afford a compleat Model to that leading Pattern of Life, *The Gentleman.*" There is not a word in this preproduction discussion of the play about the appropriateness or inappropriateness of pathos to comedy; there is not even, as there was in Dennis's essay, an insistence that comedy provoke laughter. Even in the series of articles in later numbers of the paper, after the play had appeared, the character of Bevil received most attention (much space was devoted to comparisons of him with Pamphilus, his prototype in *The Andria*). In some of the later articles, to be sure, appear comments about the sorrowful denouement; the writer objects, Steele's statement to the contrary, that the emotions aroused are not appropriate to comedy: "The Discovery at last is entirely Passionate, Melting and Tragi Comical: The Audience are sent off with a sorrowful impression, and Tears in their Eyes, not to be wip'd off by the final event." But he does not associate the appeal to the spectators' sympathy with the admirable nature of the hero.

The *St. James's Journal* was kinder to Steele, devoting a generous amount of space in three different numbers to sympathetic discussion of the play—first in a letter signed "Townly" (where the actor-managers are praised as well as the play), and later more judiciously in two letters signed ironically "Dorimant." The first letter is of little interest here, but the Dorimant letters warrant attention as discriminating contemporary appraisals of the comedy, although in them the controversial principles with which I have been chiefly concerned receive only subordinate attention. Dorimant believes *The Conscious Lovers* to be inferior to the Latin original; he finds improbabilities in the action and unnecessary episodes; he considers the character of Cimberton gross; he believes Steele represented the character of the old servant better in **The Funeral;** and though he does not find fault with Tom, he observes that the character is less closely related to the design of the play than was Davus, his prototype in Terence's comedy. On the other hand, this writer is complimentary on the subject of the relations of the Bevils, father and son: "The tender, and at the same time prudent Concern of old *Bevil,* for his Son's Interest and Satisfaction in Marriage, is very well hit; so the filial Fondness and Duty to the Father, with the Struggles of Love and Generosity to the Lady." The author thus indirectly commends the employment in comedy of exemplary characters, in this instance of characters who exhibit a "sentimental" sensitivity to the afflictions of others. He is more direct in his defense of Steele's tearful conclusion. It is significant, however, that he does not consider the inclusion of pathos in comedy (as distinct from the employment of exemplary characters) as in any way an innovation:

> . . . the tender Scene upon the Father's discovery of his Daughter, has received the most reasonable and natural Applause of eighteen successive Audiences, their Silence and their Tears. A Pleasure built upon the most sincere Delight, which no sensible Mind would exchange for the momentary *passant* Transports of an inconsiderate Laughter. An Applause which a Masterly Writer prefers to a thousand Shouts of a tumultuous and unreasonable Theatre. Some of our best Comedies, *The Fool in Fashion, The Lady's Last Stake, The Careless Husband,* have wound up their Catastrophe in this tender manner with great Success, and never-failing Applause.

Little need be said about the comments on **The Conscious Lovers** in the *Weekly Journal.* Except for a judicious appreciative essay in the issue for March 30, in which Steele's moral purpose is applauded, they represent merely another phase of that paper's long campaign against Drury Lane. Mixing derogatory judgments about the play with satirical allusions to the managers, the paper for the most part made damning pronouncements without offering substantiating arguments. Not all the allusions to the comedy are hostile, but none, except that in the issue for March 30 (and that only tangentially), provides informed comment on the critical problems posed by it. Typical of the remarks is one that anticipates Parson Adam's famous pronouncement of a later day: the writer charged that Steele wrote the play to determine "how the Publick would like *Sermons* work'd up into *Comedies.*"

Steele himself did not answer the hostile criticism, but he encouraged Benjamin Victor, then a young man who had only recently made his acquaintance, to do so. Victor's *An Epistle to Sir Richard Steele, On his Play, call'd, The Conscious Lovers* (November 29) is, in comparison with Dennis's *A Defence of Sir Fopling Flutter,* to which it purports to be an answer, a lame performance. His comments about *The Man of Mode* lack pertinency; he argues over irrelevancies not important to the fundamental question of the opposition between the two theories of comedy, the propriety, for example, of Dennis's identification of Dorimant with Rochester. Similarly he is distracted by the comparison of Bevil, Jr., with Pamphilus that had appeared in the *Freeholder's Journal:* he is at pains to demonstrate Bevil's greater virtue. But he does not neglect completely the major issues.

> Is it possible, Sir [he asks], that De—s can be so void of Shame to attempt to prove, that vicious Characters is the only Business of Comedy, and that their corrupt Examples have the same design'd Effect upon the Audience as a virtuous honourable Character. . . .

The separate principle (and Victor considers it separately) of the inclusion of pathetic incident in comedy he also defends. "It was the Opinion of all the Antients, that Love (the usual Argument of all Comedies) is there best written where it is most distress'd, and in despairing Passion; that Part of Comedy seeming best which is nearest Tragedy." At no time had Steele suggested that the pathos of comedy should approximate that of tragedy: the disciple was more devout than the master.

The defense of Steele was further strengthened by an anonymous pamphlet appearing December 13, [1723] bearing the bold title, *Sir Richard Steele, and his New* Comedy, *call'd* The Conscious Lovers, Vindicated, *From the malicious Aspersions of Mr.* John Dennis. Wherein *Mr. Dennis's vile Criticism's, in Defence of Sir* Fopling Flutter, *are Detected and Expos'd.* The unidentified author answers Dennis's arguments systematically, proceeding from point to point through Dennis's essay; but, like Victor, he often fails to discriminate between what is important to Dennis's case and what is extraneous. Some of his remarks, however, are directly pertinent, as when he explains lucidly why exemplary characters cannot be employed to arouse laughter, at the same time affirming their didactic effectiveness in comedy as models for conduct. "But cannot Comedy instruct by Virtuous Characters? Will nothing but Vice and Ridicule please; and shall Ridicule only be the Standard of Wit?" Tacitly acknowledging that Bevil's virtue somewhat exceeds probability, he defends the dramatist's right, citing Aristotle as authority, to draw characters beyond life. At this point he, of course, ignores the distinction made by orthodox critics between the characters proper to comedy and those to tragedy; but later in the essay, facing the objections made to the pathos in Steele's last act, he specifically defends the play as a comedy. Tragedies, he insists, have a fatal catastrophe; **The Conscious Lovers,** in contrast, ends happily, notwithstanding the emotion aroused in the fifth act. Employing the argument Steele had advanced in the preface to the play, he affirms the appropriateness of the emotion to comedy by reason of its origin in joy. With all his logic, however, this author seems not completely to have convinced himself. "Sir Richard Steele's new play," he concludes, "if it be not in the strictest Sense throughout a Comedy, it is an Entertainment superior to it."

The replies to Dennis in defense of Steele were thus somewhat stronger than they had been in the dispute three years before—stronger probably than Dennis had anticipated. He was angered by the town's hostile reaction to his effort to reveal the fraud he believed **The Conscious**

Lovers to be, and he displayed his anger in his second attack, *Remarks on a Play, Call'd, The Conscious Lovers, a Comedy* (January 24, 1723). To this pamphlet he prefixed a dedication to Robert Walpole and a preface, in both of which, in a manner reminiscent of *The Characters and Conduct of Sir John Edgar,* he denounces roundly the actor-managers and the "easy Patentee," reasserting his charge that they exercise a stifling, inhibitory effect on the production of dramatic poetry. It is in his "Remarks on the Preface to The Conscious Lovers," however, that he advances his most relevant and his most telling arguments. In *A Defence of Sir Fopling Flutter* his chief mark was Steele's exemplary hero, but here it is the pathos of Steele's final act—the pathos that Steele defended in his preface. Dennis's charge is, fundamentally, that Steele confused two genres by introducing into comedy emotions proper only to tragedy. "When Sir *Richard* says, that any thing that has its Foundation in Happiness and Success must be the Subject of Comedy, he confounds Comedy with that Species of Tragedy which has a happy Catastrophe." Steele's argument that comedy would be improved by introducing "a joy too exquisite for laughter" is untenable because comedy cannot be dissociated from the joy that does produce laughter: joy itself is an undifferentiated emotion common to all forms of literature; only when it is expressed as laughter is it characteristic of comedy. So goes his argument—and it is a strong one—the conclusion of which is that *The Conscious Lovers* is no comedy at all. Here he says nothing directly about the exemplary characters. They are, to be sure, the agents through whom the spectators' emotions of pity are enlisted, and, as Dennis doubtless understood, their deficiencies in laughter-provoking qualities required the substitution of some appeal in place of the traditional comic one. It is significant, however, that he does not openly associate the pathos with the model characters.

That portion of *The Remarks on the Conscious Lovers* devoted to the play itself, because it is specific rather than universal in application, adds little to the debate on comic theory. Many of Dennis's objections to improbabilities of plot and character are, nevertheless, strong ones: he finds inconsistencies in action and inadequacies in motivation. Most vehemently he objects, as would be anticipated, to Bevil, Jr., charging that his character is "made up of Qualities, either incoherent and contradictory, as Religion and Dissimulation, Morality and Fraud; or most ridiculously consistent, as Circumspection and Folly." Some of his supporting arguments are, it is true, unreasonably dogmatic, but others of them are compelling.

Indubitably the longest of the critical essays on *The Conscious Lovers* was the last of the contemporary ones, the anonymous *The Censor Censured: or, The* CONSCIOUS LOVERS *Examin'd: in a* DIALOGUE *between Sir* DICKY MARPLOT AND JACK FREEMAN. INTO WHICH MR. DENNIS *is introduced by way of* POSTSCRIPT: *with some* CONVERSATIONS *on his late* REMARKS. The author repeats in mediocre dialogue the current criticisms of the play, chiefly those hostile to it, adding little that is new. Following the *Freeholder's Journal* and Dennis's *Remarks,* he compares *The Conscious Lovers* at length with its Roman original, to the disadvantage of the moderniza-

tion. "Sir Dicky Marplot" is an enthusiastic, naïve fool, who cannot tolerate criticism of this play on which he has worked for three years. Dennis is introduced only to repeat the objections to the comedy's inconsistencies and improbabilities that he had presented in his *Remarks.* The pamphlet is repetitive in this, as in nearly all its parts; but it does emphasize anew that the preproduction expectations of *The Conscious Lovers* chiefly concerned the exemplary characters, the author recalling in his preface that

> we were taught to expect, that Vertue, long banish'd the Scenes, was once more to make a flourishing Figure on the Stage, adorn'd with all the gay Simplicity of sprightly Innocence. Thus she was to have the force of Precept and Example too; and thus at once she was to instruct and please.

The fact of the pamphlet's ambitious scale—its eighty-eight pages of dialogue—is striking testimony to the critical interest aroused by the comedy.

Few plays have attracted more attention on their first appearance than *The Conscious Lovers;* certainly few have aroused critical controversies that were sharper and more clearly defined. To dismiss that controversy as one merely over sentimental comedy—even sentimental comedy known by another name—is, as I hope I have demonstrated, seriously to oversimplify. What gave the play its advance reputation as a new form of comedy was Steele's insistence that his chief character would provide a pattern for the conduct of the Christian gentleman. Only after the play appeared was there discussion of the "sentimental" element, the appeal to the spectators' sympathy, and never were the exemplary characters and the pathos identified as a single indissoluable unit.

The production of the play marked the virtual end of Steele's attempts to reform the English stage, the task for which, as he insisted, he was appointed to Drury Lane. In the play he presented his final plea for a reformed drama—a plea that was not without great effectiveness, as the comedy of the later part of the century bears witness. Whatever had been his failures as an administrative head of Drury Lane, he accomplished one of the theatrical objectives he had set for himself in providing the stage with an enormously successful play that was without moral offense. The condition of the stage had been deplored in his patent: "instead of exhibiting such representations of human life as may tend to the encouragement and honour of Religion and Virtue, and discountenancing Vice, the English STAGE hath been the complaint of the sober, intelligent, and religious part of our people. . . ." Steele had been commanded to make the drama an incentive to virtuous behavior. *The Conscious Lovers,* in which there appear "representations of human life" that certainly were intended for "the encouragement and honour of Religion and Virtue, and discountenancing Vice," was his most effective answer to that command. The method he employed provoked serious criticism, but his play, nevertheless, represents an effective attempt at moral reform of the stage. (pp. 204-13)

John Loftis, in his Steele at Drury Lane, *University of California Press, 1952, 260 p.*

Calhoun Winton (essay date 1964)

[*Winton is an American educator and biographer who wrote a two-volume study of Steele entitled* Captain Steele: The Early Career of Richard Steele *(1964) and* Sir Richard Steele, M.P.: The Later Career *(1970). In the following excerpt from the first volume of this biography, Winton describes the success of Steele's literary innovations in the* Tatler.]

Those Londoners of coffeehouse and salon who stumbled all unknowingly into literary history by reading the first issue of *The Tatler* that April day (the twelfth, old style, precisely) in 1709 found themselves looking at a folio half-sheet, printed on both sides and resembling, for twentieth-century eyes, an oversized handbill. It bore a proper Latin motto (but no English translation) from Juvenal's First Satire: *Quicquid agunt homines . . . nostri farrago libelli:* Whatever men do is grist for our mill. If the readers therefore expected scandal and Juvenalian satire they were misled, for the anonymous author who called himself Isaac Bickerstaff was not of Juvenal's satiric school. Though the prevailing tone of pamphlet and periodical was rancorous in those days, this Bickerstaff seemed downright good-humored. The paper, he announced, was "principally intended for the use of politic persons, who are so public-spirited as to neglect their own affairs to look into the transactions of state."

> Now these gentlemen, for the most part, being men of strong zeal and weak intellects, it is both a charitable and necessary work to offer something, whereby such worthy and well-affected members of the commonwealth may be instructed, after their reading, what to think; which shall be the end and purpose of this my paper; wherein I shall from time to time report and consider all matters of what kind soever that shall occur to me, and publish such my advices and reflections every Tuesday, Thursday, and Saturday in the week. . . . I have also resolved to have something which may be of entertainment to the fair sex, in honour of whom I have taken the title of this paper.

(pp. 101-02)

A new paper could not survive on novelty alone, a thousand had fallen at Bickerstaff's side. Steele identified and combined the appeals of various periodicals in one. The question-and-answer and the hoax letter, for example, appeared, sometimes separate, sometimes combined, transfigured as the letter to the editor, a device which Steele exploited; shrewd editors have done the same ever since. News was included to attract readers; Steele felt that as Gazetteer he had access to superior news sources: the diplomatic reports. For various reasons this expedient did not work and the news sections gradually disappeared from *The Tatler.* The principal appeals, however, were just those Bickerstaff had announced in the first issue: variety, entertainment for the ladies and information for the men, and actually both for both. This is Horace's *prodesse aut delectare,* instruction and entertainment, in a new format attractive to the widest audience. Ostensibly the audience addressed was the inner circle of wit and learning, those who knew of and laughed at the Partridge-Bickerstaff hoax. But Steele was speaking over the heads of these to

the vastly larger circle in London and the provinces and even the colonies (William Byrd in Virginia was a faithful reader of *The Tatler*) who wanted to be told how to act, what to read, what, as Bickerstaff had put it, to think; who wanted to learn these things outside of church or chapel and yet who were suspicious of the libertinism associated with the literary life since Charles II's reign. A recent student of the rise of fiction, Mr. Ian Watt, has put the matter this way [in his *The Rise of the Novel,* 1957]:

> This compromise, between the wits and the less educated, between the belles-lettres and religious instruction, is perhaps the most important trend in eighteenth-century literature, and finds . . . expression in the most famous literary innovations of the century, the establishment of the *Tatler* in 1709 and of the *Spectator* in 1711.

The compromise, of course, was an effect. When Steele began *The Tatler,* he was simply following his nose, combining his strong inclination to ethical instruction (as displayed earlier in the plays and *The Christian Hero*) with the knowledge of audience tastes and popular interest he had acquired at first hand over the years in the taverns and theaters of London. As an Irishman he knew the excitement fashionable London life awakened in the outsider, like the country wife in Wycherley's play. But though these outsiders were attracted by London society, they were suspicious of it; the country squire, the merchant, the Dissenter, the parson, all these stock butts of the comedy in Restoration plays must be mollified and transformed into subscribers to a London periodical, for the inner circle was too small. Bickerstaff proceeds to this directly by way, significantly enough, of a review of *The Country Wife,* recently revived. "As I just now hinted," he writes in *Tatler* No. 3, "I own myself of the Society for Reformation of Manners." This, one might think, would be exactly designed to drive the London audience away. Not so; Steele knew that the London *beau monde,* and every other *beau monde,* liked best of all to read of itself. He followed the declaration of his membership in the SRM with the warning, "After this . . . if a fine lady thinks fit to giggle at church, or a great beau come in drunk to a play, either shall be sure to hear of it in my ensuing paper: for merely as a well-bred man, I cannot bear these enormities." There would always be, he knew, giggling ladies and drunken beaux.

Modern literary criticism is ill-equipped to deal with essays and periodical publications; categories that operate well enough with lyric poetry appear meaningless when applied to newspapers and magazines. Some theorists, indeed, are quite willing to conclude that the periodical is not a literary form at all and therefore, presumably, should be avoided by anyone having a due concern for his sensibilities. Over against such a conclusion, however, are generations, now centuries, of readers and, recently, scholars like Mr. Watt who have recognized that the better eighteenth-century periodical was, if not literature, certainly a powerful literary force. And of course, the medium in which at one time or another almost every significant writer of the century chose to work. If one then decides to defend the periodical, the nearest way out for the critic is to select a part which can be analyzed and to ascribe the quality of the whole to that part: thus *The Spectator* is good because it contains Addison's series of essays on the imagination, a subject that fits modern critical categories precisely. This approach evades entirely the question of the cumulative effect of a good periodical; why does one agree that the *American Mercury* was a good magazine in the nineteen-twenties? It was not solely because it included within its pages *Rackety-Rax*.

Steele's *Tatler* and its successor, *The Spectator,* proved to be revolutionary departures in English literature principally, perhaps, because of their tone, the attitude toward the audience, rather than their specific content. Almost everything *in* both papers had been anticipated somewhere, in some periodical, even the famous club motif. Steele had the instincts of a great editor, it is true, and the combination of ingredients, the pleasing variety, had and still has much to do with *The Tatler's* success. But it may have been the tone, lightly learned, good-humored, confident, a bit patronizing, sometimes pedantic, that, early arrived at and consistently maintained, gave the papers their true character and authority. Bickerstaff and Mr. Spectator would tell the world—and the world would listen! (pp. 103-06)

From the beginning a major theme of *The Tatler,* as it was to be of *The Spectator,* was the reform of manners, a subject difficult to treat without appearing either pedantic or obvious. The virtues Steele advocated in this reform are the ordinary, homely ones he speaks of elsewhere: good sense, decency, kindness, simple generosity; and his tone is good-natured, often jocular. As here, in an early defense of the pedestrian (*Tatler,* No. 144), he writes:

> Thus, in spite of all order, justice, and decorum, we, the greater number of the Queen's loyal subjects, for no reason in the world but because we want money, do not share alike in the division of her Majesty's highroad. The horses and slaves of the rich take up the whole street, while we peripatetics are very glad to watch an opportunity to whisk across a passage, very thankful that we are not run over for interrupting the machine that carries in it a person neither more handsome, wise, nor valiant, than the meanest of us. For this reason, were I to propose a tax, it should certainly be upon coaches and chairs: for no man living can assign a reason why one man should have half a street to carry him at his ease, and perhaps only in pursuit of pleasures, when as good a man as himself wants room for his own person to pass upon the most necessary and urgent occasion.

This is clear enough, but what is one to add? Are we to trace the echo to its classical source and ascribe the sentiment to Steele's reading of Juvenal in his schooldays? Or place this essay in the history of ideas and show how advocacy of the homely virtues is related to the rise of benevolism, the ethic of the good-willing man, in European Protestantism? Or trace Steele's call for decency, good sense, and fair play back to his orphaned childhood? Such comments seem relevant but superfluous in *The Tatler's* clear light. So it was with dueling. Steele . . . wrote as well as anyone has on the subject of this curious mole of nature and probably contributed to the eventual elimination of

dueling in the English-speaking world. His essays on dueling were often quoted by later reformers. But the elimination of dueling was, after all, only a half-skip in civilization's grand march. One can comment a minor virtue into extinction, or even maintain that the virtues Steele advocates, generosity, kindness, decency, and the rest, are not to be dignified by the term. But their presence or absence in the so-called human may be more significant than we have realized; George Orwell, at any rate, has thought so in our time.

In *The Tatler* Addison and Steele found a wider audience for their views on dramatic reform, the same views they had been expressing by precept and example for several years. The Italian opera is no better than it should be. Immorality, Restoration style, has no place on the London stage. "It is not the business of a good play to make every man a hero; but it certainly gives him a livelier sense of virtue and merit than he had when he entered the theatre. This rational pleasure (as I always call it) has for many years been very little tasted; but I am glad to find, that the true spirit of it is reviving again amongst us. . . ." Addison and Steele seem to array themselves on the side of Collier and Defoe against "profaneness and immorality" but, as John Loftis has pointed out [in his *Comedy and Society from Congreve to Fielding,* 1959], Collier and Defoe were interested in the abolition of the stage, while the essayists sought to reconcile the newly powerful mercantile community with the theater. Some reform was certain to come; it was a question of whether the theaters would be closed altogether or would set a reformed middle course. Addison and Steele were concerned that the latter counsel prevail, as it did. (pp. 110-12)

[By 1710,] *The Tatler* had settled into the format of the periodical essay; instead, that is, of several separate sections in each issue, as originally planned, Steele would present an essay on one subject or a few subjects, using the mask of Isaac Bickerstaff. News reporting as such was almost completely gone; No. 210 contains the last bit, a report of the Whig [James] Stanhope's victory in Spain, and the partisan motivations for this inclusion are so obvious as not to require comment. Steele's essays are almost always purposive; he has a rhetorical object in mind, if not the righting of the political scheme of things, then the reform of manners, or of the drama. In No. 182, for example, Bickerstaff discusses the pleasures of theater-going, the high quality of [Colley] Cibber's and [Robert] Wilks's acting, and the proper subjects of drama, alluding to the forthcoming dramatic work of a "young poet" under his tutelage. There is reason to believe that Bickerstaff's young poet is Richard Steele and the drama *The Conscious Lovers,* not actually produced until 1722. This *Tatler* may then properly be called a *ballon d'essai.* (p. 122)

In a year and a half, Steele could reflect, the paper had established itself as far and away the outstanding periodical in English. No other editor had such talented contributors; Steele himself was writing better than he ever had and Addison was at the peak of his powers. In eighteen months Steele's image had been transformed in the London mind from that of a minor playwright and Kit-Cat follower to that of Isaac Bickerstaff, Censor of Great Britain, editor of the best-known paper in the land.

On the other hand, Steele's incursions into politics, though always a part of the paper, had become more frequent and annoying to Tory readers; circulation may have declined. By [1711] . . . , Steele was certainly aware that the paper was suffering from its identification with the Whigs. Perhaps the discreet Addison suggested that it was time to retire Isaac Bickerstaff in favor of someone new, someone not so closely associated with the fallen Junto as the Censor of Great Britain.

On 2 January 1711 Steele published *Tatler* No. 271, ending the series without warning and with only the unsatisfactory explanation that "The printer having informed me, that there are as many of these papers printed as will make four volumes, I am now come to the end of my ambition in this matter, and have nothing further to say to the world under the character of Isaac Bickerstaff." The last *Tatler* finds Steele meditating on the disparity between professions and actions, conscious as in the days of *The Christian Hero* of his own shortcomings.

> The general purpose of the whole has been to recommend truth, innocence, honour, and virtue, as the chief ornaments of life; but I considered, that severity of manners was absolutely necessary to him who would censure others, and for that reason, and that only, chose to talk in a mask. I shall not carry my humility so far as to call myself a vicious man; but at the same time must confess, my life is at best but pardonable. And with no greater character than this, a man would make but an indifferent progress in attacking prevailing and fashionable vices, which Mr. Bickerstaff has done with a freedom of spirit that would have lost both its beauty and efficacy, had it been pretended to by Mr. Steele.

A graceful compliment to Addison, a brief statement acknowledging the paper's politics ("I could not be cold enough to conceal my opinion"), a few random remarks, Richard Steele signs his name and *The Tatler* is done.

Richard Steele had thus revealed himself as the author of the most popular periodical in the English-speaking world; what would its readers have known about the author himself? Though of course long known to the intimate London world of court and coffeehouse as the author of amusing comedies and the creator of Isaac Bickerstaff, Richard Steele himself was a stranger to most of his readers in the provinces and colonies. As Gazetteer he had acquired important experience in editing and writing, but because of the nature of the position he had written anonymously; anonymity, he explained in the last issue of *The Tatler,* had also seemed proper in the conduct of that periodical. Isaac Bickerstaff's tastes, opinions, and crotchets were quoted, imitated, and discussed on all sides, but the person and personality of Richard Steele were little known to most of *The Tatler's* subscribers. . . . Beyond the London literary world, Richard Steele as Richard Steele was a minor figure once again. (pp. 127-29)

Calhoun Winton, in his Captain Steele: The Early Career of Richard Steele, *The Johns Hopkins Press, 1964, 225 p.]*

Calhoun Winton   (essay date 1970)

[*In the excerpt below from the second half of Winton's biography of Steele, he discusses the controversy that surrounded the staging of Steele's* Conscious Lovers.]

The Conscious Lovers opened at Drury Lane on Wednesday, 7 November [1722]. A "greater Concourse of People was never known to be assembled," according to one newspaper's account. Those who were fortunate enough to get into Wren's theater saw Steele watching from a box in the center gallery, accompanied by his young friend Benjamin Victor, who many years later would recall that Steele was pleased with all the portrayals except that of Griffin as Cimberton. The actor-managers no doubt were stirred to heightened performances by the great concourse of people out front who had paid the higher admission price; applause was prolonged and enthusiastic, a famous general was observed shedding tears at Indiana's pathetic dilemma ("I'll warrant he'll fight ne'er the worse for that," Steele commented in the preface to the printed play)—it was a great opening night. (p. 217)

A critical controversy about the play sprang into being in the periodical press and this encouraged attendance. The controversy, however, was not over the presentation of the pathetic on stage . . . but about the play's derivation from Terence and about the nature of instruction on the stage. To the first charge, that he had adapted the plot from Terence's *Andria,* Steele cheerfully pleaded guilty. He took it for granted that his audience, or the educated members of his audience, would recognize his source and, as in Pope's *Imitations of Horace,* derive added pleasure from the echo of the Latin classic. "I am extremely surpriz'd," he wrote in the preface to the printed version, "to find . . . That what I valued my self so much upon, the Translation of [Terence], should be imputed to me as a Reproach." To the other charge, that he had violated classical decorum by seeking to instruct through a mixture of the comic and the pathetic, Steele again admits his guilt. Steele has this to say about the reunion scene of the long-lost Indiana and her father: "[Anything] that has its Foundation in Happiness and Success, must be allow'd to be the Object of Comedy; and sure it must be an Improvement of it, to introduce a Joy too exquisite for Laughter, that can have no Spring but in Delight, which is the Case of this young Lady." The syntax is broken-backed but the meaning is tolerably clear: the basis of comedy is happiness and success. Situations may be presented which are beyond laughter, that is to say, pathetic situations, if they culminate in happiness and success. Though attacked on this point by classical critics such as John Dennis, who objected to the mixture of genres, Steele in his theoretical statement was directing the attention of his readers to the self-evident: that English drama had been mixing genres for a long time, quite oblivious of classical rule or precedent. Shakespeare and Beaumont and Fletcher had mingled comic and pathetic without a nod to the critics' gallery, and John Dryden had done so as well, though Dryden had felt compelled now and again to defend his practice.

Addison and Steele, whose collaborations include the Tatler *(1709-11), the* Spectator *(1711-12), and the* Guardian *(1713), in a painting dating from about 1712.*

A more truly controversial point is Steele's contention that the end or intention of his play is instruction, in a direct sense. A play is, or can be, a guide to action: "[F]or the greatest Effect of a Play in reading [i.e., in reading a play] is to excite the Reader to go see it; and when he does so, it is then a Play has the Effect of Example and Precept." This was a theme which Steele had treated many times in his writings: the educative aspect of literature. The Horatian *aut prodesse aut delectare* is in the background here—Steele quotes Cicero to add support to his assertion—but the impulse is in the spirit of the Enlightenment rather than of Augustan Rome. Steele in invoking Cicero is employing what Peter Gay has termed [in his *The Enlightenment: An Interpretation,* 1966] the "useful and beloved past" for the improvement of the present and the future. Since a play affects the playgoer more directly than a book affects the reader, the drama, in Steele's view, is to be a prime instrument in the reform of society, but all literature is capable of guiding society along the upward road to a better day. Domestic situations such as those presented in **The Conscious Lovers** are especially suitable for edification, or so Steele had long contended. Years earlier, in **The Spectator** (No. 428), he had called for literature on new topics, for example, the misfortunes of being in need of money:

When we are come into Domestick Life in this manner, to awaken Caution and Attendance to the main Point, it would not be amiss to give now and then a Touch of Tragedy, and describe that most dreadful of all Humane Conditions, the Case of Bankrupcy; how Plenty, Credit, Chearfulness, full Hopes, and easie Possessions, are in an Instant turned into Penury, faint Aspects, Diffidence, Sorrow, and Misery; how the Man, who with an open Hand the Day before could administer to the Extremities of others, is shunn'd to Day by the Friend of his bosom.

Or, as Diderot was to put the theme more pungently years later [in his *Rameau's Nephew and Other Works,* 1956]: "The worst of it is the constrained posture in which need holds you. The needy man doesn't walk like the rest, he skips, twists, cringes, crawls." Domestic situations, the drama of the commonplace, are better suited for instruction than the sorrows of kings and the ambition of princes. In an amusing instance of life imitating art, Steele, who had known well enough the sorrows of need, followed his own precepts, illustrated the afflictions of domestic poverty in *The Conscious Lovers*—and was rewarded with a shower of money. The example could scarcely have been more apposite.

As is usual in Steele's writings, there are autobiographical echoes here and there in the play. Indiana's name is reminiscent of Steele's Aunt Bellindia, and both names are reminders of the wealth of the Indies which Indiana's father sought in fiction and Steele's grandfather Richard in fact, that quick wealth which could cut through life's problems with such ease. Myrtle's duel returns, of course, to a theme with which Steele had been preoccupied since his own duel with Kelly twenty-two years before. The pathos of Indiana's situation derives from the plight of an unmarried young woman without financial resources in a society which placed great, and increasing, importance on the size of the dowry or portion the bride could bring to a marriage settlement. With two unmarried daughters Steele had reflected on the specific aspects of such a situation.

The play was good theater, with a well-constructed plot, crisp dialogue, and meaty parts for Steele's friends, the actors and actresses he had known since the turn of the century. Anne Oldfield, who had played Rowe's pathetic heroines, could coax tears from the sternest audience. The pert, witty servant Tom was an ideal part for [Colley] Cibber.

The happy ending of *The Conscious Lovers'* opening night was a result of more than the money it brought Steele. For once in his life, of greater importance perhaps, was the renewal of his literary fame, the revival of his reputation as a writer rather than as a controversial Member of Parliament. Although the play is perhaps in the second rank of his works, among his many interesting but flawed productions, and although he received a stern critical drubbing from several quarters, the play was warmly defended by other critics and received that vote of confidence ultimately reassuring to the dramatic author, large and enthusiastic audiences. (pp. 218-22)

> *Calhoun Winton, in his* Sir Richard Steele, M.P.: The Later Career, *The Johns Hopkins Press, 1970, 265 p.*

Jean H. Hagstrum   (essay date 1980)

[*Hagstrum is an American educator whose works include an edition of* Samuel Johnson's Literary Criticism *(1952). In the excerpt below, he examines Steele's conception of love and marriage as evidenced in his personal letters to his wife, his* Tatler *and* Spectator *essays, and his final drama,* The Conscious Lovers.]

Johnson said that Addison in his poetry "thinks justly; but he thinks faintly." Can the same be said of Addison's literary twin, Richard Steele—that his emotions, though proper and decent, were lukewarm and callow? Only perhaps if one concentrates on *The Conscious Lovers,* formerly overrated because it was regarded as the *locus classicus* of sentimental feeling; but surely not if one considers those elegant and moving vignettes of common life in *The Tatler* or the exquisite and sincere letters of devotion to his wife.

Steele's literary career fulfills many of the tendencies that had been gathering force from the Restoration on: these he brings to a kind of synthesizing focus, adding the panache of his own lovable and whimsical personality. Though dashing and cavalier, Steele was a devout Christian, and he brought to the surface what many have felt in listening to the music of Bach and in contemplating the Passion and its implications for human behavior. In his *Christian Hero* (1701), his first prose work, written while he was on active duty as an ensign of the Guards and addressed to "Men of Wit and Gallantry," Steele does not scruple to rhapsodize about the crucifixion, suggesting to us who are students of the term "pathetic" that the sufferings of Christ perhaps constitute one of the fountainheads of that concept: "How his Wounds blacken! His Body writhes, and Heart heaves with Pity, and with Agony!" Turning from the religiously rhapsodic to the ethical, we see in *The Ladies Library* (1714) a Steele determined to fix the conduct of women. Out of the sentiments of the greatest English divines, he compiles a code of strict but not puritanical ethics. He attempts to establish a countertradition to the belles lettres of France and England that traduce and insult the female sex and that make it difficult to believe that the authors have ever had mothers, sisters, or wives. In other literary forms he tried to redefine heroism in terms of benevolent action and became a leading—perhaps *the* leading—opponent of the duel. Although far from being the reformer of the status of woman that François Poulain de la Barre was in France or Defoe and Mary Astell in England, he did contribute greatly to the evolution of feminist thought in the large audience he commanded.

It has been said that the *Pamela* sequel and *Amelia* are the first literary treatments of the good estate of marriage. But at least three decades before the novels of Richardson and Fielding began appearing, Steele had been exalting married love in his frank, guileless, and endearing letters to his second wife, Mary Scurlock, the "Dear Prue" of the correspondence. These were not, however, published until John Nichols brought them out in 1787—too late to influence the course of eighteenth-century sentiment but in time to impress at least one great Romantic poet, Coleridge, who adverted to them often. It is a pity they are not better known, for they belong to the great tradition of eighteenth-century letters—Pope's, Gray's, Walpole's, Cowper's—and their "frank and open demonstrations and assertions of love over a long period of years," in the words of Lawrence Stone, "are in striking contrast to the formal relations that were so carefully maintained in the sixteenth and early seventeenth centuries." Their charm lies in the fact that their author had no notion whatever of publication—which in no way distracts from their distinction in having been produced by a typical and complex sensibility, one that was at once the product and refiner of the tradition I have been elucidating.

What the principals were like in real life need not concern us here, since my task is to regard them as lovers being mythologized in the art—even the artless art—of the personal letter. The letters take on some dramatic force by the contrast of lover and beloved. He is careless about money and likes to drink with boon companions. (In Michaelmas term, 1716, there were no less than eight actions for debt taken against Steele in the courts . . . , and the shortest letter written to his wife was "Sober or not, I am / Ever Yours.") Prue is penurious, excessively prudential (hence the nickname), quarrelsome ("Two or Three Quarrells will dispatch Me quite") and she punishes him by denying him her favors ("You advise Me to take care of my soul, I do not [know] what you can think of Yours when you have, and do withhold from me your body"). But these contrasts merely add a fillip of reality to the devotion that reigns—to his love of her that continues to grow from 9 August 1707, when the letters commenced, to 23 June 1718, when they ended. Prue died on 26 December 1718, aged forty, the mother of one son and two daughters, and was buried 30 December in the south transept of West-minster Abbey opposite the monument to Dryden—a far from meaningless juxtaposition if we remember not the poet's satires and comedies but his love poetry and heroic plays.

Tracing the professions of loyalty and affection for the woman whom Steele regarded as possessing "wit and Beauty" and also a "Good Understanding," we note that their love is rich enough to have its paradoxes and that it is continually being refreshed by the living object—that it is guided by an unobtrusive religion, is fashionable in its forms of expression, and is both traditional and contempo-rary in its resonances. His is a "Generous passion" for her that is leveled with daily life and quotidian discourse: "I shall affect plainnesse and sincerity in my discourse to you, as much as other Lovers do perplexity and rapture. Instead of saying, I shall die for you, I professe I should be glad to Lead my life with you." Steele loves his Prue, but he loves virtue as well, and he dislikes "low images of Love" as a "Blind Being." Sometimes his passion takes on the vocabulary of the Longinian sublime, and he refers to "the pleasing Transport" that accompanies his thought of her "Youth Beauty and Innocence." If he is sublime, he is also tender and "pathetic": his eyes are ready to "flow with Tendernesse," and he has a "gushing Heart." After the marriage, love must coexist with suffering and the ex-asperations I have already noted. But nothing can quench the flame, which now burns brightly for her "Good sense" and her "True greatnesse of mind," the latter surely a noteworthy phrase since in the application of the language of the heroic play to daily life Steele anticipates what Rich-ardson was to do with obsessive frequency. During her long separation from him (November 1716 to December 1717, when Lady Steele was in South Wales attending to her properties), his affection remained "ardent." He is a "Slave of Beauty," but he is intellectually more admiring than ever ("You are the Head of Us"); and he bows gladly to her rule in practical affairs. When he imagines her re-turn, he thinks of agreeable clothes, cheerful conversation with a witty and handsome woman free of the worries of kitchen and nursery. Such are some of the emotions pro-duced in Steele by his lady—"Poor Dear Angry Pleased Pretty Witty Silly Eve[ry]thing Prue." The dominant emotion that suffuses the letters—"Love esteem and friendship and all that is soft"—embodies many venerable traditions about love, perhaps the dearest and closest to Steele being that of love in Milton's Eden: he wrote to Prue less than a month before they married that "the Union of minds in pure affection is renewing the First

State of Man." Such sense of identification with both Mil-ton and the sentimental movement places the correspon-dence fully in the central current of this book.

In the love letters Steele addressed his wife only and ex-pressed the private affections of his heart, revealing as he did so how much even these are guided by the *Zeitgeist* and by antecedent artistic formulations. In **The Tatler** pa-pers Steele is a public man, who has joined with his "fel-low-labourer[s], the Reformers of Manners," to civilize a nation. England must be reformed from the nation of Wycherley, a society in which "love and wenching were the business of life" (no. 3), to a modern Christian state in which there prevails a gentle, civilized view of uxorial love and domestic happiness. The stage was of course one means of effecting reform, and Steele anticipated the view of Goethe's young Wilhelm Meister when he wrote in **Tatler** 8 that the theater can create "a polite and moral gentry." The periodical essay was perhaps an even more effective weapon than the drama; and Steele's vignettes of family life, his short stories in prose with their tender por-trayals of family joys and family woes, were designed, like the characters in Shakespeare's plays, to create "strong impressions of honour and humanity" (no. 8). Since news-papers in our own day will doubtless continue to portray sentimental scenes from domestic life as one of their sta-ples, one could wish they possessed the style, wit, and moral passion of Steele, which make forgivable his addic-tion to the tearful and cloying.

Steele's essays tell of the woes of lovers, parents, children; exploit the drama of the domestic scene; and emphasize the differences between the sexes in order to stimulate mu-tual love and respect. These several themes alternate in the columns of **The Tatler** from April 1709 to January 1710/11, the last number. In no. 45 (23 July 1709) he tells the story of the "unhappy Teraminta," a kept woman who passes life gorgeously dressed but immured, her only pur-pose in life being to satisfy the brutish appetites of her keeper. She pines away "in the solitude and severity of a nun, but the conscience and guilt of a harlot." No. 82 (18 October 1709) gives two tales of "exquisite distress," the first of a wife who died on the body of her husband which is washed ashore—Steele's version of Ovid's Alcyone and Ceyx, the subject at the end of the century of a drawing by Romney and a relief sculpture by Thomas Banks; and the other of a bridegroom discharging in jest a pistol he did not know was loaded and so slaying his bride just after the ceremony—a story that sounds like unadulterated melodrama in bare summary but that actually is unfolded with understated and piercing sentiment. ("Poor good old man!—" the grieving bridegroom writes to the father about his only daughter's death, "if it be possible, do not curse me.") Because Steele wants to portray real love and life known to his readers, he delicately satirizes, in no. 85, the vogue of extravagant love—romances set in Spain—and so prepares for the realistic fictions of Defoe, Richard-son, and Fielding and for the approving criticism of John-son. Now and then, as in no. 68 (15 September 1709), he calls attention to family pathos in Shakespeare, like the ir-resistible sorrow of Macduff in *Macbeth,* who cries out, "What, both children! Both, both my children gone!" In no. 149 he attacks the cruel and ill-natured private tyrant, the husband, and invokes *Paradise Lost;* the picture of Eve being lovingly instructed by Adam . . . In no. 172 (16 May 1710) he asserts the extremely important idea that between the sexes there is difference but equality. "There is a sort of sex in souls," he says, in direct contradiction of what had been proclaimed by late seventeenth-century reformers. But this unlikeness in the psyche (men inclining toward wisdom, women toward prudence) ought not to be regarded as a reason for inequality: "Our minds have different, not superior qualities to theirs." Steele is far from being consistent, since wisdom *is* in fact superior to prudence; but his comment may reflect a high regard for a quality he lacked and his wife possessed in abundance. Sensibility is not always presented as an unmixed blessing, since it can lead to "an unmanly gentleness of mind," the price one pays, apparently, for achieving "the softnesses of humanity" (181, 6 June 1710). Tears then give way to alcohol, and only the "generous and warming" wine can relieve the distress of contemplating the untimely death of beauty and innocence. In no. 198 (15 July 1710) Caelia, a lovely and virtuous girl, dismisses a husband who is faithless and who schemes to have her seduced. Infamy and innocence cannot dwell together, as Richardson will proclaim often in *Clarissa.* The modern woman whom Steele was delineating is too much a person of pride and integrity to remain in daily intercourse with a villain. Such a view constitutes a break with Jeremy Taylor, who believed that the wife had a mission to perform in reclaiming the wayward man and even with the Apostle Paul, who believed that the husband was sanctified in the wife. When he portrays men and women, Steele's sentimentality seldom offends modern taste: in fact he strikes us as being humane, witty, and sensible. But in enforcing filial piety, he can be intolerably mawkish and not a little silly. One cannot call *Spectator* 449 (5 August 1712) morbid, but it is scarcely healthy or vigorous: "Certain it is, that there is no Kind of Affection so pure and angelick as that of a Father to a Daughter. He beholds her both with, and without Regard to her Sex. In Love to our Wives there is Desire, to our Sons there is Ambition; but in that to our Daughters, there is something which there are no Words to express." To a father, therefore, the Fidelia of this essay gives up all, rejecting every one of her suitors to care for him. But even here Steele may have been saved by his whimsy, and one hopes that he actually rescues Fidelia from a monstrously bland devotion with a concluding stroke of irony: "What adds to the Entertainment of the good old Man is, that *Fidelia,* where Merit and Fortune cannot be overlook'd by Epistolary Lovers, reads over the Accounts of her Conquests, plays on her Spinet the gayest Airs, (and while she is doing so, you would think her formed only for Gallantry) to intimate to him the Pleasures she despises for his Sake."

Steele's inability to be persuasive in portraying parents and children in **The Tatler** carries over into **The Conscious Lovers,** his best-known but perhaps not his best play. It must be considered briefly, if only because of its great influence and popular success. The play was successful on the stage because it portrayed the sensibility that was gaining the day and because it addressed itself to a subject that concerned almost everyone, the possible conflict between duty to one's heart and to one's parents. As a work of art,

Steele's play is less than satisfactory partly because successful reconciliation of that conflict was in Steele's day virtually impossible. How could one possibly be faithful at once to the desires of the heart and the desires of a father if these were in conflict? (pp. 165-71)

Let us consider how in the play Steele resolves a potential conflict and what lessons he enforces in the process. The complication is that Bevil Senior, considering the wealth involved, wants his son to marry Lucinda Sealand, whom the young man does not love but his friend Myrtle does. Bevi' Junior is in love with Indiana, but his filial piety is such that he cannot disobey his father. That piety does not always look disinterested, since the son is a bit too anxious to preserve and augment his already considerable wealth. Steele, a friend of merchant wealth, of course wants the relations of father and son to seem exemplary, but perhaps the good old servant Humphrey is right in saying that "their fear of giving each other Pain, is attended with constant mutual Uneasiness." The comment is revealing: strain must have developed when one tried to live out the new sentimental morality and reconcile it with the realities of bourgeois life. So loyal is Bevil Junior to his father's wishes that he never speaks to Indiana of the state of his heart but, instead, opens the sluices of charity to relieve her distress. An interesting and teasing association, this— between love and charity, an association that suggests that in the culture itself sex may often have lurked behind sensibility. When the two meet, they talk of esteem, a love-transcending quality which she calls "the Merit of the Soul" and he says is something only "great Souls" can possess. Steele is obviously doing what many of his successors did, attempting to transfer heroism from the military camp and the court to middle-class life. But one wonders if such sentiments—along with Indiana's professed admiration of Griselda in the opera and Bevil Junior's praise of reflection as superior to sensation and his rhapsodies about charity—are not partly uttered *faute de mieux.* Had the young people been free of the restraints they were under, they might have been making love. Of course, this love even under restraint contrasts most favorably to the foolish modesty of Mrs. Sealand, Lucinda's mother, and the animality of the oafish pedant Cimberton, whom she wishes to foist on her daughter. When the recognition scene establishes Indiana as another daughter of the rich merchant Sealand, Bevil Senior is fully reconciled to the marriage; and the conflict of duties is ended by a kind of deus ex machina solution. Thus Steele really evades the issue and has . . . created not comic laughter but only easily won joy—a mistaken aesthetic that obviates probability, instruction, and amusement. Parson Adams rightly called the play almost "solemn enough for a sermon" (*Joseph Andrews*), and the title word "conscious" refers partly to a kind of self-approving awareness that attends good behavior. But it refers primarily to love-sensibility, which suffuses the whole being with delicious, though potentially embarrassing, sensations.

In a fairly early letter, Richardson's Lovelace describes one of his victims as a "conscious girl." Of what did her "consciousness" consist and how was it manifested? She blushed, she was *"sensible all over,"* she was still innocent but at the same time encouraged the rake's amorous advances (*Clarissa*). Richardson's full meaning of "conscious" is only potentially present in Steele, but the ingredients are there. Beneath the moralistic and highly proper social surface, physical love blushes and finally blooms. Bevil Junior and Indiana embody the gentle goodness and tempered affection based unmistakably on physical love that lay at the heart of Steele's sentimental formula and was expressed more attractively in the letters and essays I have earlier discussed. It is not impossible that the title adjective and all that it implies is the most enduring contribution to subsequent culture of Steele's once famous play. (pp. 171-72)

> Jean H. Hagstrum, "Sentimental Love and Marriage: 'Esteem Enliven'd by Desire'," in his Sex and Sensibility: Ideal and Erotic Love from Milton to Mozart, *The University of Chicago Press, 1980, pp. 160-85.*

F. W. Bateson   (essay date 1986)

[*Bateson was an English critic, scholar, and editor. Below, he maintains that although Steele exercised a greater influence on the* Tatler *than his partner Addison, his contributions to the* Spectator *were "second-rate" compared to Addison's.*]

The crucial innovations in a literature occur when some sub-literary form—such as the folk-song, the popular sermon, the melodramatic romance, to give three familiar examples—ceases to be 'trash' and becomes the vehicle of aesthetic experience. The ultimate causes of such a metamorphosis are usually traceable to some cataclysm in the particular society where it occurs, or at any rate in some change in its ruling class or dominant groups. But between the social revolution and the emergence of the new literary form which is its by-product a temporal interval must apparently occur. Augustan satire was essentially an after-effect on the literary plane of what might be called the Royalist resistance movement to the Commonwealth; but though its political sources go back to the 1640s the satire itself does not find effective literary expression before Butler's *Hudibras* (Part I, 1662). Restoration comedy, which came to its maturity in the 1670s, was the product of a second wave in the anti-Puritan reaction that followed the return of Charles II from France. The eighteenth-century periodical essay, on the other hand, was the result of a reaction *against* that reaction. Addison and Steele were both Whigs, and the emergence of *The Tatler,* twenty years after the Glorious Revolution that had expelled the Stuarts and established a constitutional monarchy, was its aesthetic after-product. The sub-literature out of which the periodical essay evolved was, of course, the polemical journalism of the later seventeenth century. But the political function of that journalism had ceased with the discrediting of the Jacobite cause. The stage was now set, therefore, for a higher journalism, which could rebuke or reform the individual rather than the nation, one that was moral and social in its objectives rather than political, and with some innocent entertainment not altogether precluded. And under these new conditions the sub-literature of Restoration journalism became Augustan literature. Steele may be called the engineer of the transition—

though there had been one or two periodicals of amusement before *The Tatler* (those of Ned Ward and Peter Motteux, for example, and the curious 'Scandal Club' in Defoe's *Review*)—but its hero, its genius, was Addison. (pp. 117-18)

There is nothing Addisonian . . . in anything [Steele] wrote. His letters to his 'Prue' (whose real name was Mary) convince us that he was an affectionate husband. That she was an heiress—as his first wife had also been, who died only two years after she had become Mrs Steele—and a 'cried-up beauty' (as Kneller's portrait demonstrates) must be conceded. And the interval between the death of the first wife and the marriage to the second was perhaps too short (about six months). But the long series of letters now in the British Museum to his 'absolute governess' show that the absence of subtlety and refinement was compensated for by a natural sincerity and kindness of heart. Steele is much more likeable than Addison; he is not in the same class as a writer. And he is quite without the fineness of touch and delicacy of feeling, both as man and as writer, that characterize Addison.

It may seem paradoxical to accuse Steele of coarseness, since he was continually pounding the moral drum. But there is a crudity in the critical gospel that he preaches that convicts him of a lack of literary sensibility. The paper on Etherege's *The Man of Mode* (**The Spectator,** no 65) is a typical Puritan denunciation; it concludes as follows:

> To speak plainly of this whole Work, I think nothing but being lost to a Sense of Innocence and Virtue can make any one see this Comedy, without observing more frequent Occasion to move Sorrow and Indignation, than Mirth and Laughter. At the same time I allow it to be Nature, but it is Nature in its utmost Corruption and Degeneracy.

Steel's sentimental comedies—of which the first, *The Funeral* (1701), is much the best—are practical dramatic applications of this formula. Everything possible is done to gloss over the corruptness of human nature, and the spectators are incited to enjoy their tears over any corruptions that remain.

Steele's place in the text-books is probably a higher one than he deserves. If he is to be defended the merit to insist on is a certain sturdy independence. The kind of sentimental comedy that he practised is different from that of his immediate predecessors—Colley Cibber's, for example, or George Farquhar's—because it is clearly not motivated by mere box-office considerations. Steele wanted to *say* something. Unfortunately he had not the specific literary talent required to develop his intuitions; his last comedy, *The Conscious Lovers* (1722), is undoubtedly his worst just as the later essays are also inferior to the early ones.

But Steele did invent the periodical essay. Addison was in Ireland, the secretary of the Lord Lieutenant, when Steele launched *The Tatler* (no 1, 12 April 1709) and he has no share in the innovation on the exploitation of which his own reputation now rests. If Steele owed anything to anybody—apart from his own nose for a possibly profitable speculation (the furnaces that he built a few years earlier to produce a 'philosopher's stone' had not been profitable)—it was to Swift. (pp. 127-28)

Swift's voice is continually making itself heard in the early numbers of *The Tatler,* which bear something of the same relation to the newspapers of the time that Bickerstaff's *Predictions for the Year 1708* bear to the contemporary almanacs. The dry ironic tone is as unmistakable as the continuous suggestion of parody. It must be remembered that the original sheets of *The Tatler* looked exactly like the common-or-garden newspaper. Like *The Daily Courant, The Observator* and *The Flying Post,* it was printed in double columns on both sides of a single folio sheet of paper. It came out, like *The Evening Post, The Post Boy* and Defoe's *Review,* three times a week—on Tuesdays, Thursdays and Saturdays. If there was any difference it was that *The Tatler* was more carelessly printed and on even worse paper than its less literary competitors.

The disguise of a mock-newspaper has all the outward signs of Swift's satiric technique. The title may even be due to Swift. To *tattle* meant more at the time than to gossip; it included the probability that the gossip was false and malicious—a sense immortalized in Mr Tattle of Congreve's *Love for Love* (1695), one of the most popular plays of the period and, as it happens, one specially commended by Steele in no 1. To Swift the news reported in newspapers was precisely *tattle,* whereas Steele, much of whose income at this time was derived from his official post as Gazeteer or editor of *The London Gazette,* can hardly have been as sceptical of the contents of newspapers. Elsewhere too, in these early numbers, though the pen was always Steele's, the words are sometimes Swift's. The promise made in no 4 to publish a treatise against operas, with 'a very elaborate digression upon the London cries, wherein he (a great critic) has shown from reason and philosophy why oysters are cried, card-matches sung, and turnips and all other vegetables neither cried, sung nor said but sold with an accent and tone neither natural to man or beast' has been identified by Swift's latest editor as essentially Swiftian. The list could easily be extended.

There are good things in the early numbers of *The Tatler,* but it is formless and too heterogeneous in its subject-matter. The initial formula was to use White's Chocolate-House as the source of 'accounts of gallantry, pleasure and entertainment', with Will's Coffee-House, where Dryden had lorded it ten years earlier, for poetry, the Grecian in the Strand for learning, and St James's Coffee-House for foreign and domestic news. And 'what else I shall offer' from Mr Bickerstaff's own apartment. Steele was living at the time in Bury Street, Piccadilly, with all the coffee-houses at a convenient distance. He was of the genial, sociable temperament that one associates with those of Anglo-Irish origin (he was born in Dublin), and a coffee-house (where stronger liquors than coffee or chocolate were also obtainable) was his natural element. But the retailer of coffee-house news was finding it difficult to double the part with that of Bickerstaff, the eccentric astrologer (who has a familiar spirit called Pacolet in his service). It was fortunate that Addison came to his rescue at this point. (pp. 128-30)

Addison's first contribution to *The Tatler* was the account

of 'the Distress of the News-Writers' in no 18. The exact number of papers or parts of papers for which he was responsible is not known. It was certainly more than the 62 papers (out of a total of 271) printed by Tickell, Addison's literary executor, in the collected edition of Addison's writings that was published in 1721, immediately after his death. Nevertheless, measured quantitatively *The Tatler* is undoubtedly mainly Steele's. It also includes most of his best writing, such as the touching account of his father's death in no 181:

> The first sense of sorrow I ever knew was upon the death of my father, at which time I was not quite five years of age; but was rather amazed at what all the house meant, than possessed with a real understanding why nobody was willing to play with me. I remember I went into the room where his body lay, and my mother sat weeping alone by it. I had my battledore in my hand, and fell a-beating the coffin, and calling Papa; for, I know not how, I had some slight idea that he was locked up there. My mother catched me in her arms, and, transported beyond all patience of the silent grief she was before in, she almost smothered me in her embraces and told me in a flood of tears, 'Papa could not hear me, and would play with me no more, for they were going to put him under ground, whence he could never come to us again.' She was a very beautiful woman, of a noble spirit . . .

Such autobiographical passages are unfortunately rare, and most of the essays—on duelling, on fashionable visits, on the education of girls, on the evils of drinking—now have a merely historical interest. Addison's beneficent influence can be recognized in the trend away from disconnected episodes based on the separate coffee-houses and with each number now becoming a single coherent essay. But for the modern reader there is too much Steele, especially too much of Steele the moralist, and too little of Addison and Swift.

Between Steele's terminating *The Tatler* (2 January 1711) and the first number of *The Spectator* (1 March 1711) the interval in time was short. The crucial difference—apart from the change from three numbers a week to six—was that the supply of 'copy' was now divided equally and on equal terms between Addison and Steele, instead of Steele paying Addison for whatever material he provided. Altogether there were 555 numbers to 6 December 1712, the last number being again signed by Steele who pays a proper tribute to Addison in it, though again as in the last paper of *The Tatler* without mentioning his name. Addison contributed 251 essays; Steele's total is also 251 essays. (Friends and correspondents, some of them not identifiable now, provided the other 53 papers.) Qualitatively, however, Steele's essays are not in the same class. The coarseness of spiritual fibre almost always present in Steele's work is exemplified in three heavy-handed essays in the Sir Roger de Coverley series. The perverse widow (no 113) who still fascinates the elderly Sir Roger is drawn with spirit, but the comedy is much too obvious. In no 118 Steele returns to her and the dangerous influence of confidants, but here the point has to be reinforced by Sir Roger's game-keeper who is discovered sitting by the side of his inamorata by 'a transparent fountain' in which his Betty is reflected. Sir Roger and the Spectator overhear the game-keeper addressing the reflection:

> Oh thou dear Picture, if thou could'st remain there in the Absence of that fair Creature whom you represent in the Water, how willingly could I stand here satisfied for ever. . . .

And so on for half an unconvincing page. Apparently Betty has been listening to the spiteful gossip of Kate Willow about the game-keeper and Susan Holliday. The modern reader cannot help comparing Sir Roger's pompous game-keeper with the idiom of Lady Chatterley's lover.

Steele shows himself a competent enough journalist in **The Spectator,** but rarely much more than that. The moralizing is what **The Tatler** has prepared for us—the art of pleasing, the right choice in marriage, the relationship between parents and children, and similar topics—and though Steele's attitude is always humane the actual presentation shows no advance. Steele had been deprived of his Gazeteership by Harley and the items of foreign news that are a distracting element in **The Tatler** were no longer available for **The Spectator.** Their place tends to be taken, however, by letters sometimes written by Steele himself and sometimes—to judge by specimens still extant at Blenheim Palace—by genuine letters from readers that Steele has touched up. As literature most of the numbers for which he was responsible are at best second-rate. **The Spectator** survives in spite of Steele and because of Addison. The judgement is one that it would be futile to question. (pp. 130-32)

> *F. W. Bateson, "Addison, Steele and the Periodical Essay," in* Dryden to Johnson, *edited by Roger Lonsdale, revised edition, Sphere Reference, 1986, pp. 117-35.*

FURTHER READING

Achurch, Robert Waller. "Richard Steele, Gazetteer and Bickerstaff." In *Studies in the Early English Periodical,* edited by Richmond P. Bond, pp. 49-72. Chapel Hill: University of North Carolina Press, 1957.

　　Traces the change in the composition and conduct of Steele's *Tatler* as the frequency and quantity of its news diminished.

Adams, W. Davenport. "Steele's *Tatler.*" In his *Famous Books: Sketches in the Highways and Byeways of English Literature,* pp. 274-98. London: Virtue, Spalding, and Co., 1875.

　　Describes the general simplicity of Steele's graceful and buoyant writing style as superior to that of Addison.

Drake, Nathan. "Observations on the Effects of the *Tatler, Spectator,* and *Guardian,* on the Taste, Literature, and Morals of the Age." In his *Essays, Biographical, Critical, and Historical, Illustrative of the "Tatler," "Spectator," and "Guardian,"* Vol. III, pp. 380-401. London: C. Whittingham, 1805.

　　Comments on how the periodicals of Addison and Steele benefitted the moral and intellectual development of British society.

Dunham, W. H. "Some Forerunners of the *Tatler* and the *Spectator.*" *Modern Language Notes* XXXIII, No. 1 (January 1918): 95-101.

　　Explores the debt that the *Tatler* owes to earlier periodicals which had to some extent developed the character sketches that Steele further refined.

Ehrenpreis, Irvin. Review of *Richard Steele's Periodical Journalism 1714-16,* edited by Rae Blanchard. *The Review of English Studies* 12, No. 47 (August 1961): 299-300.

　　Maintains that Steele's heavy, blunt political satire and carelessly written essays are a "disappointing contrast" to Blanchard's expertise in editing this compilation of essays.

Furtwangler, Albert. "Mr. Spectator, Sir Roger, and Good Humour." *University of Toronto Quarterly* 46, No. 1 (Fall 1976): 31-50.

　　Analyzes Addison and Steele's approach to developing the characters of Mr. Spectator and Sir Roger de Coverly in the *Spectator.*

————. "The Making of Mr. Spectator." *Modern Language Quarterly* 38, No. 1 (March 1977): 21-39.

　　Examines how Addison and Steele created the character of Mr. Spectator based on their previous collaboration in the *Tatler.*

Graham, Walter. "Some Predecessors of the *Tatler.*" *The Journal of English and Germanic Philology* XXIV (1925): 548-54.

　　Asserts that some of the most popular devices in the *Tatler* can be found in the periodicals that preceded Steele's serial.

Humphreys, A. R. *Steele, Addison and their Periodical Essays.* London: Longmans, Green and Co., 1959, 46 p.

　　Discusses the literary achievements of Steele and Addison based on their contributions to the *Tatler* and the *Spectator.*

Irving, William Henry. "Augustan Attitudes—Steele and Addison." In his *The Providence of Wit in the English Letter Writers,* pp. 164-77. Durham, N.C.: Duke University Press, 1955.

　　Considers the evolution of the plain style of letter writing as a genre in the *Tatler* and the *Spectator.*

Kelsall, Malcolm. "Terence and Steele." In *Essays on the Eighteenth-Century English Stage,* edited by Kenneth Richards and Peter Thomson, pp. 11-27. London: Methuen and Co., 1972.

　　Compares the theme of *humanitas* in Terence's *Andria* to that of Steele's imitation, *The Conscious Lovers.*

Kenny, Shirley Strum. *The Plays of Richard Steele* by Richard Steele, edited by Shirley Strum Kenny. Oxford: Clarendon Press, 1971, 443 p.

　　Offers introductions to Steele's four comedies as well as critical commentary on each play.

Loftis, John. "Richard Steele's Censorium." *The Huntington Library Quarterly* XIV, No. 1 (November 1950): 43-66.

　　Summarizes the history of the Censorium, a private theater in which Steele attempted to implement theatrical reform by replacing productions he considered immoral with more tasteful presentations.

Macaulay, Thomas Babington. *Life and Writings of Addison.* Boston: Houghton, Mifflin and Company, 1896, 223 p.
    Compares Steele's essays for the *Tatler* to "light wines which, though deficient in body and flavor, are yet a pleasant small drink if not kept too long or carried too far," in a digression of some length.

Milic, Louis T. "The Reputation of Richard Steele: What Happened?" *Eighteenth-Century Life* I, No. 4 (June 1975): 81-7.
    Reviews several critical perceptions of Steele to determine why his literary reputation has suffered since the eighteenth century.

Scott, R. McNair. "An Aspect of Addison and Steele." *The London Mercury* XXVII, No. 162 (April 1933): 524-29.
    Claims that the essays on which Steele and Addison collaborated helped mold the "best of Cavalier and Puritan" into the model of an eighteenth-century gentleman.

Smith, William Henry. "Life of Steele." *Blackwood's Edinburgh Magazine* DCVIII, No. XCIX (June 1866): 726-46.
    Presents a detailed biographical sketch of Steele.

St. Teresa de Jesús

1515-1582

(Born Teresa Sánchez de Cepeda y Ahumada; also known as St. Teresa of Avila) Spanish prose writer and poet.

One of the most significant figures in the sixteenth-century Spanish mystic movement, St. Teresa de Jesús is also highly regarded as an accomplished prose writer. Her autobiography *El libro de su vida* (1562; *The Life of the Mother Teresa of Jesus*) is, with Miguel de Cervantes's *Don Quixote* (1602), one of the two most widely read books in Spain. Lauded for simple and clear expression of difficult theological ideas and for their compelling depiction of spiritual experiences, Teresa's *Life* and other writings gave an eloquent voice to the strain of mysticism that pervaded Spanish Catholicism and influenced the work of numerous others, including the noted Spanish mystic poet St. John of the Cross.

Teresa was born in Avila, to a merchant, Alonso Sánchez de Cepeda, and his second wife, Beatriz de Ahumada y Tapia. Cepeda was a pious man who imposed an austere existence upon his family, especially his wife. According to Teresa, her mother's only indulgence was reading chivalric romances, and she often shared these stories with her children. Biographers speculate that it was through these accounts of chivalry that Teresa and her brother Rodrigo became intrigued by the adventures of Christian crusaders; as Teresa later recorded in her autobiography, on one occasion she and her brother attempted to leave home to conduct a crusade in "the land of the Moors" but were intercepted and returned home. She also reports that as an adolescent she engaged in "youthful frivolities" which prompted her father to enroll her in the Augustinian convent of Santa María de Gracia when she was sixteen. One year later she was forced to leave the convent because of illness. During her recuperation she developed a desire to live a life of religious devotion, and in 1536 she entered the convent of Encarnación de Avila as a novice in the Carmelite order. Two years later, Teresa suffered a second, more severe, bout of illness, which left her bedridden for several years. During her long illness she read a number of religious works, including the *Third Spiritual Primer* (1527) of Francisco de Osuna, a devotional work concerning the nature of prayer which, according to Helmut Hatzfeld "laid in Teresa the very foundations for her later development as a mystic." She also read St. Augustine's *Confessions* (401), which significantly influenced the form of her *Life*.

For a decade after her recovery, Teresa underwent an agonizing spiritual struggle. She reports that she began to see in the Carmelites' formulaic religious practices a marked divergence from the fervent devotions and spiritual communion described in Francisco's *Primer*. Then, in 1555, Teresa underwent a conversion experience. Viewing a statue of Christ on the cross and meditating on his suffering, she sensed the presence of God; she later wrote, "I could

not possibly doubt that He was within me or that I was wholly engulfed in Him." Convinced that she had been granted a mystical union with God as a result of her intense meditation and prayer, she began to advocate a more contemplative, ascetic life for the Carmelites and to plan for the establishment of reformed Carmelite convents. Teresa's confessors, concerned that her claims to divine union might arouse the suspicions of the Inquisition and believing that her command of Catholic doctrine would prevent possible accusations of subverting Church authority, urged her to write an account of these experiences. Completed in 1562, this project became the first part of her autobiography, relating her childhood up through her conversion experience and the founding of the first reformed, or Discalced, convent.

Between 1563 and 1576 Teresa travelled throughout Spain, establishing Discalced Carmelite convents. During this period Teresa formed a friendship with St. John of the Cross, who became her counterpart in the monastic branch of the Carmelite Order. In 1576 she took a brief respite from her travels but continued writing, producing several works, among which were *El libro de las fundaciones de Santa Teresa de Jesús* (1576; *The Book of the*

Foundations), a continuation of her autobiography with an account of the Carmelite reform, and *El castillo interior, o las moradas* (1577; *The Interior Castle; or, The Mansions*), an allegory of the process of spiritual maturation. After 1577 members of the Catholic church and clergy became antagonistic toward Teresa's reforms. For the remaining five years of her life, she sought to placate the opposition and warned her followers against forsaking the teachings of the reformed Carmelite order. In 1582, during a series of journeys to various Discalced convents, Teresa became seriously ill. As she prepared to return to Avila, her superior, Father Antonio de Jesús Heredia, kidnapped Teresa and her travelling companions, taking them to Alba so that Teresa would be present to bless the birth of the heir of the powerful Duke of Alba. Teresa's condition deteriorated so severely during the course of the trip that the group tried to stop, but because of opposition to the Discalced movement they were refused shelter even at Carmelite houses. Teresa died shortly after reaching Alba.

The central theme of Teresa's works is the human need to become united with God. Although it is ostensibly an autobiography, Teresa's *Life* explains the mystics' methods and doctrine for achieving this mystical intercourse. She argues that a life of devotion to prayer and holiness will lead to the granting of a special communion with God. To substantiate this claim, she relates what has become her most renowned mystic experience, later depicted by Gianlorenzo Bernini in his sculpture *The Ecstasy of St. Teresa.* Teresa reported that, on this occasion, an angel stood at her left side and plunged a flaming spear representing the holiness of God into her breast, producing a pain so intense "that it caused me some moaning but the sweetness caused by this great pain was also so superlative that there was no desire to lose it since the soul is not satisfied by anything less than God." In *The Interior Castle,* which is considered to be Teresa's most important work, she likens the process of contemplation and prayer by which the individual finds unity with God to a journey through a crystal castle. As the pilgrim advances through the seven levels of the castle by means of prayer and contemplation, the path becomes increasingly difficult but the rewards more sublime until, at the seventh and innermost chamber, union with God is attained. *The Book of the Foundations, El camino de perfección* (1565; *The Way of Perfection*), and her correspondence contain more practical instructions to her followers and give concrete suggestions for a holy life. Critics have extolled Teresa's simple and direct writing style as well as the power, depth, and variety of her images, often citing her analogy of watering a garden in the *Life* and the castle imagery in *The Interior Castle* as her two most effective metaphors. Through the use of frequent digressions, incomplete sentences, extended parentheses, and unfinished explanations, Teresa seemingly engages her readers in a personal conversation, a quality which has also been admired by commentators.

Long revered for her importance as a writer of spiritual and devotional works, Teresa has received much critical attention as a literary figure during the twentieth century. Numerous scholars have praised her wit and entertaining prose style while recognizing her skill in clarifying enig-

matic theories. In recent years studies of Teresa's works have focused on more complex issues, including the influence of gender in her autobiography, the psychological implications of her writings and her mystic visions, as well as the rhetorical goals of her works. Critics such as Helmut A. Hatzfeld and Joseph Chorpenning have discussed the brilliant and complex imagery contained in Teresa's works, especially in the *Life* and *The Interior Castle.* Such studies have illuminated the subtle complexity of Teresa's work, leading to an increased appreciation of her skill as a writer of prose and the recognition that her works are, in the words of Evelyn Underhill, "at once among the glories of Spanish literature, and the best and most exact of guides to the mysteries of the inner life."

PRINCIPAL WORKS

*El libro de su vida (autobiography) 1562
  [*The Life of the Mother Teresa of Jesus,* 1611]
*El camino de perfección (treatise) 1565
  [*The Way of Perfection;* published in *The Way of Perfection and Conceptions of Divine Love,* 1852]
*Conceptos del amor de dios sobre algunas palabras de los cantares de Salomón (treatise) 1574
  [*Conceptions of Divine Love;* published in *The Way of Perfection and Conceptions of Divine Love,* 1852]
*El libro de las fundaciones de Santa Teresa de Jesús (autobiography) 1576
  [*The Second Part of the Life of the Holy Mother S. Teresa of Jesus; or, The History of the Foundations,* 1669; also published as *The Book of the Foundations,* 1853]
*El castillo interior, o las moradas (treatise) 1577
  [*The Interior Castle; or, The Mansions,* 1852]
Los libros de la Madre Teresa de Jesús (treatises, autobiography, essays, letters, and poetry) 1588
Obras de Santa Teresa de Jesus. 9 vols. (treatises, autobiographies, essays, letters, and poetry) 1915-24
The Complete Works of Saint Teresa of Jesus. 3 vols. (treatises, autobiographies, essays, and poetry) 1946
The Letters of Saint Teresa of Jesus (letters) 1951
The Collected Works of St. Teresa of Avila. 3 vols. (treatises, autobiographies, essays, letters, and poetry) 1976-85

---

*Represents completion of manuscript version. *El camino de perfección* was first published in 1583, *El libro de las fundaciones* in 1610. The remainder of Teresa's works, with the exception of excised portions of the *Conceptos del amor de dios,* were first published in the 1588 collected edition listed above.

James Fitzmaurice-Kelly   (essay date 1924)

[*Fitzmaurice-Kelly was an English scholar who wrote numerous books on Spanish literature, including* A New History of Spanish Literature *(1926), which was long regarded as the most accessible English text on the subject. In the following excerpt, he discusses St. Teresa's literary achievement.*]

[Santa Teresa] was born at Ávila on March 28, 1515. She was not cast into an atmosphere of morbid pietism. Her ancestors were mostly fighting men: of her seven brothers, six were soldiers who made a name for themselves in the New World. 'My father', says the saint, 'was very much given to the reading of good books'; her mother, she says in another passage, was much addicted to reading books of chivalry. Brought up in this atmosphere, it is not surprising that in collaboration with her brother Rodrigo, she should have written a chivalresque romance in her childhood. It would have been interesting to know how the saint, in this crude juvenile effort, disposed of her invincible knights and charming ladies, her colossal giants and astute dwarfs. But the childish effort has not survived, though we are informed that those who read it thought it extremely ingenious. This is not very credible, for it is precisely the ingenious note which is lacking in Santa Teresa's maturer work. She was soon called away from these early excursions into literature. Good man as he was, her father had no notion of playing the part of Jephthah the Gileadite in however modified a form, and when Teresa wished to enter the Carmelite Convent of the Incarnation at Ávila, he strenuously opposed the project. He resigned himself to the inevitable when the girl, though only sixteen, ran away from home in 1531. The rest of her life may be followed in a score of books in which her practical sense, her adroit diplomacy, her organizing faculties are duly celebrated. For those more interested in her solitary and enthusiastic youth, with its alternations of dejection and buoyancy of spirit, the drama of her checks, victories and indomitable struggles—these may be best read in that fascinating autobiography which was never intended for the public eye. In the *Libro de su vida,* in the *Libro de las fundaciones,* and in her copious correspondence we see the 'wonderful woman' in every aspect of her multiform character: confidential in the *Libro de su vida;* intellectual and aloof in the *Libro de las fundaciones;* personal, reproving, encouraging, cajoling, maternal—perhaps even a little fussy—in her innumerable letters. One derives from these three sources the impression that she combines in an extraordinary degree a practical faculty and positive sense with a power of subjective vision and poetic imagination. This singular combination of gifts, apparently incompatible, constitutes the rare originality of her genius and has for us a more permanent interest than her practical talent. Others might have reformed a religious order, others might have founded seventeen convents and fifteen monasteries. No one but Santa Teresa could have written the *Camino de perfección,* the *Conceptos del amor de Dios,* and, above all, the *Moradas* or *Castillo interior.* Here she deserves the epithet, so often applied to her, of 'our seraphic mother', here she recounts the amazing spiritual adventures of her lofty and romantic spirit, here she condenses all her unparalleled experiences of the inner life, leading her readers onwards step by step through the seven vestibules of her mystic castle till she conducts them at last to the ultimate annihilation of self and absorption in the Divine Essence.

Luckily for the world, her manuscripts came into the hands of Luis de Leon, himself a great writer, who instantly recognized a spirit akin to his own. He treated them with the most profound respect, always reading them, as he tells us, with increased admiration, never modifying a word, collating all copies with their originals, esteeming that in many passages he perceived a superhuman talent. In these mystic masterpieces, the saint reveals herself as a poet. She is never so much a poet as when she writes in prose. Her style is the expression of her unique personality. She turns away from art, she eschews rhetoric. Her vocabulary, varied, supple, and archaic (even at the time when she used it) is a model of the speech of the best society in Old Castile. You may find writers more correct, more elegant, more skilful in marshalling battalions of insubordinate words: you will only find in Spanish literature one writer who equals her in graphic force and in convincing simplicity. And it is that common trait—the trait of exquisite naturalness—which has led Froude to place Santa Teresa on the same level as Cervantes. Like Cervantes, Santa Teresa was a poet: but a poet only in prose. Both were poets who lacked the accomplishment of verse. She implicitly rejects the title of a poet in her *Vida* where, referring obviously to herself, she says: 'I know one who, though not a poet, improvized certain stanzas, heartfelt and expressive of her pain. They were not the product of her own understanding; but to enjoy more keenly that bliss which so sweet a pain caused her, she complained of it in that way to God'. The saint wrote verses very sparingly, not more than fourteen or fifteen poems have survived, perhaps not as many as a dozen, if we choose to be exacting as to evidence for authenticity. She burst into song on rare occasions, spontaneously, much as a blithe child will sing a simple song in sheer light-heartedness. It is as though 'the morning stars sang together', as though we had fragments of the mysterious song in the Book of the Revelation (xiv. 3) that none could learn 'but the hundred and forty and four thousand, which were redeemed from the earth'. The saint never enters upon the province of conscious art; she had a horror of rhetoric which would have commended her to Verlaine; her natural taste was for the simpler popular forms as in the Shepherd's Carol: **'Hoy nos viene a redimir',** well Englished by Mr. Arthur Symons:

> To-day, a shepherd and our kin,
> O Gil, to ransom us is sent,
> And he is God Omnipotent.
>
> For us hath He cast down the pride
> And prison wall of Satanas;
> But He is of the kin of Bras,
> Of Menga, also of Llorent.
> O is not God Omnipotent?
>
> If He is God, how then is He
> Come hither and here crucified?
> —With His dying sin also died,
> Enduring death the innocent,
> Gil, how is God Omnipotent!
>
> Why, I have seen Him born, pardie,
> And of a most sweet shepherdess.
> —If He is God, how can He be
> With such poor folk as these content?
> —Seest not He is Omnipotent?
>
> Give over idle parleyings,
> And let us serve Him, you and I,
> And since He came on earth to die,

Let us die with Him too, Llorent,
For He is God Omnipotent.

This little carol in dialogue exhibits Santa Teresa in a most characteristic mood. I am not unaware that the authenticity of this poem has been questioned. But I think I can reassure you on that head, for an autograph copy of the first three stanzas in the saint's handwriting has recently been discovered in Florence. The absence of the fourth stanza need not perplex us, nor exclude the simple little poem from the canon. For the saint never troubled to collect her verses, and was not always able to remember them. For instance, in writing to her brother, Lorenzo de Cepeda (January 2, 1577), she mentions a poem of hers **'O hermosura que excedéis'**, quotes three stanzas and then breaks off with the remark: 'I do not remember any more.'

Her personal taste was all for the popular forms of verse; but she was the child of her own time, and, being born at the beginning of the sixteenth century, just as she had a liking for *Amadis de Gaula,* she had a weakness for the alembicated songs of the *Cancioneros.* Doubtless, like her disciple Catalina de Jesús, she delighted in the celebrated lines of Escrivá—*Ven muerte tan escondida*—admired by Cervantes and by Calderon. Some echo of them and perhaps of some verses by Francisco Lopez de Villalobos may be caught in Santa Teresa's poem beginning:

> Vivo san vivir en mi,
> y tan alta vida espero,
> que muero porque no muero.

I do not say that these lines are the most typical of the saint's usual manner; they are more subtle than she is apt to be in verse, and are an interesting anticipation of the *conceptismo* represented by Quevedo and Gracian in the following century. At any rate, this composition, written at Salamanca in 1571, as we know from the saint's colleague Sor Isabel de Jesús, is the most famous of all Santa Teresa's verses; much of it is known by heart throughout the peninsula, and its wide popularity is such that its inclusion imposes itself on the most autocratic anthologist. It is generally known as Santa Teresa's 'Gloss'; and, as far as I know, there does not exist any adequate rendering of the poem in English. (pp. 74-83)

> *James Fitzmaurice-Kelly, "Two Mystic Poets," in his* Some Masters of Spanish Verse, *Oxford University Press, London, 1924, pp. 73-93.*

Evelyn Underhill   (essay date 1925)

[*Underhill was an English poet and critic who wrote several important works on mysticism. In the following excerpt, she discusses Teresa's works in the context of the sixteenth-century Spanish mystic movement.*]

Formed in part by the Ignatian spirit and method, and receiving through St. Peter the influence of Franciscan mysticism, St. Teresa (1515-82) was also touched by all the other mystical forces and persons active in sixteenth-century Spain; so that any real account of Spanish mysticism must give to her the central place. She first learnt the art of meditation from the writings of the Franciscan friar

Osuna (*c.* 1540); she corresponded with the Blessed John of Avila, the "Apostle of Andalusia" (1500-69), and a close acquaintance of the early Jesuits. St. John of the Cross (1542-91), one of the few supreme Christian contemplatives, was her devoted colleague and friend. The richness and charm of St. Teresa's character can still be felt in her works—more read, perhaps, than those of any other mystic. She is the classic example of that complete flowering of personality in which the life of contemplation does not tend to specialism, but supports and enhances a strenuous, active career. To write a series of works which are at once among the glories of Spanish literature, and the best and most exact of guides to the mysteries of the inner life; to practise, and describe with an unequalled realism, the highest degrees of prayer and contemplation; to found numerous convents in the face of apparently insuperable difficulties; to reform a great religious Order in spite of the opposition of those pious conservatives whom she was accustomed to call pussy-cats; to control at once the financial and spiritual situations of her enterprise, and to do all this in spite of persistent ill-health in a spirit of unfailing common sense, of gaiety, of dedicated love—this, which is far from exhausting the list of St. Teresa's activities, seems a sufficient programme for one soul.

The chief events of her life are well known, and need only be given briefly here. A girl of the aristocratic class, romantic and ardent in temperament, fond of all activities, of pleasure and social intercourse, she was nevertheless drawn early to religion; and became a novice in the Carmelite Convent of the Incarnation at Avila before she was twenty years of age. Four years later she fell seriously ill, was paralysed for two years, and emerged with her first spiritual ardour much reduced. For a time she gave up contemplative prayer, in which she had already made some progress, and acquiesced in the lax religious life of her convent. A struggle now began, and lasted for over twelve years, between Teresa's mystical vocation and her very human love of active life. This conflict testifies to the breadth and essential sanity of her mind, capable of a wide range of inward and outward interest and response. She has described vividly in the early chapters of her autobiography the alternations of her divided will, never able to give up the life of prayer and self-oblation, yet never willing entirely to capitulate to its imperious demands.

> On the one side God was calling me, on the other I was following the world. All the things of God gave me great pleasure, and I was a prisoner to the things of the world. It seemed as if I wished to reconcile two contradictions so much at variance with one another as are the life of the spirit and the joys, pleasures and amusements of sense. . . . I passed nearly twenty years on this stormy sea, falling and rising, but rising to no good purpose seeing that I went and fell again.

Her real state was hidden from her companions, who, seeing her love of helping souls, and her many acts of devotion, held her in special honour; a fact which increased her shame and self-contempt. At last, with the beginning of middle-age, the struggle reached its term; states of recollection and peace gradually began to predominate over the longing for outward distractions, and, as she says, her "prayer began to be solid like a house"—a truly Teresian phrase, bringing before us her profound distrust of emotional fancies, her craving for an unadorned reality.

Her forty-first year saw the end of the period of conflict; and Teresa's full mystical life at last began. Prepared in the hiddenness during the purifying years of temptation, it developed swiftly. In two years she had passed through those degrees of prayer called "quiet" and "union," which are so marvellously described in the *Life,* and reached the heights of ecstatic contemplation. It is unnecessary to describe the long series of "visions" and "voices," the trances and states of rapturous absorption which would now come upon her, even in public, to her great distress; and which at first puzzled and alarmed her spiritual advisers. These were simply the abnormal means by which an exceptionally ardent and imaginative nature realized and expressed its overwhelming experience of God. St. Teresa's own frank and detailed account of them, and of the tests by which she tried to avoid delusion, is—thanks to her remarkable genius for self-analysis—one of the most important psychological documents which we possess. It was at this time that she was first helped by the sober wisdom and experience of the early Jesuit fathers, and the Ignatian spirituality made its great contribution to the developing mysticism of Spain.

The steady growth of her contemplative power brought with it the inevitable longing for a life of greater austerity and seclusion; impossible to achieve in the Convent of the Incarnation, where the nuns were unenclosed, and saw much of their friends in the world. More and more the laxity of the Rule displeased and distressed her, though it was not until the year 1560 that she first realized her call to found a convent in poverty, where the life of self-denial might be fully lived. The active and creative side of Teresa's character, in abeyance during the first intense and largely educative years of her mystical life, now again asserted itself, but in complete subjection to her spiritual ideals. After great difficulty, she was able in 1562, when forty-seven years of age, to found the Convent of St. Joseph at Avila; a small and poor house, where the primitive Rule of Mount Carmel was strictly observed.

This period of St. Teresa's career was also that of her fullest and most continuous mystical experience: which, far from interfering with her practical undertakings, illuminated and supported them from within. The very object of her soul's union with God was, as she said in a memorable passage, "Work! work! work!" Her prayers, visions, and states of enraptured communion made her "more courageous and more free"; and gave her fresh energy and determination to deal with the obstacles which threatened again and again to wreck her enterprise.

> In the very grievous trials, persecutions, and contradictions of these months, God gave me great courage; and the more grievous they were, the greater the courage, without weariness in suffering.

That balanced and completed life of work and contemplation in which we seem to glimpse the sort of free response to the material and spiritual orders which awaits the maturity of man, was now hers. The spiritual and practical sides of her nature were completely harmonized. She could turn from directions about the finances of the community or the right sweeping down of the house, to deal in a manner equally wise and precise with the most delicate problems of the soul. Entirely given up from this time to the reforming and spiritualizing of the convents of her Order, and the educating of individual souls, St. Teresa is a classic example of the place which the mystic can and should fill in the life of the Church; and completely answers the charges of spiritual selfishness and aloofness from practical problems sometimes brought against its contemplative saints. Indeed, it was often in physical hardships—the long journeys which she confesses she disliked, or the deprivation even of needful warmth and food—that she found the material of her inward joys.

> We were (she says of her adventurous foundation of a convent in Toledo) for some days with no other furniture but two straw mattresses and one blanket, not even a withered leaf to fry a sardine with, till someone, I know not who, moved by our Lord, put a faggot in the church, with which we helped ourselves. At night it was cold, and we felt it. . . . The poverty we were in seemed to me as the source of a sweet contemplation.

The books through which her vivid spirit still reaches and affects us were written in the intervals of her many enterprises and journeys, as foundress and reformer of religious houses. Thanks to her innate literary power—for she ranks among the great prose writers of Spain—and to her frankness and psychological insight, these books, helped by her vivid and intimate letters of which a large number have been preserved, reveal Teresa's personality to us as few of the mystics have been revealed.

Two are autobiographical. The *Life,* dealing largely with her mystical experiences, was written at the wish of her directors. It brings the story of her development to the point at which she founded her first convent and began her active career, when she was about forty years old. This book, with its wonderfully clear and detailed account of the visionary and ecstatic phenomena which accompanied the education of her soul, has been ever since the *locus classicus* for those who desire to know what the higher degrees of mystical prayer, and the states of consciousness leading to and completed in ecstasy, feel like to those who experience them. The *Book of Foundations* deals with the ruling interests and events of her career as reformer and foundress; telling the story of the sixteen reformed convents of nuns which she established—often in circumstances of great difficulty—during the last fifteen years of her life. This work alone, so full of human interest and spiritual ardour, and abounding in examples of Teresian courage, wit, and common sense, is enough to establish her place among the great women of the Christian Church.

St. Teresa's other books contain the substance of her teaching on prayer and contemplation. *The Way of Perfection* was written for the sisters of St. Joseph's at Avila in the year 1566; *The Interior Castle,* her fullest and most orderly account of the spiritual life, in 1577. The brilliant and romantic girl, torn between the claims of two worlds, the exalted and courageous woman of prayer, with her unique combination of ecstasy and practicality, was now an experienced old nun. Physically worn out by ill-health, and the long and trying journeys undertaken for her reform, she had only five years to live. She was well versed in all the follies and self-deceptions of the religious temperament; had borne persecution, misunderstanding, and obstruction from the ecclesiastical authorities, had known failure as well as success. She knew all the exhaustion and desolations of the spiritual life, and the hard lot of the teacher who must often through her own interior darkness continue to help others toward the light.

> No foundation was made without trouble. . . . What it is to have to contend against many minds! . . . Inwardly ill at ease, my soul was in very great dryness and darkness. . . . My health is generally weak, but I saw clearly that our Lord gives me strength. . . . I never refrained from making a foundation for fear of trouble, though I felt a great dislike to journeys, especially long ones. . . . It was my want of health that most frequently wearied me. . . . The weather was severe, and I, so old and sickly!

Phrases like these, scattered through the accounts of her superhuman activities, remind us of the ceaseless external tension within which her own spiritual life achieved maturity, and some of its greatest moments were experienced by her. That life had indeed become one of constant and perfect intercourse with God—that deep and active union which some of the mystics have called the "spiritual marriage" or "transforming union" of the soul; and which she herself describes in the last chapters of *The Interior Castle.* Thus the difference between St. Teresa's first great book and her last, is the difference between the diary of the discoverer, and the considered instructions of the expert. *The Interior Castle* teaches the gradual unfolding of the spiritual consciousness under the image of the successive habitations which the key of prayer unlocks for the soul. It is full of Teresa's own bracing spirit; her dislike of all pretensions, all seeking for consolations, all idle and dreamy enjoyments, all spiritual conceit.

> The soul must be virile, not like those soldiers who lie down on their stomachs to drink when they are being led into battle. It must not dream of sweetness and enjoyments at the beginning of its career. Manna does not fall in the first habitations—we must press on further if we want to gather it! Then alone will the soul find all things to its taste, when it has learned to will only that which God wills. How comic our pretensions are! We are still immersed in difficulties and imperfections, we have virtues that can barely toddle, others hardly born; and we are not ashamed to demand sweetness in prayer, we grumble at dryness! May you never behave like that, sisters. Embrace the Cross—the rest is a mere extra. If God gives it you, thank Him meekly!

The very spirit of Spanish mysticism, militant, austere, practical, is in these words; and this realistic and active conception of the soul's true business and God's true demand on it, which had steadily developed during the course of her own mystical life, now follows her even to

the recesses of that "Seventh Habitation" where the divine union is achieved. For her that union means the total transfiguration of character: every power and aspect of the self enhanced, and dedicated to the redemptive purposes of God. She turns from the trances, ecstasies, visions, all that wealth of abnormal experiences which had accompanied the growth of her own soul. The ideal she now puts before her pupils is far indeed from that of the quietist.

> What is the good, my daughters, of being deeply recollected in solitude, and multiplying acts of love, and promising our Lord to do wonders in His service, if, when we come out of our prayer, the least thing makes us do the exact opposite? . . . The repose which those souls enjoy whom I speak of now is inward only; they have, and desire to have, less outwardly. For to what end, do you think, the soul sends from this Seventh Habitation, and as it were from her very deeps, aspirations into all the other habitations of this spiritual castle? Do you think these messages to faculties, senses and body, have no other end but to invite them to sleep? No, no, no! Rather to employ them more than ever. . . . Moreover, the company the soul now enjoys gives her a strength she never had before. If, as David says, one becomes holy with the holy, who can doubt that this soul, who is now become *one thing* with the Mighty God by this high union of spirit with Spirit, shares His strength? It is hence that the saints have drawn that courage which made them capable of suffering and dying for their God.

>   (pp. 172-81)

> *Evelyn Underhill, "Spanish Mysticism," in her* The Mystics of the Church, *James Clarke & Co. Ltd., 1925, pp. 168-86.*

E. Allison Peers   (essay date 1927)

[*Peers was an English scholar and educator. Specializing in the Spanish mystics and Romantics, he founded the quarterly* Bulletin of Spanish Studies *and published numerous books including* Spanish Mysticism *(1924) and* Studies of the Spanish Mystics *(1927). Peers has also written several studies of Saint Teresa, and in the following excerpt, he considers the style of Teresa's poetry and prose.*]

The principal writings of St. Teresa extend over a period of rather less than twenty years. Her *Life (Libro de su vida)*, which is mainly an account of her spiritual progress, was written between 1562 and 1565, the version now extant being a revision of an earlier story of her life, finished in the year 1562. In 1564 comes the *Constitutions,* a work of small importance for our purpose, and in the following year the *Way of Perfection (Camino de perfección)*, which, though it contains much mystical wisdom, is the most suitable of St. Teresa's books for more general devotional reading. The little known but beautiful *Conceptions of the Love of God* were written between 1567 and 1575, and the *Exclamations* probably in 1569. St. Teresa's next and last great work, however, the *Mansions* (or *Moradas,* also known, especially in English, as the *Interior Castle*),was not written till 1577. It was composed very rapidly, for the most part in the convents of Toledo and Avila, by the command of Padre Gracián and Don Alonso Velázquez, afterwards Bishop of Osma. There had previously been published another notable work, the ***Book of the Foundations,*** which, as its title implies, is mainly concerned with the foundations of the Reform; the ***Relations,*** or Reports, written by St. Teresa to her Directors on her spiritual life, bear dates between 1560 and 1579. The minor works, written at various times, include a number of poems, hymns and other verses, and . . . numerous letters . . . , of which nearly five hundred are extant. (pp. 151-52)

There are those who, whether out of devotion to St. Teresa or from other motives, have desired to pay her the supreme literary honour to which any Spanish mystical author could aspire. They have credited her with the superb sonnet "To Christ Crucified". . . . External evidence alone renders her authorship highly improbable. The sonnet is found in none of the collections of poems attributed to St. Teresa, nor in any form which of itself suggests her authorship. It was not thought of as hers till more than two hundred years after her death. The form of the poem, too, is over-complicated for St. Teresa, who never (except possibly once, and in lines that are doubtfully hers) uses any Italian metre, preferring the traditional popular measures of Spain. The attribution to St. Francis Javier depends on a Latin paraphrase of the poem (or what may be such) which is found in his letters. But, as has been abundantly demonstrated, many other hypotheses than that which it is sought to prove are deducible from the discovery of the Latin hymn. Other suggested authors are St. Ignatius of Loyola (the attribution to whom, however, is a late one), Fray Pedro de los Reyes, and (a quite recent suggestion) Fray Miguel de Guevara. The last guess seems the least unlikely, since the sonnet appears as his own work in a book undoubtedly his; and though the date of this is not earlier than 1638, the theory is the most significant contribution to the discussion which has as yet been put forward.

Whoever may have written the poem, we need no external proofs to convince us that it is not St. Teresa's. The sentiments, it is true, might well have been uttered by her; the masterly execution, however, places her authorship beyond the bounds of probability. Poet, indeed, she was, but her true medium was not verse, but prose. Very many passages in her prose works glow with the divine fire, a flame kindled first of all in the heart of the Divine Love. In prose she has free play: the torrent of inspired thoughts flows swiftly along, cutting a way for itself, unhindered, through landscapes of surpassing beauty. But, when she wrote verse, her inspiration was checked and pent up by restraints which she had never learned to master. So her lines go haltingly: her stanzas are weak and jingling. Hymns for use on special occasions she could write, and not infrequently did write, with tolerable success. Their poetic quality, however, is soon and surely estimated. Their only charms are an occasional striking simplicity and artlessness, a facility of expression, an apt refrain—the charms of the popular ballad. (pp. 202-03)

[St. Teresa] never claimed the title of poet—in all proba-

bility never dreamed that she would figure in Spanish literature. She did not even think of herself as a writer, nor aim at consciously artistic composition. "My style is so heavy," begins the ***Book of the Foundations,*** "that in spite of my wishes I fear I shall weary others and myself as well." Most of her books were written unwillingly, under obedience; many of them at irregular intervals and amid various kinds of distraction; all of them with a moral and spiritual aim and no other. Of form she recks little. "It is a long time," she will remark unconcernedly, "since I wrote the last pages, and I have had no opportunity to return to the book, so that I cannot remember what I said unless I read it all over. To save time I shall have to write what comes from my mind, without any proper connection." This gives one a fair idea of how her works were written—in odd moments, whether of inspiration or merely of temporary leisure, with no thought to anything save that they should be profitable to those who read them. In one of the mystical passages of the ***Life,*** there is a pathetic little phrase, the simple eloquence of which needs no elaboration. "This,"—referring to a metaphorical passage—"can be well understood by such as have intelligence, and they will be able to apply it more clearly than I can explain it,—*and I grow tired.*"

We shall no more expect, then, to find artistic perfection in her prose than in her verse. Not merely is she unlearned in philosophy, but (according to her own self-estimate) she has none of the qualities which make a writer. She refers constantly to her ignorance, her weakness of memory, her stupidity, and frankly confesses herself incapable of expressing in words what she would. She declares again and again that for every reason, save that she has been *commanded* to write, she is totally unfitted for doing so. "Why do they want me to write?" she said to Gracián, when he importuned her to write the book now known as the ***Mansions.*** "Let learned men who have studied write, for I am stupid and shall not know what I say. I shall put down one word after another and simply do harm. There are enough books written on prayer: for the love of God, let them leave me to my distaff and the choir and the offices of religion, like the other sisters. I am not a writer: have neither the health nor the head for it."

If her works, then, have come down to us as literature, it is as literature *malgré elle.* "My memory is so poor" (*por tener yo poca memoria*) ends the preface to the ***Foundations.***

> My memory is so poor, that I think many important things will be left out, and others will be told which could well be spared: in fact it will be of a piece with my scanty abilities and rudeness of style (*mi poco ingenio y grosería*), and the little peace I get for writing.
>
> I am like one who hears a voice from afar off, but although hearing the voice cannot distinguish the words; for at times I do not understand what I say, yet it is the Lord's pleasure that it should be well said, and if at times I talk nonsense that is because it is natural to me to do nothing well (*no acertar en nada*).
>
> Just as birds who are taught to speak know only

what they are shown or what they hear, and repeat that many times, exactly so am I.

> The Lord knows how full of confusion I am in writing on some of these subjects (*El Señor sabe la confusión con que escribo mucho de lo que escribo*): may He be praised for His patience in bearing with me.

Nevertheless, even the most exacting critic can take lessons of one kind or another from this "confused" writer.

The most striking characteristic of St. Teresa's writings from the standpoint of literature is the richness and variety of her images. This can only be explained in one way. Throughout her life, even in moments of leisure and recreation, her imagination was ever in her Master's hands, to be shaped and moulded by Him for His glory. Not only could a visit to the Duchess of Alba (an occasion long to be remembered) furnish her with illustrations to a theme: half an hour's walk would yield her parables enough for a book. She, at least, can draw rich spiritual profit from Nature. The *palmito,* which Andalucian children grub up, strip of its leaves and eat, becomes to her a symbol of the mystic life. The first attempt of some tiny bird to leave its nest suggests the need of the soul for a wise director. Some straws blowing in the wind are utilized in a description of the Prayer of Quiet, and again in an account of the sixth Mansions. The sky seems to attract St. Teresa less than it attracts the "two Luises," and in general she draws less profit from the great sights of Nature—mountains, valleys, roads, forests and the like—than from Nature's accidents. A wayside ditch starts a train of thought upon mortal sins and false virtues, and a mud wall supplies an illustration of humility. And the familiar ass—let us quote St. Teresa's own words: "I think the soul is like a little donkey, at pasture, which crops its food and eats almost without thinking of it."

This fondness for images grew upon St. Teresa with age, and it is in her *Mansions* that we find the most pregnant of them all. Especially lavish is she of similitudes drawn from living creatures. Here, again, she prefers the smaller to the greater. There is little in her works of horses, dogs, or cows—much of birds and of insects. "I believe," she says, "that in each tiny creature that God has made, be it but a little ant, there is more than we understand." And an apocryphal passage on the earthworm seems to us so characteristic of St. Teresa's manner that were it not for strong internal evidence to the contrary we should regard as wholly genuine the letter in which it occurs.

Birds, bees and butterflies figure again and again in the Saint's expositions, until they seem to become an almost essential part of them. The powers of the soul in the Prayer of Quiet are beautifully compared to doves, which, "not content with the food that is given them from the dove-cote without effort on their part, go and seek food elsewhere, and have such ill-success that they return." From time to time the bird strays from its nest, striving by reason and imaginings to attain to heights impossible to its strength; then it is that "the Lord comes and takes this little bird and puts it back in the nest that it may rest there." The soul of the mystic, indeed, is not unlike a bird "which flies here and there finding no place to rest."

The bee teaches industry and humility, prudence and ambition—a comprehensive symbolism!

> Let humility ever be at work, like the bee in the hive making honey: without this, all is lost. But let us consider that the bee does not neglect to fly out in search of flowers, and even so should the soul leave the hive of self-knowledge and soar upward from time to time to meditate upon the greatness and majesty of God.

> Let the soul remain in fruition of that favour [the Prayer of Quiet], and recollected like the prudent bee; for if no bees entered the hive, but all of them left it to wander about after each other, the honey could with difficulty be made.

As to the butterfly, it is used so many times that quotation is impossible. But a classic example may come under this heading. One day, St. Teresa learns of the process by which silk is produced. She has never heard this before, and it makes a deep impression upon her. But the idea which germinates is a spiritual one; it takes root in her mind, springs up and grows, and before long finds expression in one of the noblest passages of the *Mansions*. . . . (pp. 210-15)

Like many greater writers, St. Teresa had the habit of thinking in images, and it is partly her apt and lavish use of them which makes her so easy, and even entertaining, to read. Again and again a simple comparison makes some abstract matter perfectly clear, and St. Teresa, though apparently confusing her metaphors, can pass from picture to picture without sacrificing any of her clearness. Look, for example, at the passage in the early part of the *Mansions* where the novice (one had almost said the "traveller") is urged before proceeding farther to consider the dreadful effects of sin. Here we have first an amassing of metaphors, then a playing upon two or three of them. At one point it is hard to say if the soul is a stream or a tree, but the thought beneath the images is never lost.

> Before we go farther I wish you to consider what happens when mortal sin invades this beautiful, resplendent castle, this pearl of the east, this tree of life, planted in the living waters of life—that is, in God. There is no gloom so murky, no darkness so black, but that this is vastly more so. You need only know that the very sun, which is still within the soul, and which gave it such splendour and beauty, is as if it were not, for all the soul knows of Him, though it is as meet to enjoy His fulness as is the crystal to shine in the sun . . . .

> Like as all the streams which flow from a crystal spring are themselves crystal-clear, so is also the soul in grace; its works are well-pleasing in the eyes both of God and of man, for they flow from the source of life in which the soul is planted as it were a tree. Did it not proceed thence it would bear neither leafage nor fruit, for the waters sustain it, and water it, and cause it to bear good fruit. And thus from the soul which through its sins leaves the living waters and grows in a dark and noisome pool all that proceeds is foul and filthy like itself. You must note here that it is not the source—not the brilliant sun within the

soul—that loses its beauty and splendour, for that it has always and nothing can take it away. It is as if a perfectly black cloth had been thrown over a crystal which was in the sunshine; the sun may shine on it indeed, but its brilliance cannot reach the crystal.

Another illustration may be taken from the same chapter: the subject is the virtues of true humility. Here we have, not a sustained figure, but a succession of images chosen singly by the writer, each to make one point. To attempt to place the metaphors (which are italicized below) in one composite picture leads to absurdity; we must either invent a succession of pictures, or else turn the metaphors into plain, imageless prose:

> I repeat, then, that it is good—nay, it is excellent—to *enter the room of humility* first, rather than to fly to the other rooms, for *this is the right road. If we can travel along this safely and easily, why need we ask for wings with which to fly?* Let us seek to make the greatest progress in the way we are going. . . . I think we shall never know ourselves until we have endeavoured to know God, for . . . by considering His humility, we shall find how far we are ourselves from being humble.
>
> There are two advantages in so doing. First, it is clear that *anything white placed near black seems far whiter,* and that *black seems the darker against white.* Secondly, our understanding and will become nobler and more inclined to all good, when they turn from themselves to God; we do ourselves despite *if we never rise above the mire of our own wretchedness.* As we were saying of those in mortal sin, *how dark and noisome are the streams of their lives;* so here . . . while *we are sunk in earthly misery, the stream of our life will never leave the mire* of fear, weakness and cowardice.

The second great quality of St. Teresa's style is its simplicity and directness. She may, indeed, when a girl, have composed a chivalric romance, as her biographer Ribera would have us believe, but there is no trace, in her maturer works, of the peculiarly extravagant affectations which marked this class of fiction. Rather there is an abhorrence and a conscious avoidance of anything not straightforward and simple. Her style is as devoid of pedantry and oratory as of affectation. She aimed at writing exactly as though she were speaking, that is, as the ordinary person spoke in the Old Castile of the sixteenth century. A Spanish critic, in an excellent little monograph on St. Teresa's language [D. Antonio Sánchez Moguel, *El lenguaje de Santa Teresa de Jesús*], remarks that in all her work there are fewer than twenty words which can properly be called learned (*cultas*), thus: éxtasis, paroxismo, hipocresía, pusilánime. And even these words she wrote in their popular, everyday forms: estasi, parajismo, yproquesia, pusilamine. She frequently used popular, incorrect constructions or forms of words; Latinisms, Gallicisms and Italianisms, on the other hand, abundant as they were in her contemporaries' works, she completely eschewed. The two concomitants of familiar Spanish conversation—especially among women—are an excess of diminutives and a continual—frequently an effective—recourse to the superlative. Both diminutives and superlatives abound in St. Teresa, and this fact, together with the abnormal length of her sentences, and a conversational tendency to ellipsis, makes her one of the hardest writers to translate with any adequacy, though by no means the hardest to read. Her most eloquent pages are not those in which any subtle art of hers conceals art. They are those in which the torrent of her inspired thought has risen so overmasteringly as to overflow its usual bounds; in which her love has poured forth in floods of words and the writer has committed them to paper as rapidly as they formed in her mind. From her very heart she wrote as from her heart she spoke: that was all her skill. (pp. 216-18)

> *E. Allison Peers, "St. Teresa," in his* Studies of the Spanish Mystics, *Vol. I,* The Sheldon Press, *1927, pp. 133-226.*

E. A. Ryan   (essay date 1944)

[*In the following excerpt from a review of Thomas Walsh's biography of Teresa,* St. Teresa of Avila *(1943) and David Lewis's translation of* El libro de su vida *(1943), Ryan suggests that Teresa's works represent a coherent assimilation and synthesis of the tenets of mystical theology.*]

One of the trends of Christian spirituality at the beginning of the modern period (from 1500 on) was to systematization. This should be attributed to the revival of learning and to the comparative ease of access to the spiritual literature of the past which came in ever-increasing volume from the newly invented printing press. With such a mass of spiritual reading at hand, souls felt the need of guides to the essentials.

Often enough enthusiasts for St. Teresa of Spain have failed to see that she was in this matter quite in accord with her times. She has been praised as the most original of all Christians or at least of all Spanish Christians. It has been said that nothing borrowed can be found in her works. All is bright and shiny and new. This opinion does not lack some arguments to support it. St. Teresa certainly had no formal education and she did not know the languages required for laborious research into the literature of past spirituality. Moreover no one may deny her brilliant genius, her breadth of understanding, her remarkable intuition and the abundance of divine light which flooded her soul.

Pius X, however, in a letter to the Carmelites dated March 7, 1914, took an opposite view. He noted, with the greatest theologians of the age of Teresa, that *"quae de mystica theologia Patres Ecclesiae passim et obscure tradidissent, ea concinne in unum corpus ab hac virgine esse redacta"* (mystical theology, which had been taught without system and obscurely by the Fathers of the Church, was by this Virgin reduced to a harmonious body of doctrine). St. Teresa's genius was for assimilation and synthesis rather than for originality. If she expressed Catholic Spain so well, it was because she owed some of the richest elements of her personality to her race and century. She was never content to remain ignorant. If she could read neither Latin nor Greek, she could pick the brains of her confessors and of other learned men. Above all she read and meditated on the substantial Spanish treatises, particularly those of the Franciscans Osuna and Laredo. This gave her the traditional spiritual doctrine which was tested in due course in the laboratory of her own soul. Later on, when writing her experiences, she transmitted what she had learned and controlled to the Church of the future. She was passing along the heritage of the Middle Ages. She was not an innovator. Her writings stem from the very heart of Catholic tradition; and through her confessors, Franciscans, Jesuits, Dominicans and Carmelites, she was able to keep abreast of progressive spiritual thought in that erudite century.

Like all true Christian spirituality, that of Teresa centers on the God-man and is not a little suspicious of those who are anxious to transcend the life and passion of Christ. In her life, as well as in her teaching, mortifications and mystical experiences are never a self-sufficient norm. Ecstasy, for her, is good if the soul receives virtues during it. Revelations can be of divine origin only if they lead to spiritual action. Teresa was a realist. Those who look upon the life of prayer and contemplation as an escape should not look to Teresa for corroboration. Giving herself unreservedly to divine love, she found that it never grew insipid and, unlike voluptuousness, it never dried up the heart. For Teresa those who make human love the highest quest are the real escapists. It is divine love which gives a principle of

"St. Teresa in Ecstasy" by Gehard Seghers.

balance and energy, joyful certitude, and victory over suffering, separation and death.

Another service Teresa rendered to spirituality was the clarification of mystical terminology. Her junior contemporary, St. Robert Bellarmine, remarked that mystical authors are praised by some and blamed by others because what they say is understood in different ways. Teresa did much to remove this confusion. She had the genius to evolve a fixed classification of the mystical states which she then exploited in each of her works with the aid of new metaphors and allegories.

Some psychologists for whom mysticism is merely a form of eroticism have analyzed Teresa's vocabulary and reached uncomplimentary conclusions. These are based on mistaken notions. For the psychologists in question were blissfully ignorant of the Biblical and traditional origins of Teresa's erotic expressions. They also failed to observe that she uses them in conjunction with a great number of others drawn from nature and the Bible. In all this there is nothing personal. She is systematizing the terminology of the Spanish authors she knew. Metaphors were necessary to express what they had to say and they merely continued and passed on the traditional expressions. (pp. 141-42)

> *E. A. Ryan, in a review of "Saint Teresa of Avila" and "Life of Saint Teresa of Jesus," in* THOUGHT, *Vol. XIX, No. 72, March, 1944, pp. 141-43.*

Joseph F. Chorpenning   (essay date 1979)

[*Chorpenning is an American scholar and critic. In the following excerpt, he explores Teresa's use of the castle symbol in* Castillo interior.]

Since Alfred Morel-Fatio's inventory and study of "Les Lectures de Sainte Thérèse," the question of the sources of St. Teresa's metaphors and symbols has teased scholars. The provenance of the interior castle symbol especially has been the focus of scholarly attention. St. Teresa herself explains its origin in this way at the beginning of the *Castillo interior* (its full title is the *Moradas del castillo interior*): "Estando hoy suplicando a nuestro Señor hablase por mí—porque yo no atinava a cosa que decir ni cómo comenzar a cumplir esta obediencia [she was commanded to compose the *Castillo* under obedience]—se me ofreció lo que ahora diré para comenzar con algún fundamento, que es considerar nuestra alma como un castillo todo de un diamante u muy claro cristal, adonde hay muchos aposentos, ansí como en el cielo hay muchas moradas." Some eleven years after the composition of the *Castillo* (1577), Fray Diego de Yepes, St. Teresa's former confessor and later biographer, in a letter to Fray Luis de León, the first editor of the saint's works, claims that St. Teresa told him that the symbol was of divine origin, having come to her in a vision. Regardless of the testimony of the saint herself, or of that she allegedly gave Yepes, the symbol is not independent of literary sources. Scholars such as Rodolphe Hoornaert, Gaston Etchegoyen, and, more recently, Robert Ricard have found it or an analogue, for example, in Ludolph of Saxony's *Vita Christi*, Fray Francisco de

Osuna's *Tercer abecedario espiritual* and *Ley de amor santo,* and Fray Bernardino de Laredo's *Subida del monte Sión,* all books with which St. Teresa was familiar. Consequently, although the difficulty of locating the immediate literary sources of this symbol has been surmounted, it is virtually impossible to say that it is derivative of this or that single work. In fact, as Ricard has concluded after closely inspecting the numerous possible origins of this symbol, St. Teresa fused divers sources "dans une synthèse organique."

Up to this point, then, studies of the castle symbol by and large have been devoted to trying to track down its exact sources, and little, if any, attention has been paid to other matters related to it. For instance, closely related to St. Teresa's adoption of the architectural symbol of the castle from her immediate literary sources is the way she uses it in the *Castillo interior,* i.e., her literary and theological method of associating each part of the spiritual doctrine that she wished to present in this work with a part of the structure of the castle symbol, which she also borrows from the literary and theological tradition that preceded her. In the great amount of critical literature on the castle symbol, no mention is made of this relationship. Similarly, even in Helmut Hatzfeld's discussion of the literary method of the *Castillo* in his book *Santa Teresa de Ávila,* one looks in vain for commentary on this aspect of the *Castillo.* The purpose of this paper is to correct this state of affairs by providing a commentary on this unjustly neglected facet of the *Castillo interior.* Our commentary begins with a brief survey of the remote and immediate precedents for the *Castillo's* method, namely, the use of architectural symbols in theological writings during the Patristic period and Middle Ages and in the works of Ludolph, Osuna, and Laredo that have been identified as sources for the Castle symbol in this work, respectively. Next, it examines why and how St. Teresa used the Castle symbol in the *Castillo.* And it concludes by arguing that an appreciation of the *Castillo's* method is indispensable or understanding its place in the history of theology, another aspect of this work that has been neglected.

The tradition of using architectural symbols in theological writing during the Patristic period and Middle Ages has been masterfully surveyed by Henri de Lubac in his seminal *Exégèse médiévale: les quatr sens de l'Écriture,* a work to which Ricard refers us for the "antécédents lointains" of the castle symbol, but whose broader implications for the study of the *Castillo* he overlooks. De Lubac points out that, although architectural symbols were used in theological writing before the Middle Ages, it was during the medieval period that their use became most widespread. Furthermore, he seems to distinguish between two different, though not mutually exclusive, uses of these symbols. The first use that De Lubac discusses is in Biblical exegesis, i.e., in commentaries on the architectural symbols found in the Bible itself (Noah's ark, Solomon's temple, the city of Jerusalem, etc.). During the Patristic period, and for that matter well into the Middle Ages (e.g., Hugh of St. Victor's *De arca Noe morali* and *De arca Noe mystica*), these symbols are given various interpretations in exegesis. The second use that De Lubac describes is in writings other than those directly concerned with the ex-

planation of Biblical architectural symbols: spiritual, doctrinal, or theoretical (as, e.g., in works expounding different theories of exegesis) works. This latter is the principal way architectural symbols are used during the Middle Ages, and that which is germane to our discussion. As Christian doctrine, moral teaching, and spirituality become increasingly complicated, it was necessary to define and organize this material. To this end the medievals adopted architectural symbols. The symbols most frequently employed were the city, the castle, the house, and the temple. The method of the medieval masters was to associate, say, each article of faith, or each stage of the spiritual life, with an appropriate part of the building. To cite an example relevant to our discussion: for Hugh of St. Victor the soul is a city, whose spiritual progress is portrayed as the city of Jerusalem—its wall is discipline, built of virtues, its gate, the Catholic faith, etc. In this way the architectural symbol served to guide man through the vast and trackless world of the human soul.

The spiritual writers that immediately preceded St. Teresa and served as her sources for the castle symbol, Ludolph, Osuna, and Laredo, avail themselves fully of the variety of architectural symbols and their application found in the theological writings of the Patristic and medieval periods. Ludolph, Osuna, and Laredo use the architectural symbols of the castle, the city, and fortress to organize systematic presentations and explanations of interior realities, whether principles of the spiritual life or the structure of the soul itself. For example, in the third chapter of the fourth *tratado* of the *Tercer abecedario espiritual,* which, in her copy of this work, St. Teresa marked with crosses and marginal lines, Osuna visualizes the soul as a castle, whose three doors are its three principal powers, the intellect, the emotions, and the will. These are the three areas, Osuna says, where the soul is most liable to be attacked by the devil. This same method is used in every text from the writings of these three authors that scholars have proposed as a possible source for the castle symbol in the *Castillo.* St. Teresa not only borrows the castle symbol from her predecessors but also the way she uses it, with one difference: in the works of Ludolph, Osuna, and Laredo, and even in St. Teresa's own works prior to the *Castillo,* the architectural symbol is not the organizing principle of the work as a whole, as that of Osuna's *Tercer abecedario espiritual* is the alphabet. In the *Castillo* St. Teresa uses the architectural symbol of the castle not as part of another methodology but as *the* method of her work.

Before proceeding to see how St. Teresa uses the architectural symbol of the castle to structure her *Castillo,* I would like to discuss briefly why she chose this type of symbol. In order to ascertain this information, several not totally unrelated factors must be taken into consideration. In the first place, since composing her *Vida* (final form, 1567), St. Teresa had developed considerably in her mystical evolution, and she felt the need to report on the higher mystical stages not included in her autobiography. The *Castillo* would allow her to work out completely her *sistema místico.* The symbol of the castle, which St. Teresa imagines as composed of seven mansions, enabled her to list and to explain what in her experience were the seven stages of the spiritual life, or of nearness to God, who dwells within the seventh mansion. Following the example set by her predecessors, she associates each stage with a part of the architecture of the castle, its successive sets of rooms, thus distinguishing one phase from another. . . . Secondly, St. Teresa was commanded to write the **Castillo** by her superiors because it was feared that the manuscripts of her **Vida,** which were in the possession of the Inquisition, might not be able to be retrieved and that this portion of her doctrine might be irrevocably lost. And, thirdly, in the **Castillo** St. Teresa wished to instruct her "hermanas y hijas las monjas carmelitas descalzas," to whom it is addressed, in the spiritual life.

This last factor suggests for our consideration a facet of the method of using an architectural symbol to order a discourse which is of no small interest in the case of the **Castillo,** its affinity with what Frances Yates has described as the "art of memory." According to Yates, during Antiquity memory was a rhetorical art; the Middle Ages transformed it into a didactic and ethical art. The reason Yates gives for this transformation is exactly that which De Lubac gives for why the medievals turned to architectural symbols: to define, organize, and classify the increasingly complicated material of Christian doctrine, moral teaching, and spirituality. The principal basis for this art is the imaginative organization of space and of spatially arranged imagery. Its method is identical to that described by De Lubac: one visualizes some kind of structure in space made of recognizable parts standing in fixed relations to one another and then associates or "places" what one wishes to remember with the various parts of the structure. One can thus commit to memory virtues and vices, stages and principles of the spiritual life, etc., by relating each in succession to one of the envisioned parts of the building. The significance of all this for the **Castillo** is fairly obvious. One of the reasons St. Teresa composed the **Castillo** was pedagogical. Presumably, then, she intended that the spiritual doctrine in which she was instructing her sisters be appropriated or committed to memory in the fullest sense of the word. Her use of the spatial architectural image of the castle to expound her doctrine must have helped them considerably in this task. The art of memory thus becomes the other side of the coin to the method of using an architectural symbol to order discourse in the **Castillo.**

To sum up, each of the three aforementioned factors in one way or another had a bearing on St. Teresa's selection of the method of using the architectural symbol of the castle to structure the **Castillo:** the castle symbol provided St. Teresa with a medium for recalling what she had written in her **Vida,** for elaborating upon this material and systematizing it, and for communicating it to her sisters in a manner in which it could be easily apprehended.

Having seen why St. Teresa chose the castle symbol, let us now see how she uses it. The symbol is introduced at the beginning of the first chapter of the first mansion or set of rooms. The arrangement of the "muchas moradas" is specified as follows: "unas en lo alto, otras en bajo, otras a los lados, y en el centro y mitad de todas éstas tiene la más principal, que es adonde pasan las cosas de mucho secreto entre Dios y el alma." At the end of the work, St.

Teresa adds: "Aunque no se trata de más de siete moradas, en cada una de éstas hay muchas, en lo bajo y alto y a los lados, con lindos jardines y fuentes y laberintos. . . . " The castle with its seven mansions is the soul. The foundation of this edifice is humility; its door is prayer and meditation. The immense mansions in the interior of the castle signify the almost infinite richness of the soul made in the image of God and enriched by grace. As we move through each set of rooms, we follow the seven successive stages in the evolution of the interior life. The first mansion is that of humility, by which the soul gains self-knowledge; the second that of the practice of prayer, whereby the soul is made more alert than in the first mansion and anxious to penetrate further into the castle; and the third that of the exemplary life, in which the soul is most desirous not to offend God. In the fourth mansion the soul experiences the prayer of quiet; in the fifth spiritual bethrothal and the prayer of (incipient) union. The soul entering the sixth mansion has been wounded with love for her Spouse and seeks more opportunities of being alone with him. Lastly, the seventh mansion is that of the spiritual marriage, which inseparably joins the soul with her Spouse. The correspondences between the different aspects of the stages of the spiritual life and the parts of the castle are delineated with more detail in the first sets of mansions than they are in the later ones. The saint herself says that this is so because no comparison is valid for the wholly mystical and supernatural phases of the spiritual life, pointing up the limitations of human language in trying to express an essentially ineffable experience. As Hatzfeld has indicated, even though the link between some of the mansions and the castle image may sometimes be thin, "The main link with the Castle is always this, that in the seventh mansion the Lord and Groom is waiting."

At this time a *caveat* seems to be in order. Emphasizing, as we are here, the systematic character of the **Castillo,** we may be inclined to assume that, because of the method she has chosen in the **Castillo,** St. Teresa moves from one point to another without digression. Nothing could be further from the truth: from start to finish she tends to ramble. Though surely the most carefully planned and arranged of all of St. Teresa's works, the **Castillo** sometimes fails to maintain its precision of method. Occasionally, the single symbol of the castle cannot bear the weight of the doctrine loaded upon it, and other images must be introduced to clarify the saint's meaning. While in no way do I wish to imply that I disparage this improvisation (the very attempt to communicate the ineffable is itself admirable!), it must, I think, be frankly admitted that its combination with the systematization of the work creates a tension within it. This tension is none other than that between the affective and the intellectual, which, as Louis Martz has noted, is "everywhere evident in meditative treatises and in religious poetry" during the sixteenth and seventeenth centuries as a result of the effort to reconcile these two forces, a point I shall return to in the next, and final, section of this paper. This tension is a healthy one: it ensures a balance between these two sides of human nature. St. Teresa was cognizant of this tension, as she frequently brings herself back to her main point by calling to mind the castle symbol. E. Allison Peers perceptively remarked on this aspect of the **Castillo:** "A scholastic writer, or, for that matter, anyone with a scientific mind, would have carried the logical arrangement of the general plan into every chapter. Such a procedure, however, would have left no outlet for St. Teresa's natural spontaneity: it is difficult, indeed, to say how far experiential mysticism can ever lend itself to inflexible scientific rule without endangering its own spirit."

The rediscovery of Aristotle during the twelfth and thirteenth centuries marked a turning point in the history of theology. Up to this time theology was closely linked to the spiritual life: it was primarily a meditation on the Bible, geared toward spiritual growth and nourishing the spiritual life. Now theologians were given a framework for establishing theology as a science, and a distinction came to be made between theology as science and theology as spirituality, between theology as rational knowledge and theology as love/mysticism, between the intellectual side of theology and its affective side. By the sixteenth and seventeenth centuries this distinction had become a commonplace in spiritual literature. The consequence of this dichotomy, which, incidentally, perdures to the present day, is that a rift opened up between theologians and masters of the spiritual life. This rift is certainly in evidence in sixteenth-century Spain, where, as Marcel Bataillon's *Erasmo y España: Estudios sobre la historia espiritual del siglo XVI* affirms, there was much tension between theologians and spiritual writers. In fact, the latter were actually forced to rally to the defense of the spiritual life. This was the milieu in which St. Teresa conceived and wrote her works, for, as Francisco Márquez Villanueva has observed apropos of the saint's writings [in his *Espiritualidad y literatura en el siglo XVI*], "el tema de la defensa de la vida espiritual constituye una de las grandes generatrices de su obra."

With the appearance of innumerable religious treatises during the sixteenth and seventeenth centuries that methodized spiritual exercises and systematized the spiritual life in mind, Martz has asserted that the central aim of Catholic spirituality during this period was to teach the devout individual how to maintain a proper balance and proportion between the affective and the intellectual sides of his nature. In other words, its goal was to effect some sort of reconciliation between theology as rational knowledge and theology as love/mysticism. According to classical scholastic theology, the scientific character of theology consists in its systematization, and the role of reason is confined to clarity of exposition. In many of the spiritual treatises of the sixteenth and seventeenth centuries, a rapprochement between theology as science and theology as spirituality was brought about, because in these works their principally affective content is organized, structured, and presented in a clear, well-ordered fashion.

As far as I know, St. Teresa's *Castillo* has not previously been explicitly related to this context. I would like to suggest that the *Castillo,* St. Teresa's masterwork, is her response to the crisis precipitated in sixteenth-century Spain by the fissure between theologians and devotees of an affective piety. By adopting the method of using an architectural symbol to order her writing, St. Teresa was able to approach systematically spirituality, and thus bridge the gap between theology as science and theology as spirituality. Moreover, she excelled in this enterprise: she brought order to the whole ground of spiritual experience, from the practice of oral prayer to the mystical marriage, to an unprecedented degree. No previous author had ever attempted an exact description of the different phases of the spiritual life, let alone tried to classify them.

A little over fifty years ago, Pedro Sáinz Rodríguez called the *Castillo* "el *Organo* del misticismo cristiano." To appreciate fully this title, one must understand the *Castillo's* method, which is the product of a long literary and theological tradition, because it is responsible in no small part for the unique position which Sáinz Rodríguez wishes to indicate by this title that this work occupies in the history of Christian spirituality and, we might add, in the history of theology, a fact not hitherto adverted to. (pp. 121-33)

> *Joseph F. Chorpenning, "The Literary and Theological Method of the 'Castillo Interior',"* in Journal of Hispanic Philology, *Vol. III, No. 2, Winter, 1979, pp. 121-33. Footnotes and page references have been deleted.*

Elizabeth Teresa Howe   (essay date 1980)

[*In the following excerpt, Howe discusses* Conceptos del amor de Dios *(also called* Meditaciones*) as it reflects Teresa's mystical theology and literary style.*]

The mystical writer faces a difficult problem when attempting to translate into human, finite language the ineffable experience of union with an infinite God. Although the conundrum is never completely solved, mystics try through a variety of means to break through the limits of language in order to convey to others something of their mystical experience. In doing so, they often turn to the language of secular literature, utilizing comparisons drawn from the sensible world in order to describe their apprehension of a spiritual reality. Understandably, Scripture offers a rich source of imagery from which Christian mystical writers draw. Central among those Biblical books which have influenced mystical letters throughout the centuries is the Canticle of Canticles, a work which [according to Dom Jean de Monléon] is "peut-être consideré comme le chef d'oeuvre de la littérature universelle."

Exegesis of the Canticle offers possibilities for interpretation ranging from the literal to the allegorical, leading [C. Tresmontant in his "Commentaire du *Cantique des Cantiques*"] to describe it as "l'un des livres les plus controversés de toute l'Ecriture." Some have found in its verses an encomium to human, carnal love. Others read a mystical poem describing the individual soul's quest for and attainment of union with God on earth. Still others choose a middle ground which finds an allegory of Christ's love for the Church. From the time of Origen, mystics have regarded the Canticle as a poetic dialogue of pure love which readily lends itself to mystical interpretation. The unique function of the Canticle in mystical literature is best summarized by James A. Montgomery [in "The Song of Songs in Early and Medieval Christian Use" in *The Song of Songs: a Symposium*]:

> The Song has by no means been the cause and origin of this mystic and often erotic expression of spiritual longings and relations. That spiritual passion is germane to every religion of mystical character and found its voice within the Church without regard to the canonical book. Only the Song became an authoritative thesaurus of word and thought for the mystic's vocabulary, and its lot in the Canon has approved itself to those souls who have known how to use it.

In the Canticle, therefore, mystics who read the work as an allegory for the soul pursuing and pursued by the Divine Lover discover an analogous expression for their profoundest experience of union with God.

The method and content utilized in incorporating the Canticle of Canticles into the mystical work reflect both the educational background and the didactic forum of the individual mystic. Thus, while Origen explains the meaning of the verses by using the fourfold method, and Saint Bernard of Clairvaux elucidates its message through the medium of the sermon, San Juan de la Cruz crystallizes his mystical experience in a lyrical paraphrase, entitled the *Cántico espiritual.* The specific form, whether poem, prose treatise, or sermon, and the lyrical, exegetical, or meditative focus of each work thus reveal a great deal about the background and doctrine of each mystical writer as well as the circumstances in which each composes his work.

No less than her predecessors and counterparts in the mystical tradition, Santa Teresa de Jesús was fascinated by the Canticle of Canticles. Her predilection for comparing the final stages of mystical union to marriage may explain part of her attraction to it, for she states in *Las moradas* that "although it may be a rude comparison, I find no other that can make more understandable what I claim than the sacrament of matrimony." If, as Mary Anita Ewer claims [in her *Survey of Mystical Symbolism*], "the Divine Nuptials form in some sense, a focus of all other mystical symbolisms and of the mystical life itself," then few better examples of the beauty of pure love, human or divine, can be found than that afforded by the Canticle of Canticles.

Historical circumstances, however, were to make St. Teresa's study of the Canticle a difficult undertaking. No less an authority than the eminent Biblical scholar Fray Luis de León had run afoul of the Inquisition because of his vernacular translation of the book. In 1559 the Inquisition proscribed all translations of the Scriptures into the vulgar tongues, and in some cases special permission was required simply in order to read any version of the Bible save the Vulgate. Such constraints explain the care which St. Teresa's confessor, Padre Báñez, exercised in editing her *Meditacions* so as to obtain the permission of the Inquisitors for distribution of her work as well as Fray Luis' omission of it from his *princeps* edition of her complete works compiled shortly after her death. Added to the obstacles imposed by the Holy Tribunal is St. Teresa's own professed ignorance of Latin, so that her knowledge of the Canticle is fragmentary at best, limited to those lines which might appear in the Divine Office or to verses which served as subjects for sermons. Her personal reflections on some verses of the Canticle which form the *Meditaciones*

sobre el Cantar de los Cantares thus reflect the historical and personal limitations imposed by the circumstances in which the saint found herself.

Mention of the work first appears in a letter written in August of 1575, which alludes to a "small book." According to the chronology provided by Efrén de la Madre de Dios in the introduction to the complete works, however, the first redaction probably was written in 1566. Its destruction by fire at the suggestion of St. Teresa's confessor occurred sometime after 1580, but some copies survived and were passed from hand to hand. Various emendations followed with the second complete redaction appearing in 1574. Reference to the work in the *Moradas* indicates that composition of the *Meditaciones* predates this work. The meditations thus fit chronologically and doctrinally somewhere between the *Vida* and *Las moradas* which were completed in 1562 and 1577 respectively. On the other hand, they are contemporaneous with the *Camino de perfección.* Although they cannot compare in eloquence with *Las moradas* or in personal insight and humanity with the *Vida,* they are often linked stylistically and thematically with the *Camino de perfección.* In a word, the work is a brief compendium of her thought and thought patterns concerning the mystic way. As such it provides a concentrated example of the author's ideas and her manner of expressing them.

As is true of most of her works, St. Teresa writes "for the consolation of the sisters whom Our Lord carries by this road, and even for [her own]." Because of her intended audience and her own professed lack of erudition, the style of her *Meditaciones* is colloquial with none of the pretensions of scholarly writing. Although her observation that "the Fathers wrote many expositions" of the Canticle suggests some familiarity with the commentaries written by her predecessors, she does not cite any directly in her own work. [Howe adds in a footnote: "She does cite Saint Bernard in the *Vida.*"] Rather than an erudite exegesis of the Canticle of Canticles, therefore, St. Teresa offers her readers very personal meditations, which convey a great body of mystical doctrine through the medium of an ingenuous style.

That St. Teresa does not intend a thorough exegesis of the Canticle becomes readily apparent to her readers not only through her own caveats at the outset, but also through the limited number of verses on which she chooses to comment. Although originally written with no divisions, the *Meditaciones* have subsequently been arranged by later editors into seven chapters, the ostensible subject of each being a verse from the Canticle of Canticles. Thus, the first three chapters have as their theme the opening lines of the Canticle ("Let the Lord kiss me with the kiss of his mouth") and the fourth considers the remainder of the verse ("for your breasts are better than wine"). Chapters five, six and seven deal respectively with Canticle ii.3 ("I sat down under the shadow of Him whom I desired, and his fruit is sweet to my palate"), Canticle ii.4 ("The King brought me into the cellar of wine and set in order charity in me") and Canticle ii.5 ("Stay me up with flowers, compass me about with apples, because I languish with love"). In addition, the author cites Canticle iv.7 ("You are all fair, my love"), Canticle vi.9 ("Who is this who is like the sun?"), and Canticle viii.5 ("Under the apple tree I raised you up") in passing. Over half of the work, therefore, considers a single sentence of the Biblical source, while the remainder meditates on a scant two or three lines.

Although St. Teresa cites the opening verse of the Canticle early in the **Meditaciones,** she does not develop her thoughts concerning it at the outset, but, rather, turns her attention to related problems. She points out the difficulty facing any who would plumb the depths of the faith, but reassures her readers that "when the Lord wants to give understanding, His Majesty does it without our labor." For herself as well as for most cloistered nuns, the Canticle poses special problems both because no translation is available to them and because of the allegorical style in which it is written. To illustrate the pitfalls confronting reader and preacher alike who choose to consider the Canticle, St. Teresa offers an anecdote, which is not only humorous but also effective in driving home her point:

> For a fact, I recall hearing a religious preach a very admirable sermon, the greater part of which described these gifts resulting from the Bride's converse with God. And there was so much laughter and what he said was so badly taken, because he was speaking about love (it being the Mandatum [Holy Thursday] sermon which treats no other subject) that I was astounded.

Despite her chagrin at the preacher's disastrous results, she is able to reflect on the cause: "We are so poorly experienced in the love of God that it does not seem possible to us for a soul to deal thus with God." Her own experience has taught her, however, that it is indeed possible for a soul to know God intimately in union as the Bride knows the Bridegroom in the Canticle. Because of her own spiritual experiences, therefore, she dares to meditate on the Canticle even at the risk of being considered a presumptuous woman. Even though she has opened the **Meditaciones** by suggesting that women understand less of the mysteries of the faith than men, she modifies that notion at the conclusion of the chapter by remarking "that neither are we women supposed to refrain from enjoying the riches of the Lord." Quite simply, she claims to write only what God has given her to understand, a sentiment which echoes a similar observation in the **Vida.**

Although these opening remarks seem to bear little relation to the Canticle, they do reveal a number of characteristics of St. Teresa's style and concerns. The digressive, anecdotal narrative, so often repeated in the longer works, is the hallmark of an author who averred that she never reread what she had written. The exclamatory phrases which punctuate the text ("Oh, bless me Lord, what miserable creatures we are!" or "Oh, my Lord, that of all the goods that you bestow on us we should take such poor advantage [of them]") add a charming, personal tone to her relation and, in addition, reflect the meditative nature of her work. Yet, the style also subtly masks a reply to those critics who objected to a cloistered nun expounding on spiritual subjects. Even while she acknowledges the superior expositions of the Canticle written by learned doctors, St. Teresa humbly yet fearlessly offers her own remarks concerning the work. God's graces are given as readily to women as to men, she observes. Confident of the source of her inspiration, she states her resolution: "And so I begin with the favor of this divine King of mine and with the leave that he grants me."

Following these opening remarks, St. Teresa returns to the subject of her meditations by citing once again the initial verse of the Canticle. Her immediate response to the desired kiss is one of unworthiness expressed in a series of exclamations and rhetorical questions in which she describes herself as a "worm" and "a fool." In spite of the protestations of unworthiness, however, she proceeds with a commentary on the first verse by observing that "the kiss is a sign of peace and great friendship between two people." She likens understanding the full import of the requested kiss of the Canticle to a worthy reception of the Eucharist. Only one who loves God deeply appreciates the significance of the kiss just as only one in a state of grace receives the Eucharist meritoriously. In the sinful, on the other hand, both actions arouse fear.

Both the reference to the Eucharist and an earlier one to the Incarnation recall a similar comparison made by Saint Bernard of Clairvaux in his *Sermons* on the Canticle:

> The mouth that kisses signifies the Word who assumes human nature; the nature assumed receives the kiss; the kiss however, that takes its being both from the giver and the receiver, is a person that is formed by both, none other than "the one mediator between God and mankind, himself a man, Christ Jesus."

In the case of both mystics, interpretations of the kiss as symbolic of the Incarnation continue the exegetical tradition of an allegorical reading of the Canticle summarized by A. Robert [in *Le Cantique des Cantiques*]:

> By the Incarnation, the Word contracts a physical union with human nature and a moral union with the Church: the latter union being the end of the former. Thus, the first spouse of Christ is his humanity; the second, the Church; the third, the Blessed Virgin; and the fourth, the soul.

Although St. Teresa intimates a familiarity with the works of other commentators on the Canticle as well as with those of Saint Bernard, she does not indicate clearly here that she has any other source in mind. Like Saint Bernard, however, she will extend the meaning of the kiss to encompass those states of advanced mystical union enjoyed by very few. Thus, Gaston Etchegoyen's observation [in his *L'Amour divin: Essai sur les sources de Sainte Thérèse*] that "the kiss requested by the Bride represents for St. Teresa the Incarnation of Christ and the grace of the Eucharist" is only partially correct. As this study of the **Meditaciones** will show, St. Teresa broadens the significance of the kiss considerably.

From the description of the kiss as "a sign of peace and great friendship," St. Teresa passes to a consideration of the "peace that the worldly possess," a sign not of God's love and peace, but, rather, of the false peace of Satan. The worldly peace, which she considers no peace at all, must be met by "perpetual war" if the soul desires the "kiss of his mouth." The jarring note of war juxtaposed with the peace of the Canticle's kiss casts the soul's initial petition in the mold of the early stages of mystical progress. By comparing the trails of the purgative state to warfare, St. Teresa continues imagery which she also uses in the *Vida* and which she will reiterate in her masterpiece, *Las moradas.* The controlling image of the *Moradas,* in fact, casts the work in military terms, premised as it is on the interior castle, the fortress of the soul.

The extended admonition to avoid the false peace of the devil leads the author back to the kiss image by circuitous yet logical degrees. Contrasting the kiss of the Canticle with another Biblical kiss, St. Teresa advises her readers to "awaken fear in your soul so that you may not be lulled by that kiss of false peace which the world gives: believe that it is [the kiss] of Judas." It is an apt comparison. Just as Judas' kiss was a betrayal not only of Christ but also of the graces given him by God, so, too, the soul's turning from the pursuit of perfection is a betrayal of God's call to union. Hence, the mystic must keep in mind the kiss of the Canticle, because "the Bride indicates the peace she requests by saying: 'Kiss me with the kiss of your mouth'."

St. Teresa concludes the commentary on the kiss in the third chapter. The soul's true desire is the "holy peace" represented by the kiss of the Canticle. In contrast to the world's false peace, this kiss "is to join with the will of God, so that there may be no division between Him and her, but, rather, that it may be one and the same will." While *juntarse* ("to join") suggests union, what the author actually describes in this reference is conversion to the mystic way. Unlike those drawn to the false peace of the world, those who receive the holy peace of the Bridegroom's kiss "enjoy this favor by many signs. One is to despise all earthly things, esteeming them as worthless as they are, [second] not to wish for their own well-being, because they now understand its vanity, [third] not to exult except with those who love their Lord." The lessons described correspond to those learned by the initiate in the purgative way, who, once commencing the journey to union, is adjured to forswear the allurements of the world in order to seek God alone.

St. Teresa's explanation of the kiss and its effects, therefore, seems to echo that described by Saint Bernard when he cautions initiates to seek first to kiss just the feet of the Bridegroom, for only by stages may the soul advance to the actual *osculo oris sui.* At the conclusion of the third chapter, however, St. Teresa reiterates her request: "So, my Lord, I ask you for nothing in this life except that you 'kiss me with the kiss of your mouth'," thus implying that the kiss may also foreshadow union. When she refers to the "kiss [*osculo*] that the Bride asked for" in the *Moradas,* the context assures the reader that it certainly represents union and not purgation. E. Allison Peers stresses [in his *Studies of the Spanish Mystics*] that in Teresian mystical doctrine, Spiritual Betrothal and Marriage follow union. Thus, while the kiss refers to union, it does not represent these final states, because "the Union of Marriage is, as its name implies, no passing, occasionally repeated experience, but an almost continuous one."

In spite of her later reading of the *beso* ("kiss") in the

Moradas as a symbol of union, in the *Meditaciones* St. Teresa confines her interpretation to the initial stages of the mystic way. When she considers the remaining verse of the Canticle ("your breasts are better and more fragrant than wine"), the equation of kiss with purgative way becomes more evident. By comparing the repose implied by the "breasts" to the prayer of quiet in which "the soul feels a gentleness within itself," she underscores the ordering of stages in mystical progress. In the *Vida,* where she first discusses the prayer of quiet, it is a state which follows the trials and "wars" of purgation. A similar ordering of imagery is evident in the briefer *Meditaciones* where the "wars" of "false peace" engendered by the worldly kiss precede the repose of the prayer of quiet. The *Meditaciones* thus imitates the imagery while reiterating the doctrine of the earlier work. Subsequent descriptions of the soul as "engulfed," "amazed and absorbed," and "saturated" also recall imagery in the *Vida* where the second method of watering the garden of the soul forms an extended simile for the prayer of quiet. Similarly, association of water imagery with the prayer of quiet anticipates the *Moradas* where St. Teresa likens the state to a basin slowly filling up with water from a hidden source.

Two interrelated images emerge as a consequence of her meditation on the verse. While "it seems [to the soul] that it remains suspended in those divine arms and beside that sacred side and those [divine] breasts" it is sustained by "that divine milk." The effect wrought on the soul by its sustenance at the breast of the Bridegroom is one of "celestial intoxication . . . and drunkeness." Extending the comparison further in a touching and somewhat surprising direction, she writes:

> Just as a child does not understand how it grows or how it nurses—that is, even without it suckling or doing anything, many times milk is put in its mouth—so it is here, that the soul of itself knows nothing, neither does it do anything, nor does it know or is able to comprehend how or where that great blessing came to it.

She thus captures not only the passive nature of the prayer of quiet but also the gentleness of the Bridegroom in his dealings with the soul. When she remarks that "it does not know what to compare it to except to the mother's caress who greatly loves the child and raises and caresses it," she draws attention to the maternal qualities of the *Esposo* embodied in the Canticle's reference to the "breasts" while also anticipating one of Covarrubias' etymologies for *regalo* ("gift" or "caress") [D. Sebastián Covarrubias Orozco, *Tesoro de la lengua castellana o española*].

In this respect she echoes Saint Bernard, who says of the Bridegroom that "these two breasts are two proofs of his native kindness; his patience in awaiting the sinner and his welcoming mercy for the penitent." Saint Bernard also extends the comparison to encompass the suckling child. Nevertheless although both mystics use similar imagery, the focus of their message differs significantly. For St. Teresa the Bridegroom's breasts represent the prayer of quiet. Saint Bernard, however, equates them with spiritual doctrine disseminated by the Church. He also shifts the focus from the breasts of the Bridegroom to those of the Bride, leading Nicholas J. Perella to explain [in *The Kiss*

Sacred and Profane] that "the bride conceives and her breasts grow full with the milk that will be fed to the children she is to bear . . . [who] are the good works born of and carried out in Charity." For Saint Bernard, therefore, the soul's repose and its sustenance at the Bridegroom's breast mirror the Church's mission of forgiveness and evangelization. St. Teresa's interpretation, while seemingly more circumscribed, does not completely exclude the evangelizing mission envisioned by her predecessor, a fact which becomes evident as she discusses the mystic way in greater detail.

St. Teresa makes clear that attainment of the Bridegroom's love is possible here and now when she reminds her readers that "the Lord does not save for the next life the prize of loving Him: He commences payment in this life." The coveted prize is union with the Beloved foreshadowed by the embrace of the Canticle. Paraphrasing Canticle ii.16, the author hopes "that I may gaze on my Beloved and my Beloved on me," indicating, by her use of the subjunctive, anticipation rather than realization of the desired union. By repeating the reference to *beso* at the conclusion of this chapter, St. Teresa unequivocally equates the kiss with union, inquiring rhetorically: "What more do I desire of You in this life than to be so joined to You that there may be no division between You and me?"

Explanation of the prayer of quiet extends into the next chapter when she considers Canticle ii.3. Recalling not only the wider context of the verse but also other Biblical sources as well as traditional imagery, St. Teresa layers disparate images and so creates a statement of subtle complexity. With a passing reference to the apple tree of the Canticle (ii.3) as the source of the shade cast on the Bride, the author next alludes to the sun as symbolic of God, then recalls related passages from Scripture. In the prayer of quiet the soul "feels itself to be completely engulfed and protected by a shadow and a sort of cloud of Divinity." It is a situation that creates a paradoxical state in which the soul escapes the debilitating "weariness" engendered by worldly concerns yet conversely experiences a contradictory sort of rest "that it even tires [the soul] to have to breathe." Even as she describes the physical and spiritual aspects of the prayer of union, she also suggests earlier mystical writers. Thus, the "cloud of Divinity" evokes the medieval classic *The Cloud of Unknowing,* a work with which St. Teresa was probably not directly acquainted. The cloud also suggests the divine darkness described by Pseudo-Dionysius in a mystical work well known to her through her readings of other Spanish mystics. Through her use of the verb *engolfar* ("to engulf"), St. Teresa recalls the soul's "inebriation" at the breast of the Beloved while also foreshadowing the "absorption" characteristic of ecstatic union. Finally, the apple tree which shades the Bride of the Canticle serves an ambivalent symbolic function. Traditionally, of course, the apple tree has been understood as the forbidden tree of Eden even though the Genesis account does not specify it as such. In the Canticle of Canticles, however, such an assignation is implied in the verse: "sub arbore malo suscitavi te; ibi corrupta est mater tua ibi violata est genetrix tua." Nevertheless, in Canticle ii.3 the apple tree is used as a simile for the Bridegroom.

To St. Teresa, who was fond of meditating on the Passion, the apple tree also symbolizes the cross whose fruits the soul enjoys because Christ "[has watered] this tree with His precious blood with such admirable love."

While some of her predecessors in the spiritual life erroneously considered the prayer of quiet the apogee of the mystical flight, St. Teresa writes that "our most holy King still has much to give." The additional favors to be granted in the more advanced mystical stage of union form the basis of the meditation on the verse: "The King placed me in the wine cellar and ordered charity in me." From the illumination of the passive stage of the prayer of quiet, the soul moves to the initial unitive experience of ecstatic union symbolized by inebriation:

> He puts [the soul] in the wine cellar so that [it] may leave there enriched beyond measure. It would seem that the King wishes that there be nothing left for Him to give except that it may drink according to its desire and that it may become intoxicated by drinking from all of these wines dispensed by God. Let it rejoice in these pleasures, wonder at His greatness; and fear not to lose its life by drinking so much that it may be beyond the frailty of its nature. Let it die in that paradise of delights. Blessed be such a death that so enlivens!

The inebriation of the soul in the King's wine cellar closely resembles the effects of the prayer of quiet where the soul is "so amazed and absorbed that it does not seem to be in itself, but rather in a state of divine inebriation that it knows not what it wants, nor what it says, nor what it asks for." In the *Meditaciones* as well as in other works, however, St. Teresa distinguishes between the two states. Thus, her further explanation of "blessed intoxication" stresses that "all the powers [of the soul are] dead or asleep." In addition, her comparison of love to "an arrow shot by the will" which creates "this holy absorption" recalls the description of her ecstatic wound of love in the *Vida.*

Although the choice of terms to describe the prayer of quiet and ecstatic union is similar in the *Meditaciones,* in other works she appears to distinguish more clearly between *embevecimiento* ("absorption") and *embriaguez* ("intoxication") or *borrachez* ("inebriation" or "drunkenness"). Covarrubias' definition of *embeber* as "to take into oneself some liquid, just as the sponge imbibes water or some other liquid" seems appropriate to a description of the prayer of quiet, where the soul experiences the fullness of God's grace in a passive way. Yet, when Covarrubias says of *embevecido* that "it is so called because that thought imbibes within itself the imagination without moving on to other things, or it is like the inebriated or drunkard who does not realize what he is doing," he underscores the similarity between related terms evident in St. Teresa's works, for the "drunkard [is] he who partakes of wine." In the *Moradas,* however, St. Teresa confines *embevecimiento* to the prayer of quiet, a more appropriate metaphor when one considers her further comparison of the same state to a spring silently filling up from a hidden source. *Embriaguez* or *borrachez divina,* on the other hand, describes ecstatic union in which the powers of the soul "easily lose themselves." Union results in such profound joy that the soul longs to die in order to prolong the experience. While all the "powers of the soul [are] dead or asleep," love remains intensely alive. It is an ineffable experience beyond both understanding and description in which, paradoxically, "the soul understands—without understanding how it understands."

Evident in St. Teresa's description of ecstasy are a number of elements common to the mystical experience. For example, "Blessed be such a death, that so enlivens!" echoes the sentiments expressed in her gloss of the poem "Vivo sin vivir en mi" ("I live without living in myself!"). The mystic realizes that an unending ecstatic union is possible only in eternity. The noetic quality suffusing the mystic's apprehension of a reality beyond ordinary human understanding also characterizes ecstasy. St. Teresa thus underscores the mutual love between soul and God by balancing the unbounded generosity of the Bridegroom against the unbridled desire of the soul to drink its fill in the wine cellar.

The remainder of the chapter enumerates the gifts showered on the soul in mystical union. Like the Blessed Virgin who accepted without question the angel's explanation of God's overshadowing presence at the Annunciation, the mystic receives the Bridegroom's gifts without understanding how. By applying to the soul two other verses of the Canticle (ii.7 and vi.9), St. Teresa continues the analogy of the mystic with the Blessed Virgin, for the Bridegroom's words to the Bride, "you are all beautiful, my love" traditionally describe both the soul in union and the Blessed Virgin. Similarly, the soul encrusted with the virtues and graces of mystical union is startled into inquiring of itself: "Who is this who is like the sun?" While both verses form part of the Office of the Blessed Virgin, they also describe the mystic in union. Just as the Bride of the Canticle prefigures the Church, so, too, does she symbolize Mary in her acceptance of the divine will and the individual soul in its union with God.

In the seventh and final chapter of the *Meditaciones,* St. Teresa turns her attention to Canticle ii.5. The wound of love sustained in ecstatic union brings with it a "gentleness. . . so excessive that it undoes the soul so that it does not seem that it can still live and [so it asks for] flowers." She remarks on the paradoxical sense of dying life experienced in ecstasy. On the one hand, the body's physical appearance resembles death, for "when it is in rapture, the body remains as if dead often without being able to do anything," while the soul experiences an intense yet brief union with the Bridegroom. On the other hand, the soul's reanimation of the body brings with it a pang of longing for the exhilaration of union and its consummate joy. Thus, the soul may long to remain forever with the Bridegroom in union, yet accepts the necessity to continue its worldly existence sustained by grace and anxious to serve "[him] whom it sees that it owes so much."

The flowers which the soul requests represent the "great works in the service of our Lord." Referring to the Gospel account of Martha and Mary, St. Teresa stresses that mystical favors are not to be hoarded but, rather, are to be used "in order to profit many others." While the allusion to Martha and Mary appears in Saint Bernard's *Sermons* as well, it also appeals to St. Teresa in other contexts. Distinguishing between the prayer of quiet and the more advanced stage of unitive prayer, she points out that in union "[the soul] can also be Martha (so that it is almost working jointly in an active and contemplative life)." Similarly, in the *Moradas* she repeats the need for Martha and Mary to "work together to house the Lord." As traditional symbols of the active and contemplative lives respectively, Martha and Mary are often cast in a false dichotomy by those who stress the "better part" chosen by Mary. Such is Saint Bernard's interpretation of the Biblical figures. St. Teresa, however, rejects an emphasis on contemplation at the expense of the activity necessary not only to the good order of the particular religious house but also to the edification of the Christian community as a whole.

In yet another Gospel allusion, which was one of her favorites, she turns to the example of the Samaritan woman (John iv) who "went . . . with that divine inebriation shouting through the streets." Like Martha and Mary, the Samaritan woman embodies the active and contemplative principles of the religious life. Although she enjoyed an intimate conversation with Christ who promised her the "fons aquae salientis in vitam aeternam" (John iv.14), she did not keep the good news to herself but shared it with her neighbors. The mystic can do no less. Whether the contact with God spans the brief moments of the Samaritan woman's colloquy at the well or the prolonged friendship with Christ enjoyed by Martha and Mary, the mystic must transform the gifts received from the Bridegroom into the fruit of good works. This is the ultimate test of the veracity of mystic experience.

Although the graces she alludes to in this meditation are the mystic's goal, she cautions initiates against a too precipitous ascent to the final state. Reviewing the intermediate stages of advancement, she admonishes those who would "leap toward [union]" to sustain themselves a while longer "with the milk that [she spoke of] at the beginning." At the same time, she recalls the apple tree, equating it with "the tree of the Cross." Even as the mystic soul receives the favors of ecstatic union, it must also be willing to be "surrounded by crosses, works, and persecutions." With these few closing thoughts, St. Teresa concludes her meditations, declining to expound further because "it would be presumptuous."

Absent from the *Meditaciones* is a description of the ultimate state of spiritual marriage. In the last section of the *Moradas,* on the other hand, she distinguishes between union and spiritual betrothal:

> Although union is the joining of two things in one, in short, they can be parted and each thing remains by itself, as we ordinarily see; this favor of the Lord passes quickly and afterwards the soul finds itself without that companionship. I mean insofar as it can understand. In this other favor of the Lord [spiritual betrothal] it is not so, because the soul always remains with its God in that center.

While it is possible that she had not experienced the state at the time she wrote the *Meditaciones,* it is equally possible that she considered the Canticle itself the preeminent example of spiritual marriage so that direct reference to the state in her work would be superfluous. When she reiterates at the conclusion of the meditations that "my intention was, when I began it, to give you to understand how you could regale yourselves when you might hear some words of the Canticle and to think . . . [about] the great mysteries which they contain," she indicates that she has explored as much of the Biblical work as she intended at the outset. She leaves to her readers the task of deepening their understanding of the mysteries which the Canticle contains.

Just as the *Meditaciones sobre el Cantar* may be profitably studied as a compendium of the salient points of Teresian doctrine, so, too, do they offer the reader a summary of her style. The author cloaks her mystical teaching in ingenuous prose praised by a succession of literary critics for its simplicity, clarity, precision, harmony, terseness, virility and vigor. She avoids all artifice and pretensions to scholarship while writing in the direct, colloquial language of her native Castile complete with the phonetic misspellings and the mispronunciations of the unlettered. As Ramón Menéndez Pidal describes it [in his *La lengua de Cristóbal Colón*]: "Teresian language always demonstrates a disinclination for or an opposition to all that one might call 'literature'. " Certainly her criticism of "the erudite" underscores her disavowal of literary pretension both in this work and in others. Similarly, her frequent apostrophes to God, her use of diminutives, and her anecdotal proclivities all bespeak a colloquial style.

Since the responsibilities of her office as foundress and later prioress occupied much of her time, St. Teresa was able to write only at moments snatched from a busy schedule. Her writing "au courant de la plume," as Juan Domínguez Berrueta describes it [in *Sainte Thérèse et la vie mystique*], precluded rereading what she had already written, resulting in a tendency to repeat herself as well as a penchant for digression from the main point. The digression on war and false peace in the second chapter, although eventually tied to the kiss is, nevertheless, a case in point. Her many ellipses, incomplete sentences, extended parentheses, unfinished explanations, and verbless orations lead Menéndez Pidal to invert the equation and exclaim in both admiration and consternation, "she speaks through writing."

The tendency to digress appears early in the *Meditaciones.* Although she assures her readers that she will comment on various verses of the Canticle in the prologue, she begins in earnest only midway through the work. Aware that she is straying from the point, she repeatedly brings herself and the reader back to the main theme with a phrase such as "returning to what I began to say." Similes based on everyday life provide examples to dramatize a doctrinal point, as when she warns of the dangers of venial sins: "If a person is alive, [and if] they prick her a little with a pin or a little thorn no matter how small it may be, doesn't she feel it?"

Paired with the commonplace examples of daily conventual life are vestiges of her powerful, elemental imagery developed more fully in other works. Although water is a fa-

vorite image in her major works—used to signify the various stages of the mystical life—it is only cursorily treated in the *Meditaciones.* Early in the work there is a faint echo of the extended comparison from the *Vida* which describes the stages of mystical prayer: "If we plant a bush or a sapling and water it each day, it will grow so large that in order to uproot it later we shall need a shovel and a hoe." In this reference, however, the reader is warned of the insidious nature of faults and venial sins which gradually take root in the garden of the soul. They cannot be allowed to take deep root or proliferate like weeds lest great effort be necessary later to remove them. In her allusions to the Samaritan woman as well as to the "divine intoxication," her vocabulary also suggests the waters of the *Vida* and the *Moradas.* Although the bellicose imagery frequently utilized in the *Vida* and the *Moradas* also appears here, the Canticle description of the Bride as "terribilis ut castrorum acies ordinata" is absent from the *Meditaciones.* Since it forms part of the Office of the Blessed Virgin along with Canticle vi.9, it is an intriguing omission on St. Teresa's part.

The long digression warning against the wiles of the devil reflects similar admonitions in her other works, while her allusion to eye union and her use of the oxymoron "dying life" are conventions she shares with other mystics. Love compared to an arrow hurled by the will echoes not only the "fiery dart" of Richard of St. Victor's *Benjamin Major,* but also the "golden dart" thrust by the cherub "through her heart" in the *Vida.* Both style and individual images thus tie the *Meditaciones* to St. Teresa's other mystical works.

Composed as they were between her two major works, the *Vida* and *Las moradas,* they also provide an interesting bridge between her better known treatises. The meditations contain the salient points of mystical teaching set forth in the *Vida* but in a more structured form. For example, by ordering her meditations around selected verses of the Canticle, St. Teresa demonstrates the progressive stages of the mystical way in a somewhat orderly fashion reflected in the much more structured form taken later in *Las moradas.* Nevertheless, she loses nothing of her spontaneity, for the elements which mark her colloquial style are much in evidence. Still present in the *Meditaciones,* therefore, are the digressions, exclamations, and striking yet homely similes found in both the *Vida* and *Las moradas.* Absent, however, are dominant images such as water or the castle around which the longer mystical passages of the major works are constructed. Finally, while neither an exhaustive commentary on nor a strictly allegorical exegesis of the Canticle of Canticles, St. Teresa's *Meditaciones* does show her familiarity with some verses of the Biblical source, her ability to write in simple, direct terms about mystical union, and her spiritual and literary affinity with her mystical predecessors. The work represents, therefore, a microcosm of the Teresian mystique. (pp. 47-63)

Elizabeth Teresa Howe, "St. Teresa's 'Meditaciones' and the Mystic Tradition of the Canticle of Canticles," in Renascence, *Vol. XXXIII, No. 1, Autumn, 1980, pp. 47-64.*

Gari Laguardia   (essay date 1980)

[*In the following excerpt, Laguardia provides an analysis of the* Life, *viewing the text as Teresa's attempt to reconcile "the problematic opposition between desire and the 'father.'"*]

Santa Teresa of Avila has always been ranked as one of the great figures of Spanish literature. Yet her position as a writer, as opposed to an icon, has been consistently problematical. Many years ago, in a seminal article [in *Teresa la santa*], Américo Castro remarked that Teresa's readers and commentators were either her pious devotees, philologists interested in her colloquial style as a specimen of sixteenth-century Spanish language, or psychologists who considered her writings as a psychopathological case history. With the exception of Castro's article and perhaps one or two other studies, this situation still prevails. As a result, Teresa's texts function primarily as pretexts for discourses on one or another phenomenon that is basically extrinsic to her own discourse.

Teresa's most widely read text, the **Libro de su vida,** will be studied to reveal its fundamental literary expression. It will be seen that Teresa's selection of incidents, her ordering of these, and her imagery in general are tailored to the solution of a fundamental and difficult human problem. In this regard, Castro's most judicious insight into her writings serves nicely as a preface to my own reading of her text. In Castro's opinion, Teresa's most valuable contribution as a writer was to insert into a well-established fund of mystical discourse her own feminine temperament "que no renuncia a nada, cuando pretende renunciar a todo." In this essay I will illustrate how and why this process functions in her autobiography.

As a confessional autobiography, Santa Teresa's **Libro de su vida** seems vague. The reader who turns to Teresa's text expecting the type of revelations found in other works of the same genre—those of Saint Augustine or Rousseau, for example—is bound to be disappointed. While Teresa is fond of berating herself for her sins, she gives the reader few specific examples that would justify her bad conscience. In view of the fact that her *Life* is divided roughly into two sections, the chapters which deal with her life previous to her divinely inspired conversion on the one hand, and those that describe her new life of grace on the other, it is surprising that she does not take the opportunity to utilize the first section as an exemplary catalogue of sinful activity. On the contrary, those chapters which concern her life before taking up her religious vocation are the vaguest of all.

Even though we are given to understand that the life described in the first nine chapters of the text is ridden with sin, Teresa's ambivalence about such sins is remarkable. She repeatedly implies that she was not to blame for those sins, and shifts the culpability elsewhere: to her cousins, to books of chivalry, to her father, and to her confessors. While on occasion Teresa does admit responsibility for one sinful lapse or another, most of the time such admissions are followed by a retraction. (p. 523)

This Teresian ambiguity, which arises out of her refusal to accept full responsibility for her acts even as she recog-

nizes these as constituting part of her being, is tantamount to a fundamental denial. While Teresa ruefully realizes that her desire is "sinful," she is not willing to give up. This tension produces a resentment which in turn constantly demands the recognition and justification of those very desires. To circumvent this problem Teresa must transfer her expression of desire to a semantic sphere where it can articulate itself freely, unfettered by any sinful connotation. This re-arrangement of signifiers is the central literary problem of her self-revelation. Since Teresa's voice is not satisfied by mere expression, but requires a justifying response, her problem becomes one of finding a "reader" who would not only decipher her code, but who would respond sympathetically to her veiled confession. To Teresa's perennial chagrin such powers are beyond the reach of her father, don Alonso de Cepeda, and her various confessors.

Teresa's portrayal of don Alonso's responses to her actions illustrates this point. On one occasion we are told that Teresa's youthful "frivolities," *vanidades* were not accomplished so surreptitiously that her father did not suspect her of misbehavior. Indeed, in Teresa's opinion, it was don Alonso's suspicion that provoked him to enroll her in a convent school as a corrective measure for her errant behavior. However, Teresa never grants her father knowledge that extends beyond mere suspicion. . . . As she will do on other occasions in her narrative, Teresa characterizes her father as a bad "reader" of her discourse: in final measure he cannot penetrate and decipher her code. Unable to "read" her discourse, don Alonso is consequently barred from participating in the intimate dialogue that Teresa so insistently desires. Eventually Teresa will discover that God is the reader and listener for whom she has been searching. In contrast with don Alonso, whose suspicions do not lead to knowledge of his daughter's desires, Teresa presents us with her spiritual father: "¡Oh Dios mio, que daño hace . . . pensar que ha de haber cosa secreta que sea contra Vos!"

Unable to communicate her desires to her father, or to society, Teresa is obliged to create an imaginary setting where such communication can take place. Although parallel to her earthly circumstances, this imaginary world is separate from them by definition. We shall see that this world is inhabited by figures who approve her wishes, but who in fact are displacements of Alonso de Cepeda, the chief obstacle and object of Teresa's earthly desire. The most prominent of these figures is, of course, God. Being privy to Teresa's most intimate secrets he can respond to her desire in a way that don Alonso could not.

Yet Teresa must face the problem that on earth, in the flesh, her desires are sinful. Consequently, it is necessary to "split" her ego, so to speak, in order to maintain the privileged purity of her divine intercourse. This is why Teresa refuses to admit to any specific sensual transgression. In so doing she avoids contaminating her celestial representation with any concept of "sin." Thus, as readers, we merely perceive a vague shadow of sinful activity: Teresa the sinner reduced to a pure "manner of speaking." Teresa is progressively alienated from this shadow, and in opposition to it weaves her dialectic of desire in a willfully created sphere of signification: "Vivo sin vivir en mi."

The process whereby Teresa the sinner becomes Teresa the Saint emerges transparently if we juxtapose two famous scenes from her autobiography: a terrible seizure which left her in a coma shortly after she entered the convent, and the renowned transverberation where an angel plunges a flaming dart into her heart. These two events, apparently unconnected, separated by some twenty-four chapters of Teresa's text, in fact constitute the opposing centers around which Teresa constructs her apotheosis. If we examine the narrative material which surrounds each scene we find that from one event to another we are following a long concatenation of imagery which in the end betrays the reason for Teresa's creation and at the same time exemplifies the fundamental procedures of her narrative.

The physical infirmities which culminated in the terrible seizure (parasismo) began to manifest themselves after don Alonso placed the young Teresa in a convent school following the incident with her cousins. At first, convent life was not at all appealing to Teresa. She tells us she was "enemiguisima de ser monja . . ." Eventually, however, she decides that becoming a nun is the best way to fulfill her desire. At this point, her father, who never intended her stay at the convent to be permanent, once again obstructs his daughter's wishes. Don Alonso, who originally sent her away, now refuses to accede to Teresa's insistence on becoming a nun: "Era tanto lo que me quería, que en ninguna manera lo pude acabar con él, ni bastaron ruegos de personas que procuré le hablasen. Lo que más se pudo acabar con él fué que *después de sus días haría lo que quisiese*" (my emphasis). Teresa would follow her father's injunction in a very fundamental way years later upon his death. In the meantime she ignored it, running away from home to a convent. Her description of this momentous event is revealing insofar as it boldly anticipates the basic transference that will permit the elaboration of her desire: " . . . cuando sali de casa de mi padre, no creo será más el sentimiento cuando me muera; porque me parece cada hueso se me apartaba por sí . . . como no había amor de Dios que quitase el amor del padre y parientes, era todo haciéndome una fuerza tan grande, que si el Señor no me ayudara, no bastaran mis consideraciones para ir adelante. Aquí me dió ánimo contra mí . . . "

Teresa's first years at the convent were plagued with physical infirmities. These were, to a degree, patterned on those of a nun who was "enferma de grandísima enfermedad, y muy penosa, porque eran unas bocas en el vientre, que se le habían hecho de opilaciones, por donde echaba lo que comía." Years later, during the transverberation, the angel's spear "me llegaba a las entrañas. Al sacarle, me parecía las llevaba consigo, y me dejaba toda abrasada en amor grande de Dios." Here we can observe an essential aspect of Teresa's representation. Between one description and another there is similarity: an observed event serves as a point of departure for a concatenated elaboration which at length can be defined by that contextual similarity. The full resonance of the patent similarity between the anonymous nun's sufferings and the ecstasy of the trans-

verberation remains obscure without intercalating other elements of the lengthy concatenation. Describing the agony of the nun, Teresa remarks that such patient suffering made her envious to the point where she asked God to make her ill. She assumed that suffering would make her blessed, and since she was determined to gain "bienes eternos," she was willing to obtain them "por cualquier medio." Her determination is sparked by the significant fact that she did not feel that she had yet achieved the love of God. God, as He is wont to do throughout her narrative, grants Teresa her wish: she becomes ill. Although Teresa feels constrained to deny that her illness is similar to the nun's, since what she ate did not seep out of an ulcerated stomach, she does finally achieve substantial identity with the nun—not through divinely inspired ulceration—but through daily purges administered by doctors procured by don Alonso. This *vía purgativa,* which will find its privileged representation in the transverberation, has a more immediate metaphorical parallel. The narration of her painful physical purgation coincides with the Saint's first meditations on the great moral laxative—confession. Teresa's elaboration of this parallel allows us to define with relative precision the nature of the noxious elements which she feels obliged to cast out. When the Saint describes the beginning of her purgative process it is highly significant that she should choose to speak about confession by means of a long excursus on the sin of one of her confessors.

The confessor's sin was that he lived with a woman in concubinage. Confronted with the fact, Teresa reverses the relationship between confessor and penitent. . . . In Teresa's judgment the confessor's sin is symbolized by a copper amulet that the man carried at the insistence of his lover. Teresa believes that this amulet represents the demoniacal will of the concubine to submit the priest to her sinful wishes. Determined to rid the confessor of this baneful influence, Teresa assumes the role of confessor, as well as of "lover": " . . . comencé a mostrarle más amor. Mi intención buena era. . . . Tratábale muy de ordinario de Dios. Esto debía aprovecharle, aunque más creo le hizo al caso el quererme mucho; porque por hacerme placer, me vino a dar el idolillo, el cual hice echar luego en un rio." It is striking that the representation of such an exchange of roles and functions should correspond so closely to the purgative symbolism already applied by Teresa to her own person. Like excrement, the amulet is a physical index of something toxic. Yet the amulet is more specific because the Saint's discourse has defined it as a symbol of obsessively *illicit sexual relations.*

Here Teresa's confessional and prophylactic anxieties acquire a clarifying specificity. When she narrated this episode, Teresa was probably aware of this, too. Ordinarily quick to declare herself a miserable sinner, Teresa hastens to assure the reader several times over that she did not participate in the confessor's sinful activity: " . . . cosa que yo entendiera era pecado mortal, no la hiciera entonces." Concluding the story, Teresa covers over the insecurity betrayed by her disclaimer with the statement: "Murió muy bien y muy quitado de aquella ocasión: parece quiso el Señor que por estos medios se salvase." Teresa here has become the prophylactic agent, and to her mind this has met with God's approval. The procedure whereby she casts the amulet, a concrete image of sin, (illicit sexual relations) into the river is essentially the same procedure she will use to cleanse herself of the image of sin throughout the text.

Following the significant excursus about the wayward confessor, Teresa continues her concatenation by resuming the narration of her adolescent illness: "A los dos meses, a poder de medicinas me tenía casi acabada la vida; y el rigor del *mal de corazón* . . . era mucho más recio . . . me parecía con *dientes* agudos me asian de él . . . me había dado una *purga* cada día, estaba *tan abrasada* que se me comenzaron a encojer los nervios con *dolores* tan *incomportables,* que día ni noche ningún sosiego podía tener; una tristeza muy profunda" (my emphasis). The result of these "purges" is quite different from the one administered by the angel in the "transverberation." In that case the sensation of the flaming spear's prophylaxis was so great that it made Teresa moan in painful ecstasy. . . . Both descriptions are homologous, yet the denotation bestowed on each by the Saint differs considerably. The reason for this becomes clear if we remember that the two parallel scenes share the marginal presence of the paternal figure. In the first instance, the figure is that of the father of flesh and blood, don Alonso; in the second, it is that of the spiritual Father, God. We might recall, in this regard, that it was don Alonso who insisted on the "cures" that were to have such painful results, and that the angel's purging lance represents the will of another "father," God.

Teresa's dialectical articulation becomes transparent when we observe that from one incident to the other her ego assumes the role of a transient entity. Exiled from her home by what is basically a guilty conscience, Teresa wanders resentfully about the world of her imagination, searching for a new home. Teresa's guilty conscience must be emphasized because it is the factor which first impedes any return, and then provokes the resentment which demands the re-creation of a home, one provisionally purged of the old love object and denoted as superior and more satisfying. This process is confirmed by the resolution of Teresa's illness. Don Alonso's efforts to relieve his daughter's suffering have no effect whatsoever. The treatments he obtains for her progressively worsen her condition, or so she would have us believe. When Teresa feels that her sickness has entered the critical stage, she begs to be allowed the purgative of confession. But don Alonso refuses to allow this. The memory of this provokes a resentful outburst from Teresa: " . . . por no me dar pena, mi padre no me dejó. ¡Oh amor de carne demasiado, que aunque sea de tan católico padre y tan avisado, que lo era harto, que no fué ignorancia, me pudiera hacer gran daño! Dióme aquella noche un parasismo, que me duró estar sin ningún sentido cuatro días, poco menos."

Teresa's reproach of her father is severe. The "great harm" to which don Alonso exposed his daughter is no doubt perdition, the result of dying without the proper absolution obtained by confession. Yet, we might inquire what merciful God would allow an agonizing subject to suffer damnation in such circumstances, particularly when the subject frequently visited the confessional. The burden of sin must have been very great. That, however, is not the real substance conveyed by Teresa's discourse in this fragment. The message encoded in her outburst can be more properly understood if we juxtapose the "gran daño" with the momentous event which followed don Alonso's rejection of his daughter's wishes, the "parasismo." The Saint's seizure constitutes an effective response to her father's putatively damaging actions. Teresa's representation of her seizure is in essence a rejection of the "name" her father's word bestows upon his daughter's needs. Don Alonso interprets his daughter's needs from a perspective anchored in circumstantial reality. In short, she is gravely ill and should follow a regimen most appropriate to achieving a cure. The problem is that Teresa's corporal needs are inseparable from a desire that cannot obtain satisfaction in the "real world," because very simply, that desire corresponds to what is "forbidden." Consequently, don Alonso carries Teresa to the margin of perdition in a dual manner. His mere presence and insistence on the "real" serves as a concrete emblem that recalls what should be forgotten. Thus the Saint's guilty conscience is compelled to seek out a spiritual prophylaxis. As if this were not enough, don Alonso's disturbing presence refuses to facilitate the metaphorical elaboration which would permit a resolution to the problematics of Teresa's desire. This "double bind" will eventually oblige the Saint to diminish her father until she is given the opportunity to revive him in a sphere of signification where he can respond properly to her demand for love. In view of the untenable situation she faces, Teresa's response to her father's insistence is appropriately a fundamental negation: she lapses into a coma.

Teresa's "parasismo" is a critical juncture in her autobiographical text because upon her recovery, with the exception of one important episode, her life ceases to relate in any significant way to the physical presence of her father. Don Alonso no longer constitutes an obstacle. He emerges instead as an instrument utilized by her to create paternal metaphors which become progressively distant from the man of flesh and blood. It is not by chance that Teresa claims that Saint Joseph is responsible for the recuperation of her physical faculties, so ravaged by her seizure that she had to walk on hands and knees "como gata." One can hardly imagine a more suitable figure to replace what don Alonso, in the Saint's implicit opinion, had taken away. Saint Joseph is, after all, the stand-in father of the Holy Family and in this function is obviously asexual. . . . The first "miracle" undergone by the Saint is, then, mediated by a paternal construct. The fact that this father image is asexual indicates that Teresa's discourse has found new signifiers to replace those too closely tied to an atavistic presence.

Upon his death, don Alonso himself will leap over the bar which separates the signifier from the signified. Acquiring the denotation of "angel" he will become one more manageable signifier in Teresa's discourse. As she narrates her father's last days Teresa distracts the reader with a series of reproaches directed against herself and convents that are lax in discipline. All the while she permits herself to assume a role, in reference to her father, similar to the one she played with the wayward confessor. As don Alonso lay dying, his daughter hurried home to console him and prepare him for death: "Díjele yo que pues era tan devoto de cuando el Señor llevaba la cruz a cuestas, que pensase Su Majestad le quería dar a sentir algo de lo que había pasado con aquel dolor. Consolóse tanto, que me parece *nunca más le oí quejar*" (my emphasis). Alleviating her father's suffering to the point where, not without irony, she never hears him complain again, the Saint achieves two things. First, by doing for don Alonso what he was unable to do for her in similar circumstances she supersedes her father. In final measure, she appropriates the role of bearer of the edifying word. Reversing the relationship of father and daughter in such a way, the Saint assumes the authority to manipulate the signifiers of desire in her own way. Second, by removing don Alonso's pain, Teresa portrays herself as a prophylactic agent. These two facets of the Saint's representation of her father's final agony denote this scene as a homologue of the story of the wayward confessor. Although the pain of the dying don Alonso may not be directly equivalent to the confessor's copper amulet, the denotation that accrues to that object is present here by means of the concatenated homologue.

Don Alonso's death finally allows the Saint to construct a more or less definitive formulation of her father's image. At this point Teresa's resentment and guilty conscience are dissolved and absorbed into a revived desire: "Estuvo tres días muy falto de sentido. El día que murió se le tornó el Señor tan entero, que nos espantábamos y le tuvo hasta que a la mitad del credo . . . expiró. Quedó como un *ángel;* así me parecía a mí lo era él . . ." (my emphasis). On another occasion the Saint will remind her readers that we on earth are not angels, that we have bodies and that wanting to be angels while on earth verges on blasphemy. Although the Saint recognizes that the other world where all desires are requited does not coincide with her corporeality ("No es posible ser aquí ángeles que no es nuestra naturaleza" [*Conceptos del amor de Dios*]), this fact does not prevent *her* from entering into intimate relations with that realm of angelic spirits "siempre abrasados en amor" (*El castillo interior*).

Some years after don Alonso's death, a problem arose between Teresa and one of her confessors. He wanted her to stop maintaining certain friendships, but she was unwilling to forego them. She took the problem to God and as she prayed she was seized by "un arrebatamiento tan súbito que casi me sacó de mí." Then, during this, her first "rapture" (*arrobamiento*), God Himself accedes to Teresa's wishes with the following laconic command: "Ya no quiero que tengas conversación con hombres, sino con *ángeles*" (my emphasis). What such "conversation" involves becomes clear in the transverberation. It is worth recalling at this juncture Teresa's resentment when don Alonso refused his ailing daughter the solace of confessional conversation. That resentment exploded in the terrible "parasismo." At that point also don Alonso obstructed his daughter's desires by refusing to certify her "death." ("Esta hija no es para enterrar," he is reputed to have replied to those who were sure she had died.) He thus refused to grant his daughter entry into that world where "los que . . . allá viven . . . parecerme aquellos verdaderamente los vivos,

y los que acá viven tan muertos, que *todo el mundo me parece no me hace compañía,* en especial cuando tengo aquellos ímpetus" (my emphasis). In this context the resonance of God's command is indeed wide and includes, most significantly, don Alonso's injunction of many years before when he told his daughter that she could not do as she wished until after his death.

It is therefore not surprising that when one of Teresa's confessors insists that the Saint follow a certain regimen, a discipline that her desire requires and rejects at the same time, Teresa should suffer her first "arrobamiento." That "rapture," we now realize, was prefigured by the "seizure" that arose in response to don Alonso when he imposed another regimen upon his daughter. But in the world of "raptures," the signifiers that convey the meaning of the discourse have arranged themselves in a way that allows desire its infinite elaboration. Here Teresa is not obliged to lapse into the silence of a coma. On the contrary, she is filled with loquacious visions. The law of conscience which so often obstructed the peregrine word of desire can no longer resist its thrust, and is absorbed by it. The transverberation is one of the results of success of the Saint's discourse. But this is not enough—the Saint's desire is limitless. If she wants to leave herself and live outside herself it is not in order to be left abjectly alone, but rather to be received into God's abode, serving Him as lover even as she becomes Him. This abode is defined by the Saint not as paradise somewhere in the great beyond, but as "esta morada interior, adonde está Dios en nuestra alma" (*El castillo interior*) a place where labors are rewarded by the pleasures of enjoying "estos toques de su amor, tan suaves y penetrativos."

We have now observed that a series of varied situations in Teresa's *Vida*—illnesses, raptures, reminiscences, divine and earthly dialogues—are structured around the problematic opposition between desire and the "father." It is this opposition which the Saint attempts to resolve semantically by a series of symbolic displacements enacted through the encounters between the main protagonists of her discourse: herself, her father, her confessors, and God. In the signifying chain of Teresa's discourse, the figure of the father is elaborated until it finds a formula which allows it to become absorbed into her desire.

The objection may arise that such a reading is only a repetition of supposedly discredited psychoanalytic onslaughts on the Saint. While my conclusions are, indeed, compatible with psychoanalytical theory, it does not follow as might be claimed in some quarters, that by virtue of this fact this essay is redundant or extraliterary. A perusal of the relatively few clinical oriented considerations of Teresa demonstrates that those studies focus on Teresa as an illustrative specimen of a particular pathological syndrome: hysteria. Once the clinical picture is established little effort is expended trying to demonstrate how this is integral to the articulation of the Saint's expression. Here, on the contrary, I have defined a salient aspect of her discourse and uncovered the literary process by which such a factor develops itself dialectically. True enough, this factor which could be figuratively described as the "lost word" corresponds to the "oedipus complex" in its feminine form (or, as it were, the "Electra complex"). What merits underscoring, however, is that the mere presence of such a complex is only of contingent interest to the critic, as is Teresa's eroticism. What converts Teresa's text into a valuable and edifying discourse is the manner in which the writer represents her ego in its search for the "lost word" and how through the articulation of the discourse she reclaims it and succeeds in installing herself in an intimate relationship with it. In such a way, the text, viewed in opposition to the dissembling narrator, grants the reader an exemplary accession to truth. That is, a series of ploys, strategies, and motives which propose to veil and pretend are instead turned upon themselves and utilized to uncover that which they were meant to hide. Thus we are given a glimpse of language vindicating itself as an instrument of truth. There is little more that can be expected from a writer.

Interestingly, the above reading complements a theory increasingly advanced about Teresa ever since it was conclusively demonstrated that on her father's side she was a decendant of *conversos.* According to this line of thought, Teresa's creation of a privileged interior world, in essence, arose out of the rejection by the larger society of those who were not "old Christians." While this theory is plausible, even seductive, the textual evidence adduced to support it has not been extensive. However, my own reading of Teresa's autobiography underlines the type of tension that would be aggravated by precisely such an anxiety. If we consider the figure of don Alonso as the most important signifier of her ancestry, the drama between Teresa and her father, so full of anxiety and ambivalence, can also be read as a meditation which tries to adjust a "stained lineage" (according to conceptions common to sixteenth-century Spain) to the point where such a "stain" disappears and becomes instead a superior and select category. Such an interpretation would neither contradict nor supersede the one elaborated in this essay. It would merely underscore the "overdetermination" of Teresa's discourse. In short, coming to terms with herself meant adjusting her ego vis-à-vis a continuous series of referents, centered on her father, but occupying different points on the spectrum of identity.

I should point out, in closing, that the subtleties and complexities of Teresa's discourse have hardly been exhausted in this essay. But it seems that they will remain undiscovered unless her readers ignore the layers of mystification that have come to surround her figure and writings and confront her discourse directly. In this essay there was no overt intention of denying Teresa's mysticism per se, or of putting into question any theological transcendence that might be attributed to her. However, in light of what has been presented here it appears that it is more fruitful to assume that the fundamental referent of Teresa's discourse is not necessarily an "ineffable" experience, but rather, as her text has shown us, a series of experienced structures that seek definition and adequate representation through language. (pp. 523-30)

Gari Laguardia, "Santa Teresa and the Problem of Desire," in Hispania, *Vol. 63, No. 3, September, 1980, pp. 523-31.*

Mary C. Sullivan   (essay date 1983)

[Sullivan is an American scholar and educator. In the following excerpt, she discusses the rhetorical design of Teresa's Life.*]*

Teresa's *Life* is basically a deliberative rhetorical text written to persuade particular audiences to adopt a particular view; subordinate to this rhetorical purpose the author's primary means of persuasion is the "example" of her own life. During the period 1560-1565 Teresa was often asked to write autobiographical accounts of her spiritual life: in 1560, 1562, and 1563 she wrote three separate *Spiritual Relations* for her confessors and during the period, late 1562-1565, she was revising the first draft of a longer "account of my life . . . with complete clarity and truthfulness" at the expressed command of, first, Pedro Ibáñez and then Garcia de Toledo. The result of this latter effort is the *Life* as we know it. The first draft is evidently lost.

But as one examines the text one discovers that Teresa has done more than she was originally commanded and more than she herself initially and consciously intended: she has in fact subordinated the autobiographical task to a more compelling purpose that wells up within her in the course of her writing during those three years. She has placed "this story of my unruly life," this account of "my way of prayer and the favours which God has granted me," at the service of an overriding desire to teach and preach the mercy of God. Thus, in Aristotelian terms Teresa's *Life* becomes primarily a deliberative ("political") discourse, not a forensic narrative as one might have expected. Her predominant concern is not to argue the consistency or worth, or indeed any particular judgment, of her past life (to the extent that she is at all forensic in her method her sub-thesis concerning her own past actions is decidedly negative), but rather to argue to a range of audiences, with various necessary adaptations in each case, the truth of her major thesis which develops from her own personal relationship to one of her audiences: namely, that God in his mercy unfailingly favors the person who does not give up prayer (or who does not give up trying to pray), even the sinful person of whom she sees herself as a prime example.

Although Teresa's *Life* takes on the intention of preaching God's mercy, the work represents a divergence from the works William L. Howarth classifies as Autobiography as Oratory in his 1974 essay, "Some Principles of Autobiography" (*New Literary History,* 5, 263-81). Howarth sees the autobiographers he discusses under this strategy (Augustine, Bunyan, Gibbon, Henry Adams, and Malcolm X) as "men who share a common devotion to doctrine," an autobiography in this mode as one in which the "hero defines his superiority through the power of preaching": "since its purpose is didactic, [the hero's] story is allegorical, seeking to represent in a single life an idealized pattern of human behavior." On the other hand, Teresa appears to be devoted primarily not to doctrine as such, a matter in which she repeatedly disclaims competence, but to persons with their experience or inexperience. Hers is a far more intuitive, personally reliant, and inductive approach, and in this she neither claims nor insinuates any superiority over her audience; indeed her whole logical argument is built precisely and ironically on her personal inferiority, as she honestly perceives this. Her intention throughout is not to preach "an idealized pattern of human behavior" but to proclaim the astoundingly gracious pattern of divine behavior. I think William Howarth makes provision for excluding Teresa's *Life* from this category of autobiographies when he rightly denies what "many assume": namely, "that all religious lives are in this category, separated by doctrinal barriers, but essentially 'success stories' that teach the lesson of grace." Teresa's actual life may have been later judged a "success" by certain standards, but her *Life* is not proclamation of success but of trust in the strictest sense.

The human audiences explicitly addressed in the *Life* are many, but I think Roy Pascal [in his *Design and Truth in Autobiography*] is too clear-cut in his claim that Teresa wrote her autobiography "with the knowledge that it would be read by a wide public." The widespread publication which later occurred was not Teresa's original intention. Her extreme concern expressed in the accompanying letter to Garcia de Toledo can be taken as evidence of her conscious attitude throughout the project: her desire for a very limited audience of confessors and for protection of this by anonymity, and her recurring focus on the one original purpose, that of securing competent advice for her personal life. She writes to Garcia de Toledo of the manuscript she is forwarding: "I beseech your Reverence to amend it, and, if it is to be sent to Father Master Avila, to have it copied, for otherwise someone might recognize the handwriting. I am most anxious that the order shall be given for him to see it, as it was with this intention that I began to write it; and, if he thinks I am on the right road, this will be a great comfort to me, for I can only do what lies in my power."

But certainly a desire akin to what Roy Pascal suggests does arise in and overtake Teresa's text in the course of her narration. Close attention to the text reveals that though Teresa tries to keep her narrative directed to her confessors—as evident in her repeated use of "Your Reverence" or "Your Reverences" and in her including the few "others who are to see this" by pre-arrangement, "my son" Petro Ibáñez, and the intimate "we five who now love each other in Christ"—the impulse to proclamation of God's mercy and to compassionate instruction of all spiritual persons gains strength to a remarkable intensity in the course of the narrative. Beginning with Chapter VII in which she gives the fullest account of her past infidelity, Teresa becomes less and less able to refrain from speaking, for example, to or for any "nun" who may be allowed to read this book, "anyone who has not begun to pray," "others . . . who have begun some time back and never manage to finish their course," "others if they take warning by me," "those who are beginners," the soul who "will be very glad to reach a description of itself which will show clearly that it is travelling on the right road," "weak souls like myself," the whole audience of "those who read this" by chance or by subsequent decision of her confessors.

Teresa is not unaware of the audacity of what is happening in the text. She realizes that "for a person like myself to speak of such a thing [Prayer of Union] and to make any attempt to explain a matter which cannot even begin to be described in words may very well be ridiculous." But she believes God will help her for next to doing what she is bidden, her "chief aim is to cause souls to covet so sublime a blessing." In fact she goes so far as to invite a now much expanded audience: "if there are any persons (and there must be many) who have attained to the experiences of prayer which the Lord has granted to this miserable woman, and who think that they have strayed from the path and wish to discuss these matters with me, the Lord will help his servant to prevent His truth."

This wider audience no doubt existed in actuality in Teresa's day and may exist in actuality today; but in the act of writing the text of her *Life,* it is not an actual human audience but rather Teresa's creative self-projection of readers, her fictionalized assumptions about them, her self-generated invitation to companionship with them that is most decisive in determining the rhetorical design of the text. In a profound way, for most of the text, Teresa *needs* this audience in order to work through the attitude of *regret* with which she is struggling.

Numerous passages reveal the critical presence of yet another audience: God himself. The forensic, deliberative, and epideictic discourses addressed to this audience rise to crescendos throughout the entire *Life,* erupting at the most thematically intense points of the narrative as Teresa, without understanding, marvels at the wisdom of his past and present favors to her, pleads for his continued help, praises him and censures herself. As a narrator she is intensely affected by her own narration and argument, as well as by her audiences, and repeatedly breaks into prayer under the apparently fresh weight of each new realization of what she is writing. The author's rhetorical relationship with this divine audience, expressed in the contrariety (his mercifulness/her sinfulness) that is the subject matter of her *Life,* is by far the most complex and rich in the text, for in addition to the fact that the full range of rhetorical discourses is addressed to "His Majesty"—he is judge, ruler, and object of praise and apology—he is also cited as co-author of parts of the text itself, a matter I shall discuss later in this essay.

Aware of the new purpose that has become explicit as she was writing, Teresa concludes the text with the wish that God may allow its first recipient, Garcia de Toledo, to

> enlighten this miserable creature, so lacking in humility and so presumptuous as to have dared to resolve to write upon subjects so sublime. . . . I have hoped that through me some praise might be given to the Lord, a thing for which I have prayed for many years. And as no works which I have performed can accomplish this, I have ventured to put together this story of my unruly life . . . and have merely set down what has happened to me with all the simplicity and truth at my command.

But Teresa has not "merely set down what has happened to me." Had she been able to re-read her own text she would have seen that her desire to serve God by proclamation of his mercy in fact altered her text and subordinated the account of her life to this other purpose.

Just before the great central digression (Chapters XI-XXII) in which Teresa instructs the now-much-enlarged audience concerning the four kinds of prayer she then understood, we realize what is happening in Teresa the narrator. The intention widens perceptibly from desire that the account be useful for her own correction and enlightenment to desire that the account be useful for the enlightenment of others and so for God's praise. In the final paragraph of Chapter X she hopes: "May His Majesty be blessed for everything, and may He, for His name's sake, make use of me. For my Lord well knows that I have no other desire than this, that He may be praised and magnified a little when it is seen that on so foul and malodorous a dunghill He has planted a garden of sweet flowers." Here the autobiographical account begins to assume the subordinate function of exemplary evidence. Her own life story is henceforth presented as an encouraging and sufficient example for others—"It suffices as an illustration of His great mercies"; let others "consider what He has done to me, who wearied of offending His Majesty before He ceased forgiving me"—until finally in Chapter XXII, near the end of her disguised third-person instruction on the kinds of prayer she has experienced, an alleged "digression" or "interruption" which [Victor G. de la Concha in his *El arte literario de Santa Teresa*] regards as, in fact, the microstructure of the entire *Life,* she arrives at the great synecdochic passage in which she claims "no one, however wicked, can be excluded from his love since He has dealt in such a way with me and brought me to so high a state. Reflect that what I am saying is barely a fraction of what there is to say . . . and what are these joys that the Lord gives? Only a single drop of the great abundant river which He has prepared for us." Her life as narrated thus becomes a conclusive "fraction" of the evidence for her thesis; the content of the autobiographical account is but a "single drop" of the "abundant river" which becomes the major preoccupation of her text.

To understand Teresa's motive in this enhancement of purpose and so of audience one needs to notice the attitude of *regret* which runs through the entire text, and its relationship to the design of the whole. The enduring sorrow of the narrator, to almost the very last pages of her *Life,* is her belief that she has never been able and will never be able to *serve* God. She repeatedly refers to her lack of service, to her uselessness, to her unprofitableness. Early in the text she sees that "the only service I have rendered Him is to be what I am." Later she feels that the mere narration of her faults may be of use to others if they will take warning from her, but the possibility of such indirect service only increases her desire to serve by giving direct testimony to God's mercy that will be believed.

By the time Teresa nears the end of her writing and reaches the point in her narration where she records the event of the night of prayer in which she "saw the most sacred Humanity in far greater glory than I had ever seen before"—"it is this kind of vision that causes the greatest profit of all"—she is becoming a changed author, transformed by the memory of this event, and almost ready to believe that she can serve the Lord by proclamation: "I could never possibly conceal this or refrain from proclaiming aloud such great marvels." Even though she still

thinks that she has not served God, she admits and then denies that "in some measure these great afflictions experienced by my soul have resembled acts performed in Thy service."

Finally in the last chapter of her *Life* Teresa speaks of a particular mystical experience and explains as much as she ever explains the most thorough transformation of her desire to serve God which she experiences by the end of her writing of the *Life.* "On the occasion referred to," she writes, "the Lord said one special thing which has been of the greatest help to me." Teresa is characteristically superlative in her evaluation of God's favors, but there is reason for interpreting *this* favor as indeed the "greatest help" which she experiences during the period in which she is writing the final draft of the *Life.* Teresa describes at length but with simplicity of language her reaction to this experience: "there remained imprinted upon me one truth in particular . . . I understood what it is for a soul to be walking in truth in the presence of Truth Itself.And what I understood comes to this: the Lord showed me that He is Truth Itself. . . . This truth which I am referring to is truth in itself, and is without beginning or end, and upon this truth all other truths depend." The effect of this "imprinted" realization can only be inferred from the text which follows. First Teresa breaks into prayer questioning God; then she goes on listing his favors to her until she admits that there is no need for her to describe any more of them, and finally she makes the brief but, in view of the distress recorded throughout the text, peaceful claim: "I think I have never found myself distressed since I resolved to serve this Lord and Comforter of mine with all my might," for "there seems to me now to be no other reason for living than this, and it is for this that I pray to God most earnestly. I sometimes say to Him with my whole will: 'To die, Lord, or to suffer! I ask nothing else of Thee for myself but this'."

The destructive diffidence about her inability to serve God appears to have ceased, though with no implication of complacency, and a new peace now characterizes her life "which is a kind of sleep" wherein she finds "no great propensity either to joy or to sorrow." She declares confidently and plainly that her soul "has been awakened by the Lord from a condition in which I used to feel as I did because I was neither mortified nor dead to the things of the world; and His Majesty will not let me become blind again."

Immediately after this declaration, in the third last paragraph of the text, Teresa sums up her whole life to date and the *Life* with one brief sentence: "It is thus, dear Sir and Father, that I live now." The discourse proper ends very shortly after that quiet statement. Teresa delays only to beseech her confessors to pray for her, and to speak with considerable detachment about the possible futures of the manuscript.

In so complicated a text, in which a range of rhetorical purposes relates to a wide range of intended and emerging audiences, the unifying center of this diversity is the subject of the text itself, the conviction which I take to be the "master form" of Teresa's consciousness as she writes her *Life:* the absurd to her but nonetheless real contrariety which she perceived between God's behavior toward her and her behavior toward him, between his mercy and her sinfulness. The dominant linguistic phenomenon of the text is the frequent repetition of this mutually affecting polarity. Repeatedly Teresa writes, usually in the same sentence, as, for example, in the opening sentence of the *Life,* of the opposition between "the favours which the Lord has granted me" and "my grave sins and wicked life," between "mercy so great" and "treason so foul and abominable," between "my wickedness and the great goodness of God." At least one causal connection between these poles is persistently articulated. Her sins seem to evoke the corrective punishment of more gifts, and from this chastening graciousness come "the troubles which arise from being so much with One Who is so different from you." The chief pain for the person thus favored is her ever-increasing awareness of the seemingly ever-widening polarity: "How conscious it becomes of the multitude of Thy wonders and mercies, and of its own wretchedness." Given the God Teresa has characterized in her *Life,* in some sense a victorious "antagonist," this polarity as initially conceived presents a no-win situation for Teresa: there exists no hope for resolution of it through any adequate service or sufficient repayment. In the end her enduring conviction concerning this sustained contrast between "what I am" and "what He is" constitutes the primary evidence she advances for proving the thesis which transcends the narrative and transforms the personal "account of my life" into a deliberative discourse.

A recurring scriptural image illumines the nature of this transformation of the narrator's attitude and so, of her text: namely, Teresa's frequent quotation or paraphrase of Paul's autobiographic summation in Galatians 2:20, "I live now not I but Christ lives in me." Teresa comes eventually to see herself as one in whom these words are, by God's favor, a reality. This repeated text with the image of union it suggests is structurally important to the development of her final attitude, for it internalizes the positive extremity of the polarity which is her subject. God's mercifulness is now perceived as living *within* her otherwise weak and sinful life. This realization represents a peaceful reconciliation of these opposites, though not a neutralization of the enduring polarity. For example, as Teresa is about to describe the most intimate part of what the soul experiences in the fourth and highest kind of prayer which she elucidates in the *Life,* she steps forward from her carefully assumed third-person exposition into first-person description of herself at the very moment of writing. Reading this passage one realizes that the author's "voyage" itself, in Roy Pascal's sense, is going on before one's very eyes:

> As I was about to write of this (I had just communicated and had been experiencing this very prayer of which I am writing), I was wondering what it is the soul does during this time, when the Lord said these words to me: "It dies to itself wholly, daughter, in order that it may fix itself more and more upon me; it is no longer itself that lives, but I. As it cannot comprehend what it understands, it is an understanding which understands not." One who has experienced this will understand something of it; it cannot be

more clearly expressed. . . . I can only say that the soul feels close to God and that there abides within it such a certainty that it cannot possibly do other than believe.

Two important new notes are here revealed in the consciousness of the author: an emphasis on dying to or being delivered from oneself, over being useful, and the presence of "certainty." Thus, after the conclusion of the long central "digression" on prayer, when Teresa resumes in Chapter XXIII the narration of her life, she can claim, in order that, as she says, what is to come may be the better understood: "From this point onward, I am speaking of another and a new book—I mean, of another and a new life. Until now the life I have been living since I began to expound these matters concerning prayer is the life which God has been living in me—or so it has seemed to me. . . . Praised be the Lord, Who has delivered me from myself!" A series of verbs indicating darkness, fear, and, finally, discovery characterize the backward-glancing narration which follows. Here Teresa tries to describe the transition and transformation she experienced as she was directed "along paths which seemed to make me quite a different person," one in whom the "life" was now not her own.

At this point, a clearer history of the two drafts of the *Life* would be of immense help to the reader. We know that a first draft was completed sometime in the middle of 1562 and that the text we now have is the draft completed in late 1565 or very early 1566. But in the absence of a manuscript of the first draft we cannot ascertain the additions made between 1562 and 1565, so we cannot establish the chronological sequence of the writing of passages in the text. While it is conceivable that portions of the *Life* which appear earlier in the text may have been composed after portions of the *Life* which appear later in the text, and vice versa, there seems now no way of proving this, except for those passages which relate to events whose date is known. The inability to put the writing of many passages of the text in a reliable chronological sequence prevents a confident analysis of the development of the narrator as she wrote. Though the text at the autobiographical level is an account of Teresa's changing realizations, feelings, experiences, and attitudes and her reactions to these changes, there is no way to know for sure whether an attitude expressed near the end of the text or one expressed in the middle represents the final view of the author during the period in which she was putting her *Life* in its final form. One can only assume that the last pages of the text, where the encounter with Truth Itself is narrated, represent the latest Teresa and granted that this is so, such a transformation in the narrator's personal development as I have described does appear and the narrator's own discovery of that slow transformation, at least as it is presented in the *Life,* gives the *Life* its distinctive contour, out of which develop both the deliberative and epideictic discourses.

Three specific aspects of the text will serve to illustrate the modes of persuasion Teresa employs in her *Life,* her ethical, pathetic and logical arguments, respectively; she explicitly assigns co-authorship of the work to God and editorship to her confessors; in manifesting the ways of God in her own life as evidence for the mercy God will unfailingly show to others her chief metaphor is God's "hand"; and in arguing her thesis proclaiming this mercy toward sinners her chief warrant for its reliability is her own "experience."

A key passage assigning co-authorship to God occurs in the penultimate chapter where Teresa states:

> Much that I am writing here does not come out of my own head; I have been told it by this Heavenly Master of mine; and so, in places where I distinctly say "I was told this" or "The Lord told me," I am extremely scrupulous about adding or subtracting so much as a syllable. When I do not remember everything exactly, then, it must be understood that it comes from me and some of the things I say will come from me altogether. Anything that is good I do not attribute to myself, for I know there is nothing good in me save what the Lord has given me without my deserving it.

Earlier she had explained how, when she could not summon words to write about the fourth kind of prayer—"it seemed to me more impossible to say anything about it than to talk Greek"—and so had laid her writing task aside, "God enlightened my understanding, sometimes giving me words and sometimes showing me how to use them, for, as in dealing with the last kind of prayer, His Majesty seems to be pleased to say what I have neither the power nor the learning to express."

It is rhetorically significant that Teresa makes this claim. In Aristotelian terms the acceptability of one's logical argument and the persuasiveness of one's evidence in support of it are strengthened by one's ethical argument: that is, by the persuasiveness that derives from the character of the speaker as he presents himself. But Teresa's presentation of her own character is explicitly the reverse of what Aristotle advises, a fact which suggests important modifications in the development of Christian rhetoric. Rather than insure that her own character should look right, she presents in as specific detail as her confessors will allow her sins, her vanities, her deceit, her pride—nevertheless warning that she has presented her sins "in a light only too favourable." In direct violation of classical rhetorical theory, which she probably did not know, she explicitly says in various ways throughout the text: I am wicked, but, or indeed, *therefore,* believe me: "I am, in short, a woman, and not even a good one, but wicked."

It is true that the reader finds the honesty of her character implicit in the text, but Teresa is not playing games; she is not arguing the negative about herself in order covertly to affirm the positive. For her, the whole ethical force of her argument resides not in *her* goodness or trustworthiness, but in the goodness and trustworthiness of God whose authorship of the contour of her life in some way, for her, causes his co-authorship of her *Life* in its final shape. Her appeal to his co-authorship is not gratuitous in view of the way she has understood her own life. The conclusion she draws from her life is that God is the Speaker, Author, Source of the transcendent goodness, generosity, friendliness, good will which she is trying to persuade her readers to accept. Thus her subject and his co-authorship are in this sense identical.

About her own authorship of the text, Teresa is ambivalent: she never gainsays her own experience as reliable ground for what she argues, but she repeatedly expresses diffidence about her descriptions and explanations of that experience and this on two grounds: that she is an ignorant woman, unread and inarticulate, and that she is a weak, sinful woman susceptible to self-deception and blindness. On both counts she may mislead or harm other persons, possible readers. Despite all this, her confessors have commanded the writing of the book, so they must either assume final responsibility for the text, correcting it where necessary, or "tear it up."

Prior to the treatise on prayer, after beseeching her confessor to publish "what I have thus far said concerning my wicked life and sins" but *not* what she shall say from that point onwards about matters which concern prayer and her experience of prayer, she very explicitly lays out her trust in them: "as I think that Your Reverence, and others who are to see this, will do what, for love of the Lord, I am asking you, I am writing quite freely. In any other case, I should have great scruples about writing at all, except to confess my sins, about doing which I have none. For the rest, the very thought that I am a woman is enough to make my wings droop—how much more, then, the thought that I am such a wicked one!" During the same treatise she again expresses confidence in their editorial role: "I know I have no need to worry from the point of view either of learning or of spirituality, as this is going into the possession of those who will be able to judge it and will cut out anything which may be amiss." Toward the end of the treatise she once more resorts to the expected editorial vigilance of her confessors, especially of Garcia de Toledo: "I am being very bold. Your Reverence must destroy this if you think it is wrong."

Much can be made of Teresa's complaint in the *Life* that those who are "terrified of the devil . . . , especially if they are confessors, can upset people a great deal, and for several years they were such a trial to me that I marvel now that I was able to bear it," but the text as a whole clearly indicates Teresa's confidence in her editors. The fact that she implicates these readers in the role of the speaker is a necessary corollary to the way in which she has characterized herself. The entire ethical argument is an appeal to a composite of divine and human competences and virtues that will counterbalance the author's own intellectual deficiencies and moral weaknesses.

Teresa writes to persuade not the stalwart but the timid, "weak souls like myself." One aspect of the pathetic argument reflects this especially: the predominance of her references to God's "hand," associated as this metaphor is with her repeated claim that God led her "gradually," not as "He dealt with the Magdalen, doing His work in her very quickly." Whenever Teresa narrates the activity of God in her life, leading her out of fear or error into peace or understanding, she nearly always does so by using the image of the hand of God. Describing the folly of her waiting to seek spiritual direction "till I had amended my life, just as I had done when I gave up prayer," she states the situation plainly: "I needed the help of others, who would take me by the hand and raise me up. Blessed be the Lord,

Bernini's renowned sculpture, "The Ecstasy of St. Teresa."

that in the end, the first hand to raise me was His!" Teresa's skill in using vivid natural imagery has long been noted but the special rhetorical significance of this particular image lies, I think, in its persistence in the text and in the gentleness she ascribes to it. All fear, doubt, inability, and weakness are slowly overcome by the activity of the hand of God: "For some years, as far as I can see, Thou hast led me by Thy hand," even when "often, Lord, I would not take it."

The continualness of God's extended and leading hand is celebrated throughout the *Life* and the nearly constant presence of this image reinforces Teresa's claim that God is willing to lead souls "gradually," that he is inexhaustibly forgiving and seeking. Thus the prevalence of God's help under this metaphor of his "hand" is a major support for her pathetic argument, that strand of the text in which the author seeks to satisfy the frame of mind and emotional needs of her wider audience. The ordinariness and humanness of the metaphor allow her message of divine mercy to seem more personally accessible to her hearers. Their timid frame of mind is induced to consider with positive feelings that Teresa's evidence could conceivably lead to the conclusion she advocates for them, the decision she presses them to adopt: fidelity to prayer with trust in the mercy of God.

The logical argument in the text, upon which the deliberative discourse is primarily built, rests wholly on the induction that Teresa constructs on the basis of her own "experience." If there is one matter in the *Life* about which she does not claim to be diffident, confused, unsure, or ignorant, it is the reality of her own experience. Repeatedly she asserts its actuality, usefulness and even conclusiveness for her general thesis. What Teresa has learned by experience is so unshakably a part of her mind's certitude that she does not hesitate to build the entire edifice of her argument upon it. Though she repeatedly finds fault with her own writing in the book, she is not fundamentally disturbed by its weaknesses because she sees experience itself as more persuasive than the language in which it is transcribed: "Having gone through so much myself, I am sorry for those who begin with books alone, for it is extraordinary what a difference there is between understanding a thing and knowing it by experience."

One might say that whenever Teresa finds herself unable adequately to describe or explain a part of her argument she resorts to the bed-rock claim: "This I know by experience"; "you may take my word for this, for I have learned it by experience"; "I know, for I have observed it in my own experience." Yet her references to her experience are not merely assertive. Careful reflection on her experience evidently precedes and underlies these references: "I have a great deal of experience of this and I know that what I say is true, for I have observed it carefully and discussed it afterwards with spiritual persons." At one level of discourse (in so far as the autobiography is a narrative addressed to her confessors), she views the entire *Life* as a comprehensive testing of the whole of her experience; but at another level (in so far as she feels impelled to persuade a wider audience of a truth greater than her life), she views her *Life* as containing reliable evidence upon which to base the argument she presents. Throughout Teresa is careful to distinguish between the authenticity of her experiences as experiences and the reliability of theories that may be constructed on the basis of those experiences: "For it is one favour that the Lord should grant this favour, but quite another to understand what favour and what grace it is; and still another to be able to describe and explain it." She attempts to deal with her experience at all three levels: to acknowledge the fact of it; to name and define it; and to describe and explain it. But her extreme confidence is associated only with the fact of her experience; at the second and third levels she frequently punctuates her writing with acknowledgements of ignorance or of sheer inability to go on: "The way in which this that we call union comes, and the nature of it, I do not know how to explain. It is described in mystical theology, but I am unable to use the proper terms. . . . This, with all your learning, Your Reverence will understand: there is nothing more that I can say of it."

The irony of the above ellipsis is that the intervening passage contains a rather clear though brief metaphorical explanation of what must be the experience of union (the fire and the flame), an explanation in accord with the teaching of John of the Cross. Here as elsewhere Teresa gives up too soon; sometimes her reason for quitting the analysis is the all too human one of fatigue, as she once admits: "This will be understood perfectly by persons of intelligence and they will be able to apply it more effectively than I can describe it, for I am growing tired."

In constructing her argument from experience Teresa also enlists the experience of her readers, often maintaining that "anyone who has experience of it will know that all that I say is literally true," and, conversely, that "Anyone who has not had experience of [this] will think that it is not so; but my own view is that [it is the case]." In the latter instances Teresa seeks to meet the inexperience of others by her own experience, though a major point in her argument is the individuality of God's dealing with each person. She is very wary of transgressing the experience of others: "I have no desire . . . to distress those who in a short time have made more progress than ourselves by making them turn back and go at our own pace, or to make those who, thanks to the favours given them by God, are soaring like eagles move like hens with their feet tied." Teresa's own general experience is put forward only to argue the general thesis of God's unfailing mercy to all who try to pray, not to argue specific theses that grow out of her own more specific personal experiences.

The quintessence of Teresa's induction is a simple *a fortiori* argument, an inference from one example to a conclusion:

EXAMPLE:	I was and am a sinful woman who has severely failed in love, service, trust and other ways though I wished to be faithful; yet God has repeatedly favored me, forgiven me, led me gradually to prayer and truth.

INFERENCE:	If he has done and been this to me who am so unfaithful and unprofitable, there can be no conceivable person whom he will not bless and favor if that person desires and wishes to pray.
PROPOSITION:	Therefore, do not give up trying to pray no matter what seem to be the obstacles, for God's mercy is infinitely greater than the human weakness of one who tries to pray.

Though she chooses to base her generalization on only one example (her own life with God's numerous mercies to her), because she is convinced of the truth of her own extreme unworthiness she can argue that if the less likely is true (that God has been merciful to *her*), the more likely will also be true (that God will be merciful to others).

In Teresa's view the *Life* is a pedagogic work at the service of praise and gratitude to her own Teacher: her desire to teach continually unfolds from and returns to the desire to praise and thank the Author of what she has learned and passes on. For as her deliberative discourse rises above the autobiographical narrative, so her epideictic discourse praising God's mercy rises above but is intimately connected with the deliberative discourse.

Epideictic discourse has been sometimes viewed as having no real connection with serious argumentation, but Ch. Perelman and L. Olbrechts-Tyteca argue convincingly that "epideictic oratory has significance and importance for argumentation, because it strengthens the disposition toward action by increasing adherence to the values it lauds." Teresa's purpose in her *Life* is, finally, to persuade her readers to acceptance of the unfailing and incalculable mercy of God. Their lifelong adherence to this argument and to the action it calls for will confront the same interventions and obstacles Teresa has experienced in herself: human weakness, infidelity, sin, shame, and fear. Therefore Teresa strengthens the long-term effectiveness of her deliberative discourse by the continual presence in her narrative of praise of God's unfailing help and friendship and eloquent celebration of his gradual and undiverted overcoming of all such obstacles.

Often in the form of prayer to God, Teresa's epideictic discourse moves ardently through the entire *Life,* affirming the great value she finds in God's merciful goodness, in itself and in his steadfastly benevolent relations with persons like herself: "Blessed be He for ever, who has had so much care for me!" As she advocates praise of and adherence to God's mercy (for her, Value Itself), so she repeatedly demonstrates the praise of God that flows from her own gradually developed adherence to him, or as she explains, from his unfailing adherence to her: "even though I am what I am He has not failed me." Her deliberative discourse is continually amplified and enhanced by its logical extension of it into praise and invitations to praise. The laborious task of writing her account will, she says, "be a happy one if I have managed to say anything for which one single act of praise will be made to the Lord."

The epideictic discourse is addressed to all Teresa's audiences: her confessors, the wider audience who may be helped by her work, and God himself. It reaches its most lyrical expression when her speech of praise is addressed to God: here the *Life* ascends to song. Teresa is well aware that this impulse to sing overtakes her in the course of her writing. To her confessor she explains: "I am writing what comes to my soul; and at times when, as I write, the greatness of the debt I owe him rises up before me, it is only by a supreme effort that I can refrain from going on to sing praises to God." This apology follows the long prayer in which, in tears as she writes, the author is overcome by a fuller realization of the scriptural claim made in God's name: "My delight is to be with the children of men" (Proverbs 8:31). The full argument and form of her *Life* is here cast in rhetorical question and answer as she tries to deal with the puzzling simultaneity of this divine "delight" and her offenses—from which come her reasons for singing:

> the greater have been my sins, the more has the great blessing of Thy mercies shone forth in me. How many reasons have I for singing of them for ever! I beseech Thee, my God, that it may be so: May I sing of them, and that without end, since Thou hast seen good to work such exceeding great mercies in me . . . I am drawn out of myself by them continually, that I may be the better able to sing Thy praise. For so long as I am in myself, my Lord, and without Thee, I can do nothing but be cut off like the flowers in this garden, and this miserable earth will become a dunghill again as before. Permit it not, Lord. Let it not be Thy will that a soul purchased with so many trials should be lost.

To some extent this song of the narrator grows out of the existential loneliness of the truthful autobiographer, of such an autobiography and probably of any autobiography. Although Teresa tries generously to establish a sense of communion with her readers and expresses great affection for and trust in all her human audiences, she gradually realizes and accepts her aloneness as author and secondary subject of this text. Finally, Teresa sees herself as a solitary pilgrim. The increasing dominion over herself which she experiences as God's gift—"so great that I do not know if it can be understood by anyone who does not possess it, for it is a real natural detachment, achieved without labor of our own"—is of "great help to me in teaching me where our true home is and in showing me that on earth we are but pilgrims." She is like a person who "has to go and settle in another country"; on the journey Teresa finds sometimes that "those with whom I keep company, and whose presence comforts me, are those who I know live in Heaven: they, it seems to me, are the people who are really, alive, while those who live on earth are so dead that it seems as if there is no one in the world who can be a companion to me, especially when those vehement impulses come upon me."

By the end of her *Life* Teresa comes to accept the loneliness of the "great secrets" which "the Lord continued to show me . . . sometimes He does so still." The impossibility of verbally sharing and describing these more and more isolates Teresa:

> I wish I could give a description of at least the smallest part of what I learned, but, when I try to discover a way of doing so, I find it impossible . . . however skilful the imagination may be, it will not succeed in picturing or describing what that light is like, nor a single one of those things which I learned from the Lord with a joy so sovereign as to be indescribable. For all the senses rejoice in a high degree, and with a sweetness impossible to describe, for which reason it is better to say no more about it.

In such moments of aloneness, or when the obstacles to adherence in her own life seem greatest—as, for example, in Chapter XXV where Teresa recounts the two years during which her confessors severely tested her spirit and she was on one occasion "like a person stunned by all this tribulation and fear . . . and quite upset and worn out, with not the least idea what to do"—she often lifts her voice in prayer of praise:

> O my Lord, how true a Friend Thou art, and how powerful! For Thou canst do all Thou wilt and never dost Thou cease to will if we love Thee. Let all things praise Thee, Lord of the World. Oh, if someone would but proclaim throughout the world how faithful Thou art to Thy friends! . . .
>
> O my God, had I but understanding and learning and new words with which to exalt Thy works as my soul knows them! All these, my Lord, I lack, but if Thou forsakest not me, I shall never fail Thee. Let all learned men rise up against me, let all created things persecute me, let the devils torment me, but fail Thou not me, Lord, for I have already experience of the benefits which come to him who trusts in Thee and whom Thou deliverest.

The inconclusiveness about her own future revealed in this prayer is not an isolated instance of this in the text. With paradoxical insistence it pervades Teresa's entire narrative, even to the last paragraph of the *Life* where she expresses her final state of mind in a wish: "May it please the Lord, since He is powerful and can do what He will, that I may succeed in doing His will in all things, and may He not allow this soul to be lost which so often, by so many methods and devices, His Majesty has rescued from hell and drawn to himself. Amen." The *Life* ends here with radical openness to the future; the very language of the last paragraph is perfectly one with the meaning narrated and argued throughout the text: salvation is pure *gift* in dialogue with human freedom. "*May*" it be God's gift that she "*may* succeed in doing His will" and "*may* He not allow" her to be lost. Thus the conclusion of the *Life* consistently embodies the utter gratuitousness of God's mercy which has been the subject of her autobiographical narrative, deliberative discourse, and epideictic utterances. The "Amen" itself finalizes nothing, but rather opens the entire text to a yet undetermined future: "May it be so." Teresa the speaker irrevocably joins herself with her own wider human audience in having freely to receive and accept the persuasiveness of the thesis she has argued. Rhetorically, the speaker-narrator steps back from her own evidence and enters a future in which she will choose or

not choose to submit to the inference she has drawn from it. Teresa, we discover, is not and has not been safely secure inside her text: she too is outside of it, a hearer of it herself, a listener and discoverer with her human audiences.

In this respect, among others, the *Life* represents the self as a problem and a search; the work is a probing with no relaxation as its conclusion. As Roy Pascal expresses it, the true autobiography "is an active contribution" to the life, "not a closing of accounts. Its object is wisdom, not just self-knowledge or self-exposition; the latter is a means to the former." So Teresa of Avila concludes her text at the present point of achieved clarity and peace, but she does not preclude the rest of the journey toward greater clarity which is its object. In her letter to Garcia de Toledo which accompanies the manuscript she simply trusts that future with a trust strengthened by the experience of writing the *Life* but not rendered any the less trust for that: "I trust in his mercy that Your Reverence and I shall see each other in a place where we shall realize more clearly what great things he has done for us and praise him for ever and ever. Amen." Her quest goes on, not inside the text, which he may burn, but outside it. (pp. 456-71)

Mary C. Sullivan, "From Narrative to Proclamation: A Rhetorical Analysis of the Autobiography of Teresa of Avila," in THOUGHT, *Vol. LVIII, No. 231, December, 1983, pp. 453-71.*

FURTHER READING

Auclair, Marcel. *Teresa of Avila.* Translated by Kathleen Pond. N.Y.: Pantheon Books, 1953, 480 p.

> Highly regarded biography of Teresa.

Braybrooke, Neville. "The Geography of the Soul: St. Teresa and Kafka." *The Dalhousie Review* 38, No. 3 (Autumn 1958): 324-30.

> Discusses the differing treatment of the castle metaphor in Kafka's novel *The Castle* and Teresa's *Interior Castle.*

Chorpenning, Joseph F. "The Monastery, Paradise, and the Castle: Literary Images and Spiritual Development in St. Teresa of Avila." *Bulletin of Hispanic Studies* LXII, No. 3 (July 1985): 245-57.

> Examines Teresa's use of imagery as it reflects her understanding of the monastic ideal.

Dicken, E. W. Trueman. *The Crucible of Love: A Study of the Mysticism of Santa Teresa and St. John of the Cross.* N.Y.: Sheed & Ward, 1963, 548 p.

> Compares the writings of the two foremost Spanish mystics and their theories of spiritual maturity.

Elguera, Amalia. "The Legacy of St. Teresa." *The Commonweal* LXXVII, No. 11 (7 December 1962): 271-73.

> Historical overview of Teresa's life and works.

Froude, James Anthony. "Saint Teresa." In *The Spanish*

Story of the Armada and Other Essays, pp. 155-218. N.Y.: Charles Scribner's Sons, 1892.

    Biographical overview which places Teresa in the social and political context of sixteenth-century Spain.

Hatzfeld, Helmut A. *Santa Teresa de Avila.* New York: Twayne Publishers, 1969, 200 p.

    Biographical and critical overview of Teresa's life and work.

Hoornaert, Rodolphe. *Saint Teresa in Her Writings.* Translated by Joseph Leonard. London: Sheed & Ward, 1931, 410 p.

    First substantive study of Teresa as a literary figure; cited by Hatzfeld as the "best study as far as [Teresa's] literary achievements are concerned."

Lincoln, Victoria. *Teresa: A Woman.* Albany: State University of New York Press, 1984, 440 p.

    The first biography of St. Teresa from a women's studies perspective. Lincoln includes a bibliography of essential works on St. Teresa.

Mandel, Barrett J. "Truth and Reality in the *Life* of St. Teresa." *Renascence* 32, No. 3 (Spring 1980): 131-45.

    Argues for the authenticity of Teresa's visions.

McIntosh, Kathleen. "Intellect and Intuition: Tension and Synthesis in Santa Teresa of Avila." *Revista de Estudios Hispanicos* XVI, No. 1 (January 1982): 3-14.

    Contends that St. Teresa's success as a reformer where many of her contemporaries had failed was based on her "ability to achieve a synthesis between two conflicting realms of religious experience: the intellectual realm of theology . . . and the intuitive realm of mystical experience."

Mirollo, James V. "The Lives of Saints Teresa of Avila and Benvenuto of Florence." *Texas Studies in Literature and Language* 29, No. 1 (Spring 1987): 54-73.

    Suggests that the autobiographies of Benvenuto Cellini and Teresa reflect a Renaissance crisis of heroism brought on by "too many conflicting ideals to choose from and too many diverse appetites for heroism to be satisfied by any of them."

Moore, Virginia. "Saint Teresa." In her *Distinguished Women Writers,* pp. 135-43. New York: E. P. Dutton & Co., 1934.

    Biographical essay in which Moore identifies St. Teresa as a distinguished woman writer because of her "power of expression without falsification."

Morón-Arroyo, Ciriaco. "The Human Value of the Divine: St. Teresa of Jesus." In *Women Writers of the Renaissance and Reformation,* edited by Katharina M. Wilson, pp. 401-31. Athens, Ga.: University of Georgia Press, 1987.

    Biographical and critical overview.

Morris, C. Brian. "The Poetry of Santa Teresa." *Hispania* 69, No. 2 (May 1986): 244-50.

    Positive evaluation of St. Teresa's poetry.

Peers, Edgar Allison. *Mother of Carmel: A Portrait of St. Teresa of Jesus.* London: S. C. M. Press, 1945, 163 p.

    Highly regarded biography of St. Teresa.

————. "St. Teresa of Jesus: *The Interior Castle.*" In his *Behind That Wall: An Introduction to Some Classics of the Interior Life,* pp. 115-123. 1948. Reprint. Freeport, N.Y.: Books for Libraries Press, 1969.

    Appreciative overview of the spiritual advice contained in *The Interior Castle.*

Pritchett, V. S. "Santa Teresa." *New Statesman* LIV, No. 1378 (19 August 1957): 175-76.

    Review of J. M. Cohen's *The Life of Santa Teresa* in which Pritchett characterizes Teresa as a "simple, unaffected writer, rambling, garrulous, homely and racy."

Ramge, Sebastian V. *An Introduction to the Writings of Saint Teresa.* Chicago: Henry Regnery Company, 1963, 135 p.

    Examines each of St. Teresa's major works and includes a bibliography of works about St. Teresa available in English.

Sackville-West, V. *The Eagle & the Dove: A Study in Contrasts, St. Teresa of Avila/St. Thérèse of Lisieux.* London: Michael Joseph, 1943, 191 p.

    Discusses the lives and religious accomplishments of these two Carmelite nuns.

Smith, Paul Julian. "Writing Women in the Golden Age of Spain: Saint Teresa and María de Zayas." *MLN* 102, No. 2 (March 1987): 220-40.

    Analysis of Teresa's writing as a manifestation of the semiotic, which Smith defines as pre-verbal consciousness derived from "discharges of energy [in children] which orientate the body with reference to the mother."

Sullivan, John, ed. *Centenary of St. Teresa: Catholic University Symposium—October 15-17, 1982.* Washington D.C.: ICS Publications, 1984, 227 p.

    Collection of essays on Teresa's significance as a religious and literary figure.

Symons, Arthur. "The Poetry of Santa Teresa and San Juan de la Cruz." *The Contemporary Review* 75 (April 1899): 542-51.

    Contrasts the poetry of Teresa and St. John of the Cross, finding St. John's writings constructed of carefully selected images and plays on words while Teresa's poetry is improvisational and "full of joyous life."

Walsh, Thomas. "Teresian Poets." *The Catholic World* CXV, No. 685 (April 1922): 22-9.

    Discusses Teresa's influence on other Catholic mystic poets including St. John of the Cross.

Weber, Alison. "The Paradoxes of Humility: Santa Teresa's *Libro de la vida* as Double Bind." *Journal of Hispanic Philology* 11, No. 3 (Spring 1985): 211-30.

    Focuses on the paradoxical nature of the "dual requirements of confession and defense—of obedience and self-assertion" in Teresa's *Life.*

Literature Criticism from 1400 to 1800

Cumulative Indexes

This Index Includes References to Entries in These Gale Series

Contemporary Literary Criticism Presents excerpts of criticism on the works of novelists, poets, dramatists, short story writers, scriptwriters, and other creative writers who are now living or who have died since 1960.

Twentieth-Century Literary Criticism Contains critical excerpts by the most significant commentators on poets, novelists, short story writers, dramatists, and philosophers who died between 1900 and 1960.

Nineteenth-Century Literature Criticism Offers significant passages from criticism on authors who died between 1800 and 1899.

Literature Criticism from 1400 to 1800 Compiles significant passages from the most noteworthy criticism on authors of the fifteenth through eighteenth centuries.

Classical and Medieval Literature Criticism Offers excerpts of criticism on the works of world authors from classical antiquity through the fourteenth century.

Short Story Criticism Compiles excerpts of criticism on short fiction by writers of all eras and nationalities.

Poetry Criticism Presents excerpts of criticism on the works of poets from all eras, movements, and nationalities.

Drama Criticism contains excerpts of criticism on dramatists of all nationalities and periods of literary history.

Children's Literature Review Includes excerpts from reviews, criticism, and commentary on works of authors and illustrators who create books for children.

Contemporary Authors Series Encompasses five related series. *Contemporary Authors* provides biographical and bibliographical information on more than 97,000 writers of fiction, nonfiction, poetry, journalism, drama, motion pictures, and other fields. Each new volume contains sketches on authors not previously covered in the series. *Contemporary Authors New Revision Series* provides completely updated information on active authors covered in previously published volumes of *CA*. Only entries requiring significant change are revised for *CA New Revision Series*. *Contemporary Authors Permanent Series* consists of updated listings for deceased and inactive authors removed from the original volumes 9-36 when these volumes were revised. *Contemporary Authors Autobiography Series* presents specially commissioned autobiographies by leading contemporary writers. *Contemporary Authors Bibliographical Series* contains primary and secondary bibliographies as well as analytical bibliographical essays by authorities on major modern authors.

Dictionary of Literary Biography Encompasses three related series. *Dictionary of Literary Biography* furnishes illustrated overviews of authors' lives and works and places them in the larger perspective of literary history. *Dictionary of Literary Biography Documentary Series* illuminates the careers of major figures through a selection of literary documents, including letters, notebook and diary entries, interviews, book reviews, and photographs. *Dictionary of Literary Biography Yearbook* summarizes the past year's literary activity with articles on genres, major prizes, conferences, and other timely subjects and includes updated and new entries on individual authors.

Concise Dictionary of American Literary Biography A six-volume series that collects revised and updated sketches on major American authors that were originally presented in *Dictionary of Literary Biography*.

Something about the Author Series Encompasses three related series. *Something about the Author* contains well-illustrated biographical sketches on juvenile and young adult authors and illustrators from all eras. *Something about the Author Autobiography Series* presents specially commissioned autobiographies by prominent authors and illustrators of books for children and young adults.

Yesterday's Authors of Books for Children Contains heavily illustrated entries on children's writers who died before 1961. Complete in two volumes.

Literary Criticism Series
Cumulative Author Index

This index lists all author entries in the Gale Literary Criticism Series and includes cross-references to other Gale sources. References in the index are identified as follows:

Beecher, Catharine Esther
    1800-1878 . . . . **NCLC 30**
    See also DLB 1

Beecher, John   1904-1980 . . . . **CLC 6**
    See also CANR 8; CA 5-8R;
    obituary CA 105

Beer, Johann   1655-1700 . . . . **LC 5**

Beer, Patricia   1919?- . . . . **CLC 58**
    See also CANR 13; CA 61-64; DLB 40

Beerbohm, (Sir Henry) Max(imilian)
    1872-1956 . . . . **TCLC 1, 24**
    See also CA 104; DLB 34

Behan, Brendan
    1923-1964 . . . . **CLC 1, 8, 11, 15**
    See also CA 73-76; DLB 13

Behn, Aphra   1640?-1689 . . . . **LC 1**
    See also DLB 39, 80

Behrman, S(amuel) N(athaniel)
    1893-1973 . . . . **CLC 40**
    See also CAP 1; CA 15-16;
    obituary CA 45-48; DLB 7, 44

Beiswanger, George Edwin   1931-
    See Starbuck, George (Edwin)

Belasco, David   1853-1931 . . . . **TCLC 3**
    See also CA 104; DLB 7

Belcheva, Elisaveta   1893-
    See Bagryana, Elisaveta

Belinski, Vissarion Grigoryevich
    1811-1848 . . . . **NCLC 5**

Belitt, Ben   1911- . . . . **CLC 22**
    See also CAAS 4; CANR 7; CA 13-16R;
    DLB 5

Bell, Acton   1820-1849
    See Bronte, Anne

Bell, Currer   1816-1855
    See Bronte, Charlotte

Bell, James Madison   1826-1902 . . . **TCLC 43**
    See also BLC 1; CA 122, 124; DLB 50

Bell, Madison Smartt   1957- . . . . **CLC 41**
    See also CA 111

Bell, Marvin (Hartley)   1937- . . . . . **CLC 8, 31**
    See also CA 21-24R; DLB 5

Bellamy, Edward   1850-1898 . . . . . . **NCLC 4**
    See also DLB 12

Belloc, (Joseph) Hilaire (Pierre Sebastien
    Rene Swanton)
    1870-1953 . . . . **TCLC 7, 18**
    See also YABC 1; CA 106; DLB 19

Bellow, Saul
    1915- . . . . . **CLC 1, 2, 3, 6, 8, 10, 13, 15,
    25, 33, 34, 63**
    See also CA 5-8R; CABS 1; DLB 2, 28;
    DLB-Y 82; DLB-DS 3;
    CDALB 1941-1968

Belser, Reimond Karel Maria de   1929-
    See Ruyslinck, Ward

Bely, Andrey   1880-1934 . . . . **TCLC 7**
    See also CA 104

Benary-Isbert, Margot   1889-1979 . . . **CLC 12**
    See also CLR 12; CANR 4; CA 5-8R;
    obituary CA 89-92; SATA 2;
    obituary SATA 21

Benavente (y Martinez), Jacinto
    1866-1954 . . . . **TCLC 3**
    See also CA 106

Benchley, Peter (Bradford)
    1940- . . . . **CLC 4, 8**
    See also CANR 12; CA 17-20R; SATA 3

Benchley, Robert   1889-1945 . . . . **TCLC 1**
    See also CA 105; DLB 11

Benedikt, Michael   1935- . . . . **CLC 4, 14**
    See also CANR 7; CA 13-16R; DLB 5

Benet, Juan   1927- . . . . **CLC 28**

Benet, Stephen Vincent
    1898-1943 . . . . **TCLC 7**
    See also YABC 1; CA 104; DLB 4, 48

Benet, William Rose   1886-1950 . . . **TCLC 28**
    See also CA 118; DLB 45

Benford, Gregory (Albert)   1941- . . . . **CLC 52**
    See also CANR 12, 24; CA 69-72;
    DLB-Y 82

Benjamin, Walter   1892-1940 . . . . . **TCLC 39**

Benn, Gottfried   1886-1956 . . . . **TCLC 3**
    See also CA 106; DLB 56

Bennett, Alan   1934- . . . . **CLC 45**
    See also CA 103

Bennett, (Enoch) Arnold
    1867-1931 . . . . **TCLC 5, 20**
    See also CA 106; DLB 10, 34

Bennett, George Harold   1930-
    See Bennett, Hal
    See also CA 97-100

Bennett, Hal   1930- . . . . **CLC 5**
    See also Bennett, George Harold
    See also DLB 33

Bennett, Jay   1912- . . . . **CLC 35**
    See also CANR 11; CA 69-72; SAAS 4;
    SATA 27, 41

Bennett, Louise (Simone)   1919- . . . . . **CLC 28**
    See also Bennett-Coverly, Louise Simone
    See also BLC 1

Bennett-Coverly, Louise Simone   1919-
    See Bennett, Louise (Simone)
    See also CA 97-100

Benson, E(dward) F(rederic)
    1867-1940 . . . . **TCLC 27**
    See also CA 114

Benson, Jackson J.   1930- . . . . **CLC 34**
    See also CA 25-28R

Benson, Sally   1900-1972 . . . . **CLC 17**
    See also CAP 1; CA 19-20;
    obituary CA 37-40R; SATA 1, 35;
    obituary SATA 27

Benson, Stella   1892-1933 . . . . **TCLC 17**
    See also CA 117; DLB 36

Bentley, E(dmund) C(lerihew)
    1875-1956 . . . . **TCLC 12**
    See also CA 108; DLB 70

Bentley, Eric (Russell)   1916- . . . . **CLC 24**
    See also CANR 6; CA 5-8R

Berger, John (Peter)   1926- . . . . . . **CLC 2, 19**
    See also CA 81-84; DLB 14

Berger, Melvin (H.)   1927- . . . . **CLC 12**
    See also CANR 4; CA 5-8R; SAAS 2;
    SATA 5

Berger, Thomas (Louis)
    1924- . . . . **CLC 3, 5, 8, 11, 18, 38**
    See also CANR 5; CA 1-4R; DLB 2;
    DLB-Y 80

Bergman, (Ernst) Ingmar   1918- . . . . . **CLC 16**
    See also CA 81-84

Bergson, Henri   1859-1941 . . . . **TCLC 32**

Bergstein, Eleanor   1938- . . . . **CLC 4**
    See also CANR 5; CA 53-56

Berkoff, Steven   1937- . . . . **CLC 56**
    See also CA 104

Bermant, Chaim   1929- . . . . **CLC 40**
    See also CANR 6; CA 57-60

Bernanos, (Paul Louis) Georges
    1888-1948 . . . . **TCLC 3**
    See also CA 104; DLB 72

Bernard, April   19??- . . . . **CLC 59**

Bernhard, Thomas
    1931-1989 . . . . **CLC 3, 32, 61**
    See also CA 85-88,; obituary CA 127;
    DLB 85

Berriault, Gina   1926- . . . . **CLC 54**
    See also CA 116

Berrigan, Daniel J.   1921- . . . . **CLC 4**
    See also CAAS 1; CANR 11; CA 33-36R;
    DLB 5

Berrigan, Edmund Joseph Michael, Jr.
    1934-1983
    See Berrigan, Ted
    See also CANR 14; CA 61-64;
    obituary CA 110

Berrigan, Ted   1934-1983 . . . . **CLC 37**
    See also Berrigan, Edmund Joseph Michael,
    Jr.
    See also DLB 5

Berry, Chuck ˜1926- . . . . **CLC 17**

Berry, Wendell (Erdman)
    1934- . . . . **CLC 4, 6, 8, 27, 46**
    See also CA 73-76; DLB 5, 6

Berryman, John
    1914-1972 . . . . . **CLC 1, 2, 3, 4, 6, 8, 10,
    13, 25, 62**
    See also CAP 1; CA 15-16;
    obituary CA 33-36R; CABS 2; DLB 48;
    CDALB 1941-1968

Bertolucci, Bernardo   1940- . . . . **CLC 16**
    See also CA 106

Bertrand, Aloysius   1807-1841 . . . . **NCLC 31**

Bertran de Born   c. 1140-1215 . . . . . **CMLC 5**

Besant, Annie (Wood)   1847-1933 . . . **TCLC 9**
    See also CA 105

Bessie, Alvah   1904-1985 . . . . **CLC 23**
    See also CANR 2; CA 5-8R;
    obituary CA 116; DLB 26

Beti, Mongo   1932- . . . . **CLC 27**
    See also Beyidi, Alexandre
    See also BLC 1

Betjeman, (Sir) John
    1906-1984 . . . . **CLC 2, 6, 10, 34, 43**
    See also CA 9-12R; obituary CA 112;
    DLB 20; DLB-Y 84

Betti, Ugo   1892-1953 . . . . **TCLC 5**
    See also CA 104

Bowen, Elizabeth (Dorothea Cole)
1899-1973 . . . . . **CLC 1, 3, 6, 11, 15, 22;
SSC 3**
See also CAP 2; CA 17-18;
obituary CA 41-44R; DLB 15

Bowering, George 1935- . . . . **CLC 15, 47**
See also CANR 10; CA 21-24R; DLB 53

Bowering, Marilyn R(uthe) 1949- . . . **CLC 32**
See also CA 101

Bowers, Edgar 1924- . . . . **CLC 9**
See also CANR 24; CA 5-8R; DLB 5

Bowie, David 1947- . . . . **CLC 17**
See also Jones, David Robert

Bowles, Jane (Sydney)
1917-1973 . . . . **CLC 3, 68**
See also CAP 2; CA 19-20;
obituary CA 41-44R

Bowles, Paul (Frederick)
1910- . . . . **CLC 1, 2, 19, 53; SSC 3**
See also CAAS 1; CANR 1, 19; CA 1-4R;
DLB 5, 6

Box, Edgar 1925-
See Vidal, Gore

Boyd, William 1952- . . . . **CLC 28, 53**
See also CA 114, 120

Boyle, Kay 1903- . . **CLC 1, 5, 19, 58; SSC 5**
See also CAAS 1; CA 13-16R; DLB 4, 9, 48

Boyle, Patrick 19??- . . . . **CLC 19**

Boyle, Thomas Coraghessan
1948- . . . . **CLC 36, 55**
See also CA 120; DLB-Y 86

Brackenridge, Hugh Henry
1748-1816 . . . . **NCLC 7**
See also DLB 11, 37

Bradbury, Edward P. 1939-
See Moorcock, Michael

Bradbury, Malcolm (Stanley)
1932- . . . . **CLC 32, 61**
See also CANR 1; CA 1-4R; DLB 14

Bradbury, Ray(mond Douglas)
1920- . . . . **CLC 1, 3, 10, 15, 42**
See also CANR 2; CA 1-4R; SATA 11;
DLB 2, 8

Bradford, Gamaliel 1863-1932 . . . . . **TCLC 36**
See also DLB 17

Bradley, David (Henry), Jr. 1950- . . **CLC 23**
See also BLC 1; CANR 26; CA 104;
DLB 33

Bradley, John Ed 1959- . . . . **CLC 55**

Bradley, Katherine Harris 1846-1914
See Field, Michael

Bradley, Marion Zimmer 1930- . . . . . **CLC 30**
See also CANR 7; CA 57-60; DLB 8

Bradstreet, Anne 1612-1672 . . . . **LC 4**
See also DLB 24; CDALB 1640-1865

Bragg, Melvyn 1939- . . . . **CLC 10**
See also CANR 10; CA 57-60; DLB 14

Braine, John (Gerard)
1922-1986 . . . . **CLC 1, 3, 41**
See also CANR 1; CA 1-4R;
obituary CA 120; DLB 15; DLB-Y 86

Braithwaite, William Stanley 1878-1962
See also BLC 1; CA 125; DLB 50, 54

Brammer, Billy Lee 1930?-1978
See Brammer, William

Brammer, William 1930?-1978 . . . . . **CLC 31**
See also obituary CA 77-80

Brancati, Vitaliano 1907-1954 . . . . . **TCLC 12**
See also CA 109

Brancato, Robin F(idler) 1936- . . . . . **CLC 35**
See also CANR 11; CA 69-72; SATA 23

Brand, Millen 1906-1980 . . . . **CLC 7**
See also CA 21-24R; obituary CA 97-100

Branden, Barbara 19??- . . . . **CLC 44**

Brandes, Georg (Morris Cohen)
1842-1927 . . . . **TCLC 10**
See also CA 105

Brandys, Kazimierz 1916- . . . . **CLC 62**

Branley, Franklyn M(ansfield)
1915- . . . . **CLC 21**
See also CLR 13; CANR 14; CA 33-36R;
SATA 4

Brathwaite, Edward 1930- . . . . **CLC 11**
See also CANR 11; CA 25-28R; DLB 53

Brautigan, Richard (Gary)
1935-1984 . . . . **CLC 1, 3, 5, 9, 12, 34, 42**
See also CA 53-56; obituary CA 113;
SATA 56; DLB 2, 5; DLB-Y 80, 84

Braverman, Kate 1950- . . . . **CLC 67**
See also CA 89-92

Brecht, (Eugen) Bertolt (Friedrich)
1898-1956 . . . . **TCLC 1, 6, 13, 35**
See also CA 104; DLB 56

Bremer, Fredrika 1801-1865 . . . . . **NCLC 11**

Brennan, Christopher John
1870-1932 . . . . **TCLC 17**
See also CA 117

Brennan, Maeve 1917- . . . . **CLC 5**
See also CA 81-84

Brentano, Clemens (Maria)
1778-1842 . . . . **NCLC 1**
See also DLB 90

Brenton, Howard 1942- . . . . **CLC 31**
See also CA 69-72; DLB 13

Breslin, James 1930-
See Breslin, Jimmy
See also CA 73-76

Breslin, Jimmy 1930- . . . . **CLC 4, 43**
See also Breslin, James

Bresson, Robert 1907- . . . . **CLC 16**
See also CA 110

Breton, Andre 1896-1966 . . . **CLC 2, 9, 15, 54**
See also CAP 2; CA 19-20;
obituary CA 25-28R; DLB 65

Breytenbach, Breyten 1939- . . . . . **CLC 23, 37**
See also CA 113, 129

Bridgers, Sue Ellen 1942- . . . . **CLC 26**
See also CANR 11; CA 65-68; SAAS 1;
SATA 22; DLB 52

Bridges, Robert 1844-1930 . . . . **TCLC 1**
See also CA 104; DLB 19

Bridie, James 1888-1951 . . . . **TCLC 3**
See also Mavor, Osborne Henry
See also DLB 10

Brin, David 1950- . . . . **CLC 34**
See also CANR 24; CA 102

Brink, Andre (Philippus)
1935- . . . . **CLC 18, 36**
See also CA 104

Brinsmead, H(esba) F(ay) 1922- . . . . **CLC 21**
See also CANR 10; CA 21-24R; SAAS 5;
SATA 18

Brittain, Vera (Mary) 1893?-1970 . . . **CLC 23**
See also CAP 1; CA 15-16;
obituary CA 25-28R

Broch, Hermann 1886-1951 . . . . **TCLC 20**
See also CA 117; DLB 85

Brock, Rose 1923-
See Hansen, Joseph

Brodkey, Harold 1930- . . . . **CLC 56**
See also CA 111

Brodsky, Iosif Alexandrovich 1940-
See Brodsky, Joseph (Alexandrovich)
See also CA 41-44R

Brodsky, Joseph (Alexandrovich)
1940- . . . . **CLC 4, 6, 13, 36, 50**
See also Brodsky, Iosif Alexandrovich

Brodsky, Michael (Mark) 1948- . . . . **CLC 19**
See also CANR 18; CA 102

Bromell, Henry 1947- . . . . **CLC 5**
See also CANR 9; CA 53-56

Bromfield, Louis (Brucker)
1896-1956 . . . . **TCLC 11**
See also CA 107; DLB 4, 9

Broner, E(sther) M(asserman)
1930- . . . . **CLC 19**
See also CANR 8, 25; CA 17-20R; DLB 28

Bronk, William 1918- . . . . **CLC 10**
See also CANR 23; CA 89-92

Bronte, Anne 1820-1849 . . . . **NCLC 4**
See also DLB 21

Bronte, Charlotte
1816-1855 . . . . **NCLC 3, 8, 33**
See also DLB 21

Bronte, (Jane) Emily 1818-1848 . . **NCLC 16**
See also DLB 21, 32

Brooke, Frances 1724-1789 . . . . **LC 6**
See also DLB 39

Brooke, Henry 1703?-1783 . . . . **LC 1**
See also DLB 39

Brooke, Rupert (Chawner)
1887-1915 . . . . **TCLC 2, 7**
See also CA 104; DLB 19

Brooke-Rose, Christine 1926- . . . . . . **CLC 40**
See also CA 13-16R; DLB 14

Brookner, Anita 1928- . . . . . . **CLC 32, 34, 51**
See also CA 114, 120; DLB-Y 87

Brooks, Cleanth 1906- . . . . **CLC 24**
See also CA 17-20R; DLB 63

Brooks, Gwendolyn
1917- . . . . **CLC 1, 2, 4, 5, 15, 49**
See also BLC 1; CANR 1, 27; CA 1-4R;
SATA 6; DLB 5, 76; CDALB 1941-1968

Brooks, Mel 1926- . . . . **CLC 12**
See also Kaminsky, Melvin
See also CA 65-68; DLB 26

Brooks, Peter 1938- . . . . **CLC 34**
See also CANR 1; CA 45-48

Brooks, Van Wyck 1886-1963 . . . . . . **CLC 29**
See also CANR 6; CA 1-4R; DLB 45, 63

Brophy, Brigid (Antonia)
1929- .... **CLC 6, 11, 29**
See also CAAS 4; CANR 25; CA 5-8R;
DLB 14

Brosman, Catharine Savage 1934-.... **CLC 9**
See also CANR 21; CA 61-64

Broughton, T(homas) Alan 1936- ... **CLC 19**
See also CANR 2, 23; CA 45-48

Broumas, Olga 1949- .... **CLC 10**
See also CANR 20; CA 85-88

Brown, Charles Brockden
1771-1810 .... **NCLC 22**
See also DLB 37, 59, 73;
CDALB 1640-1865

Brown, Christy 1932-1981 .... **CLC 63**
See also CA 105; obituary CA 104

Brown, Claude 1937- .... **CLC 30**
See also BLC 1; CA 73-76

Brown, Dee (Alexander) 1908- .. **CLC 18, 47**
See also CAAS 6; CANR 11; CA 13-16R;
SATA 5; DLB-Y 80

Brown, George Douglas 1869-1902
See Douglas, George

Brown, George Mackay 1921-.... **CLC 5, 28**
See also CAAS 6; CANR 12; CA 21-24R;
SATA 35; DLB 14, 27

Brown, H. Rap 1943-
See Al-Amin, Jamil Abdullah

Brown, Hubert Gerold 1943-
See Al-Amin, Jamil Abdullah

Brown, Rita Mae 1944-........ **CLC 18, 43**
See also CANR 2, 11; CA 45-48

Brown, Rosellen 1939-............ **CLC 32**
See also CANR 14; CA 77-80

Brown, Sterling A(llen)
1901-1989 ....**CLC 1, 23, 59**
See also BLC 1; CANR 26; CA 85-88;
obituary CA 127; DLB 48, 51, 63

Brown, William Wells
1816?-1884............. **NCLC 2; DC 1**
See also BLC 1; DLB 3, 50

Browne, Jackson 1950- .... **CLC 21**
See also CA 120

Browning, Elizabeth Barrett
1806-1861 .... **NCLC 1, 16**
See also DLB 32

Browning, Robert
1812-1889 .... **NCLC 19; PC 2**
See also YABC 1; DLB 32

Browning, Tod 1882-1962 .... **CLC 16**
See also obituary CA 117

Bruccoli, Matthew J(oseph) 1931- .. **CLC 34**
See also CANR 7; CA 9-12R

Bruce, Lenny 1925-1966 .... **CLC 21**
See also Schneider, Leonard Alfred

Bruin, John 1924-
See Brutus, Dennis

Brunner, John (Kilian Houston)
1934- .... **CLC 8, 10**
See also CAAS 8; CANR 2; CA 1-4R

Brutus, Dennis 1924-............. **CLC 43**
See also BLC 1; CANR 2, 27; CA 49-52

Bryan, C(ourtlandt) D(ixon) B(arnes)
1936- .... **CLC 29**
See also CANR 13; CA 73-76

Bryant, William Cullen
1794-1878 .... **NCLC 6**
See also DLB 3, 43, 59; CDALB 1640-1865

Bryusov, Valery (Yakovlevich)
1873-1924 .... **TCLC 10**
See also CA 107

Buchan, John 1875-1940 .... **TCLC 41**
See also YABC 2; brief entry CA 108;
DLB 34, 70

Buchanan, George 1506-1582 .... **LC 4**

Buchheim, Lothar-Gunther 1918- .... **CLC 6**
See also CA 85-88

Buchner, (Karl) Georg
1813-1837 .... **NCLC 26**

Buchwald, Art(hur) 1925-.......... **CLC 33**
See also CANR 21; CA 5-8R; SATA 10

Buck, Pearl S(ydenstricker)
1892-1973 .... **CLC 7, 11, 18**
See also CANR 1; CA 1-4R;
obituary CA 41-44R; SATA 1, 25; DLB 9

Buckler, Ernest 1908-1984........ **CLC 13**
See also CAP 1; CA 11-12;
obituary CA 114; SATA 47

Buckley, Vincent (Thomas)
1925-1988 .... **CLC 57**
See also CA 101

Buckley, William F(rank), Jr.
1925- .... **CLC 7, 18, 37**
See also CANR 1, 24; CA 1-4R; DLB-Y 80

Buechner, (Carl) Frederick
1926- .... **CLC 2, 4, 6, 9**
See also CANR 11; CA 13-16R; DLB-Y 80

Buell, John (Edward) 1927-........ **CLC 10**
See also CA 1-4R; DLB 53

Buero Vallejo, Antonio 1916- ... **CLC 15, 46**
See also CANR 24; CA 106

Bukowski, Charles 1920-.... **CLC 2, 5, 9, 41**
See also CA 17-20R; DLB 5

Bulgakov, Mikhail (Afanas'evich)
1891-1940 .... **TCLC 2, 16**
See also CA 105

Bullins, Ed 1935- .... **CLC 1, 5, 7**
See also BLC 1; CANR 24; CA 49-52;
DLB 7, 38

**Bulwer-Lytton, (Lord) Edward (George Earle
Lytton)** 1803-1873 .... **NCLC 1**
See also Lytton, Edward Bulwer
See also DLB 21

Bunin, Ivan (Alexeyevich)
1870-1953 .... **TCLC 6; SSC 5**
See also CA 104

Bunting, Basil 1900-1985.... **CLC 10, 39, 47**
See also CANR 7; CA 53-56;
obituary CA 115; DLB 20

Bunuel, Luis 1900-1983 .... **CLC 16**
See also CA 101; obituary CA 110

Bunyan, John 1628-1688 .... **LC 4**
See also DLB 39

Burgess (Wilson, John) Anthony
1917- ..... **CLC 1, 2, 4, 5, 8, 10, 13, 15,
22, 40, 62**
See also Wilson, John (Anthony) Burgess
See also DLB 14

Burke, Edmund 1729-1797.......... **LC 7**

Burke, Kenneth (Duva) 1897- .... **CLC 2, 24**
See also CA 5-8R; DLB 45, 63

Burney, Fanny 1752-1840 .... **NCLC 12**
See also DLB 39

Burns, Robert 1759-1796............ **LC 3**

Burns, Tex 1908?-
See L'Amour, Louis (Dearborn)

Burnshaw, Stanley 1906-..... **CLC 3, 13, 44**
See also CA 9-12R; DLB 48

Burr, Anne 1937- .... **CLC 6**
See also CA 25-28R

Burroughs, Edgar Rice
1875-1950 .... **TCLC 2, 32**
See also CA 104; SATA 41; DLB 8

Burroughs, William S(eward)
1914- .... **CLC 1, 2, 5, 15, 22, 42**
See also CANR 20; CA 9-12R; DLB 2, 8,
16; DLB-Y 81

Busch, Frederick 1941- ... **CLC 7, 10, 18, 47**
See also CAAS 1; CA 33-36R; DLB 6

Bush, Ronald 19??-............... **CLC 34**

Butler, Octavia E(stelle) 1947- ..... **CLC 38**
See also CANR 12, 24; CA 73-76; DLB 33

Butler, Samuel 1612-1680 .... **LC 16**
See also DLB 101

Butler, Samuel 1835-1902 ...... **TCLC 1, 33**
See also CA 104; DLB 18, 57

Butor, Michel (Marie Francois)
1926- .... **CLC 1, 3, 8, 11, 15**
See also CA 9-12R

Buzo, Alexander 1944-............ **CLC 61**
See also CANR 17; CA 97-100

Buzzati, Dino 1906-1972 .... **CLC 36**
See also obituary CA 33-36R

Byars, Betsy 1928-............... **CLC 35**
See also CLR 1, 16; CANR 18; CA 33-36R;
SAAS 1; SATA 4, 46; DLB 52

Byatt, A(ntonia) S(usan Drabble)
1936- .... **CLC 19, 65**
See also CANR 13, 33; CA 13-16R;
DLB 14

Byrne, David 1953?-............... **CLC 26**

Byrne, John Keyes 1926-
See Leonard, Hugh
See also CA 102

Byron, George Gordon (Noel), Lord Byron
1788-1824 .... **NCLC 2, 12**

Caballero, Fernan 1796-1877..... **NCLC 10**

Cabell, James Branch 1879-1958 ... **TCLC 6**
See also CA 105; DLB 9, 78

Cable, George Washington
1844-1925 .... **TCLC 4; SSC 4**
See also CA 104; DLB 12, 74

Cabrera Infante, G(uillermo)
1929- .... **CLC 5, 25, 45**
See also CANR 29; CA 85-88

Cade, Toni   1939-
See Bambara, Toni Cade

CAEdmon   fl. 658-680 . . . . CMLC 7

Cage, John (Milton, Jr.)   1912- . . . . . CLC 41
See also CANR 9; CA 13-16R

Cain, G.   1929-
See Cabrera Infante, G(uillermo)

Cain, James M(allahan)
1892-1977 . . . . CLC 3, 11, 28
See also CANR 8; CA 17-20R;
obituary CA 73-76

Caldwell, Erskine (Preston)
1903-1987 . . . . CLC 1, 8, 14, 50, 60
See also CAAS 1; CANR 2; CA 1-4R;
obituary CA 121; DLB 9, 86

Caldwell, (Janet Miriam) Taylor (Holland)
1900-1985 . . . . CLC 2, 28, 39
See also CANR 5; CA 5-8R;
obituary CA 116

Calhoun, John Caldwell
1782-1850 . . . . NCLC 15
See also DLB 3

Calisher, Hortense   1911- . . . . CLC 2, 4, 8, 38
See also CANR 1, 22; CA 1-4R; DLB 2

Callaghan, Morley (Edward)
1903-1990 . . . . CLC 3, 14, 41, 65
See also CANR 33; CA 9-12R;
obituary CA 132; DLB 68

Calvino, Italo
1923-1985 . . . .   CLC 5, 8, 11, 22, 33, 39;
SSC 3
See also CANR 23; CA 85-88;
obituary CA 116

Cameron, Carey   1952- . . . . CLC 59

Cameron, Peter   1959- . . . . CLC 44
See also CA 125

Campana, Dino   1885-1932 . . . . TCLC 20
See also CA 117

Campbell, John W(ood), Jr.
1910-1971 . . . . CLC 32
See also CAP 2; CA 21-22;
obituary CA 29-32R; DLB 8

Campbell, (John) Ramsey   1946- . . . . CLC 42
See also CANR 7; CA 57-60

Campbell, (Ignatius) Roy (Dunnachie)
1901-1957 . . . . TCLC 5
See also CA 104; DLB 20

Campbell, Thomas   1777-1844 . . . . NCLC 19

Campbell, (William) Wilfred
1861-1918 . . . . TCLC 9
See also CA 106

Camus, Albert
1913-1960 . . .   CLC 1, 2, 4, 9, 11, 14, 32,
63
See also CA 89-92; DLB 72

Canby, Vincent   1924- . . . . CLC 13
See also CA 81-84

Canetti, Elias   1905- . . . . CLC 3, 14, 25
See also CANR 23; CA 21-24R; DLB 85

Canin, Ethan   1960- . . . . CLC 55

Cape, Judith   1916-
See Page, P(atricia) K(athleen)

Capek, Karel
1890-1938 . . . . TCLC 6, 37; DC 1
See also CA 104

Capote, Truman
1924-1984 . . . . .   CLC 1, 3, 8, 13, 19, 34,
38, 58; SSC 2
See also CANR 18; CA 5-8R;
obituary CA 113; DLB 2; DLB-Y 80, 84;
CDALB 1941-1968

Capra, Frank   1897- . . . . CLC 16
See also CA 61-64

Caputo, Philip   1941- . . . . CLC 32
See also CA 73-76

Card, Orson Scott   1951- . . . . CLC 44, 47, 50
See also CA 102

Cardenal, Ernesto   1925- . . . . CLC 31
See also CANR 2; CA 49-52

Carducci, Giosue   1835-1907 . . . . . . TCLC 32

Carew, Thomas   1595?-1640 . . . . LC 13

Carey, Ernestine Gilbreth   1908- . . . . CLC 17
See also CA 5-8R; SATA 2

Carey, Peter   1943- . . . . CLC 40, 55
See also CA 123, 127

Carleton, William   1794-1869 . . . . . . NCLC 3

Carlisle, Henry (Coffin)   1926- . . . . . . CLC 33
See also CANR 15; CA 13-16R

Carlson, Ron(ald F.)   1947- . . . . CLC 54
See also CA 105

Carlyle, Thomas   1795-1881 . . . . . . NCLC 22
See also DLB 55

Carman, (William) Bliss
1861-1929 . . . . TCLC 7
See also CA 104

Carpenter, Don(ald Richard)
1931- . . . . CLC 41
See also CANR 1; CA 45-48

Carpentier (y Valmont), Alejo
1904-1980 . . . . CLC 8, 11, 38
See also CANR 11; CA 65-68;
obituary CA 97-100

Carr, Emily   1871-1945 . . . . TCLC 32
See also DLB 68

Carr, John Dickson   1906-1977 . . . . . . CLC 3
See also CANR 3; CA 49-52;
obituary CA 69-72

Carr, Virginia Spencer   1929- . . . . CLC 34
See also CA 61-64

Carrier, Roch   1937- . . . . CLC 13
See also DLB 53

Carroll, James (P.)   1943- . . . . CLC 38
See also CA 81-84

Carroll, Jim   1951- . . . . CLC 35
See also CA 45-48

Carroll, Lewis   1832-1898 . . . . NCLC 2
See also Dodgson, Charles Lutwidge
See also CLR 2; DLB 18

Carroll, Paul Vincent   1900-1968 . . . . CLC 10
See also CA 9-12R; obituary CA 25-28R;
DLB 10

Carruth, Hayden   1921- . . . . CLC 4, 7, 10, 18
See also CANR 4; CA 9-12R; SATA 47;
DLB 5

Carter, Angela (Olive)   1940- . . . . . CLC 5, 41
See also CANR 12; CA 53-56; DLB 14

Carver, Raymond
1938-1988 . . .   CLC 22, 36, 53, 55; SSC 8
See also CANR 17; CA 33-36R;
obituary CA 126; DLB-Y 84, 88

Cary, (Arthur) Joyce (Lunel)
1888-1957 . . . . TCLC 1, 29
See also CA 104; DLB 15

Casanova de Seingalt, Giovanni Jacopo
1725-1798 . . . . LC 13

Casares, Adolfo Bioy   1914-
See Bioy Casares, Adolfo

Casely-Hayford, J(oseph) E(phraim)
1866-1930 . . . . TCLC 24
See also BLC 1; CA 123

Casey, John   1880-1964
See O'Casey, Sean

Casey, John   1939- . . . . CLC 59
See also CANR 23; CA 69-72

Casey, Michael   1947- . . . . CLC 2
See also CA 65-68; DLB 5

Casey, Patrick   1902-1934
See Thurman, Wallace

Casey, Warren   1935- . . . . CLC 12
See also Jacobs, Jim and Casey, Warren
See also CA 101

Casona, Alejandro   1903-1965 . . . . . . CLC 49
See also Alvarez, Alejandro Rodriguez

Cassavetes, John   1929-1991 . . . . CLC 20
See also CA 85-88, 127

Cassill, R(onald) V(erlin)   1919- . . . CLC 4, 23
See also CAAS 1; CANR 7; CA 9-12R;
DLB 6

Cassity, (Allen) Turner   1929- . . . . CLC 6, 42
See also CANR 11; CA 17-20R

Castaneda, Carlos   1935?- . . . . CLC 12
See also CA 25-28R

Castedo, Elena   1937- . . . . CLC 65
See also CA 132

Castellanos, Rosario   1925-1974 . . . . . CLC 66
See also CA 131; obituary CA 53-56

Castelvetro, Lodovico   1505-1571 . . . . . LC 12

Castiglione, Baldassare   1478-1529 . . . LC 12

Castro, Rosalia de   1837-1885 . . . . . NCLC 3

Cather, Willa (Sibert)
1873-1947 . . . . . . TCLC 1, 11, 31; SSC 2
See also CA 104; SATA 30; DLB 9, 54;
DLB-DS 1; CDALB 1865-1917

Catton, (Charles) Bruce
1899-1978 . . . . CLC 35
See also CANR 7; CA 5-8R;
obituary CA 81-84; SATA 2;
obituary SATA 24; DLB 17

Cauldwell, Frank   1923-
See King, Francis (Henry)

Caunitz, William   1935- . . . . CLC 34

Causley, Charles (Stanley)   1917- . . . . . CLC 7
See also CANR 5; CA 9-12R; SATA 3;
DLB 27

Caute, (John) David   1936- . . . . CLC 29
See also CAAS 4; CANR 1; CA 1-4R;
DLB 14

Cavafy, C(onstantine) P(eter)
1863-1933 . . . . TCLC 2, 7
See also CA 104

Davie, Donald (Alfred)
1922- .... CLC **5, 8, 10, 31**
See also CAAS 3; CANR 1; CA 1-4R;
DLB 27

Davies, Ray(mond Douglas) 1944- .. CLC **21**
See also CA 116

Davies, Rhys 1903-1978........... CLC **23**
See also CANR 4; CA 9-12R;
obituary CA 81-84

Davies, (William) Robertson
1913- .... CLC **2, 7, 13, 25, 42**
See also CANR 17; CA 33-36R; DLB 68

Davies, W(illiam) H(enry)
1871-1940 .... TCLC **5**
See also CA 104; DLB 19

Davis, Frank Marshall 1905-1987
See also BLC 1; CA 123, 125; DLB 51

Davis, H(arold) L(enoir)
1896-1960 .... CLC **49**
See also obituary CA 89-92; DLB 9

Davis, Rebecca (Blaine) Harding
1831-1910 .... TCLC **6**
See also CA 104; DLB 74

Davis, Richard Harding
1864-1916 .... TCLC **24**
See also CA 114; DLB 12, 23, 78, 79

Davison, Frank Dalby 1893-1970 ... CLC **15**
See also obituary CA 116

Davison, Peter 1928- .... CLC **28**
See also CAAS 4; CANR 3; CA 9-12R;
DLB 5

Davys, Mary 1674-1732............. LC **1**
See also DLB 39

Dawson, Fielding 1930- .... CLC **6**
See also CA 85-88

Day, Clarence (Shepard, Jr.)
1874-1935 .... TCLC **25**
See also CA 108; DLB 11

Day, Thomas 1748-1789............. LC **1**
See also YABC 1; DLB 39

Day Lewis, C(ecil)
1904-1972 .... CLC **1, 6, 10**
See also CAP 1; CA 15-16;
obituary CA 33-36R; DLB 15, 20

Dazai Osamu 1909-1948 .... TCLC **11**
See also Tsushima Shuji

De Crayencour, Marguerite 1903-1987
See Yourcenar, Marguerite

Deer, Sandra 1940-................ CLC **45**

De Ferrari, Gabriella 19??- .... CLC **65**

Defoe, Daniel 1660?-1731 .... LC **1**
See also SATA 22; DLB 39

De Hartog, Jan 1914-............... CLC **19**
See also CANR 1; CA 1-4R

Deighton, Len 1929-....... CLC **4, 7, 22, 46**
See also Deighton, Leonard Cyril
See also DLB 87

Deighton, Leonard Cyril 1929-
See Deighton, Len
See also CANR 19; CA 9-12R

De la Mare, Walter (John)
1873-1956 .... TCLC **4**
See also CLR 23; CA 110; SATA 16;
DLB 19

Delaney, Shelagh 1939- .... CLC **29**
See also CA 17-20R; DLB 13

Delany, Mary (Granville Pendarves)
1700-1788 .... LC **12**

Delany, Samuel R(ay, Jr.)
1942- .... CLC **8, 14, 38**
See also BLC 1; CANR 27; CA 81-84;
DLB 8, 33

de la Ramee, Marie Louise 1839-1908
See Ouida
See also SATA 20

De la Roche, Mazo 1885-1961 ..... CLC **14**
See also CA 85-88; DLB 68

Delbanco, Nicholas (Franklin)
1942- .... CLC **6, 13**
See also CAAS 2; CA 17-20R; DLB 6

del Castillo, Michel 1933- .... CLC **38**
See also CA 109

Deledda, Grazia 1871-1936 .... TCLC **23**
See also CA 123

Delibes (Setien), Miguel 1920- ... CLC **8, 18**
See also CANR 1; CA 45-48

DeLillo, Don
1936- .... CLC **8, 10, 13, 27, 39, 54**
See also CANR 21; CA 81-84; DLB 6

De Lisser, H(erbert) G(eorge)
1878-1944 .... TCLC **12**
See also CA 109

Deloria, Vine (Victor), Jr. 1933-.... CLC **21**
See also CANR 5, 20; CA 53-56; SATA 21

Del Vecchio, John M(ichael)
1947- .... CLC **29**
See also CA 110

de Man, Paul 1919-1983 .... CLC **55**
See also obituary CA 111; DLB 67

De Marinis, Rick 1934-............ CLC **54**
See also CANR 9, 25; CA 57-60

Demby, William 1922-............ CLC **53**
See also BLC 1; CA 81-84; DLB 33

Denby, Edwin (Orr) 1903-1983..... CLC **48**
See also obituary CA 110

Dennis, John 1657-1734........... LC **11**

Dennis, Nigel (Forbes) 1912-........ CLC **8**
See also CA 25-28R; obituary CA 129;
DLB 13, 15

De Palma, Brian 1940-............ CLC **20**
See also CA 109

De Quincey, Thomas 1785-1859 ... NCLC **4**

Deren, Eleanora 1908-1961
See Deren, Maya
See also obituary CA 111

Deren, Maya 1908-1961.......... CLC **16**
See also Deren, Eleanora

Derleth, August (William)
1909-1971 .... CLC **31**
See also CANR 4; CA 1-4R;
obituary CA 29-32R; SATA 5; DLB 9

Derrida, Jacques 1930-............ CLC **24**
See also CA 124, 127

Desai, Anita 1937- .... CLC **19, 37**
See also CA 81-84

De Saint-Luc, Jean 1909-1981
See Glassco, John

De Sica, Vittorio 1902-1974 .... CLC **20**
See also obituary CA 117

Desnos, Robert 1900-1945........ TCLC **22**
See also CA 121

Destouches, Louis-Ferdinand-Auguste
1894-1961
See Celine, Louis-Ferdinand
See also CA 85-88

Deutsch, Babette 1895-1982 .... CLC **18**
See also CANR 4; CA 1-4R;
obituary CA 108; SATA 1;
obituary SATA 33; DLB 45

Devenant, William 1606-1649 .... LC **13**

Devkota, Laxmiprasad
1909-1959 .... TCLC **23**
See also CA 123

DeVoto, Bernard (Augustine)
1897-1955 .... TCLC **29**
See also CA 113; DLB 9

De Vries, Peter
1910- .... CLC **1, 2, 3, 7, 10, 28, 46**
See also CA 17-20R; DLB 6; DLB-Y 82

Dexter, Pete 1943-............. CLC **34, 55**
See also CA 127

Diamano, Silmang 1906-
See Senghor, Leopold Sedar

Diamond, Neil (Leslie) 1941-....... CLC **30**
See also CA 108

Dick, Philip K(indred)
1928-1982 .... CLC **10, 30**
See also CANR 2, 16; CA 49-52;
obituary CA 106; DLB 8

Dickens, Charles
1812-1870 .... NCLC **3, 8, 18, 26**
See also SATA 15; DLB 21, 55, 70

Dickey, James (Lafayette)
1923- .... CLC **1, 2, 4, 7, 10, 15, 47**
See also CANR 10; CA 9-12R; CABS 2;
DLB 5; DLB-Y 82; DLB-DS 7

Dickey, William 1928-........... CLC **3, 28**
See also CANR 24; CA 9-12R; DLB 5

Dickinson, Charles 1952-........... CLC **49**

Dickinson, Emily (Elizabeth)
1830-1886 .... NCLC **21**; PC **1**
See also SATA 29; DLB 1;
CDALB 1865-1917

Dickinson, Peter (Malcolm de Brissac)
1927- .... CLC **12, 35**
See also CA 41-44R; SATA 5; DLB 87

Didion, Joan 1934-..... CLC **1, 3, 8, 14, 32**
See also CANR 14; CA 5-8R; DLB 2;
DLB-Y 81, 86; CDALB 1968-1987

Dillard, Annie 1945-............. CLC **9, 60**
See also CANR 3; CA 49-52; SATA 10;
DLB-Y 80

Dillard, R(ichard) H(enry) W(ilde)
1937- .... CLC **5**
See also CAAS 7; CANR 10; CA 21-24R;
DLB 5

Dillon, Eilis 1920-................ CLC **17**
See also CLR 26; CAAS 3; CANR 4;
CA 9-12R; SATA 2

Gilbert, (Sir) W(illiam) S(chwenck)
 1836-1911 . . . . TCLC 3
 See also CA 104; SATA 36

Gilbreth, Ernestine 1908-
 See Carey, Ernestine Gilbreth

Gilbreth, Frank B(unker), Jr.
 1911- . . . . CLC 17
 See also CA 9-12R; SATA 2

Gilchrist, Ellen 1935- . . . . CLC 34, 48
 See also CA 113, 116

Giles, Molly 1942- . . . . CLC 39
 See also CA 126

Gilliam, Terry (Vance) 1940-
 See Monty Python
 See also CA 108, 113

Gilliatt, Penelope (Ann Douglass)
 1932- . . . . CLC 2, 10, 13, 53
 See also CA 13-16R; DLB 14

Gilman, Charlotte (Anna) Perkins (Stetson)
 1860-1935 . . . . TCLC 9, 37
 See also CA 106

Gilmour, David 1944-
 See Pink Floyd

Gilpin, William 1724-1804 . . . . . . NCLC 30

Gilroy, Frank D(aniel) 1925- . . . . CLC 2
 See also CA 81-84; DLB 7

Ginsberg, Allen
 1926- . . . . CLC 1, 2, 3, 4, 6, 13, 36
 See also CANR 2; CA 1-4R; DLB 5, 16;
 CDALB 1941-1968

Ginzburg, Natalia 1916- . . . . . . CLC 5, 11, 54
 See also CA 85-88

Giono, Jean 1895-1970 . . . . CLC 4, 11
 See also CANR 2; CA 45-48;
 obituary CA 29-32R; DLB 72

Giovanni, Nikki 1943- . . . . . CLC 2, 4, 19, 64
 See also BLC 2; CLR 6; CAAS 6;
 CANR 18; CA 29-32R; SATA 24;
 DLB 5, 41

Giovene, Andrea 1904- . . . . CLC 7
 See also CA 85-88

Gippius, Zinaida (Nikolayevna) 1869-1945
 See Hippius, Zinaida
 See also CA 106

Giraudoux, (Hippolyte) Jean
 1882-1944 . . . . TCLC 2, 7
 See also CA 104; DLB 65

Gironella, Jose Maria 1917- . . . . CLC 11
 See also CA 101

Gissing, George (Robert)
 1857-1903 . . . . TCLC 3, 24
 See also CA 105; DLB 18

Gladkov, Fyodor (Vasilyevich)
 1883-1958 . . . . TCLC 27

Glanville, Brian (Lester) 1931- . . . . . . CLC 6
 See also CANR 3; CA 5-8R; SATA 42;
 DLB 15

Glasgow, Ellen (Anderson Gholson)
 1873?-1945 . . . . TCLC 2, 7
 See also CA 104; DLB 9, 12

Glassco, John 1909-1981 . . . . CLC 9
 See also CANR 15; CA 13-16R;
 obituary CA 102; DLB 68

Glasser, Ronald J. 1940?- . . . . CLC 37

Glendinning, Victoria 1937- . . . . CLC 50
 See also CA 120

Glissant, Edouard 1928- . . . . CLC 10, 68

Gloag, Julian 1930- . . . . CLC 40
 See also CANR 10; CA 65-68

Gluck, Louise (Elisabeth)
 1943- . . . . CLC 7, 22, 44
 See also CA 33-36R; DLB 5

Gobineau, Joseph Arthur (Comte) de
 1816-1882 . . . . NCLC 17

Godard, Jean-Luc 1930- . . . . CLC 20
 See also CA 93-96

Godden, (Margaret) Rumer 1907-. . . CLC 53
 See also CLR 20; CANR 4, 27; CA 7-8R;
 SATA 3, 36

Godwin, Gail 1937- . . . . CLC 5, 8, 22, 31
 See also CANR 15; CA 29-32R; DLB 6

Godwin, William 1756-1836. . . . . . NCLC 14
 See also DLB 39

Goethe, Johann Wolfgang von
 1749-1832 . . . . NCLC 4, 22

Gogarty, Oliver St. John
 1878-1957 . . . . TCLC 15
 See also CA 109; DLB 15, 19

Gogol, Nikolai (Vasilyevich)
 1809-1852 . . . . . NCLC 5, 15, 31; DC 1;
                                          SSC 4
 See also CAAS 1, 4

Goines, Donald 1937?-1974
 See also BLC 2; CA 124; obituary CA 114;
 DLB 33

Gokceli, Yasar Kemal 1923-
 See Kemal, Yashar

Gold, Herbert 1924- . . . . CLC 4, 7, 14, 42
 See also CANR 17; CA 9-12R; DLB 2;
 DLB-Y 81

Goldbarth, Albert 1948- . . . . CLC 5, 38
 See also CANR 6; CA 53-56

Goldberg, Anatol 1910-1982 . . . . CLC 34
 See also obituary CA 117

Goldemberg, Isaac 1945- . . . . CLC 52
 See also CANR 11; CA 69-72

Golding, William (Gerald)
 1911- . . . . . CLC 1, 2, 3, 8, 10, 17, 27, 58
 See also CANR 13; CA 5-8R; DLB 15

Goldman, Emma 1869-1940 . . . . . . TCLC 13
 See also CA 110

Goldman, William (W.) 1931- . . . . CLC 1, 48
 See also CA 9-12R; DLB 44

Goldmann, Lucien 1913-1970 . . . . . . CLC 24
 See also CAP 2; CA 25-28

Goldoni, Carlo 1707-1793 . . . . LC 4

Goldsberry, Steven 1949- . . . . CLC 34

Goldsmith, Oliver 1728?-1774 . . . . LC 2
 See also SATA 26; DLB 39

Gombrowicz, Witold
 1904-1969 . . . . CLC 4, 7, 11, 49
 See also CAP 2; CA 19-20;
 obituary CA 25-28R

Gomez de la Serna, Ramon
 1888-1963 . . . . CLC 9
 See also obituary CA 116

Goncharov, Ivan Alexandrovich
 1812-1891 . . . . NCLC 1

Goncourt, Edmond (Louis Antoine Huot) de
 1822-1896 . . . . NCLC 7

Goncourt, Jules (Alfred Huot) de
 1830-1870 . . . . NCLC 7

Gontier, Fernande 19??- . . . . CLC 50

Goodman, Paul 1911-1972. . . . CLC 1, 2, 4, 7
 See also CAP 2; CA 19-20;
 obituary CA 37-40R

Gordimer, Nadine
 1923- . . . . CLC 3, 5, 7, 10, 18, 33, 51
 See also CANR 3; CA 5-8R

Gordon, Adam Lindsay
 1833-1870 . . . . NCLC 21

Gordon, Caroline
 1895-1981 . . . . CLC 6, 13, 29
 See also CAP 1; CA 11-12;
 obituary CA 103; DLB 4, 9; DLB-Y 81

Gordon, Charles William 1860-1937
 See Conner, Ralph
 See also CA 109

Gordon, Mary (Catherine)
 1949- . . . . CLC 13, 22
 See also CA 102; DLB 6; DLB-Y 81

Gordon, Sol 1923- . . . . CLC 26
 See also CANR 4; CA 53-56; SATA 11

Gordone, Charles 1925- . . . . CLC 1, 4
 See also CA 93-96; DLB 7

Gorenko, Anna Andreyevna 1889?-1966
 See Akhmatova, Anna

Gorky, Maxim 1868-1936 . . . . TCLC 8
 See also Peshkov, Alexei Maximovich

Goryan, Sirak 1908-1981
 See Saroyan, William

Gosse, Edmund (William)
 1849-1928 . . . . TCLC 28
 See also CA 117; DLB 57

Gotlieb, Phyllis (Fay Bloom)
 1926- . . . . CLC 18
 See also CANR 7; CA 13-16R; DLB 88

Gould, Lois 1938?- . . . . CLC 4, 10
 See also CA 77-80

Gourmont, Remy de 1858-1915. . . . TCLC 17
 See also CA 109

Govier, Katherine 1948- . . . . CLC 51
 See also CANR 18; CA 101

Goyen, (Charles) William
 1915-1983 . . . . CLC 5, 8, 14, 40
 See also CANR 6; CA 5-8R;
 obituary CA 110; DLB 2; DLB-Y 83

Goytisolo, Juan 1931- . . . . CLC 5, 10, 23
 See also CA 85-88

Gozzi, (Conte) Carlo 1720-1806 . . NCLC 23

Grabbe, Christian Dietrich
 1801-1836 . . . . NCLC 2

Grace, Patricia 1937- . . . . CLC 56

Gracian y Morales, Baltasar
 1601-1658 . . . . LC 15

Gracq, Julien 1910- . . . . CLC 11, 48
 See also Poirier, Louis
 See also DLB 83

Haggard, (Sir) H(enry) Rider
  1856-1925 . . . . TCLC 11
  See also CA 108; SATA 16; DLB 70

Haig-Brown, Roderick L(angmere)
  1908-1976 . . . . CLC 21
  See also CANR 4; CA 5-8R;
    obituary CA 69-72; SATA 12; DLB 88

Hailey, Arthur 1920- . . . . CLC 5
  See also CANR 2; CA 1-4R; DLB-Y 82

Hailey, Elizabeth Forsythe 1938- . . . CLC 40
  See also CAAS 1; CANR 15; CA 93-96

Haines, John 1924- . . . . CLC 58
  See also CANR 13; CA 19-20R; DLB 5

Haldeman, Joe 1943- . . . . CLC 61
  See also CA 53-56; DLB 8

Haley, Alex (Palmer) 1921- . . . . . . CLC 8, 12
  See also BLC 2; CA 77-80; DLB 38

Haliburton, Thomas Chandler
  1796-1865 . . . . NCLC 15
  See also DLB 11

Hall, Donald (Andrew, Jr.)
  1928- . . . . CLC 1, 13, 37, 59
  See also CAAS 7; CANR 2; CA 5-8R;
    SATA 23; DLB 5

Hall, James Norman 1887-1951 . . . TCLC 23
  See also CA 123; SATA 21

Hall, (Marguerite) Radclyffe
  1886-1943 . . . . TCLC 12
  See also CA 110

Hall, Rodney 1935- . . . . CLC 51
  See also CA 109

Halpern, Daniel 1945- . . . . CLC 14
  See also CA 33-36R

Hamburger, Michael (Peter Leopold)
  1924- . . . . CLC 5, 14
  See also CAAS 4; CANR 2; CA 5-8R;
    DLB 27

Hamill, Pete 1935- . . . . CLC 10
  See also CANR 18; CA 25-28R

Hamilton, Edmond 1904-1977 . . . . CLC 1
  See also CANR 3; CA 1-4R; DLB 8

Hamilton, Gail 1911-
  See Corcoran, Barbara

Hamilton, Ian 1938- . . . . CLC 55
  See also CA 106; DLB 40

Hamilton, Mollie 1909?-
  See Kaye, M(ary) M(argaret)

Hamilton, (Anthony Walter) Patrick
  1904-1962 . . . . CLC 51
  See also obituary CA 113; DLB 10

Hamilton, Virginia (Esther) 1936- . . . CLC 26
  See also CLR 1, 11; CANR 20; CA 25-28R;
    SATA 4; DLB 33, 52

Hammett, (Samuel) Dashiell
  1894-1961 . . . . CLC 3, 5, 10, 19, 47
  See also CA 81-84; DLB-DS 6

Hammon, Jupiter 1711?-1800? . . . . NCLC 5
  See also BLC 2; DLB 31, 50, 31, 50

Hamner, Earl (Henry), Jr. 1923- . . . CLC 12
  See also CA 73-76; DLB 6

Hampton, Christopher (James)
  1946- . . . . CLC 4
  See also CA 25-28R; DLB 13

Hamsun, Knut 1859-1952 . . . . . . TCLC 2, 14
  See also Pedersen, Knut

Handke, Peter 1942- . . CLC 5, 8, 10, 15, 38
  See also CA 77-80; DLB 85

Hanley, James 1901-1985 . . . CLC 3, 5, 8, 13
  See also CA 73-76; obituary CA 117

Hannah, Barry 1942- . . . . CLC 23, 38
  See also CA 108, 110; DLB 6

Hansberry, Lorraine (Vivian)
  1930-1965 . . . . CLC 17, 62
  See also BLC 2; CA 109;
    obituary CA 25-28R; CABS 3; DLB 7, 38;
    CDALB 1941-1968

Hansen, Joseph 1923- . . . . CLC 38
  See also CANR 16; CA 29-32R

Hansen, Martin 1909-1955 . . . . TCLC 32

Hanson, Kenneth O(stlin) 1922- . . . . CLC 13
  See also CANR 7; CA 53-56

Hardenberg, Friedrich (Leopold Freiherr) von
  1772-1801
  See Novalis

Hardwick, Elizabeth 1916- . . . . CLC 13
  See also CANR 3; CA 5-8R; DLB 6

Hardy, Thomas
  1840-1928 . . . TCLC 4, 10, 18, 32; SSC 2
  See also CA 104, 123; SATA 25; DLB 18,
  19

Hare, David 1947- . . . . CLC 29, 58
  See also CA 97-100; DLB 13

Harlan, Louis R(udolph) 1922- . . . . . CLC 34
  See also CANR 25; CA 21-24R

Harling, Robert 1951?- . . . . CLC 53

Harmon, William (Ruth) 1938- . . . . . CLC 38
  See also CANR 14; CA 33-36R

Harper, Frances Ellen Watkins
  1825-1911 . . . . TCLC 14
  See also BLC 2; CA 125;
    brief entry CA 111; DLB 50

Harper, Michael S(teven) 1938- . . CLC 7, 22
  See also CANR 24; CA 33-36R; DLB 41

Harris, Christie (Lucy Irwin)
  1907- . . . . CLC 12
  See also CANR 6; CA 5-8R; SATA 6;
    DLB 88

Harris, Frank 1856-1931 . . . . TCLC 24
  See also CAAS 1; CA 109

Harris, George Washington
  1814-1869 . . . . NCLC 23
  See also DLB 3, 11

Harris, Joel Chandler 1848-1908 . . . TCLC 2
  See also YABC 1; CA 104; DLB 11, 23, 42,
  78, 91

Harris, John (Wyndham Parkes Lucas)
  Beynon 1903-1969 . . . . CLC 19
  See also Wyndham, John
  See also CA 102; obituary CA 89-92

Harris, MacDonald 1921- . . . . CLC 9
  See also Heiney, Donald (William)

Harris, Mark 1922- . . . . CLC 19
  See also CAAS 3; CANR 2; CA 5-8R;
    DLB 2; DLB-Y 80

Harris, (Theodore) Wilson 1921- . . . . CLC 25
  See also CANR 11, 27; CA 65-68

Harrison, Harry (Max) 1925- . . . . . . CLC 42
  See also CANR 5, 21; CA 1-4R; SATA 4;
    DLB 8

Harrison, James (Thomas) 1937- . . . CLC 66
  See also Harrison, Jim
  See also CANR 8; CA 13-16R

Harrison, Jim 1937- . . . . CLC 6, 14, 33
  See also Harrison, James (Thomas)
  See also DLB-Y 82

Harrison, Tony 1937- . . . . CLC 43
  See also CA 65-68; DLB 40

Harriss, Will(ard Irvin) 1922- . . . . . . CLC 34
  See also CA 111

Hart, Moss 1904-1961 . . . . CLC 66
  See also Conrad, Robert Arnold
  See also obituary CA 89-92; DLB 7

Harte, (Francis) Bret(t)
  1836?-1902 . . . . TCLC 1, 25; SSC 8
  See also brief entry CA 104; SATA 26;
    DLB 12, 64, 74, 79; CDALB 1865-1917

Hartley, L(eslie) P(oles)
  1895-1972 . . . . CLC 2, 22
  See also CA 45-48; obituary CA 37-40R;
    DLB 15

Hartman, Geoffrey H. 1929- . . . . CLC 27
  See also CA 117, 125; DLB 67

Haruf, Kent 19??- . . . . CLC 34

Harwood, Ronald 1934- . . . . CLC 32
  See also CANR 4; CA 1-4R; DLB 13

Hasek, Jaroslav (Matej Frantisek)
  1883-1923 . . . . TCLC 4
  See also CA 104, 129

Hass, Robert 1941- . . . . CLC 18, 39
  See also CANR 30; CA 111

Hastings, Selina 19??- . . . . CLC 44

Hauptmann, Gerhart (Johann Robert)
  1862-1946 . . . . TCLC 4
  See also CA 104; DLB 66

Havel, Vaclav 1936- . . . . CLC 25, 58, 65
  See also CA 104

Haviaras, Stratis 1935- . . . . CLC 33
  See also CA 105

Hawes, Stephen 1475?-1523? . . . . LC 17

Hawkes, John (Clendennin Burne, Jr.)
  1925- . . . . . . CLC 1, 2, 3, 4, 7, 9, 14, 15,
                                              27, 49
  See also CANR 2; CA 1-4R; DLB 2, 7;
    DLB-Y 80

Hawking, Stephen (William)
  1948- . . . . CLC 63
  See also CA 126, 129

Hawthorne, Julian 1846-1934 . . . . . TCLC 25

Hawthorne, Nathaniel
  1804-1864 . . . NCLC 2, 10, 17, 23; SSC 3
  See also YABC 2; DLB 1, 74;
    CDALB 1640-1865

Hayashi Fumiko 1904-1951 . . . . TCLC 27

Haycraft, Anna 19??-
  See Ellis, Alice Thomas
  See also CA 122

McKay, Claude 1889-1948
See McKay, Festus Claudius

McKay, Festus Claudius 1889-1948
See also BLC 2; CA 124; brief entry CA 104

McKuen, Rod 1933- .... CLC 1, 3
See also CA 41-44R

McLuhan, (Herbert) Marshall
1911-1980 .... CLC 37
See also CANR 12; CA 9-12R;
obituary CA 102; DLB 88

McManus, Declan Patrick 1955-
See Costello, Elvis

McMillan, Terry 1951- .... CLC 50, 61

McMurtry, Larry (Jeff)
1936- .... CLC 2, 3, 7, 11, 27, 44
See also CANR 19; CA 5-8R; DLB 2;
DLB-Y 80, 87; CDALB 1968-1987

McNally, Terrence 1939- ...... CLC 4, 7, 41
See also CANR 2; CA 45-48; DLB 7

McPhee, John 1931- .... CLC 36
See also CANR 20; CA 65-68

McPherson, James Alan 1943- ..... CLC 19
See also CANR 24; CA 25-28R; DLB 38

McPherson, William 1939- .... CLC 34
See also CA 57-60

McSweeney, Kerry 19??- .... CLC 34

Mead, Margaret 1901-1978 .... CLC 37
See also CANR 4; CA 1-4R;
obituary CA 81-84; SATA 20

Meaker, M. J. 1927-
See Kerr, M. E.; Meaker, Marijane

Meaker, Marijane 1927-
See Kerr, M. E.
See also CA 107; SATA 20

Medoff, Mark (Howard) 1940- ... CLC 6, 23
See also CANR 5; CA 53-56; DLB 7

Megged, Aharon 1920- .... CLC 9
See also CANR 1; CA 49-52

Mehta, Ved (Parkash) 1934- .... CLC 37
See also CANR 2, 23; CA 1-4R

Mellor, John 1953?-
See The Clash

Meltzer, Milton 1915- .... CLC 26
See also CLR 13; CA 13-16R; SAAS 1;
SATA 1, 50; DLB 61

Melville, Herman
1819-1891 ...... NCLC 3, 12, 29; SSC 1
See also SATA 59; DLB 3, 74;
CDALB 1640-1865

Membreno, Alejandro 1972- .... CLC 59

Mencken, H(enry) L(ouis)
1880-1956 .... TCLC 13
See also CA 105, 125; DLB 11, 29, 63;
CDALB 1917-1929

Mercer, David 1928-1980 .... CLC 5
See also CANR 23; CA 9-12R;
obituary CA 102; DLB 13

Meredith, George 1828-1909 ...... TCLC 17
See also CA 117; DLB 18, 35, 57

Meredith, George 1858-1924 ...... TCLC 43

Meredith, William (Morris)
1919- .... CLC 4, 13, 22, 55
See also CANR 6; CA 9-12R; DLB 5

Merezhkovsky, Dmitri
1865-1941 .... TCLC 29

Merimee, Prosper
1803-1870 .... NCLC 6; SSC 7

Merkin, Daphne 1954- .... CLC 44
See also CANR 123

Merrill, James (Ingram)
1926- .... CLC 2, 3, 6, 8, 13, 18, 34
See also CANR 10; CA 13-16R; DLB 5;
DLB-Y 85

Merton, Thomas (James)
1915-1968 .... CLC 1, 3, 11, 34
See also CANR 22; CA 5-8R;
obituary CA 25-28R; DLB 48; DLB-Y 81

Merwin, W(illiam) S(tanley)
1927- ...... CLC 1, 2, 3, 5, 8, 13, 18, 45
See also CANR 15; CA 13-16R; DLB 5

Metcalf, John 1938- .... CLC 37
See also CA 113; DLB 60

Mew, Charlotte (Mary)
1870-1928 .... TCLC 8
See also CA 105; DLB 19

Mewshaw, Michael 1943- .... CLC 9
See also CANR 7; CA 53-56; DLB-Y 80

Meyer-Meyrink, Gustav 1868-1932
See Meyrink, Gustav
See also CA 117

Meyers, Jeffrey 1939- .... CLC 39
See also CA 73-76

**Meynell, Alice (Christiana Gertrude
Thompson)** 1847-1922 .... TCLC 6
See also CA 104; DLB 19

Meyrink, Gustav 1868-1932 ...... TCLC 21
See also Meyer-Meyrink, Gustav

Michaels, Leonard 1933- .... CLC 6, 25
See also CANR 21; CA 61-64

Michaux, Henri 1899-1984 ...... CLC 8, 19
See also CA 85-88; obituary CA 114

Michelangelo 1475-1564 .... LC 12

Michelet, Jules 1798-1874 ...... NCLC 31

Michener, James A(lbert)
1907- .... CLC 1, 5, 11, 29, 60
See also CANR 21; CA 5-8R; DLB 6

Mickiewicz, Adam 1798-1855 ..... NCLC 3

Middleton, Christopher 1926- ...... CLC 13
See also CANR 29; CA 13-16R; DLB 40

Middleton, Stanley 1919- .... CLC 7, 38
See also CANR 21; CA 25-28R; DLB 14

Migueis, Jose Rodrigues 1901- ..... CLC 10

Mikszath, Kalman 1847-1910 ..... TCLC 31

Miles, Josephine (Louise)
1911-1985 .... CLC 1, 2, 14, 34, 39
See also CANR 2; CA 1-4R;
obituary CA 116; DLB 48

Mill, John Stuart 1806-1873 ..... NCLC 11
See also DLB 55

Millar, Kenneth 1915-1983 .... CLC 14
See also Macdonald, Ross
See also CANR 16; CA 9-12R;
obituary CA 110; DLB 2; DLB-Y 83;
DLB-DS 6

Millay, Edna St. Vincent
1892-1950 .... TCLC 4
See also CA 103; DLB 45;
CDALB 1917-1929

Miller, Arthur
1915- ...... CLC 1, 2, 6, 10, 15, 26, 47;
DC 1
See also CANR 2, 30; CA 1-4R; CABS 3;
DLB 7; CDALB 1941-1968

Miller, Henry (Valentine)
1891-1980 .... CLC 1, 2, 4, 9, 14, 43
See also CA 9-12R; obituary CA 97-100;
DLB 4, 9; DLB-Y 80; CDALB 1929-1941

Miller, Jason 1939?- .... CLC 2
See also CA 73-76; DLB 7

Miller, Sue 19??- .... CLC 44

Miller, Walter M(ichael), Jr.
1923- .... CLC 4, 30
See also CA 85-88; DLB 8

Millett, Kate 1934- .... CLC 67
See also CANR 32; CA 73-76

Millhauser, Steven 1943- .... CLC 21, 54
See also CA 108, 110, 111; DLB 2

Millin, Sarah Gertrude 1889-1968 .. CLC 49
See also CA 102; obituary CA 93-96

Milne, A(lan) A(lexander)
1882-1956 .... TCLC 6
See also CLR 1, 26; YABC 1; CA 104, 133;
DLB 10, 77, 100

Milner, Ron(ald) 1938- .... CLC 56
See also BLC 3; CANR 24; CA 73-76;
DLB 38

Milosz Czeslaw
1911- .... CLC 5, 11, 22, 31, 56
See also CANR 23; CA 81-84

Milton, John 1608-1674 .... LC 9

Miner, Valerie (Jane) 1947- .... CLC 40
See also CA 97-100

Minot, Susan 1956- .... CLC 44

Minus, Ed 1938- .... CLC 39

Miro (Ferrer), Gabriel (Francisco Victor)
1879-1930 .... TCLC 5
See also CA 104

Mishima, Yukio
1925-1970 .... CLC 2, 4, 6, 9, 27; DC 1;
SSC 4
See also Hiraoka, Kimitake

Mistral, Gabriela 1889-1957 .... TCLC 2
See also CA 104

Mitchell, James Leslie 1901-1935
See Gibbon, Lewis Grassic
See also CA 104; DLB 15

Mitchell, Joni 1943- .... CLC 12
See also CA 112

Mitchell (Marsh), Margaret (Munnerlyn)
1900-1949 .... TCLC 11
See also CA 109, 125; DLB 9

Mitchell, S. Weir 1829-1914 ...... TCLC 36

Mitchell, W(illiam) O(rmond)
1914- .... CLC 25
See also CANR 15; CA 77-80; DLB 88

Mitford, Mary Russell 1787-1855 .. NCLC 4

Mitford, Nancy 1904-1973 .... CLC 44
See also CA 9-12R

Miyamoto Yuriko   1899-1951 . . . . . TCLC **37**

Mo, Timothy   1950- . . . . CLC **46**
See also CA 117

Modarressi, Taghi   1931- . . . . CLC **44**
See also CA 121

Modiano, Patrick (Jean)   1945- . . . . . CLC **18**
See also CANR 17; CA 85-88; DLB 83

Mofolo, Thomas (Mokopu)
1876-1948 . . . . TCLC **22**
See also BLC 3; brief entry CA 121

Mohr, Nicholasa   1935- . . . . CLC **12**
See also CLR 22; CANR 1; CA 49-52;
SAAS 8; SATA 8

Mojtabai, A(nn) G(race)
1938- . . . . CLC **5, 9, 15, 29**
See also CA 85-88

Moliere   1622-1673 . . . . LC **10**

Molnar, Ferenc   1878-1952 . . . . TCLC **20**
See also CA 109

Momaday, N(avarre) Scott
1934- . . . . CLC **2, 19**
See also CANR 14; CA 25-28R; SATA 30,
48

Monroe, Harriet   1860-1936 . . . . TCLC **12**
See also CA 109; DLB 54, 91

Montagu, Elizabeth   1720-1800 . . . . NCLC **7**

Montagu, Lady Mary (Pierrepont) Wortley
1689-1762 . . . . LC **9**

Montague, John (Patrick)
1929- . . . . CLC **13, 46**
See also CANR 9; CA 9-12R; DLB 40

Montaigne, Michel (Eyquem) de
1533-1592 . . . . LC **8**

Montale, Eugenio   1896-1981 . . . CLC **7, 9, 18**
See also CANR 30; CA 17-20R;
obituary CA 104

Montesquieu, Charles-Louis de Secondat
1689-1755 . . . . LC **7**

Montgomery, Marion (H., Jr.)
1925- . . . . CLC **7**
See also CANR 3; CA 1-4R; DLB 6

Montgomery, Robert Bruce   1921-1978
See Crispin, Edmund
See also CA 104

Montherlant, Henri (Milon) de
1896-1972 . . . . CLC **8, 19**
See also CA 85-88; obituary CA 37-40R;
DLB 72

Monty Python . . . . CLC **21**

Moodie, Susanna (Strickland)
1803-1885 . . . . NCLC **14**

Mooney, Ted   1951- . . . . CLC **25**

Moorcock, Michael (John)
1939- . . . . CLC **5, 27, 58**
See also CAAS 5; CANR 2, 17; CA 45-48;
DLB 14

Moore, Brian
1921- . . . . CLC **1, 3, 5, 7, 8, 19, 32**
See also CANR 1, 25; CA 1-4R

Moore, George (Augustus)
1852-1933 . . . . TCLC **7**
See also CA 104; DLB 10, 18, 57

Moore, Lorrie   1957- . . . . CLC **39, 45, 68**
See also Moore, Marie Lorena

Moore, Marianne (Craig)
1887-1972 . . . CLC **1, 2, 4, 8, 10, 13, 19,**
47
See also CANR 3; CA 1-4R;
obituary CA 33-36R; SATA 20; DLB 45;
CDALB 1929-1941

Moore, Marie Lorena   1957-
See Moore, Lorrie
See also CA 116

Moore, Thomas   1779-1852 . . . . NCLC **6**

Morand, Paul   1888-1976 . . . . CLC **41**
See also obituary CA 69-72; DLB 65

Morante, Elsa   1918-1985 . . . . CLC **8, 47**
See also CA 85-88; obituary CA 117

Moravia, Alberto
1907- . . . . CLC **2, 7, 11, 18, 27, 46**
See also Pincherle, Alberto

More, Hannah   1745-1833 . . . . NCLC **27**

More, Henry   1614-1687 . . . . LC **9**

More, Sir Thomas   1478-1535 . . . . . . LC **10**

Moreas, Jean   1856-1910 . . . . TCLC **18**

Morgan, Berry   1919- . . . . CLC **6**
See also CA 49-52; DLB 6

Morgan, Edwin (George)   1920- . . . . . CLC **31**
See also CANR 3; CA 7-8R; DLB 27

Morgan, (George) Frederick
1922- . . . . CLC **23**
See also CANR 21; CA 17-20R

Morgan, Janet   1945- . . . . CLC **39**
See also CA 65-68

Morgan, Lady   1776?-1859 . . . . NCLC **29**

Morgan, Robin   1941- . . . . CLC **2**
See also CA 69-72

Morgan, Seth   1949-1990 . . . . CLC **65**
See also CA 132

Morgenstern, Christian (Otto Josef Wolfgang)
1871-1914 . . . . TCLC **8**
See also CA 105

Moricz, Zsigmond   1879-1942 . . . . . TCLC **33**

Morike, Eduard (Friedrich)
1804-1875 . . . . NCLC **10**

Mori Ogai   1862-1922 . . . . TCLC **14**
See also Mori Rintaro

Mori Rintaro   1862-1922
See Mori Ogai
See also CA 110

Moritz, Karl Philipp   1756-1793 . . . . . . LC **2**

Morris, Julian   1916-
See West, Morris L.

Morris, Steveland Judkins   1950-
See Wonder, Stevie
See also CA 111

Morris, William   1834-1896 . . . . NCLC **4**
See also DLB 18, 35, 57

Morris, Wright (Marion)
1910- . . . . CLC **1, 3, 7, 18, 37**
See also CANR 21; CA 9-12R; DLB 2;
DLB-Y 81

Morrison, James Douglas   1943-1971
See Morrison, Jim
See also CA 73-76

Morrison, Jim   1943-1971 . . . . CLC **17**
See also Morrison, James Douglas

Morrison, Toni   1931- . . . . . CLC **4, 10, 22, 55**
See also BLC 3; CANR 27; CA 29-32R;
SATA 57; DLB 6, 33; DLB-Y 81;
CDALB 1968-1987; AAYA 1

Morrison, Van   1945- . . . . CLC **21**
See also CA 116

Mortimer, John (Clifford)
1923- . . . . CLC **28, 43**
See also CANR 21; CA 13-16R; DLB 13

Mortimer, Penelope (Ruth)   1918- . . . . CLC **5**
See also CA 57-60

Mosher, Howard Frank   19??- . . . . . . CLC **62**

Mosley, Nicholas   1923- . . . . CLC **43**
See also CA 69-72; DLB 14

Moss, Howard
1922-1987 . . . . CLC **7, 14, 45, 50**
See also CANR 1; CA 1-4R;
obituary CA 123; DLB 5

Motion, Andrew (Peter)   1952- . . . . . . CLC **47**
See also DLB 40

Motley, Willard (Francis)
1912-1965 . . . . CLC **18**
See also CA 117; obituary CA 106; DLB 76

Mott, Michael (Charles Alston)
1930- . . . . CLC **15, 34**
See also CAAS 7; CANR 7, 29; CA 5-8R

Mowat, Farley (McGill)   1921- . . . . . . CLC **26**
See also CLR 20; CANR 4, 24; CA 1-4R;
SATA 3, 55; DLB 68; AAYA 1

Mphahlele, Es'kia   1919-
See Mphahlele, Ezekiel

Mphahlele, Ezekiel   1919- . . . . CLC **25**
See also BLC 3; CANR 26; CA 81-84

Mqhayi, S(amuel) E(dward) K(rune Loliwe)
1875-1945 . . . . TCLC **25**
See also BLC 3

Mrozek, Slawomir   1930- . . . . CLC **3, 13**
See also CAAS 10; CANR 29; CA 13-16R

Mtwa, Percy   19??- . . . . CLC **47**

Mueller, Lisel   1924- . . . . CLC **13, 51**
See also CA 93-96

Muir, Edwin   1887-1959 . . . . TCLC **2**
See also CA 104; DLB 20

Muir, John   1838-1914 . . . . TCLC **28**

Mujica Lainez, Manuel
1910-1984 . . . . CLC **31**
See also CA 81-84; obituary CA 112

Mukherjee, Bharati   1940- . . . . CLC **53**
See also CA 107; DLB 60

Muldoon, Paul   1951- . . . . CLC **32**
See also CA 113, 129; DLB 40

Mulisch, Harry (Kurt Victor)
1927- . . . . CLC **42**
See also CANR 6, 26; CA 9-12R

Mull, Martin   1943- . . . . CLC **17**
See also CA 105

Munford, Robert   1737?-1783 . . . . LC **5**
See also DLB 31

Munro, Alice (Laidlaw)
1931- . . . . CLC **6, 10, 19, 50; SSC 3**
See also CA 33-36R; SATA 29; DLB 53

Munro, H(ector) H(ugh)   1870-1916
See Saki
See also CA 104; DLB 34

Owl, Sebastian   1939-
    See Thompson, Hunter S(tockton)

Oz, Amos   1939- ... CLC **5, 8, 11, 27, 33, 54**
    See also CANR 27; CA 53-56

Ozick, Cynthia   1928- ......CLC **3, 7, 28, 62**
    See also CANR 23; CA 17-20R; DLB 28;
    DLB-Y 82

Ozu, Yasujiro   1903-1963 .... CLC **16**
    See also CA 112

Pa Chin   1904- .... CLC **18**
    See also Li Fei-kan

Pack, Robert   1929- .... CLC **13**
    See also CANR 3; CA 1-4R; DLB 5

Padgett, Lewis   1915-1958
    See Kuttner, Henry

Padilla, Heberto   1932- .... CLC **38**
    See also CA 123

Page, Jimmy   1944- .... CLC **12**

Page, Louise   1955- .... CLC **40**

Page, P(atricia) K(athleen)
    1916- .... CLC **7, 18**
    See also CANR 4, 22; CA 53-56; DLB 68

Paget, Violet   1856-1935
    See Lee, Vernon
    See also CA 104

Paglia, Camille   1947- .... CLC **68**

Palamas, Kostes   1859-1943 .... TCLC **5**
    See also CA 105

Palazzeschi, Aldo   1885-1974 ...... CLC **11**
    See also CA 89-92; obituary CA 53-56

Paley, Grace   1922- .... CLC **4, 6, 37; SSC 8**
    See also CANR 13; CA 25-28R; DLB 28

Palin, Michael   1943- .... CLC **21**
    See also Monty Python
    See also CA 107

Palliser, Charles   1948?- .... CLC **65**

Palma, Ricardo   1833-1919 .... TCLC **29**
    See also CANR 123

Pancake, Breece Dexter   1952-1979
    See Pancake, Breece D'J

Pancake, Breece D'J   1952-1979 .... CLC **29**
    See also obituary CA 109

Papadiamantis, Alexandros
    1851-1911 .... TCLC **29**

Papini, Giovanni   1881-1956 ...... TCLC **22**
    See also CA 121

Paracelsus   1493-1541 .... LC **14**

Parini, Jay (Lee)   1948- .... CLC **54**
    See also CA 97-100

Parker, Dorothy (Rothschild)
    1893-1967 .... CLC **15, 68; SSC 2**
    See also CAP 2; CA 19-20;
    obituary CA 25-28R; DLB 11, 45. 86

Parker, Robert B(rown)   1932- ...... CLC **27**
    See also CANR 1, 26; CA 49-52

Parkin, Frank   1940- .... CLC **43**

Parkman, Francis   1823-1893 ..... NCLC **12**
    See also DLB 1, 30

Parks, Gordon (Alexander Buchanan)
    1912- .... CLC **1, 16**
    See also BLC 3; CANR 26; CA 41-44R;
    SATA 8; DLB 33

Parnell, Thomas   1679-1718 .... LC **3**

Parra, Nicanor   1914- .... CLC **2**
    See also CA 85-88

Pasolini, Pier Paolo
    1922-1975 .... CLC **20, 37**
    See also CA 93-96; obituary CA 61-64

Pastan, Linda (Olenik)   1932- ...... CLC **27**
    See also CANR 18; CA 61-64; DLB 5

Pasternak, Boris
    1890-1960 .... CLC **7, 10, 18, 63**
    See also CA 127; obituary CA 116

Patchen, Kenneth   1911-1972 ... CLC **1, 2, 18**
    See also CANR 3; CA 1-4R;
    obituary CA 33-36R; DLB 16, 48

Pater, Walter (Horatio)
    1839-1894 .... NCLC **7**
    See also DLB 57

Paterson, Andrew Barton
    1864-1941 .... TCLC **32**

Paterson, Katherine (Womeldorf)
    1932- .... CLC **12, 30**
    See also CLR 7; CANR 28; CA 21-24R;
    SATA 13, 53; DLB 52; AAYA 1

Patmore, Coventry Kersey Dighton
    1823-1896 .... NCLC **9**
    See also DLB 35

Paton, Alan (Stewart)
    1903-1988 .... CLC **4, 10, 25, 55**
    See also CANR 22; CAP 1; CA 15-16;
    obituary CA 125; SATA 11

Paulding, James Kirke   1778-1860.. NCLC **2**
    See also DLB 3, 59, 74

Paulin, Tom   1949- .... CLC **37**
    See also CA 123; DLB 40

Paustovsky, Konstantin (Georgievich)
    1892-1968 .... CLC **40**
    See also CA 93-96; obituary CA 25-28R

Paustowsky, Konstantin (Georgievich)
    1892-1968
    See Paustovsky, Konstantin (Georgievich)

Pavese, Cesare   1908-1950 .... TCLC **3**
    See also CA 104

Pavic, Milorad   1929- .... CLC **60**

Payne, Alan   1932-
    See Jakes, John (William)

Paz, Octavio
    1914- ...... CLC **3, 4, 6, 10, 19, 51, 65;
                                       PC 1**
    See also CANR 32; CA 73-76

p'Bitek, Okot   1931-1982
    See also BLC 3; CA 124; obituary CA 107

Peacock, Molly   1947- .... CLC **60**
    See also CA 103

Peacock, Thomas Love
    1785-1886 .... NCLC **22**

Peake, Mervyn   1911-1968 .... CLC **7, 54**
    See also CANR 3; CA 5-8R;
    obituary CA 25-28R; SATA 23; DLB 15

Pearce, (Ann) Philippa   1920- .... CLC **21**
    See also Christie, (Ann) Philippa
    See also CLR 9; CA 5-8R; SATA 1

Pearl, Eric   1934-
    See Elman, Richard

Pearson, T(homas) R(eid)   1956- .... CLC **39**
    See also CA 120, 130

Peck, John   1941- .... CLC **3**
    See also CANR 3; CA 49-52

Peck, Richard   1934- .... CLC **21**
    See also CLR 15; CANR 19; CA 85-88;
    SAAS 2; SATA 18; AAYA 1

Peck, Robert Newton   1928- .... CLC **17**
    See also CA 81-84; SAAS 1; SATA 21;
    AAYA 3

Peckinpah, (David) Sam(uel)
    1925-1984 .... CLC **20**
    See also CA 109; obituary CA 114

Pedersen, Knut   1859-1952
    See Hamsun, Knut
    See also CA 104, 109, 119

Peguy, Charles (Pierre)
    1873-1914 .... TCLC **10**
    See also CA 107

Pepys, Samuel   1633-1703 .... LC **11**

Percy, Walker
    1916-1990 ... CLC **2, 3, 6, 8, 14, 18, 47,
                                            65**
    See also CANR 1, 23; CA 1-4R;
    obituary CA 131; DLB 2; DLB-Y 80

Perec, Georges   1936-1982 .... CLC **56**
    See also DLB 83

Pereda, Jose Maria de
    1833-1906 .... TCLC **16**

Perelman, S(idney) J(oseph)
    1904-1979 ... CLC **3, 5, 9, 15, 23, 44, 49**
    See also CANR 18; CA 73-76;
    obituary CA 89-92; DLB 11, 44

Peret, Benjamin   1899-1959 .... TCLC **20**
    See also CA 117

Peretz, Isaac Leib   1852?-1915..... TCLC **16**
    See also CA 109

Perez, Galdos Benito   1853-1920 ... TCLC **27**
    See also CA 125

Perrault, Charles   1628-1703 .... LC **2**
    See also SATA 25

Perse, St.-John   1887-1975 .... CLC **4, 11, 46**
    See also Leger, (Marie-Rene) Alexis
    Saint-Leger

Pesetsky, Bette   1932- .... CLC **28**

Peshkov, Alexei Maximovich   1868-1936
    See Gorky, Maxim
    See also CA 105

Pessoa, Fernando (Antonio Nogueira)
    1888-1935 .... TCLC **27**
    See also CA 125

Peterkin, Julia (Mood)   1880-1961... CLC **31**
    See also CA 102; DLB 9

Peters, Joan K.   1945- .... CLC **39**

Peters, Robert L(ouis)   1924- .... CLC **7**
    See also CAAS 8; CA 13-16R

Petofi, Sandor   1823-1849 .... NCLC **21**

Petrakis, Harry Mark   1923- .... CLC **3**
    See also CANR 4, 30; CA 9-12R

Petrov, Evgeny   1902-1942 .... TCLC **21**

Petry, Ann (Lane)   1908- ...... CLC **1, 7, 18**
    See also CLR 12; CAAS 6; CANR 4;
    CA 5-8R; SATA 5; DLB 76

Roethke, Theodore (Huebner)
1908-1963 ...... **CLC 1, 3, 8, 11, 19, 46**
See also CA 81-84; CABS 2; SAAS 1;
DLB 5; CDALB 1941-1968

Rogers, Sam 1943-
See Shepard, Sam

Rogers, Thomas (Hunton) 1931- .... **CLC 57**
See also CA 89-92

Rogers, Will(iam Penn Adair)
1879-1935 .... **TCLC 8**
See also CA 105; DLB 11

Rogin, Gilbert 1929- .... **CLC 18**
See also CANR 15; CA 65-68

Rohan, Koda 1867-1947......... **TCLC 22**
See also CA 121

Rohmer, Eric 1920- .... **CLC 16**
See also Scherer, Jean-Marie Maurice

Rohmer, Sax 1883-1959......... **TCLC 28**
See also Ward, Arthur Henry Sarsfield
See also CA 108; DLB 70

Roiphe, Anne (Richardson)
1935- .... **CLC 3, 9**
See also CA 89-92; DLB-Y 80

Rolfe, Frederick (William Serafino Austin
Lewis Mary) 1860-1913..... **TCLC 12**
See also CA 107; DLB 34

Rolland, Romain 1866-1944...... **TCLC 23**
See also CA 118; DLB 65

Rolvaag, O(le) E(dvart)
1876-1931 .... **TCLC 17**
See also CA 117; DLB 9

Romains, Jules 1885-1972 .... **CLC 7**
See also CA 85-88

Romero, Jose Ruben 1890-1952 ... **TCLC 14**
See also CA 114

Ronsard, Pierre de 1524-1585........ **LC 6**

Rooke, Leon 1934- .... **CLC 25, 34**
See also CANR 23; CA 25-28R

Roper, William 1498-1578.......... **LC 10**

Rosa, Joao Guimaraes 1908-1967... **CLC 23**
See also obituary CA 89-92

Rosen, Richard (Dean) 1949-....... **CLC 39**
See also CA 77-80

Rosenberg, Isaac 1890-1918....... **TCLC 12**
See also CA 107; DLB 20

Rosenblatt, Joe 1933-............. **CLC 15**
See also Rosenblatt, Joseph

Rosenblatt, Joseph 1933-
See Rosenblatt, Joe
See also CA 89-92

Rosenfeld, Samuel 1896-1963
See Tzara, Tristan
See also obituary CA 89-92

Rosenthal, M(acha) L(ouis) 1917-... **CLC 28**
See also CAAS 6; CANR 4; CA 1-4R;
SATA 59; DLB 5

Ross, (James) Sinclair 1908-....... **CLC 13**
See also CA 73-76; DLB 88

Rossetti, Christina Georgina
1830-1894 .... **NCLC 2**
See also SATA 20; DLB 35

Rossetti, Dante Gabriel
1828-1882 .... **NCLC 4**
See also DLB 35

Rossetti, Gabriel Charles Dante 1828-1882
See Rossetti, Dante Gabriel

Rossner, Judith (Perelman)
1935- .... **CLC 6, 9, 29**
See also CANR 18; CA 17-20R; DLB 6

Rostand, Edmond (Eugene Alexis)
1868-1918 .... **TCLC 6, 37**
See also CA 104, 126

Roth, Henry 1906-........... **CLC 2, 6, 11**
See also CAP 1; CA 11-12; DLB 28

Roth, Joseph 1894-1939......... **TCLC 33**
See also DLB 85

Roth, Philip (Milton)
1933- ...... **CLC 1, 2, 3, 4, 6, 9, 15, 22,**
31, 47, 66
See also CANR 1, 22; CA 1-4R; DLB 2, 28;
DLB-Y 82; CDALB 1968-1988

Rothenberg, James 1931-........ **CLC 57**

Rothenberg, Jerome 1931-....... **CLC 6, 57**
See also CANR 1; CA 45-48; DLB 5

Roumain, Jacques 1907-1944...... **TCLC 19**
See also BLC 3; CA 117, 125

Rourke, Constance (Mayfield)
1885-1941 .... **TCLC 12**
See also YABC 1; CA 107

Rousseau, Jean-Baptiste 1671-1741 ... **LC 9**

Rousseau, Jean-Jacques 1712-1778... **LC 14**

Roussel, Raymond 1877-1933 ..... **TCLC 20**
See also CA 117

Rovit, Earl (Herbert) 1927-......... **CLC 7**
See also CANR 12; CA 5-8R

Rowe, Nicholas 1674-1718.......... **LC 8**

Rowson, Susanna Haswell
1762-1824 .... **NCLC 5**
See also DLB 37

Roy, Gabrielle 1909-1983....... **CLC 10, 14**
See also CANR 5; CA 53-56;
obituary CA 110; DLB 68

Rozewicz, Tadeusz 1921-........ **CLC 9, 23**
See also CA 108

Ruark, Gibbons 1941- .... **CLC 3**
See also CANR 14; CA 33-36R

Rubens, Bernice 192?- .... **CLC 19, 31**
See also CA 25-28R; DLB 14

Rudkin, (James) David 1936- ...... **CLC 14**
See also CA 89-92; DLB 13

Rudnik, Raphael 1933-............. **CLC 7**
See also CA 29-32R

Ruiz, Jose Martinez 1874-1967
See Azorin

Rukeyser, Muriel
1913-1980 .... **CLC 6, 10, 15, 27**
See also CANR 26; CA 5-8R;
obituary CA 93-96; obituary SATA 22;
DLB 48

Rule, Jane (Vance) 1931-.......... **CLC 27**
See also CANR 12; CA 25-28R; DLB 60

Rulfo, Juan 1918-1986............. **CLC 8**
See also CANR 26; CA 85-88;
obituary CA 118

Runyon, (Alfred) Damon
1880-1946 .... **TCLC 10**
See also CA 107; DLB 11

Rush, Norman 1933-............. **CLC 44**
See also CA 121, 126

Rushdie, (Ahmed) Salman
1947- .... **CLC 23, 31, 55, 59**
See also CA 108, 111

Rushforth, Peter (Scott) 1945- ..... **CLC 19**
See also CA 101

Ruskin, John 1819-1900......... **TCLC 20**
See also CA 114; SATA 24; DLB 55

Russ, Joanna 1937-............... **CLC 15**
See also CANR 11; CA 25-28R; DLB 8

Russell, George William 1867-1935
See A. E.
See also CA 104

Russell, (Henry) Ken(neth Alfred)
1927- .... **CLC 16**
See also CA 105

Russell, Mary Annette Beauchamp 1866-1941
See Elizabeth

Russell, Willy 1947-.............. **CLC 60**

Rutherford, Mark 1831-1913...... **TCLC 25**
See also CA 121; DLB 18

Ruyslinck, Ward 1929-............. **CLC 14**

Ryan, Cornelius (John) 1920-1974 ... **CLC 7**
See also CA 69-72; obituary CA 53-56

Ryan, Michael 1946-.............. **CLC 65**
See also CA 49-52; DLB-Y 82

Rybakov, Anatoli 1911?- .... **CLC 23, 53**
See also CA 126

Ryder, Jonathan 1927-
See Ludlum, Robert

Ryga, George 1932-.............. **CLC 14**
See also CA 101; obituary CA 124; DLB 60

Séviné, Marquise de Marie de
Rabutin-Chantal 1626-1696..... **LC 11**

Saba, Umberto 1883-1957........ **TCLC 33**

Sabato, Ernesto 1911- .... **CLC 10, 23**
See also CA 97-100

Sacher-Masoch, Leopold von
1836?-1895................. **NCLC 31**

Sachs, Marilyn (Stickle) 1927- ..... **CLC 35**
See also CLR 2; CANR 13; CA 17-20R;
SAAS 2; SATA 3, 52

Sachs, Nelly 1891-1970 .... **CLC 14**
See also CAP 2; CA 17-18;
obituary CA 25-28R

Sackler, Howard (Oliver)
1929-1982 .... **CLC 14**
See also CA 61-64; obituary CA 108; DLB 7

Sacks, Oliver 1933- .... **CLC 67**
See also CANR 28; CA 53-56

Sade, Donatien Alphonse Francois, Comte de
1740-1814 .... **NCLC 3**

Sadoff, Ira 1945-.................. **CLC 9**
See also CANR 5, 21; CA 53-56

Safire, William 1929-............. **CLC 10**
See also CA 17-20R

Sagan, Carl (Edward) 1934-....... **CLC 30**
See also CANR 11; CA 25-28R; SATA 58

Sagan, Francoise
1935- .... **CLC 3, 6, 9, 17, 36**
See also Quoirez, Francoise
See also CANR 6; DLB 83

Author Index

Smith, A(rthur) J(ames) M(arshall)
1902-1980 . . . . CLC 15
See also CANR 4; CA 1-4R;
obituary CA 102; DLB 88

Smith, Betty (Wehner) 1896-1972. . . CLC 19
See also CA 5-8R; obituary CA 33-36R;
SATA 6; DLB-Y 82

Smith, Cecil Lewis Troughton 1899-1966
See Forester, C(ecil) S(cott)

Smith, Charlotte (Turner)
1749-1806 . . . . NCLC 23
See also DLB 39

Smith, Clark Ashton 1893-1961 . . . . CLC 43

Smith, Dave 1942- . . . . CLC 22, 42
See also Smith, David (Jeddie)
See also CAAS 7; CANR 1; DLB 5

Smith, David (Jeddie) 1942-
See Smith, Dave
See also CANR 1; CA 49-52

Smith, Florence Margaret 1902-1971
See Smith, Stevie
See also CAP 2; CA 17-18;
obituary CA 29-32R

Smith, Iain Crichton 1928- . . . . CLC 64
See also DLB 40

Smith, John 1580?-1631 . . . . LC 9
See also DLB 24, 30

Smith, Lee 1944- . . . . CLC 25
See also CA 114, 119; DLB-Y 83

Smith, Martin Cruz 1942- . . . . CLC 25
See also CANR 6; CA 85-88

Smith, Martin William 1942-
See Smith, Martin Cruz

Smith, Mary-Ann Tirone 1944- . . . . . CLC 39
See also CA 118

Smith, Patti 1946- . . . . CLC 12
See also CA 93-96

Smith, Pauline (Urmson)
1882-1959 . . . . TCLC 25
See also CA 29-32R; SATA 27

Smith, Rosamond 1938-
See Oates, Joyce Carol

Smith, Sara Mahala Redway 1900-1972
See Benson, Sally

Smith, Stevie 1902-1971. . . . CLC 3, 8, 25, 44
See also Smith, Florence Margaret
See also DLB 20

Smith, Wilbur (Addison) 1933- . . . . . CLC 33
See also CANR 7; CA 13-16R

Smith, William Jay 1918- . . . . CLC 6
See also CA 5-8R; SATA 2; DLB 5

Smolenskin, Peretz 1842-1885. . . . NCLC 30

Smollett, Tobias (George) 1721-1771 . . LC 2
See also DLB 39

Snodgrass, W(illiam) D(e Witt)
1926- . . . . CLC 2, 6, 10, 18, 68
See also CANR 6; CA 1-4R; DLB 5

Snow, C(harles) P(ercy)
1905-1980 . . . . CLC 1, 4, 6, 9, 13, 19
See also CA 5-8R; obituary CA 101;
DLB 15, 77

Snyder, Gary (Sherman)
1930- . . . . CLC 1, 2, 5, 9, 32
See also CANR 30; CA 17-20R; DLB 5, 16

Snyder, Zilpha Keatley 1927- . . . . . . CLC 17
See also CA 9-12R; SAAS 2; SATA 1, 28

Sobol, Joshua 19??- . . . . CLC 60

Soderberg. Hjalmar 1869-1941 . . . . TCLC 39

Sodergran, Edith 1892-1923. . . . . . TCLC 31

Sokolov, Raymond 1941- . . . . CLC 7
See also CA 85-88

Sologub, Fyodor 1863-1927 . . . . TCLC 9
See also Teternikov, Fyodor Kuzmich
See also CA 104

Solomos, Dionysios 1798-1857 . . . NCLC 15

Solwoska, Mara 1929-
See French, Marilyn
See also CANR 3; CA 69-72

Solzhenitsyn, Aleksandr I(sayevich)
1918- . . . CLC 1, 2, 4, 7, 9, 10, 18, 26, 34
See also CA 69-72

Somers, Jane 1919-
See Lessing, Doris (May)

Sommer, Scott 1951- . . . . CLC 25
See also CA 106

Sondheim, Stephen (Joshua)
1930- . . . . CLC 30, 39
See also CA 103

Sontag, Susan 1933- . . . CLC 1, 2, 10, 13, 31
See also CA 17-20R; DLB 2, 67

Sophocles
c. 496? B.C.-c. 406? B.C. . . . . . CMLC 2;
DC 1

Sorrentino, Gilbert
1929- . . . . CLC 3, 7, 14, 22, 40
See also CANR 14; CA 77-80; DLB 5;
DLB-Y 80

Soto, Gary 1952- . . . . CLC 32
See also CA 119, 125; DLB 82

Soupault, Philippe 1897-1990 . . . . . . CLC 68
See also CA 116; obituary CA 131

Souster, (Holmes) Raymond
1921- . . . . CLC 5, 14
See also CANR 13; CA 13-16R; DLB 88

Southern, Terry 1926- . . . . CLC 7
See also CANR 1; CA 1-4R; DLB 2

Southey, Robert 1774-1843 . . . . NCLC 8
See also SATA 54

Southworth, Emma Dorothy Eliza Nevitte
1819-1899 . . . . NCLC 26

Soyinka, Wole 1934- . . CLC 3, 5, 14, 36, 44
See also BLC 3; CANR 27; CA 13-16R;
DLB-Y 86

Spackman, W(illiam) M(ode)
1905- . . . . CLC 46
See also CA 81-84

Spacks, Barry 1931- . . . . CLC 14
See also CA 29-32R

Spanidou, Irini 1946- . . . . CLC 44

Spark, Muriel (Sarah)
1918- . . . . CLC 2, 3, 5, 8, 13, 18, 40
See also CANR 12; CA 5-8R; DLB 15

Spencer, Elizabeth 1921- . . . . CLC 22
See also CA 13-16R; SATA 14; DLB 6

Spencer, Scott 1945- . . . . CLC 30
See also CA 113; DLB-Y 86

Spender, Stephen (Harold)
1909- . . . . CLC 1, 2, 5, 10, 41
See also CA 9-12R; DLB 20

Spengler, Oswald 1880-1936 . . . . . . TCLC 25
See also CA 118

Spenser, Edmund 1552?-1599 . . . . LC 5

Spicer, Jack 1925-1965 . . . . CLC 8, 18
See also CA 85-88; DLB 5, 16

Spielberg, Peter 1929- . . . . CLC 6
See also CANR 4; CA 5-8R; DLB-Y 81

Spielberg, Steven 1947- . . . . CLC 20
See also CA 77-80; SATA 32

Spillane, Frank Morrison 1918-
See Spillane, Mickey
See also CA 25-28R

Spillane, Mickey 1918- . . . . CLC 3, 13
See also Spillane, Frank Morrison

Spinoza, Benedictus de 1632-1677 . . . . LC 9

Spinrad, Norman (Richard) 1940- . . . CLC 46
See also CANR 20; CA 37-40R; DLB 8

Spitteler, Carl (Friedrich Georg)
1845-1924 . . . . TCLC 12
See also CA 109

Spivack, Kathleen (Romola Drucker)
1938- . . . . CLC 6
See also CA 49-52

Spoto, Donald 1941- . . . . CLC 39
See also CANR 11; CA 65-68

Springsteen, Bruce 1949- . . . . CLC 17
See also CA 111

Spurling, Hilary 1940- . . . . CLC 34
See also CANR 25; CA 104

Squires, (James) Radcliffe 1917- . . . . CLC 51
See also CANR 6, 21; CA 1-4R

Stael-Holstein, Anne Louise Germaine Necker,
Baronne de 1766-1817 . . . . NCLC 3

Stafford, Jean 1915-1979 . . . CLC 4, 7, 19, 68
See also CANR 3; CA 1-4R;
obituary CA 85-88; obituary SATA 22;
DLB 2

Stafford, William (Edgar)
1914- . . . . CLC 4, 7, 29
See also CAAS 3; CANR 5, 22; CA 5-8R;
DLB 5

Stannard, Martin 1947- . . . . CLC 44

Stanton, Maura 1946- . . . . CLC 9
See also CANR 15; CA 89-92

Stapledon, (William) Olaf
1886-1950 . . . . TCLC 22
See also CA 111; DLB 15

Starbuck, George (Edwin) 1931- . . . . CLC 53
See also CANR 23; CA 21-22R

Stark, Richard 1933-
See Westlake, Donald E(dwin)

Stead, Christina (Ellen)
1902-1983 . . . . CLC 2, 5, 8, 32
See also CA 13-16R; obituary CA 109

Steele, Sir Richard 1672-1729 . . . . . . LC 18
See also DLB 84, 101

Steele, Timothy (Reid) 1948- . . . . . . CLC 45
See also CANR 16; CA 93-96

Author Index

Wesker, Arnold 1932- .... CLC 3, 5, 42
See also CAAS 7; CANR 1; CA 1-4R;
DLB 13

Wesley, Richard (Errol) 1945-....... CLC 7
See also CA 57-60; DLB 38

Wessel, Johan Herman 1742-1785 .... LC 7

West, Anthony (Panther)
1914-1987 .... CLC 50
See also CANR 3, 19; CA 45-48; DLB 15

West, Jessamyn 1907-1984 ...... CLC 7, 17
See also CA 9-12R; obituary CA 112;
obituary SATA 37; DLB 6; DLB-Y 84

West, Morris L(anglo) 1916-..... CLC 6, 33
See also CA 5-8R; obituary CA 124

West, Nathanael 1903?-1940 .... TCLC 1, 14
See also Weinstein, Nathan Wallenstein
See also CA 125, 140; DLB 4, 9, 28

West, Paul 1930- .... CLC 7, 14
See also CAAS 7; CANR 22; CA 13-16R;
DLB 14

West, Rebecca 1892-1983 .. CLC 7, 9, 31, 50
See also CANR 19; CA 5-8R;
obituary CA 109; DLB 36; DLB-Y 83

Westall, Robert (Atkinson) 1929-... CLC 17
See also CLR 13; CANR 18; CA 69-72;
SAAS 2; SATA 23

Westlake, Donald E(dwin)
1933- .... CLC 7, 33
See also CANR 16; CA 17-20R

Westmacott, Mary 1890-1976
See Christie, (Dame) Agatha (Mary
Clarissa)

Whalen, Philip 1923- .... CLC 6, 29
See also CANR 5; CA 9-12R; DLB 16

Wharton, Edith (Newbold Jones)
1862-1937 .... TCLC 3, 9, 27; SSC 6
See also CA 104; DLB 4, 9, 12, 78;
CDALB 1865-1917

Wharton, William 1925-........ CLC 18, 37
See also CA 93-96; DLB-Y 80

Wheatley (Peters), Phillis
1753?-1784............... LC 3; PC 3
See also BLC 3; DLB 31, 50;
CDALB 1640-1865

Wheelock, John Hall 1886-1978.... CLC 14
See also CANR 14; CA 13-16R;
obituary CA 77-80; DLB 45

Whelan, John 1900-
See O'Faolain, Sean

Whitaker, Rodney 1925-
See Trevanian

White, E(lwyn) B(rooks)
1899-1985 .... CLC 10, 34, 39
See also CLR 1; CANR 16; CA 13-16R;
obituary CA 116; SATA 2, 29, 44;
obituary SATA 44; DLB 11, 22

White, Edmund III 1940-........... CLC 27
See also CANR 3, 19; CA 45-48

White, Patrick (Victor Martindale)
1912-1990 ..... CLC 3, 4, 5, 7, 9, 18, 65
See also CA 81-84; obituary CA 132

White, T(erence) H(anbury)
1906-1964 .... CLC 30
See also CA 73-76; SATA 12

White, Terence de Vere 1912-...... CLC 49
See also CANR 3; CA 49-52

White, Walter (Francis)
1893-1955 .... TCLC 15
See also BLC 3; CA 115, 124; DLB 51

White, William Hale 1831-1913
See Rutherford, Mark
See also CA 121

Whitehead, E(dward) A(nthony)
1933- .... CLC 5
See also CA 65-68

Whitemore, Hugh 1936-.......... CLC 37

Whitman, Sarah Helen
1803-1878 .... NCLC 19
See also DLB 1

Whitman, Walt
1819-1892 .... NCLC 4, 31; PC 3
See also SATA 20; DLB 3, 64;
CDALB 1640-1865

Whitney, Phyllis A(yame) 1903-.... CLC 42
See also CANR 3, 25; CA 1-4R; SATA 1,
30

Whittemore, (Edward) Reed (Jr.)
1919- .... CLC 4
See also CAAS 8; CANR 4; CA 9-12R;
DLB 5

Whittier, John Greenleaf
1807-1892 .... NCLC 8
See also DLB 1; CDALB 1640-1865

Wicker, Thomas Grey 1926-
See Wicker, Tom
See also CANR 21; CA 65-68

Wicker, Tom 1926-................ CLC 7
See also Wicker, Thomas Grey

Wideman, John Edgar
1941- .... CLC 5, 34, 36, 67
See also BLC 3; CANR 14; CA 85-88;
DLB 33

Wiebe, Rudy (H.) 1934-...... CLC 6, 11, 14
See also CA 37-40R; DLB 60

Wieland, Christoph Martin
1733-1813 .... NCLC 17

Wieners, John 1934-............... CLC 7
See also CA 13-16R; DLB 16

Wiesel, Elie(zer) 1928-..... CLC 3, 5, 11, 37
See also CAAS 4; CANR 8; CA 5-8R;
SATA 56; DLB 83; DLB-Y 87

Wiggins, Marianne 1948-.......... CLC 57

Wight, James Alfred 1916-
See Herriot, James
See also CA 77-80; SATA 44

Wilbur, Richard (Purdy)
1921- .... CLC 3, 6, 9, 14, 53
See also CANR 2; CA 1-4R; CABS 2;
SATA 9; DLB 5

Wild, Peter 1940-................ CLC 14
See also CA 37-40R; DLB 5

Wilde, Oscar (Fingal O'Flahertie Wills)
1854-1900 .... TCLC 1, 8, 23, 41
See also CA 119; brief entry CA 104;
SATA 24; DLB 10, 19, 34, 57

Wilder, Billy 1906-............... CLC 20
See also Wilder, Samuel
See also DLB 26

Wilder, Samuel 1906-
See Wilder, Billy
See also CA 89-92

Wilder, Thornton (Niven)
1897-1975 ..... CLC 1, 5, 6, 10, 15, 35;
DC 1
See also CA 13-16R; obituary CA 61-64;
DLB 4, 7, 9

Wiley, Richard 1944-............. CLC 44
See also CA 121, 129

Wilhelm, Kate 1928-.............. CLC 7
See also CAAS 5; CANR 17; CA 37-40R;
DLB 8

Willard, Nancy 1936-........... CLC 7, 37
See also CLR 5; CANR 10; CA 89-92;
SATA 30, 37; DLB 5, 52

Williams, C(harles) K(enneth)
1936- .... CLC 33, 56
See also CA 37-40R; DLB 5

Williams, Charles (Walter Stansby)
1886-1945 .... TCLC 1, 11
See also CA 104

Williams, Ella Gwendolen Rees 1890-1979
See Rhys, Jean

Williams, (George) Emlyn
1905-1987 .... CLC 15
See also CA 104, 123; DLB 10, 77

Williams, Hugo 1942-............. CLC 42
See also CA 17-20R; DLB 40

Williams, John A(lfred) 1925-.... CLC 5, 13
See also BLC 3; CAAS 3; CANR 6, 26;
CA 53-56; DLB 2, 33

Williams, Jonathan (Chamberlain)
1929- .... CLC 13
See also CANR 8; CA 9-12R; DLB 5

Williams, Joy 1944-.............. CLC 31
See also CANR 22; CA 41-44R

Williams, Norman 1952- .... CLC 39
See also CA 118

Williams, Paulette 1948-
See Shange, Ntozake

Williams, Sherley Anne 1944-
See also BLC 3; CANR 25; CA 73-76;
DLB 41

Williams, Shirley 1944-
See Williams, Sherley Anne

Williams, Tennessee
1911-1983 .... CLC 1, 2, 5, 7, 8, 11, 15,
19, 30, 39, 45
See also CA 5-8R; obituary CA 108; DLB 7;
DLB-Y 83; DLB-DS 4;
CDALB 1941-1968

Williams, Thomas (Alonzo) 1926-... CLC 14
See also CANR 2; CA 1-4R

Williams, Thomas Lanier 1911-1983
See Williams, Tennessee

Williams, William Carlos
1883-1963 ... CLC 1, 2, 5, 9, 13, 22, 42,
67
See also CA 89-92; DLB 4, 16, 54, 86;
CDALB 1917-1929

Williamson, David 1932- .... CLC 56

Williamson, Jack 1908-........... CLC 29
See also Williamson, John Stewart
See also DLB 8

Williamson, John Stewart 1908-
See Williamson, Jack
See also CANR 123; CA 17-20R

Willingham, Calder (Baynard, Jr.)
1922- . . . . CLC **5, 51**
See also CANR 3; CA 5-8R; DLB 2, 44

Wilson, A(ndrew) N(orman) 1950- . . CLC **33**
See also CA 112, 122; DLB 14

Wilson, Andrew 1948-
See Wilson, Snoo

Wilson, Angus (Frank Johnstone)
1913- . . . . CLC **2, 3, 5, 25, 34**
See also CANR 21; CA 5-8R; DLB 15

Wilson, August 1945- . . . . CLC **39, 50, 63**
See also BLC 3; CA 115, 122

Wilson, Brian 1942- . . . . CLC **12**

Wilson, Colin 1931- . . . . CLC **3, 14**
See also CAAS 5; CANR 1, 122; CA 1-4R;
DLB 14

Wilson, Edmund
1895-1972 . . . . CLC **1, 2, 3, 8, 24**
See also CANR 1; CA 1-4R;
obituary CA 37-40R; DLB 63

Wilson, Ethel Davis (Bryant)
1888-1980 . . . . CLC **13**
See also CA 102; DLB 68

Wilson, Harriet 1827?-?
See also BLC 3; DLB 50

Wilson, John 1785-1854 . . . . NCLC **5**

Wilson, John (Anthony) Burgess 1917-
See Burgess, Anthony
See also CANR 2; CA 1-4R

Wilson, Lanford 1937- . . . . CLC **7, 14, 36**
See also CA 17-20R; DLB 7

Wilson, Robert (M.) 1944- . . . . CLC **7, 9**
See also CANR 2; CA 49-52

Wilson, Sloan 1920- . . . . CLC **32**
See also CANR 1; CA 1-4R

Wilson, Snoo 1948- . . . . CLC **33**
See also CA 69-72

Wilson, William S(mith) 1932- . . . . . CLC **49**
See also CA 81-84

**Winchilsea, Anne (Kingsmill) Finch, Countess
of** 1661-1720 . . . . LC **3**

Wingrove, David 1954- . . . . CLC **68**
See also CA 133

Winters, Janet Lewis 1899-
See Lewis (Winters), Janet
See also CAP 1; CA 9-10

Winters, (Arthur) Yvor
1900-1968 . . . . CLC **4, 8, 32**
See also CAP 1; CA 11-12;
obituary CA 25-28R; DLB 48

Winterson, Jeannette 1959- . . . . CLC **64**

Wiseman, Frederick 1930- . . . . CLC **20**

Wister, Owen 1860-1938 . . . . TCLC **21**
See also CA 108; DLB 9, 78

Witkiewicz, Stanislaw Ignacy
1885-1939 . . . . TCLC **8**
See also CA 105; DLB 83

Wittig, Monique 1935?- . . . . CLC **22**
See also CA 116; DLB 83

Wittlin, Joseph 1896-1976 . . . . CLC **25**
See also Wittlin, Jozef

Wittlin, Jozef 1896-1976
See Wittlin, Joseph
See also CANR 3; CA 49-52;
obituary CA 65-68

Wodehouse, (Sir) P(elham) G(renville)
1881-1975 . . . CLC **1, 2, 5, 10, 22; SSC 2**
See also CANR 3; CA 45-48;
obituary CA 57-60; SATA 22; DLB 34

Woiwode, Larry (Alfred) 1941- . . . CLC **6, 10**
See also CANR 16; CA 73-76; DLB 6

Wojciechowska, Maia (Teresa)
1927- . . . . CLC **26**
See also CLR 1; CANR 4; CA 9-12R;
SAAS 1; SATA 1, 28

Wolf, Christa 1929- . . . . CLC **14, 29, 58**
See also CA 85-88; DLB 75

Wolfe, Gene (Rodman) 1931- . . . . CLC **25**
See also CAAS 9; CANR 6; CA 57-60;
DLB 8

Wolfe, George C. 1954- . . . . CLC **49**

Wolfe, Thomas (Clayton)
1900-1938 . . . . TCLC **4, 13, 29**
See also CA 104; DLB 9; DLB-Y 85;
DLB-DS 2

Wolfe, Thomas Kennerly, Jr. 1931-
See Wolfe, Tom
See also CANR 9; CA 13-16R

Wolfe, Tom 1931- . . . CLC **1, 2, 9, 15, 35, 51**
See also Wolfe, Thomas Kennerly, Jr.

Wolff, Geoffrey (Ansell) 1937- . . . . . CLC **41**
See also CA 29-32R

Wolff, Tobias (Jonathan Ansell)
1945- . . . . CLC **39, 64**
See also CA 114, 117

Wolfram von Eschenbach
c. 1170-c. 1220 . . . . CMLC **5**

Wolitzer, Hilma 1930- . . . . CLC **17**
See also CANR 18; CA 65-68; SATA 31

Wollstonecraft Godwin, Mary
1759-1797 . . . . LC **5**
See also DLB 39

Wonder, Stevie 1950- . . . . CLC **12**
See also Morris, Steveland Judkins

Wong, Jade Snow 1922- . . . . CLC **17**
See also CA 109

Woodcott, Keith 1934-
See Brunner, John (Kilian Houston)

Woolf, (Adeline) Virginia
1882-1941 . . . . TCLC **1, 5, 20, 43; SSC 7**
See also CA 130; brief entry CA 104;
DLB 36, 100

Woollcott, Alexander (Humphreys)
1887-1943 . . . . TCLC **5**
See also CA 105; DLB 29

Wordsworth, Dorothy
1771-1855 . . . . NCLC **25**

Wordsworth, William 1770-1850 . . NCLC **12**

Wouk, Herman 1915- . . . . CLC **1, 9, 38**
See also CANR 6; CA 5-8R; DLB-Y 82

Wright, Charles 1935- . . . . CLC **6, 13, 28**
See also BLC 3; CAAS 7; CANR 26;
CA 29-32R; DLB-Y 82

Wright, Charles (Stevenson) 1932- . . . CLC **49**
See also CA 9-12R; DLB 33

Wright, James (Arlington)
1927-1980 . . . . CLC **3, 5, 10, 28**
See also CANR 4; CA 49-52;
obituary CA 97-100; DLB 5

Wright, Judith 1915- . . . . CLC **11, 53**
See also CA 13-16R; SATA 14

Wright, L(aurali) R. 1939- . . . . CLC **44**

Wright, Richard (Nathaniel)
1908-1960 . . . CLC **1, 3, 4, 9, 14, 21, 48;
SSC 2**
See also BLC 3; CA 108; DLB 76;
DLB-DS 2; CDALB 1929-1941; AAYA 5

Wright, Richard B(ruce) 1937- . . . . . . CLC **6**
See also CA 85-88; DLB 53

Wright, Rick 1945-
See Pink Floyd

Wright, Stephen 1946- . . . . CLC **33**

Wright, Willard Huntington 1888-1939
See Van Dine, S. S.
See also CA 115

Wright, William 1930- . . . . CLC **44**
See also CANR 7, 23; CA 53-56

Wu Ch'eng-en 1500?-1582? . . . . LC **7**

Wu Ching-tzu 1701-1754 . . . . LC **2**

Wurlitzer, Rudolph 1938?- . . . . . CLC **2, 4, 15**
See also CA 85-88

Wycherley, William 1640?-1716 . . . . . . LC **8**
See also DLB 80

Wylie (Benet), Elinor (Morton Hoyt)
1885-1928 . . . . TCLC **8**
See also CA 105; DLB 9, 45

Wylie, Philip (Gordon) 1902-1971 . . . CLC **43**
See also CAP 2; CA 21-22;
obituary CA 33-36R; DLB 9

Wyndham, John 1903-1969 . . . . CLC **19**
See also Harris, John (Wyndham Parkes
Lucas) Beynon

Wyss, Johann David 1743-1818 . . NCLC **10**
See also SATA 27, 29

X, Malcolm 1925-1965
See Little, Malcolm

Yanovsky, Vassily S(emenovich)
1906-1989 . . . . CLC **2, 18**
See also CA 97-100; obituary CA 129

Yates, Richard 1926- . . . . CLC **7, 8, 23**
See also CANR 10; CA 5-8R; DLB 2;
DLB-Y 81

Yeats, William Butler
1865-1939 . . . . TCLC **1, 11, 18, 31**
See also CANR 10; CA 104; DLB 10, 19

Yehoshua, A(braham) B.
1936- . . . . CLC **13, 31**
See also CA 33-36R

Yep, Laurence (Michael) 1948- . . . . . CLC **35**
See also CLR 3, 17; CANR 1; CA 49-52;
SATA 7; DLB 52

Yerby, Frank G(arvin) 1916- . . . CLC **1, 7, 22**
See also BLC 3; CANR 16; CA 9-12R;
DLB 76

Yevtushenko, Yevgeny (Alexandrovich)
1933- . . . . CLC **1, 3, 13, 26, 51**
See also CA 81-84

Author Index

Literary Criticism Series
Cumulative Topic Index

This index lists all topic entries in the Gale Literary Criticism Series *Contemporary Literary Criticism, Literature Criticism from 1400 to 1800, Nineteenth-Century Literature Criticism,* and *Twentieth-Century Literary Criticism.*

LC Cumulative Nationality Index

AFGHAN
Bābur **18**

AMERICAN
Bradstreet, Anne **4**
Edwards, Jonathan **7**
Eliot, John **5**
Knight, Sarah Kemble **7**
Munford, Robert **5**
Taylor, Edward **11**
Wheatley, Phillis **3**

ANGLO-AFRICAN
Equiano, Olaudah **16**

CANADIAN
Marie de l'Incarnation **10**

CHINESE
Lo Kuan-chung **12**
P'u Sung-ling **3**
Ts'ao Hsueh-ch'in **1**
Wu Ch'eng-En **7**
Wu-Ching-tzu **2**

DANO-NORWEGIAN
Holberg, Ludvig **6**
Wessel, Johan Herman **7**

DUTCH
Erasmus, Desiderius **16**
Lipsius, Justus **16**
Spinoza, Benedictus de **9**

ENGLISH
Addison, Joseph **18**
Andrewes, Lancelot **5**
Arbuthnot, John **1**
Aubin, Penelope **9**

Bacon, Sir Francis **18**
Behn, Aphra **1**
Brooke, Frances **6**
Bunyan, John **4**
Burke, Edmund **7**
Butler, Samuel **16**
Carew, Thomas **13**
Caxton, William **17**
Charles I **13**
Chatterton, Thomas **3**
Chaucer, Geoffrey **17**
Churchill, Charles **3**
Cleland, John **2**
Collier, Jeremy **6**
Collins, William **4**
Congreve, William **5**
Davenant, William **13**
Davys, Mary **1**
Day, Thomas **1**
Defoe, Daniel **1**
Delany, Mary **12**
Dennis, John **11**
Donne, John **10**
Drayton, Michael **8**
Dryden, John **3**
Elyot, Sir Thomas **11**
Fanshawe, Anne, Lady **11**
Fielding, Henry **1**
Fielding, Sarah **1**
Foxe, John **14**
Garrick, David **15**
Goldsmith, Oliver **2**
Gray, Thomas **4**
Hawes, Stephen **17**
Haywood, Eliza **1**
Henry VIII **10**
Herrick, Robert **13**
Howell, James **13**
Hunter, Robert **7**

Johnson, Samuel **15**
Jonson, Ben **6**
Julian of Norwich **6**
Kempe, Margery **6**
Killegrew, Anne **4**
Lanyer, Aemilia **10**
Locke, John **7**
Lyttelton, George **10**
Malory, Thomas **11**
Manley, Mary Delariviere **1**
Marvell, Andrew **4**
Milton, John **9**
Montagu, Mary Wortley, Lady **9**
More, Henry **9**
More, Sir Thomas **10**
Parnell, Thomas **3**
Pepys, Samuel **11**
Pix, Mary **8**
Pope, Alexander **3**
Prior, Matthew **4**
Reynolds, Sir Joshua **15**
Richardson, Samuel **1**
Roper, William **10**
Rowe, Nicholas **8**
Sheridan, Frances **7**
Smart, Christopher **3**
Smith, John **9**
Spenser, Edmund **5**
Steele, Sir Richard **18**
Sterne, Laurence **2**
Swift, Jonathan **1**
Trotter, Catharine **8**
Walpole, Horace **2**
Warton, Thomas **15**
Winchilsea, Anne Finch, Lady **3**
Wollstonecraft, Mary **5**
Wycherley, William **8**
Young, Edward **3**

LC Cumulative Title Index

Title Index

Title Index

Title Index

Title Index

Title Index

The Logick Primer, Some Logical Notions to Initiate the Indians in Knowledge of the Rule of Reason; and to Know How to Make Use Thereof (*The Logick Primer*) (Eliot) **5**:132, 134-35

Londinopolis; An Historical Discourse or Perlustration of the City of London (Howell) **13**:424

"London: A Poem, In Imitation of the Third Satire of Juvenal" (Johnson) **15**:187-90, 194, 206, 288, 291-95, 302-05

London Journal (Boswell)
See *Boswell's London Journal*

The Long Road of Learning (Christine de Pizan)
See *Le livre du chemin de long estude*

"A Long Story" (Gray) **4**:301, 312, 315-17, 333-34

"Longing for Heaven" (Bradstreet) **4**:85, 112

"A Looking-Glasse" (Carew) **13**:28

"Lord Daer" (Burns)
See "Meeting with Lord Daer"

"The Loss of his Mistresses" (Herrick) **13**:337

The Lost Lover; or, A Jealous Husband (Manley) **1**:315

Love and Honor (Davenant) **13**:175-77, 181, 192, 196, 215

Love at a Loss; or, Most Votes Carry It (Trotter) **8**:355, 357, 361, 368-69, 372-74

"Love Banish'd Heav'n, in Earth Was Held in Scorne" (Drayton)
See "Sonnet 23"

"Love-Begotten Daughter" (Burns)
See "A Poet's Welcome to His Love-Begotten Daughter"

"Love Disarm'd" (Prior) **4**:459

Love Elegies (Donne)
See *Elegies*

Love for Love (Congreve) **5**:66, 68, 70-1, 74, 76, 78-9, 81, 83, 84, 86-90, 92, 94, 96-101, 105-06, 109, 111

"Love, in a Humor, Play'd the Prodigall" (Drayton)
See "Sonnet 7"

Love in a Wood; or, St. James's Park (Wycherley) **8**:384, 388, 390-92, 395, 397, 402, 407, 410, 432-34

Love in Excess; or, The Fatal Enquiry (Haywood) **1**:284-85, 290, 292, 295-300

"Love in Fantastic Triumph Sat" (Behn) **1**:31, 38

Love in Several Masques (Fielding) **1**:250

Love is the Best Doctor (Molière)
See *L'amour médecin*

Love Letters between a Nobleman and His Sister (Behn) **1**:34, 43, 48

Love-Letters from King Henry VIII. to Anne Boleyn (Henry VIII) **10**:119

Love Letters to a Gentleman (Behn) **1**:38

"The Love of Fame" (Young)
See "The Universal Passion; or, The Love of Fame"

Love, the Greater Labyrinth (Juana Ines de la Cruz)
See *Amor es más laberinto*

Love Triumphant (Dryden) **3**:230

The Lover (Steele) **18**:354

"Lover and the Maiden" (Erasmus) **16**:140

"A Lover's Anger" (Prior) **4**:460

"Lovers infinitenesse" ("If yet I have not all thy love") (Donne) **10**:36, 82

Lovers' Spite (Molière)
See *Le dépit amoureux*

The Lovers Watch (Behn) **1**:41

"Loves Alchymie" (Donne) **10**:82

"Loves Deitie" (Donne) **10**:26, 81

"Loves growth" (Donne) **10**:18, 57

"Loves Usury" (Donne) **10**:52

"Lu p'an" (P'u Sung-ling) **3**:350

"Lucia" (Young) **3**:472

"Lucius" (Prior) **4**:455

The Luckey Chance; or, An Alderman's Bargain (Behn) **1**:27-9, 34, 37, 40-1, 47-8

The Lucky Mistake (Behn) **1**:32, 46, 51-2

Luminalia (Davenant) **13**:189

Luminis Naturalis (Bacon) **18**:187

"Lung-fei hsiang Kung" ("Minister Dragon's Flight") (P'u Sung-ling) **3**:350

Lung-hu feng-yün hui (Lo) **12**:282

"Le lutrin" (Boileau-Despreaux) **3**:16-17, 19, 21-2, 24, 29, 37-43

"The Luxury of Vain Imagination" (Johnson)
See *The Rambler, 89*

"Lycidas" (Milton) **9**:177, 197, 199, 203-11, 213, 229-30, 238-41, 243

Lycidus (Behn) **1**:41

The Lyfe of Sir Thomas Moore, Knighte (Roper)
See *The Mirrour of Vertue in Worldly Greatnes; or, The Life of syr Thomas More Knight*

The Lying-in Room (Holberg)
See *Barselstuen*

The Lying Lover (Steele) **18**:314-15, 330, 333, 338-40, 346, 348, 353-54, 359, 364-66, 371

The Lying Valet (Garrick) **15**:98, 100-01, 113, 121, 124

Det lykkelige skibbrud (Holberg) **6**:263, 278

Lykken bedre end Forstanden (Wessel) **7**:390

"La Lyre" (Ronsard) **6**:427-28

"A Lyrick to Mirth" (Herrick) **13**:365

Macbeth (Davenant) **13**:185-87, 212 214-16

Macbeth (Johnson)
See *Miscellaneous Observations on the Tragedy of Macbeth*

"MacFlecknoe; or, A Satire upon the Trew-Blew-Protestant Poet, T. S." (Dryden) **3**:189, 192, 199, 205, 212, 222, 231, 242

"Macphersons' Farewell" (Burns) **3**:60

"The Mad Maid's Song" (Herrick) **13**:319-20, 324, 326, 332, 336-37

Madagascar; With Other Poems (Davenant) **13**:204-05

La madre amorosa (Goldoni) **4**:260

Magazin zur Erfahrungsseelenkunde (Moritz) **2**:236

The Magic Bird's Nest (Grimmelshausen)
See *Das wunderbarliche Vogelnest (I and II)*

Magnalia naturae praecipue quoad usus humanos (*Great Works of Nature for the Particular Use of Mankind*) (Bacon) **18**:152

The Magnetic Lady (Jonson) **6**:306, 311, 314, 327, 339

The Magnificent Lovers (Molière)
See *Les amants magnifiques*

Mahomet (Defoe) **1**:162

Mahomet (Voltaire) **14**:328, 397

Mahomet and Irene (Johnson)
See *Irene: A Tragedy*

The Maiden Queen (Dryden)
See *Secret Love; or, The Maiden Queen*

"Mailie's Dying Words and Elegy" (Burns)

See "The Death and Dying Words of Poor Mailie"

"Le maître chat; ou, Le chat botté" (Perrault) **2**:254, 257-58, 260, 266-71, 280-81, 284

Le malade imaginaire (*The Imaginary Invalid*) (Molière) **10**:270, 272, 274-75, 282-83, 285-86, 290-91, 299, 304, 306, 313, 318, 327-29, 336, 339

The Male Coquette (*The Modern Fine Gentleman*) (Garrick) **15**:98, 101-03

Malpiglio (Tasso) **5**:407

Mamusse wunneetupanatamwe Up-Biblum God Naneeswe Nukkone Testament Kah Wonk Wusku Testament (*The Holy Bible: Containing the Old Testament and the New*) (Eliot) **5**:124, 126-28, 130-32, 134

Man (Marat)
See *A Philosophical Essay on Man, Being an Attempt to Investigate the Principles and Laws of the Reciprocal Influence of the Soul on the Body*

The Man in the Moone (Drayton) **8**:14, 17, 27, 32, 34, 36-7

"Man Naturally God's Enemies" (Edwards) **7**:98

The Man of Discretion (Gracián y Morales)
See *El Discreto*

"Man of Lawe's Tale" (Chaucer)
See "Man of Law's Tale"

"Man of Law's Prologue" (Chaucer) **17**:214

"Man of Law's Tale" ("Man of Lawe's Tale") (Chaucer) **17**:60, 63, 83, 119, 176, 196, 205, 232, 237

"Man Was Made to Mourn" (Burns) **3**:48, 52, 67, 74, 87

The Man with Forty Ecus (Voltaire)
See *L'homme aux quarante écus*

"Manciple's Tale" (Chaucer) **17**:173

Mandragola (Machiavelli)
See *Commedia di Callimaco: E di Lucretia*

The Mandrake (Grimmelshausen)
See *Das Galgen-Männlin*

Manductio ad Stoicam philosophiam (Lipsius)
See *Manductionis ad ph:losophiam stoicam libri tres*

Manductionis ad philosophiam stoicam libri tres (*Manductio ad Stoicam philosophiam*; *Stoic Philosophy*) (Lipsius) **16**:257-58

Manifest (Sigüenza y Góngora)
See *Manifesto philosophico contra los cometas despojados del imperio que tenian sobre los timidos*

Manifesto philosophico contra los cometas despojados del imperio que tenian sobre los timidos (*Manifest*) (Sigüenza y Góngora) **8**:341-42

"Manliness" (Donne) **10**:95

"Manne, Womanne, Syr Rogerre" (Collins) **4**:214, 229, 231, 237, 239-43

"Man's Injustice toward Providence" (Winchilsea) **3**:451

The Man's the Master (Davenant) **13**:186-87, 189

Manual of Metaphysics (More) **9**:297

Manual of the Christian Knight (Erasmus)
See *Enchiridion militis christiani*

The Manual Oracle and Art of Prudence (Gracián y Morales)
See *Oráculo manual y arte de prudencia*

Map of the Bay and the Rivers, with an Annexed Relation of the Countries and Nations That Inhabit Them (Smith)

Title Index

Title Index

Title Index

ISBN 0-8103-7960-0